America Reads   Seventh Edition

England
in Literature

America Reads Seventh Edition

Beginnings in Literature
Alan L. Madsen
Sarah Durand Wood
Philip M. Connors

Discoveries in Literature
Edmund J. Farrell
Ruth S. Cohen
L. Jane Christensen

Explorations in Literature
Ruth S. Cohen
Nancy C. Millett
Raymond J. Rodrigues

Patterns in Literature
Edmund J. Farrell
Ouida H. Clapp
Karen J. Kuehner

Traditions in Literature
James E. Miller, Jr.
Helen McDonnell
Russell J. Hogan

The United States in Literature
The Red Badge of Courage Edition
Three Long Stories Edition
James E. Miller, Jr.
Carlota Cárdenas de Dwyer
Kerry M. Wood

England in Literature
Macbeth Edition
Hamlet Edition
Helen McDonnell
John Pfordresher
Gladys V. Veidemanis

Testbooks

Guidebooks

America Reads Seventh Edition

England
in Literature

Helen McDonnell

John Pfordresher

Gladys V. Veidemanis

Scott, Foresman and Company

Editorial Offices: Glenview, Illinois
Regional Offices: Palo Alto, California
                Tucker, Georgia
                Glenview, Illinois
                Oakland, New Jersey
                Dallas, Texas

Helen McDonnell   English Supervisor of the Ocean Township Junior and Senior High Schools, Oakhurst, New Jersey. Formerly Chairman of the Committee on Comparative and World Literature, NCTE. Formerly member of the Commission on Literature, NCTE. Editor of *Nobel Parade* and coauthor of titles in the America Reads, Fountainhead, and Gateway Series, Scott, Foresman and Company.

John Pfordresher   Professor of English, Georgetown University, Washington, D.C. Editor of *Variorum Edition of the Idylls of the King* and coauthor of *Matthew Arnold, Prose Writings: The Critical Heritage*. Author of articles in *The English Journal, Studies in Short Fiction,* and *Studies in Bibliography*. Coauthor of titles in the America Reads and Fountainhead Series, Scott, Foresman and Company.

Gladys V. Veidemanis   Chairman of the Department of English at North High School in Oshkosh, Wisconsin. Coauthor of *Language: Structure and Use (10),* Scott, Foresman and Company. Wisconsin High-School Teacher of the Year (1983-1984). Member of the National Advisory Panel for the British Broadcasting Corporation's *The Shakespeare Plays*.

Cover photo: Detail of the Bayeux Tapestry.
© Erich Lessing / MAGNUM

Initial letter designs that appear in Table of Contents and with units by Eliza Lee Schulte.

Pronunciation key and dictionary entries are from *Scott, Foresman Advanced Dictionary* by E. L. Thorndike and Clarence L. Barnhart. Copyright © 1983 Scott, Foresman and Company.

ISBN: 0-673-27007-6 (*Hamlet*)
ISBN: 0-673-27008-4 (*Macbeth*)

45678910-RRW-A-959493929190898887
45678910-RRW-B-959493929190898887

Contents

Unit 1
450–1100
The Anglo-Saxons

Time Line	**1**	
Background	**2**	
The *Beowulf*-poet	**6**	
	7	*Beowulf*/translated by Charles W. Kennedy
Comment: The Nature of Grendel	**8**	
Reader's Note: The Poetry of *Beowulf*	**11**	
Reader's Note: Translating *Beowulf*	**22**	
Comment: Heroic Morality	**31**	
Comment: The Treasure of Sutton Hoo	**34**	
Poems from the Exeter Book	**42**	
	42	**The Wife's Lament**/translated by Charles W. Kennedy
	43	**The Husband's Message**/translated by Burton Raffel
	45	**Anglo-Saxon Riddles**/translated by J. Duncan Spaeth and Michael Alexander
Bede	**47**	
	48	from ***The Ecclesiastical History of the English People***/translated by Leo Sherley-Price
Celtic Literature in Wales and Ireland	**52**	
	52	from **The Stanzas of the Graves**/translated by Gwyn Jones
	53	**Eagle of Pengwern**/translated by Gwyn Williams
	53	**Pangur Ban**/translated by Robin Flower
	54	**Summer is Gone**/translated by Kuno Meyer
	54	**The Viking Terror**/translated by Frank O'Connor
The Changing English Language	**55**	
Unit 1 Review	**57**	
Content Review	**57**	
Concept Review	**57**	**The Seafarer**/translated by Burton Raffel
Composition Review	**59**	

Unit 2
1100–1500

The Medieval Period

Time Line	**61**	
Background	**62**	
Popular Ballads	**66**	
	67	Edward
	68	Sir Patrick Spence
	69	Get Up and Bar the Door
	70	The Demon Lover
Geoffrey Chaucer	**72**	
	73	from *The Canterbury Tales*/translated by Nevill Coghill
	74	The Prologue
Comment: Medieval Tourists	**77**	
	88	The Pardoner's Prologue
	90	The Pardoner's Tale
	95	The Wife of Bath's Prologue
	103	The Wife of Bath's Tale
Comment: A Medieval Valentine	**107**	
Sir Thomas Malory	**110**	
	112	The Day of Destiny, from *Morte Darthur*
The Changing English Language	**117**	
Unit 2 Review	**119**	
Content Review	**119**	
Concept Review	**119**	from *Sir Gawain and the Green Knight*/translated by Brian Stone
Composition Review	**123**	

Unit 3 · *The* *enaissance*

1500–1660

Time Line	**125**	
Background	**126**	
Sir Thomas Wyatt	**132**	
	132	**Whoso List to Hunt**
	133	**Varium et Mutabile**
	133	**He Is Not Dead That Sometime Hath a Fall**
Henry Howard, Earl of Surrey	**134**	
	134	**A Lover's Vow**
	135	**Alas, So All Things Now Do Hold Their Peace**
Reader's Note: Sonnets and Sonnet Sequences	**135**	
Comment: Elizabeth Young and Old	**136**	**When I was Fair and Young**/Elizabeth I
	137	**Gloriana Dying**/Sylvia Townsend Warner
Sir Walter Raleigh	**138**	
	139	**Sir Walter Raleigh to His Son**
	139	**To Queen Elizabeth**
	140	**What Is Our Life?**
	140	**Even Such Is Time**
Comment: The Death of Raleigh	**140**	
Christopher Marlowe	**141**	
	142	**The Passionate Shepherd to His Love**
	142	**The Nymph's Reply to the Shepherd**/ Sir Walter Raleigh
Edmund Spenser	**143**	
	144	from *The Faerie Queene*, Canto I
Reader's Note: The Spenserian Stanza	**145**	
Reader's Note: Allegory	**147**	
	148	from *Amoretti*, Sonnet 30
	148	from *Amoretti*, Sonnet 75
Sir Philip Sidney	**149**	
	150	from *Arcadia*
	150	from *Astrophel and Stella*, Sonnet 31
Comment: Sidney's Metaphor	**150**	**i carry your heart**/E. E. Cummings
	151	**Oft Have I Mused**
	151	**Thou Blind Man's Mark**

Thomas Campion	152	
	152	**When to Her Lute Corinna Sings**
	153	**Now Winter Nights Enlarge**
	153	**The Man of Life Upright**
Thomas Nashe	154	
	154	**Autumn**
	155	**A Litany in Time of Plague**
William Shakespeare	156	
	156	**Sonnet 18**
	157	**Sonnet 29**
	158	**Sonnet 30**
	158	**Sonnet 71**
	158	**Sonnet 73**
	158	**Sonnet 116**
	159	**Sonnet 130**

The Seventh Edition of *England in Literature* is available in two editions, one containing *Hamlet,* the other *Macbeth.* Thus two listings appear in the Table of Contents and in the Index, although only one of the plays will be found in this book.

	160	***Hamlet, Prince of Denmark***
	161	Act One
	176	Act Two
Comment: Shakespeare's Theater—The Globe	183	
	189	Act Three
	203	Act Four
Comment: Hamlet, Prince of Denmark	208	
	216	Act Five
	160	***Macbeth***
	162	Act One
	177	Act Two
	187	Act Three
Comment: The Witch-Scenes in *Macbeth*	198	
	202	Act Four
	215	Act Five
Comment: Shakespeare's Theater—The Globe	217	
	230	**Genesis, Chapters 1–3,** from *The King James Bible*
	234	**The Twenty-third Psalm,** from *The Great Bible*
	234	**The Twenty-third Psalm,** from *The King James Bible*
	234	**The Twenty-third Psalm,** from *The Bay Psalm Book*
	234	**The Twenty-third Psalm,** from *The New English Bible*
Sir Francis Bacon	235	
	235	**Of Studies**

John Donne **237**

238 Song

238 The Bait

239 A Valediction: Forbidding Mourning

Reader's Note: "A Valediction" **240**

241 from *Holy Sonnets,* Sonnet 10

241 from *Holy Sonnets,* Sonnet 14

241 Meditation 17

Ben Jonson **243**

244 To Cynthia

244 Still to Be Neat

244 On My First Son

245 Song, to Celia

245 On My First Daughter

Comment: Ben Jonson's Vision of His Son **245**

Robert Herrick **246**

246 The Argument of His Book

247 To the Virgins, to Make Much of Time

247 Delight in Disorder

247 Upon Julia's Clothes

Richard Lovelace **248**

249 To Althea, from Prison

249 To Lucasta, on Going to the Wars

Andrew Marvell **250**

250 To His Coy Mistress

Reader's Note: "To His Coy Mistress" **251**

252 Bermudas

George Herbert **253**

254 Avarice

254 Love (III)

255 Easter Wings

255 Virtue

John Milton **256**

257 On His Having Arrived at the Age of Twenty-Three

257 On His Blindness

258 from *Paradise Lost,* Book I

The Changing English Language **265**

Unit 3 Review **266**

Content Review **266**

Concept Review **267** from *Richard II,* Act Three/William Shakespeare

Composition Review **271**

Unit 4
1660–1780

The ge of Reason

Time Line	**273**	
Background	**274**	
John Dryden	**278**	
	279	**I Feed a Flame Within**
	279	**Song Sung by Venus in Honor of Britannia**
	280	from **Mac Flecknoe**
	281	**To the Memory of Mr. Oldham**
Reader's Note: Dryden and the Heroic Couplet	**281**	
Samuel Pepys	**282**	
	283	from *The Diary*
Jonathan Swift	**290**	
	291	**A Satirical Elegy on the Death of a Late Famous General**
	292	**A Description of a City Shower**
	294	**A Voyage to Brobdingnag, from** *Gulliver's Travels*
Comment: Size and Scale in *Gulliver's Travels*	**299**	
	307	**A Modest Proposal**
Joseph Addison	**312**	
	312	**Will Wimble, from** *The Spectator*
Sir Richard Steele	**315**	
	315	**Alexander Selkirk, from** *The Englishman*
Alexander Pope	**318**	
	319	from *The Rape of the Lock*
Reader's Note: *The Rape of the Lock* as a Mock Epic	**321**	
	326	**Epistle to Miss Blount**
	327	from *An Essay on Man*
Samuel Johnson	**328**	
	329	from the *Dictionary of the English Language*
	331	**Johnson's Letter to Chesterfield**
	332	from *The Life of Milton*
	335	**On the Death of Dr. Robert Levet**
James Boswell	**337**	
	338	from *The Life of Samuel Johnson, LL.D.*
Thomas Gray	**344**	
	344	**Elegy Written in a Country Churchyard**
	347	**Sonnet on the Death of Richard West**

The Changing English Language **348**

Unit 4 Review **349**
Content Review **349**
Concept Review **349**   from *A Journal of the Plague Year*/Daniel Defoe
Composition Review **353**

Unit 5
1780–1830

The **Romantics**

Time Line **355**
Background **356**
Robert Burns **360**
361   To a Mouse
361   John Anderson, My Jo
362   A Red, Red Rose
362   Auld Lang Syne
William Blake **363**
364   Introduction, from *Songs of Innocence*
364   Introduction, from *Songs of Experience*
Comment: Blake's Obscurities **364**
365   The Lamb, from *Songs of Innocence*
365   The Tyger, from *Songs of Experience*
366   Holy Thursday, from *Songs of Innocence*
366   Holy Thursday, from *Songs of Experience*
367   The Divine Image, from *Songs of Innocence*
367   The Human Abstract, from *Songs of Experience*
368   Proverbs of Hell, from *The Marriage of Heaven and Hell*
370   A New Jerusalem, from *Milton*
William Wordsworth **371**
372   Lines Composed a Few Miles Above Tintern Abbey
375   My Heart Leaps Up

	375	Composed upon Westminster Bridge, September 3, 1802
	376	It Is a Beauteous Evening
	376	The World Is Too Much with Us
	376	London, 1802
	377	Ode on Intimations of Immortality from Recollections of Early Childhood
Samuel Taylor Coleridge	383	
	384	Frost at Midnight
	385	Kubla Khan
Comment: Coleridge's Remarks about "Kubla Khan"	386	
George Gordon, Lord Byron	387	
	388	She Walks in Beauty
	388	So We'll Go No More A-Roving
	388	When We Two Parted
	390	from *Don Juan,* Canto I
Percy Bysshe Shelley	397	
	398	To Wordsworth
	398	Music, When Soft Voices Die
	398	England in 1819
	399	Ozymandias
	400	Ode to the West Wind
John Keats	402	
	403	On First Looking into Chapman's Homer
Comment: Did Keats Make a Blunder?	403	
	403	When I Have Fears
	404	La Belle Dame Sans Merci
	406	Ode to a Nightingale
	408	Ode on a Grecian Urn
Reader's Note: "Ode on a Grecian Urn"	409	
	410	To Autumn
	411	This Living Hand
Thomas De Quincey	412	
	413	On the Knocking at the Gate in *Macbeth*
Mary Shelley	416	
	417	from *Frankenstein*
Comment: The Gothic Novel	429	
The Changing English Language	431	
Unit 5 Review	432	
Content Review	432	
Concept Review	432	from *The Prelude,* Book I/William Wordsworth
Composition Review	435	

Unit 6
1830–1880

The **V***ictorians*

Time Line	**437**	
Background	**438**	
Alfred, Lord Tennyson	**442**	
	443	The Kraken
	443	The Lady of Shalott
Reader's Note: "The Lady of Shalott"	**444**	
	446	Ulysses
	448	Tears, Idle Tears
	448	from *In Memoriam:* 7, 27, 34, 54, 56, 106, 119
	452	The Passing of Arthur, from *Idylls of the King*
Reader's Note: "The Passing of Arthur"	**454**	
Robert Browning	**460**	
	461	Porphyria's Lover
	462	My Last Duchess
Reader's Note: The Dramatic Monologue	**463**	
	464	Prospice
Elizabeth Barrett Browning	**465**	
	465	from *Sonnets from the Portuguese:* 1, 28, 43
Matthew Arnold	**467**	
	468	Isolation
	468	Self-Dependence
	469	Dover Beach
Reader's Note: "Dover Beach"	**470**	
Charles Dickens	**472**	
	473	from *David Copperfield*
Comment: G. K. Chesterton on *David Copperfield*	**483**	
George Eliot	**489**	
	490	from *The Mill on the Floss*
John Ruskin	**499**	
	500	from *Praeterita*
The Changing English Language	**505**	
Unit 6 Review	**506**	
Content Review	**506**	
Concept Review	**506**	from *The Autobiography*/John Stuart Mill
Composition Review	**509**	

Unit 7

1880–1915

New Directions

Time Line 511	
Background 512	
Thomas Hardy 516	
516	**The Withered Arm**
Comment: Hardy's Geography 521	
536	**The Man He Killed**
536	**"Ah, Are You Digging on My Grave?"**
538	**In Time of "The Breaking of Nations"**
538	**Snow in the Suburbs**
Gerard Manley Hopkins 540	
541	**Pied Beauty**
542	**God's Grandeur**
543	**Spring and Fall: To a Young Child**
544	**Thou Art Indeed Just, Lord**
A. E. Housman 546	
547	**When I Was One-and-Twenty**
548	**Loveliest of Trees**
549	**To an Athlete Dying Young**
William Butler Yeats 550	
551	**When You Are Old**
Comment: Yeats and Ronsard 551	
Comment: Yeats on the source of "Innisfree" 552	
552	**The Lake Isle of Innisfree**
553	**Adam's Curse**
553	**Brown Penny**
555	**The Wild Swans at Coole**
556	**Sailing to Byzantium**
Reader's Note: "Sailing to Byzantium" 558	
559	**The Second Coming**
Reader's Note: "The Second Coming" 559	
560	**The Sorrow of Love (1892)**
560	**The Sorrow of Love (1927)**
Reader's Note: Yeats's Revision of "The Sorrow of Love" 561	

	562	**Girl's Song**
	562	**Young Man's Song**
	563	**Swift's Epitaph**
Joseph Conrad	**564**	
	565	**Youth**
Rudyard Kipling	**584**	
	584	**Mary Postgate**
H. G. Wells	**594**	
	594	**The Door in the Wall**
Saki	**605**	
	606	**Tobermory**
George Bernard Shaw	**611**	
	612	*Pygmalion*
	613	Act One
	619	Act Two
	633	Act Three
	641	Act Four
	646	Act Five
Comment: Shaw and Smollett	**649**	
	657	Epilogue
The Changing English Language	**665**	
Unit 7 Review	**666**	
Content Review	**666**	
Concept Review	**666**	from *The Importance of Being Earnest*/ Oscar Wilde
Composition Review	**669**	

Unit 8
1915–

The wentieth Century

Time Line	**671**	
Background	**672**	
Siegfried Sassoon	**676**	
	676	**Base Details**
	677	**Suicide in the Trenches**
	677	**Does It Matter?**

Wilfred Owen **678**

678 Dulce et Decorum Est

679 Anthem for Doomed Youth

679 Arms and the Boy

Comment: The Language of Heroism **680**

680 Disabled

Vera Brittain **682**

683 from *Testament of Youth*

T. S. Eliot **697**

698 The Hollow Men

Reader's Note: "The Hollow Men" **700**

700 Journey of the Magi

James Joyce **702**

702 Araby

Katherine Mansfield **707**

707 The Doll's House

Virginia Woolf **712**

713 Great Men's Houses

D. H. Lawrence **717**

718 Tickets, Please

726 The Piano

727 Piano

727 Snake

729 Intimates

Evelyn Waugh **730**

730 Winner Takes All

W. H. Auden **740**

741 The Unknown Citizen

742 Who's Who

743 Musée des Beaux Arts

744 In Memory of W. B. Yeats

Louis MacNeice **746**

746 The British Museum Reading Room

747 The Snow Man

Sylvia Townsend Warner **748**

749 The Phoenix

George Orwell **752**

753 Shooting an Elephant

757 from *Such, Such Were the Joys*

Stevie Smith **763**

764 The Frog Prince

765 Not Waving but Drowning

Dylan Thomas **766**

767 Fern Hill

Reader's Note: "Fern Hill" **769**

769 Do Not Go Gentle into That Good Night

Graham Greene **771**
771 **A Shocking Accident**
Frank O'Connor **776**
776 **My Oedipus Complex**
Philip Larkin **783**
783 **At Grass**
784 **Homage to a Government**
785 **The Explosion**
Ted Hughes **786**
786 **Pike**
787 **Bullfrog**
788 **Fern**
John Mortimer **789**
789 *The Dock Brief*
789 Scene One
800 Scene Two

The Changing English Language **807**
Unit 8 Review **808**
Content Review **808**
Concept Review **808** **Eveline**/James Joyce
Composition Review **811**

Definitions of Literary Terms **812**
Composition Guide **821**
Prewriting **821**
Revising **822**
Analyzing Literature **823**
Making Comparisons and Contrasts **824**
Evaluating Your Evidence **826**
Defending Your Position **827**
Developing Your Style **828**
Glossary **830**

Index of Vocabulary Exercises **854**
Index of Composition Assignments **854**
Index of Features **856**
Index of Authors and Titles **857**
Acknowledgments **861**

Items included in *Definitions of Literary Terms* are printed in **boldface** in editorial material on their first appearance and when necessary for reference.

Dates appear at the end of most selections. The date on the right is the date of publication; the date on the left is the date of composition. (The date following *Pygmalion* is that of the first English performance.)

Detail of the Bayeux Tapestry showing Saxon infantry at the Battle of Hastings.

Reign of Arthur?

- Roman withdrawal from Britain begins
- Sutton Hoo ship burial
- Lindisfarne founded

Beowulf composed

- Battle of Mount Badon

- Anglo-Saxon invasion begins

- Death of Hygelac, Beowulf's kinsman

Caedmon begins • writing poetry

- St. Patrick begins his Irish mission

Iona founded •

Synod of Whitby •

Bede • concludes his *History*

Roman Christian • missionaries arrive

Jarrow founded •

400   500   600   700

The Anglo-Saxons

Vikings invade •
East Anglia

• Vikings seize Normandy

• The Book
of Kells

• Battle of Clontarf

• Battle of Brunanburh

Reign of
Alfred the Great

Battle of Hastings •

Battle of Maldon •

Battle of Edington •

Vikings raid •
Lindisfarne

Domesday Book •

Beowulf manuscript

Anglo-Saxon Chronicle begins •

800   900   1000   1100

For the first eleven hundred years of its recorded history (55 B.C.–A.D. 1066), the island of Britain suffered a series of invasions. Warmed by the waters of the Gulf Stream, the southern part of the island invites the outsider with its mild climate and rich, easily-tilled soil. The long, irregular coastline, broken frequently by bays and rivers, provides safe anchorage for an invading fleet, which can then use the rivers to penetrate deep into the island's interior. Though each successive invasion brought bloodshed and sorrow, each also brought a new people with a new culture. Through conflict and amalgamation these different peoples created a nation.

Cave dwellers lived in the island 250,000 years ago. Invaders from the Iberian peninsula (modern Spain and Portugal) overwhelmed their fragile culture about 2000 B.C., creating a society sophisticated enough to erect Stonehenge, the circle of megaliths—huge upright stones—on Salisbury Plain. Then a new people appeared, the Celts. Migrating from further east, the Celtic peoples spread throughout Europe during the first millenium B.C. They occupied Austria, Switzerland, southern Germany, France, and Belgium, first reaching the British Isles around 600 B.C. The Celts built walled farms and hut villages. They used bronze (and later, iron) tools and grew crops. Separate Celtic tribes, each with its own king, warred with each other, erecting timber and stone fortresses and riding to battle in two-wheeled chariots. Their priests—called *druids*—conducted sacrificial rites in forest shrines.

In 55 B.C. Rome, already dominating the Mediterranean world, first tried to conquer Britain. In that year and the next Julius Caesar raided the is-land to punish the Britons for helping the Continental Celts in their struggle with the Romans. The account he later wrote of his raids begins the recorded history of Britain. Nearly a hundred years later, in A.D. 43, the emperor Claudius successfully invaded the island. Despite the rebellion led a few years later by Boudicca (or Boadicea), queen of one of the British tribes, the Romans eventually subdued most of Britain. The defeated tribes were driven into the highlands of Wales and Scotland. To keep them there, the Romans garrisoned the province of Britannia with three legions, and early in the second century the emperor Hadrian built a wall seventy-three miles long to protect the northern border.

Roman Britain became a prosperous colony with a population of three to four million people. Mining and manufacturing were carried on. Over one hundred towns served as administrative centers. Some of these had large buildings—meeting halls, law courts, temples, amphitheaters, and public baths—as well as elaborate sanitation systems. Straight, well-made Roman roads connected the towns. But Roman Britain was primarily a rural society. The sites of over six hundred large country villas have been discovered; there may have been as many as eight hundred.

The Romans ruled Britain for nearly four hundred years, but with the decline of Rome itself after the year 300, life in the province became more troubled. Warriors from Ireland, Scotland, and Germany periodically raided the British coast looking for plunder and taking slaves. (St. Patrick, a Briton, first reached Ireland as the captive of a group of these raiders.) In 410 Rome fell to an army of German barbarians, and the emperor Honorius sent a letter to the Roman Britons an-

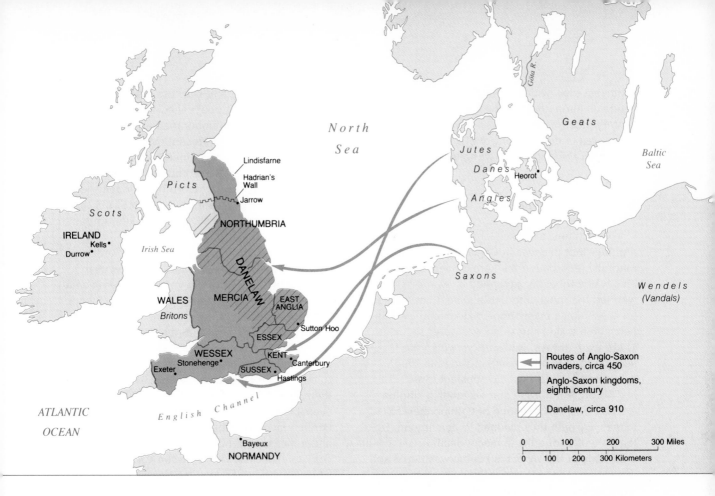

Within the map:

North Sea

Geats

Jutes

Danes · Heorot

Angles

Baltic Sea

Picts

Lindisfarne

Hadrian's Wall

Jarrow

Scots

IRELAND
Kells ·
Durrow ·

Irish Sea

NORTHUMBRIA

DANELAW

Saxons

Wendels
(Vandals)

WALES
Britons

MERCIA

EAST ANGLIA

· Sutton Hoo

ESSEX

WESSEX
Stonehenge ·

Exeter ·

KENT

· Canterbury

SUSSEX ·

Hastings

ATLANTIC OCEAN

English Channel

· Bayeux
NORMANDY

Göta R.

→ Routes of Anglo-Saxon invaders, circa 450

Anglo-Saxon kingdoms, eighth century

Danelaw, circa 910

0   100   200   300 Miles
0 100 200 300 Kilometers

---

nouncing that they must now see to their own defense.

The period after the Roman withdrawal is one of the most obscure in British history. Some of the Romanized Britons still thought of themselves as citizens of the empire; they still spoke Latin. There was an attempt to maintain the forms of provincial economic and political life. But soon towns were being abandoned, manufacturing declined, and tribal warfare reappeared. The Celtic language, with some words adapted from Latin, became once again the dominant tongue. Weak and divided, Britain once more stood open to foreign aggression.

To the east, across a relatively short span of sea, lay the coast of the European mainland, inhabited by a number of Germanic tribes, including the Angles, the Saxons, and the Jutes (see map above). They were vigorous warriors and skilled seamen, but their low-lying homelands, which had poor soil and were subject to frequent flooding from the North Sea, were inadequate for a growing population. Men of the Germanic tribes often served as mercenary soldiers. The Romans

had hired them to fight alongside the men of their legions against other barbarians. Tradition holds that two Jutish chieftains, Hengist and Horsa, were hired by the British king Vortigern to defend Britain's eastern seacoast. By 441 the tribesmen had a firm foothold at the mouth of the Thames, and groups of Angles, Saxons, and Jutes were spreading throughout eastern, central, and southern Britain, driving the Celtic inhabitants before them and settling their own people on the conquered land. As had happened during the Roman occupation, the defeated fled west into the highlands of Wales. It is among these people that the legend of Arthur arose. He may have been a Romanized Briton who for a time—in the late fifth and early sixth century—led his countrymen to victory over the Germanic tribesmen. But he was apparently defeated at last, though the earliest tradition about Arthur surrounds his fate with mystery: "The world's enigma, Arthur's grave" (see page 53).

In some areas of the northeast, the Anglo-Saxon peoples may have managed, after conquest, to coexist with the Britons, but in the southeast they evidently expelled the former inhabitants altogether. By the middle of the sixth century most of the southern lowland part of the island was under the control of a people we now call—after the Angles—the English.

Anglo-Saxon England

The culture of these Germanic settlers, during their first decades in England, seems to be faithfully recorded in the heroic poem *Beowulf.* This was a tribal society, ruled by warrior kings who led their men into battle. Defeat and capture for these kings meant immediate death. Even in peacetime a king's position was never secure. There were always rival warriors within the tribe seeking to take power, and outside the tribe neighboring kings posed a constant threat.

To protect himself and his lands a king gathered around him a retinue of fighting men called *thanes.* By oath they pledged to defend him. Defeat in battle for a thane meant death or slavery at the hands of the victors, so battle was fierce and unyielding. The king rewarded faithful service with treasure: rings, gold, and, especially, weapons. These gifts were more than payment, they were awards, a form of honor due to faithful thanes.

In this warrior society, the wealth given by a king usually came from robbing someone else. Bloodshed was common. Any offense caused by one thane had to be avenged, and one's king and fellow thanes had to come to one's aid. Hence there were endless feuds both between individuals and between tribes. Sometimes one party to a feud would be driven from the tribe, as is the case for the melancholy writer of "The Husband's Message."

King, thanes, wives, and servants gathered together in the royal quarters. These were not the stone-built castles of the medieval period, but rather a small cluster of wooden buildings surrounded by a stockade fence. The main structure was the mead-hall. *Mead* (mēd) is a fermented drink made from water, honey, malt, and yeast. Modern archaeologists have found the remains of one mead-hall that is eighty feet long, forty feet wide, its walls made of wooden planks over five inches thick, their bases sunk eight feet into the ground. Here king and warriors feasted, entertained by a singing poet called a *scop.* He composed his poetry extemporaneously—recounting both past history and present events. The scop was more than an entertainer. Fame and honor mattered greatly to these people, and it was the scop who preserved a record of their achievements for later generations. As in *Beowulf,* the warriors slept in the hall, while the king retired to a smaller outbuilding.

These relatively primitive warrior bands now spread over much of England, and took over some of the old Roman towns and governmental procedures, such as taxing, conscripting men for local armies, and building defensive dikes. The country was divided into a number of petty kingdoms. Soon, more ambitious kings began to assert an authority over other rulers, each claiming to be a ruling king, or *bretwalda.* The first of them, Aethelbert, who ruled from 560 to 616, seems to have already dreamed of a nationwide confederation of tribes which would bring unity and a measure of peace to the land. This system worked especially well between 632 and 796 when a series of *bretwaldas* from the Midland kingdom of Mercia (see map, page 3) reduced disorder and Anglo-Saxon culture could flourish for a time.

These efforts at achieving a form of unity and a modicum of peace found aid in the developing power and influence of the Christian church. Even in Roman days there had been Christian communities in Britain, though the invasion of pagan Germanic tribes nearly destroyed them. But in 597 St. Augustine, sent from Rome to convert England, reached King Aethelbert's kingdom in Kent, and during the next forty years Christian missionaries, despite setbacks, were able to convert most of the Anglo-Saxon kings and their people to Christianity.

The spread of Christianity was crucial for the development of Anglo-Saxon culture. The Church brought contact with the culture of the distant and ancient Mediterranean world. To the illiterate Germanic tribes it brought the essential skill for advanced culture—writing. Soon Anglo-Saxon monasteries were copying books from Rome, and beginning to produce the illuminated manuscripts for which they are so famous. The Church also served as an early force for unity and peace, trying to teach new values to these Germanic warrior-kings—compassion and cooperation, instead of arrogance and violence.

Anglo-Saxon culture reached a peak during the rule of the Mercian *bretwaldas* of the eighth century. From this era come most of the 30,000 lines of Anglo-Saxon poetry that have survived, as well as important works in prose such as Bede's Latin history of England. It is an era in which Anglo-Saxon and Christian cultures combined to form a new synthesis. This is dramatically evident for instance in the transfer of the complex, interlaced patterns of ornament, once used to decorate the regalia of pagan warrior-kings (see pages 34–35), to illuminate Bible manuscripts like the Lindisfarne Gospels or the Book of Durrow (see pages 49 and 45). This same synthesis appears in a poem such as "The Seafarer," where the worlds of thane and monk come together.

The Viking Era

The achievements of the eighth century were finally interrupted, however, by the appearance of yet another wave of invaders—the Vikings. They crossed the North Sea from Denmark and Norway, at first only a few boats seeking to plunder coastal monasteries and towns. These early raids of the 780s and 790s gave way to regular attacks after 835. Starting in 865, entire armies appeared, with fleets of up to 250 ships commanded by Danish kings. Between 867 and 877 the Vikings invaded and took over most of the northeast and central portions of England. Part or all of the Anglo-Saxon kingdoms of Northumbria, East Anglia, Mercia, and Essex were absorbed into the Danelaw (see map, page 3), a region where Danish rather than Anglo-Saxon law was in force.

The most successful English opponent of the Vikings was Alfred the Great (849–899). He ruled the one surviving Anglo-Saxon kingdom, Wessex, in southern England. To prevent the Vikings from seizing Wessex the way they had the Danelaw, he built what was essentially the first English navy, a fleet of longboats, each manned by sixty oarsmen. To repel unexpected attacks, he constructed fortified towns—*burhs* (bergs)—in a grid pattern throughout Wessex, manned by standing garrisons. After a series of setbacks, Alfred decisively

Manuscript illumination depicting Alfred the Great.

defeated the Vikings at Edington in 878, forcing them to retire within the Danelaw. In the uneasy peace that followed, Alfred was able to foster a second great era of Anglo-Saxon literary culture at his court, where along with the scholars he had invited from the continent, he studied and translated Latin works (including Bede's history of England) into Anglo-Saxon.

Alfred's successors were able to contain the Vikings, but essentially the England of the tenth century was divided between Scandinavian peoples in the north and east, and the surviving Anglo-Saxon peoples in the southeast and south. The struggle for control of this severed land was only halted for good by another invasion—that of the Norman, William the Conqueror.

The Anglo-Saxons dominated the history of England for 600 years. Over that period, so full of strife and confusion, this hardy people nevertheless managed to build some of the foundations for the culture of their land. They provided its language; began its literature; established traditions in law, government, and religion. They were the first Englishmen.

The *Beowulf*-Poet

Beowulf (bā′ō wŭlf) is the first masterpiece in English literature. But who wrote it and when? For what audience was it written and for what purpose? These are questions for which there will probably never be finally convincing answers. Even a close study of the poem, along with a more general consideration of the Anglo-Saxon culture it comes from, still leaves questions.

Although written in England, *Beowulf* describes the adventures of a hero who came from the southern part of what is now Sweden, to aid a people living in what is now Denmark. The poem contains scarcely a reference to England. However, it does name a known, historical figure, a Swedish king, Hygelac (hij′ə lak), who died in battle in 521. It must be that the stories *Beowulf* tells were a part of a culture which some Germanic tribe brought with them when they invaded and then settled in England, perhaps after Hygelac's death.

Around 725, according to the best modern estimates, someone took the **folk epic** of Beowulf as it had been orally transmitted by the Germanic tribes, and wrote it down in Anglo-Saxon. The *Beowulf*-poet has an absolute knowledge of the customs, the traditions, and the values of Anglo-Saxon society. But he is far more learned than the earlier *scops,* since he also knows something about the Hebrew scriptures (referring to the story of Cain and Abel). He may also have known something of Latin literature, since his poem seems to echo some passages from Virgil's *Aeneid.*

Modern readers debate the skill of the *Beowulf*-poet. Some think he was a naive, awkward writer. For example, the poem tells of two phases in Beowulf's life, his youth and his last days. They argue that there is only a loose connection between the two parts, and that the second half is less successful as poetry. Others, by contrast, insist that the two phases of the hero's life exactly balance each other and argue that the *Beowulf*-poet skillfully interrelates the two halves of his work.

Another debate continues over the *Beowulf*-poet's relationship to Christianity. The poem certainly does come from a Christianized culture. Yet, oddly, the poem never names either the pagan gods or Jesus. At Beowulf's death his most faithful follower simply says, " ' . . . long he shall lie / In the kindly care of the Lord of all.' "(lines 1827–1828). But is this a reference to the Christian Lord, or to the Northern god Odin?

The Old English scholar J. R. R. Tolkien argues that the *Beowulf*-poet was writing an intentionally *archaic* poem—that he knew about Christianity, and consequently would no longer name the heathen gods, but that because he was writing about the past he did not introduce any explicit references to the New Testament, even though its spirit helps to shape the way he thinks about life and death.

By simply examining what the *Beowulf*-poet wrote, it is possible to reach some conclusions. First, he is a writer in love with words and language. The poetry of *Beowulf* is densely packed, vigorous, full of sound. Further, the story it tells touches the receptive reader at the deepest levels. While the tales he narrates deal with heroic adventures somewhat akin to fairy tales (with their fire-breathing dragons), the *Beowulf*-poet is ultimately interested in the problems that trouble us most: the nature of success, true friendship, the final value to be found in life and in death. This poet has distinct, serious, and persuasive conclusions about these topics, which grow out of a story as richly suggestive as some of the greatest myths.

The tale of Beowulf's adventures begins with the legendary Scyld, founder of the Danish royal line. The child Scyld mysteriously comes to the Danish people sailing alone over the sea. As a young man he leads them through a series of battles in which they capture the mead-halls of surrounding tribes, subduing them and forcing them to pay tribute to the Danes. Thus Scyld establishes a pattern for success as a ruler. At his death the Danes return him to his mysterious source, setting his body, amid a heap of the treasures he has won, adrift at sea.

*B*eowulf

translated by **Charles W. Kennedy**

(The Danish Court and the Raids of Grendel)

Lo! we have listened to many a lay
Of the Spear-Danes'[1] fame, their splendor of
    old,
Their mighty princes, and martial deeds!
Many a mead-hall Scyld, son of Sceaf,[2]
5 Snatched from the forces of savage foes.
From a friendless foundling, feeble and
    wretched,
He grew to a terror as time brought change.
He throve under heaven in power and pride
Till alien peoples beyond the ocean
10 Paid toll and tribute. A good king he! . . .
'Tis by earning honor a man must rise
In every state. Then his hour struck,
And Scyld passed on to the peace of God.
    As their leader had bidden, whose word
    was law
15 In the Scylding realm[3] which he long had
    ruled,
His loving comrades carried him down
To the shore of ocean; a ring-prowed ship,
Straining at anchor and sheeted with ice,
Rode in the harbor, a prince's pride.
20 Therein they laid him, their well-loved lord,
Their ring-bestower, in the ship's embrace,
The mighty prince at the foot of the mast
Amid much treasure and many a gem
From far-off lands. No lordlier ship
25 Have I ever heard of, with weapons heaped,
With battle-armor, with bills and byrnies.[4]
On the ruler's breast lay a royal treasure
As the ship put out on the unknown deep.
With no less adornment they dressed him
    round
30 Or gift of treasure, than once they gave
Who launched him first on the lonely sea
While still but a child. A golden standard
They raised above him, high over head,
Let the wave take him on trackless seas.
35 Mournful their mood and heavy their hearts;
Nor wise man nor warrior knows for a truth
Unto what haven that cargo came. . . .

In the next lines, omitted here, the poet traces

the subsequent line of Danish kings, descended from Scyld: first his son Beowulf (not the hero of this poem, but a warrior of more ancient times); then his grandson Healfdene (hā'alf den ə). In time one of Healfdene's four children, Hrothgar (hrōth'gär), takes command of the kingdom. Following the young Scyld's earlier example, he begins by gathering about him a band of warriors.

To Hrothgar was granted glory in war,
Success in battle; retainers bold
40 Obeyed him gladly; his band increased
To a mighty host. Then his mind was moved
To have men fashion a high-built hall,
A mightier mead-hall than man had known,
Wherein to portion to old and young
45 All goodly treasure that God had given,
Save only the folk-land,[5] and lives of men.
His word was published to many a people
Far and wide o'er the ways of earth
To rear a folk-stead richly adorned;
50 The task was speeded, the time soon came
That the famous mead-hall was finished and
    done.
To distant nations its name was known,
The Hall of the Hart;[6] and the king kept well
His pledge and promise to deal out gifts,
55 Rings at the banquet. The great hall rose
High and horn-gabled,[7] holding its place. . . .
    Then an evil spirit who dwelt in the
    darkness
Endured it ill that he heard each day
The din of revelry ring through the hall,

---

1. ***Spear-Danes.*** The poet supplies the Danish people with various epithets (descriptive names) in the course of the poem, partly to help his lines alliterate, and perhaps partly as an attempt at characterization. In addition to "Spear-Danes," he calls them "Ring-Danes," "Bright-Danes," as well as "South-," "East-," and "West-Danes."
2. ***Scyld*** (shild), **son of Sceaf** (shāf), founder of the Danish line of kings, the *Scyldingas*, "descendants of Scyld." The Danish people are also referred to as "Scyldings." Scyld's name means "Shield, son of Sheaf," or perhaps "Shield with a sheaf."
3. ***Scylding realm***, Denmark.
4. ***bills and byrnies***, swords and shirts of chain mail.
5. ***folk-land***, common land (the public land owned by the community). Germanic tribal law reserved this land for grazing.
6. ***Hall of the Hart***, *Heorot* (hā'ə rot), Hrothgar's mead-hall. The hart (or stag) was a symbol of Germanic kingship. The head of the scepter found at Sutton Hoo (see pages 34–35) was a stag.
7. ***horn-gabled***, perhaps with roof ornaments carved to resemble a stag's antlers, or perhaps simply "wide-gabled."

60 The sound of the harp, and the scop's sweet
        song. . . .[8]
   They called him Grendel, a demon grim
   Haunting the fen-lands, holding the moors,
   Ranging the wastes, where the wretched
        wight
   Made his lair with the monster kin;
65 He bore the curse of the seed of Cain[9]
   Whereby God punished the grievous guilt
   Of Abel's murder. Nor ever had Cain
   Cause to boast of that deed of blood;
   God banished him far from the fields of men;
70 Of his blood was begotten an evil brood,
   Marauding monsters and menacing trolls,
   Goblins and giants who battled with God
   A long time. Grimly He gave them reward!
      Then at the nightfall the fiend drew near
75 Where the timbered mead-hall towered on
        high,
   To spy how the Danes fared after the feast.
   Within the wine-hall he found the warriors
   Fast in slumber, forgetting grief,
   Forgetting the woe of the world of men.
80 Grim and greedy the gruesome monster,
   Fierce and furious, launched attack,
   Slew thirty spearmen asleep in the hall,
   Sped away gloating, gripping the spoil,
   Dragging the dead men home to his den.
85 Then in the dawn with the coming of
        daybreak
   The war-might of Grendel was widely
        known.

   Mirth was stilled by the sound of weeping;
   The wail of the mourner awoke with day.
   And the peerless hero, the honored prince,[10]
90 Weighed down with woe and heavy of heart,
   Sat sorely grieving for slaughtered thanes,[11]
   As they traced the track of the cursed
        monster.
   From that day onward the deadly feud
   Was a long-enduring and loathsome strife.
95   Not longer was it than one night later
   The fiend returning renewed attack
   With heart firm-fixed in the hateful war,
   Feeling no rue for the grievous wrong.
   'Twas easy thereafter to mark the men
100 Who sought their slumber elsewhere afar,
   Found beds in the bowers, since Grendel's
        hate
   Was so baldly blazoned in baleful signs.
   He held himself at a safer distance
   Who escaped the clutch of the demon's
        claw.
105 So Grendel raided and ravaged the realm,

---

8. scop's sweet song. The *scop* (skop) was the tribe's storyteller, chanting his tales to the sound of the harp.
9. seed of Cain. In Genesis, Cain murders his brother Abel and is driven into the wilderness by God. According to legend his offspring included a variety of monsters. The poet mentions *eotenas*, "etans" (cannibal giants like trolls), *ylfe* "elves" (beautiful but evil in Germanic legend), and *orc-nēas*, "goblins" (animated corpses like zombies). Grendel may have been a creature of this last type (see note below).
10. honored prince, Hrothgar.
11. thanes, warriors. A thane ranked between an earl (a nobleman) and an ordinary freeman.

Comment: The Nature of Grendel

   Grendel's nature is, of course, diabolical from a Christian point of view: he is a member of the race of Cain, from whom all misshapen and unnatural beings were spawned, such as ogres and elves. He is a creature dwelling in the outer darkness, a giant, a cannibal. When he crawls off to die, he is said to join the rout of devils in Hell. However, he also appears to have roots in Scandinavian **folklore.** In Old Norse literature, monsters of his type make their appearance chiefly as *draugar*,[1] or animated corpses. They are ordinary folk who have been buried upright in cairns,[2] according to Norse custom, but if they harbor a grievance after death they will refuse to stay put and will roam about at night wreaking aimless vengeance. They are articulate and usually angry, in contrast to the silent zombies of Haiti. A draugr is supernaturally strong and invulnerable (being already dead) and will often have a mother called a *ketta,* or "she-cat," who is even more monstrous than he. Grendel, then, appears to be a blend of the *draugr* figure and a devilish monster from the world of Christian folklore.

From *Beowulf: A Dual-Language Edition*, translated by Howell D. Chickering, Jr. Garden City: Anchor Books, 1977

1. *draugar* (drou´gär), plural of *draugr* (drou´gər).
2. *cairns* (kernz, karnz). A cairn is a pile of stones serving as a memorial, tomb, or landmark.

One against all, in an evil war
Till the best of buildings was empty and still.
'Twas a weary while! Twelve winters' time
The lord of the Scyldings had suffered woe,
110 Sore affliction and deep distress.
And the malice of Grendel, in mournful lays,
Was widely sung by the sons of men,
The hateful feud that he fought with
       Hrothgar—
Year after year of struggle and strife,
115 An endless scourging, a scorning of peace
With any man of the Danish might.
No strength could move him to stay his
       hand,
Or pay for his murders;[12] the wise knew well
They could hope for no halting of savage
       assault.
120 Like a dark death-shadow the ravaging
       demon,
Nightlong prowling the misty moors,
Ensnared the warriors, wary or weak.
No man can say how these shades of hell
Come and go on their grisly rounds. . . .
125   The son of Healfdene was heavy-hearted,
Sorrowfully brooding in sore distress,
Finding no help in a hopeless strife;
Too bitter the struggle that stunned the
       people,
The long oppression, loathsome and grim.

The Geats (yā′əts) lived in southwestern Sweden. Hygelac, their king as the story begins, is
historical. He was famous for his unusual height.
("Even when he was twelve years old, no horse
could carry him," claims an eighth-century *Book
of Monsters*.) He died in battle while raiding the
European mainland in 521. Beowulf, as Hygelac's
thane, owes the king obedience. But hearing of
Grendel's attacks on the neighboring Danes, he
decides to go to their rescue, sailing from the valley of the Göta river in Sweden to the Danish island of Zealand, where Hrothgar has erected his
mead-hall, Heorot (see map, page 3).

(The Coming of Beowulf)

130   Then tales of the terrible deeds of Grendel
Reached Hygelac's thane in his home with
       the Geats;
Of living strong men he was the strongest,

Fearless and gallant and great of heart.
He gave command for a goodly vessel
135 Fitted and furnished; he fain would sail
Over the swan-road to seek the king
Who suffered so sorely for need of men.
And his bold retainers found little to blame
In his daring venture, dear though he was;
140 They viewed the omens, and urged him on.
Brave was the band he had gathered about
       him,
Fourteen stalwarts seasoned and bold,
Seeking the shore where the ship lay
       waiting,
A sea-skilled mariner sighting the landmarks.
145 Came the hour of boarding; the boat was
       riding
The waves of the harbor under the hill.
The eager mariners mounted the prow;
Billows were breaking, sea against sand.
In the ship's hold snugly they stowed their
       trappings,
150 Gleaming armor and battle-gear;
Launched the vessel, the well-braced bark,
Seaward bound on a joyous journey.
Over breaking billows, with bellying sail
And foamy beak, like a flying bird
155 The ship sped on, till the next day's sun
Showed sea-cliffs shining, towering hills
And stretching headlands. The sea was
       crossed,
The voyage ended, the vessel moored.
And the Weder people[13] waded ashore
160 With clatter of trappings and coats of mail;
Gave thanks to God that His grace had
       granted
Sea-paths safe for their ocean-journey.
   Then the Scylding coast guard watched
       from the sea-cliff
Warriors bearing their shining shields,
165 Their gleaming war-gear, ashore from the
       ship.
His mind was puzzled, he wondered much

---

12. murders. The poet here ironically refers to the Danes' inability to force Grendel to pay *wergild* ("man-payment"), or
compensation, to the families of the warriors he has murdered.
In Anglo-Saxon and Germanic law, a fixed price in money was
placed on the life of every individual in the tribe, from the churl
(the lowest-ranking freeman) to the king. This money was paid
by the killer's family to that of the victim to avoid blood feud.
13. Weder people, Weder-Géatas, "Storm-Geats," an epithet
for Beowulf's people.

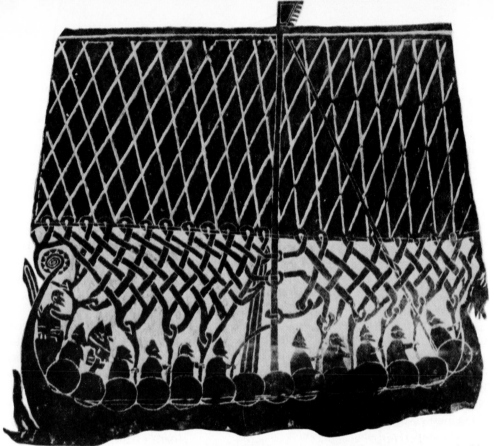

Carving of a Viking ship from a runic stone (a monument carved with runes, the letters of an ancient Germanic alphabet used from the A.D. 200s to the 1200s) located on the island of Gotland, off Sweden.

What men they were. On his good horse
  mounted,
Hrothgar's thane made haste to the beach,
Boldly brandished his mighty spear
170 With manful challenge: "What men are you,
Carrying weapons and clad in steel,
Who thus come driving across the deep
On the ocean-lanes in your lofty ship?
Long have I served as the Scylding outpost,
175 Held watch and ward at the ocean's edge
Lest foreign foemen with hostile fleet
Should come to harry our Danish home,
And never more openly sailed to these
  shores
Men without password, or leave to land.
180 I have never laid eyes upon earl on earth
More stalwart and sturdy than one of your
  troop,
A hero in armor; no hall-thane he
Tricked out with weapons, unless looks belie
  him
And noble bearing. But now I must know

185 Your birth and breeding, nor may you come
In cunning stealth upon Danish soil.
You distant-dwellers, you far seafarers,
Hearken, and ponder words that are plain:
'Tis best you hasten to have me know
190 Who your kindred and whence you come."
  The lord of the seamen gave swift reply,
The prince of the Weders unlocked his
  word-hoard:
"We are sprung of a strain of the Geatish
  stock,
Hygelac's comrades and hearth-companions.
195 My father was famous in many a folk-land,
A leader noble, Ecgtheow[14] his name! . . .
With loyal purpose we seek your lord,
The prince of your people, great Healfdene's
  son. . . .
You know if it's true, as we've heard it told,
200 That among the Scyldings some secret scather,

(*The text of* Beowulf *continues on page 12.*)

14. *Ecgtheow*, (edj'thā ō).

Reader's Note: The Poetry of *Beowulf*

To celebrate Beowulf's victory over Grendel, one of Hrothgar's thanes steps forward,

A minstrel mindful of saga and lay.
He wove his words in a winsome pattern,
Hymning the burden of Beowulf's feat,
Clothing the story in skillful verse.

This is the way the Anglo-Saxon minstrel, or *scop,* composed poetry—spontaneously, in oral form, before an audience. The audience usually knew the story already and, as the poet says, the scop's art was to "clothe" it in "skillful verse," shaping the words and the details of the story to fit the occasion. The *Beowulf-* poet could read and write, but he worked in the traditions of this older, oral poetry, as did the writers of the other Anglo-Saxon poetry which survives.

How were the scops able to stand in front of a crowd and compose acceptable poetry for hours at a time? First, they knew intimately a body of stories they had heard from earlier scops—the history and legends of their tribe. Probably they knew long passages of these earlier tellings by memory.

Second, they used a form of verse that is simple, direct, and relatively flexible, admirably fitted to oral composition. Printed above are a few lines from *Beowulf*[1] that serve to illustrate how Anglo-Saxon verse works. The symbol ð, called *edh* (eth), stands for the *th* sound.

Each line, as you can see, breaks in the middle. This pause is called a **caesura** (si zhŭr′ə, si zyŭr′ə). Thus each line of verse divides into two half-lines, the basic building-blocks of An-glo-Saxon poetry. Each half-line contains two stressed syllables and any number of un-stressed syllables; thus there are four strong beats to each line. Note the absence of rhym-ing. In Anglo-Saxon poetry a different type of repetition is used—that of the initial sound in several words of the line. This is called **allitera-tion.** Normally, alliterating consonants appear in the stressed syllables, one or two in the first half-line, and one in the second. Vowels in this

ALLITERATING WORDS

Fyrst forð ġewāt;
bāt under beorge.
on stefn stigon, —
sund wið sande;

flota wæs on ȳðum,
Beornas ġearwe
strēamas wundon,

HALF LINE

CAESURA

scheme can also alliterate. (Any vowel was considered as alliterating with any other.) Read a few lines aloud to yourself and you will begin to get a feel for its rhythm.

But **meter** is only one device which helped the scop to compose on the spot. Where was he to find the words which would fit his meter, and his alliterative **rhyme scheme**? First, the scop had what Anglo-Saxons called a *word-hoard,* a great store of words to choose from. Their language was rich in synonyms: *beorn, freca,* and *wiga* all mean "warrior," but with different **connotations,** derived from their origi-nal meanings as terms for "bear," "wolf," and "fighter." In addition, the scops had developed a special vocabulary for poetry over the centur-ies, words and phrases which fit neatly togeth-er. Alternate forms were available to fit a par-ticular context. For example, if the scop began a line with a stressed syllable starting with an *h* sound, he could say "on the sea" by the phrase *on hranrāde* ("on the whale-road"); whereas if he began with an *s* sound he could use *on seglrāde* ("on the sail-road").

Most of the compound words used in *Beo-wulf,* like "shield-bearer," are easily under-stood. But sometimes a more farfetched, rid-dling kind of descriptive comparison appears, for instance in the phrase "candle of heaven" (line 1060), used to describe the sun. This is a **kenning,** two or more words which name something by a metaphor. There are many of them in Anglo-Saxon poetry: "whale-road" for ocean, "peace-weaver" for woman, "light of battle" for sword.

---

1. A literal translation is: "Time forth went; floater was on waves, / boat under cliff. Warriors eager / on prow climbed; streams eddied, / sea against sand . . . " See lines 145–148 in your text.

Some stealthy demon in dead of night,
With grisly horror and fiendish hate
Is spreading unheard-of havoc and death.
Mayhap I can counsel the good, old king
205 What way he can master the merciless fiend,
If his coil of evil is ever to end
And feverish care grow cooler and fade—
Or else ever after his doom shall be
Distress and sorrow while still there stands
210 This best of halls on its lofty height.''
    Then from the saddle the coast guard
        spoke,
The fearless sentry: ''A seasoned warrior
Must know the difference between words
        and deeds,
If his wits are with him. I take your word
215 That your band is loyal to the lord of the
        Scyldings.
Now go your way with your weapons and
        armor,
And I will guide you; I'll give command
That my good retainers may guard your
        ship, . . .''
    Then the Geats marched on; behind at her
        mooring,
220 Fastened at anchor, their broad-beamed boat
Safely rode on her swinging cable.
Boar-heads[15] glittered on glistening helmets
Above their cheek-guards, gleaming with
        gold;
Bright and fire-hardened the boar held watch
225 Over the column of marching men.
Onward they hurried in eager haste
Till their eyes caught sight of the high-built
        hall,
Splendid with gold, the seat of the king,
Most stately of structures under the sun;
230 Its light shone out over many a land.
The coast guard showed them the shining
        hall,
The home of heroes; made plain the path;
Turned his horse; gave tongue to words:
''It is time to leave you! The mighty Lord
235 In His mercy shield you and hold you safe
In your bold adventure. I'll back to the sea
And hold my watch against hostile horde.''

(Beowulf's Welcome at Hrothgar's Court)

The street had paving of colored stone;
The path was plain to the marching men.

240 Bright were their byrnies, hard and
        hand-linked;
In their shining armor the chain mail sang
As the troop in their war-gear tramped to the
        hall.
The sea-weary sailors set down their shields,
Their wide, bright bucklers along the wall,
245 And sank to the bench. Their byrnies rang.
Their stout spears stood in a stack together
Shod with iron and shaped of ash.
'Twas a well-armed troop! Then a stately
        warrior
Questioned the strangers about their kin:
250 ''Whence come you bearing your burnished
        shields,
Your steel-gray harness and visored helms,
Your heap of spears? I am Hrothgar's
        herald,
His servant-thane. I have never seen
        strangers,
So great a number, of nobler mien.
255 Not exiles, I ween, but high-minded heroes
In greatness of heart have you sought out
        Hrothgar.''
Then bold under helmet the hero made
        answer,
Mighty of heart: ''We are Hygelac's men,
His board-companions; Beowulf is my name.
260 I will state my mission to Healfdene's son,
The noble leader, your lordly prince,
If he will grant approach to his gracious
        presence.''
And Wulfgar answered, the Wendel prince,[16]
Renowned for merit in many a land,
265 For war-might and wisdom: ''I will learn the
        wish
Of the Scylding leader, the lord of the
        Danes,
Our honored ruler and giver of rings,
Concerning your mission, and soon report
The answer our leader thinks good to give.''
270   He swiftly strode to where Hrothgar sat
Old and gray with his earls[17] about him;

---

15. **Boar-heads.** Germanic tribesmen regularly used the boar's head as a magical decoration for their helmets. The boar, sacred to the Norse god Frey, is a desperate fighter when cornered.
16. **Wulfgar . . . the Wendel prince.** Hrothgar's herald may have been one of the Vandals, a Germanic tribe living south of the Baltic between the Vistula and Oder rivers (see map, page 3).
17. **earls,** his chief men.

Crossed the floor and stood face to face
With the Danish king; he knew courtly
    custom.
Wulfgar saluted his lord and friend:
275 "Men from afar have fared to our land
Over ocean's margin—men of the Geats,
Their leader called Beowulf—seeking a
    boon,
The holding of parley, my prince, with thee.
O gracious Hrothgar, refuse not the favor!
280 In their splendid war-gear they merit well
The esteem of earls; he's a stalwart leader
Who led this troop to the land of the
    Danes."
    Hrothgar spoke, the lord of the Scyldings:
"Their leader I knew when he still was a
    lad. . . .
285 Seafaring men who have voyaged to
    Geatland
With gifts of treasure as token of peace,
Say that his hand-grip has thirty men's
    strength.
God, in His mercy, has sent him to save
    us—
So springs my hope—from Grendel's
    assaults.
290 For his gallant courage I'll load him with
    gifts!
Make haste now, marshal the men to the
    hall,
And give them welcome to Danish ground."
    Then to the door went the well-known
    warrior,
Spoke from the threshold welcoming words:
295 "The Danish leader, my lord, declares
That he knows your kinship; right welcome
    you come,
You stout sea-rovers, to Danish soil.
Enter now, in your shining armor
And vizored helmets, to Hrothgar's hall.
300 But leave your shields and the shafts of
    slaughter
To wait the issue and weighing of words."
    Then the bold one rose with his band
    around him,
A splendid massing of mighty thanes;
A few stood guard as the Geat gave bidding
305 Over the weapons stacked by the wall.
They followed in haste on the heels of their
    leader

Under Heorot's roof. Full ready and bold
The helmeted warrior strode to the hearth;
Beowulf spoke; his byrny glittered,
310 His war-net woven by cunning of smith:
"Hail! King Hrothgar! I am Hygelac's thane,
Hygelac's kinsman. Many a deed
Of honor and daring I've done in my youth.
This business of Grendel was brought to my
    ears
315 On my native soil. The seafarers say
This best of buildings, this boasted hall,
Stands dark and deserted when sun is set,
When darkening shadows gather with dusk.
The best of my people, prudent and brave,
320 Urged me, King Hrothgar, to seek you out;
They had in remembrance my courage and
    might.
Many had seen me come safe from the
    conflict,
Bloody from battle; five foes I bound
Of the giant kindred, and crushed their clan.
325 Hard-driven in danger and darkness of night
I slew the nicors[18] that swam the sea,
Avenged the woe they had caused the
    Weders,
And ended their evil—they needed the
    lesson!
And now with Grendel, the fearful fiend,
330 Single-handed I'll settle the strife!
Prince of the Danes, protector of Scyldings,
Lord of nations, and leader of men,
I beg one favor—refuse me not,
Since I come thus faring from far-off lands—
335 That I may alone with my loyal earls,
With this hardy company, cleanse Hart-Hall.
I have heard that the demon in proud disdain
Spurns all weapons; and I too scorn—
May Hygelac's heart have joy of the deed—
340 To bear my sword, or sheltering shield,
Or yellow buckler, to battle the fiend.
With hand-grip only I'll grapple with
    Grendel;
Foe against foe I'll fight to the death,
And the one who is taken must trust to
    God's grace! . . .
345 If death shall call me, he'll carry away
My gory flesh to his fen-retreat
To gorge at leisure and gulp me down,

---

18. *nicors,* water demons, animal in shape.

Soiling the marshes with stains of blood.
There'll be little need longer to care for my
   body!
350 If the battle slays me, to Hygelac send
This best of corselets that covers my breast,
   . . .
Finest of byrnies. Fate goes as Fate must!''
   Hrothgar spoke, the lord of the Scyldings:
"Deed of daring and dream of honor
355 Bring you, friend Beowulf, knowing our
   need! . . .
It is sorrow sore to recite to another
The wrongs that Grendel has wrought in the
   hall,
His savage hatred and sudden assaults.
My war-troop is weakened, my hall-band is
   wasted;
360 Fate swept them away into Grendel's grip.
But God may easily bring to an end
The ruinous deeds of the ravaging foe.
Full often my warriors over their ale-cups
Boldly boasted, when drunk with beer,
365 They would bide in the beer-hall the coming
   of battle,
The fury of Grendel, with flashing swords.
Then in the dawn, when the daylight
   strengthened,
The hall stood reddened and reeking with
   gore,
Bench-boards wet with the blood of battle;
370 And I had the fewer of faithful fighters,
Beloved retainers, whom Death had taken.
Sit now at the banquet, unbend your mood,
Speak of great deeds as your heart may spur
   you!''
   Then in the beer-hall were benches made
   ready
375 For the Geatish heroes. Noble of heart,
Proud and stalwart, they sat them down
And a beer-thane served them; bore in his
   hands
The patterned ale-cup, pouring the mead,
While the scop's sweet singing was heard in
   the hall.
380 There was joy of heroes, a host at ease,
A welcome meeting of Weder and Dane.

(Unferth Taunts Beowulf)

Then out spoke Unferth, Ecglaf's son,[19]
Who sat at the feet of the Scylding lord,

Picking a quarrel—for Beowulf's quest,
385 His bold sea-voyaging, irked him sore;
He bore it ill that any man other
In all the earth should ever achieve
More fame under heaven than he himself:
"Are you the Beowulf that strove with
   Breca[20]
390 In a swimming match in the open sea,
Both of you wantonly tempting the waves,
Risking your lives on the lonely deep
For a silly boast? No man could dissuade
   you,
Nor friend nor foe, from the foolhardy
   venture
395 Of ocean-swimming; with outstretched arms
You clasped the sea-stream, measured her
   streets,
With plowing shoulders parted the waves.
The sea-flood boiled with its wintry surges,
Seven nights you toiled in the tossing sea;
400 His strength was the greater, his swimming
   the stronger! . . .
Therefore, I ween, worse fate shall befall,
Stout as you are in the struggle of war,
In deeds of battle, if you dare to abide
Encounter with Grendel at coming of night.''
405   Beowulf spoke, the son of Ecgtheow:
"My good friend Unferth, addled with beer
Much have you made of the deeds of Breca!
I count it true that I had more courage,
More strength in swimming than any other
   man.
410 In our youth we boasted—we were both of
   us boys—
We would risk our lives in the raging sea.
And we made it good! We gripped in our
   hands
Naked swords, as we swam in the waves,
Guarding us well from the whales' assault.
415 In the breaking seas he could not outstrip
   me,
Nor would I leave him. For five nights long
Side by side we strove in the waters
Till racing combers wrenched us apart,

---

19. **Unferth, Ecglaf's** (edj'lafs) **son.** Unferth's name can be interpreted as "Peacebreaker." His role is a familiar one in heroic poetry, that of the king's rude retainer whose mockery provokes the hero to reveal himself. Something very like the Unferth episode occurs in Book VIII of the *Odyssey*.
20. **Breca** (brek'ə).

Freezing squalls, and the falling night,
420 And a bitter north wind's icy blast.
Rough were the waves; the wrath of the
 sea-fish
Was fiercely roused; but my firm-linked
 byrny,
The gold-adorned corselet that covered my
 breast,
Gave firm defense from the clutching foe.
425 Down to the bottom a savage sea-beast
Fiercely dragged me and held me fast
In a deadly grip; none the less it was granted
 me
To pierce the monster with point of steel.
Death swept it away with the swing of my
 sword.
430 The grisly sea-beasts again and again
Beset me sore; but I served them home
With my faithful blade as was well-befitting.
They failed of their pleasure to feast their fill
Crowding round my corpse on the
 ocean-bottom!
435 Bloody with wounds, at the break of day,
They lay on the sea-bench slain with the
 sword.
No more would they cumber the mariner's
 course
On the ocean deep. From the east came the
 sun,
Bright beacon of God, and the seas
 subsided;
440 I beheld the headlands, the windy walls.
Fate often delivers an undoomed earl
If his spirit be gallant! And so I was granted
To slay with the sword-edge nine of the
 nicors.
I have never heard tell of more terrible strife
445 Under dome of heaven in darkness of night,
Nor of man harder pressed on the paths of
 ocean.
But I freed my life from the grip of the foe
Though spent with the struggle. The billows
 bore me,
The swirling currents and surging seas,
450 To the land of the Finns.[21] And little I've
 heard
Of any such valiant adventures from you!
Neither Breca nor you in the press of battle
Ever showed such daring with dripping
 swords—

Though I boast not of it! But you stained
 your blade
455 With blood of your brothers, your closest of
 kin;
And for that you'll endure damnation in hell,
Sharp as you are! I say for a truth,
Son of Ecglaf, never had Grendel
Wrought such havoc and woe in the hall,
460 That horrid demon so harried your king,
If your heart were as brave as you'd have
 men think!
But Grendel has found that he never need fear
Revenge from your people, or valiant attack
From the Victor-Scyldings; he takes his toll,
465 Sparing none of the Danish stock.
He slays and slaughters and works his will
Fearing no hurt at the hands of the Danes!
But soon will I show him the stuff of the
 Geats,
Their courage in battle and strength in the
 strife;
470 Then let him who may go bold to the
 mead-hall
When the next day dawns on the dwellings
 of men,
And the sun in splendor shines warm from
 the south.''
Glad of heart was the giver of treasure,[22]
Hoary-headed and hardy in war;
475 The lordly leader had hope of help
As he listened to Beowulf's bold resolve.
 There was revel of heroes and high
 carouse,
Their speech was happy; and Hrothgar's
 queen,
Of gentle manners, in jewelled splendor
480 Gave courtly greeting to all the guests. . . .

(Beowulf Slays Grendel)

In the hall as of old were brave words
 spoken,
There was noise of revel; happy the host
Till the son of Healfdene would go to his
 rest.
He knew that the monster would meet in the
 hall

---

21. **Finns,** probably the Lapps, inhabitants of Finmarken,
around the North Cape in the northern extremity of Norway and
considerably above the Arctic Circle.
22. **giver of treasure,** Hrothgar.

485 Relentless struggle when light of the sun
Was dusky with gloom of the gathering
night,
And shadow-shapes crept in the covering
dark,
Dim under heaven. The host arose.
Hrothgar graciously greeted his guest,
490 Gave rule of the wine-hall, and wished him
well,
Praised the warrior in parting words:
"Never to any man, early or late,
Since first I could brandish buckler and
sword,
Have I trusted this ale-hall save only to you!
495 Be mindful of glory, show forth your
strength,
Keep watch against foe! No wish of your
heart
Shall go unfulfilled if you live through the
fight."
Then Hrothgar withdrew with his host of
retainers, . . .
The Geatish hero put all his hope
500 In his fearless might and the mercy of God!
He stripped from his shoulders the byrny of
steel,
Doffed helmet from head; into hand of thane
Gave inlaid iron, the best of blades;
Bade him keep well the weapons of war.
505 Beowulf uttered a gallant boast,
The stalwart Geat, ere he sought his bed:
"I count myself nowise weaker in war
Or grapple of battle than Grendel himself.
Therefore I scorn to slay him with sword,
510 Deal deadly wound, as I well might do!
Nothing he knows of a noble fighting,
Of thrusting and hewing and hacking of
shield,
Fierce as he is in the fury of war.
In the shades of darkness we'll spurn the
sword
515 If he dares without weapon to do or to die.
And God in His wisdom shall glory assign,
The ruling Lord, as He deems it right."
Then the bold in battle bowed down to his
rest,
Cheek pressed pillow; the peerless thanes
520 Were stretched in slumber around their lord.
Not one had hope of return to his home,

To the stronghold or land where he lived as
a boy.
For they knew how death had befallen the
Danes,
How many were slain as they slept in the
wine-hall. . . .
525 Then through the shades of enshrouding
night
The fiend came stealing; the archers slept
Whose duty was holding the horn-decked
hall—
Though one was watching—full well they
knew
No evil demon could drag them down
530 To shades under ground if God were not
willing.
But the hero watched awaiting the foe,
Abiding in anger the issue of war.
From the stretching moors, from the misty
hollows,
Grendel came creeping, accursed of God,
535 A murderous ravager minded to snare
Spoil of heroes in high-built hall.
Under clouded heavens he held his way
Till there rose before him the high-roofed
house,
Wine-hall of warriors gleaming with gold.
540 Nor was it the first of his fierce assaults
On the home of Hrothgar; but never before
Had he found worse fate or hardier
hall-thanes!
Storming the building he burst the portal,
Though fastened of iron, with fiendish
strength;
545 Forced open the entrance in savage fury
And rushed in rage o'er the shining floor.
A baleful glare from his eyes was gleaming
Most like to a flame. He found in the hall
Many a warrior sealed in slumber,
550 A host of kinsmen. His heart rejoiced;
The savage monster was minded to sever
Lives from bodies ere break of day,
To feast his fill of the flesh of men.
But he was not fated to glut his greed
555 With more of mankind when the night was
ended!
The hardy kinsman of Hygelac waited
To see how the monster would make his
attack.

The demon delayed not, but quickly
  clutched
A sleeping thane in his swift assault,
560 Tore him in pieces, bit through the bones,
Gulped the blood, and gobbled the flesh,
Greedily gorged on the lifeless corpse,
The hands and the feet. Then the fiend
  stepped nearer,
Sprang on the Sea-Geat lying outstretched,
565 Clasping him close with his monstrous claw.
But Beowulf grappled and gripped him hard,
Struggled up on his elbow; the shepherd of
  sins
Soon found that never before had he felt
In any man other in all the earth
570 A mightier hand-grip; his mood was
  humbled,
His courage fled; but he found no escape!
He was fain to be gone; he would flee to the
  darkness,
The fellowship of devils. Far different his
  fate
From that which befell him in former days!
575 The hardy hero, Hygelac's kinsman,
Remembered the boast he had made at the
  banquet;
He sprang to his feet, clutched Grendel fast,
Though fingers were cracking, the fiend
  pulling free.
The earl pressed after; the monster was
  minded
580 To win his freedom and flee to the fens.
He knew that his fingers were fast in the
  grip
Of a savage foe. Sorry the venture,
The raid that the ravager made on the hall.
  There was din in Heorot. For all the
  Danes,
585 The city-dwellers, the stalwart Scyldings,
That was a bitter spilling of beer!
The walls resounded, the fight was fierce,
Savage the strife as the warriors struggled.
The wonder was that the lofty wine-hall
590 Withstood the struggle, nor crashed to earth,
The house so fair; it was firmly fastened
Within and without with iron bands
Cunningly smithied; though men have said
That many a mead-bench gleaming with gold
595 Sprang from its sill as the warriors strove.
The Scylding wise men had never weened

That any ravage could wreck the building,
Firmly fashioned and finished with bone,
Or any cunning compass its fall,
600 Till the time when the swelter and surge of
  fire
Should swallow it up in a swirl of flame.[23]
  Continuous tumult filled the hall;
A terror fell on the Danish folk
As they heard through the wall the horrible
  wailing,
605 The groans of Grendel, the foe of God
Howling his hideous hymn of pain,
The hell-thane shrieking in sore defeat.
He was fast in the grip of the man who was
  greatest
Of mortal men in the strength of his might,
610 Who would never rest while the wretch was
  living,
Counting his life-days a menace to man.
  Many an earl of Beowulf brandished
His ancient iron to guard his lord,
To shelter safely the peerless prince.
615 They had no knowledge, those daring
  thanes,
When they drew their weapons to hack and
  hew,
To thrust to the heart, that the sharpest
  sword,
The choicest iron in all the world,
Could work no harm to the hideous foe.
620 On every sword he had laid a spell,
On every blade; but a bitter death
Was to be his fate; far was the journey
The monster made to the home of fiends.
  Then he who had wrought such wrong to
  men,
625 With grim delight as he warred with God,
Soon found that his strength was feeble and
  failing
In the crushing hold of Hygelac's thane.
Each loathed the other while life should last!
There Grendel suffered a grievous hurt,
630 A wound in the shoulder, gaping and wide;
Sinews snapped and bone-joints broke,
And Beowulf gained the glory of battle.
Grendel, fated, fled to the fens,
To his joyless dwelling, sick unto death.

---

23. swirl of flame. This is one of a number of allusions in the
poem to the later burning of Heorot.

635 He knew in his heart that his hours were
        numbered,
His days at an end. For all the Danes
Their wish was fulfilled in the fall of
        Grendel.
The stranger from far, the stalwart and
        strong,
Had purged of evil the hall of Hrothgar,
640 And cleansed of crime; the heart of the hero

Joyed in the deed his daring had done.
The lord of the Geats made good to the
        East-Danes
The boast he had uttered; he ended their ill,
And all the sorrow they suffered long
645 And needs must suffer—a foul offense.
The token was clear when the bold in battle
Laid down the shoulder and dripping claw—
Grendel's arm—in the gabled hall!

Discussion

1. In lines 38-55 the *Beowulf*-poet portrays a successful king. Through Hrothgar's achievements, the poet suggests his own system of values. What seems to matter most to people in his society?

2. What does Grendel look like? Does the poet describe him in detail or leave him to the reader's imagination? Cite some lines where a detail of Grendel's appearance is used to create horror.

3. What are Beowulf's motives in aiding Hrothgar? Explain how they suggest an Anglo-Saxon idea of heroism.

4. During the account of the fight between Beowulf and Grendel, the narrative **point of view** keeps shifting. Look closely at the passages which begin at lines 533, 556, 602, 624, 636, and 640, and determine whose viewpoint appears in each. Then discuss the consequences of this shifting perspective.

5. Beowulf chooses to fight Grendel alone and unarmed. What are his reasons?

(The Joy of the Danes)

When morning came, as they tell the tale,
650 Many a warrior hastened to hall,
Folk-leaders faring from far and near
Over wide-running ways, to gaze at the
        wonder,
The trail of the demon. Nor seemed his
        death
A matter of sorrow to any man
655 Who viewed the tracks of the vanquished
        monster
As he slunk weary-hearted away from the
        hall,
Doomed and defeated and marking his flight
With bloody prints to the nicors' pool.
The crimson currents bubbled and heaved
660 In eddying reaches reddened with gore;
The surges boiled with the fiery blood.
But the monster had sunk from the sight of
        men.
In that fenny covert the cursed fiend
Not long thereafter laid down his life,
665 His heathen spirit; and hell received him.
    Then all the comrades, the old and young,

The brave of heart, in a blithesome band
Came riding their horses home from the
        mere.
Beowulf's prowess was praised in song;
670 And many men stated that south or north,
Over all the world, or between the seas,
Or under the heaven, no hero was greater.
    Then spoke Hrothgar; hasting to hall
He stood at the steps, stared up at the roof
675 High and gold-gleaming; saw Grendel's
        hand:
"Thanks be to God for this glorious sight!
I have suffered much evil, much outrage
        from Grendel,
But the God of glory works wonder on
        wonder.
I had no hope of a haven from sorrow
680 While this best of houses stood badged with
        blood,
A woe far-reaching for all the wise
Who weened that they never could hold the
        hall
Against the assaults of devils and demons.

But now with God's help this hero has
    compassed
685 A deed our cunning could no way contrive.
I will keep you, Beowulf, close to my heart
In firm affection; as son to father
Hold fast henceforth to this foster-kinship.
You shall know not want of treasure or
    wealth
690 Or goodly gift that your wish may crave,
While I have power. For poorer deeds
I have granted guerdon,[24] and graced with
    honor
Weaker warriors, feebler in fight.
You have done such deeds that your fame
    shall flourish
695 Through all the ages! God grant you still
All goodly grace as He gave before.''
    Beowulf spoke, the son of Ecgtheow:
''By favor of God we won the fight,
Did the deed of valor, and boldly dared
700 The might of the monster. I would you could
    see
The fiend himself lying dead before you!
I thought to grip him in stubborn grasp
And bind him down on the bed of death,
There to lie straining in struggle for life,
705 While I gripped him fast lest he vanish
    away.

But I might not hold him or hinder his going
For God did not grant it, my fingers failed.
Too savage the strain of his fiendish
    strength!
To save his life he left shoulder and claw,
710 The arm of the monster, to mark his track,
But he bought no comfort; no whit thereby
Shall the wretched ravager racked with sin,
The loathsome spoiler, prolong his life.
A deep wound holds him in deadly grip,
715 In baleful bondage; and black with crime
The demon shall wait for the day of doom
When the God of glory shall give decree.''
    Then slower of speech was the son of
    Ecglaf,
More wary of boasting of warlike deeds,
720 While the nobles gazed at the grisly claw,
The fiend's hand fastened by hero's might
On the lofty roof. Most like to steel
Were the hardened nails, the heathen's
    hand-spurs,
Horrible, monstrous; and many men said
725 No tempered sword, no excellent iron,
Could have harmed the monster or hacked
    away
The demon's battle-claw dripping with
    blood.

---

24. *guerdon,* reward.

The Snettisham Torque, 1st century, B.C. A torque (or
torc) is an ornament to be worn around the neck.

(The Feast)

In joyful haste was Heorot decked
And a willing host of women and men
730 Gaily dressed and adorned the guest-hall.
Splendid hangings with sheen of gold
Shone on the walls, a glorious sight
To eyes that delight to behold such wonders.
The shining building was wholly shattered
735 Though braced and fastened with iron bands;
Hinges were riven; the roof alone
Remained unharmed when the horrid
　　monster,
Foul with evil, slunk off in flight. . . .
　　Soon was the time when the son of
　　Healfdene
740 Went to the wine-hall; he fain would join
With happy heart in the joy of feasting.
I never have heard of a mightier muster
Of proud retainers around their prince. . . .
Upon Beowulf, then, as a token of triumph,
745 Hrothgar bestowed a standard of gold,
A banner embroidered, a byrny and helm.
In sight of many, a costly sword
Before the hero was borne on high; . . .
On the crest of the helmet a crowning
　　wreath,
750 Woven of wire-work, warded the head
Lest tempered swordblade, sharp from the
　　file,
Deal deadly wound when the shielded
　　warrior
Went forth to battle against the foe.
Eight horses also with plated headstalls
755 The lord of heroes bade lead into hall;
On one was a saddle skillfully fashioned
And set with jewels, the battle-seat
Of the king himself, when the son of
　　Healfdene
Would fain take part in the play of swords;
760 Never in fray had his valor failed,
His kingly courage, when corpses were
　　falling. . . .
　　Then on the ale-bench to each of the earls
Who embarked with Beowulf, sailing the
　　sea-paths,
The lord of princes dealt ancient heirlooms,
765 Gift of treasure, and guerdon of gold
To requite his slaughter whom Grendel slew,
As he would have slain others, but all-wise
　　God

And the hero's courage had conquered Fate.
　. . .
Stewards poured wine from wondrous
　　vessels;
770 And Wealhtheow,[25] wearing a golden crown,
Came forth in state where the two were
　　sitting,
Courteous comrades, uncle and nephew,[26]
Each true to the other in ties of peace. . . .
Wealhtheow spoke to the warrior host:
775 "Take, dear Beowulf, collar and corselet,
Wear these treasures with right good will!
Thrive and prosper and prove your might!
Befriend my boys with your kindly counsel;
I will remember and I will repay.
780 You have earned the undying honor of
　　heroes
In regions reaching as far and wide
As the windy walls that the sea encircles.
May Fate show favor while life shall last!
I wish you wealth to your heart's content;
785 In your days of glory be good to my sons!
Here each hero is true to other,
Gentle of spirit, loyal to lord,
Friendly thanes and a folk united,
Wine-cheered warriors who do my will."

(The Troll-Wife Avenges Grendel)

790 Then she went to her seat. At the fairest
　　of feasts
Men drank of the wine-cup, knowing not
　　Fate,
Nor the fearful doom that befell the earls
When darkness gathered, and gracious
　　Hrothgar
Sought his dwelling and sank to rest.
795 A host of heroes guarded the hall
As they oft had done in the days of old.
They stripped the benches and spread the
　　floor
With beds and bolsters. But one of the
　　beer-thanes
Bowed to his hall-rest doomed to death.
800 They set at their heads their shining shields,
Their battle-bucklers; and there on the bench

---

25. Wealhtheow (wāʹal thā ō), Hrothgar's wife, the queen of the Danes.
26. uncle and nephew, Hrothgar and Hrothulf, the son of Hrothgar's younger brother Halga.

Above each hero his towering helmet,
His spear and corselet hung close at hand.
It was ever their wont to be ready for war
805 At home or in field, as it ever befell
That their lord had need. 'Twas a noble
    race!
    Then they sank to slumber. But one paid
    dear
For his evening rest, as had often happened
When Grendel haunted the lordly hall
810 And wrought such ruin, till his end was
    come,
Death for his sins; it was easily seen,
Though the monster was slain, an avenger
    survived
Prolonging the feud, though the fiend had
    perished.
The mother of Grendel, a monstrous hag,
815 Brooded over her misery, doomed to dwell
In evil waters and icy streams. . . .
But rabid and raging his mother resolved
On a dreadful revenge for the death of her
    son!
    She stole to the hall where the Danes were
    sleeping,
820 And horror fell on the host of earls
When the dam of Grendel burst in the door.
But the terror was less as the war-craft is
    weaker,
A woman's strength, than the might of a
    man . . .
As soon as discovered, the hag was in haste
825 To fly to the open, to flee for her life.
One of the warriors she swiftly seized,
Clutched him fast and made off to the fens.
He was of heroes the dearest to Hrothgar,
The best of comrades between two seas;
830 The warrior brave, the stouthearted
    spearman,
She slew in his sleep. Nor was Beowulf
    there;
But after the banquet another abode
Had been assigned to the glorious Geat.
There was tumult in Heorot. She tore from
    its place
835 The bloodstained claw. Care was renewed!
It was no good bargain when both in turn
Must pay the price with the lives of friends!
    Then the white-haired warrior, the aged
    king,

Was numb with sorrow, knowing his thane
840 No longer was living, his dearest man dead.
Beowulf, the brave, was speedily
    summoned. . . .
The hero came tramping into the hall
With his chosen band—the boards
    resounded—
Greeted the leader, the Ingwine[27] lord,
845 And asked if the night had been peaceful and
    pleasant.
    Hrothgar spoke, the lord of the Scyldings:
"Ask not of pleasure; pain is renewed
For the Danish people. Æschere[28] is dead!
    . . .
He was my comrade, closest of counsellors,
850 My shoulder-companion as side by side
We fought for our lives in the welter of war,
In the shock of battle when boar-helms
    crashed.
As an earl should be, a prince without peer,
Such was Æschere, slain in the hall
855 By the wandering demon! I know not
    whither
She fled to shelter, proud of her spoil,
Gorged to the full. She avenged the feud. . . .
    Oft in the hall I have heard my people,
Comrades and counselors, telling a tale
860 Of evil spirits their eyes have sighted,
Two mighty marauders who haunt the
    moors.
One shape, as clearly as men could see,
Seemed woman's likeness, and one seemed
    man,
An outcast wretch of another world,
865 And huger far than a human form.
Grendel my countrymen called him, not·
    knowing
What monster-brood spawned him, what sire
    begot.
Wild and lonely the land they live in,
Windswept ridges and wolf-retreats,
870 Dread tracts of fen where the falling torrent
Downward dips into gloom and shadow
Under the dusk of the darkening cliff.
Not far in miles lies the lonely mere
Where trees firm-rooted and hung with frost
(The text of Beowulf *continues on page 24.)*

---

27. Ingwine (ing'wi nə), literally, "friends of Ing," an epithet for
the Danes. Ing was an epithet of the Norse god Frey.
28. Æschere (ash'her rə).

Reader's Note: Translating *Beowulf*

At first glance, most modern readers of English would think that a passage from *Beowulf,* like that below, is in a foreign language. A closer look, however, suggests something a little different. In the first line is the word *lond,* in the second *wulf,* in the third *strēam.* A little guesswork will suggest modern English equivalents for these words. The lines below are translated by Charles Kennedy on pages 21–24 (lines 868–884). Four other translations of this same passage appear on page 23. Notice how these five translations differ.

> Hīe dȳgel lond
> warigeað, wulf-hleoþu,   windi*ge* næssas,
> frēcne fen-gelād,   ðǣr fyrgen-strēam
> under næssa genipu   niþer gewīteð,
> flōd under foldan.   Nis þæt feor heonon
> mīl-gemearces,   þæt se mere stan[*d*]eð
> ofer þǣm hongiað   hrinde bearwas,
> wudu wyrtum fæst   wæter oferhelmað.
> Þǣr mæg nihta gehwǣm   nīð-wundor sēon,
> fȳr on flōde.   Nō þæs frōd leofað
> gumena bearna   þæt þone grund wite.
> Ðēah þe hǣð-stapa   hundum geswenced,
> heorot hornum trum   holt-wudu sēce,
> feorran geflȳmed,   ǣr hē feorh seleð,
> aldor on ōfre,   ǣr hē in wille,
> hafelan [*hȳdan*].   Nis þæt hēoru stōw!

In line 12 of the Anglo-Saxon, the poet uses the kenning *hǣð-stapa* to describe a male deer. Both Spaeth and Kennedy choose a very literal, only slightly modernized version of the original words: "heather-stepper." Crossley-Holland uses a slightly different form: "moor stalker." These odd phrases can puzzle some readers, so to make it easier Alexander stretches the kenning out until it becomes a whole image: "The hart that roams the heath ..." Now its meaning may be clearer, but the translation doesn't sound very much like the original. Raffel avoids the difficulty, and the poetic force, of the kenning altogether—in his version it becomes just "A deer."

At the beginning of line 10 in the Anglo-Saxon is the phrase *fȳr on flōde,* part of a description of the frightful lake where Grendel and his mother live. The word *on* can be translated in various ways, and so, depending upon whose translation you turn to, the fire is "beneath" (Spaeth), "in" (Kennedy and Alexander), or "on" (Crossley-Holland) the water. Again Raffel ingeniously turns to a different solution: "At night that lake / Burns like a torch."

As the irregular line lengths suggest, all these translators try not only to convey the ideas, but also the quality of the poetry in *Beowulf.* While you may not be able to understand the third line of the Anglo-Saxon here, it is easy enough to notice the alliteration created by the repeated initial *f* sound, as well as the caesura, the gap in the middle of the line that indicates a pause. Now the question is, can the translators somehow imitate these sounds and rhythms in a form the modern reader can understand? Alexander's translation is very close to the order and the literal meaning of the original words: "and treacherous fen-paths: a torrent of water." There are four *t* sounds here, but only two in stressed syllables. There is alliteration, then, but it is not very pronounced. Spaeth employs a different solution, intertwining the repetition of the *m* and *s* sounds: "Ledges of mist, where mountain torrents . . ."

Every good translation makes a statement of some kind about the text it translates. For example, when Raffel uses a plain word like "deer" he emphasizes fact and action; when Kennedy uses "hart" he suggests a more elevated and remote world. Spaeth's "To die on the brink ere he brave the plunge" is certainly different from Alexander's "will die there / sooner than swim"; the one echoes an older tradition of poetic speech, while the other sounds almost like slang.

J. Duncan Spaeth (1921)

Lonely and waste is the land they inhabit,
Wolf-cliffs wild and windy headlands,
Ledges of mist, where mountain torrents
Downward plunge to dark abysses,
5 And flow unseen. Not far from here
O'er the moorland in miles, a mere expands.
Spray-frosted trees o'erspread it, and hang
O'er the water with roots fast wedged in the
     rocks.
There nightly is seen, beneath the flood,
10 A marvelous light. There lives not the man
Has fathomed the depth of the dismal mere.
Though the heather-stepper, the strong-horned
     stag,
Seek this cover, forspent with the chase,
Tracked by the hounds, he will turn at bay,
15 To die on the brink ere he brave the plunge,
Hide his head in the haunted pool.

From *Old English Poetry*, translated by J. Duncan Spaeth. Princeton: Princeton University Press, 1921.

Kevin Crossley-Holland (1968)

. . .These two live
in a little-known country, wolf-slopes, windswept
     headlands,
perilous paths across the boggy moors, where a
     mountain stream
plunges under the mist-covered cliffs,
5 rushes through a fissure. It is not far from here,
if measured in miles, that the lake stands
shadowed by trees stiff with hoar-frost.
A wood, firmly-rooted, frowns over the water.
There, night after night, a fearful wonder may be
     seen—
10 fire on the water; no man alive
is so wise as to know the nature of its depths.
Although the moor-stalker, the stag with strong
     horns,
when harried by hounds will make for the wood,
pursued from afar, he will succumb
15 to the hounds on the brink, rather than plunge in
and save his head. That is not a pleasant place.

From *Beowulf*, translated by Kevin Crossley-Holland. Translation copyright © 1968 by Kevin Crossley-Holland. Introduction copyright © 1968 by Bruce Mitchell. Reprinted by permission of Farrar, Straus & Giroux, Inc. and Macmillan, London and Basingstoke.

Burton Raffel (1963)

They live in secret places, windy
Cliffs, wolf-dens where water pours
From the rocks, then runs underground, where
     mist
Steams like black clouds, and the groves of trees
5 Growing out over their lake are all covered
With frozen spray, and wind down snakelike
Roots that reach as far as the water
And help keep it dark. At night that lake
Burns like a torch. No one knows its bottom,
10 No wisdom reaches such depths. A deer,
Hunted through the woods by packs of hounds,
A stag with great horns, though driven through
     the forest
From faraway places, prefers to die
On those shores, refuses to save its life
15 In that water. It isn't far, nor is it
A pleasant spot!

From *Beowulf* translated by Burton Raffel. Copyright © 1963 by Burton Raffel. Reprinted by arrangement with New American Library, Inc., New York.

Michael Alexander (1973)

          Mysterious is the region
they live in—of wolf-fells, wind-picked moors
and treacherous fen-paths: a torrent of water
pours down dark cliffs and plunges into the earth,
5 an underground flood. It is not far from here,
in terms of miles, that the Mere lies,
overcast with dark, crag-rooted trees
that hang in groves hoary with frost.
An uncanny sight may be seen at night there
10 —the fire in the water! The wit of living men
is not enough to know its bottom.
The hart that roams the heath, when hounds have
     pressed him
long and hard, may hide in the forest
his antlered head; but the hart will die there
15 sooner than swim and save his life;
he will sell it on the brink there, for it is not a
     safe place.

From *Beowulf*, translated by Michael Alexander (Penguin Classics 1973) pages 94–95. Copyright © 1973 by Michael Alexander. Reprinted by permission of Penguin Books Ltd.

875 Overshroud the wave with shadowing gloom.
And there a portent appears each night,
A flame in the water; no man so wise
Who knows the bound of its bottomless
    depth.
The heather-stepper, the horned stag,
880 The antlered hart hard driven by hounds,
Invading that forest in flight from afar
Will turn at bay and die on the brink
Ere ever he'll plunge in that haunted pool.
'Tis an eerie spot! Its tossing spray
885 Mounts dark to heaven when high winds stir
The driving storm, and the sky is murky,
And with foul weather the heavens weep.
On your arm only rests all our hope!
Not yet have you tempted those terrible
    reaches,
890 The region that shelters that sinful wight.
Go if you dare! I will give requital
With ancient treasure and twisted gold,
As I formerly gave in guerdon of battle,
If out of that combat you come alive.''
895   Beowulf spoke, the son of Ecgtheow:
"Sorrow not, brave one! Better for man
To avenge a friend than much to mourn.
All men must die; let him who may
Win glory ere death. That guerdon is best
900 For a noble man when his name survives
    him.
Then let us rise up, O ward of the realm,
And haste us forth to behold the track
Of Grendel's dam.²⁹ And I give you pledge
She shall not in safety escape to cover,
905 To earthy cavern, or forest fastness,
Or gulf of ocean, go where she may.
This day with patience endure the burden
Of every woe, as I know you will.''
Up sprang the ancient, gave thanks to God
910 For the heartening words the hero had
    spoken.

(Beowulf Slays the Troll-Wife)

   Quickly a horse was bridled for Hrothgar,
A mettlesome charger with braided mane;
In royal splendor the king rode forth
Mid the trampling tread of a troop of
    shieldmen.
915 The tracks lay clear where the fiend had
    fared

Over plain and bottom and woodland path,
Through murky moorland making her way
With the lifeless body, the best of thanes
Who of old with Hrothgar had guarded the
    hall.
920 By a narrow path the king pressed on
Through rocky upland and rugged ravine,
A lonely journey, past looming headlands,
The lair of monster and lurking troll.
Tried retainers, a trusty few,
925 Advanced with Hrothgar to view the ground.
Sudden they came on a dismal covert
Of trees that hung over hoary stone,
Over churning water and bloodstained wave.
Then for the Danes was the woe the deeper,
930 The sorrow sharper for Scylding earls,
When they first caught sight, on the rocky
    sea-cliff,
Of slaughtered Æschere's severed head.
The water boiled in a bloody swirling
With seething gore as the spearmen gazed.
935 The trumpet sounded a martial strain;
The shield-troop halted. Their eyes beheld
The swimming forms of strange sea-dragons,
Dim serpent shapes in the watery depths,
Sea-beasts sunning on headland slopes;
940 Snakelike monsters that oft at sunrise
On evil errands scour the sea.
Startled by tumult and trumpet's blare,
Enraged and savage, they swam away;
But one the lord of the Geats brought low,
945 Stripped of his sea-strength, despoiled of
    life,
As the bitter bow-bolt pierced his heart.
His watery-speed grew slower, and ceased,
And he floated, caught in the clutch of
    death.
Then they hauled him in with sharp-hooked
    boar-spears,
950 By sheer strength grappled and dragged him
    ashore,
A wondrous wave-beast; and all the array
Gathered to gaze at the grisly guest.
   Beowulf donned his armor for battle,
Heeded not danger; the hand-braided byrny,
955 Broad of shoulder and richly bedecked,
Must stand the ordeal of the watery depths.
Well could that corselet defend the frame

---

29. *dam,* mother.

Lest hostile thrust should pierce to the
    heart.
Or blows of battle beat down the life.
960 A gleaming helmet guarded his head
As he planned his plunge to the depths of
    the pool
Through the heaving waters—a helm
    adorned
With lavish inlay and lordly chains,
Ancient work of the weapon-smith
965 Skillfully fashioned, beset with the boar,
That no blade of battle might bite it through.
Not the least or the worst of his
    war-equipment
Was the sword the herald of Hrothgar
    loaned
In his hour of need—Hrunting[30] its name—
970 An ancient heirloom, trusty and tried;
Its blade was iron, with etched design,
Tempered in blood of many a battle.
Never in fight had it failed the hand
That drew it daring the perils of war,
975 The rush of the foe. Not the first time then
That its edge must venture on valiant deeds.
    . . .
Beowulf spoke, the son of Ecgtheow:
"O gracious ruler, gold-giver to men,
As I now set forth to attempt this feat,
980 Great son of Healfdene, hold well in mind
The solemn pledge we plighted of old,
That if doing your service I meet my death
You will mark my fall with a father's love.
Protect my kinsmen, my trusty comrades,
985 If battle take me. And all the treasure
You have heaped on me bestow upon
    Hygelac. . . ."
    After these words the prince of the
    Weders
Awaited no answer, but turned to the task,
Straightway plunged in the swirling pool.
990 Nigh unto a day he endured the depths
Ere he first had view of the vast sea-bottom.
Soon she found, who had haunted the flood,
A ravening hag, for a hundred half-years,
Greedy and grim, that a man was groping
995 In daring search through the sea-troll's
    home.
Swift she grappled and grasped the warrior
With horrid grip, but could work no harm,
No hurt to his body; the ring-locked byrny

Cloaked his life from her clutching claw;
1000 Nor could she tear through the tempered
    mail
With her savage fingers. The she-wolf bore
The ring-prince down through the watery
    depths
To her den at the bottom; nor could Beowulf
    draw
His blade for battle, though brave his mood.
1005 Many a sea-beast, strange sea-monsters,
Tasked him hard with their menacing tusks,
Broke his byrny and smote him sore.
    Then he found himself in a fearsome hall
Where water came not to work him hurt,
1010 But the flood was stayed by the sheltering
    roof.
There in the glow of firelight gleaming
The hero had view of the huge sea-troll.
He swung his war-sword with all his
    strength,
Withheld not the blow, and the savage blade
1015 Sang on her head its hymn of hate.
But the bold one found that the battle-flasher
Would bite no longer, nor harm her life.
The sword-edge failed at his sorest need.
Often of old with ease it had suffered
1020 The clash of battle, cleaving the helm,
The fated warrior's woven mail.
That time was first for the treasured blade
That its glory failed in the press of the fray.
But fixed of purpose and firm of mood
1025 Hygelac's earl was mindful of honor;
In wrath, undaunted, he dashed to earth
The jewelled sword with its scrolled design,
The blade of steel; staked all on strength,
On the might of his hand, as a man must do
1030 Who thinks to win in the welter of battle
Enduring glory; he fears not death.
The Geat-prince joyed in the straining
    struggle,
Stalwart-hearted and stirred to wrath,
Gripped the shoulder of Grendel's dam
1035 And headlong hurled the hag to the ground.
But she quickly clutched him and drew him
    close,
Countered the onset with savage claw.
The warrior staggered, for all his strength,

---

30. herald of Hrothgar . . . Hrunting (hrŭn'ting). Hrothgar's herald here is Unferth, now reconciled to Beowulf. *Hrunting* may
mean "Thruster."

Dismayed and shaken and borne to earth.
1040 She knelt upon him and drew her dagger,
With broad bright blade, to avenge her son,
Her only issue. But the corselet's steel
Shielded his breast and sheltered his life
Withstanding entrance of point and edge.

. . .

1045 Swift the hero sprang to his feet;
Saw mid the war-gear a stately sword,
An ancient war-brand of biting edge,
Choicest of weapons worthy and strong,
The work of giants, a warrior's joy,
1050 So heavy no hand but his own could hold it,
Bear to battle or wield in war.
Then the Scylding warrior, savage and grim,
Seized the ring-hilt and swung the sword,
Struck with fury, despairing of life,
1055 Thrust at the throat, broke through the
        bone-rings;
The stout blade stabbed through her fated
        flesh.
She sank in death; the sword was bloody;
The hero joyed in the work of his hand.
The gleaming radiance shimmered and shone
1060 As the candle of heaven shines clear from
        the sky.
Wrathful and resolute Hygelac's thane
Surveyed the span of the spacious hall;
Grimly gripping the hilted sword
With upraised weapon he turned to the wall.

. . .

1065 And there before him bereft of life
He saw the broken body of Grendel
Stilled in battle, and stretched in death,
As the struggle in Heorot smote him down.
The corpse sprang wide as he struck the
        blow,
1070 The hard sword-stroke that severed the
        head.
Then the tried retainers, who there with
        Hrothgar
Watched the face of the foaming pool,
Saw that the churning reaches were
        reddened,
The eddying surges stained with blood.
1075 And the gray, old spearmen spoke of the
        hero,
Having no hope he would ever return
Crowned with triumph and cheered with
        spoil.

Many were sure that the savage sea-wolf
Had slain their leader. At last came noon.
1080 The stalwart Scyldings forsook the headland;
Their proud gold-giver departed home.
But the Geats sat grieving and sick in spirit,
Stared at the water with longing eyes,
Having no hope they would ever behold
1085 Their gracious leader and lord again.
Then the great sword, eaten with blood of
        battle,
Began to soften and waste away
In iron icicles, wonder of wonders,
Melting away most like to ice
1090 When the Father looses the fetters of frost,
Slackens the bondage that binds the wave,
Strong in power of times and seasons;
He is true God! Of the goodly treasures
From the sea-cave Beowulf took but two,
1095 The monster's head and the precious hilt
Blazing with gems; but the blade had melted,
The sword dissolved, in the deadly heat,
The venomous blood of the fallen fiend. . . .

(Beowulf Returns to Heorot)

With sturdy strokes the lord of the seamen
1100 To land came swimming, rejoiced in his
        spoil,
Had joy of the burden he brought from the
        depths.
And his mighty thanes came forward to meet
        him,
Gave thanks to God they were granted to
        see
Their well-loved leader both sound and safe.
1105 From the stalwart hero his helmet and byrny
Were quickly loosened; the lake lay still,
Its motionless reaches reddened with blood.

. . .

From the sea-cliff's brim the warriors bore
The head of Grendel, with heavy toil;
1110 Four of the stoutest, with all their strength,
Could hardly carry on swaying spear
Grendel's head to the gold-decked hall.
Swift they strode, the daring and dauntless,
Fourteen Geats, to the Hall of the Hart;
1115 And proud in the midst of his marching men
Their leader measured the path to the
        mead-hall.
The hero entered, the hardy in battle,

The great in glory, to greet the king;
And Grendel's head by the hair was carried
1120 Across the floor where the feasters drank—
A terrible sight for lord and for lady—
A gruesome vision whereon men gazed!
　Beowulf spoke, the son of Ecgtheow:
"O son of Healfdene, lord of the Scyldings!
1125 This sea-spoil wondrous, whereon you stare,
We joyously bring you in token of triumph!
Barely with life surviving the battle,
The war under water, I wrought the deed
Weary and spent; and death had been swift
1130 Had God not granted His sheltering strength.
My strong-edged Hrunting, stoutest of
　　blades,
Availed me nothing. But God revealed—
Often His arm has aided the friendless—
The fairest of weapons hanging on wall,
1135 An ancient broadsword; I seized the blade,
Slew in the struggle, as fortune availed,
The cavern-warders. But the war-brand old,
The battle-blade with its scrolled design,
Dissolved in the gush of the venomous gore;
1140 The hilt alone I brought from the battle.
The record of ruin, and slaughter of Danes,
These wrongs I avenged, as was fitting and
　　right.
Now I can promise you, prince of the
　　Scyldings,
Henceforth in Heorot rest without rue
1145 For you and your nobles; nor need you
　　dread
Slaughter of follower, stalwart or stripling,
Or death of earl, as of old you did.''
Into the hand of the aged leader,
The gray-haired hero, he gave the hilt,
1150 The work of giants, the wonder of gold. . . .
　Hrothgar spoke, beholding the hilt,
The ancient relic whereon was etched
An olden record of struggle and strife,
The flood[31] that ravaged the giant race,
1155 The rushing deluge of ruin and death.
That evil kindred were alien to God,
But the Ruler avenged with the wrath of the
　　deep! . . .
Then out spoke Hrothgar, Healfdene's son,
And all the retainers were silent and still:
1160 "Well may he say, whose judgment is just,
Recalling to memory men of the past,
That this earl was born of a better stock!

Your fame, friend Beowulf, is blazoned
　　abroad
Over all wide ways, and to every people.
1165 In manful fashion have you showed your
　　strength,
Your might and wisdom. My word I will keep,
The plighted friendship we formerly pledged.
Long shall you stand as a stay to your
　　people. . . .
　'Tis a wondrous marvel how mighty God
1170 In gracious spirit bestows on men
The gift of wisdom, and goodly lands,
And princely power! He rules over all!
He suffers a man of lordly line
To set his heart on his own desires,
1175 Awards him fullness of worldly joy,
A fair homeland, and the sway of cities,
The wide dominion of many a realm,
An ample kingdom, till, cursed with folly,
The thoughts of his heart take no heed of his
　　end.
1180 He lives in luxury, knowing not want,
Knowing no shadow of sickness or age;
No haunting sorrow darkens his spirit,
No hatred or discord deepens to war;
The world is sweet, to his every desire,
1185 And evil assails not—until in his heart
Pride overpowering gathers and grows!
The warder slumbers, the guard of his spirit;
Too sound is that sleep, too sluggish the
　　weight
Of worldly affairs, too pressing the Foe,
1190 The Archer who looses the arrows of sin.
　Then is his heart pierced, under his helm,
His soul in his bosom, with bitter dart.
He has no defense for the fierce assaults
Of the loathsome Fiend. What he long has
　　cherished
1195 Seems all too little! In anger and greed
He gives no guerdon of plated rings.
Since God has granted him glory and wealth
He forgets the future, unmindful of Fate.
But it comes to pass in the day appointed
1200 His feeble body withers and fails;
Death descends, and another seizes
His hoarded riches and rashly spends
The princely treasure, imprudent of heart.

---

31. flood, Noah's flood, which also destroyed the giant race
mentioned in Genesis 6:4.

Beloved Beowulf, best of warriors,
1205 Avoid such evil and seek the good,
The heavenly wisdom. Beware of pride!
Now for a time you shall feel the fullness
And know the glory of strength, but soon
Sickness or sword shall strip you of might,
1210 Or clutch of fire, or clasp of flood,
Or flight of arrow, or bite of blade,
Or relentless age; or the light of the eye
Shall darken and dim, and death on a
sudden,
O lordly ruler, shall lay you low.
1215   A hundred half-years I've been head of
the Ring-Danes,
Defending the folk against many a tribe
With spear-point and sword in the surges of
battle
Till not one was hostile 'neath heaven's
expanse.
But a loathsome change swept over the land,
1220 Grief after gladness, when Grendel came,
That evil invader, that ancient foe!
Great sorrow of soul from his malice I
suffered;
But thanks be to God who has spared me to
see
His bloody head at the battle's end!
1225 Join now in the banquet; have joy of the
feast,
O mighty in battle! And the morrow shall
bring
Exchange of treasure in ample store."
   Happy of heart the Geat leader hastened,
Took seat at the board as the good king
bade.
1230 Once more, as of old, brave heroes made
merry
And tumult of revelry rose in the hall.
   Then dark over men the night shadows
deepened;
The host all arose, for Hrothgar was minded,
The gray, old Scylding, to go to his rest.
1235 On Beowulf too, after labor of battle,
Came limitless longing and craving for sleep.
A hall-thane graciously guided the hero,
Weary and worn, to the place prepared,
Serving his wishes and every want
1240 As befitted a mariner come from afar.
The stout-hearted warrior sank to his rest;
The lofty building, splendid and spacious,

Towered above him. His sleep was sound
Till the black-coated raven, blithesome of
spirit,
1245 Hailed the coming of Heaven's bliss.

(The Parting of Beowulf and Hrothgar)

   Then over the shadows uprose the sun.
The Geats were in haste, and eager of heart
To depart to their people. Beowulf longed
To embark in his boat, to set sail for his
home.
1250 The hero tendered the good sword Hrunting
To the son of Ecglaf, bidding him bear
The lovely blade; gave thanks for the loan,
Called it a faithful friend in the fray,
Bitter in battle. The greathearted hero
1255 Spoke no word in blame of the blade!
Arrayed in war-gear, and ready for sea,
The warriors bestirred them; and, dear to
the Danes,
Beowulf sought the high seat of the king.
The gallant in war gave greeting to Hrothgar;
1260 Beowulf spoke, the son of Ecgtheow:
"It is time at last to tell of our longing!
Our homes are far, and our hearts are fain
To seek again Hygelac over the sea.
You have welcomed us royally, harbored us
well
1265 As a man could wish; if I ever can win
Your affection more fully, O leader of
heroes,
Swift shall you find me to serve you again!"
   Hrothgar addressed him, uttered his
answer:
"Truly, these words has the Lord of wisdom
1270 Set in your heart, for I never have
hearkened
To speech so sage from a man so young.
You have strength, and prudence, and
wisdom of word! . . .
The Sea-Geats could have no happier choice
If you would be willing to rule the realm,
1275 As king to hold guard o'er the hoard and the
heroes.
The longer I know you, the better I like you,
Beloved Beowulf! You have brought it to
pass
That between our peoples a lasting peace
Shall bind the Geats to the Danish-born;
1280 And strife shall vanish, and war shall cease,

And former feuds, while I rule this realm.''
Then the son of Healfdene, shelter of
earls,
Bestowed twelve gifts on the hero in hall,
Bade him in safety with bounty of treasure
1285 Seek his dear people, and soon return.
The peerless leader, the Scylding lord,
Kissed the good thane and clasped to his
bosom
While tears welled fast from the old man's
eyes.
Both chances he weighed in his wise, old
heart,
1290 But greatly doubted if ever again
They should meet at council or drinking of
mead.

Nor could Hrothgar master—so dear was
the man—
His swelling sorrow; a yearning love
For the dauntless hero, deep in his heart,
1295 Burned through his blood. Beowulf, the
brave,
Prizing his treasure and proud of the gold,
Turned away, treading the grassy plain.
The ring-stemmed sea-goer, riding at anchor,
Awaited her lord. There was loud acclaim
1300 Of Hrothgar's gifts, as they went their way.
He was a king without failing or fault,
Till old age, master of all mankind,
Stripped him of power and pride of strength.

Discussion

1. Why does the poet go into such a detailed description of the rewards Hrothgar gives to Beowulf?

2. In the accounts of Beowulf's victories over both Grendel and his mother, another man dies before Beowulf is victorious (see lines 558 ff. and 826 ff.). This puzzles some readers who think Beowulf should have prevented these deaths. What do you think?

3. Now that you have read about Beowulf's successful battle with Grendel's mother, reconsider his earlier account of the five-day swimming race with Breca (lines 410–450). Why did the poet insert that account early in the poem?

4. The poem has an unusually long description of Grendel's lair (lines 868–887). What purposes does this passage serve? Turn to

"Translating *Beowulf*" on pages 22–23. Compare and contrast the different translations of this scene. Which most stresses action? Which emphasizes traditional poetic language? Which most successfully evokes dread?

5. In the fight with Grendel's mother the poet stresses Beowulf's need for a sword: lines 967 ff. describe the sword Hrunting he takes with him; while lines 1046 ff. describe his lucky discovery of a second weapon. Since she is weaker than her son (see lines 822–823), why does Beowulf need this weapon to kill Grendel's mother?

6. What are the essential themes in Hrothgar's famous speech to Beowulf (lines 1160–1227)? In what ways is this speech appropriate for this moment in the story?

(Beowulf Returns to Geatland)

Then down to the sea came the band of
the brave,
1305 The host of young heroes in harness of war,
In their woven mail; and the coast-warden
viewed
The heroes' return, as he heeded their
coming!
No uncivil greeting he gave from the sea-cliff
As they strode to ship in their glistening
steel;

1310 But rode toward them and called their return
A welcome sight for their Weder kin.
There on the sand the ring-stemmed ship,
The broad-bosomed bark, was loaded with
war-gear,
With horses and treasure; the mast towered
high
1315 Over the riches of Hrothgar's hoard.
A battle-sword Beowulf gave to the
boat-warden

Hilted with gold; and thereafter in hall
He had the more honor because of the
    heirloom,
The shining treasure. The ship was
    launched.
1320 Cleaving the combers of open sea
They dropped the shoreline of Denmark
    astern.
A stretching sea-cloth, a bellying sail,
Was bent on the mast; there was groaning of
    timbers;
A gale was blowing; the boat drove on.
1325 The foamy-necked plunger plowed through
    the billows,
The ring-stemmed ship through the breaking
    seas,
Till at last they sighted the sea-cliffs of
    Geatland,
The well-known headlands; and, whipped by
    the wind,
The boat drove shoreward and beached on
    the sand. . . .
1330   Then the hero strode with his stalwart
    band
Across the stretches of sandy beach,
The wide sea-shingle. The world-candle
    shone,
The hot sun hasting on high from the south.
Marching together they made their way
1335 To where in his stronghold the stout young
    king, . . .
Dispensed his treasure. Soon Hygelac heard
Of the landing of Beowulf, bulwark of men,
That his shoulder-companion had come to
    his court
Sound and safe from the strife of battle.
1340   The hall was prepared, as the prince gave
    bidding,
Places made ready for much travelled men.
And he who came safe from the surges of
    battle
Sat by the side of the king himself, . . .
In friendly fashion in high-built hall
1345 Hygelac questioned his comrade and thane;
For an eager longing burned in his breast
To hear from the Sea-Geats the tale of their
    travels. . . .

Beowulf now tells the king of his battles with
Grendel and Grendel's mother, and of the rewards his victory has won. He concludes:

"These riches I bring you, ruler of heroes,
And warmly tender with right good will.
1350 Save for you, king Hygelac, few are my
    kinsmen,
Few are the favors but come from you."
   Then he bade men bring the boar-crested
    headpiece,
The towering helmet, and steel-gray sark,[32]
The splendid war-sword, and spoke this
    word:
1355 "The good king Hrothgar gave me this gift,
This battle-armor, and first to you
Bade tell the tale of his friendly favor. . . .
Well may you wear it! Have joy of it all."

     . . .

   Then the battle-bold king, the bulwark of
    heroes,
1360 Bade bring a battle-sword banded with gold,
The heirloom of Hrethel;[33] no sharper steel,
No lovelier treasure, belonged to the Geats.
He laid the war-blade on Beowulf's lap,
Gave him a hall and a stately seat
1365 And hides[34] seven thousand. Inherited lands
Both held by birth-fee, home and estate.
But one held rule o'er the spacious realm,
And higher therein his order and rank.

(The Fire-Dragon and the Treasure)

   It later befell in the years that followed
1370 After Hygelac sank in the surges of war, . . .
That the kingdom came into Beowulf's hand.
For fifty winters he governed it well,
Aged and wise with the wisdom of years,
Till a fire-drake[35] flying in darkness of night
1375 Began to ravage and work his will.
On the upland heath he guarded a hoard,
A stone barrow lofty. Under it lay
A path concealed from the sight of men.
There a thief broke in on the heathen
    treasure,

---

32. sark, shirt (here, of mail).
33. Hrethel (hreth'əl), king of the Geats, father of Hygelac,
grandfather of Beowulf.
34. hides. The *hide* (roughly, as much land as could be worked
by one plow in a single year) varied from 40 to 120 acres. Seven
thousand hides is a huge piece of land.
35. fire-drake, a fire-breathing dragon.

Comment: Heroic Morality

In his *Germania,* the Roman historian Tacitus (A.D. 55?–120?) gave a detailed and generally reliable account of the customs of the Germanic tribes from among whom came the Anglo-Saxon peoples that would later populate England:

"On the field of battle it is a disgrace to a chief to be surpassed in courage by his followers, and to the followers not to equal the courage of their chief. And to leave a battle alive after their chief has fallen means lifelong infamy and shame. To defend and protect him, and to let him get the credit for their own acts of heroism, are the most solemn obligations of their allegiance. The chiefs fight for victory, the followers for their chief. Many noble youths, if the land of their birth is stagnating in a long period of peace and inactivity, deliberately seek out other tribes which have some war in hand.

For the Germans have no taste for peace; renown is more easily won among perils, and a large body of retainers cannot be kept together except by means of violence and war. They are always making demands on the generosity of their chief, asking for a coveted war horse or a spear stained with the blood of a defeated enemy. Their meals, for which plentiful if homely fare is provided, count in lieu of pay. The wherewithal for this openhandedness comes from war and plunder. A German is not so easily prevailed upon to plough the land and wait patiently for harvest as to challenge a foe and earn wounds for his reward. He thinks it tame and spiritless to accumulate slowly by the sweat of his brow what can be got quickly by the loss of a little blood."

From *The Agricola and The Germania* of Tacitus, translated by H. Mattingly, revised by S. A. Handford. New York: Penguin Books, 1948, 1970.

1380 Laid hand on a flagon all fretted with gold,
As the dragon discovered, though cozened in
    sleep
By the pilferer's cunning. The people soon
    found
That the mood of the dragon was roused to
    wrath! . . .
    For three hundred winters this waster of
    peoples
1385 Held the huge treasure-hall under the earth
Till the robber aroused him to anger and
    rage,
Stole the rich beaker and bore to his master,
Imploring his lord for a compact of peace.
So the hoard was robbed and its riches
    plundered;
1390 To the wretch was granted the boon that he
    begged;
And his liege-lord first had view of the
    treasure,
The ancient work of the men of old.
Then the worm awakened and war was
    kindled,
The rush of the monster along the rock,
1395 When the fierce one found the tracks of the
    foe; . . .

Swiftly the fire-drake sought through the
    plain
The man who wrought him this wrong in his
    sleep.
Inflamed and savage he circled the mound,
But the waste was deserted—no man was in
    sight.
1400 The worm's mood was kindled to battle and
    war;
Time and again he returned to the barrow
Seeking the treasure-cup. Soon he was sure
That a man had plundered the precious gold.
Enraged and restless the hoard-warden
    waited
1405 The gloom of evening. The guard of the
    mound
Was swollen with anger; the fierce one
    resolved
To requite with fire the theft of the cup.
Then the day was sped as the worm desired;
Lurking no longer within his wall
1410 He sallied forth surrounded with fire,
Encircled with flame. For the folk of the
    land
The beginning was dread as the ending was
    grievous

That came so quickly upon their lord.
   Then the baleful stranger belched fire and
     flame,
1415 Burned the bright dwellings—the glow of the
     blaze
Filled hearts with horror. The hostile
     flier
Was minded to leave there nothing alive.
From near and from far the war of the
     dragon,
The might of the monster, was widely
     revealed
1420 So that all could see how the ravaging
     scather
Hated and humbled the Geatish folk.
Then he hastened back ere the break of
     dawn
To his secret den and the spoil of gold.
He had compassed the land with a flame of
     fire,
1425 A blaze of burning; he trusted the wall,
The sheltering mound, and the strength of
     his might—
But his trust betrayed him! The terrible news
Was brought to Beowulf, told for a truth,
That his home was consumed in the surges
     of fire. . . .
1430 Dark thoughts stirred in his surging bosom,
Welled in his breast, as was not his wont.
The flame of the dragon had levelled the
     fortress,
The people's stronghold washed by the
     wave.
But the king of warriors, prince of the
     Weders,
1435 Exacted an ample revenge for it all.
The lord of warriors and leader of earls
Bade work him of iron a wondrous shield,
Knowing full well that wood could not serve
     him
Nor linden[36] defend him against the flame.
1440 The stalwart hero was doomed to suffer
The destined end of his days on earth;
Likewise the worm, though for many a
     winter
He had held his watch o'er the wealth of the
     hoard.
The ring-prince scorned to assault the
     dragon
1445 With a mighty army, or host of men.

He feared not the combat, nor counted of
     worth
The might of the worm, his courage and
     craft,
Since often aforetime, beset in the fray,
He had safely issued from many an onset,
1450 Many a combat and, crowned with success,
Purged of evil the hall of Hrothgar
And crushed out Grendel's loathsome kin.
     . . .
With eleven comrades, kindled to rage
The Geat lord went to gaze on the dragon.
1455 Full well he knew how the feud arose,
The fearful affliction; for into his hold
From hand of finder the flagon had come.
The thirteenth man in the hurrying throng
Was the sorrowful captive who caused the
     feud.
1460 With woeful spirit and all unwilling
Needs must he guide them, for he only knew
Where the earth-hall stood near the breaking
     billows
Filled with jewels and beaten gold.
The monstrous warden, waiting for battle,
1465 Watched and guarded the hoarded wealth.
No easy bargain for any of men
To seize that treasure! The stalwart king,
Gold-friend of Geats, took seat on the
     headland,
Hailed his comrades and wished them well.
1470 Sad was his spirit, restless and ready,
And the march of Fate immeasurably near;
Fate that would strike, seek his soul's
     treasure,
And deal asunder the spirit and flesh.
Not long was his life encased in the body!
1475   Beowulf spoke, the son of Ecgtheow:
"Many an ordeal I endured in youth,
And many a battle. I remember it all. . . .
   For all the rich gifts that Hygelac gave me
I repaid him in battle with shining sword,
1480 As chance was given. He granted me land,
A gracious dwelling and goodly estate. . . .
I was always before him alone in the van.
So shall I bear me while life-days last,
While the sword holds out that has served
     me well, . . .

---

36. *linden*, a shield of linden wood.

1485 With hand and hard blade, I must fight for
the treasure.'' . . .

(Beowulf and Wiglaf Slay the Dragon)

The king for the last time greeted his
comrades,
Bold helmet-bearers and faithful friends:
"I would bear no sword nor weapon to
battle
With the evil worm, if I knew how else
1490 I could close with the fiend, as I grappled
with Grendel.
From the worm I look for a welling of fire,
A belching of venom, and therefore I bear
Shield and byrny. Not one foot's space
Will I flee from the monster, the ward of the
mound.
1495 It shall fare with us both in the fight at the
wall
As Fate shall allot, the lord of mankind.
Though bold in spirit, I make no boast
As I go to fight with the flying serpent.
Clad in your corselets and trappings of war,
1500 By the side of the barrow abide you to see
Which of us twain may best after battle
Survive his wounds. Not yours the
adventure,
Nor the mission of any, save mine alone,
To measure his strength with the monstrous
dragon
1505 And play the part of a valiant earl.
By deeds of daring I'll gain the gold
Or death in battle shall break your lord.''
Then the stalwart rose with his shield
upon him,
Bold under helmet, bearing his sark
1510 Under the stone-cliff; he trusted the strength
Of his single might. Not so does a coward!
He who survived through many a struggle,
Many a combat and crashing of troops,
Saw where a stone-arch stood by the wall
1515 And a gushing stream broke out from the
barrow.
Hot with fire was the flow of its surge,
Nor could any abide near the hoard
unburned,
Nor endure its depths, for the flame of the
dragon.
Then the lord of the Geats in the grip of his
fury

1520 Gave shout of defiance; the strong-heart
stormed.
His voice rang out with the rage of battle,
Resounding under the hoary stone.
Hate was aroused; the hoard-warden knew
'Twas the voice of a man. No more was
there time
1525 To sue for peace; the breath of the serpent,
A blast of venom, burst from the rock.
The ground resounded; the lord of the Geats
Under the barrow swung up his shield
To face the dragon; the coiling foe
1530 Was gathered to strike in the deadly strife.
The stalwart hero had drawn his sword,
His ancient heirloom of tempered edge;
In the heart of each was fear of the other!
The shelter of kinsmen stood stout of heart
1535 Under towering shield as the great worm
coiled;
Clad in his war-gear he waited the rush.
In twisting folds the flame-breathing dragon
Sped to its fate. The shield of the prince
For a lesser while guarded his life and his
body
1540 Than heart had hoped. For the first time
then,
It was not his portion to prosper in war;
Fate did not grant him glory in battle!
Then lifted his arm the lord of the Geats
And smote the worm with his ancient sword
1545 But the brown edge failed as it fell on bone,
And cut less deep than the king had need
In his sore distress. Savage in mood
The ward of the barrow countered the blow
With a blast of fire; wide sprang the flame.
. . .
1550　Not long was the lull. Swiftly the battlers
Renewed their grapple. The guard of the
hoard
Grew fiercer in fury. His venomous breath
Beat in his breast. Enveloped in flame
The folk-leader suffered a sore distress.
1555 No succoring band of shoulder-companions,
No sons of warriors aided him then
By valor in battle. They fled to the forest
To save their lives; but a sorrowful spirit
Welled in the breast of one of the band.
1560 The call of kinship can never be stilled
In the heart of a man who is trusty and true.
(The text of Beowulf continues on page 36.)

Comment: The Treasure of Sutton Hoo

In the late spring of 1939, archaeologists began excavating a large burial mound on an estate called Sutton Hoo, on the east coast of England in the area once known as East Anglia (see map, page 3). The mound was the largest in a group of earth mounds or barrows that lay on a steep hundred-foot slope overlooking the inlet where the River Deben flows into the North Sea. As the painstaking work continued, the diggers realized they had uncovered the richest hoard of early Anglo-Saxon objects ever found. A jeweled sword, a richly deco-

rated shield and helmet, gold coins, silver bowls, and, above all, nineteen pieces of magnificently wrought gold jewelry set with thousands of elaborately cut garnets—these objects must have been the treasure of a mighty king. The great gold buckle alone weighs over fourteen ounces. With these objects were found an iron standard-frame and a two-foot carved whetstone, the symbols of sovereignty of an East Anglian king.

The treasure, scattered and corroded by time, lay within the hull of what had once been an eighty-nine-foot wooden ship. Only the iron bolts and nails remained, but the outline of the ship was plainly visible in the sand. No trace of a body was found; the ship was evidently a cenotaph or memorial to a king[1] whose bones lay elsewhere. From the evidence offered by the coins placed with the hoard—perhaps intended as payment for the ghostly oarsmen who were to convey the king to the next world—it is thought that the burial must have been made between the years A.D. 625 and 660. Ship burials were fairly numerous among the pagan Vikings of Europe at a later period, but rare in Anglo-Saxon England. The Sutton Hoo find was hailed as the most exciting ar-

1. Some scholars think the king may have been Redwald, mentioned by Bede in his story of the conversion of King Edwin (see page 48). Redwald had been converted to Christianity, but lapsed into pagan practices. This would account for the combination of Christian and pagan elements in the cenotaph.

chaeological discovery of the century in Britain.

In August 1939 a local Coroner's Jury was called upon to decide the legal status of the Sutton Hoo finds—whether they should be considered as treasure-trove and therefore the property of the Crown, or whether they belonged to Mrs. Pretty, the owner of the Sutton Hoo estate. If the artifacts had been secretly hidden, with the intent of recovering them later, they would become Crown property. But if it could be shown that they had been publicly buried with no intention of ever recovering them, they would remain the property of Mrs. Pretty.

The evidence presented to the jury consisted of the description in *Beowulf* of Scyld Sceafing's ship-passing and the story of the final disposal of the dragon's hoard in the account of Beowulf's funeral. The jury easily concluded on the basis of this evidence that the Sutton Hoo treasures must have been buried at a public ceremony and been intended to remain forever undisturbed. Thus they became the property of Mrs. Pretty, who then generously presented them to the British Museum, where they are now on public display.

The opening section of *Beowulf* is said to be the earliest existing documentary evidence of a ship funeral. But the description of the rich treasures that were placed in the ship had generally been looked upon as poetic fancy. The find at Sutton Hoo confirmed the historical accuracy of the *Beowulf* description of a heroic society rich in gold and other beautifully wrought objects.

Beowulf may have been composed at a time when the spectacular Sutton Hoo ship burial was still remembered. Some scholars even think the poem may have been intended as a compliment to a king of East Anglia; there is evidence pointing to the possibility that an ancestor of the East Anglian royal line was a member of the Geatish or South Swedish tribe to which Beowulf belonged.

The articles found at Sutton Hoo indicate not only that Anglo-Saxon culture of the seventh century was far more advanced than had previously been imagined, but also that the Anglo-Saxons traded widely. The helmet and shield are Swedish. The blade of the sword was probably forged in the Rhineland. The silver bowls and spoons came from the Near East and the gold coins from France.

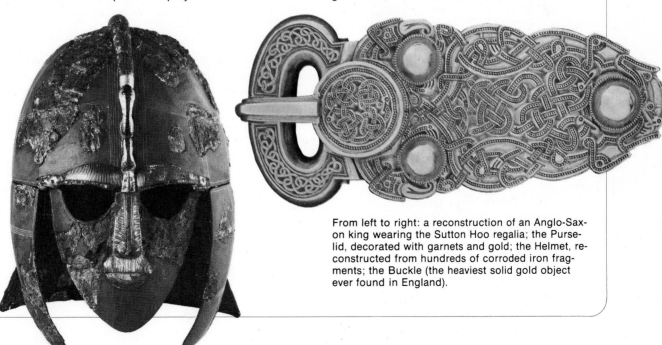

From left to right: a reconstruction of an Anglo-Saxon king wearing the Sutton Hoo regalia; the Purse-lid, decorated with garnets and gold; the Helmet, reconstructed from hundreds of corroded iron fragments; the Buckle (the heaviest solid gold object ever found in England).

His name was Wiglaf, Weohstan's son,
A prince of the Scylfings, a peerless thane,
Ælfhere's kinsman;[37] he saw his king
1565 Under his helmet smitten with heat.
He thought of the gifts which his lord had
    given,
The wealth and the land of the Wægmunding
    line
And all the folk-rights his father had owned;
Nor could he hold back, but snatched up his
    buckler,
1570 His linden shield and his ancient sword. . . .
    Wiglaf spoke in sorrow of soul,
With bitter reproach rebuking his comrades:
"I remember the time, as we drank in the
    mead-hall,
When we swore to our lord who bestowed
    these rings
1575 That we would repay for the war-gear and
    armor,
The hard swords and helmets, if need like
    this
Should ever befall him. He chose us out
From all the host for this high adventure.
            . . .
Now is the day that our lord has need
1580 Of the strength and courage of stalwart men.
Let us haste to succor his sore distress
In the horrible heat and the merciless flame.
God knows I had rather the fire should
    enfold
My body and limbs with my gold-friend and
    lord. . . .
1585 One helmet and sword, one byrny and
    shield,
Shall serve for us both in the storm of
    strife."
Then Wiglaf dashed through the deadly reek
In his battle-helmet to help his lord.
Brief were his words: "Beloved Beowulf,
1590 Summon your strength, remember the vow
You made of old in the years of youth
Not to allow your glory to lessen
As long as you lived. With resolute heart,
And dauntless daring, defend your life
1595 With all your force. I fight at your side!"
    Once again the worm, when the words
    were spoken,
The hideous foe in a horror of flame,
Rushed in rage at the hated men.

Wiglaf's buckler was burned to the boss
1600 In the billows of fire; his byrny of mail
Gave the young hero no help or defense.
But he stoutly pressed on under shield of his
    kinsman
When his own was consumed in the
    scorching flame.
Then the king once more was mindful of
    glory,
1605 Swung his great sword-blade with all his
    might
And drove it home on the dragon's head.
But Nægling[38] broke, it failed in the battle,
The blade of Beowulf, ancient and gray. . . .
    A third time then the terrible scather,
1610 The monstrous dragon inflamed with the
    feud,
Rushed on the king when the opening
    offered,
Fierce and flaming; fastened its fangs
In Beowulf's throat; he was bloodied with
    gore;
His lifeblood streamed from the welling
    wound.
1615   As they tell the tale, in the king's sore
    need
His shoulder-companion showed forth his
    valor,
His craft and courage, and native strength.
To the head of the dragon he paid no heed,
Though his hand was burned as he helped
    his king.
1620 A little lower the stalwart struck
At the evil beast, and his blade drove home
Plated and gleaming. The fire began
To lessen and wane. The king of the Weders
Summoned his wits; he drew the dagger
1625 He wore on his corselet, cutting and keen,
And slit asunder the worm with the blow.
So they felled the foe and wrought their
    revenge;
The kinsmen together had killed the dragon.

---

37. Wiglaf . . . kinsman. Wiglaf's father Weohstan (wā′ō stan)
was apparently both a prince of the Scylfings (shilf′ings), the
ruling family among the Swedes, and a member of the Wægmunding (wag′mŭn ding) family (see lines 1567–1568), the
Geatish clan to which Beowulf belonged. It has been conjec-
tured that Weohstan was a Swedish exile in Geatland (as the result of a blood feud) who had settled on Waegmunding lands.
Ælfhere (alf′her rə) is not otherwise known.
38. Nægling (nag′ling). The name of Beowulf's sword is related
to *nægl,* "nail."

So a man should be when the need is bitter!
1630 That was the last fight Beowulf fought;
That was the end of his work in the world.

(Beowulf's Death)

The wound which the dragon had dealt
    him began
To swell and burn; and soon he could feel
The baneful venom inflaming his breast.
1635 The wise, old warrior sank down by the wall
And stared at the work of the giants of old,
The arches of stone and the standing
    columns
Upholding the ancient earth-hall within.
His loyal thane, the kindest of comrades,
1640 Saw Beowulf bloody and broken in war;
In his hands bore water and bathed his
    leader,
And loosened the helm from his dear lord's
    head.
    Beowulf spoke, though his hurt was sore,
The wounds of battle grievous and grim.
1645 Full well he weened that his life was ended,
And all the joy of his years on earth;
That his days were done, and Death most
    near:
"My armor and sword I would leave to my
    son
Had Fate but granted, born of my body,
1650 An heir to follow me after I'm gone.
For fifty winters I've ruled this realm,
And never a lord of a neighboring land
Dared strike with terror or seek with sword.
In my life I abode by the lot assigned,
1655 Kept well what was mine, courted no
    quarrels,
Swore no false oaths. And now for all this
Though my hurt is grievous, my heart is
    glad.
When life leaves body, the Lord of mankind
Cannot lay to my charge the killing of
    kinsmen!
1660 Go quickly, dear Wiglaf, to gaze on the gold
Beneath the hoar stone. The dragon lies still
In the slumber of death, despoiled of his
    hoard.
Make haste that my eyes may behold the
    treasure,
The gleaming jewels, the goodly store,

1665 And, glad of the gold, more peacefully leave
The life and the realm I have ruled so long."
    Then Weohstan's son, as they tell the tale,
Clad in his corselet and trappings of war,
Hearkened at once to his wounded lord.
1670 Under roof of the barrow he broke his way.
Proud in triumph he stood by the seat,
Saw glittering jewels and gold on the ground,
The den of the dragon, the old dawn-flier,
And all the wonders along the walls.
1675 Great bowls and flagons of bygone men
Lay all unburnished and barren of gems,
Many a helmet ancient and rusted,
Many an arm-ring cunningly wrought.
Treasure and gold, though hid in the ground,
1680 Override man's wishes, hide them who will!
High o'er the hoard he beheld a banner,
Greatest of wonders, woven with skill,
All wrought of gold; its radiance lighted
The vasty ground and the glittering gems.
    . . .
1685 As I've heard the tale, the hero unaided
Rifled those riches of giants of old,
The hoard in the barrow, and heaped in his
    arms
Beakers and platters, picked what he would
And took the banner, the brightest of signs.
    . . .
1690 In haste returning enriched with spoil.
He feared, and wondered if still he would
    find
The lord of the Weders alive on the plain,
Broken and weary and smitten with wounds.
With his freight of treasure he found the
    prince,
1695 His dear lord, bloody and nigh unto death.
With water he bathed him till words broke
    forth
From the hoard of his heart and, aged and
    sad,
Beowulf spoke, as he gazed on the gold:
"For this goodly treasure whereon I gaze
1700 I give my thanks to the Lord of all,
To the Prince of glory, Eternal God,
Who granted me grace to gain for my people
Such dower of riches before my death.
I gave my life for this golden hoard.
1705 Heed well the wants, the need of my people;
My hour is come, and my end is near.
Bid warriors build, when they burn my
    body,

A stately barrow on the headland's height.
It shall be for remembrance among my
        people
1710 As it towers high on the Cape of the Whale,
And sailors shall know it as Beowulf's
        Barrow,
Seafaring mariners driving their ships
Through fogs of ocean from far countries.''
Then the great-hearted king unclasped from
        his throat
1715 A collar of gold, and gave to his thane;
Gave the young hero his gold-decked
        helmet,
His ring and his byrny, and wished him well.
''You are the last of the Wægmunding line.
All my kinsmen, earls in their glory,
1720 Fate has sent to their final doom,
And I must follow.'' These words were the
        last
The old king spoke ere the pyre received
        him,
The leaping flames of the funeral blaze,
And his breath went forth from his bosom,
        his soul
1725 Went forth from the flesh, to the joys of the
        just. . . .
    Not long was it then till the laggards in
        battle
Came forth from the forest, ten craven in
        fight,
Who had dared not face the attack of the foe
In their lord's great need. The shirkers in
        shame
1730 Came wearing their bucklers and trappings
        of war
Where the old man lay. They looked upon
        Wiglaf.
Weary he sat by the side of his leader
Attempting with water to waken his lord.
It availed him little; the wish was vain! . . .
1735 He reproached the cowards whose courage
        had failed: . . .
''Lo! he may say who would speak the truth
That the lord who gave you these goodly
        rings,
This warlike armor wherein you stand—
When oft on the ale-bench he dealt to his
        hall-men
1740 Helmet and byrny, endowing his thanes
With the fairest he found from near or from
        far—

That he grievously wasted these trappings of
        war
When battle befell him. The king of the folk
Had no need to boast of his friends in the
        fight.
1745 But the God of victory granted him strength
To avenge himself with the edge of the
        sword
When he needed valor. Of little avail
The help I brought in the bitter battle!
Yet still I strove, though beyond my
        strength,
1750 To aid my kinsman. And ever the weaker
The savage foe when I struck with my
        sword;
Ever the weaker the welling flame!
Too few defenders surrounded our ruler
When the hour of evil and terror befell.
1755 Now granting of treasure and giving of
        swords,
Inherited land-right and joy of the home,
Shall cease from your kindred. And each of
        your clan
Shall fail of his birthright when men from
        afar
Hear tell of your flight and your dastardly
        deed.
1760 Death is better for every earl
Than life besmirched with the brand of
        shame!''

(The Messenger Foretells the Doom of the Geats)
    Then Wiglaf bade tell the tidings of battle
Up over the cliff in the camp of the host
Where the linden-bearers all morning long
1765 Sat wretched in spirit, and ready for both,
The return, or the death, of their dear-loved
        lord.
Not long did he hide, who rode up the
        headland,
The news of their sorrow, but spoke before
        all:
''Our leader lies low, the lord of the Weders,
1770 The king of the Geats, on the couch of
        death.
He sleeps his last sleep by the deeds of the
        worm.
The dreadful dragon is stretched beside him
Slain with dagger-wounds. Not by the sword

Could he quell the monster or lay him low.

     . . .

1775 Let us go quickly to look on the king
Who brought us treasure, and bear his
    corpse
To the funeral pyre. The precious hoard
Shall burn with the hero. There lies the heap
Of untold treasure so grimly gained,
1780 Jewels and gems he bought with his blood
At the end of life. All these at the last
The flames shall veil and the brands devour.
No man for remembrance shall take from the
    treasure,
Nor beauteous maiden adorn her breast
1785 With gleaming jewel; bereft of gold
And tragic-hearted many shall tread
A foreign soil, now their lord has ceased
From laughter and revel and rapture of joy.
Many a spear in the cold of morning
1790 Shall be borne in hand uplifted on high.
No sound of harp shall waken the warrior,
But the dusky raven despoiling the dead
Shall clamor and cry and call to the eagle
What fare he found at the carrion-feast
1795 The while with the wolf he worried the
    corpses.'' . . .
They went with tears to behold the wonder.
They found the friend, who had dealt them
    treasure
In former days, on the bed of death,
Stretched out lifeless upon the sand. . . .
1800 They had sighted first, where it lay
    outstretched,
The monstrous wonder, the loathsome
    worm,
The horrible fire-drake, hideous-hued,
Scorched with the flame. The spread of its
    length
Was fifty foot-measures! Oft in the night
1805 It sported in air, then sinking to earth
Returned to its den. Now moveless in death
It had seen the last of its earthly lair.
Beside the dragon were bowls and beakers,
Platters lying, and precious swords
1810 Eaten with rust, where the hoard had rested
A thousand winters in the womb of earth.

    . . .

Then spoke Wiglaf, Weohstan's son:
"Often for one man many must sorrow
As has now befallen the folk of the Geats.

1815 We could not persuade the king by our
    counsel,
Our well-loved leader, to shun assault
On the dreadful dragon guarding the gold;
To let him lie where he long had lurked
In his secret lair till the world shall end.
1820 But Beowulf, dauntless, pressed to his
    doom. . . .
Let us haste once more to behold the
    treasure,
The gleaming wonders beneath the wall.
I will show the way that you all may see
And closely scan the rings and the gold.
1825 Let the bier be ready, the pyre prepared,
When we come again to carry our lord,
Our leader beloved, where long he shall lie
In the kindly care of the Lord of all.''

(Beowulf's Funeral)

    Then the son of Weohstan, stalwart in
    war,
1830 Bade send command to the heads of homes
To bring from afar the wood for the burning
Where the good king lay: "Now glede[39] shall
    devour,
As dark flame waxes, the warrior prince
Who has often withstood the shower of steel
1835 When the storm of arrows, sped from the
    string,
Broke over shield, and shaft did service,
With feather-fittings guiding the barb.''
    Then the wise son of Weohstan chose
    from the host
Seven thanes of the king, the best of the
    band;
1840 Eight heroes together they hied to the
    barrow
In under the roof of the fearful foe;
One of the warriors leading the way
Bore in his hand a burning brand.
They cast no lots who should loot the
    treasure
1845 When they saw unguarded the gold in the
    hall
Lying there useless; little they scrupled
As quickly they plundered the precious
    store.

---

39. *glede* (glēd), glowing coal, ember.

Over the sea-cliff into the ocean
They tumbled the dragon, the deadly worm,
1850 Let the sea-tide swallow the guarder of gold.
Then a wagon was loaded with well-wrought
      treasure,
A countless number of every kind;
And the aged warrior, the white-haired king,
Was borne on high to the Cape of the
      Whale.
1855   The Geat folk fashioned a peerless pyre
Hung round with helmets and battle-boards,
With gleaming byrnies as Beowulf bade.
In sorrow of soul they laid on the pyre
Their mighty leader, their well-loved lord.
1860 The warriors kindled the bale on the barrow,
Wakened the greatest of funeral fires.
Dark o'er the blaze the wood-smoke
      mounted;
The winds were still, and the sound of
      weeping
Rose with the roar of the surging flame
1865 Till the heat of the fire had broken the body.
With hearts that were heavy they chanted
      their sorrow,
Singing a dirge for the death of their lord;
And an aged woman with upbound locks
Lamented for Beowulf, wailing in woe.
1870 Over and over she uttered her dread
Of sorrow to come, of bloodshed and
      slaughter,
Terror of battle, and bondage, and shame.
The smoke of the bale-fire rose to the sky!
   The men of the Weder folk fashioned a
      mound

1875 Broad and high on the brow of the cliff,
Seen from afar by seafaring men.
Ten days they worked on the warrior's
      barrow
Inclosing the ash of the funeral flame
With a wall as worthy as wisdom could
      shape.
1880 They bore to the barrow the rings and the
      gems,
The wealth of the hoard the heroes had
      plundered.
The olden treasure they gave to the earth,
The gold to the ground, where it still
      remains
As useless to men as it was of yore.
1885 Then round the mound rode the brave in
      battle,
The sons of warriors, twelve in a band,
Bemoaning their sorrow and mourning their
      king.
They sang their dirge and spoke of the hero
Vaunting his valor and venturous deeds.
1890 So is it proper a man should praise
His friendly lord with a loving heart,
When his soul must forth from the fleeting
      flesh.
So the folk of the Geats, the friends of his
      hearth,
Bemoaned the fall of their mighty lord;
1895 Said he was kindest of worldly kings,
Mildest, most gentle, most eager for fame.
c. 725

Discussion

1. There are a number of parallels between Beowulf's youthful fight with Grendel and his last battle with the dragon. Compare and contrast these critical features: **(a)** the cause of each monster's attack on humanity; **(b)** Beowulf's motives in countering that attack; **(c)** Beowulf's preparations for battle; **(d)** the symbolic details of the fight as it progresses; **(e)** its conclusion.

2. Compare the fidelity of Beowulf's men in the three major battles he fights. What pattern emerges?

3. At the end of the poem, does the attitude towards the rewards of treasure shift?

4. For what reasons do Beowulf and his men plan and carry out the elaborate funeral at the poem's end?

5. Now that you have finished, reconsider why the *Beowulf*-poet began with Scyld's funeral.

6. The last thing said of Beowulf is that he was "... most eager for fame" (line 1896). Is this a characteristic, within the context of the poem, to be admired? Did it lead to Beowulf's downfall?

Vocabulary
Context, Dictionary

A. The following words come directly from Anglo-Saxon. Using context clues, write down a definition for each on a separate sheet of paper. Then check your definition against the one in the Glossary.

1. boon (line 277)
2. weened (line 682)
3. combers (line 1320)
4. scather (line 1420)

B. The following words may look familiar, but each also has at least one archaic sense. Using the Glossary, learn the archaic meaning of each, and then use the word in a sentence that illustrates its archaic meaning.

1. coil (line 206)
2. mere (line 668)
3. brand (line 1047)
4. bale (line 1860)

C. The following words appear frequently in descriptions of ancient warfare. Use the Glossary to help you write a brief explanation of the historical sources for each.

1. blazon (line 102)
2. stalwart (line 142)
3. brandish (line 169)
4. guerdon (line 692)
5. besmirched (line 1761)

Composition

1. Have the characteristics of good leadership changed since the days of Beowulf? To answer this question, begin in listing for yourself the strengths and weaknesses of Scyld, Hrothgar, Hygelac, and Beowulf as kings.

In an essay, describe their shared characteristics and evaluate how relevant they are to the requirements for the modern leader.

2. There are only two significant female characters in *Beowulf,* Hrothgar's wife Wealhtheow, and Grendel's mother. Locate in the poem the actions they perform that most clearly define the roles that they play in their respective worlds.

Write an essay describing what these characters do, and speculating on the reasons for the relative unimportance of female characters in this poem.

3. The people of *Beowulf* don't talk *to* each other, they make formal speeches *at* each other. This is characteristic of **epic** poetry. Imagine to yourself a very different kind of encounter, a moment during Beowulf's last day at Heorot when he suddenly meets Hrothgar alone. What do you think would be the conversation between the young warrior and the aging king.

When you have an idea of the topics they discuss, write out their conversation in the form of a **dialogue.**

4. In the description of Grendel's lair (lines 868–887) the poet imagines the proper place for a monster to live. Look over that passage again, and pick out the scene's most important characteristics.

Then transform them into modern terms by writing a description of what you imagine to be the appropriate hiding place for a contemporary monster.

5. To define how Wiglaf serves an important function at the end of *Beowulf,* go over the scenes in which he appears, and consider how they would change if he were not there.

In an analytic essay, explain to your reader through the use of these examples Wiglaf's crucial role in concluding the action of the poem.

6. To prepare a character sketch of Beowulf, locate the passages that describe his physical attributes and most clearly define his character.

Using them as a basis, write an essay that points out his positive and negative qualities. (See *Prewriting* in Composition Guide.)

*P*oems from the Exeter Book

Around the year 1070, Leofric, the first bishop of Exeter, presented to the cathedral library an old manuscript that the library catalogue describes as "a big English book about every sort of thing, wrought in song-wise." Into this book, monks had copied (sometimes carelessly) a miscellaneous collection of Anglo-Saxon poems, including "The Wife's Lament," "The Husband's Message," and "The Seafarer," as well as ninety-five verse riddles.

Exeter, located near the mouth of the river Exe in southwestern England (see map, page 3), had been sacked a number of times by Viking raiders; but when Leofric established his bishopric there, the city and its fortifications were rebuilt. But though the cathedral and its library were secure from the Vikings, the chances of a thousand years nevertheless had their effects on the ancient volume, since called the Exeter Book. The front was used at one time as a cutting-board and as a beer mat, and the back fourteen pages were burned through with a brand.

Many of the poems in the Exeter Book are classed as **elegies.** This word has its origin in a Greek term meaning "a lament." Greek and Roman poets wrote elegies both on the deaths of individuals and also, inspired by a more general melancholy, on the fact that all things must pass.

These same themes are central to Anglo-Saxon poetry. Grief for the lost heroic leader overshadows *Beowulf* from the death of Scyld to the funeral for Beowulf himself. Some passages, such as Wiglaf's speech in lines 1769–1795, could stand alone as elegiac lyric poems.

There are a number of such Anglo-Saxon elegies. All of them, though they are relatively brief in length, use the same meter and alliterative rhyme scheme found in *Beowulf*. Sometimes, as in "The Seafarer" (page 57), the sorrows of life find a solution in a more permanent realm. At other times, as in "The Wife's Lament" (see below), grief seems unending.

Despite their titles (given them by a nineteenth-century editor), "The Wife's Lament" and "The Husband's Message" are not companion pieces. They do not appear together in the Exeter Book.

"The Wife's Lament" is spoken by a woman whose husband and his plotting kinsmen have banished to a distant forest cave. The tone of the poem is angry and despairing.

"The Husband's Message," by contrast, is not particularly "elegiac" in tone. Using the same convention that is employed in Anglo-Saxon riddles (see page 45), the speaker in the poem is the message staff on which the poem is carved. The man who sends it has been exiled as a result of a feud. Now he tells his wife to take ship and join him when she hears "the sad cuckoo calling in the grove." His message ends with a series of *runes,* an alphabet used by the Germanic peoples, for which various interpretations have been offered.

*T*he Wife's Lament

translated by **Charles W. Kennedy**

A song I sing of sorrow unceasing,
The tale of my trouble, the weight of my
    woe,
Woe of the present, and woe of the past,
Woe never-ending of exile and grief,
5 But never since girlhood greater than now.

First, the pang when my lord departed,
Far from his people, beyond the sea;
Bitter the heartache at break of dawn,

From *An Anthology of Old English Poetry,* translated by Charles W. Kennedy. New York: Oxford University Press, 1960.

The longing for rumor in what far land
10 So weary a time my loved one tarried.
Far I wandered then, friendless and
      homeless,
Seeking for help in my heavy need.
   With secret plotting his kinsmen purposed
To wedge us apart, wide worlds between,
15 And bitter hate. I was sick at heart.
Harshly my lord bade lodge me here.
In all this land I had few to love me,
Few that were loyal, few that were friends.
Wherefore my spirit is heavy with sorrow
20 To learn my beloved, my dear man and mate
Bowed by ill-fortune and bitter in heart,
Is masking his purpose and planning a
      wrong.
With blithe hearts often of old we boasted
That nought should part us save death alone;
25 All that has failed and our former love
Is now as if it had never been!
Far or near where I fly there follows
The hate of him who was once so dear.
   In this forest-grove they have fixed my
      abode
30 Under an oak in a cavern of earth,
An old cave-dwelling of ancient days,
Where my heart is crushed by the weight of
      my woe.
Gloomy its depths and the cliffs that
      o'erhang it,
Grim are its confines with thorns
      overgrown—
35 A joyless dwelling where daily the longing
For an absent loved one brings anguish of
      heart.
   Lovers there are who may live their love,
Joyously keeping the couch of bliss,
While I in my earth-cave under the oak
40 Pace to and fro in the lonely dawn.
Here must I sit through the summer-long
      day,
Here must I weep in affliction and woe;
Yet never, indeed, shall my heart know rest
From all its anguish, and all its ache,
45 Wherewith life's burdens have brought me
      low.
   Ever man's years are subject to sorrow,
His heart's thoughts bitter, though his
      bearing be blithe;
Troubled his spirit, beset with distress—

Whether all wealth of the world be his lot,
50 Or hunted by Fate in a far country
My beloved is sitting soul-weary and sad,
Swept by the storm, and stiff with the frost,
In a wretched cell under rocky cliffs
By severing waters encircled about—
55 Sharpest of sorrows my lover must suffer
Remembering always a happier home.
Woeful his fate whose doom is to wait
With longing heart for an absent love.
8th century

The Husband's Message

translated by **Burton Raffel**

A tree grew me; I was green, and wood.
That came first. I was cut and sent
Away from my home, holding wily
Words, carried out on the ocean,
5 Riding a boat's back. I crossed
Stormy seas, seeking the thresholds
Where my master's message was meant to
      travel
And be known. And now the knotted planks
Of a ship have brought me here, and you
10 Shall read my lord's heart and hear
His soul's thought. I promise a glowing
Faith shall be what you find. Read.
   See: this wood has come to make you
Remember the hands that carved it, to take
      you
15 Back to the love and the pledges you shared,
You two, in that buried time when you both
Could walk unharmed across this festive
Town, the land yours, and you
Each other's. Your people fought, and the
      feud
20 Brought him exile. Now he asks you

"The Husband's Message" Reprinted from *Prairie Schooner*,
Vol. XXXII, No. 2, translated by Burton Raffel, by permission of
University of Nebraska Press. Copyright © 1958 by the University of Nebraska Press.

To listen for the sad cuckoo calling
In the grove: when its song has reached the
    edge
Of the woods, he wants you to come to him
    over
The waves, letting nothing lead you
25 Aside and no man living stop you.
    Go down to the sea, the gull's home,
And come to a ship that can carry you
    south,
Away, out on the water to where
Your husband and lord longs for your
    coming.
30 Nothing the world can send him, he says
Through me, could bring him more delight
Than for Almighty God to grant him you,
And for you and he together to bless
His soldiers and friends with treasure, with
    hammered
35 Bracelets and rings. For though his home
Is with strangers, he lives in a lovely land
And is rich: shining gold surrounds him.

And though my master was driven from
    here,
Rushing madly down to his ship
40 And onto the sea, alone, only
Alive because he fled, and glad
To escape, yet now he is served and
    followed,
Loved and obeyed by many. He has beaten
Misery: there's nothing more he wants,
45 Oh prince's daughter, no precious gems,
No stallions, no mead-hall pleasure, no
    treasure
On earth, but you, you to enjoy
In spite of the ancient oath that parted you.
And I fit together an S and an R,
50 And E, an A, a W and D,
In an oath to prove that your pledge is
    sacred
To him, and his faith as steady as his heart.
As long as life shall be in him, he'll long
To fulfill the vows and the love you shared.
8th century

Discussion

1. Several words are repeated in the first section of "The Wife's Lament" (lines 1–28): *woe* (lines 2, 3, and 4); *far* (lines 7, 9, and 11); *few* (lines 17 and 18). What effect does this repetition create?

2. In her solitude, the narrator in "The Wife's Lament" does not know anything about her distant beloved. List the conjectures she makes about him, and discuss what they imply about the way she thinks.

3. As in the Anglo-Saxon riddles (see page 45), "The Husband's Message" employs a non-human narrator—the wooden staff on which the exiled husband has carved his message. Does the device heighten or reduce the poignancy of the feeling conveyed by the poem?

4. What has happened to the exiled husband since a feud forced him to flee? How does the cuckoo's call (line 21) serve as a sign?

5. Characterize in your own words the kind of love expressed in "The Husband's Message."

Composition

The runic message at the end of "The Husband's Message" (lines 49–50) has never been successfully decoded. The translator here gives English letters that are rough equivalents for the original runes. Using these English letters, and your own imagination, create what you think would be an appropriate reading of this cryptogram.

Then in an essay explain your reading and why it would fit into the conclusion of the poem.

Anglo-Saxon Riddles

translated by **J. Duncan Spaeth** and **Michael Alexander**

Among the contents of the Exeter Book (see page 42) are ninety-five verse riddles. Riddles, along with myths, fables, folk tales, and proverbs, display the beginnings of human thought and literary expression. Like these other forms, the riddle is found worldwide. The riddle is basically a **metaphor.** A short riddle, like Number 68, is based on a single **analogy.** In a longer riddle, like Number 21, the comparison between two things simply receives more elaborate development, usually in the form of an extended **personification.** The subject of the riddle frequently speaks in its own voice (as in Numbers 5, 16, 21, and 80), teasing the reader with a series of clues, and at times concluding with a challenge to solve the puzzle. *Beowulf* gives us the world of the hero; the elegies share profound human emotion. In the Anglo-Saxon riddles we find the details of everyday life more than a thousand years ago. (The Exeter Book offers no solutions for its riddles, but suggested answers for the ones included here appear upside down at the bottom of the next page.)

5

Wounded I am, and weary with fighting;
Gashed by the iron, gored by the point of it,
Sick of battle-work, battered and scarred.
Many a fearful fight have I seen, when
5 Hope there was none, or help in the thick of
    it,
Ere I was down and fordone in the fray.
Offspring of hammers, hardest of
    battle-blades,
Smithied in forges, fell on me savagely,
Doomed to bear the brunt and the shock of
    it,
10 Fierce encounter of clashing foes.
Leech[1] cannot heal my hurts with his
    simples,[2]
Salves for my sores have I sought in vain.
Blade-cuts dolorous, deep in the side of me,
Daily and nightly redouble my wounds.

16

I war with the wind, with the waves I
    wrestle;
I must battle with both when the bottom I
    seek,
My strange habitation by surges o'er-roofed.
I am strong in the strife, while still I remain;
5 As soon as I stir, they are stronger than I.
They wrench and they wrest, till I run from
    my foes;

The Man, symbol of St. Matthew, from the seventh-century Book of Durrow.

1. **Leech,** an archaic term for "doctor."
2. **simples,** plants or herbs used in medicine.

What was put in my keeping they carry
    away.
If my back be not broken, I baffle them still;
The rocks are my helpers, when hard I am
    pressed;
10 Grimly I grip them. Guess what I'm called.

21

My beak is below, I burrow and nose
Under the ground. I go as I'm guided
By my master the farmer, old foe of the
    forest;
Bent and bowed, at my back he walks,
5 Forward pushing me over the field;
Sows on my path where I've passed along.
I came from the wood, a wagon carried me;
I was fitted with skill, I am full of wonders.
As grubbing I go, there's green on one side,
10 But black on the other my path is seen.
A curious prong pierces my back;
Beneath me in front, another grows down
And forward pointing is fixed to my head.
I tear and gash the ground with my teeth,
15 If my master steer me with skill from
    behind.

47

I heard of a wonder, of words moth-eaten;
that is a strange thing, I thought, weird
that a man's song be swallowed by a worm,
his binded sentences, his bedside stand-by
5 rustled in the night—and the robber-guest
not one whit the wiser for the words he had
    mumbled.

68

The wave, over the wave, a weird thing I
    saw,
through-wrought, and wonderfully ornate:
a wonder on the wave—water became bone.

80

I am puff-breasted, proud-crested,
a head I have, and a high tail,
eyes & ears and one foot,
both my sides, a back that's hollow,
5 a very stout beak, a steeple neck
and a home above men.
                  Harsh are my sufferings
when that which makes the forest tremble
    takes and shakes me.
Here I stand under streaming rain
10 and blinding sleet, stoned by hail;
freezes the frost and falls the snow
on me stuck-bellied. And I stick it all out
for I cannot change the chance that made
    me.
8th–10th century

Numbers 5, 16, and 21, from *Early English Poems* selected and edited by Henry S. Pancoast and John Duncan Spaeth. All rights reserved. Reprinted by permission of Holt, Rinehart and Winston, Publishers.

Numbers 47, 68, and 80, from *The Earliest English Poems*, translated by Michael Alexander (Penguin Classics, Second Edition, 1977). Copyright © 1966, 1977 by Michael Alexander. Reprinted by permission of Penguin Books Ltd.

Discussion

1. Single out the clues in each riddle which you think most clearly suggest a solution.
2. List the ways these poems perceive life as a struggle. Why might this be expected in Anglo-Saxon society?

Answers: 5—a shield; 16—an anchor; 21—a plow; 47—a bookworm; 68—ice; 80—a weathercock.

Bede 673-735

Bede, author of the most important history of early England, was born in the Anglo-Saxon kingdom of Northumbria (see map, page 3) in 673. Bede was apparently orphaned early. When Bede was seven, his relatives put him under the supervision of the monks at Wearmouth Abbey, and two years later, in 682, he transferred to the newly built abbey of Jarrow, where he was to spend the rest of his life.

Jarrow was the creation of Benedict Biscop (628-690), an ambitious, aristocratic abbot who traveled to Rome and throughout western Europe acquiring manuscripts, pictures, and sacred vestments for his monastery. When he returned he brought, along with these treasures, skilled stonecutters and makers of stained glass, to build and ornament his new abbey and train native craftsmen. But it was through Bede that he made his greatest contribution in English culture.

From boyhood Bede studied in the library Benedict created at Jarrow. Then in 703, the year of his ordination to the priesthood, Bede began to write. During the ensuing 28 years he completed forty books: commentaries on the Bible; lives of abbots, martyrs, and saints; books on philosophy and poetry—a literary achievement unequaled since the days of Augustine (354-430).

Bede's masterpiece, completed in 731, when he was 51 years old, is his *Ecclesiastical History of the English People*, describing the growth of the Christian church in England from the attack of Julius Caesar in 55 B.C. to Bede's own day. He used modern historical methods. He examined past records of events, securing copies, for example, of official letters on file in Canterbury and Rome. He gathered eyewitness accounts from churchmen all over England and at the beginning of his book carefully listed all of his sources. Modern research has tended to verify the accuracy of his account. Bede's *History* is the most important work of its kind to be written between Classical times and the Renaissance.

It is written in Latin, the language he habitually spoke, wrote, and taught in; his prose is natural and direct. Late in the ninth century, scholars at the court of King Alfred translated it into Anglo-Saxon. Already the *History* seemed to them one of the central works of their culture, worthy of reproduction into a language more people could read. That high estimate has remained into our own day.

As this passage begins Paulinus, a Christian missionary, is trying to convert the pagan Edwin, King of Northumbria. Paulinus has not been able, in Bede's words, "to bring the king's proud mind to accept the humility of the way of salvation." Then one day Edwin recalls a peculiar experience from his youth, when fleeing the persecution of his predecessor, King Ethelfrid, he had taken refuge in the court of Redwald, King of East Anglia (see note, page 34).

from The Ecclesiastical History of the English People

translated by **Leo Sherley-Price**

(The Conversion of Edwin)

. . . When his predecessor was persecuting him, Edwin wandered as an unknown fugitive for many years through many lands and kingdoms, until at length he came to Redwald, and asked him for protection against the plots of his powerful enemy. Redwald gave him a ready welcome, and promised to do everything he asked, but as soon as Ethelfrid heard that he had arrived in that province, and that he and his companions were living at the king's court as his friends, he sent messengers to offer Redwald a large sum of money to murder him. Obtaining no satisfaction, he sent a second and third time, offering even heavier bribes, and threatening war if his demand were refused. At length Redwald, either intimidated by his threats or corrupted by his bribes, agreed to his demand and promised either to kill Edwin, or to surrender him to Ethelfrid's messengers. This plot was discovered by a loyal friend of Edwin, who went to his room early one night when he was about to retire, and calling him out, warned him of the king's wicked intentions, adding: "If you are willing, I will act as your guide out of this province, and take you immediately to some place where neither Redwald nor Ethelfrid can find you." Edwin replied: "Thank you for your goodwill, but I cannot act as you suggest. I cannot break the agreement that I have made with so great a king, who has so far done me no harm, nor showed any hostility towards me. If I must die, I would rather die by his hand than by an hand less noble. For what refuge remains for me, who have already wandered for so many years in every corner of Britain, trying to escape the hatred of my enemies?" When his friend had left, Edwin remained, sitting sadly alone outside the palace, burdened with many gloomy thoughts, and not knowing what to do, or where to turn.

He had remained a considerable time in silence, grieving and desperate, when suddenly, at dead of night, he saw a man approaching whose face and clothes were strange to him, and whose unexpected arrival caused him considerable alarm. But the stranger came up and greeted him, asking why he was sitting sadly on a stone, watchful and alone, at an hour when everyone else was asleep. Edwin asked what concern it might be of his whether he passed the night indoors or outside. In reply, the man said: "Don't think that I am unaware why you are sad and sleepless and why you are keeping watch alone. I know very well who you are, what your troubles are, and what coming evils you dread. But tell me this: what reward will you give the man who can deliver you from your troubles, and persuade Redwald not to harm you or betray you to death at the hands of your enemies?" Edwin answered that he would give any reward in his power in return for such an outstanding service. Then the other went on: "And what if he also promised that you should become king, defeat your enemies, and enjoy greater power than any of your predecessors who have ever ruled the English nation?" Heartened by these enquiries, Edwin readily promised that, in return for such blessings, he would give ample proofs of his gratitude. The stranger then asked a third question. "If the man who can truthfully foretell such good fortune can also give you better and wiser guidance for your life and salvation ·than anything known to your parents and kinsfolk, will you promise to obey and follow his salutary advice?" Edwin at once promised that he would faithfully follow the guidance of anyone who could save him out of so many troubles and raise him to a throne. On this assurance, the man who addressed him laid his right hand on Edwin's head, saying: "When you receive this sign,

From *Bede: A History of the English Church and People,* translated by Leo Sherley-Price. Reprinted by permission of Penguin Books Ltd.

The illustration on the facing page is a cruciform "carpet page" from the Lindisfarne Gospels, dating from around A.D. 700.

Celtic Literature in Wales and Ireland

After the retreat of the Roman legions, Celtic Britons struggled to defend their land against Anglo-Saxon tribes. During the sixth century, driven north and west, they fought a series of ultimately futile battles with the invaders. Their poets subsequently recorded, in clusters of three-line stanzas, the names of the heroes who died then. These "Stanzas of the Graves" served primarily as mnemonic devices—to aid the bards in recalling names that otherwise might be forgotten. They are probably the oldest surviving Welsh poems. Some of the names they record subsequently became the heroes of Arthurian legend: Bedwyr—Bedivere; Gwalchmai—Gawain; March—King Mark; and Arthur himself. This reference to Arthur is the earliest now known, but already it seems to suggest the growth of legend and mystery around him. His grave is "The world's enigma. . . ."

With the ultimate success of the Anglo-Saxon conquerors, surviving Britons fled south and west, carrying with them vivid memories of their past defeats. In Wales their bards now began to compose heroic tales about the past. Unlike the Anglo-Saxon story of *Beowulf,* these were a mixture of prose narrative and lyric reflection. The prose narratives have disappeared, but some of the lyrics survive. They express intense emotion—usually tragic grief at loss and death. The "Eagle of Pengwern" comes from a longer work composed about 850 which describes a disaster suffered two hundred years earlier. In this poem the woman Heledd laments the death of her brother Cynddylan and the destruction of their town Trenn, luckless in defeat but "shining" from the fame of Cynddylan's heroism.

Because of the early and rapid spread of Christianity in Ireland, Latin was already in use there by the fifth century, and poetry in the vernacular Irish language from the sixth century still survives—the oldest vernacular literature in western Europe. Like the Welsh, Irish bards created narratives in prose and verse recording the exploits of national heroes. The greatest of these, the *Tain* (tôn), celebrating the battles of the hero Cuchulain (kə hul'ən), may have been orally composed between A.D. 500 and 700. From the seventh century comes a new sort of poetry, short lyrics with regular meter and **end rhyme**—probably derived from Latin models, but already speaking in an authentically Irish voice.

from The Stanzas of the Graves

translated by **Gwyn Jones**

1

The graves the rain makes wet and sleek,
Not men who turned the other cheek,
Cerwyd, and Cywryd, and Caw.

4

Siawn's grave is on Hirerw Mound,
5 Between the earth and his oaken shroud,
A treacherous smiler, bitter, proud.

9

Whose grave is this? [. . .]
Crazed as a wild boar in mortal strife,
He'd smile on you as he spilled your life.

10

10 At Camlan[1] the grave of Osfran's son,
After many a bloody fight.
Bedwyr's grave's on Tryfan height.

11

Gwalchmai is in Perydon ground,
His grave reproaches all mankind;
15 Cynon in Llanbadarn find.

12

A grave for March, a grave for Gwythur,
A grave for Gwgawn Red-glaive;[2]
The world's enigma, Arthur's grave.

9th–10th century

---

1. **Camlan,** site of Arthur's last battle.
2. *glaive* (glāv), sword.

Eagle of Pengwern

translated by **Gwyn Williams**

Eagle of Pengwern, grey-crested, tonight
    its shriek is high,
    eager for flesh I loved.
Eagle of Pengwern, grey-crested, tonight
5   its call is high,
    eager for Cynddylan's flesh.
Eagle of Pengwern, grey-crested, tonight
    its claw is high,
    eager for flesh I love.
10 Eagle of Pengwern, it called far tonight,
    it kept watch on men's blood;
    Trenn shall be called a luckless town.
Eagle of Pengwern, it calls far tonight,
    it feasts on men's blood;
15   Trenn shall be called a shining town.

c. 850

Pangur Ban

translated by **Robin Flower**

I and Pangur Ban, my cat,
'Tis a like task we are at;
Hunting mice is his delight,
Hunting words I sit all night.

5 Better far than praise of men
'Tis to sit with book and pen;
Pangur bears me no ill will,
He too plies his simple skill.

'Tis a merry thing to see
10 At our tasks how glad are we,
When at home we sit and find
Entertainment to our mind.

The Great Chi-Rho from the Book of Kells, an Irish illuminated manuscript dating from around A.D. 800.

Oftentimes a mouse will stray
In the hero Pangur's way;
15 Oftentimes my keen thought set
Takes a meaning in its net.

'Gainst the wall he sets his eye
Full and fierce and sharp and sly;
'Gainst the wall of knowledge I
20 All my little wisdom try.

When a mouse darts from its den,
O how glad is Pangur then!
O what gladness do I prove
When I solve the doubts I love!

25 So in peace our tasks we ply,
Pangur Ban, my cat, and I;
In our arts we find our bliss,
I have mine and he has his.

Practice every day has made
30 Pangur perfect in his trade;
I get wisdom day and night
Turning darkness into light.
9th century

*S*ummer Is Gone

translated by **Kuno Meyer**

My tidings for you: the stag bells,
Winter snows, summer is gone.

Wind high and cold, low the sun,
Short his course, sea running high.

5 Deep-red the bracken, its shape all gone—
The wild-goose has raised his wonted cry.

Cold has caught the wings of birds;
Season of ice—these are my tidings.
9th century

*T*he Viking Terror

translated by **Frank O'Connor**

Since tonight the wind is high,
The sea's white mane a fury,
I need not fear the hordes of hell
Coursing the Irish Channel.
9th century

From *A Book of Ireland* edited by Frank O'Connor. Copyright © 1959 William Collins Sons and Company Limited. Reprinted by permission.

The Oseberg Ship, not a warship but a royal barge of the ninth century used for the burial of a Norwegian queen.

Discussion

1. In "Eagle of Pengwern" the poet employs both repetition and variation. What effect does the repetition have? What effect does the variation have?

2. For what reasons might the poet in "Pangur Ban" make a comparison between scholarship and mousing? Is the comparison effective?

3. How are images of nature used in "The Viking Terror" and "Summer Is Gone" to convey emotion?

The Changing English Language

The English language has developed and continues to evolve as the people who speak it have been affected by social conditions, political events, and contacts with other cultures. This series of articles will explore the nature of the changes which our language has undergone, and the events and forces which have brought about those changes.

The first inhabitants of the British Isles whose language we know about were the Celts. Beginning in 55 B.C., the Roman general Julius Caesar led a series of unsuccessful attacks on the British Celts. About a hundred years later, in A.D. 43, Romans began settling in Britain. For the next four hundred years, Britain was part of the Roman Empire, and camps of the Latin-speaking Roman legions dotted the countryside. Their influence can still be seen in the names of such English towns as Lancaster, Manchester, and Worcester, the suffixes -caster, -chester, and -cester being derived from castrum, the Latin word for camp.

Early in the fifth century, when the Roman Empire began to disintegrate, the Romans were forced to withdraw their troops from Britain. Left without the defenses of the Roman legions, the Celts were soon attacked by Germanic tribes from across the North Sea—Jutes, Angles, and Saxons—whose homelands were along the Danish peninsula and the northwest coast of Germany. The invaders drove some of the Celts to Brittany across the sea and many others into what are now Wales and Cornwall. The Celtic language survives today as Welsh, the language of Wales; Irish, the Celtic language of Ireland; Scots Gaelic, the ancient tongue of the Highlands; and Breton, the Celtic language still spoken in Brittany.

The invading tribes of Germanic people spoke dialects of the language now called Old English or sometimes Anglo-Saxon. The largest group, the Angles, settled the lands from the Thames River to the north of England. It is from this group that the names England (Angleland) and English (Anglisc) are derived, although most of the literature written in the dialect of this northern area has been lost. The Saxons, who lived south of the Thames, spoke the variety of Old English in which most of the surviving documents of the period are written. In Kent were the Jutes; only a very few texts in the Kentish dialect have been preserved.

In 597, Augustine and other missionaries arrived from Rome, bringing Christianity and initiating the introduction of Latin words into Old English. The largest number of such words were those related to the new religion; among them were *altar, candle, hymn, organ, pope, priest,* and *temple,* which today differ only slightly from their Old English forms. Contact with the Roman church also led to the adoption of words describing clothing (e.g., our modern *sock, cap*), foods (e.g., *beet, pear*), plants and trees (*pine, lily*), and words related to education (*school, Latin, verse, meter*), as well as many others.

Beginning in the eighth century, Old English was further modified by contact with the Scandinavian languages. The inhabitants of the Scandinavian peninsula and Denmark, once close neighbors of the early Anglo-Saxons and similar to them both in blood and in language, began a series of raids on England that culminated in the eleventh century when Cnut, king of Denmark, conquered all of England and seized the English throne. For the next twenty-five years, Danish kings ruled England.

During the nearly three hundred years of Scandinavian attacks, a considerable number of Scandinavians also settled peacefully in England, especially in the northern and eastern sections. Evidence of the extent of such settlement survives in place names. A map today shows more than six hundred names such as Grimsby, Rugby, and Derby, formed from the Danish word *byr* meaning farm or town. There are also names like Thistlethwaite and Braithwaite from *thveit* meaning "isolated piece of land."

Since Old English and the language of the invaders were quite similar, there was a ready intermingling of forms of speech. In some cases, when the languages had different words to describe the same thing, the English word survived. In other cases, such Scandinavian words as *egg* and *systir* (sister) replace their Old English equivalents. The Scandinavian pronouns *they, their,* and *them* were substituted for the Old English equivalents *hie, hiera,* and *him.* Occasionally, Old English words which had fallen into disuse were revived because of Scandinavian parallels.

You saw a brief passage in Old English in the note on the poetry of *Beowulf.* Another passage appears in the note on translating *Beowulf,* followed by a variety of translations. You may recog-

The first page of the *Beowulf* manuscript.

nize a few words of the Anglo-Saxon; still, we who speak modern English must constantly remind ourselves when we see Old English that this was not a truly foreign language but the not-far-removed ancestor of our own tongue.

Our difficulty in reading Old English becomes more understandable when we realize that it was quite different in grammatical structure from the English we speak and write today. Modern English depends heavily upon the arrangement of words in a sentence to give meaning; it relies only slightly on word endings to indicate number, gender, and case (e.g., whether a noun is the object of a verb or its subject). For example, when we read

1. The king greeted the foreigner.
2. The foreigner greeted the king.

we know that in the first sentence, *king* is the subject of the verb *greeted,* and in the second sentence, *king* is the object of the verb, even though there is no change in the spelling of *king* as the function of the word changes. In Old English, "the king," when used as the grammatical subject (as in sentence 1) would be written as *se cyning;* as the object (as in sentence 2), it would be *þæm cyninge.* Old English was what linguists call a highly inflected language, which means that the meaning of a sentence depended on changes in the spelling of nouns, pronouns, adjectives, and verbs. Although modern English still makes use of inflections, there are far fewer inflected forms than there were in Anglo-Saxon times.

Old English verbs were of two types: "strong" and "weak." In strong verbs, the vowels changed in the principal part, as they do in modern *sing, sang, sung;* weak verbs indicated change of time by adding *d* or *t,* as do the majority of verbs today (*look, looked, looked*).

Apart from grammatical differences, some of the strangeness which Old English presents to a modern reader is due to differences in spelling and vocabulary. Old English used two characters, þ and ð, to represent the sound *th,* so that *wiþ* is our modern word *with,* and *ða* is the equivalent of *then.* The sound *sh* was represented in Old English by *sc,* and the sound of *k* was represented by *c.* Words like *scip, bæð, nacod,* and *þæt,* which look strange to us, were most likely pronounced in Anglo-Saxon times almost as we pronounce them today: *ship, bath, naked,* and *that.*

Fewer than a fourth of the words in modern English are derived from Old English, but among those are the most commonly used nouns, pronouns, verbs, connectives, and articles.

Why don't we still speak Anglo-Saxon? What forces made English take the form it has today? Later articles in this book will trace the political and social forces that influenced—and continue to influence—the evolution of the English language.

The Anglo-Saxons

Content Review

1. What does Beowulf seek in his adventure to Hrothgar's hall?

2. How does Beowulf's last foe differ from those he defeated earlier?

3. Describe the type of verse used for *Beowulf.*

4. Name the technical term for phrases such as "ring-giver" and "whale-road."

5. What theme dominates the Anglo-Saxon elegies?

6. Briefly restate the message in "The Husband's Message."

7. How does a riddle resemble a metaphor?

8. What function does the priest Coifi have in Bede's account of King Edwin's conversion?

9. What early tradition about King Arthur's fate is referred to in "The Stanzas of the Graves."

10. What is the basic comparison made in "Pangur Ban"?

Concept Review: Interpretation of New Material

The poem below comes from the Exeter Book (see page 42). It is the **monologue** of an old sailor.

The Seafarer   translated by **Burton Raffel**

This tale is true, and mine. It tells
How the sea took me, swept me back
And forth in sorrow and fear and pain,
Showed me suffering in a hundred ships,
5 In a thousand ports, and in me. It tells
Of smashing surf when I sweated in the cold
Of an anxious watch, perched in the bow
As it dashed under cliffs. My feet were cast
In icy bands, bound with frost,
10 With frozen chains, and hardship groaned
Around my heart. Hunger tore
At my sea-weary soul. No man sheltered
On the quiet fairness of earth can feel
How wretched I was, drifting through winter
15 On an ice-cold sea, whirled in sorrow,
Alone in a world blown clear of love,
Hung with icicles. The hailstorms flew.
The only sound was the roaring sea,
The freezing waves. The song of the swan
20 Might serve for pleasure, the cry of the
    sea-fowl,
The death-noise of birds instead of laughter,

The mewing of gulls instead of mead.
Storms beat on the rocky cliffs and were
    echoed
By icy-feathered terns and the eagle's screams;
25 No kinsman could offer comfort there,
To a soul left drowning in desolation.
   And who could believe, knowing but
The passion of cities, swelled proud with wine
And no taste of misfortune, how often, how
    wearily,
30 I put myself back on the paths of the sea.
Night would blacken; it would snow from the
    north;
Frost bound the earth and hail would fall,
The coldest seeds. And how my heart
Would begin to beat, knowing once more
35 The salt waves tossing and the towering sea!
The time for journeys would come and my soul

Called me eagerly out, sent me over
The horizon, seeking foreigners' homes.
   But there isn't a man on earth so proud,
40 So born to greatness, so bold with his youth,
Grown so brave, or so graced by God,
That he feels no fear as the sails unfurl,
Wondering what Fate has willed and will do.
No harps ring in his heart, no rewards,
45 No passion for women, no worldly pleasures,
Nothing, only the ocean's heave;
But longing wraps itself around him.
Orchards blossom, the towns bloom,
Fields grow lovely as the world springs fresh,
50 And all these admonish that willing mind
Leaping to journeys, always set
In thoughts travelling on a quickening tide.
So summer's sentinel, the cuckoo, sings
In his murmuring voice, and our hearts mourn
55 As he urges. Who could understand,
In ignorant ease, what we others suffer
As the paths of exile stretch endlessly on?
   And yet my heart wanders away,
My soul roams with the sea, the whales'
60 Home, wandering to the widest corners
Of the world, returning ravenous with desire,
Flying solitary, screaming, exciting me
To the open ocean, breaking oaths
On the curve of a wave.
                              Thus the joys of God
65 Are fervent with life, where life itself
Fades quickly into the earth. The wealth
Of the world neither reaches to Heaven nor
   remains.
No man has ever faced the dawn
Certain which of Fate's three threats
70 Would fall: illness, or age, or an enemy's
Sword, snatching the life from his soul.
The praise the living pour on the dead
Flowers from reputation: plant
An earthly life of profit reaped
75 Even from hatred and rancor, of bravery
Flung in the devil's face, and death
Can only bring you earthly praise
And a song to celebrate a place
With the angels, life eternally blessed
80 In the hosts of Heaven.
                              The days are gone
When the kingdoms of earth flourished in
   glory;

Now there are no rulers, no emperors,
No givers of gold, as once there were,
When wonderful things were worked among
   them
85 And they lived in lordly magnificence.
Those powers have vanished, those pleasures
   are dead,
The weakest survives and the world continues,
Kept spinning by toil. All glory is tarnished,
The world's honor ages and shrinks,
90 Bent like the men who mold it. Their faces
Blanch as time advances, their beards
Wither and they mourn the memory of friends,
The sons of princes, sown in the dust.
The soul stripped of its flesh knows nothing
95 Of sweetness or sour, feels no pain,
Bends neither its hand nor its brain. A brother
Opens his palms and pours down gold
On his kinsman's grave, strewing his coffin
With treasures intended for Heaven, but
   nothing
100 Golden shakes the wrath of God
For a soul overflowing with sin, and nothing
Hidden on earth rises to Heaven.
   We all fear God. He turns the earth,
He set it swinging firmly in space,
105 Gave life to the world and light to the sky.
Death leaps at the fools who forget their God.
He who lives humbly has angels from Heaven
To carry him courage and strength and belief.
A man must conquer pride, not kill it,
110 Be firm with his fellows, chaste for himself,
Treat all the world as the world deserves,
With love or with hate but never with harm,
Though an enemy seek to scorch him in hell,
Or set the flames of a funeral pyre
115 Under his lord. Fate is stronger
And God mightier than any man's mind.
Our thoughts should turn to where our home
   is,
Consider the ways of coming there,
Then strive for sure permission for us
120 To rise to that eternal joy,
That life born in the love of God
And the hope of Heaven. Praise the Holy
Grace of He who honored us,
Eternal, unchanging creator of earth. Amen.
8th century

On a separate sheet of paper, write your answers to the following questions. Do not write in your book.

1. Rewrite only the alliterating words from the following lines: "Wandering to the widest corners / Of the world."

2. What are some of the hardships and difficulties the speaker has known in his years at sea? Cite lines in which these hardships are vividly described.

3. Point out lines in which the narrator mentions the joys of seafaring. In your opinion which lines best summarize the fascination of the sea?

4. What do the words "whales' home" (lines 59–60) refer to? Is this an example of (a) an elegy; (b) a kenning; (c) a riddle; (d) a caesura?

5. What is the break or pause in the middle of the following line called: "How wretched I was, drifting through winter"? (a) scop; (b) kenning; (c) riddle; (d) caesura.

6. What three threats does the speaker say every person faces with the dawn?

7. The phrase "givers of gold" (line 83) probably means which of the following? (a) jewelers; (b) kings; (c) warriors; (d) priests.

8. What is the speaker's attitude toward worldly glory?

9. What does the speaker mean when he says, "A man must conquer pride, not kill it" (line 109)?

10. What is the predominant tone of the poem? (a) melancholy; (b) joyful; (c) fierce; (d) confident.

Composition Review

You may choose any *one* of the following assignments. Assume that you are writing for your classmates.

1. Jot down different ways in which people help each other in *Beowulf.*

Use these examples as illustrations for an essay describing human interdependence in the poem.

2. Some readers think that the monsters in *Beowulf* turn an otherwise serious work into a story for children. To effectively argue for or against this position, first decide how you will justify your own view and then write down the probable objections of an opponent.

Use these arguments as the basis of an essay supporting your view.

3. Locate passages in which Beowulf and the speaker in "The Seafarer" discuss death. Look for similiarities and differences in what they say.

In a comparison/contrast essay, use examples of their own words to define what death means for each of them.

4. In your own words enumerate the important characteristics of the Anglo-Saxon **elegy,** and then determine how they appear (or are absent) in "The Wife's Lament," "The Husband's Message," and "The Seafarer."

Using this information, write an essay describing how each of these poems illustrates (or departs from) the characteristics of the elegy.

5. Set down in a single sentence what Edwin's thane means by comparing human life to the flight of a sparrow through a mead-hall. Next, list for yourself other Anglo-Saxon writings in which this same theme appears.

Write an essay describing how (and suggesting why) such a vision of human life keeps reappearing in the literature of this era.

6. Review "The Seafarer," the Anglo-Saxon riddles, and the Welsh and Irish poems for images from nature. List the moods they evoke in you as you read them.

In an essay describe the kinds of imagery from nature that appear in these poems, and how they suggest specific types of thought and feeling.

View of London, detail of an illustration from *Poems of Charles d'Orléans*, early fifteenth century.

• First Crusade

• Earliest record of a
miracle play

History of the •
Kings of Britain

Reign of Stephen

• Henry II marries
Eleanor of Aquitaine

• Murder of
Thomas Becket

• Founding of
Oxford University

The Third Crusade •

• Founding of
Cambridge University

• Magna Carta

• Salisbury Cathedral
begun

The Model Parliament •

1100　　　　　　　　**1150**　　　　　　　　**1200**　　　　　　　　**1250**　　　　　　　　**1300**

The Medieval Period

1350	1400	1450	1500

- Battle of Bannockburn

Sir Gawain and the Green Knight •

• Death of Joan of Arc

Henry VII marries • Elizabeth of York

Battle of Sluys •

Death of the • Black Prince

• Battle of Agincourt

• Caxton's press

Battle of Crécy •

Peasants' Revolt •

• Malory: *Morte Darthur*

• Langland: *Vision of Piers Plowman*

• Paston letters begin

The Black Death • reaches England

• Battle of Poitiers

• Death of Chaucer

Battle of • Bosworth Field

Wycliffe's Bible •

Background: The Medieval Period 1100-1500

ven before the Norman Conquest in 1066, ties existed between the court of England and that of the Duchy of Normandy in northern France. In 1002 King Aethelred of England married Emma, daughter of the duke of Normandy. Their son, Edward the Confessor, half-Norman in blood, was wholly Norman in outlook. Before becoming king of England in 1042, he had spent thirty years at the Norman court, learning the French language and customs and making French friends. As king he welcomed Norman courtiers and churchmen; his court even adopted the Norman style of dress.

When Edward died without an heir in January, 1066, his throne was claimed by both the Englishman Harold Godwinson, the choice of the Witan, the king's council, and William, Duke of Normandy, who maintained, apparently with justification, that Edward had declared him heir to the English throne. After a hasty coronation Harold marched north to battle the Viking army of another claimant, King Harold Hardrada (the Ruthless) of Norway, whom he defeated and killed at Stamford Bridge near York on September 25. Three days later William landed at Pevesney Bay on England's southeastern coast with an army estimated at between 4,000 and 7,000 men, the landless younger sons of the Norman nobility and other well-born adventurers from throughout Europe. According to a contemporary chronicle, "As soon as his men were fit for service, they constructed a castle at Hastings. When King Harold was informed of this, he gathered together a great host, and came to oppose (William) at the gray apple tree, and William came upon him unexpectedly, before his army was set in order. Nevertheless the king fought against him most resolutely with those men who wished to stand by him, and there was great slaughter on both sides. King Harold was slain, and Leofwine, his brother, and Earl Gurth, his brother, and many good men. The French had possession of the place of slaughter."

Norman England

Although Harold was dead, England was not subdued without a lengthy struggle, during which most of the Anglo-Saxon nobility was wiped out. Claiming that every bit of England belonged to him, William proceeded to redistribute lands belonging to 4,000–5,000 Anglo-Saxon nobles among around 180 of his followers, in exchange for a solemn oath of loyalty to him and the promise of military service. Thus all the landowners in England became vassals—tenants—of the king.

In 1086 William carried out a survey of his entire kingdom, arousing great resentment among his English subjects. Using sworn testimony, William's agents recorded most of the land in England, together with the name of the person who owned it, its size, its value, the number and type of workers employed on it, and so on. "So thoroughly did (William) have the enquiry carried out," complains a contemporary chronicle, "that there was not a single "hide" (120 acres) of land . . . not even one ox, nor one cow, nor one pig which escaped notice in his survey." This survey, officially referred to as "the description of England," was popularly called "Domesday (Doomsday) Book," because there was no appeal from its judgment.

William's policy of consolidating governmental power in the kingship was continued during the reigns of his two sons, William Rufus (1087–

1100) and Henry I (1100–1135). But when Henry died without a male heir, the throne was contested by his daughter Matilda, and his nephew, Stephen of Blois. With the support of the Church, Stephen became king, but his mild rule soon led to anarchy. "Every great man built him(self) castles and held them against the King," says a contemporary chronicle; ". . . and when the castles were built, they filled them with devils and wicked men. By night and by day they seized those whom they believed to have any wealth, whether they were men or women; and in order to get their gold and silver, they put them into prison, and tortured them with unspeakable tortures." Things grew worse throughout the "nineteen terrible winters" of Stephen's reign, and were only remedied during that of his successor, Matilda's brilliant son Henry II (1154–1189), called "Plantagenet" from the French name for the broom plant, his father's heraldic emblem.

The Normans introduced into England both the system of land tenure based upon military service, called *feudalism*, and the knight, the mounted warrior who became the chief symbol of the code of chivalry. Far more than merely etiquette, chivalry was more nearly an aristocratic world-view. Its ideals affected the whole conduct of the lives of the nobility. That those ideals were more often professed than practiced did not lessen their influence. Chivalry did soften some of the harshness of medieval life. It bound the often lawless warrior by a code, the violation of which meant loss of honor. In combination with a wave of devotion to the Virgin Mary that swept across Europe late in the eleventh century, it raised the status of woman and gained her a larger role both in life and literature.

Chivalry developed during the twelfth century, the period of the Crusades and of the great flowering of Arthurian romance. In 1095, not long after the Norman Conquest, England became involved in the First Crusade. Inspired by religious fervor, nobles and commoners alike undertook the long and dangerous journey to Palestine, whose Christian shrines had been in the hands of Moslem Turks since 1071. The Arthurian cycle was created from a confused mixture of elements, including scraps of history relating to an apparently real military leader of the late fifth or early sixth century, as well as elements drawn from the

mythological tales of the Welsh and other Celtic people. The first complete account of the rise and fall of Arthur's kingdom was contained in *The History of the Kings of Britain,* written in 1136 by Geoffrey of Monmouth. Both in the original Latin version and a French translation, Geoffrey's book was immensely popular, so that toward the end of the twelfth century one writer exclaims, "Whither has not flying fame spread and familiarized the name of Arthur the Briton, even as far as Christendom extends."

Higher education had its beginning in England under the Normans. As early as 1117, docu-

King Arthur, an illustration from the *Chronicle of Peter of Langtoft* (died c. 1307).

ments mention a school at Oxford, and by 1133 its size and reputation had grown sufficiently for a theologian, Robert Pullen, to travel there from Paris to lecture.

English literature during the Norman period was largely confined to versified Bible stories and sermons, composed by the clergy to instruct the illiterate common people. These people had an oral literature of their own, however. The popular ballads probably began to be composed during this period. Folk drama, in the form of harvest festivals and other seasonal rituals, must also have had a part in their lives.

Literary drama, extinct since the Classical period, had begun its modern evolution as early as A.D. 900, with the inclusion of a brief bit of dialogue in the liturgy of the Easter mass. As time passed, this brief dialogue was expanded, and similar dialogues appeared in the liturgies for other religious feasts. Eventually attendance became so large that the proceedings were moved outside the church itself and into the churchyard, where secular elements began to be introduced. To the playlets dealing with the life of Christ were added others, often with more characters and a greater length, presenting episodes from the Bible and the lives of the saints. These plays were called *miracle* or *mystery* plays.

England Under the Plantagenets

The first task of Henry II when he assumed the throne was to subdue the great feudal lords of England and Normandy, who had grown so powerful during Stephen's weak reign. He immediately raised an army and re-established the power of the monarchy. A brilliant and tireless administrator, he reformed the judicial system and ran the operations of government so efficiently that at his death he left a surplus in the treasury (the last English king for over 300 years to do so). The latter part of Henry's reign was darkened by conflict with his wife, Eleanor of Aquitaine, his sons, and his friend, Thomas Becket, the Archbishop of Canterbury. The long and bitter struggle between Henry and Becket over the issue of the legal rights of the clergy reached its climax on December 30, 1170, when Becket was killed by four of Henry's knights, but apparently without the king's knowledge. Becket's death was a disaster for Henry, both personally and politically. England was horrified by the murder of its leading priest, who was immediately acclaimed a martyr. Excommunicated by an outraged Church, Henry attempted reconciliation by restoring clerical rights, and even went as a pilgrim to Becket's shrine at Canterbury.

Henry's son Richard Coeur de Lion (the Lion-Heart) spent most of his reign outside of England. Having fought against the brilliant Moslem leader Saladin in the Third Crusade, he was captured on his return home and held for ransom by the Holy Roman Emperor. While Richard was absent, his brother John tried unsuccessfully to seize the throne, with the help of the king of France. Suc-

ceeding to the throne after his brother's death in 1199, John managed to alienate his nobles, the clergy, his late ally the King of France, and the Pope. His autocratic rule, his personal excesses, and his heavy taxation finally led the nobles to rise against him. On June 15, 1215, he was forced to sign Magna Carta, "the Great Charter," that limits the power of the king and is the foundation of the representative English government. Among other reforms, it defined and safeguarded the basic rights of nobles, clergy, and freemen; it established habeas corpus (a protection against unjust imprisonment) and trial by jury; and it gave the general council (the forerunner of Parliament) power over expenditures.

It was in 1295 that Edward I summoned the first English Parliament to include, in addition to the nobility and the clergy, two representatives "from every city, borough, and leading town." The appearance of members of the middle class in Parliament was an indication of the growing wealth and power of English cities like London and Norwich.

In 1337 England became involved in the Hundred Years' War with France. The issue was English control of large parts of France. The French possessions of the Norman kings of England had been vastly increased by the marriage of Henry II and Eleanor of Aquitaine in 1152. The English king held half of France, possessions extending from the English Channel to the Pyrenees. The early battles of the war were all great English victories: Sluys (1340), where the great French fleet was nearly destroyed; Crécy (1346), where English longbowmen slaughtered French knights; Poitiers (1356), where the French king himself was taken prisoner. But eventually the French recovered, partly due to the inspiration of Joan of Arc (1412–1431). The fighting dragged on until 1453, when the French were finally victorious and England lost all her French possessions except the Channel port of Calais.

New weapons like the crossbow (and more importantly, cannon, which were first used at Crécy) weakened feudalism by lessening the military importance of the mounted knight and, later, of the castle. Another factor hastening feudalism's decline was the appearance of the Black Death, or bubonic plague, which in 1348 and 1349 devastated England, killing perhaps a third of the population. In the disorder that resulted, many serfs escaped their feudal bondage by running away to London and other population centers. Wages rose dramatically, despite government attempts to freeze them. Later, desperate for money to continue the endless war with France, the government tried to impose a poll-tax (a fixed tax levied on every adult, regardless of income). This led to riots in the cities, and, eventually, in 1381, to a major rebellion, the Peasants' Revolt. The principal leader was Wat Tyler, an eloquent adventurer who had served in the French wars. When the rioters reached London, killing, burning, and pillaging along the way, they seemed on the point of enforcing their demands, which included the abolition of serfdom. But the death of Tyler led to the collapse of the revolt.

Feudalism was not the only major institution to be weakened in the fourteenth century. The authority of the Church suffered when a quarrel over the papal succession in 1378 led to the division in the Church known as the Great Schism, which lasted until 1417. During this period there were two, and briefly, even three rival popes. A further blow to Church authority occurred in 1381, when John Wycliffe's English translation of the Bible appeared. The Church had always opposed translating the Latin of the Scriptures into the vernacular languages of Europe, fearing the spread of heresy. Wycliffe's defiance is regarded as one of the first steps toward the Reformation of the fifteenth century.

The end of the Hundred Years' War in 1415 brought only a brief peace. In 1455 began the Wars of the Roses, the bloody, thirty-year dynastic struggle between the Houses of Lancaster and York, supporters of rival claimants to the English throne. (The conflict derives its name from the heraldic emblems of the two Houses, the red rose of Lancaster and the white rose of York.) The struggle only ended in 1485, when the Yorkist king, Richard III, faced his Lancastrian rival, Henry Tudor, Earl of Richmond, at the battle of Bosworth Field. Richard was defeated and killed, and the victor, crowned Henry VII, married Elizabeth of York, uniting the two Houses and establishing the Tudor dynasty that ruled for the next century.

Literature did well under the Plantagenets. During the period 1250–1350, the upper classes began to adopt English as their language. They were entertained by the romances of Arthur, while the common people composed ballads about a hero of their own, Robin Hood. The alliterative verse form of the Anglo-Saxons had largely disappeared, replaced by the French system of end rhyme. (The alliterative form survived longest in the northern part of the country; the author of *Sir Gawain and the Green Knight,* Chaucer's great contemporary, still employed it.) The miracle plays gradually evolved into cycles of plays presented on the feast of Corpus Christi in large towns like Coventry and York.

As he threatens young King Richard II, Wat Tyler is killed by one of Richard's men. A miniature from a fifteenth-century manuscript of Froissart's *Chronicles.*

After the death of Chaucer, English literature declined. The fifteenth century is an imitative and transitional period, during which many writers tried, not always successfully, to imitate Chaucer. Although there were some attempts at innovation, not until the next century did any of them really succeed. The single exception was the appearance of Caxton's edition of Sir Thomas Malory's *Morte Darthur,* the first great masterpiece of English prose.

Popular Ballads

A **ballad** is a narrative poem, usually brief and anonymous, that is part of the oral tradition of a people. Because the English and Scottish popular ballads were sung for centuries before they were written down, exactly when or how they originated and developed is unknown. From references in old documents and the character of the ballads themselves, it seems that most were probably composed in the Scottish border region in the late Middle Ages. At least some of the ballads were probably composed to commemorate events of importance to particular communities. As generations of singers passed on the song, a word was changed here and there, stanzas were omitted, and differing versions of the same ballad often appeared.

However, certain basic characteristics did develop. Because the listeners were most interested in rapid and dramatic action, the story was more important than the characters or setting. As a rule, background material was sketched in briefly, and the action moved swiftly to its climax. Usually the tone was tragic. Ballads often ended in death by accident, murder, or suicide, or with the return of the dead.

Certain technical characteristics were also common to the ballad. The repetition of words, phrases, or lines was employed for melodic effect, to provide emphasis, and to heighten emotion. Incremental repetition, or the repetition of lines containing some small addition, or *increment,* is used to build to a climax. Many of the oldest ballads also make use of a refrain. Both types of repetition may be observed in the opening lines of "Lord Randal":

"O where ha you been, Lord Randal, my
    son?
And where ha you been, my handsome
    young man?"
"I ha been at the greenwood; mother, mak
    my bed soon,
For I'm wearied wi hunting, and fain wad lie
    down."
"An wha met ye there, Lord Randal, my son?
"An wha met you there, my handsome young
    man?"

"O I met wi my true-love; mother, mak my
    bed soon,
For I'm wearied wi huntin, and fain wad lie
    down."

All English ballads are divided into stanzas. The most frequently used stanza form, the so-called **ballad stanza,** consists of four iambic lines with four accents in the first and third lines, three in the rhyming second and fourth lines. When read, the meter of ballads often seems crude and irregular. This is because ballads were meant to be sung, and the rhythms of song differ from those of speech.

The attitude of writers toward the popular ballads has altered over the centuries. Sir Philip Sidney (see page 149) in his *Apology for Poetry* (1595) feels he must apologize for his preference: "Certainly I must confess my own barbarousness, I never heard the old song of Percy and Douglas (the ballad of "Chevy Chase") that I found not my heart moved more than with a trumpet, and yet is sung by some blind crowder (fiddler), with no rougher voice than rude style."

Joseph Addison (see page 312), writing in *The Spectator* (1711), while condescending, is not apologetic for his liking, seeing it as a universal taste: ". . . it is impossible that anything [like the ballads] should be universally tasted and approved by a multitude, though they are only the rabble of a nation, which hath not in it some peculiar aptness to please and gratify the mind of man."

The first important collection of ballads was made by Bishop Thomas Percy (1729–1811). As a young man he had found a manuscript collection of poetry dating from about 1650. Though it was damaged (servants had torn out leaves to use in lighting fires), 191 poems survived, including a number of broadside ballads (see headnote, page 70). This became the chief source for Percy's *Reliques of Ancient English Poetry* (1765).

One of those inspired by Percy's *Reliques* was the novelist Sir Walter Scott (1771–1832), who published ten years of ballad-collecting as *Minstrelsy of the Scottish Border* (1802).

Edward

"Why dois your brand sae drap wi bluid,[1]
    Edward, Edward,
Why dois your brand sae drap wi bluid,
    And why sae sad gang° yee° O?''   go/you
5 "O I hae° killed my hauke° sae guid,° have/hawk/good
    Mither,° mither,   mother
O I hae killed my hauke sae guid,
    And I had nae mair bot hee[2] O.

"Your haukis bluid was nevir° sae reid,° never/red
10   Edward, Edward,
Your haukis bluid was nevir sae reid,
    My deir° son I tell thee O.''   dear
"O I hae killed my reid-roan steid,[3]
    Mither, mither,
15 O I hae killed my reid-roan steid,
    That erst° was sae fair and frie° O.'' once/free

"Your steid was auld,° and ye hae gat mair, old
    Edward, Edward,
Your steid was auld, and ye hae gat mair,
20   Sum other dule ye drie[4] O.''
"O I hae killed my fadir° deir,   father
    Mither, mither,
O I hae killed my fadir deir,
    Alas, and wae° is mee O!''   woe

25 "And whatten penance[5] wul° ye drie for that, will
    Edward, Edward?
And whatten penance wul ye drie for that?
    My deir son, now tell me O.''
"Ile° set my feit° in yonder boat, I will/feet
30   Mither, mither,
Ile set my feit in yonder boat,
    And Ile fare ovir° the sea O.'' over

"And what wul ye doe wi your towirs and
    your ha,[6]
    Edward, Edward,
35 And what wul ye doe wi your towirs and
    your ha,
    That were sae fair to see O?''
"Ile let thame stand tul they doun fa,[7]
    Mither, mither,
Ile let thame stand tul they doun fa,
40   For here nevir mair maun° I bee O.'' must
"And what wul ye leive° to your bairns° leave/children
    and your wife,
    Edward, Edward?
And what wul ye leive to your bairns and
    your wife,
    Whan ye gang ovir the sea O?''
45 "The warldis room,[8] late° them beg let
    thrae° life,   through
    Mither, mither,
The warldis room, late them beg thrae life,
    For thame nevir mair wul I see O.''

"And what wul ye leive to your ain° mither own
    deir?
50   Edward, Edward?
And what wul ye leive to your ain mither deir?
    My deir son, now tell me O.''
"The curse of hell frae° me sall ye beir,[9] from
    Mither, mither,
55 The curse of hell frae me sall ye beir,
    Sic counseils[10] ye gave to me O.''

from *Reliques of Ancient English Poetry*, 1765

---

1. ***dois . . . bluid,*** does your sword so drip with blood.
2. ***nae . . . hee,*** no more but him.
3. ***reid-roan steid,*** red-roan horse. "Red-roan" means a red coat mottled with white or gray.
4. ***Sum . . . drie,*** some other sorrow you suffer.
5. ***whatten penance,*** what kind of penance. A penance is a punishment borne to show sorrow for wrongdoing.
6. ***wi . . . ha,*** with your towers and your hall.
7. ***thame . . . fa,*** them stand till they down fall.
8. ***worldis room,*** world is room (large enough).
9. ***sall ye beir,*** shall you bear.
10. ***Sic counseils,*** such counsels (advice).

Although no mention of Sir Patrick Spence can be found in old Scottish or English records, most authorities agree that this ballad records an actual event. While there is disagreement as to what event the ballad commemorates, evidence points toward the ill-fated return voyage of the ship that in 1281 had carried Margaret, daughter of King Alexander III of Scotland, to Norway, to marry Eric, King of Norway.

*S*ir Patrick Spence

The king sits in Dumferling¹ toune,°   *town*
  Drinking the blude-reid° wine: *blood-red*
"O whar° will I get guid° sailor,   *where/good*
  To sail this schip° of mine?"   *ship*

5 Up and spak° an eldern knicht,²   *spoke*
  Sat at the kings richt kne°:   *right knee*
"Sir Patrick Spence is the best sailor
  That sails upon the se."

The king has written a braid letter,³
10   And signed it wi his hand,
And sent it to Sir Patrick Spence,
  Was walking on the sand.

The first line that Sir Patrick red,
  A loud lauch° lauched he;   *laugh*
15 The next line that Sir Patrick red,
  The teir° blinded his ee.   *tear*

"O wha° is this has don this deid,°   *who/deed*
  This ill deid don to me,
To send me out this time o' the yeir,°   *year*
20   To sail upon the se!

"Mak hast, mak haste, my mirry° men all,   *merry*
  Our guid schip sails the morne":
"O say na sae,° my master deir,°   *so/dear*
  For I feir° a deadlie storme.   *fear*

25 "Late late yestreen° I saw the new   *last evening*
    moone,
  Wi the auld° moone in hir arme,⁴   *old*
And I feir, I feir, my deir master,
  That we will cum to harme."

O our Scots nobles wer richt laith⁵
30   To weet° their cork-heild schoone;⁶   *wet*
But lang owre a'⁷ the play wer playd,
  Their hats they swam aboone.⁸

O lang, lang may their ladies sit,
  Wi their fans into their hand,
35 Or eir° they se Sir Patrick Spence   *before*
  Cum sailing to the land.

O lang, lang may the ladies stand,
  Wi their gold kems° in their hair,   *combs*
Waiting for thair ain° deir lords,   *own*
40   For they'll se thame na mair.°   *them no more*

Haf owre,° haf owre to Aberdour,⁹   *halfway over*
  It's fiftie fadom deip,°   *deep*
And thair° lies guid Sir Patrick Spence,   *there*
  Wi the Scots lords at his feit.°   *feet*

from *Reliques of Ancient English Poetry*, 1765

---

1. **Dumferling,** Dumfermline, one of the royal residences of the Scottish monarchy. It lies in the county of Fife north of Edinburgh.
2. **eldern knicht,** old knight
3. **braid letter.** A braid (broad) letter was not a royal command, but rather an informal request, though couched in such terms that it would be nearly impossible to refuse.
4. **the new moone . . . in hir arme.** The bad omen in such a sight lay in the fact that the new moon was seen *late* in the evening. The "auld moone in hir arme" is a reference to the semi-luminous surface of the moon visible between the horns of the new moon.
5. **wer richt laith,** were right loath (very unwilling).
6. **cork-heild schoone,** cork-heeled shoes.
7. **lang owre a',** long ere (before) all.
8. **aboone,** above. Either the shoes were *aboone* (because their wearers were floating head downward); or the hats were *aboone* (floating on the surface of the water).
9. **Aberdour,** a port on the north shore of the Firth of Forth, some ten miles from Dunfermline. "Haf owre to Aberdour" means halfway home on the sea voyage from Norway. This is the approximate position of the island of Papa Stronsay, where one folklorist reports that there is a tumulus, an ancient grave mound, that is known now, "and has always been known," as the grave of Sir Patrick Spence.

Get Up and Bar the Door

It fell about the Martinmas time,[1]
  And a gay time it was then,
When our goodwife got puddings[2]
    to make,
  And she's boild them in the pan.

5 The wind sae cauld° blew south   *so cold*
    and north,
  And blew into the floor;
Quoth our goodman to our goodwife,
  "Gae° out and bar the door."   *go*

"My hand is in my hussyfskap,[3]
10 Goodman, as ye may see;
An it shoud nae° be barrd this hundred year,   *should not*
  It's no be barrd for me."

They made a paction[4] tween them twa,°   *between them two*
  They made it firm and sure,
15 That the first word whaeer shoud speak,
  Shoud rise and bar the door.

Then by there came two gentlemen,
  At twelve o clock at night,
And they could neither see house nor hall,
20 Nor coal nor candlelight.

"Now whether is this a rich man's house,
  Or whether is it a poor?"
But neer° a word wad ane° o them   *never/would any*
    speak,
  For barring of the door.

25 And first they[5] ate the white puddings,
  And then they ate the black;
Tho muckle° thought the goodwife to   *though much*
    hersel,
  Yet neer a word she spake.

A fifteenth-century tapestry (possibly intended as a cushion cover) that humorously depicts a busy housewife.

Then said the one unto the other,
30 "Here, man, tak ye my knife;
Do ye tak aff the auld° man's beard,   *old*
  And I'll kiss the goodwife."

"But there's nae water in the house,
  And what shall we do than?"
35 "What ails ye at the pudding-broo,[6]
  That boils into the pan?"

O up then started our goodman,
  An angry man was he:
"Will ye kiss my wife before my een,°   *eyes*
40 And scad me wi pudding-bree?"

Then up and started our goodwife,
  Gied° three skips on the floor: *gave*
"Goodman, you've spoken the foremost
    word,
  Get up and bar the door."

from *The Ancient and Modern Scots Songs,* 1769

---

1. **Martinmas time.** Martinmas is the feast of St. Martin, November 11.
2. **puddings,** sausages.
3. **hussyfskap,** (hŭs'if skap), housewife's work.
4. **paction,** agreement.
5. **they,** the "two gentlemen."
6. **pudding-broo,** the hot broth in which the sausages are cooking.

In the sixteenth and seventeenth century, ballads were often published on single large sheets (printed on only one side) that were called *broadsides.* In addition to popular ballads, a variety of materials appeared in broadsides: political speeches, accounts of marvels, accident reports, the last words of prisoners on the gallows. The seventeenth-century diarist Samuel Pepys (see page 282) made a large collection of broadsides.

A version of "The Demon Lover" that ap- peared in a seventeenth-century broadside and was part of Pepys's collection was entitled: "A Warning for Married Women, being an example of Mrs. Jane Reynolds (a West-country woman), born near Plymouth, who, having plighted her troth to a Seaman, was afterwards married to a Carpenter, and at last carried away by a Spirit, the manner how shall presently be recited." While they were most popular in the sixteenth century, broadsides continued to be printed into the nineteenth century.

The Demon Lover

"O where have you been, my long, long
    love,
  This long seven years and more?"
"O I'm come to seek my former vows
  Ye granted me before."

5 "O hold your tongue of your former vows,
  For they will breed sad strife;
O hold your tongue of your former vows
  For I am become a wife."

He turn'd him right and round about,
10   And the tear blinded his ee;°   eye
"I wad never hae trodden on Irish ground,
  If it had not been for thee.

"I might have had a king's daughter,
  Far, far beyond the sea;
15 I might have had a king's daughter,
  Had it not been for love o' thee."

"If ye might have had a king's daughter,
  Yersell° ye had to blame;   yourself
Ye might have taken the king's daughter,
20   For ye kend° that I was nane.°   knew/none

"If I was to leave my husband dear,
  And my two babes also,
O what have you to take me to,
  If with you I should go?"

25 "I hae° seven ships upon the sea,   have
  The eighth brought me to land;
With four-and-twenty bold mariners,
  And music on every hand."

She has taken up her two little babes,
30   Kiss'd them baith° cheek and chin;   both
"O fair ye weel,° my ain° two babes,   well/own
  For I'll never see you again."

She set her foot upon the ship,
  No mariners could she behold;
35 But the sails were o' the taffetie,
  And the masts o' the beaten gold.

She had not sail'd a league, a league,
  A league but barely three,
When dismal grew his countenance,
40   And drumlie° grew his ee.   gloomy

They had not sailed a league, a league,
  A league but barely three,
Until she espied his cloven foot,
  And she wept right bitterlie.

45 "O hold your tongue of your weeping," says
    he,
  "Of your weeping now let me be;
I will show you how the lilies grow
  On the banks of Italy."

"O what hills are yon, yon pleasant hills,
50 That the sun shines sweetly on?"
"O yon are the hills of heaven," he said,
  "Where you will never win."

"O whaten° a mountain is yon," she   *what kind of*
  said,
  "All so dreary wi' frost and snow?"

55 "O yon is the mountain of hell," he cried,
  "Where you and I will go."

He struck the tapmast° wi' his hand,   *topmast*
  The foremast wi' his knee;
And he brak° that gallant ship in twain,   *broke*
60 And sank her in the sea.

        from *Minstrelsy of the Scottish Border,* 1812

Discussion

1. (a) "Edward" is an unusual ballad in that it provides a surprise midway through and another at the end. What are these surprises? **(b)** Who, in your opinion, is the greater sinner, Edward or his mother? Explain. **(c)** "Edward" is ranked with the greatest of the folk ballads. What about it may have led to that reputation?

2. (a) What does the "blude-reid wine" in line 2 of "Sir Patrick Spence" add to the poem's emotional tone? What would be the effect of using "clear white wine" instead? **(b)** What other hints does the ballad contain that the voyage will come to a tragic end? **(c)** The news of the deaths of Sir Patrick and his crew is revealed indirectly, through the description of the ladies who are awaiting the return of their lords. To appreciate the artistry of this ballad, reread it, skipping these lines (lines 33–40). What is lost?

3. (a) In "Get Up and Bar the Door," who wins the argument between husband and wife? How do you know? **(b)** Why would the husband be more likely than the wife to object to what the two "gentlemen" plan to do? **(c)** Is this ballad dated, or can its humor be appreciated by modern readers? Why?

4. (a) What makes the woman in "The Demon Lover" decide to go away with her old sweetheart? Has she earned her fate? Discuss. **(b)** What is the first definite evidence of the supernatural in the ballad? Why is there no evidence closer to the beginning? **(c)** There are some indications that the man was really the woman's long-lost lover. What are they? There are other indications that he was a devil or demon. What are they? Which do you think he was, lover or demon? Explain.

Composition

1. Literature frequently provides details of the daily life of the age in which it was composed. Examine "Edward" and "Get Up and Bar the Door" for details of everyday life in the Middle Ages.

Compare and contrast the picture these two ballads provide of everyday life. Which ballad pictures aristocratic life? Which ballad pictures the life of the common people? (See *Making Comparisons and Contrasts* in Composition Guide.)

2. Folk beliefs and superstitions have an important place in many ballads. Examine "Sir Patrick Spence" and "The Demon Lover" for evidence of such beliefs.

Write a paper in which you discuss the folk beliefs that occur in these ballads.

3. Select a topic from recent history that would be appropriate for a modern folk ballad and think about how you would develop it—who would be involved in your dialogue, which phrases would be repeated, etc.

Write a paper in which you describe your topic and the methods and details you would use to develop it. (Note: You are not being asked to write a ballad, but to provide the material from which a ballad is made.)

4. With the help of your librarian or a music teacher, locate some modern ballads. Select a few that you feel would interest your classmates and copy them.

Write a paper explaining how they are similar to or different from the ballads in this unit.

eoffrey Chaucer 1340?–1400

Although we are uncertain as to the exact date of the birth of Geoffrey Chaucer, the first great English poet, we do know a surprising amount about his life and public career. In fact, over 300 references to him and to his family have been found in the official records of the time. Chaucer's father was a prosperous London wine merchant who had been in Flanders in 1338 with the retinue of King Edward III. The first reference to Geoffrey Chaucer occurs in 1357, when he is listed as a page in the household of the wife of Prince Lionel, a son of Edward III. Chaucer's service in that household indicates that his family had sufficient social status for him to receive a courtly education. Throughout the rest of his lifetime, Chaucer was in some way connected with members of the royal family.

Sometime in or before 1366, Chaucer married Philippa Roet, a lady-in-waiting to the Queen. Chaucer rose socially through his marriage. In 1368 he became one of the King's esquires, which in those days meant that he worked in the administrative department of the King's government. One of his duties was to act as a government envoy on foreign diplomatic missions, carrying on such work as that performed by embassies of our day.

Chaucer's diplomatic missions took him first to France and later to Italy. While in France he came in contact with French literature, and from his very earliest writings through 1370 a French influence is noticeable. To the French period can be assigned his translation of *The Romance of the Rose* (a long, allegorical poem written in French about a century earlier) and an original poem, *The Book of the Duchess,* occasioned by the death of Blanche, the first wife of John of Gaunt, Duke of Lancaster.

In 1372 Chaucer was sent to Genoa to arrange a commercial treaty. As he became acquainted with Italian life and culture, he discovered that a new interest in the learning of the past, in the literature of Greece and Rome, was sweeping over the Italian towns—the Renaissance had begun. Chaucer became acquainted with the classical authors and with the newer Italian works of Dante and Petrarch, perhaps with the tales of Boccaccio. In Chaucer's own writing the French models of his earlier years gave way to this Italian influence. To the Italian period can be assigned *The House of Fame, The Legend of Good Women,* and *The Parliament of Fowls.*

After his return to London, Chaucer became a customs official at the port of London (on condition that he kept his records in his own hand). As one of the benefits of this position the government provided him with free lodgings above Aldgate, one of the gates in the wall around London (on condition that he kept his home in good repair). There he liked to retire "as an hermyte," he says, after his working day was done, to write or read (for he loved the world of books as much as the world of men), or to look down upon the colorful throng that passed through the gateway beneath him.

Chaucer lost or gave up his comptrollership and left his home above Aldgate in 1386—the year in which it is believed he began composing *The Canterbury Tales.* His move may have been occasioned by the illness and death of Philippa, which occurred in 1386 or 1387. He retired to live in Kent, serving as justice of the peace for the shire and later representing it in Parliament. When he died in 1400, he was buried in Westminster Abbey in a section which later became established as the Poets' Corner.

from **The Canterbury Tales**   translated by **Nevill Coghill**

Chaucer's unfinished masterpiece, *The Canterbury Tales,* is one of the great works of world literature. More than ten years in the writing, it is an ingenious concoction of character sketches, stories, humor, **satire,** and conversation—all in the course of a pilgrimage to the shrine of St. Thomas Becket in Canterbury, undertaken by twenty-nine intrepid pilgrims (and Chaucer).

Representing a cross section of the population of fourteenth-century England, the pilgrims range in rank from a knight to a poor plowman. Only the very highest and lowest ranks—the nobility and the serfs—are missing. En route to Canterbury, the pilgrims eat, drink, sightsee, and talk—more than anything else they talk, and in so doing reveal more than they realize about themselves. Chaucer introduces each of his pilgrims in *The Prologue,* then lets us know still more about them through the stories they tell, which range from sermons and courtly **romances** to scurrilous *fabliaux* (brief stories, usually humorous, often off-color), and through the "links"—the conversations and squabbles they engage in between stories.

Although Chaucer intended to include 120 stories (two told by each pilgrim each way on their journey), he managed only twenty-four, some of these incomplete. There is evidence that he was reassigning some stories when his work broke off. For instance, the Skipper refers to himself as a woman, and the Sergeant at the Law says he will speak in prose, then tells a tale in verse.

(The passage below is the opening
of *The Prologue* in Chaucer's English:)
  Whan that Aprille with his shoures soote
The droghte of March hath perced to the roote,
And bathed every veyne in swich licour
Of which vertu engendred is the flour;
5 Whan Zephirus eek with his sweete breeth
Inspired hath in every holt and heeth
The tendre croppes, and the yonge sonne
Hath in the Ram his halve cours yronne,
And smale foweles maken melodye,
10 That slepen al the nyght with open ye
(So priketh hem nature in hir corages);
Thanne longen folk to goon on pilgrimages,
And palmeres for to seken straunge strondes,
To ferne halwes, kowthe in sondry londes;
15 And specially from every shires ende
Of Engelond to Caunterbury they wende,
The hooly blisful martir for to seke,
That hem hath holpen whan that they were seeke.

An ampulla for oil or holy water from Canterbury, a pilgrim's souvenir of a visit to the shrine of St. Thomas Becket, which was noted for its healing powers (see lines 15–18 of *The Prologue*).

The Prologue

When in April the sweet showers fall
And pierce the drought of March to the
    root, and all
The veins are bathed in liquor of such power
As brings about the engendering of the
    flower,
5 When also Zephyrus[1] with his sweet breath
Exhales an air in every grove and heath
Upon the tender shoots, and the young sun
His half-course in the sign of the *Ram* has
    run,[2]
And the small fowl are making melody
10 That sleep away the night with open eye
(So nature pricks them and their heart
    engages)
Then people long to go on pilgrimages
And palmers[3] long to seek the stranger
    strands
Of far-off saints, hallowed in sundry lands,
15 And specially, from every shire's end
Of England, down to Canterbury they wend
To seek the holy blissful martyr,[4] quick
To give his help to them when they were
    sick.
    It happened in that season that one day
20 In Southwark, at *The Tabard*,[5] as I lay
Ready to go on pilgrimage and start
For Canterbury, most devout at heart,
At night there came into that hostelry
Some nine and twenty in a company
25 Of sundry folk happening then to fall
In fellowship, and they were pilgrims all
That towards Canterbury meant to ride.
The rooms and stables of the inn were wide;
They made us easy, all was of the best.
30 And, briefly, when the sun had gone to rest,
I'd spoken to them all upon the trip
And was soon one with them in fellowship,
Pledged to rise early and to take the way
To Canterbury, as you heard me say.
35   But none the less, while I have time and
    space,
Before my story takes a further pace,
It seems a reasonable thing to say
What their condition was, the full array
Of each of them, as it appeared to me,

40 According to profession and degree,
And what apparel they were riding in;
And at a Knight I therefore will begin.

There was a *Knight,* a most distinguished man,
Who from the day on which he first began
45 To ride abroad had followed chivalry,
Truth, honor, generousness, and courtesy.
He had done nobly in his sovereign's war
And ridden into battle, no man more,
As well in Christian as in heathen places,
50 And ever honored for his noble graces.
    When we took Alexandria,[6] he was there.
He often sat at table in the chair
Of honor, above all nations, when in Prussia.
In Lithuania he had ridden, and Russia,
55 No Christian man so often, of his rank.
When, in Granada, Algeciras sank
Under assault, he had been there, and in
North Africa, raiding Benamarin;
In Anatolia he had been as well
60 And fought when Ayas and Attalia fell,
For all along the Mediterranean coast
He had embarked with many a noble host.
In fifteen mortal battles he had been
And jousted for our faith at Tramissene
65 Thrice in the lists, and always killed his man.
This same distinguished knight had led the van
Once with the Bey of Balat,[7] doing work
For him against another heathen Turk;

From Geoffrey Chaucer: *The Canterbury Tales,* translated by Nevill Coghill. (Penguin Classics, Revised edition 1977). Copyright 1951 by Nevill Coghill. Copyright © Nevill Coghill, 1958, 1960, 1975, 1977. Reprinted by permission of Penguin Books Ltd.

1. *Zephyrus,* the west wind.
2. *young sun . . . has run.* Since the Ram, the first sign of the Zodiac, begins its run about March 21, Chaucer dates the pilgrimage in early April.
3. *palmers,* pilgrims to the Holy Land wore the image of crossed palm leaves as their emblem.
4. *martyr,* St. Thomas Becket, murdered in Canterbury Cathedral in 1170. His tomb was a favorite destination for medieval English pilgrims.
5. *Southwark, at The Tabard.* The Tabard was a famous inn at the beginning of the road from London to Canterbury, located in a suburb south of London.
6. *Alexandria.* Here and in the following lines the narrator refers to battles against the major non-Christian enemies of Chaucer's era.
7. *Bey of Balat.* A bey was a governor of a province or district in the Ottoman Empire.

He was of sovereign value in all eyes.
70 And though so much distinguished, he was
    wise
And in his bearing modest as a maid.
He never yet a boorish thing had said
In all his life to any, come what might;
He was a true, a perfect gentle-knight.
75   Speaking of his equipment, he possessed
Fine horses, but he was not gaily dressed.
He wore a fustian tunic stained and dark
With smudges where his armor had left mark;
Just home from service, he had joined our
    ranks
80 To do his pilgrimage and render thanks.

The Squire, from the Ellesmere Chaucer.

He had his son with him, a fine young
    Squire,[8]
A lover and cadet, a lad of fire
With locks as curly as if they had been
    pressed.
He was some twenty years of age, I guessed.
85 In stature he was of a moderate length,
With wonderful agility and strength.
He'd seen some service with the cavalry
In Flanders and Artois and Picardy[9]
And had done valiantly in little space
90 Of time, in hope to win his lady's grace.

He was embroidered like a meadow bright
And full of freshest flowers, red and white.
Singing he was, or fluting all the day;
He was as fresh as is the month of May.
95 Short was his gown, the sleeves were long
    and wide;
He knew the way to sit a horse and ride.
He could make songs and poems and recite,
Knew how to joust and dance, to draw and
    write.
He loved so hotly that till dawn grew pale
100 He slept as little as a nightingale.
Courteous he was, lowly and serviceable,
And carved to serve his father at the table.

There was a Yeoman[10] with him at his
    side,
No other servant; so he chose to ride.
105 This Yeoman wore a coat and hood of
    green,
And peacock-feathered arrows, bright and
    keen
And neatly sheathed, hung at his belt the
    while
—For he could dress his gear in yeoman
    style,
His arrows never drooped their feathers
    low—
110 And in his hand he bore a mighty bow.
His head was like a nut, his face was brown.
He knew the whole of woodcraft up and
    down.
A saucy brace was on his arm to ward
It from the bowstring, and a shield and
    sword
115 Hung at one side, and at the other slipped
A jaunty dirk, spear-sharp and
    well-equipped.
A medal of St. Christopher[11] he wore
Of shining silver on his breast, and bore
A hunting-horn, well slung and burnished
    clean,
120 That dangled from a baldrick of bright green.
He was a proper forester, I guess.

---

8. Squire, a young man learning to be a knight through service.
9. Flanders and Artois and Picardy, battles much closer to home than those the Knight has seen.
10. Yeoman. A freeman and a commoner, servant to the Knight.
11. St. Christopher, patron of travelers and foresters.

The Prioress, from the Ellesmere Chaucer.

And bitterly she wept if one were dead
Or someone took a stick and made it smart;
She was all sentiment and tender heart.
155 Her veil was gathered in a seemly way,
Her nose was elegant, her eyes glass-gray;
Her mouth was very small, but soft and red,
Her forehead, certainly, was fair of spread,
Almost a span across the brows, I own;
160 She was indeed by no means undergrown.
Her cloak, I noticed, had a graceful charm.
She wore a coral trinket on her arm,
A set of beads, the gaudies tricked in green,[16]
Whence hung a golden brooch of brightest
   sheen
165 On which there first was graven a crowned A,
And lower, *Amor vincit omnia.*[17]
   Another *Nun*, the secretary at her cell,
Was riding with her, and *three Priests*[18] as well.

   A *Monk* there was, one of the finest sort
170 Who rode the country; hunting was his sport.
A manly man, to be an Abbot[19] able;
Many a dainty horse he had in stable.
His bridle, when he rode, a man might hear
Jingling in a whistling wind as clear,
175 Aye, and as loud as does the chapel bell
Where my lord Monk was Prior of the cell.[20]
The Rule of good St. Benet or St. Maur[21]
As old and strict he tended to ignore;
He let go by the things of yesterday
180 And took the modern world's more spacious
   way.
   He did not rate that text at a plucked hen
Which says that hunters are not holy men

   There also was a *Nun*, a Prioress,[12]
Her way of smiling very simple and coy.
Her greatest oath was only "By St. Loy!"[13]
125 And she was known as Madam Eglantyne.[14]
And well she sang a service, with a fine
Intoning through her nose, as was most seemly,
And she spoke daintily in French, extremely,
After the school of Stratford-atte-Bowe;[15]
130 French in the Paris style she did not know.
At meat her manners were well taught withal;
No morsel from her lips did she let fall,
Nor dipped her fingers in the sauce too deep;
But she could carry a morsel up and keep
135 The smallest drop from falling on her breast.
For courtliness she had a special zest,
And she would wipe her upper lip so clean
That not a trace of grease was to be seen
Upon the cup when she had drunk; to eat,
140 She reached a hand sedately for the meat.
She certainly was very entertaining,
Pleasant and friendly in her ways, and
   straining
To counterfeit a courtly kind of grace,
A stately bearing fitting to her place,
145 And to seem dignified in all her dealings.
As for her sympathies and tender feelings,
She was so charitably solicitous
She used to weep if she but saw a mouse
Caught in a trap, if it were dead or bleeding.
150 And she had little dogs she would be feeding
With roasted flesh, or milk, or fine white bread.

12. **Prioress,** religious woman who runs a convent.
13. **St. Loy.** This saint refused to swear on sacred relics. To swear by him was to swear mildly or not at all.
14. **Eglantyne,** sweet briar.
15. **daintily . . . Stratford-atte-Bowe,** inferior French learned in an English convent. (See "Medieval Tourists," page 77.)
16. **A set . . . green,** coral rosary beads with every larger tenth bead ("gaudies") made from a green stone.
17. **Amor . . . omnia.** "Love overcomes all." The phrase might be used for sacred or secular love. [Latin]
18. **three priests.** Since the addition of three priests would bring the total of the pilgrims up to thirty-one (instead of the twenty-nine mentioned in line 24), their appearance here is probably a result of an error made in copying Chaucer's manuscript. Moreover, it is improbable that even a distinguished churchwoman like the Prioress would have been accompanied by so large a party. So the probability is that Chaucer intended only *one* priest.
19. **Abbot,** director of a monastery.
20. **Prior of the cell,** head of a subordinate monastery.
21. **The Rule . . . St. Maur,** ancient laws governing the life of a monk, first established by St. Benedict and his disciple St. Maur.

Comment: Medieval Tourists

By Chaucer's time, as can be seen from his remark about the Prioress (who spoke her French "after the school of Stratford-atte-Bowe"), French had become, even for the well-born, a foreign language. It was no longer learned at home, but had to be taught. According to historian Paul Johnson, "From the late fourteenth century we get the first French-conversation manuals for the use of English travelers. One, entitled *La Maniere de language qui t'enseignera bien a droit parler et escrire doulx françois* [*A Manual of Language That Will Teach You to Speak French Correctly and Write It Smoothly*], and dating from 1396, tells the Englishman what to say while on the road or at an inn. It unconsciously gives the English racial view of the French: how to instruct lazy, incompetent, and venal [greedy] French hostlers [stablemen] in their duties; how to tell French innkeepers to clean up their filthy and vermin-ridden bedrooms, and to serve food which is wholesome and not messed about. . . . It differs only in detail—certainly not in fundamental attitudes—from the phrase books supplied to the English Grand Tourists in the eighteenth century."

Paul Johnson, *The Offshore Islanders.* New York: Holt, Rinehart and Winston, 1972, page 110.

And that a monk uncloistered is a mere
Fish out of water, flapping on the pier,
185 That is to say a monk out of his cloister.
That was a text he held not worth an oyster;
And I agreed and said his views were sound;
Was he to study till his head went round
Poring over books in cloisters? Must he toil
190 As Austin bade and till the very soil?
Was he to leave the world upon the shelf?
Let Austin[22] have his labor to himself.
This Monk was therefore a good man to horse;
Greyhounds he had, as swift as birds, to course.
195 Hunting a hare or riding at a fence
Was all his fun, he spared for no expense.
I saw his sleeves were garnished at the hand
With fine gray fur, the finest in the land,
And on his hood, to fasten it at his chin
200 He had a wrought-gold cunningly fashioned pin;
Into a lover's knot it seemed to pass.
His head was bald and shone like looking glass;
So did his face, as if it had been greased.
He was a fat and personable priest;
205 His prominent eyeballs never seemed to settle.
They glittered like the flames beneath a kettle;
Supple his boots, his horse in fine condition.
He was a prelate fit for exhibition,
He was not pale like a tormented soul.
210 He liked a fat swan best, and roasted whole.
His palfrey was as brown as is a berry.

There was a *Friar,* a wanton one and merry,
A Limiter,[23] a very festive fellow.
In all Four Orders[24] there was none so mellow,
215 So glib with gallant phrase and well-turned speech.
He'd fixed up many a marriage, giving each
Of his young women what he could afford her.[25]
He was a noble pillar to his Order.
Highly beloved and intimate was he
220 With County folk[26] within his boundary,
And city dames of honor and possessions;
For he was qualified to hear confessions,
Or so he said, with more than priestly scope;
He had a special licence from the Pope.
225 Sweetly he heard his penitents at shrift[27]
With pleasant absolution, for a gift.
He was an easy man in penance-giving
Where he could hope to make a decent living;

22. **Austin.** St. Augustine (A.D. 354–430) advised monks to engage in manual labor.
23. **Limiter.** Within a specific district ("limitatio") such a friar would beg for donations, preach, and bury the dead.
24. **Four Orders,** the four groups of begging friars: Dominicans, Franciscans, Carmelites, Augustinians.
25. **He'd fixed . . . afford her.** He found husbands, and perhaps dowries, for women whom he had himself seduced.
26. **County folk,** the local gentry, the socially prominent and well-to-do.
27. **shrift,** confession of sins.

It's a sure sign whenever gifts are given
230 To a poor Order that a man's well shriven,
And should he give enough he knew in verity
The penitent repented in sincerity.
For many a fellow is so hard of heart
He cannot weep, for all his inward smart.
235 Therefore instead of weeping and of prayer
One should give silver for a poor Friar's care.
He kept his tippet[28] stuffed with pins for curls,
And pocketknives, to give to pretty girls.
And certainly his voice was gay and sturdy,
240 For he sang well and played the
        hurdy-gurdy.[29]
At singsongs he was champion of the hour.
His neck was whiter than a lily flower
But strong enough to butt a bruiser down.
He knew the taverns well in every town
245 And every innkeeper and barmaid too
Better than lepers, beggars and that crew,
For in so eminent a man as he
It was not fitting with the dignity
Of his position, dealing with a scum
250 Of wretched lepers; nothing good can come
Of commerce with such slum-and-gutter
        dwellers,
But only with the rich and victual-sellers.
But anywhere a profit might accrue
Courteous he was and lowly of service too.
255 Natural gifts like his were hard to match.
He was the finest beggar of his batch,
And, for his begging-district, paid a rent;
His brethren did no poaching where he went.
For though a widow mightn't have a shoe,
260 So pleasant was his holy how-d'ye-do
He got his farthing from her just the same
Before he left, and so his income came
To more than he laid out. And how he
        romped,
Just like a puppy! He was ever prompt
265 To arbitrate disputes on settling days[30]
(For a small fee) in many helpful ways,
Not then appearing as your cloistered scholar
With threadbare habit hardly worth a dollar,
But much more like a Doctor[31] or a Pope.
270 Of double-worsted was the semi-cope[32]
Upon his shoulders, and the swelling fold
About him, like a bell about its mold
When it is casting, rounded out his dress.
He lisped a little out of wantonness
275 To make his English sweet upon his tongue.

When he had played his harp, or having sung,
His eyes would twinkle in his head as bright
As any star upon a frosty night.
This worthy's name was Hubert, it appeared.

The Merchant, from the Ellesmere Chaucer.

280 There was a *Merchant* with a forking beard
And motley[33] dress; high on his horse he sat,
Upon his head a Flemish beaver hat
And on his feet daintily buckled boots.
He told of his opinions and pursuits
285 In solemn tones, he harped on his increase
Of capital; there should be sea-police
(He thought) upon the Harwich-Holland
        ranges;[34]
He was expert at dabbling in exchanges.
This estimable Merchant so had set
290 His wits to work, none knew he was in debt,
He was so stately in administration,
In loans and bargains and negotiation.
He was an excellent fellow all the same;
To tell the truth I do not know his name.

---

28. *tippet,* a narrow part of hood or sleeve used as a pocket.
29. *hurdy-gurdy.* Chaucer's term, "rote," refers to a stringed instrument.
30. *settling days,* days on which disputes could be settled by independent negotiators out of court. Friars often acted in this capacity and received "gifts" for their services. In Chaucer's day this was officially forbidden.
31. *Doctor,* a university professor.
32. *semi-cope,* a short cope. A cope was a type of cloak, intended to be worn out-of-doors.
33. *motley,* here, cloth woven with a figured design.
34. *sea-police . . . Harwich-Holland ranges.* He wants ships sailing the England-to-Holland route protected at any cost.

295 An *Oxford Cleric*,[35] still a student though,
One who had taken logic long ago,
Was there; his horse was thinner than a rake,
And he was not too fat, I undertake,
But had a hollow look, a sober stare;
300 The thread upon his overcoat was bare.
He had found no preferment in the church
And he was too unworldly to make search
For secular employment. By his bed
He preferred having twenty books in red
305 And black, of Aristotle's philosophy,[36]
Than costly clothes, fiddle or psaltery.[37]
Though a philosopher, as I have told,
He had not found the stone for making gold.[38]
Whatever money from his friends he took
310 He spent on learning or another book
And prayed for them most earnestly,
   returning
Thanks to them thus for paying for his
   learning.
His only care was study, and indeed
He never spoke a word more than was need,
315 Formal at that, respectful in the extreme,
Short, to the point, and lofty in his theme.
A tone of moral virtue filled his speech
And gladly would he learn, and gladly teach.

A *Sergeant at the Law*[39] who paid his calls,
320 Wary and wise, for clients at St. Paul's[40]
There also was, of noted excellence.
Discreet he was, a man to reverence,
Or so he seemed, his sayings were so wise.
He often had been Justice of Assize
325 By letters patent,[41] and in full commission.
His fame and learning and his high position
Had won him many a robe and many a fee.
There was no such conveyancer[42] as he;
All was fee-simple[43] to his strong digestion,
330 Not one conveyance could be called in
   question.
Though there was nowhere one so busy as he,
He was less busy than he seemed to be.
He knew of every judgment, case and crime
Ever recorded since King William's time.[44]
335 He could dictate defences or draft deeds;
No one could pinch a comma from his screeds[45]
And he knew every statute off by rote.
He wore a homely parti-colored coat,
Girt with a silken belt of pinstripe stuff;
340 Of his appearance I have said enough.

The Franklin, from the Ellesmere Chaucer.

There was a *Franklin*[46] with him, it appeared;
White as a daisy petal was his beard.
A sanguine man, high-colored and benign,
He loved a morning sop of cake in wine.
345 He lived for pleasure and had always done,

35. *Cleric,* any divinity student; not necessarily a priest.
36. *twenty books . . . Aristotle's philosophy.* Aristotle (384–322 B.C.) was a Greek philosopher whose works had a great influence on medieval thought. Private libraries of the size possessed by the Cleric were extremely uncommon in Chaucer's day; it is not surprising that his expenditures on books left him little for food or clothing.
37. *psaltery,* stringed instrument played with the hand.
38. *stone for making gold.* In alchemy the philosopher's stone was supposed to turn ordinary metals into gold. No one ever found it.
39. *Sergeant at the Law,* one of the king's legal servants. There were only twenty such men in Chaucer's day. They were chosen from lawyers with over 16 years' experience, and sat as judges both in London and in the traveling courts, the assizes (line 324) which met at various country towns.
40. *St. Paul's,* Old St. Paul's Cathedral (destroyed by the Fire of London in 1666). During the afternoon, when the courts were closed, lawyers would meet clients on church porches to discuss business.
41. *letters patent,* official documents from the king empowering an individual to act as Judge of the Assize.
42. *conveyancer.* The Sergeant is an expert on real-estate law.
43. *fee-simple,* land owned outright. The Sergeant is obtaining as much of this as he can.
44. *King William's time,* era of William the Conqueror (1066–1087), when systematic legal records were first kept.
45. *screeds,* writing.
46. *Franklin.* Literally the term means "free man." Here we have a wealthy landowner.

For he was Epicurus'[47] very son,
In whose opinion sensual delight
Was the one true felicity in sight.
As noted as St. Julian[48] was for bounty
350 He made his household free to all the County.
His bread, his ale were finest of the fine
And no one had a better stock of wine.
His house was never short of bakemeat pies,
Of fish and flesh, and these in such supplies
355 It positively snowed with meat and drink
And all the dainties that a man could think.
According to the seasons of the year
Changes of dish were ordered to appear.
He kept fat partridges in coops, beyond,
360 Many a bream and pike were in his pond.
Woe to the cook unless the sauce was hot
And sharp, or if he wasn't on the spot!
And in his hall a table stood arrayed
And ready all day long, with places laid.
365 As Justice at the Sessions none stood higher;[49]
He often had been Member for the Shire.[50]
A dagger and a little purse of silk
Hung at his girdle, white as morning milk.
As Sheriff[51] he checked audit, every entry.
370 He was a model among landed gentry.

    A Haberdasher, a Dyer, a Carpenter,
    A Weaver, and a Carpet-maker were
    Among our ranks, all in the livery
    Of one impressive guild-fraternity.[52]
375 They were so trim and fresh their gear
        would pass
    For new. Their knives were not tricked out
        with brass
    But wrought with purest silver, which
        avouches
    A like display on girdles and on pouches.
    Each seemed a worthy burgess, fit to grace
380 A guild-hall with a seat upon the dais.[53]
    Their wisdom would have justified a plan
    To make each one of them an alderman;[54]
    They had the capital and revenue,
    Besides their wives declared it was their
        due.
385 And if they did not think so, then they
        ought;
    To be called "Madam" is a glorious
        thought,
    And so is going to church and being seen
    Having your mantle carried, like a queen.

They had a *Cook* with them who stood
    alone
390 For boiling chicken with a marrowbone,
Sharp flavoring-powder and a spice for savor.
He could distinguish London ale by flavor,
And he could roast and seethe and broil and
    fry,
Make good thick soup and bake a tasty pie.
395 But what a pity—so it seemed to me,
That he should have an ulcer on his knee.
As for blancmange,[55] he made it with the best.

There was a *Skipper* hailing from far west;
He came from Dartmouth, so I understood.
400 He rode a farmer's horse as best he could,
In a woolen gown that reached his knee.
A dagger on a lanyard falling free
Hung from his neck under his arm and down.
The summer heat had tanned his color brown,
405 And certainly he was an excellent fellow.
Many a draught of vintage, red and yellow,
He'd drawn at Bordeaux,[56] while the trader
    snored.
The nicer rules of conscience he ignored.
If, when he fought, the enemy vessel sank,
410 He sent his prisoners home; they walked the
    plank.
As for his skill in reckoning his tides,
Currents and many another risk besides,
Moons, harbors, pilots, he had such dispatch
That none from Hull to Carthage[57] was his
    match.
415 Hardy he was, prudent in undertaking;
His beard in many a tempest had its shaking,
And he knew all the havens as they were

---

47. Epicurus, Greek philosopher (342?–270 b.c.) whose ideas seemed to urge pursuit of pleasure.
48. St. Julian, patron of hospitality.
49. Justice . . . higher. When the Justices of the Peace sat in session, he presided.
50. Member . . . Shire, member of Parliament for his county.
51. Sheriff, royal administrator who collected taxes and delivered them to the king's exchequer.
52. guild-fraternity. Since these men came from different trades, this probably refers to a social or religious guild to which they all belonged.
53. guild-hall . . . dais, worthy to preside at meetings of the guild.
54. alderman, leading member of a town council.
55. blancmange. In Chaucer's day, blancmange (blə mänzh′) referred to a kind of chicken stew.
56. Bordeaux (bôr dō′), a seaport in southwestern France. The region near Bordeaux is famous for both its red and white wines.
57. Hull to Carthage. These and subsequent references indicate how widely the Skipper has traveled.

From Gottland to the Cape of Finisterre,[58]
And every creek in Brittany and Spain;
420 The barge he owned was called *The
      Maudelayne.*[59]

A *Doctor* too emerged as we proceeded;
No one alive could talk as well as he did
On points of medicine and of surgery,
For, being grounded in astronomy,[60]
425 He watched his patient closely for the hours
When, by his horoscope, he knew the powers
Of favorable planets, then ascendent,
Worked on the images for his dependent.[61]
The cause of every malady you'd got
430 He knew, and whether dry, cold, moist or
      hot;[62]
He knew their seat, their humor and condition.
He was a perfect practicing physician.
These causes being known for what they
      were,
He gave the man his medicine then and there.
435 All his apothecaries in a tribe
Were ready with the drugs he would prescribe
And each made money from the other's guile;
They had been friendly for a goodish while.
He was well-versed in Aesculapius[63] too
440 And what Hippocrates and Rufus knew
And Dioscorides, now dead and gone,
Galen and Rhazes, Hali, Serapion,
Averroes, Avicenna, Constantine,
Scotch Bernard, John of Gaddesden,
      Gilbertine.
445 In his own diet he observed some measure;
There were no superfluities for pleasure,
Only digestives, nutritives, and such.
He did not read the Bible very much.[64]
In blood-red garments, slashed with bluish
      gray
450 And lined with taffeta, he rode his way;
Yet he was rather close as to expenses
And kept the gold he won in pestilences.[65]
Gold stimulates the heart, or so we're told.
He therefore had a special love of gold.

455 A worthy *woman* from beside *Bath* city
Was with us, somewhat deaf, which was a
      pity.
In making cloth she showed so great a bent
She bettered those of Ypres and of Ghent.[66]
In all the parish not a dame dared stir

460 Towards the altar steps in front of her,
And if indeed they did, so wrath was she
As to be quite put out of charity.
Her kerchiefs were of finely woven ground;
I dared have sworn they weighed a good ten
      pound,
465 The ones she wore on Sunday, on her head.
Her hose were of the finest scarlet red
And gartered tight; her shoes were soft and
      new.
Bold was her face, handsome, and red in hue.
A worthy woman all her life, what's more
470 She'd had five husbands, all at the church
      door,[67]
Apart from other company in youth;
No need just now to speak of that, forsooth.
And she had thrice been to Jerusalem,
Seen many strange rivers and passed over
      them;
475 She'd been to Rome and also to Boulogne,
St. James of Compostella and Cologne,[68]
And she was skilled in wandering by the way.
She had gap-teeth, set widely, truth to say.
Easily on an ambling horse she sat
480 Well wimpled up,[69] and on her head a hat
As broad as is a buckler or a shield;
She had a flowing mantle that concealed

---

58. Gottland . . . Finisterre. Gottland is an island in the Baltic Sea off Sweden; the Cape of Finisterre is part of Brittany, in northwestern France.

59. The Maudelayne. A real ship of this name from Dartmouth paid customs duties in 1379 and 1391, and Chaucer may have had its master in mind in creating the Skipper.

60. astronomy. Here, astrology. It was believed that the position of the planets determined the best time to treat a patient.

61. images . . . dependent. These "images" may have been wax figures of the dependent (the patient) such as those used in witchcraft, or charms inscribed with astrological symbols.

62. dry . . . hot. In the Middle Ages people thought the human body was composed of the four elements: earth, air, fire, and water. Sickness came from too much of any one element. Character traits, too, could be explained by a slight excess of an element: too much fire produced a hot temper, etc. Such traits were called *humors* (line 431).

63. Aesculapius. This and the names that follow belong to eminent medical authorities from ancient times to Chaucer's day. The Doctor was well-read in his profession.

64. read . . . much. Doctors had a reputation for free-thinking and impiety.

65. pestilences, plagues.

66. Ypres . . . Ghent, Flemish cities famous for their weavers, and markets for the wool trade.

67. at the church door. In Chaucer's day marriage services were held at the church door, and the subsequent nuptial Mass inside.

68. Rome . . . Cologne. The Wife has visited most of the important shrines in Italy, France, Spain, and Germany.

69. well wimpled up. A linen garment covered her head, neck, and the sides of her face.

Large hips, her heels spurred sharply under
   that.
In company she liked to laugh and chat
485 And knew the remedies for love's mischances,
An art in which she knew the oldest dances.

A holy-minded man of good renown
There was, and poor, the *Parson* to a town,
Yet he was rich in holy thought and work.
490 He also was a learned man, a clerk,
Who truly knew Christ's gospel and would
   preach it
Devoutly to parishioners, and teach it.
Benign and wonderfully diligent,
And patient when adversity was sent
495 (For so he proved in much adversity)
He hated cursing to extort a fee,
Nay rather he preferred beyond a doubt
Giving to poor parishioners round about
Both from church offerings and his property;
500 He could in little find sufficiency.
Wide was his parish, with houses far asunder,
Yet he neglected not in rain or thunder,
In sickness or in grief, to pay a call
On the remotest, whether great or small,
505 Upon his feet, and in his hand a stave.
This noble example to his sheep he gave
That first he wrought, and afterwards he
   taught;
And it was from the Gospel he had caught
Those words, and he would add this figure
   too,
510 That if gold rust, what then will iron do?
For if a priest be foul in whom we trust
No wonder that a common man should
   rust; . . .
The true example that a priest should give
Is one of cleanness, how the sheep should
   live.
515 He did not set his benefice[70] to hire
And leave his sheep encumbered in the mire
Or run to London to earn easy bread
By singing masses for the wealthy dead,
Or find some Brotherhood and get enrolled.[71]
520 He stayed at home and watched over his fold
So that no wolf should make the sheep
   miscarry.
He was a shepherd and no mercenary.[72]
Holy and virtuous he was, but then
Never contemptuous of sinful men,

525 Never disdainful, never too proud or fine,
But was discreet in teaching and benign.
His business was to show a fair behavior
And draw men thus to Heaven and their Savior,
Unless indeed a man were obstinate;
530 And such, whether of high or low estate,
He put to sharp rebuke, to say the least.
I think there never was a better priest.
He sought no pomp or glory in his dealings,
No scrupulosity had spiced his feelings.
535 Christ and His Twelve Apostles and their lore
He taught, but followed it himself before.

There was a *Plowman* with him there, his
   brother;
Many a load of dung one time or other
He must have carted through the morning
   dew.
540 He was an honest worker, good and true,
Living in peace and perfect charity,
And, as the gospel bade him, so did he,
Loving God best with all his heart and mind
And then his neighbor as himself, repined
545 At no misfortune, slacked for no content,
For steadily about his work he went
To thrash his corn, to dig or to manure
Or make a ditch; and he would help the poor
For love of Christ and never take a penny
550 If he could help it, and, as prompt as any,
He paid his tithes in full when they were due
On what he owned, and on his earnings too.
He wore a tabard smock and rode a mare.

There was a *Reeve*, also a *Miller*, there,
555 A College *Manciple* from the Inns of Court,
A papal *Pardoner* and, in close consort,
A Church-Court *Summoner*, riding at a trot,
And finally myself—that was the lot.

The *Miller* was a chap of sixteen stone,[73]
560 A great stout fellow big in brawn and bone.
He did well out of them, for he could go
And win the ram at any wrestling show.
Broad, knotty and short-shouldered, he
   would boast

---

70. *benefice,* a Church office and its income.
71. *find . . . enrolled.* The Parson refuses the easy work of the
paid chaplain for a London guild.
72. *shepherd . . . mercenary.* The reference here is to Jesus'
parable of the hireling shepherd (John 10:12–13).
73. *sixteen stone,* two hundred twenty-four pounds.

The Miller and Chaucer, from the Ellesmere Chaucer.

He could heave any door off hinge and post,
565 Or take a run and break it with his head.
His beard, like any sow or fox, was red
And broad as well, as though it were a
    spade;
And, at its very tip, his nose displayed
A wart on which there stood a tuft of hair
570 Red as the bristles in an old sow's ear.
His nostrils were as black as they were wide.
He had a sword and buckler at his side,
His mighty mouth was like a furnace door.
A wrangler and buffoon, he had a store
575 Of tavern stories, filthy in the main.
His was a master-hand at stealing grain.
He felt it with his thumb and thus he knew
Its quality and took three times his due—
A thumb of gold,[74] by God, to gauge an oat!
580 He wore a hood of blue and a white coat.
He liked to play his bagpipes up and down
And that was how he brought us out of
    town.

The *Manciple* came from the Inner Temple;[75]
All caterers might follow his example
585 In buying victuals; he was never rash
Whether he bought on credit or paid cash.
He used to watch the market most precisely
And got in first, and so he did quite nicely.
Now isn't it a marvel of God's grace
590 That an illiterate fellow can outpace
The wisdom of a heap of learned men?
His masters—he had more than thirty then—
All versed in the abstrusest legal knowledge,
Could have produced a dozen from their
    College
595 Fit to be stewards in land and rents and game
To any Peer in England you could name,
And show him how to live on what he had

74. **thumb of gold.** Unscrupulous millers would secretly press
their thumbs down on their scales when weighing grain to take
more for themselves.
75. **Manciple . . . from the Inner Temple.** London lawyers
formed themselves into societies which inhabited buildings
once owned by the ancient society of Knights of the Temple.
They hired administrators, called manciples, to purchase food
for their meals.

Debt-free (unless of course the Peer were
    mad)
Or be as frugal as he might desire,
600 And make them fit to help about the Shire
In any legal case there was to try;
And yet this Manciple could wipe their eye.[76]

    The *Reeve*[77] was old and choleric and thin;
His beard was shaven closely to the skin,
605 His shorn hair came abruptly to a stop
Above his ears, and he was docked on top
Just like a priest in front; his legs were lean,
Like sticks they were, no calf was to be seen.
He kept his bins and garners very trim;
610 No auditor could gain a point on him.
And he could judge by watching drought and
    rain
The yield he might expect from seed and
    grain.
His master's sheep, his animals and hens,
Pigs, horses, dairies, stores and cattle-pens
615 Were wholly trusted to his government.
He had been under contract to present
The accounts, right from his master's
    earliest years.
No one had ever caught him in arrears.
No bailiff,[78] serf or herdsman dared to kick,
620 He knew their dodges, knew their every
    trick;
Feared like the plague he was, by those
    beneath.
He had a lovely dwelling on a heath,
Shadowed in green by trees above the sward.
A better hand at bargains than his lord,
625 He had grown rich and had a store of treasure
Well tucked away, yet out it came to pleasure
His lord with subtle loans or gifts of goods,
To earn his thanks and even coats and hoods.
When young he'd learnt a useful trade and
    still
630 He was a carpenter of first-rate skill.
The stallion-cob he rode at a slow trot
Was dapple-gray and bore the name of Scot.
He wore an overcoat of bluish shade
And rather long; he had a rusty blade
635 Slung at his side. He came, as I heard tell,
From Norfolk, near a place called Baldeswell.
His coat was tucked under his belt and
    splayed.
He rode the hindmost of our cavalcade.

There was a *Summoner*[79] with us at that Inn,
640 His face on fire, like a cherubin,[80]
For he had carbuncles.[81] His eyes were narrow,
He was as hot and lecherous as a sparrow.
Black scabby brows he had, and a thin beard.
Children were afraid when he appeared.
645 No quicksilver, lead ointment, tartar creams,
No brimstone, no boracic, so it seems,
Could make a salve that had the power to bite,
Clean up or cure his whelks[82] of knobby white
Or purge the pimples sitting on his cheeks.
650 Garlic he loved, and onions too, and leeks,
And drinking strong red wine till all was hazy.
Then he would shout and jabber as if crazy,
And wouldn't speak a word except in Latin
When he was drunk, such tags as he was pat in;
655 He only had a few, say two or three,
That he had mugged up out of some decree;
No wonder, for he heard them every day.
And, as you know, a man can teach a jay
To call out "Walter" better than the Pope.
660 But had you tried to test his wits and grope
For more, you'd have found nothing in the
    bag.
Then *"Questio quid juris"*[83] was his tag.
He was a noble varlet and a kind one,
You'd meet none better if you went to find
    one.
665 Why, he'd allow—just for a quart of wine—
Any good lad to keep a concubine
A twelvemonth and dispense him altogether!
And he had finches of his own to feather.[84]
And if he found some rascal with a maid
670 He would instruct him not to be afraid
In such a case of the Archdeacon's curse
(Unless the rascal's soul were in his purse)
For in his purse the punishment should be.

---

76. wipe their eye, knock the conceit out of them.
77. Reeve, a minor official on a country estate who served as
an intermediary between the lord of the manor and his serfs.
78. bailiff, a servant of the lord of the manor whose job was to
help direct the maintenance of farms. Traditionally a superior to
the reeve.
79. Summoner, a paid messenger who summoned "sinners" to
appear before an ecclesiastical court.
80. cherubin, a member of one of the nine orders of angles. In
medieval art the cherubim are generally depicted with flame-col-
ored faces.
81. carbuncles, pimples.
82. whelks, pimples.
83. "Questio quid juris." "The question is, what part of the law
applies?" [Latin]
84. Yet . . . feather. The Summoner indulged in the same sins
he is just said to have excused in others.

"Purse is the good Archdeacon's Hell," said he.

675 But well I know he lied in what he said;
A curse should put a guilty man in dread,
For curses kill, as shriving brings, salvation.
We should beware of excommunication.
Thus, as he pleased, the man could bring duress

680 On any young fellow in the diocese.
He knew their secrets, they did what he said.
He wore a garland set upon his head
Large as the holly-bush upon a stake
Outside an ale-house,[85] and he had a cake,

685 A round one, which it was his joke to wield
As if it were intended for a shield.

He and a gentle *Pardoner*[86] rode together,
A bird from Charing Cross[87] of the same feather,
Just back from visiting the Court of Rome.

690 He loudly sang *"Come hither, love, come home!"*
The Summoner sang deep seconds to this song,
No trumpet ever sounded half so strong.
This Pardoner had hair as yellow as wax,
Hanging down smoothly like a hank of flax.

695 In driblets fell his locks behind his head
Down to his shoulders which they overspread;
Thinly they fell, like rat-tails, one by one.
He wore no hood upon his head, for fun;
The hood inside his wallet[88] had been stowed,

700 He aimed at riding in the latest mode;
But for a little cap his head was bare
And he had bulging eyeballs, like a hare.
He'd sewed a holy relic on his cap;
His wallet lay before him on his lap,

705 Brimful of pardons come from Rome, all hot.
He had the same small voice a goat has got.
His chin no beard had harbored, nor would harbor,
Smoother than ever chin was left by barber.
I judge he was a gelding, or a mare.

710 As to his trade, from Berwick down to Ware
There was no pardoner of equal grace,
For in his trunk he had a pillow-case
Which he asserted was Our Lady's veil.
He said he had a gobbet[89] of the sail

715 Saint Peter had the time when he made bold
To walk the waves, till Jesu Christ took hold.

He had a cross of metal set with stones
And, in a glass, a rubble of pigs' bones.
And with these relics, any time he found

720 Some poor upcountry parson to astound,
In one short day, in money down, he drew
More than the parson in a month or two,
And by his flatteries and prevarication
Made monkeys of the priest and congregation.

725 But still to do him justice first and last
In church he was a noble ecclesiast.
How well he read a lesson or told a story!
But best of all he sang an Offertory,[90]
For well he knew that when that song was sung

730 He'd have to preach and tune his honey-tongue
And (well he could) win silver from the crowd.
That's why he sang so merrily and loud.
    Now I have told you shortly, in a clause,
The rank, the array, the number and the cause

735 Of our assembly in this company
In Southwark, at that high-class hostelry
Known as *The Tabard*, close beside *The Bell*.
And now the time has come for me to tell
How we behaved that evening; I'll begin

740 After we had alighted at the Inn,
Then I'll report our journey, stage by stage,
All the remainder of our pilgrimage.
But first I beg of you, in courtesy,
Not to condemn me as unmannerly

745 If I speak plainly and with no concealings
And give account of all their words and dealings,
Using their very phrases as they fell.
For certainly, as you all know so well,
He who repeats a tale after a man

750 Is bound to say, as nearly as he can,
Each single word, if he remembers it,
However rudely spoken or unfit,

---

85. *Large . . . ale-house.* A tavern was customarily identified by such a bush on a stake.

86. *Pardoner.* In the Middle Ages sinners under sentence of an extended penance could purchase a remittance of their penance duties from official pardoners. This soon led to corrupt practices, the ignorant believing they could buy complete forgiveness for a sin. Fake pardoners were only too willing to exploit such people.

87. *Charing Cross*, district of London in which was located the hospital of the Blessed Mary of Rouncivalle. In Chaucer's time unauthorized pardons were sold by persons claiming they were collecting money for the hospital, and Pardoners of Rouncivalle were often satirized.

88. *wallet*, pack.

89. *gobbet*, piece.

90. *Offertory*, a portion of the liturgy of the Mass.

Tavern scene, Italian miniature, late fourteenth century.

The wine was strong and we were glad to
    drink.
A very striking man our Host withal,
770 And fit to be a marshal in a hall.
His eyes were bright, his girth a little wide;
There is no finer burgess in Cheapside.[92]
Bold in his speech, yet wise and full of tact,
There was no manly attribute he lacked,
775 What's more he was a merry-hearted man.
After our meal he jokingly began
To talk of sport, and, among other things
After we'd settled up our reckonings,
He said as follows: "Truly, gentlemen,
780 You're very welcome and I can't think when
—Upon my word I'm telling you no lie—
I've seen a gathering here that looked so spry,
No, not this year, as in this tavern now.
I'd think you up some fun if I knew how.
785 And, as it happens, a thought has just occurred
To please you, costing nothing, on my word.
You're off to Canterbury—well, God speed!
Blessed St. Thomas answer to your need!
And I don't doubt, before the journey's done
790 You mean to while the time in tales and fun.
Indeed, there's little pleasure for your bones
Riding along and all as dumb as stones.
So let me then propose for your enjoyment,
Just as I said, a suitable employment.
795 And if my notion suits and you agree
And promise to submit yourselves to me
Playing your parts exactly as I say
Tomorrow as you ride along the way,
Then by my father's soul (and he is dead)
800 If you don't like it you can have my head!
Hold up your hands, and not another word."
    Well, our opinion was not long deferred,
It seemed not worth a serious debate;
We all agreed to it at any rate
805 And bade him issue what commands he
    would.
"My lords," he said, "now listen for your
    good,
And please don't treat my notion with
    disdain.
This is the point. I'll make it short and plain.
Each one of you shall help to make things slip

Or else the tale he tells will be untrue,
The things pretended and the phrases new.
755 He may not flinch although it were his
    brother,
He may as well say one word as another.
And Christ Himself spoke broad in Holy Writ,
Yet there is no scurrility in it,
And Plato says, for those with power to read,
760 "The word should be as cousin to the deed."[91]
Further I beg you to forgive it me
If I neglect the order and degree
And what is due to rank in what I've
    planned.
I'm short of wit as you will understand.

765   Our *Host* gave us great welcome; everyone
Was given a place and supper was begun.
He served the finest victuals you could think,

---

91. *Plato . . . deed.* The reference here is to a passage in the *Ti-maeus*, one of the dialogues of the Greek philosopher Plato (427?–347? B.C.).
92. *burgess in Cheapside,* citizen of a district in London.

810 By telling two stories on the outward trip
To Canterbury, that's what I intend,
And, on the homeward way to journey's end
Another two, tales from the days of old;
And then the man whose story is best told,
815 That is to say who gives the fullest measure
Of good morality and general pleasure,
He shall be given a supper, paid by all,
Here in this tavern, in this very hall,
When we come back again from Canterbury.
820 And in the hope to keep you bright and merry
I'll go along with you myself and ride
All at my own expense and serve as guide.
I'll be the judge, and those who won't obey
Shall pay for what we spend upon the way.
825 Now if you all agree to what you've heard
Tell me at once without another word,
And I will make arrangements early for it.''
    Of course we all agreed, in fact we swore it
Delightedly, and made entreaty too
830 That he should act as he proposed to do,
Become our Governor in short, and be
Judge of our tales and general referee,
And set the supper at a certain price.
We promised to be ruled by his advice

835 Come high, come low; unanimously thus
We set him up in judgment over us.
More wine was fetched, the business being
    done;
We drank it off and up went everyone
To bed without a moment of delay.
840   Early next morning at the spring of day
Up rose our Host and roused us like a cock,
Gathering us together in a flock,
And off we rode at slightly faster pace
Than walking to St. Thomas's watering place;[93]
845 And there our Host drew up, began to ease
His horse, and said, "Now, listen if you please,
My lords! Remember what you promised me.
If evensong and matins will agree[94]
Let's see who shall be first to tell a tale.
850 And as I hope to drink good wine and ale
I'll be your judge. The rebel who disobeys,
However much the journey costs, he pays.
Now draw for cut and then we can depart;
The man who draws the shortest cut shall
    start. . . .''

93. **St. Thomas's watering-place,** a brook on the pilgrimage route to Canterbury.
94. **If evensong . . . agree.** If you feel in the morning (matins) as you did the night before (evensong).

Discussion

1. The Knight and the Squire belong to the age of chivalry, and the Yeoman who accompanies them has apparently also seen military service. (a) What characteristics of the Knight qualify him to be praised as "a true, a perfect gentle-knight"? How do his clothes hint at his virtues? (b) By contrast, what motivates the Squire? How do his clothes suggest this? (c) Which details in the Yeoman's description suggest that he has been a soldier? Which suggest that he follows a different occupation in peacetime?

2. Which details about the Prioress suggest that, despite her religious vocation, she retains some worldly traits?

3. Chaucer depicts the Parson as the ideal priest. Which character details contribute to this impression?

4. In what ways are the Merchant, Oxford Cleric, Sergeant at the Law, and Doctor typical of their professions?

5. (a) How do the Skipper and Miller cheat others? Could they trick the Reeve? Why? (b) Given these examples, would you call Chaucer's age more corrupt than ours? Explain.

6. Scholars have discovered that there was a real-life Host of an inn called The Tabard in Southwark. His name was Harry Bailly, the name Chaucer assigns to his Host in The Cook's Prologue. This discovery has led to the belief that some of the other pilgrims had real-life originals. Select one for whom you think this may be true, and explain why you think so.

7. In lines 743–764 Chaucer disclaims responsibility for anything offensive in what he is about to present. (a) How do you feel about his statement that an author "Is bound to say, as nearly as he can, / Each single word, if he remembers it, / However rudely spoken or unfit"? (b) What might have been Chaucer's reason for ending this passage with the line "I'm short of wit as you will understand"?

Vocabulary
Context, Dictionary

A. Use context as an aid in interpreting the italicized word in each of the following passages; then on a separate sheet of paper use the italicized word in a sentence of your own that shows you understand the meaning of the word. You may use your Glossary if you are not entirely certain of the meaning. Be sure you can pronounce and spell all italicized words.

1. "When in April the sweet showers fall / And pierce the drought of March to the root, and all / The veins are bathed in liquor of such power / As brings about the *engendering* of the flower. . . ."

2. "Our Host gave us great welcome; everyone / Was given a place and supper was begun. / He served the finest *victuals* you could think. . . ."

3. "As for her sympathies and tender feelings, / She was so charitably *solicitous* / She used to weep if she but saw a mouse / Caught in a trap, if it were dead or bleeding."

4. "I saw his sleeves were *garnished* at the hand / With fine gray fur, the finest in the land. . . ."

B. Use your Glossary to answer the following questions on your paper.

1. (a) The word *boorish* may come from either of two languages. What are they? **(b)** What did the word originally mean?

2. What specific epidemic disease can *pestilence* refer to?

3. What is the meaning of the Latin word from which *eminent* comes?

4. Give the Old French and Latin words from which *accrue* comes.

Composition

1. Assume that in Chaucer's day there were news media of some sort and that you worked for one of them.

Write an interview with one of the pilgrims. (Remember to write questions that allow you to create interesting and revealing responses for the pilgrim you have chosen.)

2. Imagine you are one of the pilgrims. Reflect on what Chaucer says about the pilgrim you have chosen to be and try to see how such a person would view the world.

Write a letter home, describing the pilgrimage and some of your fellow travelers.

The Pardoner's Prologue

"My lords," he said, "in churches where
    I preach
I cultivate a haughty kind of speech
And ring it out as roundly as a bell;
I've got it all by heart, the tale I tell.
5 I have a text, it always is the same
And always has been, since I learnt the game,
Old as the hills and fresher than the grass,
Radix malorum est cupiditas.[1]
    "But first I make pronouncement whence
    I come,
10 Show them my bulls[2] in detail and in sum,
And flaunt the papal seal for their inspection

---

1. *Radix . . . cupiditas.* "Avarice is the root of all evil." [Latin]
2. *bulls,* important papal documents or letters.

As warrant for my bodily protection,
That none may have the impudence to irk
Or hinder me in Christ's most holy work.
15 Then I tell stories, as occasion calls,
Showing forth bulls from popes and cardinals,
From patriarchs and bishops; as I do,
I speak some words in Latin—just a few—
To put a saffron tinge³ upon my preaching
20 And stir devotion with a spice of teaching.
Then I bring all my long glass bottles out
Cram-full of bones and ragged bits of clout,⁴
Relics they are, at least for such are known.
Then, cased in metal, I've a shoulder bone,
25 Belonging to a sheep, a holy Jew's.⁵
'Good men,' I say, 'take heed, for here is
    news.
Take but this bone and dip it in a well;
If cow or calf, if sheep or ox should swell
From eating snakes or that a snake has stung,
30 Take water from that well and wash its tongue,
And it will then recover. Furthermore,
Where there is pox or scab or other sore,
All animals that water at that well
Are cured at once. Take note of what I tell.
35 If the good man—the owner of the stock—
Goes once a week, before the crow of cock,
Fasting, and takes a draught of water too,
Why then, according to that holy Jew,
He'll find his cattle multiply and sell.
40   " 'And it's a cure for jealousy as well;
For though a man be given to jealous wrath,
Use but this water when you make his broth,
And never again will he mistrust his wife,
Though he knew all about her sinful life,
45 Though two or three clergy had enjoyed her
    love.
    " 'Now look; I have a mitten here, a glove.
Whoever wears this mitten on his hand
Will multiply his grain. He sows his land
And up will come abundant wheat or oats,
50 Providing that he offers pence or groats.
    " 'Good men and women, here's a word
        of warning;
If there is anyone in church this morning
Guilty of sin, so far beyond expression
Horrible, that he dare not make confession,
55 Or any woman, whether young or old,
That's cuckolded her husband, be she told
That such as she shall have no power or grace
To offer to my relics in this place.

But those who can acquit themselves of blame
60 Can all come up and offer in God's name,
And I will shrive them by the authority
Committed in this papal bull to me.'
    "That trick's been worth a hundred
        marks⁶ a year
Since I became a Pardoner, never fear.
65 Then, priestlike in my pulpit, with a frown,
I stand, and when the yokels have sat down,
I preach, as you have heard me say before,
And tell a hundred lying mockeries more.
I take great pains, and stretching out my neck

The Pardoner, from the Ellesmere Chaucer.

70 To east and west I crane about and peck
Just like a pigeon sitting on a barn.
My hands and tongue together spin the yarn
And all my antics are a joy to see.
The curse of avarice and cupidity
75 Is all my sermon, for it frees the pelf.
Out come the pence, and specially for myself,

---

3. *saffron tinge.* The yellow spice saffron is used to color and
flavor food.
4. *clout,* cloth.
5. *a holy Jew's,* presumably some Old Testament figure, possibly the patriarch Jacob.
6. *marks.* The mark was worth 13 shillings and fourpence, or
two-thirds of a pound sterling. In Chaucer's time, the purchasing value of money was at least thirty times what it is today.

For my exclusive purpose is to win
And not at all to castigate their sin.
Once dead what matter how their souls may
    fare?
80 They can go blackberrying,[7] for all I care! . . .
    "But let me briefly make my purpose plain;
I preach for nothing but for greed of gain
And use the same old text, as bold as brass,
Radix malorum est cupiditas.
85 And thus I preach against the very vice
I make my living out of—avarice.
And yet however guilty of that sin
Myself, with others I have power to win
Them from it, I can bring them to repent;
90 But that is not my principal intent.
Covetousness is both the root and stuff
Of all I preach. That ought to be enough.
    "Well, then I give examples thick and fast
From bygone times, old stories from the past;
95 A yokel mind loves stories from of old,
Being the kind it can repeat and hold.
What! Do you think, as long as I can preach
And get their silver for the things I teach,
That I will live in poverty, from choice?
100 That's not the counsel of my inner voice!
No! Let me preach and beg from kirk[8] to kirk

And never do an honest job of work,
No, nor make baskets, like St. Paul,[9] to gain
A livelihood. I do not preach in vain.
105 There's no apostle I would counterfeit;
I mean to have money, wool and cheese and
    wheat
Though it were given me by the poorest lad
Or poorest village widow, though she had
A string of starving children, all agape.
110 No, let me drink the liquor of the grape
And keep a jolly wench in every town!
    "But listen, gentlemen; to bring things down
To a conclusion, would you like a tale?
Now as I've drunk a draught of corn-ripe ale,
115 By God it stands to reason I can strike
On some good story that you all will like.
For though I am a wholly vicious man
Don't think I can't tell moral tales. I can!
Here's one I often preach when out for
    winning;
120 Now please be quiet. Here is the beginning."

---

7. They . . . blackberrying, go wandering at large.
8. kirk, church.
9. make baskets . . . St. Paul. The reference is not to St. Paul
the Apostle, but to St. Paul the Hermit, who spent most of his
very long life in the Egyptian desert. He died around 347 and is
traditionally regarded as the first Christian hermit.

The Pardoner's Tale

    . . . It's of three rioters I have to tell
Who, long before the morning service bell,
Were sitting in a tavern for a drink.
And as they sat, they heard the hand-bell clink
5 Before a coffin going to the grave;
One of them called the little tavern-knave[1]
And said "Go and find out at once—look
    spry!—
Whose corpse is in that coffin passing by;
And see you get the name correctly too."
10 "Sir," said the boy, "no need, I promise you;
Two hours before you came here I was told.
He was a friend of yours in days of old,
And suddenly, last night, the man was slain,
Upon his bench, face up, dead drunk again.

15 There came a privy thief, they call him Death,
Who kills us all round here, and in a breath
He speared him through the heart, he never
    stirred.
And then Death went his way without a word.
He's killed a thousand in the present plague,
20 And, sir, it doesn't do to be too vague
If you should meet him; you had best be wary.
Be on your guard with such an adversary,
Be primed to meet him everywhere you go,
That's what my mother said. It's all I know."
25   The publican joined in with, "By St. Mary,
What the child says is right; you'd best be wary,

---

1. knave, servant.

This very year he killed, in a large village
A mile away, man, woman, serf at tillage,
Page in the household, children—all there
       were.
30 Yes, I imagine that he lives round there.
It's well to be prepared in these alarms,
He might do you dishonor!'' ''Huh, God's
       arms!''
The rioter said, ''Is he so fierce to meet?
I'll search for him, by Jesus, street by street.
35 God's blessed bones! I'll register a vow!
Here, chaps! The three of us together now,
Hold up your hands, like me, and we'll be
       brothers
In this affair, and each defend the others,
And we will kill this traitor Death, I say!
40 Away with him as he has made away
With all our friends. God's dignity! Tonight!''
    They made their bargain, swore with
       appetite,
These three, to live and die for one another
As brother-born might swear to his born
       brother.
45 And up they started in their drunken rage
And made towards this village which the page
And publican had spoken of before.
Many and grisly were the oaths they swore,
Tearing Christ's blessed body to a shred;
50 ''If we can only catch him, Death is dead!''
    When they had gone not fully half a mile,
Just as they were about to cross a stile,
They came upon a very poor old man
Who humbly greeted them and thus began,
55 ''God look to you, my lords, and give you
       quiet!''
To which the proudest of these men of riot
Gave back the answer, ''What, old fool?
       Give place!
Why are you all wrapped up except your face?
Why live so long? Isn't it time to die?''
60 The old, old fellow looked him in the eye
And said, ''Because I never yet have found,
Though I have walked to India, searching
       round
Village and city on my pilgrimage,
One who would change his youth to have
       my age.
65 And so my age is mine and must be still
Upon me, for such time as God may will.
    ''Not even Death, alas, will take my life;

So, like a wretched prisoner at strife
Within himself, I walk alone and wait
70 About the earth, which is my mother's gate,[2]
Knock-knocking with my staff from night to
       noon
And crying, 'Mother, open to me soon!
Look at me, mother, won't you let me in?
See how I wither, flesh and blood and skin!
75 Alas! When will these bones be laid to rest?
Mother, I would exchange—for that were best—
The wardrobe in my chamber, standing there
So long, for yours! Aye, for a shirt of hair[3]
To wrap me in!' She has refused her grace,
80 Whence comes the pallor of my withered face.
    ''But it dishonored you when you began
To speak so roughly, sir, to an old man,
Unless he had injured you in word or deed.
It says in holy writ, as you may read,
85 'Thou shalt rise up before the hoary head
And honor it.' And therefore be it said
'Do no more harm to an old man than you,
Being now young, would have another do
When you are old'—if you should live till then.
90 And so may God be with you, gentlemen,
For I must go whither I have to go.''
    ''By God,'' the gambler said, ''you shan't
       do so,
You don't get off so easy, by St. John!
I heard you mention, just a moment gone,
95 A certain traitor Death who singles out
And kills the fine young fellows hereabout.
And you're his spy, by God! You wait a bit.
Say where he is or you shall pay for it,
By God and by the Holy Sacrament!
100 I say you've joined together by consent
To kill us younger folk, you thieving swine!''
    ''Well, sirs,'' he said, ''if it be your design
To find out Death, turn up this crooked way
Towards that grove. I left him there today
105 Under a tree, and there you'll find him
       waiting.
He isn't one to hide for all your prating.
You see that oak? He won't be far to find.
And God protect you that redeemed mankind,
Aye, and amend you!'' Thus that ancient man.
110 At once the three young rioters began
To run, and reached the tree, and there they
       found

---

2. **mother's gate,** the grave, the entrance to ''mother earth.''
3. **shirt of hair,** a garment worn by penitents.

A pile of golden florins[4] on the ground,
New-coined, eight bushels of them as they
    thought.
No longer was it Death those fellows sought,
115 For they were all so thrilled to see the sight,
The florins were so beautiful and bright,
That down they sat beside the precious pile.
The wickedest spoke first after a while.
"Brothers," he said, "you listen to what I say.
120 I'm pretty sharp although I joke away.
It's clear that Fortune has bestowed this
    treasure
To let us live in jollity and pleasure.
Light come, light go! We'll spend it as we
    ought.
God's precious dignity! Who would have
    thought
125 This morning was to be our lucky day?
    "If one could only get the gold away,
Back to my house, or else to yours, perhaps—
For as you know, the gold is ours, chaps—
We'd all be at the top of fortune, hey?
130 But certainly it can't be done by day.
People would call us robbers—a strong gang,
So our own property would make us hang.
No, we must bring this treasure back by night
Some prudent way, and keep it out of sight.
135 And so as a solution I propose
We draw for lots and see the way it goes.
The one who draws the longest, lucky man,
Shall run to town as quickly as he can
To fetch us bread and wine—but keep things
    dark—
140 While two remain in hiding here to mark
Our heap of treasure. If there's no delay,
When night comes down we'll carry it away,
All three of us, wherever we have planned."
    He gathered lots and hid them in his hand
145 Bidding them draw for where the luck
    should fall.
It fell upon the youngest of them all,
And off he ran at once towards the town.
    As soon as he had gone the first sat down
And thus began a parley with the other:
150 "You know that you can trust me as a
    brother;
Now let me tell you where your profit lies;
You know our friend has gone to get supplies
And here's a lot of gold that is to be
Divided equally amongst us three.

155 Nevertheless, if I could shape things thus
So that we shared it out—the two of us—
Wouldn't you take it as a friendly act?"
    "But how?" the other said. "He knows
    the fact
That all the gold was left with me and you;
160 What can we tell him? What are we to do?"
    "Is it a bargain," said the first, "or no?
For I can tell you in a word or so
What's to be done to bring the thing about."
    "Trust me," the other said, "you needn't
    doubt
165 My word. I won't betray you, I'll be true."
    "Well," said his friend, "you see that we
    are two,
And two are twice as powerful as one.
Now look; when he comes back, get up in
    fun
To have a wrestle; then, as you attack,
170 I'll up and put my dagger through his back
While you and he are struggling, as in game;
Then draw your dagger too and do the same.
Then all this money will be ours to spend,
Divided equally of course, dear friend.
175 Then we can gratify our lusts and fill
The day with dicing at our own sweet will."
Thus these two miscreants agreed to slay
The third and youngest, as you heard me say.
    The youngest, as he ran towards the town,
180 Kept turning over, rolling up and down
Within his heart the beauty of those bright
New florins, saying, "Lord, to think I might
Have all that treasure to myself alone!
Could there be anyone beneath the throne
185 Of God so happy as I then should be?"
    And so the Fiend, our common enemy,
Was given power to put it in his thought
That there was always poison to be bought,
And that with poison he could kill his friends.
190 To men in such a state the Devil sends
Thoughts of this kind, and has a full
    permission
To lure them on to sorrow and perdition;
For this young man was utterly content
To kill them both and never to repent.
195 And on he ran, he had no thought to tarry,
Came to the town, found an apothecary
And said, "Sell me some poison if you will,

---

4. *florins,* coins worth a third of a pound sterling.

I have a lot of rats I want to kill
And there's a polecat too about my yard
200 That takes my chickens and it hits me hard;
But I'll get even, as is only right,
With vermin that destroy a man by night.''
   The chemist answered, ''I've a preparation
Which you shall have, and by my soul's
   salvation
205 If any living creature eat or drink
A mouthful, ere he has the time to think,
Though he took less than makes a grain of
   wheat,
You'll see him fall down dying at your feet;
Yes, die he must, and in so short a while
210 You'd hardly have the time to walk a mile,
The poison is so strong, you understand.''
   This cursed fellow grabbed into his hand
The box of poison and away he ran
Into a neighboring street, and found a man
215 Who lent him three large bottles. He
   withdrew
And deftly poured the poison into two.
He kept the third one clean, as well he might,
For his own drink, meaning to work all night
Stacking the gold and carrying it away.
220 And when this rioter, this devil's clay,
Had filled his bottles up with wine, all three,
Back to rejoin his comrades sauntered he.
   Why make a sermon of it? Why waste
   breath?
Exactly in the way they'd planned his death
225 They fell on him and slew him, two to one.
Then said the first of them when this was
   done,
''Now for a drink. Sit down and let's be
   merry,
For later on there'll be the corpse to bury.''
And, as it happened, reaching for a sup,
230 He took a bottle full of poison up
And drank; and his companion, nothing loth,
Drank from it also, and they perished both.
   There is, in Avicenna's long relation[5]
Concerning poison and its operation,
235 Trust me, no ghastlier section to transcend
What these two wretches suffered at their
   end.
Thus these two murderers received their
   due,
So did the treacherous young poisoner too.

O cursed sin! O blackguardly excess!
240 O treacherous homicide! O wickedness!
O gluttony that lusted on and diced!
O blasphemy that took the name of Christ
With habit-hardened oaths that pride began!
Alas, how comes it that a mortal man,
245 That thou, to thy Creator, Him that wrought
   thee,
That paid His precious blood for thee and
   bought thee,
Art so unnatural and false within?
   Dearly beloved, God forgive your sin
And keep you from the vice of avarice!
250 My holy pardon frees you all of this,
Provided that you make the right approaches,
That is with sterling, rings, or silver brooches.
Bow down your heads under this holy bull!
Come on, you women, offer up your wool!
255 I'll write your name into my ledger; so!
Into the bliss of Heaven you shall go.
For I'll absolve you by my holy power,
You that make offering, clean as at the hour
When you were born. . . . That, sirs, is how
   I preach
260 And Jesu Christ, soul's healer, aye, the leech
Of every soul, grant pardon and relieve you
Of sin, for that is best, I won't deceive you.
   One thing I should have mentioned in my
   tale,
Dear people. I've some relics in my bale
265 And pardons too, as full and fine, I hope,
As any in England, given me by the Pope.
If there be one among you that is willing
To have my absolution for a shilling
Devoutly given, come! and do not harden
270 Your hearts but kneel in humbleness for
   pardon;
Or else, receive my pardon as we go.
You can renew it every town or so
Always provided that you still renew
Each time, and in good money, what is due.
275 It is an honor to you to have found
A pardoner with his credentials sound
Who can absolve you as you ply the spur
In any accident that may occur.
For instance—we are all at Fortune's beck—
280 Your horse may throw you down and break
   your neck.

---

5. *Avicenna's long relation,* a work on medicine by an Arabian
physician (A.D. 980–1037).

What a security it is to all
To have me here among you and at call
With pardon for the lowly and the great
When soul leaves body for the future state!
285 And I advise our Host here to begin,
The most enveloped of you all in sin.
Come forward, Host, you shall be first to pay.
And kiss my holy relics right away.
Only a groat. Come on, unbuckle your
    purse!''
290 ''No, no,'' said he, ''not I, and may the curse
Of Christ descend upon me if I do!
You'll have me kissing your old breeches too
And swear they were the relic of a saint. . . .''
    The Pardoner said nothing, not a word;

295 He was so angry that he couldn't speak.
    ''Well,'' said our Host, ''if you're for showing
      pique,
I'll joke no more, not with an angry man.''
    The worthy Knight immediately began,
Seeing the fun was getting rather rough,
300 And said, ''No more, we've all had quite
      enough.
Now, Master Pardoner, perk up, look cheerly!
And you, Sir Host, whom I esteem so dearly,
I beg of you to kiss the Pardoner.
    ''Come, Pardoner, draw nearer, my dear
      sir.
305 Let's laugh again and keep the ball in play.''
They kissed, and we continued on our way.

Discussion

1. How sound is the psychology used by the Pardoner to extort money? See, for example, lines 51–62 of his *Prologue,* describing the trick ''worth a hundred marks a year'' to him.

2. How do the Revelers' actions reinforce the points the Pardoner is making?

3. The Old Man whom the three Revelers encounter has been called one the most striking figures in all poetry. Most critics think that he is a symbolic figure. What do you think he might symbolize?

4. *The Pardoner's Tale* has been called one of the greatest short stories ever written. Explain why you agree or disagree with this assessment.

5. The Pardoner admits (*Prologue,* line 83) that he always uses the same text or moral in his sermon. What is the irony in his use of this text?

6. After revealing all his tricks to the other pilgrims and relating his tale, the Pardoner offers to sell them the same pardon he has already admitted is worthless. How do you account for this?

7. Some critics claim that the Pardoner is the only pilgrim whom Chaucer thoroughly detests. Do you agree? Give the evidence on which you base your opinion.

Composition

1. Imagine the Pardoner preaching in the pulpit, either from the standpoint of a parishioner who believes him to be a holy and honorable man, or from the standpoint of one who sees through his tricks.

Write a brief description of the Pardoner preaching, from whichever standpoint you have chosen.

2. The Pardoner says all his sermons are based on one text, ''Avarice is the root of all evil.''

Devise an anecdote or a very short story to illustrate this text. (Or, if you prefer, substitute a word of your own choice for *avarice.*)

3. F. N. Robinson, a distinguished editor of Chaucer, wrote: ''In spite of his contemptible nature, physical and moral, the Pardoner is one of the most intellectual figures among the pilgrims and his performance is worthy of his powers.''

React to this comment in a brief composition. (See *Evaluating Your Evidence* in Composition Guide.)

_T_he Wife of Bath's Prologue

The Wife of Bath,
from the Ellesmere Chaucer.

"If there were no authority on earth
Except experience, mine, for what it's worth,
And that's enough for me, all goes to show
That marriage is a misery and a woe;
5 For let me say, if I may make so bold,
My lords, since when I was but twelve years
    old,
Thanks be to God Eternal evermore,
Five husbands have I had at the church door;
Yes, it's a fact that I have had so many,
10 All worthy in their way, as good as any. . . .
Welcome the sixth, whenever he appears.
I can't keep continent for years and years.
No sooner than one husband's dead and gone
Some other Christian man shall take me on,
15 For then, so says the Apostle,[1] I am free
To wed, o' God's name, where it pleases me.
Wedding's no sin, so far as I can learn.
Better it is to marry than to burn. . . .
Show me a time or text where God disparages,
20 Or sets a prohibition upon marriages
Expressly, let me have it! Show it me!
And where did He command virginity?
I know as well as you do, never doubt it,
All the Apostle Paul has said about it;
25 He said that as for precepts he had none.

One may advise a woman to be one;[2]
Advice is no commandment in my view.
He left it in our judgment what to do. . . .
And as for being married, he lets me do it
30 Out of indulgence, so there's nothing to it
In marrying me, suppose my husband dead;
There's nothing bigamous in such a bed. . . .
    "I grant it you. I'll never say a word
Decrying maidenhood although preferred
35 To frequent marriage; there are those who
    mean
To live in their virginity, as clean
In body as in soul, and never mate.
I'll make no boast about my own estate.
As in a noble household, we are told,
40 Not every dish and vessel's made of gold,
Some are of wood, yet earn their master's
    praise,
God calls His folk to Him in many ways.
To each of them God gave His proper gift,
Some this, some that, and left them to make
    shift.

---

1. **Apostle,** St. Paul. In the passages that follow, the Wife
quotes scripture freely—but not always accurately—to support
her arguments.
2. **one,** that is, a virgin.

45 Virginity is indeed a great perfection,
And married continence, for God's dilection,
But Christ, who of perfection is the well,
Bade not that everyone should go and sell
All that he had and give it to the poor
50 To follow in His footsteps, that is sure.
He spoke to those that would live perfectly,
And by your leave, my lords, that's not for me.
I will bestow the flower of life, the honey,
Upon the acts and fruit of matrimony.
55   ". . . I'll have a husband yet
Who shall be both my debtor and my slave
And bear his tribulation to the grave
Upon his flesh, as long as I'm his wife.
For mine shall be the power all his life
60 Over his proper body, and not he,
Thus the Apostle Paul has told it me,
And bade our husbands they should love us
    well;
There's a command on which I like to dwell
    . . ."
  The Pardoner started up, and thereupon
65 "Madam," he said, "by God and by St. John,
That's noble preaching no one could surpass!
I was about to take a wife; alas!
Am I to buy it on my flesh so dear?
There'll be no marrying for me this year!"
70   "You wait," she said, "my story's not
    begun.
You'll taste another brew before I've done;
You'll find it doesn't taste as good as ale.
And when I've finished telling you my tale
Of tribulation in the married life
75 In which I've been an expert as a wife
That is to say, myself have been the whip.
So please yourself whether you want to sip
At that same cask of marriage I shall broach;
Be cautious before making the approach. . . ."
80   "Madam, I put it to you as a prayer,"
The Pardoner said, "go on as you began!
Tell us your tale, spare not for any man.
Instruct us younger men in your technique."
"Gladly," she answered, "if I am to speak.
85 But still I hope the company won't reprove me
Though I should speak as fantasy may move
    me,
And please don't be offended at my views;
They're really only offered to amuse.
  "Now, gentlemen, I'll on and tell my tale
90 And as I hope to drink good wine and ale

I'll tell the truth. Those husbands that I had,
Three of them were good and two were bad.
The three that I call 'good' were rich and old. . . .
I managed them so well by my technique
95 Each was delighted to go out and seek
And buy some pretty things for me to wear,
Happy if I as much as spoke them fair.
God knows how spitefully I used to scold
    them.
  "Listen, I'll tell you how I used to hold them,
100 You knowing women, who can understand.
First put them in the wrong, and out of hand.
No one can be so bold—I mean no man—
At lies and swearing as a woman can.
This is no news, as you'll have realized,
105 To knowing ones, but to the misadvised.
A knowing wife if she is worth her salt
Can always prove her husband is at fault,
And even though the fellow may have heard
Some story told him by a little bird
110 She knows enough to prove the bird is crazy
And get her maid to witness she's a daisy,
With full agreement, scarce solicited.
But listen. Here's the sort of thing I said:
  " 'Now, sir old dotard, what is that you say?
115 Why is my neighbor's wife so smart and gay?
She is respected everywhere she goes.
I sit at home and have no decent clothes.
Why haunt her house? What are you doing
    there?
Are you so amorous? Is she so fair?
120 What, whispering secrets to our maid? For
    shame,
Sir ancient lecher! Time you dropped that
    game.
And if I see my gossip or a friend
You scold me like a devil! There's no end
If I as much as stroll towards his house.
125 Then you come home as drunken as a mouse,
You mount your throne and preach, chapter
    and verse
—All nonsense—and you tell me it's a curse
To marry a poor woman—she's expensive;
Or if her family's wealthy and extensive
130 You say it's torture to endure her pride
And melancholy airs, and more beside. . . .
  " 'You say that some desire us for our
    wealth,
Some for our shapeliness, our looks, our
    health,

Some for our singing, others for our dancing,
135 Some for our gentleness and dalliant glancing,
And some because our hands are soft and
small;
By your account the devil gets us all. . . .
That's what you say as you stump off to bed,
You brute! You say no man of sense would
wed,
140 That is, not if he wants to go to Heaven.
Wild thunderbolts and fire from the seven
Planets³ descend and break your withered
neck!
" 'You say that buildings falling into wreck,
And smoke, and scolding women, are the
three
145 Things that will drive a man from home.
Dear me!
What ails the poor old man to grumble so?
" 'We women hide our faults to let them
show
Once we are safely married, so you say.
There's a fine proverb for a popinjay!⁴
150 " 'You say that oxen, asses, hounds, and
horses
Can be tried out on various ploys and
courses;
And basins too, and dishes when you buy
them,
Spoons, chairs, and furnishings, a man can
try them
As he can try a suit of clothes, no doubt,
155 But no one ever tries a woman out
Until he's married her; old dotard crow!
And then you say she lets her vices show.
" 'You also say we count it for a crime
Unless you praise our beauty all the time,
160 Unless you're always poring on our faces
And call us pretty names in public places;
Or if you fail to treat me to a feast
Upon my birthday—presents at the least—
Or to respect my nurse and her grey hairs,
165 Or be polite to all my maids upstairs
And to my father's cronies and his spies.
That's what you say, old barrelful of lies!
" 'Then there's our young apprentice,
handsome Johnny;
Because he has crisp hair that shines as
bonny
170 As finest gold, and squires me up and down
You show your low suspicions in a frown.

I wouldn't have him, not if you died tomorrow!
" 'And tell me this, God punish you with
sorrow,
Why do you hide the keys of coffer doors?
175 It's just as much my property as yours.
Do you want to make an idiot of your wife?
Now, by the Lord that gave me soul and
life, . . .
I think you'd like to lock me in your coffer!
"Go where you please, dear wife," you
ought to offer,
180 "Amuse yourself! I shan't give ear to malice,
I know you for a virtuous wife, Dame Alice."
We cannot love a husband who takes charge
Of where we go. We like to be at large. . . .
" 'And when a woman tries a mild display
185 In dress or costly ornament, you say
It is a danger to her chastity,
And then, bad luck to you, start making free
With Bible tags in the Apostle's name;⁵
"And in like manner, chastely and with shame,
190 You women should adorn yourselves," said
he,
"And not with braided hair or jewelry
With pearl or golden ornament." What next!
I'll pay as much attention to your text
And rubric in such things as would a gnat.
195 " 'And once you said that I was like a cat,
For if you singe a cat it will not roam
And that's the way to keep a cat at home.
But when she feels her fur is sleek and gay
She can't be kept indoors for half a day
200 But off she takes herself as dusk is falling
To show her fur and go a-caterwauling.
Which means if I feel gay, as you suppose,
I shall run out to show my poor old clothes.
" 'Silly old fool! You and your private spies!
205 Go on, beg Argus⁶ with his hundred eyes
To be my bodyguard, that's better still!
But yet he shan't, I say, against my will.
I'll pull him by the beard, believe you me!
" 'And once you said that principally three

---

3. **seven/Planets,** the seven "wandering stars" studied by ancient astronomers: the sun, the moon, Mercury, Venus, Mars, Jupiter, and Saturn.
4. **popinjay,** parrot.
5. **Apostle's name.** The reference is to Timothy I 2:9. Note that the Wife is accusing her husband of using the same tactics that she constantly uses herself.
6. **Argus,** in Greek legend, a hundred-eyed giant who never closed all his eyes in sleep at the same time and therefore kept constant watch.

210 Misfortunes[7] trouble earth, east, west and
north,
And no man living could endure a fourth.
My dear sir shrew, Jesu cut short your life!
You preach away and say a hateful wife
Is reckoned to be one of these misfortunes.
215 Is there no other trouble that importunes
The world and that your parables could
condemn?
Must an unhappy wife be one of them?
" 'Then you compared a woman's love to
Hell,
To barren land where water will not dwell,
220 And you compared it to a quenchless fire,
The more it burns the more is its desire
To burn up everything that burnt can be.
You say that just as worms destroy a tree
A wife destroys her husband and contrives,
225 As husbands know, the ruin of their lives.'
"Such was the way, my lords, you
understand
I kept my older husbands well in hand.
I told them they were drunk and their
unfitness
To judge my conduct forced me to take
witness
230 That they were lying. Johnny and my niece
Would back me up. O Lord, I wrecked their
peace,
Innocent as they were, without remorse!
For I could bite and whinney like a horse
And launch complaints when things were all
my fault;
235 I'd have been lost if I had called a halt.
First to the mill is first to grind your corn;
I attacked first and they were overborne,
Glad to apologize and even suing
Pardon for what they'd never thought of
doing.
240 "I'd tackle one for wenching, out of hand,
Although so ill the man could hardly stand,
Yet he felt flattered in his heart because
He thought it showed how fond of him I was.
I swore that all my walking out at night
245 Was just to keep his wenching well in sight.
That was a dodge that made me shake with
mirth;
But all such wit is given us at birth.
Lies, tears, and spinning are the things God
gives

By nature to a woman, while she lives.
250 So there's one thing at least that I can boast,
That in the end I always ruled the roast;
Cunning or force was sure to make them
stumble,
And always keeping up a steady grumble. . . .
"I then would say, 'My dear, just take a
peep!
255 What a meek look on Willikin our sheep!
Come nearer, husband, let me kiss your cheek;
You should be just as patient, just as meek;
Sweeten your heart. Your conscience needs
a probe.
You're fond of preaching patience out of Job,[8]
260 And so be patient; practice what you preach,
And if you don't, my dear, we'll have to
teach
You that it's nice to have a quiet life.
One of us must be master, man or wife,
And since a man's more reasonable, he
265 Should be the patient one, you must agree . . .
"That's how my first three husbands were
undone.
Now let me tell you of my last but one.
"He was a reveller, was number four;
That is to say he kept a paramour.
270 Young, strong, and stubborn, I was full of rage
And jolly as a magpie in a cage.
Play me the harp and I would dance and
sing,
Believe me, like a nightingale in spring,
If I had had a draught of sweetened wine. . . .
275 ". . . Whenever it comes back to me,
When I recall my youth and jollity,
It fairly warms the cockles of my heart!
This very day I feel a pleasure start,
Yes, I can feel it tickling at the root.
280 Lord, how it does me good! I've had my fruit,
I've had my world and time, I've had my
fling!
But age that comes to poison everything
Has taken all my beauty and my pith.
Well, let it go, the devil go therewith!
285 The flour is gone, there is no more to say,

---

7. *three/Misfortunes.* She is alluding to Proverbs 30:21–23:
"For three things the earth is disquieted, and for four which it
cannot bear: for a servant when he reigneth; and a fool when
he is filled with meat; for an odious woman when she is married; and an handmaid that is heir to her mistress."
8. *Job,* Old Testament figure who keeps faith with God despite
many sufferings.

And I must sell the bran as best I may;
But still I mean to find my way to fun. . . .
Now let me tell you of my last but one.
　　"I told you how it filled my heart with spite
290 To see another woman his delight,
By God and all His saints I made it good!
I carved him out a cross of the same wood,
Not with my body in a filthy way,
But certainly by seeming rather gay
295 To others, frying him in his own grease
Of jealousy and rage; he got no peace.
By God on earth I was his purgatory,[9]
For which I hope his soul may be in glory.
God knows he sang a sorry tune, he flinched,
300 And bitterly enough, when the shoe pinched.
And God and he alone can say how grim,
How many were the ways I tortured him.
　　"He died when I came back from Jordan
　　　Stream[10]
And he lies buried under the rood-beam,[11]
305 Albeit that his tomb can scarce supply us
With such a show as that of King Darius
—Apelles[12] sculped it in a sumptuous taste—
But costly burial would have been mere
　　waste.
Farewell to him, God give his spirit rest!
310 He's in his grave, he's nailed up in his chest.
　　"Now of my fifth, last husband let me tell.
God never let his soul be sent to Hell!
And yet he was my worst, and many a blow
He struck me still can ache along my row
315 Of ribs, and will until my dying day. . . .
Though he had beaten me in every bone
He still could wheedle me to love, I own.
I think I loved him best, I'll tell no lie.
He was disdainful in his love, that's why.
320 We women have a curious fantasy
In such affairs, or so it seems to me.
When something's difficult, or can't be had,
We crave and cry for it all day like mad.
Forbid a thing, we pine for it all night,
325 Press fast upon us and we take to flight;
We use disdain in offering our wares.
A throng of buyers sends prices up at fairs,
Cheap goods have little value, they suppose;
And that's a thing that every woman knows.
330 　　"My fifth and last—God keep his soul in
　　　health!
The one I took for love and not for wealth,
Had been at Oxford not so long before

But had left school and gone to lodge next
　　door,
Yes, it was to my godmother's he'd gone.
335 God bless her soul! *Her* name was Alison.
She knew my heart and more of what I thought
Than did the parish priest, and so she ought!
　　　. . .
　　"And so one time it happened that in Lent,
As I so often did, I rose and went
340 To see her, ever wanting to be gay
And go a-strolling, March, April, and May,
From house to house for chat and village
　　malice.
　　"Johnny (the boy from Oxford) and Dame
　　　Alice
And I myself, into the fields we went.
345 My husband was in London all that Lent;
All the more fun for me—I only mean
The fun of seeing people and being seen
By cocky lads; for how was I to know
Where or what graces Fortune might bestow?
350 And so I made a round of visitations,
Went to processions, festivals, orations,
Preachments and pilgrimages, watched the
　　carriages
They use for plays and pageants, went to
　　marriages,
And always wore my gayest scarlet dress.
355 　　"These worms, these moths, these mites,
　　　I must confess,
Got little chance to eat it, by the way.
Why not? Because I wore it every day.
　　"Now let me tell you all that came to pass.
We sauntered in the meadows through the
　　grass
360 Toying and dallying to such extent,
Johnny and I, that I grew provident
And I suggested, were I ever free
And made a widow, he should marry me.
And certainly—I do not mean to boast—
365 I ever was more provident than most
In marriage matters and in other such.
I never think a mouse is up to much

---

9. *purgatory,* in the belief of some Christians, a place of temporary punishment for sin after death.
10. *When I . . . Jordan Stream,* when she returned from one of her pilgrimages to the Holy Land.
11. *rood-beam,* a beam usually between the chancel and the nave of a church, on which was placed a rood or crucifix. Burial within the chancel itself would have been more expensive.
12. *Apelles,* a famous Greek artist of the fourth century B.C.

That only has one hole in all the house;
If that should fail, well, it's goodbye the
    mouse.
370   "I let him think I was as one enchanted
(That was a trick my godmother implanted)
And told him I had dreamt the night away
Thinking of him, and dreamt that as I lay
He tried to kill me. Blood had drenched the
    bed.
375   'But still it was a lucky dream,' I said,
'For blood betokens gold as I recall.'
It was a lie. I hadn't dreamt at all.
'Twas from my godmother I learnt my lore
In matters such as that, and many more.
380   "Well, let me see . . . what had I to
    explain?
Aha! By God, I've got the thread again.
    "When my fourth husband lay upon his
    bier
I wept all day and looked as drear as drear,
As widows must, for it is quite in place,
385   And with a handkerchief I hid my face.
Now that I felt provided with a mate
I wept but little, I need hardly state.
    "To church they bore my husband on the
    morrow
With all the neighbors round him venting
    sorrow,
390   And one of them of course was handsome
    Johnny.
So help me God, I thought he looked so
    bonny
Behind the coffin! Heavens, what a pair
Of legs he had! Such feet, so clean and fair!
I gave my whole heart up, for him to hold.
395   He was, I think, some twenty winters old,
And I was forty then, to tell the truth.
But still, I always had a coltish tooth.
Yes, I'm gap-toothed; it suits me well I feel,
It is the print of Venus[13] and her seal.
400   So help me God I was a lusty one,
Fair, young and well-to-do, and full of fun! . . .
    "What shall I say? Before the month was
    gone
This gay young student, my delightful John,
Had married me in solemn festival.
405   I handed him the money, lands, and all
That ever had been given me before;
This I repented later, more and more.
None of my pleasures would he let me seek.

By God, he smote me once upon the cheek
410   Because I tore a page out of his book,
And that's the reason why I'm deaf. But look,
Stubborn I was, just like a lioness;
As to my tongue, a very wrangleress.
I went off gadding as I had before
415   From house to house, however much he swore.
Because of that he used to preach and scold,
Drag Roman history up from days of old,
How one Simplicius Gallus left his wife,
Deserting her completely all his life,
420   Only for poking out her head one day
Without a hat, upon the public way.
    "Some other Roman—I forget his name—
Because his wife went to a summer's game
Without his knowledge, left her in the lurch.
425   "And he would take the Bible up and
    search
For proverbs in Ecclesiasticus,[14]
Particularly one that has it thus:
'Suffer no wicked woman to gad about.'
And then would come the saying (need you
    doubt?)
430   *A man who seeks to build his house of sallows,*
A man who spurs a blind horse over fallows,
Or lets his wife make pilgrimage to Hallows,
Is worthy to be hanged upon the gallows.[15]
But all for naught. I didn't give a hen
435   For all his proverbs and his wise old men.
Nor would I take rebuke at any price;
I hate a man who points me out my vice,
And so, God knows, do many more than I.
That drove him raging mad, you may rely.
440   No more would I forbear him, I can promise.
    "Now let me tell you truly by St. Thomas
About that book and why I tore the page
And how he smote me deaf in very rage.
    "He had a book, he kept it on his shelf,
445   And night and day he read it to himself
And laughed aloud, although it was quite
    serious.

---

13. **gap-toothed . . . Venus.** It was believed that people who were gap-toothed (with their front teeth set wide apart) had amorous natures.
14. **Ecclesiasticus,** one of the books of the Apocrypha, material included in the Vulgate, but not in Jewish or Protestant Bibles. The reference is to Ecclesiasticus 25:25: "Give neither a wicked woman liberty to gad abroad."
15. **A man . . . gallows,** a proverbial saying that apparently reflects Johnny's opinion of the Wife's pilgrimages. *Sallows* are willow twigs; *fallows* are fields that have been plowed but left unseeded; *hallows* are saints, or (as here) their shrines.

He called it *Theophrastus and Valerius.*[16] . . .
　"It was a book that dealt with wicked wives;
He knew more legends of them and their lives
450 Than there are good ones mentioned in the
　　Bible.
For take my word for it, there is no libel
On women that the clergy will not paint,
Except when writing of a woman-saint,
But never good of other women, though.
455 Who called the lion savage?[17] Do you know?
By God, if women had but written stories
Like those the clergy keep in oratories,
More had been written of man's wickedness
Than all the sons of Adam could redress. . . .
460 　"Now to my purpose as I told you; look,
Here's how I got a beating for a book.
One evening Johnny, glowering with ire,
Sat with his book and read it by the fire.
And first he read of Eve whose wickedness
465 Brought all mankind to sorrow and distress,
Root-cause why Jesus Christ Himself was
　　slain
And gave His blood to buy us back again.
Aye, there's the text where you expressly
　　find
That woman brought the loss of all mankind.
470 　"He read me then how Samson[18] as he
　　slept
Was shorn of all his hair by her he kept,
And by that treachery Samson lost his eyes.
And then he read me, if I tell no lies,
All about Hercules and Deianire;[19]
475 She tricked him into setting himself on fire.
　"He left out nothing of the miseries
Occasioned by his wives to Socrates. . . .[20]
　"And then he told how one Latumius
Lamented to his comrade Arrius
480 That in his orchard-plot there grew a tree
On which his wives had hanged themselves,
　　all three,
Or so he said, out of some spite or other;
To which this Arrius replied, 'Dear brother,
Give me a cutting from that blessed tree
485 And planted in my garden it shall be!' . . .
　"Who could imagine, who could figure out
The torture in my heart? It reached the top
And when I saw that he would never stop
Reading this cursed book, all night no doubt,
490 I suddenly grabbed and tore three pages out
Where he was reading, at the very place,

And fisted such a buffet in his face
That backwards down into our fire he fell.
　"Then like a maddened lion, with a yell
495 He started up and smote me on the head,
And down I fell upon the floor for dead.
　"And when he saw how motionless I lay
He was aghast and would have fled away,
But in the end I started to come to.
500 'O have you murdered me, you robber, you,
To get my land?' I said. 'Was that the game?
Before I'm dead I'll kiss you all the same.'
　"He came up close and kneeling gently
　　down
He said, 'My love, my dearest Alison,
505 So help me God, I never again will hit
You, love; and if I did, you asked for it.
Forgive me!' But for all he was so meek
I up at once and smote him on the cheek
And said, 'Take that to level up the score!
510 Now let me die. I can't speak any more.'
　"We had a mort of trouble and heavy
　　weather
But in the end we made it up together.
He gave the bridle over to my hand,
Gave me the government of house and land,
515 Of tongue and fist, indeed of all he'd got.
I made him burn that book upon the spot.
And when I'd mastered him, and out of
　　deadlock
Secured myself the sovereignty in wedlock,
And when he said, 'My own and truest wife,
520 Do as you please for all the rest of life,
But guard your honor and my good estate,'
From that day forward there was no debate.
So help me God I was as kind to him
As any wife from Denmark to the rim
525 Of India, and as true. And he to me.
And I pray God that sits in majesty
To bless his soul and fill it with his glory.
Now, if you'll listen, I will tell my story."

---

16. *Theophrastus and Valerius,* a satire on matrimony attributed to Walter Map, a wit and cynic who lived about A.D. 1200.
17. *Who . . . savage?* In one of Aesop's fables, a lion, seeing a
picture of a lion being killed by a man, points out that all depends on the point of view; a lion would paint a man being
killed by a lion.
18. *Samson,* Old Testament figure betrayed by a woman.
19. *Hercules and Deianire.* The classical hero Hercules was unfaithful to his wife, Deianire. She revenged herself by giving him
a poisoned shirt which caused him such pain that he preferred
to build a funeral pyre and die in its flames.
20. *Socrates.* The Greek philosopher Socrates (469?–399 B.C.)
was legendary as a hen-pecked husband.

The Friar laughed when he had heard all this.

530 "Well, Ma'am," he said, "as God may send
      me bliss,
This is a long preamble to a tale!"
But when the Summoner heard the Friar rail,
"Just look!" he cried, "by the two arms of
      God!
These meddling friars are always on the prod!

535 Don't we all know a friar and a fly
Go buzzing into every dish and pie!
What do you mean with your 'preambulation'?
Amble yourself, trot, do a meditation!
You're spoiling all our fun with your
      commotion."

540 The Friar smiled and said, "Is that your
      motion?
I promise on my word before I go
To find occasion for a tale or so
About a summoner that will make us laugh."
"Well, damn your eyes, and on my own
      behalf,"

545 The Summoner answered, "mine be damned
      as well
If I can't think of several tales to tell
About the friars that will make you mourn
Before we get as far as Sittingbourne.
Have you no patience? Look, he's in a huff!"

550 Our Host called out, "Be quiet, that's
      enough!
Shut up, and let the woman tell her tale.
You must be drunk, you've taken too much
      ale.
Now, Ma'am, you go ahead and no demur."
"All right," she said, "it's just as you prefer,

555 If I have license from this worthy friar."
"Nothing," said he, "that I should more
      desire."

A Flemish parade shield of the late fifteenth century. This shield was intended only for display at a tournament, not for combat. It expresses the medieval ideal of courtly love. With death in battle perhaps awaiting him, the knight kneels in homage to his lady. The scroll above him carries his vow: "Vous ou La Mort" (You or Death).

The Wife of Bath's Tale

When good King Arthur ruled in ancient
    days,
(A king that every Briton loves to praise)
This was a land brimful of fairy folk.
The Elf Queen and her courtiers joined and
    broke
5 Their elfin dance on many a green mead,
Or so was the opinion once, I read,
Hundreds of years ago, in days of yore.
But no one now sees fairies any more,
For now the saintly charity and prayer
10 Of holy friars seem to have purged the air;
They search the countryside through field
    and stream
As thick as motes that speckle a sunbeam,
Blessing the halls, the chambers, kitchens,
    bowers,
Cities and boroughs, castles, courts, and
    towers,
15 Thorpes,[1] barns and stables, outhouses and
    dairies,
And that's the reason why there are no
    fairies. . . .
    Now it so happened, I began to say,
Long, long ago in good King Arthur's day,
There was a knight who was a lusty liver.
20 One day as he came riding from the river
He saw a maiden walking all forlorn
Ahead of him, alone as she was born.
And of that maiden, spite of all she said,
By very force he took her maidenhead.
25 This act of violence made such a stir,
So much petitioning of the king for her,
That he condemned the knight to lose his head
By course of law. He was as good as dead
(It seems that then the statutes took that view)
30 But that the queen, and other ladies too,
Implored the king to exercise his grace
So ceaselessly, he gave the queen the case
And granted her his life, and she could choose
Whether to show him mercy or refuse.
35   The queen returned him thanks with all
    her might,
And then she sent a summons to the knight
At her convenience, and expressed her will:
"You stand, for such is the position still,

In no way certain of your life," said she,
40 "Yet you shall live if you can answer me:
What is the thing that women most desire?
Beware the axe and say as I require.
    "If you can't answer on the moment, though,
I will concede you this: you are to go
45 A twelvemonth and a day to seek and learn
Sufficient answer, then you shall return.
I shall take gages[2] from you to extort
Surrender of your body to the court."
    Sad was the knight and sorrowfully sighed,
50 But there! All other choices were denied,
And in the end he chose to go away
And to return after a year and day
Armed with such answer as there might be
    sent
To him by God. He took his leave and went.
55   He knocked at every house, searched
    every place,
Yes, anywhere that offered hope of grace.
What could it be that women wanted most?
But all the same he never touched a coast,
Country, or town in which there seemed to be
60 Any two people willing to agree. . . .
    Some say the things we most desire are
    these:
Freedom to do exactly as we please,
With no one to reprove our faults and lies,
Rather to have one call us good and wise.
65 Truly there's not a woman in ten score
Who has a fault, and someone rubs the sore,
But she will kick if what he says is true;
You try it out and you will find so too.
However vicious we may be within
70 We like to be thought wise and void of sin.
Others assert we women find it sweet
When we are thought dependable, discreet
And secret, firm of purpose and controlled,
Never betraying things that we are told.
75 But that's not worth the handle of a rake;
Women conceal a thing? For Heaven's sake!
Remember Midas?[3] Will you hear the tale?

---

1. **Thorpes,** agricultural villages.
2. **gages,** pledges, guarantees.
3. **Midas.** The source is Ovid's *Metamorphoses*, in which, however, the secret is known by Midas' barber, not his wife.

Among some other little things, now stale,
Ovid relates that under his long hair
80 The unhappy Midas grew a splendid pair
Of ass's ears; as subtly as he might,
He kept his foul deformity from sight;
Save for his wife, there was not one that knew.
He loved her best, and trusted in her too.
85 He begged her not to tell a living creature
That he possessed so horrible a feature.
And she—she swore, were all the world to
    win,
She would not do such villainy and sin
As saddle her husband with so foul a name;
90 Besides to speak would be to share the shame.
Nevertheless she thought she would have died
Keeping this secret bottled up inside;
It seemed to swell her heart and she, no
    doubt,
Thought it was on the point of bursting out.
95   Fearing to speak of it to woman or man
Down to a reedy marsh she quickly ran
And reached the sedge. Her heart was all on
    fire
And, as a bittern bumbles in the mire,
She whispered to the water, near the ground,
100 "Betray me not, O water, with thy sound!
To thee alone I tell it: it appears
My husband has a pair of ass's ears!
Ah! My heart's well again, the secret's out!
I could no longer keep it, not a doubt."
105 And so you see, although we may hold fast
A little while, it must come out at last,
We can't keep secrets; as for Midas, well,
Read Ovid for his story; he will tell.
    This knight that I am telling you about
110 Perceived at last he never would find out
What it could be that women loved the best.
Faint was the soul within his sorrowful
    breast
As home he went, he dared no longer stay;
His year was up and now it was the day.
115   As he rode home in a dejected mood,
Suddenly, at the margin of a wood,
He saw a dance upon the leafy floor
Of four and twenty ladies,[4] nay, and more.
Eagerly he approached, in hope to learn
120 Some words of wisdom ere he should return;
But lo! Before he came to where they were,
Dancers and dance all vanished into air!
There wasn't a living creature to be seen

Save one old woman crouched upon the
    green.
125 A fouler-looking creature I suppose
Could scarcely be imagined. She arose
And said, "Sir knight, there's no way on
    from here.
Tell me what you are looking for, my dear,
For peradventure that were best for you;
130 We old, old women know a thing or two."
    "Dear Mother," said the knight, "alack
    the day!
I am as good as dead if I can't say
What thing it is that women most desire;
If you could tell me I would pay your hire."
135 "Give me your hand," she said, "and swear
    to do
Whatever I shall next require of you
—If so to do should lie within your might—
And you shall know the answer before night."
"Upon my honor," he answered, "I agree."
140 "Then," said the crone, "I dare to guarantee
Your life is safe; I shall make good my claim.
Upon my life the queen will say the same.
Show me the very proudest of them all
In costly coverchief or jewelled caul[5]
145 That dare say no to what I have to teach.
Let us go forward without further speech."
And then she crooned her gospel in his ear
And told him to be glad and not to fear.
    They came to court. This knight, in full
    array,
150 Stood forth and said, "O Queen, I've kept
    my day
And kept my word and have my answer ready."
    There sat the noble matrons and the heady
Young girls, and widows too, that have the
    grace
Of wisdom, all assembled in that place,
155 And there the queen herself was throned to
    hear
And judge his answer. Then the knight drew
    near
And silence was commanded through the hall.
    The queen then bade the knight to tell
    them all
What thing it was that women wanted most.
160 He stood not silent like a beast or post,

---

4. *dance . . . ladies,* the fairy ring, a familiar element in Celtic folklore.
5. *caul,* a netted cap worn by women.

The knight and the hag on their wedding night, an illustration by Edward Burne-Jones (1833–1898) for *The Wife of Bath's Tale* in the edition of Chaucer's works published by William Morris (1834–1896) at the Kelmscott Press.

But gave his answer with the ringing word
Of a man's voice and the assembly heard:
  "My liege and lady, in general," said he,
"A woman wants the selfsame sovereignty
165 Over her husband as over her lover,
And master him; he must not be above her.
That is your greatest wish, whether you kill
Or spare me; please yourself. I wait your
    will."
  In all the court not one that shook her head
170 Or contradicted what the knight had said;
Maid, wife, and widow cried, "He's saved
    his life!"
  And on the word up started the old wife,
The one the knight saw sitting on the green,
And cried, "Your mercy, sovereign lady
    queen!

175 Before the court disperses, do me right!
'Twas I who taught this answer to the knight,
For which he swore, and pledged his honor
    to it,
That the first thing I asked of him he'd do it,
So far as it should lie within his might.
180 Before this court I ask you then, sir knight,
To keep your word and take me for your
    wife;
For well you know that I have saved your
    life.
If this be false, deny it on your sword!"
  "Alas!" he said, "Old lady, by the Lord
185 I know indeed that such was my behest,
But for God's love think of a new request,
Take all my goods, but leave my body free."
"A curse on us," she said, "if I agree!

I may be foul, I may be poor and old,
190 Yet will not choose to be, for all the gold
That's bedded in the earth or lies above,
Less than your wife, nay, than your very
    love!"
    "My love?" said he. "By heaven, my
    damnation!
Alas that any of my race and station
195 Should ever make so foul a misalliance!"
Yet in the end his pleading and defiance
All went for nothing, he was forced to wed.
He takes his ancient wife and goes to bed.
    Now peradventure some may well suspect
200 A lack of care in me since I neglect
To tell of the rejoicings and display
Made at the feast upon their wedding day.
I have but a short answer to let fall;
I say there was no joy or feast at all,
205 Nothing but heaviness of heart and sorrow.
He married her in private on the morrow
And all day long stayed hidden like an owl,
It was such torture that his wife looked foul.
    Great was the anguish churning in his head
210 When he and she were piloted to bed;
He wallowed back and forth in desperate
    style.
His ancient wife lay smiling all the while;
At last she said "Bless us! Is this, my dear,
How knights and wives get on together here?
215 Are these the laws of good King Arthur's
    house?
Are knights of his all so contemptuous?
I am your own beloved and your wife,
And I am she, indeed, that saved your life;
And certainly I never did you wrong.
220 Then why, this first of nights, so sad a song?
You're carrying on as if you were half-witted!
Say, for God's love, what sin have I
    committed?
I'll put things right if you will tell me how."
    "Put right?" he cried. "That never can be
    now!
225 Nothing can ever be put right again!
You're old, and so abominably plain,
So poor to start with, so lowbred to follow;
It's little wonder if I twist and wallow!
God, that my heart would burst within my
    breast!"
230   "Is that," said she, "the cause of your
    unrest?"

    "Yes, certainly," he said, "and can you
    wonder?"
    "I could set right what you suppose a
    blunder,
That's if I cared to, in a day or two,
If I were shown more courtesy by you.
235 Just now," she said, "you spoke of gentle
    birth,
Such as descends from ancient wealth and
    worth.
If that's the claim you make for gentlemen
Such arrogance is hardly worth a hen.
Whoever loves to work for virtuous ends,
240 Public and private, and who most intends
To do what deeds of gentleness he can,
Take him to be the greatest gentleman.
Christ wills we take our gentleness from Him,
Not from a wealth of ancestry long dim,
245 Though they bequeath their whole
    establishment
By which we claim to be of high descent.
Our fathers cannot make us a bequest
Of all those virtues that became them best
And earned for them the name of gentlemen,
250 But bade us follow them as best we can. . . .
For of our parents nothing can we claim
Save temporal things, and these may hurt
    and maim.
    "But everyone knows this as well as I;
For if gentility were implanted by
255 The natural course of lineage down the line,
Public or private, could it cease to shine
In doing the fair work of gentle deed?
No vice or villainy could then bear seed. . . .
    "Gentility is only the renown
260 For bounty that your fathers handed down,
Quite foreign to your person, not your own;
Gentility must come from God alone.
That we are gentle comes to us by grace
And by no means is it bequeathed with
    place. . . .
265 And therefore, my dear husband, I conclude
That even if my ancestors were rude,
Yet God on high—and so I hope He will—
Can grant me grace to live in virtue still,
A gentlewoman only when beginning
270 To live in virtue and to shrink from sinning.
    "As for my poverty which you reprove,
Almighty God Himself in whom we move,
(The Wife of Bath's Tale *concludes on page 108.*)

Comment: A Fifteenth-Century Valentine

The letter below, which is the earliest extant valentine, comes from the Paston Letters, a collection of correspondence written between about 1420 and 1530. The Pastons were a wealthy family living in Norfolk, a county in eastern England. Most of the letters deal with questions of property, which even enter into affairs of the heart, as the letter below, written by Margery Brews to John Paston in February, 1477, poignantly indicates. The question is whether John cares enough to marry her with a rather small dowry. (He did.) The spelling has been modernized.

A fourteenth-century French miniature showing a knight wooing a peasant girl.

my mother to no cost nor business for that cause a good while after, which causes my heart to be full heavy; and that if you come and the matter take to none effect, then should I be much more sorry and full of heaviness.

And as for myself, I have done and understand in the matter that (i.e., all that) I can or may, as God knows. And I let you plainly understand that my father will no more money part withal in that behalf but one hundred pounds and fifty marks, which is right far from the accomplishment of your desire. Wherefore, if that you could be content with that good (i.e., that amount of dowry),

Right worshipful and well-beloved Valentine, in my most humble wise (way) I recommend me unto you, &c. And heartily I thank you for the letter which that you sent me by John Beckerton, whereby I understand and know that you be purposed to come to Topcroft (Margery's home) in short time, and without any errand or matter but only to have a conclusion of the matter (i.e., her dowry) betwixt my father and you. I would be most glad of any creature alive so that the matter might grow to effect. And there as you say, an (if) you come and find the matter no more toward than you did aforetime you would no more put my father and my lady

and my poor person, I would be the merriest maiden on ground. And if you think not your-self so satisfied, or that you might have much more good, as I have understood by you afore, good, true, and loving Valentine, that you take no such labor upon you as to come more for that matter; but let it pass, and never more to be spoken of, as I may be your true lover and bedewoman during my life (i.e., pray for him while she lives).

No more unto you at this time, but Almighty Jesus preserve you both body and soul, &c.

By your Valentine, MARGERY BREWS

Believe, and have our being, chose a life
Of poverty, and every man or wife,
275 Nay, every child can see our Heavenly King
Would never stoop to choose a shameful thing.
No shame in poverty if the heart is gay,
As Seneca[6] and all the learned say.
He who accepts his poverty unhurt
280 I'd say is rich although he lacked a shirt.
But truly poor are they who whine and fret
And covet what they cannot hope to get.
And he that, having nothing, covets not,
Is rich, though you may think he is a sot. . . .
285 And since it's no offense, let me be plain;
Do not rebuke my poverty again.
     "Lastly you taxed me, sir, with being old.
Yet even if you never had been told
By ancient books, you gentlemen engage
290 Yourselves in honor to respect old age.
To call an old man 'father' shows good
     breeding,
And this could be supported from my reading.
     "You say I'm old and fouler than a fen.
You need not fear to be a cuckold, then.
295 Filth and old age, I'm sure you will agree,
Are powerful wardens upon chastity.
Nevertheless, well knowing your delights,
I shall fulfil your worldly appetites.
     "You have two choices; which one will
     you try?
300 To have me old and ugly till I die,
But still a loyal, true, and humble wife
That never will displease you all her life,
Or would you rather I were young and pretty
And take your chance what happens in a
     city
305 Where friends will visit you because of me,
Yes, and in other places too, maybe.
Which would you have? The choice is all
     your own."
The knight thought long, and with a piteous
     groan
At last he said, with all the care in life,
310 "My lady and my love, my dearest wife,
I leave the matter to your wise decision.

You make the choice yourself, for the
     provision
Of what may be agreeable and rich
In honor to us both, I don't care which;
315 Whatever pleases you suffices me."
     "And have I won the mastery?" said she,
"Since I'm to choose and rule as I think fit?"
"Certainly, wife," he answered her, "that's
     it."
"Kiss me," she cried. "No quarrels! On my
     oath
320 And word of honor, you shall find me both,
That is, both fair and faithful as a wife;
May I go howling mad and take my life
Unless I prove to be as good and true
As ever wife was since the world was new!
325 And if tomorrow when the sun's above
I seem less fair than any lady-love,
Than any queen or empress east or west,
Do with my life and death as you think best.
Cast up the curtain, husband. Look at me!"
330   And when indeed the knight had looked to
     see,
Lo, she was young and lovely, rich in charms.
In ecstasy he caught her in his arms,
His heart went bathing in a bath of blisses
And melted in a hundred thousand kisses,
335 And she responded in the fullest measure
With all that could delight or give him
     pleasure.
     So they lived ever after to the end
In perfect bliss; and may Christ Jesus send
Us husbands meek and young and fresh in
     bed,
340 And grace to overbid them when we wed.
And—Jesu hear my prayer!—cut short the
     lives
Of those who won't be governed by their
     wives;
And all old, angry niggards of their pence,
God send them soon a very pestilence!
c. 1385–1400

---

6. *Seneca* (4? B.C.–A.D. 65), Roman Stoic philosopher and writer.

Discussion

1. The Wife, at the beginning of her *Prologue,* says "please don't be offended at my views; / They're really only offered to amuse" (lines 87–88). Does she really mean it? What is her purpose in this long speech?

2. From the Wife's point of view, what is a good husband? How does she keep him that way?

3. While the Wife's fourth husband was in London on business, she tells us she "Went to processions, festivals, orations, / Preachments and pilgrimages" (lines 351–352). Why did she go? For what reason, do you think, is she currently traveling to Canterbury?

4. What point of view does the fifth husband's book take on the woman question? How does that book argue its case? How does the Wife defeat the book?

5. In what ways does the story the Wife tells fit her personality and attitudes? Consider, in particular, the secret which the old hag tells the guilty knight, and the knight's solution to the problem of choosing an ugly, loyal wife or a beautiful, unfaithful one.

6. Some critics maintain that as the Wife tells her tale, she becomes so engrossed in it that she comes to identify herself with the old woman. Point out instances where the old woman speaks or acts as though she were the Wife of Bath.

7. Do you find yourself more inclined to like or to dislike the Wife of Bath? Justify your answer.

Composition

1. Chaucer often uses brief "links"—short sections of dialogue involving several of the pilgrims—to bridge the larger divisions of *The Canterbury Tales.* Examples of Chaucer's links are the remarks of the Host, the Knight, and the Pardoner at the end of *The Pardoner's Tale* (lines 285–306) and those of the Summoner and the Friar following *The Wife of Bath's Prologue* (lines 529–556).

Prepare a link of your own (it may be in prose) in which several pilgrims react to *The Wife of Bath's Tale.*

2. Assume that the Wife of Bath has been asked to deliver a brief address in support of women's rights.

Prepare a speech for her (in prose), trying to capture some of the vigor of her observations in *The Canterbury Tales.*

3. The Wife of Bath is outrageous, but so lively that most readers find her irresistible.

Find a modern parallel for her and write a short paper in which you describe that person.

Vocabulary
Affixes, Roots

Use the Glossary to answer the following questions about the structure of the words in the list below. Read each clue, then write on your paper the matching word from the list. (You will not use all the words.) Be sure you can spell and pronounce each word.

bequeath	extort
disperse	continent
caterwaul	preamble

1. Which word has two roots that describe something that might keep you awake?

2. Which has a root that might describe a sightseeing activity?

3. Which has a prefix and root that might describe what happens to a crowd sprayed with tear gas?

4. Which has a prefix and root that might describe what a prison does with inmates?

5. Which has a root that might describe an exercise motion?

Sir Thomas Malory 1395?–1471

William Caxton established the first printing press in England at Westminster in 1476. One of the first books he printed was a retelling of the adventures of King Arthur and his knights of the Round Table. The book was distinguished by the lively, cadenced prose style of its author, Sir Thomas Malory. Although today we know the work as *Morte Darthur (The Death of Arthur),* from one of the adventures it contains, on the title page of Caxton's edition it is called *The Birth, Life and Acts of King Arthur, of his Noble Knights of the Round Table, their marvelous enquests and adventures, the achieving of the San Greal and in the end Le Morte Darthur with the Dolorous Death and Departing out of this World of them All*—surely an all-inclusive title. Only one complete copy of Caxton's first edition, dated 1485, survives today (at the Pierpont Morgan Library in New York).

Malory's book ends with the following passage:

I PRAYE YOU ALL JENTYLMEN AND JENTYLWYMEN THAT REDETH THIS BOOK OF ARTHUR AND HIS KNYGHTES FROM THE BEGYNNYNG TO THE ENDYNGE, PRAYE FOR ME WHYLE I AM ON LYVE THAT GOD SENDE ME GOOD DELYVERAUNCE. AND WHAN I AM DEED, I PRAYE YOU ALL PRAYE FOR MY SOULE.

FOR THIS BOOK WAS ENDED THE NINTH YERE OF THE REYGNE OF KING EDWARD THE FOURTH, BY SYR THOMAS MALEORÉ, KNYGHT, AS JESU HELPE HYM FOR HYS GRETE MYGHT, AS HE IS THE SERVAUNT OF JESU BOTHE DAY AND NYGHT.

The scattered details scholars have been able to discover of Malory's life help explain his prayer for "good deliverance." He was in Newgate Prison when he wrote the book, and he remained there until his death on March 14, 1471.

In 1433 or 1434, on the death of his father, Malory inherited the family estates in Warwickshire and Leicestershire. Later events indicate that he made the Warwickshire property his home, for in 1436 he served under the Earl of Warwick at the siege of Calais in the Hundred Years' War, and in 1445 he represented Warwickshire in Parliament.

Malory's troubles began in the 1450s when, in a period of less than ten years, he was accused, among other things, of lying in ambush with a band of men in an attempt to murder the Duke of Buckingham; of breaking down the doors of the Cistercian Abbey at Coombe with a hundred men, frightening the monks, and ransacking the abbot's chests; of stealing seven cows, two calves, and 335 sheep; and of assault and kidnaping, extortion, and jailbreaking. The latter charge certainly was true, for in July, 1451, Malory escaped from Coleshill Prison by swimming the moat, and in October, 1454, he broke out of Colchester Castle in the company of a group of armed men. Most of Malory's activities, especially those in which he was accompanied by numbers of other men, sound less like the acts of a felon and more like the armed sorties that took place just before and during the Wars of the Roses.

However, in 1462 Malory was out of jail and with the Earl of Warwick and King Edward IV (of the House of York, who assumed the throne in 1461), fighting against the Scots and French who were supporting the deposed Henry VI (of the House of Lancaster, who had ruled from 1422 to 1461, in a reign broken by periods of madness). Note that Malory's early imprisonments occurred during Henry's reign.

Later, when for political reasons the Earl of Warwick changed sides, shifting his allegiance to the House of Lancaster, Malory followed suit. He was specifically excluded, by name, from the general pardon which Edward extended to the Lancastrians in 1468, and then or shortly thereafter was imprisoned at Newgate, where he remained until his death. Despite his advanced age, the Yorkists must have felt he was too dangerous to be at large.

Fortunately for succeeding generations,

Newgate happened to be located just across the road from the Grey Friars monastery. The monastery had a collection of manuscripts, about twenty of them being legends of Arthur, mostly in French. Perhaps this was where Malory obtained the "books of French" that he mentions as his source.

Malory's *Morte Darthur* is the most complete

Arthur's last battle at Camlan, a fourteenth-century French illustration. Mordred is shown at the bottom left and Arthur at the bottom right.

single version of the tales of King Arthur and his court that has been written in English. It represents the drawing together, arranging, and clarifying of tales from various English and French versions, many of them contradictory. The historical sources of the Arthurian legend remain obscure. Arthur was probably a Celtic chieftain who lived in Britain during the fifth century and fought the invading Anglo-Saxons, Picts, and Scots. Twelfth-century accounts of Arthur which are extant mention the Round Table and a following of a few knights.

Sometime during the height of the Middle Ages the Celtic folk hero Arthur became associated with the code of chivalry and with medieval French romances about Lancelot and the Holy Grail. Through these diverse sources Ar-

thur ultimately emerged in song and story as the embodiment of the ideal knight. It is this Arthur that Malory tried to record, so that men who lived in the days when chivalry was a lost ideal might recall fondly the glamorous yesterdays of knighthood.

"The Day of Destiny" describes the end of King Arthur's reign and the dissolution of the order which he, along with his Knights of the Round Table, has established. This end grows out of the corruption within the royal court itself. Arthur's illegitimate son Mordred seeks to kill his father. Knowing of the secret love between Arthur's wife, Queen Guinevere (gwin'ə-vir), and his best friend, Sir Lancelot, one night Mordred leads a band of knights to Guinevere's chamber. They find the Queen with Lancelot.

Although he is reluctant, Arthur feels obligated to obey the law of the land and to burn his wife at the stake. However, at the last minute Lancelot rescues her, killing the two knights Gaherys and Gareth, who were guarding her. Lancelot subsequently flees to a castle in France and Arthur forgives Guinevere; but Gawain (gä'wān, gä'win), the brother of the dead knights, demands vengeance on Lancelot.

His hatred forces Arthur to lead his men on an attack against Lancelot's French fortress. In the ensuing battles Lancelot seriously wounds Gawain but refuses to kill him.

Meanwhile, Mordred senses his chance. With Arthur away in France, he leads a rebellion in England, claiming the throne and trying to seize Guinevere as his queen. She flees to the Tower of London and Arthur, lifting the siege on Lancelot's castle, returns to defend his crown.

At Dover Arthur's forces battle Mordred for the first time, and Gawain is fatally wounded. Before his death he writes a letter to Lancelot ending their feud and asking Lancelot to return to England to help Arthur. After a second, inconclusive battle with Mordred's forces, Arthur regroups his men and moves westward.

from *Morte Darthur*

The Day of Destiny

And quickly King Arthur moved himself with his army along the coastline westward, toward Salisbury. And there was a day assigned betwixt King Arthur and Sir Mordred, that they should meet upon a field beside Salisbury and not far from the coast. And this day was assigned as Monday after Trinity Sunday,[1] whereof King Arthur was passing glad that he might be avenged upon Sir Mordred.

Then Sir Mordred stirred up a crowd of people around London, for those from Kent, Sussex and Surrey, Essex, Suffolk, and Norfolk stayed for the most part with Sir Mordred. And many a full noble knight drew unto him and also to the King; but they that loved Sir Lancelot drew unto Sir Mordred.

So upon Trinity Sunday at night King Arthur dreamed a wonderful dream, and in his dream it seemed that he saw upon a platform a chair, and the chair was fixed to a wheel,[2] and there upon sat King Arthur in richest cloth of gold that might be made. And the King dreamed there was under him, far below him, a hideous deep black water, and therein were all kinds of serpents and dragons and wild beasts foul and horrible. And suddenly the King dreamed that the wheel turned up side down, and he fell among the serpents, and every beast took him by a limb. And then the King cried out as he lay in his bed,

"Help! help!"

And then knights, squires, and yeomen awaked the King, and then he was so amazed that he knew not where he was. And so he remained awake until it was nearly day, and then he fell into a slumber again, neither sleeping nor completely awake.

Then it seemed to the King that there came Sir Gawain unto him with a number of fair ladies with him. So when King Arthur saw him he said,

"Welcome, my sister's son, I thought you had died! And now I see thee alive, great is my debt to Almighty Jesus. Ah, fair nephew, who be these ladies that come hither with you?"

"Sir," said Sir Gawain, "all these be fair ladies for whom I have fought for, when I was a living man. And all these are those that I did battle for in righteous quarrels, and God hath given them that aid for their earnest prayers; and because I did battle for them for their rights, they brought me hither unto you. Thus hath God given me leave for to warn you of your death: for if ye fight tomorrow with Sir Mordred, as ye both have agreed, doubt ye not ye shall be slain, and the greatest part of your people on both sides. And for the great concern and good that Almighty Jesus has had for you, and for pity of you and many other good men that shall be slain, God hath sent me to you of His special grace to give you warning that in no way ye do battle tomorrow, but instead that ye make a treaty for a month and a day. And request this urgently, so that tomorrow you can delay. For within a month shall come Sir Lancelot with all his noble knights, and rescue you loyally, and slay Sir Mordred and all that ever will stay with him."

Then Sir Gawain and all the ladies vanished, and at once the King called upon his knights, squires, and yeomen, and charged them quickly to fetch his noble lords and wise bishops unto him. And when they were come the King told them of his vision; that Sir Gawain had told him and warned him that if he fought on the morn, he should be slain. Then the King commanded Sir Lucan the Butler and his brother Sir Bedivere the Bold, with two bishops with them, and charged them in any way to make a treaty for a month and a day with Sir Mordred:

"And spare not, offer him lands and goods as much as ye think reasonable."

So then they departed and came to Sir Mordred where he had a grim host of a hundred thousand, and there they entreated Sir Mordred a

---

From Part IV of *The Most Piteous Tale of the Morte Darthur Saunz Guerdon,* slightly modernized, from the Winchester MS. version in *The Works of Thomas Malory* edited by Eugène Vinaver (Oxford University Press, 1947, 1967).

1. *Trinity Sunday,* the eighth Sunday after Easter.
2. *wheel,* the wheel of fortune, symbolizing the rapid changes of human destiny; it was a favorite medieval image.

long time. And at the last Sir Mordred agreed for to take over Cornwall and Kent during King Arthur's lifetime; and after that all England, after the days of King Arthur.

Then were they agreed that King Arthur and Sir Mordred should meet betwixt both their hosts, and each of them should bring fourteen persons. And so they came with this word unto Arthur. Then he said,

"I am glad that this is done"; and so he went into the field.

And when King Arthur departed he warned all his host that if they saw any sword drawn, "look ye come on fiercely and slay that traitor, Sir Mordred, for I in no way trust him." In like manner Sir Mordred warned his host that "and ye see any manner of sword drawn, look that ye come on fiercely and so slay all that before you stand, for in no way will I trust in this treaty." And in the same way said Sir Mordred unto his host: "for I know well my father will be avenged upon me."

And so they met as they had arranged, and were agreed and accorded thoroughly. And wine was fetched, and they drank together. Just then came an adder out of a little heath-bush, and it stung a knight in the foot. And so when the knight felt himself so stung, he looked down and saw the adder; and at once he drew his sword to slay the adder, and thought of no other harm. And when the host on both sides saw that sword drawn, then they blew trumpets and horns, and shouted grimly, and so both hosts attacked each other. And King Arthur mounted his horse and said, "Alas, this unhappy day!" and so rode to his men, and Sir Mordred in like wise.

And never since was there seen a more grievous battle in no Christian land, for there was only slashing and riding, thrusting and striking, and many a grim word was there spoken of one to the other, and many a deadly stroke. But ever King Arthur rode through the battle against Sir Mordred many times and acted full nobly, as a noble king should do, and at all times he never hesitated. And Sir Mordred did his utmost that day and put himself in great peril.

And thus they fought all the day long, and never ceased 'till the noble knights were fallen on the cold earth. And yet they fought still 'till it was near night, and by then was there a hundred thou-

sand lay dead upon the earth. Then was King Arthur wild with wrath beyond measure, when he saw his people so slain because of him.

And so he looked about himself and could see no more of all his host and of good knights left no more alive but two knights: Sir Lucan the Butler and his brother, Sir Bedivere; and yet they were very badly wounded.

"Jesus have mercy!" said the King, "where are all my noble knights gone? Alas, that ever I should see this grievous day! For now," said

The combat of Arthur and Mordred at Camlan, an illustration from the fifteenth-century *St. Albans Chronicle*.

King Arthur, "I am come to mine end. But would to God," said he, "that I knew now where were that traitor Sir Mordred that hath caused all this mischief."

Then King Arthur looked about and was aware where stood Sir Mordred leaning upon his sword among a great heap of dead men.

"Now give me my spear," said King Arthur

unto Sir Lucan, "for yonder I have seen the traitor that all this woe hath wrought."

"Sir, let him be," said Sir Lucan, "for he brings misfortune. And if ye pass this unfortunate day ye shall be right well revenged. And, good lord, remember ye of your night's dream and what the spirit of Sir Gawain told you last night, and God of His great goodness hath preserved you hitherto. And for God's sake, my lord, leave this battle, for, blessed be God, ye have won the field: for yet be here three alive, and with Sir Mordred is not one alive. And therefore if ye leave now, this wicked day of destiny is past!"

"Now come death, come life," said the King, "now I see him yonder alone, he shall never escape my hands! For at a better advantage shall I never have him."

"God speed you well!" said Sir Bedivere.

Then the King took his spear in both his hands, and ran towards Sir Mordred, crying out and saying,

"Traitor, now is thy death-day come!"

And when Sir Mordred saw King Arthur he ran towards him with his sword drawn in his hands, and there King Arthur struck Sir Mordred under the shield, with a thrust of his spear, through and beyond the body more than a foot. And when Sir Mordred felt that he had his death's wound he thrust himself with the might that he had up to the hand guard of King Arthur's spear, and then he smote his father, King Arthur, with his sword holding it in both his hands, upon the side of the head, so that the sword pierced the helmet and the outer membrane of the brain. And with that Sir Mordred dashed down stark dead to the earth.

And noble King Arthur fell in a swoon to the earth, and there he swooned several times, and Sir Lucan and Sir Bedivere several times lifted him up. And so weakly betwixt them they led him to a little chapel not far from the sea, and when the King was there, he thought himself reasonably eased.

Then heard they people cry in the field.

"Now go thou, Sir Lucan," said the King, "and help me to learn what means that noise in the field."

So Sir Lucan departed, though he was grievously wounded in many places; and as he rode he saw and noticed by the moonlight how the plunderers and robbers were come into the field to plunder and to rob many a full noble knight of brooches and bracelets and of many a good ring and many a rich jewel. And those that were not yet dead, there they slew them for their armor and their gold.

When Sir Lucan understood this he came to the King as soon as he might, and told him all which he had heard and seen.

"Therefore by my advice," said Sir Lucan, "it is best that we bring you to some town."

"I would that it were so," said the King, "but I may not stand, my head fails so. . . . Ah, Sir Lancelot!" said King Arthur, "this day have I missed thee! And alas, that ever I was against thee! For now I have my death, whereof Sir Gawain warned me in my dream."

Then Sir Lucan took up the King on one side and Sir Bedivere the other side, and in the lifting up the King swooned, and in the lifting Sir Lucan fell in a swoon, and part of his guts fell out of his body, and with that the noble knight's heart burst. And when the King awoke he beheld Sir Lucan, how he lay foaming at the mouth and part of his guts lay at his feet.

"Alas," said the King, "this is to me a very sad sight, to see this noble duke die so for my sake, for he would have helped me that had more need of help than I! Alas, that he would not complain for himself, for his heart was so set to help me. Now Jesu have mercy upon his soul!"

Then Sir Bedivere wept for the death of his brother.

"Now leave this mourning and this weeping, gentle knight," said the King, "for all this will not help me. For know thou well, if I might live myself, the death of Sir Lucan would grieve me evermore. But my time passeth on fast," said the King. "Therefore," said King Arthur unto Sir Bedivere, "take thou here Excalibur, my good sword, and go with it to the yonder water side; and when thou comest there, I charge thee throw my sword in that water, and come again and tell me what thou seest there."

"My lord," said Sir Bedivere, "your commandment shall be done, and lightly bring you word again."

So Sir Bedivere departed. And on the way he beheld that noble sword, and the pommel and the haft was all precious stones. And then he said to himself, "If I throw this rich sword in the water, of this shall never come good, but harm and loss." And then Sir Bedivere hid Excalibur under a tree, and so as soon as he might he came again unto the King and said he had been at the water and had thrown the sword into the water.

"What saw thou there?" said the King.

"Sir," he said, "I saw nothing but waves and wind."

"That is untruly said by thee," said the King. "And therefore go thou lightly again, and do my commandment; as thou art to me beloved and dear, spare not, but throw it in."

Sir Bedivere returns King Arthur's sword, Excalibur, to the Lady of the Lake, an illustration from a fourteenth-century French manuscript of an Arthurian romance.

Then Sir Bedivere returned again and took the sword in his hand; and yet he thought it a sin and shame to throw away that noble sword. And so again he hid the sword and returned again and told the King that he had been at the water and done his commandment.

"What sawest thou there?" said the King.

"Sir," he said, "I saw nothing but lapping waters and darkening waves."

"Ah, traitor unto me and untrue," said King Arthur, "now hast thou betrayed me twice! Who would believe that thou hast been to me so beloved and dear, and also named so noble a knight, that thou would betray me for the wealth of this sword? But now go again lightly; for thy long tarrying putteth me in great jeopardy of my life, for I am growing cold. And if thou do not

now as I bid thee, if ever I may see thee, I shall slay thee by mine own hands, for thou wouldst for my rich sword see me dead."

Then Sir Bedivere departed and went to the sword and lightly took it up, and so he went unto the water side. And there he bound the belt about the hilt, and threw the sword as far into the water as he might. And there came an arm and an hand above the water, and took it and seized it, and shook it thrice and brandished, and then vanished with the sword into the water.

So Sir Bedivere came again to the King and told him what he saw.

"Alas," said the King, "help me hence, for I dread me I have tarried over long."

Then Sir Bedivere took the King upon his back and so went with him to the water side. And when they were there, even close by the bank floated a little barge with many fair ladies on it, and among them all was a queen, and all of them had black hoods. And all of them wept and shrieked when they saw King Arthur.

"Now put me into that barge," said the King.

And so he did softly, and there received him three ladies with great mourning. And so they set him down, and in one of their laps King Arthur laid his head. And then the queen said,

"Ah, my dear brother! Why have ye tarried so long from me? Alas, this wound on your head hath caught overmuch cold!"

And then they rowed away from the land, and Sir Bedivere beheld all those ladies go away from him. Then Sir Bedivere cried out and said,

"Ah, my lord Arthur, what shall become of me, now ye go from me and leave me here alone among mine enemies?"

"Comfort thyself," said the King, "and do as well as thou mayest, for in me is no trust for to trust in. For I must go into the vale of Avilion[3] to heal me of my grievous wound. And if thou hear never more of me, pray for my soul!"

But ever the queen and ladies wept and shrieked, that it was pitiful to hear. As soon as Sir Bedivere had lost sight of the barge he wept and wailed, and so entered the forest and traveled all night.

---

3. **Avilion** (ə vil′yən) or Avalon (av′ə lon), "the isle of apples," one of the paradisal islands of Celtic mythology.

And in the morning he was aware, betwixt two wan woods, of a chapel and a hermitage. Then was Sir Bedivere fearful, and thither he went, and when he came into the chapel he saw where lay a hermit groveling on all fours, close there by a tomb was new dug. When the hermit saw Sir Bedivere he knew him well, for he was but little before Bishop of Canterbury that Sir Mordred put to flight.

"Sir," said Sir Bedivere, "what man is there here buried that ye pray so earnestly for?"

"Fair son," said the hermit, "I know not truly but only guess. But this same night, at midnight, there came a number of ladies and brought here a dead corpse and prayed me to bury him. And here they offered a hundred candles, and they gave me a thousand coins."

"Alas!" said Sir Bedivere, "that was my lord King Arthur, which lieth here buried in this chapel."

Then Sir Bedivere swooned, and when he awoke he prayed the hermit that he might stay with him still, there to live with fasting and prayers:

"For from hence will I never go," said Sir Bedivere, "by my will, but all days of my life stay here to pray for my lord Arthur."

"Sir, ye are welcome to me," said the hermit, "for I know you better than you think that I do: for ye are Sir Bedivere the Bold, and the full noble Duke Sir Lucan the Butler was your brother."

Then Sir Bedivere told the hermit all as ye have heard before, and so he remained with the hermit that was before the Bishop of Canterbury. And there Sir Bedivere put upon himself poor clothes, and served the hermit full lowly in fasting and in prayers.

Thus of Arthur I find no more written in books that have been written, nothing more of the very certainty of his brave death I never read . . .

Yet some men say in many parts of England that King Arthur is not dead, but had by the will of Our Lord Jesu gone into another place; and men say that he shall come again, and he shall win the Holy Cross. Yet I will not say that it shall be so, but rather would I say: here in this world he changed his life. And many men say that there is written upon the tomb this:

HIC IACET ARTHURUS,
REX QUONDAM REXQUE FUTURUS.

Here lies Arthur, King Once and King That Will Be.
1468–1470   1485

Discussion

1. What do you think is the meaning of Arthur's first dream on the night before the battle? In what way is it related to his second dream of that night?

2. How does the truce between Arthur and Mordred come to be broken? What does this imply about Arthur's efforts to avoid the battle? What biblical significance might there be in the appearance of the adder?

3. Arthur insists on fighting Mordred after the battle has ended. What does this tell us about his character?

4. What do the plunderers Sir Lucan sees on the battlefield suggest about England's future after Arthur's death?

5. What is the result of Sir Bedivere's delay in throwing Excalibur into the lake?

6. What can we deduce about Arthur from the behavior of the three ladies?

7. Why might people in some parts of England refuse to believe that Arthur was dead? Could this belief persist today? Explain.

Composition

Over the centuries, the Arthurian legends have inspired a variety of writers and delighted all sorts of readers.

In a brief essay discuss the reasons for the enduring popularity of the story of Arthur.

The Changing English Language

The Norman invasion in 1066 had abrupt and dramatic consequences for the English language. Naturally enough, Norman French was the official language of the governing classes of England; within a short time it was also adopted by the English nobility, as the English and Norman upper classes gradually intermingled. However, English remained the language of the masses, and the social distinction between those who spoke French and those who spoke English persisted until the beginning of the thirteenth century.

The continued use of French by the upper classes was promoted by the close ties between England and France. After the Conquest, the Anglo-Norman kings retained their titles as Dukes of Normandy, and, through contractual marriages between English and Norman nobility, Englishmen began to acquire land and conduct business in Normandy. Had the political ties across the English Channel remained unbroken, it is possible that all of us today might be speaking some form of French. However, shortly after 1200, relations between Normandy and England deteriorated. Families which held land in both countries were forced to surrender their rights in one or the other. In consequence, the nobles of Norman descent who chose to retain their landholdings in England began to think of France as an alien land and of themselves as Englishmen. A growing suspicion of things "foreign" by those descendants of the original Norman invaders who had become firmly invested in England created a growing nationalistic spirit and an increased tolerance of things English, including the language.

The revival of the English language was also aided by the rise of a middle class of tradesmen

A medieval bookshop, from a fourteenth-century manuscript.

and craftsmen, together with a slow but general improvement in economic and social conditions for the mass of native Englishmen. As the English-speaking majority gradually became more influential, the use of English in government and trade became both natural and necessary. Early in the fourteenth century writers began turning from Latin and French (which were considered the languages of scholarship and literature respectively) to English. In 1362 English was declared, by royal decree, the official language of the courts of law.

By 1400 English was totally restored as the language of the realm, but it had been substantially altered and expanded by three and a half centuries of contact with French. For the first two centuries (1066-1250) the incursion of French vocabulary was relatively slight. Words adopted from the French during this period reflect the relationships between the ruling and subordinate classes (*noble, dame, servant, messenger*) or religious concerns (*sermon, communion, confession, clergy, convent*). By 1250, when ties between England and Normandy had loosened and English nationalism was making itself felt, many more French words began to be assimilated into English—particularly words associated with government, law, and business, such as *crown, state, reign, authority, tax, judge, pardon.* Also notable are the number of words from literature (*poet, tragedy, story*), art (the word *art* itself, *music*), medicine (*physician, pain*), fashion (*gown, boot, robe*), and those concerning food (*beef, bacon, olives*) and social life (*dance, recreation*), which were borrowed from French during this period. The dimensions of the change in cultural outlook which accompanied the changes in language during this period can perhaps be inferred from these and the numerous other additions to English vocabulary, concerned as they are, in the main, with beauty, style, comfort, and the good life.

The structure of the language, too, was changing. Between 1066 and 1400 Old English, originally a highly inflected language, became greatly simplified. Inflections were dropped or were merged into the few surviving forms which are familiar today (for instance, *sing, sang, sung*). The Old English verb *help*, for example, had originally four principal parts (*healpan, healp, hulpon, -holpen*) with five or more additional endings to indicate person and number. Today, of course, it has only two principal parts (*help, helped*), with one additional ending (*-s*) in the present tense. As the Old English inflections and endings gradually disappeared, the grammatical relationships which they expressed were taken over by the pattern and order of words, so that English became an increasingly phrasal language.

During approximately the same period of time, the distinct Anglo-Saxon dialects merged and evolved into four Middle English dialect groups. The most prominent of these was East Midland, the dialect spoken by the people between the Thames and the Humber rivers. This area included the city of London, rapidly developing as a center of government and commerce. Because of London's importance, the East Midland dialect gradually came to be looked on as "the King's English." Around 1370 Geoffrey Chaucer wrote in this dialect, giving it literary status; and when William Caxton introduced printing to England a century later, he used the speech of London as his standard. The speech of the East Midland area thus became a sort of early "standard English" from which both modern English and American English are directly descended.

The changes in the English language which occurred during the three or four centuries following the Norman Conquest were so all-encompassing that few if any of Chaucer's contemporaries would have been able to comprehend the Old English of *Beowulf.* Dramatic as these changes were, they did not take place swiftly; they evolved slowly over the course of generations, and were the result of complex political and social changes in a turbulent age.

The *edieval Period*

Content Review

1. Do you find the people you encounter in medieval literature strikingly different from the people of our own day? Give specific examples to support your conclusions. In particular, you might consider the so-called "battle of the sexes," heroism in the face of danger, and jealousy in love.

2. Compare King Arthur with Beowulf. What similarities and differences do you see in these two warrior heroes?

3. We would expect to find many instances of superstition and belief in the supernatural in medieval literature. Specifically, what are they and in which works do they occur?

4. In this unit you have studied ballads, nar-rative poetry *(Canterbury Tales),* and prose fiction. Do you think that any one type is better than the others in presenting a picture of medieval England, or do they supplement one another? Explain.

5. If you were asked to name the three most memorable characters from this unit, whom would you select? Remember that they can come from any of the three types of literature mentioned in the previous question.

6. Think back over the various characters you have met in this unit. Would any of them be an appropriate role model for today's youth? Explain.

Concept Review: Interpretation of New Material

from Sir Gawain and the Green Knight

translated by **Brian Stone**

The following excerpt is from a medieval **ro-mance**—a story of knights and their deeds—by an author whose name is unknown. He was probably Chaucer's contemporary, but because he lived in a provincial center far from Chaucer's world of London and the court, the poet worked in an older tradition of alliterative me-ter that had its roots in Anglo-Saxon verse. In the following scene King Arthur and his knights of the Round Table are celebrating in Camelot during the Christmas season. Their banquet is interrupted by a giant knight of fierce appearance, on horseback, his body and clothes all "glittering green." The horseman has asked for "good sport," and since he is not wearing armor, and carries no weapons except an axe, Arthur assumes that the stranger seeks "unarmored combat." The Green Knight is speaking as the scene opens.

Sir Gawain, an illuminated capital from a fourteenth-century French manuscript.

From *Sir Gawain and the Green Knight,* translated by Brian Stone (Penguin Classics, 1974), pp. 31-37. Copyright © Brian Stone, 1959, 1964, 1974. Reprinted by permission of Penguin Books Ltd.

1

"No, it is not combat I crave, for come to that,
On this bench only beardless boys are sitting.
If I were hasped[1] in armor on a high steed,
No man among you could match me, your
    might being meager.
5 So I crave in this court a Christmas game,
For it is Yuletide and New Year, and young
    men abound here.
If any in this household is so hardy in spirit,
Of such mettlesome mind and so madly rash
As to strike a strong blow in return for another,
10 I shall offer to him this fine axe freely;
This axe, which is heavy enough, to handle as
    he please.
And I shall bide the first blow, as bare as I sit
    here.
If some intrepid man is tempted to try what I
    suggest,
Let him leap towards me and lay hold of this
    weapon,
15 Acquiring clear possession of it, no claim from
    me ensuing.
Then shall I stand up to his stroke, quite still
    on this floor—
So long as I shall have leave to launch a return
    blow
        Unchecked.
        Yet he shall have a year
        And a day's reprieve,[2] I direct.
20   Now hasten and let me hear
        Who answers, to what effect."

2

If he had astonished them at the start, yet
    stiller now
Were the henchmen[3] in hall, both high and low.
The rider wrenched himself round in his saddle
25 And rolled his red eyes about roughly and
    strangely,
Bending[4] his brows, bristling and bright, on all,
His beard swaying as he strained to see who
    would rise.
When none came to accord with him, he
    coughed aloud,
Then pulled himself up proudly, and spoke as
    follows:
30 "What, is this Arthur's house, the honor of which

Is bruited abroad so abundantly?
Has your pride disappeared? Your prowess gone?
Your victories, your valor, your vaunts, where
    are they?
The revel and renown of the Round Table
35 Is now overwhelmed by a word from one man's
    voice,
For all flinch for fear from a fight not begun!"
Upon this, he laughed so loudly that the lord[5]
    grieved.
His fair features filled with blood
        For a shame.
        He raged as roaring gale;
40   His followers felt the same.
        The King, not one to quail,
        To that cavalier then came.

3

"By heaven," then said Arthur, "What you ask
    is foolish,
But as you firmly seek folly, find it you shall.
45 No good man here is aghast at your great words.
Hand me your axe now, for heaven's sake,
And I shall bestow the boon you bid us give."
He sprang towards him swiftly, seized it from
    his hand,
And fiercely the other fellow footed the floor.[6]
50 Now Arthur had his axe, and holding it by the
    haft
Swung it about sternly, as if to strike with it.
The strong man stood before him, stretched to
    his full height,
Higher than any in the hall by a head and more.
Stern of face he stood there, stroking his beard,
55 Turning down his tunic in a tranquil manner,
Less unmanned and dismayed by the mighty
    strokes
Than if a banqueter at the bench[7] had brought
    him a drink
        Of wine.
        Then Gawain at Guinevere's[8] side

---

1. *hasped,* fastened.
2. *year . . . reprieve,* the usual period for a legal contract.
3. *henchmen,* trusted followers.
4. *Bending,* directing.
5. *lord,* King Arthur.
6. *footed the floor,* jumped off his horse.
7. *banqueter . . . bench,* a man at his seat.
8. *Gawain* (gä′wän, gä′win), nephew of Arthur and his noblest
knight, **Guinevere** (gwin′ə vir), Arthur's queen.

Bowed and spoke his design:

60 "Before all, King, confide
This fight to me. May it be mine."

4

"If you would, worthy lord," said Gawain to the
king,
"Bid me stir from this seat and stand beside you,
Allowing me without lese-majesty[9] to leave the
table,
65 And if my liege lady were not displeased thereby,
I should come there to counsel you before this
court of nobles.
For it appears unmeet[10] to me, as manners go,
When your hall hears uttered such a haughty
request,
Though you gladly agree, for you to grant it
yourself,
70 When on the benches about you many such
bold men sit,
Under heaven, I hold, the highest-mettled,
There being no braver knights when battle is
joined.
I am the weakest, the most wanting in wisdom,
I know,
And my life, if lost, would be least missed, truly.
75 Only through your being my uncle, am I to be
valued;
No bounty but your blood in my body do I
know.[11]
And since this affair is too foolish to fall to you,
And I first asked it of you, make it over to me;
And if I fail to speak fittingly, let this full court
judge
Without blame."
80 Then wisely they whispered of it,
And after, all said the same:
That the crowned king should be quit,[12]
And Gawain given the game.

5

Then the King commanded the courtly knight
to rise.
85 He directly uprose, approached courteously,
Knelt low to his liege lord, laid hold of the
weapon;
And he graciously let him have it, lifted up his
hand

And gave him God's blessing, gladly urging him
To be strong in spirit and stout of sinew.
90 "Cousin, take care," said the King, "To chop once,
And if you strike with success, certainly I think
You will take the return blow without trouble in
time."
Gripping the great axe, Gawain goes to the man
Who awaits him unwavering, not quailing at all.
95 Then said to Sir Gawain the stout knight in green,
"Let us affirm our pact freshly, before going
farther.
I beg you, bold sir, to be so good
As to tell me your true name, as I trust you to."
"In good faith," said the good knight, "Gawain
is my name,
100 And whatever happens after, I offer you this blow,
And in twelve months' time I shall take the
return blow
With whatever weapon you wish, and with no
one else
Shall I strive."
The other with pledge replied,
"I'm the merriest man alive
105 It's a blow from you I must bide,
Sir Gawain, so may I thrive."

6

"By God," said the Green Knight, "Sir Gawain,
I rejoice
That I shall have from your hand what I have
asked for here.
And you have gladly gone over, in good discourse,
110 The convenant I requested of the King in full,
Except that you shall assent, swearing in truth,
To seek me yourself, in such place as you think
To find me under the firmament,[13] and fetch
your payment
For what you deal me today before this
dignified gathering."
115 "How shall I hunt for you? How find your
home?"
Said Gawain, "By God that made me, I go in
ignorance;

---

9. *lese-majesty,* offense against the dignity of a ruler, severe
discourtesy.
10. *unmeet,* unsuitable, improper.
11. *No bounty . . . know,* that is, the only good in my body
comes from your blood.
12. *quit,* excused from the contest.
13. *firmament,* heavens, sky.

Nor, knight, do I know your name or your court.
But instruct me truly thereof, and tell me your
    name,
And I shall wear out my wits to find my way
    there;
120 Here is my oath on it, in absolute honor!"
"That is enough this New Year,[14] no more is
    needed,"
Said the gallant in green to Gawain the
    courteous,
"To tell you the truth, when I have taken the
    blow
After you have duly dealt it, I shall directly
    inform you
125 About my house and my home and my own
    name.
Then you may keep your covenant, and call on
    me,
And if I waft you no words, then well may you
    prosper,
Stay long in your own land and look for no
    further
      Trial.
      Now grip your weapon grim;
130   Let us see your fighting style."
      "Gladly," said Gawain to him,
      Stroking the steel the while.

7

On the ground the Green Knight graciously
    stood,
With head slightly slanting to expose the flesh.
135 His long and lovely locks he laid over his
    crown,
Baring the naked neck for the business now
    due.
Gawain gripped his axe and gathered it on high,
Advanced the left foot before him on the ground,
And slashed swiftly down on the exposed part,
140 So that the sharp blade sheared through,
    shattering the bones,
Sank deep in the sleek flesh, split it in two,
And the scintillating steel struck the ground.
The fair head fell from the neck, struck the floor,
And people spurned it as it rolled around.
145 Blood spurted from the body, bright against
    the green.
Yet the fellow did not fall, nor falter one whit,
But stoutly sprang forward on legs still sturdy,

The Green Knight's decapitated head magically speaks,
an illustration from the manuscript of *Sir Gawain and
the Green Knight.*

Roughly reached out among the ranks of nobles,
Seized his splendid head and straightway lifted
    it.
150 Then he strode to his steed, snatched the bridle,
Stepped into the stirrup and swung aloft,
Holding his head in his hand by the hair.
He settled himself in the saddle as steadily
As if nothing had happened to him, though he
    had
      No head.
155   He twisted his trunk about,
      That gruesome body that bled;
      He caused much dread and doubt
      By the time his say was said.
c.1380–1400

---

14. **New Year,** a time associated with friendship and piety.

On a separate piece of paper, write your answers to the following questions. Do not write in your book.

1. Where does this scene take place?

2. Who proposes the "Christmas game" in the first stanza?

3. What is the attitude of the knights and ladies toward the Green Knight in stanza 2?

4. How would you characterize the Green Knight's statements in stanza 2?

5. What effect do the Green Knight's words have on Arthur?

6. Rewrite *only* the alliterative words in the following line: "When your hall hears uttered such a haughty request."

7. What kind of character does Gawain reveal in stanza 4?

8. In stanza 6, when does the Green Knight promise to reveal his name and home to Gawain?

9. What evidence of the supernatural is there in the last stanza?

10. Among the Green Knight's outstanding characteristics is: **(a)** humility; **(b)** dishonesty; **(c)** arrogance; **(d)** devotion.

Composition Review

You may choose any *one* of the following assignments. Assume that you are writing for your classmates.

1. Knighthood was one of the preeminent institutions of the Middle Ages. Among its professed ideals were courage, loyalty, piety, and respect for women. A number of knights appear in the selections in this unit: Chaucer's Knight and Squire, the knight in *The Wife of Bath's Tale,* Sir Patrick Spence, Arthur and his Round Table (in both Malory and the *Gawain*-poet).

Select one or more of these characters and write a brief paper examining how he reflects (or departs from) the code of knighthood.

2. The theme of death appears in a number of the selections in this unit. *The Pardoner's Tale,* "Edward," "Sir Patrick Spence," "The Demon Lover," and *The Day of Destiny* treat it.

Write a brief paper discussing the treatment of the theme of death in one or more of these selections.

3. Arthur and his court are presented in both Malory and the *Gawain*-poet, but there are a number of significant differences in the way the two writers treat this subject.

Compare and contrast the description of Arthur's court that appears in *The Day of Destiny* and *Sir Gawain and the Green Knight.*

4. The Prioress and the Wife of Bath are the preeminent women among the pilgrims, and seem intended as a contrast.

Compare and contrast the characters of the Prioress (lines 122-166) and the Wife of Bath (lines 455-486) as they are described in *The Prologue* to *The Canterbury Tales.*

Detail of *A Procession of Queen Elizabeth I*, attributed to Robert Peake the Elder, painted c. 1600.

Columbus to
West Indies

Cabot to North America

Vasco da Gama
to India

Cortez in Mexico

Henry VIII:
Defense of the Seven Sacraments

Copernicus's theory

Book of Common Prayer

Act of Supremacy

Golding's *Ovid*

Surrey's
Virgil

1500   1525   1550

Unit 3 1500–1660

The  enaissance

The Globe Theater opens •

Execution of Charles I •

• Holinshed: *Chronicles*

Browne: *Religio Medici* •

Hakluyt: *Voyages* •

• Shakespeare: *Hamlet*

Defeat of the Armada •

Puritans close the theaters •

Spenser: •
The Faerie Queene

Sidney: •
Astrophel and Stella

Battle of Naseby •

• Shakespeare: *Macbeth*

• Marlowe:
Dr. Faustus

Herrick: Hesperides •

Bacon: *Essays* •

• Drake's voyage

Background: The Renaissance 1500–1660

In the opening years of the fourteenth century, there developed in Italy an interest in the manuscripts that had survived from ancient Greece and Rome. As more and more of these were unearthed in libraries and monasteries, Italy fell under the spell of the intellectual movement we have come to call the Renaissance—the rebirth of scholarship based on classical learning and philosophy. Spreading westward across Europe, the phenomenon of the Renaissance touched England lightly and fleetingly during Chaucer's time. This early contact was negligible, however, largely because external wars and internal strife ravaged the country for almost a century and a half, from 1337 to 1485.

As the Renaissance developed in Italy and other European countries, it began to take on added dimensions. Perhaps stimulated by the discovery that the men and women of ancient Greece and Rome were intelligent, cultured, and creative, the Renaissance gradually became also a rebirth of the human spirit, a realization of the human potential for development. This realization led eventually to many discoveries—geographical, religious, and scientific, as well as artistic and philosophical. Both the Age of Discovery of new lands, including the exploration of America, and the Protestant Reformation had their origins in the Renaissance spirit. To the same spirit may be attributed Copernicus's assertion that the earth was not the center of the universe.

The Renaissance in England

The Renaissance in England may be divided into three parts: the rise of the Renaissance un-

der the early Tudor monarchs (1500–1558), the height of the Renaissance under Elizabeth I (1558–1603), and the decline of the Renaissance under the Stuart monarchs (1603–1649).

In 1485, with the end of the Wars of the Roses and the crowning of Henry VII, domestic unrest ended. Henry immediately set about unifying the country, strengthening the crown, and replenishing the royal treasury.

Under the reign of his son, Henry VIII (1509–1547), England was ripe for the intellectual ferment of the Renaissance. The population had begun to increase rapidly, feudalism was on its deathbed, and there was a steady movement of population to the larger towns and cities, especially London. The population of London, only 93,000 in 1563, had by 1605 more than doubled, to 224,000. Part of this growth came about because of the enclosure laws, which meant that large open areas, originally available to everyone, were fenced in, and many agricultural workers, no longer able to pay the higher rents for arable land, moved to the cities where there was a better chance to find work.

The invention of the printing press, together with improved methods of manufacturing paper, made possible the rapid spread of knowledge. In 1476, during the Wars of the Roses, William Caxton had set up England's first printing press at Westminster, a part of London. By 1640, that press and others had printed more than 26,000 different works and editions. It is estimated that by 1530 more than half the population of England was literate.

Renaissance learning made its tardy entry into England near the end of the fifteenth century, carried home by scholars who had traveled in Italy. Earliest among these was the Oxford

Group, which introduced what became known as the "New Learning" (or humanism) to Oxford University in the 1490s and 1500s. Leaders of this group were William Grocyn (c. 1446–1519), Thomas Linacre (1460–1524), and John Colet (1466–1519). A decade later, the great Dutch humanist, Desiderius Erasmus, was teaching Greek at Cambridge University.

Learning flourished not only at Oxford and Cambridge, but at the lower educational levels too. In 1510 John Colet, one of the original Oxford Group, now Dean of St. Paul's Cathedral, used his inheritance to establish the cathedral school of St. Paul's, the first preparatory school to be devoted to teaching the new learning. Other private schools followed rapidly.

The first major impact of the Renaissance on English literature is observable in the poetry of Wyatt and Surrey, who introduced and Anglicized the sonnet, an Italian verse form that has proved to be popular in English. Surrey is credited also with inventing English blank verse. Other verse forms, borrowed from the Italian and the French, had a lesser impact. Elaborate Renaissance conventions of love poetry were also transplanted, finding their outlet chiefly in sonnets and sonnet sequences.

Though the non-native influence was strong insofar as poetry was concerned, the native drama continued to develop and gain popularity. Miracle and morality plays remained a favorite form of entertainment, while a new dramatic form, the interlude, developed. One of the important ancestors of Elizabethan drama, the interlude was a short play designed to be presented between the courses of a banquet.

While the Renaissance was gathering strength in England, two events occurred that diminished the influence of the Church. The first was Martin Luther's posting of his Ninety-five Theses on a church door in Wittenberg, Germany, in 1517, an act that heralded the Reformation. The second event was brought about by the desire of Henry VIII for a male heir and his wish to divorce Catherine of Aragon, who had borne only one child, Mary. When the Pope refused to end the marriage, Henry, with an eye also to seizing the vast holdings of the Church, overthrew papal jurisdiction, married Anne Boleyn, and was declared, with Parliament's help, head of the Church of England, sometimes called the Anglican Church. Thus England became a Protestant nation.

The Oath of Supremacy, affirming the King as head of both Church and State, was required of those in the service of the Church or the King, as well as those in the learned professions and those attending Oxford or Cambridge Universities. The oath led to ruined careers or martyrdom for many Catholics, who regarded the Pope as the head of the Church.

The problem of succession to the throne continued to trouble Henry. Anne Boleyn gave him one child, Elizabeth, before she was convicted and executed for adultery. Her successor, Jane

Portrait of Henry VIII by court painter Hans Holbein, a great master of realism, 1542.

Seymour, died in childbirth, leaving a sickly son, Edward. Henry's next three marriages—to Anne of Cleves, Catherine Howard, and Catherine Parr—were childless. Three of his children, by three different queens, ruled England.

During the reign of Henry's successor, the child king Edward VI, the movement toward Protestantism continued. However, Queen Mary, the next monarch, was a devout Catholic. Her attempts to restore Catholicism to the country resulted in internal turmoil and much bloodshed.

The Height of the Renaissance

Under the reign of Elizabeth I (1558–1603), the next monarch, order was restored and England entered upon her most glorious age. Only twenty-five when she assumed the throne, Elizabeth, who never married, was to rule wisely and well for forty-five years.

That England welcomed its new queen is apparent in a contemporary document. Holinshed's *Chronicle* has this to say about Elizabeth's coronation in 1558:

On her entering the city of London, she was received of the people with prayers, wishes, welcomings, cries, and tender words, all which argued a wonderful earnest love of most obedient subjects towards their sovereign. And on the other side, her grace, by holding up her hands, and merry countenance to such as stood far off, and most tender and gentle language to those that stood nigh unto her grace, did declare herself no less thankfully to receive her people's good will, than they lovingly offered it to her. And it was not only to those her subjects who were of noble birth that she showed herself thus very gracious, but also to the poorest sort. How many nosegays did her grace receive at poor women's hands! How oftentimes stayed she her chariot, when she saw any simple body offer to speak to her grace! A branch of rosemary given her grace with a supplication about Fleet Bridge, was seen in her chariot till her grace came to Westminster, not without the marvellous wondering of such as knew the presenter, and noted the queen's most gracious receiving and keeping the same. Therefore may the poor and needy look for great hope at her grace's hand, who hath shown so loving a carefulness for them.

Through her policy of middle-of-the-road Protestantism, Elizabeth held in check throughout her reign the proponents of Catholicism on one hand and the growing numbers of Puritan extremists on the other. A master politician, wise in the choice of her counselors, Elizabeth established a strong central government that received the loyal support of her subjects. In 1570, when the Pope excommunicated Elizabeth, his act had the unexpected result of uniting England still more strongly behind its queen. Mary Queen of Scots was a Catholic and heir to the throne after Elizabeth. As such, she represented an invitation to rebellion from within and aggression from without on the part of persons interested in toppling England's Protestant monarchy. Persuaded by her advisers that her cousin's death was a political necessity, Elizabeth set in motion a chain of events that led to Mary's beheading in 1587.

Interested in education, Queen Elizabeth established one hundred free grammar schools in all parts of the country. (Her Stuart successors, James and Charles, were responsible for almost three hundred more.) These schools were open to both sexes of all ranks. Eager to educate their children, many people took advantage of the free schools; this may well have been one of the reasons for England's advancement. The growing middle class wanted schools in order to educate its children; as these children were educated, the middle class itself grew in power, its influence growing proportionately in the House of Commons.

In 1579, Gresham College was founded in London to cater to the needs of the middle class. Unlike the classical curriculum offered by Oxford

and Cambridge, its curriculum included law, medicine, and other practical courses suited to the bustling world of London.

During Elizabeth's reign, England began to gain supremacy on the seas. Riches came from ventures like those of the pirate-patriot Sir Francis Drake, whom Elizabeth commissioned to intercept Spanish treasure ships on the high seas. Drake's voyage around the world (1577-1580) resulted in his returning to England with a treasure taken from the Spanish—much of which went to swell Elizabeth's treasury. Naturally, this displeased King Philip II of Spain. On Drake's return the Queen herself went aboard his ship, the *Golden Hind,* and knighted him then and there.

Threatened by the Armada, an invasion fleet sent by her long-time enemy, Philip of Spain, Elizabeth sent the English navy out to destroy the enemy ships. Her words upon that occasion are noteworthy: ". . . I know I have the body of a weak feeble woman, but I have the heart and stomach of a king—and a king of England, too, and think foul scorn that . . . Spain or any Prince of Europe should dare to invade the borders of my realm." The defeat of the Armada in 1588 meant that England would remain Protestant and that it would emerge as a dominant sea power.

Elizabeth's reign was an age of courtiers. The queen loved music and dancing, and her court entertainments were notable. Educated in both classical and modern languages, Elizabeth was not only a master politician, but also a poet (see page 136). Many of the men of her court did live up to the Renaissance ideal (as expressed in *Hamlet*) of courtier, soldier, and scholar. Most famous of the courtier poets were Sir Walter Raleigh and Sir Philip Sidney. Edmund Spenser, unsuccessfully seeking the monarch's favor, wrote *The Faerie Queene,* a long allegorical epic in which Gloriana, the Faerie Queene, represented Elizabeth.

The bustling activity of the court with its swarms of royal agents, foreign ambassadors, churchmen, scholars, poets, actors, musicians, cooks, porters, and chambermaids was faithfully reproduced in the city of London as a whole.

Action between the British *Royal Ark* (right) and the flagship of the Spanish Armada off the Isle of Wight as shown in a painting by Vroom. Because the British here abandoned the custom of grappling and boarding for the practice of standing off and firing, they revolutionized naval warfare, and became the masters of the sea.

Here carts and coaches, laughing and quarreling throngs of men, women, and children jostled up and down the streets to such an extent that posts had to be set up to keep houses from falling down.

Elizabeth's tastes as well as those of her subjects ran the gamut from public hangings, witch burnings, bearbaitings, and bawdy jokes on up into the rarer atmosphere of exquisite jewels, silks, and brocades, stately dances, and elevated discussions of Christian theology, Greek philosophy, and Italian poetry. Just as Elizabeth could slap and spit at her associates one moment and discuss the elegancies of Italian poetry the next, so her subjects could stop in at the Paris Garden where mastiffs tore at Harry Hunks, the bear, and then pass on to the Globe Theater next door, where Romeo's words dropped gently into Juliet's ears.

Lyric poetry and song also flourished in Elizabethan England, as courtier and commoner alike found in song an outlet for the exuberant Renaissance spirit. Most famous of the songwriters was Thomas Campion, whose five collections of songs with lute accompaniment were printed and made available to Elizabethans at all social levels. Another source of popular music was the drama. Songs were an integral part not only of comedies, but on occasion also of tragedies.

Beyond question the Elizabethan period was the golden age of English drama, including among its dramatists Christopher Marlowe, William Shakespeare, and Ben Jonson, along with more than a dozen other first-rate playwrights. Under the skillful handling of these dramatists, blank verse, introduced into the language by Surrey, became the main vehicle for tragedy and comedy. *Hamlet, Macbeth,* and Shakespeare's other tragedies were cast in blank verse, as were his comedies.

Native English drama, which had existed at least since medieval times, was the wellspring of Elizabethan drama. Although Classical drama had been known earlier, its initial influence came in the 1560s, with the translation of Latin drama, especially the revenge tragedies of Seneca and the comedies of Plautus and Terence. Somehow everything came together, and Elizabethan England saw the theater develop to an unprecedented degree. The plays of the great dramatists contained something for everyone: low comedy for the uneducated, elevated philosophical concepts for the educated, and strong story lines to engage the attention of everyone.

Because the public theaters attracted large audiences from all levels of society, pickpockets and other criminals were drawn there. As Puritan influence grew in England, more and more complaints were made about the ungodliness of the theaters, and they were occasionally closed. In time of plague, too, their operations were suspended, and the acting companies went on tour.

The Puritan influence that forced the occasional closing of the theaters was symptomatic of what was to come. Renaissance exuberance was the exuberance of youth, and as Elizabethan poets warned, youth cannot last forever. Queen Elizabeth's moderate Protestantism and personal presence had maintained England's domestic stability. In 1600, however, when the new century began, Elizabeth was in her late sixties, an aging queen not in the best of health. Despite the urging of her counselors, not until she was dying in 1603 did the childless Elizabeth name her successor, King James of Scotland, the son of Mary Queen of Scots.

The Decline of the Renaissance

James I, the first Stuart king, had little first-hand knowledge of England, nor was he the kind of leader to rouse patriotic fervor and loyalty in his new subjects. Elizabeth had managed to maintain religious balance between Protestants and Catholics, but under the Stuarts, James and his son Charles I, who succeeded him, that balance was lost. Both monarchs were firm Anglicans (members of the Church of England), opposed to Puritanism. James's active persecution of the Puritans, in fact, led to the founding of Plymouth in New England in 1620.

There was growing religious and political unrest under James. In 1604, under the leadership of Robert Catesby and Guy Fawkes, a group of Catholics conceived the idea of blowing up the Parliament building while both Houses were assembled for the opening of Parliament, and King James and his family were in attendance. By November, 1605, the Gunpowder Plot, as it has come to be called, had resulted in the concealment of vast quantities of explosives in the cellar of the Parliament building. At almost the last moment, however, the plot was discovered and government agents seized Guy Fawkes in the cellar. The other conspirators were pursued, and those who were not killed were tried, found guilty, and executed. Today in England, November 5 is celebrated as Guy Fawkes Day with fireworks and bonfires.

Both James and Charles also engaged in struggles with Parliament, notably the House of Commons, over finances and what they believed to be their divine right to rule absolutely. The increasing strength of the predominantly Puritan middle class in the House of Commons made confrontation inevitable. This did not occur until the reign of Charles, who settled his disputes with his Parliaments by high-handedly dismissing them. In 1642, civil war erupted, with the king and his supporters, called Royalists or Cavaliers, ranged against the Parliamentary forces, called Puritans or Roundheads, led by Oliver Cromwell. The king was defeated, tried, found guilty of treason, and beheaded in 1649. England was declared to be no longer a monarchy, but a commonwealth under the jurisdiction of Parliament.

At the beginning of the Stuart period, poetry was only a little less exuberant, a little more cynical and introspective than it had been earlier under Elizabeth. A major development was the growth of a group of *metaphysical* poets, led by John Donne. For emphasis, they used "strong" or harsh lines, overriding regular meter; they employed strained metaphors (or *conceits*); and they were intellectual rather than romantic, even in their love poetry.

A number of young Cavaliers, loyal to the king, wrote lyrics about love and loyalty, but even in the love poems it is evident that the freshness of the Elizabethan era had passed. Among the best of these poets were Richard Lovelace and Robert Herrick.

King James performed a great service to literature as well as to the Protestant cause when he commissioned a new English translation of the Bible. Completed in 1611, the King James Bible influenced English prose for generations.

Drama continued to flourish in England under the Stuarts. Shakespeare's great tragedies

Portrait of James I by Van Somer, with the Banqueting House, Whitehall, in the background, 1619–1620.

were written during the reign of King James, and Shakespeare's acting company, taken under the patronage of the king, became known as the King's Men. The theater did in fact remain a popular form of entertainment until the Puritan government closed all playhouses in 1649.

The greatest of the Puritan poets, and one of the greatest English poets, was John Milton, Latin Secretary to the Puritan Commonwealth. While in this position his sight began to fail; eventually he became blind. Sightless, he composed *Paradise Lost*, his greatest work and the most successful English epic. He chose for his subject the fall of man.

In 1660, the monarchy was restored, with Charles II (the son of the executed Charles I) on the throne. Theaters were reopened and, at least for a while, a mood of gaiety reigned.

Sir Thomas Wyatt 1503–1542

Thomas Wyatt was born in Allington Castle, Kent, and spent most of his adult life at court and abroad in the service of King Henry VIII. Wyatt was one of the first writers to bring to England from Italy and France the themes and forms of Renaissance poetry.

Educated at St. John's College, Cambridge, Wyatt went on to a career as courtier and diplomat, serving as Clerk of the King's Jewels, as Ambassador to Spain, as Ambassador to Emperor Charles V, and as a member of a number of diplomatic missions to France and Italy.

Twice imprisoned by Henry, he was twice pardoned and restored to royal favor. Apparently Wyatt had been in love with his first cousin, Anne Boleyn, who later became the second wife of Henry VIII and the mother of the future Queen Elizabeth I. In 1536, when Elizabeth was two years old, Anne Boleyn was charged with adultery and executed. Although Wyatt was imprisoned in the Tower of London for a time, he was exonerated and freed. Continuing in Henry's service, he survived a second imprisonment in 1541, this time on charges of treason, and died of a fever contracted while he was en route to yet another diplomatic mission.

From his travels abroad, Wyatt had firsthand contact with the sonnet and other verse forms.

Although he is known for introducing the Italian sonnet into England, his best poetry is probably in the native English lyric tradition.

Few of Wyatt's poems were published in his lifetime, typical of an age when courtiers privately circulated their poems in manuscript. In 1557, however, fifteen years after his death, *Tottel's Miscellany,* an important collection of early English Renaissance poetry, was published; 97 of its 276 poems are by Wyatt.

The three Wyatt poems that follow show his versatility and lyrical gifts. "Whoso List to Hunt," the first of these, is an example of the adaptation of the Italian sonnet form to English.

*W*hoso List to Hunt

Whoso list[1] to hunt, I know where is an hind,[2]
But as for me, alas, I may no more.
The vain travail hath wearied me so sore,
I am of them that farthest come behind.
5 Yet may I, by no means, my wearied mind
Draw from the deer; but as she fleeth afore,
Fainting I follow. I leave off therefore,
Since in a net I seek to hold the wind.

Whoso list her hunt, I put him out of doubt,
10 As well as I, may spend his time in vain.
And graven with diamonds in letters plain
There is written, her fair neck round about,
"*Noli me tangere,*[3] for Caesar's I am,
And wild for to hold, though I seem tame."

1557

---

1. *list,* likes.
2. *hind,* female deer.
3. *Noli me tangere,* do not touch me. [Latin] Tradition has it that the subject of this sonnet was Anne Boleyn, Wyatt's first cousin, with whom he was reputed to be in love. Anne was the wife of Henry VIII and Queen of England.

Varium et Mutabile[1]

Is it possible
   That so high debate,
   So sharp, so sore, and of such rate,
   Should end so soon and was begun so late?
5 Is it possible?

Is it possible
   So cruel intent,
   So hasty heat and so soon spent,
   From love to hate, and thence for to relent?
10 Is it possible?

Is it possible
   That any may find
   Within one heart so diverse mind,
   To change or turn as weather and wind?
15 Is it possible?

Is it possible
   To spy it in an eye
   That turns as oft as chance on die?[2]
   The truth whereof can any try?
20 Is it possible?

It is possible
   For to turn so oft,
   To bring that lowest that was most aloft,
   And to fall highest, yet to light soft.[3]
25 It is possible.

All is possible,
   Who so list believe;
   Trust therefore first, and after preve,[4]
   As men wed ladies by license and leave,
30 All is possible.   1557

---

1. *Varium et Mutabile,* fickle and changeable. [Latin] From the Latin poet Virgil's *Aeneid:* "Varium et mutabile semper / Femina"—Woman is always fickle and changing.
2. *die,* one of a pair of dice.
3. *fall . . . soft,* to fall from a great height, yet land softly.
4. *preve,* prove.

He Is Not Dead That Sometime Hath a Fall

He is not dead that sometime hath a fall;
   The sun returneth that was under the
      cloud;
And when fortune hath spit out all her gall,[1]
   I trust good luck to me shall be allowed.
5 For I have seen a ship into haven[2] fall
   After the storm hath broke both mast and
      shroud;
And eke[3] the willow that stoopeth with the
      wind
Doth rise again, and greater wood doth bind.[4]
           1557

---

1. *gall,* bitterness, hate.
2. *haven,* harbor or port.
3. *eke,* also, moreover.
4. *greater . . . bind.* Larger trees are restrained from motion ("bind") and therefore break rather than bend with the wind. There may also be a suggestion that the supple branches of the willow will be used to bind together branches from bigger trees that broke because they could not bend with the wind.

Discussion

1. The typical writer of a **sonnet** liked to speak in elaborate **metaphors,** in which one set of terms stands for another. What is the central metaphor in Wyatt's "Whoso List to Hunt"?

2. (a) Stanzas three and four are keys to determining the meaning of "Varium et Mutabile." What is described in them as changeable? (b) What then might the first two stanzas be about? (c) The last two stanzas give the answer to the question posed in the first four; according to the speaker, what *is* possible?

3. Would you say that "He Is Not Dead That Sometime Hath a Fall" was prompted by a good or a bad experience? Explain.

Henry Howard,
Earl of Surrey 1517–1547

Of noble lineage (his father was the Duke of Norfolk and a close adviser to Henry VIII), Surrey received a private education at home. When Surrey was only fifteen, he traveled to France and remained for several months at the French court.

Surrey's first military service occurred in 1536, when he accompanied his father to the north of England to suppress a revolt against Henry VIII. In 1537 he was imprisoned for striking at court a man who accused him of having been sympathetic to the rebels.

Released from prison, he showed his family pride and high spirits to such an extent that in 1539 he was referred to as "the most foolish proud boy in England." In the same year he commanded Henry's forces in Norfolk, and in 1541 he was honored by being made a Knight of the Garter. The strange alliances and misfortunes of Henry's court first touched Surrey personally in 1542 when he was present at the execution of his cousin Catherine Howard, Henry VIII's fifth wife. That same year his quick temper involved him in trouble again and he was briefly imprisoned for challenging another courtier to a duel.

He served in the military in France, where he distinguished himself for bravery and was wounded on the battlefield. In 1546 he and his father were arrested on several charges of treason, and in January, 1547, he was beheaded—just a little more than one week before Henry died.

Although it may seem difficult for one man to have experienced so much in a short life, Surrey was also an accomplished poet. He is represented in *Tottel's Miscellany* (1557) by forty poems. It was he who introduced the English or Shakespearean sonnet form, more natural to the English language than the Italian form. Surrey's poetry is more polished than Wyatt's, but it is generally thought to be less forceful and original in content.

A Lover's Vow

Set me whereas the sun doth parch the green,
Or where his beams may not dissolve the ice,
In temperate heat, where he is felt and seen;
With proud people, in presence sad and wise,
5 Set me in base, or yet in high degree;
In the long night, or in the shortest day;
In clear weather, or where mists thickest be;
In lusty youth, or when my hairs be gray;
Set me in earth, in heaven, or yet in hell;
10 In hill, in dale, or in the foaming flood;
Thrall,[1] or at large—alive whereso I dwell;
Sick or in health, in ill fame or in good;
Yours will I be, and with that only thought
Comfort myself when that my hap[2] is naught.

1557

---

1. **Thrall,** enslaved.
2. **hap,** good fortune.

A las, So All Things Now Do Hold Their Peace[1]

Alas! so all things now do hold their peace,
Heaven and earth disturbèd in no thing;
The beasts, the air, the birds their song do cease,
The nightès chare[2] the stars about doth bring.
5 Calm is the sea, the waves work less and less;
So am not I, whom love, alas, doth wring,
Bringing before my face the great increase
Of my desires, whereat I weep and sing,
In joy and woe, as in a doubtful ease.
10 For my sweet thoughts sometime do
       pleasure bring,
But by and by the cause of my disease[3]
Gives me a pang that inwardly doth sting,
When that I think what grief it is again
To live and lack the thing should rid my pain.

1557

---

1. A version of a sonnet by Petrarch, an Italian poet who lived 1304–1374.
2. *chare,* chariot.
3. *disease,* uneasiness, discomfort.

Discussion

1. The last two lines of Surrey's "A Lover's Vow" appear to explain the somewhat frenzied tone of the preceding lines. What is the explanation, and how persuasive is it?

2. (a) In "Alas, So All Things Now Do Hold Their Peace," what is the cause of the lover's uneasiness? (b) Does the speaker appear to be more serious in this sonnet or in "A Lover's Vow"? Justify your answer by referring to the poems.

Reader's Note: Sonnets and Sonnet Sequences

Imported into England from Italy, the **sonnet** takes two major forms in English poetry: the Italian or Petrarchan (named for Petrarch, its greatest Italian practitioner), and the English or Shakespearean (named for its greatest English practitioner). Both types consist of fourteen lines written in **iambic pentameter:** ten syllables to a line, with the stress on every second syllable. For variety, occasionally the poet adds an extra syllable, subtracts one, or shifts the stress.

Although the number of lines and the **meter** are the same in both the Italian and English sonnets, the two differ in **rhyme scheme** and in the organization of subject matter. In its purest form, the Italian sonnet states its idea (called the *problem* or *proposition*) in its first eight lines and resolves it (the *resolution* or *conclusion*) in the last six lines. The rhyme scheme of the Italian sonnet supports this thought division, the first eight lines always rhyming *abba abba,* the last six lines using a mixture of three rhymes: *cde cde* (the most common), *cc dd ee,* or other combinations.

Unlike the Italian sonnet, the English sonnet in its purest form states its idea in the first twelve lines and resolves it in the last two. Customarily the idea is repeated in a different form every four lines (or is stated in the first four lines and then amplified in four-line groups), and the rhyme scheme conforms to this thought division: *abab cdcd efef,* and the concluding couplet, *gg.*

From the Italian models come a number of the conventions of the sonnet, one of which is an exaggerated description of the beauty of the beloved. She is usually blonde and fair, with a peaches-and-cream complexion and cherry-red lips—and she is disdainful. Common themes are fame, mutability (changes worked by time), and the coldness of the beloved. A poet generally felt obligated to work within these conventions, but he tried to achieve originality in spite of them.

Comment: Elizabeth Young and Old

The woman who gave her name to one of the greatest periods in England's history—the Elizabethan Age—was in every respect a remarkable human being. Too often we view her from the regal or historical perspective, failing to consider the personality behind all the pomp and ceremony.

Wit, song, and dance made Elizabeth's court a lively place. Not only did she herself enjoy writing poetry, but she enjoyed being honored in the poems of her courtiers. In fact, it was said that one route to preferment at court was to write good verse. For some this was so; for others it was not. "When I Was Fair and Young" is an example of Elizabeth's verse style.

"Gloriana Dying" was one of the last poems of Sylvia Townsend Warner (1893–1978), a twentieth-century English poet, novelist, and short-story writer. This poem is a **dramatic monologue** spoken by the dying Queen Elizabeth, often referred to as "Gloriana" by her subjects. In her last illness, Elizabeth grew fearful of her long, wakeful nights, and refused to go to bed, snatching at sleep during the day in a chair, or on cushions on the floor.

Queen Elizabeth I

When I Was Fair and Young

When I was fair and young, and favor
    gracèd me,
  Of many was I sought, their mistress for
    to be;
But I did scorn them all, and answered them
    therefore,
  "Go, go, go, seek some otherwhere,
5   Impòrtune me no more!"

How many weeping eyes I made to pine
    with woe,
  How many sighing hearts, I have no skill
    to show;
Yet I the prouder grew, and answered them
    therefore,
  "Go, go, go, seek some otherwhere,
10   Impòrtune me no more!"

Then spake fair Venus' son, that proud
    victorious boy,[1]
  And said, "Fine dame, since that you be
    so coy,
I will so pluck your plumes that you shall
    say no more,
  'Go, go, go, seek some otherwhere,
15   Impòrtune me no more!' "

When he had spake these words, such
    change grew in my breast,
  That neither night nor day since that, I
    could take any rest,
Then lo! I did repent that I had said before,
  "Go, go, go, seek some otherwhere,
20   Impòrtune me no more!"

1579?   c. 1590

---

1. **Venus' son . . . boy.** Cupid and his mother Venus were the patrons of lovers in Classical mythology.

Sylvia Townsend Warner

Gloriana Dying

None shall gainsay me. I will lie on the floor.
Hitherto from horseback, throne, balcony,
I have looked down upon your looking up.
Those sands are run. Now I reverse the glass
5 And bid henceforth your homage downward,
          falling
Obedient and unheeded as leaves in autumn
To quilt the wakeful study I must make
Examining my kingdom from below.
How tall my people are! Like a race of trees
10 They sway, sigh, nod heads, rustle above me,
And their attentive eyes are distant as
          starshine.
I have still cherished the handsome and
          well-made:
No queen has better masts within her forests
Growing, nor prouder and more restive minds
15 Scabbarded in the loyalty of subjects;
No virgin has had better worship than I.
No, no! Leave me alone, woman! I will not·
Be put into a bed. Do you suppose
That I who've ridden through all weathers,
          danced
20 Under a treasury's weight of jewels, sat
Myself to stone through sermons and addresses,
Shall come to harm by sleeping on a floor?
Not that I sleep. A bed were good enough
If that were in my mind. But I am here
25 For a deep study and contemplation,
And as Persephone,[1] and the red vixen,[2]
Go underground to sharpen their wits,
I have left my dais to learn a new policy
Through watching of your feet, and as the Indian
30 Lays all his listening body along the earth
I lie in wait for the reverberation
Of things to come and dangers threatening.
Is that the Bishop praying? Let him pray on.
If his knees tire his faith can cushion them.
35 How the poor man grieves Heaven with
          news of me!
Deposuit superbos.[3] But no hand
Other than my own has put me down —

Not feebleness enforced on brain or limb,
Not fear, misgiving, fantasy, age, palsy,
40 Has felled me. I lie here by my own will,
And by the curiosity of a queen.
I dare say there is not in all England
One who lies closer to the ground than I.
Not the traitor in the condemned hold
45 Whose few straws edge away from under his
          weight
Of ironed fatality; not the shepherd
Huddled for cold under the hawthorn bush,
Nor the long, dreaming country lad who lies
Scorching his book before the dying brand.[4]

1980

---

1. *Persephone,* (pər sef'ə nē) in Greek myths the daughter of Zeus and Demeter, made queen of the lower world by Hades, but allowed to spend part of each year on earth.
2. *vixen,* a female fox.
3. *Deposuit superbos,* he has put down the proud. [Latin] The Bishop is reading from "The Magnificat," the Latin text of the song of the Virgin Mary recorded in Luke 1:46–55.
4. *brand,* a piece of burning wood.

"Gloriana Dying" from *Twelve Poems* by Sylvia Townsend Warner. Copyright © 1980 by Susanna Pinney and William Maxwell. Reprinted by permission of the author's Literary Estate and Chatto & Windus.

Discussion

1. (a) What is the **tone** of "When I Was Fair and Young"? (b) In the last stanza, what has occurred in the speaker's life? (c) Do you think that Queen Elizabeth intended this poem to be autobiographical? Explain.

2. In "Gloriana Dying," Queen Elizabeth is speaking. (a) What is unusual about her position? (b) How does she feel about it? (c) Why does she not wish to be moved? (d) One reader has remarked on the similarities between Elizabeth's personality as described in "When I Was Fair and Young" and in "Gloriana Dying." What are some of these similarities?

Sir Walter Raleigh 1552?–1618

Sir Walter Raleigh lived to the fullest the Renaissance ideal of the complete courtier—soldier, statesman, and poet—and was in addition philosopher, historian, explorer, and colonizer. His life ended in a way that was all too common in his times—on the headsman's block on trumped-up charges of treason.

Born in Devonshire about 1552, Raleigh enrolled in Oriel College, Oxford, about 1568, leaving a year later to become a soldier with the Huguenot (French Protestant) army in France. In 1575 he was a member of the Middle Temple of the Inns of Court, apparently on the way to a career in law. However, by 1578 he was fighting with the Dutch against Spain, and then in the Irish campaigns. In the early 1580s he came to Queen Elizabeth's attention and rose rapidly in her favor, becoming her adviser in 1583. He was elevated to knighthood in 1584. In that year, too, with Elizabeth's help he sponsored the first attempt to colonize Virginia, named for Elizabeth, the Virgin Queen.

In 1585 he was in charge of preparations to repel the expected Spanish invasion—indeed, throughout his life he was violently opposed to Spain, especially to Spanish colonization in the New World. Raleigh became Captain of Elizabeth's Guardsmen in 1588, an appointment that made him responsible for her physical safety, an extremely important post in those troubled, often violent times.

By the late 1580s the Earl of Essex had begun to supplant Raleigh as the Queen's favorite, and in 1592 Raleigh incurred royal disfavor by secretly marrying Elizabeth Throckmorton, one of the Queen's maids of honor. When the marriage was discovered, the erring couple were imprisoned in the Tower of London but were released near the end of the year. Although Raleigh never fully regained Elizabeth's favor, he continued to lead an adventurous life in her service. In 1595 he participated in an exploratory voyage to Guyana; in 1596 he was wounded fighting the Spanish in Cadiz, and in the same year he testified against the Earl of Essex at the latter's trial for treason.

Elizabeth was aging, and Raleigh opposed the naming of James as her successor. From the time that James I became king of England in 1603, Raleigh, who was considered dangerous, was in trouble. Almost immediately he was accused of conspiracy against the King, convicted on charges of treason, and sentenced to death. He was pardoned three days before his execution, but kept in prison in the Tower of London, where his wife and son were permitted to join him. There he spent his time writing his *History of the World,* and conducting scientific experiments. In 1616 James I, still holding the sentence of death over Raleigh, permitted him to head a treasure-hunting expedition to Guyana, held by the Spaniards, on condition that he not fight them. But a battle did erupt (though Raleigh was on shipboard at the time); the English were defeated and Raleigh's son killed. The ill-fated expedition returned to England with its leader suffering from malaria.

Upon his return to England, Raleigh was arrested and, on October 29, 1618, beheaded on the old charges of treason. It is said that he asked for the beheading to be done quickly because he felt malarial chills coming on and did not want his enemies to think that he was trembling with fear.

Sir Walter Raleigh to His Son

Three things there be that prosper up apace
And flourish, whilst they grow asunder far,
But on a day, they meet all in one place,
And when they meet, they one another mar;
5 And they be these: the wood, the weed, the
  wag.[1]
The wood is that which makes the gallow tree;
The weed is that which strings the
  hangman's bag;
The wag, my pretty knave, betokeneth thee.

Mark well, dear boy, whilst these assemble not,
10 Green springs the tree, hemp grows, the wag
  is wild;
But when they meet, it makes the timber rot,
It frets the halter, and it chokes the child.
Then bless thee, and beware, and let us pray
We part not with thee at this meeting day.
c. 1600

---

1. **wag,** a mischievous boy, probably a shortening of *waghalter,* one who is likely to swing in the hangman's halter (or noose).

To Queen Elizabeth

Our passions are most like to floods and streams,
The shallow murmur, but the deep are dumb;
So, when affections yield discourse, it seems
The bottom is but shallow whence they come.
5   They that are rich in words must needs
      discover
    That they are poor in that which makes a
      lover.

Wrong not, dear empress of my heart,
    The merit of true passion
With thinking that he feels no smart
10   That sues for no compassion;
Since, if my plaints serve not to prove
    The conquest of your beauty,
They come not from defect of love
    But from excess of duty.

15 For knowing that I sue to serve
    A saint of such perfection
As all desire, yet none deserve,
    A place in her affection,
I rather choose to want[1] relief
20   Than venture the revealing;
When glory recommends the grief,
    Despair distrusts the healing.

Thus those desires that aim too high
    For any mortal lover,
25 When reason cannot make them die
    Discretion doth them cover.
Yet, when discretion doth bereave
    The plaints that they should utter,
Then your discretion may perceive
30   That silence is a suitor.

Silence in love bewrays[2] more woe
    Than words, though ne'er so witty;
A beggar that is dumb, you know,
    Deserveth double pity.
35 Then misconceive not, dearest heart,
    My true though secret passion;
He smarteth[3] most that hides his smart
    And sues for no compassion.
1592?   1655

---

1. **want,** lack.
2. **bewrays,** betrays, reveals.
3. **smarteth,** hurts.

What Is Our Life?

What is our life? a play of passion;
Our mirth, the music of division;[1]
Our mothers' wombs the tiring-houses[2] be
Where we are dressed for this short comedy.
5 Heaven the judicious sharp spectator is,
That sits and marks still[3] who doth act amiss;
Our graves that hide us from the searching sun
Are like drawn curtains when the play is done.
Thus march we playing to our latest rest;
10 Only we die in earnest—that's no jest.

1612

---

1. *music of division,* music played between acts or other divisions of a play.
2. *tiring-houses,* dressing rooms.
3. *still,* continuously.

Even Such Is Time

Even such is time, which takes in trust
Our youth, our joys, and all we have,
And pays us but with age and dust,
Who in the dark and silent grave
5 When we have wandered all our ways
Shuts up the story of our days,
And from which earth, and grave, and dust
The Lord shall raise me up, I trust.

1628

Discussion

1. **(a)** According to tradition, Raleigh once spread out his cloak for Queen Elizabeth to walk on. Is "To Queen Elizabeth" reminiscent of this same Raleigh? Explain. **(b)** How do you think Queen Elizabeth might have responded to this poem? Why?

2. In "Sir Walter Raleigh to His Son," Raleigh uses **alliteration** to call attention to the important items he enumerates in line 5: "the wood, the weed, the wag." **(a)** To what does each of the items refer? Of what, then, is Raleigh warning his son? **(b)** What is the tone of the poem? What does it reveal about Raleigh's feelings for his son?

3. **(a)** What images from the theater do you find in "What Is Our Life"? **(b)** Relate the last line ("Only we die in earnest—that's no jest") to the rest of the poem.

4. **(a)** Is "Even Such Is Time" a poem of complaint, a philosophical poem, a religious poem, or something else? Explain. **(b)** Discuss how suitable it might be for Raleigh's own epitaph.

Comment: The Death of Raleigh

A scaffold was erected in the old palace yard, upon which after fourteen years reprievement, [Sir Walter Raleigh's] head was cut off; at which time, such abundance of blood issued from his veins, that showed he had stock of nature enough left to have continued him many years in life, though now above three score years old, if it had not been taken away by the hand of violence. And this was the end of the great Sir Walter Raleigh: great sometimes in the favor of Queen Elizabeth, and next to Sir Frances Drake, the great scourge and hate of the Spaniard. . . .

From *Aubrey's Brief Lives,* edited by Oliver Lawson Dick. Copyright 1949 by Oliver Lawson Dick. Reprinted by permission of the publishers, Martin Secker & Warburg Limited and the University of Michigan Press. [First published in 1690.]

Christopher Marlowe
1564–1593

Christopher Marlowe led a short and stormy life, much of which is still shrouded in mystery. The son of a Canterbury shoemaker, he attended King's School, Canterbury, and later Corpus Christi College, Cambridge, holding for six years a scholarship usually awarded to someone intending to enter the ministry.

While still at Cambridge, Marlowe became a government agent (or spy), probably working directly for Sir Francis Walsingham, Queen Elizabeth's Secretary of State. Although he received his B.A. without difficulty, in 1587 the university was about to deny his M.A., possibly because of rumors that he planned to join Catholic emigrés from England at Douay, Belgium, immediately after graduation. However, Elizabeth's Privy Council intervened because of services (unknown to this day) that Marlowe had rendered her, "because it is not Her Majesty's pleasure that anyone employed as he had been in matters touching the benefit of his country should be defamed by those that are ignorant in the affairs he went about." Needless to say, Marlowe received his degree.

In a manner that foreshadowed his own death a few years later, Marlowe became involved in a brawl with William Bradley. Another poet, Thomas Watson, intervened and killed Bradley. Although both men were taken into custody, Watson pleaded self-defense and both were released.

By 1591, Marlowe was established as a playwright and was sharing London lodgings with Thomas Kyd, another playwright. Marlowe's plays cannot be dated with certainty, but he probably had written or was in the process of writing *Tamburlaine, Doctor Faustus,* and *The Jew of Malta,* his three greatest tragedies. He had also become friendly with Sir Walter Raleigh and other courtiers.

On May 12, 1593, Kyd was arrested and, under torture, claimed that Marlowe was the author of some atheistical papers found in their lodgings. Called before the Privy Council on May 20, Marlowe was questioned and released, but was required to appear before them daily. On May 30, while the case was still pending, Marlowe was at the inn of the Widow Bull in Deptford with Ingram Frizer, who was in the employ of Thomas Walsingham, and two other men. According to testimony, they quarreled over the bill and Frizer stabbed Marlowe in self-defense, killing him instantly.

Marlowe's major achievement lay in adapting **blank verse** to the stage. Ben Jonson expressed his admiration when he referred to "Marlowe's mighty line." Marlowe's ability to compress thought, image, and idea into superb lines of blank verse paved the way for Shakespeare and later practitioners of the art. In addition, Marlowe is known for the towering heroes of his dramas, all of them strong and overpowering until tragedy strikes.

In a far lighter mood, Marlowe wrote what is probably the most famous poem to emerge from Elizabethan England; "The Passionate Shepherd to His Love" has generated many responses (and parodies). The best of these, "The Nymph's Reply to the Shepherd," written by Sir Walter Raleigh, appears with it.

The Passionate Shepherd to His Love

Come live with me and be my love,
And we will all the pleasures prove
That hills and valleys, dales and fields,
Or woods, or steepy mountain yields.

5   And we will sit upon the rocks,
Seeing the shepherds feed their flocks,
By shallow rivers to whose falls
Melodious birds sing madrigals.[1]

And I will make thee beds of roses
10   And a thousand fragrant posies,
A cap of flowers, and a kirtle[2]
Embroidered all with leaves of myrtle;

A gown made of the finest wool
Which from our pretty lambs we pull;
15   Fair lined slippers for the cold,
With buckles of the purest gold;

A belt of straw and ivy buds,
With coral clasps and amber studs—
And if these pleasures may thee move,
20   Come live with me and be my love.

The shepherd swains shall dance and sing
For thy delight each May morning—
If these delights thy mind may move,
Then live with me and be my love.

1599

---

1. **madrigals,** poems set to music, songs.
2. **kirtle,** a skirt or dress.

The Nymph's Reply to the Shepherd[1]

If all the world and love were young,
And truth in every shepherd's tongue,
These pretty pleasures might me move
To live with thee and be thy love.

5   Time drives the flocks from field to fold,
When rivers rage and rocks grow cold;
And Philomel[2] becometh dumb;
The rest complain of cares to come.

The flowers do fade, and wanton fields
10   To wayward winter reckoning yields;
A honey tongue, a heart of gall,
Is fancy's spring, but sorrow's fall.

Thy gowns, thy shoes, thy bed of roses,
Thy cap, thy kirtle, and thy posies,
15   Soon break, soon wither, soon forgotten,
In folly ripe, in reason rotten.

Thy belt of straw and ivy buds,
Thy coral clasps and amber studs,
All these in me no means can move
20   To come to thee and be thy love.

But could youth last and love still breed,
Had joys no date nor age no need,
Then these delights my mind might move
To live with thee and be thy love.

1600

---

1. a **nymph** is a young and beautiful woman.
2. **Philomel,** the nightingale.

Discussion

1. What sorts of "delights" does the Shepherd offer the young woman—sophisticated, simple, or what?
2. (a) Under what circumstances does the Nymph say she would consent to be the Shepherd's love? (b) Do you think she really means this, or is she just being coy?

Composition

Imagine that you wish to write a script for a modern version of the shepherd-nymph exchange. Think about the setting, and the instructions you want to give your actors.

Write the script in prose dialogue or poetry, in formal or informal language. (See *Revising* in Composition Guide.)

Edmund Spenser 1552–1599

Unlike the courtier poets, who were satisfied to have their verses circulated in manuscript form, Edmund Spenser wrote for publication—and for the royal favor he hoped would be his through publication.

Coming from an impoverished background (his father was a journeyman clothmaker), Spenser was a "poor boy"—a scholarship student at the Merchant Tailors' School, then under the direction of Richard Mulcaster, one of the great educators of the age. Spenser went on to Pembroke Hall, Cambridge, as a "sizar," a scholarship student who had servant duties to perform; poverty continued to dog his footsteps throughout his life.

After taking his B.A. (1573) and M.A. (1576), Spenser served as secretary to the Bishop of Rochester, then in 1579 entered the service of the Earl of Leicester. His appointment there was short-lived, for in 1580 he was sent to Ireland as secretary to its new governor, Lord Grey of Wilton. Except for several visits to England, Spenser remained in Ireland for the rest of his life.

In 1579, before he left England, Spenser had published *The Shepheardes Calender,* rich in classical **allusions** and written in deliberately archaic language. He had also begun his masterpiece, *The Faerie Queene,* a long allegorical poem dedicated to Queen Elizabeth. Not until 1590, and then with the help of Sir Walter Raleigh, was any part of this poem published. Raleigh had visited Spenser at his home, Kilcolman Castle, and the two returned to England together. When the first three books were published, Queen Elizabeth awarded him a pension.

Returning to Ireland, Spenser fell in love with Elizabeth Boyle, to whom he dedicated his sonnet cycle, *Amoretti* (1594)—the title means "little love poems"—which tells the story of their romance. To celebrate their marriage, he composed a beautiful marriage hymn, *Epithalamion* (1594). In 1595 three more books of *The Faerie Queene* were published. These were followed in the same year by another marriage hymn, *Prothalamion,* commissioned by the Earl of Worcester in honor of the double marriage of his two eldest daughters.

Meantime, conditions in Ireland were deteriorating rapidly, and in October, 1598, Spenser's home was burned by the rebels; Spenser and his wife barely escaped with their lives. Sent to London in December, 1598, to plead for reinforcements for the English garrison in Ireland, Spenser became ill. He died in London on January 13, 1599, under conditions suggesting dire poverty. The Earl of Essex paid for his funeral, and he was laid to rest near Chaucer, whom he had long admired, in the Poets' Corner in Westminster Abbey.

Edmund Spenser's plan for his allegorical epic, *The Faerie Queene* (published 1590-1595), was remarkably elaborate: there were to be twelve books, each book to be devoted to one of the twelve virtues of chivalry, such as Holiness, Temperance, Chastity. Spenser completed only half of his projected plan, or a total of six books with twelve cantos each. Even so, the poem is the longest noteworthy poem in the English language.

In order to illustrate moral virtues, Spenser fashioned his poem as an allegory, letting his characters stand for particular abstract qualities. But the allegorical purposes fused with political and other purposes, and the charac-

(Introduction continues on page 144.)

ters became identifiable not only with virtues but with historical personages. The Faerie Queene herself, Gloriana, is a guiding presence throughout the work who dispatches her knights on errands and quests in the service of virtue. Gloriana represents glory in a general sense, but she also represents Queen Elizabeth.

The Faerie Queene opens with a description of a knight riding his steed across a plain. He is followed by a lovely lady who is attended by a dwarf carrying her "needments" on his back. The knight is venturing forth to prove his power in battle and thus to win the favor of his queen and the admiration of the lady. This strange group soon loses its way and comes by accident upon an ominous-looking cave. Inside lurks an ugly monster, half serpent, half woman—"most loathsome, filthy, foul."

from *The Faerie Queene*

The Knight Slays a Monster
(from Canto I)

14

But full of fire and greedy hardiment,[1]
   The youthful knight could not for aught be
     stayed,
   But forth unto the darksome hole he went,
   And looked in: his glistering armor made
5   A little glooming light, much like a shade,
   By which he saw the ugly monster plain,
   Half like a serpent horribly displayed,
   But th'other half did woman's shape retain,
Most loathsome, filthy, foul, and full of vile
     disdain.

15

10 And as she lay upon the dirty ground,
   Her huge long tail her den all overspread,
   Yet was in knots and many broughtes[2]
     upwound,
   Pointed with mortal sting. Of her there bred
   A thousand young ones, which she daily fed,
15   Sucking upon her poisonous dugs, each one
   Of sundry shapes, yet all ill favored:
   Soon as that uncouth light upon them shone,
Into her mouth they crept, and sudden all
     were gone.

16

Their dam upstart, out of her den affrayed,[3]
20   And rushed forth, hurling her hideous tail
   About her cursed head, whose folds displayed
   Were stretched now forth at length
     without entrail.[4]
   She looked about, and seeing one in mail
   Armed to point,[5] sought back to turn again;
25   For light she hated as the deadly bale,
   Ay wont in desert darkness to remain,
Where plain none might her see, nor she see
     any plain.

---

1. **greedy hardiment,** eager courage.
2. **broughtes,** coils.
3. **affrayed,** frightened away.
4. **entrail,** coiling, folding
5. **to point,** completely.

17

Which when the valiant Elf[6] perceived, he leapt
  As lion fierce upon the flying prey,
30 And with his trenchant blade her boldly kept
  From turning back, and forced her to stay:
  Therewith enraged she loudly 'gan to bray,
  And turning fierce, her speckled tail
    advanced,
  Threatening her angry sting, him to dismay:
35 Who naught aghast, his mighty hand
    enhanced:[7]
The stroke down from her head unto her
    shoulder glanced.

18

Much daunted with that dint,[8] her sense was
    dazed,
  Yet kindling rage, herself she gathered
    round,
  And all at once her beastly body raised
40 With doubled forces high above the ground:
  Then wrapping up her wreathed stern
    around,
  Leaped fierce upon his shield, and her
    huge train[9]
  All suddenly about his body wound,
  That hand or foot to stir he strove in vain:
45 God help the man so wrapped in Error's
    endless train.[10]

19

His Lady sad to see his sore constraint,
  Cried out, "Now, now, Sir knight, show
    what ye be.
  Add faith unto your force, and be not faint:
  Strangle her, else she sure will strangle
    thee."
50 That when he heard, in great perplexity,
  His gall did grate for grief[11] and high disdain,
  And knitting all his force got one hand free,
  Wherewith he gripped her gorge with so
    great pain,
That soon to loose her wicked bands did her
    constrain.

20

55 Therewith she spewed out of her filthy maw
  A flood of poison horrible and black,
  Full of great lumps of flesh and gobbets raw,
  Which stunk so vilely, that it forced him slack
  His grasping hold, and from her turn him
    back:
60 Her vomit full of books and papers was,
  With loathly frogs and toads, which eyes
    did lack,
  And creeping sought way in the weedy grass:
Her filthy parbreake[12] all the place defiled
    has.

---

6. **Elf,** the knight; he was described as coming from Faerie.
7. **enhanced,** lifted.
8. **dint,** blow.
9. **train,** long trailing tail.
10. **train,** snare.
11. **His gall . . . grief,** his anger was stirred.
12. **parbreake,** vomit.

Reader's Note: The Spenserian Stanza

Edmund Spenser devised a special stanza
for *The Faerie Queene*. It has a total of nine
lines, the first eight in iambic pentameter (five
feet of unaccented-accented syllables), and the
last an **alexandrine,** made of *iambic hexameter*
(i.e., with one additional foot). The rhyme
scheme is highly interlocking: *ababbcbcc*. The
tightness of the form, and especially the final-
ty of the long last line, tends to make each
stanza self-contained. The result, when used in
narrative poetry (at least in Spenser's hands),
is a sequence of densely packed, richly woven
images, almost like miniatures flashing by one
at a time, vividly present and then gone.

21

As when old father Nilus 'gins to swell
65   With timely pride above the Egyptian vale,
His fatty waves do fertile slime outwell,
And overflow each plain and lowly dale:
But when his later spring 'gins to avale,[13]
Huge heaps of mud he leaves, wherein
    there breed
70   Ten thousand kinds of creatures, partly male
And partly female of his fruitful seed;
Such ugly monstrous shapes elsewhere may
    no man reed.[14]

22

The same so sore annoyed has the knight,
That well nigh choked with the deadly stink,
75   His forces fail, nor can no longer fight.
Whose courage when the fiend perceived
    to shrink,
She poured forth out of her hellish sink
Her fruitful cursed spawn of serpents small,
Deformed monsters, foul, and black as ink,
80   Which swarming all about his legs did crawl,
And him encumbered sore, but could not
    hurt at all.

23

As gentle Shepherd in sweet eventide,
When ruddy Phoebus[15] 'gins to welke[16] in
    west,
High on an hill, his flock to viewen wide,
85   Marks which do bite their hasty supper best;
A cloud of cumbrous[17] gnats do him molest,
All striving to infix their feeble stings,
That from their 'noyance he no where can
    rest,
But with his clownish hands their tender
    wings
90 He brusheth oft, and oft doth mar their
    murmurings.

24

Thus ill bestead,[18] and fearful more of shame,
Than of the certain peril he stood in,
Half furious unto his foe he came,
Resolved in mind all suddenly to win,
95   Or soon to lose, before he once would lin;[19]
And struck at her with more than manly force,
That from her body full of filthy sin
He raft[20] her hateful head without remorse;
A stream of coal-black blood forth gushed
    from her corse.[21]

25

100 Her scattered brood, soon as their Parent dear
They saw so rudely falling to the ground,
Groaning full deadly, all with troublous fear,
Gathered themselves about her body round,
Weening their wonted entrance to have found
105   At her wide mouth: but being there withstood
They flocked all about her bleeding wound,
And sucked up their dying mother's blood,
Making her death their life, and eke[22] her
    hurt their good.

26

That detestable sight him much amazed,
110   To see th'unkindly Imps of heaven accursed,
Devour their dam; on whom while so he
    gazed,
Having all satisfied their bloody thirst,
Their bellies swollen he saw with fullness
    burst,
And bowels gushing forth: well worthy end
115   Of such as drunk her life, the which them
    nursed:
Now needeth him no longer labor spend,
His foes have slain themselves, with whom
    he should contend.

---

13. *avale,* subside.
14. *reed,* see.
15. *Phoebus* (fē'bəs), Apollo, the Greek god of the sun.
16. *welke,* diminish.
17. *cumbrous,* bothersome, annoying.
18. *bestead,* situated.
19. *lin,* stop.
20. *raft,* took off.
21. *corse,* body.
22. *eke,* also.

27

His Lady seeing all that chanced, from far
    Approached in haste to greet his victory,
120   And said, "Fair knight, born under happy
        star,
    Who see your vanquished foes before you lie:
    Well worthy be you of that Armory,[23]
    Wherein you have great glory won this day,
    And proved your strength on a strong
        enemy,
125   Your first adventure: many such I pray,
And henceforth ever wish, that like succeed
        it may."

28

Then mounted he upon his Steed again,
    And with the Lady backward sought to
        wend;
    That path he kept, which beaten was most
        plain,
130   Nor ever would to any byway bend,
    But still did follow one unto the end,
    The which at last out of the wood them
        brought.
    So forward on his way (with God to friend)[24]
    He passed forth, and new adventure sought;
135 Long way he traveled, before he heard of
        aught.

1590

---

23. *Armory,* i.e., the armor of a Christian man (a reference to Ephesians 6:13–14).
24. *to friend,* as a friend.

Discussion

1. (a) Many readers of *The Faerie Queene* have noted its dreamlike quality. What elements in the passage suggest a dream? **(b)** Are the characters individuals or types?

2. The knight represents Holiness; the lady, Truth; the monster, Error. Holiness, with the aid of Truth, crushes Error. Look at the passage as **allegory**. **(a)** In stanza 16, why is the monster afraid of light? **(b)** Discuss the children of the monster—their creation and their death—in allegorical terms.

3. The form, **imagery,** and language of *The Faerie Queene* are in large part the secret of its success. **(a)** What is the effect in the Spenserian stanza of the long last line? Does it convey a sense of rapidity and openness, or the opposite? How does this sense affect the narrative flow? **(b)** Stanzas 25 and 26 present a repulsive sight of the monster's children thriving on their mother's death and then expiring. Examine the imagery and diction to discover how Spenser achieves this effect. **(c)** Show how the Shepherd metaphor in stanza 23 functions in the passage—that is, if the shepherd represents the knight, what do the swarming gnats represent?

Reader's Note: Allegory

An **allegory** is a narrative in which the characters, events, or settings stand for something other than simply themselves. Very frequently they represent abstract ideas such as Faith, Honor, Virtue, but sometimes political, religious, or professional attitudes, beliefs, or personages. Allegory is not, therefore, a literary type in the sense of "sonnet" or "short story." It is, rather, a strategy or technique that can be used in any literary type, poetry or prose. The most famous allegories in English literature are the medieval morality play, *Everyman,* Edmund Spenser's long poem, *The Faerie Queene,* and John Bunyan's prose narrative, *Pilgrim's Progress.*

from *Amoretti*

30

My love is like to ice, and I to fire:
How comes it then that this her cold so great
Is not dissolved through my so hot desire,
But harder grows the more I her entreat?
5 Or how comes it that my exceeding heat
Is not allayed by her heart-frozen cold,
But that I burn much more in boiling sweat,
And feel my flames augmented manifold?
What more miraculous thing may be told,
10 That fire, which all things melts, should
    harden ice,
And ice, which is congealed with senseless
    cold,
Should kindle fire by wonderful device?
Such is the power of love in gentle mind,
That it can alter all the course of kind.[1]

1595

1. *kind,* nature.

75

One day I wrote her name upon the strand,
But came the waves and washèd it away:
Again I wrote it with a second hand,
But came the tide and made my pains his prey.
5 "Vain man," said she, "that dost in vain assay
A mortal thing so to immortalize,
For I myself shall like to this decay,
And eke[1] my name be wipèd out likewise."
"Not so," quoth I, "let baser things devise
10 To die in dust, but you shall live in fame;
My verse your virtues rare shall eternize,
And in the heavens write your glorious name.
Where, whenas death shall all the world
    subdue,
Our love shall live, and later life renew."

1595

1. *eke,* also.

Portrait of unidentified man against a background of flames by Nicholas Hilliard, who introduced the art of the miniature into England.

Discussion

1. A **paradox** is a statement that seems to say two opposite things. What is paradoxical about the central metaphor (fire and ice) of sonnet 30?

2. **(a)** Who is speaking in lines 5–8 of sonnet 75? **(b)** Who is speaking in lines 9–14, and what is he promising?

Sir Philip Sidney 1554–1586

Sir Philip Sidney may be said to epitomize the ideal Renaissance courtier. Of high birth, he received an education that accorded with his background: Shrewsbury School, followed in 1568 by Christ Church College, Oxford, which he left in 1571 without taking his degree, probably because of an outbreak of plague.

For the next several years Sidney traveled on the European continent, including in his itinerary Paris, where he served for several months as Gentleman of the Bedchamber to King Charles IX of France, in which position of honor he undoubtedly learned much about French politics and statesmanship.

Following the Massacre of St. Bartholomew (occurring on August 23, 1572, the eve of the saint's feast) when thousands of French Protestants were killed, Sidney left Paris. For the next several years he traveled in Germany, Hungary, Italy, and the Netherlands, managing to study music and astronomy along the way, and to have his portrait (apparently lost) painted in Venice by Veronese. All of this was done before he was twenty-one.

In 1575 Sidney returned to England and to Elizabeth's court. He accompanied Elizabeth on a visit to the estate of the Earl of Essex, where he met the Earl's thirteen-year-old daughter, Penelope Devereux, whom he later immortalized as the Stella of his sonnet sequence, *Astrophel and Stella,* usually regarded as his greatest literary achievement. This sequence was published posthumously in 1591 and led to a vogue for sonnet sequences, about twenty-five of which have survived.

After a brief assignment as ambassador to Germany, Sidney returned to court in 1580 and possibly incurred Elizabeth's displeasure by writing her a letter opposing her proposed marriage to the Duke of Anjou. Temporarily unwelcome at court, Sidney spent some time with his sister, the Countess of Pembroke, completing for her a prose romance, the *Arcadia,* that he had begun about 1577.

Regarded as the second of Sidney's major literary achievements, this book was published in 1590, in revised form, as *The Countess of Pembroke's Arcadia.* Though written chiefly in prose, it did contain some poems. Lost for more than three hundred years, two manuscript copies of Sidney's original *Arcadia* were found in 1907; several others have since been located.

Sidney's third major literary achievement was a pamphlet titled *An Apology for Poetry,* written around 1583 but first published in 1595. It is usually considered the single most outstanding work of Elizabethan literary theory and criticism.

In 1583 Sidney was knighted and married Frances Walsingham, the daughter of Sir Francis Walsingham, Elizabeth's Secretary of State. In 1585 Sidney was making plans to sail with Sir Francis Drake on a voyage of discovery to the New World when Queen Elizabeth intervened, sending him to the Netherlands to join the Protestant forces there.

In September, 1586, in a minor skirmish, Sidney received a bullet wound in the left thigh. Tradition has it that after he was wounded Sidney gave the last of his water to a dying foot soldier, saying that the soldier had greater need of it than he. Medical care was still primitive, and Sidney died of his wound twenty-six days later.

from *Arcadia*

My true love hath my heart, and I have his,
By just exchange one for the other given:
I hold his dear, and mine he cannot miss;
There never was a bargain better driven.
5 His heart in me keeps me and him in one;
My heart in him his thoughts and senses
    guides:
He loves my heart, for once it was his own;
I cherish his, because in me it bides.
His heart his wound received from my sight;
10 My heart was wounded with his wounded
    heart;
For, as from me on him his hurt did light,
So still me-thought in me his hurt did smart:
Both equal hurt, in this change sought our bliss:
My true love hath my heart and I have his.
1580   1590

from *Astrophel and Stella*

31

With how sad steps, Oh Moon, thou climb'st
    the skies!
How silently, and with how wan a face!
What, may it be that even in heavenly place
That busy archer[1] his sharp arrows tries?
5 Sure, if that long-with-love-acquainted eyes
Can judge of love, thou feel'st a lover's case,
I read it in thy looks—thy languished grace
To me, that feel the like, thy state descries.[2]
Then, even of fellowship, Oh Moon, tell me,
10 Is constant love deemed there but want of wit?
Are beauties there as proud as here they be?
Do they above love to be loved, and yet
Those lovers scorn whom that love doth
    possess?
Do they call virtue there ungratefulness?[3]
                1591

---

1. **archer,** Cupid.
2. **descries,** reveals.
3. **Do . . . ungratefulness?** Do they call ungratefulness a virtue there?

Comment: Sidney's Metaphor

The modern American poet E. E. Cummings (1894–1962) has written a poem astonishingly close in meaning and **metaphor** to Sidney's "My true love hath my heart."

A shepherd, black-thread embroidery, late 16th century.

E. E. Cummings

i carry your heart

i carry your heart with me(i carry it in
my heart)i am never without it(anywhere
i go you go,my dear;and whatever is done
by only me is your doing,my darling)
                  i fear
5 no fate(for you are my fate,my sweet)i want
no world(for beautiful you are my world,my
    true)
and it's you are whatever a moon has always
    meant
and whatever a sun will always sing is you

here is the deepest secret nobody knows
10 (here is the root of the root and the bud of
    the bud
and the sky of the sky of a tree called
    life;which grows
higher than soul can hope or mind can hide)
and this is the wonder that's keeping the
    stars apart

i carry your heart(i carry it in my heart)
                1952

"i carry your heart" by E. E. Cummings from his volume *Complete Poems 1913–1962.* Copyright 1952 by E. E. Cummings. Reprinted by permission of Harcourt Brace Jovanovich, Inc. and Granada Publishing Ltd.

Oft Have I Mused

Oft have I mused, but now at length I find
Why those that die, men say they do depart.
Depart!—a word so gentle, to my mind
Weakly did seem to paint Death's ugly dart.
5 But now the stars, with their strange course,
    do bind
Me one to leave, with whom I leave my heart:
I hear a cry of spirits faint and blind,
That, parting thus, my chiefest part I part.
Part of my life, the loathèd part to me,
10 Lives to impart my weary clay some breath:
But that good part, wherein all comforts be,
Now dead, doth show departure is a death—
Yea, worse than death: death parts both woe
    and joy;
From joy I part, still living in annoy.
1582   1591

Miniature of an unknown young man by Isaac Oliver, c. 1590.

Thou Blind Man's Mark

Thou blind man's mark,[1] thou fool's
    self-chosen snare,
Fond fancy's scum, and dregs of scattered
    thought;
Band[2] of all evils, cradle of causeless care;
Thou web of will, whose end is never wrought;
5 Desire! Desire! I have too dearly bought,
With price of mangled mind, thy worthless ware;
Too long, too long, asleep thou hast me brought,
Who should my mind to higher things prepare.
But yet in vain thou hast my ruin sought;
10 In vain thou mad'st me to vain things aspire;
In vain thou kindlest all thy smoky fire;
For Virtue hath this better lesson taught—
Within myself to seek my only hire,
Desiring naught but how to kill Desire.
1581   1598

---

1. *mark,* target.
2. *Band,* cloth used for swaddling, or wrapping, an infant.

Discussion

1. What does sonnet 31 imply about the speaker's experience with love?

2. Both "My true love hath my heart" and "i carry your heart" make use of a single **conceit** (a fanciful and sometimes farfetched metaphor) in which there is much play on the word "heart." **(a)** How are the two poems alike and how do they differ in developing this conceit? **(b)** Explain line 5 in the Sidney poem: "His heart in me keeps me and him in one." **(c)** Explain lines 3–4 in the Cummings poem: "whatever is done / by only me is your doing, my darling."

3. **(a)** To whom or what is "Thou Blind Man's Mark" addressed? How do you know? **(b)** What is it about?

4. "Oft Have I Mused" says that parting from a loved one is a kind of death. Discuss the similarities and differences between death and parting as described in this poem.

Thomas Campion 1567–1620

A page of music to the poem printed below from Campion's *A Book of Airs* (1601).

Representative of the rising middle class rather than of aristocratic circles, Thomas Campion attended Cambridge and was a law student, but then became a physician as well as an extremely talented poet and composer. In 1591, five of his lyrics were included, without attribution to him, in an unauthorized edition of Sidney's *Astrophel and Stella.* His next appearance in print was in 1595, with *Poemata,* a collection of poems in Latin. Throughout his lifetime he respected classical verse forms, often trying the same idea in both Latin and English verse.

Campion's greatest claim to fame, however, rests on his songs and the music he composed for them. Many of these songs remain as fresh and musical today as they were when they were composed nearly four centuries ago. Called simply *A Book of Airs,* the first of these collections was published in 1601 in collaboration with another songwriter. The lovely lyric, "When to Her Lute Corinna Sings," belongs to this 1601 collection, as does "The Man of Life Upright," marked by its gentle understatement.

About 1613 *Two Books of Airs* was published, followed about 1617 by *The Third and Fourth Book of Airs;* all of these were written by Campion. "Now Winter Nights Enlarge,"

with its description of how Elizabethans spent their winter evenings, belongs to these later collections.

In addition to his songs and Latin verses, Campion wrote four **masques,** elaborate musical productions performed by ladies and gentlemen for the entertainment of courtly society. One of these written in 1605 for Queen Anne, the wife of King James I, called for an orchestra of lutes, cornets, harpsichords, and viols. As the three lyrics that follow show, Campion was a versatile artist, and the musicality of his works is evident even when they are printed without the melodies he wrote for them.

When to Her Lute Corinna Sings

When to her lute Corinna sings,
Her voice revives the leaden strings,
And doth in highest notes appear
As any challenged echo clear;
5 But when she doth of mourning speak,
Even with her sighs the strings do break.

And as her lute doth live or die,
Led by her passion, so must I:
For when of pleasure she doth sing,
10 My thoughts enjoy a sudden spring;
But if she doth of sorrow speak,
Even from my heart the strings do break.

1601

Now Winter Nights Enlarge

Now winter nights enlarge
    The number of their hours,
And clouds their storms discharge
    Upon the airy towers.
5 Let now the chimneys blaze,
    And cups o'erflow with wine;
Let well-tuned words amaze
    With harmony divine.
Now yellow waxen lights
10   Shall wait on honey Love,
While youthful revels, masques,[1] and courtly
    sights
    Sleep's leaden spells remove.

This time doth well dispense
    With[2] lovers' long discourse.
15 Much speech hath some defense
    Though beauty no remorse.
All do not all things well:
    Some measures comely tread,
Some knotted riddles tell,
20   Some poems smoothly read.
The Summer hath his joys,
    And Winter his delights;
Though Love and all his pleasures are but
    toys,
    They shorten tedious nights.

1617

---

1. *masques,* amateur dramatic entertainments with costumes
and scenery.
2. *dispense / With,* allow.

The Man of Life Upright

The man of life upright,
    Whose guiltless heart is free
From all dishonest deeds,
    Or thought of vanity;

5 The man whose silent days
    In harmless joys are spent,
Whom hopes cannot delude,
    Nor sorrow discontent;

That man needs neither towers
10   Nor armor for defense,
Nor secret vaults to fly
    From thunder's violence.

He only can behold
    With unaffrighted eyes
15 The horrors of the deep
    And terrors of the skies.

Thus, scorning all the cares
    That fate or fortune brings,
He makes the heav'n his book,
20   His wisdom heav'nly things,

Good thoughts his only friends,
    His wealth a well-spent age,
The earth his sober inn
    And quiet pilgrimage.

1601

Discussion

1. In what respects is "When to Her Lute" a love poem?

2. Could the person described in "The Man of Life Upright" live in today's world? Justify your answer.

3. "Now Winter Nights Enlarge" describes a world that existed long before anyone could even imagine that someday television would be invented. (a) What did people do then to amuse themselves during the long winter evenings? (b) Were their entertainments really so different from our own? Explain.

Thomas Nashe 1567?–1601

The son of a clergyman, Nashe was educated at St. John's College, Cambridge, then traveled in France and Italy before establishing himself in London in 1588. Along with Christopher Marlowe, he was part of a circle of wild-living, ambitious authors known as the University Wits.

Nashe's best-known work is *The Unfortunate Traveler* (1594), usually regarded as the first English picaresque (adventure) novel. He was also the author of a number of pamphlets, many of them scurrilous, and became involved in a pamphlet war with Gabriel Harvey that ended in censorship of their works.

This was not Nashe's first brush with the law. Earlier he had enlisted Ben Jonson to collaborate with him on a comedy, *The Isle of Dogs* (1597), which was so heavy-handed in its satire that Queen Elizabeth's Privy Council, finding it contained "very seditious and slanderous matter," stopped the performance, closed the theaters, indicted the authors on charges of sedition, and managed to arrest Ben Jonson. Nashe had slipped quietly away to Yarmouth, where he hid for some time.

A woodcut showing Thomas Nashe in chains, from a book that attacks him.

The two lyrics included here come from a masque-like play called *Summer's Last Will and Testament,* written by Nashe for the Archbishop of Canterbury and performed at his palace in Croydon in October, 1592. Once again the plague was raging in London, and Nashe took advantage of the opportunity to connect this outbreak with the death of summer.

*A*utumn

Autumn hath all the summer's fruitful treasure;
Gone is our sport, fled is poor Croydon's[1]
    pleasure.
Short days, sharp days, long nights come on
    apace,
Ah, who shall hide us from the winter's face?
5 Cold doth increase, the sickness will not cease,
And here we lie, God knows, with little ease.
    From winter, plague, and pestilence, good
        Lord, deliver us!

London doth mourn, Lambeth[2] is quite forlorn;
Trades[3] cry, woe worth that ever they were born.
10 The want of term[4] is town and city's harm;

Close chambers we do want, to keep us warm.
Long banishèd must we live from our friends;
This low-built house[5] will bring us to our ends.
    From winter, plague, and pestilence, good
        Lord, deliver us!
1592   1600

---

1. Croydon's, the Archbishop of Canterbury's summer residence, outside London.
2. Lambeth, location of the Archbishop's London residence.
3. Trades, tradespeople.
4. want of term, lack of a conclusion to the plague; there may also be a reference to the Michaelmas school term, which occurred in the autumn.
5. low-built house, the palace of the Archbishop, built in a low and unhealthy location.

A Litany[1] *in Time of Plague*

Adieu, farewell, earth's bliss;
This world uncertain is:
Fond[2] are life's lustful joys;
Death proves them all but toys;
5 None from his darts can fly;
I am sick, I must die.
　　Lord, have mercy on us!

Rich men, trust not in wealth,
Gold cannot buy you health;
10 Physic[3] himself must fade;
All things to end are made;
The plague full swift goes by;
I am sick, I must die.
　　Lord, have mercy on us!

15 Beauty is but a flower
Which wrinkles will devour;
Brightness falls from the air;
Queens have died young and fair;
Dust hath closed Helen's eye;[4]
20 I am sick, I must die.
　　Lord, have mercy on us!

Strength stoops unto the grave,
Worms feed on Hector[5] brave;
Swords may not fight with fate;
25 Earth still holds ope her gate;
Come, come! the bells do cry[6]—
I am sick, I must die.
　　Lord, have mercy on us!

Wit with his wantonness
30 Tasteth death's bitterness;
Hell's executioner
Hath no ears for to hear
What vain art can reply;
I am sick, I must die.
35　　Lord, have mercy on us!

Woodcut of the plague, part of a pamphlet that listed the deaths in the 1592 plague and asked for God's help.

Haste, therefore, each degree[7]
To welcome destiny;
Heaven is our heritage;
Earth but a player's stage;
40 Mount we unto the sky;
I am sick, I must die.
　　Lord, have mercy on us!

1592　　　　　　　　　　　　　1600

1. *Litany,* a prayer consisting of a repeated series of words.
2. *Fond,* foolish.
3. *Physic,* medicine.
4. *Dust . . . eye.* Death has claimed Helen of Troy, supposedly the most beautiful woman in the world.
5. *Hector,* the bravest of the Trojan warriors, killed by Achilles.
6. *the bells do cry,* church bells tolling a death, or perhaps the bells rung by those assigned to cart away the dead.
7. *degree,* social rank or class.

Discussion

1. "A Litany in Time of Plague" may be read as a lament for the end of summer, or as a philosophical lyric that says death will come eventually to all—the rich, the beautiful, the strong, the clever. Which interpretation do you prefer, and why?

2. Which poem strikes you as more melancholy, "A Litany in Time of Plague" or "Autumn"? Why?

William Shakespeare 1564–1616

More than two hundred contemporary references to Shakespeare have been located among church records, legal records, documents in the Public Record Office, and miscellaneous repositories. When these are assembled, we have at least the skeleton outline of his life, beginning with his baptism on April 26, 1564, in Trinity Church, Stratford-on-Avon, and ending with his burial there on April 25, 1616.

Shakespeare's father, John, was a prosperous glove maker of Stratford who, after holding minor municipal offices, was elected high bailiff (the equivalent of mayor) of Stratford. Shakespeare's mother, Mary Arden, came from an affluent family of landowners.

Shakespeare probably received his early education at the excellent Stratford Grammar School, supervised by an Oxford graduate, where he would have learned Latin and a smattering of Greek. In 1582 Shakespeare married Anne Hathaway, who lived in a neighboring hamlet. Susanna, their first child, was born in 1583, followed in 1585 by twins, a boy and a girl, named Hamnet and Judith.

From 1585 to 1592 we have no record of Shakespeare's life. One story, that he was for a time a schoolmaster in the country, has not been proved. At some point in this period, Shakespeare must have moved to London and begun a theatrical career. The next reference to him, an unfavorable one, comes from a pamphlet called *A Groatsworth of Wit* (1592), written by Robert Greene. Addressed by Greene to his fellow University Wits who, like him, had been struggling to earn a living as journalists and playwrights, the pamphlet refers to Shakespeare unflatteringly, calling him "an upstart crow, beautified with our feathers, that with his tiger's heart wrapped in a player's hide supposes he is as well able to bombast out a blank verse as the rest of you; and being an absolute *Johannes fac totum,* is in his own conceit the only Shake-scene in a country."

Apparently Shakespeare, whose background was not that of a University Wit but of a "player" (actor), had been taking some playwriting business away from Greene and his friends, possibly updating plays they had once worked on. The "tiger's heart" phrase is an oblique reference to a line in Shakespeare's *Henry VI, Part 3;* "O tiger's heart wrapped in a woman's hide"; *"Johannes fac totum"* means "jack-of-all-trades," probably because Shakespeare was acting and writing; "Shake-scene" is an obvi-

Shakespeare's Sonnets

18

Shall I compare thee to a summer's day?
Thou art more lovely and more temperate:
Rough winds do shake the darling buds of May,
And summer's lease hath all too short a date:
5 Sometime too hot the eye of heaven shines,
And often is his gold complexion dimmed,
And every fair from fair sometimes declines,
By chance or nature's changing course untrimmed;[1]
But thy eternal summer shall not fade,
10 Nor lose possession of that fair thou owest,[2]
Nor shall Death brag thou wander'st in his shade,
When in eternal lines to time thou growest.
    So long as men can breathe, or eyes can see,
    So long lives this, and this gives life to thee.

1609

---

1. *untrimmed,* reduced; shorn of beauty.
2. *fair thou owest,* beauty you possess.

This bust, sculpted by Geraert Janssen, stands in Trinity Church where Shakespeare is buried. It is believed to be a good likeness of the poet.

ous play on the poet's name. From 1592 to the end of Shakespeare's life, there are many references to him and to his literary output.

Shakespeare's major activity lay in the field of drama. He became a full shareholder in his acting company (the Lord Chamberlain's Men, later the King's Men), he was part-owner of the Globe Theater and later of Blackfriars Theater, and in 1597 he purchased property in Stratford, including New Place, one of the largest houses in the town. He probably retired there about 1610,

traveling to London when necessary to take care of his theatrical business.

Although some of Shakespeare's plays were published during his lifetime, not until after his death was any attempt made to collect them in a single volume. This work was overseen by John Hemings and Henry Condell, fellow actors and close friends of Shakespeare; the First Folio, the first edition of Shakespeare's collected plays, appeared in 1623.

In all, 154 sonnets belong to Shakespeare's sonnet sequence. The sonnets were probably written in the 1590s but were first published in 1609. They tell a fragmentary story involving a young man, a "dark lady," and the poet himself, together with a "rival poet." In sonnets 1–126, the young man has the principal role, while in the remainder the dark lady becomes prominent. Scholars and critics have made many attempts to untangle all the mysteries of Shakespeare's sonnets, as they may shed light on his life, but generally to no avail. It is important to remember that Shakespeare's sonnets were written at a time when such sequences were fashionable, and thus the sonnets may be more an exercise in literary convention than in autobiography.

29

When in disgrace with fortune and men's eyes,
I all alone beweep my outcast state,
And trouble deaf heaven with my bootless[1]
   cries,
And look upon myself and curse my fate,
5 Wishing me like to one more rich in hope,
Featured like him, like him with friends
   possessed,
Desiring this man's art and that man's scope,
With what I most enjoy contented least—
Yet in these thoughts myself almost
   despising,

10 Haply I think on thee, and then my state,
Like to the lark at break of day arising
From sullen earth, sings hymns at heaven's
   gate.
   For thy sweet love remembered such
     wealth brings
   That then I scorn to change my state with
     kings.

1609

---

1. *bootless,* useless.

30

When to the sessions[1] of sweet silent thought
I summon up remembrance of things past,
I sigh the lack of many a thing I sought,
And with old woes new wail my dear time's
    waste:
5 Then can I drown an eye, unused to flow,
For precious friends hid in death's dateless[2]
    night,
And weep afresh love's long since canceled woe,
And moan the expense[3] of many a vanished
    sight:
Then can I grieve at grievances foregone,[4]
10 And heavily from woe to woe tell o'er
The sad account of forebemoanèd moan,
Which I new pay as if not paid before.
    But if the while I think on thee, dear friend,
    All losses are restored and sorrows end.

                       1609

---

1. **sessions,** literally, the sittings of a law court.
2. **dateless,** endless.
3. **expense,** loss.
4. **foregone,** past.

73

That time of year thou mayst in me behold
When yellow leaves, or none, or few, do hang
Upon those boughs which shake against the cold,
Bare ruined choirs[1] where late the sweet
    birds sang.
5 In me thou see'st the twilight of such day
As after sunset fadeth in the west,
Which by and by black night doth take away,
Death's second self, that seals up[2] all in rest.
In me thou see'st the glowing of such fire,
10 That on the ashes of his youth doth lie
As the deathbed whereon it must expire,
Consumed with that which it was nourished by.
    This thou perceivest, which makes thy
      love more strong,
    To love that well which thou must leave
      ere long.

                       1609

---

1. **choirs,** part of a cathedral where services are held.
2. **seals up,** ends, concludes.

71

No longer mourn for me when I am dead
Than you shall hear the surly sullen bell[1]
Give warning to the world that I am fled
From this vile world, with vilest worms to
    dwell:
5 Nay, if you read this line, remember not
The hand that writ it; for I love you so,
That I in your sweet thoughts would be forgot,
If thinking on me then should make you woe.
Oh, if, I say, you look upon this verse
10 When I perhaps compounded am with clay,
Do not so much as my poor name rehearse,
But let your love even with my life decay;
    Lest the wise world should look into your
      moan,
    And mock you with me after I am gone.

                       1609

---

1. **bell,** the bell tolled as someone was dying, in order that
those who heard it might pray for the departing soul.

116

Let me not to the marriage of true minds
Admit impediments. Love is not love
Which alters when it alteration finds,
Or bends with the remover to remove.[1]
5 Oh no! It is an ever-fixèd mark,
That looks on tempests and is never shaken;
It is the star to every wandering bark,
Whose worth's unknown, although his height
    be taken.
Love's not Time's fool, though rosy lips and
    cheeks
10 Within his bending sickle's compass come;
Love alters not with his brief hours and weeks,
But bears it out even to the edge of doom.
    If this be error and upon me proved,
    I never writ, nor no man ever loved.

                       1609

---

1. **Or bends . . . remove,** or changes when the loved one is in-
constant.

130

My mistress' eyes are nothing like the sun;
Coral is far more red than her lips' red;
If snow be white, why then her breasts are dun;
If hairs be wires, black wires grow on her head;
5 I have seen roses damasked,[1] red and white,
But no such roses see I in her cheeks;
And in some perfumes is there more delight
Than in the breath that from my mistress reeks;
I love to hear her speak, yet well I know
10 That music hath a far more pleasing sound;

I grant I never saw a goddess go;[2]
My mistress, when she walks, treads on the
    ground.
  And yet, by heaven, I think my love as rare
  As any she[3] belied with false compare.

1609

---

1. **damasked,** mingled.
2. **go,** walk.
3. **any she,** any woman.

Discussion

1. **(a)** In sonnet 18, does the speaker find more similarities or differences between the person he is addressing and a summer's day? **(b)** In the last line, to what does "this" refer, and how does it give life to the beloved? **(c)** Considering how long ago this sonnet was written, how true is the sentiment expressed in the last six lines? Explain.

2. Sonnets 29 and 30 are sequential. **(a)** What is the situation of the speaker in 29? **(b)** In 30? **(c)** Despite the different situations, how are the two similar?

3. How sincere is the advice given by the speaker in sonnet 71? Explain.

4. Sonnet 73 is a superb example of the English sonnet, with its theme being developed in three stages (lines 1-4, 5-8, 9-12) and brought to a conclusion in the final couplet. By specific references to the sonnet, show how the theme is developed.

5. Comment upon the effectiveness of the closing couplet in sonnet 116.

6. Sonnet 130 is in a way an anti-sonnet. **(a)** What does it do to each of the following conventions of the sonnet: the beauty of the beloved; her golden hair, blue eyes, rosy cheeks, and red lips; her sweet breath; her melodious voice; her graceful walk? **(b)** What then does the concluding couplet do to the meaning of the entire sonnet? To the conventions of the sonnet?

Vocabulary
Combined Skills

Use your Glossary to answer the following questions about the structure of the words listed below. Read each clue and then write on a separate sheet of paper the matching word from the list. Then write a one-word synonym for each word.

allay	discourse	compound
delude	travail	encumber
remorse		

1. Which word has a Latin root that means a kind of exercise?

2. Which word has a prefix and root the literal meanings of which when joined together might describe what one does to individual ingredients to make a stew?

3. Which word has a prefix and root whose literal meanings describe what a dog might do if attacked?

4. Which word has a root that describes something that anchors a tent rope?

5. Which word has an Old English prefix and root, the literal meanings of which you might use in an informal phrase telling someone to stop bothering you?

6. Which has a root that describes what keeps an animal in the zoo?

7. Which has a root the literal meaning of which might describe what a child does?

*M*acbeth William Shakespeare

In 1955 Glen Byam Shaw directed a production of *Macbeth* at Stratford-upon-Avon. Photographs of this production, taken by Angus McBean, are used here to illustrate the play. Macbeth is played by Laurence Olivier, Lady Macbeth by Vivien Leigh.

CHARACTERS

DUNCAN, *king of Scotland*

MALCOLM
DONALBAIN   *his sons*

MACBETH
BANQUO   *generals of the king's army*

MACDUFF
LENNOX
ROSS
MENTEITH   *noblemen of Scotland*
ANGUS
CAITHNESS

FLEANCE, *son to Banquo*
SIWARD, *Earl of Northumberland,*
  general of the English forces

YOUNG SIWARD, *his son*
SEYTON, *an officer attending on Macbeth*
BOY, *son to Macduff*
AN ENGLISH DOCTOR
A SCOTTISH DOCTOR
A CAPTAIN
A PORTER
AN OLD MAN
THREE MURDERERS
LADY MACBETH
LADY MACDUFF
GENTLEWOMAN *attending on Lady Macbeth*
HECATE
THREE WITCHES
APPARITIONS
LORDS, GENTLEMEN, OFFICERS, SOLDIERS,
  ATTENDANTS, AND MESSENGERS

Before you turn to the reading of *Macbeth,* imagine yourself in London about the year 1606. Queen Elizabeth has been dead almost three years and her Scottish cousin, James Stuart, now wears the crown. It is about two o'clock on a summer afternoon, and as you look south across the Thames, you see flags waving from the tops of several public buildings. All Londoners know that these flags indicate performance of plays in the buildings on which they flutter.

The cries of street vendors and the chatter of shop apprentices fade into the distance as you approach the Bankside, the south bank of the Thames, by boat. You hear the beating of drums and the sounding of trumpets, the signal that the play will soon begin. The boatman waits his turn to approach the steps just a short distance from the south gate to London Bridge, the same bridge that Chaucer's pilgrims had crossed, back in the fourteenth century. It is now topped with the eight heads of the recently executed conspirators in the Gunpowder Plot.

As you gain the street again, you are swept along in the crowd. Caught in the mainstream, you are carried almost to within the door of the nearest theater. Glancing above the main entrance, you see prominently displayed a sign with the figure of Hercules supporting the world and know that you are at The Globe. You manage to clear the crowd and to read the red-lettered playbill tacked upon the board.

You pay your entrance penny and pass through the main door. Pushing through the crowded vestibule, you find yourself inside an octagonal auditorium, open to the air except for the thatched roof projecting over the stage and over three tiers of galleries, which line the walls. The stage itself extends to the center of the open area, called the "yard," which is now rapidly filling with "groundlings" or standing spectators. Elbowing each other for standing room and exchanging coarse jests are "sixpenny mechanics," apprentices in greasy leather jackets, and servants wearing their masters' badges. You pay a penny more and are admitted to the gallery sections. For good seats in the lower galleries, called the "twopenny rooms," you pay another twopence.

The trumpets sound again. The crowd begins to quiet. The five or six gallants seated upon the stage continue to play cards and to converse with two or three others sitting in the sideboxes. Just now a boy comes upon the stage bearing a placard on which is written, "A Desert Place." A rumble of thunder is heard, three witches come upon the stage, and the play begins.

Act One

Scene 1.

A desert place. (Played on the Tarras, possibly with the use of the Music Gallery above for one of the three witches.) Thunder and lightning. Enter three WITCHES.

FIRST WITCH. When shall we three meet again
    In thunder, lightning, or in rain?
SECOND WITCH. When the hurlyburly's done,
    When the battle's lost and won.
5 **THIRD WITCH.** That will be ere the set of sun.
FIRST WITCH. Where the place?
SECOND WITCH.   Upon the heath.
THIRD WITCH. There to meet with Macbeth.
FIRST WITCH. I come, Graymalkin!°
SECOND WITCH. Paddock° calls.
10 **THIRD WITCH.** Anon.
ALL. Fair is foul, and foul is fair,[1]
    Hover through the fog and filthy air.[2]

                                       (Exeunt.)

Scene 2.

A camp near Forres.° (Played on the Platform.) Alarum within.° Enter DUNCAN, MALCOLM, DONALBAIN, LENNOX, *with* ATTENDANTS, *meeting a bleeding* CAPTAIN.

DUNCAN.[3] What bloody° man is that? He can report,
    As seemeth by his plight, of the revolt
    The newest state.
MALCOLM.   This is the sergeant°
    Who like a good and hardy soldier fought
5   'Gainst my captivity.[4] Hail, brave friend!
    Say to the King the knowledge of the broil
    As thou didst leave it.
CAPTAIN.   Doubtful it stood,
    As two spent swimmers that do cling together
    And choke their art.° The merciless Macdonwald—
10   Worthy to be a rebel, for to that
    The multiplying villainies of nature
    Do swarm upon him—from the western isles°
    Of kerns° and gallowglasses° is supplied;
    And Fortune, on his damnèd quarrel smiling,

Graymalkin: a gray cat.
Paddock: a toad.

1. *Line 11:* What does this line mean? Be alert for characters and events which illustrate this apparent contradiction.
2. What is the purpose of this scene? In some stage presentations it has been omitted. If you were staging *Macbeth*, would you include it? Why or why not?
Forres: a town north of Edinburgh.
Alarum within: offstage noises indicating that a battle is going on. An alarum usually consisted of confused sounds of trumpets, drums, clash of arms, and men yelling.
3. In reading the speeches of Duncan, consider whether he has the characteristics of a strong king.
bloody: Blood is one of the significant motifs that recur in the play. Others are sleeplessness, animal and bird imagery, clothing metaphors (usually of borrowed or ill-fitting garments), darkness and light, hell and devils, and reversal of accepted values. Note throughout what purpose these motifs might serve.
sergeant: In Shakespeare's day, military ranks were not distinguished so clearly as they are now; although the officer is "Captain" in the stage directions and speech headings, Malcolm may not be incorrect in addressing him as "sergeant."
4. About how old do you guess Malcolm is? As the play progresses, keep this age in mind to see if events support or refute it.
choke their art: hinder their ability to swim.
the western isles: Ireland and the Hebrides.
kerns: lightly-armed Irish foot soldiers.
gallowglasses. Irish foot soldiers armed with axes.

Notes from *On Producing Shakespeare* by Ronald Watkins. First published London 1950 by Michael Joseph, Ltd. Second edition Copyright © 1964 by Benjamin Blom, Inc. Distributed by Arno Press Inc. Reprinted by permission.

15   Showed like a rebel's whore.° But all's too weak;
     For brave Macbeth—well he deserves that name—
     Disdaining Fortune, with his brandished steel,
     Which smoked with bloody execution,
     Like valor's minion° carvéd out his passage
20   Till he faced the slave;°
     Which ne'er shook hands, nor bade farewell to him,
     Till he unseamed him from the nave to the chaps,°
     And fixed his head upon our battlements.
     DUNCAN. O valiant cousin! Worthy gentleman!
25 **CAPTAIN.** As whence the sun 'gins his reflection
     Shipwrecking storms and direful thunders break,
     So from that spring whence comfort seemed to come
     Discomfort swells. Mark, King of Scotland, mark:
     No sooner justice had, with valor armed,
30   Compelled these skipping kerns to trust their heels,
     But the Norweyan° lord, surveying vantage,
     With furbished arms and new supplies of men,
     Began a fresh assault.

Fortune . . . whore: Fortune falsely seemed to favor Macdonwald. (Fortune was often described as a harlot who was fickle and granted her favors to anyone, regardless of worth.)
minion: darling or favorite.
slave: Macdonwald.
unseamed him . . . chaps: split him from navel to jaws.

Norweyan: Norwegian.

DUNCAN.   Dismayed not this
Our captains, Macbeth and Banquo?
CAPTAIN.   Yes—
35 As sparrows eagles, or the hare the lion.
If I say sooth, I must report they were
As cannons overcharged with double cracks,° so they

Doubly redoubled strokes upon the foe;
Except they meant to bathe in reeking wounds,
40 Or memorize another Golgotha,°
I cannot tell.[5]
But I am faint; my gashes cry for help.

DUNCAN. So well thy words become thee as thy wounds;
They smack of honor both. Go get him surgeons.

                        (*Exit* CAPTAIN, *attended.*)

45 Who comes here?

                        (*Enter* ROSS.)

MALCOLM.   The worthy thane° of Ross.

LENNOX. What a haste looks through his eyes! So should he look
That seems to speak things strange.
ROSS.   God save the King!
DUNCAN. Whence cam'st thou, worthy thane?
ROSS.   From Fife, great
    King,
Where the Norweyan banners flout the sky
50 And fan our people cold. Norway himself°
With terrible numbers,

Assisted by that most disloyal traitor,
The thane of Cawdor, began a dismal conflict,
Till that Bellona's bridegroom,° lapped in proof,°
55 Confronted him with self-comparisons,°
Point against point rebellious, arm 'gainst arm,

Curbing his lavish spirit; and, to conclude,
The victory fell on us.
DUNCAN.   Great happiness!
ROSS.   That now
Sweno, the Norways' King, craves composition;°

60 Nor would we deign him burial of his men
Till he disbursed, at Saint Colme's Inch,°
Ten thousand dollars° to our general use.

DUNCAN. No more that thane of Cawdor shall deceive
Our bosom interest.° Go pronounce his present death,
And with his former title greet Macbeth.

ROSS. I'll see it done.
DUNCAN. What he hath lost noble Macbeth hath won.

                        (*Exeunt.*)

Scene 3.

A heath° near Forres. (Played on the Platform and in the Study.)
Thunder. Enter the three WITCHES.

FIRST WITCH. Where hast thou been, sister?
SECOND WITCH. Killing swine.
THIRD WITCH. Sister, where thou?
FIRST WITCH. A sailor's wife had chestnuts in her lap,
5   And munched, and munched, and munched—"Give me," quoth
      I.
    "Aroint thee,° witch!" the rump-fed ronyon° cries.
    Her husband's to Aleppo° gone, master o' the *Tiger*,
    But in a sieve I'll thither sail,
    And, like a rat without a tail,°
10   I'll do, I'll do, and I'll do.
SECOND WITCH. I'll give thee a wind.
FIRST WITCH. Thou'rt kind.
THIRD WITCH. And I another.
FIRST WITCH. I myself have all the other,
15   And the very ports they blow,
    All the quarters that they know
    I' the shipman's card.°
    I will drain him dry as hay;
    Sleep shall neither night nor day
20   Hang upon his penthouse lid;°
    He shall live a man forbid;°
    Weary sev'nights° nine times nine
    Shall he dwindle, peak, and pine;
    Though his bark cannot be lost,
25   Yet it shall be tempest-tossed.[6]
    Look what I have.
SECOND WITCH. Show me, show me.
FIRST WITCH. Here I have a pilot's thumb,
    Wrecked as homeward he did come.

(Drum within.)

30 THIRD WITCH. A drum, a drum!
    Macbeth doth come!
ALL. The weird sisters, hand in hand
    Posters of° the sea and land,
    Thus do go about, about;
35   Thrice to thine, and thrice to mine,
    And thrice again to make up nine.°
    Peace! the charm's wound up.°

(Enter MACBETH *and* BANQUO.*)*

MACBETH. So foul and fair a day I have not seen.[7]
BANQUO. How far is 't called to Forres?° What are these
40   So withered, and so wild in their attire,
    That look not like the inhabitants o' the earth,
    And yet are on 't? Live you?° Or are you aught

(The heath-set in the Study might contain gaunt bushes, their shape indicating that the wind is blowing strongly toward the point of Macbeth's entry. The grave-trap may be open—perhaps disguised with a stone or a turf-bank—ready to receive one of the disappearing sisters.)

Aroint thee: begone.
rump-fed ronyon: mangy creature, fed on refuse.
Aleppo: city in NW Syria, famous as a trading center.
without a tail: It was believed that witches could change themselves into animals, but could be detected by some deformity.

shipman's card: compass card or chart.

penthouse lid: eyelid.
forbid: accursed.
sev'nights: weeks

6. Lines 24–25: What do these lines indicate about the extent of the witches' power?

Posters of: travelers over.
(The weird sisters . . . nine: This incantation might accompany a ritual dance with which the witches mark out in the center of the Platform a charmed circle for Macbeth to step into.)
(Peace! . . . up: They retreat hastily to the perimeter outside the Stage-Post on the opposite side from the door of Macbeth's entry.)
7. Line 38: What earlier lines is Macbeth echoing? What does he mean? Why might Shakespeare have given him this line?
(How . . . Forres? Shouted through fog to the distant figures.)
(Live you? Spoken at close range.)

That man may question? You seem to understand me,
By each at once her choppy finger laying
45   Upon her skinny lips.[8] You should be women,
And yet your beards forbid me to interpret
That you are so.
MACBETH.   Speak, if you can; what are you?°
FIRST WITCH. All hail, Macbeth! hail to thee, thane of Glamis!°
SECOND WITCH. All hail, Macbeth! hail to thee, thane of Cawdor!
50 THIRD WITCH. All hail, Macbeth, that shalt be king hereafter!
BANQUO. Good sir, why do you start,[9] and seem to fear
Things that do sound so fair? I' the name of truth,
Are ye fantastical, or that indeed
Which outwardly ye show? My noble partner
55   You greet with present grace and great prediction
Of noble having and of royal hope,
That he seems rapt withal;° to me you speak not.
If you can look into the seeds of time,
And say which grain will grow and which will not,
60   Speak then to me, who neither beg nor fear
Your favors nor your hate.

8. *Lines 44–45:* The witches gesture ''silence'' in response to Banquo's question, yet they answer Macbeth at once. What does this show about the nature of their spell?
(Speak . . . you? As he enters, Macbeth might move into the charmed circle the witches have made, reacting from the spell with a shudder. Banquo's course would be in front of the circle. Macbeth would then speak from the circle.)
Glamis: (glämz)
9. Why *does* Macbeth start? As you read on, compare his reaction to the witches' prophecies with Banquo's reaction. What do the reactions of the two men reveal? What might this suggest about the future action of the play?
rapt withal: completely lost in thought.

FIRST WITCH. Hail!

SECOND WITCH. Hail!

THIRD WITCH. Hail!

65 **FIRST WITCH.** Lesser than Macbeth, and greater.

SECOND WITCH. Not so happy, yet much happier.

THIRD WITCH. Thou shalt get° kings, though thou be none.   ***get:*** beget.
    So all hail, Macbeth and Banquo!

FIRST WITCH. Banquo and Macbeth, all hail!

70 **MACBETH.** Stay, you imperfect speakers, tell me more.
    By Sinel's° death I know I am thane of Glamis;   ***Sinel:*** Macbeth's father. Macbeth had
    But how of Cawdor? The thane of Cawdor lives,   inherited the title.
    A prosperous gentleman. And to be king
    Stands not within the prospect of belief,
75   No more than to be Cawdor. Say from whence
    You owe this strange intelligence? Or why
    Upon this blasted heath you stop our way
    With such prophetic greeting? Speak, I charge you.

                        (WITCHES vanish.)°   ***(vanish:*** through the grave-trap in the
Study.)

BANQUO. The earth hath bubbles, as the water has,
80   And these are of them. Whither are they vanished?

MACBETH. Into the air, and what seemed corporal melted
    As breath into the wind. Would they had stayed!

BANQUO. Were such things here as we do speak about?
    Or have we eaten on the insane root°   ***insane root:*** a root that causes
85   That takes the reason prisoner?   hallucinations or insanity.

MACBETH. Your children shall be kings.

BANQUO.   You shall be king.

MACBETH. And thane of Cawdor, too; went it not so?

BANQUO. To the selfsame tune and words. Who's here?

                        (Enter ROSS *and* ANGUS.)

ROSS. The King hath happily received, Macbeth,
90   The news of thy success; and when he reads
    Thy personal venture in the rebels' fight,
    His wonders and his praises do contend
    Which should be thine or his. Silenced° with that,   ***Silenced:*** speechless with admiration.
    In viewing o'er the rest o' the selfsame day,
95   He finds thee in the stout Norweyan ranks,
    Nothing afeared of what thyself didst make,   ***Nothing . . . death:*** Macbeth killed, but
    Strange images of death.° As thick as hail   did not fear death for himself.
    Came post with post,° and everyone did bear   ***post with post:*** one newsbearer after
    Thy praises in his kingdom's great defense,   another.
100   And poured them down before him.

ANGUS.   We are sent
    To give thee from our royal master thanks;
    Only to herald thee into his sight,
    Not pay thee.

ROSS.   And, for an earnest° of a greater honor,   ***earnest:*** pledge; promise.
    He bade me, from him, call thee thane of Cawdor;
105   In which addition, hail, most worthy thane!
    For it is thine.

BANQUO.   What, can the devil speak true?

MACBETH. The thane of Cawdor lives; why do you dress me
In borrowed robes?

ANGUS.   Who was the thane lives yet;
But under heavy judgment bears that life
110   Which he deserves to lose. Whether he was combined
With those of Norway, or did line° the rebel
With hidden help and vantage, or that with both
He labored in his country's wreck, I know not;
But treasons capital, confessed and proved,
115   Have overthrown him.

MACBETH (*aside*).   Glamis, and thane of Cawdor!
The greatest is behind.°[10] (*To* ROSS *and* ANGUS) Thanks for your
    pains.
(*To* BANQUO) Do you not hope your children shall be kings,
When those that gave the thane of Cawdor to me
Promised no less to them?

BANQUO.   That, trusted home,
120   Might yet enkindle you unto the crown,°
Besides the thane of Cawdor. But 'tis strange;
And oftentimes, to win us to our harm,
The instruments of darkness tell us truths,
Win us with honest trifles, to betray's
125   In deepest consequence.
Cousins, a word, I pray you.

MACBETH (*aside*).   Two truths are told,
As happy prologues to the swelling act
Of the imperial theme.—I thank you, gentlemen.
(*Aside*) This supernatural soliciting
130   Cannot be ill, cannot be good; if ill,
Why hath it given me earnest of success,
Commencing in a truth? I am thane of Cawdor;
If good, why do I yield to that suggestion
Whose horrid image doth unfix my hair
135   And make my seated heart knock at my ribs,
Against the use of nature? Present fears
Are less than horrible imaginings;
My thought, whose murder yet is but fantastical,
Shakes so my single state of man that function
140   Is smothered in surmise, and nothing is
But what is not.°[11]

BANQUO.   Look, how our partner's rapt.

MACBETH (*aside*). If chance will have me king, why, chance
    may crown me,
Without my stir.

BANQUO.   New honors come upon him,
Like our strange garments,° cleave not to their mold
145   But with the aid of use.

line: support.

behind: to come.
10. What has Ross said earlier that would allow Macbeth to say, "The greatest is behind"—even if he had not had the confrontation with the witches? Contrast Macbeth's reactions with Banquo's.

That . . . crown: Complete belief in the witches may arouse in you the ambition to become king. (Note the word "enkindle.")

My thought . . . is not: My thought, in which the murder is still only a fantasy, so disturbs me that all power of action is smothered by imagination, and only unreal imaginings seem real to me.
11. Note the ambivalent feelings Macbeth expresses in this aside. Which side of his nature seems to predominate here?

strange garments: new clothes.

MACBETH (aside).   Come what come may,
  Time and the hour runs through the roughest day.[12]
BANQUO. Worthy Macbeth, we stay upon your leisure.°
MACBETH. Give me your favor; my dull brain was wrought
  With things forgotten. Kind gentlemen, your pains
150 Are registered where every day I turn
  The leaf to read them.° Let us toward the King.
  Think upon what hath chanced, and, at more time,
  The interim having weighed it, let us speak
  Our free hearts each to other.[13]
BANQUO.   Very gladly.
155 MACBETH. Till then, enough. Come, friends.

                                    (Exeunt.)

Scene 4.

Forres. The palace. (Played on the Platform.) Flourish.° Enter
DUNCAN, MALCOLM, DONALBAIN, LENNOX, *and* ATTENDANTS.

DUNCAN. Is execution done on Cawdor? Are not
  Those in commission yet returned?
MALCOLM.   My liege,
  They are not yet come back. But I have spoke
  With one that saw him die; who did report
5 That very frankly he confessed his treasons,
  Implored your Highness' pardon, and set forth
  A deep repentance. Nothing in his life
  Became him like the leaving it; he died
  As one that had been studied in his death
10 To throw away the dearest thing he owed,
  As 'twere a careless trifle.
DUNCAN.   There's no art
  To find the mind's construction in the face.°
  He was a gentleman on whom I built
  An absolute trust.[14]
              (*Enter* MACBETH, BANQUO, ROSS, *and* ANGUS.)
                    O worthiest cousin!
15 The sin of my ingratitude even now
  Was heavy on me; thou art so far before
  The swiftest wing of recompense is slow
  To overtake thee. Would thou hadst less deserved,
  That the proportion both of thanks and payment
20 Might have been mine! Only I have left to say,
  More is thy due than more than all can pay.[15]
MACBETH. The service and the loyalty I owe,
  In doing it, pays itself. Your Highness' part
  Is to receive our duties; and our duties
25 Are to your throne and state, children and servants,
  Which do but what they should, by doing every thing
  Safe toward your love and honor.[16]

DUNCAN.   Welcome hither;
    I have begun to plant thee, and will labor
    To make thee full of growing.[17] Noble Banquo,
30 That hast no less deserved, nor must be known
    No less to have done so, let me enfold thee
    And hold thee to my heart.
BANQUO.   There if I grow,
    The harvest is your own.
DUNCAN.   My plenteous joys,
    Wanton in fullness, seek to hide themselves
35 In drops of sorrow.[18] Sons, kinsmen, thanes,
    And you whose places are the nearest, know
    We will establish our estate upon°
    Our eldest, Malcolm, whom we name hereafter
    The Prince of Cumberland;[19] which honor must
40 Not unaccompanied invest him only,
    But signs of nobleness, like stars, shall shine
    On all deservers. From hence to Inverness,°
    And bind us further to you.
MACBETH. The rest is labor which is not used for you.°
45 I'll be myself the harbinger, and make joyful
    The hearing of my wife with your approach;
    So humbly take my leave.
DUNCAN.   My worthy Cawdor!
MACBETH (aside). The Prince of Cumberland! that is a step
    On which I must fall down, or else o'erleap,
50 For in my way it lies. Stars, hide your fires;
    Let not light see my black and deep desires;
    The eye wink at the hand; yet let that be
    Which the eye fears, when it is done, to see.[20]

                                                    (Exit.)

DUNCAN. True, worthy Banquo; he is full so valiant,[21]
55 And in his commendations I am fed;
    It is a banquet to me. Let's after him,
    Whose care is gone before to bid us welcome.
    It is a peerless kinsman.

                                (Flourish. Exeunt.)

Scene 5.
Inverness. MACBETH's *castle. (Played in the Chamber.) Enter* LADY
MACBETH, *reading a letter.*

LADY MACBETH. "They met me in the day of success; and I have
    learned by the perfectest report they have more in them than mor-
    tal knowledge. When I burned in desire to question them further,
    they made themselves air, into which they vanished. Whiles I
5   stood rapt in the wonder of it, came missives° from the King,
    who all-hailed me 'Thane of Cawdor'; by which title, before, these
    weird sisters saluted me, and referred me to the coming-on of

17. *I have begun . . . growing:* What
does Duncan mean?

18. *My plenteous joys . . . sorrow:*
What does Duncan say in his physical
reaction?
establish . . . upon: name as heir to
the throne.

19. *Lines 35–39a:* How should the
actor playing Macbeth react here? Why
might Duncan pick this moment and
this company to name Malcolm his
successor?
Inverness: Macbeth's castle.

The rest . . . you: Resting is work for
me, when I am doing nothing to help
you.

20. *Lines 48–53:* Is Macbeth's reaction
at all surprising? Is it justified? What
does his speech suggest may be his
"black and deep desires"?
21. To whom is Duncan referring?
What do you think Banquo has just
been saying to Duncan?

missives: messages.

time, with 'Hail, king that shalt be!' This have I thought good to
deliver thee, my dearest partner of greatness, that thou mightst
10 not lose the dues of rejoicing, by being ignorant of what greatness
is promised thee. Lay it to thy heart, and farewell.''²²
Glamis thou art, and Cawdor; and shalt be
What thou art promised. Yet do I fear thy nature;
It is too full o' the milk of human kindness
15 To catch the nearest way.²³ Thou wouldst be great;
Art not without ambition, but without
The illness° should attend it. What thou wouldst highly,
That wouldst thou holily; wouldst not play false,
And yet wouldst wrongly win. Thou 'ldst have, great Glamis,
20 That which cries, ''Thus thou must do, if thou have it'';
And that which rather thou dost fear to do
Than wishest should be undone. Hie thee hither,
That I may pour my spirits in thine ear,
And chastise with the valor of my tongue
25 All that impedes thee from the golden round,°
Which fate and metaphysical aid doth seem
To have thee crowned withal.²⁴

(*Enter a* MESSENGER.)
What is your tidings?
MESSENGER. The King comes here tonight.
LADY MACBETH.   Thou'rt mad to say it!²⁵
Is not thy master with him? Who, were't so,
30 Would have informed for preparation.
MESSENGER. So please you, it is true; our thane is coming;
One of my fellows had the speed of him,°
Who, almost dead for breath, had scarcely more
Than would make up his message.
LADY MACBETH.   Give him tending;
35 He brings great news.²⁶

(*Exit* MESSENGER.)
The raven° himself is hoarse
That croaks the fatal entrance of Duncan
Under my battlements. Come, you spirits
That tend on mortal thoughts,° unsex me here,
And fill me from the crown to the toe top-full
40 Of direst cruelty! make thick my blood;
Stop up the access and passage to remorse,
That no compunctious visitings of nature°
Shake my fell²⁷ purpose, nor keep peace between
The effect and it!° Come to my woman's breasts,
45 And take my milk for gall, you murdering ministers,
Wherever in your sightless substances
You wait on nature's mischief! Come, thick night,
And pall° thee in the dunnest° smoke of hell,
That my keen knife see not the wound it makes,²⁸

22. What does the letter reveal about their relationship? Which phrases in the letter are especially significant?

23. How does Lady Macbeth's first reaction to the witches' prophecies differ from Macbeth's?
illness: unscrupulousness.

golden round: the crown.

24. In what ways does Lady Macbeth's description of her husband reinforce your impression of the ambivalence of his character?

25. In what tone of voice would she say this? What would be her tone in the next sentence? Why?

had the speed of him: outdistanced him.

26. *Line 35a:* What thought has just occurred to Lady Macbeth?

raven: Long believed to be a bird of ill omen, the raven was said to foretell death by its croaking.

mortal thoughts: murderous thoughts.

compunctious . . . nature: natural feelings of compassion.
27. The word *fell* has many meanings. What ''reverberations'' does it set up in your mind? Which meaning(s) applies?
keep peace . . . and it: come between my intention and my carrying out of it.

pall: wrap.
dunnest: darkest; murkiest.
28. At this point, who does Lady Macbeth think will commit the murder?

50   Nor heaven peep through the blanket of the dark,
      To cry, "Hold, hold!"[29]

                              (Enter MACBETH.*)*
                  Great Glamis! Worthy Cawdor!
      Greater than both, by the all-hail hereafter!
      Thy letters have transported me beyond
      This ignorant present, and I feel now
55   The future in the instant.
      MACBETH.   My dearest love,
      Duncan comes here tonight.
      LADY MACBETH.   And when goes hence?
      MACBETH. Tomorrow, as he purposes.[30]
      LADY MACBETH.   O never
      Shall sun that morrow see!
      Your face, my thane, is as a book where men
60   May read strange matters. To beguile the time,
      Look like the time;° bear welcome in your eye,
      Your hand, your tongue. Look like the innocent flower,
      But be the serpent under 't. He that's coming
      Must be provided for;[31] and you shall put
65   This night's great business into my dispatch,°
      Which shall to all our nights and days to come
      Give solely sovereign sway and masterdom.
      MACBETH. We will speak further.[32]
      LADY MACBETH.   Only look up clear;
      To alter favor ever is to fear°—
70   Leave all the rest to me.

                                   (Exeunt.)

Scene 6.

Before MACBETH'*s castle. (Played on the Platform.) Hautboys°*
and torches. Enter DUNCAN, MALCOLM, DONALBAIN, BANQUO,
LENNOX, MACDUFF, ROSS, ANGUS, *and* ATTENDANTS.

      DUNCAN. This castle hath a pleasant seat; the air
      Nimbly and sweetly recommends itself
      Unto our gentle senses.[33]
      BANQUO.   This guest of summer,
      The temple-haunting martlet,° does approve,°
5   By his loved mansionry, that the heaven's breath
      Smells wooingly here. No jutty, frieze,
      Buttress, nor coign of vantage but this bird
      Hath made his pendent bed and procreant cradle;
      Where they most breed and haunt, I have observed,
10   The air is delicate.[34]
                              (Enter LADY MACBETH.*)*
      DUNCAN.   See, see, our honored hostess!
      The love that follows us sometime is our trouble,
      Which still we thank as love. Herein I teach you

29. *Lines 35–51a:* What is Lady
Macbeth trying to do in this speech?
What conflict in her character is
revealed by the conflict between her
expressed desires and the nurturing
metaphor she uses?

30. How does Macbeth say this?
(Firmly? tentatively?)

To beguile . . . time: to deceive the
world, appear as it demands or
expects.

31. In what senses does she use the
phrase "provided for"?
dispatch: care.

32. Is Macbeth completely convinced?

To alter . . . fear: to change facial
expression shows fear.

Hautboys: a band of oboelike
instruments, generally used by
Shakespeare in connection with a
procession or a banquet.

33. Note that almost all Duncan's lines
may be read in an ominous, ironic
sense.
martlet: martin, a bird of the swallow
family.
approve: demonstrate.

34. *Lines 1–10:* Contrast these lines
with Lady Macbeth's reference to the
raven in Act One, Scene 5, 35b–37a.

How you shall bid God 'ild° us for your pains,
And thank us for your trouble.°

LADY MACBETH.   All our service
15 In every point twice done and then done double[35]
Were poor and single business to contend
Against those honors deep and broad wherewith
Your Majesty loads our house; for those of old,
And the late dignities heaped up to them,
20 We rest your hermits.°

DUCAN.   Where's the thane of Cawdor?
We coursed him at the heels, and had a purpose
To be his purveyor;° but he rides well,
And his great love, sharp as his spur, hath holp him
To his home before us. Fair and noble hostess,
25 We are your guests tonight.

LADY MACBETH.   Your servants ever
Have theirs, themselves, and what is theirs, in compt,
To make their audit at your Highness' pleasure,
Still to return your own.°

DUNCAN.   Give me your hand;
Conduct me to mine host. We love him highly,
30 And shall continue our graces toward him.
By your leave, hostess.

                                    (Exeunt.)

Scene 7.
Outside a banqueting hall in MACBETH's *castle. (Played on the
Platform.) Hautboys and torches. Enter a* SEWER,° *and divers*
SERVANTS *with dishes and service, and pass over the stage. Then
enter* MACBETH.

MACBETH. If it were done when 'tis done, then 'twere well
It were done quickly; if the assassination
Could trammel up the consequence, and catch
With his surcease° success; that but this blow
5 Might be the be-all and the end-all here,
But here, upon this bank and shoal of time,
We'd jump° the life to come. But in these cases
We still have judgment here; that we but teach
Bloody instructions,[36] which, being taught, return
10 To plague the inventor; this even-handed justice
Commends the ingredients of our poisoned chalice
To our own lips. He's here in double trust:
First, as I am his kinsman and his subject,
Strong both against the deed; then, as his host,
15 Who should against his murderer shut the door,
Not bear the knife myself. Besides, this Duncan
Hath borne his faculties° so meek, hath been
So clear in his great office, that his virtues

God 'ild: literally "God yield," used in returning thanks.
The love . . . your trouble: Duncan means that, since he is there because he loves them, they should thank him even for the trouble he causes them.
35. What might be ironic in these lines?

We rest your hermits: Like hermits, we will pray for you.

purveyor: forerunner.

Your servants . . . own: Since we are your servants, all that we have is subject to account and ready to be delivered to you.

Sewer: servant who arranges the dining table. (Stage business: ". . . the comedy gang of the company make a brief appearance, one no doubt unpunctual, another caught tasting the dish he carries. They will form up for inspection by the Sewer, before marching into the banquet-hall [the Chamber]: noises of merriment from inside will become suddenly louder and more hilarious as they disappear, and will be hushed all at once as an unseen door bangs shut. Macbeth comes swiftly onto the empty Platform in the sudden silence."—Watkins)
surcease: death.
jump: risk.
36. This soliloquy has been a rich source of titles for mystery books, such as *Bloody Instructions* (line 9). How many suitable titles can you find?

faculties: royal power.

Will plead like angels, trumpet-tongued, against
20 The deep damnation of his taking-off,°
And pity, like a naked, new-born babe,
Striding the blast,° or heaven's cherubim, horsed
Upon the sightless couriers of the air,°
Shall blow the horrid deed in every eye,
25 That tears shall drown the wind. I have no spur
To prick the sides of my intent, but only
Vaulting ambition, which o'erleaps itself
And falls on the other.°37

(Enter LADY MACBETH.*)*
            How now! what news?

30 LADY MACBETH. He has almost supped; why have you left the chamber?
MACBETH. Hath he asked for me?
LADY MACBETH.   Know you not he has?
MACBETH. We will proceed no further in this business.
He hath honored me of late; and I have bought
Golden opinions from all sorts of people,
Which would be worn now in their newest gloss,
35 Not cast aside so soon.38
LADY MACBETH.39   Was the hope drunk
Wherein you dressed yourself? Hath it slept since?
And wakes it now, to look so green and pale
At what it did so freely? From this time
Such I account thy love. Art thou afeard
40 To be the same in thine own act and valor

taking-off: murder.
Striding the blast: riding the wind.
couriers of the air: winds.
I have . . . the other: I have nothing to stimulate me to the execution of my purpose but ambition, which is apt to overreach itself. ("Overreaching" is expressed here by the image of a person meaning ʋo vault into his saddle who takes too great a leap and falls on the other side of his horse.)

37. In what specific ways does this soliloquy support Lady Macbeth's estimate of Macbeth?

38. What does Macbeth give as his reason for not proceeding with the murder? Is this explanation in accord, with what he said in his soliloquy (lines 1–28)? If not, why does he offer a different reason to his wife?
39. Trace through the arguments by which she works to convince her husband to go through with the murder. Is this a plausible scene? Why or why not?

As thou art in desire? Wouldst thou have that
Which thou esteem'st the ornament of life,°
And live a coward in thine own esteem,
Letting "I dare not" wait upon "I would,"
45   Like the poor cat i' the adage?°

MACBETH.   Prithee, peace.
I dare do all that may become a man;
Who dares do more is none.[40]

LADY MACBETH.   What beast was't, then,
That made you break this enterprise to me?[41]
When you durst do it, then you were a man;
50   And, to be more than what you were, you would
Be so much more the man. Nor time nor place
Did then adhere,° and yet you would make both;
They have made themselves, and that their fitness now
Does unmake you. I have given suck, and know
55   How tender 'tis to love the babe that milks me;
I would, while it was smiling in my face,
Have plucked my nipple from his boneless gums,
And dashed the brains out,[42] had I so sworn as you
Have done to this.

MACBETH.   If we should fail?

LADY MACBETH.   We fail![43]
60   But screw your courage to the sticking-place,°
And we'll not fail.[44] When Duncan is asleep—
Whereto the rather shall this day's hard journey
Soundly invite him—his two chamberlains
Will I with wine and wassail so convince
65   That memory, the warder of the brain,
Shall be a fume, and the receipt of reason
A limbeck only.° When in swinish sleep
Their drenched natures lie as in a death,
What cannot you and I perform upon
70   The unguarded Duncan?[45] What not put upon
His spongy° officers, who shall bear the guilt
Of our great quell?°

MACBETH.   Bring forth men-children only
For thy undaunted mettle should compose
Nothing but males. Will it not be received,
75   When we have marked with blood those sleepy two
Of his own chamber and used their very daggers,
That they have done 't?

LADY MACBETH.   Who dares receive it other,
As we shall make our griefs and clamor roar
Upon his death?

MACBETH.   I am settled, and bend up
80   Each corporal agent to this terrible feat.°
Away, and mock the time with fairest show;
False face must hide what the false heart doth know.[46]

                                   (Exeunt.)

---

ornament of life: the crown.

cat . . . adage: The adage is "The cat would eat fish, but would not wet her feet."

40. How does Macbeth say this: pleadingly? mildly? defensively? angrily?

41. Did he explicitly "break it" to her, or did he merely suggest it?

Nor time . . . adhere: There was no suitable time or place to commit the murder.

42. *Lines 54–59a:* To what earlier speech by Lady Macbeth do these lines bear a resemblance?

43. Editors of *Macbeth* have punctuated this line variously as either "We fail!" or "We fail?" How would the change in punctuation affect the meaning?

But screw . . . place: The image is drawn from the mechanical device used to prepare a crossbow for firing.

44. Lady Macbeth has been angry. How does her tone change here? Why?

memory . . . only: memory and reason both will dissipate, like the vapor of the alcohol they drink. This complicated image compares the human brain to the apparatus used in distilling alcohol.

45. Who does Lady Macbeth now say will commit the murder?

spongy: drunken.

quell: murder.

bend up . . . feat: direct all my bodily powers to executing the murder.

46. Macbeth has made up his mind to commit the murder. Has he convinced himself that what he is about to do is morally justified?

Act Two

Scene 1.

Court of MACBETH's *castle. (Played on the Platform.) Enter*
BANQUO, *and* FLEANCE *bearing a torch before him.*

BANQUO. How goes the night, boy?
FLEANCE. The moon is down; I have not heard the clock.
BANQUO. And she goes down at twelve.
FLEANCE.   I take 't, 'tis later, sir.
BANQUO. Hold, take my sword. There's husbandry° in heaven;
5   Their candles are all out. Take thee that,⁴⁷ too.
    A heavy summons lies like lead upon me,
    And yet I would not sleep; merciful powers,
    Restrain in me the curséd thoughts that nature
    Gives way to in repose!⁴⁸
                        (Enter MACBETH, *and a* SERVANT *with a torch.)*
                        Give me my sword.
10   Who's there?
MACBETH. A friend.
BANQUO. What, sir, not yet at rest? The King's abed.
    He hath been in unusual pleasure, and
    Sent forth great largess to your offices.°
15   This diamond he greets your wife withal,⁴⁹
    By the name of most kind hostess; and shut up
    In measureless content.°
MACBETH.   Being unprepared,
    Our will became the servant to defect,
    Which else should free have wrought.°
BANQUO.   All's well.
20   I dreamt last night of the three weird sisters;
    To you they have showed some truth.
MACBETH.   I think not of them;
    Yet, when we can entreat an hour to serve,
    We would spend it in some words upon that business,
    If you would grant the time.
BANQUO.   At your kind'st leisure.
25 **MACBETH.** If you shall cleave to my consent, when 'tis,°
    It shall make honor for you.
BANQUO.   So I lose none
    In seeking to augment it, but still keep
    My bosom franchised and allegiance clear,
    I shall be counseled.°⁵⁰
MACBETH.   Good repose the while!
30 **BANQUO.** Thanks, sir. The like to you!
                        (Exeunt BANQUO *and* FLEANCE.)*
MACBETH. Go bid thy mistress, when my drink is ready,
    She strike upon the bell. Get thee to bed.
                        (Exit SERVANT.)*

    Is this a dagger which I see before me,

husbandry: economy.
47. What might "that" be?

48. What is bothering Banquo? What might his "cursed thoughts" be?

great largess . . . offices: many gifts of money to be distributed among your servants.
49. Why does Shakespeare have Banquo instead of Duncan give the diamond?
shut up . . . content: has ended his day greatly contented.
Being unprepared . . . wrought: The unexpectedness of Duncan's visit has prevented us from entertaining him as we would have liked.

If you . . . when 'tis: If you ally yourself with me, when the time comes.
So I . . . counseled: As long as I do not lose my honor in trying to increase it, and keep myself free and my loyalty to Duncan unstained, I will listen to you.

50. *Lines 26–29:* Why might Banquo be suspicious at this point? What do these lines tell you about his character?

The handle toward my hand? Come, let me clutch thee.
35 I have thee not, and yet I see thee still.
Art thou not, fatal vision, sensible
To feeling as to sight? Or art thou but
A dagger of the mind, a false creation,
Proceeding from the heat-oppressèd brain?[51]
40 I see thee yet, in form as palpable
As this which now I draw.
Thou marshal'st me° the way that I was going,
And such an instrument I was to use.
Mine eyes are made the fools o' the other senses,
45 Or else worth all the rest; I see thee still,
And on thy blade and dudgeon° gouts of blood,
Which was not so before. There's no such thing;
It is the bloody business which informs°
Thus to mine eyes. Now o'er the one half world
50 Nature seems dead, and wicked dreams abuse
The curtained sleep; witchcraft celebrates
Pale Hecate's° offerings, and withered murder,
Alarumed by his sentinel, the wolf,
Whose howl's his watch, thus with his stealthy pace,
55 With Tarquin's° ravishing strides, toward his design
Moves like a ghost. Thou sure and firm-set earth,
Hear not my steps, which way they walk, for fear
Thy very stones prate of my whereabout,
And take the present horror from the time,
60 Which now suits with it. Whiles I threat, he lives;
Words to the heat of deeds too cold breath gives.

(*A bell rings.*)

I go, and it is done; the bell invites me.
Hear it not, Duncan; for it is a knell
That summons thee to heaven or to hell.

(*Exit.*)°

51. (a) If you were directing a stage production of *Macbeth,* would you have the dagger physically appear before Macbeth, or would you have him address the empty air?
  (b) What does the imaginary dagger reveal about Macbeth's character in general, and his feelings about the murder specifically?
Thou marshal'st me: you conduct, lead me.
dudgeon: hilt.

informs: appears.

Hecate: goddess of witchcraft.

Tarquin: one of the tyrannical kings of early Rome, who ravished the chaste Lucrece.

(Macbeth exits through the Study, which presumably leads to Duncan's chamber.)

Scene 2.

The same. (Played in the Study and on the Platform.) Enter LADY MACBETH.°

LADY MACBETH. That which hath made them drunk hath made me
    bold;
  What hath quenched them hath given me fire. Hark! Peace!
  It was the owl that shrieked, the fatal bellman,°
  Which gives the stern'st good-night. He is about it.
5 The doors are open; and the surfeited grooms
  Do mock their charge with snores. I have drugged their pos-
    sets,°
  That death and nature do contend about them,
  Whether they live or die.
MACBETH (*within*). Who's there? What, ho!°
10 LADY MACBETH. Alack, I am afraid they have awaked,
  And 'tis not done. The attempt and not the deed
  Confounds us. Hark! I laid their daggers ready;
  He could not miss 'em. Had he not resembled
  My father as he slept, I had done 't.[52]

                        (Enter MACBETH.)°
                      My husband!

15 MACBETH. I have done the deed. Didst thou not hear a noise?
LADY MACBETH. I heard the owl scream and the crickets cry.
  Did not you speak?
MACBETH.   When?
LADY MACBETH.   Now.
MACBETH.   As I descended?
LADY MACBETH. Aye.
MACBETH. Hark!
20 Who lies i' the second chamber?
LADY MACBETH.   Donalbain.
MACBETH (*looking on his hands*). This is a sorry sight.
LADY MACBETH. A foolish thought, to say a sorry sight.
MACBETH. There's one did laugh in 's sleep, and one cried,
    "Murder!"[53]
  That they did wake each other; I stood and heard them;
25 But they did say their prayers, and addressed them
  Again to sleep.
LADY MACBETH. There are two° lodged together.
MACBETH. One cried, "God bless us!" and "Amen" the other,
  As they had seen me with these hangman's hands.°
  Listening their fear, I could not say, "Amen,"
30 When they did say, "God bless us!"
LADY MACBETH.   Consider it not so deeply.
MACBETH. But wherefore could not I pronounce "Amen"?
  I had most need of blessing, and "Amen"
  Stuck in my throat.
LADY MACBETH.   These deeds must not be thought
  After these ways; so, it will make us mad.

(Lady Macbeth enters in the Study. Through the center door might be seen the beginning of a flight of stairs leading to Duncan's apartment.)

owl . . . bellman: The screech of an owl was often interpreted as an omen of death. In Elizabethan times, the passing bell was rung to indicate that someone was dying (see John Donne, "Meditation 17," page 241).
possets: drinks made of hot milk curdled with wine or ale.

(Macbeth may momentarily appear on the Tarras as he speaks this line.)

52. Is Lady Macbeth's weakness here expected? How do you account for it? What might be her tone here: frightened? irritated? angry? shaken?

(Macbeth descends the stairs into the Study.)

53. Is Macbeth responding to Lady Macbeth here? Where should the actor's attention be directed as he speaks? Think about this as the scene continues.

two: Malcolm and Donalbain.

hangman's hands: In Elizabethan England, the hangman also had to "draw"—remove the entrails from—some of his victims.

35　MACBETH. Methought I heard a voice cry, "Sleep no more!
　　Macbeth does murder sleep," the innocent sleep,
　　Sleep that knits up the raveled sleave° of care,
　　The death of each day's life, sore labor's bath,
　　Balm of hurt minds, great nature's second course,
40　Chief nourisher in life's feast—
　　LADY MACBETH.　　　　　　　　What do you mean?
　　MACBETH. Still it cried, "Sleep no more!" to all the house;
　　"Glamis hath murdered sleep, and therefore Cawdor
　　Shall sleep no more; Macbeth shall sleep no more."
　　LADY MACBETH. Who was it that thus cried? Why, worthy thane,
45　You do unbend your noble strength, to think
　　So brainsickly of things.⁵⁴ Go get some water,
　　And wash this filthy witness from your hand.
　　Why did you bring these daggers from the place?
　　They must lie there. Go carry them, and smear
50　The sleepy grooms with blood.
　　MACBETH.　　　　　　　　　　I'll go no more;
　　I am afraid to think what I have done;
　　Look on 't again I dare not.
　　LADY MACBETH.　　　　　　Infirm of purpose!
　　Give me the daggers. The sleeping and the dead
　　Are but as pictures; 'tis the eye of childhood
55　That fears a painted devil. If he do bleed,
　　I'll gild the faces of the grooms withal;
　　For it must seem their guilt.°⁵⁵

　　　　　　　　　　　　(Exit. Knocking within.)

　　MACBETH.　　　　　　　Whence is that knocking?
　　How is 't with me, when every noise appals me?
　　What hands are here? Ha! they pluck out mine eyes.
60　Will all great Neptune's ocean wash this blood
　　Clean from my hand? No, this my hand will rather
　　The multitudinous seas incarnadine,°
　　Making the green one red.°

　　　　　　　　　　(Re-enter LADY MACBETH.)

　　LADY MACBETH. My hands are of your color; but I shame
65　To wear a heart so white. (Knocking within.) I hear a knocking
　　At the south entry; retire we to our chamber;
　　A little water clears us of this deed.
　　How easy is it, then!⁵⁶ Your constancy
　　Hath left you unattended.° (Knocking within.) Hark! more knock-
　　　　ing.
70　Get on your nightgown,° lest occasion call us,
　　And show us to be watchers.° Be not lost
　　So poorly in your thoughts.⁵⁷
　　MACBETH. To know my deed, 'twere best not know myself.°

　　　　　　　　　　　　　(Knocking within.)

　　Wake Duncan with thy knocking! I would thou couldst!

　　　　　　　　　　　　　(Exeunt.)⁵⁸

raveled sleave: tangled thread.

54. At what point does Macbeth again become aware of Lady Macbeth?

I'll gild . . . guilt: a pun on the words *gild* and *guilt.* The pun would have been more obvious to an Elizabethan audience, for *gold* was often used synonymously with *red.*
55. *Lines 15–57:* What is Macbeth's state of mind after the murder? Lady Macbeth's? What mistake has Macbeth made? What is illogical about Lady Macbeth's proposed method of remedying it? How do you account for her failure to think straight?

incarnadine: redden.
Making . . . red: making the green sea red.

56. *Lines 64–68a:* Both now have blood on their hands. Do you agree that "a little water" can "clear them" of the murder? In what sense might it? In what sense not? Contrast Lady Macbeth's words with Macbeth's in lines 60–63.
Your constancy . . . unattended: Your composure has left you.
nightgown: dressing gown.
watchers: awake.
57. How has Macbeth been reacting? In what manner does Lady Macbeth say "Be not lost . . ."?
To know . . . myself: It is better to be lost in my thoughts than to be aware of what I have done.
58. At what pace should this scene be played? What clues in the dialogue tell you?

Scene 3.

The same. (Played in the Study and on the Platform.) Knocking within. Enter a PORTER.

PORTER. Here's a knocking indeed! If a man were porter of hell-gate, he should have old° turning the key. *(Knocking within.)* Knock, knock, knock! Who's there, i' the name of Beelzebub?° Here's a farmer, that hanged himself on the expectation of plenty.° Come
5 in time; have napkins enow° about you; here you'll sweat for 't. *(Knocking within.)* Knock, knock! Who's there, in the other devil's name? Faith, here's an equivocator[59] that could swear in both the scales against either scale; who committed treason enough for God's sake, yet could not equivocate to heaven. O come
10 in, equivocator. *(Knocking within.)* Knock, knock, knock! Who's there? Faith, here's an English tailor come hither for stealing out of a French hose.° Come in, tailor; here you may roast your goose.° *(Knocking within.)* Knock, knock; never at quiet! What are you? But this place is too cold for hell. I'll devil-porter it
15 no further. I had thought to have let in some of all professions that go the primrose way to the everlasting bonfire.° *(Knocking within.)* Anon, anon! I pray you, remember the porter.°

(Opens the gate.)

(Enter MACDUFF *and* LENNOX.*)*

MACDUFF. Was it so late, friend, ere you went to bed,
That you do lie so late?

20 PORTER. 'Faith, sir, we were carousing till the second cock:° and drink, sir, is a great provoker of three things.

MACDUFF. What three things does drink especially provoke?

PORTER. Marry, sir, nose-painting, sleep, and urine. Lechery, sir, it provokes, and unprovokes; it provokes the desire, but it takes
25 away the performance: therefore, much drink may be said to be an equivocator with lechery: it makes him, and it mars him; it sets him on, and it takes him off; it persuades him, and disheartens him; makes him stand to, and not stand to; in conclusion, equivocates him in a sleep, and, giving him the lie, leaves him.

30 MACDUFF. I believe drink gave thee the lie last night.

PORTER. That it did, sir, i' the very throat on me; but I requited him for his lie; and, I think, being too strong for him, though he took up my legs sometime, yet I made a shift to cast him.[60]

MACDUFF. Is thy master stirring?

(Enter MACBETH.*)*

35 Our knocking has awakened him; here he comes.

LENNOX. Good-morrow, noble sir.

MACBETH.   Good-morrow, both.

MACDUFF. Is the King stirring, worthy thane?

MACBETH.   Not yet.

MACDUFF. He did command me to call timely° on him;
I have almost slipped the hour.

MACBETH.   I'll bring you to him.

---

old: dialect for "plenty of."
Beelzebub: the Devil.

expectation of plenty: because he tried illegally to earn an excess profit on his crops.
napkins enow: enough handkerchiefs to wipe off the sweat caused by the heat of Hell.
59. This is usually taken as an allusion to the trial of the Jesuit Henry Garnet for treason in the spring of 1606, and to the doctrine of equivocation used in his defense: that a lie was not a lie if the speaker had in mind a different meaning which made the statement true. Watch for examples of equivocation which follow.
stealing . . . hose: Tailors were often accused of stealing cloth. Since French hose (breeches) at this period were short and tight, it would take a clever tailor to cut them smaller and steal the excess cloth.
goose: a pressing iron used by a tailor. There may also be a play on the expression "cook your goose."
primrose . . . bonfire: path of pleasure leading to everlasting damnation in Hell.
remember the porter: here he holds out his hand for a tip.
second cock: about three o'clock in the morning.

60. Many of the expressions in this passage refer to wrestling. "Gave thee the lie" means "floored you and put you to sleep." "Took up my leg" means "got my feet off the ground." "Cast" is a pun meaning both "throw down" and "vomit."

What is the dramatic effect of having this comical scene follow immediately the encounter between Macbeth and Lady Macbeth after the murder?
timely: early.

MACDUFF. I know this is a joyful trouble to you;
    But yet 'tis one.

MACBETH. The labor we delight in physics° pain.   **physics:** cures.
    This is the door.

MACDUFF.   I'll make so bold to call,
    For 'tis my limited° service.   *(Exit.)*   **limited:** appointed.

45 **LENNOX.** Goes the King hence today?

MACBETH.   He does; he did appoint so.

LENNOX. The night has been unruly; where we lay,
    Our chimneys were blown down; and, as they say,
    Lamentings heard i' the air; strange screams of death,
    And prophesying with accents terrible
50   Of dire combustion and confused events
    New hatched to the woeful time; the obscure bird°   **obscure bird:** the owl.
    Clamored the livelong night. Some say the earth
    Was feverous and did shake.

MACBETH.   'Twas a rough night.[61]   **61.** How would Macbeth say this?

LENNOX. My young remembrance cannot parallel
55   A fellow to it.

                      (Re-enter MACDUFF.*)*

MACDUFF. O horror, horror, horror! Tongue nor heart
    Cannot conceive nor name thee![62]   **62.** Is Macduff's response a plausible one?

MACBETH ⎱
LENNOX ⎰   What's the matter?

MACDUFF. Confusion now hath made his masterpiece!
    Most sacrilegious murder hath broke ope
60   The Lord's anointed temple,° and stole thence   **Lord's . . . temple:** an allusion to the
    The life o' the building!   idea that the king is God's representative. The metaphorical temple is the king's body.

MACBETH.   What is 't you say? The life?[63]   **63.** Is Macbeth's response a plausible one?

LENNOX. Mean you his Majesty?

MACDUFF. Approach the chamber, and destroy your sight
    With a new Gorgon.° Do not bid me speak;   **Gorgon:** a horrible monster of Greek legend. Whoever looked at her was turned to stone.
65   See, and then speak yourselves.

              (Exeunt MACBETH *and* LENNOX.*)*
              Awake, awake!
    Ring the alarum-bell. Murder and treason!
    Banquo and Donalbain! Malcolm! awake!
    Shake off this downy sleep, death's counterfeit,
    And look on death itself! Up, up, and see
70   The great doom's image!° Malcolm! Banquo!   **great doom's image:** a sight as awful as Judgment Day.
    As from your graves rise up, and walk like sprites,
    To countenance this horror! Ring the bell.
    (Bell rings.)

             (Enter LADY MACBETH.*)*

LADY MACBETH. What's the business,
    That such a hideous trumpet calls to parley
75   The sleepers of the house? Speak, speak!

MACDUFF.   O gentle lady,
    'Tis not for you to hear what I can speak;

The repetition, in a woman's ear,
Would murder as it fell.

(*Enter* BANQUO.)

O Banquo, Banquo,
Our royal master's murdered!

LADY MACBETH.   Woe, alas!
80   What, in our house?[64]

BANQUO.   Too cruel anywhere.
Dear Duff, I prithee, contradict thyself,
And say it is not so.[65]

(*Re-enter* MACBETH *and* LENNOX, *with* ROSS.)

MACBETH. Had I but died an hour before this chance,
I had lived a blessed time; for, from this instant,
85   There's nothing serious in mortality;°
All is but toys; renown and grace is dead;
The wine of life is drawn, and the mere lees
Is left this vault° to brag of.[66]

(*Enter* MALCOLM *and* DONALBAIN.)

DONALBAIN. What is amiss?

MACBETH.   You are, and do not know 't.
90   The spring, the head, the fountain of your blood
Is stopped; the very source of it is stopped.

MACDUFF. Your royal father's murdered.

MALCOLM.   Oh, by whom?[67]

LENNOX. Those of his chamber, as it seemed, had done 't;
Their hands and faces were all badged° with blood;
95   So were their daggers, which unwiped we found
Upon their pillows.
They stared, and were distracted; no man's life
Was to be trusted with them.

MACBETH. Oh, yet I do repent me of my fury,
100   That I did kill them.[68]

MACDUFF.   Wherefore did you so?

MACBETH. Who can be wise, amazed, temperate and furious,
Loyal and neutral, in a moment? No man.
The expedition° of my violent love
Outrun the pauser, reason. Here lay Duncan,
105   His silver skin laced with his golden blood;
And his gashed stabs looked like a breach in nature
For ruin's wasteful entrance; there, the murderers,
Steeped in the colors of their trade, their daggers
Unmannerly breeched with gore. Who could refrain,
110   That had a heart to love, and in that heart
Courage to make 's love known?

LADY MACBETH.   Help me hence, ho![69]

MACDUFF. Look to the lady.

MALCOLM (*aside to* DONALBAIN). Why do we hold our tongues,
That most may claim this argument for ours?°

DONALBAIN (*aside to* MALCOLM). What should be spoken here,
        where our fate,

64. Is Lady Macbeth's response what you would expect? How do you account for it?

65. Is Banquo surprised at what has happened? What does he think of Lady Macbeth's response?

mortality: human life.

this vault: the universe.
66. How many meanings can you read into this speech? Consider what it might mean to the assembled lords, to Macbeth himself, and to the reader.

67. How might Malcolm say this?

badged: marked; splotched.

68. How should the actor playing Macduff react to this announcement? the actor playing Banquo?

expedition: haste.
(". . . a fine wild scene with the thanes in dishabille; the servants half naked. The fainting lady is one focal point upstage and surrounded by thanes and servants, so as not to distract from the whispered conversation of Malcolm and Donalbain, right forward at the center of the octagon; Macbeth no doubt prominent on the perimeter, outside one of the Stage-Posts, with a grim eye of menace on the two princes. . . ."—Watkins)

69. Some commentators maintain that Lady Macbeth really faints; others claim she only pretends to. Which theory seems more likely? Justify your answer in terms of what you know about Macbeth and Lady Macbeth, and the dialogue immediately preceding.
That most . . . ours: who are most concerned.

115 Hid in an auger-hole,° may rush, and seize us?
    Let's away;
    Our tears are not yet brewed.
MALCOLM *(aside to* DONALBAIN*).* Nor our strong sorrow
    Upon the foot of motion.
BANQUO.   Look to the lady;
                   (LADY MACBETH *is carried out.*)
    And when we have our naked frailties hid,°
120   That suffer in exposure, let us meet,
    And question this most bloody piece of work,
    To know it further. Fears and scruples° shake us;
    In the great hand of God I stand, and thence
    Against the undivulged pretense I fight
125   Of treasonous malice.°[70]
MACDUFF.   And so do I.
ALL.   So all.
MACBETH. Let's briefly put on manly readiness,°
    And meet i' the hall together.
ALL.   Well contented.
            (*Exeunt all but* MALCOLM *and* DONALBAIN.)
MALCOLM. What will you do? Let's not consort with them.
    To show an unfelt sorrow is an office
130   Which the false man does easy.[71] I'll to England.
DONALBAIN. To Ireland, I; our separated fortune
    Shall keep us both the safer; where we are,
    There's daggers in men's smiles; the near in blood,
    The nearer bloody.°
MALCOLM.   This murderous shaft that's shot
135   Hath not yet lighted, and our safest way
    Is to avoid the aim. Therefore to horse;
    And let us not be dainty of° leave-taking,
    But shift away; there's warrant in that theft
    Which steals itself, when there's no mercy left.°
                      (*Exeunt.*)[72]

auger-hole: obscure hiding place.

when . . . hid: gotten dressed.

scruples: doubts.
Against . . . malice: I will fight against the unknown purpose which prompted this act of treason.
70. Why did Shakespeare give this speech to Banquo rather than to Macduff?

put . . . readiness: get dressed.

71. How does Malcolm's speech relate to "Foul is fair"?

the near . . . bloody: the closer the kinship to Duncan, the greater the chance of being murdered.

dainty of: ceremonious about.

there's warrant . . . left: we are justified in stealing away in these merciless times.
72. What initially makes Malcolm and Donalbain suspicious? (Macbeth's windy remarks? what Banquo and Macduff have just said? or what?)

Scene 4.

Outside MACBETH'S *castle. (Played on the Platform.) Enter* ROSS *and an* OLD MAN.

OLD MAN. Threescore and ten I can remember well;
    Within the volume of which time I have seen
    Hours dreadful and things strange; but this sore night
    Hath trifled° former knowings.
ROSS.   Ah, good father,
5   Thou seest, the heavens, as troubled with man's act,
    Threaten his bloody stage; by the clock, 'tis day,
    And yet dark night strangles the traveling lamp.°

trifled: made trivial.

traveling lamp: the sun.

Is 't night's predominance, or the day's shame,
That darkness does the face of earth entomb,
10 When living light should kiss it?
OLD MAN.   'Tis unnatural,[73]
Even like the deed that's done. On Tuesday last
A falcon, towering in her pride of place,
Was by a mousing owl hawked at and killed.[74]
ROSS. And Duncan's horses—a thing most strange and certain—
15 Beauteous and swift, the minions° of their race,
Turned wild in nature—broke their stalls, flung out,
Contending 'gainst obedience, as they would make
War with mankind.
OLD MAN.   'Tis said they eat each other.
ROSS. They did so, to the amazement of mine eyes,
20 That looked upon it.

                              (Enter MACDUFF.)
                  Here comes the good Macduff.
How goes the world, sir, now?
MACDUFF.   Why, see you not?
ROSS. Is 't known who did this more than bloody deed?
MACDUFF. Those that Macbeth hath slain.
ROSS.   Alas, the day!
What good could they pretend?°
MACDUFF.   They were suborned.°
25 Malcolm and Donalbain, the King's two sons,
Are stol'n away and fled; which puts upon them
Suspicion of the deed.
ROSS.   'Gainst nature still!
Thriftless ambition, that will ravin up°
Thine own life's means!° Then 'tis most like
30 The sovereignty will fall upon Macbeth.
MACDUFF. He is already named, and gone to Scone°
To be invested.
ROSS.   Where is Duncan's body?
MACDUFF. Carried to Colmekill,°
The sacred storehouse of his predecessors,
35 And guardian of their bones.
ROSS.   Will you to Scone?
MACDUFF. No, cousin, I'll to Fife.
ROSS.   Well, I will thither.
MACDUFF. Well, may you see things well done there; adieu!
Lest our old robes sit easier than our new![75]
ROSS. Farewell, father.
40 OLD MAN. God's benison° go with you; and with those
That would make good of bad, and friends of foes!

                              (Exeunt.)[76]

73. The Elizabethans saw nature as existing in a strictly ordered state. Ross and the Old Man describe events which indicate that the order in nature is awry. Be alert for further indications of unnatural workings in the universe. What might they reflect?
74. What is the symbolic meaning of the falcon-owl incident? Watch for specific symbolic significance in other unnatural acts mentioned.

minions: darlings.

What . . . pretend: What profit could they have aimed at?
suborned: hired or bribed.

ravin up: devour.
own life's means: parent.

Scone: ancient residence of Scottish kings.

Colmekill (kōm'kil): Iona Island.

75. Why might Macduff be suspicious of Macbeth?

benison: blessing.

76. What is the dramatic purpose of this scene?

Act Three

Scene 1.

Forres. The palace. (Played on the Platform and in the Study.) Enter
BANQUO.

BANQUO. Thou hast it now—King, Cawdor, Glamis, all[77]—
  As the weird women promised; and, I fear,
  Thou play'dst most foully for 't. Yet it was said
  It should not stand in thy posterity,
5 But that myself should be the root and father
  Of many kings. If there come truth from them—
  As upon thee, Macbeth, their speeches shine—
  Why, by the verities on thee made good,
  May they not be my oracles as well,
10 And set me up in hope? But hush! no more.[78]
  (Sennet° sounded. Enter MACBETH, *as king,*
    LADY MACBETH, *as queen,* LENNOX, ROSS, LORDS, LADIES,
    and ATTENDANTS.)
MACBETH. Here's our chief guest.
LADY MACBETH.   If he had been forgotten,
  It had been as a gap in our great feast,
  And all-thing unbecoming.
MACBETH. Tonight we hold a solemn supper, sir,
15 And I'll request your presence.
BANQUO.   Let your Highness
  Command upon me; to the which my duties
  Are with a most indissoluble tie
  Forever knit.[79]
MACBETH. Ride you this afternoon?
20 BANQUO. Aye, my good lord.
MACBETH. We should have else desired your good advice,
  Which still hath been both grave and prosperous,°
  In this day's council; but we'll take tomorrow.
  Is 't far you ride?[80]
25 BANQUO. As far, my lord, as will fill up the time
  'Twixt this and supper. Go not my horse the better,
  I must become a borrower of the night
  For a dark hour or twain.
MACBETH.   Fail not our feast.
BANQUO. My lord, I will not.
30 MACBETH. We hear our bloody cousins are bestowed
  In England and in Ireland, not confessing
  Their cruel parricide, filling their hearers
  With strange invention;[81] but of that tomorrow,
  When therewithal we shall have cause of state
35 Craving us jointly.° Hie you to horse; adieu,
  Till you return at night. Goes Fleance with you?[82]
BANQUO. Aye, my good lord; our time does call upon 's.
MACBETH. I wish your horses swift and sure of foot;

77. How much time has passed by now?

78. Banquo alone of the lords knows about the witches' prophecies, but he has said nothing about them. Why hasn't he? Does he have any plans for immediate action?
Sennet: musical piece played by cornets, generally used to grace a formal procession. It indicates here that Macbeth has achieved the object of his ambition.

79. In what tone does Banquo speak?

Which . . . prosperous: which always has been thoughtful and fruitful.

80. Why does Macbeth ask this question (and later ones) about Banquo's plans?

81. How should the actor playing Banquo react when Macbeth tells him about Malcolm and Donalbain?
cause . . . jointly: affairs of state demanding the attention of both of us.
82. In what tone of voice does Macbeth ask this question?

And so I do commend you to their backs.

40 Farewell. *(Exit* BANQUO.*)*
Let every man be master of his time
Till seven at night. To make society
The sweeter welcome, we will keep ourself
Till supper-time alone; while then, God be with you.
(Exeunt all but MACBETH *and an* ATTENDANT.*)*

45 Sirrah, a word with you; attend those men
Our pleasure?

ATTENDANT. They are, my lord, without the palace gate.

MACBETH. Bring them before us.
(Exit ATTENDANT.*)*
                              To be thus is nothing,
But to be safely thus.—Our fears in Banquo

50 Stick deep; and in his royalty of nature
Reigns that which would be feared. 'Tis much he dares;
And, to that dauntless temper of his mind,
He hath a wisdom that doth guide his valor
To act in safety. There is none but he

55 Whose being I do fear; and, under him,
My Genius is rebuked; as, it is said,
Mark Antony's was by Caesar.° He chid the sisters
When first they put the name of king upon me,
And bade them speak to him; then prophetlike

60 They hailed him father to a line of kings.
Upon my head they placed a fruitless crown,
And put a barren scepter in my gripe,
Thence to be wrenched with an unlineal hand,[83]
No son of mine succeeding. If 't be so,

65 For Banquo's issue have I filed° my mind;
For them the gracious Duncan have I murdered;
Put rancors in the vessel of my peace
Only for them; and mine eternal jewel
Given to the common enemy of man,°

70 To make them kings, the seed of Banquo kings!
Rather than so, come fate into the list,°
And champion me to the utterance!° [84] Who's there?
(Re-enter ATTENDANT, *with two* MURDERERS.*)*
Now go to the door, and stay there till we call.
(Exit ATTENDANT.*)*
Was it not yesterday we spoke together?

75 FIRST MURDERER. It was, so please your Highness.

MACBETH.   Well, then, now
Have you considered of my speeches? Know
That it was he in the times past which held you
So under fortune,° which you thought had been
Our innocent self; this I made good to you

80 In our last conference, passed in probation° with you,
How you were borne in hand,° how crossed, the instruments,
Who wrought with them, and all things else that might

("There can be no better background for this soliloquy than the royal 'state' on which Macbeth sits in his King's robes, wearing his fruitless crown, and grasping his barren sceptre. The setting is more properly one of circumstance than of locality."— Watkins)

There is none . . . Caesar: Macbeth's insatiable ambition is silently rebuked by Banquo's innate loyalty. Mark Antony feared Octavius Caesar as a political, not personal, enemy, and this is how Macbeth regards Banquo.

83. *Wrenched* has connotations of violence. How has Macbeth interpreted Banquo's loyalty and his silence about the witches' prophecies? What does he fear Banquo may do?
filed: defiled.

mine eternal . . . man: given my soul to the Devil.

list: battlefield.
champion . . . utterance: fight me to the death.
84. *Lines 47–72:* How does this soliloquy compare with the earlier one (Act One, Scene 7, 1–28) in which he contemplated the murder of Duncan?

Know . . . fortune: It is sometimes assumed that the First and Second Murderers are former retainers of Banquo's.
passed in probation: gave detailed proof.
borne in hand: deceived.

To half a soul and to a notion crazed°
Say, "Thus did Banquo."

FIRST MURDERER.   You made it known to us.

85 **MACBETH.** I did so, and went further, which is now
Our point of second meeting. Do you find
Your patience so predominant in your nature
That you can let this go? Are you so gospeled°
To pray for this good man and for his issue,

90 Whose heavy hand hath bowed you to the grave
And beggared yours forever?

FIRST MURDERER.   We are men, my liege.

MACBETH. Aye, in the catalogue ye go for men;
As hounds and greyhounds, mongrels, spaniels, curs,
Shoughs, water-rugs, and demi-wolves are clept°

95 All by the name of dogs. The valued file°
Distinguishes the swift, the slow, the subtle,
The housekeeper, the hunter, every one
According to the gift which bounteous nature
Hath in him closed, whereby he does receive

100 Particular addition, from the bill
That writes them all alike;° and so of men.
Now if you have a station in the file,
Not i' the worst rank of manhood, say 't;
And I will put that business in your bosoms

105 Whose execution takes your enemy off,
Grapples you to the heart and love of us,
Who wear our health but sickly in his life,
Which in his death were perfect.

SECOND MURDERER.   I am one, my liege,
Whom the vile blows and buffets of the world

110 Have so incensed that I am reckless what
I do to spite the world.

FIRST MURDERER.   And I another
So weary with disasters, tugged with° fortune,
That I would set my life on any chance,
To mend it, or be rid on 't.

MACBETH.   Both of you

115 Know Banquo was your enemy.

BOTH MURDERERS.   True, my lord.

MACBETH. So is he mine; and in such bloody distance°
That every minute of his being thrusts
Against my near'st of life;° and though I could
With barefaced power sweep him from my sight

120 And bid my will avouch it,° yet I must not,
For certain friends that are both his and mine,
Whose loves I may not drop, but wail his fall°
Who I myself struck down; and thence it is
That I to your assistance do make love,

125 Masking the business from the common eye
For sundry weighty reasons.

notion crazed: half-wit.

gospeled: religious.

Shoughs . . . clept: shaggy dogs, water dogs, and half-wolves are called.
valued file: list according to worth.

Particular . . . alike: specific qualifications along with the general attributes.

tugged with: pulled about by.

such bloody distance: with such hostility.

thrusts . . . life: threatens my very existence.

bid . . . avouch it: justify it as an act of royal will.

but . . . fall: I must pretend to lament his death.

SECOND MURDERER.   We shall, my lord,
  Perform what you command us.
FIRST MURDERER.   Though our lives—
MACBETH. Your spirits shine through you. Within this hour at
    most
  I will advise you where to plant yourselves;
130 Acquaint you with the perfect spy o' the time,°
  The moment on 't; for 't must be done tonight,
  And something from the palace; always thought
  That I require a clearness.° And with him—
  To leave no rubs nor botches in the work—
135 Fleance his son, that keeps him company,
  Whose absence is no less material to me
  Than is his father's, must embrace the fate
  Of that dark hour. Resolve yourselves° apart;
  I'll come to you anon.
BOTH MURDERERS.   We are resolved, my lord.
140 **MACBETH.** I'll call upon you straight; abide within.
                              (*Exeunt* MURDERERS.)
  It is concluded. Banquo, thy soul's flight,
  If it find heaven, must find it out tonight.
                                        (*Exit.*)

Acquaint . . . time: Critics still puzzle over the exact meaning of this passage. A plausible interpretation is that Macbeth will give them the most accurate report available as to the time when they should begin watching for Banquo.
clearness: freedom from suspicion.

Resolve yourselves: make up your minds.

Scene 2.
The palace. (Played in the Chamber.) Enter LADY MACBETH *and a* SERVANT.

LADY MACBETH. Is Banquo gone from court?
SERVANT. Aye, madam, but returns again tonight.
LADY MACBETH. Say to the King I would attend his leisure
  For a few words.
SERVANT.   Madam, I will.   (*Exit.*)
LADY MACBETH.   Naught's had, all's spent,
5 Where our desire is got without content.
  'Tis safer to be that which we destroy
  Than by destruction dwell in doubtful joy.[85]
                              (*Enter* MACBETH.)
  How now, my lord! why do you keep alone,
  Of sorriest fancies your companions making,
10 Using those thoughts which should indeed have died
  With them they think on? Things without all remedy
  Should be without regard; what's done is done.
MACBETH. We have scotched° the snake, not killed it;
  She'll close and be herself, whilst our poor malice
15 Remains in danger of her former tooth.
  But let the frame of things° disjoint, both the worlds suffer,°
  Ere we will eat our meal in fear, and sleep
  In the affliction of these terrible dreams
  That shake us nightly; better be with the dead,

85. In what way has Lady Macbeth changed?

scotched: cut, gashed.

frame of things: the universe.
both . . . suffer: earth and heaven perish.

20   Whom we, to gain our peace, have sent to peace,
     Than on the torture of the mind to lie
     In restless ecstasy.° Duncan is in his grave;

restless ecstasy: suffering, torment.

     After life's fitful fever he sleeps well.
     Treason has done his worst; nor steel, nor poison,
25   Malice domestic,° foreign levy,° nothing,
     Can touch him further.[86]

Malice domestic: civil war.
levy: invasion.
86. *Lines 4–26:* How do you judge Macbeth and Lady Macbeth now feel about the murder of Duncan?

LADY MACBETH.   Come on,
     Gentle my lord, sleek o'er your rugged looks;
     Be bright and jovial among your guests tonight.
MACBETH. So shall I, love; and so, I pray, be you.
30   Let your remembrance apply to Banquo;
     Present him eminence,° both with eye and tongue;
     Unsafe the while, that we

Present him eminence: show him special favor.

     Must lave our honors in these flattering streams,
     And make our faces vizards° to our hearts,
35   Disguising what they are.°

vizards: masks.

LADY MACBETH.   You must leave this.
MACBETH. Oh, full of scorpions is my mind, dear wife!
     Thou know'st that Banquo, and his Fleance, lives.

Unsafe . . . are: We are unsafe so long as we must flatter and appear to be what we are not.

LADY MACBETH. But in them nature's copy's not eterne.°
MACBETH. There's comfort yet; they are assailable;
40   Then be thou jocund. Ere the bat hath flown
     His cloistered flight, ere to black Hecate's summons

But . . . eterne: They will not live forever.

The shard-borne beetle° with his drowsy hums
Hath rung night's yawning peal, there shall be done
A deed of dreadful note.
LADY MACBETH.   What's to be done?[87]
45 **MACBETH.** Be innocent of the knowledge, dearest chuck,
Till thou applaud the deed. Come, seeling° night,
Scarf up° the tender eye of pitiful day;
And with thy bloody and invisible hand
Cancel and tear to pieces that great bond°
50 Which keeps me pale! Light thickens, and the crow
Makes wing to the rooky wood;
Good things of day begin to droop and drowse,
Whiles night's black agents to their preys do rouse.
Thou marvel'st at my words; but hold thee still;
55 Things bad begun make strong themselves by ill.
So, prithee, go with me.   *(Exeunt.)*[88]

Scene 3.
A park near the palace. (Played on the Platform.) Enter three
MURDERERS.[89]
FIRST MURDERER. But who did bid thee join with us?
THIRD MURDERER.   Macbeth.
SECOND MURDERER. He needs not our mistrust, since he delivers
Our offices and what we have to do
To the direction just.°
FIRST MURDERER.   Then stand with us.°
5 The west yet glimmers with some streaks of day;
Now spurs the lated traveler apace
To gain the timely inn; and near approaches
The subject of our watch.
THIRD MURDERER.   Hark! I hear horses.
BANQUO *(within).* Give us a light there, ho!
SECOND MURDERER.   Then 'tis he; the rest
10 That are within the note of expectation°
Already are i' the court.
FIRST MURDERER.   His horses go about.°
THIRD MURDERER. Almost a mile; but he does usually,
So all men do, from hence to the palace gate
Make it their walk.
SECOND MURDERER. A light, a light!
                    (Enter BANQUO, *and* FLEANCE *with a torch.)*
THIRD MURDERER.   'Tis he.
15 **FIRST MURDERER.** Stand to 't.
BANQUO. It will be rain tonight.
FIRST MURDERER.   Let it come down.
                         (They set upon BANQUO.)
BANQUO. Oh, treachery! Fly, good Fleance, fly, fly, fly!
Thou mayest revenge. O slave!
                    (Dies. FLEANCE *escapes.)*

shard-borne beetle: Critics suggest two possible meanings: (1) a dung beetle; (2) a beetle that is borne on (flies with) shards, or horny wing cases.
87. Who is now taking the lead in planning?
seeling: blinding. To seel is a technical term used in falconry for sewing up the eyelids of a young hawk to make him used to the hood. (Macbeth is now speaking from the Tarras outside Lady Macbeth's chamber.)
Scarf up: blindfold.
great bond: Banquo's bond of life (?).

88. Compare the planning of Banquo's murder with the planning of Duncan's. What indications are there that the relationship between Macbeth and his wife has changed?

89. How many murderers were present in Macbeth's first interview with them? Why might Macbeth involve a third murderer in the plot?
    The third murderer has been variously identified as: a confidential servant of Macbeth's; the character called Attendant in Scene 1; Ross; Macbeth himself. On the basis of evidence in the play, which seems most likely? (Watkins points out: "There is a purely mechanical reason why a third murderer is necessary: Banquo's body must be carried off, and it takes two to carry him off expeditiously; not only that, but the light struck from the hand of Fleance must also be removed before the change of locality to the ensuing banquet scene. One of the trio must pick up the light.")

He needs not . . . just: We need not distrust him, since he reports accurately what we are to do.
(Then stand with us: The murderers might use the Stage-Posts for their ambush.)

note of expectation: list of expected guests.

go about: take the long way to the castle. (Shakespeare had to find some plausible excuse for not bringing the horses onstage.)

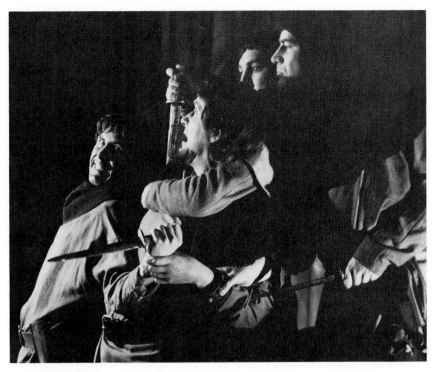

THIRD MURDERER. Who did strike out the light?

FIRST MURDERER.   Was 't not the
   way?

20 **THIRD MURDERER.** There's but one down; the son is fled.

SECOND MURDERER.   We
   have lost
   Best half of our affair.

FIRST MURDERER. Well, let's away, and say how much is done.

$$\textit{(Exeunt.)}^{90}$$

90. What are some of the circumstances that contributed to Fleance's escape?

Scene 4.

Hall in the palace. (Played on the Platform and in the Study.) A banquet prepared. Enter MACBETH, LADY MACBETH, ROSS, LENNOX, LORDS, *and* ATTENDANTS.

MACBETH. You know your own degrees;° sit down. At first
   And last the hearty welcome.

LORDS.   Thanks to your Majesty.

MACBETH. Ourself will mingle with society
   And play the humble host.

5 Our hostess keeps her state,° but in best time
   We will require her welcome.

LADY MACBETH. Pronounce it for me, sir, to all our friends;
   For my heart speaks they are welcome.

(FIRST MURDERER *appears at the door.*)

MACBETH. See, they encounter thee with their hearts' thanks.

10 Both sides are even. Here I'll sit i' the midst.°
   Be large in mirth; anon we'll drink a measure

degrees: rank. Guests at state banquets were seated according to rank.

keeps her state. remains seated on her throne (in the Study).

i' the midst: Macbeth's place at the table is in the middle facing the audience.

The table round. (*Moves toward* MURDERER *at door.*)° There's
  blood upon thy face.
MURDERER. 'Tis Banquo's then.
MACBETH. 'Tis better thee without than he within.°
15 Is he dispatched?
MURDERER. My lord, his throat is cut; that I did for him.
MACBETH. Thou art the best o' the cutthroats; yet he's good
  That did the like for Fleance. If thou didst it,
  Thou art the nonpareil.°
MURDERER.   Most royal sir,
20 Fleance is 'scaped.
MACBETH (*aside*).[91] Then comes my fit again; I had else been
    perfect,
  Whole as the marble, founded as the rock,
  As broad and general as the casing° air.
  But now I am cabined, cribbed, confined, bound in
25 To saucy doubts and fears. But Banquo's safe?
MURDERER. Aye, my good lord; safe in a ditch he bides,
  With twenty trenchèd gashes on his head,
  The least a death to nature.
MACBETH.   Thanks for that;
  There the grown serpent lies. The worm that's fled
30 Hath nature that in time will venom breed,
  No teeth for the present. Get thee gone; tomorrow
  We'll hear ourselves° again.   (*Exit* MURDERER.)
LADY MACBETH.   My royal lord,
  You do not give the cheer; the feast is sold
  That is not often vouched, while 'tis a-making,
35 'Tis given with welcome; to feed were best at home;
  From thence the sauce to meat is ceremony;
  Meeting were bare without it.°
MACBETH.   Sweet remembrancer!
  Now good digestion wait on appetite,
  And health on both!
LENNOX.   May't please your Highness sit.
    (*The* GHOST OF BANQUO *enters, and sits in* MACBETH's *place.*)[92]
40 MACBETH. Here had we now our country's honor roofed,°
  Were the gracèd person of our Banquo present;
  Who may I rather challenge for unkindness
  Than pity for mischance!°
ROSS.   His absence, sir,
  Lays blame upon his promise. Please 't your Highness
45 To grace us with your royal company.
MACBETH. The table's full.
LENNOX.   Here is a place reserved, sir.
MACBETH. Where?
LENNOX. Here, my good lord. What is 't that moves your Highness?
50 MACBETH. Which of you have done this?
LORDS.   What, my good lord?

(Moves . . . door: Because of the size
of the Platform, this whispered
conversation could plausibly take
place at one side, outside one of the
Stage-Posts.)
'Tis better . . . within: The blood is
better on you than in him.

nonpareil: one without equal.

91. Macbeth must react in some way
before he speaks. What would be
appropriate?

casing: enveloping.

hear ourselves: talk it over.

the feast is . . . it: Unless a host keeps
his guests assured of their welcome,
the meal is like one bought at an inn,
and one might as well dine at home.
When one is away from home,
ceremony should accompany the meal.

92. Watch for the point when Macbeth
becomes aware of the ghost.
   If you were staging a modern
production, would you have the ghost
physically on stage? Explain.
Here had . . . roofed: We would have
all our country's most honored men
here.
Who may I . . . mischance: Who is, I
hope, absent because he has chosen
not to attend rather than because he
has been prevented from coming by
some misfortune.

MACBETH. Thou canst not say I did it; never shake
Thy gory locks at me.[93]

ROSS. Gentlemen, rise; his Highness is not well.

LADY MACBETH. Sit, worthy friends. My lord is often thus,
And hath been from his youth. Pray you, keep seat;
55 The fit is momentary; upon a thought°
He will again be well. If much you note him,
You shall offend him and extend his passion;°
Feed, and regard him not.[94] Are you a man?

MACBETH. Aye, and a bold one, that dare look on that
60 Which might appal the devil.

LADY MACBETH.   O proper stuff!
This is the very painting of your fear;
This is the air-drawn dagger which, you said,
Led you to Duncan.[95] Oh, these flaws and starts,
Imposters to° true fear, would well become
65 A woman's story at a winter's fire,
Authorized by her grandam. Shame itself!
Why do you make such faces? When all's done,
You look but on a stool.[96]

MACBETH. Prithee, see there! behold! look! lo! how say you?
70 Why, what care I? If thou canst nod, speak, too.
If charnel houses and our graves must send
Those that we bury back, our monuments
Shall be the maws of kites.°   (GHOST *vanishes.*)

LADY MACBETH.   What, quite unmanned in folly?

MACBETH. If I stand here, I saw him.

LADY MACBETH.   Fie, for shame!

75 **MACBETH.** Blood hath been shed ere now, i' the olden time,
Ere humane statue purged the gentle weal;°
Aye, and since, too, murders have been performed
Too terrible for the ear. The time has been,
That, when the brains were out, the man would die,
80 And there an end; but now they rise again,
With twenty mortal murders on their crowns,°
And push us from our stools; this is more strange
Than such a murder is.

LADY MACBETH.   My worthy lord,
Your noble friends do lack you.

MACBETH.   I do forget.
85 Do not muse at me, my most worthy friends;
I have a strange infirmity, which is nothing
To those that know me. Come, love and health to all;
Then I'll sit down. Give me some wine; fill full.
I drink to the general joy o' the whole table,
90 And to our dear friend Banquo, whom we miss;
Would he were here! To all, and him, we thirst,°
And all to all.

LORDS.   Our duties, and the pledge.

                    (*Re-enter* GHOST.)

93. To whom is Macbeth speaking? What is the "it" he denies doing?

upon a thought: in a moment.
extend his passion: prolong his fit.

94. *Lines 53–58a:* What tone of voice would Lady Macbeth use here? To whom does she then say "Are you a man?" How would her tone change here?

95. Where on the stage would Macbeth and Lady Macbeth be positioned at this point?
Imposters to: imitations of.

96. Does Lady Macbeth see the ghost?

If charnel . . . kites: If morgues and graves cannot keep our bodies buried, our burial place should be the stomachs of birds of prey.

Ere . . . weal: before laws purged violence from society.

mortal . . . crowns: deadly wounds on their heads.

thirst: wish to drink.

MACBETH. Avaunt! and quit my sight! Let the earth hide thee!
   Thy bones are marrowless, thy blood is cold;
95 Thou has no speculation° in those eyes
   Which thou dost glare with!

LADY MACBETH.   Think of this, good peers,
   But as a thing of custom; 'tis no other;
   Only it spoils the pleasure of the time.[97]

MACBETH. What man dare, I dare.
100 Approach thou like the rugged Russian bear,
   The armed rhinoceros, or the Hyrcan tiger;
   Take any shape but that, and my firm nerves
   Shall never tremble. Or be alive again,
   And dare me to the desert with thy sword;

speculation: light of living intelligence.

97. Who hears Macbeth's tirades? How do Macbeth and Lady Macbeth explain his behavior? Do you think the lords accept the explanation?

105 If trembling I inhabit then,° protest me
The baby of a girl.° Hence, horrible shadow!
Unreal mockery, hence!

                         (GHOST *vanishes.*)[98]

                Why, so; being gone,
I am a man again. Pray you, sit still.

LADY MACBETH. You have displaced the mirth, broke the good meeting,
110 With most admired° disorder.

MACBETH.   Can such things be,
And overcome us like a summer's cloud,
Without our special wonder? You make me strange
Even to the disposition that I owe,°
When now I think you can behold such sights,
115 And keep the natural ruby of your cheeks,
When mine is blanched with fear.

ROSS.   What sights, my lord?

LADY MACBETH. I pray you, speak not; he grows worse and worse;
Question enrages him. At once, good night;
Stand not upon the order of your going,°
120 But go at once.

LENNOX.   Good night; and better health
Attend his Majesty!

LADY MACBETH.   A kind good-night to all![99]

       (*Exeunt all but* MACBETH *and* LADY MACBETH.)

MACBETH. It will have blood; they say, blood will have blood.
Stones have been known to move and trees to speak;
Augurs and understood relations have
125 By magot-pies and choughs and rooks brought forth
The secret'st man of blood.° What is the night?

LADY MACBETH. Almost at odds with morning, which is which.

MACBETH. How say'st thou, that Macduff denies his person
At our great bidding?

LADY MACBETH.   Did you send to him, sir?

130 **MACBETH.** I hear it by the way; but I will send.
There's not a one of them but in his house
I keep a servant feed.° I will tomorrow,
And betimes I will, to the weird sisters.°
More shall they speak; for now I am bent to know,
135 By the worst means, the worst. For mine own good,
All causes shall give way; I am in blood
Stepped in so far that, should I wade no more,
Returning were as tedious as go o'er.
Strange things I have in head, that will to hand;
140 Which must be acted ere they may be scanned.°

LADY MACBETH. You lack the season of all natures, sleep.

MACBETH. Come, we'll to sleep. My strange and self-abuse
Is the initiate fear that wants hard use;°
We are yet but young in deed.[100]

                                (*Exeunt.*)

If . . . then: If I then still tremble.
The baby of a girl: puny infant of an immature mother. (Some editors interpret it as "a girl's doll.")

98. Who has seen the ghost? What similar hallucination occurs earlier in the play, and what purpose do both incidents serve?

admired: wondered at.

You make . . . owe: You make me wonder at my own disposition.

Stand not . . . going: Do not wait to leave in formal order.

99. Macbeth has not explicitly told Lady Macbeth of his plot to murder Banquo. At what point in this scene do you think she realizes what has happened? How might an actress convey this knowledge to an audience?

Augurs . . . blood: Through talking birds, omens correctly interpreted have led to the discovery of the most secretive of murderers. Magot-pies are magpies; choughs, a type of crow.

feed: paid [in fee] to spy.

I will . . . sisters: I will send for Macduff tomorrow, and very early I will go to the witches.

Which . . . scanned: which must be done before they can be discussed or considered.
My strange . . . use: My peculiar actions arise from the fact that I am a novice at crime, not yet hardened.
100. (a) Do you agree with Macbeth's explanation for his agitation and sleeplessness? How well would you say he knows himself?
(b) What should the pace and mood be for this part of the scene?

MACBETH—ACT THREE, SCENE 4 **197**

Comment: The Witch Scenes in *Macbeth*

A. C. Bradley

On the one hand the Witches are credited by some critics with far too great an influence upon the action; sometimes they are described as goddesses, or even as fates, whom Macbeth is powerless to resist. On the other hand, we are told that, great as is their influence on the action, it is so because they are merely symbolic representations of the unconscious or half-conscious guilt in Macbeth.

As to the former, Shakespeare took as material for his purposes, the ideas about witchcraft that he found existing in people around him and in books like Reginald Scot's *Discovery* (1584). And he used these ideas without changing their substance at all. He selected and improved, avoiding the merely ridiculous, dismissing the sexually loathsome or stimulating, rehandling and heightening whatever could touch the imagination with fear, horror, and mysterious attraction. The Witches, that is to say, are not goddesses, or fates, or, in any way whatever, supernatural beings. They are old women, poor and ragged, skinny and hideous, full of vulgar spite, occupied in killing their neighbors' swine or revenging themselves on sailors' wives who have refused them chestnuts. There is not a syllable in *Macbeth* to imply that they are anything but women. But they have received from evil spirits certain supernatural powers.

Next, while the influence of the Witches' prophecies on Macbeth is very great, it is quite clearly shown to be an influence and nothing more. There is no sign whatever in the play that Shakespeare meant the actions of Macbeth to be forced on him by an external power. The prophecies of the Witches are presented simply as dangerous circumstances with which Macbeth has to deal. Macbeth is, in the ordinary sense, perfectly free in regard to them. That the influence of the first prophecies upon him came as much from himself as from them, is made abundantly clear by the obviously in-

tentional contrast between him and Banquo. Banquo, ambitious but perfectly honest, is scarcely even startled by them, and he remains throughout the scene indifferent to them. But when Macbeth heard them he was not an innocent man. Precisely how far his mind was guilty may be a question; but no innocent man would have started, as he did, with a start of *fear* at the mere prophecy of a crown, or have conceived thereupon *immediately* the thought of murder. Either this thought was not new to him, or he had cherished at least some vaguer dishonorable dream. In either case not only was he free to accept or resist the temptation, but the temptation was already within him. And we are admitting, again, too much when we use the word "temptation" in reference to the first prophecies of the Witches. Speaking strictly we must affirm that he was tempted only by himself. *He* speaks indeed of their "supernatural soliciting"; but in fact they did not solicit. They merely announced events: they hailed him as Thane of Glamis, Thane of Cawdor, and King hereafter. No connection of these announcements with any actions of his was even hinted by them.

When Macbeth sees the Witches again, after the murders of Duncan and Banquo, we observe, however, a striking change. They no longer need to go and meet him; he seeks them out. He has committed himself to his course of evil. Now accordingly they do "solicit." They prophesy, but they also give advice: they bid him be bloody, bold, and secure. We have no hope that he will reject their advice; but so far are they from having, even now, any power to compel him to accept it, that they make careful preparations to deceive him into doing so. And, almost as though to intimate how entirely the responsibility for his deeds still lies with Macbeth, Shakespeare makes his first act after this interview one for which his

From Lecture IX in *Shakespearean Tragedy* by A. C. Bradley. Copyright © by A. C. Bradley. Reprinted by permission of St. Martin's Press, Inc. and Macmillan, London and Basingstoke.

tempters gave him not a hint—the slaughter of Macduff's wife and children.

To all this we must add that Macbeth himself nowhere betrays a suspicion that his action is, or has been, thrust on him by an external power. He curses the Witches for deceiving him, but he never attempts to shift to them the burden of his guilt.

We may deal more briefly with the opposite interpretation. According to it the Witches and their prophecies are to be taken merely as symbolical representations of thoughts and desires which have slumbered in Macbeth's breast and now rise into consciousness and confront him. With this idea, which springs from the wish to get rid of a mere external supernaturalism, and to find a psychological and spiritual meaning in that which the groundlings probably received as hard facts, one may feel sympathy. But it is evident that it is rather a "philosophy" of the Witches than an immediate dramatic apprehension of them; and even so it will be found both incomplete and, in other respects, inadequate.

It is incomplete because it cannot possibly be applied to all the facts. Let us grant that it will apply to the most important prophecy, that of the crown; and that the later warning which Macbeth receives, to beware of Macduff, also answers to something in his own breast and "harps his fear aright." But there we have to stop. Macbeth had evidently no suspicion of that treachery in Cawdor through which he himself became Thane; and who will suggest that he had any idea, however subconscious, about Birnam Wood or the man not born of woman?

The theory under consideration is inadequate here chiefly because it is much too narrow. The Witches and their prophecies, if they are to be taken symbolically, must represent not only the evil slumbering in the hero's soul, but all those obscurer influences of the evil around him in the world which aid his own ambition and the incitements of his wife. Such influences, even if we put aside all belief in evil

The three witches posed with Lady Macbeth in a Wisdom Bridge Theater production of *Kabuki Macbeth* (Chicago, 1981).

"spirits," are as certain, momentous, and terrifying facts as the presence of inchoate evil in the soul itself; and if we exclude all reference to these facts from our idea of the Witches, it will be greatly impoverished and will certainly fail to correspond with the imaginative effect. The words of the Witches are fatal to the hero only because there is in him something which leaps into light at the sound of them; but they are at the same time the witness of forces which never cease to work in the world around him, and, on the instant of his surrender to them, entangle him inextricably in the web of Fate. If the inward connection is once realized (and Shakespeare has left us no excuse for missing it), we need not fear, and indeed shall scarcely be able, to exaggerate the effect of the Witch scenes in heightening and deepening the sense of fear, horror, and mystery which pervades the atmosphere of tragedy.

Scene 5.

A heath.[101] (*Perhaps* HECATE *on the Tarras, with the three* WITCHES *below.*) *Thunder. Enter the three* WITCHES, *meeting* HECATE.

FIRST WITCH. Why, how now, Hecate! you look angerly.

HECATE. Have I not reason, beldams as you are,
    Saucy and overbold? How did you dare
    To trade and traffic with Macbeth
5   In riddles and affairs of death;
    And I, the mistress of your charms,
    The close contriver of all harms,
    Was never called to bear my part,
    Or show the glory of our art?
10   And, which is worse, all you have done
    Hath been but for a wayward son,
    Spiteful and wrathful, who, as others do,
    Loves for his own ends, not for you.
    But make amends now. Get you gone,
15   And at the pit of Acheron°
    Meet me i' the morning. Thither he
    Will come to know his destiny.
    Your vessels and your spells provide,
    Your charms and everything beside.
20   I am for the air; this night I'll spend
    Unto a dismal and a fatal end;
    Great business must be wrought ere noon.
    Upon the corner of the moon
    There hangs a vaporous drop profound;
25   I'll catch it ere it come to ground;
    And that, distilled by magic sleights,
    Shall raise such artificial sprites
    As by the strength of their illusion
    Shall draw him on to his confusion.
30   He shall spurn fate, scorn death, and bear
    His hopes 'bove wisdom, grace, and fear;
    And you all know security°
    Is mortals' chiefest enemy.
        (*Music and a song within, "Come away, come away," etc.*)
    Hark! I am called; my little spirit, see,
35   Sits in a foggy cloud, and stays for me.   (*Exit.*)

FIRST WITCH. Come, let's make haste; she'll soon be back again.
                    (*Exeunt.*)

Scene 6.

Forres. The palace. (Played on the Tarras.) Enter LENNOX *and another* LORD.

LENNOX. My former speeches have but hit your thoughts,
    Which can interpret further;° only, I say,
    Things have been strangely borne.° The gracious Duncan

---

101. It is generally accepted that this scene was not written by Shakespeare. Do you see anything in the style of the writing which may have led to this opinion?

Acheron: a river in Hell.

security: overconfidence.

My former . . . further: My earlier speeches have only given you ideas, from which you can draw your own conclusions.
borne: conducted.

Was pitied of Macbeth; marry, he was dead.
5 And the right-valiant Banquo walked too late;
Whom, you may say, if 't please you, Fleance killed,
For Fleance fled; men must not walk too late.
Who cannot want the thought how monstrous
It was for Malcolm and for Donalbain
10 To kill their gracious father? Damnèd fact!
How it did grieve Macbeth! Did he not straight
In pious rage the two delinquents tear,
That were the slaves of drink and thralls of sleep?
Was not that nobly done? Aye, and wisely, too;
15 For 'twould have angered any heart alive
To hear the men deny 't. So that, I say,
He has borne all things well. And I do think
That had he Duncan's sons under his key—
As, an 't please heaven, he shall not—they should find
20 What 'twere to kill a father; so should Fleance.
But, peace! for from broad words° and 'cause he failed
His presence at the tyrant's feast, I hear
Macduff lives in disgrace; sir, can you tell
Where he bestows himself?[102]

LORD.   The son of Duncan,
25 From whom this tyrant holds the due of birth,
Lives in the English court, and is received
Of the most pious Edward° with such grace
That the malevolence of fortune nothing
Takes from his high respect. Thither Macduff
30 Is gone to pray the holy King, upon his aid
To wake Northumberland and warlike Siward;
That by the help of these—with Him above
To ratify the work—we may again
Give to our tables meat, sleep to our nights,
35 Free from our feasts and banquets bloody knives,
Do faithful homage and receive free honors,
All which we pine for now; and this report
Hath so exasperate the King that he
Prepares for some attempt of war.

LENNOX.   Sent he to Macduff?°
40 LORD. He did; and with an absolute "Sir, not I,"
The cloudy° messenger turns me his back,
And hums, as who should say, "You'll rue the time
That clogs° me with this answer."

LENNOX.   And that well might
Advise him° to a caution, to hold what distance
45 His wisdom can provide. Some holy angel
Fly to the court of England and unfold
His message ere he come, that a swift blessing
May soon return to this our suffering country
Under a hand accursed!

LORD.   I'll send my prayers with him. (Exeunt.)[103]

from broad words: because he spoke frankly.

102. Note the indirect suggestions in Lennox's speech. Why is he less than forthright?
 At what points does his tone of voice change? What is the dramatic effect of these changes?
Edward: Edward the Confessor, King of England 1042-1066.

Sent he . . . ? Did he send for Macduff?

cloudy: sullen.

clogs: obstructs.

him: Macduff.
103. What is the dramatic purpose of this scene? What earlier scene does it parallel?
 Some scholars believe this scene should follow Act Four, Scene 1, where it seems to make better sense. It may have been shifted to its present position when Scene 5 was added, to avoid having two scenes with the witches come together.

Act Four

Scene 1.
A cavern.° In the middle, a boiling caldron. Thunder. Enter the three
WITCHES.

FIRST WITCH. Thrice the brinded cat hath mewed.
SECOND WITCH. Thrice and once the hedgepig° whined.
THIRD WITCH. Harpier° cries, " 'Tis time, 'tis time."
FIRST WITCH. Round about the caldron go;
5   In the poisoned entrails throw.
    Toad, that under cold stone
    Days and nights has thirty-one
    Sweltered venom sleeping got,
    Boil thou first i' the charmed pot.
10 **ALL.** Double, double toil and trouble;
    Fire burn and caldron bubble.
    SECOND WITCH. Fillet of a fenny snake,
    In the caldron boil and bake;
    Eye of newt and toe of frog,
15 Wool of bat and tongue of dog,
    Adder's fork and blind-worm's° sting,
    Lizard's leg and howlet's wing,°
    For a charm of powerful trouble,
    Like a hell-broth boil and bubble.
20 **ALL.** Double, double toil and trouble;
    Fire burn and caldron bubble.
    THIRD WITCH. Scale of dragon, tooth of wolf,
    Witches' mummy, maw and gulf°
    Of the ravined° salt-sea shark,
25 Root of hemlock digged i' the dark,
    Liver of blaspheming Jew,
    Gall of goat, and slips of yew°
    Slivered in the moon's eclipse,
    Nose of Turk and Tartar's lips,
30 Finger of birth-strangled babe
    Ditch-delivered by a drab,°
    Make the gruel thick and slab;°
    Add thereto a tiger's chaudron,°
    For the ingredients of our caldron.
35 **ALL.** Double, double toil and trouble;
    Fire burn and caldron bubble.
    SECOND WITCH. Cool it with a baboon's blood,
    Then the charm is firm and good.
          (Enter HECATE *to the other three* WITCHES.)°
    HECATE. Oh, well done! I commend your pains;
40 And everyone shall share i' the gains.
    And now about the caldron sing,
    Like elves and fairies in a ring,

Glosses

(cavern: probably set in the Study.)

hedgepig: hedgehog.

Harpier: the Third Witch's familiar spirit.

blind-worm: a small snakelike lizard, thought to be poisonous.
howlet's wing: the wing of a small owl.

maw and gulf: stomach and gullet.

ravined: ravenous.

yew: evergreen tree, thought to be poisonous.

drab: whore.

slab: slimy.

chaudron: entrails.

The appearance of Hecate is believed to be a later addition, not by Shakespeare—perhaps to provide an excuse for a dance and a song.

Enchanting all that you put in.
(Music and a song, "Black spirits," etc.)

(HECATE *retires.*)

SECOND WITCH. By the pricking of my thumbs,
45   Something wicked this way comes.
             Open, locks,
             Whoever knocks!

(Enter MACBETH.*)*

MACBETH. How now, you secret, black, and midnight hags!
        What is 't you do?[104]

ALL.   A deed without a name.

50 **MACBETH.** I conjure you, by that which you profess,
        Howe'er you come to know it, answer me.
        Though you untie the winds and let them fight
        Against the churches; though the yesty° waves
        Confound and swallow navigation up;
55   Though bladed corn be lodged° and trees blown down;
        Though castles topple on their warders' heads;
        Though palaces and pyramids do slope
        Their heads to their foundations; though the treasure

104. How has Macbeth's attitude toward the witches changed since his first meeting with them (Act One, Scene 3)? What might this suggest about changes in his character?

yesty: foamy.

Though . . . lodged: Though grain, still green, be beaten down.

Of nature's germens° tumble all together,
60   Even till destruction sicken;° answer me
To what I ask you.

FIRST WITCH.   Speak.

SECOND WITCH.   Demand.

THIRD WITCH.   We'll answer.

FIRST WITCH. Say, if thou'dst rather hear it from our mouths,
Or from our masters?

MACBETH.   Call 'em; let me see 'em.

FIRST WITCH. Pour in sow's blood, that hath eaten
65   Her nine farrow; grease that's sweaten
From the murderer's gibbet throw
Into the flame.

ALL.   Come, high or low;
Thyself and office deftly show!

          (*Thunder.* FIRST APPARITION: *an armed Head.*)[105]

MACBETH. Tell me, thou unknown power—

FIRST WITCH.   He knows thy
70   thought;
Hear his speech, but say thou naught.

FIRST APPARITION. Macbeth! Macbeth! Macbeth! beware Macduff;
Beware the thane of Fife. Dismiss me. Enough.°

                    (*Descends.*)

MACBETH. Whate'er thou art, for thy good caution, thanks;
Thou hast harped° my fear aright; but one word more—

75 **FIRST WITCH.** He will not be commanded; here's another,
More potent than the first.

          (*Thunder.* SECOND APPARITION: *a bloody Child.*)°

SECOND APPARITION.   Macbeth! Macbeth! Macbeth!

MACBETH. Had I three ears, I 'ld hear thee.

SECOND APPARITION. Be bloody, bold, and resolute; laugh to scorn
80   The power of man, for none of woman born
Shall harm Macbeth.

                    (*Descends.*)

MACBETH. Then live, Macduff; what need I fear of thee?
But yet I'll make assurance double sure,
And take a bond of fate,° thou shalt not live;
85   That I may tell pale-hearted fear it lies,
And sleep in spite of thunder.
(*Thunder.* THIRD APPARITION: *a Child crowned, with a tree in
his hand.*)°
                    What is this,
That rises like the issue of a king,
And wears upon his baby-brow the round
And top of sovereignty?

ALL.   Listen, but speak not to 't.

90 **THIRD APPARITION.** Be lion-mettled, proud, and take no care
Who chafes, who frets, or where conspirers are.
Macbeth shall never vanquished be until
Great Birnam wood to high Dunsinane hill

nature's germens: the seeds or elements through which nature operates.
sicken: is surfeited.

105. In Shakespeare's time, the apparition of a helmeted head came up (presumably from Hell below) through the caldron, which was placed over a trap door. If you were directing a modern production, how would you solve the problems of staging the appearance of the apparitions? What modern equipment might you use?
Dismiss . . . Enough: Note that this is the only apparition that does not equivocate with Macbeth. (Explained in Act Five, Scene 8.)

harped: guessed.

bloody Child: Macduff as a child. (Explained in Act Five, Scene 8.)

take . . . fate: make sure that fate's promise is fulfilled.

Child . . . hand: Malcolm. (Explained in Act Five, Scene 4.)

Shall come against him.

                               (Descends.)

MACBETH.   That will never be;

95 Who can impress° the forest, bid the tree

  Unfix his earth-bound root? Sweet bodements!° good!

  Rebellion's head, rise never till the wood

  Of Birnam rise, and our high-placed Macbeth

  Shall live the lease of nature, pay his breath

100 To time and mortal custom.° Yet my heart

  Throbs to know one thing; tell me, if your art

  Can tell so much—shall Banquo's issue ever

  Reign in this kingdom?

ALL.   Seek to know no more.

MACBETH. I will be satisfied; deny me this,

105 And an eternal curse fall on you! Let me know.

  Why sinks that caldron? and what noise° is this?

                               (Hautboys.)

FIRST WITCH. Show!

SECOND WITCH. Show!

THIRD WITCH. Show!

110 **ALL.** Show his eyes, and grieve his heart;

  Come like shadows, so depart!

  (A show of EIGHT KINGS,° *the last with a glass° in his hand;*

  BANQUO'S GHOST *following.)*

MACBETH. Thou art too like the spirit of Banquo; down!

  Thy crown does sear mine eyeballs.° And thy hair,

  Thou other gold-bound brow, is like the first.

115 A third is like the former. Filthy hags!

  Why do you show me this? A fourth! Start, eyes!

  What, will the line stretch out to the crack of doom?

  Another yet! A seventh! I'll see no more;

  And yet the eighth appears, who bears a glass

120 Which shows me many more; and some I see

  That twofold balls and treble scepters° carry.

  Horrible sight! Now, I see, 'tis true;

  For the blood-boltered° Banquo smiles upon me,

  And points at them for his. *(*APPARITIONS *vanish.)* What, is this

    so?

125 **FIRST WITCH.** Aye, sir, all this is so; but why

  Stands Macbeth thus amazedly?

  Come, sisters, cheer we up his sprites,

  And show the best of our delights.

  I'll charm the air to give a sound,

130 While you perform your antic round;°

  That this great King may kindly say

  Our duties did his welcome pay.

  (Music. The WITCHES *dance, and then vanish, with* HECATE.*)*

MACBETH. Where are they? Gone? Let this pernicious hour

  Stand aye accursed in the calendar!

135 Come in, without there!°

impress: conscript; force to serve as soldiers.
bodements: prophecies.

pay his breath . . . custom: die a natural death.

noise: music.

A show . . . Kings: The eight Stuart kings of Scotland, descending from Banquo and succeeding down to James I, the present king, walk in turn across the back of the stage.
glass: a magic mirror showing the future.
Thou . . . eyeballs: Spoken as the first king passes. Macbeth continues to comment as each king passes in turn.

twofold . . . scepters: The balls or orbs and scepters symbolize the sovereignty of England and Scotland, and the kingdoms of England, Scotland, and Ireland which were united for the first time under James I, eighth of Stuart kings.
blood-boltered: having hair matted with blood.

antic round: grotesque [or ancient?] round dance.

Lines 125–135: This passage is also considered to be a later interpolation, not by Shakespeare.

(Enter LENNOX.)

LENNOX. What's your Grace's will?

MACBETH. Saw you the weird sisters?

LENNOX. No, my lord.

MACBETH. Came they not by you?

LENNOX. No, indeed, my lord.

MACBETH. Infected be the air whereon they ride;
And damned all those that trust them![106] I did hear

140 The galloping of horse; who was 't came by?

LENNOX. 'Tis two or three, my lord, that bring you word
Macduff is fled to England.

MACBETH. Fled to England!

LENNOX. Aye, my good lord.

MACBETH *(aside).* Time, thou anticipatest my dread exploits;

145 The flighty purpose never is o'ertook
Unless the deed go with it; from this moment
The very firstlings of my heart shall be
The firstlings of my hand.° And even now,
To crown my thoughts with acts, be it thought and done.

150 The castle of Macduff I will surprise;
Seize upon Fife; give to the edge o' the sword
His wife, his babes, and all unfortunate souls
That trace him in his line. No boasting like a fool;
This deed I'll do before this purpose cool.

155 But no more sights!—Where are these gentlemen?
Come, bring me where they are.

(Exeunt.)

Scene 2.

Fife. MACDUFF's *castle. (Played in the Chamber.) Enter* LADY
MACDUFF, *her* SON, *and* ROSS.

LADY MACDUFF. What had he done, to make him fly the land?[107]

ROSS. You must have patience, madam.

LADY MACDUFF. He had none;
His flight was madness. When our actions do not,
Our fears do make us traitors.

ROSS. You know not

5 Whether it was his wisdom or his fear.

LADY MACDUFF. Wisdom! to leave his wife, to leave his babes,
His mansion and his titles in a place
From whence himself does fly? He loves us not;
He wants the natural touch;° for the poor wren,

10 The most diminutive of birds, will fight,
Her young ones in her nest, against the owl.
All is the fear and nothing is the love;
As little is the wisdom, where the flight
So runs against all reason.

ROSS. My dearest coz,°

15 I pray you, school° yourself; but, for your husband,

106. What is the irony of this line?

The flighty . . . hand: One must act at once if one is to accomplish one's purpose. From now on I shall put my thoughts into immediate action.

107. What message has Ross apparently just brought to Lady Macduff?

He wants . . . touch: He lacks natural human affection.

coz: cousin.

school: control.

He is noble, wise, judicious, and best knows
The fits o' the season.° I dare not speak much further;
But cruel are the times, when we are traitors
And do not know ourselves,° when we hold rumor
20 From what we fear,° yet know not what we fear,
But float upon a wild and violent sea
Each way and move. I take my leave of you;
Shall not be long but I'll be here again;
Things at the worst will cease, or else climb upward
25 To what they were before. My pretty cousin,°
Blessing upon you!
LADY MACDUFF. Fathered he is, and yet he's fatherless.
ROSS. I am so much a fool, should I stay longer,
It would be my disgrace and your discomfort;°
30 I take my leave at once.

(*Exit* ROSS.)

LADY MACDUFF.   Sirrah,° your father's dead;
And what will you do now? How will you live?
SON. As birds do, mother.
LADY MACDUFF.   What, with worms and flies?
SON. With what I get, I mean; and so do they.
LADY MACDUFF. Poor bird! thou'ldst never fear the net nor lime,°
35 The pitfall nor the gin.°
SON. Why should I, mother? Poor birds they are not set for.
My father is not dead, for all your saying.
LADY MACDUFF. Yes, he is dead; how wilt thou do for a father?
SON. Nay, how will you do for a husband?
40 LADY MACDUFF. Why, I can buy me twenty at any market.
SON. Then you'll buy 'em to sell again.

fits . . . season: violence of the times.

do not . . . ourselves: do not know ourselves (or each other) to be traitors. **hold rumor . . . fear:** believe rumors that grow out of fears.

My . . . cousin: Macduff's small son.

It would be . . . discomfort: Ross feels like weeping; in Shakespeare's time it was considered disgraceful for a man to weep. **Sirrah:** ordinary form of address used in speaking to children and servants.

lime: birdlime, a sticky substance used to catch birds. **gin:** snare.

LADY MACDUFF. Thou speak'st with all thy wit; and yet, i' faith,
With wit enough for thee.

SON. Was my father a traitor, mother?

45 **LADY MACDUFF.** Aye, that he was.

SON. What is a traitor?

LADY MACDUFF. Why, one that swears and lies.°

SON. And be all traitors that do so?

LADY MACDUFF. Every one that does so is a traitor, and must
be hanged.

50 **SON.** And must they all be hanged that swear and lie?

LADY MACDUFF. Every one.

SON. Who must hang them?

LADY MACDUFF. Why, the honest men.

SON. Then the liars and swearers are fools, for there are liars and
55 swearers enow to beat the honest men and hang up them.

LADY MACDUFF. Now, God help thee, poor monkey! But how wilt
thou do for a father?

SON. If he were dead, you'ld weep for him; if you would not, it were
a good sign that I should quickly have a new father.

60 **LADY MACDUFF.** Poor prattler, how thou talk'st![108]

                                (Enter a MESSENGER.*)*[109]

MESSENGER. Bless you, fair dame! I am not to you known,
Though in your state of honor I am perfect.°
I doubt° some danger does approach you nearly.
If you will take a homely man's advice,
65 Be not found here; hence, with your little ones.
To fright you thus, methinks I am too savage;
To do worse to you were fell cruelty,
Which is too nigh your person. Heaven preserve you!
I dare abide no longer.   *(Exit.)*

LADY MACDUFF.   Whither should I fly?
70 I have done no harm. But I remember now
I am in this earthly world, where to do harm
Is often laudable, to do good sometime
Accounted dangerous folly; why, then, alas,
Do I put up that womanly defense,
75 To say I have done no harm?   *(Enter* MURDERERS.*)*
                 What are these faces?

FIRST MURDERER. Where is your husband?

LADY MACDUFF. I hope in no place so unsanctified
Where such as thou mayst find him.

FIRST MURDERER.   He's a traitor.

SON. Thou liest, thou shag-eared° villain!

FIRST MURDERER.   What, you egg!
                               (Stabbing him)
80 Young fry of treachery!

SON.   He has killed me, mother;
Run away, I pray you!   *(Dies.)*
(Exit LADY MACDUFF, *crying "Murder!" Exeunt* MURDERERS,
following her.)[110]

---

swears and lies: swears allegiance and then breaks his oath.

108. *Macbeth* has only two humorous scenes: the broad comedy of the drunken porter, and the light comedy of this scene. What was Shakespeare's dramatic purpose in placing Lady Macduff's scene here?

109. It has been suggested that the messenger may have been sent by Lady Macbeth. Does this seem possible? Be alert for possible clues later in the play.
in your . . . perfect: I know of your honorable rank.
doubt: suspect.

shag-eared: often said to mean *shaggy-haired,* but Elizabethan criminals sometimes had their ears slit, and this could be the meaning.

110. Trace the murders committed by Macbeth up to this point in terms of their justifiability. What is revealed about changes in his character?

Scene 3.°

England. Before the King's palace. (Played on the Platform and in the Study.) Enter MALCOLM *and* MACDUFF.

MALCOLM. Let us seek out some desolate shade, and there
   Weep our sad bosoms empty.

MACDUFF.   Let us rather
   Hold fast the mortal sword and, like good men,
   Bestride our downfall'n birthdom.° Each new morn

5   New widows howl, new orphans cry, new sorrows
   Strike heaven on the face,¹¹¹ that it resounds
   As if it felt with Scotland and yelled out
   Like syllable of dolor.

MALCOLM.   What I believe, I'll wail;
   What know, believe; and what I can redress,

10   As I shall find the time to friend,° I will.
   What you have spoke, it may be so perchance;
   This tyrant, whose sole name blisters our tongues,
   Was once thought honest; you have loved him well.
   He hath not touched you yet. I am young; but something

15   You may deserve of him through me,° and wisdom
   To offer up a weak poor innocent lamb
   To appease an angry god.

MACDUFF. I am not treacherous.

MALCOLM.   But Macbeth is.
   A good and virtuous nature may recoil

20   In an imperial charge.° But I shall crave your pardon;
   That which you are my thoughts cannot transpose;°
   Angels are bright still, though the brightest fell;
   Though all things foul would wear the brows of grace,
   Yet grace must still look so.

MACDUFF.   I have lost my hopes.

25 MALCOLM. Perchance even there where I did find my doubts,
   Why in that rawness left you wife and child,
   Those precious motives, those strong knots of love,
   Without leave-taking? I pray you,
   Let not my jealousies be your dishonors,

30   But mine own safeties.° You may be rightly just,
   Whatever I shall think.

MACDUFF.   Bleed, bleed, poor country!
   Great tyranny! lay thou thy basis sure,
   For goodness dare not check thee; wear thou thy wrongs;
   The title is affeered!° Fare thee well, lord.

35   I would not be the villain that thou think'st
   For the whole space that's in the tyrant's grasp,
   And the rich East to boot.

MALCOLM.   Be not offended;
   I speak not as in absolute fear of you.
   I think our country sinks beneath the yoke;

40   It weeps, it bleeds; and each new day a gash

(The unusual length of Scene 3 may be explained by the fact that it was customary to give the chief actor a rest during the fourth act, or thereabouts, of a tragedy.)

Bestride . . . birthdom: defend our fallen fatherland.

111. What is the irony in Macduff's saying this?

to friend: suitable.

but something . . . me: but you may win favor from Macbeth by betraying me.

recoil . . . charge: reverse itself through loyalty to the king. *transpose:* change.

Let not . . . safeties: I am suspicious not to dishonor you but because I wish to assure my own safety.

The title . . . affeered: Your title of tyranny is confirmed.

Is added to her wounds. I think withal
There would be hands uplifted in my right;
And here from gracious England° have I offer
Of goodly thousands; but, for all this,
45 When I shall tread upon the tyrant's head,
Or wear it on my sword, yet my poor country
Shall have more vices than it had before,
More suffer, and more sundry ways than ever,
By him that shall succeed.

MACDUFF.   What should he be?

50 **MALCOLM.** It is myself I mean; in whom I know
All the particulars of vice so grafted
That, when they shall be opened, black Macbeth
Will seem as pure as snow, and the poor state
Esteem him as a lamb, being compared
55 With my confineless harms.°

MACDUFF.   Not in the legions
Of horrid hell can come a devil more damned
In evils to top Macbeth.

MALCOLM   I grant him bloody,
Luxurious,° avaricious, false, deceitful,
Sudden,° malicious, smacking of every sin
60 That has a name; but there's no bottom, none,
In my voluptuousness. Your wives, your daughters,
Your matrons and your maids, could not fill up
The cistern of my lust; and my desire.
All continent impediments would o'erbear
65 That did oppose my will. Better Macbeth
Than such an one to reign.[112]

MACDUFF.   Boundless intemperance
In nature is a tyranny; it hath been
The untimely emptying of the happy throne
And fall of many kings. But fear not yet
70 To take upon you what is yours; you may
Convey° your pleasures in a spacious plenty,
And yet seem cold, the time° you may so hoodwink.
We have willing dames enough; there cannot be
That vulture in you, to devour so many
75 As will to greatness dedicate themselves,
Finding it so inclined.

MALCOLM.   With this there grows
In my most ill-composed affection° such
A stanchless° avarice that, were I king,
I should cut off the nobles for their lands,
80 Desire his jewels and this other's house;
And my more-having would be as a sauce
To make me hunger more; that I should forge
Quarrels unjust against the good and loyal,
Destroying them for wealth.

MACDUFF.   This avarice

England: the king of England.

confineless harms: unlimited evil.

Luxurious: lustful.
Sudden: violent.

112. Why does Malcolm makes this confession?

Convey: obtain secretly.
the time: the world.

ill-composed affection: evil disposition.
stanchless: insatiable.

85   Sticks deeper, grows with more pernicious root
        Than summer-seeming° lust, and it hath been
        The sword of our slain kings. Yet do not fear;
        Scotland hath foisons° to fill up your will,
        Of your mere own. All these are portable,
90   With other graces weighed.°
    MALCOLM. But I have none; the king-becoming graces,
        As justice, verity, temperance, stableness,
        Bounty, perseverance, mercy, lowliness,
        Devotion, patience, courage, fortitude,
95   I have no relish of them, but abound
        In the division of each several crime,
        Acting it many ways. Nay, had I power, I should
        Pour the sweet milk of concord into hell,
        Uproar the universal peace, confound
100   All unity on earth.
    MACDUFF.   O Scotland, Scotland!
    MALCOLM. If such a one be fit to govern, speak;
        I am as I have spoken.
    MACDUFF.   Fit to govern!
        No, not to live. O nation miserable,
        With an untitled tyrant bloody-sceptered,
105   When shalt thou see thy wholesome days again,
        Since that the truest issue of thy throne
        By his own interdiction° stands accursed,
        And does blaspheme his breed? Thy royal father
        Was a most sainted king. The queen that bore thee,
110   Oftener upon her knees than on her feet,
        Died every day she lived.° Fare thee well!
        These evils thou repeat'st upon thyself
        Have banished me from Scotland. O my breast,
        Thy hope ends here!
    MALCOLM.   Macduff, this noble passion,
115   Child of integrity, hath from my soul
        Wiped the black scruples, reconciled my thoughts,
        To thy good truth and honor. Devilish Macbeth
        By many of these trains° hath sought to win me
        Into his power, and modest wisdom plucks me
120   From overcredulous haste. But God above
        Deal between thee and me! For even now
        I put myself to thy direction, and
        Unspeak mine own detraction, here abjure
        The taints and blames I laid upon myself,
125   For strangers to my nature. I am yet
        Unknown to woman, never was forsworn,
        Scarcely have coveted what was mine own,
        At no time broke my faith, would not betray
        The devil to his fellow, and delight
130   No less in truth than life; my first false speaking
        Was this upon myself. What I am truly

summer-seeming: short-lived.

foisons: plenty.

All these . . . weighed: These weaknesses are bearable, considering your other virtues.

interdiction: decree.

Died . . . lived: prepared for death by daily prayers and self-sacrifice.

trains: devices.

Is thine and my poor country's to command;
Whither indeed, before thy here-approach,
Old Siward, with ten thousand warlike men,
135   Already at a point,° was setting forth.
Now we'll together; and the chance of goodness
Be like our warranted quarrel!° Why are you silent?
MACDUFF. Such welcome and unwelcome things at once
'Tis hard to reconcile.

(Enter a DOCTOR.*)*

140   MALCOLM. Well, more anon.—Comes the King forth, I pray you?
DOCTOR. Aye, sir; there are a crew of wretched souls
That stay his cure.° There malady convinces
The great assay of art;° but at his touch—
Such sanctity hath heaven given his hand—
145   They presently amend.
MALCOLM.   I thank you, doctor.

(Exit DOCTOR.*)*

MACDUFF. What's the disease he means?
MALCOLM.   'Tis called the evil:°
A most miraculous work in this good King;
Which often, since my here-remain in England,
I have seen him do. How he solicits heaven,
150   Himself best knows; but strangely-visited people,
All swoln and ulcerous, pitiful to the eye,
The mere despair of surgery, he cures,
Hanging a golden stamp about their necks,
Put on with holy prayers. And 'tis spoken,
155   To the succeeding royalty he leaves
The healing benediction. With this strange virtue,
He hath a heavenly gift of prophecy,
And sundry blessings hang about his throne,
That speak him full of grace.

(Enter ROSS.*)*

MACDUFF.   See, who comes here?
160   MALCOLM. My countryman; but yet I know him not.
MACDUFF. My ever-gentle cousin, welcome hither.
MALCOLM. I know him now. Good God, betimes remove
The means that makes us strangers!
ROSS.   Sir, amen.
MACDUFF. Stands Scotland where it did?
ROSS.   Alas, poor country!
165   Almost afraid to know itself. It cannot
Be called our mother, but our grave; where nothing,
But who knows nothing, is once seen to smile;
Where sighs and groans and shrieks that rend the air
Are made, not marked; where violent sorrow seems
170   A modern ecstasy.° The dead man's knell
Is there scarce asked for who; and good men's lives
Expire before the flowers in their caps,
Dying or ere they sicken.

at a point: prepared.

and the chance . . . quarrel: and may our chance of success be as strong as the justness of our cause.

stay his cure: wait for him to cure them.
convinces . . . art: defies cure by any medical skill.

the evil: scrofula, a disease characterized by swelling of the lymphatic glands. It was called "the king's evil" because of a belief that it could be healed by the touch of a king. This curing power was first attributed to Edward the Confessor and later to his successors. This passage was obviously intended to flatter James I, who believed he had this power.

A modern ecstasy: ordinary feeling.

MACDUFF.   Oh, relation
Too nice,° and yet too true!
MALCOLM.   What's the newest grief?
175 ROSS. That of an hour's age doth hiss the speaker;°
Each minute teems° a new one.
MACDUFF.   How does my wife?
ROSS. Why, well.[113]
MACDUFF.   And all my children?
ROSS.   Well, too.
MACDUFF. The tyrant has not battered at their peace?
ROSS. No; they were well at peace when I did leave 'em.
180 MACDUFF. Be not a niggard of your speech; how goes 't?
ROSS. When I came hither to transport the tidings,
Which I have heavily borne, there ran a rumor
Of many worthy fellows that were out;°
Which was to my belief witnessed the rather,
185 For that I saw the tyrant's power afoot.
Now is the time of help; your eye in Scotland
Would create soldiers, make our women fight,
To doff their dire distresses.
MALCOLM.   Be 't their comfort
We are coming thither. Gracious England hath
190 Lent us good Siward and ten thousand men;
An older and a better soldier none
That Christendom gives out.
ROSS.   Would I could answer
This comfort with the like! But I have words
That would be howled out in the desert air,
195 Where hearing should not latch° them.
MACDUFF.   What concern they?
The general cause? Or is it a fee-grief°
Due to some single breast?
ROSS.   No mind that's honest
But in it shares some woe; though the main part
Pertains to you alone.
MACDUFF.   If it be mine,
200 Keep it not from me; quickly let me have it.
ROSS. Let not your ears despise my tongue forever,
Which shall possess them with the heaviest sound
That ever yet they heard.
MACDUFF.   Hum! I guess at it.
ROSS. Your castle is surprised; your wife and babes
205 Savagely slaughtered.[114] To relate the manner
Were, on the quarry° of these murdered deer,
To add the death of you.
MALCOLM.   Merciful heaven!
What, man! ne'er pull your hat upon your brows;
Give sorrow words: the grief that does not speak
210 Whispers the o'er-fraught heart, and bids it break.

relation too nice: report too exact.

doth hiss the speaker: causes the speaker to be hissed because he is already out of date.
teems: brings forth.
113. How does Ross speak: quickly, or hesitantly?

out: in arms.

latch: catch the sound of.

fee-grief: private grief.

114. What has happened that might prompt Ross now to tell Macduff the truth about his wife and children?
quarry: heap of dead bodies.

MACDUFF. My children, too?

ROSS. Wife, children, servants, all
That could be found.

MACDUFF. And I must be from thence!
My wife killed, too?

ROSS. I have said.

MALCOLM. Be comforted;
Let's make us medicines of our great revenge,
215 To cure his deadly grief.

MACDUFF. He has no children.[115] All my pretty ones?
Did you say all? O hell-kite! All?
What, all my pretty chickens and their dam
At one fell swoop?

220 **MALCOLM.** Dispute it like a man.

MACDUFF. I shall do so;
But I must also feel it as a man.
I cannot but remember such things were,
That were most precious to me. Did heaven look on
And would not take their part? Sinful Macduff,
225 They were all struck for thee! Naught, that I am,
Not for their own demerits, but for mine,
Fell slaughter on their souls. Heaven rest them now!

115. To whom is Macduff referring? What does he mean? (Several interpretations are possible.)

MALCOLM. Be this the whetstone of your sword; let grief
    Convert to anger; blunt not the heart, enrage it.

230 **MACDUFF.** Oh, I could play the woman with mine eyes
    And braggart with my tongue! But, gentle heavens,
    Cut short all intermission; front to front
    Bring thou this fiend of Scotland and myself;
    Within my sword's length set him; if he 'scape,

235   Heaven forgive him, too!

MALCOLM.   This tune goes manly.
    Come, go we to the King; our power is ready;
    Our lack is nothing but our leave.° Macbeth
    Is ripe for shaking, and the powers above
    Put on their instruments. Receive what cheer you may;

240   The night is long that never finds the day.

                             (Exeunt.)[116]

Our lack . . . leave: We only need the King's permission to depart.

116. Why do you think Shakespeare had Macduff learn of Lady Macduff's murder *after* he had convinced Malcolm of his loyalty?

Act Five

Scene 1.

Dunsinane. Anteroom in the castle. (Played in the Chamber.) Enter a DOCTOR OF PHYSIC° *and a* WAITING-GENTLEWOMAN.

Physic: medicine.

DOCTOR. I have two nights watched with you, but can perceive no truth in your report. When was it she last walked?[117]

GENTLEWOMAN. Since his Majesty went into the field, I have seen her rise from her bed, throw her nightgown upon her, unlock
5 her closet, take forth paper, fold it, write upon 't, read it, afterwards seal it, and again return to bed; yet all this while in a most fast sleep.

DOCTOR. A great perturbation in nature, to receive at once the benefit of sleep, and do the effects of watching! In this slumbery
10 agitation, besides her walking and other actual performances, what, at any time, have you heard her say?

GENTLEWOMAN. That, sir, which I will not report after her.

DOCTOR. You may to me; and 'tis most meet you should.

GENTLEWOMAN. Neither to you nor anyone, having no witness to
15 confirm my speech.

                    (Enter LADY MACBETH, *with a taper.)*

Lo, you, here she comes! This is her very guise; and, upon my life, fast asleep. Observe her; stand close.

DOCTOR. How came she by that light?

GENTLEWOMAN. Why, it stood by her; she has light by her contin-
20 ually, 'tis her command.

DOCTOR. You see, her eyes are open.

GENTLEWOMAN. Aye, but their sense is shut.

117. Note that this scene is largely in prose—perhaps because the disjointed remarks of Lady Macbeth's sleepwalking do not seem suitable for poetry; the Doctor and Gentlewoman, who speak on a less intense emotional plane, could not very well be given poetry to speak while Lady Macbeth was present.

DOCTOR. What is it she does now? Look how she rubs her hands.

GENTLEWOMAN. It is an accustomed action with her, to seem thus
washing her hands. I have known her continue in this a quarter of
an hour.

LADY MACBETH. Yet here's a spot.

DOCTOR. Hark! she speaks. I will set down what comes from her, to
satisfy my remembrance the more strongly.

LADY MACBETH. Out, damned spot! out, I say!—One; two. Why,
then 'tis time to do 't.—Hell is murky! Fie, my lord, fie! a soldier,
and afeard? What need we fear who knows it, when none can call
our power to account?—Yet who would have thought the old man
to have had so much blood in him?

DOCTOR. Do you mark that?

LADY MACBETH. The thane of Fife had a wife; where is she now?—
What, will these hands ne'er be clean?—No more o' that, my lord,
no more o' that; you mar all with this starting.

DOCTOR. Go to, go to; you have known what you should not.

GENTLEWOMAN. She has spoke what she should not, I am sure of
that. Heaven knows what she has known.

LADY MACBETH. Here's the smell of the blood still; all the perfumes
of Arabia will not sweeten this little hand. Oh, oh, oh!

DOCTOR. What a sigh is there! The heart is sorely charged.

GENTLEWOMAN. I would not have such a heart in my bosom for the
dignity of the whole body.

DOCTOR. Well, well, well—

GENTLEWOMAN. Pray God it be, sir.

DOCTOR. This disease is beyond my practice; yet I have known
those which have walked in their sleep who have died holily in
their beds.

LADY MACBETH. Wash your hands, put on your nightgown; look not
so pale.—I tell you yet again, Banquo's buried; he cannot come
out on 's grave.

DOCTOR. Even so?

LADY MACBETH. To bed, to bed! There's knocking at the gate. Come,
come, come, come, give me your hand. What's done cannot be
undone.—To bed, to bed, to bed![118]

DOCTOR. Will she go now to bed?

(Exit LADY MACBETH.*)*

GENTLEWOMAN. Directly.

DOCTOR. Foul whisperings are abroad! unnatural deeds
Do breed unnatural troubles; infected minds
To their deaf pillows will discharge their secrets.
More needs she the divine than the physician.
God, God forgive us all! Look after her;
Remove from her the means of all annoyance,°
And still keep eyes upon her. So, good night.
My mind she has mated,° and amazed my sight.
I think, but dare not speak.

GENTLEWOMAN.   Good night, good doctor.

(Exeunt.)[119]

118. (a) Can you connect each phrase
of Lady Macbeth's speeches with some
specific aspect of the crimes in which
she has been involved?
    (b) Lady Macbeth is obviously in
process of emotional collapse. Have
there been signs earlier in the play that
this might happen? Note especially her
speeches at her last appearance, the
end of Act Three, Scene 4.

annoyance: injury to herself.

mated: confounded.

119. How convincingly has
Shakespeare portrayed emotional
illness?

Comment: Shakespeare's Theater—The Globe

After 1599, Shakespeare probably wrote most of his plays with London's Globe Theater in mind. According to the conjectures of scholars, the outside diameter of the theater was about 84 feet, and its three tiers of seats, plus an open area for standees, could accommodate about 2000 spectators.

The main acting area was the Platform, which extended out into the audience and was probably some 24 feet across the front, 41 feet across the widest part at the back, and 29 feet deep. At the back of the Platform was a recess known as the Study which was usually used for interior scenes. At either side of the Study were large permanent doors, similar to the street doors of Elizabethan town houses. These were the main stage entrances. In the floor of the Platform were a number of trap doors leading to the area below stage known as Hell. From these traps arose apparitions, smoke, and fog, and through them actors descended when the action required them to go underground.

On the second level there was another cur-tained recess called the Chamber, generally used for domestic settings, especially scenes involving women. In front of the Chamber was a narrow balcony called the Tarras (terrace) which connected with two small bay windows or window stages that flanked it. The Tarras was often used in conjunction with the Platform—for example, to represent a hill, battlements, or a gallery from which observers watched action below.

The third level contained a narrow musicians' gallery which could also be used as an acting area. Above it was a canopied roof supported by two large stage posts that rose from the Platform. Sound effects such as thunder or battle "alarums" were produced in the Huts above the Canopy. The Huts also housed a pulley system used for lowering apparitions or objects supposed to appear from midair.

This entire three-story structure which formed the back of the stage and gave the effect of a large Elizabethan town house was known as the Tiring House. It was the Globe's permanent set.

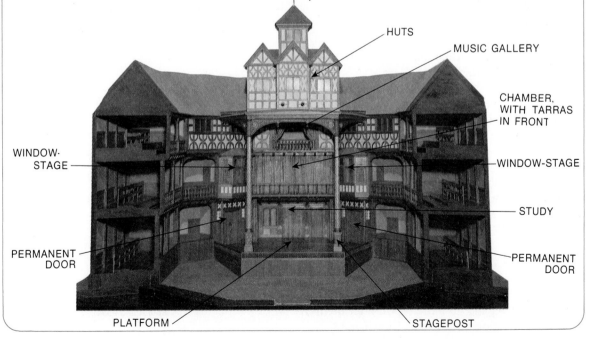

HUTS

MUSIC GALLERY

CHAMBER, WITH TARRAS IN FRONT

WINDOW-STAGE

WINDOW-STAGE

STUDY

PERMANENT DOOR

PERMANENT DOOR

PLATFORM

STAGEPOST

Scene 2.[120]

The country near Dunsinane. (Played on the Platform.) Drum and colors. Enter MENTEITH, CAITHNESS, ANGUS, LENNOX, *and* SOLDIERS.

MENTEITH. The English power is near, led on by Malcolm,
His uncle Siward, and the good Macduff.
Revenges burn in them; for their dear causes
Would to the bleeding and the grim alarm
5   Excite the mortified man.°
ANGUS.   Near Birnam wood
Shall we well meet them; that way are they coming.
CAITHNESS. Who knows if Donalbain be with his brother?
LENNOX. For certain, sir, he is not. I have a file
Of all the gentry: there is Siward's son,[121]
10 And many unrough° youths that even now
Protest their first of manhood.°
MENTEITH.   What does the tyrant?
CAITHNESS. Great Dunsinane he strongly fortifies.
Some say he's mad; others that lesser hate him
Do call it valiant fury; but, for certain,
15 He cannot buckle his distempered cause
Within the belt of rule.°
ANGUS.   Now does he feel
His secret murders sticking on his hands;
Now minutely revolts upbraid his faith-breach;°
Those he commands move only in command,
20 Nothing in love; now does he feel his title
Hang loose about him, like a giant's robe
Upon a dwarfish thief.
MENTEITH.   Who then shall blame
His pestered senses to recoil and start,
When all that is within him does condemn
25 Itself for being there?
CAITHNESS.   Well, march we on,
To give obedience where 'tis truly owed.
Meet we the medicine of the sickly weal,
And with him pour we in our country's purge
Each drop of us.°
LENNOX.   Or so much as it needs,
30 To dew the sovereign flower and drown the weeds.
Make we our march towards Birnam.

                    (Exeunt, marching.)

Scene 3.

Dunsinane. A room in the castle. (Played in the Chamber.) Enter MACBETH, DOCTOR, *and* ATTENDANTS.

MACBETH. Bring me no more reports; let them° fly all.
Till Birnam wood remove to Dunsinane,

---

120. Note that this act is made up of a series of short scenes which take place alternately at Dunsinane Castle and on the battlefields. On the stage of the Globe, this could easily be managed. If you were making a film of *Macbeth*, how would you handle the frequent shifts? How might they be dealt with in a modern stage production?

their dear causes . . . man: their deeply-felt causes would arouse a dead man to bloody battle.

121. Follow young Siward's activities. Why did Shakespeare introduce this episode?
unrough: beardless.
Protest . . . manhood: call themselves men for the first time.

He cannot . . . rule: He cannot control the situation.

Now . . . faith-breach: Every minute, those who revolt against him blame his faithlessness.

Meet we . . . us: We go to meet Malcolm, who will heal the sickness of our country, and to offer our lives in the curing process.

them: the thanes.

I cannot taint° with fear. What's the boy Malcolm?
Was he not born of woman? The spirits that know
All mortal consequences have pronounced me thus:
"Fear not, Macbeth; no man that's born of woman
Shall e'er have power upon thee." Then fly, false thanes,
and mingle with the English epicures.°
The mind I sway by° and the heart I bear
Shall never sag with doubt nor shake with fear.

(Enter a SERVANT.)

The devil damn thee black, thou cream-faced loon!
Where got'st thou that goose look?

SERVANT. There is ten thousand—

MACBETH.   Geese, villain?

SERVANT.   Soldiers, sir.

MACBETH. Go prick thy face, and over-red° thy fear,
Thou lily-livered boy. What soldiers, patch?°
Death of thy soul! those linen cheeks of thine
Are counselors to fear. What soldiers, whey-face?

SERVANT. The English force, so please you.

MACBETH. Take thy face hence.

(Exit SERVANT.)

                                        Seyton!—I am sick at heart,
When I behold—Seyton, I say!—This push°
Will cheer me ever, or disseat me now.
I have lived long enough; my way of life
Is fall'n into the sear, the yellow leaf;
And that which should accompany old age,
As honor, love, obedience, troops of friends,
I must not look to have; but, in their stead,
Curses, not loud but deep, mouth-honor, breath,
Which the poor heart would fain deny, and dare not.
Seyton!¹²²

(Enter SEYTON.)

SEYTON. What is your gracious pleasure?

MACBETH.   What news more?

SEYTON. All is confirmed, my lord, which was reported.

MACBETH. I'll fight till from my bones my flesh be hacked.
Give me my armor.

SEYTON.   'Tis not needed yet.

MACBETH. I'll put it on.
Send out moe horses, skirr° the country round;
Hang those that talk of fear. Give me mine armor.
How does your patient, doctor?¹²³

DOCTOR.   Not so sick, my lord,
As she is troubled with thick-coming fancies,
That keep her from her rest.

MACBETH.   Cure her of that.
Canst thou not minister to a mind diseased,
Pluck from the memory a rooted sorrow,
Raze out the written troubles of the brain,

---

taint: become infected.

epicures: lovers of luxury.

I sway by: I am directed by.

over-red: redden. The implication is that the servant's blood has gone to his lower body on account of his fear. He is pale, and there is no blood in his liver, where his courage should have resided—hence, *lily-livered.*
patch: fool.

push: attack.

122. What *appears* to be Macbeth's emotional state at the beginning of the scene? How is he actually feeling? What tells you?

skirr: scour.

123. What do Macbeth's remarks about his wife's illness reveal about the state of their relationship at this point?

And with some sweet oblivious antidote
Cleanse the stuffed bosom of that perilous stuff°
45 Which weighs upon the heart?

DOCTOR.   Therein the patient
Must minister to himself.

MACBETH. Throw physic to the dogs; I'll none of it.
Come, put mine armor on; give me my staff.
Seyton, send out.° Doctor, the thanes fly from me.
50 Come sir, dispatch. If thou couldst, doctor, cast
The water of my land,° find her disease,
And purge it to a sound and pristine health,
I would applaud thee to the very echo,
That should applaud again.—Pull 't off,° I say.—
55 What rhubarb, senna, or what purgative drug,
Would scour these English hence? Hear'st thou of them?

DOCTOR. Aye, my good lord; your royal preparation
Makes us hear something.

MACBETH.   Bring it° after me.
I will not be afraid of death and bane
60 Till Birnam forest come to Dunsinane.

DOCTOR (aside). Were I from Dunsinane away and clear,
Profit again should hardly draw me here.

                                        (Exeunt.)

Scene 4.

*Country near Birnam wood. (Played on the Platform.) Drum and
colors. Enter* MALCOLM, OLD SIWARD *and his* SON, MACDUFF, MEN-
TEITH, CAITHNESS, ANGUS, LENNOX, ROSS, *and* SOLDIERS, *marching.*

MALCOLM. Cousins, I hope the days are near at hand
That chambers will be safe.°

MENTEITH.   We doubt it nothing.

SIWARD. What wood is this before us?

MENTEITH.   The wood of Birnam.

MALCOLM. Let every soldier hew him down a bough,
5   And bear 't before him; thereby shall we shadow
The numbers of our host, and make discovery°
Err in report of us.°

SOLDIERS.   It shall be done.

SIWARD. We learn no other but the confident tyrant
Keeps still in Dunsinane, and will endure
10 Our setting down before 't.°

MALCOLM.   'Tis his main hope;
For where there is advantage to be given,
Both more and less° have given him the revolt,
And none serve with him but constrainéd things
Whose hearts are absent, too.

MACDUFF.   Let our just censures

---

stuff: Some scholars think this word is a printer's error and should be *grief.*

send out: send out more scouts.

cast . . . land: diagnose my country's illness.

Pull 't off: referring to some part of his armor.

it: the armor.

That chambers . . . safe: when people can sleep safely.

discovery: Macbeth's scouts.

Lines 3–7: Here the equivocations of the apparitions begin to be revealed.

setting down. . . : laying siege to it.

Both more and less: both nobles and common people.

15   Attend the true event,° and put we on
   Industrious soldiership.
   SIWARD.   The time approaches
   That will with due decision make us know
   What we shall say we have and what we owe.
   Thoughts speculative their unsure hopes relate,
20   But certain issue strokes must arbitrate;°
   Toward which advance the war.

                              (Exeunt, marching.)

Let . . . event: Let our judgment await the actual outcome of the battle.

Thoughts . . . arbitrate: We are now speculating on the basis of our hopes; only after the battle will we know the real outcome.

Scene 5.

Dunsinane. Within the castle. (Played on the Tarras and in the Chamber.) Enter° MACBETH, SEYTON, and SOLDIERS, with drum and colors.

(They enter on the Tarras.)

MACBETH. Hang out our banners on the outward walls;
   The cry is still "They come!" Our castle's strength
   Will laugh a seige to scorn; here let them lie
   Till famine and the ague eat them up.
5   Were they not forced° with those that should be ours,
   We might have met them dareful, beard to beard,
   And beat them backward home.

forced: reinforced.

                         (A cry of women within.)
                 What is that noise?
SEYTON. It is the cry of women, my good lord.

                               (Exit.)°

(Exits into the Chamber.)

MACBETH. I have almost forgot the taste of fears.
10   The time has been[124] my senses would have cooled
   To hear a night-shriek, and my fell of hair°
   Would at a dismal treatise° rouse and stir
   As life were in 't. I have supped full with horrors;
   Direness, familiar to my slaughterous thoughts,
15   Cannot once start me.

124. When was the time he refers to? What does the rest of the speech suggest about changes in his character?
fell of hair: hair of his head.
dismal treatise: horrible story.

                        (Re-enter SEYTON.)°

(He re-enters from the Chamber.)

       Wherefore was that cry?
SEYTON. The Queen, my lord, is dead.
MACBETH.[125] She should have died hereafter;
   There would have been a time for such a word.
   Tomorrow, and tomorrow, and tomorrow,
20   Creeps in this petty pace from day to day,
   To the last syllable of recorded time,
   And all our yesterdays have lighted fools
   The way to dusty death. Out, out, brief candle!
   Life's but a walking shadow, a poor player
25   That struts and frets his hour upon the stage
   And then is heard no more; it is a tale
   Told by an idiot, full of sound and fury,
   Signifying nothing.[126]

125. How might Macbeth react before he speaks?

126. What does Macbeth mean by "She should have died hereafter"? Which lines in the soliloquy are most helpful in providing clues? What does the soliloquy say about life in general? about Macbeth's life specifically?

                        (Enter a MESSENGER.)

Thou comest to use thy tongue; thy story quickly.
30 **MESSENGER.** Gracious my lord,
I should report that which I say I saw,
But know not how to do it.
MACBETH.   Well, say, sir.
MESSENGER. As I did stand my watch upon the hill,
I looked toward Birnam, and anon, methought,
35 The wood began to move.
MACBETH.   Liar and slave!
MESSENGER. Let me endure your wrath, if 't be not so.
Within this three mile may you see it coming;
I say, a moving grove.
MACBETH.   If thou speak'st false,
Upon the next tree shalt thou hang alive,
40 Till famine cling° thee; if thy speech be sooth,
I care not if thou dost for me as much.
I pull in resolution,° and begin
To doubt the equivocation° of the fiend
That lies like truth: "Fear not, till Birnam wood
45 Do come to Dunsinane"; and now a wood
Comes toward Dunsinane. Arm, arm, and out!¹²⁷
If this which he avouches does appear,
There is nor flying hence nor tarrying here.
I 'gin to be aweary of the sun,
50 And wish the estate o' the world were now undone.
Ring the alarum-bell! Blow, wind! come, wrack!°
At least we'll die with harness on our back.

                                    (*Exeunt.*)

cling: shrivel up.

I pull in resolution: I weaken in
confidence. With these words begins
Macbeth's awareness that he has been
duped by the witches.
doubt the equivocation: fear the
deception.
127. *Line 46:* Compare these words
with lines 2–7 of this scene. What has
caused Macbeth to change his plans?

wrack: ruin; destruction.

Scene 6.
*Dunsinane. Before the castle. (Played on the Platform.) Drum and
colors. Enter* MALCOLM, OLD SIWARD, MACDUFF, *and their* ARMY,
with boughs.
MALCOLM. Now near enough; your leavy screens throw down,
And show like those you are. You, worthy uncle,
Shall, with my cousin, your right noble son,
Lead our first battle;° worthy Macduff and we
5 Shall take upon 's what else remains to do,
According to our order.
SIWARD.   Fare you well.
Do we but find the tyrant's power tonight,
Let us be beaten, if we cannot fight.
MACDUFF. Make all our trumpets speak; give them all breath,
10 Those clamorous harbingers of blood and death.

                                    (*Exeunt.*)

battle: division of troops.

Scene 7.

Another part of the field. (Played on the Platform.) Alarums. Enter
MACBETH.

MACBETH. They have tied me to a stake; I cannot fly,
  But, bearlike, I must fight the course.° What's he
  That was not born of woman? Such a one
  Am I to fear, or none.

(Enter YOUNG SIWARD.*)*

5 YOUNG SIWARD. What is thy name?
MACBETH.   Thou'lt be afraid to hear it.
YOUNG SIWARD. No; though thou call'st thyself a hotter name
  Than any is in hell.
MACBETH.   My name's Macbeth.
YOUNG SIWARD. The devil himself could not pronounce a title
  More hateful to mine ear.
MACBETH.   No, nor more fearful.
10 YOUNG SIWARD. Thou liest, abhorréd tyrant; with my sword
  I'll prove the lie thou speak'st.

(They fight, and YOUNG SIWARD *is slain.)*

MACBETH. Thou wast born of woman.
  But swords I smile at, weapons laugh to scorn,
  Brandished by man that's of a woman born.

(Exit.)

(Alarums. Enter MACDUFF.*)*

MACDUFF. That way the noise is. Tyrant, show thy face!
15   If thou be'st slain and with no stroke of mine,
  My wife and children's ghosts will haunt me still.
  I cannot strike at wretched kerns, whose arms
  Are hired to bear their staves; either thou, Macbeth,
  Or else my sword with an unbattered edge
20   I sheathe again undeeded. There thou shouldst be;
  By this great clatter, one of greatest note
  Seems bruited.° Let me find him, fortune!
  And more I beg not.   *(Exit. Alarums.)*

(Enter MALCOLM *and* OLD SIWARD.*)*

SIWARD. This way, my lord; the castle's gently rendered;°
25   The tyrant's people on both sides do fight;
  The noble thanes do bravely in the war;
  The day almost itself professes yours,
  And little is to do.
MALCOLM.   We have met with foes
  That strike beside us.
SIWARD.   Enter, sir, the castle.

(Exeunt. Alarums.)

(At this point, the Study curtains may have been thrown open to reveal the gate of Macbeth's castle, with perhaps a portcullis hanging under the Tarras. Macbeth stands at bay before the gates.)
They have . . . course: In bearbaiting, a popular sport in Shakespeare's time, a bear was tied to a stake and forced to fight rounds with dogs set upon it in relays.

bruited: announced by a great noise.

rendered: surrendered.
(The formal entry into the castle, after surrender, might be made through gates visible in the Study. Victorious soldiers might appear in the window-stages and dip the tyrant's banners, planting those of Malcolm and Siward on the Tarras. Macbeth's next entry and that of Macduff would probably be made through the two stage-doors on the Platform.)

Scene 8.

Another part of the field. (Played on the Platform.) Enter
MACBETH.

MACBETH. Why should I play the Roman fool and die
  On mine own sword?° Whiles I see lives,° the gashes
  Do better upon them.

                              (Enter MACDUFF.*)*

MACDUFF.   Turn, hell-hound, turn!
MACBETH. Of all men else I have avoided thee.
5   But get thee back; my soul is too much charged
  With blood of thine already.
MACDUFF.   I have no words;
  My voice is in my sword, thou bloodier villain
  Than terms can give thee out!

                              (They fight.)

MACBETH.   Thou losest labor;
  As easy mayst thou the intrenchant° air
10   With thy keen sword impress as make me bleed.
  Let fall thy blade on vulnerable crests;
  I bear a charmèd life, which must not yield
  To one of woman born.
MACDUFF.   Despair thy charm;
  And let the angel whom thou still hast served
15   Tell thee Macduff was from his mother's womb
  Untimely ripped.
MACBETH. Accursèd be that tongue that tells me so,
  For it hath cowed my better part of man!
  And be these juggling fiends no more believed
20   That palter with us in a double sense;
  That keep the word of promise to our ear,
  And break it to our hope. I'll not fight with thee.
MACDUFF. Then yield thee, coward,
  And live to be the show and gaze o' the time.
25   We'll have thee, as our rarer monsters are,
  Painted upon a pole,° and underwrit,
  "Here may you see the tyrant."
MACBETH.   I will not yield,
  To kiss the ground before young Malcolm's feet,
  And to be baited with the rabble's curse.
30   Though Birnam wood be come to Dunsinane,
  And thou opposed, being of no woman born,
  Yet I will try the last. Before my body
  I throw my warlike shield. Lay on, Macduff,
  And damned be him that first cries, "Hold, enough!"¹²⁸

                    (Exeunt, fighting. Alarums.)
          (Retreat. Flourish. Enter, with drum and
          colors. MALCOLM, OLD SIWARD, ROSS, *the*
              other THANES, *and* SOLDIERS.*)*
35 MALCOLM. I would the friends we miss were safe arrived.

Why . . . sword: The Romans considered suicide more honorable than capture.
lives: living persons.

intrenchant: invulnerable.

Painted . . . pole: your picture painted on a board which will be suspended on a pole.

128. *Lines 27–34:* How do Macbeth's last lines in the play relate to his character as described by the Captain in Act One, Scene 2?

SIWARD. Some must go off;° and yet, by these I see,
So great a day as this is cheaply bought.

MALCOLM. Macduff is missing, and your noble son.

ROSS. Your son, my lord, has paid a soldier's debt;
40 He only lived but till he was a man;
The which no sooner had his prowess confirmed
In the unshrinking station where he fought,
But like a man he died.

SIWARD.   Then he is dead?[129]

ROSS. Aye, and brought off the field; your cause of sorrow
45 Must not be measured by his worth, for then
It hath no end.

SIWARD.   Had he his hurts before?

ROSS. Aye, on the front.

SIWARD.   Why then, God's soldier be he![130]
Had I as many sons as I have hairs,
I would not wish them to a fairer death;
50 And so, his knell is knolled.

MALCOLM.   He's worth more sorrow,
And that I'll spend for him.

SIWARD.   He's worth no more.
They say he parted well, and paid his score;
And so, God be with him! Here comes newer comfort.

                    (*Re-enter* MACDUFF, *with* MACBETH's *head.*)

go off: die.

129. Compare Siward's reaction to his son's death (a) to the way Macbeth reacted at the news of Duncan's death (Act Two, Scene 3); and (b) to Macduff's reaction when he heard of the murder of his family.

130. Why does Siward say this?

MACDUFF. Hail, King! for so thou art. Behold, where stands
55   The usurper's curséd head. The time is free;
    I see thee compassed with thy kingdom's pearl,°
    That speak my salutation in their minds;
    Whose voices I desire aloud with mine—
    Hail, King of Scotland!
ALL.   Hail, King of Scotland!
60 **MALCOLM.** We shall not spend a large expense of time
    Before we reckon with your several loves,
    And make us even with you. My thanes and kinsmen,
    Henceforth be earls, the first that ever Scotland
    In such an honor named. What's more to do,
65   Which would be planted newly with the time,
    As calling home our exiled friends abroad
    That fled the snares of watchful tyranny;
    Producing forth the cruel ministers
    Of this dead butcher and his fiendlike queen,
70   Who, as 'tis thought, by self and violent hands
    Took off her life;[131] this, and what needful else
    That calls upon us, by the grace of Grace
    We will perform in measure, time, and place;
    So, thanks to all at once and to each one,
75   Whom we invite to see us crowned at Scone.

                              (Flourish. Exeunt.)

compassed . . . pearl: surrounded by the nobles of your kingdom.

131. *Lines 69–71:* What other indications are there that Lady Macbeth has committed suicide?

(Watkins: "The finale a fully crowded scene. Malcolm center, with Macduff and Siward near him; the Thanes grouped by the two Stage-Posts; some soldiers around the perimeter, others on the Tarras with Macbeth's head and banners. The departure is processional through the Castle gates in the Study, to the accompaniment of a Flourish. The tyrant's head remains when all others have withdrawn into the Tiring-House.")

Discussion

1. The undoing or downfall of the main character in a tragedy is usually brought about through a tragic flaw in his character, or through a tragic error. What brought about Macbeth's downfall? Lady Macbeth's?

2. Tragedy is often said to arouse feelings of pity and fear in its audience. Is this true of the play *Macbeth*? Explain.

3. Compare Macbeth and Lady Macbeth as they appear in Act One with the way they appear in Act Five. How has each of them changed with respect to strength of character? How do you account for this?

4. Lady Macbeth fades out of the play almost completely (except for the sleepwalking scene) after Act Three. What dramatic effect is achieved by her absence and her final reappearance?

5. Do you agree with Malcolm's dismissal of Macbeth and Lady Macbeth as "this dead butcher and his fiendlike queen"? Explain.

6. What sort of king was Duncan? (Note what he says, what he does, and what others say about him.) Is Shakespeare's portrayal of his character consistent?

7. Duncan said of the traitorous Thane of Cawdor: "There's no art / To find the mind's construction in the face." The ability to go beneath the surface to interpret character and motivation—in others and in oneself—is universally important, on the stage and off. **(a)** How sound a judge was Lady Macbeth of Macbeth's character? **(b)** How sound a judge was Macbeth of Lady Macbeth's character? **(c)** How well did Macbeth and Lady Macbeth understand themselves and their own psychological limitations?

8. In literature, characters are frequently used as **foils;** that is, the characteristics of one point up by contrast the characteristics of another. **(a)** What traits of Macbeth are thrown into relief by contrast with Duncan? with young Siward? with Malcolm? **(b)** What characteristics of Lady Macbeth are pointed up by contrast with Lady Macduff?

Vocabulary
Etymologies

Use your Glossary to answer on a separate sheet of paper the following questions about the italicized words.

1. **(a)** What is the meaning of *bait* in this phrase: "I will not yield, / . . . to be *baited* with the rabble's curse"? **(b)** From what specific Scandinavian language does the word derive?

2. **(a)** From what language does the word *jovial* come? **(b)** Give the English spelling of the planet that is mentioned in the history of the word.

3. **(a)** Through what two languages did *parley* pass before entering into English? **(b)** Do the words listed at the end of the entry derive from the same source as *parley*? (You may have to check the entry for *doublet* to answer this question.)

4. Of what word for an element or material is *mettle* a different form?

5. **(a)** To what other word is *harbinger* closely related? **(b)** Use a one-word synonym to give the word's present meaning.

6. **(a)** What is the meaning of the root word in *disburse*? **(b)** What is the present meaning of the word?

7. Give two meanings for *confound* that are no longer used in ordinary language.

Composition

You may choose any *one* of the following assignments. Assume that you are writing for your classmates.

1. Commentators have pointed out that three forces are at work to destroy Macbeth: flaws in his own character, the forces of evil or the Devil as represented by the Three Weird Sisters, and Lady Macbeth. Select the force that you think was most responsible for his downfall. Go through the play to find evidence to support your view. Keep a record of your evidence, then outline it to make the most persuasive case you can.

Write a paper in which you show how the force you have chosen is predominant. You may wish to note that the other forces exist, but that the one you select is the major one. (See *Defending Your Position* in Composition Guide.)

2. To *equivocate* means "to use ambiguous expressions, especially to mislead." Go through the play and list examples of such misleading ambiguity. Try to gather your examples under three or four headings, and then use these categories to organize an outline.

Discuss equivocation as a theme in *Macbeth,* citing specific examples from the text.

3. Assume that Macbeth and Lady Macbeth have both been taken prisoner, and that a decision has been made to execute the one found more guilty and to free the other. Assume that you are the prosecutor and prepare the case against either Lady Macbeth or Macbeth. In order to do this you need to think of every scrap of evidence that will convict whichever character you have chosen to prosecute.

Once your evidence is assembled and organized, write a summary of the prosecution's case.

4. Select any symbol or unifying device and trace its use throughout the play, keeping track of the various uses by means of a list or outline. Suggestions: blood, birds, reality-illusion, sleep and sleeplessness, night and darkness. However, you are not limited to these.

Discuss your chosen symbol or device in a paper. Cite examples. (See *Analyzing Literature* in Composition Guide.)

5. Imagine that you are preparing a filmscript for a short scene (or part of a scene) from *Macbeth.* Think about acting suggestions and directions for camera angles, lighting, sets, and so forth.

Write the filmscript, making the settings, directions, and so forth as detailed as possible.

6. After Macbeth is upset by seeing Duncan's blood on his hands (Act Two, Scene 2), he frequently makes references to blood in his speeches. Track down as many of these references as you can find and select the most significant.

In a paper, explain what these references reveal about the deterioration of Macbeth's character.

No complete translation of the Bible was made into English until the late fourteenth century, when John Wycliffe, a theologian and church reformer who was condemned as a heretic, oversaw a translation. Other "unauthorized" translations appeared in the early sixteenth century, including versions by William Tyndale and Miles Coverdale. Finally, in 1539, the "Great Bible" appeared, under the auspices of the reigning monarch, Henry VIII. This was the first English Bible with official endorsement.

In 1604, James I convened a conference at Hampton Court at which plans were laid for a new version of the Bible by a group of translators. Some fifty or so theologians and scholars began work in various centers of learning (Oxford, Cambridge, Westminster), making extensive use of previous translations, especially those of Tyndale and Wycliffe. The work was issued in 1611 as the "Authorized Version" and has fixed itself so firmly in the imagination of the English-speaking world that no other translation seems able to challenge it.

The King James Bible has been called "the noblest monument of English prose," and deserves the epithet because of the sheer brilliance of its language. The King James version preserves the old language and plain style of the earlier English versions, in contrast to the ornamental style characteristic of some prose in the early seventeenth century. Its extensive use of concrete terms and images, its straightforward phrases and sentences, its balance and parallelism in many passages—all make for a dignified simplicity eminently compatible with religious feeling and ritual. Indeed, the language of the King James Bible has so profoundly affected succeeding generations of writers and has so thoroughly stamped itself in the minds of ordinary people that today it forms a basic part of our everyday speech.

For a comparison of translations of the Bible, see the various versions of the Twenty-third Psalm on page 234.

from T*he King James Bible*

Genesis, Chapters 1–3

In the beginning God created the heaven and the earth. And the earth was without form, and void; and darkness was upon the face of the deep. And the Spirit of God moved upon the face of the waters. And God said, "Let there be light": and there was light. And God saw the light, that it was good: and God divided the light from the darkness. And God called the light Day, and the darkness he called Night. And the evening and the morning were the first day.

And God said, "Let there be a firmament in the midst of the waters, and let it divide the waters from the waters." And God made the firmament, and divided the waters which were under the firmament from the waters which were above the firmament: and it was so. And God called the firmament Heaven. And the evening and the morning were the second day.

And God said, "Let the waters under the heaven be gathered together unto one place, and let the dry land appear": and it was so. And God called the dry land Earth; and the gathering together of the waters called he Seas: and God saw that it was good. And God said, "Let the earth bring forth grass, the herb yielding seed, and the fruit tree yielding fruit after his kind, whose seed is in itself, upon the earth": and it was so. And the earth brought forth grass, and herb yielding seed after his kind, and the tree yielding fruit, whose seed was in itself, after his kind: and God saw that it was good. And the evening and the morning were the third day.

Adam Naming the Beasts
by William Blake, 1810.

And God said, "Let there be lights in the firmament of the heaven to divide the day from the night; and let them be for signs, and for seasons, and for days, and years: and let them be for lights in the firmament of the heaven to give light upon the earth": and it was so. And God made two great lights; the greater light to rule the day, and the lesser light to rule the night: he made the stars also. And God set them in the firmament of the heaven to give light upon the earth. And to rule over the day and over the night, and to divide the light from the darkness: and God saw that it was good. And the evening and the morning were the fourth day.

And God said, "Let the waters bring forth abundantly the moving creature that hath life, and fowl that may fly above the earth in the open firmament of heaven." And God created great whales, and every living creature that moveth, which the waters brought forth abundantly, after their kind, and every winged fowl after his kind: and God saw that it was good. And God blessed them, saying, "Be fruitful, and multiply, and fill the waters in the seas, and let fowl multiply in the earth." And the evening and the morning were the fifth day.

And God said, "Let the earth bring forth the living creature after his kind, cattle, and creeping thing, and beast of the earth after his kind": and it was so. And God made the beast of the earth after his kind, and cattle after their kind, and every thing that creepeth upon the earth after his kind: and God saw that it was good.

And God said, "Let us make man in our

image, after our likeness; and let them have dominion over the fish of the sea, and over the fowl of the air, and over the cattle, and over all the earth, and over every creeping thing that creepeth upon the earth.'' So God created man in his own image, in the image of God created he him; male and female created he them. And God blessed them, and God said unto them, ''Be fruitful, and multiply, and replenish the earth, and subdue it: and have dominion over the fish of the sea, and over the fowl of the air, and over every living thing that moveth upon the earth.''

And God said, ''Behold, I have given you every herb bearing seed, which is upon the face of all the earth, and every tree, in the which is the fruit of a tree yielding seed; to you it shall be for meat. And to every beast of the earth, and to every fowl of the air, and to every thing that creepeth upon the earth, wherein there is life, I have given every green herb for meat'': and it was so.

And God saw every thing that he had made, and behold, it was very good. And the evening and the morning were the sixth day.

Thus the heavens and the earth were finished, and all the host of them. And on the seventh day God ended his work which he had made; and he rested on the seventh day from all his work which he had made. And God blessed the seventh day, and sanctified it: because that in it he had rested from all his work which God created and made.

The Creation of Adam and Eve

These are the generations of the heavens and of the earth when they were created, in the day that the Lord God made the earth and the heavens, and every plant of the field before it was in the earth, and every herb of the field before it grew: for the Lord God had not caused it to rain upon the earth, and there was not a man to till the ground. But there went up a mist from the earth, and watered the whole face of the ground. And the Lord God formed man of the dust of the ground, and breathed into his nostrils the breath of life; and man became a living soul.

And the Lord God planted a garden eastward in Eden; and there he put the man whom he had formed. And out of the ground made the Lord God to grow every tree that is pleasant to the sight, and good for food; the tree of life also in the midst of the garden, and the tree of knowledge of good and evil. . . .

And the Lord God took the man, and put him into the garden of Eden to dress it and to keep it. And the Lord God commanded the man, saying, ''Of every tree of the garden thou mayest freely eat: but of the tree of the knowledge of good and evil, thou shalt not eat of it: for in the day that thou eatest thereof thou shalt surely die.''

And the Lord God said, ''It is not good that the man should be alone; I will make him an helpmeet for him.'' And out of the ground the Lord God formed every beast of the field, and every fowl of the air; and brought them unto Adam to see what he would call them: and whatsoever Adam called every living creature, that was the name thereof. And Adam gave names to all cattle, and to the fowl of the air, and to every beast of the field; but for Adam there was not found an helpmeet for him.

And the Lord God caused a deep sleep to fall upon Adam, and he slept: and he took one of his ribs, and closed up the flesh instead thereof; and the rib, which the Lord God had taken from man, made he a woman, and brought her unto the man.

And Adam said, ''This is now bone of my bones, and flesh of my flesh: she shall be called Woman, because she was taken out of Man.''

Therefore shall a man leave his father and his mother, and shall cleave unto his wife: and they shall be one flesh. And they were both naked, the man and his wife, and were not ashamed.

Forbidden Fruit

Now the serpent was more subtil than any beast of the field which the Lord God had made.

And he said unto the woman, ''Yea, hath God said, 'Ye shall not eat of every tree of the garden'?''

And the woman said unto the serpent, ''We may eat of the fruit of the trees of the garden: but of the fruit of the tree which is in the midst of the garden, God hath said, 'Ye shall not eat of it, neither shall ye touch it, lest ye die.' ''

And the serpent said unto the woman, ''Ye shall not surely die: for God doth know that in the day ye eat thereof, then your eyes shall be opened, and ye shall be as gods, knowing good and evil.''

And when the woman saw that the tree was good for food, and that it was pleasant to the eyes, and a tree to be desired to make one wise, she took of the fruit thereof, and did eat, and gave also unto her husband with her; and he did eat. And the eyes of them both were opened, and they knew that they were naked; and they sewed fig leaves together, and made themselves aprons.

And they heard the voice of the Lord God walking in the garden in the cool of the day: and Adam and his wife hid themselves from the presence of the Lord God amongst the trees of the garden.

And the Lord God called unto Adam, and said unto him, ''Where art thou?''

And he said, ''I heard thy voice in the garden, and I was afraid, because I was naked; and I hid myself.''

And he said, ''Who told thee that thou wast naked? Has thou eaten of the tree, whereof I commanded thee that thou shouldest not eat?''

And the man said, ''The woman whom thou gavest to be with me, she gave me of the tree, and I did eat.''

And the Lord God said unto the woman, ''What is this that thou hast done?''

And the woman said, ''The serpent beguiled me, and I did eat.''

And the Lord God said unto the serpent, ''Because thou hast done this, thou art cursed above all cattle, and above every beast of the field; upon thy belly shalt thou go, and dust shalt thou eat all the days of thy life: and I will put enmity between thee and the woman, and between thy seed and her seed; it shall bruise thy head, and thou shalt bruise his heel.''

Unto the woman he said, ''I will greatly multiply thy sorrow and thy conception; in sorrow thou shalt bring forth children; and thy desire shall be to thy husband, and he shall rule over thee.''

And unto Adam he said, ''Because thou hast hearkened unto the voice of thy wife, and hast eaten of the tree, of which I commanded thee, saying, 'Thou shalt not eat of it': cursed is the ground for thy sake; in sorrow shalt thou eat of it all the days of thy life. Thorns also and thistles shall it bring forth to thee; and thou shalt eat the herb of the field; in the sweat of thy face shalt thou eat bread, till thou return unto the ground; for out of it wast thou taken: for dust thou art, and unto dust shalt thou return.''

And Adam called his wife's name Eve; because she was the mother of all living. Unto Adam also and to his wife did the Lord God make coats of skins, and clothed them.

And the Lord God said, ''Behold, the man is become as one of us, to know good and evil: and now, lest he put forth his hand, and take also of the tree of life, and eat, and live for ever'': therefore the Lord God sent him forth from the garden of Eden, to till the ground from whence he was taken. So he drove out the man; and he placed at the east of the garden of Eden Cherubims, and a flaming sword which turned every way, to keep the way of the tree of life.

1611

Discussion

1. Imagine that a child, beginning to be fully conscious of the world that surrounds it, asks: ''Who created the world? How? Why? How long did it take? What about whales? How about man himself?'' Show how the opening of Genesis answers these questions.

2. According to Genesis, why did God create man? woman?

3. Analyze the behavior of Adam and Eve after they eat the forbidden fruit, and indicate how they have changed.

4. The repetition of certain words and phrases gives these passages a richness and solemnity. What are some of these words and phrases?

5. Find a passage you consider particularly effective and explore the reasons for its effectiveness. For example, analyze: ''In the beginning God created the heaven and the earth.''

> The Bible has been the best seller of all time, and translations of it have been numerous. The achievement of the King James version can best be judged by comparing it with some of the others. Here are four versions of the Twenty-third Psalm: the King James translation, one published before it, and two published later.

from **The Great Bible** (1539)

The Lord is my shepherd; therefore can I lack nothing. He shall feed me in a green pasture, and lead me forth beside the waters of comfort. He shall convert my soul, and bring me forth in the paths of righteousness for his name's sake. Yea, though I walk through the valley of the shadow of death, I will fear no evil, for thou art with me. Thy rod and thy staff comfort me. Thou shalt prepare a table before me against them that trouble me; thou has anointed my head with oil, and my cup shall be full. But thy loving-kindness and mercy shall follow me all the days of my life and I will dwell in the house of the Lord forever.

from **The King James Bible** (1611)

The Lord is my shepherd: I shall not want.
He maketh me to lie down in green pastures:
   he leadeth me beside the still waters.
He restoreth my soul: he leadeth me in the
   paths of righteousness for his name's sake.
Yea, though I walk through the valley of the
   shadow of death, I will fear no evil: for thou
   art with me; thy rod and thy staff they
   comfort me.
Thou preparest a table before me in the
   presence of mine enemies: thou anointest my
   head with oil; my cup runneth over.
Surely goodness and mercy shall follow me all
   the days of my life: and I will dwell in the
   house of the Lord forever.

from **The Bay Psalm Book** (1640)[1]

The Lord to me a shepherd is,
   want therefore shall not I.
He in the folds of tender grass,
   doth cause me down to lie:
To waters calm me gently leads,
   Restore my soul doth he:
He doth in paths of righteousness
   for his name's sake lead me.
Yea though in valley of death's shade
   I walk, none ill I'll fear:
Because thou art with me, thy rod
   and staff my comfort are.
For me a table thou hast spread,
   in presence of my foes:
Thou dost anoint my head with oil,
   my cup it overflows.
Goodness and mercy surely shall
   all my days follow me:
And in the Lord's house I shall dwell
   so long as days shall be.

from **The New English Bible** (1970)

The LORD is my shepherd; I shall want nothing.
   He makes me lie down in green pastures,
and leads me beside the waters of peace;
   he renews life within me,
and for his name's sake guides me in the
right path.
Even though I walk through a valley dark as
death
I fear no evil, for thou art with me,
thy staff and thy crook are my comfort.

Thou spreadest a table for me in the sight of
   my enemies;
   thou hast richly bathed my head with oil,
      and my cup runs over.
Goodness and love unfailing, these will
follow me
   all the days of my life,
   and I shall dwell in the house of the LORD
   my whole life long.

---

1. The Bay Psalm Book was the first book published in the American Colonies.

From *The New English Bible.* Copyright © The Delegates of the Oxford University Press and the Syndics of the Cambridge University Press 1961, 1970. Reprinted by permission.

Sir Francis Bacon 1561–1626

A brilliant child, Bacon entered Trinity College, Cambridge, in 1573, when he was only twelve. Leaving there in 1575, he was admitted to Gray's Inn to study law in 1576. When he was sixteen, he traveled to Paris in the entourage of the British Ambassador, going on to other parts of France, Italy, and Spain, in what had become the typical European tour for promising young men of good family.

In 1579 the death of Bacon's father, who was Lord Keeper of the Great Seal to Queen Elizabeth, recalled him to England. He began his political career in 1584 by being elected to Parliament; he was re-elected a number of times. Bypassed during the reign of Elizabeth, Bacon rose rapidly under James; he was knighted in 1603, became Solicitor General in 1607, Attorney General in 1613, a member of the Privy Council in 1616, Lord Keeper of the Great Seal (his father's position) in 1617, and Lord Chancellor in 1618, at which time he was created Baron Verulam, and in 1621 Viscount St. Albans.

Bacon's political career ended that same year, when he was charged with misconduct in office, admitted his guilt, and was fined, stripped of his office, and barred from sitting in Parliament. Retiring to the family estate, Bacon continued the writing and scientific experiments he had begun much earlier in life. In 1626, while he was conducting an experiment to determine whether stuffing a chicken with snow would prevent it from spoiling, he contracted a chill that developed into bronchitis, from which he died.

Although Bacon won fame as a philosopher and scientist, our interest in him is as an author, particularly an essayist. From 1597 to 1625 he published, in three collections, a total of fifty-eight essays and was responsible for introducing the essay form into England. His essays were short, treated a variety of subjects of universal interest, and contained sentences so memorable that many are still quoted today, centuries after they were written.

Bacon is known also for other works, among them *The New Atlantis* (1626), which might be considered an early example of science fiction, in which he describes an ideal state. Of particular interest is the portion dealing with Solomon's House, dedicated to the study of science, which is said to have led to the founding of the Royal Society (for the study of science) some years later. In 1620 *Novum Organum* (The New Instrument) was published; written in Latin, the language of learning, it influenced future scientific research through its advocacy of the inductive method of inquiry. The essay you are about to read, "Of Studies," is frequently quoted and is an example of how much thought Bacon can include in a short piece of writing.

Of Studies

Studies serve for delight, for ornament, and for ability. Their chief use for delight is in privateness and retiring; for ornament, is in discourse; and for ability, is in the judgment and disposition of business; for expert[1] men can execute, and perhaps judge of particulars, one by one; but the general counsels, and the plots and marshaling of affairs come best from those that are learned. To

---

1. **expert,** experienced; practical.

spend too much time in studies is sloth; to use them too much for ornament is affectation; to make judgment wholly by their rules is the humor[2] of a scholar. They perfect nature, and are perfected by experience; for natural abilities are like natural plants, that need pruning by study; and studies themselves do give forth directions too much at large, except they be bounded in by experience. Crafty[3] men contemn studies, simple men admire them, and wise men use them; for they teach not their own use; but that is a wisdom without them and above them, won by observation.

Read not to contradict and confute, nor to believe and take for granted, nor to find talk and discourse, but to weigh and consider. Some books are to be tasted, others to be swallowed, and some few to be chewed and digested; that is, some books are to be read only in parts; others to be read but not curiously,[4] and some few to be read wholly, and with diligence and attention. Some books also may be read by deputy, and extracts made of them by others; but that would be only in the less important arguments and the meaner sort of books; else distilled books are, like common distilled waters, flashy[5] things.

Reading maketh a full man; conference[6] a ready man; and writing an exact man. And, therefore, if a man write little, he had need have a great memory; if he confer little, he had need have a present wit;[7] and if he read little, he had need have much cunning, to seem to know what he doth not. Histories make men wise; poets, witty; the mathematics, subtile; natural philosophy, deep; moral, grave; logic and rhetoric, able to contend: *Abeunt studia in mores!*[8] Nay, there is no stand or impediment in the wit but may be wrought out by fit studies; like as diseases of the body may have appropriate exercises. Bowling is good for the stone and reins,[9] shooting for the lungs and breast, gentle walking for the stomach, riding for the head, and the like. So if a man's wit be wandering, let him study mathematics; for in demonstrations, if his wit be called away never so little, he must begin again. If his wit be not apt to distinguish or find differences, let him study the schoolmen,[10] for they are *cymini sectores!*[11] If he be not apt to beat over matters, and to call up one thing to prove and illustrate another, let him study the lawyers' cases. So every defect of the mind may have a special receipt.

1625

2. *humor,* whim, disposition.
3. *Crafty,* skilled in crafts; practical.
4. *curiously,* thoroughly.
5. *flashy,* tasteless, flat.
6. *conference,* conversation.
7. *present wit,* quick intelligence. The word *wit* is used throughout the essay in this sense.
8. *Abeunt . . . mores!* Studies develop into habits. [Latin]
9. *stone and reins,* kidney stone. Reins are kidneys.
10. *schoolmen,* medieval scholars.
11. *cymini sectores,* hairsplitters (literally, splitters of cumin-seeds.) [Latin]

Discussion

1. This **essay** is so closely written that to understand and appreciate it fully you must stop and consider the meaning of almost every sentence. Explain in your own words the following: **(a)** Studies serve for delight, for ornament, and for ability. **(b)** To spend too much time in studies is sloth; to use them too much for ornament is affectation; to make judgment wholly by their rules is the humor of a scholar. **(c)** Reading maketh a full man; conference a ready man; and writing an exact man.

2. Discuss books that you would put in the following categories: "Some books are to be tasted, others to be swallowed, and some few to be chewed and digested."

Composition

Bacon wrote many other essays, some of the titles of which are "Of Parents and Children," "Of Truth," "Of Envy," and "Of Cunning." Look up the titles of other essays written by Bacon.

Select one of the above titles, or one you found yourself, and write a short essay. Try to achieve a style that is formal and concise. (See *Developing Your Style* in Composition Guide.)

John Donne 1572–1631

John Donne, one of the great poets and preachers of his age, has left his mark on modern poetry. Born into a Catholic family, Donne was sent to Hart Hall, Oxford, when he was twelve; he also spent some time at Trinity College, Cambridge, and in 1591 was studying law at Lincoln's Inn, in London. In 1596 he participated with Essex and Raleigh in the raid on Cadiz, and in 1597 he voyaged with Essex to the Azores and Spain.

Back in England, attempting to establish himself in a career, Donne became secretary to Sir Thomas Egerton, Lord Keeper of the Great Seal. There he met Egerton's niece, Anne More, fell in love with her, and married her secretly in 1601. When her father learned of the marriage, he was so infuriated that he ruined Donne's career and had him imprisoned. There is a story that from prison Donne wrote the following note to Anne: "John Donne, Anne Donne, Undone."

After his release from prison, Donne lived with Anne in relative poverty. Although he and his father-in-law became reconciled in 1608, not until 1610 did he secure the sort of position for which he was equipped by both intellect and education, becoming secretary to Sir Robert Drury.

As early as 1603, and possibly even earlier, Donne had become an Anglican. After he had written some anti-Catholic pamphlets for Thomas Morton, the Dean of Gloucester, he was asked to take Anglican holy orders to become a priest but refused. In 1615, however, at the urging of King James himself, Donne entered the Anglican priesthood. He became chaplain to the King, then rose rapidly until in 1621 he became Dean of St. Paul's Cathedral, London. A few years earlier, in 1617, Anne had died in childbirth, leaving Donne with seven children (she had borne twelve). Stating that he did not want his children to have a stepmother, Donne did not marry again.

In general, Donne's writing parallels his life. Until he met and fell in love with Anne, he had many love affairs, and his early poetry reflects those affairs and his cynical attitude toward women. After his marriage, he wrote Anne some of the most sincere love poems in the English language. Later, after he became a clergyman, he wrote both religious poetry and religious prose. Some 160 of his sermons have survived, and he was regarded as the foremost preacher of his day.

As he grew older, Donne became concerned with death and the dissolution of the human body. Perhaps the sins of his youth troubled him, perhaps he missed Anne, perhaps his own failing health was a cause of concern. Near the end of his life, he had his portrait painted in his burial shroud, to remind him of his approaching death.

Donne is credited with developing what is called **metaphysical poetry.** This is poetry that relies for its effect on conceits, metaphors in which a very ingenious and complex comparison is made. Intellectual, strong, often violating traditional rules of scansion, metaphysical poetry requires work on the part of the reader—but the sudden insights it provides more than justify the effort.

Song

Go and catch a falling star,
   Get with child a mandrake root,[1]
Tell me where all past years are,
   Or who cleft the devil's foot;
5 Teach me to hear mermaids singing,
Or to keep off envy's stinging,
     And find
     What wind
Serves to advance an honest mind.

10 If thou be'st born to strange sights,
   Things invisible to see,
Ride ten thousand days and nights,
   Till age snow white hairs on thee,
Thou, when thou return'st, will tell me

15 All strange wonders that befell thee,
     And swear
     Nowhere
Lives a woman true, and fair.

If thou find'st one, let me know;
20   Such a pilgrimage were sweet.
Yet do not; I would not go,
   Though at next door we might meet.
Though she were true when you met her,
And last till you write your letter,
25   Yet she
     Will be
False, ere I come, to two or three.

1633

---

1. **Get . . . mandrake root.** Mandrake is a European herb with a forked root, fancied to resemble the figure of a man. (Recognizing the resemblance as well as the impossibility of a plant's reproducing as humans do, Donne includes this in his catalogue of fantastic achievements.)

The Bait

Come live with me, and be my love,
And we will some new pleasures prove
Of golden sands, and crystal brooks,
With silken lines, and silver hooks.

5 There will the river whispering run
Warmed by thy eyes, more than the sun.
And there th' enamoured fish will stay,
Begging themselves they may betray.

When thou wilt swim in that live bath,
10 Each fish, which every channel hath,
Will amorously to thee swim,
Gladder to catch thee, than thou him.

If thou, to be so seen, be'st loath,
By sun, or moon, thou darkenest both,
15 And if myself have leave to see,
I need not their light, having thee.

Let others freeze with angling reeds,
And cut their legs, with shells and weeds,
Or treacherously poor fish beset,
20 With strangling snare, or windowy net:

Let coarse bold hands, from slimy nest
The bedded fish in banks out-wrest,
Or curious traitors, sleavesilk flies
Bewitch poor fishes' wandering eyes.

25 For thee, thou need'st no such deceit,
For thou thyself art thine own bait;
That fish, that is not catched thereby,
Alas, is wiser far than I.

1633

A Valediction:[1] Forbidding Mourning

As virtuous men pass mildly away,
    And whisper to their souls to go,
Whilst some of their sad friends do say
    The breath goes now, and some say, No;

5 So let us melt, and make no noise,
    No tear-floods, nor sigh-tempests move,
'Twere profanation of our joys
    To tell the laity our love.

Moving of th' earth brings harms and fears,
10   Men reckon what it did and meant,
But trepidation of the spheres,
    Though greater far, is innocent.[2]

Dull sublunary[3] lovers' love
    (Whose soul is sense)[4] cannot admit
15 Absence, because it doth remove
    Those things which elemented[5] it.

But we by a love so much refined
    That our selves know not what it is,
Inter-assuréd of the mind,
20   Care less, eyes, lips, and hands to miss.

Our two souls therefore, which are one,
    Though I must go, endure not yet
A breach, but an expansion,
    Like gold to airy thinness beat.

25 If they be two, they are two so
    As stiff twin compasses[6] are two;
Thy soul, the fixed foot, makes no show
    To move, but doth, if th' other do.

And though it in the center sit,
30   Yet when the other far doth roam,
It leans and hearkens after it,
    And grows erect, as that comes home.

Such wilt thou be to me, who must
    Like th' other foot, obliquely run;
35 Thy firmness makes my circle[7] just,
    And makes me end where I begun.

1633

Albrecht Dürer, *Melancholy I,* Collection of The Art Institute of Chicago. This engraving shows the figure of Melancholy holding a compass.

---

1. **Valediction,** a bidding farewell.
2. **trepidation . . . innocent.** Movements of the heavenly spheres, though greater than those of an earthquake, provoke no fears in (nor danger to) man.
3. **sublunary,** beneath the moon, i.e., earthly and subject to change.
4. **(Whose soul is sense),** whose essence is not mind or spirit.
5. **elemented,** composed.
6. **compasses.** The image is of the instrument used for describing a circle. One branch or leg of the compass is held steady, as a pivot, while the other leg is rotated to draw the circle.
7. **circle.** The circle was a symbol of perfection.

Discussion

1. **(a)** What quality do all the instructions in Donne's "Song" share? **(b)** What is the state of mind of the speaker of the poem, and what do you think has happened to him? **(c)** What is the tone of the poem?

2. Reread "The Passionate Shepherd to His Love" (page 142), and then discuss the differences introduced in "The Bait."

3. How do the lovers of "A Valediction" differ from the "dull sublunary lovers" of stanza 4?

4. Explain the next-to-last line of "A Valediction": "Thy firmness makes my circle just."

5. "A Valediction" employs one of the most unusual **conceits** (ingenious metaphors) in all literature: "If they be . . . . I begun" (lines 25-36). Explain the conceit.

Reader's Note: "A Valediction"

Donne wrote this poem to his wife, Anne, just before he left on an extended trip to France. Since Anne was expecting another child, she could not accompany him. According to Donne's biographer, Sir Izaak Walton, Anne had a premonition of impending tragedy. Events later proved her correct, for the child was born dead. Donne, while in France, saw a vision of Anne walking across the bedroom with a dead child in her arms.

"A Valediction" is a farewell message that forbids Anne to mourn Donne's absence. Having established his purpose, Donne needs a reason to support that purpose, and he needs suitable metaphors to express that reason. His reason is simple: he and Anne are inseparable because their souls are so intermixed that they have become one (line 21); therefore, even though he must go far away, he and she, being connected by that soul, are not really parted. Here he uses two **conceits** (ingenious metaphors) to explain why: (1) like gold beaten to airy thinness (line 24), their combined soul will expand, without separation or break, to cover the distance (lines 22–23); or (2) their combined soul is like a pair of compasses, with Anne, the fixed foot, leaning toward Donne, the roaming foot, as he travels, steadying him on his journey and straightening again as he comes home (lines 25-36).

To strengthen his argument, Donne contrasts his and Anne's love (in which they share a single soul) with ordinary love ("dull sublunary lovers' love," line 13), which cannot admit absence because its "soul" is physical ("sense" or sensation, line 14), and therefore when one of the lovers is gone, he (or she) is physically removed from the other (lines 15–16).

The love of Donne and Anne is also on a higher level, like the concentric spheres of the Ptolemaic system of astronomy (lines 11–12); "tear-floods" and "sigh-tempests" (line 6) would profane it (lines 7–8). Therefore, at parting they should "melt, and make no noise" (line 5), just as "virtuous men pass mildly away, / And whisper to their souls to go" (lines 1–2). Note that Donne does not separate these men from their souls; note also that lines 1–8 are a simile, the first part introduced by "As" (line 1), the second by "So" (line 5).

Finally, the word "melt" (line 5) may be troublesome. However, an intricate relationship is expressed in lines 4–6, in which "melt" and "tear-floods" (line 6) match, and "breath" (line 4) and "sigh-tempests" (line 6) match; in both pairs the second word represents a superfluity of the first.

Thus, in a series of sometimes outrageous comparisons—conceits, similes, and metaphors drawn from meteorology, theology, geology, Ptolemaic astronomy, metallurgy, and geometry—Donne tells Anne that there is no need to mourn his departure, for their love is so great and their souls so intermingled that they will not really be separated by his journey.

from *H*oly Sonnets

10

Death, be not proud, though some have
    called thee
Mighty and dreadful, for thou art not so;
For those whom thou think'st thou dost
    overthrow
Die not, poor Death, nor yet canst thou kill me.
5 From rest and sleep, which but thy pictures be,
Much pleasure; then from thee much more
    must flow,
And soonest our best men with thee do go,
Rest of their bones, and soul's delivery.
Thou art slave to fate, chance, kings, and
    desperate men,
10 And dost with poison, war, and sickness dwell,
And poppy[1] or charms can make us sleep as
    well,
And better than thy stroke; why swell'st[2]
    thou then?
One short sleep past, we wake eternally,
And death shall be no more; Death, thou
    shalt die.   1633

14

Batter my heart, three-personed God;[3] for you
As yet but knock, breathe, shine, and seek
    to mend;
That I may rise and stand, o'erthrow me,
    and bend
Your force to break, blow, burn, and make
    me new.
5 I, like an usurped town, to another due,
Labor to admit you, but O, to no end;
Reason, your viceroy in me, me should defend,
But is captived, and proves weak or untrue.
Yet dearly I love you, and would be loved fain,
10 But am betrothed unto your enemy.
Divorce me, untie or break that knot again;
Take me to you, imprison me, for I,
Except you enthral me, never shall be free,
Nor ever chaste, except you ravish me.
                        1633

---

1. *poppy,* the source of various narcotic drugs.
2. *swell'st,* puff up with pride.
3. *three-personed God,* the Trinity of the Father, the Son, and the Holy Spirit.

Discussion

1. In sonnet 10, the speaker scorns Death. **(a)** How does he cast aspersions on Death's powers? **(b)** What is meant by the last line, "And death shall be no more; Death, thou shalt die"?

2. Sonnet 14 follows both the rhyme scheme and thought division of the Petrarchan sonnet. **(a)** What is the problem stated in the first eight lines? **(b)** Who is the "enemy" mentioned in line 10? **(c)** In the last six lines, how does the speaker ask to have his problem resolved?

---

*M*editation 17

Nunc lento sonitu dicunt, Morieris.
(Now this bell tolling softly for another,
says to me, Thou must die.)

Perchance he for whom this bell tolls may be so ill as that he knows not it tolls for him; and perchance I may think myself so much better than I am, as that they who are about me and see

my state, may have caused it to toll for me, and I know not that. The church is catholic, universal, so are all her actions; all that she does belongs to all. When she baptizes a child, that action concerns me; for that child is thereby connected to that head which is my head too, and ingrafted into that body whereof I am a member.[1] And when she buries a man, that action concerns me. All mankind is of one author and is one volume;

---

1. *head . . . member.* That is, the Christian church is the head of all people, as well as a body made up of its members.

Statue of John Donne in his burial shroud.

every book shall lie open to one another. As therefore the bell that rings to a sermon calls not upon the preacher only, but upon the congregation to come, so this bell calls us all; but how much more me, who am brought so near the door by this sickness.

There was a contention as far as a suit[2] (in which piety and dignity, religion and estimation,[3] were mingled) which of the religious orders should ring to prayers first in the morning; and it was determined that they should ring first that rose earliest. If we understand aright the dignity of this bell that tolls for our evening prayer, we would be glad to make it ours by rising early, in that application, that it might be ours as well as his whose indeed it is. The bell doth toll for him that thinks it doth; and though it intermit again, yet from that minute that that occasion wrought upon him, he is united to God. Who casts not up his eye to the sun when it rises? But who takes off his eye from a comet when that breaks out? Who bends not his ear to any bell which upon any occasion rings? But who can remove it from that bell which is passing a piece of himself out of this world? No man is an island, entire of itself; every man is a piece of the continent, a part of the main. If a clod be washed away by the sea, Europe is the less, as well as if a promontory were, as well as if a manor of thy friend's or of thine own were. Any man's death diminishes me because I am involved in mankind; and therefore never send to know for whom the bell tolls; it tolls for thee. . . .

1624

when one man dies, one chapter is not torn out of the book, but translated into a better language, and every chapter must be so translated. God employs several translators; some pieces are translated by age, some by sickness, some by war, some by justice; but God's hand is in every translation, and his hand shall bind up all our scattered leaves again for that library where

---

2. *contention . . . suit,* a controversy that went as far as a lawsuit.
3. *estimation,* self-esteem.

Discussion

1. At the time Donne wrote "Meditation 17," he was recovering from a serious illness, so in one sense the selection is autobiographical. How might that fact have influenced the entire piece?

2. Discuss the meaning and effectiveness of the two main metaphors: man as a chapter in a book and man as a piece of a continent.

3. Explain in your own words: ". . . never send to know for whom the bell tolls; it tolls for thee."

Ben Jonson 1572–1637

Soon after Ben Jonson was born, his father died, and his mother took as her second husband a master bricklayer. With financial help, Ben was able to attend the Westminster School in London, where he studied under William Camden. From that scholar he probably acquired his taste for classical learning.

Too poor to attend either Oxford or Cambridge, Jonson worked for a time with his stepfather as a bricklayer, then went off to Flanders to fight against the Spanish. In front of both armies, Jonson killed one of the enemy in single combat.

In 1595 or thereabouts, Jonson returned to England. By this time he was married, and he sought employment as an actor and playwright. Induced by Thomas Nashe to collaborate on *The Isle of Dogs* (1597), his first venture into playwriting, Jonson was jailed for a time when the play was judged to have stirred up discontent against the government. His next attempt, *Every Man in His Humor* (1598), in which Shakespeare played a role, was a great success. In this comedy Jonson introduced into the English theater the concept of "humors," the idea that each comic character has a humor, or personality trait, that controls his actions. Shakespeare and other contemporary dramatists were influenced by this idea.

Jonson's quick temper soon got him into further trouble. Before the year was out, he had argued with another actor, Gabriel Spencer, whom he killed in a duel. Imprisoned again, he escaped hanging by reciting his "neck verse"—in an age that valued scholarship, any man who was able to translate a passage of Latin into English could plead benefit of clergy to secure a trial in a church court, where punishments were less harsh than in the secular courts. Jonson's classical knowledge stood him in good stead in this instance, but he was branded on the left thumb to show that he was a convicted felon.

By this time, however, Jonson was on the way to becoming a successful playwright.

Among his best comedies are *Volpone* (1606), a further development of his humor theory, and *The Alchemist* (1610). In addition, he ventured into the field of classical tragedy with *Sejanus* (1603), which was not a success, and he wrote many masques, most of them for court performance. Some of his best lyrics were written for the masques.

Jonson was friendly with Shakespeare, Raleigh, and Donne, and King James made him poet laureate. A number of young poets, including Herrick and Lovelace (who follow Jonson in this unit), respecting Jonson's talents, called themselves the "Sons of Ben."

Jonson's old age was difficult. After the death of King James, he was no longer called upon to write court masques; in 1628 he suffered a paralyzing stroke, and he may well have been in financial need. When he died in 1637, he was buried in Poets' Corner, Westminster Abbey. Ironically, there is some controversy over whether the first word in the inscription on the slab that marks his grave is in Latin: "Orare (pray for) Ben Jonson"; or in English: "O rare Ben Jonson."

Some of Jonson's lyrics follow. Two are songs from his plays; one, "Song, to Celia," is a complete reworking of various lines from classical poetry; two are epitaphs for a son and daughter—the son died of plague in 1603, aged seven, and the daughter died in infancy.

Still to Be Neat

Still[1] to be neat, still to be dressed,
As[2] you were going to a feast;
Still to be powdered, still perfumed:
Lady, it is to be presumed,
5 Though art's hid causes are not found,
All is not sweet, all is not sound.

Give me a look, give me a face,
That makes simplicity a grace;
Robes loosely flowing, hair as free:
10 Such sweet neglect more taketh me
Than all th' adulteries[3] of art;
They strike mine eyes, but not my heart.

1609

---

1. **Still,** always.
2. **As,** as if, as though.
3. **adulteries,** deceits.

To Cynthia

Queen and huntress, chaste and fair,
Now the sun is laid to sleep,
Seated in thy silver chair,
State in wonted[1] manner keep:
5　Hesperus entreats thy light,
　Goddess excellently bright.

Earth, let not thy envious shade
Dare itself to interpose;[2]
Cynthia's shining orb was made
10 Heaven to clear,[3] when day did close:
　Bless us then with wishèd sight,
　Goddess excellently bright.

Lay thy bow of pearl apart,
And thy crystal shining quiver;
15 Give unto the flying hart[4]
Space to breathe, how short soever:
　Thou that mak'st a day of night,
　Goddess excellently bright.

1600

---

1. **wonted,** habitual.
2. **Earth . . . interpose,** an eclipse was thought to be a warning of coming evil.
3. **clear,** brighten.
4. **hart,** male deer.

On My First Son

Farewell, thou child of my right hand,[1] and joy;
　My sin was too much hope of thee, loved boy.
Seven years thou wert lent to me, and I thee pay,
　Exacted by thy fate, on the just day.[2]
5 O, could I lose all father,[3] now! For why
　Will man lament the state he should envy?
To have so soon 'scaped world's and flesh's rage,
　And, if no other misery, yet age!
Rest in soft peace; and, asked, say: Here
　doth lie
10　Ben Jonson his best piece of poetry[4]—
For whose sake, henceforth, all his vows be
　such,
　As what he loves may never like too much.[5]

1616

---

1. **child of my right hand,** the meaning of the Hebrew name Benjamin. Jonson's eldest son, who died of the plague in 1603, was also named Benjamin.
2. **just day,** the boy died on his seventh birthday; may also refer to the Day of Judgment.
3. **lose all father,** abandon the bonds between father and son so he would not feel his grief so keenly.
4. **his best piece of poetry,** his greatest creation, the most nearly perfect thing he made.
5. **As what . . . too much,** that what he loves may never please him too much (and therefore his grief will be less).

Song, to Celia

Drink to me only with thine eyes,
    And I will pledge with mine;
Or leave a kiss but in the cup,
    And I'll not look for wine.
5 The thirst that from the soul doth rise
    Doth ask a drink divine;
But might I of Jove's nectar[1] sup,
    I would not change for thine.

I sent thee late a rosy wreath,
10   Not so much honoring thee
As giving it a hope, that there
    It could not withered be.
But thou thereon didst only breathe,
    And sent'st it back to me;
15 Since when it grows, and smells, I swear,
    Not of itself but thee.

1616

---

1. *nectar,* the drink of the gods.

On My First Daughter

Here lies, to each her parents' ruth,[1]
Mary, the daughter of their youth;
Yet all heaven's gifts being heaven's due,
It makes the father less to rue.[2]
5 At six months' end she parted hence
With safety of her innocence;
Whose soul heaven's queen, whose name
    she bears,
In comfort of her mother's tears,
Hath placed amongst her virgin-train:
10 Where, while that severed doth remain,[3]
This grave partakes the fleshly birth;
Which cover lightly, gentle earth!

1616

---

1. *ruth,* grief or pity.
2. *rue,* regret.
3. *severed doth remain,* body and soul, separated at death, will be reunited at the Resurrection.

Comment: Ben Jonson's Vision of His Son

At that time [plague] was in London, [Jonson] being in the country at Sir Robert Cotton's house with old Camden, he saw in a vision his eldest son, then a child and at London, appear unto him with the mark of a bloody cross on his forehead, as if it had been cutted with a sword; at which amazed he prayed unto God, and in the morning he came to Mr. Camden's chamber to tell him, who persuaded him it was but an apprehension of his fantasy at which he should not be disjected. In the mean time comes there letters from his wife of the death of that boy in the plague. He appeared to him (he said) of a manly shape, and of that growth that he thinks he shall be at the resurrection.

From *Notes of Ben Jonson's Conversations with William Drummond of Hawthornden,* edited by David Laing, 1842.

Discussion

1. In "To Cynthia," Cynthia has two major functions: goddess of the hunt and goddess of the moon. How are the two intertwined in the third stanza, and which does the speaker ask to have prevail?

2. (a) Does the speaker in "Still to Be Neat" prefer artificiality or naturalness in a woman? Explain. (b) Comment upon the meaning and effectiveness of the last line of the poem.

3. "To Celia" is one of the most famous of all lyrics. It consists of two extended metaphors, one in the first stanza and the other in the second. (a) What are they? (b) Which do you think is more effective? Why?

4. (a) In "On My First Son," comment upon the effectiveness of the epitaph, "Here doth lie / Ben Jonson his best piece of poetry." (b) Using direct references to the poem, discuss the extent of the speaker's grief.

5. (a) Compare the depth of emotion expressed in "On My First Daughter" with that expressed in "On My First Son." (b) Discuss the extent to which the age of the two children may have affected Jonson's grief.

Robert Herrick 1591–1674

A Londoner by birth and disposition, Herrick spent nearly thirty years of his life as a country parson in remote Devonshire. As a youth, Herrick was apprenticed to his uncle, Sir William Herrick, a goldsmith and jeweler to the king. It seems that Herrick remained with his uncle until 1613, when he entered Cambridge at the age of twenty-two. He received his B.A. in 1617 and his M.A. in 1620. He was ordained in 1623 and six years later left his beloved London to become a vicar.

At first dissatisfied with the rustic ways of Devonshire, Herrick gradually adjusted and, in many of his lyrics, preserved for future generations the quaint customs of his own corner of southwest England. Herrick, who never married, addressed many of his poems to a series of imaginary mistresses, all of the names taken from classical poetry. A true "Son of Ben," he was at home with the classics, and his poems show an artful simplicity that is the result of constant polishing.

When the Puritans came to power, Herrick lost his parish and in 1647 returned to London—with his poetry. In 1648 his poems were published, in a volume divided into two parts. The first part, *Hesperides,* contained his secular poems, more than eleven hundred of them; the second part, *Noble Numbers,* contained his religious poems, numbering about three hundred. Herrick's work went almost unnoticed; it was not "rediscovered" until the nineteenth century.

In 1662, after the restoration of the monarchy, Herrick again became a vicar. He returned to his parish in Devonshire and lived there for twelve years, until his death in 1674.

Herrick is generally regarded as the best of the Cavalier poets and the "Sons of Ben." All of the Herrick poems that follow were published in *Hesperides* in 1648. "The Argument of His Book" is the first poem in the collection.

The Argument[1] *of His Book*

I sing of brooks, of blossoms, birds, and bowers,
Of April, May, of June, and July flowers.
I sing of Maypoles, hock carts, wassails, wakes,[2]
Of bridegrooms, brides, and of their bridal cakes.
5 I write of youth, of love, and have access
By these to sing of cleanly wantonness.[3]
I sing of dews, of rains, and, piece by piece,
Of balm, of oil, of spice, and ambergris.[4]
I sing of times trans-shifting, and I write
10 How roses first came red and lilies white.
I write of groves, of twilights, and I sing

The court of Mab and of the Fairy King.[5]
I write of hell; I sing (and ever shall)
Of heaven, and hope to have it after all.

1648

---

1. **Argument,** subject matter, summary of the contents.
2. **hock . . . wakes.** Hock carts carried home the last load of the harvest; *wassails* are revels or parties; *wakes* refer to parish festivals.
3. **cleanly wantonness,** good fun.
4. **ambergris,** an ingredient used in making perfumes.
5. **Mab . . . King.** Mab is Queen of the Fairies, and Oberon is the Fairy King.

To the Virgins, to Make Much of Time

Gather ye rosebuds while ye may,
   Old time is still a-flying;
And this same flower that smiles today,
   Tomorrow will be dying.

5 The glorious lamp of heaven, the sun,
   The higher he's a-getting,
The sooner will his race be run,
   And nearer he's to setting.

    That age is best which is the first,
10   When youth and blood are warmer;
But being spent, the worse, and worst
   Times still succeed the former.

Then be not coy, but use your time,
   And, while ye may, go marry;
15 For, having lost but once your prime,
   You may forever tarry.

1648

Delight in Disorder

A sweet disorder in the dress
Kindles in clothes a wantonness.[1]
A lawn[2] about the shoulders thrown
Into a fine distraction;
5 An erring[3] lace, which here and there
Enthralls the crimson stomacher,[4]
A cuff neglectful, and thereby
Ribbons to flow confusèdly;
A winning wave, deserving note,
10 In the tempestuous petticoat;
A careless shoestring, in whose tie
I see a wild civility;
Do more bewitch me than when art
Is too precise in every part.

1648

1. **wantonness,** gaiety.
2. **lawn,** linen scarf.
3. **erring,** wandering, straying.
4. **stomacher,** cloth laced across the front of a dress.

Upon Julia's Clothes

Whenas in silks my Julia goes,
Then, then, methinks, how sweetly flows
That liquefaction of her clothes.

Next, when I cast mine eyes, and see
5 That brave[1] vibration, each way free,
O, how that glittering taketh me!

1648

1. **brave,** bright, splendid.

Discussion

1. When did you become aware "The Argument of His Book" was a **sonnet**—or were you aware of that fact? How does its subject matter differ from that of the conventional sonnet? its rhyme scheme?

2. **(a)** What is the advice given to young women in "To the Virgins, to Make Much of Time"? **(b)** Is the advice as sound today as it was then? Why?

3. Is "Upon Julia's Clothes" more about Julia or her silk dress? Explain.

4. Is the speaker in "Delight in Disorder" saying that he prefers a slovenly woman? Explain.

Richard Lovelace 1618–1657

Possessed of all the attributes needed to be a success at Queen Elizabeth's court, Lovelace was unfortunately born a century too late, into a world in which the courtly characteristics he possessed worked more to his detriment than to his advantage. Born into a wealthy family in Kent and heir to great estates, Lovelace was educated at Charterhouse and at Gloucester Hall, Oxford. Tradition has it that when King Charles and Queen Henrietta Maria visited in Oxford in 1636, they were so taken with Lovelace's handsome face and fine manners that they had him given his M.A. on the spot.

After college, Lovelace served at the court of Charles and Henrietta Maria, and he remained steadfastly loyal to his King even when that loyalty cost him his freedom and estates. Without doubt, he is the most romantic—and one of the most unfortunate—of the Cavalier poets. Interested in the arts, Lovelace was an amateur painter and musician as well as poet, but he tended at first to follow the Elizabethan tradition of considering his poetry merely the recreational activity of a highborn gentleman.

After the fall of Charles, Lovelace had the courage to present in 1642 to a very unsympathetic House of Commons a petition in the King's favor. His bravery resulted in his being imprisoned for seven weeks; he used the time to write "To Althea, from Prison," a poem that probably did not endear him to the Puritan cause. Freed, Lovelace left England to fight with the French against the Spaniards. After being wounded at the seige of Dunkirk in 1646, he returned to England, only to be imprisoned again as an enemy of the Puritan Commonwealth. He used his prison time wisely, to prepare his poems for publication; they appeared in 1649 in a volume titled *Lucasta*.

The latter years of Lovelace's life were not happy ones. When he was freed, his estates and their revenues were gone, and he was a poor man. He died of consumption in 1657. In 1659 a posthumous volume of his later poems appeared, titled appropriately enough, *Lucasta: Posthume Poems*.

To Althea, from Prison

When Love with unconfinèd wings
    Hovers within my gates,
And my divine Althea brings
    To whisper at the grates;
5 When I lie tangled in her hair
    And fettered to her eye,
The birds that wanton in the air
    Know no such liberty.

When flowing cups run swiftly round,
10   With no allaying Thames,[1]
Our careless heads with roses bound,
    Our hearts with loyal flames;
When thirsty grief in wine we steep,
    When healths and drafts go free,
15 Fishes that tipple in the deep
    Know no such liberty.

When, like committed linnets, I
    With shriller throat will sing
The sweetness, mercy, majesty,
20   And glories of my King;
When I shall voice aloud how good
    He is, how great should be,
Enlargèd winds, that curl the flood,
    Know no such liberty.

25 Stone walls do not a prison make,
    Nor iron bars a cage;
Minds innocent and quiet take
    That for an hermitage;
If I have freedom in my love
30   And in my soul am free,
Angels alone, that soar above,
    Enjoy such liberty.

1649

---

1. *no allaying Thames,* no diluting water from the Thames River.

To Lucasta, on Going to the Wars

Tell me not, sweet, I am unkind,
    That from the nunnery
Of thy chaste breast and quiet mind
    To war and arms I fly.

5 True, a new mistress now I chase,
    The first foe in the field;
And with a stronger faith embrace
    A sword, a horse, a shield.

Yet this inconstancy is such
10   As thou too shalt adore;
I could not love thee, dear, so much,
    Loved I not honor more.

1649

Discussion

1. What might Lucasta's reaction be to the poem addressed to her?

2. Despite its easy lyricism, "To Althea, from Prison" is a poem about three important things: love, imprisonment, and loyalty. What is the speaker's attitude toward each?

3. What metaphors can you identify in these poems?

Andrew Marvell 1621–1678

One of the few politically active people to lose nothing during the turbulent years of the Revolution, the Puritan Commonwealth, and the Restoration, Andrew Marvell succeeded in winning the trust of both sides. Born in Winestead-in-Holderness, Yorkshire, he received his early education at Hull Grammar School and called Hull his home for most of his life.

At twelve, Marvell was sent to Cambridge, receiving his B.A. degree from Trinity College in 1639 and staying on there until 1641. By the time he left Cambridge he knew Latin, Greek, Hebrew, Arabic, Syrian, Chaldean, and Persian, a remarkable achievement for one so young.

In 1642 Marvell left England for four years of travel on the European continent, visiting Holland, France, Switzerland, Italy, and Spain, and en route learning Dutch, French, Italian, and Spanish. Returning to England, he found employment in 1650 as tutor to the daughter of Lord Fairfax. For two years he lived at Nun Appleton, Fairfax's country estate in Yorkshire. To these years belong a number of pastoral poems and Marvell's lifelong feeling for the joys of the countryside.

In 1653 Marvell, who had become acquainted with John Milton, was recommended by Milton to become his assistant. During this period

Marvell also got to know John Oxenbridge; earlier, Oxenbridge had been a Puritan minister in the Bermudas, and from him Marvell derived much of the background for his poem "Bermudas."

Finally, after four years, in 1657 Marvell became Milton's assistant, and a close friendship developed between the two men. In 1659, Marvell became member of Parliament for Hull, continuing to be re-elected until his death. When the monarchy was restored in 1660, Marvell interceded for Milton and helped to save him from imprisonment or execution.

*T*o *His Coy Mistress*

1

Had we but world enough, and time,[1]
This coyness, lady, were no crime.
We would sit down, and think which way
To walk, and pass our long love's day.
5 Thou by the Indian Ganges' side
Shouldst rubies find; I by the tide
Of Humber[2] would complain.[3] I would
Love you ten years before the flood,[4]
And you should, if you please, refuse
10 Till the conversion of the Jews.[5]

My vegetable[6] love should grow
Vaster than empires and more slow;
An hundred years should go to praise
Thine eyes, and on thy forehead gaze;
15 Two hundred to adore each breast,
But thirty thousand to the rest;

---

1. *time.* Note that the poem opens with a situation contrary to fact.
2. *Humber,* the river that flows through Marvell's home town of Hull.
3. *complain,* i.e., sing plaintive love songs.
4. *flood,* the Biblical flood.
5. *conversion of the Jews.* It was a popular belief that this would occur just before the Last Judgment and the end of the world.
6. *vegetable,* not in the modern sense, but in the sense of living growth.

An age at least to every part,
And the last age should show your heart.
For, lady, you deserve this state;[7]
20 Nor would I love at lower rate.

2

But[8] at my back I always hear
Time's wingèd chariot hurrying near;
And yonder all before us lie
Deserts of vast eternity.
25 Thy beauty shall no more be found,
Nor in thy marble vault shall sound
My echoing song; then worms shall try
That long preserved virginity,
And your quaint[9] honor turn to dust.
30 And into ashes all my lust:
The grave's a fine and private place,
But none, I think, do there embrace.

3

Now therefore,[10] while the youthful hue
Sits on thy skin like morning dew,

35 And while thy willing soul transpires[11]
At every pore with instant fires,
Now let us sport us while we may,
And now, like amorous birds of prey,
Rather at once our time devour
40 Than languish in his slow-chapped[12] power,
Let us roll all our strength and all
Our sweetness up into one ball,
And tear our pleasures with rough strife
Thorough[13] the iron gates of life;
45 Thus, though we cannot make our sun
Stand still, yet we will make him run.[14]
c. 1650   1681

---

7. state, dignity.
8. But. This word reverses the situation contrary to fact of stanza 1, and returns to the real world.
9. quaint, fastidious, out-of-fashion.
10. Now therefore. With these words, the speaker proposes a scheme of action.
11. transpires, breathes out.
12. slow-chapped, slow-jawed.
13. Thorough, through.
14. Thus, though . . . run. Since the sun will not stand still for us, let us make him run to keep up with us.

Reader's Note: "To His Coy Mistress"

On the surface a love poem of the **carpe diem** type, urging the speaker's mistress to seize love while she is young enough to enjoy it, this poem is developed in a far more intellectual manner than, for example, Marlowe's "The Passionate Shepherd" (page 142) or Herrick's "To the Virgins" (page 247).

The first line sets up a condition contrary to fact: "*Had* we but world enough and time," meaning that in fact the lovers have neither. The rest of the first stanza provides an elaborate, farfetched, geographical and historical list of the things the lovers would do *if* time and place (eternity and infinity) permitted.

Another three-letter word, "But," matching the "Had" of line 1, opens the second stanza and introduces the world as it really is. Time does not stop, but hurries on, taking youth and life with it. Indisputable is the chilling reality of

lines 31 and 32, "The grave's . . . embrace."

Still another three-letter word, "Now," opens the third movement of the poem. Recognizing the world as it is, the lovers should take advantage of their present moment of youth to defeat their enemy, time. Note the references to time here: like "birds of prey," the lovers should "at once our time devour" (line 39), rather than "Languish in his slow-chapped power" (line 40); in other words, they should reverse the normal process. This idea of reversal is amplified in the closing couplet: "though we cannot make our sun [which measures their time] / Stand still, yet we will make him run" (lines 45–46) in order to keep up with them. Taken as an entity, therefore, the poem becomes a challenge to the enemy (time) as well as an invitation to the mistress.

Readers are to imagine that this song of thanksgiving is being sung by a small group of Puritans who have recently reached Bermuda after a long sea journey from England. Since Bermuda offered religious freedom to its colonists, these Puritans could now worship as they pleased, without government restraint.

Bermudas

Where the remote Bermudas ride
In the ocean's bosom unespied,
From a small boat that rowed along
The listening winds received this song:

5 "What should we do but sing His praise
That led us through the watery maze
Unto an isle so long unknown,
And yet far kinder than our own?[1]
Where He the huge sea-monsters wracks[2]
10 That lift the deep upon their backs,
He lands us on a grassy stage,
Safe from the storms' and prelates' rage.[3]
He gave us this eternal spring
Which here enamels everything,
15 And sends the fowls to us in care
On daily visits through the air.
He hangs in shades the orange bright
Like golden lamps in a green night,
And does in the pomegranates close
20 Jewels more rich than Ormus[4] shows.
He makes the figs our mouths to meet
And throws the melons at our feet;
But apples[5] plants of such a price,
No tree could ever bear them twice.
25 With cedars chosen by His hand
From Lebanon[6] He stores the land;
And makes the hollow seas that roar
Proclaim the ambergris[7] on shore.
He cast (of which we rather boast)
30 The Gospel's pearl upon our coast;
And in these rocks for us did frame
A temple where to sound His name.
Oh, let our voice His praise exalt

Till it arrive at heaven's vault,
35 Which thence, perhaps, rebounding may
Echo beyond the Mexique bay!"[8]

Thus sung they in the English boat
A holy and a cheerful note;
And all the way, to guide their chime,
40 With falling oars they kept the time.

1681

---

1. **our own,** England.
2. **wracks,** controls, destroys.
3. **prelates' rage,** the anger of Anglican bishops.
4. **Ormus,** Ormuz, an ancient seaport of Persia noted for its wealth.
5. **apples,** pineapples.
6. **cedars . . . Lebanon,** trees like the famous ones in Lebanon.
7. **ambergris,** a substance found in whales, used in making perfume.
8. **Mexique bay,** the Gulf of Mexico.

Discussion

1. **(a)** The first stanza of "To His Coy Mistress" sounds like a traditional love poem urging the lady to make the most of time. However, something disturbing happens in the second stanza (lines 21–32). What is it? **(b)** Relate the last two lines to the rest of the poem.

2. "Bermudas" is a peaceful and joyous poem. **(a)** What hints does it contain as to why the Puritans were so pleased with their new home? **(b)** Try reading the song (stanza 2, lines 5–36) without the first and third stanzas of the poem. What do they add to it?

George Herbert
1593–1633

George Herbert at Bemerton
by William Dyce, 1861.

In his infancy George Herbert, the fifth of seven sons, was dedicated to a life in the church by his mother, a not uncommon career for the younger sons of large, noble families. His father died when Herbert was three. John Donne was a family friend, and certainly Herbert was influenced by that great churchman.

After attending the Westminster School in London, Herbert went on to Trinity College, Cambridge, with the intent of entering the ministry. When he was sixteen he wrote his mother from Cambridge, "My poor abilities in poetry shall be all and ever consecrated to God's glory." After he received his M.A. in 1616, he stayed on at Cambridge, presumably to complete his studies for the ministry.

In 1620, however, Herbert was chosen Orator of Cambridge, a position of honor that normally led to political preferment and high political office. Through this position he became friendly with many powerful nobles and King James himself. At this point, if not sooner, began the struggle between the two facets of his personality, one pulling him toward the church, the other pulling him toward King James's court, where he knew he would be welcomed for his family background (five of his brothers were already in public or diplomatic service), his intellectual achievements, and his attractive personality. In June, 1624, he took a six-month leave of absence from Cambridge to seek preferment at court.

Despite promises, nothing materialized from his time at court. With the death in 1625 of James, he lost his most powerful patron. After a brief period of retirement, in 1626 he took a minor office in the church. In 1627 his mother died, and later that year he resigned as Orator of Cambridge. Herbert had already shown signs of tuberculosis, and he needed to strengthen himself before making any further commitments. In 1629 he was well enough to marry, and in 1630, yielding to his religious vocation, he was ordained and became rector of Bemerton, near Salisbury.

The three years of life that remained to him were probably the happiest he had known, as he took care of his parishioners, completed the religious poems published after his death as *The Temple* (1633), and wrote *A Priest to the Temple, or the Country Parson* (1652), recording in prose his life at Bemerton. Just before his death, Herbert sent the manuscript of *The Temple* to a minister friend with instructions to burn it unless he felt the poems might "turn to the advantage of any dejected poor soul." Fortunately for posterity, the friend recognized the value of the manuscript.

Contained in *The Temple* are more than 160 poems, written in a variety of patterns, but all connected in some way with religion or the religious experience. As the title indicates, the intent of the book is to honor and praise God.

Though cast in the form of an English sonnet, this poem concerns itself with a subject far different from the traditional subject matter for sonnets.

This poem, written in the form of a dialogue, celebrates the Holy Eucharist (Communion), which is described as a banquet at which Jesus (Love) is the host who insists the speaker stay to a dinner of salvation.

*A*varice

Money, thou bane[1] of bliss, and source of woe,
  Whence com'st thou, that thou art so
    fresh and fine?
  I know thy parentage is base and low:
Man found thee poor and dirty in a mine.
5 Surely thou didst so little contribute
  To this great kingdom, which thou now
    hast got,
  That he was fain,[2] when thou wert destitute,
To dig thee out of thy dark cave and grot:[3]
Then forcing thee by fire he made thee bright:
10   Nay, thou hast got the face of man; for we
  Have with our stamp and seal transferred
    our right:
Thou art the man, and man but dross[4] to thee.
  Man calleth thee his wealth, who made
    thee rich;
  And while he digs out thee, falls in the ditch.

1633

---

1. **bane,** ruin.
2. **fain,** willing.
3. **grot,** grotto.
4. **dross,** waste or scum that comes to the surface of melting metals.

*L*ove (III)

Love bade me welcome: yet my soul drew back,
  Guilty of dust and sin.
But quick-eyed Love,[1] observing me grow slack[2]
  From my first entrance in,
5 Drew nearer to me, sweetly questioning,
  If I lacked any thing.

"A guest," I answered, "worthy to be
    here":
  Love said, "You shall be he."
"I the unkind, ungrateful? Ah my dear,
10   I cannot look on thee."
Love took my hand, and smiling did reply,
  "Who made the eyes but I?"

"Truth Lord, but I have marred them: let
    my shame
  Go where it doth deserve."
15 "And know you not," says Love, "who
    bore the blame?"
  "My dear, then I will serve."
"You must sit down," says Love, "and
    taste my meat."[3]
  So I did sit and eat.

1633

---

1. **quick-eyed Love,** divine love; contrasted with the blindness of Cupid, or erotic love.
2. **slack,** backward.
3. **meat,** food in general, a meal; here refers to Holy Communion.

Easter Wings

Lord, who createdst man in wealth and store,[1]
  Though foolishly he lost the same,
    Decaying more and more
      Till he became
5   Most poor:
        With thee
      O let me rise
    As larks, harmoniously,
  And sing this day thy victories:
10 Then shall the fall further the flight in me.

My tender age in sorrow did begin;
  And still with sicknesses and shame
    Thou didst so punish sin,
      That I became
15   Most thin.
        With thee
      Let me combine,
    And feel this day thy victory;
  For, if I imp[2] my wing on thine,
20 Affliction shall advance the flight in me.

1633

---

1. *store,* abundance.
2. *imp* a technical term used in falconry. Additional feathers were grafted (imped) onto a falcon's wings to improve its ability to fly.

Virtue

Sweet day, so cool, so calm, so bright,
  The bridal of the earth and sky:
The dew shall weep thy fall tonight;
  For thou must die.

5 Sweet rose, whose hue, angry and brave,[1]
  Bids the rash gazer wipe his eye:
Thy root is ever in its grave,
  And thou must die.

Sweet spring, full of sweet days and roses,
10   A box where sweets[2] compacted lie;
My music shows ye have your closes,[3]
  And all must die.

Only a sweet and virtuous soul,
  Like seasoned timber, never gives;
15 But though the whole world turn to coal,[4]
  Then chiefly lives.

1633

---

1. *angry and brave,* red and splendid.
2. *sweets,* perfumes.
3. *closes,* ending cadences of a song.
4. *coal,* become a cinder at the Last Judgment.

Discussion

1. **(a)** Explain what the speaker in "Avarice" means by lines 10 and 11. **(b)** What is the meaning of the concluding couplet? How does it sum up the meaning of the rest of the poem?

2. **(a)** What relation does the third stanza of "Virtue" have to the first two stanzas? **(b)** How does the fourth stanza relate to the earlier ones?

3. Explore the ways in which Herbert makes the shape of "Easter Wings" reflect its content, and vice versa.

4. One reader has commented that "Love III" deals with repentance and forgiveness. Explain why you agree or disagree.

John Milton 1608–1674

John Milton was born and brought up in London, the son of a well-to-do scrivener (notary) who also dabbled in real estate. Sent to St. Paul's School, Milton applied himself so energetically to his studies that by 1625 he had mastered Greek, Latin, and Hebrew, as well as a number of modern European languages. Going on to Christ College, Cambridge, he received his B.A. in 1629 and his M.A. in 1632.

The course of Milton's life was shaped by two unrelated events. First, because of his Puritan leanings, he decided against a career in the Anglican church. Second, Milton became blind in 1651, when he was forty-three.

Having decided not to stay at Cambridge to study divinity, Milton spent six years in private study at his father's country house at Horton, Buckinghamshire, reading omnivorously in the varied languages he had mastered. By this time Milton had written several masques and a number of poems in Latin and English, some of which had been published. In 1637 "Lycidas," a pastoral elegy, was included in a volume of poems honoring Edward King, a Cambridge classmate of Milton's who had been drowned in a shipwreck in the Irish Sea.

Early in 1638 Milton began a tour of Europe that lasted for more than a year. He returned to England in 1639, earlier than he had originally intended, because of the troubled political situation there. Setting up residence in London, he busied himself with his writing and with tutoring his two nephews; later he added several other boys, all of them boarding with him. By this time Milton was seriously considering the epic poem he intended to write, trying to come up with a suitable subject for it.

In 1642 Milton married Mary Powell, who came from a Royalist family. She died in childbirth in 1652, leaving Milton with three small daughters. In the meantime, in March, 1649, after he had published a pamphlet justifying the execution of King Charles, Milton was named Latin Secretary in the Council of State of the Puritan government. Warned that he would lose his sight if he continued to do close work,

he decided the cause was important enough for him to risk his vision. He became totally blind in 1651, the year before his wife died. In 1656 Milton took a second wife, Katherine Woodcock, who died in childbirth in 1658.

With the end of the Puritan regime and the restoration of the Stuart line of kings Milton, who had been a strong supporter of the Puritans and of the execution of Charles I, was regarded as a dangerous enemy. Perhaps because of his age and blindness, perhaps because of the intercession of Andrew Marvell, who had worked as his assistant but was friendly with the Restoration government, Milton escaped execution or lengthy imprisonment, but he was heavily fined and lost most of his property.

No longer active politically, Milton was finally free to write the epic poem he had set aside for so long. He probably began writing *Paradise Lost* about 1660, completing it in 1665. Because he was blind, he dictated the poem to his three daughters, who served as secretaries. In 1663 he married Elizabeth Minshull, who survived him. *Paradise Lost* was published in 1667, followed in 1671 by a single volume containing its shorter sequel, *Paradise Regained,* and a closet drama (not intended for stage production), *Samson Agonistes.* In 1674 Milton died of complications following an attack of gout.

On His Having Arrived at the Age of Twenty-Three

How soon hath Time, the subtle thief of youth,
Stolen on his wing my three and twentieth
    year!
My hasting days fly on with full career,
But my late spring no bud or blossom showeth.[1]
5 Perhaps my semblance[2] might deceive the truth,
That I to manhood am arrived so near;
And inward ripeness doth much less appear,
That some more timely-happy spirits endueth.[3]
Yet be it less or more, or soon or slow,
10 It shall be still in strictest measure even[4]

To that same lot, however mean or high,
Toward which Time leads me, and the will
    of Heaven;
All is, if I have grace to use it so,
As ever in my great Task-Master's eye.

1631   1645

---

1. **showeth,** shows.
2. **semblance,** youthful appearance.
3. **endueth,** endows.
4. **even,** adequate; i.e., his "inward ripeness," or inner readiness, will be adequate to whatever destiny Time and Heaven are leading him.

On His Blindness

When I consider how my light is spent,
Ere half my days, in this dark world and wide,
And that one talent[1] which is death to hide
Lodged with me useless, though my soul
    more bent
5 To serve therewith my Maker, and present
My true account, lest He, returning, chide;
"Doth God exact day-labor, light denied?"
I fondly[2] ask. But Patience, to prevent

That murmur, soon replies: "God doth not need
10 Either man's work or His own gifts; who best
Bear His mild yoke, they serve Him best.
    His state
Is kingly: thousands at His bidding speed,
And post o'er land and ocean without rest:
They also serve who only stand and wait."

1652   1673

---

1. **talent,** the gift of writing. This refers to Jesus's parable of the "unprofitable servant," condemned for burying his one talent, or coin, instead of spending it. (Matt. 25:15–30)
2. **fondly,** foolishly.

Discussion

1. **(a)** In "On His Having Arrived at the Age of Twenty-Three," how is Time the subtle thief of youth? **(b)** In what respects does Milton claim to be less mature than others his age? **(c)** What consolation does he refer to in the last six lines?

2. **(a)** In "On His Blindness," what does Milton mean by "Doth God exact day-labor, light denied" (line 7)? **(b)** What solace does he find in the final line, "They also serve who only stand and wait"? **(c)** Who in today's world might also derive solace from this line?

3. Compare "On His Blindness" with the sonnet written at the age of twenty-three (more than two decades earlier), both of which are concerned with Milton's achievements.

Like all **epic** poems, Milton's *Paradise Lost* is a long narrative of events on a grand scale. In the case of *Paradise Lost,* the scale is one of the grandest possible, for the poem has as its setting the entire universe. The main characters are God, His Son, Adam and Eve, and Satan. And the theme is the fall of man as embodied in the biblical story of the temptation of Adam and Eve and their expulsion from Paradise.

As if inspired by the earthly event of civil war in his own time and place, Milton envisions a civil war in Heaven, arising over God's appointment of His Son to the seat of honor and power at His right hand. Satan, one of the archangels, desires the exalted position for himself, and with a third of the other angels he wages war against God and His followers. God's forces prove superior; Satan and his rebel host are sent plunging down into Hell, the place that God had prepared for them, as far removed from Heaven as possible.

From this point on Satan vows eternal vengeance. He has heard of God's plan to fashion a new creature called man and to place him in a new region called the world. Why not strike back at God through the corruption of this latest creature of His handiwork?

The story of Satan's meeting with Adam and Eve in the Garden of Eden follows, in the main, the Bible story. Satan tempts Eve, who in turn persuades Adam to eat the forbidden fruit of the Tree of Knowledge. For this disobedience, Adam and Eve are driven from Paradise out into the world. The twelfth and last book of the poem closes with the pair standing hand in hand upon the threshold of the world. Paradise, "so late their happy home," lies behind them. Sadly and penitently they face the future, their punishment softened only by the promise of the ultimate redemption of man by Christ.

Milton began his epic **in medias res,** or "in the middle of the action," waiting until later in the poem to provide a narrative of the earlier events of his story. Thus in Book I the reader is confronted with the terrifying scenes of Satan and his "horrid crew . . . rolling in the fiery gulf" of Hell and of Satan hurling thundering speeches of defiance at the Almighty.

from Paradise Lost

from **Book I**

Of man's first disobedience, and the fruit
Of that forbidden tree, whose mortal taste
Brought death into the world, and all our
    woe,
With loss of Eden, till one greater Man[1]
5 Restore us, and regain the blissful seat,
Sing Heavenly Muse,[2] that on the secret top
Of Oreb, or of Sinai,[3] didst inspire
That shepherd,[4] who first taught the chosen
    seed,[5]
In the beginning[6] how the heavens and earth
10 Rose out of Chaos; Or if Sion hill[7]
Delight thee more, and Siloa's brook[8] that
    flowed

Fast by the oracle of God; I thence
Invoke thy aid to my adventurous song,
That with no middle flight intends to soar

---

1. *Man,* the Messiah.
2. *Heavenly Muse.* Milton does not name his muse directly here, but later (Book VII) calls her Urania, meaning "Heavenly," which is the name of the Muse of Astronomy, though Milton is careful to state there is no connection between his muse and the pagan Nine Muses.
3. *Oreb . . . Sinai,* twin peaks in Arabia.
4. *shepherd,* Moses, who on Mt. Sinai received the Word of God.
5. *chosen seed,* the Israelites.
6. *beginning,* a punning reference to the Book of Genesis, supposedly composed by Moses.
7. *Sion hill,* the height upon which Jerusalem was built.
8. *Siloa's brook,* the stream which flowed near the hill on which the temple was erected in Jerusalem.

The fallen angels by M. Burgess after John Baptist Medina, from John Milton's *Paradise Lost*, London, 1688, the first illustrated edition.

15 Above the Aonian mount,[9] while it pursues
Things unattempted yet in prose or rhyme.
And chiefly Thou, O Spirit, that dost prefer
Before all temples the upright heart and pure,
Instruct me, for Thou knowest; Thou from
    the first
20 Wast present, and, with mighty wings
    outspread,
Dovelike sat'st brooding on the vast Abyss
And mad'st it pregnant: What in me is dark
Illumine, what is low raise and support;
That to the height of this great argument
25 I may assert Eternal Providence,
And justify the ways of God to men.[10]
    Say first,[11] for Heaven hides nothing from
    thy view,
Nor the deep tract of Hell, say first what cause
Moved our grand Parents in that happy state,
30 Favored of Heaven so highly, to fall off
From their Creator, and transgress His will
For one restraint, lords of the world besides?
Who first seduced them to that foul revolt?[12]
The infernal Serpent; he it was whose guile
35 Stirred up with envy and revenge, deceived
The mother of mankind, what time his pride[13]
Had cast him out from Heaven, with all his
    host
Of rebel Angels, by whose aid aspiring
To set himself in glory above his peers,
40 He trusted to have equaled the Most High,
If He opposed; and with ambitious aim
Against the throne and monarchy of God
Raised impious war in Heaven and battle proud
With vain attempt. Him the Almighty Power
45 Hurled headlong flaming from the ethereal sky
With hideous ruin and combustion down
To bottomless perdition, there to dwell
In adamantine chains and penal fire,
Who durst defy the Omnipotent to arms.
50 Nine times the space that measures day and
    night
To mortal men, he with his horrid crew
Lay vanquished, rolling in the fiery gulf,
Confounded though immortal. But his doom
Reserved him to more wrath; for now the
    thought
55 Both of lost happiness and lasting pain
Torments him; round he throws his baleful eyes,
That witnessed[14] huge affliction and dismay
Mixed with obdúrate pride and steadfast hate:

At once as far as angels' ken he views
60 The dismal situation waste and wild;
A dungeon horrible, on all sides round
As one great furnace flamed, yet from those
    flames
No light, but rather darkness visible[15]
Served only to discover sights of woe,
65 Regions of sorrow, doleful shades, where peace
And rest can never dwell, hope never comes
That comes to all;[16] but torture without end
Still urges, and a fiery deluge, fed
With ever-burning sulphur unconsumed:
70 Such place Eternal Justice had prepared
For those rebellious, here their prison ordained
In utter darkness, and their portion set
As far removed from God and light of Heaven
As from the center thrice to the utmost pole.
75 O how unlike the place from whence they fell!
There the companions of his fall, o'erwhelmed
With floods and whirlwinds of tempestuous
    fire,
He soon discerns, and weltering[17] by his side
One next himself in power, and next in crime,
80 Long after known in Palestine, and named
Beelzebub.[18] To whom the Arch-Enemy,
And thence in Heaven called Satan,[19] with
    bold words
Breaking the horrid silence thus began:

Addressing Beelzebub, Satan boldly declares that though he has been thrown into Hell, he will continue to fight God with all his might. Beelzebub is afraid that God is too strong to be overcome. Satan, chiding him for his fears, begins to make plans.

---

9. **Aonian** (ā ō′ni ən) **mount,** Mount Helicon, representing Greek poetry, which Milton, by writing a Christian poem, endeavored to surpass.
10. **men.** This concludes the invocation (lines 1-26).
11. **Say first.** Here begins the epic question.
12. **revolt.** The epic question ends here.
13. **pride,** Satan's sin, the most deadly of the Seven Deadly Sins.
14. **witnessed,** gave evidence of.
15. **darkness visible.** It was thought that the flames of hell gave no light.
16. **to all.** The greatest torment of Hell was the total absence of hope of salvation.
17. **weltering,** tossing.
18. **Beelzebub** (bi el′zə bub), from Hebrew meaning "Lord of Flies." In the time of Jesus, Beelzebub was "prince of the demons." (Matthew 12:24; Luke 11:15) In certain medieval literature he was a chief associate of Satan.
19. **Satan,** "the Adversary."

"Seest thou yon dreary plain, forlorn and
    wild,
85 The seat of desolation, void of light,
Save what the glimmering of these livid
    flames
Casts pale and dreadful? Thither let us tend
From off the tossing of these fiery waves,
There rest, if any rest can harbor there,
90 And reassembling our afflicted powers,
Consult how we may henceforth most offend
Our Enemy,[20] our own loss how repair,
How overcome this dire calamity,
What reinforcement we may gain from hope;
95 If not, what resolution from despair."
    Thus Satan, talking to his nearest mate,
With head uplift above the wave, and eyes
That sparkling blazed; his other parts besides
Prone on the flood, extended long and large,
100 Lay floating many a rood,[21] in bulk as huge
As whom the fables name of monstrous size,
Titanian, or Earth-born,[22] that warred on Jove,
Briareos or Typhon,[23] whom the den
By ancient Tarsus held, or that sea-beast
105 Leviathan,[24] which God of all His works
Created hugest that swim the ocean-stream:
Him, haply slumbering on the Norway foam,
The pilot of some small night-foundered skiff,
Deeming some island, oft, as seamen tell,
110 With fixèd anchor in his scaly rind
Moors by his side under the lee, while night
Invests the sea, and wishèd morn delays:
So stretched out huge in length the
    Arch-Fiend lay
Chained on the burning lake; nor ever thence
115 Had risen or heaved his head, but that the will
And high permission of all-ruling Heaven
Left him at large to his own dark designs,
That with reiterated crimes he might
Heap on himself damnation, while he sought
120 Evil to others, and enraged might see
How all his malice served but to bring forth
Infinite goodness, grace, and mercy shown
On Man by him seduced, but on himself
Treble confusion, wrath, and vengeance poured.
125 Forthwith upright he rears from off the pool
His mighty stature; on each hand the flames,
Driven backward, slope their pointing spires,
    and rolled
In billows, leave in the midst a horrid vale.
Then with expanded wings he steers his flight

130 Aloft, incumbent on the dusky air
That felt unusual weight, till on dry land
He lights, if it were land that ever burned
With solid, as the lake with liquid fire;
And such appeared in hue, as when the force
135 Of subterranean wind transports a hill
Torn from Pelorus,[25] or the shattered side
Of thundering Etna, whose combustible
And fueled entrails thence conceiving fire,
Sublimed with mineral fury, aid the winds,
140 And leave a singèd bottom all involved
With stench and smoke: Such resting found
    the sole
Of unblest feet. Him followed his next mate,
Both glorying to have scaped the Stygian
    flood[26]
As gods, and by their own recovered strength,
145 Not by the sufferance of Supernal Power.
    "Is this the region, this the soil, the clime,"
Said then the lost Archangel, "this the seat
That we must change for Heaven, this
    mournful gloom
For that celestial light? Be it so, since He
150 Who now is sovereign can dispose and bid
What shall be right: Farthest from Him is best,
Whom reason hath equaled, force hath made
    supreme
Above His equals.[27] Farewell, happy fields,
Where joy for ever dwells: Hail, horrors! hail,
155 Infernal world! and thou, profoundest Hell,
Receive thy new possessor: One who brings
A mind not to be changed by place or time.
The mind is its own place, and in itself
Can make a Heaven of Hell, a Hell of Heaven.
160 What matter where, if I be still the same,
And what I should be, all but less than He
Whom thunder hath made greater? Here at least

---

20. Enemy, God.
21. rood, usually seven or eight yards.
22. Earth-born. Both the Titans (giants descended from Heaven) and the earth-born (giants) "warred on Jove."
23. Briareos (bri ar'i əs) **or Typhon** (tī'fən), in Greek mythology, two monsters, the first with a hundred hands, the second with a hundred fire-breathing heads, who attempted to overthrow the dynasty of Jove. Typhon lived in Cilicia (sə lish'ə), of which Tarsus (tär'səs) (line 104) was the capital.
24. Leviathan, huge sea-monster mentioned in the Bible.
25. Pelorus (pə lor'əs), the northeastern promontory of Sicily near the volcano of Mount Etna (line 137).
26. Stygian (stij'i ən) **flood,** the river Styx, one of the four rivers in Hades.
27. equals. Note that Satan equates his reason with that of God, and attributes his defeat to the larger number of angels that remained loyal to God.

We shall be free; the Almighty hath not built
Here for His envy, will not drive us hence:
165 Here we may reign secure, and in my choice
To reign is worth ambition though in Hell:
Better to reign in Hell, than serve in Heaven.
But wherefore let we then our faithful friends,
The associates and copartners of our loss,
170 Lie thus astonished on the oblivious pool,
And call them not to share with us their part
In this unhappy mansion, or once more
With rallied arms to try what may be yet
Regained in Heaven, or what more lost in Hell?''
175   So Satan spake, and him Beelzebub
Thus answered: ''Leader of those armies bright,
Which, but the Omnipotent, none could have
    foiled,
If once they hear that voice, their liveliest
    pledge
Of hope in fears and dangers, heard so oft
180 In worst extremes, and on the perilous edge
Of battle when it raged, in all assaults
Their surest signal, they will soon resume
New courage and revive, though now they lie
Groveling and prostrate on yon lake of fire,
185 As we erewhile, astounded and amazed;
No wonder, fallen such a pernicious height.''
    He scarce had ceased when the superior
        Fiend
Was moving toward the shore; his
        ponderous shield,
Ethereal temper, massy, large, and round,
190 Behind him cast; the broad circumference
Hung on his shoulders like the moon, whose
        orb
Through optic glass the Tuscan artist views
At evening from the top of Fesole,
Or in Valdarno,[28] to descry new lands,
195 Rivers, or mountains in her spotty globe.
His spear, to equal which the tallest pine
Hewn on Norwegian hills, to be the mast
Of some great ammiral,[29] were but a wand,
He walked with to support uneasy steps
200 Over the burning marl, not like those steps
On Heaven's azure; and the torrid clime
Smote on him sore besides, vaulted with fire;
Nathless[30] he so endured, till on the beach
Of that inflaméd sea, he stood and called
205 His legions, Angel forms, who lay entranced
Thick as autumnal leaves that strow the brooks
In Vallombrosa,[31] where the Etrurian shades

High over-arched embower; or scattered sedge
Afloat, when with fierce winds Orion[32] armed
210 Hath vexed the Red Sea coast, whose waves
        o'erthrew
Busiris and his Memphian chivalry,
While with perfidious hatred they pursued
The sojourners of Goshen,[33] who beheld
From the safe shore their floating carcasses
215 And broken chariot wheels—so thick
        bestrewn,
Abject and lost, lay these, covering the flood,
Under amazement of their hideous change.
He called so loud that all the hollow deep
Of Hell resounded: ''Princes, Potentates,
220 Warriors, the Flower of Heaven, once
        yours, now lost,
If such astonishment as this can seize
Eternal Spirits; or have ye chosen this place
After the toil of battle to repose
Your wearied virtue, for the ease you find
225 To slumber here, as in the vales of Heaven?
Or in this abject posture have ye sworn
To adore the Conqueror? Who now beholds
Cherub and Seraph rolling in the flood
With scattered arms and ensigns, till anon
230 His swift pursuers from Heaven gates discern
The advantage, and descending, tread us down
Thus drooping, or with linkéd thunderbolts
Transfix us to the bottom of this gulf.
Awake, arise, or be forever fallen!''

First to rise from the burning lake are the
leaders of the fallen angels. Followed by the
multitude, they wing their way to the plain
and assemble in military formation before
their ''dread Commander,'' Satan.

28. **optic . . . Valdarno.** The optic glass is the telescope of Galileo, whom Milton refers to as Tuscan because he lived in Tuscany, a region in central Italy which includes Florence. Fesole (Fiesole, fē e′zō lā) is a city on a hill near Florence. Valdarno (val där′no) is the valley of the River Arno in which Florence is situated.
29. **ammiral,** admiral, the flagship bearing the admiral of the fleet.
30. **Nathless,** nevertheless.
31. **Vallombrosa** (val lom brō′sə), a valley twenty miles east of Florence. Florence and the surrounding country are in ancient Etruria (i trür′iə) (line 207).
32. **Orion,** in Greek mythology, a hunter who became a constellation after his death. When the constellation rises late (in November), it is supposed to cause storms.
33. **Goshen** (gō′shən). Busiris was a mythical king of Egypt (Goshen). Milton considers him the Pharaoh who with his cavalry pursued the children of Israel into the Red Sea (Exodus 14).

He, above the rest
In shape and gesture proudly eminent,
Stood like a tower; his form had yet not lost
All her original brightness, nor appeared
Less than Archangel ruined, and the excess
240 Of glory obscured: As when the sun new-risen
Looks through the horizontal misty air
Shorn of his beams, or from behind the moon,
In dim eclipse, disastrous twilight sheds
On half the nations, and with fear of change
245 Perplexes monarchs. Darkened so, yet shone
Above them all the Archangel; but his face
Deep scars of thunder had entrenched, and care
Sat on his faded cheek, but under brows

Of dauntless courage, and considerate pride
250 Waiting revenge: Cruel his eye, but cast
Signs of remorse and passion, to behold
The fellows of his crime, the followers rather
(Far other once beheld in bliss), condemned
Forever now to have their lot in pain.

In his speech to the army, Satan
announces his intention of seeking revenge
by fraud or guile, not force. Book I ends
with the building of the palace of
Pandemonium (that is, "All Demons"), and
with preparations for a council of war.

1667

Discussion

Understanding Structure

Paradise Lost is the greatest **epic** in the English language. Although it observes the conventions of the classical epic, pagan elements have been Christianized. To appreciate the excerpt you have just read, you should become aware of its epic conventions.

1. "Of man's first disobedience . . . ways of God to men" (lines 1–26) constitutes the **invocation,** which, in the classical tradition, begins the epic. In them the poet invokes the aid of a muse and states the theme of his work. **(a)** What muse does Milton invoke? Why? **(b)** What is the theme of the epic?

2. "Say first . . . revolt" (lines 27–33) poses the epic question, the question that the epic will deal with. In *Paradise Lost,* the epic question has two parts. What are they?

3. To aid in the visualization and understanding of scenes, persons, and events, the epic employs many **similes.** Because we are dealing with the introductory phases of the poem, only one appears in the first hundred lines. What is it?

4. The epic achieves much of its effect by the use of the epic simile, which consists of multiple comparisons, and is introduced by "like," "as," or, more commonly, "as whom," "as when," "as where," etc. The first of these epic similes, referred to as the Leviathan Simi-

le, occurs in lines 101-112 *(As whom . . . morn delays).* **(a)** To what beings is Satan being compared? **(b)** Which image remains the strongest in your mind? Why? **(c)** There are three more of these epic similes in the selection. List them and explain the function of each.

5. Epic speeches are usually in elevated language, are usually introduced by the name of the person(s) being addressed, and are often boastful. Reread the following speeches and indicate the presence or absence of elevated language, epithets, and boastfulness: Satan to Beelzebub (lines 146–174); Beelzebub to Satan (lines 176–187); Satan to his followers (lines 219–234).

6. A classical epic always includes detailed descriptions of the armor and weapons of the combatants and descriptions of their battles. Find the equivalent in *Paradise Lost.*

Comprehending Meaning and Artistry

1. In the invocation, Milton asks to be able to "assert Eternal Providence" (line 25)—meaning that God controls everything. **(a)** How do the lines "So stretched out . . . vengeance poured" (113–124) support Milton's assertion? **(b)** Account then for the following lines: "Both

(Discussion continues on page 264.)

glorying to have 'scaped the Stygian flood / As gods, and by their own recovered strength, / Not by the sufferance of Supernal Power'' (143–145).

2. Summarize briefly the action of the excerpts listed in the first question, parts **a** and **b**.

3. All readers must marvel at the range of visual detail that the blind Milton incorporated in his epic. Find a quiet place where you can read without interruption, and reread the following passages so that you may visualize the images: **(a)** The description of Hell (lines 61–69) and scattered references elsewhere. What are the most striking images? **(b)** The descriptions of Satan (lines 96–101; 126–128; 187–202; 235–250). Condense these into a single-sentence description of him.

4. *Paradise Lost* abounds in quotable lines. Explain in your own words the meaning of the following: **(a)** ''The mind is its own place, and in itself / Can make a Heaven of Hell, a Hell of Heaven'' (lines 158–159). **(b)** ''Better to reign in Hell than serve in Heaven'' (line 167).

5. Milton did not intend that Satan be the protagonist of *Paradise Lost,* as the later books of his epic show. He did, however, paint Satan's character so strongly that generations of readers have become fascinated by him. Using what you have gleaned from the excerpts you have read, discuss the character traits of Satan that make him seem almost an antihero (a **protagonist** with character traits opposed to those of the conventional hero).

Vocabulary
Context, Dictionary

A. Using context as an aid, write the most appropriate definition for each italicized word on a separate sheet of paper.

1. ''Read not to contradict and *confute,* nor to believe and take for granted, nor to find talk and discourse, but to weigh and consider.'' **(a)** prove true; **(b)** prove false; **(c)** applaud.

2. ''Hail Horrors! hail / *Infernal* world! and thou profoundest Hell / Receive thy new possessor.'' **(a)** hellish; **(b)** heavenly; **(c)** peaceful.

3. ''And God said unto them, 'Be fruitful, and multiply, and *replenish* the earth.' '' **(a)** waste; **(b)** plunder; **(c)** refill.

B. Use your Glossary to answer the following questions about the words listed below. Read each clue and then write the matching word from the list on your paper.

fetter	oracle
nectar	torrid

1. Which comes from a word related to a part of the body?

2. Which can mean an answer, a place, or a person?

3. Which refers to a substance gathered by bees?

Composition

1. Satan's sin, the deadliest of all sins, was pride. First, list some of Satan's actions that demonstrate his pride. Then, list some examples of his statements that reveal his pride.

Write a short composition in which you point out evidence of his pride and discuss the effects of it on him and his followers.

2. *Paradise Lost* abounds in images of light and darkness, perhaps suggested or supported by Milton's consciousness of his own blindness. List some of these images.

Write a short paper in which you discuss images of light and darkness. Be sure to draw on your list of examples for evidence to support your argument. (See *Evaluating Your Evidence* in Composition Guide.)

3. Find a complete edition of *Paradise Lost.* Your school librarian might be able to help you. Compare one of the other eleven books of *Paradise Lost* with that of the excerpt from Book I that you have just read. You might find Book IX, dealing with the temptation of Adam and Eve, especially interesting.

Write a paper in which you compare the language or action of the excerpt from Book I with an excerpt from one of the other eleven books.

The Changing English Language

The last years of the fifteenth century mark the end of the Middle English period and the beginning of what is called the early Modern English period. The development of the language during the sixteenth century seems at first both paradoxical and chaotic. On the one hand, there was a movement to make the language more uniform; on the other hand, it continued to be, in both its spoken and written forms, more plastic than it is now.

Some of the confusion during the sixteenth century was due to the persistence of regional dialects. Contributing to the problem of regional variations was the lack of any standard system of spelling and pronunciation. A writer spelled according to his own tastes, and a reader had to have a certain amount of agility and imagination. The word *fellow*, for example, was spelled variously as *fallow, felowe, felow, fallowe*.

During the sixteenth century the first attempts to "improve" and regulate the language were made. Among the forces promoting regulation was the printing press, which eliminated the vagaries and mistakes in handwritten manuscripts and greatly enlarged the number of books and pamphlets available. With the growth of printing came a renewed interest in education (a word, by the way, first used in English in 1531). By Shakespeare's time about half the population of London could at least read, and that number continued to grow.

Among the tens of thousands of items run off the presses during the later part of the century were numerous "how to" books on spelling and usage, and many pamphlets and introductions defending the English vernacular over Latin as the language for all occasions. The preoccupation with a uniform language grew out of the strong sense of national identity; the experimentation with new vocabulary and new means of expression grew out of the adventurous spirit of the Elizabethans and also out of the concern for ele-

gance and style; there was a realization that, in the newly flexible social structure, an elegant style could contribute to upward social mobility.

Of necessity the language had to grow to accommodate the new discoveries being made in scholarship and science. During the later years of the sixteenth century, English vocabulary was tremendously expanded by energetic and sometimes indiscriminate adaptation of words from Latin, Greek, French, Italian, and Spanish to supply terms the native idiom lacked. (Experts estimate that more than ten thousand words were added to English during this period.) So widespread was the importation of foreign terms that the first dictionaries printed in England were listings not of English but of foreign terms.

Latin and Greek contributed thousands of words, among them *antipathy, catastrophe, external, erupt, halo, anachronism, encyclopedia, appendix, emphasis, submerge, strenuous, inflate, infringement.* From French came *bigot, alloy,* and *detail,* while *balcony, cameo, stanza,* and *violin* were borrowed from Italian. Spanish and Portuguese added *alligator, negro, potato, tobacco, cannibal,* and many others. Together with, and partially in reaction to, this habit of borrowing and experimenting with foreign terms, there arose a movement to revive and adapt Old English words, adding to the language such forms as *wolfish, briny, astound, doom, filch,* and *freak.* It was largely through scholarly writing and literature that most of the new terms gained admittance to the language. The poets of the period— particularly Spenser and Shakespeare—were notorious coiners and borrowers of words.

In contrast to the tremendous embellishment of its vocabulary, the grammatical structure of English underwent relatively few changes in the sixteenth century. Some time in the last part of the century, a shift in the pronunciation of long vowels settled the pronunciation of English close to what it is today.

The  *enaissance*

Content Review

1. The introduction to this unit mentions that the exuberance of early Renaissance poetry gave way to a more cynical and introspective outlook as the Renaissance waned. Select three or four poets whose works may be used to demonstrate these changes, and explain how at least one poem by each typifies exuberance, cynicism, or introspection.

2. One of the major achievements of Renaissance literature was the introduction and development of the sonnet. Among its major practitioners were Wyatt, Surrey, Sidney, Spenser, Shakespeare, Donne, and Milton. Select any three sonnets, each written by a different author from this group, and discuss similarities and differences in structure and content.

3. Many of the selections in this unit treat the *carpe diem* theme, which translated from Latin to English means "seize [enjoy] the day," and in poetry usually functions to urge the young to take advantage of love while they may, before their youth and beauty have succumbed to the swift and inexorable passage of time. The first examples in this unit are the paired poems, "The Passionate Shepherd to His Love" and "The Nymph's Reply" (p. 142). Find two or three of the others and compare their treatment of the theme with those of the Marlowe and Raleigh poems.

4. "Poetry with ingenious comparisons, far-fetched assertions, and extraordinarily clever phrasing may be interesting but cannot be sincere as genuine love poetry because it does not express deep feeling or profound emotion." Defend or attack this statement, using examples from the poetry of the Renaissance period.

5. The Renaissance has been described as consisting of "a rebirth of the human spirit, a realization of the human potential for development." Select one major author from this unit and discuss how his works illustrate that Renaissance ideal.

6. It has been said that Shakespeare stands at the pinnacle of Renaissance artistry. Support or attack this claim, using as your basis the works included in this unit.

7. The Renaissance in England produced many poems that either were set to music or were written as songs. Although Campion is recognized as the foremost composer of songs, there were other poets who wrote lyrics that were just as musical, though they did not compose the music for them. Nashe is one of these, Jonson another, and there are poems throughout the unit that rank with these for musical qualities. Select several of these, by the poets mentioned or any others, and discuss the elements that make them suitable for lyrics.

8. Religion had its place in Renaissance poetry, especially in the works of Herbert and in Donne's "Holy Sonnets." Discuss the sincerity and the content of several of these works. As an alternative, discuss the relationship one of these poets shows in his works between himself and his God.

9. If you were asked to prepare your own Renaissance unit, which authors would you omit? To which would you give more space? Less space? Discuss.

10. From the poetry you have read in this unit, do you think the attitude of male to female (or vice versa) differed greatly in Renaissance England from what it is in America today? Discuss, being sure to make specific references to some of the works in the unit.

The scene you are about to read comes from *Richard II,* one of Shakespeare's history plays. King Richard's rule is being challenged by his cousin Henry Bolingbroke, Duke of Hereford. As the following scene opens Richard has returned to his kingdom from a war in Ireland. He finds Bolingbroke, whom he had earlier ex- iled, back in England at the head of a large army leading a rebellion. The Elizabethans, in general, believed that a king received his right to rule directly from God, and not from the people governed. A king was considered to be God's deputy on earth, and therefore rebellion was a moral as well as a political issue.

from Richard II, Act Three • *William Shakespeare*

CHARACTERS:
KING RICHARD II
DUKE OF AUMERLE, son to the Duke of York
BISHOP OF CARLISLE
EARL OF SALISBURY
SIR STEPHEN SCROOP

Scene 2.
The coast of Wales, near Barkloughly castle. Drum: flourish and colors. Enter the KING, AUMERLE, *the* BISHOP OF CARLISLE, *with Soldiers.*

K. RICH. Barkloughly castle call they this at hand?
AUM. Yea, my lord. How brooks[1] your grace the air,
    After your late[2] tossing on the breaking seas?
K. RICH. Needs must I like it well: I weep for joy
5   To stand upon my kingdom once again.
    Dear earth, I do salute thee with my hand,
    Though rebels wound thee with their horses' hoofs:
    As a long-parted mother with her child
    Plays fondly with her tears and smiles in meeting,
10   So, weeping, smiling, greet I thee, my earth,
    And do thee favors with my royal hands.
    Feed not thy sovereign's foe, my gentle earth,
    Nor with thy sweets comfort his ravenous[3] sense;
    But let thy spiders, that suck up thy venom,
15   And heavy-gaited toads lie in their way,
    Doing annoyance to the treacherous feet
    Which with usurping[4] steps do trample thee:

    Yield stinging nettles to mine enemies;
    And when they from thy bosom pluck a flower,
20   Guard it, I pray thee, with a lurking adder[5]
    Whose double[6] tongue may with a mortal touch
    Throw death upon thy sovereign's enemies.
    Mock not my senseless conjuration,[7] lords:
    This earth shall have a feeling and these stones
25   Prove armed soldiers, ere her native[8] king
    Shall falter under foul rebellion's arms.
CAR. Fear not, my lord: that Power that made you king
    Hath power to keep you king in spite of all.
    The means that heaven yields must be embraced,
30   And not neglected; else, if heaven would,
    And we will not, heaven's offer we refuse,
    The proffered means of succour and redress.
AUM. He means, my lord, that we are too remiss;[9]
    Whilst Bolingbroke, through our security,[10]
35   Grows strong and great in substance and in power.
K. RICH. Discomfortable[11] cousin! know'st thou not
    That when the searching eye of heaven[12] is hid,
    Behind the globe, that lights the lower world,[13]

---

1. *brooks,* enjoys.
2. *late,* recent.
3. *ravenous,* greedy.
4. *usurping,* seizing by force.
5. *adder,* poisonous snake.
6. *double,* forked.
7. *senseless conjuration,* appeal to unfeeling things.
8. *native,* entitled to the crown by birth.
9. *remiss,* careless.
10. *security,* confidence.
11. *Discomfortable,* uncomforting.
12. *searching eye of heaven,* the sun.
13. *that lights the lower world.* This clause modifies *eye of heaven.*

Then thieves and robbers range abroad unseen
40 In murders and in outrage, boldly here;
But when from under this terrestrial ball
He fires the proud tops of the eastern pines
And darts his light through every guilty hole,
Then murders, treasons and detested sins,
45 The cloak of night being plucked from off their
        backs,
Stand bare and naked, trembling at them
        selves?
So when this thief, this traitor, Bolingbroke,
Who all this while hath revelled in the night
Whilst we were wand'ring with the antipodes,[14]
50 Shall see us rising in our throne, the east,
His treasons will sit blushing in his face,
Not able to endure the sight of day,
But self-affrighted tremble at his sin.
Not all the water in the rough rude sea
55 Can wash the balm[15] off from an anointed king;
The breath of worldly men cannot depose
The deputy elected by the Lord:
For every man that Bolingbroke hath pressed[16]
To lift shrewd steel against our golden crown,
60 God for his Richard hath in heavenly pay
A glorious angel: then, if angels fight,
Weak men must fall, for heaven still guards the
        right.

            (Enter SALISBURY.)
Welcome, my lord: how far off lies your power?
SAL. Nor near[17] nor farther off, my gracious lord,
65 Than this weak arm: discomfort[18] guides my
        tongue
And bids me speak of nothing but despair.
One day too late, I fear me, noble lord,
Hath clouded all thy happy days on earth:
O, call back yesterday, bid time return,
70 And thou shalt have twelve thousand fighting
        men!
To-day, to-day, unhappy day, too late,
O'erthrows thy joys, friends, fortune and thy
        state:
For all the Welshmen, hearing thou wert dead,
Are gone to Bolingbroke, dispersed and fled.
75 **AUM.** Comfort, my liege: why looks your grace so
        pale?
K. RICH. But now the blood of twenty thousand
        men
Did triumph in my face, and they are fled;
And, till so much blood thither come again,
Have I not reason to look pale and dead?

80 All souls that will be safe fly from my side,
For time hath set a blot upon my pride.
AUM. Comfort, my liege; remember who you are.
K. RICH. I had forgot myself: am I not king?
Awake, thou coward majesty! thou sleepest.
85 Is not the king's name twenty thousand names?
Arm, arm, my name! a puny subject strikes
At thy great glory. Look not to the ground,
Ye favorites of a king: are we not high?
High be our thoughts: I know my uncle York
90 Hath power enough to serve our turn. But who
        comes here?

            (Enter SCROOP.)
SCROOP. More health and happiness betide[19] my
        liege
That can my care-tuned tongue deliver him!
K. RICH. Mine ear is open and my heart prepared:
The worst is worldly loss thou canst unfold.
95 Say, is my kingdom lost? why, 'twas my care;
And what loss is it to be rid of care?
Strives Bolingbroke to be as great as we?
Greater he shall not be; if he serve God,
We'll serve Him too and be his fellow so:
100 Revolt our subjects? that we cannot mend;
They break their faith to God as well as us:
Cry woe, destruction, ruin and decay;
The worst is death, and death will have his day.
SCROOP. Glad am I that your highness is so armed
105 To bear the tidings of calamity.
Like an unseasonable stormy day,
Which makes the silver rivers drown their
        shores,
As if the world were all dissolved to tears,
So high above his limits swells the rage
110 Of Bolingbroke, covering your fearful land
With hard bright steel and hearts harder than
        steel.
White-beards have armed their thin and hairless
        scalps
Against thy majesty; boys, with women's voices,
Strive to speak big and clap[20] their female[21]
        joints
115 In stiff unwieldy arms against thy crown:

---

14. *antipodes,* opposite points on the globe.
15. *balm,* consecrated oil used in anointing a king.
16. *pressed,* forced into the ranks.
17. *near,* nearer.
18. *discomfort,* discouragement.
19. *betide,* happen to.
20. *clap,* thrust.
21. *female,* youthful.

Richard Chamberlain in a Seattle Repertory Theatre production of *Richard II.*

Thy very beadsmen[22] learn to bend their bows
Of double-fatal[23] yew against thy state;
Yea, distaff-women manage[24] rusty bills[25]
Against thy seat: both young and old rebel,
120 And all goes worse than I have power to tell.
   K. RICH. Too well, too well thou tell'st a tale so ill.
Where is the Earl of Wiltshire? where is Bagot?
What is become of Bushy? where is Green?
That they have let the dangerous enemy
125 Measure our confines with such peaceful[26] steps?
If we prevail, their heads shall pay for it:
I warrant they have made peace with Boling-broke.
   SCROOP. Peace have they made with him indeed, my lord.
   K. RICH. O villains, vipers, damned without redemption!
130 Dogs, easily won to fawn on any man!
Snakes, in my heart-blood warmed, that sting my heart!
Three Judases, each one thrice worse than Judas!
Would they make peace? terrible hell make war
Upon their spotted souls for this offense!
135   **SCROOP.** Sweet love, I see, changing his property,[27]
Turns to the sourest and most deadly hate:
Again uncurse their souls; their peace is made
With heads, and not with hands: those whom you curse
Have felt the worst of death's destroying wound
140 And lie full low, graved in the hollow ground.
   AUM. Is Bushy, Green, and the Earl of Wiltshire dead?
   SCROOP. Ay, all of them at Bristow lost their heads.
   AUM. Where is the duke my father with his power?
   K. RICH. No matter where; of comfort no man speak:
145 Let's talk of graves, of worms and epitaphs;
Make dust our paper and with rainy eyes
Write sorrow on the bosom of the earth,
Let's choose executors[28] and talk of wills:
And yet not so, for what can we bequeath
150 Save our deposed bodies to the ground?
Our lands, our lives and all are Bolingbroke's,
And nothing can we call our own but death
And that small model[29] of the barren earth
Which serves as paste and cover to our bones,

155 For God's sake, let us sit upon the ground
And tell sad stories of the death of kings:
How some have been deposed; some slain in war;
Some haunted by the ghosts they have deposed;
Some poisoned by their wives; some sleeping killed;
160 All murdered: for within the hollow crown
That rounds the mortal temples of a king
Keeps Death his court[30] and there the antic[31] sits,
Scoffing his state and grinning at his[32] pomp,
Allowing him a breath,[33] a little scene,
165 To monarchize, be feared and kill with looks,
Infusing him with self and vain conceit,
As if this flesh which walls about our life
Were brass impregnable, and humored[34] thus
Comes at the last and with a little pin
170 Bores through his castle wall, and farewell king!
Cover your heads and mock not flesh and blood
With solemn reverence: throw away respect,
Tradition, form and ceremonious duty,
For you have but mistook me all this while:
175 I live with bread like you, feel want,
Taste grief, need friends: subjected[35] thus,
How can you say to me, I am a king?

---

22. **beadsmen,** people whose duty it was to pray for the king.
23. **double-fatal.** The wood was used for bows and the berry as poison.
24. **manage,** wield.
25. **bills,** weapons.
26. **peaceful,** unopposed.
27. **property,** distinctive quality.
28. **executors,** persons named to carry out the provisions of a will.
29. **model,** the body or the grave mound.
30. **Keeps Death his court,** death presides over the king's court.
31. **antic,** grotesque figure.
32. **his,** the king's.
33. **breath,** breathing space, moment.
34. **humored,** Death's having satisfied his humor or whim.
35. **subjected,** made subject to grief, want, etc. (with pun on "being treated like a subject").

On a separate sheet of paper, write your answers to the following questions. Do not write in your book.

1. Does Richard's rival to the throne appear in this scene?

2. In the simile in lines 8–10, to what does Richard compare himself and his greeting to the earth?

3. Who or what is the "Power" referred to by the Bishop of Carlisle in line 27?

4. To what object does Richard compare himself in the metaphor in line 50?

5. What has happened to the Earl of Salisbury's forces?

6. To what is the rage of Bolingbroke compared in the simile in lines 106–111?

7. List the persons and things to which Richard compares those who have betrayed him in lines 129–132.

8. In the metaphor in lines 146–147, dust is said to be "paper." What is the implement that is to write upon that "paper"?

9. What is the "castle wall" that is bored through with a pin in lines 169–170? What then happens to the king?

10. How would you describe the tone of Richard's final speech?

Composition Review

You may choose any *one* of the following assignments. Assume that you are writing for your classmates.

1. At the first mention of the monster in *The Faerie Queene* (line 7) and Satan in *Paradise Lost* (line 34) both are described as what sort of creature? Look up both scenes and list some similarities and differences between the two creatures.

Write a paper in which you compare and contrast the two, including in your discussion the images of darkness and light and what these images represent.

2. Samuel Taylor Coleridge has said of Hamlet that he is an intellectual, called upon to act deliberately for human and divine reasons, who keeps resolving to act and yet always delays action. Go back to the play to find evidence to support or refute this interpretation.

Write a paper in which you agree or disagree with Coleridge's analysis, and give reasons to support your answer.

3. *Macbeth* is, first of all, a play about the murder of a king. This act destroys harmony not only in the character of Macbeth, but also in the society at large. Go back and look at the play, keeping in mind the relationship between kingship, order, and anarchy.

Discuss in a composition Macbeth as an agent of disintegration and disorder. Give examples from the play to support your case.

4. Lovelace and Herrick are only two of the Cavalier poets. Others are Sir John Suckling, George Wither, and Edmund Waller. Find some of their poems and read them, keeping in mind the works of Lovelace and Herrick that you have already read. Be sure to keep track of the titles of the poems and the books in which you find them.

Write a paper in which you compare the poems of Herrick and Lovelace with those of one or more of the other Cavalier poets you have discovered on your own.

5. Death is ever-present in the literature of the Renaissance, whether prose, poetry, or drama. Do some research in the library into the average life span of people in the sixteenth and seventeenth centuries. See what you can discover about infant-mortality rates and mothers dying in childbirth in the same period.

Write about the various attitudes toward death in Donne's "Death Be Not Proud" (Holy Sonnet no. 10) and "Meditation 17," and Jonson's "On My First Son" and "On My First Daughter."

6. Based on the works you have read in this unit, make a list of the qualities and features that would characterize one of the following: **(a)** a Renaissance courtier; **(b)** a Renaissance woman; **(c)** a Renaissance sonneteer.

Using your imagination, write a description based on your list. Make reference to specific works to give life and authenticity to your portrait.

7. "Mutability" was the Renaissance term for the changes worked by time. The term included ideas such as fickleness, luck, and fate.

Discuss the attitudes toward time expressed in Herrick's "To the Virgins, to Make Much of Time," Milton's "On His Having Arrived at the Age of Twenty-Three," and Marvell's "To His Coy Mistress."

Detail of *Canvassing for Votes* by William Hogarth, number 2 of *An Election* series, painted 1754. A farmer is bribed for his vote outside an inn.

The Fire of London •

• Hobbes: *Leviathan*

The Puritan
Commonwealth

• Bunyan: *Pilgrim's Progress*

Pope: *An Essay* •
on Criticism

• Royal Society founded

• Theaters reopened

• Newton: *Principia*

Restoration of •
Stuart Monarchy

The Glorious Revolution •

Pope: *The Rape* •
of the Lock

• The Diary of
Samuel Pepys

Locke: *Essay Concerning* •
Human Understanding

The Great Plague •

1650   **1675**   **1700**

The  *ge of Reason*

- Pope: *The Dunciad*

- Swift: *A Modest Proposal*

- Swift: *Gulliver's Travels*

Defoe: *A Journal of the Plague Year*

- Pope: *An Essay on Man*

Richardson: *Pamela* •

Fielding: *Tom Jones* •

- Gray: *Elegy Written in a Country Churchyard*

- British Museum opens

- The Lisbon earthquake
- Johnson's *Dictionary*
  - Sterne: *Tristram Shandy*

- Percy: *Reliques*

- Johnson and Boswell meet

Royal Academy founded •

First edition of • *Encyclopedia Britannica*

Goldsmith: *She Stoops to Conquer* •

- Paine: *Common Sense*

- Smith: *Wealth of Nations*

American Revolution

- Sheridan: *The School for Scandal*

725   1750   1775   1800

Background: The Age of Reason 1660–1780

In Europe in the late seventeenth and eighteenth centuries, there was a general intellectual and literary movement known as the Enlightenment. This movement was characterized by rationalism, that is, by the principle or habit of accepting reason as the supreme authority in matters of opinion, belief, or conduct. Intellectual freedom and relative freedom from prejudice and superstition in religion and politics were ideals typical of the age; as in all ages, behavior often did not match ideals.

In England this movement is more commonly known as the Age of Reason. The English version of this general European movement tended to give an equal place to experience and reason in examining the human condition, and was therefore less strictly "rational" than the French or other Continental versions. It is important to remember that in England many of the most important writers of the period were opposed to the rationalist ideals of social progress and human perfectability.

It was an age, in Europe at least, in which people were concerned with manners and morals, with understanding themselves, their immediate world, and their relations with one another. It was a period influenced by John Locke's *Essay Concerning Human Understanding* (1690), which argued that "our business here is not to know all things, but those which concern our conduct." It was an age that advocated the use of scientific method to test old theories and to develop new knowledge.

The Early Years, 1660–1700

When in 1660 the Puritan regime was toppled and King Charles II returned triumphantly to the throne, it was to an England generally delighted to have its monarchy restored. Samuel Pepys, who was with the official party that brought the king home in the Restoration of 1660, recorded the event in his diary. He also recorded another event he witnessed soon after: the hanging of a Puritan involved in the execution of Charles I, the new king's father.

The Restoration brought many changes to England. Once again the Anglican Church became the Established Church, and the Puritans were ousted from both governmental and church positions. Soon after his return, Charles permitted the theaters, closed by the Puritans, to reopen, and he himself sponsored one acting company, the King's Players, while his brother James, the Duke of York, sponsored another.

Not everything ran smoothly, however. Charles had been in exile in France for a number of years, and he brought back some French customs that shocked the more pious people of his realm. Soon a spirit of licentiousness characterized the behavior of the Court and the nobility. Additionally, Charles attempted to restore some of the privileges of the Catholics, and himself became a Catholic on his deathbed in 1685. Since Charles left no children, his brother, who was a Catholic, succeeded him as James II. Afraid of the reemergence of Catholicism, the country watched and waited. The Duke of Monmouth, illegitimate son of Charles II, led an uprising against James II in 1685. The rebellion failed. When James's second wife gave birth to a son, a Catholic line seemed virtually assured.

By his first marriage, however, James had two daughters, both of whom had been raised as Protestants. The elder, Mary, who was married to the Protestant William of Orange, ruler of the United Provinces of Holland, had been next in line for the English throne until the birth of

James's son. Through secret negotiations, William and Mary were offered the throne as joint rulers and, in 1688, William crossed the English Channel with a small army. Immediately the English flocked to his support, and James prudently escaped to France. As a result of the Glorious Revolution of 1688 (so called because it involved no bloodshed), William and Mary were crowned in 1689. After Mary's death, William was the sole ruler until he died in 1702. As a condition to their rule, William and Mary accepted a Bill of Rights, passed by Parliament, which limited the power of the crown and reaffirmed the supremacy of Parliament.

Not all the activity in England between 1660 and 1700 was political, and not all of Charles's activities met with public or private disapproval. In 1662 he chartered the Royal Society, thus making official the scientific activities and investigations it had been carrying on for some time. The Society made two important contributions besides its scientific work: it required the use of the scientific method in all of its investigations, and it insisted that reports be written in clear, simple prose.

Several years after Charles was crowned, London underwent two disasters in rapid succession. In 1665 plague ran rampant through the city, killing 70,000 of its inhabitants. Soon after the disease abated, fire broke out in June, 1666, and raged uncontrolled for five days. By the time it was extinguished, 13,000 houses and nearly a hundred churches had been destroyed; two-thirds of the population was homeless. An excerpt from Daniel Defoe's fictional account of the plague appears on pages 349–352. Samuel Pepys's eyewitness account of the fire, taken from the pages of his *Diary,* appears on pages 283–289.

London was rebuilt with wider streets and more solidly constructed buildings. Many of the most beautiful of these, among them St. Paul's Cathedral and the lovely small church of St. Mary-le-Bow, were designed by Sir Christopher Wren, who became England's leading architect.

In literature, changes took place that had begun with Ben Jonson's use of classical models early in the seventeenth century. Love sonnets were replaced by satirical verses aimed at correcting individuals and society. The closed or

heroic couplet, consisting of two lines of rhyming iambic pentameter, lent itself naturally to satire and was popularized by John Dryden and later brought to perfection by Alexander Pope. Prose became less ornate and, with the introduction of literary periodicals, the periodical essay, short

Portrait of Sir Christopher Wren holding the plans of St. Paul's Cathedral, apparently begun by Antonio Verrio and completed by Godfrey Kneller and James Thornhill.

and intended for consumption by the middle class, became the vogue. Most of the authors in this unit, beginning with Dryden, contributed to these periodicals.

With the reopening of the theaters, drama too underwent several changes. The boy actors who had played female roles in Elizabethan drama were replaced by actresses, although some members of the clergy and upper classes considered acting an unsuitable career for a woman. Accompanying this change was the development of the comedy of manners, or Restoration comedy, such as William Wycherley's *The Country Wife* (1675) and William Congreve's *The Way of the World* (1700). This was a sophisticated type of drama that featured multiple plots involving intrigue and infidelity, and deriving much of its humor from characters who tried to adopt manners suitable to a different station in life. Soon these plays became so scandalous that Restoration comedy became synonymous with licentiousness.

In 1652, the opening of the first coffeehouse in London had provided a place where men could meet their friends, drink coffee, smoke, and talk. By the end of the century several thousand coffeehouses were in existence. Here the rising middle class could rub shoulders with writers and members of the upper classes.

The Middle Years, 1700–1744

Queen Anne, the younger sister of Queen Mary, ruled from 1702–1714. When she died without an heir, the throne went to George I of the German state of Hanover. George, the great-grandson of James I, possessed Stuart blood, was a Protestant, and was acceptable to the Parliament, even though he spoke German and spent as much time as he could in Hanover. The same was true of his son, George II, who ruled from 1727 to 1760.

Accompanying the changes in monarchs was a growth in the power of the prime minister and his cabinet until, under the first two Hanoverian kings, the country was in effect ruled by the ministry. England now had two political parties: the Tories, who favored royal power and the established Church of England and opposed change, and the Whigs, who favored reforms, progress, and parliamentary rather than royal power. During part of Anne's reign and all of the reigns of George I and George II the Whigs wielded most of the power. They favored the new mercantile middle class living in London and other cities and therefore fostered trade and contributed to the growth of the cities and international commerce.

During the early years of the century the middle class, which had already begun to merge with the landed gentry through intermarriage and common concerns for wealth and property, moved into a position of social dominance. The middle class exercised a growing influence on literature. Their new wealth now permitted them to buy books, and writers turned from the demands of aristocratic patrons to the open market, hoping to make a living there. Middle-class readers preferred to read about people like themselves, so tragedies gave way to realistic novels such as Samuel Richardson's *Pamela* (1740) or Henry Fielding's *Tom Jones* (1749).

The working class meanwhile—the ever-increasing number of people working in mines and factories and at heavy labor, whose voices began to be heard in the eighteenth century—benefited little if any from England's new riches. The same was true even for great numbers of people who considered themselves middle class.

In London, for example, which received the bulk of the great population shift from country to town, the inequality in the distribution of wealth was appalling. In the streets the silks and brocades and powdered wigs, the gilded coaches and sedan chairs of the rich moved against a background of rags, filth, stench, and crime. Beaux and belles attended plays at Drury Lane Theater, heard Italian operas, sipped wine in the arbors of Vauxhall or Ranelagh Gardens, or watched fireworks, while hundreds of people wondered where their next meal was coming from. Sir Joshua Reynolds and Thomas Gainsborough turned out elegant portraits of prosperous ladies and gentlemen, while William Hogarth savagely satirized the wealthy and protested against the lot of the poor in paintings and graphic works.

For most English people the poverty and uncertainty of life were such that, as Samuel Johnson said, "He that sees before him to his third dinner, has a long prospect." While the Enlightenment may have swept Europe, it had little effect on the rights of women or on their education. Women were not generally educated, and they had limited property rights.

Coffeehouses and literary periodicals catered to the middle-class audience; in fact, the great insurance firm of Lloyd's of London drew its name, as well as its origin, from Lloyd's Coffeehouse. Richard Steele's periodical *The Tatler* (1709–1711) was organized so that its contents seemed to emanate from the coffeehouses. This periodical and *The Spectator* (1711–1712), published by Steele and Joseph Addison, aimed at improving the morals and manners of their readers and were successful in both areas.

After the Glorious Revolution of 1688, a reaction to the moral laxity of the Restoration set in. By 1700 this reaction was felt in the theater and elsewhere. Richard Steele, also a dramatist and a partner in the Drury Lane Theater, popularized a new type of moral comedy that came to be known as sentimental comedy and helped to make the theater respectable again.

Perhaps the greatest moralist of them all, Jonathan Swift, put his satirical pen to use in exposing and ridiculing individual and social evils of his day. His *A Modest Proposal* (page 307) portrayed in biting satire the plight of the Irish people; in *Gulliver's Travels* (page 294) his chief targets were governmental and personal hypocrisy and vice. Without doubt, Swift was the greatest prose satirist of the Age of Reason.

In the hands of Alexander Pope the closed couplet reached perfection. Pope "played" the twenty syllables of the couplet the way a master musician plays his instrument, demonstrating in his own verse the precept he advocated in his *Essay on Criticism:* " 'Tis not enough no harshness gives offense, / The sound must seem an echo to the sense." Pope's *The Rape of the Lock* (pages 319–325) is the greatest English mock epic, just as he himself is considered the greatest English satirical poet.

Until the Age of Reason, authors had sought wealthy patrons, usually from the nobility, to subsidize their work. However, one of the results of the Puritan regime was the weakening of the patronage system. During the Restoration and Hanoverian periods constant changes occurred in the peerage, depending on the political mood of the times, so that few of the nobility became patrons. Playwriting produced an income, and Dryden and other authors made use of that source. Being named Poet Laureate also provided money, but that honor was politically reversible, as Dryden learned. Political appointments helped, but they took time away from writing, and they too were temporary, as Addison and Steele discovered. A fourth method remained—payment from publishers, and the most profitable way to publish a book was through subscription—advertising, and receiving advance payment for, a deluxe edition of a projected work, which would then be published in both deluxe and ordinary editions; the subscription payments supported the author while completing the project. Dryden used this system successfully for his translation of Virgil, as did Pope for his translation of Homer. Pope was, in fact, the first English author to support himself entirely by his pen.

The Late Years, 1744–1780

By 1744 the Hanoverian line of kings had established itself in England. In 1760 George III, the first of this line to be born in England and to speak English as his first language, became king; he ruled for sixty years, until 1820. George III is known in America as the king against whom the American Revolution was fought. The first two Georges had supported the Whig party; George III supported the Tories. He also attempted, largely without success, to regain some of the royal powers that through the years had been assumed by Parliament.

The great man of letters of this period was Samuel Johnson. Besides writing periodical essays, poetry, pamphlets, travel journals, criticism, and one heroic tragedy, Johnson successfully completed three major projects, any one of them a lifetime's work for most people. He compiled the first truly comprehensive English dictionary (see page 329); he edited a complete edition of Shakespeare, including both textual and critical notes; and he wrote *Lives of the Poets,* critical biographies of fifty-two of England's poets (see the *Life of Milton,* page 332).

Although many of the ideas and literary modes of the Age of Reason lasted through the eighteenth century, by its second half changes had begun to occur. Thomas Gray, who used verse forms other than the heroic couplet, was a forerunner of the Romantic Age. So too were his air of gentle melancholy and his interest in wild landscapes, older English, Welsh, and Norse poetry, and the common man.

John Dryden 1631–1700

Born into a Puritan family, Dryden showed in his own life the religious turmoil of the age. First espousing the Anglican faith, he became a Catholic upon the accession of King James II. With the Glorious Revolution of 1688 and the coming to power of the Protestant monarchs William and Mary in 1689, he kept his Catholic faith but lost his profitable Court appointments as Poet Laureate and Historiographer Royal. He was forced to return solely to writing for his living.

Dryden left his mark on the literature of his age and succeeding ages in a number of areas: he was a successful dramatist; he was responsible for popularizing the closed couplet in poetry; he wrote excellent literary criticism; he was a clever political satirist; and he was a talented translator.

After attending Westminster School and receiving his B.A. from Trinity College, Cambridge, Dryden settled in London and probably held a minor position in the Cromwell government. An early poem, *Heroic Stanzas on the Death of Cromwell* (1659) was followed a year later by *Astraea Redux,* which celebrates the Restoration of the Stuart line to the throne of England.

With the Restoration and the reopening of the theaters, Dryden turned to playwriting as a source of income; between 1663 and 1681 he averaged a play a year in production. The Restoration was kind to Dryden in many ways. By 1662 he was sufficiently well known to be elected to the Royal Society, a group founded in 1660 and dedicated to promoting scientific inquiry. For the rest of his life he retained an interest in science, which appeared in his poems. He also credited the proceedings of the Royal Society for his clear and accurate prose style. In 1663 Dryden married well, taking for his wife Lady Elizabeth Howard, daughter of the Earl of Berkshire and sister of Sir Robert Howard, with whom Dryden collaborated on a play.

Four years later, in 1667, Dryden's *Annus Mirabilis* was published, a poem commemorating three events of the previous year: the end of the plague, the Great Fire of London, and the Dutch War. The next year he was made Poet Laureate, followed two years later by Historiographer Royal. These Court appointments brought him added income.

Dryden's venture into political satire began in 1681, with the publication of *Absalom and Achitophel,* a poem in closed couplets, written after an unsuccessful attempt by Charles's illegitimate son, the Duke of Monmouth, to seize the throne. *Mac Flecknoe* (1682), an excerpt from which follows, is a prime example of literary satire.

With the accession of William and Mary, Dryden lost his royal appointments. By an ironic twist of fate, these appointments went to Thomas Shadwell who, as the butt of Dryden's satire in *Mac Flecknoe,* had been crowned the new King of Nonsense.

Dryden began, in his early sixties, a new and successful career as a translator. Among the authors he translated were Juvenal, Persius, and Virgil. His translation of Virgil's *Aeneid,* published in 1697, was extremely popular.

In his declining years Dryden, respected as the supreme literary figure of his day, spent much of his time at Will's Coffeehouse, to which younger authors and would-be authors came to listen to his conversation and learn from him. Among these was Alexander Pope, aged twelve, whose veneration for Dryden lasted throughout his lifetime.

This song is from Dryden's play *Secret-Love.*

I Feed a Flame Within

I feed a flame within which so torments me
That it both pains my heart, and yet
    contents me:
'Tis such a pleasing smart, and I so love it,
That I had rather die, than once remove it.

5 Yet he for whom I grieve shall never know it,
My tongue does not betray, nor my eyes
    show it:
Not a sigh nor a tear my pain discloses,
But they fall silently like dew on roses.

Thus to prevent my love from being cruel,
10 My heart's the sacrifice as 'tis the fuel:
And while I suffer this to give him quiet,
My faith rewards my love, though he deny it.

On his eyes will I gaze, and there delight me;
While I conceal my love, no frown can fright
    me:
15 To be more happy I dare not aspire;
Nor can I fall more low, mounting no higher.

1668

This song is from Dryden's play *King Arthur.*

Song Sung by Venus in Honor of Britannia[1]

Fairest isle, all isles excelling,
    Seat of pleasures and of loves;
Venus here will choose her dwelling,
    And forsake her Cyprian groves.[2]

5 Cupid[3] from his favorite nation
    Care and envy will remove;
Jealousy, that poisons passion,
    And despair, that dies for love.

Gentle murmurs, sweet complaining,
10   Sighs that blow the fire of love;
Soft repulses, kind disdaining,
    Shall be all the pains you prove.

Every swain shall pay his duty,
    Grateful every nymph shall prove;
15 And as these excel in beauty,
    Those shall be renowned for love.

1691

---

1. *Venus . . . Britannia.* Venus is the Greek goddess of love; Britannia is England.
2. *Cyprian groves.* Venus supposedly rose from the sea off Cyprus and established her temple there.
3. *Cupid,* the son of Venus and the child-god of love.

Discussion

1. (a) According to the speaker of "I Feed a Flame Within," why does she conceal her love? (b) Explain the meaning of "My heart's the sacrifice as 'tis the fuel" (line 10).

2. (a) How does "Song Sung by Venus in Honor of Britannia" honor Britannia? (b) As a result of Venus's dwelling in England, in what will the women ("nymphs") excel? For what will the men ("swains") be renowned?

One of Dryden's most effective **satires**, *Mac Flecknoe* has as its target Thomas Shadwell, who earned Dryden's ire by praising *The Rehearsal,* a play in which Dryden was parodied and ridiculed. Flecknoe was an Irish poet, notorious for his poor poetry, who died in 1678.

Calling Shadwell the son of Flecknoe (in Gaelic *Mac* means "son of"), Dryden proceeds to use his cutting wit at Shadwell's expense. The complete poem, from which an excerpt is published here, is 217 lines in length.

from Mac Flecknoe

All human things are subject to decay,
And when fate summons, monarchs must obey.
This Flecknoe found, who, like Augustus,[1]
    young
Was called to empire, and had governed long;
5 In prose and verse was owned, without dispute,
Through all the realms of Nonsense, absolute.
This agèd prince, now flourishing in peace,
And blessed with issue of a large increase;
Worn out with business, did at length debate
10 To settle the succession of the State;
And, pondering which of all his sons was fit
To reign, and wage immortal war with wit,
Cried: " 'Tis resolved; for nature pleads,
    that he
Should only rule, who most resembles me.
15 Sh——[2] alone my perfect image bears,
Mature in dullness from his tender years:
Sh—— alone, of all my sons, is he
Who stands confirmed in full stupidity.
The rest to some faint meaning make pretense,
20 But Sh—— never deviates into sense.
Some beams of wit on other souls may fall,
Strike through, and make a lucid interval;
But Sh——'s genuine night admits no ray,
His rising fogs prevail upon the day.

25 Besides, his goodly fabric[3] fills the eye,
And seems designed for thoughtless majesty;
Thoughtless as monarch oaks that shade the
    plain,
And, spread in solemn state, supinely reign.
Heywood and Shirley[4] were but types[5] of
    thee,
30 Thou last great prophet of tautology.[6]

1682

---

1. Augustus, the first emperor of Rome (27 B.C. to A.D. 14); he became emperor at the age of thirty-six.
2. Sh——, Shadwell. Satirists commonly used only the initial or the first two letters of the victim's name.
3. goodly fabric, bulky body, a reference to Shadwell's obesity.
4. Heywood and Shirley, popular playwrights of the early seventeenth century.
5. types, prototypes, prefigurings.
6. tautology, needless repetition, redundancy.

Discussion

1. (a) Why does Flecknoe select Shadwell as his successor? (b) Suppose you were Shadwell reading this poem. How would you feel about it? about its author?

2. (a) In "To the Memory of Mr. Oldham," what parallels does Dryden perceive between Mr. Oldham and himself? what differences? (b) What words in lines 19–21 contribute to the development of a single image? What does this image illustrate? (c) Compare this poem with A. E. Housman's "To an Athlete Dying Young" (page 549). What themes and imagery do they share?

To the Memory of Mr. Oldham

Farewell, too little and too lately known,
Whom I began to think and call my own;
For sure our souls were near allied, and thine
Cast in the same poetic mold with mine.
5 One common note on either lyre did strike,
And knaves and fools we both abhorred alike:
To the same goal did both our studies drive,
The last set out the soonest did arrive.[1]
Thus Nisus[2] fell upon the slippery place,
10 While his young friend performed and won
    the race.
O early ripe! to thy abundant store
What could advancing age have added more?
It might (what Nature never gives the young)
Have taught the numbers[3] of thy native tongue.
15 But Satire needs not those, and Wit will shine
Through the harsh cadence[4] of a rugged line.
A noble error, and but seldom made,
When poets are by too much force betrayed.
Thy generous fruits, though gathered ere
    their prime

20 Still showed a quickness; and maturing time
But mellows what we write to the dull
    sweets of Rhyme.
Once more, hail and farewell;[5] farewell, thou
    young,
But ah too short, Marcellus[6] of our tongue;
Thy brows with ivy, and with laurels[7] bound;
25 But Fate and gloomy Night encompass thee
    around.

                         1684

---

1. *The last . . . arrive.* Oldham, born in 1653, was 22 years younger than Dryden, but gained fame for his satirical poetry before Dryden.
2. *Nisus.* Virgil (*Aeneid* V, 315–39) describes a race in which two friends compete. Nisus is ahead until he accidentally slips. He then trips another contender so his friend Euryalus can win.
3. *numbers,* ability to write in meter.
4. *harsh cadence,* irregular meter.
5. *hail and farewell,* translation of *ave atque vale,* a Latin phrase used when friends part.
6. *Marcellus,* nephew and promising heir of Caesar Augustus, who died at the age of nineteen.
7. *ivy . . . laurels,* the wreath awarded to a poet.

Reader's Note: Dryden and the Heroic Couplet

Although the use of the rhyming iambic pentameter **couplet** was not original with him, it was Dryden who used it so effectively that it became the preferred way to write for the next three generations of poets.

Dryden's predecessors developed the habit of finishing some unit of thought with the last word of the couplet's second line. The advantage of this practice is the highly condensed content of these "closed" couplets.

Within the two lines of the **heroic couplet** (so called from its use in the heroic poetry—both epic and tragedy—of the seventeenth century) Dryden and his successors like Swift and Pope explored a number of intriguing structural possibilities. The two lines could be used in parallel forms to reinforce an idea, as in this description of aging and death (drawn, as both examples here will be, from *Mac Flecknoe):*

All human things are subject to decay,
And when fate summons, monarchs must
    obey.

                  (lines 1–2)

The pair of lines could be used just as easily to express contrast, as in this description of Shadwell's soul, which no beams of wit can penetrate and enlighten:

But Sh_____'s genuine night admits no
    ray,
His rising fogs prevail upon the day.

               (lines 23–24)

These are the most obvious devices. Ingenious poets of Dryden's era found many ways to work in this form.

Samuel Pepys 1633–1703

Pepys (pēps) was born in London and lived there most of his life. He was educated at St. Paul's School and went to Magdalene College, Cambridge, on a scholarship, receiving both a B.A. and an M.A. At twenty-two he married Elizabeth St. Michel, the beautiful but poor daughter of a French Huguenot.

What has given Pepys his literary reputation is his private *Diary,* written in a sort of short-hand code (all 3,012 pages of it), covering a period of nearly ten years, from January 1, 1660, to May 31, 1669. Failing vision caused him to give it up. Evidently Pepys did not intend the *Diary* for anyone's eyes but his own, for he includes in it not only the public events at Court and in London, but also his own most private thoughts and actions.

Thanks to two accidents the original manuscript of the *Diary* was preserved and then rediscovered. When Pepys died in 1703, his will provided that all his books, papers, and collections were to go to Magdalene College; his *Diary,* set aside thirty-four years earlier, was among those papers. In 1818, the diary of John Evelyn, with whom Pepys had been friendly, was published. The references it made to Pepys aroused interest in him. Pepys's *Diary* was located, but deciphering the shorthand code required three years. In 1825 an abridged version was published; in the years since then more and more of it has come out. An unabridged, annotated edition is now available.

In 1660, the year that Pepys began the *Diary,* he became secretary to his distant cousin Edward Montagu, who as Admiral of the Navy was in charge of bringing King Charles II home from France. Pepys, who was with him, recorded the events in his *Diary.* Soon after, Charles awarded Montagu the title of Earl of Sandwich and Pepys's fortunes rose too. He was made Clerk of the Acts in the Navy Office, a position of considerable honor that included a good salary and a fine, rent-free home.

For the next nine years, Pepys faithfully recorded in code in his *Diary* the events, major and minor, of his life. Since he was active in public affairs, these include much of the history of the age: the return and coronation of Charles II; the hanging of Thomas Harrison, one of the Puritans responsible for executing Charles I; the severe outbreak of plague in 1665, during which most Court officials deserted London (Pepys stayed on because of the Dutch War and his responsibilities at the Navy Office); the Great Fire of London in 1666; the reopening of the theaters. In addition, Pepys recorded the daily events of his domestic life in great detail, so that we come to know his wife, his servants, his Navy Office associates, his neighbors, and his many friends. Thus, when we read the *Diary* we derive a twofold enjoyment: first, of history in the making, and then of Pepys's reaction to it, as well as to the more trivial episodes of life.

Readers of Pepys's *Diary* tend to remember him for the more gossipy and personal passages that reveal him as a man rather than as a competent administrator and friend of many of the great of his age. For much of his adult life he held a position equivalent to that of a modern Secretary of the Navy; he was on excellent terms with and respected by King Charles II, King James II, and other high-ranking courtiers, as well as with Sir Isaac Newton and other scientists; and he had hosts of friends, all of whom seemed to respect him.

The portion of Pepys's *Diary* included here deals largely with the Great Fire of London, which started on September 2, 1666, and raged out of control for almost a week. Before it was extinguished, it had destroyed two-thirds of London. More than thirteen thousand houses were burned, plus other buildings, including eighty-nine churches. Miraculously, only six people lost their lives, but 250,000 were homeless, camping out in makeshift tents in the fields adjacent to London. It is difficult to comprehend what the burning of London meant in its day. Pepys helps us to realize some of this through his vivid eyewitness descriptions. One thing, however, he does not tell us, for he did not know it: never again was London paralyzed by the plague, for the fire destroyed the rats that carried the plague as well as the old buildings that harbored them.

(See map, page 285.)

from The Diary

September 2, 1666 (Lord's day). Some of our maids sitting up late last night to get things ready against our feast today, Jane called us up about three in the morning, to tell us of a great fire they saw in the City.[1] So I rose and slipped on my nightgown, and went to her window; and thought it to be on the backside of Mark Lane at the farthest; but, being unused to such fires as followed, I thought it far enough off; and so went to bed again, and to sleep. About seven rose again to dress myself, and there looked out at the window, and saw the fire not so much as it was, and further off. So to my closet[2] to set things to rights, after yesterday's cleaning. By and by Jane [Pepys's maid] comes and tells me that she hears that above 300 houses have been burned down tonight by the fire we saw, and that it is now burning down all Fish Street, by London Bridge. So I made myself ready presently, and walked to the Tower;[3] and there got up upon one of the high places, Sir J. Robinson's little son going up with me; and there I did see the houses at that end of the bridge all on fire, and an infinite great fire on this and the other side the end of the bridge; which, among other people, did trouble me for poor little Michell and our Sarah on the bridge.[4] So down with my heart full of trouble, to the Lieutenant of the Tower, who tells me that it begun this morning in the King's baker's house in Pudding Lane, and that it hath burned St. Magnus's Church and most part of Fish Street already. So I down to the waterside, and there got a boat,[5] and through bridge and there saw a lamentable fire. Poor Michell's house, as far as the Old Swan, already burned that way, and the fire running further, that, in a very little time, it got as far as the Steelyard,[6] while I was there. Everybody endeavoring to remove their goods, and flinging into the river, or bringing them into lighters[7] that lay off; poor people staying in their houses as long as till the very fire touched them, and then running into boats, or clambering from one pair of stairs, by the waterside, to another. And, among other things, the poor pigeons, I perceive, were loath to leave their houses, but hovered about the windows and balconies, till some of them burned their wings, and fell down.

Having stayed, and in an hour's time seen the fire rage every way; and nobody, to my sight,

---

1. **the City,** the area within the medieval walls of London; the business district.
2. **closet,** study.
3. **Tower,** the Tower of London, an ancient fort on the Thames.
4. **on the bridge.** In Pepys's time, London Bridge was covered with houses and shops.
5. **boat.** Small boats rowed by "watermen" were a common form of transportation in the city.
6. **the Steelyard.** A German trading area established west of London Bridge on the north side of the Thames.
7. **lighters,** small, flat-bottomed boats.

endeavoring to quench it, but to remove their goods, and leave all to the fire, and having seen it get as far as the Steelyard, and the wind mighty high, and driving it into the city: and everything, after so long a drought, proving combustible, even the very stones of churches; and, among other things, the poor steeple by which pretty Mrs.—— lives, and whereof my old schoolfellow Elborough is parson, taken fire in the very top, and there burned till it fell down; I to Whitehall, with a gentleman with me who desired to go off from the Tower, to see the fire, in my boat; to Whitehall,[8] and there up to the King's closet in the Chapel, where people come about me, and I did give them an account dismayed them all, and word was carried into the King. So I was called for, and did tell the King and Duke of York what I saw; and, that unless his Majesty did command houses to be pulled down, nothing could stop the fire. They seemed much troubled, and the King commanded me to go to my Lord Mayor[9] from him, and command him to spare no houses, but to pull down before the fire every way. The Duke of York bid me tell him, that if he would have any more soldiers, he shall; and so did my Lord Arlington afterwards, as a great secret. Here meeting with Captain Cocke, I in his coach, which he lent me, and Creed with me to Paul's;[10] and there walked along Watling Street, as well as I could, every creature coming away loaden with goods to save, and, here and there, sick people carried away in beds. Extraordinary good goods carried in carts and on backs. At last met my Lord Mayor in Canning Street, like a man spent, with a handkerchief about his neck. To the King's message, he cried like a fainting woman, "Lord! what can I do? I am spent; people will not obey me. I have been pulling down houses; but the fire overtakes us faster than we can do it." That he needed no more soldiers; and that, for himself, he must go and refresh himself, having been up all night. So he left me, and I him, and walked home, seeing people all almost distracted, and no manner of means used to quench the fire. The houses, too, so very thick thereabouts, and full of matter for burning, as pitch and tar, in Thames Street; and warehouses of oil, and wines, and brandy, and other things. Here I saw Mr. Isaake Houblon, that handsome man, prettily dressed and dirty at his door at Dowgate, receiv-ing some of his brothers' things, whose houses were on fire; and, as he says, have been removed twice already; and he doubts (as it soon proved) that they must be, in a little time, removed from his house also, which was a sad consideration. And to see the churches all filling with goods by people who themselves should have been quietly there at this time.

By this time, it was about twelve o'clock; and so home, and there find my guests, which was Mr. Wood and his wife Barbary Shelden, and also Mr. Moone; she mighty fine, and her husband, for aught I see, a likely man. But Mr. Moone's design and mine, which was to look over my closet, and please him with the sight thereof, which he hath long desired, was wholly disappointed; for we were in great trouble and disturbance at this fire, not knowing what to think of it. However, we had an extraordinary good dinner, and as merry as at this time we could be.

While at dinner, Mrs. Batelier come to enquire after Mr. Woolfe and Stanes (who, it seems, are related to them) whose houses in Fish Street are all burned, and they in a sad condition. She would not stay in the fright.

As soon as dined, I and Moone away, and walked through the City, the streets full of nothing but people and horses and carts loaden with goods, ready to run over one another, and removing goods from one burned house to another. They now removing out of Canning Street, which received goods in the morning, into Lombard Street, and further; and among others, I now saw my little goldsmith Stokes receiving some friend's goods, whose house itself was burned the day after. We parted at Paul's; he home, and I to Paul's Wharf, where I had appointed a boat to attend me, and took in Mr. Carcasse and his brother, whom I met in the street, and carried them below and above bridge too and again to see the fire, which was now got further, both below and above, and no likelihood of stopping it. Met with the King and Duke of York in their barge, and with them to Queenhithe, and there called Sir

---

8. **Whitehall,** king's residence and offices in London, upriver from the Tower and the fire.
9. **Lord Mayor,** of London.
10. **Paul's.** Pepys travels back towards the fire, to one of the largest churches in London, which the fire is soon to destroy.

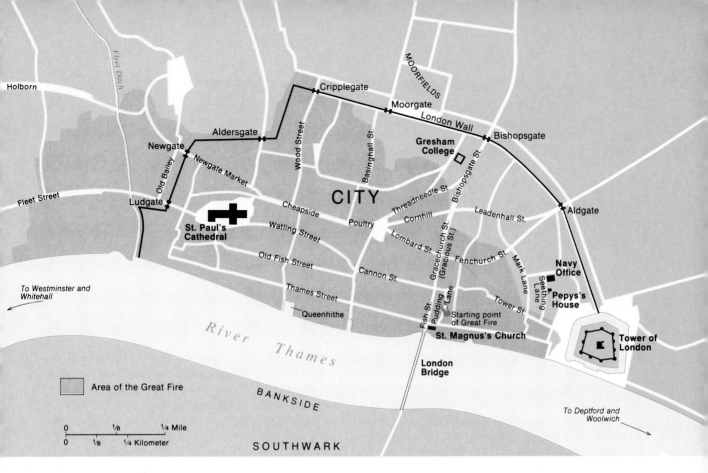

Richard Browne to them. Their order was only to pull down houses apace, and so below bridge at the waterside; but little was or could be done, the fire coming upon them so fast. Good hopes there was of stopping it at the Three Cranes above, and at Buttulph's Wharf below bridge, if care be used; but the wind carries it into the city, so as we know not, by the waterside, what it do there. River full of lighters and boats taking in goods, and good goods swimming in the water; and only I observed that hardly one lighter or boat in three that had the goods of a house in, but there was a pair of virginals[11] in it. Having seen as much as I could now, I away to Whitehall by appointment, and there walked to St. James's Park; and there met my wife, and Creed, and Wood, and his wife, and walked to my boat; and there upon the water again, and to the fire up and down, it still increasing, and the wind great. So near the fire as we could for smoke; and all over the Thames, with one's face in the wind, you were almost burned with a shower of fire-drops. This is very true; so as houses were burned by these drops and flakes of fire, three or four, nay, five or six houses, one from another. When we could endure no more

upon the water, we to a little ale house on the Bankside, over against the Three Cranes, and there stayed till it was dark almost and saw the fire grow; and, as it grew darker, appeared more and more; and in corners and upon steeples, and between churches and houses, as far as we could see up the hill of the city, in a most horrid, malicious, bloody flame, not like the fine flame of an ordinary fire. Barbary and her husband away before us. We stayed till, it being darkish, we saw the fire as only one entire arch of fire from this to the other side the bridge, and in a bow up the hill for an arch of above a mile long; it made me weep to see it. The churches, houses, and all on fire, and flaming at once; and a horrid noise the flames made, and the cracking of houses at their ruin. So home with a sad heart, and there find everybody discoursing and lamenting the fire; and poor Tom Hater come with some few of his goods saved out of his house, which was burned upon Fish Street Hill. I invited him to lie at my house, and did receive his goods; but was deceived in his lying there, the news coming every moment of the

---

11. **virginals,** small legless pianos.

growth of the fire; so as we were forced to begin to pack up our own goods, and prepare for their removal; and did by moonshine, it being brave, dry, and moonshine and warm weather, carry much of my goods into the garden; and Mr. Hater and I did remove my money and iron chests into my cellar, as thinking that the safest place. And got my bags of gold into my office, ready to carry away, and my chief papers of accounts also there, and my tallies into a box by themselves. So great was our fear, as Sir W. Batten hath carts come out of the country to fetch away his goods this night. We did put Mr. Hater, poor man! to bed a little; but he got but very little rest, so much noise being in my house, taking down of goods.

September 3. About four o'clock in the morning, my Lady Batten sent me a cart to carry away all my money and plate and best things to Sir W. Rider's at Bednall Green; which I did, riding myself in my nightgown in the cart; and, Lord! to see how the streets and the highways are crowded with people, running and riding and getting of carts at any rate to fetch away things. I find Sir W. Rider tired with being called up all night and receiving things from several friends. His house full of goods, and much of Sir. W. Batten and Sir W. Penn's. I am eased at my heart to have my treasure so well secured. Then home with much ado to find a way. Nor any sleep all this night to me nor my poor wife. But then, and all this day, she and I and all my people[12] laboring to get away the rest of our things, and did get Mr. Tooker to get me a lighter to take them in, and we did carry them (myself some) over Tower Hill, which was by this time full of people's goods, bringing their goods thither. And down to the lighter, which lay at the next quay above the Towerdock. And here was my neighbor's wife, Mrs. ——, with her pretty child and some few of her things, which I did willingly give way to be saved with mine. But there was no passing with anything through the postern, the crowd was so great. At night, lay down a little upon a quilt of W. Hewer in the office (all my own things being packed up or gone); and after me, my poor wife did the like— we having fed upon the remains of yesterday's dinner, having no fire nor dishes, nor any opportunity of dressing anything.

September 4. Up by break of day to get away the remainder of my things, which I did by a lighter at the Iron Gate; and my hands so few, that it was the afternoon before we could get them all away.

Sir W. Penn and I to Tower Street, and there met the fire burning three or four doors beyond Mr. Howells; whose goods, poor man (his trays and dishes, shovels etc., were flung all along Tower Street in the kennels,[13] and people working therewith from one end to the other), the fire coming on in that narrow street, on both sides, with infinite fury. Sir W. Batten, not knowing how to remove his wine, did dig a pit in the garden and laid it in there; and I took the opportunity

---

12. my people, Pepys's servants.
13. kennels, ditch down the center of the road.

of laying all the papers of my office that I could not otherwise dispose of. And in the evening Sir W. Penn and I did dig another and put our wine in it, and I my Parmesan cheese as well as my wine and some other things.

This night Mrs. Turner, who, poor woman, was removing her goods all this day—good goods, into the garden, and knew not how to dispose of them—and her husband supped with my wife and I at night in the office, upon a shoulder of mutton from the cook's, without any napkin or anything, in a sad manner but were merry. Only, now and then walking into the garden and saw how horridly the sky looks, all on a fire in the night, was enough to put us out of our wits; and indeed it was extremely dreadful, for it looks just as if it was at us, and the whole heaven on fire. I after supper walked in the dark down to Tower Street, and there saw it all on fire at the Trinity house on that side and the Dolphin Tavern on this side, which was very near us—and the fire with extraordinary vehemence. Now begins the practice of blowing up of houses in Tower Street, those next the Tower, which at first did frighten people more than anything; but it stopped the fire where it was done—it bringing down the houses to the ground in the same places they stood, and then it was easy to quench what little fire was in it, though it kindled nothing almost. W. Hewer this day went to see how his mother did, and comes late home, but telling us how he hath been forced to remove her to Islington, her house in Pye Corner being burned. So that it is got so far

that way and all the Old Bailey, and was running down to Fleet Street. And Paul's is burned, and all Cheapside. I wrote to my father this night; but the posthouse[14] being burned, the letter could not go.

September 5. I lay down in the office again upon W. Hewer's quilt, being mighty weary, and sore in my feet with going till I was hardly able to stand. About two in the morning my wife calls me up, and tells me of new cries of "Fire!"—it being come to Barking Church, which is the bottom of our land. I up; and finding it so, resolved presently to take her away, and did, and took my gold (which was about £2350). W. Hewer, and Jane down by Proundy's boat to Woolwich; but, Lord! what a sad sight it was by moonlight, to see the whole city almost on fire, that you might see it plain at Woolwich, as if you were by it. There, when I come, I find the gates[15] shut, but no guard kept at all; which troubled me, because of discourse now begun, that there is plot in it,[16] and that the French had done it. I got the gates open, and to Mr. Shelden's, where I locked up my gold, and charged my wife and W. Hewer never to leave the room without one of them in it, night or day. So back again, by the way seeing my goods well in the lighters at Deptford, and watched well by people. Home, and whereas I expected to have seen our house on fire, it being now about seven o'clock, it was not. But to the fire, and

14. *posthouse,* post office.
15. *gates,* to the dockyard.
16. *plot in it,* i.e., the fire.

there find greater hopes than I expected; for my confidence of finding our office on fire was such, that I durst not ask anybody how it was with us, till I come and saw it not burned. But, going to the fire, I find, by the blowing up of houses, and the great help given by the workmen out of the King's yards, sent up by Sir W. Penn, there is a good stop given to it, as well as at Mark Lane end as ours; it having only burned the dial of Barking Church, and part of the porch, and was there quenched. I up to the top of Barking steeple, and there saw the saddest sight of desolation that I ever saw; everywhere great fires, oil-cellars, and brimstone, and other things burning. I became afeard to stay there long, and therefore down again as fast as I could, the fire being spread as far as I could see it; and to Sir W. Penn's, and there eat a piece of cold meat, having eaten nothing since Sunday, but the remains of Sunday's dinner. Here I met with Mr. Young and Whistler; and, having removed all my things, and received good hopes that the fire at our end is stopped, they and I walked into the town, and find Fenchurch Street, Gracious Street, and Lombard Street all in dust. The Exchange[17] a sad sight, nothing standing there, of all the statues or pillars, but Sir Thomas Gresham's picture in the corner. Walked into Moorfields, our feet ready to burn, walking through the town among the hot coals, and find that full of people, and poor wretches carrying their goods there, and everybody keeping his goods together by themselves; and a great blessing it is to them that it is fair weather for them to keep abroad night and day; drank there, and paid twopence for a plain penny loaf. Thence homeward, having passed through Cheapside, and Newgate Market, all burned; and seen Anthony Joyce's house in fire; and took up, which I keep by me, a piece of glass of Mercer's Chapel in the street, where much more was, so melted and buckled with the heat of the fire like parchment. I also did see a poor cat taken out of a hole in a chimney, joining to the wall of the Exchange, with the hair all burned off the body, and yet alive. So home at night, and find there good hopes of saving our office; but great endeavors of watching all night, and having men ready; and so we lodged them in the office, and had drink and bread and cheese for them. And I lay down and slept a good night about midnight;

though, when I rose, I heard that there had been a great alarm of French and Dutch[18] being risen, which proved nothing. But it is a strange thing to see how long this time did look since Sunday, having been always full of variety of actions, and little sleep, that it looked like a week or more, and I had forgot almost the day of the week.

September 6. Up about five o'clock, and there met Mr. Gawden at the gate of the office (I intending to go out, as I used every now and then to do, to see how the fire is) to call our men to Bishopsgate, where no fire had yet been near, and there is now one broke out—which did give great grounds to people, and to me too, to think that there is some kind of plot in this (on which many by this time have been taken, and it hath been dangerous for any stranger to walk in the streets); but I went with the men and we did put it out in a little time, so that that was well again. It was pretty to see how hard the women did work in the kennels sweeping of water; but then they would scold for drink and be as drunk as devils. I saw good butts of sugar broke open in the street, and people go and take handfuls out and put into beer and drink it. And now all being pretty well, I took boat and over to Southwark, and took boat on the other side the bridge and so to Westminster, thinking to shift myself,[19] being all in dirt from top to bottom. But could not there find any place to buy a shirt or pair of gloves, Westminster Hall being full of people's goods—those in Westminster having removed all their goods, and the Exchequer money put into vessels to carry to Nonsuch.[20] But to the Swan, and there was trimmed. And then to Whitehall, but saw nobody, and so home. A sad sight to see how the River looks—no houses nor church near it to the Temple—where it stopped. At home did go with Sir W. Batten and our neighbor Knightly (who, with one more, was the only man of any fashion left in all the neighborhood hereabouts, they all removing their goods and leaving their houses to the mercy of the fire) to Sir R. Ford's, and there dined, in an earthen platter a fried breast of mutton, a great many of us. But very merry; and

---

17. *the Exchange,* a large building in which merchants met to discuss business; built in 1576 by Sir Thomas Gresham.
18. *French and Dutch,* England's enemies at the time.
19. *shift myself,* change clothes.
20. *Nonsuch,* a royal palace in Surrey.

indeed as good a meal, though as ugly a one, as ever I had in my life. Thence down to Deptford, and there with great satisfaction landed all my goods at Sir G. Carteret's, safe, and nothing missed I could see, or hurt. This being done to my great content, I home; and to Sir W. Batten's, and there with Sir R. Ford, Mr. Knightly, and one Withers, a professed lying rogue, supped well; and mighty merry and our fears over. From them to the office and there slept, with the office full of laborers, who talked and slept and walked all night long there. But strange it was to see Clothworkers Hall on fire these three days and nights in one body of Flame—it being the cellar, full of Oil.

September 7. Up by five o'clock and, blessed be God, find all well, and by water to Paul's Wharf. Walked thence and saw all the town burned, and a miserable sight of Paul's church, with all the roofs fallen and the body of the choir fallen into St. Faith's[21]—Paul's school also—Ludgate—Fleet Street—my father's house, and the church, and a good part of the Temple the like. So to Creeds lodging near the New Exchange, and there find him laid down upon a bed—the house all unfurnished, there being fears of the fire's coming to them. There borrowed a shirt of him—and washed. To Sir W. Coventry at St. James's, who lay without Curtains, having removed all his goods—as the King at Whitehall and everybody had done and was doing. He hopes we shall have no public distractions upon this fire, which is what everybody fears—because of the talk of the French having a hand in it. And it is a proper time for discontents—but all men's minds are full of care to protect themselves and save their goods. The militia is in arms everywhere.

This day our merchants first met at Gresham College, which by proclamation is to be their Exchange. Strange to hear what is bid for houses all up and down here—a friend of Sir W. Riders having £150 for what he used to let for £40/per annum. Much dispute where the Custom House shall be; thereby the growth of the City again to be foreseen. My Lord Treasurer, they say, and others, would have it at the other end of the town. I home late to Sir W. Penn, who did give me a bed—but without curtains or hangings, all being down. So here I went the first time into a naked bed, only my drawers on—and did sleep pretty well; but still, both sleeping and waking, had a fear of fire in my heart, that I took little rest.

1666   1825

---

21. **St. Faith's,** a chapel under St. Paul's Cathedral.

Discussion

1. Pepys's *Diary* is important for what it tells us of the historical events of his time.
(a) Which episodes or details about the fire of London are clearest in your mind? **(b)** During the fire, how does Pepys conduct himself as a public official, husband, and friend?

2. Pepys's *Diary* is also important for what it tells us about him. Even in a section like the one you have just read, which deals with historical events, we can surmise quite a bit about his daily life and about what others thought of him. **(a)** What does his everyday home life seem to be like? **(b)** How do the King and the Duke of York seem to feel about him? **(c)** What do Sir William Penn and Pepys's other titled friends think of him? **(d)** What do his other friends and neighbors think of him?

Composition

Imagine that you are, like Pepys, a resident of seventeenth-century London, but that your house has been destroyed by the Great Fire. Using the map of London and the illustration of the fire, imagine yourself in a particular location or street.

Write a **narrative** in which you describe how you first notice the oncoming danger, what you do to save your house and its "goods," and your feelings after the fire has been brought under control and you return to the ruins. As a conclusion, tell what you think those fortunate enough to escape the fire should do for people like you.

Jonathan Swift 1667–1745

Born into an age that saw satire as one means of improving the human condition, Swift became England's greatest prose satirist. Of his satire Swift wrote to poet Alexander Pope, "the chief end I propose to myself in all my labors is to vex the world rather than divert it."

Although his parents were English, Swift was born in Ireland, and circumstances compelled him to spend most of his life there, though he really wanted to live in or near London. His father died before his birth. Swift's uncle undertook his education, putting him in a boarding school in Kilkenny when he was six; at fifteen he went to Trinity College, Dublin, where he received his B.A. in 1686.

Leaving Ireland, Swift went to work as secretary to a distant relative, Sir William Temple, at Moor Park in England. As part of his duties he tutored Esther Johnson, Temple's ward, then only eight years old. She later became the "Stella" of his letters and poems. In 1694 Swift returned to Ireland long enough to be ordained an Anglican priest and spend a short time in a parish near Belfast. However, he soon went back to his former employer in England and remained there until Temple died in 1699, leaving one thousand pounds each to Swift and Esther.

Faced with the need to seek other employment, Swift returned again to Ireland, this time as domestic chaplain to Lord Berkeley, Lord Justice of Ireland. Soon Esther and Rebecca Dingley, her companion, followed him to Ireland. In 1700 he was given the parish of Laracor, near Dublin. For almost ten years, though officially he resided in Ireland, he spent a great deal of time in England, becoming friendly with Addison, Steele, and other authors.

After becoming embroiled in English politics, Swift changed his party from Whig to Tory in 1710, taking over the editorship of the *Examiner,* the official publication of the Tories. In 1713 he was named Dean of St. Patrick's Cathedral, Dublin, a great disappointment to him, for he had been hoping to receive a church in England. From 1710 to 1713, while he was in England, Swift wrote playfully affectionate letters, sometimes two a day, to Stella (Esther) in Dublin. After his death these were published as *Journal to Stella.*

When, in 1714, the Tories lost power, Swift retired to Dublin. Taking an increasing interest in Irish problems, in 1724 he wrote and had published a series of satirical letters against a projected English scheme to debase the Irish coinage. He signed these letters M. B. Drapier, from which they became known as the *Drapier's Letters.* They so incensed the English government that an award of three hundred pounds was offered for their author; no one revealed Swift's identity.

Gulliver's Travels, Swift's masterpiece on which he had worked for a number of years, was published anonymously in 1726 and immediately became a best seller and the talk of England. In 1728 Stella died; upon her death Swift settled a pension on Rebecca Dingley. Swift's last major publication, probably his bitterest piece of satire, was his *Modest Proposal,* published in 1729.

For most of his adult life, Swift had suffered from an inner ear disorder that caused dizziness and nausea and impaired his hearing. In or before 1727 he was totally deaf. About 1740 his mental faculties began to fail, and in 1742 he was declared of unsound mind. He died in 1745 and was buried in St. Patrick's Cathedral in Dublin.

At the height of his success as a writer of political pamphlets, Swift had in 1711 attacked the most celebrated and popular general in the British army, the Duke of Marlborough. While granting his great military skill, Swift accused the duke of prolonging the War of the Spanish Succession to make money for himself and several other prominent Whigs. Shortly thereafter Marlborough was dismissed. When he died (June 16, 1722), Swift wrote the following poem. It is perhaps just as well that the poem was not published until 1764, nineteen years after Swift's death.

Duke of Marlborough marching into Germany. Queen Anne playing card by J. Spofforth.

A Satirical Elegy on the Death of a Late Famous General

His Grace! impossible! what, dead!
Of old age, too, and in his bed!
And could that Mighty Warrior fall?
And so inglorious, after all!
5   Well, since he's gone, no matter how,
The last loud trump[1] must wake him now;
And, trust me, as the noise grows stronger,
He'd wish to sleep a little longer.
And could he be indeed so old
10 As by the newspapers we're told?
Threescore, I think, is pretty high;
'Twas time in conscience he should die.
This world he cumbered long enough;
He burnt his candle to the snuff;
15 And that's the reason, some folks think,
He left behind so great a stink.[2]
Behold his funeral appears,
Nor widow's sighs, nor orphan's tears,
Wont[3] at such times each heart to pierce,
20 Attend the progress of his hearse.
But what of that, his friends may say,
He had those honors in his day.
True to his profit and his pride,
He made them weep before he died.

25   Come hither, all ye empty things,
Ye bubbles raised by breath of kings;
Who float upon the tide of state,
Come hither, and behold your fate.
Let Pride be taught by this rebuke,
30 How very mean a thing's a Duke;
From all his ill-got honors flung,
Turned to the dirt from whence he sprung.
1722   1764

---

1. *trump,* trumpet signaling the Last Judgment.
2. *stink.* When a candle burned down all the way, its smoldering wick had a foul smell.
3. *wont,* accustomed.

Discussion

1. From the way Swift writes the first few lines of "A Satirical Elegy,"—the exclamations, the questions—what appears to have happened just before the poem begins? What kind of **tone** does this give the poem as a whole?

2. Why does the poem's speaker think the late general would prefer to sleep through the Last Judgment (lines 7–8)?

3. What images does the speaker use in the last stanza to describe the general? What do they suggest about the dead man?

A *Description of a City Shower*

Careful observers may foretell the hour
(By sure prognostics) when to dread a shower:
While rain depends,[1] the pensive cat gives o'er
Her frolics, and pursues her tail no more.
5 Returning home at night, you'll find the sink[2]
Strike your offended sense with double stink.
If you be wise, then go not far to dine;
You'll spend in coach hire more than save in
    wine.
A coming shower your shooting corns presage,
10 Old achés throb, your hollow tooth will rage.
Sauntering in coffeehouse is Dulman seen;
He damns the climate and complains of spleen.[3]
   Meanwhile the South, rising with dabbled
    wings,
A sable cloud athwart the welkin[4] flings,
15 That swilled more liquor than it could contain,
And, like a drunkard, gives it up again.
Brisk Susan[5] whips her linen from the rope,
While the first drizzling shower is borne aslope:
Such is that sprinkling which some careless
    quean[6]
20 Flirts on you from her mop, but not so clean:
You fly, invoke the gods; then turning, stop
To rail; she singing, still whirls on her mop.
Not yet the dust had shunned the unequal
    strife,
But, aided by the wind, fought still for life,
25 And wafted with its foe by violent gust,
'Twas doubtful which was rain and which
    was dust.
Ah! where must needy poet seek for aid,
When dust and rain at once his coat invade?
Sole coat, where dust cemented by the rain
30 Erects the nap, and leaves a mingled stain.
   Now in contiguous drops the flood comes
    down,
Threatening with deluge this devoted[7] town.
To shops in crowds the daggled[8] females fly,
Pretend to cheapen[9] goods, but nothing buy.

35 The Templar[10] spruce, while every spout's
    abroach,
Stays till 'tis fair, yet seems to call a coach.
The tucked-up sempstress walks with hasty
    strides,
While streams run down her oiled umbrella's
    sides.
Here various kinds, by various fortunes led,
40 Commence acquaintance underneath a shed.
Triumphant Tories and desponding Whigs[11]
Forget their feuds, and join to save their wigs.
Boxed in a chair[12] the beau impatient sits,
While spouts run clattering o'er the roof by fits,
45 And ever and anon with frightful din
The leather[13] sounds; he trembles from within.
So when Troy chairmen bore the wooden
    steed,[14]
Pregnant with Greeks impatient to be freed
(Those bully Greeks, who, as the moderns do,
50 Instead of paying chairmen, run them
    through),[15]
Laocoön[16] struck the outside with his spear,

---

1. *depends,* literally, hangs overhead, i.e., is imminent.
2. *sink,* sewer.
3. *Dulman . . . spleen,* Dulman (dull man) describes a type. Spleen (melancholy) was commonly attributed to rainy weather.
4. *welkin,* sky.
5. *Susan,* a servant.
6. *quean,* wench.
7. *devoted,* doomed.
8. *daggled,* mud-spattered.
9. *cheapen,* bargain over.
10. *Templar,* law student.
11. *Tories, Whigs,* two leading political parties. The former had just won power.
12. *chair,* sedan chair, an enclosed seat carried on poles by two men. A common form of city transportation for the rich.
13. *leather,* roof of the sedan chair.
14. *Troy chairmen . . . steed,* humorous reference to the Trojan horse, a hollow wooden image that the Greeks used to sneak some hidden warriors into Troy.
15. *run them through,* with swords.
16. *Laocoön,* Trojan priest who sensed the Greek plot and struck the Trojan horse with his spear. His comrades ignored his warning.

And each imprisoned hero quaked for fear.
  Now from all parts the swelling kennels[17]
    flow,
And bear their trophies with them as they go:
55 Filth of all hues and odors seem to tell
  What street they sailed from, by their sight
    and smell.
They, as each torrent drives with rapid force,
From Smithfield or St. Pulchre's shape their
    course,
And in huge confluence joined at Snow Hill
    ridge,
60 Fall from the conduit prone to Holborn Bridge.
Sweepings from butchers' stalls, dung, guts,
    and blood,
Drowned puppies, stinking sprats,[18] all
    drenched in mud,
Dead cats, and turnip tops, come tumbling
    down the flood.

                      1710

---

17. *kennels*, street gutters.
18. *sprats*, herrings.

Discussion

1. Each of the four verse paragraphs of "A Description of a City Shower" describes some phase of the shower. Which phase does each describe, and how effectively?

2. This poem contains some gentle **satire.** Explain who or what is being satirized in the passages dealing with the following: the needy poet (lines 27–30), the daggled females (lines 33–34), the Templar (lines 35–36), the beau (lines 43–46).

3. Swift lived in London whenever he could. Does this poem suggest why?

In the first book of *Gulliver's Travels*, Lemuel Gulliver finds himself in the land of the Lilliputians, tiny people only one-tenth his size. Swift uses these tiny people to satirize the pretensions of the English and their customs.

As the second book opens, Gulliver has again gone to sea as a ship's doctor; his ship has just weathered a storm that has blown it so far off course that no one has any idea where the ship is.

from Gulliver's Travels

A Voyage to Brobdingnag

On the 16th day of June, 1703, a boy on the topmast discovered land. On the 17th we came in full view of a great island or continent (for we knew not whether) on the south side whereof was a small neck of land jutting out into the sea, and a creek too shallow to hold a ship of above one hundred tons. We cast anchor within a league of this creek, and our Captain sent a dozen of his men well armed in the longboat, with vessels for water if any could be found. I desired his leave to go with them that I might see the country and make what discoveries I could. When we came to land we saw no river or spring, nor any sign of inhabitants. Our men therefore wandered on the shore to find out some fresh water near the sea, and I walked alone about a mile on the other side, where I observed the country all barren and rocky. I now began to be weary, and seeing nothing to entertain my curiosity, I returned gently down towards the creek; and the sea being full in my view, I saw our men already got into the boat, and rowing for life to the ship. I was going to hollow[1] after them, although it had been to little purpose, when I observed a huge creature walking after them in the sea as fast as he could; he waded not much deeper than his knees and took prodigious strides, but our men had the start of him half a league, and the sea thereabouts being full of sharp-pointed rocks, the monster was not able to overtake the boat. This I was afterwards told, for I durst not stay to see the issue of that adventure, but ran as fast as I could the way I first went, and then climbed up a steep hill, which gave me some prospect of the country. I found it fully cultivated; but that which first surprised me was the length of the grass, which, in those grounds that seemed to be kept for hay, was about twenty foot high.

I fell into a highroad, for so I took it to be, although it served to the inhabitants only as a footpath through a field of barley. Here I walked on for some time, but could see little on either side, it being now near harvest, and the corn[2] rising at least forty foot. I was an hour walking to the end of this field, which was fenced in with a hedge of at least one hundred and twenty foot high, and the trees so lofty that I could make no computation of their altitude. There was a stile[3] to pass from this field into the next: it had four steps, and a stone to cross over when you came to the utmost. It was impossible for me to climb this stile, because every step was six foot high, and the upper stone above twenty. I was endeavoring to find some gap in the hedge when I discovered one of the inhabitants in the next field advancing towards the stile, of the same size with him whom I saw in the sea pursuing our boat. He appeared as tall as an ordinary spire-steeple, and took about ten yards at every stride, as near as I could guess. I was struck with the utmost fear and astonishment, and ran to hide myself in the corn, from whence I saw him at the top of the stile, looking back into the next field on the right

---

1. *hollow,* call out or exclaim.
2. *corn,* the principal grain of any country; here it means wheat.
3. *stile,* a set of steps for ascending and descending.

hand; and heard him call in a voice many degrees louder than a speaking trumpet; but the noise was so high in the air that at first I certainly thought it was thunder. Whereupon seven monsters like himself came towards him with reaping hooks in their hands, each hook about the largeness of six scythes. These people were not so well clad as the first, whose servants or laborers they seemed to be. For, upon some words he spoke, they went to reap the corn in the field where I lay. I kept from them at as great a distance as I could, but was forced to move with extreme difficulty, for the stalks of the corn were sometimes not above a foot distant, so that I could hardly squeeze my body betwixt them. However, I made a shift to go forward till I came to a part of the field where the corn had been laid by the rain and wind; here it was impossible for me to advance a step, for the stalks were so interwoven that I could not creep through, and the beards of the fallen ears so strong and pointed that they pierced through my clothes into my flesh. At the same time I heard the reapers not above an hundred yards behind me. Being quite dispirited with toil, and wholly overcome by grief and despair, I lay down between two ridges and heartily wished I might there end my days. I bemoaned my desolate widow and fatherless children; I lamented my own folly and willfulness in attempting a second voyage against the advice of all my friends and relations. In this terrible agitation of mind, I could not forbear thinking of Lilliput,[4] whose inhabitants looked upon me as the greatest prodigy that ever appeared in the world; where I was able to draw an imperial fleet in my hand, and perform those other actions which will be recorded forever in the chronicles of that empire, while posterity shall hardly believe them, although attested by millions. I reflected what a mortification it must prove to me to appear as inconsiderable in this nation as one single Lilliputian would be among us. But this I conceived was to be the least of my misfortunes; for as human creatures are observed to be more savage and cruel in proportion to their bulk, what could I expect but to be a morsel in the mouth of the first among these enormous barbarians who should happen to seize me? Undoubtedly philosophers are in the right when they tell us that nothing is great or little otherwise than by comparison. It might have pleased for-

tune to let the Lilliputians find some nation where the people were as diminutive with respect to them as they were to me. And who knows but that even this prodigious race of mortals might be equally overmatched in some distant part of the world, whereof we have yet no discovery?

Scared and confounded as I was, I could not forbear going on with these reflections; when one of the reapers approaching within ten yards of the ridge where I lay, made me apprehend that with the next step I should be squashed to death under his foot, or cut in two with his reaping hook. And therefore when he was again about to move, I screamed as loud as fear could make me. Whereupon the huge creature trod short, and looking round about under him for some time, at last espied me as I lay on the ground. He considered a while with the caution of one who endeavors to lay hold on a small dangerous animal in such a manner that it shall not be able either to scratch or to bite him, as I myself have sometimes done with a weasel in England. At length he ventured to take me up behind by the middle between his forefinger and thumb, and brought me within three yards of his eyes, that he might behold my shape more perfectly. I guessed his meaning, and my good fortune gave me so much presence of mind that I resolved not to struggle in the least as he held me in the air about sixty foot from the ground, although he grievously pinched my sides, for fear I should slip through his fingers. All I ventured was to raise mine eyes towards the sun, and place my hands together in a supplicating posture, and to speak some words in an humble melancholy tone, suitable to the condition I then was in. For I apprehended every moment that he would dash me against the ground, as we usually do any little hateful animal which we have a mind to destroy. But my good star would have it that he appeared pleased with my voice and gestures, and began to look upon me as a curiosity, much wondering to hear me pronounce articulate words, although he could not understand them. In the meantime I was not able to forbear groaning and shedding tears and turning my head towards my sides, letting him know, as well as I could, how cruelly I was hurt by the pressure of

---

4. Lilliput, the country of the tiny people where Gulliver was shipwrecked on his first voyage.

his thumb and finger. He seemed to apprehend my meaning; for, lifting up the lappet[5] of his coat, he put me gently into it, and immediately ran along with me to his master, who was a substantial farmer, and the same person I had first seen in the field.

The farmer having (as I supposed by their talk) received such an account of me as his servant could give him, took a piece of a small straw about the size of a walking staff, and therewith lifted up the lappets of my coat, which it seems he thought to be some kind of covering that nature had given me. He blew my hairs aside to take a better view of my face. He called his hinds[6] about him, and asked them (as I afterwards learned) whether they had ever seen in the fields any little creature that resembled me. He then placed me softly on the ground upon all four; but I got immediately up, and walked slowly backwards and forwards, to let those people see I had no intent to run away. They all sat down in a circle about me, the better to observe my motions. I pulled off my hat, and made a low bow towards the farmer; I fell on my knees, and lifted up my hands and eyes, and spoke several words as loud as I could; I took a purse of gold out of my pocket, and humbly presented it to him. He received it on the palm of his hand, then applied it close to his eye to see what it was, and afterwards turned it several times with the point of a pin (which he took out of his sleeve), but could make nothing of it. Whereupon I made a sign that he should place his hand on the ground; I then took the purse, and opening it, poured all the gold into his palm. There were six Spanish pieces of four pistoles each, beside twenty or thirty smaller coins. I saw him wet the tip of his little finger upon his tongue, and take up one of my largest pieces, and then another; but he seemed to be wholly ignorant what they were. He made me a sign to put them again into my purse, and the purse again into my pocket, which after offering to him several times, I thought it best to do.

The farmer by this time was convinced I must be a rational creature. He spoke often to me, but the sound of his voice pierced my ears like that of a water mill, yet his words were articulate enough. I answered as loud as I could in several languages, and he often laid his ear within two yards of me, but all in vain, for we were wholly unintelligible to each other. He then sent his servants to their work, and taking his handkerchief out of his pocket, he doubled and spread it on his hand, which he placed flat on the ground with the palm upwards, making me a sign to step into it, as I could easily do, for it was not above a foot in thickness. I thought it my part to obey, and for fear of falling, laid myself at full length upon the handkerchief, with the remainder of which he lapped me up to the head for further security, and in this manner carried me home to his house. There he called his wife, and showed me to her; but she screamed and ran back as women in England do at the sight of a toad or a spider. However, when she had a while seen my behavior, and how well I observed the signs her husband made, she was soon reconciled, and by degrees grew extremely tender of me.

> Gulliver is given into the care of the farmer's nine-year-old daughter, Glumdalclitch, who teaches him the language. The farmer decides to make money by displaying Gulliver in the large towns and capital of the country. The Queen sends for him, is pleased with Gulliver, and purchases him. At his suggestion, she retains Glumdalclitch to care for Gulliver. He is presented to the King, who takes an interest in him.

His Majesty sent for three great scholars who were then in their weekly waiting (according to the custom in that country). These gentlemen, after they had a while examined my shape with much nicety, were of different opinions concerning me. They all agreed that I could not be produced according to the regular laws of nature, because I was not framed with a capacity of preserving my life, either by swiftness, or climbing of trees, or digging holes in the earth. They observed by my teeth, which they viewed with great exactness, that I was a carnivorous animal; yet most quadrupeds being an overmatch for me, and field mice, with some others, too nimble, they could not imagine how I should be able to support myself, unless I fed upon snails and other

---

5. *lappet,* flap.
6. *hinds,* servants.

insects; which they offered, by many learned arguments, to evince that I could not possibly do. One of them seemed to think that I might be an embryo, or abortive birth. But this opinion was rejected by the other two, who observed my limbs to be perfect and finished, and that I had lived several years, as it was manifest from my beard, the stumps whereof they plainly discovered through a magnifying glass. They would not allow me to be a dwarf, because my littleness was beyond all degrees of comparison; for the Queen's favorite dwarf, the smallest ever known in that kingdom, was nearly thirty foot high. After much debate, they concluded unanimously that I was only *relplum scalcath,* which is interpreted literally, *lusus naturae,*[7] a determination exactly agreeable to the modern philosophy of Europe, whose professors, disdaining the old evasion of *occult causes,* whereby the followers of Aristotle endeavor in vain to disguise their ignorance, have invented this wonderful solution of all difficulties, to the unspeakable advancement of human knowledge.

After this decisive conclusion, I entreated to be heard a word or two. I applied myself to the King, and assured his Majesty that I came from a country which abounded with several millions of both sexes, and of my own stature, where the animals, trees, and houses were all in proportion, and where by consequence I might be as able to defend myself, and to find sustenance, as any of his Majesty's subjects could do here; which I took for a full answer to those gentlemen's arguments. To this they only replied with a smile of contempt, saying that the farmer had instructed me very well in my lesson. The King, who had a much better understanding, dismissing his learned men, sent for the farmer, who by good fortune was not yet gone out of town; having therefore first examined him privately, and then confronted him with me and the young girl, his Majesty began to think that what we told him might possibly be true. He desired the Queen to order that a particular care should be taken of me, and was of opinion that Glumdalclitch should still continue in her office of tending me, because he observed we had a great affection for each other. A convenient apartment was provided for her at Court; she had a sort of governess appointed to take care of her education, a maid to dress her,

and two other servants for menial offices; but the care of me was wholly appropriated to herself. The Queen commanded her own cabinetmaker to contrive a box that might serve me for a bedchamber, after the model that Glumdalclitch and I should agree upon. This man was a most ingenious artist, and according to my directions, in three weeks finished for me a wooden chamber of sixteen foot square and twelve high, with sash windows, a door, and two closets, like a London bedchamber. The board that made the ceiling was to be lifted up and down by two hinges, to put in a bed ready furnished by her Majesty's upholsterer, which Glumdalclitch took out every day to air, made it with her own hands, and letting it down at night, locked up the roof over me. A nice[8] workman, who was famous for little curiosities, undertook to make me two chairs, with backs and frames, of a substance not unlike ivory, and two tables, with a cabinet to put my things in. The room was quilted on all sides, as well as the floor and the ceiling, to prevent any accident from the carelessness of those who carried me, and to break the force of a jolt when I went in a coach. I desired a lock for my door to prevent rats and mice from coming in: the smith, after several attempts, made the smallest that ever was seen among them, for I have known a larger at the gate of a gentleman's house in England. I made a shift[9] to keep the key in a pocket of my own, fearing Glumdalclitch might lose it. The Queen likewise ordered the thinnest silks that could be gotten, to make me clothes, not much thicker than an English blanket, very cumbersome till I was accustomed to them. They were after the fashion of the kingdom, partly resembling the Persian, and partly the Chinese, and are a very grave, decent habit.

The Queen became so fond of my company that she could not dine without me. I had a table placed upon the same at which her Majesty ate, just at her left elbow, and a chair to sit on. Glumdalclitch stood upon a stool on the floor, near my table, to assist and take care of me. I had an entire set of silver dishes and plates, and other necessaries, which, in proportion to those of the Queen, were not much bigger than what I have

---

7. *lusus naturae,* a sport, or freak of nature. [Latin]
8. *nice,* precise or exact.
9. *made a shift,* arranged or contrived.

seen of the same kind in a London toyshop, for the furniture of a baby-house: these my little nurse kept in her pocket in a silver box and gave me at meals as I wanted them, always cleaning them herself. No person dined with the Queen but the two Princesses Royal, the elder sixteen years old, and the younger at that time thirteen and a month. Her Majesty used to put a bit of meat upon one of my dishes, out of which I carved for myself; and her diversion was to see me eat in miniature. For the Queen (who had indeed but a weak stomach) took up at one mouthful as much as a dozen English farmers could eat at a meal, which to me was for some time a very nauseous sight. She would craunch[10] the wing of a lark, bones and all, between her teeth, although it were nine times as large as that of a full-grown turkey; and put a bit of bread into her mouth as big as two twelve-penny loaves. She drank out of a golden cup, above a hogshead at a draught. Her knives were twice as long as a scythe set straight upon the handle. The spoons, forks, and other instruments were all in the same proportion. I remember when Glumdalclitch carried me out of curiosity to see some of the tables at Court, where ten or a dozen of these enormous knives and forks were lifted up together, I thought I had never till then beheld so terrible a sight.

It is the custom that every Wednesday (which, as I have before observed, was their Sabbath) the King and Queen, with the royal issue of both sexes, dine together in the apartment of his Majesty, to whom I was now become a favorite; and at these times my little chair and table were placed at his left hand, before one of the salt-cellars. This prince took a pleasure in conversing with me, inquiring into the manners, religion, laws, government, and learning of Europe; wherein I gave him the best account I was able. His apprehension was so clear, and his judgment so exact, that he made very wise reflections and observations upon all I said. But I confess that after I had been a little too copious in talking of my own beloved country, of our trade and wars by sea and land, of our schisms in religion and parties in the state, the prejudices of his education prevailed so far that he could not forbear taking me up in his right hand, and stroking me gently with the other, after an hearty fit of laughing,

asked me whether I were a Whig or a Tory. Then turning to his first minister, who waited behind him with a white staff, near as tall as the mainmast of the *Royal Sovereign*,[11] he observed how contemptible a thing was human grandeur, which could be mimicked by such diminutive insects as I: "and yet," said he, "I dare engage, these creatures have their titles and distinctions of honor; they contrive little nests and burrows, that they call houses and cities; they make a figure in dress and equipage;[12] they love, they fight, they dispute, they cheat, they betray." And thus he continued on, while my color came and went several times with indignation to hear our noble country, the mistress of arts and arms, the scourge of France, the arbitress of Europe, the seat of virtue, piety, honor, and truth, the pride and envy of the world, so contemptuously treated.

But as I was not in a condition to resent injuries, so, upon mature thoughts, I began to doubt whether I were injured or no. For, after having been accustomed several months to the sight and converse of this people, and observed every object upon which I cast my eyes to be of proportionable magnitude, the horror I had first conceived from their bulk and aspect was so far worn off that if I had then beheld a company of English lords and ladies in their finery and birthday clothes,[13] acting their several parts in the most courtly manner of strutting and bowing and prating, to say the truth, I should have been strongly tempted to laugh as much at them as this King and his grandees did at me. Neither indeed could I forbear smiling at myself when the Queen used to place me upon her hand towards a looking glass, by which both our persons appeared before me in full view together; and there could be nothing more ridiculous than the comparison; so that I really began to imagine myself dwindled many degrees below my usual size. . . .

I was frequently rallied by the Queen upon account of my fearfulness, and she used to ask me whether the people of my country were as great cowards as myself. The occasion was this. The kingdom is much pestered with flies in sum-

---

10. *craunch,* crunch.
11. *Royal Sovereign,* one of the largest ships in the Royal Navy.
12. *equipage,* carriage with its horses, driver, and servants.
13. *birthday clothes,* fashionable London traditionally dressed with splendor for royal birthdays.

Comment: Size and Scale in *Gulliver's Travels*

Samuel Johnson had the following to say of *Gulliver's Travels:* "When once you have thought of big men and little men, it is very easy to do all the rest." Perhaps Johnson was right, but there is more to thinking "of big men and little men" than first meets the eye. Take, for instance, the problem of scale. The Lilliputians were one-tenth Gulliver's size, the Brobdingnagians were twelve times his size.

Consider for a moment what the size of the Brobdingnagians means. Swift's scale of twelve to one corresponds to the number of inches in a foot, and probably this ratio was intentional. To better comprehend the power of Swift's invention, try to picture for yourself the size of a six-foot (by Brobdingnagian standards) Brobdingnagian. To us he would be seventy-two feet tall, the height of a six- or seven-story building.

Or try the concept in reverse: you are $\frac{1}{12}$ the size of Brobdingnagians. Compute $\frac{1}{12}$ of your height; for most of us this is five or six inches. Now measure against your leg how high this would be (just slightly above the ankle bone).

Next, picture yourself that height, looking up as far as you can see at the creature towering above you, and picture a world built to his scale. Imagine what an ordinary chair or table would look like, or a picture on a television screen. Realize too that with eyes adapted to your "miniature" world, you would see blemishes you never believed possible, that an ordinary eyelash would be frightening because of its length (nearly a foot long by your minuscule standards).

As a further exercise, imagine your everyday world from a different perspective. Try getting down on the floor and examining the room from that perspective—you'll see what the underside of most of your furniture looks like. Now, try to imagine being Gulliver's size in Brobdingnag and seeing those items from his scale. You will perhaps agree with Johnson that, "when once you have thought of big men and little men, it is very easy to do all the rest"—provided you can also think of a world built to that scale.

---

mer, and these odious insects, each of them as big as a Dunstable lark, hardly gave me any rest while I sat at dinner, with their continual humming and buzzing about my ears. They would sometimes alight upon my victuals, and leave their loathsome excrement or spawn behind, which to me was very visible, although not to the natives of that country, whose large optics were not so acute as mine in viewing smaller objects. Sometimes they would fix upon my nose or forehead, where they stung me to the quick, smelling very offensively; and I could easily trace that viscous matter, which our naturalists tell us enables those creatures to walk with their feet upwards upon a ceiling. I had much ado to defend myself against these destable animals, and could not forbear starting when they came on my face. It was the common practice of the dwarf to catch a number of these insects in his hand, as schoolboys do among us, and let them out suddenly under my nose, on purpose to frighten me, and divert the

Queen. My remedy was to cut them in pieces with my knife as they flew in the air, wherein my dexterity was much admired.

I remember one morning when Glumdalclitch had set me in my box upon a window, as she usually did in fair days to give me air (for I durst not venture to let the box be hung on a nail out of the window, as we do with cages in England), after I had lifted up one of my sashes, and sat down at my table to eat a piece of sweet cake for my breakfast, above twenty wasps, allured by the smell, came flying into the room, humming louder than the drones of as many bagpipes. Some of them seized my cake, and carried it piecemeal away; others flew about my head and face, confounding me with the noise, and putting me in the utmost terror of their stings. However, I had the courage to rise and draw my hanger,[14] and attack them in the air. I dispatched four of them, but the

---

14. *hanger*, sword.

rest got away, and I presently shut my window. These insects were as large as partridges; I took out their stings, found them an inch and a half long, and as sharp as needles. I carefully preserved them all, and having since shown them with some other curiosities in several parts of Europe, upon my return to England I gave three of them to Gresham College,[15] and kept the fourth for myself. . . .

But the greatest danger I ever underwent in that kingdom was from a monkey, who belonged to one of the clerks of the kitchen. Glumdalclitch had locked me up in her closet,[16] while she went somewhere upon business or a visit. The weather being very warm, the closet window was left open, as well as the windows in the door of my bigger box, in which I usually lived, because of its largeness and conveniency. As I sat quietly meditating at my table, I heard something bounce in at the closet window, and skip about from one side to the other, whereat, although I was much alarmed, yet I ventured to look out, but stirred not from my seat; and then I saw this frolicsome animal, frisking and leaping up and down, till at last he came to my box, which he seemed to view with great pleasure and curiosity, peeping in at the door and every window. I retreated to the farther corner of my room, or box, but the monkey looking in at every side, put me into such a fright that I wanted presence of mind to conceal myself under the bed, as I might easily have done. After some time spent in peeping, grinning, and chattering, he at last espied me, and reaching one of his paws in at the door, as a cat does when she plays with a mouse, although I often shifted place to avoid him, he at length seized the lappet of my coat (which, being made of that country cloth, was very thick and strong) and dragged me out. He took me up in his right forefoot, and held me as a nurse does a child she is going to suckle, just as I have seen the same sort of creature do with a kitten in Europe: and when I offered to struggle, he squeezed me so hard that I thought it more prudent to submit. I have good reason to believe that he took me for a young one of his own species, by his often stroking my face very gently with his other paw. In these diversions he was interrupted by a noise at the closet door, as if somebody were opening it, whereupon he suddenly leaped up to the window at which he had

come in, and thence upon the leads[17] and gutters, walking upon three legs, and holding me in the fourth, till he clambered up to a roof that was next to ours. I heard Glumdalclitch give a shriek at the moment he was carrying me out. The poor girl was almost distracted: that quarter of the palace was all in an uproar; the servants ran for ladders; the monkey was seen by hundreds in the court, sitting upon the ridge of a building, holding me like a baby in one of his forepaws and feeding me with the other, by cramming into my mouth some victuals[18] he had squeezed out of the bag on one side of his chaps, and patting me when I would not eat; whereat many of the rabble below could not forbear laughing; neither do I think they justly ought to be blamed, for without question the sight was ridiculous enough to everybody but myself. Some of the people threw up stones, hoping to drive the monkey down; but this was strictly forbidden, or else very probably my brains had been dashed out.

15. **Gresham College,** where the Royal Society, a scientific association, held its meetings.
16. **closet,** a small room used as an office or study.
17. **leads,** roof.
18. **victuals,** (vit′ls) food or provisions.

The ladders were now applied, and mounted by several men; which the monkey observing, and finding himself almost encompassed, not being able to make speed enough with his three legs, let me drop on a ridge tile, and made his escape. Here I sat for some time three hundred yards from the ground, expecting every moment to be blown down by the wind, or to fall by my own giddiness, and come tumbling over and over from the ridge to the eaves. But an honest lad, one of my nurse's footmen, climbed up, and putting me into his breeches pocket, brought me down safe.

I was almost choked with the filthy stuff the monkey had crammed down my throat; but my dear little nurse picked it out of my mouth with a small needle, and then I fell a vomiting, which gave me great relief. Yet I was so weak and bruised in the sides with the squeezes given me by this odious animal that I was forced to keep my bed a fortnight. The King, Queen, and all the Court sent every day to inquire after my health, and her Majesty made me several visits during my sickness. The monkey was killed, and an order made that no such animal should be kept about the palace. . . .

I desired the Queen's woman to save for me the combings of her Majesty's hair, whereof in time I got a good quantity; and consulting with my friend the cabinetmaker, who had received general orders to do little jobs for me, I directed him to make two chair frames, no larger than those I had in my box, and then to bore little holes with a fine awl round those parts where I designed the backs and seats; through these holes I wove the strongest hairs I could pick out, just after the manner of cane chairs in England. When they were finished, I made a present of them to her Majesty, who kept them in her cabinet, and used to show them for curiosities, as indeed they were the wonder of every one that beheld them. The Queen would have made me sit upon one of these chairs, but I absolutely refused to obey her, protesting I would rather die a thousand deaths than place a dishonorable part of my body on those precious hairs that once adorned her Majesty's head. Of these hairs (as I had always a mechanical genius) I likewise made a neat little purse above five foot long, with her Majesty's name deciphered in gold letters, which I gave to

Glumdalclitch by the Queen's consent. To say the truth, it was more for show than use, being not of strength to bear the weight of the larger coins; and therefore she kept nothing in it but some little toys that girls are fond of.

The King, who delighted in music, had frequent consorts[19] at court, to which I was sometimes carried, and set in my box on a table to hear them; but the noise was so great that I could hardly distinguish the tunes. I am confident that all the drums and trumpets of a royal army, beating and sounding together just at your ears, could not equal it. My practice was to have my box removed from the places where the performers sat, as far as I could, then to shut the doors and windows of it, and draw the window curtains, after which I found their music not disagreeable.

I had learned in my youth to play a little upon the spinet. Glumdalclitch kept one in her chamber, and a master attended twice a week to teach her: I call it a spinet, because it somewhat resembled that instrument, and was played upon in the same manner. A fancy came into my head that I would entertain the King and Queen with an English tune upon this instrument. But this appeared extremely difficult: for the spinet was near sixty foot long, each key being almost a foot wide; so that, with my arms extended, I could not reach to above five keys, and to press them down required a good smart stroke with my fist, which would be too great a labor and to no purpose. The method I contrived was this: I prepared two round sticks about the bigness of common cudgels; they were thicker at one end than the other, and I covered the thicker ends with a piece of a mouse's skin, that by rapping on them I might neither damage the tops of the keys, nor interrupt the sound. Before the spinet a bench was placed, about four foot below the keys, and I was put upon the bench. I ran sideling[20] upon it that way and this, as fast as I could, banging the proper keys with my two sticks; and made a shift to play a jig, to the great satisfaction of both their Majesties: but it was the most violent exercise I ever underwent, and yet I could not strike above sixteen keys, nor, consequently, play the bass and

---

19. *consorts,* concerts.
20. *sideling,* sideways.

treble together, as other artists do; which was a great disadvantage to my performance.

Gulliver spends some time telling the King about the society, economy, and government of England and the wars she has engaged in. As he does so, he unconsciously praises one abuse after another. The King takes careful notes of everything Gulliver says.

His Majesty in other audience was at the pains to recapitulate the sum of all I had spoken; compared the questions he made with the answers I had given; then taking me into his hands, and stroking me gently, delivered himself in these words, which I shall never forget nor the manner he spoke them in. "My little friend Grildrig,[21] you have made a most admirable panegyric[22] upon your country. You have clearly proved that ignorance, idleness, and vice are the proper ingredients for qualifying a legislator. That laws are best explained, interpreted, and applied by those whose interests and abilities lie in perverting, confounding, and eluding them. I observe among you some lines of an institution which in its original might have been tolerable; but these half erased, and the rest wholly blurred and blotted by corruptions. It doth not appear from all you have said how any one virtue is required towards the procurement of any one station among you; much less that men are ennobled on account of their virtue, that priests are advanced for their piety or learning, soldiers for their conduct or valor, judges for their integrity, senators for the love of their country, or counselors for their wisdom. As for yourself," continued the King, "who have spent the greatest part of your life in traveling, I am well disposed to hope you may hitherto have escaped many vices of your country. But by what I have gathered from your own relation, and the answers I have with much pains wringed and extorted from you, I cannot but conclude the bulk of your natives to be the most pernicious race of little odious vermin that nature ever suffered to crawl upon the surface of the earth."

Nothing but an extreme love of truth could have hindered me from concealing this part of my story. It was in vain to discover my resentments, which were always turned into ridicule; and I was forced to rest with patience while my noble and most beloved country was so injuriously treated. I am heartily sorry as any of my readers can possibly be that such an occasion was given, but this prince happened to be so curious and inquisitive upon every particular that it could not consist either with gratitude or good manners to refuse giving him what satisfaction I was able. Yet thus much I may be allowed to say in my own vindication: that I artfully eluded many of his questions, and gave to every point a more favorable turn by many degrees than the strictness of truth would allow. For I have always borne that laudable partiality to my own country, which Dionysius Halicarnassensis[23] with so much justice recommends to an historian. I would hide the frailties and deformities of my political mother, and place her virtues and beauties in the most advantageous light. This was my sincere endeavor in those many discourses I had with that mighty monarch, although it unfortunately failed of success.

But great allowances should be given to a King who lives wholly secluded from the rest of the world, and must therefore be altogether unacquainted with the manners and customs that most prevail in other nations: the want of which knowledge will ever produce many *prejudices,* and a certain *narrowness of thinking,* from which we and the politer countries of Europe are wholly exempted. And it would be hard indeed if so remote a prince's notions of virtue and vice were to be offered as a standard for all mankind.

To confirm what I have now said, and further, to show the miserable effects of a *confined education,* I shall here insert a passage which will hardly obtain belief. In hopes to ingratiate myself farther into his Majesty's favor, I told him of an invention discovered between three and four hundred years ago, to make a certain powder, into an heap of which the smallest spark of fire falling would kindle the whole in a moment, although it were as big as a mountain, and make it all fly up in the air together, with a noise and

---

21. **Grildrig,** the name given to Gulliver in Brobdingnag. It means "manikin."
22. **panegyric,** speech or writing in praise of something.
23. **Dionysius Halicarnassensis** (dĭ′ə nĭsh′ē əs hal′ə kăr nas′sen sis), a Greek writer in the time of Augustus who wrote a history of Rome.

agitation greater than thunder. That a proper quantity of this powder rammed into an hollow tube of brass or iron, according to its bigness, would drive a ball of iron or lead with such violence and speed as nothing was able to sustain its force. That the largest balls thus discharged would not only destroy whole ranks of an army at once, but batter the strongest walls to the ground; sink down ships with a thousand men in each, to the bottom of the sea; and, when linked together by a chain, would cut through masts and rigging; divide hundreds of bodies in the middle, and lay all waste before them. That we often put this powder into large hollow balls of iron, and discharged them by an engine into some city we were besieging; which would rip up the pavements, tear the houses to pieces, burst and throw splinters on every side, dashing out the brains of all who came near. That I knew the ingredients very well, which were cheap and common; I understood the manner of compounding them, and could direct his workmen how to make those

tubes of a size proportionable to all other things in his Majesty's kingdom, and the largest need not be above two hundred foot long; twenty or thirty of which tubes, charged with the proper quantity of powder and balls, would batter down the walls of the strongest town in his dominions in a few hours; or destroy the whole metropolis, if ever it should pretend to dispute his absolute commands. This I humbly offered to his Majesty as a small tribute of acknowledgment in return of so many marks that I had received of his royal favor and protection.

The King was struck with horror at the description I had given of those terrible engines and the proposal I had made. He was amazed how so impotent and groveling an insect as I (these were his expressions) could entertain such inhuman ideas, and in so familiar a manner as to appear wholly unmoved at all the scenes of blood and desolation which I had painted as the common effects of those destructive machines; whereof he said some evil genius, enemy to mankind, must have been the first contriver. As for himself, he protested that although few things delighted him so much as new discoveries in art or in nature, yet he would rather lose half his kingdom than be privy to such a secret, which he commanded me, as I valued my life, never to mention any more.

A strange effect of *narrow principles* and *short views!* that a prince possessed of every quality which procures veneration, love, and esteem; of strong parts, great wisdom, and profound learning; endued with admirable talents for government, and almost adored by his subjects; should from a *nice, unnecessary scruple,* whereof in Europe we can have no conception, let slip an opportunity put into his hands that would have made him absolute master of the lives, the liberties, and the fortunes of his people. Neither do I say this with the least intention to detract from the many virtues of that excellent King, whose character I am sensible will on this account be very much lessened in the opinion of an English reader: but I take this defect among them to have risen from their ignorance; they not having hitherto reduced politics into a science, as the more acute wits of Europe had done. For I remember very well, in a discourse one day with the King, when I happened to say there were several thousand books among us written upon the art of government, it gave him (directly contrary to my intention) a very mean opinion of our understandings. He professed both to abominate and despise all *mystery, refinement,* and *intrigue,* either in a prince or a minister. He could not tell what I meant by *secrets of state,* where an enemy or some rival nation were not in the case. He confined the knowledge of governing within very *narrow bounds:* to common sense and reason, to justice and lenity,[24] to the speedy determination of civil and criminal causes, with some other obvious topics which are not worth considering. And he gave it for his opinion that whoever could make two ears of corn or two blades of grass to grow upon a spot of ground where only one grew before would deserve better of mankind and do more essential service to his country than the whole race of politicians put together.

Gulliver, having been in Brobdingnag about two years, is taken by the King and Queen on a tour to the south coast of the kingdom. Longing to see the ocean again, Gulliver asks permission to be carried there by a page whom he likes and who earlier had been entrusted with his care.

I shall never forget with what unwillingness Glumdalclitch consented, nor the strict charge she gave the page to be careful of me, bursting at the same time into a flood of tears, as if she had some foreboding of what was to happen. The boy took me out in my box about half an hour's walk from the palace, towards the rocks on the seashore. I ordered him to set me down, and lifting up one of my sashes, cast many a wistful melancholy look towards the sea. I found myself not very well, and told the page that I had a mind to take a nap in my hammock, which I hoped would do me good. I got in, and the boy shut the window close down, to keep out the cold. I soon fell asleep: and all I can conjecture is that while I slept, the page, thinking no danger could happen, went among the rocks to look for birds' eggs; having before observed him from my window searching about, and picking up one or two in the clefts. Be that as it will, I found myself suddenly awaked with a violent pull upon the ring which

was fastened at the top of my box for the conveniency of carriage. I felt my box raised very high in the air, and then borne forward with prodigious speed. The first jolt had like to have shaken me out of my hammock, but afterwards the motion was easy enough. I called out several times as loud as I could raise my voice, but all to no purpose. I looked towards my windows, and could see nothing but the clouds and sky. I heard a noise just over my head like the clapping of wings, and then began to perceive the woeful condition I was in; that some eagle had got the ring of my box in his beak, with an intent to let it fall on a rock, like a tortoise in a shell, and then pick out my body and devour it. For the sagacity and smell of this bird enable him to discover his quarry at a great distance, although better concealed than I could be within a two-inch board.

In a little time I observed the noise and flutter of wings to increase very fast, and my box was tossed up and down like a signpost in a windy day. I heard several bangs or buffets, as I thought, given to the eagle (for such I am certain it must have been that held the ring of my box in his beak), and then all on a sudden felt myself falling perpendicularly down for above a minute, but with such incredible swiftness that I almost lost my breath. My fall was topped by a terrible squash, that sounded louder to mine ears than the cataract of Niagara; after which I was quite in the dark for another minute, and then my box began to rise so high that I could see light from the tops of my windows. I now perceived that I was fallen into the sea. My box, by the weight of my body, the goods that were in, and the broad plates of iron fixed for strength at the four corners of the top and bottom, floated about five foot deep in water. I did then and do now suppose that the eagle which flew away with my box was pursued by two or three others, and forced to let me drop while he was defending himself against the rest, who hoped to share in the prey. The plates of iron fastened at the bottom of the box (for those were the strongest) preserved the balance while it fell, and hindered it from being broken on the surface of the water. Every joint of it was well grooved, and the door did not move on hinges, but up and down like a sash; which kept my closet so tight

---

24. *lenity,* mercy.

A Modest Pr

*For Preventing the Childre
Poor People in Ireland fro
Their Parents or Country,
Them Beneficial to the Pu*

It is a melancholy obje
through this great town,[1] or
when they see the streets,
doors crowded with begga
followed by three, four, or s
and importuning every pa
These mothers, instead of t
their honest livelihood, are
their time in strolling to be
helpless infants; who as the
thieves, for want of work
native country to fight fo
Spain, or sell themselves to

I think it is agreed by all
digious number of children
backs, or at the heels of th
quently of their fathers, is,
able state of the kingdom, a
grievance; and therefore wl
a fair, cheap, and easy met
children sound, useful mem
wealth would deserve so w
have his statue set up for
nation.

But my intention is very
fined to provide only for the
beggars: it is of a much gre
take in the whole number of
age who are born of parents
to support them as those wh
in the streets.

that very little water came in. I got with much
difficulty out of my hammock, having first ventured to draw back the slip-board on the roof
already mentioned, contrived on purpose to let in
air, for want of which I found myself almost stifled.

How often did I then wish myself with my
dear Glumdalclitch, from whom one single hour
had so far divided me! And I may say with truth
that in the midst of my own misfortune, I could
not forbear lamenting my poor nurse, the grief
she would suffer for my loss, the displeasure of
the Queen, and the ruin of her fortune. Perhaps
many travelers have not been under greater difficulties and distress than I was at this juncture,
expecting every moment to see my box dashed in
pieces, or at least overset by the first violent blast
or a rising wave. A breach in one single pane of
glass would have been immediate death, nor
could anything have preserved the windows but
the strong lattice wires placed on the outside
against accidents in traveling. I saw the water
ooze in at several crannies, although the leaks
were not considerable, and I endeavored to stop
them as well as I could. I was not able to lift up
the roof of my closet, which otherwise I certainly

should have done, and sat on the top of it, where I
might at least preserve myself from being shut
up, as I may call it, in the hold. Or, if I escaped
these dangers for a day or two, what could I
expect but a miserable death of cold and hunger!
I was four hours under these circumstances,
expecting and indeed wishing every moment to
be my last.

I have already told the reader that there were
two strong staples fixed upon that side of my box
which had no window and into which the servant,
who used to carry me on horseback, would put a
leathern belt, and buckle it about his waist. Being
in this disconsolate state, I heard, or at least
thought I heard, some kind of grating noise on
that side of my box where the staples were fixed;
and soon after I began to fancy that the box was
pulled or towed along in the sea; for I now and
then felt a sort of tugging, which made the waves
rise near the tops of my windows, leaving me
almost in the dark. This gave me some faint
hopes of relief, although I was not able to imagine
how it could be brought about. I ventured to
unscrew one of my chairs, which were always
fastened to the floor; and having made a hard
shift to screw it down again directly under the
slipping-board that I had lately opened, I
mounted on the chair, and putting my mouth as
near as I could to the hole, I called for help in a
loud voice, and in all the languages I understood.
I then fastened my handkerchief to a stick I usually carried, and thrusting it up the hole, waved it
several times in the air, that if any boat or ship
were near, the seamen might conjecture some
unhappy mortal to be shut up in the box.

I found no effect from all I could do, but plainly perceived my closet to be moved along; and in
the space of an hour or better, that side of the box
where the staples were, and had no window,
struck against something that was hard. I apprehended it to be a rock, and found myself tossed
more than ever. I plainly heard a noise upon the
cover of my closet, like that of a cable, and the
grating of it as it passed through the ring. I then
found myself hoisted up by degrees at least three
foot higher than I was before. Whereupon I again
thrust up my stick and handkerchief, calling for
help till I was almost hoarse. In return to which, I
heard a great shout repeated three times, giving
me such transports of joy as are not to be con-

ceived but by those
trampling over my
through the hole wit
tongue: "If there b
speak." I answered,
by ill fortune into th
any creature underw
was moving, to be d
was in. The voice re
was fastened to the
should immediately
cover, large enough
that was needless a

Discussion

1. *Gulliver's Tr*
of adventure and
to Brobdingnag is
the elements of ac
answer the followi
reach Brobdingna
necessary to have
location? **(b)** In wl
how small Gullive
people of Brobdin
happen to be sold
Gulliver's most dai
and how he is save
ver make from the
hair? Why do you
the story? **(f)** How
play an English jig
think Swift include
does Gulliver leave

2. Considering t

sand couple whose wives are breeders; from which number I subtract thirty thousand couple, who are able to maintain their own children (although I apprehend there cannot be so many, under the present distresses of the kingdom), but this being granted, there will remain an hundred and seventy thousand breeders. I again subtract fifty thousand for those women who miscarry, or whose children die by accident or disease within the year. There only remain one hundred and twenty thousand children of poor parents annually born. The question therefore is, How this number shall be reared and provided for? which, as I have already said, under the present situation of affairs, is utterly impossible by all the methods hitherto proposed. For we can neither employ them in handicraft or agriculture; we neither build houses (I mean in the country) nor cultivate land: they can very seldom pick up a livelihood by stealing till they arrive at six years old, except where they are of towardly[4] parts; although I confess they learn the rudiments much earlier; during which time they can, however, be properly looked upon only as probationers; as I have been informed by a principal gentleman in the county of Cavan, who protested to me that he never knew above one or two instances under the age of six, even in a part of the kingdom so renowned for the quickest proficiency in that art.

I am assured by our merchants that a boy or a girl before twelve years old is no salable commodity; and even when they come to this age they will not yield above three pounds, or three pounds and half a crown at most, on the exchange; which cannot turn to account either to the parents or kingdom, the charge of nutriment and rags having been at least four times that value.

I shall now therefore humbly propose my own thoughts, which I hope will not be liable to the least objection.

I have been assured by a very knowing American of my acquaintance in London that a young healthy child well nursed is at a year old a most delicious, nourishing, and wholesome food, whether stewed, roasted, baked, or boiled; and I make no doubt that it will equally serve in a fricassee or a ragout.[5]

I do therefore humbly offer it to public consideration that of the hundred and twenty thousand children already computed, twenty thousand may be reserved for breed, whereof only one-fourth part to be males; which is more than we allow to sheep, black cattle, or swine; and my reason is that these children are seldom the fruits of marriage, a circumstance not much regarded by our savages; therefore one male will be sufficient to serve four females. That the remaining hundred thousand may, at a year old, be offered in sale to the persons of quality and fortune through the kingdom; always advising the mother to let them suck plentifully in the last month, so as to render them plump and fat for a good table. A child will make two dishes at an entertainment for friends; and when the family dines alone, the fore or hind quarter will make a reasonable dish, and seasoned with a little pepper or salt will be very good boiled on the fourth day, especially in winter.

I have reckoned upon a medium that a child just born will weigh twelve pounds, and in a solar year, if tolerably nursed, will increase to twenty-eight pounds.

I grant this food will be somewhat dear, and therefore very proper for landlords, who, as they have already devoured most of the parents, seem to have the best title to the children.

Infant's flesh will be in season throughout the year, but more plentifully in March, and a little before and after: for we are told by a grave author, an eminent French physician,[6] that fish being a prolific diet, there are more children born in Roman Catholic countries about nine months after Lent than at any other season; therefore, reckoning a year after Lent, the markets will be more glutted than usual, because the number of popish infants is at least three to one in this kingdom: and therefore it will have one other collateral advantage, by lessening the number of papists among us.

I have already computed the charge of nursing a beggar's child (in which list I reckon all cottagers, laborers, and four-fifths of the farmers) to be about two shillings per annum, rags included; and I believe no gentleman would repine to give ten shillings for the carcass of a good fat child,

---

4. *towardly,* dutiful; easily managed.
5. *ragout* (ra gü'), a highly seasoned meat stew.
6. *grave author . . . physician,* François Rabelais (c. 1494–1553), who was anything but a "grave author."

which, as I have said, will make four dishes of excellent nutritive meat, when he has only some particular friend or his own family to dine with him. Thus the squire will learn to be a good landlord and grow popular among his tenants; the mother will have eight shillings net profit and be fit for work till she produces another child.

Those who are more thrifty (as I must confess the times require) may flay the carcass; the skin of which artificially[7] dressed will make admirable gloves for ladies and summer boots for fine gentlemen.

As to our city of Dublin, shambles[8] may be appointed for this purpose in the most convenient parts of it, and butchers we may be assured will not be wanting; although I rather recommend buying the children alive and dressing them hot from the knife as we do roasting pigs.

A very worthy person, a true lover of his country, and whose virtues I highly esteem, was lately pleased, in discoursing on this matter, to offer a refinement upon my scheme. He said that many gentlemen of this kingdom, having of late destroyed their deer, he conceived that the want of venison might be well supplied by the bodies of young lads and maidens, not exceeding fourteen years of age nor under twelve; so great a number of both sexes in every country being now ready to starve for want of work and service; and these to be disposed of by their parents, if alive, or otherwise by their nearest relations. But with due deference to so excellent a friend and so deserving a patriot, I cannot be altogether in his sentiments; for as to the males, my American acquaintance assured me from frequent experience that their flesh was generally tough and lean, like that of our schoolboys, by continual exercise, and their taste disagreeable; and to fatten them would not answer the charge. Then as to the females, it would, I think, with humble submission be a loss to the public, because they soon would become breeders themselves: and besides, it is not improbable that some scrupulous people might be apt to censure such a practice (although indeed very unjustly), as a little bordering upon cruelty; which, I confess, has always been with me the strongest objection against any project, how well soever intended.

But in order to justify my friend, he confessed that this expedient was put into his head by the famous Psalmanazar,[9] a native of the island Formosa, who came from thence to London above twenty years ago: and in conversation told my friend that in his country when any young person happened to be put to death, the executioner sold the carcass to persons of quality as a prime dainty; and that in his time the body of a plump girl of fifteen, who was crucified for an attempt to poison the emperor, was sold to his imperial majesty's prime minister of state, and other great mandarins of the court, in joints from the gibbet, at four hundred crowns. Neither indeed can I deny that if the same use were made of several plump girls in this town, who, without one single groat to their fortunes, cannot stir abroad without a chair, and appear at a playhouse and assemblies in foreign fineries which they never will pay for, the kingdom would not be the worse.

Some persons of a desponding spirit are in great concern about that vast number of poor people who are aged, diseased, or maimed; and I have been desired to employ my thoughts, what course may be taken to ease the nation of so grievous an encumbrance. But I am not in the least pain upon that matter, because it is very well known that they are every day dying and rotting, by cold and famine, and filth and vermin, as fast as can be reasonably expected. And as to the young laborers, they are now in almost as hopeful a condition: they cannot get work, and consequently pine away for want of nourishment to a degree that if at any time they are accidentally hired to common labor, they have not strength to perform it; and thus the country and themselves are happily delivered from the evils to come.

I have too long digressed and therefore shall return to my subject. I think the advantages, by the proposal which I have made, are obvious and many, as well as of the highest importance.

For first, as I have already observed, it would greatly lessen the number of papists, with whom we are yearly overrun, being the principal breeders of the nation, as well as our most dangerous enemies; and who stay at home on purpose to

---

7. *artificially,* artfully; skillfully.
8. *shambles,* slaughterhouses.
9. *Psalmanazar,* the imposter George Psalmanazar (c. 1679–1763), a Frenchman who passed himself off in England as a Formosan, and wrote a totally fictional "true" account of Formosa, in which he described cannibalism.

deliver the kingdom to the Pretender, hoping to take their advantage by the absence of so many good Protestants, who have chosen rather to leave their country than stay at home and pay tithes against their conscience to an Episcopal curate.[10]

Secondly, the poorer tenants will have something valuable of their own, which by law may be made liable to distress,[11] and help to pay their landlord's rent; their corn and cattle being already seized, and money a thing unknown.

Thirdly, whereas the maintenance of a hundred thousand children, from two years old and upwards, cannot be computed at less than ten shillings a piece per annum, the nation's stock will be thereby increased fifty thousand pounds per annum, beside the profit of a new dish introduced to the tables of all gentlemen of fortune in the kingdom who have any refinement in taste. And the money will circulate among ourselves, the goods being entirely of our own growth and manufacture.

Fourthly, the constant breeders, besides the gain of eight shillings sterling per annum by the sale of their children, will be rid of the charge of maintaining them after the first year.

Fifthly, this food would likewise bring great custom to taverns: where the vintners will certainly be so prudent as to procure the best receipts for dressing it to perfection, and consequently have their houses frequented by all the fine gentlemen, who justly value themselves upon their knowledge in good eating: and a skilful cook, who understands how to oblige his guests, will contrive to make it as expensive as they please.

Sixthly, this would be a great inducement to marriage, which all wise nations have either encouraged by rewards or enforced by laws and penalties. It would increase the care and tenderness of mothers toward their children, when they were sure of a settlement for life to the poor babes, provided in some sort by the public, to their annual profit instead of expense. We should see an honest emulation among the married women, which of them could bring the fattest child to the market. Men would become as fond of their wives during the time of their pregnancy as they are now of their mares in foal, their cows in calf, or sows when they are ready to farrow;

nor offer to beat or kick them (as is too frequent a practice) for fear of a miscarriage.

Many other advantages might be enumerated. For instance, the addition of some thousand carcasses in our exportation of barreled beef, the propagation of swine's flesh, and improvement in the art of making good bacon, so much wanted among us by the great destruction of pigs, too frequent at our tables; which are no way comparable in taste or magnificence to a well-grown, fat, yearling child, which roasted whole will make a considerable figure at a lord mayor's feast, or any other public entertainment. But this and many others I omit, being studious of brevity.

Supposing that one thousand families in this city would be constant customers for infants' flesh, besides others who might have it at merry meetings, particularly weddings and christenings, I compute that Dublin would take off annually about twenty thousand carcasses; and the rest of the kingdom (where probably they will be sold somewhat cheaper) the remaining eighty thousand.

I can think of no one objection that will possibly be raised against this proposal, unless it should be urged that the number of people will be thereby much lessened in the kingdom. This I freely own, and it was indeed one principal design in offering it to the world. I desire the reader will observe that I calculate my remedy for this one individual kingdom of Ireland, and for no other that ever was, is, or, I think, ever can be upon earth. Therefore let no man talk to me of other expedients: of taxing our absentees at five shillings a pound: of using neither clothes nor household furniture, except what is of our own growth and manufacture: of utterly rejecting the materials and instruments that promote foreign luxury: of curing the expensiveness of pride, vanity, idleness, and gaming in our women: of introducing a vein of parsimony, prudence, and temperance: of learning to love our country, in the want of which we differ even from Laplanders and the inhabitants of Topinamboo:[12] of quitting our animosities and factions, nor acting any

---

10. *Protestants . . . curate.* Swift is here attacking the absentee landlords.
11. *distress,* distraint, the legal seizure of property for payment of debts.
12. *Topinamboo,* a savage area of Brazil.

longer like the Jews, who were murdering one another at the very moment their city was taken:[13] of being a little cautious not to sell our country and conscience for nothing: of teaching landlords to have at least one degree of mercy toward their tenants: lastly, of putting a spirit of honesty, industry, and skill into our shopkeepers; who, if a resolution could now be taken to buy only our native goods, would immediately unite to cheat and exact upon us in the price, the measure, and the goodness, nor could ever yet be brought to make one fair proposal of just dealing, though often and earnestly invited to it.[14]

Therefore, I repeat, let no man talk to me of these and the like expedients, till he has at least some glimpse of hope that there will ever be some hearty and sincere attempt to put them in practice.

But as to myself, having been wearied out for many years with offering vain, idle, visionary thoughts, and at length utterly despairing of success, I fortunately fell upon this proposal; which, as it is wholly new, so it has something solid and real, of no expense and little trouble, full in our own power, and whereby we can incur no danger in disobliging England. For this kind of commodity will not bear exportation, the flesh being of too tender a consistence to admit a long continuance in salt, although perhaps I could name a country which would be glad to eat up our whole nation without it.[15]

After all, I am not so violently bent upon my own opinion as to reject any offer proposed by wise men, which shall be found equally innocent, cheap, easy, and effectual. But before something of that kind shall be advanced in contradiction to my scheme, and offering a better, I desire the author or authors will be pleased maturely to consider two points. First, as things now stand, how they will be able to find food and raiment for an hundred thousand useless mouths and backs. And, secondly, there being a round million of creatures in human figure throughout this kingdom, whose whole subsistence put into a common stock would leave them in debt two millions of pounds sterling, adding those who are beggars by profession to the bulk of farmers, cottagers, and laborers, with their wives and children, who are beggars in effect; I desire those politicians, who dislike my overture, and may perhaps be so bold as to attempt an answer, that they will first ask the parents of these mortals, whether they would not at this day think it a great happiness to have been sold for food at a year old in the manner I prescribe, and thereby have avoided such a perpetual scene of misfortunes as they have since gone through by the oppression of landlords, the impossibility of paying rent without money or trade, the want of common sustenance, with neither house nor clothes to cover them from the inclemencies of the weather, and the most inevitable prospect of entailing the like or greater miseries upon their breed for ever.

I profess, in the sincerity of my heart, that I have not the least personal interest in endeavoring to promote this necessary work, having no other motive than the public good of my country, by advancing our trade, providing for infants, relieving the poor, and giving some pleasure to the rich. I have no children by which I can propose to get a single penny; the youngest being nine years old, and my wife past childbearing.

1729

---

13. **city was taken.** While the Roman Emperor Titus was besieging Jerusalem, which he took and destroyed in A.D. 70, within the city factions of fanatics were waging bloody warfare.
14. **invited to it.** Swift had already made all these proposals in various pamphlets.
15. **a country . . . without it.** England; this is another way of saying, "The English are devouring the Irish."

Discussion

1. At what point in *A Modest Proposal* did you first realize that Swift was using **irony**? What was your reaction?

2. Paragraph four refers to "a child just dropped from its dam." The essay contains other terms usually applied only to animals. Why does Swift use this device?

3. List some of the shocking details of life in Ireland the essay casually reveals.

4. Which solution do you think Swift intends his readers to choose: the "modest proposal," or the list of alternatives on pages 310–311?

5. Who are the major targets of this satire? In what ways might the Irish themselves be responsible for their plight?

Joseph Addison 1672–1719

Addison was educated at the Charterhouse School, where he met Richard Steele and the two began a lifelong friendship. After receiving his B.A. and M.A. from Magdalen College, Oxford, Addison spent four years in Europe gaining proficiency in modern languages. Entering government service in 1704, Addison (a Whig) was a Member of Parliament from 1708 to his death, and eventually became Secretary of State.

He first achieved literary notice in 1705 with *The Campaign,* a poem celebrating Marlborough's victory in the Battle of Blenheim, and his classical tragedy *Cato* was a great success. He is best known for his part in the development of the periodical essay, his contributions to *The Tatler* and *The Spectator.*

While Addison was living in Ireland on a government assignment, he saw a copy of *The Tatler.* Suspecting it to be the work of Steele, he sent the paper a contribution and thereafter often wrote for it.

In 1711 he and Steele founded the best and most famous of the periodicals, *The Spectator,* published daily, Monday through Saturday, from March 1, 1711, to December 6, 1712. Continuing in the tradition of *The Tatler,* with its objective of improving manners and morals, *The Spectator* was, however, more Addison's than Steele's. Its anonymous Mr. Spectator reported on people, events, and ideas.

Set at the home of Sir Roger de Coverley, the "country squire" member of the Spectator Club, this **essay** deals with a problem all too common in eighteenth-century England. The **narrator** is the Spectator himself.

W*ill Wimble*

The Spectator, No. 108, July 4, 1711
Gratis anhelans, multa agendo nihil agens.[1]

As I was yesterday morning walking with Sir Roger before his house, a country fellow brought him a huge fish, which, he told him, Mr. William Wimble had caught that very morning; and that he presented it, with his service, to him, and intended to come and dine with him. At the same time he delivered a letter, which my friend read to me as soon as the messenger left him.

SIR ROGER:

I desire you to accept of a jack[2] which is the best I have caught this season. I intend to come and stay with you a week and see how the perch bite in the Black River. I observed, with some concern, the last time I saw you upon the bowling green, that your whip wanted a lash to it. I will bring half a dozen with me that I twisted last

---

1. *Gratis . . . agens,* "Out of breath to no purpose, and very busy about nothing," a quotation from a Roman writer of fables.
2. *jack,* pike (a kind of fish).

week, which I hope will serve you all the time you are in the country. I have not been out of the saddle for six days last past, having been at Eton with Sir John's eldest son. He takes to his learning hugely.

I am, Sir, your humble servant,

WILL WIMBLE

This extraordinary letter and message that accompanied it made me very curious to know the character and quality of the gentleman who sent them, which I found to be as follows:

Will Wimble is younger brother to a baronet and descended of the ancient family of the Wimbles. He is now between forty and fifty; but being bred to no business and born to no estate, he generally lives with his elder brother as superintendent of his game. He hunts a pack of dogs better than any man in the country and is very famous for finding out a hare. He is extremely well versed in all the little handicrafts of an idle man. He makes a May fly[3] to a miracle and furnishes the whole country with angle rods. As he is a good-natured, officious[4] fellow and very much esteemed upon account of his family, he is a welcome guest at every house and keeps up a good correspondence among all the gentlemen about him. He carries a tulip root in his pocket from one to another or exchanges a puppy between a couple of friends that live perhaps in the opposite sides of the county.

Will is a particular favorite of all the young heirs, whom he frequently obliges with a net that he has weaved or a setting dog that he has made himself.[5] He now and then presents a pair of garters of his own knitting to their mothers or sisters and raises a great deal of mirth among them by inquiring, as often as he meets them, *how they wear*. These gentlemenlike manufactures and obliging little humors make Will the darling of the country.

Sir Roger was proceeding in the character of him when we saw him make up to us with two or three hazel twigs in his hand that he had cut in Sir Roger's woods as he came through them, in his way to the house. I was very much pleased to observe on one side the hearty and sincere welcome with which Sir Roger received him and on the other the secret joy which his guest discovered at sight of the good old knight.

After the first salutes were over, Will desired Sir Roger to lend him one of his servants to carry a set of shuttlecocks he had with him in a little box to a lady that lived about a mile off, to whom it seems he had promised such a present for above this half year. Sir Roger's back was no sooner turned but honest Will began to tell me of a large cock pheasant that he had sprung in one of the neighboring woods, with two or three other adventures of the same nature. Odd and uncommon characters are the game that I look for and most delight in; for which reason I was as much pleased with the novelty of the person that talked to me as he could be for his life with the springing of a pheasant, and therefore listened to him with more than ordinary attention.

In the midst of his discourse the bell rung to dinner, where the gentleman I have been speaking of had the pleasure of seeing the huge jack he had caught served up for the first dish in a most sumptuous manner. Upon our sitting down to it he gave us a long account how he had hooked it, played with it, foiled it, and at length drew it out upon the bank, with several other particulars that lasted all the first course. A dish of wild fowl that came afterwards furnished conversation for the rest of the dinner, which concluded with a late invention of Will's for improving the quail pipe.[6]

Upon withdrawing into my room after dinner I was secretly touched with compassion toward the honest gentleman that had dined with us and could not but consider with a great deal of concern how so good a heart and such busy hands were wholly employed in trifles, that so much humanity should be so little beneficial to others, and so much industry so little advantageous to himself. The same temper of mind and application to affairs might have recommended him to the public esteem and have raised his fortune to another station of life. What good to his country or himself might not a trader or merchant have done with such useful though ordinary qualifications?

Will Wimble's is the case of many a younger

---

3. *May fly,* a lure used in angling.
4. *officious,* eager to please or help.
5. *made himself,* trained.
6. *quail pipe,* instrument used for imitating the sound of a quail.

brother of a great family, who had rather see their children starve like gentlemen than thrive in a trade or profession that is beneath their quality. This humor fills several parts of Europe with pride and beggary. It is the happiness of a trading nation like ours that the younger sons, though uncapable of any liberal art or profession, may be placed in such a way of life as may perhaps enable them to vie with the best of their family. Accordingly, we find several citizens that were launched into the world with narrow fortunes rising by an honest industry to greater estates than those of their elder brothers. It is not improbable but Will was formerly tried at divinity, law, or physic;[7] and that, finding his genius did not lie that way, his parents gave him up at length to his own inventions. But certainly, however improper he might have been for studies of a higher nature, he was perfectly well turned for the occupations of trade and commerce.

1711

---

7. *physic,* medicine.

Discussion

1. Why is Will an idle gentleman?
2. (a) What does he do that makes him popular in the neighborhood? (b) How does Mr. Spectator feel about these activities?
3. What is Mr. Spectator attempting to correct through this essay?

Vocabulary
Context, Dictionary

Use context and your Glossary to match the words listed with the quotes that follow. On a separate sheet of paper, write the word (or words if more than one seems to fit) next to the number for each quote.

abhorred	expedients	particles
combustible	loath	rebuke
contiguous	odious	viscous

1. "Yet I was so weak and bruised in the sides with the squeezes given me by this _____ animal, that I was forced to keep my bed a fortnight."
2. "The poor pigeons I perceive were _____ to leave their houses."
3. "Therefore let no man talk to me of other _____."
4. "And knaves and fools we both _____ alike."
5. "Now in _____ drops the flood comes down."
6. "... I could easily trace that _____ matter, which our naturalists tell us enables these creatures to walk with their feet upwards upon a ceiling."
7. "... And the wind mighty high and driving it [the fire] into the city, and everything . . . proving _____, even the very stones of churches. . . ."
8. "Let Pride be taught by this _____, / How very mean a thing's a duke."

For those quotes for which you have listed more than one word, use the following page references to locate the quote. Then put a star next to the correct word on your paper.

1. page 301;
2. page 283;
3. page 310;
4. page 281;
5. page 292;
6. page 299;
7. page 284;
8. page 291.

Sir Richard Steele 1672–1729

Flamboyant, often in debt, with a temper as quick as his wit, Steele nevertheless was a firm advocate of morality. In combination with Addison, he did much to convert England from Restoration worldliness to a new sense of personal and national decency. Born in Dublin, he attended Charterhouse School in London, where he first met Addison. He went on to Oxford but left Merton College without a degree to accept a commission in the army.

While in the army, Steele wrote *The Christian Hero* (1701), a pamphlet that praised King William III. Following this he wrote three moral comedies, none of them successful; however, these and his later successful comedies did set the vogue for sentimental comedies.

On April 12, 1709, the first issue of *The Tatler* appeared in the London coffeehouses. Issued thrice weekly under the motto, "Whatever men do is the subject of this book," it was Steele's attempt to educate the new middle class in manners and morals. On January 2, 1711, after 271 issues, *The Tatler* ceased publication.

A short time later Addison and Steele produced *The Spectator.* When that too ceased publication, Steele tried other periodicals: *The Guardian* (1713; 175 issues), *The Englishman* (1713-1714; 57 issues), *The Lover* (1714; 40 issues), and at least five others. It was *The Tatler,* however, that showed the way to its successors.

Appearing in *The Englishman,* a successor to *The Spectator,* Steele's essay deals with the man whose real-life adventure gave Daniel Defoe the idea for *Robinson Crusoe.* True to Steele's determination to educate the middle class, the essay ends with a moral.

Alexander Selkirk

The Englishman, No. 26, December 13, 1713
Talia monstrabat, relegens errata retrorsum[1] Virgil

Under the title of this paper, I do not think it foreign to my design to speak of a man born in her Majesty's dominions, and relate an adventure in his life so uncommon that it is doubtful whether the like has happened to any of the human race. The person I speak of is Alexander Selkirk, whose name is familiar to men of curiosity from the fame of his having lived four years and four months alone in the island of Juan Fernández.[2] I had the pleasure frequently to converse with the

---

1. *Talia . . . retrorsum,* "He displayed such things as he retraced his past wanderings."
2. *Juan Fernández,* a group of islands located 400 miles west of Chile.

man soon after his arrival in England in the year 1711.

It was a matter of great curiosity to hear him, as he is a man of good sense, give an account of the different revolutions in his own mind in the long solitude. When we consider how painful absence from company for the space of but one evening is to the generality of mankind, we may have a sense how painful this necessary and constant solitude was to a man bred a sailor, and ever accustomed to enjoy and suffer, eat, drink, and sleep in fellowship and company.

He was put ashore from a leaky vessel, with the captain of which he had had an irreconcilable difference; and he chose rather to take his fate in this place than in a crazy vessel, under a disagreeable commander. His portion was a sea-chest, his wearing clothes and bedding, a firelock,[3] a pound of gunpowder, a large quantity of bullets, a flint and steel, a few pounds of tobacco, a hatchet, a knife, a kettle, a Bible, and other books of devotion together with pieces that concerned navigation, and his mathematical instruments. Resentment against his officer, who had ill-used him, made him look forward on this change of life as the more eligible one, till the instant in which he saw the vessel put off; at which moment his heart yearned within him, and melted at the parting with his comrades and all human society at once.

He had in provisions for the sustenance of life but the quantity of two meals, the island abounding only in wild goats, cats, and rats. He judged it most probable that he should find more immediate and easy relief by finding shellfish on the shore than seeking game with his gun. He accordingly found great quantities of turtles, whose flesh is extremely delicious, and of which he frequently ate very plentifully on his first arrival, till it grew disagreeable to his stomach, except in jellies.

The necessities of hunger and thirst were his greatest diversions from the reflection on his lonely condition. When those appetites were satisfied, the desire of society was as strong a call upon him, and he appeared to himself least necessitous when he wanted everything; for the supports of his body were easily attained, but the eager longings for seeing again the face of man during the interval of craving bodily appetites were hardly supportable.

He grew dejected, languid, and melancholy, scarce able to refrain from doing himself violence, till by degrees, by the force of reason, and frequent reading of the Scriptures, and turning his thoughts upon the study of navigation, after the space of eighteen months he grew thoroughly reconciled to his condition. When he had made this conquest, the vigor of his health, disengagement from the world, a constant, cheerful, serene sky, and a temperate air made his life one continual feast, and his being much more joyful than it had before been irksome. He, now taking delight in everything, made the hut in which he lay, by ornaments which he cut down from a spacious wood, on the side of which it was situated, the most delicious bower, fanned with continual breezes and gentle aspirations of wind, that made his repose after the chase equal to the most sensual pleasures.

I forgot to observe that, during the time of his dissatisfaction, monsters of the deep, which frequently lay on the shore, added to the horrors of his solitude; the dreadful howling and voices seemed too terrible to be made for the human ears; but upon the recovery of his temper, he could with pleasure not only hear their voices, but approach the monsters themselves with great intrepidity. He speaks of sea lions, whose jaws and tails were capable of seizing or breaking the limbs of a man, if he approached them; but at that time his spirits and life were so high, and he could act so regularly and unconcerned, that merely from being unruffled in himself he killed them with the greatest ease imaginable; for observing that, though their jaws and tails were so terrible, yet the animals being mighty slow in working themselves around, he had nothing to do but place himself exactly opposite to their middle, and as close to them as possible, he dispatched them with his hatchet at will.

The precaution which he took against want, in case of sickness, was to lame kids when very young, so that they might recover their health, but never be capable of speed. These he had in

---

3. *firelock*, a gun.

great numbers about his hut; and when he was himself in full vigor, he could take at full speed the swiftest goat running up a promontory, and never failed of catching them but on descent.

His habitation was extremely pestered with rats, which gnawed his clothes and feet when sleeping. To defend him against them, he fed and tamed numbers of young kitlings,[4] who lay about his bed and preserved him from the enemy. When his clothes were worn out, he dried and tacked together the skins of goats, with which he clothed himself, and was inured to pass through woods, bushes, and brambles with as much carelessness and precipitance as any other animal. It happened once to him that, running on the summit of a hill, he made a stretch to seize a goat, with which under him he fell down a precipice, and lay helpless for the space of three days, the length of which time he measured by the moon's growth since his last observation. This manner of life grew so exquisitely pleasant that he never had a moment heavy on his hands; his nights were untroubled, and his days joyous, from the practice of temperance and exercise. It was his manner to use stated hours and places for exercises of devotion, which he performed aloud, in order to keep up the faculties of speech, and to utter himself with greater energy.

When I first saw him, I thought, if I had not been lent into his character and story, I could have discerned that he had been much separated from company, from his aspect and gesture; there was a strong but cheerful seriousness in his look, and a certain disregard to the ordinary things about him, as if he had been sunk in thought. When the ship which brought him off the island came in, he received them with the greatest indifference, with relation to the prospect of going off with them, but with great satisfaction in an opportunity to refresh and help them. The man frequently bewailed his return to the world, which could not, he said, with all its enjoyments, restore him to the tranquility of his solitude. Though I had frequently conversed with him, after a few months' absence he met me in the street, and though he spoke to me, I could not recollect that I had seen him; familiar converse in this town had taken off the loneliness of his aspect, and quite altered the air of his face.

This plain man's story is a memorable example that he is happiest who confines his wants to natural necessities; and he that goes further in his desires increases his wants in proportion to his acquisitions; or to use his own expression, "I am now worth eight hundred pounds, but shall never be so happy as when I was not worth a farthing."

1713

---

4. *kitlings,* young cats or kittens.

Discussion

1. How does Selkirk's reaction to his solitude change with the passage of time?

2. Contrast Selkirk's appearance when the narrator first meets him in London with his appearance when the narrator again encounters him some time later. How do you account for the change?

3. What moral does Steele draw from Selkirk's experience? Explain why you agree or disagree.

Alexander Pope 1688–1744

Despite personal handicaps that would have caused a man of lesser determination to give up, Pope rose to be the leading literary figure of his day. He was a Roman Catholic in an age when adherence to the "Old Faith" prevented him from receiving a university education, voting, or holding public office, and when the tax burden on Catholics was sufficiently high to drive many families into bankruptcy.

In addition, at the age of twelve Pope was stricken with tuberculosis of the spine, a disease that left him dwarfed, crippled, and in almost constant pain. By sheer force of will he managed to educate himself and to become admired as a poet and feared as a satirist, claiming in a late poem, "Yes, I am proud; I must be proud to see / Men not afraid of God, afraid of me."

Pope was born in London, but soon after his illness his father, a retired merchant, moved the family to Binfield, in Windsor Forest, where the rural surroundings were healthier. In 1718 Pope moved to Twickenham, near London, where he spent the rest of his life; he later became known as the "wasp of Twickenham" because of the stinging quality of his satire.

Beginning to write poetry when he was very young, Pope saw his *Pastorals* in print in 1709, when he was only twenty-one. When his *Essay on Criticism* was published two years later, he became famous. In 1712 the first version of Pope's mock epic, *The Rape of the Lock,* appeared; it was revised and expanded in 1714 (see pages 319–325).

About 1713 Pope was instrumental in forming the Scriblerus Club, a group of writers (including Swift) who met on occasion to satirize the pretensions of learned men. Shortly thereafter Pope announced a subscription for a verse translation of Homer's *Iliad.* Almost at once criticism began, led by the Whigs. Probably most of this adverse comment stemmed from Pope's friendship with Swift, at whom the Whigs were angry because of his recent defection from their party to the Tories. In any event, Pope's Catholicism was attacked, as was his competency in Greek. The stir did not interfere with subscription sales.

For two years Pope labored over his translation, the first volume of which was published in 1715. Two days later a rival translation of the *Iliad* appeared, done by Thomas Tickell, an Oxford man, probably with the assistance of Joseph Addison. Even though this translation was a failure, Pope was upset by it, for Addison had been his longtime friend. Turning to his pen, Pope wrote a scathing satirical portrait of Addison. So successful was Pope's translation of the *Iliad* that he followed it with a translation of the *Odyssey.*

Pope earned a large income through his poetry, editorial work, and translations. In an age of satire, he was often subjected to vituperative literary attacks, but he gave better than he got, cutting down his enemies with sharply honed heroic couplets. Among his later works are *The Dunciad* (in several versions); *An Essay on Man* (1733-1734), an excerpt from which follows (page 327); and *Moral Essays* (1731-1735). All of these poems are written in heroic couplets.

In writing *The Rape of the Lock,* Pope attempted to placate both sides in a real-life quarrel that had arisen when Lord Petre (the Baron in the poem) snipped off a lock of hair from the head of Arabella Fermor (Belinda in the poem). To achieve his purpose, Pope had

volved. Only one of the minor characters depicted was offended; Arabella was pleased with the attention given her. While it would have made the story complete if the real-life hero and heroine had married and lived happi-

not to be. The Baron
d richer heiress and died
year. Arabella married an-
became the mother of six

em

s winning lips to lay,
said, or seemed to say. . . .

her guardian sylph, Ariel,
explaining the life of the
with a grave warning.)

o thy protection claim,
l Ariel is my name.
crystal wilds of air,
thy ruling star
d event impend,
norning sun descend,
t what, or how, or where:
oh pious maid, beware!
hy guardian can:
st beware of man!''
k,[4] who thought she slept

his mistress with his

gested that Pope write the
en the two families.
f watch in which a pressure
atch to strike the last hour

n dressed in fine clothes for

'Twas then, Belinda, if report say true,
40 Thy eyes first opened on a billet-doux;[5]
Wounds, charms, and ardors were no sooner
     read,
But all the vision vanished from thy head.
   And now, unveiled, the toilet[6] stands displayed,
Each silver vase in mystic order laid.
45 First, robed in white, the nymph intent adores,
With head uncovered, the cosmetic powers.
A heavenly image in the glass appears,
To that she bends, to that her eye she rears;

The Toilet by Aubrey Beardsley. The Beardsley illustrations in this poem were done for an edition of *The Rape of the Lock* published in 1896.

The inferior priestess,[7] at her altar's side,
50 Trembling, begins the sacred rites of pride.
Unnumbered treasures ope at once, and here
The various offerings of the world appear;
From each she nicely culls with curious toil,
And decks the goddess with the glittering spoil.
55 This casket India's glowing gems unlocks,
And all Arabia[8] breathes from yonder box.
The tortoise here and elephant unite,

Transformed to combs, the speckled and the white.
Here files of pins extend their shining rows,
60 Puffs, powders, patches, Bibles, billet-doux.
Now awful[9] Beauty puts on all its arms;
The fair each moment rises in her charms,
Repairs her smiles, awakens every grace,
And calls forth all the wonders of her face;
65 Sees by degrees a purer blush arise,
And keener lightnings quicken in her eyes.
The busy Sylphs surround their darling care;
These set the head, and those divide the hair,
Some fold the sleeve, while others plait the
     gown;
70 And Betty's[10] praised for labors not her own.

CANTO II

(After her elaborate preparations at the dressing table, Belinda sets out, "launched on the bosom of the silver Thames," on her way to Hampton Court, one of the royal palaces near London, and the center of her delightful, sophisticated, and trivial social life.)

   This nymph, to the destruction of mankind,
Nourished two locks, which graceful hung behind
In equal curls, and well conspired to deck
With shining ringlets the smooth ivory neck.
75 Love in these labyrinths his slaves detains,
And mighty hearts are held in slender chains.
With hairy springes[11] we the birds betray,
Slight lines of hair surprise the finny prey,
Fair tresses man's imperial race ensnare,
80 And beauty draws us with a single hair.
   The adventurous Baron the bright locks
     admired;
He saw, he wished, and to the prize aspired.
Resolved to win, he meditates the way,
By force to ravish, or by fraud betray;
85 For when success a lover's toils attends,
Few ask, if fraud or force attained his ends.

---

5. *billet-doux,* love letter.
6. *toilet,* dressing table.
7. *inferior priestess,* Belinda's maid, Betty.
8. *Arabia,* source of perfumes.
9. *awful,* awesome or awe-inspiring.
10. *Betty,* Belinda's maid.
11. *springes,* nooses to catch birds.

A **mock epic** uses the form and style of an epic poem to satirize a trivial subject by making it appear ridiculous. In *The Rape of the Lock* Pope uses exaggeration as his major tool to show how trivial was the basis for the quarrel between the families of Arabella Fermor and Lord Petre.

The traditional epic opens with a statement of its **theme.** Pope states his in the first few lines: "What dire offense from amorous causes springs, / What mighty contests rise from trivial things, / I sing." True to the epic tradition, Pope invokes a Muse, a spirit that inspires the poet. Next, he poses the important epic question, which the rest of the poem will seek to answer: "In tasks so bold [snipping the lock of hair] can little men engage, / And in soft bosoms dwells such mighty rage?"

Also in the epic tradition are formal speeches, often boastful, delivered in elevated language. Pope provides these in the Baron's triumphal speech (lines 187–204), and in Belinda's reply (lines 205–234).

The war of the classical epic is here fought by the lords and ladies led respectively by the Baron and Belinda. To Belinda's weapon—a bodkin, or needle—is given the complete genealogy accorded to the hero's armor and weapons in a traditional epic (lines 257–264). The supernatural elements that intervene in the affairs of humans in traditional epics are in Pope's poem the Sylphs and Gnomes.

Finally, Pope's own device of juxtaposing in a single couplet the great with the trivial occurs throughout the poem. For example:

Here thou, great Anna, whom three realms obey,
Dost sometimes counsel take—and sometimes tea.

(lines 135–136)

Not louder shrieks to pitying Heaven are cast,
When husbands or when lapdogs breathe their last.

(lines 183–184)

Pope's purpose in joining these disparate elements is to weld the trivial to the elevated, and to extend both beyond Belinda and the Baron to the follies of the whole human race, from queens to lapdog-loving wives.

(The sylph Ariel, aware of the threat to Belinda, summons his fellow sylphs and sends them to their various stations about Belinda to guard her every precious possession.)

"This day, black omens threat the brightest Fair
That ever deserved a watchful spirit's care;
Some dire disaster, or by force, or slight;
90   But what, or where, the Fates have wrapped in night.
Whether the nymph shall break Diana's law,[12]
Or some frail china jar receive a flaw;
Or stain her honor, or her new brocade;
Forget her prayers, or miss a masquerade;
95   Or lose her heart, or necklace, at a ball;
Or whether Heaven has doomed that Shock must fall.

Haste, then, ye spirits! to your charge repair:
The fluttering fan be Zephyretta's care;
The drops[13] to thee, Brillante, we consign;
100   And, Momentilla, let the watch be thine:
Do thou, Crispissa, tend her favorite lock;
Ariel himself shall be the guard of Shock.
    "To fifty chosen Sylphs, of special note,
We trust the important charge, the petticoat:
105   Oft have we known that sevenfold fence to fail,
Though stiff with hoops, and armed with ribs of whale;
Form a strong line about the silver bound,
And guard the wide circumference around.
    "Whatever spirit, careless of his charge,

---

12. **Diana's law,** chastity. Diana was the goddess of maidenhood.
13. **drops,** pendant earrings.
14. **bodkin,** a large blunt needle with an eye.

His post neglects, or leaves the fair at large,
110 Shall feel sharp vengeance soon o'ertake his
    sins,
Be stopped in vials, or transfixed with pins;
Or plunged in lakes of bitter washes lie,
Or wedged whole ages in a bodkin's eye:
115 Gums and pomatums[15] shall his flight restrain,
While clogged he beats his silken wings in vain;
Or alum styptics[16] with contracting power
Shrink his thin essence like a rivelled flower:
Or, as Ixion[17] fixed, the wretch shall feel
120 The giddy motion of the whirling mill,
In fumes of burning chocolate shall glow,
And tremble at the sea that froths below!''
    He spoke; the spirits from the sails descend;
Some, orb in orb, around the nymph extend,
125 Some thrid[18] the mazy ringlets of her hair,
Some hang upon the pendants of her ear;
With beating hearts the dire event they wait,
Anxious, and trembling for the birth of Fate.

CANTO III

Close by those meads, for ever crowned with
    flowers,
130 Where Thames with pride surveys his rising
    towers,
There stands a structure of majestic frame,
Which from the neighboring Hampton takes its
    name.[19]
Here Britain's statesmen oft the fall foredoom
Of foreign tyrants, and of nymphs at home;
135 Here thou, great Anna![20] whom three realms
    obey,
Dost sometimes counsel take—and sometimes
    tea.
    Hither the heroes and the nymphs resort,
To taste awhile the pleasures of a court;
In various talk the instructive hours they
    passed,
140 Who gave the ball, or paid the visit last;
One speaks the glory of the British Queen,
And one describes a charming Indian screen;
A third interprets motions, looks, and eyes;
At every word a reputation dies.
145 Snuff, or the fan, supply each pause of chat,
With singing, laughing, ogling, and all that.
    Meanwhile, declining from the noon of day,
The sun obliquely shoots his burning ray;

The hungry judges soon the sentence sign,
150 And wretches hang that jurymen may dine; . . .

(Belinda joins the pleasure-seekers at Hampton
Court, and wins at a card game, ombre, over the
Baron who covets her locks. But as the game
ends, and they all partake of refreshments, the
Baron seizes his opportunity.)

    But when to mischief mortals bend their will,
How soon they find fit instruments of ill!
Just then, Clarissa drew with tempting grace
A two-edged weapon[21] from her shining case;
155 So ladies in romance assist their knight,
Present the spear, and arm him for the fight.
He takes the gift with reverence, and extends
The little engine on his fingers' ends;
This just behind Belinda's neck he spread,
160 As o'er the fragrant steams she bends her head:
Swift to the lock a thousand sprites repair,
A thousand wings, by turns, blow back the hair;
And thrice they twitched the diamond in her ear;
Thrice she looked back, and thrice the foe
    drew near.
165 Just in that instant, anxious Ariel sought
The close recesses of the virgin's thought;
As on the nosegay in her breast reclined,
He watched the ideas rising in her mind,
Sudden he viewed, in spite of all her art,
170 An earthly lover lurking at her heart.
Amazed, confused, he found his power expired,
Resigned to fate, and with a sigh retired.
    The peer now spreads the glittering forfex[22]
    wide,
To inclose the lock; now joins it, to divide.
175 Even then, before the fatal engine closed,
A wretched Sylph too fondly interposed;
Fate urged the shears, and cut the Sylph in
    twain
(But airy substance soon unites again).
The meeting points the sacred hair dissever

---

15. pomatums, perfumed ointments to keep the hair in
place.
16. alum styptics, astringents.
17. Ixion, in Greek myth, fastened to an endlessly revolving
wheel in Hades as punishment for making love to Juno,
queen of the gods.
18. thrid, thread; pass through.
19. name, Hampton Court, a royal palace near London.
20. Anna, Queen Anne (1702-1714).
21. two-edged weapon, scissors.
22. forfex, scissors.

What time would spare, from steel receives
    its date,
And monuments, like men, submit to fate!
Steel could the labor of the gods destroy,
200 And strike to dust the imperial towers of Troy;
Steel could the works of mortal pride confound,
And hew triumphal arches to the ground.
What wonder then, fair nymph! thy hairs
    should feel
The conquering force of unresisted steel?''

CANTO IV

(Confusion and hysteria result from the Baron's
dastardly deed of cutting off Belinda's lock of
hair, and Belinda delivers to the Baron a speech
of elevated indignation.)

205 ''For ever cursed be this detested day,
Which snatched my best, my favorite curl away!
Happy! ah ten times happy had I been,
If Hampton Court these eyes had never seen!
Yet am not I the first mistaken maid,
210 By love of courts to numerous ills betrayed.
Oh had I rather unadmired remained
In some lone isle, or distant northern land;
Where the gilt chariot never marks the way,
Where none learn ombre, none e'er taste
    bohea![24]
215 There kept my charms concealed from mortal
    eye,
Like roses that in deserts bloom and die.
What moved my mind with youthful lords to
    roam?
Oh had I stayed, and said my prayers at home!
'Twas this, the morning omens seemed to tell:
220 Thrice from my trembling hand the patchbox
    fell;
The tottering china shook without a wind,
Nay, Poll sat mute, and Shock was most unkind!
A Sylph too warned me of the threats of fate,
In mystic visions, now believed too late!
225 See the poor remnants of these slighted hairs!
My hands shall rend what ev'n thy rapine
    spares:
These, in two sable ringlets taught to break,

The Rape of the Lock by Aubrey Beardsley.

180 From the fair head, for ever, and for ever!
    Then flashed the living lightning from her
      eyes,
And screams of horror rend the affrighted skies.
Not louder shrieks to pitying Heaven are cast,
When husbands or when lap dogs breathe their
    last;
185 Or when rich China vessels fallen from high,
In glittering dust and painted fragments lie!
    ''Let wreaths of triumph now my temples
      twine,''
(The victor cried) ''the glorious prize is mine!
While fish in streams, or birds delight in air,
190 Or in a coach and six the British fair,
As long as *Atalantis*[23] shall be read,
Or the small pillow grace a lady's bed,
While visits shall be paid on solemn days,
When numerous wax-lights in bright order
    blaze,
195 While nymphs take treats, or assignations give,
So long my honor, name, and praise shall live!

---

23. Atalantis, a popular book of court scandal and gossip.
24. bohea, an expensive tea.

Once gave new beauties to the snowy neck.
The sister-lock now sits uncouth, alone,
230 And in its fellow's fate foresees its own;
Uncurled it hangs, the fatal shears demands;
And tempts, once more, thy sacrilegious hands.
Oh hadst thou, cruel! been content to seize
Hairs less in sight, or any hairs but these!''

CANTO V

(Such a treacherous deed as the rape of a lock
of lady's hair inevitably results in an "epic" battle.)

235 "To arms, to arms!" the fierce virago[25] cries,
And swift as lightning to the combat flies.
All side in parties, and begin the attack;
Fans clap, silks rustle, and tough whalebones
   crack;
Heroes' and heroines' shouts confusedly rise,
240 And bass, and treble voices strike the skies.
No common weapons in their hands are found,
Like gods they fight, nor dread a mortal wound.

(Belinda attacks the Baron, but to no avail.
They are both deprived of the precious lock as it
rises into the skies immortalized and transfigured
into a heavenly body.)

See fierce Belinda on the Baron flies,
With more than usual lightning in her eyes;
245 Nor feared the chief the unequal fight to try,
Who sought no more than on his foe to die.
But this bold lord, with manly strength endued,
She with one finger and a thumb subdued:
Just where the breath of life his nostrils drew,
250 A charge of snuff the wily virgin threw;
The Gnomes direct, to every atom just,
The pungent grains of titillating dust.
Sudden, with starting tears each eye o'erflows,
And the high dome re-echoes to his nose.
255 "Now meet thy fate," incensed Belinda
   cried,
And drew a deadly bodkin[26] from her side.
(The same, his ancient personage to deck,
Her great-great-grandsire wore about his neck
In three seal rings; which after, melted down,
260 Formed a vast buckle for his widow's gown:
Her infant grandame's whistle next it grew,
The bells she jingled, and the whistle blew;

The Battle of the Beaux and the Belles, Aubrey Beardsley.

Then in a bodkin graced her mother's hairs,
Which long she wore, and now Belinda wears.)
265 "Boast not my fall" (he cried) "insulting foe!
Thou by some other shalt be laid as low.
Nor think, to die dejects my lofty mind;
All that I dread is leaving you behind!
Rather than so, ah let me still survive,
270 And burn in Cupid's flames—but burn alive."
"Restore the lock!" she cries; and all around
"Restore the lock!" the vaulted roofs rebound.
Not fierce Othello in so loud a strain
Roared for the handkerchief that caused his pain.[27]
275 But see how oft ambitious aims are crossed,
And chiefs contend till all the prize is lost!
The lock, obtained with guilt, and kept with
   pain,
In every place is sought, but sought in vain:

25. *virago,* a strong, vigorous woman; amazon.
26. *bodkin,* ornamental hairpin shaped like a stiletto.
27. *Othello . . . pain,* In Shakespeare's play, Othello becomes enraged when his wife Desdemona fails to produce a highly prized handkerchief and is convinced she has given it to her supposed lover.

With such a prize no mortal must be blest,
280 So Heaven decrees! with Heaven who can
　　　contest?
　　Some thought it mounted to the lunar sphere,
Since all things lost on earth, are treasured there.
There heroes' wits are kept in ponderous vases,
And beaux' in snuffboxes and tweezer-cases.
285 There broken vows, and deathbed alms are
　　　found,
And lovers' hearts with ends of riband bound;
The courtier's promises and sick man's prayers,
The smiles of harlots, and the tears of heirs.
Cages for gnats, and chains to yoke a flea,
290 Dried butterflies, and tomes of casuistry.[28]
　　But trust the Muse—she saw it upward rise,
Though marked by none but quick poetic eyes:
(So Rome's great founder to the heavens
　　　withdrew,
To Proculus alone confessed in view.)[29]
295 A sudden star, it shot through liquid air,
And drew behind a radiant trail of hair.
Not Berenice's lock[30] first rose so bright,
The heavens bespangling with disheveled light.
The Sylphs behold it kindling as it flies,
300 And pleased pursue its progress through the
　　　skies.
　　This the beau monde[31] shall from the Mall[32]
　　　survey,
And hail with music its propitious ray.

This, the blest lover shall for Venus take,
And send up vows from Rosamonda's lake.[33]
305 This Partridge soon shall view in cloudless skies,
When next he looks through Galileo's eyes;
And hence the egregious wizard shall foredoom
The fate of Louis, and the fall of Rome.[34]
　　Then cease, bright nymph! to mourn thy
　　　ravished hair
310 Which adds new glory to the shining sphere!
Not all the tresses that fair head can boast
Shall draw such envy as the lock you lost.
For, after all the murders of your eye,
When, after millions slain, your self shall die;
315 When those fair suns shall set, as set they must,
And all those tresses shall be laid in dust;
This lock, the Muse shall consecrate to fame,
And 'midst the stars inscribe Belinda's name.
1712　　　　　　　　　　　　　　　　　1714

---

28. **tomes of casuistry,** books of oversubtle reasoning about conscience and conduct.
29. **So Rome's . . . view.** Proculus, a Roman senator, saw Romulus, the founder of Rome, taken to heaven.
30. **Berenice's lock.** The Egyptian queen Berenice dedicated a lock of her beautiful hair to Venus for the safe return of her husband from war; the hair was turned into a comet. There is a constellation known as *Coma Berenicis,* Berenice's hair.
31. **beau monde,** fashionable society.
32. **Mall,** a promenade in St. James's Park in London.
33. **Rosamonda's lake,** in St. James's Park.
34. **Partridge . . . Rome.** John Partridge (1644-1715) was an astrologer and almanac-maker who annually predicted the downfall of the King of France and of the Pope.

Discussion

1. (a) How does the Baron manage to cut off Belinda's lock despite the Sylphs? **(b)** What "chemical warfare" does Belinda use to defeat the Baron? **(c)** What finally becomes of the lock of hair?

2. (a) What devices are used to make Belinda seem like a goddess? to seem like an Amazon or other female warrior? **(b)** How does Pope make these appropriate to a mock epic?

3. The Baron's feelings about Belinda are clear. What are her feelings about him?

4. How important are the Sylphs (the supernatural elements or spirits) to the plot of the poem? to the atmosphere? Explain.

5. In what respects has the war between the sexes remained unchanged from the time of *The Rape of the Lock* to the present day? In what respects has it changed?

6. Explain how *The Rape of the Lock* could be popular with the real-life principals involved, at the same time that it pointed out the ridiculousness of their quarrel.

Composition

Imagine that you are a newspaper reporter sent to cover the loss of Belinda's lock. Take notes on the important points, and then make an outline of your story.

Write a newspaper story in which you answer all the important questions of the journalist: *who, what, where, when, why,* and *how.*

Included among the poems in Pope's 1717 collection was the "Epistle to Miss Blount." Pope used the term "epistle" to describe a letter in verse. This poem, light and affectionate in tone, was written to Teresa Blount, the sister of Pope's close friend, Martha Blount. The poem was occasioned by Teresa's return to the country after being in London for the coronation of King George I in 1714.

Epistle to Miss Blount

The Richmond Water-Walk by Thomas Gainsborough, a study made about 1785 for a never-completed painting.

As some fond virgin,[1] whom her mother's care
Drags from the town to wholesome country air,
Just when she learns to roll a melting eye,
And hear a spark,[2] yet think no danger nigh;
5 From the dear man unwilling she must sever,
Yet takes one kiss before she parts for ever;
Thus from the world fair Zephalinda[3] flew,
Saw others happy, and with sighs withdrew;
Not that their pleasures caused her discontent;
10 She sighed not that they stayed, but that she went.
  She went to plain-work,[4] and to purling brooks,
Old-fashioned halls, dull aunts, and croaking rooks;
She went from opera, park, assembly, play,
To morning walks, and prayers three hours a day;
15 To part her time 'twixt reading and bohea,[5]
To muse, and spill her solitary tea,
Or o'er cold coffee trifle with the spoon,
Count the slow clock, and dine exact at noon;[6]
Divert her eyes with pictures in the fire,
20 Hum half a tune, tell stories to the squire;
Up to her godly garret after seven,
There starve and pray, for that's the way to heaven.
  Some squire, perhaps, you take delight to rack,
Whose game is whist,[7] whose treat a toast in sack;[8]

---

1. *fond virgin,* simple young girl.
2. *spark,* handsome young man.
3. *Zephalinda,* a pet name for Miss Teresa Blount.
4. *plain-work,* sewing; as opposed to fancy-work, or embroidery.
5. *bohea,* a variety of tea.
6. *at noon,* fashionable people dined at three or four P.M.
7. *whist,* a card game.
8. *sack,* sherry, or other strong, light-colored wine.

25 Who visits with a gun, presents you birds,
   Then gives a smacking buss, and cries—no
      words!
   Or with his hounds comes hallooing from the
      stable,
   Makes love with nods, and knees beneath a
      table;
   Whose laughs are hearty, though his jests are
      coarse,
30 And loves you best of all things—but his horse.
   In some fair evening, on your elbow laid,
   You dream of triumphs in the rural shade;
   In pensive thought recall the fancied scene,
   See coronations rise on every green:
35 Before you pass the imaginary sights
   Of lords, and earls, and dukes, and gartered
      knights,
   While the spread fan o'ershades your closing
      eyes,
   Then give one flirt,[9] and all the vision flies.
   Thus vanish scepters, coronets, and balls,
40 And leave you in lone woods or empty walls!
      So when your slave,[10] at some dear idle time
   (Not plagued with headaches or the want of
      rhyme),
   Stands in the streets abstracted from the crew,
   And while he seems to study, thinks of you;
45 Just when his fancy paints[11] your sprightly eyes,
   Or sees the blush of soft Parthenia[12] rise,
   Gay[13] pats my shoulder, and you vanish quite;
   Streets, chairs, and coxcombs rush upon my
      sight:
   Vexed to be still in town, I knit my brow,
50 Look sour, and hum a tune—as you may now.
1714   1717

---

9. *flirt,* closing a fan.
10. *slave,* Pope himself.
11. *paints,* imagines.
12. *Parthenia,* a pet name for Martha Blount, Teresa's sister.
13. *Gay,* John Gay (1685-1732), English poet and dramatist, and friend of Pope's.

An Essay on Man consists of four **epistles.** This excerpt comes from the second epistle, which Pope titled "Of the Nature and State of Man with respect to Himself, as an Individual"; in other words, Pope is dealing with man from the psychological viewpoint of the eighteenth century.

from *An Essay on Man*

Know then thyself, presume not God to scan;
The proper study of mankind is Man.
Placed on this isthmus of a middle state,
A being darkly wise, and rudely great:
5 With too much knowledge for the Skeptic[1] side,
With too much weakness for the Stoic's[2] pride,
He hangs between: in doubt to act, or rest;
In doubt to deem himself a god, or beast;
In doubt his mind or body to prefer;
10 Born but to die, and reasoning but to err;
Alike in ignorance, his reason such,
Whether he thinks too little, or too much:
Chaos of thought and passion, all confused;
Still by himself abused, or disabused;
15 Created half to rise, and half to fall;
Great lord of all things, yet a prey to all;
Sole judge of truth, in endless error hurled:
The glory, jest, and riddle of the world!
                                                 1733

---

1. *Skeptic,* a person who questions the possibility or certainty of our knowledge of anything; a doubter.
2. *Stoic,* member of a school of philosophy founded in Athens which taught that one should be free from passion and unmoved by life's happenings.

Discussion

1. (a) In the "Epistle to Miss Blount," how is life in London made to seem preferable to life in the country? (b) How attractive as a potential husband is the squire (lines 23–30)? Why? (c) Compare Pope's reverie (lines 41–50) with the one he pictures for Miss Blount (lines 31–40). (d) Explain the last two lines.

2. (a) Explain the relationship of the last line of *An Essay on Man* to the rest of the excerpt. (b) Do you agree or disagree with Pope's evaluation of humanity? Discuss.

Samuel Johnson 1709–1784

One of the most remarkable men of his age, Johnson won renown as a scholar, poet, essayist, conversationalist, literary critic, and compiler of the first comprehensive English dictionary. He is also the subject of one of the greatest biographies ever written, Boswell's *Life of Johnson* (see page 338).

Born in Lichfield in Staffordshire, the son of a provincial bookseller who was rarely more than a step or two ahead of poverty, Johnson as an infant contracted scrofula (tuberculosis of the lymph glands) from his nurse. The disease marred his face and left him blind in one eye; in addition, it was probably responsible for the occasional nervous twitches that he could not suppress. Johnson attended the Lichfield Grammar School and in 1728 went on to Pembroke College, Oxford, remaining there slightly more than a year before lack of funds compelled him to leave. From 1729 to 1737 Johnson worked as a bookseller and schoolmaster. In 1735 he married a widow considerably older than he.

In 1737, having completed a tragic drama, *Irene,* Johnson went to London, accompanied by David Garrick, who had been one of his pupils and was to go on to become the most famous actor of his day. From 1737 to 1746 Johnson earned his living by writing for *The Gentleman's Magazine.*

In 1747 Johnson announced the plan for his *Dictionary of the English Language.* He completed this monumental work eight years later. In 1756 he announced his second major project: a new and complete edition of Shakespeare, which he finished in 1765. Johnson's third and last major project, his *Lives of the English Poets,* he began in 1779 and completed in 1781 (see page 332).

While the *Dictionary* was underway, Johnson continued to write to support himself and his project. From 1750 to 1752 he edited his own periodical, *The Rambler,* which ran for 208 issues; he also wrote essays, book reviews, and articles for other publications. Garrick was successful in having *Irene,* Johnson's tragedy, produced in 1749 at the Drury Lane Theater. When the *Dictionary* was finally published in 1755, Johnson's fame was assured.

During the time that Johnson was editing Shakespeare, he continued to do other literary work. From 1758 to 1760 he wrote *The Idler,* a series of essays, nearly 100 in all. In January, 1759, his *Rasselas* was published, a rare blend of Oriental novel and philosophical tale. Although King George III awarded him a pension in 1762, Johnson continued writing.

On May 16, 1763, Johnson met the young Scotsman, James Boswell, who was to become his biographer. As their friendship ripened, Boswell spent some time almost every year with Johnson. In 1764 Johnson founded the Literary Club, a group of distinguished men who met once a week at the Turk's Head Coffee House in Soho. Among its charter members were Sir Joshua Reynolds, the great portrait painter, Oliver Goldsmith, physician and author, and Edmund Burke, orator and statesman. Garrick and Boswell later became members.

In 1775 Oxford University awarded the aging Johnson an honorary doctorate. In June, 1783, Johnson suffered a stroke that temporarily left him unable to speak. He died eighteen months later, on December 13, 1784, and was buried in Westminster Abbey.

Johnson's reputation as a scholar and writer was established in 1755 with the publication of his *Dictionary*. Selling for ninety shillings and filling two large volumes, the *Dictionary* was the most comprehensive English lexicon ever published. In Italy and France similar dictionaries, prepared under the direction of national academies, represented the work of forty or more men. Johnson prepared his single-handedly, with the help of six clerks to copy out the quotations which illustrated the proper use of words.

In all, the *Dictionary* consisted of four parts: a comprehensive preface, explaining Johnson's objectives and methods and giving some background on earlier dictionaries; a history of the development of the English language; a grammar; and finally, the body of the dictionary itself, composed of an extensive, carefully selected list of words, some aids to pronunciation, some etymologies (sources of the words), definitions that were divided and numbered when the word had more than one, and the illustrative quotations.

The *Dictionary* has had a permanent effect on the English language. Below are entries from the *Dictionary,* selected either for their comprehensiveness or the personal touches they show.

from the Dictionary *of the English Language*

alliga′tor. The crocodile. This name is chiefly used for the crocodile of America, between which, and that of Africa, naturalists have laid down this difference, that one moves the upper, and the other the lower jaw; but this is now known to be chimerical, the lower jaw being equally moved by both.

bu′lly. (Skinner derives this word from *burly,* as a corruption in the pronunciation; which is very probably right; or from *bulky,* or *bull-eyed;* which are less probable. May it not come from *bull,* the pope's letter, implying the insolence of those who came invested with authority from the papal court?) A noisy, blustering, quarrelling fellow: it is generally taken for a man that has only the appearance of courage.

bu′tterfly. A beautiful insect, so named because it first appears at the beginning of the season for butter.

chi′cken. (3) A term for a young girl.

chiru′rgeon. One that cures ailments, not by internal medicines, but outward applications. It is now generally pronounced, and by many written, *surgeon.*

cough. A convulsion of the lungs, vellicated by some sharp serosity. It is pronounced *coff.*

cu′ckoo. (1) A bird which appears in the spring; and is said to suck the eggs of other birds, and lay her own to be hatched in their place; from which practice, it was usual to alarm a husband at the approach of an adulterer by calling *cuckoo,* which, by mistake, was in time applied to the husband. This bird is remarkable for the uniformity of his note, from which his name in most tongues seems to have been formed.

to cu′rtail. (*curto,* Latin. It was anciently written *curtal,* which perhaps is more proper; but dogs that had their tails cut, being called *curtal* dogs, the word was vulgarly conceived to mean originally *to cut the tail,* and was in time written according to that notion.) (1) To cut off; to cut short; to shorten.

dedica′tion. (2) A servile address to a patron.

den. (1) A cavern or hollow running horizontally, or with a small obliquity, under ground; distinct from a hole, which runs down perpendicularly.

dull. (8) Not exhilarating; not delightful; as, *to make dictionaries is* dull *work.*

e′ssay. (2) A loose sally of the mind; an irregular indigested piece; not a regular and orderly composition.

exci′se.[1] A hateful tax levied upon commodities, and adjudged not by the common judges of property, but wretches hired by those to whom excise is paid.

fa′vorite. (2) One chosen as a companion by his superior; a mean wretch whose whole business is by any means to please.

fun. (A low cant word.) Sport; high merriment; frolicksome delight.

ga′mbler. (A cant word, I suppose, for *game,* or *gamester.*) A knave whose practice it is to invite the unwary to game and cheat them.

to gi′ggle. To laugh idly; to titter; to grin with merry levity. It is retained in Scotland.

goat. A ruminant animal that seems a middle species between deer and sheep.

gob. A small quantity. A low word.

gra′vy. The serous juice that runs from flesh not much dried by the fire.

gru′bstreet. Originally the name of a street in Moorfields in London, much inhabited by writers of small histories, dictionaries, and temporary poems; whence any mean production is called *grubstreet.*

to hiss. To utter a noise like that of a serpent and some other animals. It is remarkable, that this word cannot be pronounced without making the noise which it signifies.

itch. (1) A cutaneous disease extremely contagious, which overspreads the body with small pustules filled with a thin serum, and raised as microscopes have discovered by a small animal. It is cured by sulphur.

lexico′grapher. A writer of dictionaries; a harmless drudge, that busies himself in tracing the original, and detailing the signification of words.

lunch, lu′ncheon. As much food as one's hand can hold.

ne′twork. Any thing reticulated or decussated, at equal distances, with interstices between the intersections.

oats. A grain, which in England is generally given to horses, but in Scotland supports the people.

pa′rasite. One that frequents rich tables, and earns his welcome by flattery.

pa′stern.[2] (1) The knee of an horse.

pa′tron. (1) One who countenances, supports, or protects. Commonly a wretch who supports with insolence, and is paid with flattery.

pe′nsion. An allowance made to any one without an equivalent. In England it is generally understood to mean pay given to a state hireling for treason to his country.

pe′nsioner. (2) A slave of state hired by a stipend to obey his master.

sa′tire. A poem in which wickedness or folly is censured. Proper *satire* is distinguished, by the generality of the reflections, from a *lampoon* which is aimed against a particular person; but they are too frequently confounded.

shre′wmouse. A mouse of which the bite is generally supposed venomous, and to which vulgar tradition assigns such malignity, that she is said to lame the foot over which she runs. I am informed that all these reports are calumnious, and that her feet and teeth are equally harmless with those of any other little mouse. Our ancestors however looked on her with such terror, that they are supposed to have given her name to a scolding woman, whom for her venom they call a *shrew.*

so′nnet. (1) A short poem consisting of fourteen lines, of which the rhymes are adjusted by a particular rule. It is not very suitable to the English language, and has not been used by any man of eminence since Milton.

To′ry. (A cant term, derived, I suppose, from an Irish word signifying a savage.) One who adheres to the ancient constitution of the state, and the apostolical hierarchy of the Church of England, opposed to a Whig.[3]

Whig. (2) The name of a faction.

wi′tticism. A mean attempt at wit.

to worm. (2) To deprive a dog of something, nobody knows what, under his tongue, which is said to prevent him, nobody knows why, from running mad.

1755

---

1. *excise.* Johnson's father had had trouble with the commissioners of excise, in the conduct of his business as a bookseller and maker of parchment.
2. *pastern.* In fact, part of the foot of a horse. When a lady asked Johnson how he came to define the word in this way, he answered, "Ignorance, Madam, pure ignorance." But he didn't bother to correct his definition until eighteen years later.
3. *Whig.* Johnson himself was a Tory.

When Johnson, in 1746, first proposed the idea of compiling a dictionary, he discussed the project with Lord Chesterfield, one of the most cultivated noblemen of the age and a man with some scholarly knowledge of language and literature. Chesterfield expressed interest, and in accordance with the custom of literary patronage, gave Johnson a gift of £10. Johnson then addressed to him a detailed *Plan of a Dictionary,* in which Chesterfield is referred to as the patron of the project. Chesterfield read and approved the document before it was published, and apparently promised Johnson his continued assistance and financial support. This, however, never materialized. When the *Dictionary* finally appeared in 1755, Chesterfield expressed the desire to be regarded as its patron. This is the letter Johnson wrote him.

Johnson's Letter to Chesterfield

To the Right Honorable
the Earl of Chesterfield

February 7, 1755.

My Lord,

I have lately been informed by the proprietor of *The World,*[1] that two papers, in which my *Dictionary* is recommended to the public, were written by your Lordship. To be so distinguished is an honor which, being very little accustomed to favors from the great, I know not well how to receive, or in what terms to acknowledge.

When, upon some slight encouragement, I first visited your Lordship, I was overpowered, like the rest of mankind, by the enchantment of your address; and could not forbear to wish that I might boast myself *"Le vainqueur du vainqueur de la terre,"*[2] that I might obtain that regard for which I saw the world contending; but I found my attendance so little encouraged, that neither pride nor modesty would suffer me to continue it. When I had once addressed your Lordship in public, I had exhausted all the art of pleasing which a retired and uncourtly scholar can possess. I had done all that I could; and no man is well pleased to have his all neglected, be it ever so little.

Seven years, my Lord, have now passed, since I waited in your outward rooms, or was repulsed from your door; during which time I have been pushing on my work through difficulties, of which it is useless to complain, and have

Detail from a portrait of Chesterfield painted by an unknown artist around 1742.

brought it, at last, to the verge of publication, without one act of assistance, one word of encouragement, or one smile of favor. Such treatment I did not expect, for I never had a patron before.

The shepherd in Virgil grew at last acquainted with Love, and found him a native of the rocks.[3]

Is not a patron, my Lord, one who looks with unconcern on a man struggling for life in the water, and, when he has reached ground, encum-

---

1. The World, a newspaper run by a friend of Johnson's.
2. "Le vainquer . . . de la terre." "the conqueror of the conqueror of the world." [French]
3. The shepherd . . . rocks. Johnson is referring to a passage in the *Eclogues,* a collection of pastorals by the Latin poet Virgil (70–19 B.C.), that speaks of the cruelty of love.

bers him with help? The notice which you have been pleased to take of my labors, had it been early, had been kind; but it has been delayed till I am indifferent, and cannot enjoy it; till I am solitary, and cannot impart it; till I am known, and do not want it. I hope it is no very cynical asperity not to confess obligations where no benefit has been received, or to be unwilling that the public should consider me as owing that to a patron, which Providence has enabled me to do for myself.

Having carried on my work thus far with so little obligation to any favorer of learning, I shall not be disappointed though I should conclude it, if less be possible, with less; for I have been long wakened from that dream of hope, in which I once boasted myself with so much exultation.

My Lord,
Your Lordship's most humble,
Most obedient servant,

Sam. Johnson

Discussion

1. The excerpts from the *Dictionary* provide a cross-section of Johnson's personality as well as his work. Find examples that: **(a)** illustrate his **irony; (b)** show his learning; **(c)** display the beliefs of his age; **(d)** reveal his prejudices; **(e)** show his ability to enjoy a joke at his own expense; **(f)** demonstrate his thoroughness; **(g)** indicate the timelessness of some colloquial or slang words and expressions; **(h)** have undergone great change in meaning or acceptability since Johnson's day.

2. **(a)** Which sentences and expressions in Johnson's letter to Chesterfield are most effective in expressing Johnson's pain and anger at Chesterfield's behavior? **(b)** One critic has referred to Johnson's letter as "impertinent." Explain why you agree or disagree. **(c)** Compare the *Dictionary* definition of *patron* with that in the letter. Which do you prefer? Why?

This excerpt from *The Life of Milton* (one of fifty-two critical **biographies** included in Johnson's *Lives of the Poets*) concentrates on Milton the man rather than on his poetry. Milton's appearance, habits, learning, religion, politics, and character are thoroughly described by Johnson; although he did not care for Milton's religion or politics, he admired his poetry.

from *The Life of Milton*

Milton has the reputation of having been in his youth eminently beautiful, so as to have been called the Lady of his college. His hair, which was of a light brown, parted at the foretop, and hung down upon his shoulders, according to the picture which he has given of Adam. He was, however, not of the heroic stature, but rather below the middle size, according to Mr. Richardson, who mentions him as having narrowly escaped from being "short and thick." He was vigorous and active, and delighted in the exercise of the sword, in which he is related to have been eminently skillful. His weapon was, I believe, not the rapier, but the backsword, of which he recommends the use in his book on education.

His eyes are said never to have been bright; but, if he was a dexterous fencer, they must have been once quick.

His domestic habits, so far as they are known, were those of a severe student. He drank little strong drink of any kind, and fed without excess in quantity, and in his earlier years without deli-

Henry Fuseli, *Blind Milton Dictating to His Daughters,* Collection of The Art Institute of Chicago.

cacy of choice. In his youth he studied late at night; but afterwards changed his hours, and rested in bed from nine to four in the summer, and five in winter. The course of his day was best known after he was blind. When he first rose he heard a chapter in the Hebrew Bible, and then studied till twelve; then took some exercise for an hour; then dined; then played on the organ, and sung, or heard another sing; then studied to six; then entertained his visitors till eight; then supped, and, after a pipe of tobacco and a glass of water, went to bed.

So is his life described; but this even tenor appears attainable only in colleges. He that lives in the world will sometimes have the succession of his practice broken and confused. Visitors, of whom Milton is represented to have had great numbers, will come and stay unseasonably; business, of which every man has some, must be done when others will do it.

When he did not care to rise early he had something read to him by his bedside; perhaps at this time his daughters were employed. He composed much in the morning and dictated in the day, sitting obliquely in an elbowchair, with his leg thrown over the arm.

Fortune appears not to have had much of his care. In the civil wars he lent his personal estate to the Parliament, but when, after the contest was decided, he solicited repayment, he met not only with neglect, but "sharp rebuke"; and, having tired both himself and his friends, was given up to poverty and hopeless indignation, till he shewed how able he was to do greater service. He was then made Latin secretary, with two hundred pounds a year, and had a thousand pounds for his *Defence of the People*. His widow, who after his death retired to Namtwich in Cheshire, and died about 1729, is said to have reported that he lost two thousand pounds by entrusting it to a scrivener;[1] and that, in the general depredation upon the Church, he had grasped an estate of about sixty pounds a year belonging to Westminster Abbey, which, like other sharers of the plunder of rebellion, he was afterwards obliged to return. Two thousand pounds, which he had placed in the Excise Office, were also lost. There is yet no reason to believe that he was ever reduced to indigence: his wants being few were competently supplied. He sold his library before his death, and left his family fifteen hundred pounds; on which his widow laid hold, and only gave one hundred to each of his daughters.

His literature was unquestionably great. He read all the languages which are considered either as learned or polite: Hebrew, with its two dialects, Greek, Latin, Italian, French, and Spanish. In Latin his skill was such as places him in the first rank of writers and critics; and he appears to have cultivated Italian with uncommon diligence. The books in which his daughter, who used to read to him, represented him as most delighting, after Homer, which he could almost repeat, were Ovid's *Metamorphoses* and Euripides. His Euripides is, by Mr. Cradock's kindness, now in my hands: the margin is sometimes noted; but I have found nothing remarkable.

Of the English poets he set most value upon Spenser, Shakespeare, and Cowley. Spenser was apparently his favorite; Shakespeare he may easily be supposed to like, with every other skillful reader, but I should not have expected that Cowley, whose ideas of excellence were different from his own, would have had much of his approbation. His character of Dryden, who sometimes visited him, was that he was a good rhymist, but no poet.

His theological opinions are said to have been first Calvinistical, and afterwards, perhaps when he began to hate the Presbyterians, to have extended towards Arminianism.[2] In the mixed questions of theology and government he never thinks that he can recede far enough from popery or prelacy; but what Baudius says of Erasmus seems applicable to him: "magis habuit quod fugeret, quam quod sequeretur."[3] He had determined rather what to condemn than what to approve. He has not associated himself with any denomination of Protestants: we know rather what he was not, than what he was. He was not of the Church of Rome; he was not of the Church of England.

To be of no church is dangerous. Religion, of which the rewards are distant and which is animated only by Faith and Hope, will glide by degrees out of the mind unless it be invigorated and reimpressed by external ordinances, by stated calls to worship, and the salutary influence of example. Milton, who appears to have had full conviction of the truth of Christianity, and to have regarded the Holy Scriptures with the profoundest veneration, to have been untainted by any heretical peculiarity of opinion, and to have lived in a confirmed belief of the immediate and occasional agency of Providence, yet grew old without any visible worship. In the distribution of his hours, there was no hour of prayer, either solitary or with his household; omitting public prayers, he omitted all.

Of this omission the reason has been sought, upon a supposition which ought never to be made, that men live with their own approbation, and justify their conduct to themselves. Prayer certainly was not thought superfluous by him, who represents our first parents as praying acceptably in the state of innocence, and efficaciously after their fall. That he lived without prayer can hardly be affirmed; his studies and meditations were an habitual prayer. The neglect of it in his family was probably a fault for which he condemned himself, and which he intended to correct, but that death, as too often happens, intercepted his reformation.

---

1. **scrivener,** here probably a notary.
2. **Calvinistical, Presbyterians, Arminianism,** complex theological positions. Simply put, Johnson alludes to Milton's early belief in predestination, shared by Calvin and a sect of his followers, the Presbyterians, and to Milton's later doubts about the same subject, shared by the followers of Jacobus Arminius.
3. **"magis habuit . . . sequeretur."** "He was possessed more by what he fled than by what he followed." [Latin] Erasmus (1466?–1536) expressed his humanistic outlook in frequent attacks on the medieval pieties of his time.

His political notions were those of an acrimonious and surly republican, for which it is not known that he gave any better reason than that "a popular government was the most frugal; for the trappings of a monarchy would set up an ordinary commonwealth." It is surely very shallow policy, that supposes money to be the chief good; and even this without considering that the support and expense of a Court is for the most part only a particular kind of traffic, by which money is circulated without any national impoverishment.

Milton's republicanism was, I am afraid, founded in an envious hatred of greatness, and a sullen desire of independence; in petulance impatient of control, and pride disdainful of superiority. He hated monarchs in the state and prelates in the church; for he hated all whom he was required to obey. It is to be suspected that his predominant desire was to destroy rather than establish, and that he felt not so much the love of liberty as repugnance to authority.

It has been observed that they who most loudly clamor for liberty do not most liberally grant it. What we know of Milton's character in domestic relations is, that he was severe and arbitrary. His family consisted of women; and there appears in his books something like a Turkish contempt of females, as subordinate and inferior beings. That his own daughters might not break the ranks, he suffered them to be depressed by a mean and penurious education. He thought woman made only for obedience, and man only for rebellion.

1779

Discussion

1. Where in the first two paragraphs does Johnson give his own insights rather than descriptive details?

2. How does Johnson react to the traditional description of the way Milton spent his day? What does this reaction tell us about Johnson's own life?

3. What does Johnson criticize about Milton's religion? his politics?

4. Explain why you are or are not bothered by Johnson's stating of his own ideas and prejudices in writing of Milton's life.

One of Johnson's most admirable qualities was his generosity. After his wife's death, a number of people became either temporary or permanent members of his household. For over twenty years an obscure doctor, Robert Levet, who cared mostly for the poor, lived with him. When Levet suddenly died, Johnson, nearing his own death, wrote the following poem.

On the Death of Dr. Robert Levet

Condemned to Hope's delusive mine,
  As on we toil from day to day,
By sudden blasts, or slow decline,
  Our social comforts drop away.

5 Well tried through many a varying year,
  See Levet to the grave descend;
Officious,[1] innocent, sincere,
  Of every friendless name the friend.

---

1. *Officious,* charitable.

Yet still he fills affection's eye,
10   Obscurely wise and coarsely kind;
Nor, lettered Arrogance, deny
       Thy praise to merit unrefined.

When fainting Nature called for aid,
       And hovering Death prepared the blow,
15 His vigorous remedy displayed
       The power of art without the show.

In Misery's darkest cavern known,
       His useful care was ever nigh,
Where hopeless Anguish poured his groan,
20   And lonely Want retired to die.

No summons mocked by chill delay,
       No petty gain disdained by pride,
The modest wants of every day
       The toil of every day supplied.

25 His virtues walked their narrow round,
       Nor made a pause, nor left a void;
And sure the Eternal Master found
       The single talent well employed.[2]

The busy day, the peaceful night,
30   Unfelt, uncounted, glided by;
His frame was firm, his powers were bright,
       Though now his eightieth year was nigh.

Then with no throbbing fiery pain,
       No cold gradations of decay,
35 Death broke at once the vital chain,
       And freed his soul the nearest way.

1783

---

2. *the Eternal Master . . . well employed.* In Christ's parable of the talents, those with even few natural gifts are exhorted to regard their development as a divine trust. (Matt. 25:14–30)

Discussion

1. In praising Dr. Levet, Johnson implicitly criticizes another, different kind of doctor. Using details from the poem, describe Levet's opposite.

2. In what ways does the account of Levet's last days function as an ideal for the aged Johnson?

Vocabulary
Context, Dictionary

Some of the words that you have encountered in the selections from Addison, Steele, Pope, and Johnson are italicized in the following questions. Answer these questions on a separate sheet of paper. If you need help, consult the Glossary. Give reasons for your answers.

1. If someone introduced you to a *baronet,* would you be meeting a person in the beef business, a person with a title, or someone who worked in a tavern?

2. What sort of waterway might be dug across an *isthmus* for ships to go through—a lake, a canal, a pond?

3. If someone displays *asperity,* is he or she more likely to be smiling, frowning, or nodding?

4. Is someone who is *languid* likely to prefer playing tennis, sipping a cool drink, or painting a fence?

5. If you lived in a *garret* and had been out for the evening, would you have to go upstairs or downstairs to go to bed?

6. If you knew that a report about someone was *calumnious,* would you think less of that person?

7. Are the brave or the cowardly more likely to display *intrepidity*?

8. Is someone who is *pensive* more likely to be thinking about plans for the weekend, a relationship that's ended, or a favorite kind of pie?

9. Is an act of *depredation* if discovered likely to be punished or rewarded?

10. Is a *penurious* person more likely to be a miser, a gambler, or a spendthrift?

James Boswell 1740–1795

When Boswell and Johnson first met, on May 16, 1763, Boswell, though only twenty-three, had already published poems and pamphlets anonymously, and was an accepted member of Edinburgh's literary circles. The eldest son of Alexander Boswell, Lord of Auchinleck, he had studied law for seven years in Edinburgh and Glasgow, and was soon to spend more than two years on the European Continent, completing his education. He had already begun keeping his detailed journal, which was to become the source for several books besides his biography of Johnson.

By December, 1763, when Boswell left on his Continental tour, he and Johnson had become friends. During the time Boswell was away, he studied law for a time at Utrecht, in the Netherlands, then met and became friendly with both Voltaire and Rousseau, French writers and thinkers, and with General Paoli, the Corsican patriot. More than a celebrity-seeker, Boswell was convivial, witty, and intelligent.

When Boswell returned from his travels in February, 1766, he saw Johnson almost immediately, and their friendship grew rapidly. In the twenty-one years they knew each other, however, they did not spend all that much time together, for Boswell was pursuing a separate career in Scotland. He was admitted to the bar, married, and lived in Edinburgh, visiting London about once a year to see Johnson.

In the summer of 1773 Johnson traveled to Scotland and spent three months with Boswell. The two men undertook an extended tour of the remote and primitive Hebrides, about which both wrote books. Johnson's account, *A Journey to the Western Islands of Scotland,* appeared soon after the tour; Boswell's, titled *The Journal of a Tour to the Hebrides with Samuel Johnson, LL.D.,* was published in 1785, after Johnson's death. Because it recorded Johnson's conversations with and about others without their permission, it caused an immediate stir and evoked some criticism, for people were not accustomed to such candid biography. This criticism was to recur when Boswell's *The Life of Samuel Johnson, LL.D.* was published in 1791. Boswell and Johnson continued to meet regularly until Johnson's death; in fact, in July, 1784, Boswell accompanied Johnson on a trip to Oxford.

In later life Boswell made an unsuccessful attempt at entering Scottish politics. To facilitate publishing his biography of Johnson, he moved himself and his family to London in 1786. Three years later his wife died. Boswell spent his remaining years in poor health but managed to prepare three editions of the *Life* before his death in 1795. He was buried at Auchinleck, the family estate in Scotland.

With the discovery of some of Boswell's papers at Malahide Castle in Ireland and more of them in Scotland, his writing technique has been closely studied in recent years. Either late at night or early in the morning, he made notes of his activities. Later, when he had time, he converted these into full journal entries; these entries constituted his major source for the *Life.* He painstakingly verified every date and piece of information he gleaned, sending out questionnaires and letters, interviewing people who had known Johnson, and reading Johnson's correspondence. In selecting and presenting details, he worked with a keen dramatic sense, often building to a climax in which Johnson wittily capped whatever conversation was under way. Today we recognize Boswell for the creative artist he was; modern biography owes much to him.

Probably the best introduction to Boswell's technique and Johnson's wit is the record in the *Life* of the first meeting of the two:

"At last on Monday the 16th of May, when I was sitting in Mr. Davies's back-parlor, after having drunk tea with him and Mrs. Davies, Johnson unexpectedly came into the shop; and Mr. Davies having perceived him through the glass door in the room in which we were sitting, advancing toward us, he announced his awful approach to me. . . .

"Mr. Davies mentioned my name, and respectfully introduced me to him. I was much agitated, and recollecting his prejudices against the Scotch, of which I had heard much, I said to Davies, 'Don't tell where I come from.'

" 'From Scotland,' cried Davies roguishly.

'Mr Johnson, (said I) I do indeed come from Scotland, but I cannot help it.' . . . .This speech was somewhat unlucky, for with that quickness of wit for which he was so remarkable, he . . . retorted, 'That, Sir, I find is what a very great many of your countrymen cannot help.'

"This stroke stunned me a good deal; and when we had sat down, I felt myself not a little embarrassed, and apprehensive of what might come next. . . .

"I was highly pleased with the extraordinary vigor of his conversation, and regretted that I was drawn away from it by an engagement at another place."

Thus Boswell describes their first meeting. The technique here is similar to that of the rest of the *Life*—dramatic, carefully setting the scene for Johnson's utterances and wit.

from *The Life of Samuel Johnson, LL.D.*

On London

Talking of a London life, he said, "The happiness of London is not to be conceived but by those who have been in it. I will venture to say, there is more learning and science within the circumference of ten miles from where we now sit, than in all the rest of the kingdom."

BOSWELL. "The only disadvantage is the great distance at which people live from one another."

JOHNSON. "Yes, Sir; but that is occasioned by the largeness of it, which is the cause of all the other advantages."

BOSWELL. "Sometimes I have been in the humor of wishing to retire to a desert."

JOHNSON. "Sir, you have desert enough in Scotland."

I suggested a doubt, that if I were to reside in London, the exquisite zest with which I relished it in occasional visits might go off, and I might grow tired of it.

JOHNSON. "Why, Sir, you find no man, at all intellectual, who is willing to leave London. No, Sir, when a man is tired of London, he is tired of life; for there is in London all that life can afford."

On Eating

At supper this night he talked of good eating with uncommon satisfaction. "Some people (said he) have a foolish way of not minding, or pretending not to mind, what they eat. For my part, I mind my belly very studiously, and very carefully; for I look upon it that he who does not mind his belly will hardly mind anything else."

He now appeared to me *Jean Bull philosophe*,[1] and he was, for the moment, not only serious but vehement. Yet I have heard him, upon other occasions, talk with great contempt of people who were anxious to gratify their palates; and the 206th number of his *Rambler* is a master-

---

1. *Jean Bull philosophe,* John Bull the philosopher [French]. John Bull is the personification of the British nation, the typical Englishman.

ly essay against gulosity.[2] His practice, indeed, I must acknowledge, may be considered as casting the balance of his different opinions upon this subject, for I never knew any man who relished good eating more than he did. When at table, he was totally absorbed in the business of the moment; his looks seemed riveted to his plate; nor would he, unless when in very high company, say one word, or even pay the least attention to what was said by others, till he had satisfied his appetite, which was so fierce, and indulged with such intenseness, that while in the act of eating, the veins of his forehead swelled, and generally a strong perspiration was visible. To those whose sensations were delicate, this could not but be disgusting; and it was doubtless not very suitable to the character of a philosopher, who should be distinguished by self-command. But it must be owned that Johnson, though he could be rigidly *abstemious,* was not a *temperate* man either in eating or drinking. He could refrain, but he could not use moderately. He told me that he had fasted two days without inconvenience, and that he had never been hungry but once. They who beheld with wonder how much he ate upon all occasions when his dinner was to his taste could not easily conceive what he must have meant by hunger, and not only was he remarkable for the extraordinary quantity which he ate, but he was, or affected to be, a man of very nice discernment in the science of cookery. He used to descant critically on the dishes which had been at table where he had dined or supped, and to recollect minutely what he had liked.

He about the same time was so much displeased with the performances of a nobleman's French cook, that he exclaimed with vehemence, "I'd throw such a rascal into the river"; and he then proceeded to alarm a lady at whose house he was to sup, by the following manifesto of his skill: "I, Madam, who live at a variety of good tables, am a much better judge of cookery, than any person who has a very tolerable cook, but lives much at home; for his palate is gradually adapted to the taste of his cook; whereas, Madam, in trying by a wider range, I can more exquisitely judge."

When invited to dine, even with an intimate friend, he was not pleased if something better than a plain dinner was not prepared for him. I have heard him say on such an occasion, "This was a good dinner enough, to be sure: but it was not a dinner to *ask* a man to."

On the other hand, he was wont to express, with great glee, his satisfaction when he had been entertained quite to his mind. One day when he had dined with his neighbor and landlord, in Bolt-court, Mr. Allen, the printer, whose old housekeeper had studied his taste in everything, he pronounced this eulogy: "Sir, we could not have had a better dinner, had there been a *Synod*[3] *of Cooks.*"

On the Dictionary

That he was fully aware of the arduous nature of the undertaking, he acknowledges; and shows himself perfectly sensible of it in the conclusion of this "Plan"; but he had a noble consciousness of his own abilities, which enabled him to go on with undaunted spirit.

Dr. Adams found him one day busy at his Dictionary, when the following dialogue ensued.

ADAMS. "This is a great work, Sir. How are you to get all the etymologies?"

JOHNSON. "Why, Sir, here is a shelf with Junius, and Skinner,[4] and others; and there is a Welsh gentleman who has published a collection of Welsh proverbs, who will help me with the Welsh."

ADAMS. "But, Sir, how can you do this in three years?"

JOHNSON. "Sir, I have no doubt that I can do it in three years."

ADAMS. "But the French Academy,[5] which consists of forty members, took forty years to compile their Dictionary."

JOHNSON. "Sir, thus it is. This is the proportion. Let me see; forty times forty is sixteen hundred. As three to sixteen hundred, so is the proportion of an Englishman to a Frenchman."

With so much ease and pleasantry could he

---

2. gulosity, excessive appetite, greediness.
3. Synod, council, assembly, convention.
4. Junius and Skinner. The sources of many of Johnson's etymologies for the Germanic languages. Franciscus Junius (1589–1677) was a German-born philologist who lived in England and studied Teutonic languages. Stephen Skinner (1623–1667) was a physician and philologist.
5. French Academy, a society composed of forty outstanding men and women of letters; the chief purpose of the Academy is upholding correct usage of the French language.

talk of that prodigious labor which he had undertaken to execute.

On Books and Reading

JOHNSON. "Sir, I love the acquaintance of young people; because, in the first place, I don't like to think myself growing old. In the next place, young acquaintances must last longest, if they do last; and then, Sir, young men have more virtue than old men; they have more generous sentiments in every respect. I love the young dogs of this age: they have more wit and humor and knowledge of life than we had; but then the dogs are not so good scholars. Sir, in my early years I read very hard. It is a sad reflection, but a true one, that I knew almost as much at eighteen as I do now. My judgment, to be sure, was not so good; but I had all the facts. I remember very well, when I was at Oxford, an old gentleman said to me, 'Young man, ply your book diligently now, and acquire a stock of knowledge; for when years come upon you, you will find that poring upon books will be but an irksome task.' "

JOHNSON. "Idleness is a disease which must be combated; but I would not advise a rigid adherence to a particular plan of study. I myself have never persisted in any plan for two days together. A man ought to read just as inclination leads him: for what he reads as a task will do him little good. A young man should read five hours in a day, and so may acquire a great deal of knowledge."

On Pity

JOHNSON. "Pity is not natural to man. Children are always cruel. Savages are always cruel. Pity is acquired and improved by the cultivation of reason. We may have uneasy sensations for seeing a creature in distress, without pity; for we have not pity unless we wish to relieve them. When I am on my way to dine with a friend, and finding it late, have bid the coachman make haste, if I happen to attend when he whips his horses, I may feel unpleasantly that the animals are put to pain, but I do not wish him to desist. No, sir, I wish him to drive on."

Talking of our feeling for the distresses of others:

JOHNSON. "Why, Sir, there is much noise made about it, but it is greatly exaggerated. No, Sir, we have a certain degree of feeling to prompt us to do good; more than that, Providence does not intend. It would be misery to no purpose."

BOSWELL. "But suppose now, Sir, that one of your intimate friends were apprehended for an offense for which he might be hanged."

JOHNSON. "I should do what I could to bail him, and give him any other assistance; but if he were once fairly hanged, I should not suffer."

BOSWELL. "Would you eat your dinner that day, Sir?"

JOHNSON. "Yes, Sir; and eat it as if he were eating it with me. Why, there's Baretti[6] who is to be tried for his life tomorrow, friends have risen up for him on every side; yet if he should be hanged, none of them will eat a slice of plum pudding the less. Sir, that sympathetic feeling goes a very little way in depressing the mind."

The Social Order

I described to him an impudent fellow from Scotland, who affected to be a savage, and railed at all established systems.

JOHNSON. "There is nothing surprising in this, Sir. He wants to make himself conspicuous. He would tumble in a hogsty, as long as you looked at him and called to him to come out. But let him alone, never mind him, and he'll soon give it over."

I added that the same person maintained that there was no distinction between virtue and vice.

JOHNSON. "Why, Sir, if the fellow does not think as he speaks, he is lying; and I see not what honor he can propose to himself from having the character of a liar. But if he does really think that there is no distinction between virtue and vice, why, Sir, when he leaves our houses let us count our spoons."

He again insisted on the duty of maintaining subordination of rank.

---

6. *Baretti,* a teacher of Italian and friend of Johnson's, who was tried and acquitted for murder.

Oliver Goldsmith, James Boswell, and Samuel Johnson at the Mitre Tavern, London.
Colored engraving, nineteenth century.

JOHNSON. "Sir, I would no more deprive a nobleman of his respect, than of his money. I consider myself as acting a part in the great system of society, and I do to others as I would have them to do to me. I would behave to a nobleman as I should expect he would behave to me, were I a nobleman and he Sam Johnson. Sir, there is one Mrs. Macaulay in this town, a great republican. One day when I was at her house, I put on a very grave countenance, and said to her, 'Madam, I am now become a convert to your way of thinking. I am convinced that all mankind are upon an equal footing; and to give you an unquestionable proof, Madam, that I am in earnest, here is a very sensible, civil, well-behaved fellow-citizen, your footman; I desire that he may be allowed to sit down and dine with us.' I thus, Sir, showed her the absurdity of the leveling doctrine. She has never liked me since. Sir, your levelers wish to level *down* as far as themselves; but they cannot bear leveling *up* to themselves. They would all have some people under them; why not then have some people above them?"

On Slavery

After supper I accompanied him to his apartment, and at my request he dictated to me an argument in favor of the negro who was then claiming his liberty, in an action in the Court of Session in Scotland. He had always been very zealous against slavery in every form, in which I with all deference thought that he discovered "a zeal without knowledge." Upon one occasion, when in company with some very grave men at Oxford, his toast was, "Here's to the next insurrection of the negroes in the West Indies."

His violent prejudice against our West Indian and American settlers appeared whenever there was an opportunity. Towards the conclusion of his "Taxation no Tyranny," he says "how is it that we hear the loudest yelps for liberty among the drivers of negroes?"

On Johnson's Character

His figure was large and well-formed, and his countenance of the cast of an ancient statue; yet his appearance was rendered strange and somewhat uncouth, by convulsive cramps, by the scars of that distemper which it was once imagined the royal touch could cure,[7] and by a slov-

---

7. **distemper . . . cure.** Scrofula was called the "King's Evil" because of the belief that it could be cured by the monarch's touch. Johnson's mother took him to London when he was two-and-a-half to be touched by Queen Anne, of course to no avail.

enly mode of dress. He had the use only of one eye; yet so much does mind govern, and even supply the deficiency of organs, that his visual perceptions, as far as they extended, were uncommonly quick and accurate. So morbid was his temperament, that he never knew the natural joy of a free and vigorous use of his limbs; when he walked, it was like the struggling gait of one in fetters; when he rode, he had no command or direction of his horse, but was carried as if in a balloon. That with his constitution and habits of life he should have lived seventy-five years, is a proof that an inherent *vivida vis*,[8] is a powerful preservative of the human frame.

He was prone to superstition, but not to credulity. Though his imagination might incline him to a belief of the marvelous and the mysterious, his vigorous reason examined the evidence with jealousy. He was a sincere and zealous Christian, of high Church-of-England and monarchical principles, which he would not tamely suffer to be questioned; and had, perhaps, at an early period, narrowed his mind somewhat too much, both as to religion and politics. His being impressed with the danger of extreme latitude in either, though he was of a very independent spirit, occasioned his appearing somewhat unfavorable to the prevalence of that noble freedom of sentiment which is the best possession of man. Nor can it be denied, that he had many prejudices; which, however, frequently suggested many of his pointed sayings, that rather show a playfulness of fancy than any settled malignity. He was steady and inflexible in maintaining the obligations of religion and morality; both from a regard for the order of society, and from a veneration for the Great Source of all order: correct, nay stern in his taste; hard to please, and easily offended; impetuous and irritable in his temper, but of a most humane and benevolent heart, which showed itself not only in a most liberal charity, as far as his circumstances would allow, but in a thousand instances of active benevolence.

He was afflicted with a bodily disease, which made him often restless and fretful; and with a constitutional melancholy, the clouds of which darkened the brightness of his fancy, and gave a gloomy cast to his whole course of thinking: we, therefore, ought not to wonder at his sallies of impatience and passion at any time; especially when provoked by obtrusive ignorance, or presuming petulance; and allowance must be made for his uttering hasty and satirical sallies even against his best friends. And, surely, when it is considered, that, "amidst sickness and sorrow," he exerted his faculties in so many works for the benefit of mankind and particularly that he achieved the great and admirable Dictionary of our language, we must be astonished at his resolution.

The solemn text, "of him to whom much is given, much will be required," seems to have been ever present to his mind, in a rigorous sense, and to have made him dissatisfied with his labors and acts of goodness, however comparatively great; so that the unavoidable consciousness of his superiority was, in that respect, a cause of disquiet. He suffered so much from this, and from the gloom which perpetually haunted him, and made solitude frightful, that it may be said of him, "If in this life only he had hope, he was of all men most miserable."

He loved praise, when it was brought to him; but was too proud to seek for it. He was somewhat susceptible of flattery. As he was general and unconfined in his studies, he cannot be considered as master of any one particular science; but he had accumulated a vast and various collection of learning and knowledge, which was so arranged in his mind, as to be ever in readiness to be brought forth. But his superiority over other learned men consisted chiefly in what may be called the art of thinking, the art of using his mind; a certain continual power of seizing the useful substance of all that he knew, and exhibiting it in a clear and forcible manner; so that knowledge, which we often see to be no better than lumber in men of dull understanding, was, in him true, evident, and actual wisdom.

His moral precepts are practical; for they are drawn from an intimate acquaintance with human nature. His maxims carry conviction; for they are founded on the basis of common sense, and a very attentive and minute survey of real life. His mind was so full of imagery, that he might have been perpetually a poet; yet it is remarkable, that, however rich his prose is in this respect, his poetical pieces, in general, have not much of that

---

8. *vivida vis,* life force. [Latin]

splendor, but are rather distinguished by strong sentiment, and acute observation, conveyed in harmonious and energetic verse, particularly in heroic couplets. Though usually grave, and even awful in his deportment, he possessed uncommon and peculiar powers of wit and humor; he frequently indulged himself in colloquial pleasantry; and the heartiest merriment was often enjoyed in his company; with this great advantage, that, as it was entirely free from any poisonous tincture of vice or impiety, it was salutary to those who shared in it.

He had accustomed himself to such accuracy in his common conversation, that he at all times expressed his thoughts with great force, and an elegant choice of language, the effect of which was aided by his having a loud voice, and a slow deliberate utterance. In him were united a most logical head with a most fertile imagination, which gave him an extraordinary advantage in arguing: for he could reason close or wide, as he saw best for the moment. Exulting in his intellec-

tual strength and dexterity, he could, when he pleased, be the greatest sophist that ever contended in the lists of declamation; and, from a spirit of contradiction, and a delight in showing his powers, he would often maintain the wrong side with equal warmth and ingenuity: so that, when there was an audience, his real opinions could seldom be gathered from his talk; though, when he was in company with a single friend, he would discuss a subject with genuine fairness; but he was too conscientious to make error permanent and pernicious, by deliberately writing it; and, in all his numerous works, he earnestly inculcated what appeared to him to be the truth; his piety being constant, and the ruling principle of all his conduct.

Such was Samuel Johnson, a man whose talents, acquirements, and virtues were so extraordinary, that the more his character is considered the more he will be regarded by the present age, and by posterity, with admiration and reverence.   1791

Discussion

1. In *The Life of Samuel Johnson,* Boswell's professed objective is to write Johnson's biography so that "he will be seen as he really was," to "delineate him without reserve." **(a)** What are some of the unpleasant aspects of the picture of Johnson that Boswell presents? **(b)** What admirable characteristics do you find in Boswell's Johnson?

2. What role does Boswell play in these scenes? Why does he act this way?

3. Why does Boswell sometimes report Johnson's conversations as if they were a part of a play?

4. Why do you think people desired Johnson's company?

5. Does Boswell succeed in making Johnson come alive for you? Explain.

6. How do you think Johnson felt about Boswell?

Composition

1. The American critic J. Donald Adams has commented on Johnson's *Dictionary:* "Steeped in prejudice and tinged with mulishness as some of the definitions were, they are at least always the product of a sharp and honest mind. It is one of Johnson's great—and one of his most engaging—qualities, that he never indulged in double talk, that he never soft-soaped anyone. . . . Behind this book there is a man."

In a brief essay, discuss the relevance of this statement, not only to the *Dictionary,* but to the picture of Johnson that emerges from all the writings by or about him in this section.

2. Some of the ideas Johnson expounded to Boswell are still being talked about today. For example, on the importance of reading as discussed in "Of Books and Reading"; on our feeling for the distresses of others as presented in "On Pity"; on class structure as explained in "The Social Order"; on hypocrisy as Johnson reacts to it wherever he encounters it.

Select one of these and write a brief essay in which you discuss the extent to which our ideas are similar to or different from those of Johnson's day.

Thomas Gray 1716–1771

After studying at Eton, where he formed close friendships with Horace Walpole, son of the prime minister, and Richard West, Gray went on to Cambridge in 1734, leaving in 1738 without his degree to accompany Walpole on a tour of France and Italy. In 1741, after a disagreement, Gray returned to England alone. Later he and Walpole patched up their quarrel.

Returning to Cambridge in 1742, Gray completed his studies and then made the University his home for the rest of his life, devoting himself to scholarly pursuits. He became expert in the arts, especially literature, and in history; he was, in fact, appointed Professor of Modern History in 1768. Having mastered many regular academic fields, he turned his attention to more unusual ones: pre-Elizabethan poetry and Old Welsh and Norse literature, doing some translations into English. In his interest in these older literatures and in his enjoyment of unspoiled, natural landscapes, he was a forerunner of the Romantic Age.

Shortly after his break with Walpole, Gray in 1742 lost his other close friend, Richard West. Shocked and depressed by West's untimely death, Gray developed a strong streak of melancholy that stayed with him for the rest of his life. His "Sonnet on the Death of Richard West" (page 347) displays that melancholy.

In his later years, Gray lived almost as a recluse, leaving Cambridge only occasionally to vacation in the Lake District or in Scotland, where he could admire the rugged scenery, or to read and do research in the library of the newly opened British Museum in London. Because he kept reworking his poems in an attempt to perfect them, his poetic output was small. Only in his letters, now considered among the best in an age when letter-writing was an art, does Gray show his shy, affectionate nature and gentle humor. When he died in 1771, the churchyard of Stoke Poges, a village in Buckinghamshire, said to be the setting of the "Elegy Written in a Country Churchyard," became his own final resting place.

The "Elegy" presents in carefully selected language a scene of rural serenity; introduces a note of melancholy; goes on to reflect on death, the common man, and the ironies of human destiny; and concludes with the speaker's epitaph for himself.

*E*legy Written in a Country Churchyard

The curfew tolls the knell of parting day,
  The lowing herd wind slowly o'er the lea,
The plowman homeward plods his weary way,
  And leaves the world to darkness and to me.

5 Now fades the glimmering landscape on the
    sight,

And all the air a solemn stillness holds,
Save where the beetle wheels his droning flight,
  And drowsy tinklings lull the distant folds;

Save that from yonder ivy-mantled tower
10 The moping owl does to the moon complain
Of such as, wandering near her secret bower,

Molest her ancient solitary reign.

Beneath those rugged elms, that yew-tree's
    shade,
    Where heaves the turf in many a moldering
    heap,
15 Each in his narrow cell forever laid,
    The rude forefathers of the hamlet sleep.

The breezy call of incense-breathing morn,
    The swallow twittering from the straw-built
    shed,
The cock's shrill clarion, or the echoing horn,[1]
20   No more shall rouse them from their lowly
    bed.

For them no more the blazing hearth shall burn,
    Or busy housewife ply her evening care;
No children run to lisp their sire's return,
    Or climb his knees the envied kiss to share.

25 Oft did the harvest to their sickle yield;
    Their furrow oft the stubborn glebe has broke;
How jocund did they drive their team afield!
    How bowed the woods beneath their sturdy
    stroke!

Let not Ambition mock their useful toil,
30   Their homely joys, and destiny obscure;
Nor Grandeur hear with a disdainful smile
    The short and simple annals of the poor.

The boast of heraldry, the pomp of power,
    And all that beauty, all that wealth e'er gave,
35 Awaits alike the inevitable hour:
    The paths of glory lead but to the grave.

Nor you, ye proud, impute to these the fault,
    If Memory o'er their tomb no trophies raise,
Where through the long-drawn aisle and fretted
    vault
40   The pealing anthem swells the note of praise.

Can storied urn[2] or animated[3] bust
    Back to its mansion call the fleeting breath?
Can Honor's voice provoke the silent dust,
    Or Flattery soothe the dull cold ear of Death?

45 Perhaps in this neglected spot is laid
    Some heart once pregnant with celestial fire;

Hands that the rod of empire might have swayed,
    Or waked to ecstasy the living lyre.

But Knowledge to their eyes her ample page,
50   Rich with the spoils of time, did ne'er unroll;
Chill Penury repressed their noble rage,
    And froze the genial current of the soul.

Full many a gem of purest ray serene,
    The dark unfathomed caves of ocean bear;
55 Full many a flower is born to blush unseen,
    And waste its sweetness on the desert air.

Some village Hampden,[4] that with dauntless
    breast
    The little tyrant of his fields withstood;
Some mute inglorious Milton here may rest,
60   Some Cromwell,[5] guiltless of his country's
    blood.

The applause of listening senates to command,
    The threats of pain and ruin to despise,
To scatter plenty o'er a smiling land,
    And read their history in a nation's eyes,

65 Their lot forbade; nor circumscribed alone
    Their growing virtues, but their crimes
    confined;
Forbade to wade through slaughter to a throne,
    And shut the gates of mercy on mankind;

The struggling pangs of conscious truth to hide,
70   To quench the blushes of ingenuous shame,
Or heap the shrine of Luxury and Pride
    With incense kindled at the Muse's flame.

Far from the madding crowd's ignoble strife,
    Their sober wishes never learned to stray;
75 Along the cool sequestered vale of life
    They kept the noiseless tenor of their way.

---

1. *horn,* the huntsman's horn.
2. *storied urn,* an urn decorated with pictures that tell a story.
3. *animated,* lifelike.
4. *Hampden,* John Hampden (1594–1643), member of the Puritan or Roundhead party who spoke out against royal taxes.
5. *Cromwell.* Oliver Cromwell (1599–1658) was a Puritan military leader who became Lord Protector of the Commonwealth after the execution of Charles I.

Yet even these bones from insult to protect,
  Some frail memorial still erected nigh,
With uncouth[6] rhymes and shapeless sculpture
    decked,
80 Implores the passing tribute of a sigh.

Their name, their years, spelt by the unlettered
    Muse,
  The place of fame and elegy supply;
And many a holy text around she strews,
  That teach the rustic moralist to die.

Illustration for Gray's "Elegy" by R. Bentley, 1753.

85 For who, to dumb forgetfulness a prey,
  This pleasing anxious being e'er resigned,
Left the warm precincts of the cheerful day,
  Nor cast one longing lingering look behind?

On some fond breast the parting soul relies,
90 Some pious drops the closing eye requires;
Even from the tomb the voice of Nature cries,
  Even in our ashes live their wonted fires.

For thee,[7] who mindful of the unhonored dead
  Dost in these lines their artless tale relate;
95 If chance, by lonely contemplation led,
  Some kindred spirit shall inquire thy fate,

Haply some hoary-headed swain may say,
  "Oft have we seen him at the peep of dawn
Brushing with hasty steps the dews away
100 To meet the sun upon the upland lawn,

"There at the foot of yonder nodding beech
  That wreathes its old fantastic roots so high,
His listless length at noontide would he stretch,
  And pore upon the brook that babbles by.

105 "Hard by yon wood, now smiling as in scorn,
  Muttering his wayward fancies he would
    rove;
Now drooping, woeful-wan, like one forlorn,
  Or crazed with care, or crossed in hopeless
    love.

"One morn I missed him on the customed hill,
110 Along the heath, and near his favorite tree;
Another came; nor yet beside the rill,
  Nor up the lawn, nor at the wood was he;

"The next, with dirges due, in sad array,
  Slow through the church-way path we saw
    him borne.
115 Approach and read (for thou canst read) the lay,
  Graved on the stone beneath yon aged thorn."

The Epitaph

Here rests his head upon the lap of earth,
  A youth to Fortune and to Fame unknown;
Fair Science frowned not on his humble birth,
120 *And Melancholy marked him for her own.*

Large was his bounty, and his soul sincere;
  Heaven did a recompense as largely send;
He gave to Misery all he had, a tear;
  He gained from Heaven ('twas all he wished)
    a friend.

125 *No farther seek his merits to disclose,*
  Or draw his frailties from their dread abode,
(There they alike in trembling hope repose),
  The bosom of his Father and his God.
1742–50   1751

---

6. *uncouth,* strange, odd.
7. *thee,* Gray himself.

Sonnet on the Death of Richard West[1]

In vain to me the smiling mornings shine,
  And reddening Phoebus[2] lifts his golden fire;
The birds in vain their amorous descant join,
  Or cheerful fields resume their green attire;
5 These ears, alas! for other notes repine,
  A different object do these eyes require;
My lonely anguish melts no heart but mine,
  And in my breast the imperfect joys expire.
Yet morning smiles the busy race to cheer,
10   And new-born pleasure brings to happier
    men;

The fields to all their wonted tribute bear;
  To warm their little loves the birds complain:
I fruitless mourn to him that cannot hear,
  And weep the more, because I weep in vain.

1742   1775

---

1. Richard West (1716–1742), poet and friend of Gray's, who died at the age of thirty-six.
2. Phoebus (fē′bəs), an epithet of Apollo, the Greek god of the sun, meaning "bright." Here, the sun.

Discussion

1. (a) What words in the first stanza of the "Elegy" contribute to the air of melancholy that pervades the poem? **(b)** How do the second and third stanzas add to this melancholy?

2. The fourth stanza of the "Elegy" introduces the subject of the poem, the "rude forefathers of the hamlet." **(a)** What is the speaker's attitude toward them as contrasted with his attitude toward the world? **(b)** To what extent were the rude forefathers' poverty and lack of education a handicap? **(c)** To what extent were they a blessing?

3. According to the epitaph that ends the "Elegy," how satisfactory a life did the speaker live?

4. (a) In the first four lines of the "Sonnet on the Death of Richard West," three elements of nature that should give happiness are mentioned. What are they? **(b)** Each of these natural elements is mentioned at least once again—where, and to what effect?

Vocabulary
Pronunciation Key

Following each of the sentences below are the pronunciations of two different words. One of these pronunciations is for the word that belongs in the blank. Use the pronunciation key in the Glossary to choose the correct pronunciation. Copy the letter of the correct choice on a separate sheet of paper, after the sentence number. Then write the word as it would appear in each sentence. Be sure you understand the meaning of each word.

1. "That he was fully aware of the _____ nature of the undertaking, he acknowledges. . . ." **(a)** ə sep′tik; **(b)** är′jü əs.

2. "To quench the blushes of _____ shame . . ." **(a)** in jē′nyəs; **(b)** in jen′yü əs.

3. ". . . .but he was too conscientious to make error permanent and _____, by deliberately writing it. . . ." **(a)** pər nish′əs; **(b)** pər snik′ə tē.

4. "But it must be owned that Johnson, though he could be rigidly _____, was not a temperate man either in eating or drinking." **(a)** ab stē′mē əs; **(b)** ab′stə nəns.

5. "Heaven did a _____ as largely send." **(a)** rek′əm pens; **(b)** rek′ən dīt.

6. "He used to _____ critically on the dishes which had been at table where he had dined or supped. . . ." **(a)** dis′kount; **(b)** des kant′.

7. "Some heart once pregnant with _____ fire." **(a)** sə les′chəl; **(b)** sel′ə brāt.

8. "This is a great work, Sir. How are you to get all the _____?" **(a)** et′ə mol′ə jēz; **(b)** yü kə lip′ təs əs.

The Changing English Language

The desire for order and certainty that emerged amidst the turmoil of the seventeenth century was reflected in the development of the language. Particularly in the latter half of the century, the English people, reacting against the novelties and unregulated spontaneity which characterized Elizabethan expression, began to call for an ordered, rational language.

"On the Publishing Day of *The Dunciad*," attributed to George Dalziel, 1853. Writers hostile to Alexander Pope cannot prevent *The Dunciad* from appearing.

The Royal Society, founded in 1660 by a group of learned men and scientists, objected to the Elizabethan love of verbal gymnastics on the ground that it was unscientific, and demanded of its members instead "a close, naked, natural way of speaking; positive expressions, clear senses, a native easiness, bringing as near the mathematical plainness as they can."

Those caught in the surge toward greater simplicity and precision—among them Swift, Steele, Addison, Johnson, and Lord Chesterfield—tended to disparage what they called "cant" or "low speech." These arbiters of language realized, as did many of their time, that the English language was in a muddle that the disputes over grammar of the previous centuries had failed to solve: words still had widely variant meanings, spellings, and pronunciations, and the general instability of the language was a barrier to clear communication. In the mishandling of the language the educated and well-to-do seem to have been as guilty as any.

The urge to introduce order into the language is evident in hundreds of projects undertaken during the course of the century. Johnson's ponderous two-volume *Dictionary*, great achievement though it was, offered only a partial solution to the problems of standardizing the language, and before the century ended there were many other attempts. The efforts at standardization spilled over into literary texts. One mid-eighteenth-century editor announced that Shakespeare's works were an "unweeded Garden grown to Seed," and confidently set about the cultivation and pruning he thought necessary. Another overearnest reformer named Bentley tackled Milton's poetry, and got for his pains Pope's ridicule for being a scribbler "whose unwearied pains / Made Horace dull, and humbled Milton's strains." If there was widespread agreement that the English language needed polishing, there was little agreement about how it should be done, and the controversy continued throughout the century.

While neoclassicism did much to tone down the bizarre and freakish aspects of seventeenth-century speech, it did not, in spite of its insistence on rules and rigidity, stamp out the rich variety which makes English a vital instrument of communication. Although both Johnson and Swift objected to the use of such words as *humbug, prig, doodle, bamboozle, fib, bully, fop, banter, stingy, fun, prude,* they continued in use then as they do today, evidence of the fact that people, not grammar books or dictionaries, make and perpetuate language.

The  *ge of Reason*

Content Review

1. The love poetry that characterized the Renaissance is almost totally missing from the Age of Reason. What has replaced it? Why might this have happened?

2. This unit contains four poems dealing with the deaths of people the poets had known: Dryden's "To the Memory of Mr. Old-ham," Swift's "A Satirical Elegy on the Death of a Late Famous General," Johnson's "On the Death of Dr. Robert Levet," and Gray's "Son-net on the Death of Richard West." Compare these poems with regard to the poet's intent and how well he carries it out, the devices he uses, and the form of the poem (heroic cou-plets, sonnet, and so forth).

3. Many of the selections in this unit are bitingly satirical. Do you think any of them are unjustifiably so? Explain.

4. Because the Age of Reason stressed so-cial relationships among people, a number of the selections deal with manners—the way people should behave toward one another. Dis-cuss this with regard to Pope's *The Rape of the Lock,* Johnson's "Letter to Chesterfield," and appropriate parts of Boswell's *The Life of Samuel Johnson.*

5. Much of the focus of the Age of Reason was on life in London. Discuss the attitudes to-ward that city shown in Swift's "A Description of a City Shower," Pepys's *Diary,* and Bos-well's *The Life of Samuel Johnson.*

6. The Age of Reason also presented pic-tures of country life. Compare and contrast those given in Pope's "Epistle to Miss Blount," Addison's "Will Wimble," and Gray's "Elegy Written in a Country Churchyard."

7. Compare the attitude and technique of Johnson in his *Life of Milton* with those of Boswell in *The Life of Samuel Johnson.*

8. Both Dryden and Johnson wrote about authors. Compare the excerpt from Dryden's *Mac Flecknoe* with the excerpt from Johnson's *The Life of Milton.*

9. Discuss Gulliver and Alexander Selkirk as castaways with regard to how they came to be abandoned, the sort of life each led while a castaway, and the author's intent in writing the piece.

10. Writers of the Age of Reason frequently write about public issues. Discuss the applica-bility of this statement to works by Pepys, Swift, and Defoe (see below).

Concept Review: Interpretation of New Material

from A Journal of the Plague Year • *Daniel Defoe*

Daniel Defoe (1659–1731) was only a child during the Great Plague of London in 1665, and had no detailed recollection of the events he described in *A Journal of the Plague Year* (1722). The book was written and published in response to the widespread alarm about a new outbreak of the plague that had occurred in Eur-ope in 1721. Defoe did a great deal of research to make his account of the London plague of 1665 convincing to readers concerned about a possible new outbreak in England.

1

It pleased God that I was still spared, and very hearty and sound in health, but very impatient of being pent up within doors without air, as I had been for fourteen days or thereabouts, and I could not restrain myself, but I would go to carry a letter for my brother to the post-house. Then it was indeed that I observed a profound silence in the streets. When I came to the post-house, as I went to put in my letter, I saw a man stand in one corner of the yard and talking to another at a win-dow, and a third had opened a door belonging to the office. In the middle of the yard lay a small leather purse with two keys hanging at it, with money in it, but nobody would meddle with it. I asked how long it had lain there; the man at the window said it had lain almost an hour, but that they had not meddled with it, because they did not know but the person who dropped it might come back to look for it. I had no such need of money, nor was the sum so big that I had any inclination to meddle with it, or to get the money at the hazard it might be attended with; so I seemed to go away, when the man who had opened the door said he would take it up, but so that if the right owner came for it he should be sure to have it. So he went in and fetched a pail of water, and set it down hard by the purse, then went again and fetched some gunpowder, and cast a good deal of powder upon the purse, and then made a train from that which he had thrown loose upon the purse. The train reached about two yards. After this he goes in a third time and fetches out a pair of tongs red hot, and which he had prepared, I suppose, on purpose, and first setting fire to the train of powder, that singed the purse, and also smoked the air sufficiently. But he was not content with that, but he then takes up the purse with the tongs, holding it so long till the tongs burnt through the purse, and then he shook the money out into the pail of water, so he carried it in. The money, as I remember, was about thirteen shillings and some smooth groats and brass farthings.[1] . . .

2

Passing through Tokenhouse Yard, in Lothbury, of a sudden a casement[2] violently opened just over my head, and a woman gave three frightful screeches, and then cried, "Oh! death, death, death!" in a most inimitable[3] tone, and which struck me with horror and a chillness in my very blood. There was nobody to be seen in the whole street, neither did any other window open, for people had no curiosity now in any case, nor could anybody help one another, so I went on to pass into Bell Alley.

Just in Bell Alley, on the right hand of the passage, there was a more terrible cry than that, though it was not so directed out at the window; but the whole family was in terrible fright, and I could hear women and children run screaming

about the rooms like distracted, when a garret-window opened, and somebody from a window on the other side of the alley called and asked, "What is the matter?" upon which, from the first window it was answered, "O Lord, my old master has hanged himself!" The other asked again, "Is he quite dead?" and the first answered, "Ay, ay, quite dead; quite dead and cold!" This person was a merchant and a deputy alderman, and very rich. I care not to mention the name, though I knew his name too, but that would be an hardship to the family, which is now flourishing again.

But this is but one; it is scarce credible what dreadful cases happened in particular families every day. People in the rage of the distemper, or in the torment of their swellings, which was indeed intolerable, running out of their own government,[4] raving and distracted, and often-times laying violent hands upon themselves, throwing themselves out at their windows, shooting themselves, &c.; mothers murdering their own children in their lunacy, some dying of mere grief as a passion, some of mere fright and surprise without

---

1. *groats, farthings,* coins worth a small sum.
2. *casement,* window that opens on hinges.
3. *inimitable,* impossible to imitate.
4. *government,* control.

Fleeing from the Plague, 1665.

any infection at all, others frighted into idiotism and foolish distractions, some into despair and lunacy, others into melancholy madness. . . .

3

. . . here I must observe also that the plague, as I suppose all distempers do, operated in a different manner on differing constitutions;[5] some were immediately overwhelmed with it, and it came to violent fevers, vomitings, insufferable headaches, pains in the back, and so up to ravings and ragings with those pains; others with swellings and tumors in the neck and groin, or armpits, which till they could be broke put them into insufferable agonies and torment; while others, as I have observed, were silently infected, the fever preying upon their spirits insensibly, and they seeing little of it till they fell into swooning, and faintings, and death without pain.

I am not physician enough to enter into the particular reasons and manner of these differing effects of one and the same distemper. . . . I am only relating what I know, or have heard, or believe of the particular cases, and what fell within the compass of my view; . . . but this may be added too, that though the former sort of those cases, namely, those openly visited, were the

worst for themselves as to pain . . . yet the latter had the worst state of the disease; for in the former they frequently recovered, especially if the swellings broke, but the latter was inevitable death; no cure, no help could be possible, nothing could follow but death. . . .

4

. . . the shutting up of houses, so as to confine those that were well with those that were sick, had very great inconveniences in it, and some that were very tragical. . . . But it was authorized by a law, it had the public good in view as the end chiefly aimed at, and all the private injuries that were done by the putting it in execution must be put to the account of the public benefit.

It is doubtful to this day whether, in the whole, it contributed anything to the stop of the infection. . . . Certain it is that if all the infected persons were effectually shut in, no sound person could have been infected by them, because they could not have come near them. But the case was this, and I shall only touch it here, namely, that the infection was propagated insensibly,[6] and by

5. ***constitutions***, physical makeups, natures.
6. ***propagated insensibly***, reproduced, multiplied, or passed on unknowingly.

such persons as were not visibly infected, who neither knew whom they infected or who they were infected by. . . .

5

. . . the common people, who, ignorant and stupid in their reflections, as they were brutishly wicked and thoughtless before, were now led by their fright to extremes of folly; and, as I have said before that they ran to conjurers[7] and witches, and all sorts of deceivers, to know what should become of them (who fed their fears, and kept them always alarmed and awake on purpose to delude them and pick their pockets), so they were as mad upon their running after quacks and mountebanks,[8] and every practising old woman, for medicines and remedies; storing themselves with such multitudes of pills, potions, and preservatives, as they were called, that they not only spent their money, but even poisoned themselves beforehand, for fear of the poison of the infection, and prepared their bodies for the plague, instead of preserving them against it. On the other hand, it is incredible, and scarce to be imagined, how the posts of houses and corners of streets were plastered over with doctors' bills and papers of ignorant fellows, quacking and tampering in physic, and inviting the people to come to them for remedies, which was generally set off with such flourishes as these, viz.:[9] "Infallible preventive pills against the plague." "Never-failing preservatives against the infection." "Sovereign cordials against the corruption of the air." "Exact regulations for the conduct of the body in case of an infection." "Anti-pestilential pills." "Incomparable drink against the plague, never found out before." "An universal remedy for the plague." "The only true plague-water." "The royal antidote against all kinds of infection"; and such a number more that I cannot reckon up; and if I could, would fill a book of themselves to set them down. . . .

6

It is here . . . to be observed that after the funerals became so many that people could not toll the bell, mourn or weep, or wear black for one another, as they did before; no, nor so much as make coffins for those that died; so after a while the fury of the infection appeared to be so in-creased that, in short, they shut up no houses at all. It seemed enough that all the remedies of that kind had been used till they were found fruitless, and that the plague spread itself with an irresistible fury; so that as the fire the succeeding year spread itself, and burned with such violence that the citizens, in despair, gave over their endeavors to extinguish it, so in the plague it came at last to such violence that people sat still looking at one another, and seemed quite abandoned to despair.

7

In the middle of their distress, when the condition of the city of London was so truly calamitous,[10] just then it pleased God, as it were, by His immediate hand to disarm this enemy; the poison was taken out of the sting. It was wonderful; even the physicians themselves were surprised at it. Wherever they visited they found their patients better; either they had sweated kindly, or the tumors were broke, or the carbuncles went down, and the inflammations round them changed color, or the fever was gone, or the violent headache was assuaged, or some good symptom was in the case; so that in a few days everybody was recovering, whole families that were infected and down, that had ministers praying with them, and expected death every hour, were revived and healed, and none died at all out of them.

Nor was this by any new medicine found out, or new method of cure discovered, or by any experience in the operation which the physicians or surgeons attained to; but it was evidently from the secret invisible hand of Him that had at first sent this disease as a judgment upon us; and let the atheistic part of mankind call my saying what they please, it is no enthusiasm; it was acknowledged at that time by all mankind.

1722

---

7. *conjurers*, tricksters, magicians.
8. *mountebanks*, person who sells useless medicines in public.
9. *viz.*, namely.
10. *calamitous*, disastrous.

On a separate sheet of paper, write your answers to the following questions. Do not write in your book.

1. In section 1, the man uses gunpowder and tongs to get the money in the purse (a) in order

to avoid the plague; **(b)** because it is locked; **(c)** to injure the rightful owner; **(d)** to alarm neighborhood residents.

2. The main cause of the violence described in the last paragraph of section 2 is **(a)** greed; **(b)** physical suffering; **(c)** anger; **(d)** folly.

3. When the narrator uses the phrase "the latter" in the second paragraph of section 3, he is referring to those **(a)** openly afflicted with the plague; **(b)** who did not receive medical care; **(c)** silently infected; **(d)** who escaped the plague.

4. In section 4, the narrator says that shutting up houses **(a)** had no effect on the spread of the plague; **(b)** greatly reduced the spread of plague; **(c)** increased the spread of plague; **(d)** stabilized the spread of the plague.

5. In section 5, taking "pills, potions, and preservatives" **(a)** helped to preserve people's lives; **(b)** was avoided by most people; **(c)** is disapproved of by the narrator; **(d)** weakened people's health.

6. The list at the end of section 5 provides examples of **(a)** effective medicines; **(b)** book titles; **(c)** fake remedies; **(d)** last words of the dying.

7. The fire described by Pepys took place **(a)** the year before the plague; **(b)** during the plague; **(c)** the year after the plague; **(d)** in a different century.

8. In section 6, the narrator says that the reaction to the fire and plague were similar in that people **(a)** despaired; **(b)** helped one another; **(c)** fled; **(d)** plundered.

9. In the last part of the first sentence of section 7, the plague is figuratively compared to a **(a)** housebreaker; **(b)** poisonous creature; **(c)** murderer; **(d)** traitor.

10. The dominant tone of this passage is **(a)** fearful; **(b)** angry; **(c)** factual; **(d)** puzzled.

Composition Review

You may choose any *one* of the following assignments. Assume that you are writing for your classmates.

1. Think about the appropriateness of the label "The Age of Reason" to describe the selections you have read in this unit. What seems meant by reason—rationality, common sense, reasonableness, experience, skepticism? Is rationality the ultimate value for any or all of these writers? Are there any values held to be equal, or superior, to reason by the writers of the period?

In an essay, discuss the label "The Age of Reason" in terms of the selections you have read in this unit. Cite examples to support your argument.

2. Literature underwent changes in form, content, and purpose from the beginning of the Age of Reason to its end. Consider Dryden, who comes first in the unit, and Gray, who comes last.

Discuss some of these changes, especially as they are reflected in Dryden's "To the Memory of Mr. Oldham" and Gray's "Sonnet on the Death of Richard West."

3. *Verisimilitude* means the accumulation of realistic details to make a work of fiction appear to be true. Sometimes this device is used to make the fantastic appear possible, or to make the possible seem actual. Sir Walter Scott observed that "Swift possessed the art of verisimilitude."

Compare Defoe's use of verisimilitude in *A Journal of the Plague Year* with Swift's use of it in *Gulliver's Travels,* with particular attention to the different purposes of the authors and the different kinds of books they were writing.

4. According to Addison and Steele, the objectives of their literary periodicals were "to enliven morality with wit, and to temper wit with morality."

In a short paper, discuss how any two or three selections from this unit (including, if you wish, those by Addison and Steele) carry out these objectives.

5. Two main kinds of satire are often identified: Horatian (after the Roman poet Horace), which tends to be gentle and humorous, and Juvenalian (after the Roman poet Juvenal), which tends to be harsh and biting.

Write an essay in which you discuss some examples of satire from this unit in terms of the above distinction. Be specific.

Detail of *A Morning View of Coalbrookdale* by William Williams, painted in 1777.

French Revolution

• Death of Louis XVI

• Napoleonic Wars begin

Burns: *Poems* •

• Blake: *Songs of Experience*

Blake: *Songs of Innocence* •

Wordsworth and Coleridge: *Lyrical Ballads* •

Blake: •
Jerusalem

• Beckford: Vathek

• Radcliffe:
The Mysteries of Udolpho

1780   **1790**   **1800**

The *Romantics*

Coleridge: *Biographia Literaria* •

• Scott: *Ivanhoe*

Byron: *Don Juan* •

• Byron: *Childe Harold's Pilgrimage*

• Shelley: *Prometheus Unbound*

elson's naval victory
Trafalgar

• Keats: *The Eve of St. Agnes*

• Battle of Waterloo

Keats: *Endymion* •

• Lamb: *Essays of Elia*

Peterloo Massacre •

Catholic Emancipation Act •

• Austen: *Pride and Prejudice*

1810   **1820**   **1830**

Background: The Romantics 1780–1830

As its name suggests, the Romantic Age brought a more daring, individual, and imaginative approach to both literature and life. In the late eighteenth and early nineteenth centuries, many of the most important English writers turned away from the values and ideas characteristic of the Age of Reason. The individual, rather than society, was at the center of the Romantic vision. The Romantic writers tended to be optimists who believed in the possibility of progress and social and human reform. As champions of democratic ideals, they sharply attacked all forms of tyranny and the spreading evils of industrialism, such as urban blight, a polluted environment, and the alienation of people from nature and one another.

The Romantic writers tended to believe that the eighteenth-century dedication to common sense and experience, reasonableness, and tradition, though in many ways admirable, had resulted in a limitation of vision, an inability to transcend the hard facts of the real world to glimpse an ideal one.

An Age of Revolution

The impact of the French Revolution in 1789 upon the writers of the age cannot be overemphasized. While impressed by the efforts of the American colonists to wrest power from their British rulers, the English felt personally removed from such events as Valley Forge. France, however, was only a brief passage across the English Channel. For a time, almost every important British writer responded warmly to the cry of the French for "Liberty, Equality, Fraternity." For ex-

ample, government restrictions that barred his return to France in 1793 were all that kept William Wordsworth from taking up residence in that country and siding with the revolutionaries.

Whereas the writers of the Age of Reason tended to regard evil as a basic part of human nature, the Romantic writers generally saw humanity as naturally good, but corrupted by society and its institutions of religion, education, and government. Thus, the French Revolution gave life and breath to the dreams of some Romantic writers for a society in which there would be liberty and equality for all. It also contributed later to a sense of disillusionment following the Reign of Terror in France, during which the oppressed classes became as violent and corrupt as their former rulers, thereby paving the way for Napoleon's rise to power.

One of the most significant aspects of nineteenth-century English life was the slow but steady application of the principles of democracy. England emerged from the eighteenth century a parliamentary state in which the monarchy was largely a figurehead. The English Parliament was far from a truly representative body, however, until, after years of popular agitation, Parliament finally passed the First Reform Bill of 1832, which liberalized representation in Parliament.

The Industrial Revolution took place in England from 1750–1850. During this period England changed from an agricultural to an industrial society and from home manufacturing to factory production. The Industrial Revolution helped make England prosperous and powerful, but it involved exploitation of the workers, who lived under deplorable conditions.

As the Industrial Revolution gathered force, towns became cities; more and more villagers, forced by economic necessity to seek work in the growing factories, huddled together in filthy slums. Workers—men, women, and children—labored from sunrise to sunset for meager wages. A child able to pull a cart in the suffocating coal mines or to sweep a floor in the textile factories was considered old enough to work by many employers and some parents. For the children of the poor, religious training, medical care, and education were practically nonexistent.

Gradually English society began to awaken to its obligations to the miserable and helpless. Through the efforts of reformers, the church and government assumed their responsibilities. Sunday schools were organized; hospitals were built; movements were begun to reform the prisons and regulate the conditions of child labor.

The effects of revolution abroad, the demand for a more democratic government, and a growing awareness of social injustice at home were all reflected in a new spirit that over a period of years affected practically every aspect of English life.

A New Spirit in Life and Literature

The Romantic Age in England was part of a movement that affected all the countries of Western Europe. The forms of romanticism were so many and varied, in some instances embracing contradictory values, that it is difficult to speak of the movement as a whole. It tended to align itself with the humanitarian spirit of the democratic revolutionaries; but romantics were not always democrats, and democrats were not always revolutionaries. Perhaps the safest thing to say is that romanticism represented an attempt to rediscover the mystery and wonder of the world, an attempt to go beyond ordinary reality into the deeper, less obvious, and more elusive levels of individual human existence.

The emergence and spread of the romantic spirit in England gradually became apparent in all aspects of life—fashions, manners, and morals. Simplicity and naturalness rather than artificiality and excess characterized this new spirit and lifestyle. In literature, the emergence of the Romantic spirit was particularly evident in the writers' choice of subject matter.

For most of the Romantic poets, nature was the principal source of inspiration, spiritual truth, and enlightenment. Nature, according to Samuel Taylor Coleridge in "Frost at Midnight," should be seen as embodying the "eternal language" whereby God teaches and molds the human spirit.

Poets of the Romantic Age focused on the ordinary person and common life in order to affirm the worth and dignity of all human beings, and to repudiate the evils of a class system that artificially designated a few select people as more important than others because of wealth, position, or name.

In 1765 Bishop Thomas Percy published *Reliques of Ancient English Poetry,* a collection of ballads dating back to late medieval times (see page 66). Several authors, including Thomas Gray, made translations of old Celtic and Scandinavian legends. Other writers produced Gothic novels or romances—that is, stories laid in medieval times and filled with ruined castles, mysterious doors, supernaturalism of all kinds. English people of the Romantic Age turned eagerly to all these writings about medieval times, especially to the old ballads. People longed for literature that dealt with the elemental themes of courage and valor, hatred and revenge, love and death.

Writers of the Age of Reason exposed the follies of society with satire, a sophisticated form of attack; the youthful Romantics, inspired by the revolutions in America and France and incensed by inhumane working conditions, poverty, and government corruption, spoke out in a voice of anger and outrage. In "London, 1802," Wordsworth calls England "a fen / of stagnant waters" that has lost "manners, virtue, freedom, power." Percy Shelley, in "England in 1819," characterizes the rulers as leeches "who neither see, nor feel, nor know," but who drink the life's blood of a poor and starving populace. Shelley, like many of the other Romantics, was strongly influenced by William Godwin's *Political Justice* (1793), a work that criticized the existing society and outlined a new ethic and Utopian ideal. Godwin's wife, Mary Wollstonecraft, Mary Shelley's mother, produced an outspoken feminist manifesto, *A Vindication of the Rights of Woman* (1792), and spent her short, intense life living by the ideals she advocated.

Salisbury Cathedral by John Constable, 1823.

Two Generations of Poets

In the period from 1786 to 1830, seven major poets emerged who permanently affected the nature of English language and literature. Burns, Blake, Wordsworth, and Coleridge may be regarded as the first generation of Romantic poets, writing most of their major works from 1786 to 1805. Byron, Shelley, and Keats are the second generation, producing their major works between 1810 to 1824.

Though commonly grouped with writers of the eighteenth century because of the time in which they lived and wrote, Robert Burns and William Blake were clearly forerunners of the Romantic movement in subject matter, themes, and style. Both were gifted poets, unaffiliated with any literary group, who poured out their lyrics while living lives of hard labor and obscurity.

The publication of *Poems, Chiefly in the Scottish Dialect* (1786) by Robert Burns is a landmark in English literature. Published when he was only twenty-seven, the book made Burns famous and gave the world a memorable collection of poems. His lyrics on love, nature, patriotism, the nobility of the common man, and the spontaneous emotions of the heart, are expressed in native dialect; his treatment of these themes has made him one of the best-loved poets.

As an old man, William Blake, one of the most original minds of his time, had a circle of young admirers; but during most of his life, he lived in relative obscurity in a working-class neighborhood of London. Central to Blake's vision is the concept of "contraries," the necessity of experiencing opposites, such as pain and joy, success and failure, prudence and excess, in order to understand life. Consequently, Blake produced *Songs of Innocence* and *Songs of Experience,* contrasting poems that need to be paired to yield their deepest meaning. Though Blake's talent and achievement were not widely recognized in his time, today his reputation is firmly established.

In 1798, with the publication of *Lyrical Ballads,* William Wordsworth and Samuel Taylor Coleridge gave official birth to the Romantic Age in literature, setting forth a formula for a new kind of poetry and presenting twenty-three poems that demonstrated the formula in use. The second edition of *Lyrical Ballads,* published in 1800, contained a preface in which Wordsworth stated the poetic principles that he and Coleridge believed in: first, that ordinary life is the best subject for poetry because the feelings of simple people are sincere and natural; second, that the everyday language of these people best conveys their feelings and is therefore best suited to poetry; third, that the expression of feeling is more important in poetry than the development of an action, or story; and finally, that "poetry is the spontaneous overflow of powerful feelings," and "takes its origin from emotion recollected in tranquillity." While these principles were often challenged by other writers of Wordsworth's day, they served as a formal declaration of a new spirit in English literature and became a turning point in the history of English poetry.

The important figures of the second generation of Romantic poets were Lord Byron, Percy Bysshe Shelley, and John Keats. Though highly different in personality and artistic temperament, they were similarly intense, precocious, and tragically short-lived. Though a generation older, Wordsworth and Coleridge outlived all three poets. While initially a major source of inspiration for their poetic theory and practice, Wordsworth and Coleridge turned politically conservative as they grew older, leading the young poets, especially Byron and Shelley, to denounce their one-time idols as traitors to their former principles.

During his brief lifetime, George Gordon, Lord Byron, was the most popular poet abroad as well as at home and also the most scandalous. English society eventually turned against him and he exiled himself to Europe in 1816. During the next eight years he traveled and lived in southern Europe. Reckless, bitter, and in constant revolt against society, he succeeded in producing his best work, including his masterpiece *Don Juan,* a satirical narrative that sums up his reflections on life and human nature. Though Byron always declared himself a disciple of Pope and is today regarded as the greatest satirical poet since Pope, he (more than any other poet of the age) epitomized Romanticism by his unswerving dedication to the cause of freedom and liberty and by the Romantic image he imprinted on the public imagination.

Like Byron, Shelley was rebellious, scandalous, and charismatic. The keynote of Shelley's character was his revolt against tyrannical influences, his belief that the church, state, and commerce, as organized and conducted in his time, led to superstition, selfishness, and corruption. As expressed in the preface to one of his longer poems, *Prometheus Unbound,* Shelley always had "a passion for reforming the world." But it is as a lyric poet that he is remembered.

Possibly the most famous line John Keats ever wrote was, "Beauty is truth, truth beauty," in his poem "Ode on a Grecian Urn"; this work explores the relationship between art and life and expresses the gospel of beauty that guided Keats's brilliant but brief artistic career. In spite of illness, family hardship, and a strained love affair, Keats succeeded, during a nine-month period in 1819, in writing his greatest poems.

Overall, the literature of the Romantic Age has about it a sense of the uniqueness of the individual, a deep personal earnestness, a sensuous delight in both the common and exotic things of this world, a blend of intensely felt joy and dejection, a yearning for ideal states of being, and a probing interest in mysterious and mystical experience. If the Romantic vision of the world was occasionally tinged with bitterness or outrage, it was because the Romantics confronted an increasingly mechanical and materialistic society.

Robert Burns 1759–1796

Robert Burns, the eldest of seven children, was born in a humble two-room cottage in Ayrshire, Scotland, which his father had built from native stone and clay. The history of the family was one of incessant poverty—poor land, high rents, and back-breaking physical labor. Burns worked as a plowboy on the family farm. He described his life during these early years as "the cheerless gloom of a hermit and the unceasing toil of a galley slave."

Though his formal education was limited, his father inspired in him a love of learning that led him to the works of such writers as Shakespeare, Milton, Dryden, and Pope. He also had a firm grounding in English grammar, a reading knowledge of French, and some background in mathematics and surveying. While plowing in the field, often with a book of ballads in his hands, or going about his other labors, he would recollect the Scottish songs and legends his mother had taught him and mentally compose poems and songs in his native dialect that he would write down in the evening. That his early life was not altogether cheerless can be seen in his lilting poems on love and nature.

After the death of his father in 1784, Burns and his brother took over another farm and continued the struggle with poverty. By this time, Burns had been in and out of several love affairs (he admitted that his "sweetest hours" were "spent among the lasses"), and had also fallen into habits of drinking and dissipation that were to plague him the rest of his life. At age twenty-six, discouraged by his poverty and a frustrating love affair, he determined to embark for Jamaica, but first he gathered together a few of his poems which he published under the title *Poems, Chiefly in the Scottish Dialect* (1786).

Much to his surprise, the book was an overnight success, and instead of going to Jamaica, Burns left for Edinburgh to arrange for a second edition and to find himself swept up in the fashionable literary salons of the city. Edinburgh society, however, regarded Burns as primarily a rustic novelty, and he only made matters worse by acting the part of the arrogant, overly eager literary celebrity.

In 1788 Burns married Jean Armour. Disillusioned with city life, they settled on a farm in Dumfries; the next year he was made an excise officer (collector of taxes), a position that required frequent trips of two hundred miles on horseback. His last years were miserable and depressing, marred by recurrent bouts of ill health, but he nevertheless took on the task of helping to create and preserve the songs of his nation. Before his early death at thirty-seven, he had succeeded in contributing three hundred songs to James Johnson's *The Scots Musical Museum* (1787–1803) and George Thomson's *A Select Collection of Original Scottish Airs for the Voice* (1793–1805). Burns's greatest poetic gift was his ability to express the feelings and concerns of ordinary people in a natural, flowing idiom, thus making him a poet for everyone.

*T*o a Mouse

*on turning her up in her nest
with the plow, November, 1785*

WEE, sleekit,° cow'rin', tim'rous beastie,   sleek
O, what a panic's in thy breastie!
Thou need na start awa sae hasty,
      Wi' bickering brattle!°   short race
5 I wad be laith to rin an' chase thee,
      Wi' murd'ring pattle!°   plow-spade

I'm truly sorry man's dominion
Has broken Nature's social union,
An' justifies that ill opinion
10   Which makes thee startle
At me, thy poor earth-born companion,
      An' fellow-mortal!

I doubt na, whiles,° but thou may thieve;   sometimes
What then? poor beastie, thou maun live!
15 A daimen-icker in a thrave¹
      'S a sma' request;
I'll get a blessin' wi' the lave,°   the rest
      And never miss 't!

Thy wee bit housie, too, in ruin!
20 Its silly wa's° the win's are strewin'!   simple walls
An' naething, now, to big° a new ane,   build
      O' foggage° green!   coarse grass
An' bleak December's win's ensuin',
      Baith snell° an' keen!   biting

25 Thou saw the fields laid bare and waste,
An' weary winter comin' fast,
An' cozie here, beneath the blast,
      Thou thought to dwell,
Till crash! the cruel coulter° past   plowshare
30   Out-thro' thy cell.

That wee bit heap o' leaves an' stibble
Has cost thee mony a weary nibble!
Now thou's turn'd out, for a' thy trouble,
      But house or hald,°   abode
35 To thole° the winter's sleety dribble,   endure
      An' cranreuch° cauld!   hoarfrost

But, Mousie, thou art no thy lane,°   alone
In proving foresight may be vain:

The best laid schemes o' mice an' men
      40 Gang aft a-gley,°   go awry
An' lea'e us nought but grief an' pain
      For promised joy.

Still thou art blest compared wi' me!
The present only toucheth thee:
45 But oh! I backward cast my e'e
      On prospects drear!
An' forward, tho' I canna see,
      I guess an' fear!
1785   1786

---

1. *A daimen-icker in a thrave,* an occasional ear or head of grain in a shock.

*J*ohn Anderson, My Jo

John Anderson my jo,° John,   sweetheart
      When we were first acquent,
Your locks were like the raven,
      Your bonnie brow was brent;°   smooth
5 But now your brow is beld,° John,   bald
      Your locks are like the snaw,°   snow
But blessings on your frosty pow,°   pate, head
      John Anderson my jo!

John Anderson my jo, John,
10   We clamb the hill thegither,°   together
And monie a cantie° day, John,   happy
      We've had wi' ane anither;
Now we maun totter down, John,
      And hand in hand we'll go,
15 And sleep thegither at the foot,
      John Anderson my jo!

                                    1790

A Red, Red Rose

O my luve is like a red, red rose,
  That's newly sprung in June;
O my luve is like the melodie
  That's sweetly played in tune.

5 As fair art thou, my bonnie lass,
     So deep in luve am I;
   And I will luve thee still, my dear,
     Till a' the seas gang dry.

   Till a' the seas gang dry, my dear,
10   And the rocks melt wi' the sun;
   And I will luve thee still, my dear,
     While the sands o' life shall run.

   And fare thee weel, my only luve,
     And fare thee weel a while!
15 And I will come again, my luve,
     Tho' it were ten thousand mile!
1794   1796

Auld Lang Syne

Should auld acquaintance be forgot,
  And never brought to min'?
Should auld acquaintance be forgot,
  And auld lang syne?[1]

CHORUS

5 For auld lang syne, my dear,
     For auld lang syne,
   We'll tak a cup o' kindness yet
     For auld lang syne.

   And surely ye'll be your pint-stowp,[2]
10   And surely I'll be mine!
   And we'll tak a cup o' kindness yet
     For auld lang syne.

   We twa hae run about the braes,°   hillsides
     And pu'd the gowans° fine;   daisies
15 But we've wandered monie a weary fit°   foot, step
     Sin' auld lang syne.

   We twa hae paidled° i' burn,°   paddled/brook
     From mornin' sun till dine;°   dinner time
   But seas between us braid° hae roared   broad
20   Sin' auld lang syne.

   And there's a hand, my trusty fiere,°   friend
     And gie's a hand o' thine;
   And we'll tak a right guid-willie waught[3]
     For auld lang syne.
1788   1796

---

1. **auld lang syne,** literally old long since; that is, old times, the good old days.
2. **ye'll . . . pint-stowp,** you will pay for your pint of drink.
3. **right . . . waught,** hearty goodwill draft, or drink.

Discussion

1. The first six stanzas of "To a Mouse" describe the panic of the mouse whose nest has been turned up. **(a)** Why does the poet regard the mouse's situation as truly pitiable? **(b)** According to the first two lines of the second stanza, why is the mouse justified in running away in panic from a "fellow mortal"?

2. **(a)** What philosophical idea is expressed in the last two stanzas? **(b)** Why is the speaker's plight—and that of other human beings—always likely to be worse than that of nonhuman creatures?

3. What is gained by using the problems of a mouse to make a comment on the human condition?

4. Contrast the John Anderson of the past with the person he has become in "John Anderson, My Jo."

5. What is the meaning of the climb up and down "the hill thegither"?

6. What are the speaker's feelings about her life with John Anderson?

7. What situation probably motivated the writing of "A Red, Red Rose"?

8. How old do the lovers appear to be?

9. **(a)** Point out uses of **hyperbole** in the speaker's declaration of love in "A Red, Red Rose." **(b)** Can these declarations be taken seriously?

10. Why is "Auld Lang Syne" especially appropriate for New Year's Eve, when it is often sung?

William Blake 1757–1827

During his lifetime and for half a century afterwards, William Blake's poetry and art were largely ignored, even derided as the work of a madman. When he died in 1827, reportedly while improvising hymns of praise on his deathbed, he was buried in an unmarked grave. Today he is recognized as a poet, painter, engraver, and spiritual visionary of extraordinary originality and genius who succeeded in breaking away from the formalism of his century and using his literary and artistic talents to illuminate the landscape of the spirit and imagination.

William Blake was born in London in 1757 and lived all but three of his seventy years in a working-class section of the city. Blake was educated through the efforts of his father and his own avid reading in the Bible, philosophy, and poetry. At age ten, Blake expressed an interest in becoming a painter and was enrolled in a drawing school and later apprenticed to an engraver. By 1779 he had begun to accept commissions to illustrate and engrave the works of other writers and was launched on his lifetime career as a respected craftsman. His marriage in 1782 to Catherine Boucher, whom he taught to read, write, and assist him in his engraving work, was happy. Blake's wife soothed and sustained him during his states of visionary rapture, sitting immobile for long hours at his side.

As a child Blake was deeply religious and reported having had an experience of mystic revelation when he was only four. On one occasion he informed his parents that he had seen the prophet Ezekiel in a tree and, on another occasion, said that he had seen a tree filled with angels. By the time of his marriage, Blake had become so consumed in mystical beliefs that his wife is said to have remarked: "I have very little of Mr. Blake's company. He is always in Paradise."

While his development as a painter was fairly gradual, as a poet he was precocious; already in his early teens Blake had begun writing verse that displayed a mastery of the lyric form. Between 1783 and 1793 he wrote, illustrated, and printed his most famous lyrics, *Songs of Innocence* and *Songs of Experience*. He prepared his own illustrative engravings for these poems by a process he himself developed, and either he or his wife tinted each illustration. The result was something comparable to the illuminated manuscripts of medieval times.

Absent from Blake's best-known poems are the classical allusions and formal language that characterized the work of his contemporaries; in their place are a childlike simplicity, lyricism, and visual immediacy that link him to other writers of the Romantic movement. Shortly before his death, Blake reaffirmed the artistic creed to which he was faithful all his life: "I have been very near the gates of death, and have returned very weak and an old man, feeble and tottering, but not in spirit and life, not in the real man, the imagination, which liveth forever."

Songs of Innocence first appeared in 1789. Five years later Blake published a second volume, which he titled *Songs of Innocence and Experience: Shewing the Two Contrary States of the Human Soul.* Although not all the *Songs of Innocence* have counterparts in the *Songs of Experience,* the subtitle, as well as the fact that he never published the *Songs of Experience* as a separate volume, suggest that he intended the poems to be matched.

Introduction

from *Songs of Innocence*

Piping down the valleys wild
Piping songs of pleasant glee
On a cloud I saw a child,
And he laughing said to me:

5 "Pipe a song about a Lamb!"
So I piped with merry cheer.
"Piper pipe that song again"—
So I piped, he wept to hear.

"Drop thy pipe thy happy pipe
10 Sing thy songs of happy cheer."
So I sung the same again
While he wept with joy to hear.

"Piper sit thee down and write
In a book that all may read"—
15 So he vanished from my sight,
And I plucked a hollow reed,

And I made a rural pen,
And I stained the water clear,
And I wrote my happy songs,
20 Every child may joy to hear.

1789

Introduction

from *Songs of Experience*

Hear the voice of the Bard!
Who Present, Past, and Future sees;
Whose ears have heard
The Holy Word,
5 That walked among the ancient trees;

Calling the lapsèd Soul[1]
And weeping in the evening dew;
That might control
The starry pole,
10 And fallen, fallen light renew!

"O Earth, O Earth return!
Arise from out the dewy grass;
Night is worn,
And the morn
15 Rises from the slumberous mass.

"Turn away no more:
Why wilt thou turn away
The starry floor
The wat'ry shore
20 Is given thee till the break of day."

1794

---

1. **lapsèd Soul,** soul fallen from grace after the fall of Adam and Eve.

Comment: Blake's Obscurities

Few people of his own day understood or appreciated Blake's writings or his drawings. In a letter to a Dr. Trusler whose writings he was asked to illustrate and who objected to the obscurity of his designs, he wrote: "You say that I [need] somebody to Elucidate my Ideas. What is Grand is necessarily obscure to Weak men. That which can be made Explicit to the Idiot is not worthy my care. The wisest of the Ancients considered what is not too Explicit as the fittest for Instruction, because it rouses the faculties to act. I name Moses, Solomon, Aesop, Homer, Plato."

But in the same letter he also says: "But I am happy to find a Great Majority of Fellow Mortals who can Elucidate My Visions, and Particularly they have been elucidated by Children, who have taken a greater delight in contemplating my Pictures than I even hoped. Neither Youth nor Childhood is Folly or Incapacity."

The Lamb

from *Songs of Innocence*

    Little Lamb, who made thee?
    Dost thou know who made thee?
Gave thee life, and bid thee feed
By the stream and o'er the mead;
5 Gave thee clothing of delight,
Softest clothing, woolly, bright;
Gave thee such a tender voice,
Making all the vales rejoice?
    Little Lamb, who made thee?
10   Dost thou know who made thee?

    Little Lamb, I'll tell thee,
    Little Lamb, I'll tell thee:
He is callèd by thy name,
For he calls himself a Lamb.[1]
15 He is meek, and he is mild;
He became a little child.
I a child, and thou a lamb,
We are callèd by his name.
    Little Lamb, God bless thee!
20   Little Lamb, God bless thee!

                                        1789

---

1. **Lamb,** symbol of Jesus Christ as Redeemer: "Behold the Lamb of God, which taketh away the sin of the world" (John 1 : 29).

The Tyger

from *Songs of Experience*

Tyger! Tyger! burning bright
In the forests of the night,
What immortal hand or eye
Could frame thy fearful symmetry?

5 In what distant deeps or skies
Burnt the fire of thine eyes?
On what wings dare he aspire?
What the hand dare seize the fire?

And what shoulder, and what art,
10 Could twist the sinews of thy heart?
And when thy heart began to beat,
What dread hand? and what dread feet?

What the hammer? what the chain?
In what furnace was thy brain?
15 What the anvil? what dread grasp
Dare its deadly terrors clasp?

When the stars threw down their spears,
And watered heaven with their tears,
Did he smile his work to see?
20 Did he who made the Lamb make thee?

Tyger! Tyger! burning bright
In the forests of the night,
What immortal hand or eye
Dare frame thy fearful symmetry?

                                        1794

Discussion

1. In the "Introduction" to *Songs of Innocence*, the speaker is both piper and poet. In the "Introduction" to *Songs of Experience*, there is no identifiable speaker, but the reader is instructed to listen to the voice of the bard, who is also a prophet. How is each an appropriate figure for the poems he introduces?

2. The setting of the "Introduction" to *Innocence* is probably daytime; the setting of the "Introduction" to *Experience* ranges from evening to daybreak. What do these settings suggest?

3. "The Lamb" and "The Tyger" are matched poems. How is each connected with the "Introduction" to its category?

4. The contrast between the lamb and the tiger is striking. What qualities of each are emphasized by the images of the poems?

Holy Thursday

from *Songs of Innocence*

'Twas on a Holy Thursday,[1] their innocent
    faces clean,
The children walking two and two, in red
    and blue and green,
Grey-headed beadles walked before, with
    wands[2] as white as snow,
Till into the high dome of Paul's they like
    Thames' waters flow.

5 O what a multitude they seemed, these
    flowers of London town!
Seated in companies they sit with radiance
    all their own.
The hum of multitudes was there, but
    multitudes of lambs,
Thousands of little boys and girls raising
    their innocent hands.

Now like a mighty wind they raise to heaven
    the voice of song,
10 Or like harmonious thunderings the seats of
    Heaven among.
Beneath them sit the agèd men, wise
    guardians of the poor;
Then cherish pity, lest you drive an angel
    from your door.

1789

---

1. **Holy Thursday,** Ascension Day, the fortieth day after Easter,
when children in orphanages were brought to St. Paul's Cathedral to give thanks for the charity of God, of which human charity is supposedly a reflection.
2. **wands,** rods, symbols of the beadles' authority.

Holy Thursday

from *Songs of Experience*

Is this a holy thing to see
In a rich and fruitful land,
Babes reduced to misery,
Fed with cold and usurous hand?

5 Is that trembling cry a song?
Can it be a song of joy?
And so many children poor?
It is a land of poverty!

And their sun does never shine,
10 And their fields are bleak and bare,
And their ways are filled with thorns:
It is eternal winter there.

For where-e'er the sun does shine,
And where-e'er the rain does fall,
15 Babe can never hunger there,
Nor poverty the mind appall.

1794

Discussion

1. What effect does Blake gain through the contrasting views of the children in the matched "Holy Thursday" poems?

2. Point out differences in the language and the **rhythm** of these poems that account for their distinct contrast in tone.

3. What do the "Holy Thursday" poems reveal about the life of London's poor in Blake's day?

"The Divine Image" by William Blake, from *Songs of Innocence,* 1789.

The Human Abstract

from *Songs of Experience*

Pity would be no more,
If we did not make somebody Poor;
And Mercy no more could be,
If all were as happy as we;

5 And mutual fear brings peace,
Till the selfish loves increase;
Then Cruelty knits a snare,
And spreads his baits with care.

He sits down with holy fears,
10 And waters the ground with tears;
Then Humility takes its root
Underneath his foot.

Soon spreads the dismal shade
Of Mystery over his head;
15 And the Caterpillar and Fly
Feed on the Mystery.

And it bears the fruit of Deceit,
Ruddy and sweet to eat;
And the Raven his nest has made
20 In its thickest shade.

The Gods of the earth and sea,
Sought thro' Nature to find this Tree;
But their search was all in vain:
There grows one in the Human Brain.

1794

The Divine Image

from *Songs of Innocence*

To Mercy, Pity, Peace, and Love
All pray in their distress:
And to these virtues of delight
Return their thankfulness.

5 For Mercy, Pity, Peace, and Love
Is God, our father dear,
And Mercy, Pity, Peace, and Love
Is Man, his child and care.

For Mercy has a human heart,
10 Pity a human face:
And Love, the human form divine,
And Peace, the human dress.

Then every man, of every clime,
That prays in his distress,
15 Prays to the human form divine,
Love, Mercy, Pity, Peace.

And all must love the human form,
In heathen, Turk, or Jew.
Where Mercy, Love, and Pity dwell
20 There God is dwelling too.

1789

Discussion

1. (a) Explain the meaning of the terms "The Divine Image" and "The Human Abstract" as defined by each poem. (b) What noble human ideal is expressed in the last stanza of "The Divine Image"? (c) "The Human Abstract" provides a cynical repudiation of the noble qualities attributed to humanity in "The Divine Image." Refer to specific statements in the poem that support this view.

Between 1783 and 1793, the years he was working on the *Songs of Innocence and Experience,* Blake also completed one major prose work, *The Marriage of Heaven and Hell,* which includes "Proverbs of Hell," a series of **aphorisms** containing simple and memorable images that further develop a central theme of his works: "Without contraries is no progression." What Blake means is that the interplay between opposites is a necessary condition of learning; that is, an emotion like joy cannot be fully understood without the experience of its opposite, sorrow. Similarly, the innocence of childhood needs to be balanced by the wisdom gained through experience, however painful and disenchanting.

Proverbs of Hell

from *The Marriage of Heaven and Hell*

In seed time learn, in harvest teach, in winter enjoy.
Drive your cart and your plow over the bones of the dead.
The road of excess leads to the palace of wisdom.
Prudence is a rich, ugly old maid courted by Incapacity.
5 The cut worm forgives the plow.
A fool sees not the same tree that a wise man sees.
He whose face gives no light, shall never become a star.
Eternity is in love with the productions of time.
All wholesome food is caught without a net or a trap.
10 No bird soars too high, if he soars with his own wings.
If the fool would persist in his folly he would become wise.
Shame is pride's cloak.
Excess of sorrow laughs. Excess of joy weeps.
The roaring of lions, the howling of wolves, the raging of the stormy sea, and the destructive sword,
     are portions of eternity, too great for the eye of man.
15 Let man wear the fell of the lion, woman the fleece of the sheep.
The bird a nest, the spider a web, man friendship.
What is now proved was once only imagined.
Every thing possible to be believed is an image of truth.
The fox provides for himself, but God provides for the lion.
20 Think in the morning. Act in the noon. Eat in the evening. Sleep in the night.
The tygers of wrath are wiser than the horses of instruction.
Expect poison from the standing water.
You never know what is enough unless you know what is more than enough.
The weak in courage is strong in cunning.
25 Damn braces. Bless relaxes.
The crow wished every thing was black, the owl that every thing was white.
Improvement makes strait roads; but the crooked roads without improvements are roads of Genius.
Truth can never be told so as to be understood, and not be believed.
1790–1793   1793

Nebuchadnezzar by William Blake, 1795.

Discussion

1. The "Proverbs of Hell," according to Blake, were intended to "show the nature of infernal wisdom," that is, the wisdom that can be acquired only through sometimes painful experience. Consider each proverb and decide what you think it means. Try to restate each one in your own words.

2. In general, how are human beings advised by the "Proverbs of Hell" to conduct their lives?

3. What kinds of attitudes and behavior are specifically condemned in the "Proverbs"?

4. How does the proverb that begins with "The roaring of lions, the howling of wolves" (line 14) help explain Blake's attitude toward the creature in "The Tyger"?

The following poem has long been used as the hymn of the British Labour Party, which represents the working class. Blake's confidence in the goodness of God and the redeemable nature of man are clearly evident in the poem. Many readers have interpreted the "dark Satanic Mills" (line 8) as a reference to the factories springing up in England during Blake's time in which workers slaved long hours for small pay. Other readers insist the mills are not the real ones of industrial England, but are rather the figurative mills of the mind.

Woodcut by
William Blake
to illustrate
R. J. Thornton's
*Pastorals of
Virgil*, 1821.

A New Jerusalem

from *Milton*

And did those feet[1] in ancient time
Walk upon England's mountains green?
And was the holy Lamb of God,
On England's pleasant pastures seen?

5 And did the Countenance Divine,
Shine forth upon our clouded hills?
And was Jerusalem builded here,
Among these dark Satanic Mills?

Bring me my Bow of burning gold:
10 Bring me my Arrows of desire:
Bring me my Spear: O clouds unfold!
Bring me my Chariot of fire!

I will not cease from Mental Fight,
Nor shall my Sword sleep in my hand:
15 Till we have built Jerusalem,
In England's green and pleasant Land.
1800–1809?   1809–1810

---

1. *feet,* of Jesus.

Discussion

1. What is the "ancient time" referred to in the first line? With this in mind, explain the references in lines 3–8.

2. What, by means of **metaphor,** is the poet requesting in stanza three?

3. Explain why members of the British Labour Party might find the last stanza inspiring.

4. According to the last two stanzas, what is the rightful task and role of the poet?

Composition

Although at first the Lamb and the Tyger each seem to be a **symbol** of opposites—representations of, for example, good and evil, meekness and ferocity, peace and war—they are perhaps not so much opposites as different creatures in an infinitely varied universe.

With this view in mind, write a paper in which you explain why both poems can be regarded as celebrations of the greatness of God.

William Wordsworth 1770–1850

Wordsworth was born on April 7, 1770, in Cockermouth, a village on the edge of the Lake District, a scenic mountain region in northwest England. "Fair seed-time had my soul," said Wordsworth of his childhood years spent exploring a landscape of extraordinary beauty and variety. For eight years he attended Hawkshead Grammar School, where his love of reading and poetic inclinations were strongly encouraged. Wordsworth was enrolled at St. John's College, Cambridge, in 1787 as a scholarship student. Uninspired by the classical curriculum, he devoted himself instead to independent reading, long rambles in the countryside, and extended sessions of writing poetry.

During the summer of 1790, instead of studying for his comprehensive examinations, Wordsworth undertook a walking tour of Switzerland and France from which he returned radicalized in his political thinking and fired with enthusiasm for the French Revolution. "Bliss was it in that dawn to be alive, / But to be young was very Heaven!" is his description of that period in his autobiographical poem, *The Prelude*. After graduation, Wordsworth returned to France in 1792, determined to learn French well enough to qualify as a tutor or gentleman's companion. Here he met and fell in love with Annette Vallon, who bore him a daughter, Caroline. A lack of funds forced Wordsworth's return to England in December of 1792. Cut off from a return to France by the declaration of war between Britain and France in 1793, increasingly disillusioned with the Revolution following the Reign of Terror and the advent of Napoleon, and uncertain about his personal and professional future, Wordsworth declared in *The Prelude,* "I lost / All feeling of conviction, and . . . Yielded up moral questions in despair."

Two critical developments in 1795 marked a major turning point in Wordsworth's life: a bequest of nine hundred pounds from a friend that enabled him to establish a home for his beloved sister Dorothy and himself at Racedown, and the commencement of his friendship and artistic collaboration with Samuel Taylor Coleridge, a creative association that would lead, in 1798, to the publication of a revolutionary volume of poems and ballads. Published anonymously, *Lyrical Ballads* contained twenty-three poems (nineteen by Wordsworth, four by Coleridge) published according to the following scheme: Wordsworth was to "give the charm of novelty to subjects of everyday life"; Coleridge was to let his imagination roam over more unusual and supernatural subject matter. Ironically, though the book included such poems as Coleridge's "Rime of the Ancient Mariner" and Wordsworth's "Tintern Abbey" (now considered among the finest in the English language), it was at first contemptuously received by critics and poets alike. In 1800, an expanded edition was published with a preface written by Wordsworth to explain his theory of poetry, in which he stated that "all good poetry is the spontaneous overflow of powerful feelings." He further asserted that the subject matter of poetry must be taken from "humble and rustic life" and be expressed in the language of "man speaking to man," that is, in simple, direct speech.

In 1802 Wordsworth married Mary Hutchinson, a childhood schoolmate, with whom he had five children, two of whom died in childhood. By 1810 Wordsworth's extraordinary powers of awareness had begun to fade along with his revolutionary zeal and youthful intensity.

Wordsworth composed this poem while on a walking tour with his sister Dorothy along the River Wye, which winds back and forth across the border between England and Wales on its way to the Bristol Channel. The beautiful ruin of Tintern Abbey is located in a deep valley at the river's edge. Wordsworth had previously visited the Wye in 1793, five years before this poem was published in *Lyrical Ballads*.

Lines Composed a Few Miles Above Tintern Abbey

Five years have past; five summers, with the length
Of five long winters! and again I hear
These waters, rolling from their mountain springs
With a soft inland murmur.—Once again
5 Do I behold these steep and lofty cliffs
That on a wild secluded scene impress
Thoughts of more deep seclusion and connect
The landscape with the quiet of the sky.
The day is come when I again repose
10 Here, under this dark sycamore, and view
These plots of cottage ground, these orchard tufts,
Which at this season, with their unripe fruits,
Are clad in one green hue, and lose themselves
Mid groves and copses. Once again I see
15 These hedgerows, hardly hedgerows, little lines
Of sportive wood run wild; these pastoral farms,
Green to the very door; and wreaths of smoke
Sent up, in silence, from among the trees,
With some uncertain notice, as might seem
20 Of vagrant dwellers in the houseless woods,
Or of some Hermit's cave, where by his fire
The Hermit sits alone.

These beauteous forms,
Through a long absence, have not been to me
As is a landscape to a blind man's eye;
25 But oft, in lonely rooms, and 'mid the din
Of towns and cities, I have owed to them,

In hours of weariness, sensations sweet,
Felt in the blood, and felt along the heart;
And passing even into my purer mind,
30 With tranquil restoration:—feelings too
Of unremembered pleasure, such, perhaps,
As have no slight or trivial influence
On that best portion of a good man's life,
His little, nameless, unremembered acts
35 Of kindness and of love. Nor less, I trust,
To them I may have owed another gift,
Of aspect more sublime; that blessèd mood,
In which the burthen of the mystery,
In which the heavy and the weary weight
40 Of all this unintelligible world,
Is lightened—that serene and blessèd mood,
In which the affections gently lead us on—
Until, the breath of this corporeal frame
And even the motion of our human blood
45 Almost suspended, we are laid asleep
In body, and become a living soul;
While with an eye made quiet by the power
Of harmony, and the deep power of joy,
We see into the life of things.

If this
50 Be but a vain belief, yet, oh! how oft—
In darkness and amid the many shapes
Of joyless daylight; when the fretful stir
Unprofitable, and the fever of the world,
Have hung upon the beatings of my heart—
55 How oft, in spirit, have I turned to thee,
O sylvan Wye!¹ thou wanderer through the woods,
How often has my spirit turned to thee!

---

1. **Wye**, a river that runs past Tintern Abbey.

And now, with gleams of half-extinguished
    thought,
With many recognitions dim and faint,
60 And somewhat of a sad perplexity,
The picture of the mind revives again;
While here I stand, not only with the sense
Of present pleasure, but with pleasing
    thoughts
That in this moment there is life and food
65 For future years. And so I dare to hope,
Though changed, no doubt, from what I was
    when first
I came among these hills, when like a roe[2]
I bounded o'er the mountains, by the sides
Of the deep rivers, and the lonely streams,
70 Wherever nature led: more like a man
Flying from something that he dreads than
    one
Who sought the thing he loved. For nature
    then
(The coarser pleasures of my boyish days,
And their glad animal movements all gone
    by)
75 To me was all in all.—I cannot paint
What then I was. The sounding cataract[3]
Haunted me like a passion: the tall rock,
The mountain, and the deep and gloomy
    wood,
Their colors and their forms, were then to
    me
80 An appetite; a feeling and a love,
That had no need of a remoter charm,
By thought supplied, nor any interest
Unborrowed from the eye.—That time is
    past,
And all its aching joys are now no more,
85 And all its dizzy raptures. Not for this
Faint I, nor mourn nor murmur; other gifts
Have followed; for such loss, I would
    believe,
Abundant recompense. For I have learned
To look on nature, not as in the hour
90 Of thoughtless youth, but hearing often
    times
The still, sad music of humanity,
Nor harsh nor grating, though of ample
    power
To chasten and subdue. And I have felt
A presence that disturbs me with the joy
95 Of elevated thoughts; a sense sublime

Tintern Abbey by Joseph M. W. Turner, painted around 1794.

Of something far more deeply interfused,
Whose dwelling is the light of setting suns,
And the round ocean and the living air,
And the blue sky, and in the mind of man;
100 A motion and a spirit, that impels
All thinking things, all objects of all thought,
And rolls through all things. Therefore am I
    still
A lover of the meadows and the woods,
And mountains; and of all that we behold
105 From this green earth; of all the mighty
    world
Of eye, and ear—both what they half create,
And what perceive; well pleased to
    recognize
In nature and the language of the sense
The anchor of my purest thoughts, the
    nurse,

2. *roe,* a small, agile deer.
3. *cataract,* waterfall.

110 The guide, the guardian of my heart, and
      soul
   Of all my moral being.

                              Nor perchance,
   If I were not thus taught, should I the more
   Suffer my genial spirits[4] to decay;
   For thou art with me here upon the banks
115 Of this fair river; thou my dearest Friend,[5]
   My dear, dear Friend; and in thy voice I
      catch
   The language of my former heart, and read
   My former pleasures in the shooting lights
   Of thy wild eyes. Oh! yet a little while
120 May I behold in thee what I was once,
   My dear, dear Sister! and this prayer I
      make,
   Knowing that Nature never did betray
   The heart that loved her; 'tis her privilege,
   Through all the years of this our life, to lead
125 From joy to joy; for she can so inform[6]
   The mind that is within us, so impress
   With quietness and beauty, and so feed
   With lofty thoughts, that neither evil
      tongues,
   Rash judgments, nor the sneers of selfish
      men,
130 Nor greetings where no kindness is, nor all
   The dreary intercourse of daily life,
   Shall e'er prevail against us, or disturb
   Our cheerful faith, that all which we behold
   Is full of blessings. Therefore let the moon
135 Shine on thee in the solitary walk;
   And let the misty mountain winds be free
   To blow against thee; and, in after years,
   When these wild ecstasies shall be matured
   Into a sober pleasure, when thy mind
140 Shall be a mansion for all lovely forms,
   Thy memory be as a dwelling place
   For all sweet sounds and harmonies; oh!
      then,
   If solitude, or fear, or pain, or grief,
   Should be thy portion, with what healing
      thoughts
145 Of tender joy wilt thou remember me,
   And these my exhortations! Nor,
      perchance—
   If I should be where I no more can hear
   Thy voice, nor catch from thy wild eyes
      these gleams

   Of past existence—wilt thou then forget
150 That on the banks of this delightful stream
   We stood together; and that I, so long
   A worshiper of Nature, hither came
   Unwearied in that service—rather say
   With warmer love—oh! with far deeper zeal
155 Of holier love. Nor wilt thou then forget
   That after many wanderings, many years
   Of absence, these steep woods and lofty
      cliffs,
   And this green pastoral landscape, were to
      me
   More dear, both for themselves and for thy
      sake!

                                          1798

Discussion

1. In lines 1–22, the countryside is described. What specific features of the external landscape would have to be included in a painting of this scene? Are there any signs of human habitation?

2. **(a)** Judging from lines 22–65, what three major benefits has Wordsworth derived from having once beheld the beauty of this natural scene? Overall, what "gifts" or sustenance does Wordsworth find in nature? **(b)** At what times has he felt impelled to recall this particular "picture of the mind"?

3. In lines 65–111, the poet describes two phases of his developing attitude toward nature. **(a)** What was his attitude when he first visited the Wye? **(b)** How does his present attitude differ from his feelings then?

4. In the last section of the poem, Wordsworth turns his attention to his sister Dorothy and her attitude toward nature. **(a)** At which phase of development in relation to nature does Dorothy now stand? **(b)** What are her brother's wishes for her? **(c)** How is Wordsworth's affection for his sister connected with the themes of the poem?

My Heart Leaps Up

My heart leaps up when I behold
   A rainbow in the sky:
So was it when my life began;
So is it now I am a man:
5 So be it when I shall grow old,
   Or let me die!
The Child is father of the Man;
And I could wish my days to be
Bound each to each by natural piety.[1]
1802   1807

---

1. *piety,* reverence, affection.

Composed upon Westminster Bridge, September 3, 1802

Earth has not anything to show more fair:
Dull would he be of soul who could pass by
A sight so touching in its majesty;
This City now doth, like a garment, wear
5 The beauty of the morning; silent, bare,
Ships, towers, domes, theaters, and temples
   lie
Open unto the fields, and to the sky;
All bright and glittering in the smokeless air.
Never did sun more beautifully steep
10 In his first splendor, valley, rock, or hill;
Ne'er saw I, never felt, a calm so deep!
The river glideth at his own sweet will:
Dear God! the very houses seem asleep;
And all that mighty heart is lying still!
1802   1807

Discussion

1. According to the first six lines of "My Heart Leaps Up," what condition of life was essential for Wordsworth, without which he would prefer death?

2. **(a)** "My Heart Leaps Up" is generally considered a summary of Wordsworth's philosophy. Explain, accounting for the **paradox** expressed in line 7. **(b)** What does Wordsworth mean by "days . . . / Bound . . . by natural piety"?

3. As he stands upon Westminster Bridge in the early morning, what sights and emotions touch the poet's soul?

4. Point out uses of **personification** in "Composed upon Westminster Bridge." What effect is achieved through ascribing human qualities to the city?

5. What do you think motivates the exclamation with which the poem ends?

It Is a Beauteous Evening

It is a beauteous evening, calm and free,
The holy time is quiet as a Nun
Breathless with adoration; the broad sun
Is sinking down in its tranquillity;
5   The gentleness of heaven broods o'er the Sea:
Listen! the mighty Being[1] is awake,
And doth with his eternal motion make
A sound like thunder—everlastingly.
Dear Child![2] dear Girl! that walkest with me
          here,
10 If thou appear untouched by solemn thought,
Thy nature is not therefore less divine:
Thou liest in Abraham's bosom[3] all the year,
And worship'st at the Temple's inner shrine,
God being with thee when we know it not.
1802   1807

---

1. *Being,* the ocean.
2. *Dear Child,* Wordsworth's French daughter, Caroline.
3. *in Abraham's bosom,* in the presence of God. See Luke 16:22.

The World Is Too Much with Us

The world is too much with us; late and soon,
Getting and spending, we lay waste our powers:
Little we see in Nature that is ours;
We have given our hearts away, a sordid boon!
5   This Sea that bares her bosom to the moon,
The winds that will be howling at all hours,
And are up-gathered now like sleeping flowers;
For this, for everything, we are out of tune;
It moves us not.—Great God! I'd rather be
10 A Pagan suckled in a creed outworn;
So might I, standing on this pleasant lea,
Have glimpses that would make me less forlorn;
Have sight of Proteus rising from the sea;
Or hear old Triton[1] blow his wreathèd horn.
1802-1804   1807

---

1. *Proteus* (prō'tē əs) . . . *Triton* (trīt'n), sea gods in classical mythology.

London, 1802

Milton! thou shouldst be living at this hour:
England hath need of thee: she is a fen
Of stagnant waters: altar, sword, and pen,
Fireside, the heroic wealth of hall and
          bower,
5   Have forfeited their ancient English dower
Of inward happiness. We are selfish men:
Oh! raise us up, return to us again;
And give us manners, virtue, freedom,
          power.
Thy soul was like a Star, and dwelt apart;
10 Thou hadst a voice whose sound was like
          the sea:
Pure as the naked heavens, majestic, free;
So didst thou travel on life's common way,
In cheerful godliness; and yet thy heart
The lowliest duties on herself did lay.
1802   1807

Discussion

1. (a) Describe the setting of "It Is a Beauteous Evening." What mood does this setting inspire in the poet? **(b)** What effect does Wordsworth achieve through the use of the **simile** comparing the evening to a nun?

2. (a) How is Wordsworth's response to the beauty of the evening different from that of his daughter? **(b)** What explanation does Wordsworth give for the child's attitude being different from his?

3. (a) In "London, 1802" why is England so greatly in need of Milton's return? **(b)** What is Milton being asked to restore to English life?

4. According to the poet, why is Milton the right person to inspire reform?

5. (a) In "The World Is Too Much with Us," what aspects of the "world" does Wordsworth say are "too much with us"? **(b)** With what aspects of nature are we "out of tune"?

6. According to the last six lines of the sonnet, what is the "creed" that Wordsworth says he would prefer to the materialism of his day?

7. Do the ideas in the poem apply to contemporary life? Explain.

8. How does this sonnet resemble "London, 1802" in theme and tone?

Nature was for Wordsworth a source of spiritual insight. Nowhere does he express this view so clearly as in the "Ode On Intimations of Immortality." As you read the **ode,** keep these points in mind: (1) In his childhood and youth Wordsworth had a strong intuition that the soul, which is eternal and never dies, comes into a human body at birth from a glorious heavenly home. (2) Gradually, as he grew older, he lost the vision of his childhood belief. (3) In manhood, experiences with nature have brought him comfort and renewed his belief in immortality.

Ode on Intimations of Immortality from Recollections of Early Childhood

The Child is father of the Man;
And I could wish my days to be
Bound each to each by natural piety.

1

There was a time when meadow, grove, and stream,
The earth, and every common sight,
        To me did seem
        Appareled in celestial light,
5 The glory and the freshness of a dream.
It is not now as it hath been of yore;—
        Turn wheresoe'er I may,
        By night or day,
The things which I have seen I now can see no more.

2

10   The Rainbow comes and goes,
       And lovely is the Rose,
       The Moon doth with delight
Look round her when the heavens are bare;
       Waters on a starry night
15   Are beautiful and fair;
       The sunshine is a glorious birth;
       But yet I know, where'er I go,
That there hath passed away a glory from the earth.

3

Now, while the birds thus sing a joyous song,
20   And while the young lambs bound
       As to the tabor's sound,[1]
To me alone there came a thought of grief:
A timely utterance gave that thought relief,
       And I again am strong:

---

1. *tabor's sound,* drum beat.

25 The cataracts blow their trumpets from the steep;
No more shall grief of mine the season wrong;
I hear the Echoes through the mountains throng,
The Winds come to me from the fields of sleep,
        And all the earth is gay;
30   Land and sea
Give themselves up to jollity,
And with the heart of May
Doth every Beast keep holiday—
        Thou Child of Joy,
35 Shout round me, let me hear thy shouts, thou happy Shepherd-boy!

4

Ye blessèd Creatures, I have heard the call
        Ye to each other make; I see
The heavens laugh with you in your jubilee;
        My heart is at your festival,
40   My head hath its coronal,[2]
The fullness of your bliss, I feel—I feel it all.
        Oh, evil day! if I were sullen
        While Earth herself is adorning,
        This sweet May-morning,
45   And the Children are culling
        On every side,
        In a thousand valleys far and wide,
Fresh flowers; while the sun shines warm,
And the Babe leaps up on his Mother's arm:—
50   I hear, I hear, with joy I hear!
        —But there's a Tree, of many, one,
A single Field which I have looked upon,
Both of them speak of something that is gone:
        The Pansy at my feet
55   Doth the same tale repeat:
Whither is fled the visionary gleam?
Where is it now, the glory and the dream?

5

Our birth is but a sleep and a forgetting:
The Soul that rises with us, our life's Star,[3]
60   Hath had elsewhere its setting,
        And cometh from afar:
        Not in entire forgetfulness,
        And not in utter nakedness,
But trailing clouds of glory do we come
65   From God, who is our home:
Heaven lies about us in our infancy!

---

2. *coronal,* crown of flowers.
3. *Star,* the sun.

Shades of the prison-house begin to close
        Upon the growing Boy,
But he beholds the light, and whence it flows
70   He sees it in his joy;
The Youth, who daily farther from the east
        Must travel, still is Nature's priest,
        And by the vision splendid
        Is on his way attended;
75 At length the Man perceives it die away,
And fade into the light of common day.

6

Earth fills her lap with pleasures of her own;
Yearnings she hath in her own natural kind,
And even with something of a Mother's mind,
80   And no unworthy aim,
        The homely[4] Nurse doth all she can
To make her Foster-child, her Inmate Man,
        Forget the glories he hath known,
And that imperial palace whence he came.

7

85 Behold the Child among his new-born blisses,
A six years' Darling of a pigmy size!
See, where 'mid work of his own hand he lies,
Fretted[5] by sallies of his mother's kisses,
With light upon him from his father's eyes!
90 See, at his feet, some little plan or chart,
Some fragment from his dream of human life,
Shaped by himself with newly-learnèd art;
        A wedding or a festival
        A mourning or a funeral,
95   And this hath now his heart,
        And unto this he frames his song:
        Then will he fit his tongue
To dialogues of business, love, or strife;
        But it will not be long
100   Ere this be thrown aside,
        And with new joy and pride
The little Actor cons[6] another part;
Filling from time to time his "humorous stage"[7]
With all the Persons, down to palsied Age,
105 That Life brings with her in her equipage;
        As if his whole vocation
        Were endless imitation.

---

4. homely, familiar, friendly, simple.
5. Fretted, bothered.
6. cons, learns.
7. "humorous stage," from a sonnet by Samuel Daniel (1562-1619). *Humorous* means "changeable" or "moody" here.

8

Thou, whose exterior semblance doth belie
　　　　Thy Soul's immensity;
110 Thou best Philosopher, who yet dost keep
Thy heritage, thou Eye among the blind,
That, deaf and silent, read'st the eternal deep,[8]
Haunted forever by the eternal mind—
　　　　Mighty Prophet! Seer blest!
115 　　　　On whom those truths do rest,
Which we are toiling all our lives to find,
In darkness lost, the darkness of the grave;
Thou, over whom thy Immortality
Broods like the Day, a Master o'er a Slave,
120 A Presence which is not to be put by;
Thou little Child, yet glorious in the might
Of heaven-born freedom on thy being's height,
Why with such earnest pains dost thou provoke
The years to bring the inevitable yoke,
125 Thus blindly with thy blessedness at strife?
Full soon thy Soul shall have her earthly freight,
And custom lie upon thee with a weight,
Heavy as frost, and deep almost as life!

9

　　　　Oh, joy! that in our embers
130 　　　　Is something that doth live,
　　　　That nature yet remembers
　　　　What was so fugitive!
The thought of our past years in me doth breed
Perpetual benediction: not indeed
135 For that which is most worthy to be blest;
Delight and liberty, the simple creed
Of Childhood, whether busy or at rest,
With new-fledged hope still fluttering in his breast:—
　　　　Not for these I raise
140 　　　　The song of thanks and praise;
　　　　But for those obstinate questionings
　　　　Of sense and outward things,
　　　　Fallings from us, vanishings;
　　　　Blank misgivings of a Creature
145 Moving about in worlds not realized,[9]
High instincts before which our mortal Nature
Did tremble like a guilty Thing surprised:
　　　　But for those first affections,
　　　　Those shadowy recollections,
150 　Which, be they what they may,
Are yet the fountain light of all our day,
Are yet a master light of all our seeing;

8. *eternal deep,* mysteries of eternity.
9. *not realized,* not yet truly understood.

Uphold us, cherish, and have power to make
Our noisy years seem moments in the being
155 Of the eternal Silence: truths that wake,
        To perish never;
Which neither listlessness, nor mad endeavor,
        Nor Man nor Boy,
Nor all this is at enmity with joy,
160 Can utterly abolish or destroy!
        Hence in a season of calm weather
        Though inland far we be,
Our Souls have sight of that immortal sea
        Which brought us hither,
165   Can in a moment travel thither,
And see the Children sport upon the shore,
And hear the mighty waters rolling evermore.

10

Then sing, ye Birds, sing, sing, a joyous song!
        And let the young Lambs bound
170   As to the tabor's sound!
We in thought will join your throng,
        Ye that pipe and ye that play,
        Ye that through your hearts today
        Feel the gladness of the May!
175 What though the radiance which was once so bright
Be now forever taken from my sight,
    Though nothing can bring back the hour
Of splendor in the grass, of glory in the flower;
        We will grieve not, rather find
180   Strength in what remains behind;
        In the primal sympathy
        Which having been must ever be;
        In the soothing thoughts that spring
        Out of human suffering;
185   In the faith that looks through death,
In years that bring the philosophic mind.

11

And O, ye Fountains, Meadows, Hills, and Groves,
Forebode not any severing of our loves!
Yet in my heart of hearts I feel your might;
190 I only have relinquished one delight
To live beneath your more habitual sway.
I love the Brooks which down their channels fret,
Even more than when I tripped lightly as they;
The innocent brightness of a new-born Day
195   Is lovely yet;
The Clouds that gather round the setting sun
Do take a sober coloring from an eye
That hath kept watch o'er man's mortality;

Another race hath been, and other palms are won.
200 Thanks to the human heart by which we live,
Thanks to its tenderness, its joys, and fears,
To me the meanest flower that blows can give
Thoughts that do often lie too deep for tears.
1802–1804   1807

Discussion

1. The first four stanzas of the "Intimations Ode" express a sense of loss. **(a)** To what time of life is Wordsworth referring in stanza 1? **(b)** How have his feelings changed since the days when "every common sight" seemed "appareled in celestial light"? **(c)** In stanzas 3 and 4, what incidents temporarily restore the poet's sense of joy? What is meant by "A timely utterance gave that thought relief"? **(d)** Despite this brief resurgence of joy, what causes the poet to conclude that "the visionary gleam . . . the glory and the dream" are permanently gone?

2. Stanzas 5 through 8 offer an explanation for the sense of loss Wordsworth is experiencing. **(a)** To what is the span of a human life, from birth to maturity, compared? To what is the soul compared? **(b)** Identify the stages in the journey from birth to manhood described in stanza 5. **(c)** Why, in stanza 6, does Wordsworth speak of the earth as a "homely Nurse" and of man as "her Foster-child"? What is the "imperial palace" which is man's true home?

3. Coleridge's six-year-old son Hartley was the "Darling of a pigmy size" whom Wordsworth uses to represent childhood in stanzas 7 and 8. **(a)** Wordsworth speaks of the child's immensity of soul and addresses him as a "best Philosopher" and "Mighty Prophet! Seer blest!" What is his justification for such extravagant praise? **(b)** What does he mean by referring to the child as an "Eye among the blind"? **(c)** According to lines 121–125, how is the child "at strife" with his own "blessedness"?

4. Stanzas 9 through 11 offer a consolation to the poet for his sense of loss and provide reasons for exultation. **(a)** The first four lines of stanza 9 explain the reason for the speak-er's renewed sense of joy. Why does he feel moved to "raise / The song of thanks and praise"? **(b)** What is the "splendor in the grass" (stanza 10) that can never be recaptured? Yet, "what remains behind" as a source of strength and sustenance? **(c)** What "one delight" has been "relinquished" with the passing of childhood? Is this loss offset by any gains from maturity?

5. Wordsworth prefaced the "Intimations Ode" with the last three lines of "My Heart Leaps Up." What relation is there between the short poem and the "Intimations Ode"?

6. Many lines in the poem depend on an interpretation of **metaphor** for their meaning. In your own words, state the idea expressed in each of the following lines: **(a)** "Shades of the prison-house begin to close / Upon the growing Boy" (lines 67–68). **(b)** "The Youth, who daily farther from the east / Must travel, still is Nature's priest" (lines 71–72). **(c)** "Full soon thy Soul shall have her earthly freight, / And custom lie upon thee with a weight, / Heavy as frost, and deep almost as life!" (lines 126–128).

Composition

According to an old saying, "You can't go home again," but Wordsworth, in "Tintern Abbey," demonstrates that a return visit to a favorite place, though never the same as the first, can sometimes be even more pleasurable.

In a paper, describe your own experience of returning to a childhood haunt or place you loved after a long absence. How did you feel? Were you disillusioned, or delighted in a new and different way?

Samuel Taylor Coleridge
1772–1834

Coleridge was very possibly the most versatile and stimulating mind of his generation—a poet, critic, philosopher, theologian, lecturer, journalist, and charismatic personality. He was simultaneously self-destructive, impetuous, and contradictory. Constantly self-deprecating, Coleridge helped perpetuate the widespread legend of himself as a genius incapable of finishing anything he started, irresponsible, wasteful of his talents, and in the reproachful words of Thomas Carlyle, "sunk inextricably in the depths of putrescent idleness." This is the same man, however, whom Wordsworth termed, "the most wonderful man that I have ever known," and of whom the essayist Charles Lamb stated, "never saw I his likeness, nor probably the world can again."

The youngest of twelve children of a Devonshire vicar, Coleridge was spoiled, precocious, and restless, continually lost in his dream world. After his father died when he was ten years old, Coleridge was sent to school in London, a time of loneliness and intense intellectual growth that he recalls in his poem "Frost at Midnight." At age nineteen he went up to Cambridge. Here he spent a studious year before falling into bad habits and sinking deeply into debt, a situation which, in 1793, led him impulsively to join the Fifteenth Light Dragoons under the ludicrous alias of Silas Tomkyn Comberbacke. After a few disastrous weeks his brothers succeeded in securing his discharge and he returned to Cambridge, though never to graduate.

A decisive meeting with the poet Robert Southey during the summer of 1793 resulted in a scheme for an ideal community to be established on the banks of the Susquehanna River in Pennsylvania. To further the cause, Coleridge became engaged to Sara Fricker, the sister of Southey's fiancée. Following the inevitable collapse of their Utopian dream, Coleridge went through with the marriage to Sara, though inwardly "wretched."

In one extraordinary year, 1798–1799, Coleridge began his stimulating association with Wordsworth and his sister Dorothy, wrote three of his best poems ("The Rime of the Ancient Mariner," "Kubla Khan," and the first part of "Christabel"), and was given 150 pounds a year for life, relieving him of oppressive financial burdens. The relationship between the two poets led to the refining of their poetic gifts and the publication in 1798 of *Lyrical Ballads.* By 1801, Coleridge had become a confirmed opium addict. Suffering from neuralgia and other ailments, a marriage gone sour, and the ebbing of his creative powers, he continued to deteriorate physically and emotionally, a state of mind described in "Dejection: an Ode." At thirty-five he separated from his wife; in 1810 a quarrel with Wordsworth caused a breach in their friendship until a reconciliation in 1828.

Despite his lifelong struggle against the addictive powers of opium, Coleridge's accomplishments were prodigious. His major critical effort, the *Biographia Literaria,* published in 1817, provides an account of the purpose and origin of the *Lyrical Ballads* and an analysis of the excellence and defects of Wordsworth's poetry. From 1819 until his death in 1834, Coleridge lived in London in the house of James Gillman, a surgeon, receiving many distinguished visitors from England and America and acquiring his legendary reputation as a brilliant conversationalist.

Frost at Midnight

The Frost performs its secret ministry,
Unhelped by any wind. The owlet's cry
Came loud—and hark, again! loud as before.
The inmates of my cottage, all at rest,
5 Have left me to that solitude, which suits
Abstruser musings: save that at my side
My cradled infant[1] slumbers peacefully.
'Tis calm indeed! so calm, that it disturbs
And vexes meditation with its strange
10 And extreme silentness. Sea, hill, and wood,
This populous village! Sea, and hill, and wood,
With all the numberless goings-on of life,
Inaudible as dreams! the thin blue flame
Lies on my low-burnt fire, and quivers not;
15 Only that film,[2] which fluttered on the grate,
Still flutters there, the sole unquiet thing.
Methinks its motion in this hush of nature
Gives it dim sympathies with me who live,
Making it a companionable form,
20 Whose puny flaps and freaks the idling Spirit
By its own moods interprets, everywhere
Echo or mirror seeking of itself,
And makes a toy of Thought.

               But O! how oft,
How oft, at school,[3] with most believing mind,
25 Presageful, have I gazed upon the bars,
To watch that fluttering *stranger!* and as oft
With unclosed lids, already had I dreamt
Of my sweet birthplace, and the old church
    tower,
Whose bells, the poor man's only music, rang
30 From morn to evening, all the hot fair-day,
So sweetly, that they stirred and haunted me
With a wild pleasure, falling on mine ear
Most like articulate sounds of things to come!
So gazed I, till the soothing things, I dreamt,
35 Lulled me to sleep, and sleep prolonged my
    dreams!
And so I brooded all the following morn,
Awed by the stern preceptor's[4] face, mine eye
Fixed with mock study on my swimming book:
Save if the door half opened, and I snatched
40 A hasty glance, and still my heart leaped up,
For still I hoped to see the *stranger's* face,
Townsman, or aunt, or sister more beloved,
My playmate when we both were clothed alike![5]

Dear Babe, that sleepest cradled by my side,
45 Whose gentle breathings, heard in this deep
    calm,
Fill up the interspersèd vacancies
And momentary pauses of the thought!
My babe so beautiful! it thrills my heart
With tender gladness, thus to look at thee,
50 And think that thou shalt learn far other lore,
And in far other scenes! For I was reared
In the great city, pent 'mid cloisters dim,
And saw nought lovely but the sky and stars.
But *thou,* my babe! shalt wander like a breeze
55 By lakes and sandy shores, beneath the crags
Of ancient mountain, and beneath the clouds,
Which image in their bulk both lakes and
    shores
And mountain crags: so shalt thou see and hear
The lovely shapes and sounds intelligible
60 Of that eternal language, which thy God
Utters, who from eternity doth teach
Himself in all, and all things in himself
Great universal Teacher! he shall mold
Thy spirit, and by giving make it ask.

65   Therefore all seasons shall be sweet to thee,
Whether the summer clothe the general earth
With greenness, or the redbreast sit and sing
Betwixt the tufts of snow on the bare branch
Of mossy apple tree, while the nigh thatch
70 Smokes in the sun-thaw; whether the
    eave-drops fall
Heard only in the trances of the blast,
Or if the secret ministry of frost
Shall hang them up in silent icicles,
Quietly shining to the quiet Moon.

                      1798

---

1. **My cradled infant,** Coleridge's son, Hartley.
2. **film,** a film of soot. Coleridge's note on this reads: "In all parts of the kingdom these films are called *strangers* and are supposed to portend the arrival of some absent friend."
3. **school,** Christ's Hospital, London.
4. **stern preceptor,** James Boyer, master of Christ's Hospital.
5. **when we both were clothed alike,** i.e, when both Coleridge and his sister Ann wore infant clothes.

Chinese pagoda and bridge, designed by John Nash (1752—1835).

*K*ubla Khan

In Xanadu did Kubla Khan[1]
A stately pleasure-dome decree:
Where Alph, the sacred river, ran
Through caverns measureless to man
5   Down to a sunless sea.
So twice five miles of fertile ground
With walls and towers were girdled round:
And there were gardens bright with sinuous rills,
Where blossomed many an incense-bearing tree;
10 And here were forests ancient as the hills,
Enfolding sunny spots of greenery.

But oh! that deep romantic chasm which slanted

Down the green hill athwart a cedarn cover!
A savage place! as holy and enchanted
15 As e'er beneath a waning moon was haunted
By woman wailing for her demon-lover!
And from this chasm, with ceaseless turmoil seething,
As if this earth in fast thick pants were breathing,
A mighty fountain momently[2] was forced:
20 Amid whose swift half-intermitted burst
Huge fragments vaulted like rebounding hail,
Or chaffy grain beneath the thresher's flail:
And 'mid these dancing rocks at once and ever
It flung up momently the sacred river.
25 Five miles meandering with a mazy motion
Through wood and dale the sacred river ran,
Then reached the caverns measureless to man,
And sank in tumult to a lifeless ocean:
And 'mid this tumult Kubla heard from far
30 Ancestral voices prophesying war!
   The shadow of the dome of pleasure
   Floated midway on the waves;
   Where was heard the mingled measure
   From the fountain and the caves.
35 It was a miracle of rare device,
A sunny pleasure-dome with caves of ice!

   A damsel with a dulcimer
   In a vision once I saw:
   It was an Abyssinian maid,
40   And on her dulcimer she played,
   Singing of Mount Abora.
Could I revive within me
Her symphony and song,
To such a deep delight 'twould win me,
45 That with music loud and long,
I would build that dome in air,
That sunny dome! those caves of ice,
And all who heard should see them there,
And all should cry, Beware! Beware!
50 His flashing eyes, his floating hair!
Weave a circle round him thrice,
And close your eyes with holy dread,
For he on honey-dew hath fed,
And drunk the milk of Paradise.
1797   1816

---

1. **Kubla Khan,** founded the Mongol dynasty in China in the thirteenth century.
2. **momently,** intermittently, at every moment.

Comment: Coleridge's Remarks About "Kubla Khan"[1]

The following fragment is here published at the request of a poet of great and deserved celebrity,[2] and, as far as the author's own opinions are concerned, rather as a psychological curiosity, than on the ground of any supposed *poetic* merits.

In the summer of the year 1797, the author, then in ill health, had retired to a lonely farmhouse between Porlock and Linton, on the Exmoor confines of Somerset and Devonshire. In consequence of a slight indisposition, an anodyne had been prescribed, from the effects of which he fell asleep in his chair at the moment that he was reading the following sentence, or words of the same substance, in *Purchas's Pilgrimage:* "Here the Khan Kubla commanded a palace to be built, and a stately garden thereunto. And thus ten miles of fertile ground were inclosed with a wall." The author continued for about three hours in a profound sleep, at least of the external senses, during which time he has the most vivid confidence that he could not have composed less than from two to three hundred lines; if that indeed can be called composition in which all the images rose up before him as *things,* with a parallel production of the correspondent expressions, without any sensation or consciousness of effort. On awaking he appeared to himself to have a distinct recollection of the whole, and taking his pen, ink, and paper, instantly and eagerly wrote down the lines that are here preserved. At this moment he was unfortunately called out by a person on business from Porlock, and detained by him above an hour, and on his return to his room, found, to his no small surprise and mortification, that though he still retained some vague and dim recollection of the general purport of the vision, yet, with the exception of some eight or ten scattered lines and images, all the rest had passed away like the images on the surface of a stream into which a stone has been cast. . . .

---

1. These remarks by Coleridge were prefixed to "Kubla Khan" when it was first published in *Christabel; Kubla Khan, a Vision; The Pains of Sleep* (1816). Coleridge refers to himself in the third person in these remarks.
2. *poet . . . celebrity,* Byron.

Discussion

1. (a) What do Coleridge's memories in "Frost at Midnight" suggest about his boyhood? **(b)** What differences between his own school days and Hartley's does he wish for?

2. In line 1 and line 72 of "Frost at Midnight" Coleridge refers to the "secret ministry of frost." What are the implications of this phrase, particularly the word "ministry"?

3. Though dreamlike and incomplete, "Kubla Khan" has a first section that projects an ideal concept or realm, and a second section that expresses an aspiration to reach or transcend this ideal. Describe some of the extraordinary features of the "pleasure-dome."

4. Readers of "Kubla Khan" have often commented that the poem has sinister undertones. Do you find any? What lines or phrases suggest them to you?

Vocabulary

Etymologies

Use your Glossary to answer the following questions about the etymology or history of the words given below. Read each clue and then write on your paper the matching word from the list.

bard	beadle
genial	sinuous

1. Which word comes from Old French and means a kind of official person?

2. Which comes from a word in Latin that originally meant "curve"?

3. Which refers to singers of a sort who entertained from before recorded history to the Middle Ages?

4. Which comes from a Latin word, the original form of which we use to mean someone brilliant?

George Gordon, Lord Byron
1788–1824

Strikingly handsome, with a reputation for wickedness and free thought, George Gordon, Lord Byron embodied in his life and in his writings the figure subsequently known as the "Byronic hero": a moody, turbulent individualist, self-exiled from society after exhausting all possibilities of human excitement, and tormented by remorse over secret sins committed in the past.

Byron was descended from two high-strung, undisciplined families with reputations for reckless living and violence. Byron's father, a spendthrift army captain and playboy known as "Mad Jack," dissipated the fortunes of the two heiresses he married and left his widow to rear their three-year-old child in virtual poverty. Byron's mother was tempestuous, proud, and slightly mad, a person who alternately showered her child with love, then taunted him as a "lame brat" because of the deformed right foot with which he was born.

At the age of ten, George Gordon became the sixth Lord Byron upon the death of his great-uncle, inheriting a fortune and the estate of Newstead Abbey. He was later enrolled at Harrow, where he proved to be an indifferent student, but a fine athlete and leader. When Byron entered Cambridge at seventeen, he was well read in both Latin and Greek, excelled in swimming and boxing, and had already fallen in love twice. After graduation, Byron took the customary Grand Tour of Europe. Returning to London at age twenty-three, he published the first two cantos of *Childe Harold,* which were so immediately and prodigiously popular that, as he put it, "I awoke one morning and found myself famous." He took his seat in the House of Lords and made a brilliant speech defending workers who had wrecked machinery that threatened their jobs.

Enjoying his role as the favorite of London society, Byron gained the reputation of being one who was "mad, bad, and dangerous to know." He dressed as he felt a poet should and cultivated a deliberately mysterious air. After several love affairs, he married the nobly born, very proper Annabella Milbanke in an attempt to gain some stability and respectability in his life. After one year of marriage that caused her to question her husband's sanity, his wife returned to her parents with their newborn daughter. The circumstances of the separation scandalized English society and led to Byron's decision, in 1816, to leave England for good.

"Making a public show of a very genuine misery, he swept across Europe the pageant of his bleeding heart." Thus Matthew Arnold described Byron's conduct following his moral banishment from England as he wandered across the Continent. Despite being "half mad during the time . . . between metaphysics, mountains, lakes, love unextinguishable, thoughts unutterable, and the nightmare of my own delinquencies," Byron poured out some of his greatest work.

Even today Byron remains a legend and a paradox—a fiery rebel and a conventional aristocrat, an idealist and a cynic, a scandalous playboy to his countrymen and a hero to the Greeks, to whose war of liberation from Turkish rule his money and energies were committed during the months before his death at Missolonghi on April 19, 1824, at the age of thirty-six.

She Walks in Beauty

She[1] walks in beauty, like the night
  Of cloudless climes and starry skies;
And all that's best of dark and bright
  Meet in her aspect and her eyes:
5 Thus mellowed to that tender light
  Which heaven to gaudy day denies.

One shade the more, one ray the less,
  Had half impaired the nameless grace
Which waves in every raven tress,
10   Or softly lightens o'er her face;
Where thoughts serenely sweet express
  How pure, how dear their dwelling-place.

And on that cheek, and o'er that brow,
  So soft, so calm, yet eloquent,
15 The smiles that win, the tints that glow,
  But tell of days in goodness spent,
A mind at peace with all below,
  A heart whose love is innocent!

1814   1815

---

1. **She,** Lady Wilmot Horton, Byron's beautiful young cousin by marriage, who had appeared in an evening dress of black mourning brightened with spangles.

So We'll Go No More A-Roving

So we'll go no more a-roving
  So late into the night,
Though the heart be still as loving,
  And the moon be still as bright.

5 For the sword outwears its sheath,
  And the soul wears out the breast,
And the heart must pause to breathe,
  And Love itself have rest.

Though the night was made for loving,
10   And the day returns too soon,
Yet we'll go no more a-roving
  By the light of the moon.

1817   1830

When We Two Parted

When we two parted
  In silence and tears,
Half broken-hearted
  To sever for years,
5 Pale grew thy cheek and cold,
  Colder thy kiss;
Truly that hour foretold
  Sorrow to this.

The dew of the morning
10   Sunk chill on my brow—
It felt like the warning
  Of what I feel now.
Thy vows are all broken,
  And light is thy fame;
15 I hear thy name spoken,
  And share in its shame.

They name thee before me,
  A knell to mine ear;
A shudder comes o'er me—
20   Why wert thou so dear?
They know not I knew thee,
  Who knew thee too well—
Long, long shall I rue thee,
  Too deeply to tell.

25 In secret we met—
  In silence I grieve,
That thy heart could forget,
  Thy spirit deceive.
If I should meet thee
30   After long years,
How should I greet thee?—
  With silence and tears.

1808   1816

Discussion

1. "She Walks in Beauty" expresses both a physical and spiritual ideal. **(a)** Keeping in mind that standards of beauty vary from age to age, identify what the speaker has set forth as a physical ideal. **(b)** What spiritual ideal does the woman described embody?

2. Which aspects of beauty—the physical or the spiritual—does the poem more strongly emphasize?

3. What experience does "When We Two Parted" describe?

4. **(a)** As he reflects on the parting from his beloved, what does the speaker recognize as a presentiment of future sorrow? **(b)** The speaker declares: "Long, long shall I rue thee." What circumstances have made the experience especially unhappy?

5. The second stanza of "So We'll Go No More A-Roving" explains the title. Why will there be no more roving?

6. What is the basic mood of the poem?

The Don Juan legend of the great lover had been popular in Europe for centuries before Byron's version. It first appeared in literary form in a play by the Spanish dramatist Tirso de Molina (1570?–1648). In addition to Byron's *Don Juan* (pronounced jü'ən, not hwän), a play by Molière, Mozart's opera *Don Giovanni,* and the "Don Juan in Hell" scene in Shaw's *Man and Superman* are some of the more famous treatments of the theme.

Byron confided in a letter to Thomas Moore that his poem was probably "too free for these very modest days," and indeed the first five cantos were published anonymously by Byron, who had already outraged the English public. "Confess, confess, you dog," wrote Byron in a letter, ". . . it may be bawdy but is it not good English? It may be profligate but is it not *life,* is it not *the thing?*"

To his publisher, who had asked for the plan of the poem, Byron wrote: "I had not quite fixed whether to make him end in Hell, or in an unhappy marriage, not knowing which would be the severest. The Spanish tradition says Hell: but it is probably only an Allegory of the other state."

from Don Juan

from Canto I

1

I want a hero: an uncommon want,
  When every year and month sends forth a
    new one,
Till, after cloying the gazettes with cant,
  The age discovers he is not the true one;
5 Of such as these I should not care to vaunt,
  I'll therefore take our ancient friend Don
    Juan—
We all have seen him, in the pantomime,
Sent to the devil somewhat ere his time.

6

Most epic poets plunge "in medias res"[1]
10   (Horace makes this the heroic turnpike road),
And then your hero tells, whene'er you please,
  What went before—by way of episode,
While seated after dinner at his ease,
  Beside his mistress in some soft abode,
15 Palace, or garden, paradise, or cavern,
Which serves the happy couple for a tavern.

7

That is the usual method, but not mine—
  My way is to begin with the beginning;
The regularity of my design

20   Forbids all wandering as the worst of sinning,
And therefore I shall open with a line
  (Although it cost me half an hour in spinning)
Narrating somewhat of Don Juan's father,
And also of his mother, if you'd rather.

8

25 In Seville was he born, a pleasant city,
  Famous for oranges and women—he
Who has not seen it will be much to pity,
  So says the proverb—and I quite agree;
Of all the Spanish towns is none more pretty.
30   Cadiz, perhaps—but that you soon may see—
Don Juan's parents lived beside the river,
A noble stream, and called the Guadalquivir.

9

His father's name was Jóse—*Don,* of course,
  A true Hidalgo,[2] free from every stain
35 Of Moor or Hebrew blood, he traced his source
  Through the most Gothic gentlemen of Spain;
A better cavalier ne'er mounted horse,
  Or, being mounted, e'er got down again,

---

1. **"in medias res"** (in mā'dē äs räs'), "in the middle of things," from the Latin poet Horace.
2. **Hidalgo,** a member of the lower Spanish nobility.

Than Jóse, who begot our hero, who
40 Begot—but that's to come—Well, to renew:

10

His mother was a learnèd lady, famed
    For every branch of every science known—
In every Christian language ever named,
    With virtues equalled by her wit alone:
45 She made the cleverest people quite ashamed,
    And even the good with inward envy groan,
Finding themselves so very much exceeded
In their own way by all the things that she did.

13

She knew the Latin—that is, "the Lord's
    prayer,"
50   And Greek—the alphabet—I'm nearly sure;
She read some French romances here and there,
    Although her mode of speaking was not pure;
For native Spanish she had no great care,
    At least her conversation was obscure;
55 Her thoughts were theorems, her words a
    problem,
    As if she deemed that mystery would ennoble
    'em.

15

Some women use their tongues—she *looked* a
    lecture,
    Each eye a sermon, and her brow a homily,
An all-in-all sufficient self-director,
60   Like the lamented late Sir Samuel Romilly,[3]
The Law's expounder, and the State's
    corrector,
    Whose suicide was almost an anomaly—
One sad example more, that "All is vanity,"—
(The jury brought their verdict in "Insanity.")

17

65 Oh! she was perfect past all parallel—
    Of any modern female saint's comparison;
So far above the cunning powers of hell,
    Her guardian angel had given up his garrison;
Even her minutest motions went as well
70   As those of the best time-piece made by
    Harrison:[4]
In virtues nothing earthly could surpass her,
Save thine "incomparable oil," Macassar![5]

18

Perfect she was, but as perfection is
    Insipid in this naughty world of ours,
75 Where our first parents never learned to kiss
    Till they were exiled from their earlier bowers,
Where all was peace, and innocence, and bliss
    (I wonder how they got through the twelve
    hours),
Don Jóse, like a lineal son of Eve,
80 Went plucking various fruit without her leave.

19

He was a mortal of the careless kind,
    With no great love for learning, or the
    learned,
Who chose to go where'er he had a mind,
    And never dreamed his lady was concerned;
85 The world, as usual, wickedly inclined
    To see a kingdom or a house o'erturned,
Whispered he had a mistress, some said *two*,
But for domestic quarrels *one* will do.

20

Now Donna Inez had, with all her merit,
90   A great opinion of her own good qualities;
Neglect, indeed, requires a saint to bear it,
    And such, indeed, she was in her moralities;
But then she had a devil of a spirit,
    And sometimes mixed up fancies with realities,
95 And let few opportunities escape
Of getting her liege lord into a scrape.

23

Don Jóse and his lady quarrelled—*why*,
    Not any of the many could divine,
Though several thousand people chose to try,
100   'Twas surely no concern of theirs nor mine;
I loathe that low vice—curiosity;
    But if there's anything in which I shine,
'Tis in arranging all my friends' affairs,
Not having, of my own, domestic cares.

---

3. *Sir Samuel Romilly,* an English lawyer who represented
Byron's wife in her suit for divorce; he committed suicide in
1818.
4. *Harrison,* John Harrison (1693-1776), English watchmaker
who invented the first practical marine chronometer, enabling
sailors to compute accurately their longitude at sea.
5. *Macassar,* a fragrant oil used as a hair dressing.

24

105 And so I interfered, and with the best
　　Intentions, but their treatment was not kind;
I think the foolish people were possessed,
　　For neither of them could I ever find,
Although their porter afterwards confessed—
110　　But that's no matter, and the worst's behind,
For little Juan o'er me threw, downstairs,
A pail of housemaid's water unawares.

25

A little curly-headed, good-for-nothing,
　　And mischief-making monkey from his birth;
115 His parents ne'er agreed except in doting
　　Upon the most unquiet imp on earth;
Instead of quarreling, had they been but both
　　　in
　　Their senses, they'd have sent young master
　　　forth
To school, or had him soundly whipped at
　　home.
120 To teach him manners for the time to come.

26

Don Jóse and the Donna Inez led
　　For some time an unhappy sort of life,
Wishing each other, not divorced, but dead;
　　They lived respectably as man and wife,
125 Their conduct was exceedingly well-bred,
　　And gave no outward signs of inward strife,
Until at length the smothered fire broke out,
And put the business past all kind of doubt.

27

For Inez called some druggists and physicians,
130　　And tried to prove her loving lord was *mad,*
But as he had some lucid intermissions,
　　She next decided he was only *bad;*
Yet when they asked her for her depositions,
　　No sort of explanation could be had,
135 Save that her duty both to man and God
Required this conduct—which seemed very odd.

32

Their friends had tried at reconciliation,
　　Then their relations, who made matters worse
('Twere hard to tell upon a like occasion
140　　To whom it may be best to have recourse—
I can't say much for friend or yet relation);
　　The lawyers did their utmost for divorce,

But scarce a fee was paid on either side
Before, unluckily, Don Jóse died.

33

145 He died: and most unluckily, because,
　　According to all hints I could collect
From counsel learned in those kinds of laws
　　(Although their talk's obscure and
　　　circumspect),
His death contrived to spoil a charming cause;
150　　A thousand pities also with respect
To public feeling, which on this occasion
Was manifested in a great sensation.

37

Dying intestate, Juan was sole heir
　　To a chancery[6] suit, and messuages,[7] and
　　　lands,
155 Which, with a long minority and care,
　　Promised to turn out well in proper hands:
Inez became sole guardian, which was fair,
　　And answered but to nature's just demands;
An only son left with an only mother
160 Is brought up much more wisely than another.

38

Sagest of women, even of widows, she
　　Resolved that Juan should be quite a paragon,
And worthy of the noblest pedigree
　　(His sire was of Castile, his dam from
　　　Aragon).
165 Then for accomplishments of chivalry,
　　In case our lord the king should go to war
　　　again,
He learned the arts of riding, fencing, gunnery,
And how to scale a fortress—or a nunnery.

39

But that which Donna Inez most desired,
170　　And saw into herself each day before all
The learnèd tutors whom for him she hired,
　　Was that his breeding should be strictly
　　　moral:
Much into all his studies she inquired,
　　And so they were submitted first to her, all,
175 Arts, sciences, no branch was made a mystery
To Juan's eyes, excepting natural history.

---

6. *chancery,* high court in England famous for its delays.
7. *messuages* (mes'wij əz), houses together with adjacent
buildings.

40

The languages, especially the dead,
    The sciences, and most of all the abstruse,
The arts, at least all such as could be said
180   To be the most remote from common use,
In all these he was much and deeply read;
    But not a page of anything that's loose,
Or hints continuation of the species,
Was ever suffered, lest he should grow vicious.

41

185 His classic studies made a little puzzle,
    Because of filthy loves of gods and
      goddesses,
Who in the earlier ages raised a bustle,
    But never put on pantaloons or bodices;
His reverend tutors had at times a tussle,
190   And for their Aeneids, Iliads, and Odysseys,
Were forced to make an odd sort of apology,
For Donna Inez dreaded the Mythology.

44

Juan was taught from out the best edition,
    Expurgated by learnèd men, who place,
195 Judiciously, from out the schoolboy's vision,

The grosser parts; but, fearful to deface
Too much their modest bard by this omission,
    And pitying sore this mutilated case,
They only add them all in an appendix,
200 Which saves, in fact, the trouble of an index.

45

For there we have them all "at one fell swoop,"
    Instead of being scattered through the pages;
They stand forth marshalled in a handsome
      troop,
    To meet the ingenuous youth of future ages,
205 Till some less rigid editor shall stoop
    To call them back into their separate cages,
Instead of standing staring all together,
Like garden gods—and not so decent either.

47

Sermons he read, and lectures he endured,
210   And homilies, and lives of all the saints;
To Jerome and to Chrysostom[8] inured,
    He did not take such studies for restraints;
But how faith is acquired, and then ensured,
    So well not one of the aforesaid paints

---

8. **Jerome . . . Chrysostom,** early Christian writers.

A Spanish Fiesta
(1836) by John
Frederick Lewis.

215 As Saint Augustine in his fine Confessions,⁹
Which make the reader envy his
transgressions.

48

This, too was a sealed book to little Juan—
I can't but say that his mamma was right,
If such an education was the true one.
220 She scarcely trusted him from out her sight;
Her maids were old, and if she took a new one,
You might be sure she was a perfect fright;
She did this during even her husband's life—
I recommend as much to every wife.

49

225 Young Juan waxed in godliness and grace;
At six a charming child, and at eleven
With all the promise of as fine a face
As e'er to man's maturer growth was
given—.
He studied steadily and grew apace,
230 And seemed, at least, in the right road to
heaven,
For half his days were passed at church, the
other
Between his tutors, confessor, and mother.

50

At six, I said, he was a charming child,
At twelve he was a fine, but quiet boy;
235 Although in infancy a little wild,
They tamed him down amongst them: to
destroy
His natural spirit not in vain they toiled.
At least it seemed so; and his mother's joy
Was to declare how sage, and still, and steady,
240 Her young philosopher was grown already.

54

Young Juan now was sixteen years of age,
Tall, handsome, slender, but well knit: he
seemed
Active, though not so sprightly, as a page;
And everybody but his mother deemed
245 Him almost man; but she flew in a rage
And bit her lips (for else she might have
screamed)
If any said so, for to be precocious
Was in her eyes a thing the most atrocious.

55

Amongst her numerous acquaintance, all
250 Selected for discretion and devotion,
There was the Donna Julia, whom to call
Pretty were but to give a feeble notion
Of many charms in her as natural
As sweetness to the flower, or salt to ocean,
255 Her zone to Venus, or his bow to Cupid,
(But this last simile is trite and stupid).

60

Her eye (I'm very fond of handsome eyes)
Was large and dark, suppressing half its fire
Until she spoke, then through its soft disguise
260 Flashed an expression more of pride than ire,
And love than either; and there would arise
A something in them which was not desire,
But would have been, perhaps, but for the soul
Which struggled through and chastened down
the whole.

61

265 Her glossy hair was clustered o'er a brow
Bright with intelligence, and fair, and smooth;
Her eyebrow's shape was like the aërial bow,
Her cheek all purple with the beam of youth,
Mounting, at times, to a transparent glow,
270 As if her veins ran lightning; she, in sooth,
Possessed an air and grace by no means
common;
Her stature tall—I hate a dumpy woman.

62

Wedded she was some years, and to a man
Of fifty, and such husbands are in plenty;
275 And yet, I think, instead of such a ONE
'Twere better to have TWO of
five-and-twenty,
Especially in countries near the sun:
And now I think on't, "mi vien in mente,"¹⁰
Ladies even of the most uneasy virtue
280 Prefer a spouse whose age is short of thirty.

69

Juan she saw, and, as a pretty child,
Caressed him often—such a thing might be

---

9. Saint Augustine . . . Confessions. In his *Confessions* Saint
Augustine (354–430) describes a variety of his youthful sins.
10. "mi vien in mente" (mē vē en' in men'tā), "it comes to
mind." [Italian]

Quite innocently done, and harmless styled,
    When she had twenty years, and thirteen he;
285 But I am not so sure I should have smiled
    When he was sixteen, Julia twenty-three;
These few short years make wondrous
        alterations,
Particularly amongst sunburnt nations.

70

Whate'er the cause might be, they had become
290   Changed; for the dame grew distant, the
            youth shy,
Their looks cast down, their greetings almost
        dumb,
    And much embarrassment in either eye;
There surely will be little doubt with some
    That Donna Julia knew the reason why,
295 But as for Juan, he had no more notion
Than he who never saw the sea, of ocean.

71

Yet Julia's very coldness still was kind,
    And tremulously gentle her small hand
Withdrew itself from his, but left behind
300   A little pressure, thrilling, and so bland
And slight, so very slight, that to the mind
    'Twas but a doubt; but ne'er magician's wand
Wrought change with all Armida's[11] fairy art
    Like what this light touch left on Juan's heart.

72

305 And if she met him, though she smiled no more,
    She looked a sadness sweeter than her smile,
As if her heart had deeper thoughts in store
    She must not own, but cherished more the
        while
For that compression in its burning core;
310   Even innocence itself has many a wile,
And will not dare to trust itself with truth,
And love is taught hypocrisy from youth.

75

Poor Julia's heart was in an awkward state;
    She felt it going, and resolved to make
315 The noblest efforts for herself and mate,
    For honor's, pride's, religion's, virtue's sake.
Her resolutions were most truly great,
    And almost might have made a Tarquin[12] quake:
She prayed the Virgin Mary for her grace,
320 As being the best judge of a lady's case.

76

She vowed she never would see Juan more,
    And next day paid a visit to his mother,
And looked extremely at the opening door,
    Which, by the Virgin's grace, let in another;
325 Grateful she was, and yet a little sore—
    Again it opens, it can be no other,
'Tis surely Juan now—No! I'm afraid
That night the Virgin was no further prayed.

77

She now determined that a virtuous woman
330   Should rather face and overcome temptation,
That flight was base and dastardly, and no man
    Should ever give her heart the least sensation;
That is to say, a thought beyond the common
    Preference, that we must feel upon occasion,
335 For people who are pleasanter than others,
But then they only seem so many brothers.

78

And even if by chance—and who can tell?
    The devil's so very sly—she should discover
That all within was not so very well,
340   And, if still free, that such a lover
Might please perhaps, a virtuous wife can quell
    Such thoughts, and be the better when
        they're over;
And if the man should ask, 'tis but denial:
I recommend young ladies to make trial.

79

345 And then there are such things as love divine,
    Bright and immaculate, unmixed and pure,
Such as the angels think so very fine,
    And matrons, who would be no less secure,
Platonic, perfect, "just such love as mine":
350   Thus Julia said—and thought so, to be sure,
And so I'd have her think, were I the man
On whom her reveries celestial ran.

86

So much for Julia. Now we'll turn to Juan.
    Poor little fellow! he had no idea
355 Of his own case, and never hit the true one;

---

11. Armida, a sorceress mentioned in *Jerusalem Delivered*, an
epic poem by the Italian Renaissance poet Torquato Tasso
(1544–1595).
12. a Tarquin, one of the legendary kings of ancient Rome,
noted for their lustiness.

In feelings quick as Ovid's Miss Medea,[13]
He puzzled over what he found a new one,
   But not as yet imagined it could be a
Thing quite in course, and not at all alarming,
360 Which, with a little patience, might grow
     charming.

87

Silent and pensive, idle, restless, slow,
   His home deserted for the lonely wood,
Tormented with a wound he could not know,
   His, like all deep grief, plunged in solitude:
365 I'm fond myself of solitude or so,
   But then, I beg it may be understood,
By solitude I mean a Sultan's, not
A hermit's, with a harem for a grot.

90

Young Juan wandered by the glassy brooks,
370   Thinking unutterable things; he threw
Himself at length within the leafy nooks
   Where the wild branch of the cork forest grew;
There poets find materials for their books,
   And every now and then we read them
     through,
375 So that their plan and prosody are eligible,
Unless, like Wordsworth, they prove
     unintelligible.

91

He, Juan (and not Wordsworth), so pursued
   His self-communion with his own high soul,
Until his mighty heart, in its great mood,
380   Had mitigated part, though not the whole
Of its disease; he did the best he could
   With things not very subject to control,
And turned, without perceiving his condition,
Like Coleridge, into a metaphysician.

92

385 He thought about himself, and the whole earth,
   Of man the wonderful, and of the stars,
And how the deuce they ever could have birth;
   And then he thought of earthquakes, and of
     wars,
How many miles the moon might have in girth,
390   Of air-balloons, and of the many bars
To perfect knowledge of the boundless skies—
And then he thought of Donna Julia's eyes.
1818   1819

There are 132 more stanzas in the remainder of Canto I of *Don Juan*. Between 1819 and 1823 Byron added fifteen more cantos to the poem.

---

13. Ovid's Miss Medea. In the *Metamorphoses,* Ovid presents Medea as a quick-tempered woman who took dreadful revenge on Jason for deserting her.

Discussion

1. In stanza 6, the speaker refers to one of the **epic** conventions. What is the convention? What use does he intend to make of it in his own epic, as he tells us in stanza 7?

2. In stanza 7, the speaker states that the regularity of his plans for his epic poem "Forbids all wandering as the worst of sinning," and then proceeds immediately to digress. Point out examples of "wandering" in other stanzas.

3. In stanzas 10-18 Donna Inez is described. The speaker says, "Oh! she was perfect past all parallel." What examples of her character and behavior reveal that the speaker meant just the opposite?

4. What view of marriage is conveyed through the description of Don José and Donna Inez's relationship?

5. (a) What plans does Donna Inez have for her son? What is the speaker's attitude toward these plans? **(b)** Which aspects of Don Juan's education are most sharply satirized? What comment is the speaker making about the society of his times?

6. The encounter between Donna Julia and Don Juan exploits the stock situation of comedy and farce of the beautiful young woman, married to an old husband, who gets involved with a younger man. How sincere are Donna Julia's efforts to resist temptation?

7. Most of Byron's stanzas contain some sort of "punch line." Locate a few examples. Describe the effect in terms of any of the following words: mild, sharp, stinging, savage, childish, clever, showy, profound.

Percy Bysshe Shelley

1792–1822

Like Byron, Shelley was an exceptionally controversial personality, whose reputation was marred by scandal. He was known for his personal charm, unwavering opposition to tyranny, and great gifts. Unlike Byron, whose literary reputation was legendary during his lifetime, Shelley achieved recognition only after death. By the end of the nineteenth century, however, he had become a primary force in English poetry, influencing the work of such later writers as Browning, Swinburne, Hardy, and Yeats.

Shelley was the eldest son of a well-to-do country squire who never understood nor was able to control his maverick child. During his unhappy school years, Shelley was bullied by the older boys because of his slight build and moody shyness; he became known at Eton as "mad Shelley" because of his eccentric ways. Although a brilliant student, he was always resentful of authority. At Oxford his rebelliousness and nonconformist behavior caused him severe problems, especially since he had become a convert to the radical philosophy of William Godwin. His collaboration on a pamphlet entitled *The Necessity of Atheism* resulted in his abrupt expulsion from Oxford and a further strain in his relationship with his parents.

Soon after leaving for London, Shelley eloped with sixteen-year-old Harriet Westbrooke, with whom he had two children. Three years later he fell in love with William Godwin's daughter, Mary, and eloped with her to Switzerland, ringing the final knell on his public reputation. In 1816 Harriet committed suicide and, shortly thereafter, Shelley married Mary Godwin, but he never fully recovered from the scorn the English public heaped upon him for his actions. The courts also denied him custody of his two children by Harriet.

In 1818 Shelley and Mary moved to Italy. Shelley's last four years were a time of close friendships, most notably with Byron, and highly productive work, including the writing of a tragedy, *The Cenci;* his masterpiece, *Pro-metheus Unbound;* and numerous lyrics, such as "Ode to the West Wind," "Ozymandias," "Ode to a Skylark," and "The Cloud." During the year 1821, he published his magnificent elegy for Keats, "Adonais," and *A Defense of Poetry.*

In 1822, when Shelley was approaching his thirtieth birthday, he was drowned while sailing off the Italian coast. His body washed ashore ten days later. A volume of Keats was found in one pocket and a volume of Sophocles in the other. He was cremated by friends on a funeral pyre on the beach. Byron was present and swam out to watch the flames that devoured his friend and fellow exile. Shelley's ashes were buried near Keats's grave in the Protestant Cemetery in Rome. Describing his valued friend, Byron called Shelley, "the best and least selfish man I ever knew. I never knew one who was not a beast in comparison."

Wordsworth was once a courageous spokesman for "truth and liberty" in literature and politics, a liberal activist who set an example for others in the struggle for freedom and reform; in later life Wordsworth grew very conservative, turning his back on causes he earlier espoused. Shelley, whose desire to reform the world never wavered, felt hurt and betrayed by Wordsworth's abandonment of liberal causes and ideals. In "To Wordsworth" (page 398) Shelley laments the change in his former hero.

To Wordsworth

Poet of Nature, thou hast wept to know
That things depart which never may return:
Childhood and youth, friendship and love's
    first glow,
Have fled like sweet dreams, leaving thee to
    mourn.
5 These common woes I feel. One loss is mine
Which thou too feel'st, yet I alone deplore.
Thou wert as a lone star, whose light did shine
On some frail bark in winter's midnight roar:
Thou hast like to a rock-built refuge stood
10 Above the blind and battling multitude:
In honored poverty thy voice did weave
Songs consecrate to truth and liberty,—
Deserting these, thou leavest me to grieve,
Thus having been, that thou shouldst cease to
    be.

1815   1816

Music, When Soft Voices Die

Music, when soft voices die,
Vibrates in the memory—
Odors, when sweet violets sicken,
Live within the sense they quicken.

5 Rose leaves, when the rose is dead,
Are heaped for the beloved's bed;
And so thy thoughts, when thou art gone,
Love itself shall slumber on.

1821   1824

England in 1819

An old, mad, blind, despised, and dying king[1]—
Princes, the dregs of their dull race, who flow
Through public scorn—mud from a muddy
    spring;
Rulers who neither see, nor feel, nor know,
5 But leechlike to their fainting country cling,
Till they drop, blind in blood, without a blow;
A people starved and stabbed in the untilled
    field—
An army, which liberticide and prey
Makes as a two-edged sword to all who wield;
10 Golden and sanguine laws which tempt and slay;
Religion Christless, Godless—a book sealed;
A Senate—Time's worst statute[2] unrepealed—
Are graves, from which a glorious Phantom[3]
    may
Burst, to illumine your tempestuous day.

1819   1839

---

1. **An old . . . king,** George III, who died in 1820, blind and insane.
2. **Time's worst statute,** the law restricting the civil liberties of Roman Catholics, which was not repealed until 1829.
3. **Phantom,** revolution.

Discussion

1. In "To Wordsworth," what "common woes" that Wordsworth experienced and wrote about has Shelley also known?

2. Explain the double meaning of the last line, especially of the words "been" and "be."

3. (a) What is the condition of England in "England in 1819" as Shelley views it? (b) What specific faults of the country's rulers does the sonnet identify?

4. (a) In the last two lines of the same poem, what is predicted? (b) To what does the word "graves" (line 13) refer?

5. What is the tone of "England in 1819"?

6. (a) State the central idea of "Music, When Soft Voices Die." (b) What three examples of this idea are provided in lines 1–6? (c) Describe the emotional progression in the poem, taking into account the order in which the examples are presented.

Funerary temple of Ramses II at Thebes, sketched by
David Roberts in 1838.

O*zymandias*

I met a traveler from an antique land
Who said: Two vast and trunkless legs of stone
Stand in the desert . . . Near them, on the
  sand,
Half sunk, a shattered visage lies, whose
  frown,
5 And wrinkled lip, and sneer of cold
  command,
Tell that its sculptor well those passions read
Which yet survive, stamped on these lifeless
  things,
The hand that mocked them, and the heart
  that fed:[1]
And on the pedestal these words appear:
10 "My name is Ozymandias, king of kings:
Look on my works, ye Mighty, and
  despair!"
Nothing beside remains. Round the decay
Of that colossal wreck, boundless and bare
The lone and level sands stretch far away.
1817   1818

---

1. **The hand . . . fed,** that is, the passions carved in the stone
have outlived the hand that sculpted ("mocked" or imitated)
them and the pharaoh's heart that nurtured them.

According to an early Greek historian, Ozymandias (more commonly known as Ramses II) was an Egyptian pharaoh whose huge statue bore the following inscription: "I am Ozymandias, King of Kings; if anyone wishes to know what I am and where I lie, let him surpass me in some of my exploits."

Discussion

1. Given the description by the traveler of the present condition of the statue and landscape, what **irony** is there in the inscription on the pedestal?

2. What does the line "The hand that mocked them, and the heart that fed" ironically explain about both the sculptor and the tyrant Ozymandias?

3. What comment, if any, is Shelley making on tyranny?

Of the inspiration for "Ode to the West Wind," Shelley wrote: "This poem was conceived and chiefly written in a wood that skirts the Arno, near Florence, and on a day when that tempestuous wind, whose temperature is at once mild and animating, was collecting the vapors which pour down the autumnal rains. They began, as I foresaw, at sunset with a violent tempest of hail and rain, attended by that magnificent thunder and lightning peculiar to the . . . regions."

Ode to the West Wind

1

O wild West Wind, thou breath of Autumn's
    being,
Thou, from whose unseen presence the
    leaves dead
Are driven, like ghosts from an enchanter
    fleeing,

Yellow, and black, and pale, and hectic red,
5 Pestilence-stricken multitudes: O thou,
Who chariotest to their dark wintry bed

The wingèd seeds, where they lie cold and
    low,
Each like a corpse within its grave, until
Thine azure sister of the Spring shall blow

10 Her clarion o'er the dreaming earth, and fill
(Driving sweet buds like flocks to feed in air)
With living hues and odors plain and hill:

Wild Spirit, which art moving everywhere;
Destroyer and preserver; hear, oh, hear!

2

15 Thou on whose stream, mid the steep sky's
    commotion,
Loose clouds like earth's decaying leaves
    are shed,
Shook from the tangled boughs of Heaven
    and Ocean,

Angels of rain and lightning: there are spread
On the blue surface of thine aëry surge,
20 Like the bright hair uplifted from the head

Of some fierce Maenad,[1] even from the dim
    verge
Of the horizon to the zenith's height,
The locks of the approaching storm. Thou
    dirge

Of the dying year, to which this closing night
25 Will be the dome of a vast sepulcher,
Vaulted with all thy congregated might

Of vapors, from whose solid atmosphere
Black rain, and fire, and hail will burst: oh
    hear!

3

Thou who didst waken from his summer
    dreams
30 The blue Mediterranean, where he lay,
Lulled by the coil of his crystàlline streams,

Beside a pumice isle in Baiae's bay,[2]
And saw in sleep old palaces and towers
Quivering within the wave's intenser day,

35 All overgrown with azure moss and flowers
So sweet, the sense faints picturing them!
    Thou
For whose path the Atlantic's level powers[3]

---

1. **Maenad** (mē'nad), a priestess of Dionysus, Greek god of wine, who was worshiped with savage, orgiastic rites.
2. **Baiae's** (bä'yäz) **bay.** The modern village of Baia is a seaport about ten miles from Naples in Italy.
3. **the Atlantic's level powers,** the surface of the ocean.

Cleave themselves into chasms, while far
    below
The sea-blooms and the oozy woods which
    wear
40 The sapless foliage of the ocean, know

Thy voice, and suddenly grow gray with
    fear,
And tremble and despoil themselves: oh,
    hear!

4

If I were a dead leaf thou mightest bear;
If I were a swift cloud to fly with thee;
45 A wave to pant beneath thy power, and
    share

The impulse of thy strength, only less free
Than thou, O uncontrollable! If even
I were as in my boyhood, and could be

The comrade of thy wanderings over
    Heaven,
50 As then, when to outstrip the skyey speed
Scarce seemed a vision; I would ne'er have
    striven

As thus with thee in prayer in my sore need.
Oh, lift me as a wave, a leaf, a cloud!
I fall upon the thorns of life! I bleed!

55 A heavy weight of hours has chained and
    bowed
One too like thee: tameless, and swift, and
    proud.

5

Make me thy lyre, even as the forest is:
What if my leaves are falling like its own!
The tumult of thy mighty harmonies

60 Will take from both a deep, autumnal tone,
Sweet though in sadness. Be thou, Spirit
    fierce,
My spirit! Be thou me, impetuous one!

Drive my dead thoughts over the universe
Like withered leaves to quicken a new birth!
65 And, by the incantation of this verse,

Scatter, as from an unextinguished hearth
Ashes and sparks, my words among
    mankind!
Be through my lips to unawakened earth

The trumpet of a prophecy! O Wind,
70 If Winter comes, can Spring be far behind?
1819   1820

Discussion

1. "Ode to the West Wind" is divided into five sections. What is the topic of each section?

2. What two contradictory forces does the West Wind represent? What echoes of this **paradox** do you find throughout the poem? In what sense is the West Wind a spirit "moving everywhere"?

3. In the fourth stanza the poet draws a comparison between himself and the West Wind. How are they alike? In what ways are they different?

4. The fifth stanza begins with the request, "Make me thy lyre," and concludes with the command, "Be through my lips . . . / The trumpet of a prophecy!" What change in the poet's attitude toward himself and in the tone of the poem is marked by the movement from "lyre" to "trumpet"?

5. (a) What does Shelley see in the West Wind that he envies and desires for himself as a poet? (b) In what sense would Shelley as poet, like the West Wind, function as both "destroyer" and "preserver"?

John Keats 1795–1821

John Keats was born in London, the eldest of four children. His father, a cockney stable keeper, was killed in a riding accident when John was nine; six years later his mother died of tuberculosis. From the age of eight to fifteen, Keats attended a small school at Enfield, where he distinguished himself as a brilliant student and acquired his passionate love of English poetry. At the age of fifteen, soon after his mother's death, his guardians apprenticed him to an apothecary (druggist) and surgeon. Although he spent some time working in London hospitals and qualified to practice as an apothecary, he soon abandoned this profession to devote his time to literature.

With support from the critic Leigh Hunt, the poet William Wordsworth, and the essayist Charles Lamb, Keats at age twenty-one began his literary career in earnest. According to a school friend, for Keats "the greatest men in the world were the Poets, and to rank among them was the chief object of his ambition." In the fall of 1818, Keats returned home to nurse his younger brother Tom until the latter's death, in December, from tuberculosis. Soon after, the publication of *Endymion,* his first sustained poetic effort, received unduly harsh criticism. Critics, mocking his cockney heritage and his medical training, advised him to go back to his "plaster, pills, and ointment boxes" and leave the writing of poetry to the educated and cultured. This adverse publicity kept his poetry from selling and left him almost destitute. Meanwhile, Keats fell in love with the beautiful and lively Fanny Brawne. Their intense and hopeless love affair was an added source of anguish for the passionate young man who desired marriage but found himself thwarted by financial difficulties and worsening health.

Despite sorrow and adversities, the year 1819 was for Keats one of profound growth as a poet. Uplifted by an unusually beautiful and early spring, he produced such exalted works as "The Eve of St. Agnes," "La Belle Dame Sans Merci," and his great odes. The following spring his last book was published—*Lamia, Isabella, The Eve of St. Agnes, and Other Poems* (the book found in Shelley's pocket after his drowning)—a work that one critic has called "the greatest single volume of English poetry of the nineteenth century."

Though deeply influenced by his reading of Spenser, Shakespeare, and Milton, Keats took Wordsworth as his chief poetic guide, believing with him that poetry should be the creation of concrete sensual images in the service of profound creative thought. In contrast to most of his contemporaries, he strove to subordinate his own personality in order to concentrate exclusively on the subject itself, an artistic capacity to which he gave the term, "Negative Capability."

After a desperate flight to Italy to find a warmer climate in which to regain his health, Keats died of tuberculosis on February 23, 1821, at the age of twenty-five. He lies buried in the Protestant Cemetery in Rome under the epitaph he wrote for himself, "Here lies one whose name was writ in water."

Charles Cowden Clarke, an old friend and former teacher, first introduced Keats to Greek literature when he presented him with George Chapman's spirited translation of Homer's *Iliad*. To Keats, who knew no Greek, it was a revelation and a delight; he spent the whole night reading it. About ten o'clock the next morning, Keats sent Clarke a communication. It was the following sonnet.

On First Looking into Chapman's Homer

Much have I traveled in the realms of gold,
   And many goodly states and kingdoms seen;
   Round many western islands have I been
Which bards in fealty to Apollo[1] hold.
5 Oft of one wide expanse had I been told
   That deep-browed Homer ruled as his
     demesne;[2]
   Yet did I never breathe its pure serene
Till I heard Chapman speak out loud and bold:
Then felt I like some watcher of the skies
10 When a new planet swims into his ken;
Or like stout Cortez[3] when with eagle eyes
   He stared at the Pacific—and all his men
Looked at each other with a wild surmise—
   Silent, upon a peak in Darien.[4]

1816

---

1. *Apollo,* god of poetry and music.
2. *demesne* (di mēn′), domain.
3. *Cortez.* Balboa, not Cortez, discovered the Pacific Ocean.
4. *Darien,* in Panama.

When I Have Fears

When I have fears that I may cease to be
Before my pen has gleaned my teeming brain,
Before high-pilèd books, in charact'ry,[1]
Hold like rich garners the full-ripened grain;
5 When I behold, upon the night's starred face,
Huge cloudy symbols of a high romance,
And think that I may never live to trace
Their shadows, with the magic hand of chance;
And when I feel, fair creature of an hour,
10 That I shall never look upon thee more,
Never have relish in the faery power
Of unreflecting love!—then on the shore
Of the wide world I stand alone, and think
Till Love and Fame to nothingness do sink.

1818   1848

---

1. *charact'ry,* characters or letters, that is, writing.

Comment: Did Keats Make a Blunder?

The fact that Balboa, not Cortez, first discovered the Pacific has disturbed commentators on Keats's sonnet "On First Looking into Chapman's Homer" for many years. Why does Keats, who was a voracious reader from boyhood and acquainted with most of the available literature on historic voyages, use Cortez as his symbol of discovery? Perhaps he deliberately chose Cortez to imply that one need not be "the first" to make a discovery for that discovery to have profound personal significance. After all, Keats was not the first to read Chapman's famous translation of Homer (which had been in print for two centuries), nor was his discovery of Chapman's version his first contact with Homer (he had read Pope's translation). He was talking about the satisfactions of an inner voyage, where "first" no longer counts.

Translated from the French, the title means "the beautiful lady without pity." The poem is probably based on the centuries-old ballad "True Thomas," which tells how a man was enchanted by the Queen of Elfland and lured to her home, where he had to serve her for seven years. Keats takes up that story after the seven years are over and the spell has been broken. The situation in the poem is considered to be symbolic of hopeless love and to reflect the state of Keats's own love affair.

La Belle Dame Sans Merci

1

O what can ail thee, Knight-at-arms,
    Alone and palely loitering?
The sedge has withered from the lake
    And no birds sing!

2

5 O what can ail thee, Knight-at-arms,
    So haggard, and so woebegone?
The squirrel's granary is full
    And the harvest's done.

3

I see a lily on thy brow
10   With anguish moist and fever dew,
And on thy cheeks a fading rose
    Fast withereth too.

La Belle Dame Sans Merci by
John William Waterhouse, 1893.

4

I met a Lady in the Meads,
    Full beautiful, a faery's child,
15 Her hair was long, her foot was light,
    And her eyes were wild.

5

I made a Garland for her head,
    And bracelets too, and fragrant zone;[1]
She looked at me as she did love
20   And made sweet moan.

6

I set her on my pacing steed
    And nothing else saw all day long,
For sidelong would she bend and sing
    A faery's song.

7

25 She found me roots of relish sweet,
    And honey wild, and manna dew,
And sure in language strange she said
    "I love thee true."

8

She took me to her elfin grot
30   And there she wept and sighed full sore,
And there I shut her wild wild eyes
     With kisses four.

9

And there she lullèd me asleep,
     And there I dreamed—Ah, woe betide!—
35 The latest dream I ever dreamt
     On the cold hill side.

10

I saw pale Kings, and Princes too,
     Pale warriors, death-pale were they all;
They cried, "La Belle Dame sans Merci
40   Hath thee in thrall!"

11

I saw their starved lips in the gloam
     With horrid warning gapèd wide,
And I awoke, and found me here
     On the cold hill's side.

12

45 And this is why I sojourn here,
     Alone and palely loitering;
Though the sedge is withered from the lake
     And no birds sing.

1819   1820

_____

1. *zone,* girdle.

Discussion

1. According to the first eight lines of "On First Looking into Chapman's Homer," where has Keats been able to "travel" through his reading? What "one wide expanse" had he only heard about until his discovery of Chapman's book?

2. What does the comparison with Cortez suggest about Keats's feelings after reading Chapman?

3. In "When I Have Fears," intimations of early death lead Keats to lament the future loss of three kinds of experience. What are they? What possible reason might Keats have had for mentioning them in this order?

4. Judging by lines 12–14, what is the emotional effect of these "fears" on the poet? How does he finally deal with them?

5. (a) What aspects of the Knight's behavior and appearance in "La Belle Dame Sans Merci" cause the passerby to inquire repeatedly, "O what can ail thee"? (b) How does the setting contribute to the mood of melancholy and loss?

6. Beginning with stanza 4 the Knight describes his encounter with a supernatural creature, possibly the Queen of Elfland. What images help create an atmosphere of romance and enchantment?

7. What kind of "enthrallment" does the lady impose? Is it the imprisonment of physical love, or the confinements of a world of misleading fancy? Might it be the confines of a temporal world where youth and youthful love grow into withered old age?

8. What effects has this "enthrallment" had on the Knight? What are the overtones of the last two lines of the poem in respect to his condition?

After the death of his brother Tom, Keats spent nearly a year with a friend, Charles Armitage Brown, who described the circumstances surrounding the writing of the "Ode to a Nightingale" as follows:

"In the spring a nightingale had built her nest near my house. Keats felt a tranquil and continual joy in her song; one morning he took his chair from the breakfast table to the grass plot under a plum tree, where he sat for two or three hours. When he came into the house, I perceived he had some scraps of paper in his hand, and these he was quietly thrusting behind the books. On inquiry, I found those scraps, four or five in number; the writing was not well legible, and it was difficult to arrange the stanzas. With his assistance I succeeded, and this was his 'Ode to a Nightingale.' "

The poem is a reverie inspired by the bird's song. In the first stanza the poet is just sinking into the reverie; in the last stanza he comes out of it and back to consciousness of the real world. The first and last stanzas constitute a frame for the reverie proper.

Ode to a Nightingale

My heart aches, and a drowsy numbness pains
  My sense, as though of hemlock[1] I had drunk,
Or emptied some dull opiate to the drains
  One minute past, and Lethe-wards[2] had sunk:
5 'Tis not through envy of thy happy lot,
  But being too happy in thine happiness—
    That thou, light-wingèd Dryad[3] of the trees,
    In some melodious plot
Of beechen green, and shadows numberless,
10   Singest of summer in full-throated ease.

O for a draft of vintage! that hath been
  Cooled a long age in the deep-delvèd earth,
Tasting of Flora[4] and the country green,
  Dance, and Provençal song,[5] and sunburnt mirth!
15 O for a beaker full of the warm South,
  Full of the true, the blushful Hippocrene,[6]
    With beaded bubbles winking at the brim,
    And purple-stainèd mouth;
That I might drink, and leave the world unseen,
20   And with thee fade away into the forest dim:

Fade far away, dissolve, and quite forget
  What thou among the leaves hast never known,
The weariness, the fever, and the fret
  Here, where men sit and hear each other groan;
25 Where palsy shakes a few, sad, last gray hairs,

Where youth grows pale, and specter-thin, and dies;
  Where but to think is to be full of sorrow
    And leaden-eyed despairs,
Where Beauty cannot keep her lustrous eyes,
30   Or new love pine at them beyond tomorrow.

Away! away! for I will fly to thee,
  Not charioted by Bacchus[7] and his pards,
But on the viewless[8] wings of Poesy,
  Though the dull brain perplexes and retards:
35 Already with thee! tender is the night,
  And haply the Queen-Moon is on her throne,
    Clustered around by all her starry Fays;
    But here there is no light,
Save what from heaven is with the breezes blown
40   Through verdurous glooms and winding mossy ways.

---

1. *hemlock,* a poison.
2. *Lethe-wards,* towards Lethe, the river of forgetfulness in Hades.
3. *Dryad,* a tree nymph.
4. *Flora,* goddess of the flowers and the spring.
5. *Provençal song.* Provence in southern France was famous in the Middle Ages for the songs of its troubadours.
6. *Hippocrene,* a fountain on Mt. Helicon in Greece, sacred to the Muses.
7. *Bacchus,* god of wine, who was often represented as riding in a carriage drawn by leopards (pards).
8. *viewless,* invisible.

The Enchanted Castle by Claude Lorrain, a seventeenth-century French painting supposedly remembered by Keats when he wrote "Ode to a Nightingale."

I cannot see what flowers are at my feet,
   Nor what soft incense hangs upon the boughs,
But, in embalmèd darkness, guess each sweet
   Wherewith the seasonable month endows
45 The grass, the thicket, and the fruit tree wild;
    White hawthorn, and the pastoral eglantine;
     Fast fading violets covered up in leaves;
      And mid-May's eldest child,
The coming musk-rose, full of dewy wine,
50   The murmurous haunt of flies on summer eves.

Darkling I listen; and, for many a time,
   I have been half in love with easeful Death,
Called him soft names in many a musèd rhyme,
   To take into the air my quiet breath;
55 Now more than ever seems it rich to die,
   To cease upon the midnight with no pain,
    While thou art pouring forth thy soul abroad
     In such an ecstasy!
Still wouldst thou sing, and I have ears in vain—
60   To thy high requiem become a sod.

Thou wast not born for death, immortal Bird!
   No hungry generations tread thee down;
The voice I hear this passing night was heard
   In ancient days by emperor and clown:[9]
65 Perhaps the selfsame song that found a path
   Through the sad heart of Ruth, when sick for home,
    She stood in tears amid the alien corn;[10]
     The same that oft-times hath
Charmed magic casements, opening on the foam
70   Of perilous seas, in faery lands forlorn.

Forlorn! the very word is like a bell
   To toll me back from thee to my sole self!
Adieu! the fancy cannot cheat so well
   As she is famed to do, deceiving elf.
75 Adieu! adieu! thy plaintive anthem fades
   Past the near meadows, over the still stream,
    Up the hillside; and now 'tis buried deep
     In the next valley glades:
Was it a vision, or a waking dream?
80   Fled is that music—Do I wake or sleep?
1819   1820

---

9. *clown*, peasant.
10. *Ruth . . . corn.* According to the Bible story, Ruth left her homeland to go with Naomi, her mother-in-law, to Judah, a foreign country to her, where she worked in the corn (wheat) fields (Ruth 2:1-23).

About 1800, Thomas Bruce, Earl of Elgin, brought some of the classical sculptures that had for centuries adorned the Parthenon, a temple on the Acropolis at Athens, to England. They were purchased by the government in 1816 and exhibited in the British Museum, where they became known as the Elgin marbles. Here Keats saw them and, inspired by their enduring beauty, wrote the "Ode on a Grecian Urn," which expresses the essence of his belief about the relationship of truth and beauty.

Ode on a Grecian Urn

Thou still unravished bride of quietness,
    Thou foster child of Silence and slow Time,
Sylvan historian, who canst thus express
    A flowery tale more sweetly than our
        rhyme—
5 What leaf-fringed legend haunts about thy
        shape
    Of deities or mortals, or of both,
      In Tempe[1] or the dales of Arcady?[2]
What men or gods are these? What maidens
      loath?
What mad pursuit? What struggle to escape?
10   What pipes and timbrels? What wild
        ecstasy?

Heard melodies are sweet, but those unheard
    Are sweeter; therefore, ye soft pipes, play
        on;
Not to the sensual ear, but, more endeared,
    Pipe to the spirit ditties of no tone:
15 Fair youth, beneath the trees, thou canst not
      leave

    Thy song, nor ever can those trees be bare;
      Bold lover, never, never canst thou kiss,
Though winning near the goal—yet, do not
      grieve;
She cannot fade, though thou hast not thy
      bliss,
20   Forever will thou love, and she be fair!

Ah, happy, happy boughs! that cannot shed
    Your leaves, nor ever bid the spring adieu;
And, happy melodist, unwearièd,
    Forever piping songs forever new;
25 More happy love! more happy, happy love!
    Forever warm and still to be enjoyed,
      Forever panting, and forever young;
All breathing human passion far above,
That leaves a heart high-sorrowful and cloyed,
30   A burning forehead, and a parching
      tongue.

---

1. **Tempe** (tem′pē), a beautiful valley in Thessaly in Greece.
2. **Arcady,** Arcadia, a part of ancient Greece, celebrated in pastoral poetry as the home of an ideal shepherd life.

Who are these coming to the sacrifice?
　　To what green altar, O mysterious priest,
Lead'st thou that heifer lowing at the skies,
　　And all her silken flanks with garlands
　　　　dressed?
35　What little town by river or seashore,
　　Or mountain-built with peaceful citadel,
　　　　Is emptied of this folk, this pious morn?
　　And, little town, thy streets forevermore
Will silent be; and not a soul to tell
40　　Why thou art desolate, can e'er return.

O Attic shape!³ Fair attitude! with brede⁴
　　Of marble men and maidens overwrought,
With forest branches and the trodden weed;

Thou, silent form! dost tease us out of
　　thought
45　As doth eternity: Cold Pastoral!
　　When old age shall this generation waste,
　　　　Thou shalt remain, in midst of other woe
　　Than ours, a friend to man, to whom thou
　　　　say'st,
　　"Beauty is truth, truth beauty—that is all
50　　Ye know on earth, and all ye need to
　　　　know."
　　1819   1820

3. *Attic shape,* a shape representing the simple, elegant taste of Athens.
4. *brede,* embroidery.

Reader's Note: "Ode on a Grecian Urn"

In "Ode on a Grecian Urn" Keats addresses the urn directly, calling it a "still unravished bride of quietness," a "foster child of Silence and slow Time," and a "Sylvan historian." Though ancient, the urn has remained fresh and unblemished and is awesomely silent. Since it has remained "young" through many centuries, it can only be a "foster child" of Time, who ages and destroys her natural children. The scenes portrayed are "sylvan," that is, set in a rural, forested region, and depict rustic life. According to Keats, through touch and sight the urn soundlessly communicates its "flowery tale more sweetly" than the poet's "rhyme."

The poem can be seen as developing a series of paradoxes: the young lovers, though destined never to touch, enjoy a love "Forever warm . . . Forever panting"; static carvings describe a scene of dynamic action; even in its most ideal moments, art is a reminder of death and decay. The last stanza strikes a positive note. The urn is called a "friend to man," of this and succeeding generations, that can "tease us out of thought / As doth eternity." Great art enables humanity temporarily to transcend mortal limitations, to contemplate the good, the true, and the beautiful, and to perceive life in the context of eternity.

Discussion

1. **(a)** What do you think Keats means by addressing the urn as a "still unravished bride of quietness," a "foster child of Silence and slow Time" and a "Sylvan historian"? **(b)** Describe the scenes pictured on the urn. Do they seem to be clear or indistinct?

2. **(a)** In lines 11–12, Keats says, "Heard melodies are sweet, but those unheard / Are sweeter." Explain in your own words what this might mean. **(b)** What other paradoxes are to be found in the first four stanzas?

3. What biographical note is introduced in the third stanza? What do you think the effect of this is?

4. In what other sense, besides its being made of marble, is the urn a "Cold pastoral"?

5. What truth about the human condition does the urn convey? What seems to be Keats's concept of "beauty"?

6. According to some readers, one theme of the ode is the relationship between art and life. How would you explain this theme?

7. With what similar theme are both "Ode to a Nightingale" and "Ode on a Grecian Urn" concerned? How do they differ in subject matter and tone?

The Cyder Feast, a wood engraving
by Edward Calvert, 1828.

*T*o *Autumn*

1

Season of mists and mellow fruitfulness,
  Close bosom-friend of the maturing sun;
Conspiring with him how to load and bless
    With fruit the vines that round the
      thatch-eaves run;
5 To bend with apples the mossed cottage-trees,
  And fill all fruit with ripeness to the core;
    To swell the gourd, and plump the hazel
      shells
With a sweet kernel; to set budding more,
  And still more, later flowers for the bees,
10   Until they think warm days will never cease,
    For Summer has o'er-brimmed their
      clammy cells.

2

Who hath not seen thee oft amid thy store?
  Sometimes whoever seeks abroad may find
Thee sitting careless on a granary floor,
15   Thy hair soft-lifted by the winnowing wind;
Or on a half-reaped furrow sound asleep,
  Drowsed with the fume of poppies, while thy
    hook
    Spares the next swath and all its twinéd
      flowers:
And sometimes like a gleaner thou dost keep
20   Steady thy laden head across a brook;
  Or by a cider-press, with patient look,
    Thou watchest the last oozing hours by
      hours.

3

Where are the songs of Spring? Aye, where are
    they?
  Think not of them, thou hast thy music too—
25 While barred clouds bloom the soft-dying day,
    And touch the stubble-plains with rosy hue;
Then in a wailful choir the small gnats mourn
    Among the river sallows,[1] borne aloft
      Or sinking as the light wind lives or dies;
30 And full-grown lambs loud bleat from hilly
    bourn,
  Hedge crickets sing; and now with treble soft
  The redbreast whistles from a garden croft,
    And gathering swallows twitter in the
    skies.
1819   1820

---

1. *sallows,* willows.

This poem was supposedly written for Fanny
Brawne, with whom Keats was in love.

This Living Hand

This living hand, now warm and capable
Of earnest grasping, would, if it were cold
And in the icy silence of the tomb,
So haunt thy days and chill thy dreaming nights
5 That thou wouldst wish thine own heart dry of
  blood
So in my veins red life might stream again,
And thou be conscience-calmed—see here it
  is—
I hold it towards you.
1819   1898

Discussion

1. The images of "To Autumn" are highly concrete and richly sensuous, providing not just a description of the season but a sequence of sense impressions that makes it come to life. Identify the dominant sense impressions in each of the three stanzas.

2. Discuss "To Autumn" in the context of Keats's life. What hints of melancholy, of things coming to their end, can be found in stanza 3?

3. How does "To Autumn" demonstrate Keats's theory of "Negative Capability"?

4. "This Living Hand" is probably the last lyric Keats wrote before his death. **(a)** What is the tone of the poem? **(b)** The poem implies that the woman being addressed needs to be "conscience-calmed." With what crime is she being charged?

Vocabulary
Combined Skills

A. Use context and structure as aids to interpreting the meaning of the italicized word in each passage. Then on a separate sheet of paper rewrite the phrase that contains the italicized word, substituting a synonymous word or expression for that word.

1. "Scatter, as from an *unextinguished* hearth / Ashes and sparks, my words among mankind!"

2. ". . . Near them, on the sand, / Half sunk, a shattered *visage* lies, whose frown, / And wrinkled lip, and sneer of cold command, / Tell that its sculptor well those passions read . . ."

B. Many English words include the root *sol,* which comes from the Latin word *solus,* meaning "alone." On your paper, show where this root appears in each of the following passages. You may use your Glossary.

1. "And, little town, thy streets forevermore / Will silent be; and not a soul to tell / Why thou art desolate, can e'er return."

2. "Silent and pensive, idle, restless, slow, / His home deserted for the lonely wood, / Tormented with a wound he could not know, / His, like all deep grief, plunged in solitude."

Thomas De Quincey

1785–1859

The son of a wealthy Manchester merchant, Thomas De Quincey was extraordinarily gifted and sensitive, an individual of vast knowledge. By the age of fifteen he could read, write, and speak Greek "as though it were his native tongue." At the age of seventeen, unhappy with himself and his life at school, he ran away to London, living in poverty while continuing his close reading of the English poets and keeping a diary, which he later drew on for his autobiographical writings. Following a reconciliation with his family, he attended Oxford, where he studied German literature and philosophy as well as English literature. A brilliant but erratic student, he left Oxford in 1808 without a degree because he could not face the emotional ordeal of the oral examination.

An ardent admirer of both Wordsworth and Coleridge, whom he had met in 1807, De Quincey moved to the Lake District, took a home near Wordsworth, and began a close relationship with those Romantic poets living in the area. De Quincey was among the first to recognize the importance of Wordsworth's and Coleridge's *Lyrical Ballads,* and he became an enthusiastic advocate of Romantic literature. After having been warmly accepted by Coleridge, De Quincey anonymously arranged for him to receive a gift of money. By this time De Quincey, like Coleridge, had become addicted to opium to relieve the pains of neuralgia and other ailments, some acquired during his earlier period of hardship in London.

In 1821, part of the *Confessions of an English Opium-Eater* was published in periodical form and, in the following year, in its entirety. Considered De Quincey's masterpiece, the book sold extremely well and was praised for its authentic detail and imaginative prose style. For the remainder of his life De Quincey was a prolific contributor of essays on personal, political, social, critical, historical, and even philosophical subjects to various periodicals.

De Quincey moved to Edinburgh in middle age and remained there until his death on December 8, 1859. In his commentary on the poetry of Pope, De Quincey drew a distinction between "the literature of knowledge" and "the literature of power": "The function of the first is to teach; the function of the second is to move; the first is a rudder; the second, an oar or sail." De Quincey's best work belongs to the literature of power.

The following essay by De Quincey, originally written as a magazine article, considers the scene in Shakespeare's play in which Macbeth and Lady Macbeth are startled by a loud knocking just after they have murdered King Duncan. This occurs in Act Two, at the end of scene 2 and the beginning of scene 3. The essay is a famous example of critical impressionism, in which the emphasis is on the writer's impressions and emotional responses to the subject under discussion, rather than on a rigorously developed logical argument.

On the Knocking at the Gate in Macbeth

From my boyish days I had always felt a great perplexity on one point in *Macbeth*. It was this: the knocking at the gate which succeeds to the murder of Duncan produced to my feelings an effect for which I never could account. The effect was that it reflected back upon the murderer a peculiar awfulness and a depth of solemnity; yet, however obstinately I endeavored with my understanding to comprehend this, for many years I never could see *why* it should produce such an effect.

Here I pause for one moment, to exhort the reader never to pay any attention to his understanding[1] when it stands in opposition to any other faculty of his mind. The mere understanding, however useful and indispensable, is the meanest faculty in the human mind, and the most to be distrusted; and yet the great majority of people trust to nothing else—which may do for ordinary life, but not for philosophical purposes. Of this out of ten thousand instances that I might produce I will cite one. Ask of any person whatsoever who is not previously prepared for the demand by a knowledge of perspective to draw in the rudest way the commonest appearance which depends upon the laws of that science—as, for instance, to represent the effect of two walls standing at right angles to each other, or the appearance of the houses on each side of a street as seen by a person looking down the street from one extremity. Now, in all cases, unless the person has happened to observe in pictures how it is that artists produce these effects, he will be utterly unable to make the smallest approximation to it. Yet why? For he has actually seen the effect every day of his life. The reason is that he allows his understanding to overrule his eyes. His understanding, which includes no intuitive knowledge of the laws of vision, can furnish him with no reason why a line which is known and can be proved to be a horizontal line should not *appear* a horizontal line: a line that made any angle with the perpendicular less than a right angle would seem to him to indicate that his houses were all tumbling down together. Accord-ingly, he makes the line of his houses a horizontal line, and fails of course to produce the effect demanded. Here, then, is one instance out of many in which not only the understanding is allowed to overrule the eyes, but where the understanding is positively allowed to obliterate the eyes, as it were; for not only does the man believe the evidence of his understanding in opposition to that of his eyes, but (which is monstrous) the idiot is not aware that his eyes ever gave such evidence. He does not know that he has seen (and therefore *quoad*[2] his consciousness has *not* seen) that which he *has* seen every day of his life.

But to return from this digression. My understanding could furnish no reason why the knocking at the gate in *Macbeth* should produce any effect, direct or reflected. In fact, my understanding said positively that it could *not* produce any effect. But I knew better; I felt that it did; and I waited and clung to the problem until further knowledge should enable me to solve it. At length, in 1812, Mr. Williams made his *début* on the stage of Ratcliffe Highway, and executed those unparalleled murders which have procured for him such a brilliant and undying reputation.[3] On which murders, by the way, I must observe that in one respect they have had an ill effect, by making the connoisseur in murder very fastidious in his taste, and dissatisfied with anything that has been since done in that line. All other murders look pale by the deep crimson of his; and, as an amateur once said to me in a querulous tone, "There has been absolutely nothing *doing* since his time, or nothing that's worth speaking of." But this is wrong; for it is unreasonable to expect all men to be great artists, and born with the genius of Mr. Williams. Now, it will be remembered that in the first of these murders (that of the Marrs) the same incident (of a knocking at the

---

1. **understanding,** intellect; the reasoning faculty.
2. **quoad** (kwō′ad), relative to. [Latin]
3. **Mr. Williams . . . reputation.** In fact, it was in December, 1811, that John Williams, a seaman, murdered two families in the Ratcliffe Highway, a street in the slums of the East End of London.

door soon after the work of extermination was complete) did actually occur which the genius of Shakespeare has invented; and all good judges, and the most eminent dilettanti,[4] acknowledged the felicity of Shakespeare's suggestion as soon as it was actually realized. Here, then, was a fresh proof that I had been right in relying on my own feeling, in opposition to my understanding; and again I set myself to study the problem. At length I solved it to my own satisfaction; and my solution is this: murder, in ordinary cases, where the sympathy is wholly directed to the case of the murdered person, is an incident of coarse and vulgar horror; and for this reason—that it flings the interest exclusively upon the natural but ignoble instinct by which we cleave to life: an instinct which, as being indispensable to the primal law of self-preservation, is the same in kind (though different in degree) amongst all living creatures. This instinct, therefore, because it annihilates all distinctions, and degrades the greatest of men to the level of "the poor beetle that we tread on,"[5] exhibits human nature in its most abject and humiliating attitude. Such an attitude would little suit the purposes of the poet. What then must he do? He must throw the interest on the murderer. Our sympathy must be with *him* (of course I mean a sympathy of comprehension, a sympathy by which we enter into his feelings, and are made to understand them—not a sympathy of pity or approbation). In the murdered person, all strife of thought, all flux and reflux of passion and of purpose, are crushed by one overwhelming panic; the fear of instant death smites him "with its petrific mace."[6] But in the murderer, such a murderer as a poet will condescend to, there must be raging some great storm of passion—jealousy, ambition, vengeance, hatred—which will create a hell within him; and into this hell we are to look.

In *Macbeth*, for the sake of gratifying his own enormous and teeming faculty of creation, Shakespeare has introduced two murderers: and, as usual in his hands, they are remarkably discriminated; but—though in Macbeth the strife of mind is greater than in his wife, the tiger spirit not so awake, and his feelings caught chiefly by contagion from her—yet, as both were finally involved in the guilt of murder, the murderous mind of necessity is finally to be presumed in both. This was to be expressed; and, on its own account, as well as to make it a more proportionable antagonist to the unoffending nature of their victim, "the gracious Duncan,"[7] and adequately to expound "the deep damnation of his taking off,"[8] this was to be expressed with peculiar energy. We were to be made to feel that the human nature—i.e., the divine nature of love and mercy, spread through the hearts of all creatures, and seldom utterly withdrawn from man—was gone, vanished, extinct, and that the fiendish nature had taken its place. And, as this effect is marvellously accomplished in the *dialogues* and *soliloquies* themselves, so it is finally consummated by the expedient under consideration; and it is to this that I now solicit the reader's attention. If the reader has ever witnessed a wife, daughter, or sister in a fainting fit, he may chance to have observed that the most affecting moment in such a spectacle is *that* in which a sigh and a stirring announce the recommencement of suspended life. Or, if the reader has ever been present in a vast metropolis on the day when some great national idol was carried in funeral pomp to his grave, and, chancing to walk near the course through which it passed, has felt powerfully, in the silence and desertion of the streets, and in the stagnation of ordinary business, the deep interest which at that moment was possessing the heart of man—if all at once he should hear the death-like stillness broken up by the sound of wheels rattling away from the scene, and making known that the transitory vision was dissolved, he will be aware that at no moment was his sense of the complete suspension and pause in ordinary human concerns so full and affecting as at that moment when the suspension ceases, and the goings-on of human life are suddenly resumed. All action in any direction is best expounded, measured, and made apprehensible, by reaction. Now, apply this to the case in *Macbeth*. Here, as I have said, the retiring of the

4. *dilettanti*, literally, lovers of art; here, lovers of the art of murder.
5. *"the poor beetle . . . on,"* Shakespeare, *Measure for Measure*, Act Three, Scene 1, line 78.
6. *"with its petrific mace,"* Milton, *Paradise Lost*, Book Ten, line 293. *Petrific* means "petrifying."
7. *"the gracious Duncan,"* Shakespeare, *Macbeth*, Act Three, Scene 1, line 66.
8. *"the deep . . . taking off,"* Shakespeare, *Macbeth*, Act One, Scene 7, line 20. "Taking off" means murder.

human heart and the entrance of the fiendish heart was to be expressed and made sensible. Another world has stepped in; and the murderers are taken out of the region of human things, human purposes, human desires. They are transfigured: Lady Macbeth is "unsexed";[9] Macbeth has forgot that he was born of woman; both are conformed to the image of devils; and the world of devils is suddenly revealed. But how shall this be conveyed and made palpable? In order that a new world may step in, this world must for a time disappear. The murderers and the murder must be insulated—cut off by an immeasurable gulf from the ordinary tide and succession of human affairs—locked up and sequestered in some deep recess; we must be made sensible that the world of ordinary life is suddenly arrested, laid asleep, tranced, racked into a dread armistice; time must be annihilated, relation to things without abolished; and all must pass self-withdrawn into a deep syncope and suspension of earthly passion. Hence it is that, when the deed is done, when the work of darkness is perfect, then the world of darkness passes away like a pageantry in the clouds: the knocking at the gate is heard, and it makes known audibly that the reaction has commenced; the human has made its reflux upon the fiendish; the pulses of life are beginning to beat again; and the reestablishment of the goings-on of the world in which we live first makes us profoundly sensible of the awful parenthesis that had suspended them.

O mighty poet! Thy works are not as those of other men, simply and merely great works of art, but are also like the phenomena of nature, like the sun and the sea, the stars and the flowers, like frost and snow, rain and dew, hailstorm and thunder, which are to be studied with entire submission of our own faculties, and in the perfect faith that in them there can be no too much or too little, nothing useless or inert, but that, the farther we press in our discoveries, the more we shall see proofs of design and self-supporting arrangement where the careless eye had seen nothing but accident!

1823

---

9. *"unsexed,"* a reference to *Macbeth*, Act One, Scene 5, line 38.

Discussion

1. (a) For the author of the essay, what "one point" in *Macbeth* was a source of perplexity? (b) Which does the writer trust more, intellect or feeling? What reason does he give for his preference?

2. What happened that caused De Quincey to understand the effect that the knocking had on him?

3. What is De Quincey's explanation for the emotional impact of the knocking at the gate?

4. The last paragraph is lavish in its praise of Shakespeare. What are De Quincey's reasons for stating that Shakespeare's works "are not as those of other men"?

Vocabulary
Antonyms, Synonyms

Determine the relationship between the two italicized words listed in each numbered item. Then select, from the pairs of words that follow, the words that are related in the same way as the words in the first pair. Write your choice on a separate sheet of paper. Example—*hot : cold* (the colon means "is related to") as (a) weather : storm; (b) day : night; (c) desert : sand. In the example, *hot* is the opposite of *cold;* therefore, the correct answer is day : night. There is a word in each italicized pair that you will probably have to check in the Glossary.

1. *primal : modern* as (a) advise : encourage; (b) happy : sad; (c) age : time.

2. *swarm : teem* as (a) free : captive; (b) lifeless : inactive; (c) tragedy : farce.

3. *obstinate : flexible* as (a) careful : sloppy; (b) appeal : attract; (c) principle : rule.

4. *peaceful : querulous* as (a) fitness : appropriateness; (b) childish : juvenile; (c) hidden : obvious.

5. *confusion : perplexity* as (a) rest : exercise; (b) hint : suggestion; (c) seriousness : foolishness.

Mary Shelley 1797–1851

Mary Shelley seemed destined for greatness. Her mother was Mary Wollstonecraft, a liberal thinker and radical feminist who wrote *A Vindication of the Rights of Woman.* Her father, William Godwin, was the author of *Political Justice,* a work that contributed to the political radicalization of the young writers of the era, including Wordsworth, Coleridge, and Shelley, the man with whom Mary eloped at age sixteen and later married. Today she is known mainly for her first novel *Frankenstein,* a work that caused a sensation when it was published in 1818 and which continues to assert a lasting hold on the imagination.

Mary Shelley was born on August 30, 1797. Ten days later her mother died, leaving Mary and a half sister in the care of the bereaved and impractical William Godwin. The father quickly remarried a next-door neighbor, Mrs. Mary Jane Clairmont, a widow with two children. Mary Shelley disliked her stepmother intensely but idolized her father and the mother she never knew, for whose death she blamed herself.

Mary Shelley began writing when she was a small child. By the age of nine, she could boast of having heard Coleridge recite "The Rime of the Ancient Mariner" and of hearing Thomas De Quincey relate his theories on the occult. Starting in 1812, she stayed for two years with a family in Scotland, coming home occasionally on visits. On one such visit in 1812 she met the poet Percy Shelley, who had come to serve as a disciple of William Godwin. In May of 1814 they met again and, at the end of July, eloped to Europe, leaving behind his wife Harriet and two children. The marriage was legalized two years later following Harriet's suicide. By age twenty-four, Mary Shelley was a widow who had lost three of her four children and who faced a hard struggle to support herself and her remaining child. Other than *Frankenstein,* Mary Shelley wrote travel books, four additional novels, biographical sketches, and notes on her husband's poems that scholars have found invaluable. She died in 1851 at the age of fifty-three.

In her preface to *Frankenstein,* Mary Shelley recounts the fascinating circumstances that inspired the book's creation. On a holiday to Switzerland in the summer of 1816, the Shelleys met Lord Byron, with whom they shared hours of conversation. Since the summer proved "wet and uncongenial," they were confined to the house for days on end, during which they read German ghost stories. One night Byron proposed that each of them try writing a ghost story for their mutual entertainment; Mary Shelley was the only one to complete the task.

For several days she had sought in vain for a story idea, then it came to her in a vivid dream following an evening of discussion of the experiments of Erasmus Darwin to animate lifeless matter. In her own words: "Night waned upon this talk; and even the witching hour had gone by before we retired to rest. When I placed my head on my pillow I did not sleep, nor could I be said to think. My imagination, unbidden, possessed and guided me, gifting the successive images that arose in my mind with a vividness far beyond the normal bounds of reverie. I saw—with shut eyes but acute mental vision—I saw the pale student of unhallowed arts kneeling beside the thing he had put together." The next day the actual writing of *Frankenstein* began.

In his early adolescence, Victor Frankenstein, the precocious eldest son of a distinguished family in Geneva, pours over the
works of Paracelsus and Albertus Magnus, medieval alchemists, and becomes imbued with
"a fervent longing to penetrate the secrets of
nature" and pursue a career in natural science.
During two years of intensive study at the University of Ingolstadt, Frankenstein astounds his
professors by his mastery of chemistry and research procedures and his passion to probe
"the deepest mysteries of creation." Having exhausted the resources at Ingolstadt, Frankenstein thinks of returning home to his family
and fiancée, Elizabeth, but finds his stay pro-
tracted by the following incident which he relates to his benefactor, Robert Walton. Victor
Frankenstein is speaking:

from *F*rankenstein

1

One of the phenomena which had peculiarly
attracted my attention was the structure of the
human frame, and, indeed, any animal endued
with life. Whence, I often asked myself, did the
principle of life proceed? It was a bold question,
and one which has ever been considered as a
mystery; yet with how many things are we upon
the brink of becoming acquainted, if cowardice or
carelessness did not restrain our inquiries. I
revolved these circumstances in my mind, and
determined thenceforth to apply myself more
particularly to those branches of natural philosophy which relate to physiology. Unless I had
been animated by an almost supernatural enthusiasm, my application to this study would have
been irksome, and almost intolerable. To examine the causes of life, we must first have recourse
to death. I became acquainted with the science of
anatomy: but this was not sufficient; I must also
observe the natural decay and corruption of the
human body. In my education my father had tak-
en the greatest precautions that my mind should
be impressed with no supernatural horrors. I do
not ever remember to have trembled at a tale of
superstition, or to have feared the apparition of a
spirit. Darkness had no effect upon my fancy;
and a churchyard was to me merely the recepta-
cle of bodies deprived of life, which, from being
the seat of beauty and strength, had become food
for the worm. Now I was led to examine the
cause and progress of this decay, and forced to
spend days and nights in vaults and charnel
houses.[1] My attention was fixed upon every
object the most insupportable to the delicacy of
the human feelings. I saw how the fine form of
man was degraded and wasted; I beheld the corruption of death succeed to the blooming cheek
of life; I saw how the worm inherited the wonders
of the eye and brain. I paused, examining and
analyzing all the minutiae of causation, as exem-
plified in the change from life to death, and death
to life, until from the midst of this darkness a sudden light broke in upon me—a light so brilliant
and wondrous, yet so simple, that while I became
dizzy with the immensity of the prospect which it
illustrated, I was surprised, that among so many
men of genius who had directed their inquiries
towards the same science, that I alone should be
reserved to discover so astonishing a secret.

Remember, I am not recording the vision of a
madman. The sun does not more certainly shine
in the heavens, than that which I now affirm is
true. Some miracle might have produced it, yet
the stages of the discovery were distinct and
probable. After days and nights of incredible
labor and fatigue, I succeeded in discovering the
cause of generation and life; nay, more, I became
myself capable of bestowing animation upon lifeless matter.

---

1. **charnel houses,** places where dead bodies or bones are laid.

The astonishment which I had at first experienced on this discovery soon gave place to delight and rapture. After so much time spent in painful labor, to arrive at once at the summit of my desires was the most gratifying consummation of my toils. But this discovery was so great and overwhelming that all the steps by which I had been progressively led to it were obliterated, and I beheld only the result. What had been the study and desire of the wisest men since the creation of the world was now within my grasp. Not that, like a magic scene, it all opened upon me at once: the information I had obtained was of a nature rather to direct my endeavors so soon as I should point them towards the object of my search, than to exhibit that object already accomplished. . . .

I see by your eagerness, and the wonder and hope which your eyes express, my friend, that you expect to be informed of the secret with which I am acquainted; that cannot be: listen patiently until the end of my story, and you will easily perceive why I am reserved upon that subject. I will not lead you on, unguarded and ardent as I then was, to your destruction and infallible misery. Learn from me, if not by my precepts, at least by my example, how dangerous is the acquirement of knowledge, and how much happier that man is who believes his native town to be the world, than he who aspires to become greater than his nature will allow.

When I found so astonishing a power placed within my hands, I hesitated a long time concerning the manner in which I should employ it. Although I possessed the capacity of bestowing animation, yet to prepare a frame for the reception of it, with all its intricacies of fibers, muscles, and veins, still remained a work of inconceivable difficulty and labor. I doubted at first whether I should attempt the creation of a being like myself, or one of simpler organization; but my imagination was too much exalted by my first success to permit me to doubt of my ability to give life to an animal as complex and wonderful as man. The materials at present within my command hardly appeared adequate to so arduous an undertaking; but I doubted not that I should ultimately succeed. I prepared myself for a multitude of reverses; my operations might be incessantly baffled, and at last my work be imperfect: yet,

when I considered the improvement which every day takes place in science and mechanics, I was encouraged to hope my present attempts would at least lay the foundations of future success. Nor could I consider the magnitude and complexity of my plan as any argument of its impracticability. It was with these feelings that I began the creation of a human being. As the minuteness of the parts formed a great hinderance to my speed, I resolved, contrary to my first intention, to make the being of a gigantic stature; that is to say, about eight feet in height, and proportionably large. After having formed this determination, and having spent some months in successfully collecting and arranging my materials, I began.

No one can conceive the variety of feelings which bore me onwards, like a hurricane, in the first enthusiasm of success. Life and death appeared to me ideal bounds, which I should first break through, and pour a torrent of light into our dark world. A new species would bless me as its creator and source; many happy and excellent natures would owe their being to me. No father could claim the gratitude of his child so completely as I should deserve theirs. Pursuing these reflections, I thought that if I could bestow animation upon lifeless matter, I might in process of time (although I now found it impossible) renew life where death had apparently devoted the body to corruption.

These thoughts supported my spirits, while I pursued my undertaking with unremitting ardor. My cheek had grown pale with study, and my person had become emaciated with confinement. Sometimes, on the very brink of certainty, I failed; yet still I clung to the hope which the next day or the next hour might realize. One secret which I alone possessed was the hope to which I had dedicated myself; and the moon gazed on my midnight labors, while, with unrelaxed and breathless eagerness, I pursued nature to her hiding places. Who shall conceive the horrors of my secret toil, as I dabbled among the unhallowed damps of the grave, or tortured the living animal to animate the lifeless clay? My limbs now tremble and my eyes swim with the remembrance; but then a resistless, and almost frantic, impulse urged me forward; I seemed to have lost all soul or sensation but for this one pursuit. It was indeed but a passing trance that only made me feel with renewed acuteness so soon as, the unnatural stimulus ceasing to operate, I had returned to my old habits. I collected bones from charnel houses; and disturbed, with profane fingers, the tremendous secrets of the human frame. In a solitary chamber, or rather cell, at the top of the house, and separated from all the other apartments by a gallery and staircase, I kept my workshop of filthy creation: my eyeballs were starting from their sockets in attending to the details of my employment. The dissecting room and the slaughter-house furnished many of my materials; and often did my human nature turn with loathing from my occupation, whilst, still urged on by an eagerness which perpetually increased, I brought my work near to a conclusion.

The summer months passed while I was thus engaged, heart and soul, in one pursuit. It was a most beautiful season; never did the fields bestow a more plentiful harvest, or the vines yield a more luxuriant vintage: but my eyes were insensible to the charms of nature. And the same feelings which made me neglect the scenes around me caused me also to forget those friends who were so many miles absent, and whom I had not seen for so long a time. I knew my silence disquieted them; and I well remembered the words of my father: "I know that while you are pleased with yourself, you will think of us with affection, and we shall hear regularly from you. You must pardon me if I regard any interruption in your correspondence as a proof that your other duties are equally neglected."

I knew well, therefore, what would be my father's feelings; but I could not tear my thoughts from my employment, loathsome in itself, but which had taken an irresistible hold of my imagination. I wished, as it were, to procrastinate all that related to my feelings of affection until the great object, which swallowed up every habit of my nature, should be completed.

I then thought that my father would be unjust if he ascribed my neglect to vice, or faultiness on my part; but I am now convinced that he was justified in conceiving that I should not be altogether free from blame. A human being in perfection ought always to preserve a calm and peaceful mind, and never to allow passion or a transitory desire to disturb his tranquillity. I do not think that the pursuit of knowledge is an exception to this rule. If the study to which you apply yourself has a tendency to weaken your affections, and to destroy your taste for those simple pleasures in which no alloy can possibly mix, then that study is certainly unlawful, that is to say, not befitting the human mind. If this rule were always observed; if no man allowed any pursuit whatsoever to interfere with the tranquillity of his domestic affections, Greece had not been enslaved; Caesar would have spared his country; America would have been discovered more gradually; and the empires of Mexico and Peru had not been destroyed.

But I forget that I am moralizing in the most interesting part of my tale; and your looks remind me to proceed.

My father made no reproach in his letters, and only took notice of my silence by inquiring into my occupations more particularly than before. Winter, spring, and summer passed away during my labors; but I did not watch the blossom or the expanding leaves—sights which before always yielded me supreme delight—so deeply was I engrossed in my occupation. The leaves of that year had withered before my work drew near to a close; and now every day showed me more plainly how well I had succeeded. But my enthusiasm was checked by my anxiety, and I appeared rather like one doomed by slavery to toil in the mines, or any other unwholesome trade, than an artist occupied by his favorite employment. Every night I was oppressed by a slow fever, and I became nervous to a most painful degree; the fall of a leaf startled me, and I shunned my fellow creatures as if I had been guilty of a crime. Sometimes I grew alarmed at the wreck I perceived that I had become; the energy of my purpose alone sustained me: my labors would soon end, and I believed that exercise and amusement would then drive away incipient disease; and I promised myself both of these when my creation should be complete.

It was on a dreary night of November that I beheld the accomplishment of my toils. With an anxiety that almost amounted to agony, I collected the instruments of life around me, that I might infuse a spark of being into the lifeless thing that lay at my feet. It was already one in the morning; the rain pattered dismally against the panes, and my candle was nearly burnt out, when, by the glimmer of the half-extinguished light, I saw the dull yellow eye of the creature open; it breathed hard, and a convulsive motion agitated its limbs.

How can I describe my emotions at this catastrophe, or how delineate the wretch whom with such infinite pains and care I had endeavored to form? His limbs were in proportion, and I had selected his features as beautiful. Beautiful!— Great God! His yellow skin scarcely covered the work of muscles and arteries beneath; his hair was of a lustrous black, and flowing; his teeth of a pearly whiteness; but these luxuriances only formed a more horrid contrast with his watery eyes, that seemed almost of the same color as the dun white sockets in which they were set, his shriveled complexion and straight black lips.

The different accidents of life are not so changeable as the feelings of human nature. I had worked hard for nearly two years, for the sole purpose of infusing life into an inanimate body. For this I had deprived myself of rest and health. I had desired it with an ardor that far exceeded moderation; but now that I had finished, the beauty of the dream vanished, and breathless horror and disgust filled my heart. Unable to endure the aspect of the being I had created, I rushed out of the room, and continued a long time traversing my bedchamber, unable to compose my mind to sleep. At length lassitude succeeded to the tumult I had before endured; and I threw myself on the bed in my clothes, endeavoring to seek a few moments of forgetfulness. But it was in vain: I slept, indeed, but I was disturbed by the wildest dreams. I thought I saw Elizabeth, in the bloom of health, walking in the streets of Ingolstadt. Delighted and surprised, I embraced her; but as I imprinted the first kiss on her lips, they became livid with the hue of death; her features appeared to change, and I thought that I held the corpse of my dead mother in my arms; a shroud enveloped her form, and I saw the grave-worms crawling in the folds of the flannel. I started from my sleep with horror; a cold dew covered my forehead, my teeth chattered, and every limb became convulsed: when, by the dim and yellow light of the moon, as it forced its way through the window shutters, I beheld the wretch—the miserable monster whom I had created. He held up the curtain of the bed; and his eyes, if eyes they may be called, were fixed on me. His jaws

opened, and he muttered some inarticulate sounds, while a grin wrinkled his cheeks. He might have spoken, but I did not hear; one hand was stretched out, seemingly to detain me, but I escaped, and rushed down stairs. I took refuge in the courtyard belonging to the house which I inhabited; where I remained during the rest of the night, walking up and down in the greatest agitation, listening attentively, catching and fearing each sound as if it were to announce the approach of the demoniacal corpse to which I had so miserably given life.

Oh! no mortal could support the horror of that countenance. A mummy again endued with animation could not be so hideous as that wretch. I had gazed on him while unfinished; he was ugly then; but when those muscles and joints were rendered capable of motion, it became a thing such as even Dante[2] could not have conceived.

I passed the night wretchedly. Sometimes my pulse beat so quickly and hardly that I felt the palpitation of every artery; at others, I nearly sank to the ground through languor and extreme weakness. Mingled with this horror, I felt the bitterness of disappointment; dreams that had been my food and pleasant rest for so long a space were now become a hell to me; and the change was so rapid, the overthrow so complete!

Morning, dismal and wet, at length dawned, and discovered to my sleepless and aching eyes the church of Ingolstadt, its white steeple and clock, which indicated the sixth hour. The porter opened the gates of the court, which had that night been my asylum, and I issued into the streets, pacing them with quick steps, as if I sought to avoid the wretch whom I feared every turning of the street would present to my view. I did not dare return to the apartment which I inhabited, but felt impelled to hurry on, although drenched by the rain which poured from a black and comfortless sky.

I continued walking in this manner for some time, endeavoring, by bodily exercise, to ease the load that weighed upon my mind. I traversed the streets, without any clear conception of where I was, or what I was doing. My heart palpitated in the sickness of fear; and I hurried on with irregular steps, not daring to look about me:—

---

2. **Dante**, (1265-1321) Italian poet, author of the *Inferno*.

"Like one who, on a lonely road,
  Doth walk in fear and dread,
And, having once turned round, walks on,
  And turns no more his head;
Because he knows a frightful fiend
  Doth close behind him tread."[3]

Continuing thus, I came at length opposite to the inn at which the various diligences and carriages usually stopped. Here I paused, I knew not why; but I remained some minutes with my eyes fixed on a coach that was coming towards me from the other end of the street. As it drew nearer, I observed that it was the Swiss diligence: it stopped just where I was standing, and, on the door being opened, I perceived Henry Clerval, who, on seeing me, instantly sprung out. "My dear Frankenstein," exclaimed he, "how glad I am to see you! how fortunate that you should be here at the very moment of my alighting!"

Nothing could equal my delight on seeing Clerval; his presence brought back to my thoughts my father, Elizabeth, and all those scenes of home so dear to my recollection. I grasped his hand, and in a moment forgot my horror and misfortune; I felt suddenly, and for the first time during many months, calm and serene joy. I welcomed my friend, therefore, in the most cordial manner, and we walked towards my college. Clerval continued talking for some time about our mutual friends, and his own good fortune in being permitted to come to Ingolstadt. "You may easily believe," said he, "how great was the difficulty to persuade my father that all necessary knowledge was not comprised in the noble art of bookkeeping; and, indeed, I believe I left him incredulous to the last, for his constant answer to my unwearied entreaties was the same as that of the Dutch schoolmaster in the *Vicar of Wakefield:*[4]—'I have ten thousand florins a year without Greek, I eat heartily without Greek.' But his affection for me at length overcame his dislike of learning, and he has permitted me to undertake a voyage of discovery to the land of knowledge."

"It gives me the greatest delight to see you; but tell me how you left my father, brothers, and Elizabeth."

"Very well, and very happy, only a little uneasy that they hear from you so seldom. By the by, I mean to lecture you a little upon their account myself.—But, my dear Frankenstein," continued he, stopping short, and gazing full in my face, "I did not before remark how very ill you appear; so thin and pale; you look as if you had been watching for several nights."

"You have guessed right; I have lately been so deeply engaged in one occupation that I have not allowed myself sufficient rest, as you see: but I hope, I sincerely hope, that all these employments are now at an end, and that I am at length free."

I trembled excessively; I could not endure to think of, and far less to allude to, the occurrences of the preceding night. I walked with a quick pace, and we soon arrived at my college. I then reflected, and the thought made me shiver, that the creature whom I had left in my apartment might still be there, alive, and walking about. I dreaded to behold this monster; but I feared still more that Henry should see him. Entreating him, therefore, to remain a few minutes at the bottom of the stairs, I darted up towards my own room. My hand was already on the lock of the door before I recollected myself. I then paused; and a cold shivering came over me. I threw the door forcibly open, as children are accustomed to do when they expect a specter to stand in waiting for them on the other side; but nothing appeared. I stepped fearfully in: the apartment was empty; and my bedroom was also freed from its hideous guest. I could hardly believe that so great a good fortune could have befallen me; but when I became assured that my enemy had indeed fled, I clapped my hands for joy, and ran down to Clerval.

We ascended into my room, and the servant presently brought breakfast; but I was unable to contain myself. It was not joy only that possessed me; I felt my flesh tingle with excess of sensitiveness, and my pulse beat rapidly. I was unable to remain for a single instant in the same place; I jumped over the chairs, clapped my hands, and laughed aloud. Clerval at first attributed my unusual spirits to joy on his arrival; but when he observed me more attentively he saw a wildness in my eyes for which he could not account; and

---

3. a stanza from Coleridge's "Rime of the Ancient Mariner."
4. *Vicar of Wakefield,* a novel by Oliver Goldsmith, published in 1766.

my loud, unrestrained, heartless laughter, frightened and astonished him.

"My dear Victor," cried he, "what, for God's sake, is the matter? Do not laugh in that manner. How ill you are! What is the cause of all this?"

"Do not ask me," cried I, putting my hands before my eyes, for I thought I saw the dreaded specter glide into the room; "*he* can tell.—Oh, save me! save me!" I imagined that the monster seized me; I struggled furiously, and fell down in a fit.

Poor Clerval! what must have been his feelings? A meeting, which he anticipated with such joy, so strangely turned to bitterness. But I was not the witness of his grief; for I was lifeless, and did not recover my senses for a long, long time.

2

After being away six years, Frankenstein finds his long-delayed homecoming marred by the tragic news of the murder of his youngest brother, William, by an unknown strangler whom Frankenstein, in a moment of intuition, realizes is the monster he created. In a terrible breach of justice, "poor, good" Justine Moritz, a former servant and companion, is executed for the crime, thereby deepening Frankenstein's feelings of personal guilt and despair. Crushed by sorrow and remorse, Frankenstein suffers a nervous collapse like that which followed the creation of the monster and impulsively departs to wander alone in the Alps and, finally, to ascend the summit of Montanvert Mountain. Victor Frankenstein is speaking:

It was nearly noon when I arrived at the top of the ascent. For some time I sat upon the rock that overlooks the sea of ice. A mist covered both that and the surrounding mountains. Presently a breeze dissipated the cloud, and I descended upon the glacier. The surface is very uneven, rising like the waves of a troubled sea, descending low, and interspersed by rifts that sink deep. The field of ice is almost a league in width, but I spent nearly two hours in crossing it. The opposite mountain is a bare perpendicular rock. From the side where I now stood Montanvert was exactly opposite, at the distance of a league; and above it rose Mont Blanc, in awful majesty. I remained in a recess of the rock, gazing on this wonderful and stupendous scene. The sea, or rather the vast river of ice, wound among its dependent mountains, whose aerial summits hung over its recesses. Their icy and glittering peaks shone in the sunlight over the clouds. My heart, which was before sorrowful, now swelled with something like joy; I exclaimed—"Wandering spirits, if indeed ye wander, and do not rest in your narrow beds, allow me this faint happiness, or take me, as your companion, away from the joys of life."

As I said this, I suddenly beheld the figure of a man, at some distance, advancing towards me with superhuman speed. He bounded over the crevices in the ice, among which I had walked with caution; his stature, also, as he approached, seemed to exceed that of man. I was troubled: a mist came over my eyes, and I felt a faintness seize me; but I was quickly restored by the cold gale of the mountains. I perceived, as the shape came nearer (sight tremendous and abhorred!) that it was the wretch whom I had created. I trembled with rage and horror, resolving to wait his approach, and then close with him in mortal combat. He approached; his countenance bespoke bitter anguish, combined with disdain and malignity, while its unearthly ugliness rendered it almost too horrible for human eyes. But I scarcely observed this; rage and hatred had at first deprived me of utterance, and I recovered only to overwhelm him with words expressive of furious detestation and contempt.

"Devil," I exclaimed, "do you dare approach me? and do not you fear the fierce vengeance of my arm wreaked on your miserable head? Begone, vile insect! or rather, stay, that I may trample you to dust! and, oh! that I could, with the extinction of your miserable existence, restore those victims whom you have so diabolically murdered!"

"I expected this reception," said the demon. "All men hate the wretched; how, then, must I be hated, who am miserable beyond all living things! Yet you, my creator, detest and spurn me, thy creature, to whom thou art bound by ties only dissoluble by the annihilation of one of us. You purpose to kill me. How dare you sport thus with life? Do your duty towards me, and I will do mine towards you and the rest of mankind. If you will comply with my conditions, I will leave them and

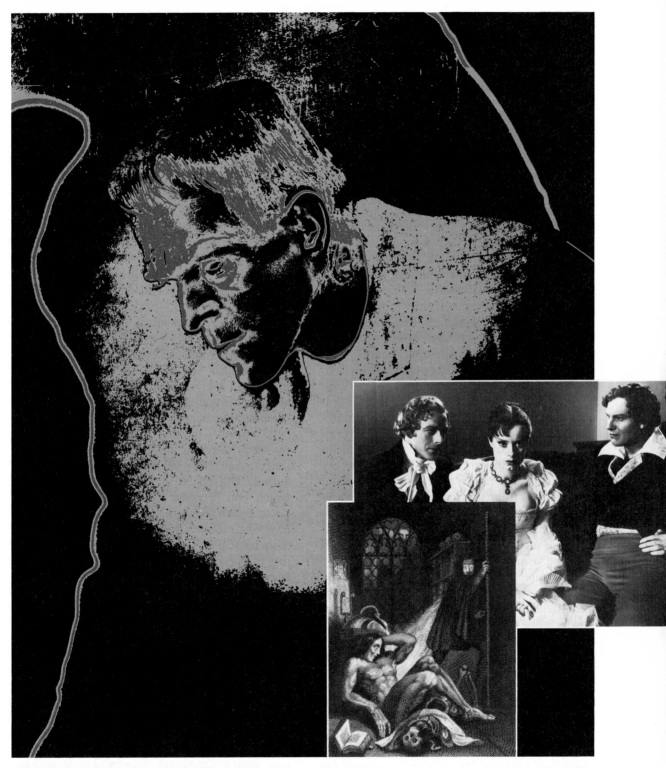

(Top) Boris Karloff as the creature in the film *Frankenstein* (1931). (Right) Elsa Lanchester as Mary Shelley in *The Bride of Frankenstein* (1935). (Bottom) Illustration from the 1832 edition of *Frankenstein*.

of which I was for ever barred, then impotent envy and bitter indignation filled me with an insatiable thirst for vengeance. I recollected my threat and resolved that it should be accomplished. . . . And now it is ended; there is my last victim!''

I was at first touched by the expressions of his misery; yet, when I called to mind what Frankenstein had said of his powers of eloquence and persuasion, and when I again cast my eyes on the lifeless form of my friend, indignation was rekindled within me. ''Wretch!'' I said, ''it is well that you come here to whine over the desolation that you have made. You throw a torch into a pile of buildings; and when they are consumed you sit among the ruins and lament the fall. Hypocritical fiend! if he whom you mourn still lived, still would he be the object, again would he become the prey, of your accursed vengeance. It is not pity that you feel; you lament only because the victim of your malignity is withdrawn from your power.''

''Oh, it is not thus—not thus,'' interrupted the being; ''yet such must be the impression conveyed to you by what appears to be the purport of my actions. Yet I seek not a fellow-feeling in my misery. No sympathy may I ever find. When I first sought it, it was the love of virtue, the feelings of happiness and affection with which my whole being overflowed, that I wished to be participated. . . . But now crime has degraded me beneath the meanest animal. No guilt, no mischief, no malignity, no misery, can be found comparable to mine. When I run over the frightful catalogue of my sins, I cannot believe that I am the same creature whose thoughts were once filled with sublime and transcendent visions of the beauty and the majesty of goodness. But it is even so; the fallen angel becomes a malignant devil. Yet even that enemy of God and man had friends and associates in his desolation; I am alone.

''You, who call Frankenstein your friend, seem to have a knowledge of my crimes and his misfortunes. But in the detail which he gave you of them he could not sum up the hours and months of misery which I endured, wasting in impotent passions. For while I destroyed his hopes, I did not satisfy my own desires. They were for ever ardent and craving; still I desired

love and fellowship, and I was still spurned. Was there no injustice in this? Am I to be thought the only criminal when all human kind sinned against me? . . . I, the miserable and the abandoned, am an abortion, to be spurned at, and kicked, and trampled on. Even now my blood boils at the recollection of this injustice.

''But it is true that I am a wretch. I have murdered the lovely and the helpless; I have strangled the innocent as they slept, and grasped to death his throat who never injured me or any other living thing. I have devoted my creator, the select specimen of all that is worthy of love and admiration among men, to misery; I have pursued him even to that irremediable ruin. There he lies, white and cold in death. You hate me; but your abhorrence cannot equal that with which I regard myself. I look on the hands which executed the deed; I think on the heart in which the imagination of it was conceived, and long for the moment when these hands will meet my eyes, when that imagination will haunt my thoughts no more.

''Fear not that I shall be the instrument of future mischief. My work is nearly complete. . . . I shall quit your vessel on the ice-raft which brought me thither, and shall seek the most northern extremity of the globe; I shall collect my funeral pile and consume to ashes this miserable frame, that its remains may afford no light to any curious and unhallowed wretch who would create such another as I have been. I shall die. I shall no longer feel the agonies which now consume me, or be the prey of feelings unsatisfied, yet unquenched. He is dead who called me into being; and when I shall be no more the very remembrance of us both will speedily vanish. I shall no longer see the sun or stars, or feel the winds play on my cheeks. Light, feeling, and sense will pass away; and in this condition must I find my happiness. Some years ago, when the images which this world affords first opened upon me, when I felt the cheering warmth of summer, and heard the rustling of the leaves and the warbling of the birds, and these were all to me, I should have wept to die; now it is my only consolation. Polluted by crimes, and torn by the bitterest remorse, where can I find rest but in death?

''Farewell! I leave you, and in you the last of

human kind whom these eyes will ever behold. Farewell, Frankenstein! If thou wert yet alive, and yet cherished a desire of revenge against me, it would be better satiated in my life than in my destruction. . . .

"But soon," he cried, with sad and solemn enthusiasm, "I shall die, and what I now feel be no longer felt. Soon these burning miseries will be extinct. I shall ascend my funeral pile triumphantly, and exult in the agony of the torturing flames. The light of that conflagration will fade away; my ashes will be swept into the sea by the winds. My spirit will sleep in peace; or if it thinks, it will not surely think thus. Farewell."

He sprung from the cabin-window, as he said this, upon the ice-raft which lay close to the vessel. He was soon borne away by the waves and lost in darkness and distance.

1817

Discussion

Section 1

1. What qualities of mind make Dr. Frankenstein's search for "the principle of life," which entails days and nights in vaults and graveyards, less horrifying to him than to the average person?

2. Frankenstein reads in Robert Walton's expression an eagerness to know his "secret"—how to animate lifeless matter. What does he tell Walton he should learn from him instead?

3. Frankenstein states he hesitated a long time before deciding how to employ his new-found power. **(a)** Why does he finally decide to create a being like himself? How are these plans later modified? **(b)** Describe the scope of Frankenstein's ambition, at this stage of his labor, for himself and for the world. **(c)** According to Frankenstein, what are the effects of his hard labor on his body, mind, and emotions? **(d)** In retrospect, does Frankenstein approve of his creation of the monster? Explain.

4. **(a)** Describe the events on the "dreary night of November" when Frankenstein beholds the results of his two years of labor. **(b)** What is the effect on Frankenstein of Clerval's arrival?

Section 2

1. Once he recognizes the figure approaching through the mist on the mountains, how does Frankenstein feel, and what does he decide to do?

2. **(a)** In describing the encounter between Frankenstein and the monster on the mountain top, what use does Mary Shelley make of the biblical story of the fall of man? **(b)** Judging from the monster's remarks, what does Mary Shelley believe to be the origin of evil in human life? **(c)** The monster forcefully rebukes Frankenstein, declaring, "Do your duty towards me. . . ." What duty does Frankenstein neglect to perform? Is the monster justified in feeling he has been wronged?

3. Why does Frankenstein agree to go with the monster to the hut on the mountain to hear his tale? Is he touched by anything the monster says to him?

Section 3

1. Describe the setting for the creation of the second monster. What are Frankenstein's feelings as he begins assembling the second creature?

2. State Frankenstein's reasons for suddenly destroying the second creature.

3. How does the monster react to the destruction of his future mate? Which of his threats is the most ominous?

Section 4

1. The monster tells Walton: "the fallen angel becomes a malignant devil." What does this statement mean, and how does it summarize the monster's moral history?

2. The monster also declares that "all human kind sinned against me." What specific examples of the injustice he has suffered does the monster cite?

3. **(a)** Is the monster's remorse over the death of Frankenstein genuine? **(b)** What ending has the monster planned for himself?

Overview

1. To what extent can it be said that Frankenstein and the monster symbolize the best and worst in each other as well as the essential duality of human nature? Can you think of other works of literature that portray the double nature of humanity, a mixture of both good and evil?

2. At times the monster's words become almost laughable in their sophistication. In your opinion, what aspects of the story are most convincing? which least so?

3. The novel has a pronounced didactic component, representing Mary Shelley's attempt to interpret and moralize on her imaginative vision. What do you regard as the moral "lessons" of the story?

4. How does the portrayal of the monster in the novel differ from the common public conception of the monster fostered by the mass media, especially film versions of the story?

5. What is Robert Walton's function in the novel?

The Changing English Language

The years prior to and including those of the Romantic Movement are notable for the beginnings of really serious attempts to improve and correct the spoken language—in other words, to set up a standard of pronunciation. In 1773 William Kendrick published the first dictionary that indicated vowel sounds, and he was quickly copied by both English and American lexicographers. Because many of these men felt that words should be pronounced as they are spelled, there was a tendency to reestablish older pronunciations, especially in respect to unaccented syllables. This was especially true in America, which was establishing an English of its own. Americans rebelled against the pronunciations of Samuel Johnson, long the accepted English authority. Although Johnson's *Dictionary* (see page 329) had indicated no pronunciations, his poetry through its meter made clear which pronunciations he regarded as standard. Thus in his poem *The Vanity of Human Wishes* the following words obviously are to be pronounced with only two syllables: *venturous, treacherous, powerful, general, history, quivering, flattering,* and *slippery.* Yet, with the possible exception of *general,* they were three-syllable words in America.

It was not until the Romantic Age that Greek began to affect the English language directly. Many new philosophic and scientific names were being added to the language. Combining two or more words or roots from Latin or Greek gave the language such words as *barometer* and *thermometer.* Another method of creating new words was adding Greek combining forms, prefixes, and suffixes such as *micro-* ("small"), *macro-* ("large"), *tele-* ("far"), *per-* ("maximum"), *-oid* ("like"), *-ic* ("smaller"), and *-ous* ("larger") to words already in use. In this manner words like *microscope, macrocosm, telepathy, peroxide, parotoid, sulphuric,* and *sulphurous* were produced.

Partly as a result of the interest of the romanticists in the Middle Ages, words belonging to the past were reintroduced into the language. The imitation of older ballads revived some archaic words found in such poems. Coleridge uses *eft-*

The title page to *Songs of Innocence,* 1789, by William Blake.

soons for *again, I wis* (from the Middle English *iwis*) for *certainly,* and *een* for *eye.* Keats uses *faeries,* the archaic spelling of *fairies, fay* in place of *faith,* and *sooth* to mean *smooth.* These words, not only old but odd, were scarcely likely to be adopted in conversation, but they served to acquaint readers with the language of England's past. In their search for color the romanticists also included slang and dialect terms, and although these forms are sparsely used in comparison with their use in literature today, they began to find acceptance in writing. Many of the romanticists liked to coin their own words; sometimes, as with *fuzzgig* and *critickasting,* these bordered on the ridiculous.

As you know, the romantic writers were concerned with bringing naturalness and simplicity back into the language. Consequently some of them felt that borrowed or foreign words should be eliminated from the language because they corrupted the mother tongue. This discrimination against foreign words was not widespread, for English had become quite stabilized.

The Romantics

Content Review

1. Compare and contrast the various views of the evils that afflict society expressed in Blake's "Holy Thursday" (from *Songs of Experience),* Wordsworth's "London, 1802," and Shelley's "England in 1819." Discuss what solutions, if any, are suggested to society's ills in these poems.

2. Compare and contrast the attitudes toward city and urban life expressed in Wordsworth's "Tintern Abbey" (lines 22–27 and 49–54), Coleridge's "Frost at Midnight" (lines 48–53), and Byron's *Don Juan* (stanza 8).

3. Judging from stanzas 90 and 91 in *Don Juan,* what was Byron's view of Wordsworth and Coleridge? What specific attitudes of these two poets does Byron seem to be satirizing? Based upon your reading of *Don Juan,* how does Byron seem to differ from these two poets?

4. Discuss the relationship between art and death as revealed by Keats in "When I Have Fears," "Ode on a Grecian Urn," and "Ode to a Nightingale."

5. Contrast the education of a youth that Byron describes in *Don Juan* with that which Wordsworth describes in *The Prelude* (Concept Review), with particular attention to the different tones of the two selections.

6. Explain why the term "The Age of Revolt" is an appropriate label for the Romantic period. Mention specific writers and their works to support your argument.

7. Compare Wordsworth's views on nature and childhood as expressed in "Tintern Abbey" and "Ode on Intimations of Immortality" with Coleridge's views in "Frost at Midnight."

8. Discuss Blake's use of **paradox** in the "Proverbs of Hell."

9. Discuss how each of the Romantic poets viewed the natural world. Use examples from each poet's work to illustrate the view of nature.

10. Explain what you consider to be the finest ideals of the Romantic Age, specific ways of viewing life and humanity that we should hold on to today.

Concept Review: Interpretation of New Material

from The Prelude, Book I • *William Wordsworth*

Wordworth referred to *The Prelude,* on which he worked for almost fifty years, as "a history of the author's mind." This excerpt describes boyhood adventures that made a profound impression on him.

1

Fair seed-time had my soul, and I grew up
Fostered alike by beauty and by fear:
Much favored in my birthplace, and no less
In that belovèd Vale[1] to which erelong
5 We were transplanted—there were we let loose
For sports of wider range. Ere I had told
Ten birthdays, when among the mountain slopes
Frost, and the breath of frosty wind, had snapped

The last autumnal crocus, 'twas my joy
10 With store of springes[2] o'er my shoulder hung
To range the open heights where woodcocks run
Along the smooth green turf. Through half the
        night,

---

1. **Vale,** Esthwaite Vale in Lancashire, near Wordworth's boyhood home.
2. **springes,** snares for catching birds.

Scudding[3] away from snare to snare, I plied
That anxious visitation—moon and stars
15 Were shining o'er my head. I was alone,
And seemed to be a trouble to the peace
That dwelt among them. Sometimes it befell
In these night wanderings, that a strong desire
O'erpowered my better reason, and the bird
20 Which was the captive of another's toil
Became my prey; and when the deed was done
I heard among the solitary hills
Low breathings coming after me, and sounds
Of undistinguishable motion, steps
25 Almost as silent as the turf they trod.

2

Nor less, when spring had warmed the
cultured Vale,
Moved we as plunderers where the mother bird
Had in high places built her lodge; though mean
Our object and inglorious, yet the end
30 Was not ignoble. Oh! when I have hung
Above the raven's nest, by knots of grass
And half-inch fissures in the slippery rock
But ill sustained, and almost (so it seemed)
Suspended by the blast that blew amain,[4]
35 Shouldering the naked crag, oh, at that time
While on the perilous ridge I hung alone,
With what strange utterance did the loud dry
wind
Blow through my ear! the sky seemed not a
sky
Of earth—and with what motion moved the
clouds!

3

40 Dust as we are, the immortal spirit grows
Like harmony in music; there is a dark
Inscrutable workmanship that reconciles
Discordant elements, makes them cling
together
In one society. How strange that all
45 The terrors, pains, and early miseries,
Regrets, vexations, lassitudes interfused
Within my mind, should e'er have borne a part,
And that a needful part, in making up
The calm existence that is mine when I
50 Am worthy of myself! Praise to the end!
Thanks to the means which Nature deigned to
employ;
Whether her fearless visitings, or those

That came with soft alarm, like hurtless light
Opening the peaceful clouds; or she may use
55 Severer interventions, ministry
More palpable, as best might suit her aim.

4

One summer evening (led by her) I found
A little boat tied to a willow tree
Within a rocky cove, its usual home.
60 Straight I unloosed her chain, and stepping in
Pushed from the shore. It was an act of stealth
And troubled pleasure, nor without the voice
Of mountain echoes did my boat move on;
Leaving behind her still, on either side,
65 Small circles glittering idly in the moon,
Until they melted all into one track
Of sparkling light. But now, like one who rows,
Proud of his skill, to reach a chosen point
With an unswerving line, I fixed my view
70 Upon the summit of a craggy ridge,
The horizon's utmost boundary; far above
Was nothing but the stars and the gray sky.
She was an elfin pinnace;[5] lustily
I dipped my oars into the silent lake,
75 And, as I rose upon the stroke, my boat
Went heaving through the water like a swan;
When, from behind that craggy steep till then
The horizon's bound, a huge peak, black and
huge,
As if with voluntary power instinct,
80 Upreared its head. I struck and struck again,
And growing still in stature the grim shape
Towered up between me and the stars, and
still,
For so it seemed, with purpose of its own
And measured motion like a living thing,
85 Strode after me. With trembling oars I turned,
And through the silent water stole my way
Back to the covert of the willow tree;
There in her mooring place I left my bark,[6]
And through the meadows homeward went, in
grave
90 And serious mood; but after I had seen
That spectacle, for many days, my brain
Worked with a dim and undetermined sense
Of unknown modes of being; o'er my thoughts

---

3. **Scudding,** moving swiftly.
4. **amain,** with full force, violently.
5. **pinnace,** a light boat or vessel.
6. **bark,** boat.

There hung a darkness, call it solitude
95 Or blank desertion. No familiar shapes
Remained, no pleasant images of trees,
Of sea or sky, no colors of green fields;
But huge and mighty forms, that do not live
Like living men, moved slowly through the
        mind
100 By day, and were a trouble to my dreams.

5

Wisdom and Spirit of the universe!
Thou Soul that art the eternity of thought
That givest to forms and images a breath
And everlasting motion, not in vain
105 By day or starlight thus from my first dawn
Of childhood didst thou intertwine for me
The passions that build up our human soul;
Not with the mean and vulgar works of man,
But with high objects, with enduring things—
110 With life and nature—purifying thus
The elements of feeling and of thought,
And sanctifying, by such discipline,
Both pain and fear, until we recognize
A grandeur in the beatings of the heart.
115 Nor was this fellowship vouchsafed[7] to me
With stinted kindness. In November days,
When vapors rolling down the valley made
A lonely scene more lonesome, among woods,
At noon and 'mid the calm of summer nights,
120 When, by the margin of the trembling lake,
Beneath the gloomy hills homeward I went
In solitude, such intercourse was mine;
Mine was it in the fields both day and night,
And by the waters, all the summer long.

6

125 And in the frosty season, when the sun
Was set, and visible for many a mile
The cottage windows blazed through twilight
        gloom,
I heeded not their summons: happy time
It was indeed for all of us—for me
130 It was a time of rapture! Clear and loud
The village clock tolled six—I wheeled about,
Proud and exulting like an untired horse

That cares not for his home. All shod with
        steel,
We hissed along the polished ice in games
135 Confederate,[8] imitative of the chase
And woodland pleasures—the resounding
        horn,
The pack loud chiming, and the hunted hare.
So through the darkness and the cold we flew,
And not a voice was idle; with the din
140 Smitten, the precipices rang aloud;
The leafless trees and every icy crag
Tinkled like iron; while far distant hills
Into the tumult sent an alien sound
Of melancholy not unnoticed, while the stars
145 Eastward were sparkling clear, and in the west
The orange sky of evening died away.
Not seldom from the uproar I retired
Into a silent bay, or sportively
Glanced sideway, leaving the tumultuous
        throng,
150 To cut across the reflex[9] of a star
That fled, and, flying still before me, gleamed
Upon the glassy plain; and oftentimes,
When we had given our bodies to the wind,
And all the shadowy banks on either side
155 Came sweeping through the darkness,
        spinning still
The rapid line of motion, then at once
Have I, reclining back upon my heels,
Stopped short; yet still the solitary cliffs
Wheeled by me—even as if the earth had
        rolled
160 With visible motion her diurnal round![10]
Behind me did they stretch in solemn train,
Feebler and feebler, and I stood and watched
Till all was tranquil as a dreamless sleep.
1805   1850

---

7. **vouchsafed,** granted or given.
8. **Confederate,** joined or allied.
9. **reflex,** reflection.
10. **diurnal round,** daily turning (on its axis).

On a separate sheet of paper, write your answers to the following questions. Do not write in your book.

1. In verse paragraph 1, what has the speaker stolen?

2. What one word makes lines 37–38 an example of **personification?**

3. In lines 40–41, what simile does the speaker use to describe the growth of the spirit?

4. What sort of existence does the speaker say all the troubles listed in lines 45–47 have resulted in?

5. What "upreared its head" in line 80?

6. To whom is verse paragraph 5 addressed?

7. In verse paragraph 5, with what did the "Wisdom and Spirit of the universe" intertwine the passions that went to make up the speaker's soul—the "works of man," or "life and nature"?

8. In the simile in lines 131–133, to what does the speaker compare himself?

9. What time of day is described in lines 144–146?

10. In a few words, summarize the speaker's attitude toward the natural world.

Composition Review

You may choose any *one* of the following assignments. Assume that you are writing for your classmates.

1. Reread Wordsworth's "The World Is Too Much with Us." Think about aspects of the modern world with which you think we are "out of tune." Make a list of examples of ways in which "we lay waste our powers."

Write your own version of Wordsworth's poem in free verse in which you show how "we have given our hearts away."

2. Reread Wordsworth's "Composed upon Westminster Bridge." Then think about a familiar scene that implies a contrast of some sort; for example, Main Street at midnight; an empty football stadium; a school without students; the announcement of bad news during a party.

Write a description of one of the above scenes or a scene of your choice. Show a distinct contrast between stillness and action, noise and silence, gaiety and somberness—or a contrasting pair of your choice. Choose words that create a clear picture and mood.

3. Make a list of character traits for one of the following: Donna Inez in *Don Juan;* Wordsworth as revealed in his autobiographical poems and sonnets; Dr. Frankenstein in Mary Shelley's *Frankenstein.* Identify dominant qualities and traits, including personality, temperament, ambitions, values, beliefs, relations with others.

Write a brief character sketch of the figure you have chosen. Be specific in describing the character.

4. Reread "La Belle Dame Sans Merci," noting the question-and-answer pattern of organization. Think of a mysterious figure who might have an intriguing story to relate; possible choices might include a weeping child, a dark-eyed boy, a lovely maid.

Write an original ballad in which you interview the mysterious figure of your choice. Start with Keats's opening line, "O what can ail thee, _____," filling in the identity of the person you are questioning. Then, in ballad stanzas, tell the story that explains your character's state of mind.

5. The Romantics regarded nature as a teacher and source of wisdom and enlightenment. Think of an experience in which nature proved to be your teacher, whether for good or bad.

Write a description of your experience. Describe the setting, the experience itself, and its meaning to you.

6. The Romantic poets glorified childhood, describing it as a time of idyllic enjoyment of nature and a state of innocence. To what extent do you share their view of nature and life?

Write a paper about childhood as the Golden Age of life. Make specific references to your own experience and to your reading of the Romantic poets.

Detail of *Work* by Ford Madox Brown, painted between 1852 and 1865.

Tennyson: *In Memoriam* •

• The Reform Bill

• Ruskin: *Modern Painters*

• The Great
Exhibition
opens

E. Bronte: *Wuthering Heights* •

C. Bronte: *Jane Eyre* •

• Newman *et al: Tracts for the Times*

Macaulay: *History of England* •

Dickens: *David Copperfield* •

The Crimean War

Dickens: *Pickwick Papers* •

E. B. Browning: *Sonnets from the Portuguese* •

1830   **1840**   **1850**

The Victorians

- R. Browning: *Men and Women*

- C. Rossetti: *Goblin Market*

- Eliot: *Middlemarch*

- Carroll: *Alice in Wonderland*

Fitzgerald: •
Rubaiyat of Omar Khayyam

- Pater: *Studies in the History of the Renaissance*

• Eliot: *The Mill on the Floss*

Darwin: •
Origin of Species

R. Browning: *The Ring and the Book* •

Tennyson: •
Idylls of the King

Hardy: *Return of the Native* •

Mill: *On Liberty* •

Arnold: *Culture and Anarchy* •

1860   **1870**   **1880**

Background: The Victorians 1830–1880

On June 20, 1837, the Lord Chamberlain and the Archbishop of Canterbury woke the eighteen-year-old Victoria to tell her that her uncle King William IV was dead and she was the Queen. That night she wrote in her diary, "I am very young and perhaps in many, though not in all things, inexperienced, but I am sure, that very few have more real good will and more real desire to do what is fit and right than I have." Victoria proved herself worthy. Her sixty-three-year reign, the longest in English history, became a symbol of stability and propriety.

The Victorian era marks the climax of England's rise to economic and military supremacy. Nineteenth-century England became the first modern, industrialized nation. It ruled the most widespread empire in world history, embracing all of Canada, Australia, and New Zealand, the lands that today constitute India and Pakistan, as well as many smaller countries in Asia, Africa, and the Caribbean. England's undisputed economic power during the middle of the nineteenth century further extended the nation's dominance—many independent countries were virtual fiefdoms, trading primarily with England and using the English pound sterling as international currency.

Although a great power in the world, internally England was anything but stable, and in the earliest decades of the Victorian era its very survival seemed dubious to many. The years of war with France, from the early days of the French Revolution (1789) to the final defeat of Napoleon (1815), permitted a small group of wealthy, landowning aristocrats who controlled the government to halt political reform. They claimed that any change might imperil the war effort and stifled dissent. "There was not a city, no, not a town," wrote Coleridge in 1809, "in which a man suspected of holding democratic principles could move abroad without receiving some unpleasant proof of the hatred in which his supposed opinions were held by the great majority of the people." With France defeated, this ruling minority strove to maintain the status quo. When thousands of workers gathered outside Manchester in August of 1819 to hear speeches on "cleanliness, sobriety, order, and peace," the local militia fired into the crowd, killing eleven and wounding four hundred. An English version of the French Revolution seemed perilously close—then, and intermittently over the next twenty years. Middle-class young men of the era, according to the novelist Charles Kingsley, thought "that the masses were their natural enemies and that they might have to fight . . . for the safety of their property and the honor of their sisters."

Such anger and fear grew out of the profound economic and social changes that swept over England between 1815 and 1850. During that period the English experienced a revolution scarcely less convulsive than the French had endured—the Industrial Revolution. It had begun in the eighteenth century, with the invention of the steam engine and of machines for spinning and weaving. After the war with France was concluded, this English industrial revolution began in earnest. In the north of England the newly mechanized textile industry expanded rapidly. One district in Yorkshire increased its textile production from 2.4 million yards in 1839 to 42 million yards in 1849. In 1848 English production of iron equaled that of the rest of the world combined. Much of this iron went into the spreading system of railroads. England opened the first stretch of commercial track in 1830. By 1839 there were 1,200 miles, and by 1850, 7,000 miles.

Increased agricultural production and improved medical techniques, coupled with a hope in the future, led to a rapidly expanding population. Despite emigration, the number of people in England doubled between 1801 and 1850. At the same time, there was a massive population shift from rural areas to the newly industrialized cities: Bradford, for example, went from a population of 13,000 in 1801 to 104,000 in 1861. To those who owned the means of production, and to those who controlled the nation politically, these immense changes sometimes seemed proof of an almost divine blessing on the nation. "The spinning jenny and the railroad, Cunard's liners and the electric telegraph, are to me," says a rather typical optimist in Kingsley's novel *Yeast*, "signs that we are, on some points at least, in harmony with the universe; that there is a mighty spirit working among us, who . . . may be the Ordering and Creating God." The historian T. B. Macaulay asserted in 1835, that the English had become, quite simply, "the greatest and the most highly civilized people that ever the world saw. . . ."

However, in his novel *Sybil* (1845) the writer and politician Benjamin Disraeli pointed out the existence in England of "two nations . . . who are as ignorant of each other's habits, thoughts, and feelings, as if they were . . . of different planets; who are formed by a different breeding, are fed by a different food, are ordered by different manners, and are not governed by the same laws." These "two nations" were the rich and the poor.

In describing the London of 1837 in *Nicholas Nickleby*, Dickens stressed this dramatic and per-

Queen Victoria and the Prince Consort and their Eldest Children in 1846, by Franz Xavier Winterhalter.

ilous dichotomy. "The rags of the squalid ballad-singer fluttered in the rich light that showed the goldsmith's treasures, pale and pinched-up faces hovered about the windows where was tempting food, hungry eyes wandered over the profusion guarded by one thin sheet of brittle glass—an

Illustration showing one of the evils of the Industrial Revolution—child labor in factories.

iron wall to them; half-naked shivering figures stopped to gaze at Chinese shawls and golden stuffs of India. . . . Life and death went hand in hand; wealth and poverty stood side by side; repletion and starvation laid them down together."

Rapid industrialization destroyed old jobs as it provided new ones. Population shifts left thousands housed in urban slums with bad water, no sanitation, and little food. Periodic depressions in markets for goods left whole factories unemployed. The English government was unequipped to handle such new and large-scale problems. In addition, many thoughtful people believed that widespread suffering and even death were inevitable. Malthus had argued in 1798 that the only

way to control population growth was starvation or self-control, while Ricardo in 1817 claimed that wages must be just high enough to permit a worker to survive. Anything more, he wrote, would wreck the system. Thus, a man as influential and powerful as Matthew Arnold's patron, Lord Lansdowne, could quite calmly predict that in the Irish famine of the 1840s, "one million of persons would die before it was over," and then persuade the government to cut back on its famine relief program; in the next two years, a million people did die.

Even for those who had a job, life as a member of the new industrial working class was difficult at best. Men, women, and children accustomed to the community life of rural towns and farms, to the varied and independent work habits of the farm and the small shop, found themselves laboring up to sixteen hours a day, six days a week, in factories without any governmental safety regulations. The work was monotonous. It turned people into "hands," as the factory owners called the anonymous workers, with no control over their lives, hired and fired at the whim of the owner or the fluctuation of the market. Looking at the disparity between classes in 1853, Ruskin argued that workers feel "that the kind of labor to which they are condemned is verily a degrading one, and makes them less than men."

The Victorian years brought with them increasing efforts to achieve political, social, and economic reforms that would reshape the country to meet the changes created by industrialization. In 1832 Parliament passed a Reform Bill that increased the electorate by fifty percent—now one Englishman in five could vote, though the bill carefully excluded workers and women from the franchise. The 1840s, the worst years of the century for unemployment, hunger, and disease, brought radical working-class agitation for the People's Charter, which demanded universal male suffrage and a Parliament in which any man could serve. Though at times Chartist agitation moved to the brink of armed confrontation, the government never responded directly to their demands. Instead, in a series of bills, Parliament repealed some of its more unjust laws, and began to legislate shorter working hours, industrial safety, urban sanitary reform, and so on. Ultimately, mounting economic prosperity reduced radical agitation, and in 1867 in a second Reform Bill, most working men gained the vote.

These years of rapid change had a great influence on the way people thought. During Victoria's reign it became clear that all things were subject to change—that change itself had become a permanent phenomenon. One way to deal with this was to trust in change, and thus developed the Victorian belief in progress.

But serious difficulties arose when one applied such thinking to religion—something that most people thought a fixed aspect of their lives. The very developments in science that were creating the marvels of modern technology now raised questions about the Bible. Lyell's *Principles of Geology* (1830) and Chamber's *Vestiges of Creation* (1844) seemed to prove the earth far older than the Bible said it was, while radical German theologians questioned the divinity of Jesus. Such challenges deeply troubled thoughtful people, who felt the need for conclusive answers.

In an era of change, confusion, and alarm, English writers felt compelled to accept social responsibilities. A college friend warned the poet Alfred Tennyson, "we cannot live in art." Tennyson accepted the challenge. For a nation raised in the warnings of the Sunday sermon, serious writing now frequently took up the burden and the authority of the preacher, both to enlighten, by suggesting new solutions to current problems, and also to inspirit, by moving the heart to new hope.

Victorians were avid readers. In their era there was little theater or music, and not only the educated elite, but many ordinary people found reading their principal source of entertainment and information. There was in the era not only an esteem, but a passion for verse. At Cambridge and Oxford promising undergraduates neglected their studies to write, read, and argue about poetry. All sorts of poems appeared: lyrics, narratives, verse dramas, epics, a bewildering variety of invention and experiment.

But the dominant form of the era, the preeminent form of middle-class expression, was the novel. Victorians bought them in hardbound volumes, as paperbound serials that appeared each month, or borrowed them from privately owned lending libraries. They liked long novels that told stories about their own world: the middle-class struggle for financial security, social acceptance, and love in marriage.

A particular form of novel that achieved great success traced the growth and development—the progress—of a central character from youth to adulthood. In so doing, the Victorians, building upon Romantic predecessors such as Wordsworth, gave a new importance to childhood, seeing it as a time of heightened perception and sensitivity, a critical period that shapes the adult personality.

Finally, there were the Victorian writers of nonfiction prose, a form of expression to which the era awarded particular significance. The Victorians discarded the informal essay of the eighteenth century for the long article on a matter of substance. These frequently appeared first in thick reviews that came out four times annually or, in later years, in monthly and weekly magazines. Later, the author would gather together such articles into a collection, or interweave them into a book. Exposition in such works was frequently not merely to explain; it was to move. In Victorian prose one finds not only the art of the orator, but that of the poet as well.

Probably never in the history of England were the rewards for authorship so great, at least for successful writers, as they were in this period. Publishers vied with each other to arrange contracts with Tennyson and Dickens, both of whom made fortunes by their pens. Readers turned to them to learn ways of thinking and modes of feeling—writers were treated as sages or prophets. Browning's every utterance was carefully considered by members of the Browning Society. More significantly, interlocking friendships joined most of the eminent writers of the day. They read aloud to each other from their latest works, shared criticism and ideas, and grew old together. "It was," as the modern historian G. M. Young writes, "a part of the felicity of the [1850s] to possess a literature which was at once topical, contemporary, and classic; to meet the Immortals on the streets, and to read them with added zest for the encounter."

Victoria outlived this generation of writers whose first works appeared when she was a young queen. Another, and a very different cluster of authors appeared, and the next unit explores the new directions they took.

Alfred, Lord Tennyson
1809–1892

When Alfred Tennyson arrived at Cambridge University in November of 1827, he was a lanky, remote eighteen-year-old who found it difficult to make friends. Though raised in a crowded country parsonage as one of eleven children, Tennyson as a boy had been given to solitude and depression. This gloom came partly from fears that the epilepsy which had driven his father to alcoholism, violence, and madness would prove hereditary. For the young Tennyson, relief came in writing; even before going to Cambridge he, along with two of his brothers, had published a small volume of poems.

Gradually, a group of Cambridge undergraduates recognized that here was a major new poet. They encouraged Tennyson in his writing and became for him a second, more supportive, family. Tennyson's closest friend from this period was Arthur Henry Hallam, the son of a wealthy historian. It was he who urged Tennyson to publish *Poems, Chiefly Lyrical* (1830). There, for the first time, apeared lyrics such as "The Kraken" that struck a distinctive new note in English literature—combining the rich language of Keats with strangely evocative symbols that resist simple explanation. These poems mark the beginning of Victorian poetry.

Soon Hallam was engaged to marry Tennyson's younger sister, Emily. Together, Tennyson and Hallam traveled to the Pyrenees in the summer of 1830 and to the Rhine two years later. Their close friendship became what R. B. Martin calls "the most emotionally intense period" Tennyson ever knew. Then, while on a trip to Vienna with his father, Hallam suddenly died of a ruptured blood vessel in the brain.

At this critical turning point in his life, Tennyson rejected the depression and madness of his family background and resolutely turned toward achievement through his art. In the two months following the news of his friend's death (October–November, 1833), he drafted "Ulysses," with its defiant cry for action, the first version of "The Passing of Arthur," whose legendary hero bears the same name as Tennyson's friend, and some of the lyrical poems that were to become *In Memoriam, A. H. H.* In these works Tennyson fuses private emotional crisis; public, moral conclusions; and symbols drawn from a wide literary heritage, both classical and native. His ability to write of both the private and the public, the present problem described in terms of materials drawn from the past, gave Tennyson the chance to powerfully integrate thought and feeling in his poetry.

The ensuing years were difficult. Tennyson lived on slender grants of money from his family, moving restlessly from one lodging to another, trying to write. His *Poems* (two volumes, 1842) and *The Princess* (1847) started to build a public reputation, but his first great success came in 1850 when, yielding to a friend's insistence, he finally published *In Memoriam,* a cycle of lyrics that laments Hallam's death and chronicles Tennyson's own struggle to regain an appetite for life.

In Memoriam enjoyed enormous public and critical success. It brought profits that enabled Tennyson to marry and live a settled life, and won him the title Poet Laureate, which he was to hold for nearly half a century.

The Kraken

Below the thunders of the upper deep;
Far, far beneath in the abysmal sea,
His ancient, dreamless, uninvaded sleep
The Kraken[1] sleepeth: faintest sunlights flee
5 About his shadowy sides: above him swell
Huge sponges of millennial growth and height;
And far away into the sickly light,
From many a wondrous grot and secret cell
Unnumbered and enormous polypi[2]
10 Winnow with giant arms the slumbering green.
There hath he lain for ages and will lie
Battening upon huge seaworms in his sleep,
Until the latter fire[3] shall heat the deep;
Then once by man and angels to be seen,
15 In roaring he shall rise and on the surface die.

1830

---

1. **Kraken,** mythical sea monster.
2. **polypi** (pol′ip ī′), octopuses, or sea serpents.
3. **latter fire,** the destruction of the earth at the Last Judgment.

Discussion

1. Where does the Kraken live?
2. How does its environment help to describe the Kraken?
3. When will the Kraken be seen by humanity?

The Lady of Shalott

PART 1

On either side the river lie
Long fields of barley and of rye,
That clothe the wold and meet the sky;
And through the field the road runs by
5   To many-towered Camelot;
And up and down the people go,
Gazing where the lilies blow
Round an island there below,
      The island of Shalott.

10 Willows whiten, aspens quiver,
Little breezes dusk and shiver
Through the wave that runs for ever
By the island in the river
      Flowing down to Camelot.
15 Four gray walls, and four gray towers,
Overlook a space of flowers,
And the silent isle embowers
      The Lady of Shalott.

By the margin, willow-veiled,
20 Slide the heavy barges trailed
By slow horses; and unhailed
The shallop flitteth silken-sailed
      Skimming down to Camelot:
But who hath seen her wave her hand?
25 Or at the casement seen her stand?
Or is she known in all the land,
      The Lady of Shalott?

Only reapers, reaping early
In among the bearded barley,
30 Hear a song that echoes cheerly
From the river winding clearly,
      Down to towered Camelot:
And by the moon the reaper weary,
Piling sheaves in uplands airy,
35 Listening, whispers " 'Tis the fairy
      Lady of Shalott."

PART 2

There she weaves by night and day
A magic web with colors gay.
She has heard a whisper say,
40 A curse is on her if she stay

To look down to Camelot.
She knows not what the curse may be,
And so she weaveth steadily,
And little other care hath she,
45   The Lady of Shalott.

And moving through a mirror clear
That hangs before her all the year,
Shadows of the world appear.
There she sees the highway near
50   Winding down to Camelot:
There the river eddy whirls,
And there the surly village churls,
And the red cloaks of market girls,
        Pass onward from Shalott.

55 Sometimes a troop of damsels glad,
An abbot on an ambling pad,
Sometimes a curly shepherd lad,
Or long-haired page in crimson clad,
        Goes by to towered Camelot;
60 And sometimes through the mirror blue
The knights come riding two and two:
She hath no loyal knight and true,
        The Lady of Shalott.

But in her web she still delights
65 To weave the mirror's magic sights,
For often through the silent nights
A funeral, with plumes and lights
        And music, went to Camelot:
Or when the moon was overhead,
70 Came two young lovers lately wed;
"I am half sick of shadows," said
        The Lady of Shalott.

PART 3

A bow-shot from her bower eaves,
He rode between the barley sheaves,
75 The sun came dazzling through the leaves,
And flamed upon the brazen greaves
        Of bold Sir Lancelot.
A red-cross knight for ever kneeled
To a lady in his shield,
80 That sparkled on the yellow field,
        Beside remote Shalott.

The gemmy bridle glittered free,
Like to some branch of stars we see

Hung in the golden Galaxy.
85 The bridle bells rang merrily
        As he rode down to Camelot:
And from his blazoned baldric slung
A mighty silver bugle hung,
And as he rode his armor rung,
90   Beside remote Shalott.

All in the blue unclouded weather
Thick-jewelled shone the saddle leather,
The helmet and the helmet feather
Burned like one burning flame together,
95   As he rode down to Camelot.
As often through the purple night,

Below the starry clusters bright,
Some bearded meteor, trailing light,
　　Moves over still Shalott.

100 His broad clear brow in sunlight glowed;
On burnished hooves his war horse trode;
From underneath his helmet flowed
His coal black curls as on he rode,
　　As he rode down to Camelot.
105 From the bank and from the river
He flashed into the crystal mirror,
"Tirra lirra," by the river
　　Sang Sir Lancelot.

She left the web, she left the loom,
110 She made three paces through the room,
She saw the water lily bloom,
She saw the helmet and the plume,
　　She looked down to Camelot.
Out flew the web and floated wide;
115 The mirror cracked from side to side;
"The curse is come upon me," cried
　　The Lady of Shalott.

PART 4

In the stormy east wind straining,
The pale yellow woods were waning,
120 The broad stream in his banks complaining.
Heavily the low sky raining
　　Over towered Camelot;
Down she came and found a boat
Beneath a willow left afloat,
125 And round about the prow she wrote
　　The Lady of Shalott.

And down the river's dim expanse
Like some bold seer in a trance,
Seeing all his own mischance—
130 With a glassy countenance
　　Did she look to Camelot.
And at the closing of the day
She loosed the chain, and down she lay;
The broad stream bore her far away,
135 　　The Lady of Shalott.

Lying, robed in snowy white
That loosely flew to left and right—
The leaves upon her falling light—
Through the noises of the night

140 She floated down to Camelot:
And as the boat head wound along
The willowy hills and fields among,
They heard her singing her last song,
　　The Lady of Shalott.

145 Heard a carol, mournful, holy,
Chanted loudly, chanted lowly,
Till her blood was frozen slowly,
And her eyes were darkened wholly,
　　Turned to towered Camelot.
150 For ere she reached upon the tide
The first house by the water-side,
Singing in her song she died,
　　The Lady of Shalott.

Under tower and balcony,
155 By garden wall and gallery,
A gleaming shape she floated by,
Dead-pale between the houses high,
　　Silent into Camelot.
Out upon the wharfs they came,
160 Knight and burgher, lord and dame,
And round the prow they read her name,
　　The Lady of Shalott.

Who is this? and what is here?
And in the lighted palace near
165 Died the sound of royal cheer;
And they crossed themselves for fear,
　　All the knights at Camelot:
But Lancelot mused a little space;
He said, "She has a lovely face;
170 God in his mercy lend her grace,
　　The Lady of Shalott."

1842

Discussion

1. One of the central themes of "The Lady of Shalott" is that of life as a journey that leads to death. Explain how the geography or physical setting of the poem is a **symbol** of this theme. Give particular attention to the river, the road, and the island.

2. What do you think is the source of the "curse" on the Lady?

3. Characterize Lancelot's reactions to the Lady. Is he true to the image on his shield?

For ten years the Greek hero Ulysses fought in the Trojan War. Then, while sailing back toward his island kingdom of Ithaca, his men offended Neptune, god of the sea, and for ten more years Ulysses had to struggle to reach home. When he finally arrived, he faced battle with rival suitors for his wife and throne. With his victory, the traditional story as told in Homer's *Odyssey* comes to an end. Many have speculated on what Ulysses might have done in later life. Tennyson, following the medieval poet Dante, concludes that after such adventures Ulysses could not rest content.

Ulysses

It little profits that an idle king,
By this still hearth, among these barren crags,
Matched with an agèd wife, I mete and dole
Unequal laws unto a savage race,
5   That hoard, and sleep, and feed, and know not
        me.
I cannot rest from travel: I will drink
Life to the lees: all times I have enjoyed
Greatly, have suffered greatly, both with those
That loved me, and alone; on shore, and when
10 Through scudding drifts the rainy Hyades[1]
Vexed the dim sea: I am become a name;
For always roaming with a hungry heart
Much have I seen and known; cities of men
And manners, climates, councils, governments,
15 Myself not least, but honored of them all;
And drunk delight of battle with my peers,
Far on the ringing plains of windy Troy.
I am part of all that I have met;
Yet all experience is an arch wherethrough
20 Gleams that untraveled world whose margin
        fades
Forever and forever when I move.
How dull it is to pause, to make an end,
To rust unburnished, not to shine in use!
As though to breathe were life! Life piled on life
25 Were all too little, and of one to me
Little remains: but every hour is saved
From that eternal silence, something more,
A bringer of new things; and vile it were
For some three suns to store and hoard myself,
30 And this gray spirit yearning in desire
To follow knowledge like a sinking star,
Beyond the utmost bound of human thought.

This is my son, mine own Telemachus,
To whom I leave the scepter and the isle—
35 Well-loved of me, discerning to fulfill
This labor, by slow prudence to make mild
A rugged people, and through soft degrees
Subdue them to the useful and the good.
Most blameless is he, centered in the sphere
40 Of common duties, decent not to fail
In offices of tenderness, and pay
Meet adoration to my household gods,
When I am gone. He works his work, I mine.
There lies the port; the vessel puffs her sail:
45 There gloom the dark, broad seas. My mariners,
Souls that have toiled, and wrought, and
        thought with me—
That ever with a frolic welcome took
The thunder and the sunshine, and opposed
Free hearts, free foreheads—you and I are old;
50 Old age hath yet his honor and his toil;
Death closes all: but something ere the end,
Some work of noble note, may yet be done,
Not unbecoming men that strove with gods.
The lights begin to twinkle from the rocks:
55 The long day wanes: the slow moon climbs: the
        deep
Moans round with many voices. Come, my
        friends,
'Tis not too late to seek a newer world.
Push off, and sitting well in order smite
The sounding furrows; for my purpose holds
60 To sail beyond the sunset, and the baths
Of all the western stars, until I die.

---

1. *rainy Hyades* (hī′ə dēz′), constellation of stars whose appearance brought rainy weather.

Ulysses Deriding Polyphemus by J. M. W. Turner, painted around 1829.

It may be that the gulfs will wash us down:
It may be we shall touch the Happy Isles,²
And see the great Achilles, whom we knew.
65 Though much is taken, much abides; and
      though
We are not now that strength which in old days
Moved earth and heaven; that which we are,
      we are;
One equal temper of heroic hearts,
Made weak by time and fate, but strong in will
70 To strive, to seek, to find, and not to yield.
1833   1842

_____

2. **To sail . . . Happy Isles.** Ulysses conceives of the world in terms of ancient geography. The stars literally plunge into the sea (lines 60–61), boats can fall off the edge of the earth into an abyss (line 62), and somewhere in the West are the Happy Islands, a paradise for heroes now dead, like Achilles who fought beside Ulysses at Troy (lines 63–64).

Discussion

1. How does Ulysses describe the people of Ithaca, his son, and his wife? What do such descriptions tell you about Ulysses' attitudes?

2. In what specific **setting** does Ulysses speak the words of the poem? What does the setting suggest about life?

3. What does Ulysses seek in his next voyage? Evaluate his decision in your own words.

Tennyson wrote this poem in the autumn of 1834, just a year after Hallam's death, during a visit to the celebrated ruins of Tintern Abbey (see Wordsworth's poem, page 372). It is a poem, said Tennyson, about "the sense of the abiding in the transient."

*T*ears, Idle Tears

Tears, idle tears, I know not what they mean,
Tears from the depth of some divine despair
Rise in the heart, and gather to the eyes,
In looking on the happy Autumn fields,
5 And thinking of the days that are no more.

Fresh as the first beam glittering on a sail,
That brings our friends up from the underworld,
Sad as the last which reddens over one
That sinks with all we love below the verge;
10 So sad, so fresh, the days that are no more.

Ah, sad and strange as in dark summer dawns
The earliest pipe of half-awakened birds

To dying ears, when unto dying eyes
The casement slowly grows a glimmering square;
15 So sad, so strange, the days that are no more.

Dear as remembered kisses after death,
And sweet as those by hopeless fancy feigned
On lips that are for others; deep as love,
Deep as first love, and wild with all regret;
20 O Death in Life, the days that are no more.
1834   1847

Discussion

1. **(a)** List the images from "Tears, Idle Tears" that illustrate how the past can be "sad," "fresh," "strange," and "deep." **(b)** How does each image aid in building up the emotion of the poem?

from *I*n Memoriam

Like the **sonnet** sequences of the Elizabethan poets (see Reader's Note, page 135), *In Memoriam* is a book-length work built up from brief **lyric** poems. However, it is something new in English poetry because, rather than simply expressing conventional love sentiments, *In Memoriam* chronicles the emotional, psychological, and intellectual growth of an individual. In 131 lyrics the poet moves from initial grief, through mounting depression, to virtual despair; and then, thanks to the help of others and the spiritual nourishment of nature, he turns toward a personal recovery based on a new vision of life.

In lyric 7, still numb from the first news of his friend's death, the speaker wanders to the door of Hallam's family home.

7

Dark house, by which once more I stand
    Here in the long unlovely street,
    Doors, where my heart was used to beat
So quickly, waiting for a hand,

5 A hand that can be clasped no more—
    Behold me, for I cannot sleep,
    And like a guilty thing I creep
At earliest morning to the door.

He is not here; but far away
10   The noise of life begins again,
   And ghastly thro' the drizzling rain
On the bald street breaks the blank day.

Grief for his friend's death joins, in the speaker's mind, with disturbing questions. Would it have been more prudent to live a less emotionally committed life, to be free from conscience, as animals are, and to never have really loved? Lyric 27 is his answer.

27

I envy not in any moods
   The captive void of noble rage,
   The linnet born within the cage,
That never knew the summer woods:

5 I envy not the beast that takes
   His license in the field of time,
   Unfettered by the sense of crime,
To whom a conscience never wakes;

Nor, what may count itself as blest,
10   The heart that never plighted troth
   But stagnates in the weeds of sloth;
Nor any want-begotten rest.

I hold it true, whate'er befall;
   I feel it, when I sorrow most;
15   'Tis better to have loved and lost
Than never to have loved at all.

Time passes. In brooding over the fact of Hallam's death, the poet begins to question the meaning and the purpose of life itself. In lyric 34, after initially reminding himself of what he ought to believe (lines 1–2), he considers what life would be like if death were the absolute end of everything.

34

My own dim life should teach me this,
   That life shall live for evermore,
   Else earth is darkness at the core,
And dust and ashes all that is;

5 This round of green, this orb of flame,
   Fantastic beauty; such as lurks
   In some wild poet, when he works
Without a conscience or an aim.

The Doubt: "Can These Dry Bones Live?" by Henry Alexander Bowler was intended to illustrate *In Memoriam*.

What then were God to such as I?
10   'T were hardly worth my while to choose
   Of things all mortal, or to use
A little patience ere I die;

'T were best at once to sink to peace,
   Like birds the charming serpent draws,
15   To drop head-foremost in the jaws
Of vacant darkness and to cease.

What sort of argument can the mind use, in opposition to such a depressing vision of reality? Lyric 54 offers one answer.

54

Oh yet we trust that somehow good
   Will be the final goal of ill,

To pangs of nature, sins of will,
Defects of doubt, and taints of blood;

5   That nothing walks with aimless feet;
That not one life shall be destroyed,
Or cast as rubbish to the void,
When God hath made the pile complete;

That not a worm is cloven in vain;
10   That not a moth with vain desire
Is shriveled in a fruitless fire,
Or but subserves another's gain.

Behold, we know not anything;
I can but trust that good shall fall
15   At last—far off—at last, to all,
And every winter change to spring.

So runs my dream: but what am I?
An infant crying in the night:
An infant crying for the light:
20   And with no language but a cry.

But this "trust"—that in each death must lie
some unseen purpose—seems refuted by
Nature since, as lyric 55 argues, "So careful of
the type she [Nature] seems, / So careless of
the single life . . . ." Tennyson was a thoughtful
reader of current scientific studies in geologi-
cal history and knew about the recent discoveries of fossils (such as the dinosaurs he alludes
to as "dragons of the prime") that greatly extended the history of the earth, cast doubt on
the factual reliability of the Bible, and suggested that the human species was but one of
millions of "types" of life on earth. Geology
and the fossil record seemed to show that no
type can be certain of permanent renewal—
not even our own. Hence, to his simplistic
assertion that at least the type survives, Nature
has a chilling response.

56

"So careful of the type?" but no.
From scarpèd cliff[1] and quarried stone
She cries, "A thousand types are gone:
I care for nothing, all shall go.

5   "Thou makest thine appeal to me:
I bring to life, I bring to death:
The spirit does but mean the breath:
I know no more." And he, shall he,

Man, her last work, who seemed so fair,
10   Such splendid purpose in his eyes,
Who rolled the psalm to wintry skies,
Who built him fanes[2] of fruitless prayer,

Who trusted God was love indeed
And love Creation's final law—
15   Though Nature, red in tooth and claw
With ravine, shrieked against his creed—

Who loved, who suffered countless ills,
Who battled for the True, the Just,
Be blown about the desert dust,
20   Or sealed within the iron hills?

No more? A monster then, a dream,
A discord. Dragons of the prime,
That tare[3] each other in their slime,
Were mellow music matched with him.

25   O life as futile, then, as frail!
O for thy voice to soothe and bless!
What hope of answer, or redress?
Behind the veil, behind the veil.

---

1. **scarpèd cliff.** The exposed strata of the cliff reveal extinct fossil species.
2. **fanes,** temples.
3. **tare,** tore.

To such doubts, initiated by Hallam's death
and complicated by the investigations of modern science, *In Memoriam* offers no simple
answers. Instead, it traces a personal growth in
trust and faith and a renewed sense of purpose
in the life of its speaker. This process reaches
one climax on New Year's Eve, 1838, when the
speaker finally feels strong enough to reject
much from the dead past and to accept the
vitality of things to come.

106

Ring out, wild bells, to the wild sky,
  The flying cloud, the frosty light:
  The year is dying in the night;
Ring out, wild bells, and let him die.

5 Ring out the old, ring in the new,
  Ring, happy bells, across the snow:
  The year is going, let him go;
Ring out the false, ring in the true.

Ring out the grief that saps the mind,
10 For those that here we see no more;
  Ring out the feud of rich and poor,
Ring in redress to all mankind.

Ring out a slowly dying cause,
  And ancient forms of party strife;
15 Ring in the nobler modes of life,
With sweeter manners, purer laws.

Ring out the want, the care, the sin,
  The faithless coldness of the times;
  Ring out, ring out my mournful rhymes,
20 But ring the fuller minstrel in.

Ring out false pride in place and blood,
  The civic slander and the spite;
  Ring in the love of truth and right,
Ring in the common love of good.

25 Ring out old shapes of foul disease;
  Ring out the narrowing lust of gold;
  Ring out the thousand wars of old,
Ring in the thousand years of peace.

Ring in the valiant man and free,
30 The larger heart, the kindlier hand;
  Ring out the darkness of the land,
Ring in the Christ that is to be.

By the end of the cycle, he has achieved a close unity with Nature, a harmony within his own spirit, and, finally, he senses the presence of his lost friend once more.

119

Doors, where my heart was used to beat
  So quickly, not as one that weeps
  I come once more; the city sleeps;
I smell the meadow in the street;

5 I hear a chirp of birds; I see
  Betwixt the black fronts long-withdrawn
  A light-blue lane of early dawn,
And think of early days and thee,

And bless thee, for thy lips are bland,
10 And bright the friendship of thine eye;
  And in my thoughts with scarce a sigh
I take the pressure of thine hand.

1850

Discussion

1. In lyric 27 the speaker compares himself to a number of figures who do *not* do something. List them, explaining the different kinds of denial they represent.

2. With what choice does lyric 34 seem to conclude?

3. Describe how lyric 56 contrasts two visions of human history, seen first by faith, then by unbelieving despair.

4. What does the speaker in lyric 106 mean by "let him die" in line 4?

5. Compare and contrast the details in lyrics 7 and 119.

The Passing of Arthur   from *Idylls of the King*

That story which the bold Sir Bedivere,
First made and latest left of all the knights,
Told, when the man was no more than a voice
In the white winter of his age, to those
5 With whom he dwelt, new faces, other minds.

For on their march to westward, Bedivere,
Who slowly paced among the slumbering host,
Heard in his tent the moanings of the King:
"I found Him in the shining of the stars,
10 I marked Him in the flowering of His fields,
But in His ways with men I find Him not.
I waged His wars, and now I pass and die.
O me! for why is all around us here
As if some lesser god had made the world,
15 But had not force to shape it as he would,
Till the High God behold it from beyond,
And enter it, and make it beautiful?
Or else as if the world were wholly fair,
But that these eyes of men are dense and dim,
20 And have not power to see it as it is.
Perchance, because we see not to the close—
For I, being simple, thought to work His will,
And have but stricken with the sword in vain;
And all whereon I leaned in wife and friend
25 Is traitor to my peace, and all my realm
Reels back into the beast, and is no more.
My God, thou hast forgotten me in my death;
Nay—God my Christ—I pass but shall not die."
Then, ere that last weird battle in the West,
30 There came on Arthur sleeping, Gawain killed

In Lancelot's war,[1] the ghost of Gawain blown
Along a wandering wind, and past his ear
Went shrilling, "Hollow, hollow all delight!
Hail, King! to-morrow thou shalt pass away.
35 Farewell! there is an isle of rest for thee.
And I am blown along a wandering wind,
And hollow, hollow, hollow all delight."
And fainter onward, like wild birds that change
Their season[2] in the night and wail their way
40 From cloud to cloud, down the long wind the
     dream
Shrilled; but in going mingled with dim cries
Far in the moonlit haze among the hills,
As of some lonely city sacked by night,
When all is lost, and wife and child with wail
45 Pass to new lords; and Arthur woke and called,
"Who spake? A dream. O light upon the wind,
Thine, Gawain, was the voice—are these dim
     cries
Thine? or doth all that haunts the waste and wild
Mourn, knowing it will go along with me?"
50 This heard the bold Sir Bedivere and spake:
"O me, my King, let pass whatever will,
Elves,[3] and the harmless glamor of the field;
But in their stead thy name and glory cling

---

1. **Lancelot's war.** Arthur's recent attack on Lancelot. See the headnote above.
2. **wild birds . . . season,** migrating birds flying north or south according to the season of the year.
3. **Elves,** elemental spirits of the wild, according to medieval folk belief; one of the peoples of Fairyland.

To all high places like a golden cloud
55 For ever; but as yet thou shalt not pass.
Light was Gawain in life, and light in death
Is Gawain, for the ghost is as the man;
And care not thou for dreams from him, but
    rise—
I hear the steps of Modred in the West,
60 And with him many of thy people, and knights
Once thine, whom thou hast loved, but grosser
    grown
Than heathen, spitting at their vows and thee.
Right well in heart they know thee for the King.
Arise, go forth and conquer as of old.''
65 Then spake King Arthur to Sir Bedivere:
''Far other is this battle in the West
Whereto we move, than when we strove in
    youth,
And brake the petty kings, and fought with
    Rome,
Or thrust the heathen from the Roman wall,
70 And shook him thro' the North. Ill doom is mine
To war against my people and my knights.
The king who fights his people fights himself.
And they my knights, who loved me once, the
    stroke
That strikes them dead is as my death to me.
75 Yet let us hence, and find or feel a way
Thro' this blind haze, which ever since I saw
One lying in the dust at Almesbury,[4]
Hath folded in the passes of the world.''

Then rose the King and moved his host by
    night,
80 And ever pushed Sir Modred, league by league,
Back to the sunset bound of Lyonesse[5]—
A land of old upheaven from the abyss
By fire, to sink into the abyss again;
Where fragments of forgotten peoples dwelt,
85 And the long mountains ended in a coast
Of ever-shifting sand, and far away
The phantom circle of a moaning sea.
There the pursuer could pursue no more,
And he that fled no further fly the King;
90 And there, that day when the great light of
    heaven
Burned at his lowest[6] in the rolling year,
On the waste sand by the waste sea they closed.
Nor ever yet had Arthur fought a fight
Like this last, dim, weird battle of the West.
95 A deathwhite mist slept over sand and sea;

Whereof the chill, to him who breathed it, drew
Down with his blood, till all his heart was cold
With formless fear. And ev'n on Arthur fell
Confusion, since he saw not whom he fought.
100 For friend and foe were shadows in the mist,
And friend slew friend not knowing whom he
    slew;
And some had visions out of golden youth,
And some beheld the faces of old ghosts
Look in upon the battle. And in the mist
105 Was many a noble deed, many a base,
And chance and craft and strength in single fights,
And ever and anon with host to host
Shocks, and the splintering spear, the hard mail
    hewn,
Shield-breakings, and the clash of brands,[7] the
    crash
110 Of battleaxes on shattered helms, and shrieks
After the Christ, of those who falling down
Looked up for heaven, and only saw the mist;
And shouts of heathen and the traitor knights,
Oaths, insult, filth, and monstrous blasphemies,
115 Sweat, writhings, anguish, laboring of the lungs
In that close mist, and cryings of the light,
Moans of the dying, and voices of the dead.
Last, as by some one deathbed after wail
Of suffering, silence follows, or thro' death
120 Or deathlike swoon, thus over all that shore,
Save for some whisper of the seething seas,
A dead hush fell; but when the dolorous day
Grew drearier toward twilight falling, came
A bitter wind, clear from the North, and blew
125 The mist aside, and with that wind the tide
Rose, and the pale King glanced across the field
Of battle: but no man was moving there;
Nor any cry of Christian heard thereon,
Nor yet of heathen; only the wan wave
130 Brake in among dead faces, to and fro
Swaying the helpless hands, and up and down
Tumbling the hollow helmets of the fallen,

---

4. One . . . Almesbury (ämz′bẽr ē). According to Tennyson,
Queen Guinevere fled to the nunnery at Almesbury. Arthur pursued her there. When she heard his steps approaching the door
of her nun's cell, she fell from her chair "And grovelled with her
face against the floor." (Guinevere, line 412)
5. Lyonesse (lī′ō nes′), a legendary country supposed to have
once been attached to the peninsula of Cornwall, but long since
sunk under the sea. Lyonesse is sometimes identified with
Cornwall itself.
6. Burned at his lowest, the time of the winter solstice.
7. brands, swords.

By the end of the medieval period Arthur's story had gone through many transformations, but its great **climax** remained his final battle and death, modified by the note of hope in his return. Like many of his contemporaries, Tennyson believed the early 1830s were the end of an era in English history; a traditional, agrarian, aristocratic world was being replaced by a new world of innovation, industrialization, and democracy. Bedivere's lament—"I, the last, go forth companionless, / And the days darken round me, and the years, / Among new men, strange faces, other minds"—articulated something many people felt. Tennyson's poem became an effort to resolve this sense of crisis by strengthening the faint hope with which Malory's account of Arthur concludes into a belief in the future.

Tennyson was, even in the 1830s, already well-read in mythology and theories of **myth,** and he added to Malory's account a more explicitly optimistic, mythic dimension. Many cultures tell the story of the hero who fails, dies, and then returns. Such stories echo the cycles of the day and the seasons, and reassure the listener that dawn and spring will come again. While Malory is vague about the time of year in which Arthur dies, Tennyson is very explicit: Arthur fights on New Year's Eve, and dies on New Year's Day. The funeral barge carrying Arthur sails into the sun in "the stillness of the dead world's winter dawn" (line 442). This parallel between Arthur's life and the yearly cycle joins a similar parallel between Arthur and the sun's daily cycle. In the account of his youthful successes, Arthur is described as having a "forehead like a rising sun" (line 385); now, at his dying hour his face looks like "the withered moon / Smote by the fresh beam of the springing east" (lines 381–382). Arthur's resemblance to the cyclic gods of earlier myths promises a more certain return.

Tennyson then adds another dimension with more than one **allusion** to Jesus. Of course for most Victorian readers, to see in Arthur a resemblance to Jesus was to evoke that trust in his return to life which their religion so consistently taught. Further, it suggested that Arthur might serve as a model for a life of public service and self-sacrifice.

Finally, Tennyson gave to his tale the typically Victorian trust in progress. In his last moments Arthur concludes, "The old order changeth, yielding place to new." To his contemporaries, fearful of the changing character of England, Tennyson's conclusions were clear and heartening.

And shivered brands that once had fought with Rome,
And rolling far along the gloomy shores
135 The voice of days of old and days to be.
Then spake King Arthur to Sir Bedivere,
And whiter than the mist that all day long
Had held the field of battle was the King:
"Hearest thou this great voice that shakes the world,
140 And wastes the narrow realm whereon we move,
And beats upon the faces of the dead,
My dead, as tho' they had not died for me?—
O Bedivere, for on my heart hath fall'n
Confusion, till I know not what I am,
145 Nor whence I am, nor whether I be King,
Behold, I seem but King among the dead."

Then spake the bold Sir Bedivere: "My King,
King everywhere! and so the dead have kings,
There also will I worship thee as King.
150 Yet still thy life is whole, and still I live
Who love thee; but who hates thee, he that brought
The heathen back among us, yonder stands,
Modred unharmed, the traitor of thine house."
Then spake the King: "My house hath been my doom.
155 But call not thou this traitor of my house
Who hath but dwelt beneath one roof with me.
My house are rather they who sware my vows,
Yea, even while they brake them, owned me King.
And well for thee, saying in my dark hour,

160 When all the purport of my throne hath failed,
That quick or dead thou holdest me for King.
King am I, whatsoever be their cry;
And one last act of knighthood shalt thou see
Yet, ere I pass.'' And uttering this the King
165 Made at the man: then Modred smote his liege
Hard on that helm which many a heathen sword
Had beaten thin; while Arthur at one blow,
Striking the last stroke with Excalibur,
Slew him, and all but slain himself, he fell.
170 So all day long the noise of battle rolled
Among the mountains by the winter sea;
Until King Arthur's Table, man by man,
Had fall'n in Lyonesse about their lord,
King Arthur. Then, because his wound was deep,
175 The bold Sir Bedivere uplifted him,
And bore him to a chapel nigh the field,
A broken chancel[8] with a broken cross,
That stood on a dark strait of barren land:
On one side lay the Ocean, and on one
180 Lay a great water, and the moon was full.
Then spake King Arthur to Sir Bedivere:
''The sequel of to-day unsolders all
The goodliest fellowship of famous knights
Whereof this world holds record. Such a sleep
185 They sleep—the men I loved. I think that we
Shall never more, at any future time,
Delight our souls with talk of knightly deeds,
Walking about the gardens and the halls
Of Camelot, as in the days that were.
190 I perish by this people which I made,—
Tho' Merlin[9] sware that I should come again
To rule once more; but, let what will be, be,
I am so deeply smitten thro' the helm
That without help I cannot last till morn.
195 Thou therefore take my brand Excalibur,
Which was my pride: for thou rememberest how
In those old days, one summer noon, an arm
Rose up from out the bosom of the lake,
Clothed in white samite,[10] mystic, wonderful,
200 Holding the sword—and how I rowed across
And took it, and have worn it, like a king;
And, wheresoever I am sung or told
In aftertime, this also shall be known;
But now delay not: take Excalibur,
205 And fling him far into the middle mere:
Watch what thou seest, and lightly bring me
        word.''
To him replied the bold Sir Bedivere:
''It is not meet, Sir King, to leave thee thus,

Aidless, alone, and smitten thro' the helm—
210 A little thing may harm a wounded man;
Yet I thy hest will all perform at full,
Watch what I see, and lightly bring thee word.''
So saying, from the ruined shrine he stept,
And in the moon athwart the place of tombs,
215 Where lay the mighty bones of ancient men,
Old knights, and over them the sea wind sang
Shrill, chill, with flakes of foam. He, stepping
        down
By zigzag paths, and juts of pointed rock,
Came on the shining levels of the lake.
220 There drew he forth the brand Excalibur,
And o'er him, drawing it, the winter moon,
Brightening the skirts of a long cloud, ran forth
And sparkled keen with frost against the hilt;
For all the haft twinkled with diamond sparks,
225 Myriads of topaz lights, and jacinth work
Of subtlest jewellery. He gazed so long
That both his eyes were dazzled as he stood,
This way and that dividing the swift mind,
In act to throw: but at the last it seemed
230 Better to leave Excalibur concealed
There in the many-knotted waterflags,
That whistled stiff and dry about the marge.
So strode he back slow to the wounded King.
Then spake King Arthur to Sir Bedivere:
235 ''Hast thou performed my mission which I gave?
What is it thou hast seen? or what hast heard?''
And answer made the bold Sir Bedivere:
''I heard the ripple washing in the reeds,
And the wild water lapping on the crag.''
240 To whom replied King Arthur, faint and pale:
''Thou has betrayed thy nature and thy name,
Not rendering true answer, as beseemed
Thy fealty, nor like a noble knight:
For surer sign had followed, either hand,
245 Or voice, or else a motion of the mere.
This is a shameful thing for men to lie.
Yet now, I charge thee, quickly go again,
As thou art lief[11] and dear, and do the thing
I bade thee, watch, and lightly bring me word.''
250 Then went Sir Bedivere the second time
Across the ridge, and paced beside the mere,
Counting the dewy pebbles, fixed in thought;

---

8. *chancel* (chan'sel), the space around the altar of a church.
9. *Merlin* (mėr'lən), a magician and prophet who was Arthur's chief advisor. At the beginning of the king's reign, Merlin had prophesied that Arthur would not die, but return to rule.
10. *samite* (sam'īt), a rich, heavy silk fabric.
11. *lief* (lēf), beloved.

But when he saw the wonder of the hilt,
How curiously and strangely chased,[12] he smote
255 His palms together, and he cried aloud:
"And if indeed I cast the brand away,
Surely a precious thing, one worthy note,
Should thus be lost for ever from the earth,
Which might have pleased the eyes of many men.
260 What good should follow this, if this were done?
What harm, undone? Deep harm to disobey,
Seeing obedience is the bond of rule.
Were it well to obey then, if a king demand
An act unprofitable, against himself?
265 The King is sick, and knows not what he does.
What record, or what relic of my lord
Should be to aftertime, but empty breath
And rumors of a doubt? But were this kept,
Stored in some treasure-house of mighty kings,
270 Some one might show it at a joust of arms,
Saying, 'King Arthur's sword, Excalibur,
Wrought by the lonely maiden of the Lake.
Nine years she wrought it, sitting in the deeps
Upon the hidden bases of the hills.'
275 So might some old man speak in the aftertime
To all the people, winning reverence.
But now much honor and much fame were lost."
So spake he, clouded with his own conceit,[13]
And hid Excalibur the second time,
280 And so strode back slow to the wounded King.
Then spoke King Arthur, breathing heavily:
"What is it thou hast seen? or what has heard?"
And answer made the bold Sir Bedivere:
"I heard the water lapping on the crag,
285 And the long ripple washing in the reeds."
To whom replied King Arthur, much in wrath:
"Ah, miserable and unkind, untrue,
Unknightly, traitor-hearted! Woe is me!
Authority forgets a dying king,
290 Laid widowed of the power in his eye
That bowed the will. I see thee what thou art,
For thou, the latest-left of all my knights,
In whom should meet the offices of all,
Thou wouldst betray me for the precious hilt;
295 Either from lust of gold, or like a girl
Valuing the giddy pleasure of the eyes.
Yet, for a man may fail in duty twice,
And the third time may prosper, get thee hence.
But, if thou spare to fling Excalibur,
300 I will arise and slay thee with my hands."
Then quickly rose Sir Bedivere, and ran,
And, leaping down the ridges lightly, plunged

Among the bulrush beds, and clutched the sword,
And strongly wheeled and threw it. The great brand
305 Made lightnings in the splendor of the moon,
And flashing round and round, and whirled in an arch,
Shot like a streamer of the northern morn,
Seen where the moving isles of winter shock
By night, with noises of the Northern Sea.[14]
310 So flashed and fell the brand Excalibur.
But ere he dipt the surface, rose an arm
Clothed in white samite, mystic, wonderful,
And caught him by the hilt, and brandished him
Three times, and drew him under in the mere.
315 And lightly went the other to the King.
Then spoke King Arthur, drawing thicker breath:
"Now see I by thine eyes that this is done.
Speak out: what is it thou hast heard, or seen?"
And answer made the bold Sir Bedivere:
320 "Sir King, I closed mine eyelids, lest the gems
Should blind my purpose, for I never saw,
Nor shall see, here or elsewhere, till I die,
Not tho' I live three lives of mortal men,
So great a miracle as yonder hilt.
325 Then with both hands I flung him, wheeling him;
But when I looked again, behold an arm,
Clothed in white samite, mystic, wonderful,
That caught him by the hilt, and brandished him
Three times, and drew him under in the mere."
330 And answer made King Arthur, breathing hard:
"My end draws nigh; 'tis time that I were gone.
Make broad thy shoulders to receive my weight,
And bear me to the margin; yet I fear
My wound hath taken cold, and I shall die."
335 So saying, from the pavement he half rose,
Slowly, with pain, reclining on his arm,
And looking wistfully with wide blue eyes
As in a picture. Him Sir Bedivere
Remorsefully regarded thro' his tears,
340 And would have spoken, but he found not words;
Then took with care, and kneeling on one knee,
O'er both his shoulders drew the languid hands,
And rising bore him thro' the place of tombs.

---

12. *chased* (chās'd), carved or engraved.
13. *conceit,* an idea or notion, often a farfetched one.
14. **Shot like a streamer . . . the Northern Sea.** The comparison here is between the flight of the sword and the aurora borealis, the "northern lights," bands of light appearing in the sky around the polar regions. The "moving isles of winter" are icebergs.

Detail of *The Last Sleep of Arthur in Avalon* by Sir Edward Burne-Jones, painted between 1881 and 1898.

But, as he walked, King Arthur panted hard,
345 Like one that feels a nightmare on his bed
When all the house is mute. So sighed the King,
Muttering and murmuring at his ear, ''Quick, quick!
I fear it is too late, and I shall die.''
But the other swiftly strode from ridge to ridge,
350 Clothed with his breath, and looking, as he walked,

Larger than human on the frozen hills.
He heard the deep behind him, and a cry
Before. His own thought drove him like a goad.
Dry clashed his harness in the icy caves
355 And barren chasms, and all to left and right
The bare black cliff clanged round him, as he based
His feet on juts of slippery crag that rang
Sharp-smitten with the dint of armed heels—
And on a sudden, lo! the level lake,

360 And the long glories of the winter moon.
Then saw they how there hove a dusky barge,
Dark as a funeral scarf from stem to stern,
Beneath them; and descending they were ware[15]
That all the decks were dense with stately
      forms,
365 Black-stoled, black-hooded, like a dream—by
      these
Three Queens with crowns of gold. And from
      them rose
A cry that shivered to the tingling stars,
And, as it were one voice, an agony
Of lamentation, like a wind that shrills
370 All night in a waste land, where no one comes,
Or hath come, since the making of the world.
Then murmured Arthur, "Place me in the
      barge."
So to the barge they came. There those three
      Queens
Put forth their hands, and took the King, and
      wept.
375 But she, that rose the tallest of them all
And fairest, laid his head upon her lap,
And loosed the shattered casque, and chafed
      his hands,
And called him by his name, complaining loud,
And dropping bitter tears against a brow
380 Striped with dark blood: for all his face was
      white
And colorless, and like the withered moon
Smote by the fresh beam of the springing east;
And all his greaves and cuisses dashed with
      drops
Of onset;[16] and the light and lustrous curls—
385 That made his forehead like a rising sun
High from the dais-throne—were parched with
      dust;
Or clotted into points and hanging loose,
Mixed with the knightly growth that fringed his lips.
So like a shattered column lay the King;
390 Not like that Arthur who, with lance in rest,
From spur to plume a star of tournament,
Shot thro' the lists at Camelot, and charged
Before the eyes of ladies and of kings.
Then loudly cried the bold Sir Bedivere:
395 "Ah! my Lord Arthur, whither shall I go?
Where shall I hide my forehead and my eyes?
For now I see the true old times are dead,
When every morning brought a noble chance,
And every chance brought out a noble knight.

400 Such times have been not since the light that led
The holy Elders with the gift of myrrh.[17]
But now the whole Round Table is dissolved
Which was an image of the mighty world,
And I, the last, go forth companionless,
405 And the days darken round me, and the years,
Among new men, strange faces, other minds."
And slowly answered Arthur from the barge:
"The old order changeth, yielding place to new,
And God fulfils himself in many ways,
410 Lest one good custom should corrupt the world.
Comfort thyself; what comfort is in me?
I have lived my life, and that which I have done
May He within himself make pure! but thou,
If thou shouldst never see my face again,
415 Pray for my soul. More things are wrought by
      prayer
Than this world dreams of. Wherefore, let thy
      voice
Rise like a fountain for me night and day.
For what are men better than sheep or goats
That nourish a blind life within the brain,
420 If, knowing God, they lift not hands of prayer
Both for themselves and those who call them
      friend?
For so the whole round earth is every way
Bound by gold chains about the feet of God.
But now farewell. I am going a long way
425 With these thou seest—if indeed I go
(For all my mind is clouded with a doubt)—
To the island-valley of Avilion;[18]
Where falls not hail, or rain, or any snow.
Nor ever wind blows loudly; but it lies
430 Deep-meadowed, happy, fair with orchard lawns
And bowery hollows crowned with summer sea,
Where I will heal me of my grievous wound."
So said he, and the barge with oar and sail
Moved from the brink, like some full-breasted
      swan
435 That, fluting a wild carol ere her death,
Ruffles her pure cold plume, and takes the flood
With swarthy webs. Long stood Sir Bedivere
Revolving many memories, till the hull
Looked one black dot against the verge of dawn,

---

15. **ware,** aware.
16. **onset,** combat; "drops / Of onset" are of blood.
17. **holy Elders . . . myrrh.** The three Magi, or priestly kings, were led by a star to the birthplace of Christ, each carrying a gift. One of the gifts was *myrrh* (mėr), a fragrant resin.
18. **Avilion** (ə vil'ē ən), or *Avalon,* one of the paradisal isles of Celtic legend, located in the West.

440 And on the mere the wailing died away.
But when that moan had past for ever more,
The stillness of the dead world's winter dawn
Amazed him, and he groaned, "The King is
gone."
And therewithal came on him the weird rhyme,
445 "From the great deep to the great deep he
goes."
Whereat he slowly turned and slowly clomb
The last hard footstep of that iron crag;
Thence marked the black hull moving yet, and
cried,
"He passes to be King among the dead,
450 And after healing of his grievous wound
He comes again; but—if he come no more—
O me, be yon dark Queens in yon black boat,
Who shrieked and wailed, the three whereat we
gazed

On that high day, when, clothed with living light,
455 They stood before his throne in silence, friends
Of Arthur, who should help him at his need?"
Then from the dawn it seemed there came, but
faint
As from beyond the limit of the world,
Like the last echo born of a great cry,
460 Sounds, as if some fair city were one voice
Around a king returning from his wars.
Thereat once more he moved about, and clomb
Ev'n to the highest he could climb, and saw,
Straining his eyes beneath an arch of hand,
465 Or thought he saw, the speck that bare the King,
Down that long water opening on the deep
Somewhere far off, pass on and on, and go
From less to less and vanish into light.
And the new sun rose bringing the new year.
1833, 1869   1869

<hr>

Discussion

1. In "The Passing of Arthur," what kind of spiritual crisis does Arthur face the night before the battle? Consider, in particular, lines 9–17.

2. In what ways does the setting of the battle in the west underscore its finality?

3. **(a)** What are Bedivere's reasons for twice refusing to throw away Excalibur? **(b)** How is he able, finally, to do it? **(c)** What do Bedivere's failures suggest?

4. In his final speech (especially lines 408–410) how does Arthur account for the failure of his realm?

5. What does Tennyson suggest about the future in the way he describes the departure of Arthur's mysterious barge?

Vocabulary
Affixes, Roots

Explain how the prefix in each of the following italicized words modifies its root and determines its meaning. If necessary, use your Glossary.

1. ". . . . Like some bold seer in a trance, / Seeing all his own *mischance* . . . ."

2. "*Perchance,* because we see not to the close . . . ."

3. ". . . . That not a moth with vain desire / Is shriveled in a fruitless fire, / Or but *subserves* another's gain."

4. "What hope of answer, or *redress* / Behind the veil . . . ?"

Composition

1. Imagine what Ulysses might be doing, thinking, and feeling a month after he sails from Ithaca.

Following Tennyson's example, write, in the form of a prose **monologue,** what Ulysses might be saying.

2. The last six stanzas of lyric 106 from *In Memoriam* express a hope for progress and improvement. Select from each stanza one example of the future the poem cries out for, and jot these examples down.

Using this informal list, write an essay describing the world of which Tennyson dreams.

Robert Browning 1812–1889

In contrast to many other successful writers of his era, Robert Browning enjoyed a happy boyhood. He was educated largely at home and spent much of his free time reading some of the six thousand books in his father's library.

At the age of twelve he sent a collection of poems off to a magazine editor (they were rejected), and by late adolescence he had decided to become a poet. His indulgent parents raised no objections, and prepared to go on supporting him indefinitely. This may have hurt Browning's early development as a writer. He was under no constraints to modify what he did to please editors or readers. He wrote just as he wished, and what he wrote struck most people as very odd. His first serious effort (a long, confessional poem) seemed to John Stuart Mill to manifest "a more intense and morbid self-consciousness than I ever knew in any sane being."

Browning responded to that just criticism; he sought to replace his youthful, subjective work with objective, dramatic poetry. He took as his subjects not his own feelings, but the diverse people and places he had read about in his father's library. Yet in his use of geographically and historically distant material, Browning was always conscious of, and speaking to, his contemporaries. His poetry is never just an escape to some lost time. "My Last Duchess" may be set in Renaissance Italy, but it is about the greed that kills love for the sake of money and power, an important subject for his middle-class audience.

Browning's poetry remained difficult for many people to read. Rather than the smooth, harmonious verse of Tennyson, Browning favored a rugged, irregular music not very different from the sound of the speaking voice. Some wondered if this was poetry at all. Then, too, Browning typically felt free to make allusions to obscure facts; such references made his poems difficult to grasp, and unnerved some readers. Browning's father continued to pay to have his son's poems published. The public remained indifferent.

But another poet, far more celebrated, did take note of Browning's efforts, and when he sent Elizabeth Barrett a letter (June 10, 1845) praising her latest book, she replied with unexpected praise for his poetry. So began a famous courtship and marriage.

The Brownings settled in Florence, Italy. Both worked hard at their poetry. In 1855 Robert published what modern readers consider one of his greatest achievements, a collection of fifty dramatic monologues titled *Men and Women*. It received mixed reviews. In June of 1861 Elizabeth died. Making a complete break from the happy past, Robert returned to London and to his writing.

And now the public reception of his poetry began to improve. His *Dramatis Personae* collection of 1864 won positive reviews. Then, between 1868 and 1869 he published his most ambitious work, *The Ring and the Book,* a 21,000-line poem in which nine different people consider an obscure Roman murder. The critics placed him in the first rank of English poets.

In the ensuing years Browning continued to write. He became a very public man, seen at London parties almost nightly, honored as a great thinker and poet. But for all his heartiness, another part of him remained lonely, still seeking, as he put it in a poem of 1883, "the loved one's face."

Porphyria's Lover

The rain set early in tonight,
    The sullen wind was soon awake,
It tore the elm-tops down for spite,
    And did its worst to vex the lake:
5   I listened with heart fit to break.
When glided in Porphyria; straight
    She shut the cold out and the storm,
And kneeled and made the cheerless grate
    Blaze up, and all the cottage warm;
10   Which done, she rose, and from her form
Withdrew the dripping cloak and shawl,
    And laid her soiled gloves by, untied
Her hat and let the damp hair fall,
    And, last, she sat down by my side
15   And called me. When no voice replied,
She put my arm about her waist,
    And made her smooth white shoulder bare,
And all her yellow hair displaced,
    And, stooping, made my cheek lie there,
20   And spread, o'er all, her yellow hair,
Murmuring how she loved me—she
    Too weak, for all her heart's endeavor,
To set its struggling passion free
    From pride, and vainer ties dissever,
25   And give herself to me forever.
But passion sometimes would prevail,
    Nor could tonight's gay feast restrain
A sudden thought of one so pale
    For love of her, and all in vain:
    So, she was come through wind and rain.
Be sure I looked up at her eyes
    Happy and proud; at last I knew
Porphyria worshiped me: surprise
    Made my heart swell, and still it grew
35   While I debated what to do.
That moment she was mine, mine, fair,
    Perfectly pure and good: I found
A thing to do, and all her hair
    In one long yellow string I wound
40   Three times her little throat around,
And strangled her. No pain felt she;
    I am quite sure she felt no pain.
As a shut bud that holds a bee,
    I warily oped her lids: again
45   Laughed the blue eyes without a stain.
And I untightened next the tress
    About her neck; her cheek once more

The Bridesmaid by Sir John Everett Millais, dated 1851.

Blushed bright beneath my burning kiss:
    I propped her head up as before,
50   Only, this time my shoulder bore
Her head, which droops upon it still:
    The smiling rosy little head,
So glad it has its utmost will,
    That all it scorned at once is fled,
55   And I, its love, am gained instead!
Porphyria's love: she guessed not how
    Her darling one wish would be heard.
And thus we sit together now,
    And all night long we have not stirred,
60   And yet God has not said a word!   1836

Discussion

1. In what ways does the speaker's description of the weather in "Porphyria's Lover" (lines 1–4) define his own mood?

2. Browning carefully balances the first thirty lines of his poem against the last thirty. Explain how these two equal parts contrast with each other.

3. To what extent do lines 36–38 explain the speaker's motive for this murder?

My Last Duchess

The time is the sixteenth century, the scene is the city of Ferrara in northern Italy. The speaker is the Duke of Ferrara.

Above: Lucretia de Medici, painted by the school of Angelo Bronzino. Below: Alphonso d'Este, Second Duke of Ferrara, painted by Girolamo da Carpi.

That's my last duchess painted on the wall,
Looking as if she were alive. I call
That piece a wonder, now: Frà Pandolf's hands
Worked busily a day, and there she stands.
5 Will 't please you sit and look at her? I said
"Frà Pandolf" by design, for never read
Strangers like you that pictured countenance,
The depth and passion of its earnest glance,
But to myself they turned (since none puts by
10 The curtain I have drawn for you, but I)
And seemed as they would ask me, if they durst,
How such a glance came there; so, not the first
Are you to turn and ask thus. Sir, 'twas not
Her husband's presence only, called that spot
15 Of joy into the Duchess' cheek: perhaps
Frà Pandolf chanced to say "Her mantle laps
Over my lady's wrist too much," or "Paint
Must never hope to reproduce the faint
Half-flush that dies along her throat": such stuff
20 Was courtesy, she thought, and cause enough
For calling up that spot of joy. She had
A heart—how shall I say?—too soon made glad,
Too easily impressed; she liked whate'er
She looked on, and her looks went everywhere.
25 Sir, 'twas all one! My favor at her breast,
The dropping of the daylight in the West,
The bough of cherries some officious fool
Broke in the orchard for her, the white mule
She rode with round the terrace—all and each
30 Would draw from her alike the approving
        speech,
Or blush, at least. She thanked men—good!
        but thanked
Somehow—I know not how—as if she ranked
My gift of a nine-hundred-years-old name
With anybody's gift. Who'd stoop to blame
35 This sort of trifling? Even had you skill
In speech—which I have not—to make your
        will
Quite clear to such an one, and say, "Just this
Or that in you disgusts me; here you miss,
Or there exceed the mark"—and if she let
40 Herself be lessoned so, nor plainly set
Her wits to yours, forsooth, and made excuse—
E'en then would be some stooping; and I choose
Never to stoop. Oh sir, she smiled, no doubt,
Whene'er I passed her; but who passed without

45 Much the same smile? This grew; I gave
    commands;
Then all smiles stopped together. There she
    stands
As if alive. Will 't please you rise? We'll meet
The company below, then. I repeat,
The Count your master's known munificence

50 Is ample warrant that no just pretense
Of mine for dowry will be disallowed;
Though his fair daughter's self, as I avowed
At starting, is my object. Nay, we'll go
Together down, sir. Notice Neptune, though,
55 Taming a sea-horse, thought a rarity,
Which Claus of Innsbruck cast in bronze for me!

1842

Discussion

1. (a) Who is listening to the Duke? Why does the listener dare not question (line 11) the expression on the painted face? **(b)** Explain the purpose of the listener's mission to the court; what gesture does the listener make to cause the Duke to say, "Nay, we'll / Together down, sir" (lines 53–54)?

2. In pinpointing that aspect of his last duchess which "disgusts" him (line 38), the Duke lists some things that made her flush with joy (lines 21–30). What do these objects of her delight suggest about this woman?

3. (a) Why is the Duke so pleased with the portrait of a woman he disliked? **(b)** In what ways does his sculpture of Neptune (lines 54–55) reflect this same sort of pleasure?

4. How do the poem's last words define the Duke's personality?

5. It is the Duke who calls attention to the picture, explains what it means to him, and who thus, indirectly, relates the fate of his "last" duchess. Why do you think he reveals all this to his listener?

Reader's Note: The Dramatic Monologue

Robert Browning perfected what we now call the **dramatic monologue.** Only one person speaks in such a poem, but that character's words create: first, a dramatic scene; second, a question or problem; and third, a listener the speaker addresses. Answering the discussion questions on "My Last Duchess" illustrates how intricately Browning can work such utterances into what seems spontaneous utterance.

Most of the time, the speaker in a dramatic monologue is attempting to achieve something by talking; the purpose is not to state the truth but to persuade. Some of Browning's most famous characters are murderers and con artists, and one of the chief pleasures in reading a dramatic monologue is discerning the gap between what a speaker says and what is actually the case. By the time the Duke says that it is only the girl herself he seeks (lines 52–53), we know too much about him to believe the assertion.

Tennyson's "Ulysses" is in most ways a dramatic monologue, and many readers find it difficult to be sure whether Ulysses' argument for renewing his travels is valid, or just a form of deceptive selfishness. How does one judge a man who describes a wife, faithful to him during a twenty-year separation, as simply "aged," and whose only words for an equally loyal son are "blameless" and "decent"?

The dramatic monologue, very much a development of the nineteenth century, stresses the relative nature of truth. In a poem of this sort the reader observes everything from the speaker's perspective, rather than seeing things as they are. The form emphasizes how people lie to each other and deceive themselves. It suggests that any viewpoint is open to challenge. In Browning's most ambitious work, *The Ring and the Book,* nine different characters examine the evidence in a murder case. Each makes a different judgment. The book as a whole asks: is there any way of overcoming subjective limits and reaching the truth? Can truth exist, independent from any individual point of view? It is a very modern problem.

The Latin word *Prospice* (pros'pi chē) means "Look Forward!" and suggests Browning's unflinching attitude toward death. The last three lines of the poem refer to Elizabeth Barrett Browning, who had died shortly before the poem was written.

Prospice

Fear death? — to feel the fog in my throat,
  The mist in my face,
When the snows begin, and the blasts denote
  I am nearing the place,
5 The power of the night, the press of the storm,
  The post of the foe;
Where he stands, the Arch Fear in a visible
    form,
  Yet the strong man must go:
For the journey is done and the summit
    attained,
10 And the barriers fall,
Though a battle's to fight ere the guerdon be
    gained,
  The reward of it all.
I was ever a fighter, so — one fight more,
  The best and the last!
15 I would hate that death bandaged my eyes, and
    forebore,

And bade me creep past.
No! let me taste the whole of it, fare like my
    peers
  The heroes of old,
Bear the brunt, in a minute pay glad life's
    arrears
20 Of pain, darkness and cold.
For sudden the worst turns the best to the brave,
  The black minute's at end,
And the elements' rage, the fiend-voices that
    rave,
  Shall dwindle, shall blend,
25 Shall change, shall become first a peace out of
    pain,
  Then a light, then thy breast,
O thou soul of my soul! I shall clasp thee again,
  And with God be the rest!

1864

Discussion

1. What **metaphor** dominates this poem?
2. How does the dominant metaphor suggest the speaker's way of looking at life and at death?

Composition

"Porphyria's Lover" originally appeared, along with another poem, under the title "Madhouse Cells." But there are all sorts of insanity.

Identify the quality and character of the madness in "Porphyria's Lover" by choosing one sentence that typifies the speaker. Then, select a sentence typical of the Duke in "My Last Duchess."

Now write an essay that defines, through an analysis of his own words, the madness of Porphyria's lover, and then consider whether a form of this insanity also afflicts the Duke.

Elizabeth Barrett Browning 1806–1861

Elizabeth Barrett Browning became, despite formidable obstacles, one of the most widely read and admired poets of her day. From her earliest years she demonstrated keen independence of spirit. The studies for young ladies of her era did not interest her. Not content with the meager education given Victorian girls, she insisted on learning Greek, Latin, French, Italian, German, and Spanish from tutors, while studying history and philosophy on her own.

What interested her most was literature. She began writing poetry at the age of eight, and in her twentieth year she published her first collection of verse.

Already, though, her health was declining. In her fifteenth year she had started taking opium at a doctor's direction to relieve what was called a "nervous disorder." Unhappily, the drug became not a cure but another problem. In 1838 she suffered a serious breakdown.

When she settled at the family home in London in 1841 it was as a permanent invalid. Elizabeth devoted what energy she had to writing, and in 1844 a two-volume collection of poems won high praise, in part for lyrics such as "The Cry of the Children" that indignantly protested the suffering of children forced to work in factories and mines. It was Robert Browning's letter praising this collection that initiated their celebrated correspondence. In "Sonnets from the Portuguese," written during 1846, Elizabeth chronicles her growing love for him. Elizabeth's father was violently opposed to even the idea of marriage, and so finally the lovers eloped, fleeing to Italy in September of 1846. Mr. Barrett refused to see them, or their son (born in 1849), ever again. Only in 1849, after several years of marriage, did she finally show "Sonnets from the Portuguese" to Robert. He prevailed upon her to publish them in 1850.

Liberated from her sickroom and stimulated by married life in Florence, Elizabeth continued to write poetry not only about love, but also about political change and social justice. Robert Browning never envied his wife's success. Her development as an artist was, however, tragically cut short by her unexpected death in 1861.

from ***Sonnets from the Portuguese***

1

I thought once how Theocritus[1] had sung
Of the sweet years, the dear and wished-for
    years,
Who each one in a gracious hand appears
To bear a gift for mortals, old or young;

---

1. Theocritus, Greek writer of the third century B.C. One of his poems personified the hours.

The Tryst by Arthur Hughes, painted 1850–1855.

5 And, as I mused it in his antique tongue,
I saw in gradual vision, through my tears,
The sweet, sad years, the melancholy years,
Those of my own life, who by turns had flung
A shadow across me. Straightway I was 'ware,
10 So weeping, how a mystic shape did move
Behind me, and drew me backward by the hair;
And a voice said in mastery, while I strove,
  "Guess now who holds thee?"—"Death," I
    said. But there
The silver answer rang, "Not Death, but Love."

28

My letters! all dead paper, mute and white!
And yet they seem alive and quivering
Against my tremulous hands which loose the
    string
And let them drop down on my knee to-night.
5 This said—he wished to have me in his sight

Once, as a friend: this fixed a day in spring
To come and touch my hand . . . a simple thing,
Yet I wept for it!—this, . . . the paper's light . . .
Said, *Dear I love thee;* and I sank and quailed
10 As if God's future thundered on my past.
This said, *I am thine*—and so its ink has paled
With lying at my heart that beat too fast.
And this . . . O Love, thy words have ill
    availed
If, what this said, I dared repeat at last!

43

How do I love thee? Let me count the ways.
I love thee to the depth and breadth and height
My soul can reach, when feeling out of sight
For the ends of Being and ideal Grace.
5 I love thee to the level of everyday's
Most quiet need, by sun and candlelight.
I love thee freely, as men strive for Right;
I love thee purely, as they turn from Praise.
I love thee with the passion put to use
10 In my old griefs, and with my childhood's faith.
I love thee with a love I seemed to lose
With my lost saints—I love thee with the
    breadth,
Smiles, tears, of all my life!—and, if God
    choose,
I shall but love thee better after death.

1845–1846   1850

Discussion

1. **(a)** What had the past years given the speaker of sonnet 1? **(b)** What does she think is the "mystic shape" of line 10? **(c)** Why does the actual identity of this "shape" surprise the reader?

2. What do you think it is that the speaker refuses to say at the end of sonnet 28?

3. **(a)** How does sonnet 43 develop the spatial metaphor of its second line? **(b)** Starting at line 10, the sonnet switches to the temporal dimension, referring to "old griefs," "childhood's faith," and "lost saints" (line 12). How does this dimension fit the catalogue listing the "ways" of love?

Matthew Arnold 1822–1888

The most complex problem of Matthew Arnold's youth was living in the shadow of his celebrated father. Thomas Arnold had taken over the direction of Rugby School in 1828 and within a few years transformed it into a model educational institution.

From his sixth year Matthew lived with his parents at Rugby, in a home swarming with bright, ambitious boys from the school. No one needed to tell him of the high expectations his parents held for his success. While Arnold was always a loving and respectful son, perhaps unconsciously he felt the need to rebel. His own academic performance was uneven—at times brilliant, at times very bad. Nevertheless, he won a scholarship to Oxford in 1841.

There he found little challenge in his studies and ample time to turn himself into a young dandy, playing whist and billiards, carefully choosing outlandish waistcoats, addressing his friends as "my dear." As one older contemporary put it, "a very gentlemanly young man with a slight tinge of the fop that does no harm when blended with talents, good nature, and high spirits."

Arnold's father died unexpectedly of a heart attack in 1842. Matthew remained at Oxford, continuing to study philosophy there until 1846. It was a period of indecision. While many of his contemporaries embarked on professional careers, Arnold remained uncommitted. In 1847 he began to serve as private secretary to Lord Lansdowne, President of the Privy Council and head of the Council on Education. Arnold's duties were light and in his free time he wrote poetry. By 1849 he could publish his first volume, *The Strayed Reveller.* The mixed response to the book kept him unsure of his calling.

Arnold felt intensely the confusion of the modern world—"everything is against one," he wrote in 1849—and he dreamed of a poetry that might help, a poetry that would "not only . . . interest, but also . . . inspirit and rejoice the reader." This he strove for in his own work.

But in moments of depression he would insist, "my poems are fragments—i.e., . . . I am fragments . . . the whole effect of my poems is vague and indeterminate." Perhaps Arnold set too high a goal for his art. Certainly, in his best lyrical poems, though he may not inspirit and rejoice, he can deeply touch the reader.

Practical matters intervened. In 1850 he proposed to Frances Wightman, and to support himself and his wife he obtained, with the help of Lord Lansdowne, a job in the civil service. For the next thirty-five years Arnold worked as an inspector of private schools for poor children. It was an exhausting job, requiring constant travel. But it permitted Arnold direct involvement in some of the social problems of his day.

Writing poetry became progressively more difficult. In 1853 he told a close friend, "I am past thirty, and three parts iced over—and my pen, it seems to me is even stiffer and more cramped than my feeling." More and more, in what free time he could find, Arnold turned to prose. He began with essays on literature, and its ability to help humanity in the spiritual crises of modern life. As time passed, his range expanded into essays and books on education, political issues, and theology. Arnold became, much like his father before him, one of the leading intellectuals of his day.

The woman addressed here in such pessimistic terms may have been a childhood friend of Arnold's named Mary Claude. By 1848 she was a beautiful and brilliant young writer and ethnologist—an anthropologist who deals with the various racial or cultural groups of people. Arnold evidently arranged to meet her in Switzerland, but she left before he arrived. During the next few months he wrote a series of lyrics in which he gave her the fictitious name of Marguerite. In the series the poem below is titled "To Marguerite—Continued."

*I*solation

Yes! in the sea of life enisled,[1]
With echoing straits between us thrown,
Dotting the shoreless watery wild,
We mortal millions live *alone*.
5 The islands feel the enclasping flow,
And then their endless bounds they know.

But when the moon their hollows lights,
And they are swept by balms of spring,
And in their glens, on starry nights,
10 The nightingales divinely sing;
And lovely notes, from shore to shore,
Across the sounds and channels pour—

Oh! then a longing like despair
Is to their farthest caverns sent;
15 For surely once, they feel, we were
Parts of a single continent!
Now round us spreads the watery plain—
Oh might our marges[2] meet again!

Who ordered, that their longing's fire
20 Should be, as soon as kindled, cooled?
Who renders vain their deep desire?—
A God, a God their severance ruled!
And bade betwixt their shores to be
The unplumbed, salt, estranging sea.   1852

---

1. **enisled,** placed apart, as on an island.
2. **marges,** borders, edges, margins.

*S*elf-Dependence

Weary of myself, and sick of asking
What I am, and what I ought to be,
At this vessel's prow I stand, which bears me
Forwards, forwards o'er the starlit sea.

5 And a look of passionate desire
O'er the sea and to the stars I send:
"Ye who from my childhood up have
          calmed me,
Calm me, ah, compose me to the end!

"Ah, once more," I cried, "ye stars, ye waters,
10 On my heart your mighty charm renew;
Still, still let me, as I gaze upon you,
Feel my soul becoming vast like you!"

From the intense, clear, star-sown vault of
          heaven,
Over the lit sea's unquiet way,
15 In the rustling night-air came the answer:
"Wouldst thou *be* as these are? *Live* as they.

"Unaffrighted by the silence round them,
Undistracted by the sights they see,
These demand not that the things without them
20 Yield them love, amusement, sympathy.

"And with joy the stars perform their shining,
And the sea its long moon-silvered roll;
For self-poised they live, nor pine with noting
All the fever of some differing soul.

25 "Bounded by themselves, and unregardful
In what state God's other works may be,
In their own tasks all their powers pouring,
These attain the mighty life you see."

O air-born voice! long since, severely clear,
30 A cry like thine in mine own heart I hear:
"Resolve to be thyself; and know that he
Who finds himself loses his misery!"
                                                1852

Pegwell Bay, Kent by William Dyce, painted 1859–1860.

Dover Beach

The sea is calm tonight,
The tide is full, the moon lies fair
Upon the straits; on the French coast the light
Gleams and is gone; the cliffs of England stand,
5 Glimmering and vast, out in the tranquil bay.
Come to the window, sweet is the night air!

Only, from the long line of spray
Where the sea meets the moon-blanched land,
Listen! you hear the grating roar
10 Of pebbles which the waves draw back, and fling,
At their return, up the high strand,
Begin, and cease, and then again begin,

The town of Dover, sheltered by the towering chalk cliffs of the English south coast, lies within sight of France. For centuries it has served as a port for travelers bound for the continent. Dover's proximity to Europe also makes it one of England's most vulnerable points, and a Norman castle built on a hill above the town stands as a reminder of the dangers to peace and security that occasionally threaten from across the narrow span of the English Channel.

Arnold and his wife visited Dover twice in 1851: in June, just after their wedding, and in October, on their way to a continental vacation. He almost certainly wrote "Dover Beach" during this period, and he clearly poured into this relatively short poem, which seems to be addressed to his wife, the ideas and feelings of the moment.

Arnold begins with the image of the ocean, and that image dominates the poem. But the way his speaker sees the ocean shifts as his ideas and his mood evolve, and it is this change in thought and feeling that constitutes the action of the poem.

At first glance, what the speaker sees is a "calm" (line 1) sea; the tide is "full" (line 2); the French coast is visible, yet at a safe distance. The protecting cliffs of England "stand, / Glimmering and vast" (line 5). He calls his listener to the window to enjoy this scene. But then a shift begins—there is the "grating roar" (line 9) of the waves. The very sounds of these words harshly contrasts with the agreeable "calm" and "full" of the first lines. And whereas the speaker first looked from a distance, seeing "the long line of spray" (line 7), he is now much closer and more involved with the scene, as he observes pebbles picked up by the waves and hurled up the shore (line 10).

With tremulous cadence slow, and bring
The eternal note of sadness in.

15 Sophocles[1] long ago
Heard it on the Aegean, and it brought
Into his mind the turbid ebb and flow
Of human misery; we
Find also in the sound a thought,
20 Hearing it by this distant northern sea.

The Sea of Faith
Was once, too, at the full, and round earth's
        shore
Lay like the folds of a bright girdle[2] furled.
But now I only hear
25 Its melancholy, long, withdrawing roar,
Retreating, to the breath
Of the night wind, down the vast edges drear
And naked shingles[3] of the world.

Ah, love, let us be true
30 To one another! for the world, which seems
To lie before us like a land of dreams,
So various, so beautiful, so new,
Hath really neither joy, nor love, nor light,
Nor certitude, nor peace, nor help for pain;
35 And we are here as on a darkling plain
Swept with confused alarms of struggle and
        flight,
Where ignorant armies clash by night.
1851   1867

---

1. **Sophocles,** Greek dramatist (495-406 B.C.).
2. *girdle,* in the traditional sense, a garment that encircles, or girds, the body; usually a loose belt around the waist.
3. *shingles,* pebble beaches.

In the sound of the waves the speaker hears the "eternal note of sadness" (line 14). To Arnold the Greek playwright Sophocles epitomized "the calm, the cheerfulness, the disinterested objectivity" lacking in the modern spirit, and his works achieved a "noble serenity which always accompanies true insight."

The note of sadness makes the poem's speaker recall what Sophocles heard in the ocean's roar: an objective, distanced vision of human suffering. But as a modern man, the speaker has a more specific, a more subjective association.

His phrase, the "Sea of Faith" (line 21), is intentionally ambiguous. It can refer to a faith in God—in Arnold's time many thoughtful people were troubled by religious doubts and at times it seemed as if an era of calm belief had been replaced by one of disturbing uncertainties. But "Faith" here also includes simple trust in other people and in society. As lines 33–34 indicate, the speaker no longer has faith in "certitude . . . peace . . . [or] help for pain" and lines 25–27 describe his sense of vulnerability, terror, and absolute solitude.

The speaker's only solution is a very modern one—a plea for love and fidelity in one other person (lines 29–30). The scene at the beginning of the poem, with its security and tranquility, seems now only a deception, a "land of dreams" (line 31). In the final lines the speaker looks at a very different ocean. The moonlight is gone. The calm of the full tide has dissolved into confusion. The waves look like warriors in a night battle, fighting in ignorance. In the poem's last words we hear the roar of the waves and understand the despair they have inspired.

Discussion

1. Explain how Arnold uses a single image to express the ideas of "Isolation."

2. (a) What is it that troubles the speaker of "Self-Dependence"? (b) Why does he address the stars? (c) What aspects of the stars, listed in lines 16–28, do you admire? Are there any you would fault? (d) Are lines 31–32 simply a return to the problems of lines 1–2, or do they resolve them?

3. In what ways does the image of the moonlit ocean change in the first four stanzas of "Dover Beach"?

4. Why does the speaker of "Dover Beach" beg his love to "be true"?

5. How does the natural scene the speaker is looking at suggest the final image of "Dover Beach"?

Charles Dickens 1812–1870

After Shakespeare, Charles Dickens is the most popular English writer. During his lifetime Dickens completed fourteen novels, two travel books, and four Christmas novellas. He left, as well, a novel unfinished at his death, and several volumes of essays and sketches associated with the three literary magazines he edited during his career.

Dickens achieved his successes on his own. His boyhood was a struggle for survival. His father, John Dickens, was charming but irresponsible. Though he sired a family of eight children, he was chronically careless about money matters. By the time young Dickens was ten, the family was penniless and living in a slum. He received a sketchy education at best. Then, in his twelfth year, his parents decided he should go to work.

They found him a job in a warehouse pasting labels on bottles of shoe polish. It was an experience he called "the secret agony of my soul." Later in life he kept the secret from all but one of his friends. Dickens never minded hard work, but already, at this young age, he felt intimations of his real abilities, and to work as a drudge six days a week seemed to stifle any chance he had for success in life. He never forgave his parents who, he felt, had cast him away.

After about half a year, sympathetic relatives rescued the Dickens family, and Charles went back to school filled with hope. At fifteen he began a career as a law clerk, and learned stenography. Soon he was using this skill to record speeches in Parliament, and by the age of twenty he had become a successful newspaper reporter.

Dickens began submitting short fictional sketches to London magazines, and one caught the eye of the publishers Chapman and Hall. They were planning to try a new form of fiction: a series of illustrated comical sketches that would appear serially each month for better than a year. They hired the young Dickens

Dickens's Dream by Robert William Buss, an unfinished painting showing the author in his study with some of the countless characters he created.

and at the end of March, 1836, the first issue of *The Pickwick Papers* appeared. By November forty thousand readers a month were snapping up their copies, and Dickens found himself an international celebrity.

Dickens wrote all of his novels for serial publication. His early novels were informal in design—Dickens felt free to introduce characters and incidents at whim, or at the bidding of the public. But at least from the time of *Dombey and Son* (1846–1848) he abandoned this informality for strictly organized novels. With few exceptions, each succeeding novel gained him a wider readership.

from *David Copperfield*

Whether I shall turn out to be the hero of my own life, or whether that station will be held by anybody else, these pages must show. To begin my life with the beginning of my life, I record that I was born (as I have been informed and believe) on a Friday, at twelve o'clock at night. It was remarked that the clock began to strike, and I began to cry, simultaneously. . . .

I was born at Blunderstone, in Suffolk, or "thereby," as they say in Scotland. I was a posthumous child. My father's eyes had closed upon the light of this world six months, when mine opened on it. There is something strange to me, even now, in the reflection that he never saw me; and something stranger yet in the shadowy remembrance that I have of my first childish associations with his white gravestone in the churchyard, and of the indefinable compassion I used to feel for it lying out alone there in the dark night, when our little parlor was warm and bright with fire and candle, and the doors of our house were—almost cruelly, it seemed to me sometimes—bolted and locked against it. . . .

The first objects that assume a distinct presence before me, as I look far back, into the blank of my infancy, are my mother with her pretty hair and youthful shape, and Peggotty with no shape at all, and eyes so dark that they seemed to darken their whole neighborhood in her face, and cheeks and arms so hard and red that I wondered the birds didn't peck her in preference to apples.

I believe I can remember these two at a little distance apart, dwarfed to my sight by stooping down or kneeling on the floor, and I going unsteadily from the one to the other. I have an impression on my mind which I cannot distinguish from actual remembrance, of the touch of Peggotty's forefinger as she used to hold it out to me, and of its being roughened by needlework, like a pocket nutmeg grater.

This may be fancy, through I think the memory of most of us can go farther back into such times than many of us suppose; just as I believe the power of observation in numbers of very young children to be quite wonderful for its close-

Dickens's work always combines the comic and the tragic. His is a comprehensive view of human life and his novels make a vigorous response to the injustice and the suffering of his era. His plots are rich with incident, complex, and full of suspense. They keep the reader turning the page. Finally, and here again the parallel with Shakespeare is compelling, his characters live. While some readers may forget details of plot and scene, the gallery of characters Dickens created remains in the memory and the imagination. His is a densely peopled world, and ultimately this is why so many readers enjoy his novels.

ness and accuracy. Indeed, I think that most grown men who are remarkable in this respect, may with greater propriety be said not to have lost the faculty, than to have acquired it; the rather, as I generally observe such men to retain a certain freshness, and gentleness, and capacity of being pleased, which are also an inheritance they have preserved from their childhood. . . .

What else do I remember? Let me see. There comes out of the cloud, our house—not new to me, but quite familiar, in its earliest remembrance. On the ground floor is Peggotty's kitchen, opening into a back yard; with a pigeon-house on a pole, in the center, without any pigeons in it; a great dog kennel in a corner, without any dog; and a quantity of fowls that look terribly tall to me, walking about, in a menacing and ferocious manner. There is one cock who gets upon a post to crow, and seems to take particular notice of me as I look at him through the kitchen window, who makes me shiver, he is so fierce. Of the geese outside the side gate who come waddling after me with their long necks stretched out when I go that way, I dream at night: as a man environed by wild beasts might dream of lions.

Here is a long passage—what an enormous perspective I make of it!—leading from Peggotty's kitchen to the front door. A dark store room opens out of it, and that is a place to be run past at night; for I don't know what may be among those tubs and jars and old tea chests, when there is nobody in there with a dimly burning light, letting a moldy air come out at the door, in which there is the smell of soap, pickles, pepper, candles, and coffee, all at one whiff. Then there are the two parlors: the parlor in which we sit of an evening, my mother and I and Peggotty—for Peggotty is quite our companion, when her work is done and we are alone—and the best parlor where we sit on a Sunday; grandly, but not so comfortably. There is something of a doleful air about that room to me, for Peggotty has told me—I don't know when, but apparently ages ago—about my father's funeral, and the company having their black cloaks put on. One Sunday night my mother reads to Peggotty and me in there, how Lazarus was raised up from the dead. And I am so frightened that they are afterwards obliged to take me out of bed, and show me the quiet churchyard out of the bedroom window, with the dead all lying in their graves at rest, below the solemn moon.

There is nothing half so green that I know anywhere, as the grass of that churchyard; nothing half so shady as its trees; nothing half so quiet as its tombstones. The sheep are feeding there, when I kneel up, early in the morning, in my little bed in a closet[1] within my mother's room, to look out at it; and I see the red light shining on the sun-dial, and think within myself, "Is the sundial glad, I wonder, that it can tell the time again?"

Here is our pew in the church. What a high-backed pew! With a window near it, out of which our house can be seen, and *is* seen many times during the morning service, by Peggotty, who likes to make herself as sure as she can that it's not being robbed, or is not in flames. But though Peggotty's eye wanders, she is much offended if mine does, and frowns to me, as I stand upon the seat, that I am to look at the clergyman. But I can't always look at him—I know him without that white thing on, and I am afraid of his wondering why I stare so, and perhaps stopping the service to inquire—and what am I to do? It's a dreadful thing to gape, but I must do something. I look at my mother, but *she* pretends not to see me. I look at a boy in the aisle, and *he* makes faces at me. I look at the sunlight coming in at the open door through the porch, and there I see a stray sheep—I don't mean a sinner, but mutton—half making up his mind to come into the church. I feel that if I looked at him any longer, I might be tempted to say something out loud; and what would become of me then! . . . I look . . . to the pulpit; and think what a good place it would be to play in, and what a castle it would make, with another boy coming up the stairs to attack it, and having the velvet cushion with the tassels thrown down on his head. In time my eyes gradually shut up; and, from seeming to hear the clergyman singing a drowsy song in the heat, I hear nothing, until I fall off the seat with a crash, and am taken out, more dead than alive, by Peggotty.

And now I see the outside of our house, with the latticed bedroom windows standing open to let in the sweet-smelling air, and the ragged old

---

1. *closet,* enclosure.

Our Pew at Church, by "Phiz" (Hablot Knight Browne).

rooks' nests still dangling in the elm trees at the bottom of the front garden. Now I am in the garden at the back, beyond the yard where the empty pigeon house and dog kennel are—a very preserve of butterflies, as I remember it, with a high fence, and a gate and padlock; where the fruit clusters on the trees, riper and richer than fruit has ever been since, in any other garden, and where my mother gathers some in a basket, while I stand by, bolting furtive gooseberries, and trying to look unmoved. A great wind rises, and the summer is gone in a moment. We are playing in the winter twilight, dancing about the parlor. When my mother is out of breath and rests herself in an elbow chair, I watch her winding her bright curls round her fingers, and straightening her waist, and nobody knows better than I do that she likes to look so well, and is proud of being so pretty.

That is among my very earliest impressions. That, and a sense that we were both a little afraid of Peggotty, and submitted ourselves in most things to her direction, were among the first opinions—if they may be so called—that I ever derived from what I saw.

Peggotty and I were sitting one night by the parlor fire, alone. I had been reading to Peggotty about crocodiles. I must have read very perspicuously, or the good soul must have been deeply interested, for I remember she had a cloudy impression, after I had done, that they were a sort of vegetable. I was tired of reading, and dead sleepy; but having leave, as a high treat, to sit up until my mother came home from spending the evening at a neighbor's, I would rather had died upon my post (of course) than have gone to bed. I had reached that stage of sleepiness when Peggotty seemed to swell and grow immensely large. I propped my eyelids open with my two forefingers, and looked perseveringly at her as she sat at work; at the little bit of wax candle she kept for her thread—how old it looked, being so wrinkled in all directions!—at the little house with a thatched roof, where the yard-measure lived; at her work box with a sliding lid, with a view of Saint Paul's Cathedral (with a pink dome) painted on the top; at the brass thimble on her finger; at herself, whom I thought lovely. I felt so sleepy, that I knew if I lost sight of anything, for a moment, I was gone.

"Peggotty," says I, suddenly, "were you ever married?"

"Lord, Master Davy," replied Peggotty. "What's put marriage in your head!"

She answered with such a start, that it quite awoke me. And then she stopped in her work, and looked at me, with her needle drawn out to its thread's length.

"But *were* you ever married, Peggotty?" says I. "You are a very handsome woman, an't you?"

I thought her in a different style from my mother, certainly; but of another school of beauty, I considered her a perfect example. . . .

"*Me* handsome, Davy!" said Peggotty. "Lawk, no, my dear! But what put marriage in your head?"

"I don't know!—You mustn't marry more than one person at a time, may you, Peggotty?"

"Certainly not," says Peggotty, with the promptest decision.

"But if you marry a person, and the person dies, why then you may marry another person, mayn't you, Peggotty?"

"You MAY," says Peggotty, "if you choose, my dear. That's a matter of opinion."

"But what is your opinion, Peggotty?" said I.

I asked her, and looked curiously at her, because she looked so curiously at me.

"My opinion is," said Peggotty, taking her eyes from me, after a little indecision and going on with her work, "that I never was married myself, Master Davy, and that I don't expect to be. That's all I know about the subject."

"You an't cross, I suppose, Peggotty, are you?" said I, after sitting quiet for a minute.

I really thought she was, she had been so short with me; but I was quite mistaken: for she laid aside her work (which was a stocking of her own), and opening her arms wide, took my curly head within them, and gave it a good squeeze. I know it was a good squeeze, because, being very plump, whenever she made any little exertion after she was dressed, some of the buttons on the back of her gown flew off. And I recollect two bursting to the opposite side of the parlor, while she was hugging me.

"Now let me hear some more about the Crorkindills," said Peggotty, who was not quite right in the name yet, "for I an't heard half enough."

I couldn't quite understand why Peggotty looked so queer, or why she was so ready to go back to the crocodiles. However, we returned to those monsters, with fresh wakefulness on my part, and we left their eggs in the sand for the sun to hatch; and we ran away from them, and baffled them by constantly turning, which they were unable to do quickly, on account of their unwieldy make; and we went into the water after them, as natives, and put sharp pieces of timber down their throats; and in short we ran the whole crocodile gauntlet. *I* did at least; but I had my doubts of Peggotty, who was thoughtfully sticking her needle into various parts of her face and arms, all the time.

We had exhausted the crocodiles, and begun with the alligators, when the garden bell rang. We went out to the door; and there was my mother, looking even unusually pretty, I thought, and with her a gentleman with beautiful black hair and whiskers, who had walked home with us from church last Sunday.

As my mother stooped down on the threshold to take me in her arms and kiss me, the gentleman said I was a more highly privileged little fellow than a monarch—or something like that; for my later understanding comes, I am sensible, to my aid here.

"What does that mean?" I asked him, over her shoulder.

He patted me on the head; but somehow, I didn't like him or his deep voice, and I was jealous that his hand should touch my mother's in touching me—which it did. I put it away, as roughly as I could.

"Oh Davy!" remonstrated my mother.

"Dear boy!" said the gentleman. "I cannot wonder at his devotion!"

I never saw such a beautiful color on my mother's face before. She gently chid me for being rude; and, keeping me close to her shawl, turned to thank the gentleman for taking so much trouble as to bring her home. She put out her hand to him as she spoke, and, as he met it with his own, she glanced, I thought, at me.

"Let us say 'good night,' my fine boy," said the gentleman, when he had bent his head—*I* saw him!—over my mother's little glove.

"Good night!" said I.

"Come! Let us be the best friends in the world!" said the gentleman, laughing. "Shake hands!"

My right hand was in my mother's left, so I gave him the other.

"Why that's the wrong hand, Davy!" laughed the gentleman.

My mother drew my right hand forward, but I was resolved, for my former reason, not to give it him, and I did not. I gave him the other, and he shook it heartily, and said I was a brave fellow, and went away.

At this minute I see him turn round in the garden, and give us a last look with his ill-omened black eyes, before the door was shut.

Peggotty, who had not said a word or moved a finger, secured the fastenings instantly, and we all went into the parlor. My mother, contrary to her usual habit, instead of coming to the elbow chair by the fire, remained at the other end of the room, and sat singing to herself.

"—Hope you have had a pleasant evening, ma'am," said Peggotty, standing as stiff as a barrel in the center of the room, with a candlestick in her hand.

"Much obliged to you, Peggotty," returned my mother, in a cheerful voice, "I have had a *very* pleasant evening."

"A stranger or so makes an agreeable change," suggested Peggotty.

"A very agreeable change indeed," returned my mother.

Peggotty continuing to stand motionless in the middle of the room, and my mother resuming her singing, I fell asleep, though I was not so sound asleep but that I could hear voices, without hearing what they said. When I half awoke from this uncomfortable doze, I found Peggotty and my mother both in tears, and both talking.

"Not such a one as this, Mr. Copperfield wouldn't have liked," said Peggotty. "That I say, and that I swear!"

"Good Heavens!" cried my mother. "You'll drive me mad! Was ever any poor girl so ill-used by her servants as I am! Why do I do myself the injustice of calling myself a girl? Have I never been married, Peggotty?"

"God knows you have, ma'am," returned Peggotty.

"Then how can you dare," said my mother—"you know I don't mean how can you dare, Peggotty, but how can you have the heart—to make me so uncomfortable and say such bitter things to me, when you are well aware that I haven't, out of this place, a single friend to turn to!"

"The more's the reason," returned Peggotty, "for saying that it won't do. No! That it won't do. No! No price could make it do. No!"—I thought Peggotty would have thrown the candlestick away, she was so emphatic with it.

"How can you be so aggravating," cried my mother, shedding more tears than before, "as to talk in such an unjust manner! How can you go on as if it was all settled and arranged, Peggotty, when I tell you over and over again, you cruel thing, that beyond the commonest civilities nothing whatever has passed! You talk of admiration. What am I to do? If people are so silly as to indulge the sentiment, is it *my* fault? What am I to do, I ask you? Would you wish me to shave my head and black my face, or disfigure myself with a burn, or a scald, or something of that sort? I dare say you would, Peggotty. I dare say you'd quite enjoy it."

Peggotty seemed to take this aspersion very much to heart, I thought.

"And my dear boy," cried my mother, coming to the elbow chair in which I was, and caressing me, "my own little Davy! Is it to be hinted to me that I am wanting in affection for my precious treasure, the dearest little fellow that ever was!"

"Nobody never went and hinted no such a thing," said Peggotty.

"You did, Peggotty!" returned my mother. "You know you did. What else was it possible to infer from what you said, you unkind creature, when you know as well as I do, that on his account only last quarter I wouldn't buy myself a new parasol, though that old green one is frayed the whole way up, and the fringe is perfectly mangy. You know it is, Peggotty. You can't deny it." Then, turning affectionately to me, with her cheek against mine, "Am I a naughty mama to you, Davy? Am I a nasty, cruel, selfish, bad mama? Say I am, my child; say 'yes,' my dear boy, and Peggotty will love you, and Peggotty's love is a great deal better than mine, Davy. *I* don't love you at all, do I?"

At this, we all fell a-crying together. I think I was the loudest of the party, but I am sure we were all sincere about it. I was quite heartbroken myself, and am afraid that in the first transports of wounded tenderness I called Peggotty a "Beast." That honest creature was in deep affliction, I remember, and must have become quite buttonless on the occasion; for a little volley of those explosives went off, when, after having made it up with my mother, she kneeled down by the elbow chair, and made it up with me.

We went to bed greatly dejected. My sobs kept waking me, for a long time; and when one very strong sob quite hoisted me up in bed, I found my mother sitting on the coverlet, and leaning over me. I fell asleep in her arms, after that, and slept soundly.

Whether it was the following Sunday when I saw the gentleman again, or whether there was any greater lapse of time before he reappeared, I cannot recall. I don't profess to be clear about dates. But there he was, in church, and he walked home with us afterwards. He came in, too, to look at a famous geranium we had, in the parlor window. It did not appear to me that he took much notice of it, but before he went he asked my mother to give him a bit of the blossom. She begged him to choose it for himself, but he refused to do that—I could not understand why—so she plucked it for him, and gave it into his hand. He said he would never, never, part with it any more; and I thought he must be quite a fool not to know that it would fall to pieces in a day or two.

Peggotty began to be less with us, of an evening, than she had always been. My mother deferred to her very much—more than usual, it occurred to me—and we were all three excellent friends; still we were different from what we used to be, and were not so comfortable among ourselves. Sometimes I fancied that Peggotty perhaps objected to my mother's wearing all the pretty dresses she had in her drawers, or to her going so often to visit at that neighbor's; but I couldn't, to my satisfaction, make out how it was.

Gradually, I became used to seeing the gentleman with the black whiskers. I liked him no better than at first, and had the same uneasy jealousy of him; but if I had any reason for it beyond a child's instinctive dislike, and a general idea that Peggotty and I could make much of my mother without any help, it certainly was not *the* reason that I might have found if I had been older. No such thing came into my mind, or near it. I could observe, in little pieces, as it were; but as to making a net of a number of these pieces, and catching anybody in it, that was, as yet, beyond me.

One autumn morning I was with my mother in the front garden, when Mr. Murdstone—I knew him by that name now—came by, on horseback. He reined up his horse to salute my mother, and said he was going to Lowestoft to see some friends who were there with a yacht, and merrily proposed to take me on the saddle before him if I would like the ride.

The air was so clear and pleasant, and the horse seemed to like the idea of the ride so much himself, as he stood snorting and pawing at the garden gate, that I had a great desire to go. . . .

Mr. Murdstone and I were soon off, and trotting along on the green turf by the side of the road. He held me quite easily with one arm, and I don't think I was restless usually; but I could not make up my mind to sit in front of him without turning my head sometimes, and looking up in his face. He had that kind of shallow black eye—I want a better word to express an eye that has no depth in it to be looked into—which, when it is abstracted, seems from some peculiarity of light to be disfigured, for a moment at a time, by a cast. Several times when I glanced at him, I observed that appearance with a sort of awe, and wondered what he was thinking about so closely. His hair and whiskers were blacker and thicker, looked at so near, than even I had given them credit for being. A squareness about the lower part of his face, and the dotted indication of the strong black beard he shaved close every day, reminded me of the waxwork that had travelled into our neighborhood some half-a-year before. This, his regular eyebrows, and the rich white, and black, and brown, of his complexion—confound his complexion, and his memory!—made me think him, in spite of my misgivings, a very handsome man. I have no doubt that my poor dear mother thought him so too.

We went to an hotel by the sea, where two gentlemen were smoking cigars in a room by themselves. Each of them was lying on at least four chairs, and had a large rough jacket on. In a corner was a heap of coats and boat-cloaks, and a flag, all bundled up together.

They both rolled on to their feet in an untidy sort of manner when we came in, and said ''Halloa, Murdstone! We thought you were dead!''

''Not yet,'' said Mr. Murdstone.

''And who's this shaver?'' said one of the gentlemen, taking hold of me.

''That's Davy,'' returned Mr. Murdstone.

''Davy who?'' said the gentleman. ''Jones?''

''Copperfield,'' said Mr. Murdstone.

''What! Bewitching Mrs. Copperfield's encumbrance?'' cried the gentleman. ''The pretty little widow?''

''Quinion,'' said Mr. Murdstone, ''take care, if you please. Somebody's sharp.''

''Who is?'' asked the gentleman, laughing.

I looked up, quickly; being curious to know.

''Only Brooks of Sheffield,''[2] said Mr. Murdstone.

---

2. **Brooks of Sheffield**, famous English makers of knives and other cutting instruments.

I was quite relieved to find it was only Brooks of Sheffield; for, at first, I really thought it was I.

There seemed to be something comical in the reputation of Mr. Brooks of Sheffield, for both the gentlemen laughed heartily when he was mentioned, and Mr. Murdstone was a good deal amused also. After some laughing, the gentleman whom he had called Quinion, said:

"And what is the opinion of Brooks of Sheffield, in reference to the projected business?"

"Why, I don't know that Brooks understands much about it at present," replied Mr. Murdstone; "but he is not generally favorable, I believe."

There was more laughter at this, and Mr. Quinion said he would ring the bell for some sherry in which to drink to Brooks. This he did; and when the wine came, he made me have a little, with a biscuit, and, before I drank it, stand up and say "Confusion to Brooks of Sheffield!" The toast was received with great applause, and such hearty laughter that it made me laugh too; at which they laughed the more. In short, we quite enjoyed ourselves. . . .

I observed all day that Mr. Murdstone was graver and steadier than the two gentlemen. They were very gay and careless. They joked freely with one another, but seldom with him. It appeared to me that he was more clever and cold than they were, and that they regarded him with something of my own feeling. I remarked that once or twice when Mr. Quinion was talking, he looked at Mr. Murdstone sideways, as if to make sure of his not being displeased; and that once when Mr. Passnidge (the other gentleman) was in high spirits, he trod upon his foot, and gave him a secret caution with his eyes, to observe Mr. Murdstone, who was sitting stern and silent. Nor do I recollect that Mr. Murdstone laughed at all that day, except at the Sheffield joke—and that, by-the-by, was his own.

We went home early in the evening. . . . When he was gone, my mother asked me all about the day I had had, and what they had said and done. I mentioned what they had said about her, and she laughed, and told me they were impudent fellows who talked nonsense—but I knew it pleased her. I knew it quite as well as I know it now. I took the opportunity of asking if she were at all acquainted with Mr. Brooks of Sheffield, but she answered No, only she supposed he must be a manufacturer in the knife and fork way.

Can I say of her face—altered as I have reason to remember it, perished as I know it is—that it is gone, when here it comes before me at this instant, as distinct as any face that I may choose to look on in a crowded street? Can I say of her innocent and girlish beauty, that it faded, and was no more, when its breath falls on my cheek now, as it fell that night? Can I say she ever changed, when my remembrance brings her back to life, thus only; and, truer to its loving youth than I have been, or man ever is, still holds fast what it cherished then?

I write of her just as she was when I had gone to bed after this talk, and she came to bid me good night. She kneeled down playfully by the side of the bed, and laying her chin upon her hands, and laughing, said:

"What was it they said, Davy? Tell me again. I can't believe it."

"'Bewitching——'" I began.

My mother put her hand upon my lips to stop me.

"It was never bewitching," she said, laughing. "It never could have been bewitching, Davy. Now I know it wasn't!"

"Yes it was. 'Bewitching Mrs. Copperfield,'" I repeated stoutly. "And 'pretty.'"

"No no, it was never pretty. Not pretty," interposed my mother, laying her fingers on my lips again.

"Yes it was. 'Pretty little widow.'"

"What foolish, impudent creatures!" cried my mother, laughing and covering her face. "What ridiculous men! An't they? Davy dear—"

"Well, Ma."

"Don't tell Peggotty; she might be angry with them. I am dreadfully angry with them myself; but I would rather Peggotty didn't know."

I promised, of course; and we kissed one another over and over again, and I soon fell fast asleep.

It seems to me, at this distance of time, as if it were the next day when Peggotty broached the striking and adventurous proposition I am about to mention; but it was probably about two months afterwards.

We were sitting as before, one evening (when

my mother was out as before), in company with the stocking and the yard-measure, and the bit of wax, and the box with Saint Paul's on the lid, and the Crocodile Book, when Peggotty, after looking at me several times, and opening her mouth as if she were going to speak, without doing it—which I thought was merely gaping, or I should have been rather alarmed—said coaxingly:

"Master Davy, how should you like to go along with me and spend a fortnight at my brother's at Yarmouth? Wouldn't *that* be a treat?"

"Is your brother an agreeable man, Peggotty?" I inquired, provisionally.

"Oh what an agreeable man he is!" cried Peggotty, holding up her hands. "Then there's the sea; and the boats and ships; and the fishermen; and the beach. . . ."

I was flushed by her summary of delights, and replied that it would indeed be a treat, but what would my mother say?

"Why then I'll as good as bet a guinea," said Peggotty, intent upon my face, "that she'll let us go. I'll ask her, if you like, as soon as ever she comes home. There now!"

"But what's she to do while we're away?" said I, putting my small elbows on the table to argue the point. "She can't live by herself."

If Peggotty were looking for a hole, all of a sudden, in the heel of that stocking, it must have been a very little one indeed, and not worth darning.

"I say! Peggotty! She can't live by herself, you know."

"Oh bless you!" said Peggotty, looking at me again at last. "Don't you know? She's going to stay for a fortnight with Mrs. Grayper. Mrs. Grayper's going to have a lot of company."

Oh! If that was it, I was quite ready to go. I waited, in the utmost impatience, until my mother came home from Mrs. Grayper's (for it was that identical neighbor), to ascertain if we could get leave to carry out this great idea. Without being nearly so much surprised as I had expected, my mother entered into it readily; and it was all arranged that night, and my board and lodging during the visit were to be paid for.

The day soon came for our going. It was such an early day that it came soon, even to me, who was in a fever of expectation, and half afraid that an earthquake or a fiery mountain, or some other great convulsion of nature, might interpose to stop the expedition. We were to go in a carrier's cart, which departed in the morning after breakfast. I would have given any money to have been allowed to wrap myself up overnight, and sleep in my hat and boots.

It touches me nearly now, although I tell it lightly, to recollect how eager I was to leave my happy home; to think how little I suspected what I did leave for ever.

I am glad to recollect that when the carrier's cart was at the gate, and my mother stood there kissing me, a grateful fondness for her and for the old place I had never turned my back upon before, made me cry. I am glad to know that my mother cried too, and that I felt her heart beat against mine.

I am glad to recollect that when the carrier began to move, my mother ran out at the gate, and called to him to stop, that she might kiss me once more. I am glad to dwell upon the earnestness and love with which she lifted up her face to mine, and did so.

As we left her standing in the road, Mr. Murdstone came up to where she was, and seemed to expostulate with her for being so moved. I was looking back round the awning of the cart, and wondered what business it was of his. Peggotty, who was also looking back on the other side, seemed anything but satisfied; as the face she brought into the cart denoted.

I sat looking at Peggotty for some time, in a reverie on this supposititious case: whether, if she were employed to lose me like the boy in the fairy tale, I should be able to track my way home again by the buttons she would shed. . . .

> Young David, in his innocence, enjoys his holiday with Peggotty's family. Time passes swiftly, and soon he must return home.

Now, all the time I had been on my visit, I had been ungrateful to my home again, and had thought little or nothing about it. But I was no sooner turned towards it, than my reproachful young conscience seemed to point that way with a steady finger; and I felt, all the more for the sinking of my spirits, that it was my nest, and that my mother was my comforter and friend.

This gained upon me as we went along; so that

the nearer we drew, and the more familiar the objects became that we passed, the more excited I was to get there, and to run into her arms. But Peggotty, instead of sharing in these transports, tried to check them (though very kindly), and looked confused and out of sorts.

Blunderstone Rookery would come, however, in spite of her, when the carrier's horse pleased—and did. How well I recollect it, on a cold grey afternoon, with a dull sky, threatening rain!

The door opened, and I looked, half laughing and half crying in my pleasant agitation, for my mother. It was not she, but a strange servant.

"Why, Peggotty!" I said ruefully, "isn't she come home!"

"Yes, yes, Master Davy," said Peggotty. "She's come home. Wait a little bit, Master Davy, and I'll—I'll tell you something."

Between her agitation, and her natural awkwardness in getting out of the cart, Peggotty was making a most extraordinary festoon of herself, but I felt too blank and strange to tell her so. When she had got down, she took me by the hand; led me, wondering, into the kitchen; and shut the door.

"Peggotty!" said I, quite frightened. "What's the matter?"

"Nothing's the matter, bless you, Master Davy dear!" she answered, assuming an air of sprightliness.

"Something's the matter, I'm sure. Where's mama?"

"Where's mama, Master Davy?" repeated Peggotty.

"Yes. Why hasn't she come out to the gate, and what have we come in here for? Oh, Peggotty!" My eyes were full, and I felt as if I were going to tumble down.

"Bless the precious boy!" cried Peggotty, taking hold of me. "What is it? Speak, my pet!"

"Not dead, too! Oh, she's not dead, Peggotty?"

Peggotty cried out No! with an astonishing volume of voice; and then sat down, and began to pant, and said I had given her a turn.

I gave her a hug to take away the turn, or to give her another turn in the right direction, and then stood before her, looking at her in anxious inquiry.

"You see, dear, I should have told you before now," said Peggotty, "but I hadn't an opportunity. I ought to have made it, perhaps, but I couldn't azackly"—that was always the substitute for exactly, in Peggotty's militia of words—"bring my mind to it."

"Go on, Peggotty," said I, more frightened than before.

"Master Davy," said Peggotty, untying her bonnet with a shaking hand, and speaking in a breathless sort of way. "What do you think? You have got a Pa!"

I trembled, and turned white. Something—I don't know what, or how—connected with the grave in the churchyard, and the raising of the dead, seemed to strike me like an unwholesome wind.

"A new one," said Peggotty.

"A new one?" I repeated.

Peggotty gave a gasp, as if she were swallowing something that was very hard, and, putting out her hand, said:

"Come and see him."

"I don't want to see him."

—"And your mama," said Peggotty.

I ceased to draw back, and we went straight to the best parlor, where she left me. On one side of the fire, sat my mother; on the other, Mr. Murdstone. My mother dropped her work, and arose hurriedly, but timidly I thought.

"Now, Clara, my dear," said Mr. Murdstone. "Recollect! control yourself, always control yourself! Davy boy, how do you do?"

I gave him my hand. After a moment of suspense, I went and kissed my mother: she kissed me, patted me gently on the shoulder, and sat down again to her work. I could not look at her, I could not look at him, I knew quite well that he was looking at us both; and I turned to the window and looked out there, at some shrubs that were drooping their heads in the cold.

As soon as I could creep away, I crept upstairs. My old dear bedroom was changed, and I was to lie a long way off. I rambled downstairs to find anything that was like itself, so altered it all seemed; and roamed into the yard. I very soon started back from there, for the empty dog kennel was filled up with a great dog—deep-mouthed and black-haired like Him—and he was very angry at the sight of me, and sprung out to get at me.

If the room to which my bed was removed, were a sentient thing that could give evidence, I might appeal to it at this day—who sleeps there now, I wonder!—to bear witness for me what a heavy heart I carried to it. I went up there, hearing the dog in the yard bark after me all the way while I climbed the stairs; and, looking as blank and strange upon the room as the room looked upon me, sat down with my small hands crossed, and thought.

I thought of the oddest things. Of the shape of the room, of the cracks in the ceiling, of the paper on the wall, of the flaws in the window glass making ripples and dimples on the prospect, of the washing stand being rickety on its three legs, and having a discontented something about it. . . . I rolled myself up in a corner of the counterpane, and cried myself to sleep.

I was awakened by somebody saying "Here he is!" and uncovering my hot head. My mother and Peggotty had come to look for me, and it was one of them who had done it.

"Davy," said my mother. "What's the matter?"

I thought it very strange that she should ask me, and answered, "Nothing." I turned over on my face, I recollect, to hide my trembling lip, which answered her with greater truth.

"Davy," said my mother. "Davy, my child!"

I dare say no words she could have uttered, would have affected me so much, then, as her calling me her child. I hid my tears in the bedclothes, and pressed her from me with my hand, when she would have raised me up.

"This is your doing, Peggotty, you cruel thing!" said my mother. "I have no doubt at all about it. How can you reconcile it to your conscience, I wonder, to prejudice my own boy against me, or against anybody who is dear to me? What do you mean by it, Peggotty?"

Poor Peggotty lifted up her hands and eyes, and only answered, in a sort of paraphrase of the grace I usually repeated after dinner, "Lord forgive you, Mrs. Copperfield, and for what you have said this minute, may you never be truly sorry!"

"It's enough to distract me," cried my mother. "In my honeymoon, too, when my most inveterate enemy might relent, one would think, and not envy me a little peace of mind and happiness. Davy, you naughty boy! Peggotty, you savage creature! Oh, dear me!" cried my mother, turning from one of us to the other, in her pettish wilful manner, "what a troublesome world this is, when one has the most right to expect it to be as agreeable as possible!"

I felt the touch of a hand that I knew was neither hers nor Peggotty's, and slipped to my feet at the bedside. It was Mr. Murdstone's hand, and he kept it on my arm as he said:

"What's this? Clara, my love, have you forgotten?—Firmness, my dear!"

"I am very sorry, Edward," said my mother. "I meant to be very good, but I am so uncomfortable."

"Indeed!" he answered. "That's a bad hearing, so soon, Clara."

"I say it's very hard I should be made so now," returned my mother, pouting; "and it is—very hard—isn't it?"

He drew her to him, whispered in her ear, and kissed her. I knew as well, when I saw my mother's head lean down upon his shoulder, and her arm touch his neck—I knew as well that he could mold her pliant nature into any form he chose, as I know, now, that he did it.

"Go you below, my love," said Mr. Murdstone. "David and I will come down, together. My friend," turning a darkening face on Peggotty, when he had watched my mother out, and dismissed her with a nod and a smile: "do you know your mistress's name?"

"She has been my mistress a long time, sir," answered Peggotty. "I ought to it."

"That's true," he answered. "But I thought I heard you, as I came upstairs, address her by a name that is not hers. She has taken mine, you know. Will you remember that?"

Peggotty, with some uneasy glances at me, curtseyed herself out of the room without replying; seeing, I suppose, that she was expected to go, and had no excuse for remaining. When we two were left alone, he shut the door, and sitting on a chair, and holding me standing before him, looked steadily into my eyes. I felt my own attracted, no less steadily, to his. As I recall our being opposed thus, face to face, I seem again to hear my heart beat fast and high.

"David," he said, making his lips thin, by

pressing them together, "if I have an obstinate horse or dog to deal with, what do you think I do?"

"I don't know."

"I beat him."

I had answered in a kind of breathless whisper, but I felt, in my silence, that my breath was shorter now.

"I make him wince, and smart. I say to myself, 'I'll conquer that fellow'; and if it were to cost him all the blood he had, I should do it. What is that upon your face?"

"Dirt," I said.

He knew it was the mark of tears as well as I. But if he had asked the question twenty times, each time with twenty blows, I believe my baby heart would have burst before I would have told him so.

"You have a good deal of intelligence for a little fellow," he said, with a grave smile that belonged to him, "and you understand me very well, I see. Wash that face, sir, and come down with me. . . ."

> Soon Mr. Murdstone's sister Jane joins the unhappy family and brother and sister begin to separate David from his mother.

There had been some talk on occasions of my going to boarding school. Mr. and Miss Murdstone had originated it, and my mother had of course agreed with them. Nothing, however, was concluded on the subject yet. In the meantime, I learnt lessons at home.

Shall I ever forget those lessons! They were presided over nominally by my mother, but really by Mr. Murdstone and his sister, who were always present, and found them a favorable occasion for giving my mother lessons in that miscalled firmness, which was the bane of both our lives. I believe I was kept at home, for that purpose. I had been apt enough to learn, and willing enough, when my mother and I had lived alone together. I can faintly remember learning the alphabet at her knee. To this day, when I look upon the fat black letters in the primer, the puzzling novelty of their shapes, and the easy good nature of O and Q and S, always seem to present themselves again before me as they used to do. But they recall no feeling of disgust or reluctance.

Comment: G. K. Chesterton on *David Copperfield*

For though there are many other aspects of *David Copperfield,* this autobiographical aspect is, after all, the greatest. It is not only both realistic and romantic; it is realistic because it is romantic. It is human nature described with the human exaggeration. We all know the stiff-necked and humorous old-fashioned nurse, so conventional and yet so original, so dependent and yet so independent. We all know the intrusive stepfather, the abstract strange male, coarse, handsome, sulky, successful, a breaker-up of homes. We know David's poor and aristocratic mother, so proud, so gratified, so desolate. But while these are real characters they are real characters lit up with the colors of youth and passion. They are real people romantically felt.

When we say the book is true to life we must stipulate that it is especially true to youth: even to boyhood. All the characters seem a little larger than they really were, for David is looking up at them. And the early pages of the book are in particular astonishingly vivid. Parts of it seem like fragments of our forgotten infancy. The dark house of childhood, the loneliness, the things half understood, the nurse with her inscrutable sulks and her more inscrutable tenderness, the sudden deportations to distant places, the seaside and its childish friendships, all this stirs in us when we read it, like something out of a previous existence. Above all, Dickens has excellently depicted the child enthroned in that humble circle which only in after years he perceives to have been humble.

G. K. Chesterton, *Charles Dickens*, New York: Dodd, Mead & Co., 1906.

On the contrary, I seem to have walked along a path of flowers as far as the Crocodile Book, and to have been cheered by the gentleness of my mother's voice and manner all the way. But these solemn lessons which succeeded those, I remember as the deathblow at my peace, and a grievous daily drudgery and misery. They were very long, very numerous, very hard—perfectly unintelligible, some of them, to me—and I was generally as much bewildered by them as I believe my poor mother was herself.

Let me remember how it used to be, and bring one morning back again.

I come into the second-best parlor after breakfast, with my books, and an exercise book, and a slate. My mother is ready for me at her writing desk, but not half so ready as Mr. Murdstone in his easy chair by the window (though he pretends to be reading a book), or as Miss Murdstone, sitting near my mother stringing steel beads. The very sight of these two has such an influence over me, that I begin to feel the words I have been at infinite pains to get into my head, all sliding away, and going I don't know where. I wonder where they *do* go, by-the-by?

I hand the first book to my mother. Perhaps it is a grammar, perhaps a history, or geography. I take a last drowning look at the page as I give it into her hand, and start off aloud at a racing pace while I have got it fresh. I trip over a word. Mr. Murdstone looks up. I trip over another word. Miss Murdstone looks up. I redden, tumble over half-a-dozen words, and stop. I think my mother would show me the book if she dared, but she does not dare, and she says softly:

"Oh, Davy, Davy!"

"Now, Clara," says Mr. Murdstone, "be firm with the boy. Don't say 'Oh, Davy, Davy!' That's childish. He knows his lesson, or he does not know it."

"He does *not* know it," Miss Murdstone interposes awfully.

"I am really afraid he does not," says my mother.

"Then you see, Clara," returns Miss Murdstone, "you should just give him the book back, and make him know it."

"Yes, certainly," says my mother; "that is what I intend to do, my dear Jane. Now, Davy, try once more, and don't be stupid."

I obey the first clause of the injunction by trying once more, but am not so successful with the second, for I am very stupid. I tumble down before I get to the old place, at a point where I was all right before, and stop to think. But I don't think about the lesson. I can't. I think of the number of yards of net in Miss Murdstone's cap, or of

the price of Mr. Murdstone's dressing gown, or any such ridiculous problem that I have no business with, and don't want to have anything at all to do with. Mr. Murdstone makes a movement of impatience which I have been expecting for a long time. Miss Murdstone does the same. My mother glances submissively at them, shuts the book, and lays it by as an arrear to be worked out when my other tasks are done.

There is a pile of these arrears very soon, and it swells like a rolling snowball. The bigger it gets, the more stupid *I* get. The case is so hopeless, and I feel that I am wallowing in such a bog of nonsense, that I give up all idea of getting out, and abandon myself to my fate. The despairing way in which my mother and I look at each other, as I blunder on, is truly melancholy. But the greatest effect in these miserable lessons is when my mother (thinking nobody is observing her) tries to give me the clue by the motion of her lips. At that instant, Miss Murdstone, who has been lying in wait for nothing else all along, says in a deep warning voice:

"Clara!"

My mother starts, colors, and smiles faintly. Mr. Murdstone comes out of his chair, takes the book, throws it at me or boxes my ears with it, and turns me out of the room by the shoulders.

Even when the lessons are done, the worst is yet to happen, in the shape of an appalling sum. This is invented for me, and delivered to me orally by Mr. Murdstone, and begins, "If I go into a cheesemonger's shop, and buy five thousand double-Gloucester cheeses at fourpence-halfpenny each, present payment" —at which I see Miss Murdstone secretly overjoyed. I pore over these cheeses without any result or enlightenment until dinner time; when . . . I have a slice of bread to help me out with the cheeses, and am considered in disgrace for the rest of the evening. . . .

The natural result of this treatment, continued, I suppose, for some six months or more, was to make me sullen, dull, and dogged. I was not made the less so, by my sense of being daily more and more shut out and alienated from my mother. I believe I should have been almost stupefied but for one circumstance.

It was this. My father had left in a little room upstairs, to which I had access (for it adjoined my own) a small collection of books which nobody else in our house ever troubled. From that blessed little room *Roderick Random, Peregrine Pickle, Humphrey Clinker, Tom Jones, The Vicar of Wakefield, Don Quixote, Gil Blas,* and *Robinson Crusoe,* came out, a glorious host, to keep me company.[3] They kept alive my fancy, and my hope of something beyond that place and time. . . . It is astonishing to me now, how I found time, in the midst of my porings and blunderings over heavier themes, to read those books as I did. It is curious to me how I could ever have consoled myself under my small troubles (which were great troubles to me), by impersonating my favorite characters in them—as I did—and by putting Mr. and Miss Murdstone into all the bad ones—which I did too. . . . I had a greedy relish for a few volumes of Voyages and Travels—I forget what, now—that were on those shelves; and for days and days I can remember to have gone about my region of our house, armed with the center-piece out of an old set of boot-trees—the perfect realization of Captain Somebody, of the Royal British Navy, in danger of being beset by savages, and resolved to sell his life at a great price. The Captain never lost dignity, from having his ears boxed with the Latin Grammar. I did; but the Captain was a Captain and a hero, in despite of all the grammars of all the languages in the world, dead or alive.

This was my only and my constant comfort. When I think of it, the picture always rises in my mind, of a summer evening, the boys at play in the churchyard, and I sitting on my bed, reading as if for life. Every barn in the neighborhood, every stone in the church, and every foot of the churchyard, had some association of its own, in my mind, connected with these books, and stood for some locality made famous in them. . . .

The reader now understands as well as I do, what I was when I came to that point of my youthful history to which I am now coming again.

One morning when I went into the parlor with my books, I found my mother looking anxious, Miss Murdstone looking firm, and Mr. Murdstone binding something round the bottom of a cane—a lithe and limber cane, which he left off binding when I came in, and poised and switched in the air.

"I tell you, Clara," said Mr. Murdstone, "I have been often flogged myself."

"To be sure; of course," said Miss Murdstone.

"Certainly, my dear Jane," faltered my mother, meekly. "But—but do you think it did Edward good?"

"Do you think it did Edward harm, Clara?" asked Mr. Murdstone, gravely.

"That's the point!" said his sister.

To this my mother returned, "Certainly, my dear Jane," and said no more.

I felt an apprehension that I was personally interested in this dialogue, and sought Mr. Murdstone's eye as it lighted on mine.

"Now, David," he said—and I saw that cast again, as he said it—"you must be far more careful today than usual." He gave the cane another poise, and another switch; and having finished his preparation of it, laid it down beside him, with an expressive look, and took up his book.

This was a good freshener to my presence of mind, as a beginning. I felt the words of my lessons slipping off, not one by one, or line by line, but by the entire page. I tried to lay hold of them; but they seemed, if I may so express it, to have put skates on, and to skim away from me with a smoothness there was no checking.

We began badly, and went on worse. I had come in, with an idea of distinguishing myself rather, conceiving that I was very well prepared; but it turned out to be quite a mistake. Book after book was added to the heap of failures, Miss Murdstone being firmly watchful of us all the time. And when we came at last to the five thousand cheeses (canes he made it that day, I remember), my mother burst out crying.

"Clara!" said Miss Murdstone, in her warning voice.

"I am not quite well, my dear Jane, I think," said my mother.

I saw him wink, solemnly, at his sister, as he rose and said, taking up the cane:

"Why, Jane, we can hardly expect Clara to bear, with perfect firmness, the worry and tor-

---

3. *Roderick Random* (1748), *Peregrine Pickle* (1751), and *Humphrey Clinker* (1771) are novels by Tobias Smollett. *Tom Jones* (1749) is a novel by Henry Fielding. *The Vicar of Wakefield* (1766) is a novel by Oliver Goldsmith. *Don Quixote* (1605) is a Spanish novel by Miguel de Cervantes. *Gil Blas* (1715) is a French novel by Le Sage. *Robinson Crusoe* (1719) is a novel by Daniel Defoe.

ment that David has occasioned her today. That would be stoical. Clara is greatly strengthened and improved, but we can hardly expect so much from her. David, you and I will go upstairs, boy.''

As he took me out at the door, my mother ran towards us. Miss Murdstone said, ''Clara! are you a perfect fool?'' and interfered. I saw my mother stop her ears then, and I heard her crying.

He walked me up to my room slowly and gravely—I am certain he had a delight in that formal parade of executing justice—and when we got there, suddenly twisted my head under his arm.

''Mr. Murdstone! Sir!'' I cried to him. ''Don't! Pray don't beat me! I have tried to learn, sir, but I can't learn when you and Miss Murdstone are by. I can't indeed!''

''Can't you, indeed, David?'' he said. ''We'll try that.''

He had my head as in a vice, but I twined round him somehow, and stopped him for a moment, entreating him not to beat me. It was only for a moment that I stopped him, for he cut me heavily an instant afterwards, and in the same instant I caught the hand with which he held me in my mouth, between my teeth, and bit it through. It sets my teeth on edge to think of it.

He beat me then, as if he would have beaten me to death. Above all the noise we made, I heard them running up the stairs, and crying out—I heard my mother crying out—and Peggotty. Then he was gone; and the door was locked outside; and I was lying, fevered and hot, and torn, and sore, and raging in my puny way, upon the floor.

How well I recollect, when I became quiet, what an unnatural stillness seemed to reign through the whole house! How well I remember, when my smart and passion began to cool, how wicked I began to feel!

I sat listening for a long while, but there was not a sound. I crawled up from the floor, and saw my face in the glass, so swollen, red, and ugly, that it almost frightened me. My stripes were sore and stiff, and made me cry afresh, when I moved; but they were nothing to the guilt I felt. It lay heavier on my breast than if I had been a most atrocious criminal, I dare say.

It had begun to grow dark, and I had shut the window (I had been lying, for the most part, with my head upon the sill, by turns crying, dozing, and looking listlessly out), when the key was turned, and Miss Murdstone came in with some bread and meat, and milk. These she put down upon the table without a word, glaring at me the while with exemplary firmness, and then retired, locking the door after her.

Long after it was dark I sat there, wondering whether anybody else would come. When this appeared improbable for that night, I undressed, and went to bed; and, there, I began to wonder fearfully what would be done to me. Whether it was a criminal act that I had committed? Whether I should be taken into custody, and sent to prison? Whether I was at all in danger of being hanged?

I never shall forget the waking, next morning; the being cheerful and fresh for the first moment, and then the being weighed down by the stale and dismal oppression of remembrance. Miss Murdstone reappeared before I was out of bed; told me, in so many words, that I was free to walk in the garden for half an hour and no longer; and retired, leaving the door open, that I might avail myself of that permission.

I did so, and did so every morning of my imprisonment, which lasted five days. If I could have seen my mother alone, I should have gone down on my knees to her and besought her forgiveness; but I saw no one, Miss Murdstone excepted, during the whole time—except at evening prayers in the parlor; to which I was escorted by Miss Murdstone after everybody else was placed; where I was stationed, a young outlaw, all alone by myself near the door; and whence I was solemnly conducted by my jailer, before anyone arose from the devotional posture. I only observed that my mother was as far off from me as she could be, and kept her face another way so that I never saw it; and that Mr. Murdstone's hand was bound up in a large linen wrapper.

The length of those five days I can convey no idea of to anyone. They occupy the place of years in my remembrance. The way in which I listened to all the incidents of the house that made themselves audible to me; the ringing of bells, the opening and shutting of doors, the murmuring of voices, the footsteps on the stairs; to any laughing, whistling, or singing, outside, which seemed more dismal than anything else to me in my solitude and disgrace—the uncertain pace of the hours, especially at night, when I would wake thinking it was morning, and find that the family were not yet gone to bed, and that all the length of night had yet to come—the depressed dreams and nightmares I had—the return of day, noon, afternoon, evening, when the boys played in the churchyard, and I watched them from a distance within the room, being ashamed to show myself at the window lest they should know I was a prisoner—the strange sensation of never hearing myself speak—the fleeting intervals of something like cheerfulness, which came with eating and drinking, and went away with it—the setting in of rain one evening, with a fresh smell, and its coming down faster and faster between me and the church, until it and gathering night seemed to quench me in gloom, and fear, and remorse—all this appears to have gone round and round for years instead of days, it is so vividly and strongly stamped on my remembrance.

On the last night of my restraint, I was awakened by hearing my own name spoken in a whisper. I started up in bed, and putting out my arms in the dark, said:

"Is that you, Peggotty?"

There was no immediate answer, but presently I heard my name again, in a tone so very mysterious and awful, that I think I should have gone into a fit, if it hadn't occurred to me that it must have come through the keyhole.

I groped my way to the door, and putting my own lips to the keyhole, whispered:

"Is that you, Peggotty, dear?"

"Yes, my own precious Davy," she replied. "Be as soft as a mouse, or the Cat'll hear us."

I understood this to mean Miss Murdstone, and was sensible of the urgency of the case; her room being close by.

"How's mama, dear Peggotty? Is she very angry with me?"

I could hear Peggotty crying softly on her side of the keyhole, as I was doing on mine, before she answered. "No. Not very."

"What is going to be done with me, Peggotty dear? Do you know?"

"School. Near London," was Peggotty's answer. I was obliged to get her to repeat it, for she spoke it the first time quite down my throat, in consequence of my having forgotten to take my mouth away from the keyhole and put my ear there; and though her words tickled me a good deal, I didn't hear them.

"When, Peggotty?"

"Tomorrow."

"Is that the reason why Miss Murdstone took the clothes out of my drawers?" which she had done, though I have forgotten to mention it.

"Yes," said Peggotty. "Box."

"Shan't I see mama?"

"Yes," said Peggotty. "Morning."

Then Peggotty fitted her mouth close to the keyhole, and delivered these words through it with as much feeling and earnestness as a keyhole has ever been the medium of communicating, I will venture to assert: shooting in each broken little sentence in a convulsive little burst of its own.

"Davy, dear. If I ain't ben azackly as intimate with you. Lately, as I used to be. It ain't because I don't love you. Just as well and more, my pretty poppet. It's because I thought it better for you. And for someone else besides. Davy, my darling, are you listening? Can you hear me?"

"Ye—ye—ye—yes, Peggotty!" I sobbed.

"My own!" said Peggotty, with infinite compassion. "What I want to say, is. That you must never forget me. For I'll never forget you. And I'll take as much care of your mama, Davy. As ever I took of you. And I won't leave her. The day may come when she'll be glad to lay her poor head. On her stupid, cross old Peggotty's arm again. And I'll write to you, my dear. Though I ain't no scholar. And I'll—I'll—" Peggotty fell to kissing the keyhole, as she couldn't kiss me . . . and we both of us kissed the keyhole with the greatest affection—I patted it with my hand, I recollect, as if it had been her honest face—and parted. From that night there grew up in my breast, a feeling for Peggotty, which I cannot very well define. She did not replace my mother; no one could do that; but she came into a vacancy in my heart, which closed upon her, and I felt towards her something I have never felt for any other human being. It was a sort of comical affection too; and yet if she had died, I cannot think what I should have done, or how I should have acted out the tragedy it would have been to me.

In the morning Miss Murdstone appeared as usual, and told me I was going to school; which was not altogether such news to me as she supposed. She also informed me that when I was dressed, I was to come downstairs into the parlor, and have my breakfast. There, I found my mother, very pale and with red eyes: into whose arms I ran, and begged her pardon from my suffering soul.

"Oh, Davy!" she said. "That you could hurt any one I love! Try to be better, pray to be better! I forgive you; but I am so grieved, Davy, that you should have such bad passions in your heart."

They had persuaded her that I was a wicked fellow, and she was more sorry for that, than for my going away. I felt it sorely. I tried to eat my parting breakfast, but my tears dropped upon my bread-and-butter, and trickled into my tea, and choked me. I saw my mother look at me sometimes, and then glance at the watchful Miss Murdstone, and then look down, or look away.

"Master Copperfield's box there!" said Miss Murdstone, when wheels were heard at the gate.

I looked for Peggotty, but it was not she; neither she nor Mr. Murdstone appeared. My former acquaintance, the carrier, was at the door; the box was taken out to his cart, and lifted in.

"Clara!" said Miss Murdstone, in her warning note.

"Ready, my dear Jane," returned my mother. "Good bye, Davy. You are going for your own good. Good bye, my child. You will come home in the holidays, and be a better boy."

"Clara!" Miss Murdstone repeated.

"Certainly, my dear Jane," replied my mother, who was holding me. "I forgive you, my dear boy. God bless you!"

"Clara!" Miss Murdstone repeated.

Miss Murdstone was good enough to take me out to the cart, and to say on the way that she hoped I would repent, before I came to a bad end; and then I got into the cart, and the lazy horse walked off with it.   1849

Discussion

1. Dickens portrays these early scenes from a child's (David's) point of view. Give examples of how Dickens shows the reader things from a child's visual perspective and a child's limited, or selective, understanding of events.

2. How do Peggotty and Mrs. Copperfield divide up the traditional functions of a mother? Why does this make David even more jealous of Mr. Murdstone?

3. The reader strongly dislikes Murdstone before that character ever betrays his true nature. Explain how David's first descriptions of Murdstone's physical appearance reveal David's growing suspicions about him.

4. What does education become under the direction of the Murdstones?

5. What does fiction mean to David as a boy? Does his story serve different purposes from the books he once read?

6. Why does David bite Mr. Murdstone? What does this act suggest about David?

7. At the start of his narrative, David raises and leaves open the question of heroism. In the excerpt you have read, do you find a hero? Explain your answer and in so doing define your understanding of the term.

Composition

1. Dickens has a remarkable ability to portray how a child sees the world. Using your own memories, or an invented scene, picture an event from a child's perspective. Keep in mind how height, inadequate understanding, and intense sensations will modify what is seen.

Then write a description of what happens from the child's point of view.

2. George Orwell describes Dickens's use of what he calls the "unnecessary detail." Orwell insists it is the inclusion of superfluous information that creates the special atmosphere in Dickens's novels. Isolate details from *David Copperfield* that you think are unnecessary for strictly narrative purposes.

In an essay explain how they affect your reading of the story.

George Eliot 1819–1880

When Mary Ann Evans began to publish fiction in 1858, she took the pen name George Eliot; this change was an emblem of the seriousness with which she addressed her new career. There were many successful women novelists in mid-Victorian England who wrote under their own names, but there existed a general assumption that they wrote "women's novels." When Evans began to publish her novels under an assumed name she was implicitly asserting her intention to rival the greatest novelists of her day.

Mary Ann Evans's father dominated her childhood. A powerful man, both physically and intellectually, Robert Evans was self-educated. He rose to serve as chief agricultural agent for a wealthy landowner. His daughter Mary Ann showed early intellectual promise and from the ages of five to sixteen she attended a series of schools for girls, in which she acquired a fervent belief in Christianity. On the death of her mother in 1836, Evans came home to keep house for her father—a task that proved increasingly restrictive, but to which she devoted herself.

At home she continued to learn, studying Italian and German, reading all of Wordsworth's poetry and, more than anything else, probing further into theology. In 1841 the family moved to Coventry where Evans met a group of radical intellectuals. Soon, she doubted God's existence. Her father required her attendance at church and, after a struggle, she obeyed. But she continued to study, publishing her own translation of a work of skeptical German theology in 1846.

The death of her father in 1849 freed Evans from domestic responsibilities but posed serious problems. Where and how was she to live? She settled in London, joining a group of free-thinking writers who respected her now formidable abilities. By 1851 she was editing *The Westminster Review,* translating German phi-

losophy, and publishing her own essays on the intellectual questions of the day.

In 1853, in the midst of this stimulating environment, she met G. E. Lewes, another writer and thinker. Soon they fell in love. Lewes was already married, but his wife had deserted him. Divorce proved impossible. Evans decided to defy convention and live with him, calling herself Mrs. Lewes and insisting that in all but law they were husband and wife. In mid-Victorian Britain they had to lead a retired life.

It was Lewes who persuaded Mary Ann Evans to write fiction. Her first novel, *Adam Bede* (1859) enjoyed immediate success. In her second novel, *The Mill on the Floss* (1860) Evans used a setting from England's past to study some of its current problems. The novel's evocative pictures of farms, grain mills, and small towns mirror the places and people Evans knew as a girl and read about in the poetry of Wordsworth. Yet in this world that she depicts she sees some of the critical problems of her era, especially the question of sexual equality. Even in childhood, the novel's heroine, Maggie Tulliver, feels the injustice of a world in which women are expected to be intellectually inferior to men. The novel traces her efforts to work against that injustice.

The Mill on the Floss (1860) describes a rural England that was disappearing even as George Eliot wrote. At the center of the novel is the Tulliver family. Mr. Tulliver owns a flour mill on the Floss River and has two hired men, Luke and Harry, to help him run it. He has been successful in business, even though he has never been formally educated, and despite the fact that he is always embroiled in law suits about property rights with a local lawyer. Mr. Tulliver's son Tom is beginning to grow up and his father, in trying to decide what to do with the boy, consults his friend Mr. Riley. Although Mr. Tulliver doesn't know it, his daughter Maggie is listening.

from *The Mill on the Floss*

The gentleman in the ample white cravat and shirt-frill, taking his brandy-and-water so pleasantly with his good friend Tulliver, is Mr. Riley, a gentleman with a waxen complexion and fat hands, rather highly educated for an auctioneer and appraiser, but large-hearted enough to show a great deal of *bonhommie*[1] towards simple country acquaintances of hospitable habits. Mr. Riley spoke of such acquaintances kindly as "people of the old school."

The conversation had come to a pause. . . .

"There's a thing I've got i' my head," said Mr. Tulliver at last, in rather a lower tone than usual, as he turned his head and looked steadfastly at his companion.

"Ah!" said Mr. Riley, in a tone of mild interest. He was a man with heavy waxen eyelids and high-arched eyebrows, looking exactly the same under all circumstances. This immovability of face, and the habit of taking a pinch of snuff before he gave an answer, made him trebly oracular to Mr. Tulliver.

"It's a very particular thing," he went on; "it's about my boy Tom."

At the sound of this name, Maggie, who was seated on a low stool close by the fire, with a large book open on her lap, shook her heavy hair back and looked up eagerly. There were few sounds that roused Maggie when she was dreaming over her book, but Tom's name served as well as the shrillest whistle: in an instant she was on the watch, with gleaming eyes, like a Skye terrier suspecting mischief, or at all events determined to fly at any one who threatened it towards Tom.

"You see, I want to put him to a new school at Midsummer," said Mr. Tulliver; "he's comin' away from the 'cademy at Ladyday,[2] an' I shall let him run loose for a quarter; but after that I want to send him to a downright good school, where they'll make a scholard of him."

"Well," said Mr. Riley, "there's no greater advantage you can give him than a good education. Not," he added, with polite significance—"not that a man can't be an excellent miller and farmer, and a shrewd sensible fellow into the bargain, without much help from the schoolmaster."

"I believe you," said Mr. Tulliver, winking, and turning his head on one side, "but that's where it is. I don't *mean* Tom to be a miller and farmer. I see no fun i' that: why, if I made him a miller an' farmer, he'd be expectin' to take to the Mill an' the land, an' a-hinting at me as it was time for me to lay by[3] an' think o' my latter end. Nay, nay, I've seen enough o' that wi' sons. I'll never pull my coat off before I go to bed. I shall give Tom an eddication an' put him to a business, as he may make a nest for himself, an' not want to push me out o' mine. Pretty well if he gets it when I'm dead an' gone. I shan't be put off wi' spoon-meat afore I've lost my teeth."

---

1. *bonhommie,* good-natured friendship.
2. *Ladyday,* March 25th, a legal holiday in England.
3. *lay by,* retire.

This was evidently a point on which Mr. Tulliver felt strongly, and the impetus which had given unusual rapidity and emphasis to his speech, showed itself still unexhausted for some minutes afterwards, in a defiant motion of the head from side to side, and an occasional "Nay, nay," like a subsiding growl.

These angry symptoms were keenly observed by Maggie, and cut her to the quick. Tom, it appeared, was supposed capable of turning his father out of doors, and of making the future in some way tragic by his wickedness. This was not to be borne; and Maggie jumped up from her stool, forgetting all about her heavy book, which fell with a bang within the fender; and going up between her father's knees, said, in a half-crying, half-indignant voice—

"Father, Tom wouldn't be naughty to you ever; I know he wouldn't."

Mrs. Tulliver was out of the room superintending a choice supper dish, and Mr. Tulliver's heart was touched; so Maggie was not scolded about the book. Mr. Riley quietly picked it up and looked at it, while the father laughed with a certain tenderness in his hard-lined face, and patted his little girl on the back, and then held her hands and kept her between his knees.

"What! they mustn't say any harm o' Tom, eh?" said Mr. Tulliver, looking at Maggie with a twinkling eye. Then, in a lower voice, turning to Mr. Riley, as though Maggie couldn't hear, "She understands what one's talking about so as never was. And you should hear her read—straight off, as if she knowed it all beforehand. And allays at her book! But it's bad—it's bad," Mr. Tulliver added, sadly, checking this blamable exultation; "a woman's no business wi' being so clever; it'll turn to trouble, I doubt. But, bless you!"—here the exultation was clearly recovering the mastery—"she'll read the books and understand 'em better nor half the folks as are growed up."

Maggie's cheeks began to flush with triumphant excitement: she thought Mr. Riley would have a respect for her now; it had been evident that he thought nothing of her before.

Mr. Riley was turning over the leaves of the book, and she could make nothing of his face, with its high-arched eyebrows; but he presently looked at her and said,

"Come, come and tell me something about this book; here are some pictures—I want to know what they mean."

Maggie with deepening color went without hesitation to Mr. Riley's elbow and looked over the book, eagerly seizing one corner, and tossing back her mane, while she said,

"O, I'll tell you what that means. It's a dreadful picture, isn't it? But I can't help looking at it. That old woman in the water's a witch—they've put her in to find out whether she's a witch or no, and if she swims she's a witch, and if she's drowned—and killed, you know—she's innocent, and not a witch, but only a poor silly old woman. But what good would it do her then, you know, when she was drowned? Only, I suppose, she'd go to heaven, and God would make it up to her. And this dreadful blacksmith with his arms akimbo, laughing—oh, isn't he ugly?—I'll tell you what he is. He's the devil *really*" (here Maggie's voice became louder and more emphatic), "and not a right blacksmith; for the devil takes the shape of wicked men, and walks about and sets people doing wicked things, and he's oftener in the shape of a bad man than any other, because, you know, if people saw he was the devil, and he roared at 'em, they'd run away, and he couldn't make 'em do what he pleased."

Mr. Tulliver had listened to this exposition of Maggie's with petrifying wonder. . . .

"Go, go!" said Mr. Tulliver, peremptorily, beginning to feel rather uncomfortable at these free remarks on the personal appearance of a being powerful enough to create lawyers; "shut up the book, and let's hear no more o' such talk. It is as I thought—the child 'ull learn more mischief nor good wi' the books. Go, go and see after your mother."

Maggie shut up the book at once, with a sense of disgrace, but not being inclined to see after her mother, she compromised the matter by going into a dark corner behind her father's chair, and nursing her doll, towards which she had an occasional fit of fondness in Tom's absence, neglecting its toilette, but lavishing so many warm kisses on it that the waxen cheeks had a wasted unhealthy appearance.

"Did you ever hear the like on't?" said Mr. Tulliver, as Maggie retired. "It's a pity but what she'd been the lad—she'd ha' been a match for the lawyers, *she* would. It's the wonderful'st thing''—here he lowered his voice—''as I picked the mother because she wasn't o'er 'cute[4]—bein' a good-looking woman too, an' come of a rare family for managing; but I picked her from her sisters o' purpose, 'cause she was a bit weak, like; for I wasn't agoin' to be told the rights o' things by my own fireside. But you see when a man's got brains himself, there's no knowing where they'll run to; an' a pleasant sort o' soft woman may go on breeding you stupid lads and 'cute wenches, till it's like as if the world was turned topsy-turvy. It's an uncommon puzzlin' thing.''

It was a heavy disappointment to Maggie that she was not allowed to go with her father in the gig when he went to fetch Tom home from the academy; but the morning was too wet, Mrs. Tulliver said, for a little girl to go out in her best bonnet. Maggie took the opposite view very strongly, and it was a direct consequence of this difference of opinion that when her mother was in the act of brushing out the reluctant black crop, Maggie suddenly rushed from under her hands and dipped her head in a basin of water standing near—in the vindictive determination that there should be no more chance of curls that day.

'''Maggie, Maggie,'' exlaimed Mrs. Tulliver, sitting stout and helpless with the brushes on her lap, ''what is to become of you if you're so naughty? I'll tell your Aunt Glegg and your Aunt Pullet when they come next week, and they'll never love you any more. O dear, O dear! look at your clean pinafore, wet from top to bottom. Folks 'ull think it's a judgment on me as I've got such a child—they'll think I've done summat wicked.''

Before this remonstrance was finished, Maggie was already out of hearing, making her way towards the great attic that ran under the old high-pitched roof, shaking the water from her black locks as she ran, like a Skye terrier escaped from his bath. This attic was Maggie's favorite retreat on a wet day, when the weather was not too cold; here she fretted out all her ill-humors, and talked aloud to the worm-eaten floors and the worm-eaten shelves, and the dark rafters festooned with cobwebs; and here she kept a Fetish[5] which she punished for all her misfortunes. This was the trunk of a large wooden doll, which once stared with the roundest of eyes above the red-

dest of cheeks; but was now entirely defaced by a long career of vicarious suffering. Three nails driven into the head commemorated as many crises in Maggie's nine years of earthly struggle; that luxury of vengeance having been suggested to her by the picture of Jael destroying Sisera in the old Bible. The last nail had been driven in with a fiercer stroke than usual, for the Fetish on that occasion represented Aunt Glegg. But immediately afterwards Maggie had reflected that if she drove many nails in, she would not be so well able to fancy that the head was hurt when she knocked it against the wall, nor to comfort it, and make believe to poultice it, when her fury was abated; for even Aunt Glegg would be pitiable when she had been hurt very much, and thoroughly humiliated, so as to beg her niece's pardon. Since then she had driven no more nails in, but had soothed herself by alternately grinding and beating the wooden head against the rough brick of the great chimneys that made two square pillars supporting the roof. That was what she did this morning on reaching the attic, sobbing all the while with a passion that expelled every other form of consciousness—even the memory of the grievance that had caused it. As at last the sobs were getting quieter, and the grinding less fierce, a sudden beam of sunshine, falling through the wire lattice across the worm-eaten shelves, made her throw away the Fetish and run to the window. The sun was really breaking out; the sound of the mill seemed cheerful again; the granary doors were open; and there was Yap, the queer white-and-brown terrier, with one ear turned back, trotting about and sniffing vaguely, as if he were in search of a companion. It was irresistible. Maggie tossed her hair back and ran downstairs, seized her bonnet without putting it on, peeped, and then dashed along the passage lest she should encounter her mother, and was quickly out in the yard, whirling round like a Pythoness,[6] and singing as she whirled, ''Yap, Yap, Tom's coming home!'' while Yap danced and barked round her,

---

4. 'cute, acute, that is, intelligent.
5. *Fetish,* in primitive cultures, an object believed to possess magical powers; Maggie's fetish, much like a voodoo doll, receives the punishments she cannot inflict on other people.
6. *Pythoness,* a priestess to the god Apollo, so named because Apollo once slew a monstrous serpent named Python. Such priestesses expressed their devotion in whirling dances.

as much as to say, if there was any noise wanted he was the dog for it.

"Hegh, hegh, Miss, you'll make yourself giddy, an' tumble down i' the dirt," said Luke, the head miller, a tall broad-shouldered man of forty, black-eyed and black-haired, subdued by a general mealiness. . . .

Maggie paused in her whirling and said, staggering a little, "O no, it doesn't make me giddy, Luke; may I go into the mill with you?"

Maggie loved to linger in the great spaces of the mill, and often came out with her black hair powdered to a soft whiteness that made her dark eyes flash out with new fire. The resolute din, the unresting motion of the great stones, giving her a dim delicious awe as at the presence of an uncontrollable force—the meal for ever pouring, pouring—the fine white powder softening all surfaces, and making the very spider-nets look like a fairy lace work—the sweet pure scent of the meal—all helped to make Maggie feel that the mill was a little world apart from her outside everyday life. . . . But the part of the mill she liked best was the topmost story—the corn-hutch, where there were the great heaps of grain, which she could sit on and slide down continually. She was in the habit of taking this recreation as she conversed with Luke, to whom she was very communicative, wishing him to think well of her understanding, as her father did.

Perhaps she felt it necessary to recover her position with him on the present occasion, for, as she sat sliding on the heap of grain near which he was busying himself, she said, at that shrill pitch which was requisite in mill-society—

"I think you never read any book but the Bible—did you, Luke?"

"Nay, Miss—an' not much o' that," said Luke, with great frankness. "I'm no reader, I aren't. . . ."

"Why, you're like my brother Tom, Luke," said Maggie, wishing to turn the conversation agreeably; "Tom's not fond of reading. I love Tom so dearly, Luke—better than anybody else in the world. When he grows up, I shall keep his house, and we shall always live together. I can tell him everything he doesn't know. But I think Tom's clever, for all he doesn't like books: he makes beautiful whipcord and rabbit pens."

"Ah," said Luke, "but he'll be fine an' vexed, as the rabbits are all dead."

"Dead!" screamed Maggie, jumping up from her sliding seat on the corn. "O dear, Luke! What! the lop-eared one, and the spotted doe that Tom spent all his money to buy?"

"As dead as moles," said Luke, fetching his comparison from the unmistakable corpses[7] nailed to the stable-wall.

"O dear, Luke," said Maggie, in a piteous tone, while the big tears rolled down her cheek; "Tom told me to take care of 'em, and I forgot. What *shall* I do?"

"Well, you see, Miss, they were in that far tool house, an' it was nobody's business to see to 'em. I reckon Master Tom told Harry to feed 'em, but there's no countin' on Harry—*he's* an offal creatur as iver come about the primises, he is. He remembers nothing but his own inside—an' I wish it 'ud gripe him."

"O, Luke, Tom told me to be sure and remember the rabbits every day; but how could I, when they didn't come into my head, you know? O, he will be so angry with me, I know he will, and so sorry about his rabbits—and so am I sorry. O, what *shall* I do?"

"Don't you fret, Miss," said Luke, soothingly, "they're nash things, them lop-eared rabbits—they'd happen ha' died, if they'd been fed. Things out o' natur niver thrive: God A'mighty doesn't like 'em. He made the rabbits' ears to lie back, an' it's nothin' but contrairiness to make 'em hing down like a mastiff dog's. Master Tom 'ull know better nor buy such things another time. Don't you fret, Miss. Will you come along home wi' me, and see my wife? I'm a-goin' this minute." The invitation offered an agreeable distraction to Maggie's grief, and her tears gradually subsided as she trotted along by Luke's side to his pleasant cottage, which stood with its apple and pear trees, and with the added dignity of a lean-to pig-sty, at the other end of the Mill fields. . . .

Tom was to arrive early in the afternoon, and there was another fluttering heart besides Maggie's when it was late enough for the sound of the gig-wheels to be expected; for if Mrs. Tulliver had a strong feeling, it was fondness for her boy.

---

7. *corpses,* moles killed because they are farm pests.

At last the sound came—that quick light bowling of the gig-wheels—and in spite of the wind, which was blowing the clouds about, and was not likely to respect Mrs. Tulliver's curls and cap-strings, she came outside the door, and even held her hand on Maggie's offending head, forgetting all the griefs of the morning.

"There he is, my sweet lad! But, Lord ha' mercy! he's got never a collar on; it's been lost on the road, I'll be bound, and spoilt the set."

Mrs. Tulliver stood with her arms open; Maggie jumped first on one leg and then on the other; while Tom descended from the gig, and said, with masculine reticence as to the tender emotions, "Hallo! Yap—what! are you there?"

Nevertheless he submitted to be kissed willingly enough, though Maggie hung on his neck in rather a strangling fashion, while his blue-grey eyes wandered towards the croft and the lambs and the river, where he promised himself that he would begin to fish the first thing tomorrow morning. He was one of those lads that grow everywhere in England, and, at twelve or thirteen years of age, look as much alike as goslings:—a lad with light-brown hair, cheeks of cream and roses, full lips, indeterminate nose and eye-brows—a physiognomy in which it seems impossible to discern anything but the generic character of boyhood; as different as possible from poor Maggie's phiz, which Nature seemed to have molded and colored with the most decided intention. But that same Nature has the deep cunning which hides itself under the appearance of openness, so that simple people think they can see through her quite well, and all the while she is secretly preparing a refutation of their confident prophecies. Under these average boyish physiognomies that she seems to turn off by the gross, she conceals some of her most rigid, inflexible purposes, some of her most unmodifiable characters; and the dark-eyed, demonstrative, rebellious girl may after all turn out to be a passive being compared with this pink-and-white bit of masculinity with the indeterminate features.

"Maggie," said Tom, confidentially, taking her into a corner, as soon as his mother was gone out to examine his box, and the warm parlor had taken off the chill he had felt from the long drive, "you don't know what I've got in *my* pockets,"

nodding his head up and down as a means of rousing her sense of mystery. . . .

"What is it?" said Maggie, in a whisper. "I can see nothing but a bit of yellow."

"Why it's . . . a . . . new . . . guess, Maggie!"

"O, I *can't* guess, Tom," said Maggie, impatiently.

"Don't be a spitfire, else I won't tell you," said Tom, thrusting his hand back into his pocket, and looking determined.

"No, Tom," said Maggie, imploringly, laying hold of the arm that was held stiffly in the pocket. "I'm not cross, Tom; it was only because I can't bear guessing. *Please* be good to me."

Tom's arm slowly relaxed, and he said, "Well, then it's a new fishline—two new uns—one for you, Maggie, all to yourself. I wouldn't go halves in the toffee and gingerbread on purpose to save the money; and Gibson and Spouncer fought with me because I wouldn't.[8] And here's hooks; see here! . . . . I say, *won't* we go and fish tomorrow down by the Round Pool? And you shall catch your own fish, Maggie, and put the worms on, and everything—won't it be fun?"

Maggie's answer was to throw her arms round Tom's neck and hug him, and hold her cheek against his without speaking, while he slowly unwound some of the line, saying, after a pause,

"Wasn't I a good brother, now, to buy you a line all to yourself? You know, I needn't have bought it, if I hadn't liked."

"Yes, very, very good . . . . I *do* love you, Tom."

Tom had put the line back in his pocket, and was looking at the hooks one by one, before he spoke again.

"And the fellows fought me, because I wouldn't give in about the toffee."

"O dear! I wish they wouldn't fight at your school, Tom. Didn't it hurt you?"

"Hurt me? no," said Tom, putting up the hooks again, taking out a large pocketknife, and slowly opening the largest blade, which he looked at meditatively as he rubbed his finger along it. Then he added—

---

8. **Gibson . . . I wouldn't,** school chums who wanted Tom to spend his pocket money on treats.

Spring by Frederick
Walker, 1864.

"I gave Spouncer a black eye, I know—that's
what he got by wanting to leather *me*; I wasn't
going to go halves because anybody leathered
me."

"O how brave you are, Tom! I think you're
like Samson. If there came a lion roaring at me, I
think you'd fight him—wouldn't you, Tom?"

"How can a lion come roaring at you, you
silly thing? There's no lions, only in the
shows."

"No; but if we were in the lion countries—I
mean in Africa, where it's very hot—the lions eat
people there. I can show it you in the book where
I read it."

"Well, I should get a gun and shoot him."

"But if you hadn't got a gun—we might have
gone out, you know, not thinking—just as we go
fishing; and then a great lion might run towards
us roaring, and we couldn't get away from him.
What should you do, Tom?"

Tom paused, and at last turned away contemptuously, saying, "But the lion *isn't* coming.
What's the use of talking?"

"But I like to fancy how it would be," said
Maggie, following him. "Just think what you
would do, Tom."

"O don't bother, Maggie! you're such a silly—I shall go and see my rabbits."

Maggie's heart began to flutter with fear. She
dared not tell the sad truth at once, but she
walked after Tom in trembling silence as he went
out, thinking how she could tell him the news so
as to soften at once his sorrow and his anger; for
Maggie dreaded Tom's anger of all things—it was
quite a different anger from her own.

"Tom," she said, timidly, when they were
out of doors, "how much money did you give for
your rabbits?"

"Two half-crowns and a sixpence," said
Tom, promptly.

"I think I've got a great deal more than that in my steel purse upstairs. I'll ask mother to give it you."

"What for?" said Tom. "I don't want *your* money, you silly thing. I've got a great deal more money than you, because I'm a boy. I always have half-sovereigns and sovereigns for my Christmas boxes, because I shall be a man, and you only have five-shilling pieces, because you're only a girl."

"Well, but, Tom—if mother would let me give you two halfcrowns and a sixpence out of my purse to put into your pocket and spend, you know; and buy some more rabbits with it?"

"More rabbits? I don't want any more."

"O, but Tom, they're all dead."

Tom stopped immediately in his walk and turned round towards Maggie. "You forgot to feed 'em, then, and Harry forgot?" he said, his color heightening for a moment, but soon subsiding. "I'll pitch into Harry—I'll have him turned away. And I don't love you, Maggie. You shan't go fishing with me tomorrow. I told you to go and see the rabbits every day." He walked on again.

"Yes, but I forgot—and I couldn't help it, indeed, Tom. I'm so very sorry," said Maggie, while the tears rushed fast.

"You're a naughty girl," said Tom severely, "and I'm sorry I bought you the fishline. I don't love you."

"O, Tom, it's very cruel," sobbed Maggie. "I'd forgive you, if *you* forgot anything—I wouldn't mind what you did—I'd forgive you and love you."

"Yes, you're a silly—but I never *do* forget things—*I* don't."

"O, please forgive me, Tom; my heart will break," said Maggie, shaking with sobs, clinging to Tom's arm, and laying her wet cheek on his shoulder.

Tom shook her off, and stopped again, saying in a peremptory tone, "Now, Maggie, you just listen. Aren't I a good brother to you?"

"Ye-ye-es," sobbed Maggie, her chin rising and falling convulsedly.

"Didn't I think about your fishline all this quarter, and mean to buy it, and saved my money o' purpose, and wouldn't go halves in the toffee, and Spouncer fought me because I wouldn't?"

"Ye-ye-es . . . and I . . . lo-lo-love you so, Tom."

"But you're a naughty girl. Last holidays you licked the paint off my lozenge box, and the holidays before that you let the boat drag my fishline down when I'd set you to watch it, and you pushed your head through my kite, all for nothing."

"But I didn't mean," said Maggie; "I couldn't help it."

"Yes, you could," said Tom, "if you'd minded what you were doing. And you're a naughty girl, and you shan't go fishing with me tomorrow."

With this terrible conclusion, Tom ran away from Maggie towards the mill, meaning to greet Luke there, and complain to him of Harry.

Maggie stood motionless, except from her sobs, for a minute or two; then she turned round and ran into the house, and up to her attic, where she sat on the floor, and laid her head against the worm-eaten shelf, with a crushing sense of misery. Tom was come home, and she had thought how happy she should be—and now he was cruel to her. What use was anything, if Tom didn't love her? O, he was very cruel! Hadn't she wanted to give him the money, and said how very sorry she was? She knew she was naughty to her mother, but she had never been naughty to Tom—had never *meant* to be naughty to him.

"O, he is cruel!" Maggie sobbed aloud, finding a wretched pleasure in the hollow resonance that came through the long empty space of the attic. She never thought of beating or grinding her Fetish; she was too miserable to be angry.

These bitter sorrows of childhood! when sorrow is all new and strange, when hope has not yet got wings to fly beyond the days and weeks, and the space from summer to summer seems measureless.

Maggie soon thought she had been hours in the attic, and it must be teatime, and they were all having their tea, and not thinking of her. Well, then, she would stay up there and starve herself—hide herself behind the tub, and stay there all night; and then they would all be frightened, and Tom would be sorry. Thus Maggie thought in the pride of her heart, as she crept behind the tub; but presently she began to cry again at the idea that they didn't mind her being there. If she went down again to Tom now—would he forgive her?—perhaps her father would be there, and he would take her part. But, then, she wanted Tom to forgive her because he loved her, not because his father told him. No, she would never go down if Tom didn't come to fetch her. This resolution lasted in great intensity for five dark minutes behind the tub; but then the need of being loved, the strongest need in poor Maggie's nature, began to wrestle with her pride, and soon threw it. She crept from behind her tub into the twilight of the long attic, but just then she heard a quick footstep on the stairs. . . .

It was Tom's step . . . that Maggie heard on the stairs, when her need of love had triumphed over her pride, and she was going down with her swollen eyes and dishevelled hair to beg for pity. At least her father would stroke her head and say, "Never mind, my wench." It is a wonderful subduer, this need of love—this hunger of the heart—as peremptory as that other hunger by which Nature forces us to submit to the yoke, and change the face of the world.

But she knew Tom's step, and her heart began to beat violently with the sudden shock of hope. He only stood still at the top of the stairs and said, "Maggie, you're to come down." But she rushed to him and clung round his neck, sobbing, "O Tom, please forgive me—I can't bear it—I will always be good—always remember things—do love me—please, dear Tom!"

We learn to restrain ourselves as we get older. We keep apart when we have quarrelled, express ourselves in well-bred phrases, and in this way preserve a dignified alienation, showing much firmness on one side, and swallowing much grief on the other. We no longer approximate in our behavior to the mere impulsiveness of the lower animals, but conduct ourselves in every respect like members of a highly civilized society. Maggie and Tom were still very much like young animals, and so she could rub her cheek against his, and kiss his ear in a random, sobbing way; and there were tender fibers in the lad that had been used to answer to Maggie's fondling; so that he behaved with a weakness quite inconsistent with his resolution to punish her as much as she deserved: he actually began to kiss her in return, and say—

"Don't cry, then, Magsie—here, eat a bit o' cake."

Maggie's sobs began to subside, and she put out her mouth for the cake and bit a piece: and then Tom bit a piece, just for company, and they ate together and rubbed each other's cheeks and brows and noses together, while they ate, with a humiliating resemblance to two friendly ponies.

"Come along, Magsie, and have tea," said Tom at last, when there was no more cake except what was downstairs.

So ended the sorrows of this day, and the next morning Maggie was trotting with her own fishing rod in one hand and a handle of the basket in the other, stepping always, by a peculiar gift, in the muddiest places, and looking darkly radiant from under her beaver bonnet because Tom was good to her. She had told Tom, however, that she should like him to put the worms on the hook for her, although she accepted his word when he assured her that worms couldn't feel (it was Tom's private opinion that it didn't much matter if they did). He knew all about worms, and fish, and those things; and what birds were mischievous, and how padlocks opened, and which way the handles of the gates were to be lifted. Maggie thought this sort of knowledge was very wonderful—much more difficult than remembering what was in the books; and she was rather in awe of Tom's superiority, for he was the only person who called her knowledge "stuff," and did not feel surprised at her cleverness. Tom, indeed, was of opinion that Maggie was a silly little thing; all girls were silly—they couldn't throw a stone so as to hit anything, couldn't do anything with a pocketknife, and were frightened at frogs. Still he was very fond of his sister, and meant always to take care of her, make her his housekeeper, and punish her when she did wrong. . . .

It was one of their happy mornings. They trotted along and sat down together, with no thought that life would ever change much for them: they would only get bigger and not go to school, and it would always be like the holidays; they would always live together and be fond of each other. And the mill with its booming—the great chestnut tree under which they played at houses—their own little river, the Ripple, where the banks seemed like home, and Tom was always seeing the water rats, while Maggie gathered the purple plumy tops of the reeds, which she forgot and dropped afterwards . . . these things would always be just the same to them.

Life did change for Tom and Maggie; and yet they were not wrong in believing that the thoughts and loves of these first years would always make part of their lives. We could never have loved the earth so well if we had had no childhood in it,—if it were not the earth where the same flowers come up again every spring that we used to gather with our tiny fingers as we sat lisping to ourselves on the grass—the same hips and haws on the autumn hedgerows—the same redbreasts that we used to call "God's birds," because they did no harm to the precious crops. What novelty is worth that sweet monotony where everything is known, and *loved* because it is known?

The wood I walk in on this mild May day, with the young yellow-brown foliage of the oaks between me and the blue sky, the white star-flowers and the blue-eyed speedwell and the ground ivy at my feet—what grove of tropic palms, what strange ferns or splendid broad pet-alled blossoms, could ever thrill such deep and delicate fibers within me as this home scene? These familiar flowers, these well remembered bird notes, this sky, with its fitful brightness, these furrowed and grassy fields, each with a sort of personality given to it by the capricious hedge-rows—such things as these are the mother tongue of our imagination, the language that is laden with all the subtle inextricable associations the fleeting hours of our childhood left behind them. Our delight in the sunshine on the deep bladed grass today, might be no more than the faint perception of wearied souls, if it were not for the sunshine and the grass in the far-off years which still live in us, and transform our perception into love.

1860

Discussion

1. In what ways does Eliot use the first scene, the conversation between Riley and Tulliver and Maggie's intrusion, to illustrate how education can serve to perpetuate injustice?

2. What does the fetish doll hidden in the attic tell us about Maggie?

3. Mr. Tulliver and Luke don't speak in polished English. Why do you think the novel so carefully records their speech? What effect does it have?

4. The narrator tells us that "Maggie and Tom were still very much like young animals." What does she mean by this? What animals do you find associated with Tom and Maggie?

5. How does the selection illustrate the narrator's conclusion: "We could never have loved the earth so well if we had had no childhood in it"?

Vocabulary
Antonyms, Synonyms

Determine whether the italicized words in each numbered item below are synonyms or antonyms. Then select, from the pairs of words that follow, the words that are related in the same way as the words in the first pair. Write your choice on a separate sheet of paper. There is a word in each italicized pair that you will probably have to check in the Glossary.

1. *oracular : wise* as **(a)** faultfinding : tolerant; **(b)** hidden : concealed; **(c)** dislike : like.

2. *petrifying : melting* as **(a)** usual : extraordinary; **(b)** humor : wit; **(c)** teasing : joking.

3. *vindictive : kind* as **(a)** shorten : lengthen; **(b)** comfort : relief; **(c)** misfortune : distress.

4. *poultice : bandage* as **(a)** unpleasant : pleasant; **(b)** appeal : request; **(c)** rudeness : politeness.

5. *peremptory : decisive* as **(a)** noise : calm; **(b)** energetic : inactive; **(c)** tired : careworn.

Composition

The narrator of *The Mill on the Floss* steps back occasionally from her story to make general statements about human experience. Skim through the selection noting some of these general statements and choose one.

In an essay explain first what the narrator has to say about the topic, and then go on to express your own ideas about what she says.

John Ruskin 1819–1900

Self-portrait by John Ruskin, 1874.

There appeared in the middle of the nineteenth century a series of outstanding prose writers. Macaulay's history, Newman's writings on religion, the essays of Matthew Arnold, Charles Dickens, and George Eliot are examples that give only a glimpse of the range and significance of Victorian prose. Perhaps the most unusual member of this group is John Ruskin. Ruskin's mind, ambitious and restless, saw the interconnectedness of things, and this resulted in his greatest triumphs as a writer as well as his later tragedy as a public figure.

Ruskin started out as an art critic. *Modern Painters,* which appeared in five volumes between 1843 and 1860, was to be a defense of the English painter Turner but also became, as Ruskin's ideas evolved, a study of the beauty of natural forms and, finally, of the interrelationship between art and life. While working on *Modern Painters,* Ruskin turned to a collateral topic, writing on architecture. *The Stones of Venice* (1851–1853) represents a turning point in his thought; he argues that what people make and how they work arise directly out of the moral character of their society. He draws a significant contrast between the life-enhancing work of the medieval craftsman and the life-destroying labor of the modern factory "hand."

While these ideas stimulated young and discontented thinkers, most Victorians simply ignored such concepts, preferring to revel in Ruskin's vivid descriptions of old Venetian buildings. But Ruskin himself was changing; he began to write books with an explicit social message. In 1860 Ruskin published his first consistent attack on industrial injustice—*Unto This Last.* Readers accustomed to Ruskin only as an art critic were furious with his social criticism: "a mad governess," one reader called him, writing a book of "windy hysterics."

Undismayed, Ruskin continued the battle and, in the 1860s and 1870s, continued publishing books and essays about nature, art, and social injustice. As the years passed, however, the indifference of his readers to the issues he saw in such a burning light, coupled with what had become a profoundly lonely and unhappy private life, brought on intermittent attacks of mental illness.

To turn his mind from the topics that stirred his indignation and thus troubled his sanity, Ruskin began in 1885 to write an autobiography he called *Praeterita,* Latin for "the past." In this book he could return to the boyhood that remained luminous and alive in his memory.

His father, James Ruskin, had been a wealthy importer of Spanish sherry. His mother spent her girlhood in an evangelical school. This training led her to dedicate her only son to God; she planned that he would become a clergyman. In his youth she denied him most of the ordinary pleasures of childhood while thoroughly training him in the study of the Bible. Under the shadow of oncoming madness, Ruskin's last book recalls, with visionary clarity, this lost world of childhood.

from Praeterita

My mother's general principles of first treatment were, to guard me with steady watchfulness from all avoidable pain or danger; and, for the rest, to let me amuse myself as I liked, provided I was neither fretful nor troublesome. But the law was, that I should find my own amusement. No toys of any kind were at first allowed;—and the pity of my Croydon aunt for my monastic poverty in this respect was boundless. On one of my birthdays, thinking to overcome my mother's resolution by splendor of temptation, she bought the most radiant Punch and Judy she could find in all the Soho bazaar—as big as a real Punch and Judy, all dressed in scarlet and gold, and that would dance, tied to the leg of a chair. I must have been greatly impressed, for I remember well the look of the two figures, as my aunt herself exhibited their virtues. My mother was obliged to accept them; but afterwards quietly told me it was not right that I should have them; and I never saw them again.

Nor did I painfully wish, what I was never permitted for an instant to hope, or even imagine, the possession of such things as one saw in toy-shops. I had a bunch of keys to play with, as long as I was capable only of pleasure in what glittered and jingled; as I grew older, I had a cart, and a ball; and when I was five or six years old, two boxes of well-cut wooden bricks. With these modest, but, I still think, entirely sufficient possessions, and being always summarily whipped if I cried, did not do as I was bid, or tumbled on the stairs, I soon attained serene and secure methods of life and motion; and could pass my days contentedly in tracing the squares and comparing the colors of my carpet;—examining the knots in the wood of the floor, or counting the bricks in the opposite houses; with rapturous intervals of excitement during the filling of the water-cart, through its leathern pipe, from the dripping iron post at the pavement edge; or the still more admirable proceedings of the turncock, when he turned and turned till a fountain sprang up in the middle of the street. But the carpet, and what patterns I could find in bed covers, dresses, or wallpapers to be examined, were my chief resources, and my attention to the particulars in these was soon so accurate, that when at three and a half I was taken to have my portrait painted by Mr. Northcote, I had not been ten minutes alone with him before I asked him why there were holes in his carpet. . . .

I think it should be related also that having, as aforesaid, been steadily whipped if I was troublesome, my formed habit of serenity was greatly pleasing to the old painter; for I sat contentedly motionless, counting the holes in his carpet, or watching him squeeze his paint out of its bladders,—a beautiful operation, indeed, to my thinking;—but I do not remember taking any interest in Mr. Northcote's application of the pigments to the canvas; my ideas of delightful art, in that respect, involving indispensably the possession of a large pot, filled with paint of the brightest green, and of a brush which would come out of it soppy. But my quietude was so pleasing to the old man that he begged my father and mother to let me sit to him for the face of a child which he was painting in a classical subject; where I was accordingly represented as reclining on a leopard skin, and having a thorn taken out of my foot by a wild man of the woods. . . .

We seldom had company, even on week days; and I was never allowed to come down to dessert, until much later in life—when I was able to crack nuts neatly. I was then permitted to come down to crack other people's nuts for them—(I hope they liked the ministration)—but never to have any myself; nor anything else of dainty kind, either then or at other times. Once at Hunter Street, I recollect my mother giving me three raisins, in the forenoon, out of the store cabinet; and I remember perfectly the first time I tasted custard, in our lodgings in Norfolk Street—where we had gone while the house was being painted, or cleaned, or something. My father was dining in the front room, and did not finish his custard; and my mother brought me the bottom of it into the back room. . . .

When Ruskin was four, his father and mother moved to Herne Hill. To the little boy what mattered most about the new house was its large back garden, with flowering fruit trees.

The differences of primal importance which I observed between the nature of this garden, and that of Eden, as I had imagined it, were, that, in this one, *all* the fruit was forbidden; and there were no companionable beasts: in other respects the little domain answered every purpose of Paradise to me; and the climate, in that cycle of our years, allowed me to pass most of my life in it. My mother never gave me more to learn than she knew I could easily get learnt, if I set myself honestly to work, by twelve o'clock. She never allowed anything to disturb me when my task was set; if it was not said rightly by twelve o'clock, I was kept in till I knew it, and in general, even when Latin Grammar came to supplement the Psalms. I was my own master for at least an hour before half-past one dinner, and for the rest of the afternoon.

My mother, herself finding her chief personal pleasure in her flowers, was often planting or pruning beside me, at least if I chose to stay beside *her*. I never thought of doing anything behind her back which I would not have done before her face; and her presence was therefore no restraint to me; but, also, no particular pleasure, for, from having always been left so much alone, I had generally my own little affairs to see after; and, on the whole, by the time I was seven years old, was already getting too independent, mentally, even of my father and mother; and, having nobody else to be dependent upon, began to lead a very small, perky, contented, conceited, Cock-Robinson-Crusoe sort of life, in the central point which it appeared to me, (as it must naturally appear to geometrical animals,) that I occupied in the universe.

This was partly the fault of my father's modesty; and partly of his pride. He had so much more confidence in my mother's judgment as to such matters than in his own, that he never ven-

Trees and Pond, attributed to John Ruskin, 1831 or 1832. This painting is in the style of Ruskin's first instructor, Charles Runciman.

tured even to help, much less to cross her, in the conduct of my education; on the other hand, in the fixed purpose of making an ecclesiastical gentleman of me, with the superfinest of manners, and access to the highest circles of fleshly and spiritual society, the visits to Croydon, where I entirely loved my aunt, and young baker-cousins, became rarer and more rare: the society of our neighbors on the hill could not be had without breaking up our regular and sweetly selfish manner of living; and on the whole, I had nothing animate to care for, in a childish way, but myself, some nests of ants, which the gardener would never leave undisturbed for me, and a sociable bird or two; though I never had the sense or perseverance to make one really tame. But that was partly because, if ever I managed to bring one to be the least trustful of me, the cats got it.

Under these circumstances, what powers of imagination I possessed, either fastened themselves on inanimate things—the sky, the leaves, and pebbles, observable within the walls of Eden,—or caught at any opportunity of flight into regions of romance, compatible with the objective realities of existence in the nineteenth century, within a mile and a quarter of Camberwell Green.

Herein my father, happily, though with no definite intention other than of pleasing me, when he found he could do so without infringing any of my mother's rules, became my guide. I was particularly fond of watching him shave; and was always allowed to come into his room in the morning (under the one in which I am now writing), to be the motionless witness of that operation. Over his dressing table hung one of his own watercolor drawings. . . .

When my father had finished shaving, he always told me a story about this picture. The custom began without any initial purpose of his, in consequence of my troublesome curiosity whether the fisherman lived in the cottage, and where he was going to in the boat. It being settled, for peace' sake, that he *did* live in the cottage, and was going in the boat to fish near the castle, the plot of the drama afterwards gradually thickened; and became, I believe, involved with that of the tragedy of *Douglas*, and of the *Castle Spectre*, in both of which pieces my father had performed in private theatricals, before my mother, and a select Edinburgh audience, when he was a boy of sixteen, and she, at grave twenty, a model housekeeper, and very scornful and religiously suspicious of theatricals. But she was never weary of telling me, in later years, how beautiful my father looked in his Highland dress, with the high black feathers.

In the afternoons, when my father returned (always punctually) from his business, he dined, at half-past four, in the front parlor, my mother sitting beside him to hear the events of the day, and give counsel and encouragement with respect to the same;—chiefly the last, for my father was apt to be vexed if orders for sherry fell the least short of their due standard, even for a day or two. I was never present at this time, however, and only avouch what I relate by hearsay and probable conjecture; for between four and six it would have been a grave misdemeanor in me if I so much as approached the parlor door.

After that, in summer time, we were all in the garden as long as the day lasted; tea under the white-heart cherry tree; or in winter and rough weather, at six o'clock in the drawing room,—I having my cup of milk, and slice of bread-and-butter, in a little recess, with a table in front of it, wholly sacred to me; and in which I remained in the evenings as an Idol in a niche, while my mother knitted, and my father read to her,—and to me, so far as I chose to listen. . . .

Such being the salutary pleasures of Herne Hill, I have next with deeper gratitude to chronicle what I owe to my mother for the resolutely consistent lessons which so exercised me in the Scriptures as to make every word of them familiar to my ear in habitual music,—yet in that familiarity reverenced, as transcending all thought, and ordaining all conduct.

This she effected, not by her own sayings or personal authority; but simply by compelling me to read the book thoroughly, for myself. As soon as I was able to read with fluency, she began a course of Bible work with me, which never ceased till I went to Oxford. She read alternate verses with me, watching, at first, every intonation of my voice, and correcting the false ones, till she made me understand the verse, if within my reach, rightly, and energetically. It might be beyond me altogether; that she did not care about; but she made sure that as soon as I got hold of it at all, I should get hold of it by the right end.

In this way she began with the first verse of Genesis, and went straight through, to the last verse of the Apocalypse; hard names, numbers, Levitical law, and all; and began again at Genesis the next day. If a name was hard, the better the exercise in pronunciation,—if a chapter was tiresome, the better lesson in patience,—if loathsome, the better lesson in faith that there was some use in its being so outspoken. After our chapters, (from two to three a day, according to their length, the first thing after breakfast, and no interruption from servants allowed,—none from visitors, who either joined in the reading or had to stay upstairs,—and none from any visitings or excursions, except real travelling,) I had to learn a few verses by heart, or repeat, to make sure I had not lost, something of what was already known; and, with the chapters thus gradually possessed from the first word to the last, I had to learn the whole body of the fine old Scottish paraphrases,[1] which are good, melodious, and forceful verse; and to which, together with the Bible itself, I owe the first cultivation of my ear in sound. . . .

But it is only by deliberate effort that I recall the long morning hours of toil, as regular as sunrise,—toil on both sides equal—by which, year after year, my mother forced me to learn these paraphrases, and chapters, (the eighth of 1st Kings being one—try it, good reader, in a leisure hour!) allowing not so much as a syllable to be missed or misplaced; while every sentence was required to be said over and over again till she was satisfied with the accent of it. I recollect a struggle between us of about three weeks, concerning the accent of the ''of'' in the lines

> ''Shall any following spring revive
> The ashes of the urn?''—

I insisting, partly in childish obstinacy, and partly in true instinct for rhythm, (being wholly careless on the subject both of urns and their contents,) on reciting it with an accent *of*. It was not, I say, till after three weeks' labor, that my mother got the accent lightened on the ''of'' and laid on the ashes, to her mind. But had it taken three years she would have done it, having once undertaken to do it. And, assuredly, had she not done it,—well, there's no knowing what would have happened; but I'm very thankful she *did*. . . .

And truly, though I have picked up the elements of a little further knowledge—in mathematics, meteorology, and the like, in after life,—and owe not a little to the teaching of many people, this maternal installation of my mind in that property of chapters[2] I count very confidently the most precious, and, on the whole, the one *essential* part of all my education.

And it is perhaps already time to mark what advantage and mischief, by the chances of life up to seven years old, had been irrevocably determined for me.

I will first count my blessings (as a not unwise friend once recommended me to do, continually; whereas I have a bad trick of always numbering the thorns in my fingers and not the bones in them).

And for best and truest beginning of all blessings, I had been taught the perfect meaning of Peace, in thought, act, and word.

I never had heard my father's or mother's voice once raised in any question with each other; nor seen an angry, or even slightly hurt or offended, glance in the eyes of either. I had never heard a servant scolded; nor even suddenly, passionately, or in any severe manner, blamed. I had never seen a moment's trouble or disorder in any household matter; nor anything whatever either done in a hurry, or undone in due time. I had no conception of such a feeling as anxiety; my father's occasional vexation in the afternoon, when he had only got an order for twelve butts[3] after expecting one for fifteen, as I have just stated, was never manifested to *me;* and itself related only to the question whether his name would be a step higher or lower in the year's list of sherry exporters; for he never spent more than half his income, and therefore found himself little incommoded by occasional variations in the total of it. I had never done any wrong that I knew of—beyond occasionally delaying the commitment to heart of some improving sentence, that I might watch a wasp on the window pane, or a bird in the cherry tree; and I had never seen any grief.

Next to this quite priceless gift of Peace, I had received the perfect understanding of the natures of Obedience and Faith. I obeyed word, or lifted finger, of father or mother, simply as a ship her helm; not only without idea of resistance, but receiving the direction as a part of my own life and force, and helpful law, as necessary to me in every moral action as the law of gravity in leaping. And my practice in Faith was soon complete: nothing was ever promised me that was not given; nothing ever threatened me that was not inflicted, and nothing ever told me that was not true. . . .

Lastly, an extreme perfection in palate and all other bodily senses, given by the utter prohibition of cake, wine, comfits, or, except in carefullest restriction, fruit; and by fine preparation of what food was given me. Such I esteem the main

---

1. **Scottish paraphrases,** verse translations from the Bible.
2. **chapters,** memorized from the Bible.
3. **butts,** barrels (of sherry).

blessings of my childhood;—next, let me count the equally dominant calamities.

First, that I had nothing to love.

My parents were—in a sort—visible powers of nature to me, no more loved than the sun and the moon: only I should have been annoyed and puzzled if either of them had gone out; (how much, now, when both are darkened!)—still less did I love God; not that I had any quarrel with Him, or fear of Him; but simply found what people told me was His service, disagreeable; and what people told me was His book, not entertaining. I had no companions to quarrel with, neither; nobody to assist, and nobody to thank. Not a servant was ever allowed to do anything for me, but what it was their duty to do; and why should I have been grateful to the cook for cooking, or the gardener for gardening,—when the one dared not give me a baked potato without asking leave, and the other would not let my ants' nests alone, because they made the walks untidy? The evil consequence of all this was not, however, what might perhaps have been expected, that I grew up selfish or unaffectionate; but that, when affection did come, it came with violence utterly rampant and unmanageable, at least by me, who never before had anything to manage.

For (second of chief calamities) I had nothing to endure. Danger or pain of any kind I knew not: my strength was never exercised, my patience never tried, and my courage never fortified. Not that I was ever afraid of anything,—either ghosts, thunder, or beasts; and one of the nearest approaches to insubordination which I was ever tempted into as a child, was in passionate effort to get leave to play with the lion's cubs in Wombwell's menagerie.

Thirdly. I was taught no precision nor etiquette of manners; it was enough if, in the little society we saw, I remained unobtrusive, and replied to a question without shyness: but the shyness came later, and increased as I grew conscious of the rudeness arising from the want of social discipline, and found it impossible to acquire, in advanced life, dexterity in any bodily exercise, skill in any pleasing accomplishment, or ease and tact in ordinary behavior.

Lastly, and chief of evils. My judgment of right and wrong, and powers of independent action, were left entirely undeveloped; because the bridle and blinkers were never taken off me. Children should have their times of being off duty, like soldiers; and when once the obedience, if required, is certain, the little creature should be very early put for periods of practice in complete command of itself; set on the barebacked horse of its own will, and left to break it by its own strength. But the ceaseless authority exercised over my youth left me, when cast out at last into the world, unable for some time to do more than drift with its vortices.

My present verdict, therefore, on the general tenor of my education at that time, must be, that it was at once too formal and too luxurious; leaving my character, at the most important moment for its construction, cramped indeed, but not disciplined; and only by protection innocent, instead of by practice virtuous. My mother saw this herself, and but too clearly, in later years; and whenever I did anything wrong, stupid, or hard-hearted,—(and I have done many things that were all three,)—always said, "It is because you were too much indulged."

1885

Discussion

1. How did the restrictions in Ruskin's early childhood train him in a particular way of looking at things? What are the advantages and disadvantages of this way of seeing?

2. If the garden at Herne Hill was, as Ruskin calls it, a sort of "Eden," what were its pleasures and its limits?

3. How did Ruskin's early study of the Bible help him later as a writer?

4. Ruskin tells us that his childhood gave him three blessings. Examine the way he describes each, and consider whether, at the same time, he implies that these were at best qualified blessings.

The Changing English Language

Polite English of the Victorian period—especially the early years—was extremely formal. Men addressed their wives as "Mrs." and husbands were treated with equal courtesy. The utmost formality was extended to strangers, thereby implying they were solemn and important people. There were certain classes of people—the ambitious businessman, the newly rich, the aspiring student—who carried this formality to absurd lengths. They spoke an exaggerated English of their own called *genteelism.*

The first and most important rule of genteelism was to avoid the common word and use instead a learned, bookish synonym. The advocates of genteelism did not help themselves to a piece of bread with jam—they assisted themselves to a portion of bread with preserves; they did not begin a meal—they commenced a collation; they did not use a toothpowder—they employed a dentrifice; they did not shut the door to a room—they closed the portal to an accommodation; and they never used *before, except,* or *about*—it was *ere, save,* and *anent.*

The rapid advance of invention and mechanization all during the Victorian Age created a need for many new words. Grammarians protested the forming of such words as *telegraph and typewriter* by scientists, inventors, and manufacturers, and felt that the making of words should be left to the etymologists.

As American English grew in the nineteenth century, it often used different words from British English to denote the same thing. Compare the following words pertaining to the railroad industry—the first of each pair is American, the second is British: *railroad—railway; conductor—guard; fireman—stoker; car—carriage; track—line; freight—goods; trunk—box;* and *check—register.* Britishers were *ill, clever,* and *homely;* Americans were *sick, smart,* and *friendly.*

As the language grew, when words were needed they were used with little regard for "correctness" in spite of the snobbery of genteelism and the protests of grammarians.

Title page of *All the Year Round,* a periodical founded and edited by Charles Dickens.

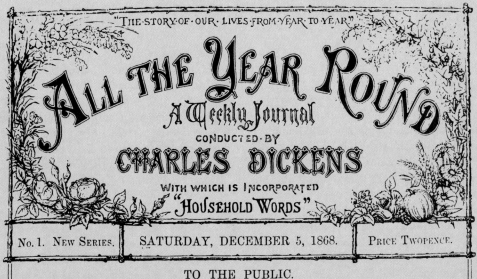

"THE·STORY·OF·OUR·LIVES·FROM·YEAR·TO·YEAR"

ALL THE YEAR ROUND

A Weekly Journal

CONDUCTED·BY

CHARLES DICKENS

WITH WHICH IS INCORPORATED

"HOUSEHOLD WORDS"

| No. 1. New Series. | SATURDAY, DECEMBER 5, 1868. | Price Twopence. |

TO THE PUBLIC.

A very unjustifiable paragraph has appeared in some newspapers, to the effect that I have relinquished the Editorship of this Publication. It is not only unjustifiable because it is wholly untrue, but because it must be either wilfully or negligently untrue, if any respect be due to the explicit terms of my repeatedly-published announcement of the present New Series under my own hand.

CHARLES DICKENS.

Content Review

1. What makes the Lady of Shalott (Tennyson) and the Duke's last Duchess (Browning) so vulnerable?

2. Compare how Tennyson's "Ring out, wild bells" (*In Memoriam,* lyric 106) and Browning's "Prospice" view death.

3. Define a dramatic monologue.

4. Describe the various reasons for living provided in Tennyson's "Ulysses," Arnold's "Dover Beach," and Elizabeth Barrett Browning's sonnet 43 from *Sonnets from the Portuguese.*

5. Define the significance of the journeys in "Ulysses" and "Self-Dependence."

6. How does the sea function as a **symbol** in Arnold's "Dover Beach"?

7. How do Maggie Tulliver and David Copperfield express their feelings of rebellion?

8. Analyze the motives for cruelty in Dickens's Mr. Murdstone.

Concept Review: Interpretation of New Material

John Stuart Mill's father, James Mill, sensed the precocious brilliance in his son and directed his unusual education. John Stuart Mill (1806-1873) fulfilled his father's expectations. He wrote a series of highly respected books on logic (1843), economics (1848), the concept of liberty (1859), and the rights of women (1869). At his death he left a manuscript of the *Autobiography.*

from The Autobiography of John Stuart Mill · *John Stuart Mill*

I have no remembrance of the time when I began to learn Greek. I have been told that it was when I was three years old. My earliest recollection on the subject, is that of committing to memory what my father termed Vocables, being lists of common Greek words, with their signification in English, which he wrote out for me on cards. Of grammar, until some years later, I learnt no more than the inflections of the nouns and verbs, but, after a course of vocables, proceeded at once to translation; and I faintly remember going through *Aesop's Fables,* the first Greek book which I read. The *Anabasis,*[1] which I remember better, was the second. I learnt no Latin until my eighth year. At that time I had read, under my father's tuition, a number of Greek prose authors. . . . But my father, in all his teaching, demanded of me not only the utmost that I could do, but much that I could by no possibility have done. What he was himself willing to undergo for the sake of my instruction, may be judged from the fact, that I went through the whole process of preparing my Greek lessons in the same room and at the same table at which he was writing: and as in those days Greek and English lexicons were not, and I could make no more use of a Greek and Latin lexicon than could be made without having yet begun to learn Latin, I was forced to have recourse to him for the meaning of every word which I did not know. This incessant interruption, he, one of the most impatient of men, submitted to, and wrote under that interruption several volumes of his History and all else that he had to write during those years.

The only thing besides Greek, that I learnt as a

---

1. **Anabasis,** a history written by Xenophon (zen′ə fən), Greek writer and military leader, which tells of a Greek army in Asia that fought its way home through enemy territory.

lesson in this part of my childhood, was arithmetic: this also my father taught me: it was the task of the evenings, and I well remember its disagreeableness. But the lessons were only a part of the daily instruction I received. Much of it consisted in the books I read by myself, and my father's discourses to me, chiefly during our walks. From 1810 to the end of 1813 we were living in Newington Green, then an almost rustic neighborhood. My father's health required considerable and constant exercise, and he walked habitually before breakfast, generally in the green lanes towards Hornsey. In these walks I always accompanied him, and with my earliest recollections of green fields and wild flowers, is mingled that of the account I gave him daily of what I had read the day before. To the best of my remembrance, this was a voluntary rather than a prescribed exercise. I made notes on slips of paper while reading, and from these, in the morning walks, I told the story to him; for the books were chiefly histories, of which I read in this manner a great number. . . . Of children's books, any more than of playthings, I had scarcely any, except an occasional gift from a relation or acquaintance: among those I had, *Robinson Crusoe* was preeminent, and continued to delight me through all my boyhood. It was no part however of my father's system to exclude books of amusement, though he allowed them very sparingly. Of such books he possessed at that time next to none, but he borrowed several for me; those which I remember are the *Arabian Nights,* Cazotte's *Arabian Tales, Don Quixote,* Miss Edgeworth's *Popular Tales,* and a book of some reputation in its day, Brooke's *Fool of Quality.*

In my eighth year I commenced learning Latin, in conjunction with a younger sister, to whom I taught it as I went on, and who afterwards repeated the lessons to my father: and from this time, other sisters and brothers being successively added as pupils, a considerable part of my day's work consisted of this preparatory teaching. It was a part which I greatly disliked; the more so, as I was held responsible for the lessons of my pupils, in almost as full a sense as for my own: I however derived from this discipline the great advantage of learning more thoroughly and retaining more lastingly the things which I was set to teach: perhaps, too, the practice it afforded in ex-

plaining difficulties to others, may even at that age have been useful. . . .

A voluntary exercise, to which throughout my boyhood I was much addicted, was what I called writing histories. I successively composed a Roman history, picked out of Hooke; an abridgement of the *Ancient Universal History;* a History of Holland, from my favorite Watson and from an anonymous compilation; and in my eleventh and twelfth year I occupied myself with writing what I flattered myself was something serious. This was no less than a history of the Roman Government, compiled (with the assistance of Hooke) from Livy and Dionysius:[2] of which I wrote as much as would have made an octavo volume. . . .

During this part of my childhood, one of my greatest amusements was experimental science; in the theoretical, however, not the practical sense of the word; not trying experiments—a kind of discipline which I have often regretted not having had—nor even seeing, but merely reading about them. I never remember being so wrapt up in any book, as I was in Joyce's *Scientific Dialogues;* and I was rather recalcitrant to my father's criticisms of the bad reasoning respecting the first principles of physics, which abounds in the early part of that work. I devoured treatises on Chemistry, especially that of my father's early friend and schoolfellow, Dr. Thomson, for years before I attended a lecture or saw an experiment.

From about the age of twelve, I entered into another and more advanced stage in my course of instruction; in which the main object was no longer the aids and appliances of thought, but the thoughts themselves. This commenced with Logic. . . . I know nothing in my education, to which I think myself more indebted for whatever capacity of thinking I have attained. The first intellectual operation in which I arrived at any proficiency, was dissecting a bad argument, and finding in what part the fallacy lay: and though whatever capacity of this sort I attained was due to the fact that it was an intellectual exercise in which I was most perseveringly drilled by my father, yet it is also true that the school logic, and the mental habits acquired in studying it, were among the principal instruments of this drilling. I am persuaded that nothing, in modern education, tends

---

2. *Livy and Dionysius,* historians of ancient Rome.

so much, when properly used, to form exact thinkers, who attach a precise meaning to words and propositions, and are not imposed on by vague, loose, or ambiguous terms. . . .

In the course of instruction which I have partially retraced, the point most superficially apparent is the great effort to give, during the years of childhood an amount of knowledge in what are considered the higher branches of education, which is seldom acquired (if acquired at all) until the age of manhood. The result of the experiment shows the ease with which this may be done, and places in a strong light the wretched waste of so many precious years as are spent in acquiring the modicum of Latin and Greek commonly taught to schoolboys; a waste, which has led so many educational reformers to entertain the ill-judged proposal of discarding these languages altogether from general education. If I had been by nature extremely quick of apprehension, or had possessed a very accurate and retentive memory, or were of a remarkably active and energetic character, the trial would not be conclusive; but in all these natural gifts I am rather below than above par; what I could do, could assuredly be done by any boy or girl of average capacity and healthy physical constitution: and if I have accomplished anything, I owe it, among other fortunate circumstances, to the fact that through the early training bestowed on me by my father, I started, I may fairly say, with an advantage of a quarter of a century over my contemporaries.

There was one cardinal point in this training, of which I have already given some indication, and which, more than anything else, was the cause of whatever good it effected. Most boys or youths who have had much knowledge drilled into them, have their mental capacities not strengthened, but overlaid by it. They are crammed with mere facts, and with the opinions or phrases of other people, and these are accepted as a substitute for the power to form opinions of their own: and thus the sons of eminent fathers, who have spared no pains in their education, so often grow up mere parroters of what they have learnt, incapable of using their minds except in the furrows traced for them. Mine, however, was not an education of cram. My father never permitted anything which I learnt to degenerate into a mere exercise of memory. He strove to make the

understanding not only go along with every step of the teaching, but, if possible, precede it. Anything which could be found out by thinking I never was told, until I had exhausted my efforts to find it out for myself. . . . A pupil from whom nothing is ever demanded which he cannot do, never does all he can.

One of the evils most liable to attend on any sort of early proficiency, and which often fatally blights its promise, my father most anxiously guarded against. This was self-conceit. He kept me, with extreme vigilance, out of the way of hearing myself praised, or of being led to make self-flattering comparisons between myself and others. From his own [dealings] with me I could derive none but a very humble opinion of myself; and the standard of comparison he always held up to me, was not what other people did, but what a man could and ought to do. He completely succeeded in preserving me from the sort of influences he so much dreaded. I was not at all aware that my attainments were anything unusual at my age. If I accidentally had my attention drawn to the fact that some other boy knew less than myself—which happened less often than might be imagined—I concluded, not that I knew much, but that he, for some reason or other, knew little, or that his knowledge was of a different kind from mine. . . .

It is evident that this, among many other of the purposes of my father's scheme of education, could not have been accomplished if he had not carefully kept me from having any great amount of [contact] with other boys. He was earnestly bent upon my escaping not only the ordinary corrupting influence which boys exercise over boys, but the contagion of vulgar modes of thought and feeling; and for this he was willing that I should pay the price of inferiority in the accomplishments which schoolboys in all countries chiefly cultivate. The deficiencies in my education were principally in the things which boys learn from being turned out to shift for themselves, and from being brought together in large numbers. From temperance and much walking, I grew up healthy and hardy, though not muscular; but I could do no feats of skill or physical strength, and knew none of the ordinary bodily exercises. It was not that play, or time for it, was refused me. Though no holidays were allowed, lest the habit of work should be broken, and a taste for idleness acquired, I had ample leisure in every day to amuse myself; but as I had no boy companions, and the animal need of physical activity was satisfied by walking, my amusements, which were mostly solitary, were in general of a quiet, if not a bookish turn, and gave little stimulus to any other kind even of mental activity than that which was already called forth by my studies: I consequently remained long, and in a less degree have always remained, inexpert in anything requiring manual dexterity; my mind as well as my hands, did its work very lamely when it was applied, or ought to have been applied, to the practical details which, as they are the chief interest of life to the majority of men, are also the things in which whatever mental capacity they have, chiefly shows itself: I was constantly meriting reproof by inattention, inobservance, and general slackness of mind in matters of daily life. My father was the extreme opposite in these particulars: his senses and mental faculties were always on the alert; he carried decision and energy of character in his whole manner and into every action of life: and this, as much as his talents, contributed to the strong impression which he always made upon those with whom he came into personal contact. But the children of energetic parents, frequently grow up unenergetic, because they lean on their parents, and the parents are energetic for them. The education which my father gave me, was in itself much more fitted for training me to *know* than to *do*.

1873

Write your answers to the following questions on a separate sheet of paper. Do not write in your book.

1. What special burdens did John Stuart Mill's father have in teaching his son Greek?

2. In his memory, what does Mill associate with his first experience of nature?

3. How did Mill acquire a book like the *Arabian Nights?*

4. Explain the "advantage" Mill enjoyed in teaching his brothers and sisters Latin.

5. At what age did Mill write "something serious" in history?

6. Why was Mill's education in science incomplete?

7. What aspect of his education trained Mill to think exactly, and to use words precisely?

8. Compare and contrast Mill's account of his education with Ruskin's account in *Praeterita* and Dickens's account in *David Copperfield.*

9. How did Mill's father save him from conceit?

10. Why was Mill incapable of "feats of skill or physical strength"?

Composition Review

You may choose any *one* of the following assignments. Assume that you are writing for your classmates.

1. Review the lyrics from *In Memoriam,* listing their references to recent scientific discoveries. In each case, note the implications the speaker finds in them.

Then write an essay that explains why science so troubles the speaker of *In Memoriam.*

2. In "The Passing of Arthur" and "My Last Duchess," both Tennyson's King and Browning's Duke address inferiors. Locate the passages in which each endeavors to exert his will over someone else, and note how he does it.

In an essay, compare and contrast the quality of their command and authority.

3. Compare the solitary childhood of David Copperfield to Maggie Tulliver's emotional intimacy with her brother Tom.

In an essay, explain which state is preferable, in your judgment.

4. To explain how Victorian parents could use education to control children, begin by selecting what you consider to be three important examples from this unit. Define for yourself the parent's goal by examining how the education was conducted in each example.

Then in an essay describe how Victorian literature attacked such efforts to use the training of children to dominate or exploit them.

Piccadilly Circus by Charles Ginner, painted in 1912.

Fabian Society founded •

First volume of the •
Oxford English Dictionary

• Hardy:
The Mayor of Casterbridge

Kipling: *Plain Tales* •
from the Hills

Hardy: *Wessex Tales* •

Death of Hopkins •

• Frazer: *The Golden Bough*

• Shaw: *The Quintessence
of Ibsenism*

• Hardy: *Tess of the D'Urbervilles*

• Yeats: *The Countess
Cathleen*

• Kipling: *Barrack-Room
Ballads*

Hardy: *Jude the Obscure* •

Kipling: *The Jungle Book* •

• Wells: *The
Time Machine*

• Wilde: *The
Importance of
Being Earnest*

Queen Victoria's •
Diamond Jubilee

• Housman: *A
Shropshire*

1880   1885   1890   1895

New Directions

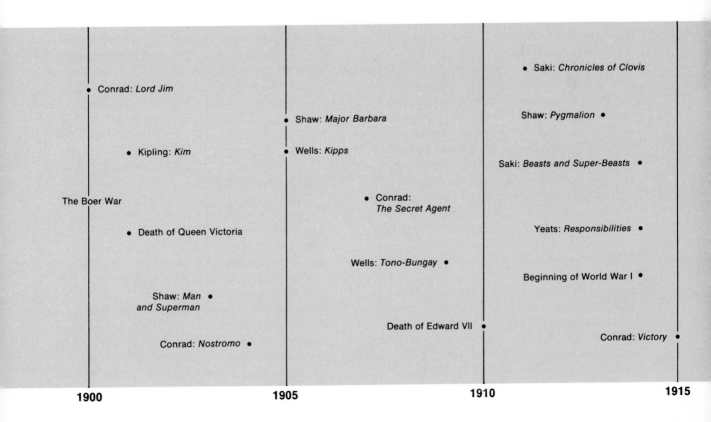

- Conrad: *Lord Jim*
- Kipling: *Kim*

The Boer War

- Death of Queen Victoria

Shaw: *Man and Superman* •

- Conrad: *Nostromo* •

- Shaw: *Major Barbara*
- Wells: *Kipps*

- Conrad: *The Secret Agent*

Wells: *Tono-Bungay* •

Death of Edward VII •

- Saki: *Chronicles of Clovis*

Shaw: *Pygmalion* •

Saki: *Beasts and Super-Beasts* •

Yeats: *Responsibilities* •

Beginning of World War I •

Conrad: *Victory* •

1900   1905   1910   1915

Background: New Directions 1880–1915

By 1880 England had become the first modern industrial empire. Its large, urban manufacturing centers, with a highly disciplined work force using advanced machine methods, produced goods that went by rail and then by steamship to consumers all over the world, protected en route by the world's largest navy. British financial power and administrative leadership dominated not only the island nation and its colonial territories, but many other countries as well, so that the English could be found in positions of authority and influence in places as distant as China, Borneo, Morocco, and Argentina. Nevertheless, England's commercial success and position of world leadership were not unaccompanied with problems.

The most persistent and visible of these problems remained the condition of the English working class. As the poet Gerard Manley Hopkins wrote, "It is a dreadful thing for the greatest and most necessary part of a very rich nation to live a hard life without dignity, knowledge, comforts, delight, or hopes in the midst of plenty—which plenty they make." Most industrial laborers still worked a six-day week, dressed poorly, and lived in substandard housing. Few had any education; fewer still went to church, since they were disillusioned with organized religion. In the 1880s and 1890s some middle-class intellectuals became convinced that only radical solutions would remedy these problems, and important writers like William Morris and George Bernard Shaw committed themselves to socialism.

Such efforts to effect radical change were hampered in part by steadily improving economic conditions during this period. Thanks to falling prices, real wages rose as much as forty percent. At the same time the government was making efforts at moderate change. In 1884 a series of voting reforms opened the franchise to virtually every adult male, thus effectively creating popular democracy in England. The Education Act of 1891 established free schools for everyone up to the age of twelve.

These crucial developments in social justice at home came at a time of new challenge from abroad. Germany, fresh from its victory in the Franco-Prussian War (1870), and the United States, recovered from its own Civil War (1861–1865), now became serious threats to English predominance. The Royal Commission on Trade and Industry (1885–1886) noted, "We are beginning to feel the effects of foreign competition in quarters where our trade formerly enjoyed a virtual monopoly." A central problem was that the machinery of England's industrial base was aging, but no one seemed to want to go to the expense of having it modernized.

British Imperialism

British investment and energy were going elsewhere, into the expansion and defense of the Empire. Even into the 1870s most people had considered British colonies like India merely as economic burdens. But with the appearance of new commercial rivals, the notion of a worldwide confederation of nations under British control, and hence ready markets for British goods, now became popular. Sometimes through gunboat diplomacy, sometimes through negotiation and formal treaty, England expanded its Empire, gaining control over territories that are now Egypt (1882), Nigeria (1885), Kenya and Uganda (1888), Zimbabwe (1889), and Sudan (1898–1899).

Some of those promoting expansion perceived in the Empire a strain of high idealism. Lord Salisbury, a British prime minister in the 1880s and 1890s, argued that colonialism could be, for the newly adopted peoples, ''a great civilizing, Christianizing force.'' In a celebrated poem Rudyard Kipling instructed the English, ''Take up the White Man's burden— / The savage wars of peace— / Fill full the mouth of Famine / And bid the sickness cease . . .'' But in the same year (1899), Joseph Conrad described imperialist adventurers far differently in his novella *Heart of Darkness:* ''To tear treasure out of the bowels of the land was their desire, with no more moral purpose at the back of it than there is in burglars breaking into a safe.'' The debate over imperialism reached a crisis in England's war with the Dutch Boer settlers over South Africa (1899–1902), a war England won, but at the expense of bitter criticism at home and abroad.

Even more divisive was the problem of English control over Ireland. Legally, Ireland was a part of England and its representatives sat in Parliament. But the Roman Catholic Irish resented their Protestant English landlords and demanded home rule. This problem was not effectively solved until 1921, with the establishment of the Irish Free State, and throughout the period before World War I Ireland experienced recurrent political turmoil. This turmoil was accompanied by a remarkable cultural awakening in Ireland. As part of an effort to recover the native culture, there was an attempt to revive the Irish language. Folklorists collected poems and tales of Irish myth and legend that survived in medieval manuscripts or in oral form in remote peasant villages. Most importantly, a series of gifted writers endeavored to create a valid Irish literature, rooted in its people, their language and traditions, and separate from the English. The most important figure in this movement, the poet William Butler Yeats, helped found the Abbey Theatre in Dublin (1904), encouraging a new native drama on Irish themes and in Irish idiom.

An important characteristic of this revival, in its efforts to regain a specifically Irish spirit, was its rejection both of Protestant and Catholic Christianity, and its celebration of the pagan mythology of early Ireland. This effort to reach back to the cultural roots of a people and their primitive connection to the land was going on in England as well, most notably in the fiction of Thomas Hardy. His efforts to discover a more elemental human experience in the lives of rural people met frequent criticism. Hardy's disregard for middle-class moral values and what detractors called his ''pessimism'' offended many readers. Hardy's defiant response was to assert that ''the soul has her eternal rights . . . she will not be darkened by statutes, nor lullabied by the music of bells.'' He insisted that his so-called ''pessimism'' was actually only a part of ''the exploration of reality'' and a ''first step towards the soul's betterment.''

A New World View

Explorations such as Hardy's were in part the consequence of the ongoing problems posed by modern science. The ideas of Charles Darwin, championed by biologists like Thomas Henry Huxley (who coined the word *agnostic*), seemed to cut through old assumptions about human nature and destiny, leaving people uncertain about themselves and their future. H. G. Wells described this new dismay: ''Science is a match that man has just got alight. He thought he was in a room—in moments of devotion, a temple—and that his light would be reflected from and display walls inscribed with wonderful secrets. . . . It is a curious sensation, now that the preliminary splutter is over and the flame burns up clear, to see . . . in place of all that human comfort and beauty he anticipated—darkness still.'' (1891) This sense of darkness and loneliness, of a mysterious universe that seems without order or purpose, pervades the literature of the period.

This new world view had an immediate effect on how people viewed social and moral questions. The confusion in a character from Conrad's novel *The Secret Agent* (1907) is typical: ''He was incapable by now of judging what could be true, possible, or even probable in this astounding universe. He was terrified out of all capacity for belief or disbelief. . . .'' This grim vision reached a sort of climax in Shaw's play *Heartbreak House,* written just before the outbreak of war in 1914:

HECTOR. And this ship that we are all in? This soul's prison we call England?

CAPTAIN SHOTOVER. The captain is in his bunk, drinking bottled ditch-water; and the crew is gambling in the forecastle. She will strike and sink and split. Do you think the laws of God will be suspended in England's favor because you were born in it?

The literature from this era of challenge, anxiety, and doubt is singularly different from that of the high Victorian period. Though many members of the generation of Tennyson and Browning were still alive, younger writers largely rejected not only their affirmations, but also the way they wrote, seeking instead new forms for new perceptions.

One striking evidence of this is the sudden re-emergence of the theater into English literature. Since the days of the Puritans there had been strong opposition to any theatrical performances in English society, and this was abetted by the Licensing Act of 1737 that permitted only three London theaters to present serious drama. Although the Act was revoked in 1843, and the numbers of theaters grew, serious plays in English do not reappear until the 1880s and 1890s. When they do, it is partly under the influence of the controversial Norwegian playwright Henrik Ibsen. Ibsen's disciple George Bernard Shaw revolutionized British theater in the 1890s with a series of what he called "Plays Unpleasant," because in them "dramatic power is used to force the spectator to face unpleasant facts." Even the fairly lighthearted *Pygmalion* (1913) is also a serious exploration of the English class system.

Much of the important writing of this period first appeared in weekly magazines, and these periodicals had an important influence on the character of fiction at the end of the century. Novels in the mid-Victorian period had been long—traditionally 900 pages. This was too long for a magazine, and the novels of this period began to shrink in length. Magazines encouraged the development of the short story (a form the Americans had perfected in the 1840s but which the British had largely ignored until the 1880s) and also of the "tale" or novella, like Hardy's "The Withered Arm" and Conrad's "Youth," far too long to be a short story, yet still too brief to be a

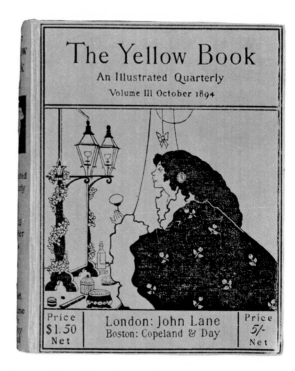

A copy of *The Yellow Book*, a famous literary periodical of the 1890s, with a cover designed by Aubrey Beardsley (1872–1898). Several of Beardsley's illustrations accompany *The Rape of the Lock* (pages 319–325).

novel. Magazines were aimed at a family readership and editors tried to maintain strict control over the content of the stories published, though writers like Hardy constantly fought against such restraints. Mid-Victorian fiction typically dealt with middle-class England, but the fiction at the century's close is more varied in its subjects. Hardy's peasant tragedies, Kipling's tales of India, Conrad's sea stories, and the scientific romances of H. G. Wells expanded fiction's reach.

Victorian writers generally, and the poets in particular, accepted the serious responsibility to speak out on the issues of the day, and endeavored to find solutions to the dilemmas of the era. This frequently led to long, complex poems in a wide variety of forms, like Tennyson's *In Memoriam*. Toward the end of the century most poets abandoned this responsibility. Hardy is typical in denying any philosophical importance for his poems. They are, he wrote, "merely what I have often explained to be only a confused heap of impressions. . . ." Consequently, it is the brief, emotionally charged lyric that dominates poetry before the First World War.

Edwardian England

Queen Victoria lived until January, 1901, in a realm radically different from the one she first knew and increasingly alien to what she most valued. Her son, nearly sixty years old when he was crowned Edward VII, reigned only nine years. Despite the brevity of the Edwardian period, it saw the development of a national conscience that expressed itself in important social legislation (including the first old-age pensions) that laid the groundwork for the English welfare state. The foremost architect of reform was the brilliant Welsh politician David Lloyd George. In a speech to the House of Commons in 1909 in defense of his budget funding these radical social programs, Lloyd George stated, "This is a war budget. It is for raising money to wage war against poverty and squalidness. I cannot help believing that before this generation has passed away, we shall have advanced a great step toward that good time when poverty, wretchedness, and the human degradation which always followed in its camp will be as remote to the people of this country as the wolves which once infested its forests."

It was also during this period that the women's suffrage movement entered a more radical phase, its supporters courting arrest and imprisonment in their struggle to win the right to vote. Militant suffragettes like Emmeline Pankhurst and her daughters Christabel and Sylvia represented a dramatic change in the public conception of a woman's role. It was a long way from the Victorian heroine who crocheted, played the piano, and swooned at the slightest provocation, to women like Lady Constance Lytton, who endured forcible feeding in prison, or Emily Wilding Davison, who was killed when she threw herself under the hooves of a horse owned by Edward's son and successor, George V, at the running of the Derby (England's most famous horse race) on June 4, 1913.

George had succeeded his father in May of 1910. Four years later, England became involved in World War I, in the words of historian Paul Johnson, "the greatest moral, spiritual, and physical catastrophe in the entire history of the English people—a catastrophe whose consequences, all wholly evil, are still with us." On the eve of the war, despite the buoyant confidence of many in England that the fighting would be over by Christmas, the British Foreign Secretary Sir Edward Grey observed with a grim foreboding, "The lamps are going out all over Europe; we shall not see them lit again in our lifetime."

Mrs. Emmeline Pankhurst (third from the left), leader of the women's suffrage movement, speaking against the government during an election campaign in the summer of 1907.

Thomas Hardy 1840–1928

Hardy was born in a thatched cottage in southern Dorsetshire, near the edge of the area he called "Egdon Heath." His father, a skilled stonemason, taught his son to play the violin and sent him to country day schools. At age 15 Hardy began to study architecture, and for the next six years he began the day, by his own account, "reading the *Iliad,* the *Aeneid,* or the Greek Testament from six to eight in the morning, would work at Gothic architecture all day, and then in the evening rush off with his fiddle under his arm . . . to play country dances. . . ."

In 1861 the twenty-one-year-old apprentice went to London to begin his career. It was a decade of intellectual ferment. Darwin's work had recently stirred troubling debates, and Browning's poetry seemed to be challenging the dominance of Tennyson's work. John Stuart Mill's *On Liberty* urged individualism of thought and decision.

Hardy seems to have willfully concealed the details of his life during these years, but it appears he fell violently and unhappily in love, perhaps several times, lost his belief in God, and found himself progressively more unsure about his own goals. He tried poetry, considered a career as an actor, and finally decided to write fiction.

In part, this was a practical decision. From the first Hardy aimed his fiction at serial publication in magazines, where it would most quickly pay the bills. However, at the same time, not forgetting an earlier dream, he resolved to keep his tales "as near to poetry in their subject as the conditions would allow." Evidently this meant for Hardy a fearless accuracy of depiction, no matter what the subject, coupled with vivid rendering. "My art," he said, "is to intensify the expression of things. . . ." The publisher Alexander Macmillan read the draft of his first novel and sent it back, saying it "meant mischief." The emotional power of Hardy's fiction disturbed readers from the start.

But he persevered, deciding "he was committed to novel-writing as a regular trade, as much as he had formerly been to architecture. . . ." After his first success, *Far from the Madding Crowd* (1874), came *The Return of the Native* (1878), *The Mayor of Casterbridge* (1885), and *Tess of the D'Urbervilles* (1891). Hardy wrote about the Dorset countryside he knew intimately, calling it *Wessex* (the name of the Anglo-Saxon kingdom once located there). He wrote about agrarian working-class people, milkmaids, stonecutters, and shepherds, as George Eliot had done, but not, as in her novels, from the distant perspective of the London intellectual. Hardy's rustics are not the object

The Withered Arm

A Lorn Milkmaid

It was an eighty-cow dairy, and the troop of milkers, regular and supernumerary, were all at work; for, though the time of year was as yet but early April, the feed lay entirely in water-mead-

of analysis or sentiment. Nor is his subject the middle-class race for success. Driven by instinctive emotions they do not fully recognize, his people act with a power that seems to place them outside conventional moral judgments. Trapped in a universe where the operations of a seemingly malign fate drive them toward tragic ends, they find no help in the conventional theological assumptions of the day. Hardy's rejection of middle-class moral values disturbed and finally shocked some readers, but as time passed his novels gained in popularity and prestige.

In 1874 he married and in 1885 built a remote country home in Dorset. From 1877 on he spent three to four months a year in fashionable society, while the rest of the time he lived in the country, "vibrating," as he put it, "at a swing between the artificial gaieties of a London season and the quaintness of a primitive rustic life."

In 1895 *Jude the Obscure* elicited such bitter critical attacks that Hardy decided to stop writing novels altogether. He had made enough money anyhow, and could afford to return to an earlier dream. In 1898 he published his first volume of poetry. Over the next twenty-nine years Hardy completed over 900 lyrics. His verse was utterly independent of the taste of his day. "My poetry was revolutionary," he said, "in the sense that I meant to avoid the jewelled line. . . ." Instead, he strove for a rough, natural voice, with rustic diction and irregular meters expressing concrete, particularized impressions of life. As the modern American poet Ezra Pound exclaimed, "Now *there* is clarity, there is the harvest of having written twenty novels first."

While he began as a younger rival to George Eliot, Hardy lived into the jazz age and the world of Freud, Einstein, and T. S. Eliot. He doesn't seem to have been surprised by the darker vision of the twentieth century. He had seen it already.

"The Withered Arm" is from Hardy's first collection of short stories, *Wessex Tales.* It begins in 1818 and climaxes in 1825, troubled times for England, when hungry, angry farm workers burned down the ricks (haystacks) of local landowners. Such arsonists, if they were caught, were hanged.

The setting is the southern part of Dorsetshire, Hardy's native countryside. The dominant landscape is "Egdon Heath," Hardy's collective name for a number of heaths (high, rolling stretches of uncultivated land) lying between Dorchester and Bournemouth. Covered with coarse grasses and low shrubs, the heath has remained largely unchanged since prehistoric times. A Roman road cuts through it, Celtic burial mounds crown some of its hilltops, and Shakespeare's King Lear may once have wandered there. In the opening chapter of his novel *The Return of the Native*, Hardy described the heath as "a place perfectly accordant with man's nature—neither ghastly, hateful, nor ugly; neither commonplace, unmeaning, nor tame; but, like man, slighted and enduring; and withal colossal and mysterious in its swarthy monotony. As with some persons who have long lived apart, solitude seemed to look out of its countenance. It had a lonely face, suggesting tragical possibilities." Near the heath is a dairy farm, an "outlying second farm" belonging to a rich local landowner, and here the story begins.

ows, and the cows were "in full pail."[1] The hour was about six in the evening, and three-fourths of the large, red, rectangular animals having been finished off, there was opportunity for a little conversation.

"He do bring home his bride tomorrow, I hear. They've come as far as Anglebury today."

The voice seemed to proceed from the belly of the cow called Cherry, but the speaker was a milking-woman, whose face was buried in the flank of that motionless beast.

"Hav' anybody seen her?" said another.

There was a negative response from the first.

---

1. *in full pail,* producing large quantities of milk.

"Though they say she's a rosy-cheeked, tisty-tosty[2] little body enough," she added; and as the milkmaid spoke she turned her face so that she could glance past her cow's tail to the other side of the barton,[3] where a thin, fading woman of thirty milked somewhat apart from the rest.

"Years younger than he, they say," continued the second, with also a glance of reflectiveness in the same direction.

"How old do you call him, then?"

"Thirty or so."

"More like forty," broke in an old milkman near, in a long white pinafore or "wropper," and with the brim of his hat tied down, so that he looked like a woman. "'A[4] was born before our Great Weir was builded, and I hadn't man's wages when I laved[5] water there."

The discussion waxed so warm that the purr of the milk streams became jerky, till a voice from another cow's belly cried with authority, "Now then, what the Turk do it matter to us about Farmer Lodge's age, or Farmer Lodge's new mis'ess? I shall have to pay him nine pound a year for the rent of every one of these milchers, whatever his age or hers. Get on with your work, or 'twill be dark afore we have done. The evening is pinking in a'ready." This speaker was the dairyman himself, by whom the milkmaids and men were employed.

Nothing more was said publicly about Farmer Lodge's wedding, but the first woman murmured under her cow to her next neighbor, "'Tis hard for *she*," signifying the thin worn milkmaid aforesaid.

"O no," said the second. "He ha'n't spoke to Rhoda Brook for years."

When the milking was done they washed their pails and hung them on a many-forked stand made as usual of the peeled limb of an oak tree, set upright in the earth and resembling a colossal antlered horn. The majority then dispersed in various directions homeward. The thin woman who had not spoken was joined by a boy of twelve or thereabout, and the twain went away up the field also.

Their course lay apart from that of the others, to a lonely spot high above the water-meads, and not far from the border of Egdon Heath, whose dark countenance was visible in the distance as they drew nigh to their home.

"They've just been saying down in barton that your father brings his young wife home from Anglebury tomorrow," the woman observed. "I shall want to send you for a few things to market, and you'll be pretty sure to meet 'em."

"Yes, mother," said the boy. "Is father married then?"

"Yes. . . . You can give her a look, and tell me what she's like, if you do see her."

"Yes, mother."

"If she's dark or fair, and if she's tall—as tall as I. And if she seems like a woman who has ever worked for a living, or one that has been always well off, and has never done anything, and shows marks of the lady on her, as I expect she do."

"Yes."

They crept up the hill in the twilight and entered the cottage. It was built of mud walls, the surface of which had been washed by many rains into channels and depressions that left none of the original flat face visible; while here and there in the thatch above a rafter showed like a bone protruding through the skin.

She was kneeling down in the chimney corner, before two pieces of turf laid together with the heather inwards, blowing at the red-hot ashes with her breath till the turves flamed. The radiance lit her pale cheek, and made her dark eyes, that had once been handsome, seem handsome anew. "Yes," she resumed, "see if she is dark or fair, and if you can, notice if her hands be white; if not, see if they look as though she had ever done housework, or are milker's hands like mine."

The boy again promised, inattentively this time, his mother not observing that he was cutting a notch with his pocketknife in the beech-backed chair.

The Young Wife

The road from Anglebury to Holmstoke is in general level; but there is one place where a sharp ascent breaks its monotony. Farmers homeward

---

2. *tisty-tosty,* plump and attractive. This, and the dialect used throughout, is that of Dorsetshire.
3. *barton,* dairy.
4. *'A,* he.
5. *laved,* dipped out (as with a ladle).

bound from the former market town, who trot all the rest of the way, walk their horses up this short incline.

The next evening while the sun was yet bright a handsome new gig, with a lemon-colored body and red wheels, was spinning westward along the level highway at the heels of a powerful mare. The driver was a yeoman[6] in the prime of life, cleanly shaven like an actor, his face being toned to that bluish-vermilion hue which so often graces a thriving farmer's features when returning home after successful dealings in the town. Beside him sat a woman, many years his junior—almost, indeed, a girl. Her face too was fresh in color, but it was of a totally different quality—soft and evanescent, like the light under a heap of rose petals.

Few people travelled this way, for it was not a main road; and the long white riband of gravel that stretched before them was empty, save of one small scarce-moving speck, which presently resolved itself into the figure of a boy, who was creeping on at a snail's pace, and continually looking behind him—the heavy bundle he carried being some excuse for, if not the reason of, his dilatoriness. When the bouncing gig party slowed at the bottom of the incline above mentioned, the pedestrian was only a few yards in front. Supporting the large bundle by putting one hand on his hip, he turned and looked straight at the farmer's wife as though he would read her through and through, pacing along abreast of the horse.

The low sun was full in her face, rendering every feature, shade, and contour distinct, from the curve of her little nostril to the color of her eyes. The farmer, though he seemed annoyed at the boy's persistent presence, did not order him to get out of the way; and thus the lad preceded

---

6. **yeoman**, a small landowner.

them, his hard gaze never leaving her, till they reached the top of the ascent, when the farmer trotted on with relief in his lineaments—having taken no outward notice of the boy whatever.

"How that poor lad stared at me!" said the young wife.

"Yes, dear; I saw that he did."

"He is one of the village, I suppose?"

"One of the neighborhood. I think he lives with his mother a mile or two off."

"He knows who we are, no doubt?"

"O yes. You must expect to be stared at just at first, my pretty Gertrude."

"I do, though I think the poor boy may have looked at us in the hope we might relieve him of his heavy load, rather than from curiosity."

"O no," said her husband offhandedly. "These country lads will carry a hundredweight once they get it on their backs; besides his pack had more size than weight in it. Now, then, another mile and I shall be able to show you our house in the distance—if it is not too dark before we get there." The wheels spun round, and particles flew from their periphery as before, till a white house of ample dimensions revealed itself, with farm buildings and ricks at the back.

Meanwhile the boy had quickened his pace, and turning up a by-lane some mile and half short of the white farmstead, ascended towards the leaner pastures, and so on to the cottage of his mother.

She had reached home after her day's milking at the outlying dairy, and was washing cabbage at the doorway in the declining light. "Hold up the net a moment," she said, without preface, as the boy came up.

He flung down his bundle, held the edge of the cabbage net, and as she filled its meshes with the dripping leaves she went on, "Well, did you see her?"

"Yes; quite plain."

"Is she ladylike?"

"Yes; and more. A lady complete."

"Is she young?"

"Well, she's growed up, and her ways be quite a woman's."

"Of course. What color is her hair and face?"

"Her hair is lightish, and her face as comely as a live doll's."

"Her eyes, then, are not dark like mine?"

"No—of a bluish turn, and her mouth is very nice and red; and when she smiles, her teeth show white."

"Is she tall?" said the woman sharply.

"I couldn't see. She was sitting down."

"Then do you go to Holmstoke church tomorrow morning: she's sure to be there. Go early and notice her walking in, and come home and tell me if she's taller than I."

"Very well, mother. But why don't you go and see for yourself?"

"*I* go to see her! I wouldn't look up at her if she were to pass my window this instant. She was with Mr. Lodge, of course. What did he say or do?"

"Just the same as usual."

"Took no notice of you?"

"None."

Next day the mother put a clean shirt on the boy, and started him off for Holmstoke church. He reached the ancient little pile when the door was just being opened, and he was the first to enter. Taking his seat by the font, he watched all the parishioners file in. The well-to-do Farmer Lodge came nearly last; and his young wife, who accompanied him, walked up the aisle with the shyness natural to a modest woman who had appeared thus for the first time. As all other eyes were fixed upon her, the youth's stare was not noticed now.

When he reached home his mother said, "Well?" before he had entered the room.

"She is not tall. She is rather short," he replied.

"Ah!" said his mother, with satisfaction.

"But she's very pretty—very. In fact, she's lovely." The youthful freshness of the yeoman's wife had evidently made an impression even on the somewhat hard nature of the boy.

"That's all I want to hear," said his mother quickly. "Now, spread the tablecloth. The hare you wired is very tender; but mind that nobody catches you. You've never told me what sort of hands she had."

"I have never seen 'em. She never took off her gloves."

"What did she wear this morning?"

"A white bonnet and a silver-colored gownd.

(*"The Withered Arm"* continues on page 522.)

Comment: Hardy's Geography

The geography of Hardy's Wessex follows that of nineteenth-century Dorsetshire closely enough that it is possible to identify many of the places mentioned in his fiction and poetry. The map below shows the portion of southern Dorsetshire that Hardy used as the principal setting for "The Withered Arm." On the right is a list of some of the places mentioned in the story with their real originals opposite:

the "outlying second farm" ... Hethfelton Farm

Anglebury .... Wareham

Great Weir .... Stony Weir

Holmstoke (house) .... Hethfelton Lodge

Holmstoke (village) .... East Stoke

Holmstoke church ..... old church, East Stoke

plantation .... Great Plantation

Casterbridge .... Dorchester

Stickleford .... Tincleton

Egdon Heath .. South Heath, Stoke Heath, etc.

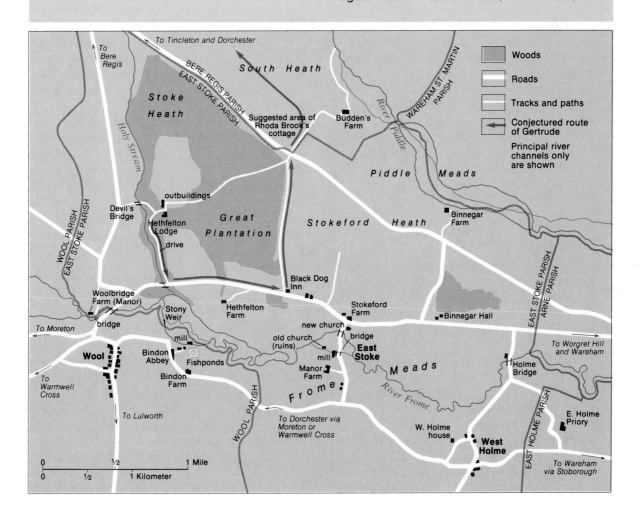

It whewed and whistled so loud when it rubbed against the pews that the lady colored up more than ever for very shame at the noise, and pulled it in to keep it from touching; but when she pushed into her seat, it whewed more than ever. Mr. Lodge, he seemed pleased, and his waistcoat stuck out, and his great golden seals hung like a lord's; but she seemed to wish her noisy gownd anywhere but on her.''

''Not she! However, that will do now.''

These descriptions of the newly married couple were continued from time to time by the boy at his mother's request, after any chance encounter he had had with them. But Rhoda Brook, though she might easily have seen young Mrs. Lodge for herself by walking a couple of miles, would never attempt an excursion towards the quarter where the farmhouse lay. Neither did she, at the daily milking in the dairyman's yard on Lodge's outlying second farm, ever speak on the subject of the recent marriage. The dairyman, who rented the cows of Lodge, and knew perfectly the tall milkmaid's history, with manly kindliness always kept the gossip in the cow barton from annoying Rhoda. But the atmosphere thereabout was full of the subject during the first days of Mrs. Lodge's arrival; and from her boy's description and the casual words of the other milkers, Rhoda Brook could raise a mental image of the unconscious Mrs. Lodge that was realistic as a photograph.

A Vision

One night, two or three weeks after the bridal return, when the boy was gone to bed, Rhoda sat a long time over the turf ashes that she had raked out in front of her to extinguish them. She contemplated so intently the new wife, as presented to her in her mind's eye over the embers, that she forgot the lapse of time. At last, wearied with her day's work, she too retired.

But the figure which had occupied her so much during this and the previous days was not to be banished at night. For the first time Gertrude Lodge visited the supplanted woman in her dreams. Rhoda Brook dreamed—since her assertion that she really saw, before falling asleep, was not to be believed—that the young wife, in the

pale silk dress and white bonnet, but with features shockingly distorted, and wrinkled as by age, was sitting upon her chest as she lay. The pressure of Mrs. Lodge's person grew heavier; the blue eyes peered cruelly into her face; and then the figure thrust forward its left hand mockingly, so as to make the wedding ring it wore glitter in Rhoda's eyes. Maddened mentally, and nearly suffocated by pressure, the sleeper struggled; the incubus, still regarding her, withdrew to the foot of the bed, only, however, to come forward by degrees, resume her seat, and flash her left hand as before.

Gasping for breath, Rhoda, in a last desperate effort, swung out her right hand, seized the confronting specter by its obtrusive left arm, and whirled it backward to the floor, starting up herself as she did so with a low cry.

''O, merciful heaven!'' she cried, sitting on the edge of the bed in a cold sweat; ''that was not a dream—she was here!''

She could feel her antagonist's arm within her grasp even now—the very flesh and bone of it, as it seemed. She looked on the floor whither she had whirled the specter, but there was nothing to be seen.

Rhoda Brook slept no more that night, and when she went milking at the next dawn they noticed how pale and haggard she looked. The milk that she drew quivered into the pail; her hand had not calmed even yet, and still retained the feel of the arm. She came home to breakfast as wearily as if it had been supper time.

''What was that noise in your chimmer, mother, last night?'' said her son. ''You fell off the bed, surely?''

''Did you hear anything fall? At what time?''

''Just when the clock struck two.''

She could not explain, and when the meal was done went silently about her household work, the boy assisting her, for he hated going afield on the farms, and she indulged his reluctance. Between eleven and twelve the garden gate clicked, and she lifted her eyes to the window. At the bottom of the garden, within the gate, stood the woman of her vision. Rhoda seemed transfixed.

''Ah, she said she would come!'' exclaimed the boy, also observing her.

''Said so—when? How does she know us?''

"I have seen and spoken to her. I talked to her yesterday."

"I told you," said the mother, flushing indignantly, "never to speak to anybody in that house, or go near the place."

"I did not speak to her till she spoke to me. And I did not go near the place. I met her in the road."

"What did you tell her?"

"Nothing. She said, 'Are you the poor boy who had to bring the heavy load from market?' And she looked at my boots, and said they would not keep my feet dry if it came on wet, because they were so cracked. I told her I lived with my mother, and we had enough to do to keep ourselves, and that's how it was; and she said then, 'I'll come and bring you some better boots, and see your mother.' She gives away things to other folks in the meads besides us."

Mrs. Lodge was by this time close to the door—not in her silk, as Rhoda had dreamt of in the bedchamber, but in a morning hat, and gown of common light material, which became her better than silk. On her arm she carried a basket.

The impression remaining from the night's experience was still strong. Brook had almost expected to see the wrinkles, the scorn, and the cruelty on her visitor's face. She would have escaped an interview, had escape been possible. There was, however, no back door to the cottage, and in an instant the boy had lifted the latch to Mrs. Lodge's gentle knock.

"I see I have come to the right house," said she, glancing at the lad, and smiling. "But I was not sure till you opened the door."

The figure and action were those of the phantom; but her voice was so indescribably sweet, her glance so winning, her smile so tender, so unlike that of Rhoda's midnight visitant, that the latter could hardly believe the evidence of her senses. She was truly glad that she had not hidden away in sheer aversion, as she had been inclined to do. In her basket Mrs. Lodge brought the pair of boots that she had promised to the boy, and other useful articles.

At these proofs of a kindly feeling towards her and hers Rhoda's heart reproached her bitterly. This innocent young thing should have her blessing and not her curse. When she left them a light seemed gone from the dwelling. Two days later

she came again to know if the boots fitted; and less than a fortnight after that paid Rhoda another call. On this occasion the boy was absent.

"I walk a good deal," said Mrs. Lodge, "and your house is the nearest outside our own parish.[7] I hope you are well. You don't look quite well."

Rhoda said she was well enough; and, indeed, though the paler of the two, there was more of the strength that endures in her well-defined features and large frame than in the soft-cheeked young woman before her. The conversation became quite confidential as regarded their powers and weaknesses; and when Mrs. Lodge was leaving, Rhoda said, "I hope you will find this air agree with you, ma'am, and not suffer from the damp of the water meads."

The younger one replied that there was not much doubt of it, her general health being usually good. "Though, now you remind me," she added, "I have one little ailment which puzzles me. It is nothing serious, but I cannot make it out."

She uncovered her left hand and arm; and their outline confronted Rhoda's gaze as the exact original of the limb she had beheld and seized in her dream. Upon the pink round surface of the arm were faint marks of an unhealthy color, as if produced by a rough grasp. Rhoda's eyes became riveted on the discolorations; she fancied that she discerned in them the shape of her own four fingers.

"How did it happen?" she said mechanically.

"I cannot tell," replied Mrs. Lodge, shaking her head. "One night when I was sound asleep, dreaming I was away in some strange place, a pain suddenly shot into my arm there, and was so keen as to awaken me. I must have struck it in the daytime, I suppose, though I don't remember doing so." She added, laughing, "I tell my dear husband that it looks just as if he had flown into a rage and struck me there. O, I daresay it will soon disappear."

"Ha, ha! Yes. . . . On what night did it come?"

Mrs. Lodge considered, and said it would be a fortnight ago on the morrow. "When I awoke I

---

7. **parish,** in Britain, the unit of local government; counties are divided into parishes.

could not remember where I was," she added, "till the clock striking two reminded me."

She had named the night and the hour of Rhoda's spectral encounter, and Brook felt like a guilty thing. The artless disclosure startled her; she did not reason on the freaks of coincidence; and all the scenery of that ghastly night returned with double vividness to her mind.

"O, can it be," she said to herself, when her visitor had departed, "that I exercise a malignant power over people against my own will?" She knew that she had been slyly called a witch since her fall; but never having understood why that particular stigma had been attached to her, it had passed disregarded. Could this be the explanation, and had such things as this ever happened before?

A Suggestion

The summer drew on, and Rhoda Brook almost dreaded to meet Mrs. Lodge again, notwithstanding that her feeling for the young wife amounted well-nigh to affection. Something in her own individuality seemed to convict Rhoda of crime. Yet a fatality sometimes would direct the steps of the latter to the outskirts of Holmstoke whenever she left her house for any other purpose than her daily work; and hence it happened that their next encounter was out of doors. Rhoda could not avoid the subject which had so mystified her, and after the first few words she stammered, "I hope your—arm is well again, ma'am?" She had perceived with consternation that Gertrude Lodge carried her left arm stiffly.

"No; it is not quite well. Indeed it is no better at all; it is rather worse. It pains me dreadfully sometimes."

"Perhaps you had better go to a doctor, ma'am."

She replied that she had already seen a doctor. Her husband had insisted upon her going to one. But the surgeon had not seemed to understand the afflicted limb at all; he had told her to bathe it in hot water, and she had bathed it, but the treatment had done no good.

"Will you let me see it?" said the milkwoman.

Mrs. Lodge pushed up her sleeve and disclosed the place, which was a few inches above the wrist. As soon as Rhoda Brook saw it, she could hardly preserve her composure. There was nothing of the nature of a wound, but the arm at that point had a shrivelled look, and the outline of the four fingers appeared more distinct than at the former time. Moreover, she fancied that they were imprinted in precisely the relative position of her clutch upon the arm in the trance; the first finger towards Gertrude's wrist, and the fourth towards her elbow.

What the impress resembled seemed to have struck Gertrude herself since their last meeting. "It looks almost like finger marks," she said; adding with a faint laugh, "my husband says it is as if some witch, or the devil himself, had taken hold of me there, and blasted the flesh."

Rhoda shivered. "That's fancy," she said hurriedly. "I wouldn't mind it, if I were you."

"I shouldn't so much mind it," said the younger, with hesitation, "if—if I hadn't a notion that it makes my husband—dislike me—no, love me less. Men think so much of personal appearance."

"Some do—he for one."

"Yes; and he was very proud of mine, at first."

"Keep your arm covered from his sight."

"Ah—he knows the disfigurement is there!" She tried to hide the tears that filled her eyes.

"Well, ma'am, I earnestly hope it will go away soon."

And so the milkwoman's mind was chained anew to the subject by a horrid sort of spell as she returned home. The sense of having been guilty of an act of malignity increased, affect as she might to ridicule her superstition. In her secret heart Rhoda did not altogether object to a slight diminution of her successor's beauty, by whatever means it had come about; but she did not wish to inflict upon her physical pain. For though this pretty young woman had rendered impossible any reparation which Lodge might have made Rhoda for his past conduct, everything like resentment at the unconscious usurpation had quite passed away from the elder's mind.

If the sweet and kindly Gertrude Lodge only knew of the dream scene in the bedchamber, what would she think? Not to inform her of it seemed treachery in the presence of her friendliness; but tell she could not of her own accord—neither could she devise a remedy.

She mused upon the matter the greater part of the night; and the next day, after the morning milking, set out to obtain another glimpse of Gertrude Lodge if she could, being held to her by a gruesome fascination. By watching the house from a distance the milkmaid was presently able to discern the farmer's wife in a ride she was taking alone—probably to join her husband in some distant field. Mrs. Lodge perceived her, and cantered in her direction.

"Good morning, Rhoda!" Gertrude said, when she had come up. "I was going to call."

Rhoda noticed that Mrs. Lodge held the reins with some difficulty.

"I hope—the bad arm," said Rhoda.

"They tell me there is possibly one way by which I might be able to find out the cause, and so perhaps the cure, of it," replied the other anxiously. "It is by going to some clever man over in Egdon Heath. They did not know if he was still alive—and I cannot remember his name at this moment; but they said that you knew more of his movements than anybody else hereabout, and could tell me if he were still to be consulted. Dear me—what was his name? But you know."

"Not Conjuror Trendle?" said her thin companion, turning pale.

"Trendle—yes. Is he alive?"

"I believe so," said Rhoda, with reluctance.

"Why do you call him *conjuror?*"

"Well—they say—they used to say he was a—he had powers other folks have not."

"O, how could my people be so superstitious as to recommend a man of that sort! I thought they meant some medical man. I shall think no more of him."

Rhoda looked relieved, and Mrs. Lodge rode on. The milkwoman had inwardly seen, from the moment she heard of her having been mentioned as a reference for this man, that there must exist a sarcastic feeling among the workfolk that a sorceress would know the whereabouts of the exorcist. They suspected her, then. A short time ago this would have given no concern to a woman of her common sense. But she had a haunting reason to be superstitious now; and she had been seized with sudden dread that this Conjuror Trendle might name her as the malignant influence which was blasting the fair person of Gertrude, and so lead her friend to hate her for ever, and to treat her as some fiend in human shape.

But all was not over. Two days after, a shadow intruded into the window pattern thrown on Rhoda Brook's floor by the afternoon sun. The woman opened the door at once, almost breathlessly.

"Are you alone?" said Gertrude. She seemed to be no less harassed and anxious than Brook herself.

"Yes," said Rhoda.

"The place on my arm seems worse, and troubles me!" the young farmer's wife went on. "It is so mysterious! I do hope it will not be an incurable wound. I have again been thinking of what they said about Conjuror Trendle. I don't really believe in such men, but I should not mind just visiting him, from curiosity—though on no account must my husband know. Is it far to where he lives?"

"Yes—five miles," said Rhoda backwardly. "In the heart of Egdon."

"Well, I should have to walk. Could not you go with me to show me the way—say tomorrow afternoon?"

"O, not I; that is—," the milkwoman murmured, with a start of dismay. Again the dread seized her that something to do with her fierce act in the dream might be revealed, and her character in the eyes of the most useful friend she had ever had be ruined irretrievably.

Mrs. Lodge urged, and Rhoda finally assented, though with much misgiving. Sad as the journey would be to her, she could not conscientiously stand in the way of a possible remedy for her patron's strange affliction. It was agreed that, to escape suspicion of their mystic intent, they should meet at the edge of the heath at the corner of a plantation[8] which was visible from the spot where they now stood.

Conjuror Trendle

By the next afternoon Rhoda would have done anything to escape this inquiry. But she had

---

8. *plantation,* a grove of planted trees.

promised to go. Moreover, there was a horrid fascination at times in becoming instrumental in throwing such possible light on her own character as would reveal her to be something greater in the occult world than she had ever herself suspected.

She started just before the time of day mentioned between them, and half-an-hour's brisk walking brought her to the southeastern extension of the Egdon tract of country, where the fir plantation was. A slight figure, cloaked and veiled, was already there. Rhoda recognized, almost with a shudder, that Mrs. Lodge bore her left arm in a sling.

They hardly spoke to each other, and immediately set out on their climb into the interior of this solemn country, which stood high above the rich alluvial soil they had left half-an-hour before. It was a long walk; thick clouds made the atmosphere dark, though it was as yet only early afternoon; and the wind howled dismally over the slopes of the heath—not improbably the same heath which had witnessed the agony of the Wessex King Ina, presented to after-ages as Lear.[9] Gertrude Lodge talked most, Rhoda replying with monosyllabic preoccupation. She had a strange dislike to walking on the side of her companion where hung the afflicted arm, moving round to the other when inadvertently near it. Much heather had been brushed by their feet when they descended upon a cart track, beside which stood the house of the man they sought.

He did not profess his remedial practices openly, or care anything about their continuance, his direct interests being those of a dealer in furze, turf, "sharp sand,"[10] and other local products. Indeed, he affected not to believe largely in his own powers, and when warts that had been shown him for cure miraculously disappeared—which it must be owned they infallibly did—he would say lightly, "O, I only drink a glass of grog upon 'em at your expense—perhaps it's all chance," and immediately turn the subject.

He was at home when they arrived, having in fact seen them descending into his valley. He was a gray-bearded man, with a reddish face, and he looked singularly at Rhoda the first moment he beheld her. Mrs. Lodge told him her errand; and then with words of self-disparagement he examined her arm.

"Medicine can't cure it," he said promptly. " 'Tis the work of an enemy."

Rhoda shrank into herself, and drew back.

"An enemy? What enemy?" asked Mrs. Lodge.

He shook his head. "That's best known to yourself," he said. "If you like, I can show the person to you, though I shall not myself know who it is. I can do no more; and don't wish to do that."

She pressed him; on which he told Rhoda to wait outside where she stood, and took Mrs. Lodge into the room. It opened immediately from the door; and, as the latter remained ajar, Rhoda Brook could see the proceedings without taking part in them. He brought a tumbler from the dresser, nearly filled it with water, and fetching an egg, prepared it in some private way; after which he broke it on the edge of the glass, so that

9. **Wessex King Ina . . . Lear.** Ina (or *Ine*), who died in A.D. 726, was a West-Saxon king. The tradition about his wandering on the heath was first mentioned by the antiquarian William Camden (1551–1623) in his *Remaines of a Greater Worke, concerning Britaine* (1605). Some nineteenth-century editors of Shakespeare noted this as a possible (though suspiciously late) source for Shakespeare's *King Lear,* which may be where Hardy encountered the idea.

10. **furze, turf, "sharp sand."** Furze is a spiny evergreen shrub used as fuel and feed for cattle; turf is peat, dried for use as fuel; sharp sand is sand generally free from foreign particles such as clay or loam.

the white went in and the yolk remained. As it was getting gloomy, he took the glass and its contents to the window, and told Gertrude to watch the mixture closely. They leant over the table together, and the milkwoman could see the opaline hue of the egg fluid changing form as it sank in the water, but she was not near enough to define the shape that it assumed.

"Do you catch the likeness of any face or figure as you look?" demanded the conjuror of the young woman.

She murmured a reply, in tones so low as to be inaudible to Rhoda, and continued to gaze intently into the glass. Rhoda turned, and walked a few steps away.

When Mrs. Lodge came out and her face was met by the light, it appeared exceedingly pale—as pale as Rhoda's—against the sad dun shades of the upland's garniture. Trendle shut the door behind her, and they at once started homeward together. But Rhoda perceived that her companion had quite changed.

"Did he charge much?" she asked tentatively.

"O no—nothing. He would not take a farthing," said Gertrude.

"And what did you see?" inquired Rhoda.

"Nothing I—care to speak of." The constraint in her manner was remarkable; her face was so rigid as to wear an oldened aspect, faintly suggestive of the face in Rhoda's bedchamber.

"Was it you who first proposed coming here?" Mrs. Lodge suddenly inquired, after a long pause. "How very odd, if you did!"

"No. But I am not sorry we have come, all things considered," she replied. For the first time a sense of triumph possessed her, and she did not altogether deplore that the young thing at her side should learn that their lives had been antagonized by other influences than their own.

The subject was no more alluded to during the long and dreary walk home. But in some way or other a story was whispered about the many-dairied lowland that winter that Mrs. Lodge's gradual loss of the use of her left arm was owing to her being "overlooked"[11] by Rhoda Brook. The latter kept her own counsel about the incubus, but her face grew sadder and thinner; and in the spring she and her boy disappeared from the neighborhood of Holmstoke.

A Second Attempt

Half a dozen years passed away, and Mr. and Mrs. Lodge's married experience sank into prosiness, and worse. The farmer was usually gloomy and silent: the woman whom he had wooed for her grace and beauty was contorted and disfigured in the left limb; moreover, she had brought him no child, which rendered it likely that he would be the last of a family who had occupied that valley for some two hundred years. He thought of Rhoda Brook and her son; and feared this might be a judgment from heaven upon him.

The once blithe-hearted and enlightened Gertrude was changing into an irritable, superstitious woman, whose whole time was given to experimenting upon her ailment with every quack remedy she came across. She was honestly attached to her husband, and was ever secretly hoping against hope to win back his heart again by regaining some at least of her personal beauty. Hence it arose that her closet was lined with bottles, packets, and ointment pots of every description—nay, bunches of mystic herbs, charms, and books of necromancy, which in her schoolgirl time she would have ridiculed as folly.

"Damned if you won't poison yourself with these apothecary messes and witch mixtures some time or other," said her husband, when his eye chanced to fall upon the multitudinous array.

She did not reply, but turned her sad, soft glance upon him in such heartswollen reproach that he looked sorry for his words, and added, "I only meant it for your good, you know, Gertrude."

"I'll clear out the whole lot, and destroy them," said she huskily, "and try such remedies no more!"

"You want somebody to cheer you," he observed. "I once thought of adopting a boy; but he is too old now. And he is gone away I don't know where."

She guessed to whom he alluded; for Rhoda Brook's story had in the course of years become known to her; though not a word had ever passed between her husband and herself on the subject.

---

11. *overlooked,* looked upon with the evil eye; bewitched.

Neither had she ever spoken to him of her visit to Conjuror Trendle, and of what was revealed to her, or she thought was revealed to her, by that solitary heathman.

She was now five-and-twenty; but she seemed older. "Six years of marriage, and only a few months of love," she sometimes whispered to herself. And then she thought of the apparent cause, and said, with a tragic glance at her withering limb, "If I could only again be as I was when he first saw me!"

She obediently destroyed her nostrums and charms; but there remained a hankering wish to try something else—some other sort of cure altogether. She had never revisited Trendle since she had been conducted to the house of the solitary by Rhoda against her will; but it now suddenly occurred to Gertrude that she would, in a last desperate effort at deliverance from this seeming curse, again seek out the man, if he yet lived. He was entitled to a certain credence, for the indistinct form he had raised in the glass had undoubtedly resembled the only woman in the world who—as she now knew, though not then—could have a reason for bearing her ill will. The visit should be paid.

This time she went alone, though she nearly got lost on the heath, and roamed a considerable distance out of her way. Trendle's house was reached at last, however. He was not indoors, and instead of waiting at the cottage, she went to where his bent figure was pointed out to her at work a long way off. Trendle remembered her, and laying down the handful of furze roots which he was gathering and throwing into a heap, he offered to accompany her in her homeward direction, as the distance was considerable and the days were short. So they walked together, his head bowed nearly to the earth, and his form of a color with it.

"You can send away warts and other excrescences, I know," she said; "why can't you send away this?" And the arm was uncovered.

"You think too much of my powers!" said Trendle; "and I am old and weak now, too. No, no; it is too much for me to attempt in my own person. What have ye tried?"

She named to him some of the hundred medicaments and counterspells which she had adopted from time to time. He shook his head.

"Some were good enough," he said approvingly; "but not many of them for such as this. This is of the nature of a blight, not of the nature of a wound; and if you ever do throw it off, it will be all at once."

"If I only could!"

"There is only one chance of doing it known to me. It has never failed in kindred afflictions—that I can declare. But it is hard to carry out, and especially for a woman."

"Tell me!" said she.

"You must touch with the limb the neck of a man who's been hanged."

She started a little at the image he had raised.

"Before he's cold—just after he's cut down," continued the conjuror impassively.

"How can that do good?"

"It will turn the blood and change the constitution. But, as I say, to do it is hard. You must go to the jail when there's a hanging, and wait for him when he's brought off the gallows. Lots have done it, though perhaps not such pretty women as you. I used to send dozens for skin complaints. But that was in former times. The last I sent was in '13–near twelve years ago."

He had no more to tell her; and, when he had put her into a straight track homeward, turned and left her, refusing all money as at first.

A Ride

The communication sank deep into Gertrude's mind. Her nature was rather a timid one; and probably of all remedies that the white wizard could have suggested there was not one which would have filled her with so much aversion as this, not to speak of the immense obstacles in the way of its adoption.

Casterbridge, the county town, was a dozen or fifteen miles off; and though in those days, when men were executed for horse stealing, arson, and burglary, an assize[12] seldom passed without a hanging, it was not likely that she could get access to the body of the criminal unaided. And the fear of her husband's anger made her

---

12. **assize,** session of the law court.

reluctant to breathe a word of Trendle's suggestion to him or to anybody about him.

She did nothing for months, and patiently bore her disfigurement as before. But her woman's nature, craving for renewed love through the medium of renewed beauty (she was but twenty-five), was ever stimulating her to try what, at any rate, could hardly do her any harm. "What came by a spell will go by a spell surely," she would say. Whenever her imagination pictured the act she shrank in terror from the possibility of it. Then the words of the conjuror, "It will turn your blood," were seen to be capable of a scientific no less than a ghastly interpretation; the mastering desire returned, and urged her on again.

There was at this time but one county paper, and that her husband only occasionally borrowed. But old-fashioned days had old-fashioned means, and news was extensively conveyed by word of mouth from market to market, or from fair to fair, so that, whenever such an event as an execution was about to take place, few within a radius of twenty miles were ignorant of the coming sight; and, so far as Holmstoke was concerned, some enthusiasts had been known to walk all the way to Casterbridge and back in one day, solely to witness the spectacle. The next assizes were in March; and when Gertrude Lodge heard that they had been held, she inquired stealthily at the inn as to the result, as soon as she could find opportunity.

She was, however, too late. The time at which the sentences were to be carried out had arrived, and to make the journey and obtain admission at such short notice required at least her husband's assistance. She dared not tell him, for she had found by delicate experiment that these smoldering village beliefs made him furious if mentioned, partly because he half entertained them himself. It was therefore necessary to wait for another opportunity.

Her determination received a fillip from learning that two epileptic children had attended from this very village of Holmstoke many years before with beneficial results, though the experiment had been strongly condemned by the neighboring clergy. April, May, June, passed; and it is no overstatement to say that by the end of the last-named month Gertrude well-nigh longed for the death of a fellow creature. Instead of her formal prayers each night, her unconscious prayer was, "O Lord, hang some guilty or innocent person soon!"

This time she made earlier inquiries, and was altogether more systematic in her proceedings. Moreover, the season was summer, between the haymaking and the harvest, and in the leisure thus afforded him her husband had been holiday-taking away from home.

The assizes were in July, and she went to the inn as before. There was to be one execution—only one—for arson.

Her greatest problem was not how to get to Casterbridge, but what means she should adopt for obtaining admission to the jail. Though access for such purposes had formerly never been denied, the custom had fallen into desuetude; and in contemplating her possible difficulties, she was again almost driven to fall back upon her husband. But, on sounding him about the assizes, he was so uncommunicative, so more than usually cold, that she did not proceed, and decided that whatever she did she would do alone.

Fortune, obdurate hitherto, showed her unexpected favor. On the Thursday before the Saturday fixed for the execution, Lodge remarked to her that he was going away from home for another day or two on business at a fair, and that he was sorry he could not take her with him.

She exhibited on this occasion so much readiness to stay at home that he looked at her in surprise. Time had been when she would have shown deep disappointment at the loss of such a jaunt. However, he lapsed into his usual taciturnity, and on the day named left Holmstoke.

It was now her turn. She at first had thought of driving, but on reflection held that driving would not do, since it would necessitate her keeping to the turnpike road, and so increase by tenfold the risk of her ghastly errand being found out. She decided to ride and avoid the beaten track, notwithstanding that in her husband's stables there was no animal just at present which by any stretch of imagination could be considered a lady's mount, in spite of his promise before marriage to always keep a mare for her. He had, however, many cart horses, fine ones of their kind; and among the rest was a serviceable creature, an equine Amazon, with a back as broad as a sofa, on which Gertrude had occasionally taken an airing when unwell. This horse she chose.

On Friday afternoon one of the men brought it round. She was dressed, and before going down looked at her shriveled arm. "Ah!" she said to it, "if it had not been for you this terrible ordeal would have been saved me!"

When strapping up the bundle in which she carried a few articles of clothing, she took occasion to say to the servant, "I take these in case I should not get back tonight from the person I am going to visit. Don't be alarmed if I am not in by ten, and close up the house as usual. I shall be at home tomorrow for certain." She meant then to tell her husband privately: the deed accomplished was not like the deed projected. He would almost certainly forgive her.

And then the pretty palpitating Gertrude Lodge went from her husband's homestead; but though her goal was Casterbridge she did not take the direct route thither through Stickleford. Her cunning course at first was in precisely the opposite direction. As soon as she was out of sight, however, she turned to the left, by a road which led into Egdon, and on entering the heath wheeled round, and set out in the true course, due westerly. A more private way down the county could not be imagined; and as to direction, she had merely to keep her horse's head to a point a little to the right of the sun. She knew that she would light upon a furze cutter or cottager of some sort from time to time, from whom she might correct her bearing.

Though the date was comparatively recent, Egdon was much less fragmentary in character than now. The attempts—successful and otherwise—at cultivation on the lower slopes, which intrude and break up the original heath into small detached heaths had not been carried far; Enclosure Acts[13] had not taken effect, and the banks and fences which now exclude the cattle of those villagers who formerly enjoyed rights of commonage thereon, and the carts of those who had turbary privileges[14] which kept them in firing all the year round, were not erected. Gertrude, therefore, rode along with no other obstacles than the prickly furze bushes, the mats of heather, the white watercourses, and the natural steeps and declivities of the ground.

Her horse was sure, if heavy-footed and slow, and though a draught animal, was easy-paced; had it been otherwise, she was not a woman who could have ventured to ride over such a bit of country with a half-dead arm. It was therefore nearly eight o'clock when she drew rein to breathe her bearer on the last outlying high point of heathland towards Casterbridge, previous to leaving Egdon for the cultivated valleys.

She halted before a pool called Rushy Pond, flanked by the ends of two hedges; a railing ran through the center of the pond, dividing it in half. Over the railing she saw the low green country; over the green trees the roofs of the town; over the roofs a white flat façade, denoting the entrance to the county jail. On the roof of this front specks were moving about; they seemed to be workmen erecting something. Her flesh crept. She descended slowly, and was soon amid cornfields[15] and pastures. In another half-hour, when it was almost dusk, Gertrude reached the White Hart, the first inn of the town on that side.

Little surprise was excited by her arrival; farmers' wives rode on horseback then more than they do now; though, for that matter, Mrs. Lodge was not imagined to be a wife at all; the innkeeper supposed her some harum-skarum young woman who had come to attend "hang-fair" next day. Neither her husband nor herself ever dealt in Casterbridge market, so that she was unknown. While dismounting she beheld a crowd of boys standing at the door of a harness-maker's shop just above the inn, looking inside it with deep interest.

"What is going on there?" she asked of the ostler.

"Making the rope for to-morrow."

She throbbed responsively, and contracted her arm.

" 'Tis sold by the inch afterwards," the man continued. "I could get you a bit, miss, for nothing, if you'd like?"

---

13. **Enclosure Acts,** parliamentary legislation enabling landlords to enclose the large open fields typical of medieval English farming, as well as commons and wasteland, into large agricultural operations. It increased farm production, but also resulted in social unrest because of the many evictions of smallholders accompanying enclosure.
14. **turbary privileges,** the right to cut peat (Latin, *turba*) on another's land.
15. **cornfields,** wheatfields.

She hastily repudiated any such wish, all the more from a curious creeping feeling that the condemned wretch's destiny was becoming interwoven with her own; and having engaged a room for the night, sat down to think.

Up to this time she had formed but the vaguest notions about her means of obtaining access to the prison. The words of the cunning man returned to her mind. He had implied that she should use her beauty, impaired though it was, as a passkey. In her inexperience she knew little about jail functionaries; she had heard of a high-sheriff and an under-sheriff, but dimly only. She knew, however, that there must be a hangman, and to the hangman she determined to apply.

A Waterside Hermit

At this date, and for several years after, there was a hangman to almost every jail. Gertrude found, on inquiry, that the Casterbridge official dwelt in a lonely cottage by a deep slow river flowing under the cliff on which the prison buildings were situate—the stream being the selfsame one, though she did not know it, which watered the Stickleford and Holmstoke meads lower down in its course.

Having changed her dress, and before she had eaten or drunk—for she could not take her ease till she had ascertained some particulars—Gertrude pursued her way by a path along the waterside to the cottage indicated. Passing thus the outskirts of the jail, she discerned on the level roof over the gateway three rectangular lines against the sky, where the specks had been moving in her distant view; she recognized what the erection was, and passed quickly on. Another hundred yards brought her to the executioner's house, which a boy pointed out. It stood close to the same stream, and was hard by a weir, the waters of which emitted a steady roar.

While she stood hesitating the door opened, and an old man came forth shading a candle with one hand. Locking the door on the outside, he turned to a flight of wooden steps fixed against the end of the cottage, and began to ascend them, this being evidently the staircase to his bedroom. Gertrude hastened forward, but by the time she reached the foot of the ladder he was at the top.

She called to him loudly enough to be heard above the roar of the weir; he looked down and said, "What d'ye want here?"

"To speak to you a minute."

The candlelight, such as it was, fell upon her imploring, pale, upturned face, and Davies (as the hangman was called) backed down the ladder. "I was just going to bed," he said; "'Early to bed and early to rise,' but I don't mind stopping a minute for such a one as you. Come into house." He reopened the door, and preceded her to the room within.

The implements of his daily work, which was that of a jobbing gardener, stood in a corner, and seeing probably that she looked rural, he said, "If you want me to undertake country work I can't come, for I never leave Casterbridge for gentle nor simple—not I. My real calling is officer of justice," he added formally.

"Yes, yes! That's it. Tomorrow!"

"Ah! I thought so. Well, what's the matter about that? 'Tis no use to come here about the knot—folks do come continually, but I tell 'em one knot is as merciful as another if ye keep it under the ear. Is the unfortunate man a relation; or, I should say, perhaps" (looking at her dress) "a person who's been in your employ?"

"No. What time is the execution?"

"The same as usual—twelve o'clock, or as soon after as the London mail coach gets in. We always wait for that, in case of a reprieve."

"O—a reprieve—I hope not!" she said involuntarily.

"Well,—hee, hee!—as a matter of business, so do I! But still, if ever a young fellow deserved to be let off, this one does; only just turned eighteen. And only present by chance when the rick was fired. Howsomever, there's not much risk of it, as they are obliged to make an example of him, there having been so much destruction of property that way lately."

"I mean," she explained, "that I want to touch him for a charm, a cure of an affliction, by the advice of a man who has proved the virtue of the remedy."

"O yes, miss! Now I understand. I've had such people come in past years. But it didn't strike me that you looked of a sort to require blood-turning. What's the complaint? The wrong kind for this, I'll be bound."

"My arm." She reluctantly showed the withered skin.

"Ah!—'tis all a-scram!" said the hangman, examining it.

"Yes," said she.

"Well," he continued, with interest, "that *is* the class o' subject, I'm bound to admit! I like the look of the wownd; it is truly as suitable for the cure as any I ever saw. 'Twas a knowing man that sent 'ee, whoever he was."

"You can contrive for me all that's necessary?" she said breathlessly.

"You should really have gone to the governor of the jail, and your doctor with 'ee, and given your name and address—that's how it used to be done, if I recollect. Still, perhaps, I can manage it for a trifling fee."

"O, thank you! I would rather do it this way, as I should like it kept private."

"Lover not to know, eh?"

"No—husband."

"Aha! Very well. I'll get 'ee a touch of the corpse."

"Where is it now?" she said, shuddering.

"It?—*he*, you mean; he's living yet. Just inside that little small winder up there in the glum." He signified the jail on the cliff above.

She thought of her husband and her friends. "Yes, of course," she said; "and how am I to proceed?"

He took her to the door. "Now, do you be waiting at the little wicket in the wall, that you'll find up there in the lane, not later than one o'clock. I will open it from the inside, as I shan't come home to dinner till he's cut down. Goodnight. Be punctual; and if you don't want anybody to know 'ee, wear a veil. Ah—once I had such a daughter as you!"

She went away, and climbed the path above, to assure herself that she would be able to find the wicket next day. Its outline was soon visible to her—a narrow opening in the outer wall of the prison precincts. The steep was so great that, having reached the wicket, she stopped a moment to breathe; and, looking back upon the waterside cot, saw the hangman again ascending his outdoor staircase. He entered the loft or chamber to which it led, and in a few minutes extinguished his light.

The town clock struck ten, and she returned to the White Hart as she had come.

A Rencounter

It was one o'clock on Saturday. Gertrude Lodge, having been admitted to the jail as above described, was sitting in a waiting room within the second gate, which stood under a classic archway of ashlar, then comparatively modern, and bearing the inscription, COUNTY JAIL: 1793. This had been the façade she saw from the heath the day before. Near at hand was a passage to the roof on which the gallows stood.

The town was thronged, and the market suspended; but Gertrude had seen scarcely a soul. Having kept her room till the hour of the appointment, she had proceeded to the spot by a way which avoided the open space below the cliff where the spectators had gathered; but she could, even now, hear the multitudinous babble of their voices, out of which rose at intervals the hoarse croak of a single voice uttering the words, "Last dying speech and confession!" There had been no reprieve, and the execution was over; but the crowd still waited to see the body taken down.

Soon the persistent woman heard a trampling overhead, then a hand beckoned to her, and, following directions, she went out and crossed the inner paved court beyond the gatehouse, her knees trembling so that she could scarcely walk. One of her arms was out of its sleeve, and only covered by her shawl.

On the spot at which she had now arrived were two trestles, and before she could think of their purpose she heard feet descending stairs somewhere at her back. Turn her head she would not, or could not, and, rigid in this position, she was conscious of a rough coffin passing her shoulder, borne by four men. It was open, and in it lay the body of a young man, wearing the smockfrock of a rustic, and fustian breeches. The corpse had been thrown into the coffin so hastily that the shirt of the smockfrock was hanging over. The burden was temporarily deposited on the trestles.

By this time the young woman's state was such that a gray mist seemed to float before her eyes, on account of which, and the veil she wore, she could scarcely discern anything: it was as though she had nearly died, but was held up by a sort of galvanism.

"Now!" said a voice close at hand, and she was just conscious that the word had been addressed to her.

By a last strenuous effort she advanced, at the same time hearing persons approaching behind her. She bared her poor curst arm; and Davies, uncovering the face of the corpse, took Gertrude's hand, and held it so that her arm lay across the dead man's neck, upon a line the color of an unripe blackberry, which surrounded it.

Gertrude shrieked: "the turn o' the blood," predicted by the conjuror, had taken place. But at that moment a second shriek rent the air of the enclosure: it was not Gertrude's, and its effect upon her was to make her start round.

Immediately behind her stood Rhoda Brook, her face drawn, and her eyes red with weeping. Behind Rhoda stood Gertrude's own husband; his countenance lined, his eyes dim, but without a tear.

"D—n you! what are you doing here?" he said hoarsely.

"Hussy—to come between us and our child now!" cried Rhoda. "This is the meaning of what Satan showed me in the vision! You are like her at last!" And clutching the bare arm of the younger woman, she pulled her unresistingly back against the wall. Immediately Brook had loosened her hold the fragile young Gertrude slid down against the feet of her husband. When he lifted her up she was unconscious.

The mere sight of the twain had been enough to suggest to her that the dead young man was Rhoda's son. At that time the relatives of an executed convict had the privilege of claiming the body for burial, if they chose to do so; and it was for this purpose that Lodge was awaiting the inquest with Rhoda. He had been summoned by her as soon as the young man was taken in the crime, and at different times since; and he had attended in court during the trial. This was the "holiday" he had been indulging in of late. The two wretched parents had wished to avoid exposure; and hence had come themselves for the body, a waggon and sheet for its conveyance and covering being in waiting outside.

Gertrude's case was so serious that it was deemed advisable to call to her the surgeon who was at hand. She was taken out of the jail into the town; but she never reached home alive. Her delicate vitality, sapped perhaps by the paralyzed arm, collapsed under the double shock that followed the severe strain, physical and mental, to which she had subjected herself during the previous twenty-four hours. Her blood had been "turned" indeed—too far. Her death took place in the town three days after.

Her husband was never seen in Casterbridge

again; once only in the old market place at Angle-bury, which he had so much frequented, and very seldom in public anywhere. Burdened at first with moodiness and remorse, he eventually changed for the better, and appeared as a chastened and thoughtful man. Soon after attending the funeral of his poor young wife he took steps towards giving up the farms in Holmstoke and the adjoining parish, and, having sold every head of his stock, he went away to Port-Bredy, at the other end of the county, living there in solitary lodgings till his death two years later of a painless decline. It was then found that he had bequeathed the whole of his not inconsiderable property to a reformatory for boys, subject to the payment of a small annuity to Rhoda Brook, if she could be found to claim it.

For some time she could not be found; but eventually she reappeared in her old parish, absolutely refusing, however, to have anything to do with the provision made for her. Her monotonous milking at the dairy was resumed, and followed for many long years, till her form became bent, and her once abundant dark hair white and worn away at the forehead—perhaps by long pressure against the cows. Here, sometimes, those who knew her experiences would stand and observe her, and wonder what sombre thoughts were beating inside that impassive, wrinkled brow, to the rhythm of the alternating milk streams.

1888

Discussion

1. As the story begins, what does Rhoda Brooke want to know about Farmer Lodge's new wife? How do her questions explain Rhoda's feelings?

2. In our first glimpse of Gertrude, she looks "soft and evanescent, like the light under a heap of rose-petals." How does this image establish our sense of her character? Is this a correct first impression?

3. What meaning do you read in Rhoda's dream?

4. Gertrude, when first aware of the strange marks on her arm, says, "I tell my dear husband that it looks just as if he had flown into a rage and struck me there." How could this odd suggestion make sense?

5. By the fourth chapter ("A Suggestion," page 525), Rhoda and Gertrude have struck up an acquaintance—in fact Rhoda has a feeling for the young wife that "amounted well-nigh to affection." How can you explain this?

6. Hardy describes the first visit to Conjuror Trendle from Rhoda's point of view. How does this give suspense to the scene? How does it influence the reader's sympathy for the characters?

7. Why does Rhoda feel a "sense of triumph" after the first visit to Trendle? Should she?

8. What characteristics of Trendle lead one to believe in his power?

9. What moral weakness makes Gertrude long "for the death of a fellow creature"? Does she have this weakness from the beginning of the tale?

10. The country people call Rhoda a witch and at the end of the story Rhoda calls Gertrude a "hussy." Do these names fit? What meaning lies in each?

11. Discuss the fate of this story's main characters. Do they deserve their fate?

Composition

By the end of "The Withered Arm" each of the four major characters is guilty of a serious error in judgment. Choose one to write about, and begin by thinking about the person's faults and what caused them.

In an essay using your conclusions, first take the role of the accuser and draw up an indictment. Then, counter it with the sorts of excuses the individual would supply to account for what he or she did. (See *Evaluating Your Evidence* in Composition Guide.)

The Man He Killed

"Had he and I but met
    By some old ancient inn,
We should have sat us down to wet
    Right many a nipperkin!¹

5 "But ranged as infantry,
    And staring face to face,
I shot at him as he at me,
    And killed him in his place.

    "I shot him dead because—
10 Because he was my foe,
Just so: my foe of course he was;
    That's clear enough; although

"He thought he'd 'list,² perhaps,
    Off-hand like—just as I—
15 Was out of work—had sold his traps³—
    No other reason why.

    "Yes; quaint and curious war is!
    You shoot a fellow down
You'd treat if met where any bar is,
20   Or help to half-a-crown."⁴   1902

---

1. *nipperkin,* a half-pint of ale.
2. *'list,* enlist.
3. *traps,* simple personal belongings.
4. *half-a-crown,* an English coin worth about sixty cents at the time of the story, though far larger in purchasing power.

"Ah, Are You Digging on My Grave?"

"Ah, are you digging on my grave
    My loved one?—planting rue?"
—"No: yesterday he went to wed
One of the brightest wealth has bred.
5 'It cannot hurt her now,' he said,
    'That I should not be true.' "

"Then who is digging on my grave?
    My nearest dearest kin?"
—"Ah, no: they sit and think, 'What use!
10 What good will planting flowers produce?
No tendance of her mound can loose
    Her spirit from Death's gin.' "¹

"But some one digs upon my grave?
    My enemy?—prodding sly?"
15 —"Nay: when she heard you had passed the Gate
That shuts on all flesh soon or late,
She thought you no more worth her hate,
    And cares not where you lie."

"Then, who is digging on my grave?
20   Say—since I have not guessed!"
—"O it is I, my mistress dear,
Your little dog, who still lives near,
And much I hope my movements here
    Have not disturbed your rest?"

25 "Ah, yes! *You* dig upon my grave . . .
    Why flashed it not on me
That one true heart was left behind!
What feeling do we ever find
To equal among human kind
30   A dog's fidelity!"

"Mistress, I dug upon your grave
    To bury a bone, in case
I should be hungry near this spot
When passing on my daily trot.
35 I am sorry, but I quite forgot
    It was your resting-place."   1914

---

1. *gin,* a snare or trap for game.

Cerne Abbas churchyard, Dorset.

In Time of "The Breaking of Nations"[1]

I

Only a man harrowing clods
   In a slow silent walk
With an old horse that stumbles and nods
   Half asleep as they stalk.

II

5 Only thin smoke without flame
   From the heaps of couch-grass;
Yet this will go onward the same
   Though Dynasties pass.

III

Yonder a maid and her wight[2]
10   Come whispering by:
War's annals will fade into night
   Ere their story die.

1916

---

1. **"The Breaking of Nations,"** an allusion to Jeremiah 51:20.
2. **wight,** an archaic word meaning "a human being."

Snow in the Suburbs

Every branch big with it,
   Bent every twig with it;
Every fork like a white web-foot;
Every street and pavement mute;
5 Some flakes have lost their way, and grope back upward, when
Meeting those meandering down they turn and descend again.
   The palings are glued together like a wall,
   And there is no waft of wind with the fleecy fall.

   A sparrow enters the tree,
10   Whereon immediately
A snow-lump thrice his own slight size
Descends on him and showers his head and eyes,
   And overturns him,
   And near inurns him,
15   And lights on a nether twig, when its brush
Starts off a volley of other lodging lumps with a rush.

   The steps are a blanched slope,
   Up which, with feeble hope,
A black cat comes, wide-eyed and thin;
20   And we take him in.

1925

Discussion

The Man He Killed

1. How wealthy do you think the speaker is? What leads you to this conclusion? In particular, does he use any words which suggest his social class?

2. Why does the speaker repeat himself in stanza three?

3. For what reasons does he go to war? Do you think these are unusual motives?

"Ah, Are You Digging on My Grave?"

1. What does the dead girl hope for? Is there an order to her questions?

2. What is ironical about the fifth stanza?

3. What does the poem imply, through the answers to each question?

In Time of "The Breaking of Nations"

1. What does the word *Only*, which begins the first two stanzas, mean in this context?

2. Together, the images of the poem make a single picture. What does this picture show literally, and what can it suggest symbolically?

3. To whom does the word *their* of line 12 refer?

Snow in the Suburbs

1. What is the effect of the repetition of the word *every* four times in the first four lines?

2. Hardy substantially revised the **diction** of "Snow in the Suburbs." Below are some examples of the language in his first draft for the poem, followed by the words he finally did use. In each case discuss the differences between them and speculate on why he opted for his final choices. Line 5: first *float*, then *grope*. Line 6: first *coming*, then *meandering*. Line 16: first *cascade*, then *volley*; first *waiting*, then *lodging*.

3. What does the unusual verb *inurns* (line 14) mean? What tone does it give to the description?

4. Why are lines 5–6 and 15–16 longer than most of the others?

5. What does the poem's last image mean?

Gerard Manley Hopkins
1844–1889

Gerard Manley Hopkins was the eldest son of an exceptional family. His father published a book on mathematics and another of his own poems, while his mother read German philosophy. Several of their children became artists, some were skilled in music, and all took seriously their devotion to the Church of England.

Hopkins's superior work at Highgate School won him admission to Oxford in 1863, where he studied classics. Already he felt a strong inclination to write poetry. Notebook jottings from his college days record his fascination with words: "Grind, gride, grid, grit, groat, grate . . . Original meaning to *strike, rub* . . . That which is produced by such means is the *grit,* the *groats* or crumbs . . ." And, following Ruskin's example, he was already studying nature with an exactness of perception that sought the specific and particular character of each cloud, each leaf.

But more profound issues intervened. Like many of his contemporaries, Hopkins questioned the religion of his family, and in October of 1866 he broke with them to join the Roman Catholic Church. After completing his Oxford studies, Hopkins joined the Jesuit order in September of 1868. In beginning a long period of training for the priesthood, he dramatically burned all his youthful poems.

During the next few years Hopkins felt it wrong to write verse, but in 1875 he seized upon the chance remark of a religious superior and wrote a long (280-line) poem commemorating the wreck of the sailing vessel *Deutschland*. Later he told a friend, "I had long had haunting my ear the echo of a new rhythm . . ." and here it burst forth. During the next few years Hopkins studied theology in Wales

Welsh Mountain Landscape by James Dickson Innes (1887–1914), painted about 1912.

and in a series of lyrics such as "Pied Beauty" and "God's Grandeur" he celebrated his ecstatic sense of the divine in nature.

After his ordination in 1877 Hopkins served as a parish priest in industrial towns such as Manchester and Liverpool. This experience, he said, "laid upon my mind a . . . truly crushing conviction, of the misery of the town life to the poor . . . of the degradation of our race, of the hollowness of this century's civilization." A more sombre note appears in poems such as "Spring and Fall" as Hopkins's sense of human suffering intensified.

From the first Hopkins's poetry was unusual. He admired many of the classic poets, but his reaction to their work was, he said, "to make me admire and do otherwise." Judging his own work he confessed, "No doubt my poetry errs on the side of oddness . . . ." But he recognized this was the consequence of his search for the particular, the distinctive in things. Hopkins shared his poems with but a very few friends, and though he dreamed of a wider audience he made little effort to have his works published.

From 1881 on he taught classical languages, first at the Jesuit seminary in Stonyhurst, then, from 1884, at the Catholic University College in Dublin. He disliked his teaching responsibilities but scrupulously fulfilled them.

His emotional life grew more troubled. His God, "the only person that I am in love with seldom, especially now, stirs my heart . . ." he told a friend, and he became haunted by the suicides of several Oxford friends, concluding "it must be . . . a dreadful feature of our days." By 1885 he felt overwhelmed by a "constant, crippling" melancholy which, he confessed, "is much like madness." From this dark period come some of Hopkins's greatest poems, sonnets such as "Thou art indeed just, Lord" in which he struggles with the encroaching tragedy of his life. These were a last, splendid gesture. Hopkins had never been very healthy and in an outbreak of typhoid fever he died in 1889.

A friend and fellow writer, Robert Bridges, saved Hopkins's poems and 29 years later, in 1918, published them to an astonished and, by then, appreciative world. (For more information on Hopkins's poetic theory see the entry **sprung rhythm** in the Definitions of Literary Terms.)

Pied Beauty

Glory be to God for dappled things—
    For skies of couple-color as a brinded[1] cow;
      For rose-moles all in stipple[2] upon trout that swim;
Fresh-firecoal chestnut-falls;[3] finches' wings;
5   Landscape plotted and pieced—fold, fallow, and plow;[4]
    And all trades, their gear and tackle and trim.

All things counter,[5] original, spare, strange;
    Whatever is fickle, freckled (who knows how?)
      With swift, slow; sweet, sour; adazzle, dim;
10 He fathers-forth whose beauty is past change:
      Praise him.

1877   1918

1. **brinded,** streaked with different colors. An early form of *brindled*.
2. **stipple.** In graphic arts, areas of color or shade are sometimes rendered by masses of tiny dots, called *stipples*.
3. **Fresh-firecoal chestnut-falls.** Newly fallen nuts stripped of their husks look like glowing coals.
4. **Landscape . . . plow.** Seen from a distance, a landscape can look as if an architect laid it out in square sections—"plotted" it out; or a tailor sewed it together out of square bits of cloth—"pieced" it together. Different sections can be set aside to be used as pastures—"folds"; to sit idly regaining fertility—"fallow"; or be placed under cultivation—"plow."
5. **counter,** contrary to expectation.

God's Grandeur

The world is charged with the grandeur of God.
 It will flame out, like shining from shook foil;
 It gathers to a greatness, like the ooze of oil
Crushed. Why do men then now not reck his rod?
5 Generations have trod, have trod, have trod;
 And all is seared with trade; bleared, smeared with toil;
 And wears man's smudge and shares man's smell: the soil
Is bare now, nor can foot feel, being shod.

And for[1] all this, nature is never spent;
10 There lives the dearest freshness deep down things;
And though the last lights off the black West went
 Oh, morning, at the brown brink eastward, springs—
Because the Holy Ghost over the bent
 World broods with warm breast and with ah! bright wings.

1877   1918

---

1. *for,* despite.

Reader's Note: Imagery in "God's Grandeur"

In an early essay Hopkins wrote, "All things . . . are charged with God, and if we know how to touch them, give off sparks and take fire . . . " The **imagery** here is electrical, and refers to a battery, or to the static electricity which can build up in cloth or hair. Touching such objects strikes sparks—shocks and surprises you. The first line of this poem expresses this idea in its image of a "charged" world. The second is related to it. Here we have an image of flaming light rays which Hopkins himself explained in a letter to a friend. "I mean foil in its sense of leaf or tinsel . . . Shaken gold foil gives off broad glares like sheet lightning and also, and this is true of nothing else, owing to its zigzag dints and creasings and network of small many cornered facets, a sort of forked lightning too."

In lines three and four the initial images of electrical sparks and lightning are replaced by their opposites. If you put a puddle of heavy oil, like olive oil, between two surfaces and squeeze them together, the oil will be crushed into a thin ooze. But if you then separate the surfaces the tension within the oil itself will pull oil droplets back together. It is this kind of internal force drawing things back together which Hopkins here contrasts with the radiating energy of the first lines. He sees both as typical of God's power, reflected in His creation.

In line four the poet wonders why people no longer fear God's authority—fear the birch rod which God, like an angry father beating his children, could use to punish evil. This "rod" also suggests the lightning rod which carries the electrical energy of the divine storm to earth and links the first lines of the poem with this passage, as the "smear" of line six and "smudge" of line seven link with the oil of line three—though in lines six and seven the oil is the defiling oil of industrial society.

The imagery of the first eight lines, then, describes a god of power and wrath, and an earth sullied by a senseless civilization. The last six lines of the sonnet turn to very different images—a spring of fresh water (line 10), sunset and sunrise (lines 11–12), with a double use of the verb "spring" in line 12, and finally, a multiple image in which God the Holy Ghost, the spiritual dimension of the Christian God, is seen as the dawn of both a new day and a new, regenerated life, and also a dove, a benevolent bird of peace hovering over the world.

Spring and Fall: To a Young Child

Márgarét, are you gríeving
Over Goldengrove unleaving?
Leáves, líke the things of man, you
With your fresh thoughts care for, can you?
5 Áh! ás the heart grows older
It will come to such sights colder
By and by, nor spare a sigh
Though worlds of wanwood leafmeal[1] lie;
And yet you wíll weep and know why.
10 Now no matter, child, the name:

Sórrow's spríngs áre the same.
Nor mouth had, no nor mind, expressed
What heart heard of, ghost guessed:
It ís the blight man was born for,
15 It is Margaret you mourn for.
1880   1918

---

1. **wanwood leafmeal**, palely colored autumn leaves (''wan'')
have fallen to the ground where they lie matted and already dis-
integrating (''leafmeal'').

Autumn Leaves, by Sir
John Everett Millais,
painted in 1856.

Chanklin, Isle of Wight
1866
the diameter is 6⅝ in.

Thou Art Indeed Just, Lord

Righteous art thou, O Lord,
when I plead with thee; yet let me talk
with thee of thy judgments: Wherefore
doth the way of the wicked prosper?
(Jeremiah 12:1)

Thou art indeed just, Lord, if I contend
With thee; but, sir, so what I plead is just.
Why do sinners' ways prosper? and why must
Disappointment all I endeavor end?
5   Wert thou my enemy, O thou my friend,
How wouldst thou worse, I wonder, than thou dost
Defeat, thwart me? Oh, the sots and thralls of lust
Do in spare hours more thrive than I that spend,
Sir, life upon thy cause. See, banks and brakes[1]
10 Now, leavèd how thick! lacèd they are again
With fretty chervil,[2] look, and fresh wind shakes
Them; birds build—but not I build; no, but strain,
Time's eunuch, and not breed one work that wakes.
Mine, O thou lord of life, send my roots rain.

1889   1918

The illustration above is a sketch by Hopkins of Shanklin in the Isle of Wight, dated 1866.

---

1. **brakes,** thickets.
2. **fretty chervil.** Chervil is an aromatic herb of the parsley family. *Fretty,* meaning "patterned like fretwork," describes its leaves.

Discussion

Pied Beauty

1. What particular characteristics of natural things does this poem celebrate? List several examples.

2. The compression of Hopkins's verse superimposes often oddly different images, one atop the other. Examine lines 2 and 3 and disentangle the individual images in each. Then, explain how Hopkins combines them, and how such a combination affects the reader.

3. Read lines 7 to 9 aloud and listen to them carefully. What rhythms do you hear? What kinds of sound do they make? How do their aural characteristics reinforce Hopkins's meaning?

4. In what way, according to "Pied Beauty," is God different from creation? Why does this characteristic merit praise?

God's Grandeur

1. What different characteristics of divine power do the first two sentences describe?

2. Examine lines 5 to 8 and analyze how Hopkins uses repetition of words, sounds, and ideas to move the reader.

3. What does Hopkins mean by the word *spent* in line 9, and the word *bent* in 13?

Spring and Fall

1. Why does the speaker, in the first four lines, express surprise at Margaret's response to autumn?

2. Why, in future years, will she become "colder" (line 6)?

3. The speaker refuses in line 10 to give the "name" of sorrow's springs. What do you think it is? Why won't he say it?

Thou art indeed just, Lord

1. Why does the speaker "contend" with the Lord; and yet call him "sir"? What human relationship do these words fit?

2. What is it that now seems to make the speaker's friend his enemy?

3. At the middle of line 9 the poem suddenly switches imagery. What sort of images dominate lines 9 to 12? How does this sudden introduction influence the development of the poem?

4. At the poem's conclusion, to whom does the speaker turn? For what does he ask?

Composition

From "God's Grandeur" select the three or four words which to your mind most exactly express how Hopkins looks at the world, its beauty and its ugliness.

Then in an essay use these same words to describe the natural world that you know personally.

A. E. Housman 1859–1936

As the oldest in a family of seven, Housman spent much of his boyhood instructing younger brothers and sisters, unconsciously anticipating the teaching role he was to take for most of his life. During these years he was very close to his mother, and under her direction he made a close study of the Bible.

Housman entered a private secondary school at age eleven. The next year brought the first major blow in his unhappy life. His mother, exhausted by the strain of childbearing and embittered by her husband's infidelities, died prematurely. Housman brooded over what he considered the injustice of her suffering.

At school he was a promising scholar of classical languages and won the prize for poetry two years in a row. In October of 1877, riding the crest of these successes, he entered Oxford on a scholarship. There he found the quality of instruction inadequate, and he soon began skipping lectures and ignoring required reading assignments, preferring to study authors of his own choosing by himself. With friends he founded and co-edited an undergraduate magazine *Ye Round Table,* to which he contributed high-spirited parodies of contemporary poetry and fiction. Privately, however, his view of himself and the world grew darker, and by 1880 he was a confirmed atheist.

In 1881 Housman failed the Oxford comprehensive examination in classics. He had clearly overestimated his own studies and foolishly ignored whole areas on which he was to be tested. He returned home, taught in a local school for a few months, and then acquired a civil service job in the Government Patent Office.

Living now in London, Housman resolved to vindicate himself, and in his free time he began on a course of intensive study of the classics. During the next ten years (1882–1892) he wrote over twenty scholarly essays, and when the post of Professor of Latin at the University of London became available in 1893, he applied, informing the College authorities of his failure at Oxford but also enclosing letters of commendation from seventeen authorities in his field. He got the job.

Housman had written poetry, on and off, since his boyhood, but beginning in 1893 a fresh burst of inspiration came to him and by 1895 he had 58 lyrics ready. Published that year at his own expense as *A Shropshire Lad,* the book enjoyed at first a very moderate success. But its reputation grew with time, and thanks to the appearance of some of its lyrics in paperback anthologies distributed to soldiers during World War I, its fame spread.

Housman's poetry is artfully simple. His subjects are the universal ones, love and death, overshadowed in his treatment by a pervasive pessimism. The "business of poetry," he once said, "is to harmonize the sadness of the universe." While the poems may allude to rural Shropshire, they do not grow out of experience. This is a stylized, literary countryside which owes more to Latin pastoral poetry than to conversations with real shepherds. But the sound of the verse does echo the music of folk ballads and song lyrics, and Housman's language is as simple and straightforward as any countryman could wish.

In his last years Housman enjoyed international acclaim for his scholarly work. But his work as a poet was essentially over. While he tried to present *Last Poems* (1922) as new work, most of its lyrics come from the years when he was first writing his *Shropshire Lad.* The inspiration of those years never returned to him.

When I Was One-and-Twenty

When I was one-and-twenty
　　I heard a wise man say,
"Give crowns and pounds and guineas
　　But not your heart away;
5　Give pearls away and rubies
　　But keep your fancy free."
But I was one-and-twenty,
　　No use to talk to me.

When I was one-and-twenty
10　I heard him say again,
"The heart out of the bosom
　　Was never given in vain;
'Tis paid with sighs a plenty
　　And sold for endless rue."
15　And I am two-and-twenty,
　　And oh, 'tis true, 'tis true.

1896

Comment: Housman on Writing His Poetry

Late in his life A. E. Housman accepted an invitation to lecture on poetry at Cambridge. At the end of his remarks he turned to the definition of the term. "Poetry," he said, ". . . seems to me more physical than intellectual . . ." and he went on to describe the physical "symptoms" which it "provokes": "Experience has taught me, when I am shaving of a morning, to keep watch over my thoughts, because, if a line of poetry strays into my memory, my skin bristles so that the razor ceases to act. This particular symptom is accompanied by a shiver down the spine . . ." Housman's description of how his poems began is equally physical: "Having drunk a pint of beer at luncheon— beer is a sedative to the brain, and my afternoons are the least intellectual portion of my life—I would go out for a walk of two or three hours. As I went along, thinking of nothing in particular, only looking at things around me and following the progress of the seasons, there would flow into my mind, with sudden and unaccountable emotion, sometimes a line or two of verse, sometimes a whole stanza at once, accompanied, not preceded, by a vague notion of the poem which they were destined to form a part of. Then there would usually be a lull of an hour or so, then perhaps the spring would bubble up again . . . When I got home I wrote them down, leaving gaps, and hoping that further inspiration might be forthcoming another day."

Excerpt from "The Name and Nature of Poetry" from *A. E. Housman Selected Prose*, edited by John Carter. Copyright © 1961 by Cambridge University Press. Reprinted by permission.

In a Shoreham Garden, by Samuel Palmer, painted about 1829.

Loveliest of Trees

Loveliest of trees, the cherry now
Is hung with bloom along the bough,
And stands about the woodland ride,
Wearing white for Eastertide.

5 Now, of my threescore years and ten,
Twenty will not come again,
And take from seventy springs a score,
It only leaves me fifty more.

And since to look at things in bloom
10 Fifty springs are little room,
About the woodlands I will go
To see the cherry hung with snow.

1896

To an Athlete Dying Young

The time you won your town the race
We chaired you through the market place;
Man and boy stood cheering by,
And home we brought you shoulder-high.

5 Today, the road all runners come,
Shoulder-high we bring you home,
And set you at your threshold down,
Townsman of a stiller town.

Smart lad, to slip betimes away
10 From fields where glory does not stay,
And early though the laurel grows
It withers quicker than the rose.

Eyes the shady night has shut
Cannot see the record cut,

15 And silence sounds no worse than cheers
After earth has stopped the ears.

Now you will not swell the rout
Of lads that wore their honors out,
Runners whom renown outran
20 And the name died before the man.

So set, before its echoes fade,
The fleet foot on the sill of shade,
And hold to the low lintel up
The still-defended challenge cup.

25 And round that early-laureled head
Will flock to gaze the strengthless dead,
And find unwithered on its curls
The garland briefer than a girl's.

1896

Discussion

When I Was One-and-Twenty

1. What kind of language does the "wise man" choose in discussing love? Note, in particular, his verbs. Why would the young man ignore him?

2. What would life be like if one followed the old man's advice?

Loveliest of Trees

1. What is it about the blossom of the cherry tree that makes it the "loveliest of trees" for this speaker? Consider, especially, the connotations of the poem's last metaphor.

2. What is the speaker doing in the second stanza? Why?

To an Athlete Dying Young

1. The poem describes two processions. Compare and contrast them.

2. What does the speaker mean by "a stiller town"? List the details he gives which describe it.

3. Why does the speaker consider the athlete a "Smart lad" (line 9)?

Composition

Housman thinks the athlete is a "smart lad" to die before someone else betters his record. Write down what you think must be the assumptions that lie behind this kind of thinking.

Using this list of assumptions as a source of ideas to affirm or deny, write an essay explaining your own way of facing the possibility that sooner or later someone else is going to do what you do a little better.

William Butler Yeats 1865–1939

As a child Yeats (yāts) divided his time between Dublin (and later, London), where his father worked as a portrait painter, and County Sligo in the West of Ireland, where he lived with his mother's family of sailors and merchants. It was from them that he first became acquainted with the oral literature of the Irish peasantry. He was a mediocre student, uninterested in most of the subjects taught. For a while, in his late teens, he tried painting as a career, but finally determined to write.

His first books, published before the end of the century, define his lifelong interests. The poems collected in *The Wanderings of Oisin* derive from his intensive study of Irish myth and folklore. For centuries Ireland had been an English colony, its economy exploited and its native culture suppressed. Yeats's early poems and his book on Irish folk tales, *The Celtic Twilight* (1893), were in part political acts. "We had in Ireland," he wrote, "imaginative stories, which the uneducated classes knew and even sang, and might we not make those stories current among the educated classes . . . and at last . . . so deepen the political passion of the nation that all . . . would accept a common design?" Yeats's plays, beginning with *The Countess Cathleen* (1892), had, for some time, this same goal.

It was through his growing involvement in Irish politics that Yeats first met the revolutionary agitator Maud Gonne. Her beauty and the power of her personality overwhelmed him. Yeats repeatedly proposed marriage but she always refused him, her sole interest fixed on achieving Irish independence.

During the same period Yeats also embarked on a lifelong spiritual quest. Dissatisfied both with his father's atheism and with orthodox religion, he searched for a hidden supernatural dimension in life, joining secret mystical societies, attending séances, and studying alchemy and esoteric philosophy. From this odd lore he acquired not only his belief in a spirit world and reincarnation, but also a body of symbolic images that gave coherence and visual power to his writing. He felt convinced these symbols derived their authority and power from their source in the "Great Memory," the collective unconsciousness of humanity that connects individuals with the *Spiritus Mundi* (Latin for "soul of the world").

In 1905 Yeats and his close friend Lady Augusta Gregory cofounded the Abbey Theatre in Dublin. Here their plays, as well as works by J. M. Synge and Sean O'Casey, created a new, specifically Irish drama that had strong influence both on the modern theater and on Irish politics.

Writing for the stage impressed Yeats with the importance of precise, spare language. The darkening sky of European history confirmed the necessity for him to cast off what he called the "overcharged color" of his early poetry. He "deliberately reshaped" his style, seeking something "hard and cold, some articulation of the Image, which is the opposite of all that I am . . . and all that my country is . . ." As Yeats's poetry dealt with the horror of the Irish fight for independence and looked forward toward an uncertain future world, it acquired the clarity and conciseness that mark twentieth-century style. In his own work Yeats thus began as one of the last romantics but evolved into a leader in modernist, experimental poetry. The evolution of Yeats's art never ceased. The poems written when he was an old man are his most audacious. In 1923 Yeats received the Nobel Prize for Literature.

When You Are Old

When you are old and gray and full of sleep,
And nodding by the fire, take down this book,
And slowly read, and dream of the soft look
Your eyes had once, and of their shadows deep;

5 How many loved your moments of glad grace,
And loved your beauty with love false or true,
But one man loved the pilgrim soul in you,
And loved the sorrows of your changing face;

And bending down beside the glowing bars,
10 Murmur, a little sadly, how Love fled
And paced upon the mountains overhead
And hid his face amid a crowd of stars.

1892

From *Collected Poems* by William Butler Yeats (New York: Macmillan, 1956). Reprinted by permission of Macmillan Publishing Company, Michael B. Yeats, Anne Yeats and Macmillan, London, Limited.

Maud Gonne (1866–1953), Irish nationalist with whom Yeats was in love and to whom a number of his poems are addressed, including "When Your Are Old" and "Adam's Curse."

Comment: Yeats and Ronsard

"When You Are Old" is, among other things, a rewriting of a sonnet by the French poet Pierre de Ronsard (1524–1585) published in 1552. Yeats's first words simply translate Ronsard's, but their conclusions are very different. When Ronsard looks into the future, he imagines that, "I shall be underground and, a ghost without bones, / By the shadows of myrtle trees I will take my rest. . ." Hoping this pathetic picture might move his beloved to regret her "proud disdain," he suddenly makes this concluding suggestion: "Live now, believe me, don't wait for tomorrow; / Gather today the roses of this life." The effect Ronsard wished his poem to have is clear. But, what does Yeats's poem seek to achieve?

Comment: Yeats on the Source of "Innisfree"

. . . Sometimes I told myself very adventurous love-stories with myself for hero, and at other times I planned out a life of lonely austerity, and at other times mixed the ideals and planned a life of lonely austerity mitigated by periodical lapses. I had still the ambition, formed in Sligo in my teens, of living in imitation of Thoreau on Innisfree, a little island in Lough Gill, and when walking through Fleet Street very homesick I heard a little tinkle of water and saw a fountain in a shop-window which balanced a little ball upon its jet, and began to remember lake water. From the sudden remembrance came my poem *Innisfree*, my first lyric with anything in its rhythm of my own music.

From *The Autobiography of William Butler Yeats*, Macmillan, 1965, page 103.

The Lake Isle of Innisfree

I will arise and go now, and go to Innisfree,
And a small cabin build there, of clay and wattles made;
Nine bean rows will I have there, a hive for the honeybee,
And live alone in the bee-loud glade.

5 And I shall have some peace there, for peace comes dropping slow,
Dropping from the veils of the morning to where the cricket sings;
There midnight's all a-glimmer, and noon a purple glow,
And evening full of the linnet's wings.[1]

I will arise and go now, for always night and day
10 I hear lake water lapping with low sounds by the shore;
While I stand on the roadway, or on the pavements gray,
I hear it in the deep heart's core.

1892

From *Collected Poems* by William Butler Yeats (New York: Macmillan, 1956). Reprinted by permission of Macmillan Publishing Company, Michael B. Yeats, Anne Yeats and Macmillan, London, Limited.

1. linnet's wings. The linnet is a small songbird.

Adam's Curse

We sat together at one summer's end,
That beautiful mild woman, your close friend,
And you[1] and I, and talked of poetry.
I said, "A line will take us hours maybe;
5 Yet if it does not seem a moment's thought,
Our stitching and unstitching has been naught.
Better go down upon your marrow-bones[2]
And scrub a kitchen pavement, or break stones
Like an old pauper, in all kinds of weather;
10 For to articulate sweet sounds together
Is to work harder than all these, and yet
Be thought an idler by the noisy set
Of bankers, schoolmasters, and clergymen
The martyrs call the world."
                And thereupon
15 That beautiful mild woman for whose sake
There's many a one shall find out all heartache
On finding that her voice is sweet and low
Replied, "To be born woman is to know—
Although they do not talk of it at school—
20 That we must labor to be beautiful."
I said, "It's certain there is no fine thing
Since Adam's fall but needs much laboring.
There have been lovers who thought love should be
So much compounded of high courtesy
25 That they would sigh and quote with learned looks
Precedents out of beautiful old books;
Yet now it seems an idle trade enough."

We sat grown quiet at the name of love;
We saw the last embers of daylight die,
30 And in the trembling blue-green of the sky
A moon, worn as if it had been a shell
Washed by time's waters as they rose and fell
About the stars and broke in days and years.

I had a thought for no one's but your ears:
35 That you were beautiful, and that I strove
To love you in the old high way of love;[3]
That it had all seemed happy, and yet we'd grown
As weary-hearted as that hollow moon.   1903

According to the story of creation in Genesis (see pages 230–233), God cursed Adam and Eve for their disobedience. Eve's portion was the pain of childbirth and the rule of her husband. Adam's curse was lifelong toil and final death: "In the sweat of thy face shalt thou eat bread, till thou return to the ground; for out of it wast thou taken: for dust thou art, and unto dust thou shalt return." (Genesis 3:17–19)

Brown Penny

I whispered, "I am too young."
And then, "I am old enough";
Wherefore I threw a penny
To find out if I might love.
5 "Go and love, go and love, young man,
If the lady be young and fair."
Ah, penny, brown penny, brown penny,
I am looped in the loops of her hair.

O love is the crooked thing,
10 There is nobody wise enough
To find out all that is in it,
For he would be thinking of love
Till the stars had run away
And the shadows eaten the moon.
15 Ah, penny, brown penny, brown penny,
One cannot begin it too soon.
                    1910

From *Collected Poems* by William Butler Yeats (New York: Macmillan, 1956). Reprinted by permission of Macmillan Publishing Company, Michael B. Yeats, Anne Yeats and Macmillan, London, Limited.

1. *you,* Maud Gonne (gun), the Irish revolutionary Yeats loved and made the subject of many early poems. Her portrait appears on page 551.
2. *marrow-bones,* knees.
3. *the old high way of love,* medieval and renaissance ideals of love and courtesy, with all the elaborate conventions accompanying them that governed aristocratic sexuality.

"Brown Penny" from *Collected Poems* by William Butler Yeats. Copyright 1912 by Macmillan Publishing Co., Inc., renewed 1940 by Bertha Georgie Yeats. Reprinted by permission of Macmillan Publishing Company, Michael B. Yeats, Anne Yeats and Macmillan, London, Limited.

Discussion

The Lake Isle of Innisfree

1. The images of line 11 depict the world in which the poem's speaker now lives. By studying what he seeks at Innisfree, infer what his present life must be like.

2. Yeats described this poem as his first lyric with the "rhythm of my own music." Repetition plays a major role in this movement. **(a)** What words does the poet repeat? **(b)** What sounds—consonants and vowels—does this poem repeat?

When You Are Old

1. Compare the two kinds of love described in the second stanza. In particular, what does the phrase "pilgrim soul" mean?

2. Lines 1-2 and 9 picture his love when she is old. What sort of old age does he predict for her?

3. Lines 9 and 12 contrast the speaker and his beloved. Analyze the opposing states described in these two images. Now, who has the "pilgrim soul"?

Adam's Curse

1. In Genesis Adam's curse describes the hard life of the farmer. Yeats lists three other kinds of labor. What are they? Why doesn't "the world" (line 14) consider these efforts true work? What is it about them that commands the poet's respect?

2. How do the images of the last two verse paragraphs embody the final part of Adam's curse (". . . dust thou art, and unto dust thou shalt return")?

Brown Penny

Images of stars (line 13) and the moon (line 14) familiar from earlier Yeats love poems, reappear here. But the brown penny is new. How does the image of the brown penny differ from those earlier images and how does it affect the tone of this poem?

Vocabulary
Dictionary

Use your Glossary to answer the following questions about the italicized words. Write your answers on a separate sheet of paper. Be sure you know the meaning, spelling, and pronunciation of each word.

1. (a) From what specific Scandinavian language does *thwart* come? **(b)** What is the spelling and meaning of the original word from which *thwart* comes?

2. What are the three Latin words given in the development of the word *fidelity*?

3. (a) What is the spelling of the Greek word from which *anarchy* comes? **(b)** What is the meaning of the prefix and root that form the Greek word?

4. Look at the entry for *blight* and tell why it is or is not an appropriate word to describe humanity in the concluding lines of Hopkins's "Spring and Fall."

5. What religious meanings does the word *revelation* have?

6. (a) What do the Latin root words in *artifice* mean? **(b)** How many syllables does the word have? **(c)** Write one rhyme word each for the first and third syllables.

The Wild Swans at Coole[1]

The trees are in their autumn beauty,
The woodland paths are dry,
Under the October twilight the water
Mirrors a still sky;
5 Upon the brimming water among the
    stones
Are nine-and-fifty swans.

The nineteenth autumn has come
    upon me
Since I first made my count;
I saw, before I had well finished,
10 All suddenly mount
And scatter wheeling in great broken
    rings
Upon their clamorous wings.

I have looked upon those brilliant
    creatures,
And now my heart is sore.
15 All's changed since I, hearing at
    twilight,
The first time on this shore,
The bell-beat of their wings above my
    head,
Trod with a lighter tread.

Unwearied still, lover by lover,
20 They paddle in the cold
Companionable streams or climb the
    air;
Their hearts have not grown old;
Passion or conquest, wander where they will,
Attend upon them still.

25 But now they drift on the still water,
Mysterious, beautiful;
Among what rushes will they build,
By what lake's edge or pool
Delight men's eyes when I awake some day
30 To find they have flown away?

1917

"Swan, Rush, and Iris," a design for wallpaper by Walter Crane, 1877.

1. *Coole* (kül). Coole Park was the country estate of Yeats's wealthy friend Lady Augusta Gregory (1852-1932), the Irish playwright and folklorist.

*S*ailing to Byzantium[1]

A sixteenth–century illustration of Istanbul.

I

That is no country for old men. The young
In one another's arms, birds in the trees,
—Those dying generations—at their song,
The salmon-falls, the mackerel-crowded seas,
5 Fish, flesh, or fowl, commend all summer long
Whatever is begotten, born, and dies.
Caught in that sensual music all neglect
Monuments of unaging intellect.

II

An aged man is but a paltry thing,
10 A tattered coat upon a stick, unless
Soul clap its hands and sing, and louder sing
For every tatter in its mortal dress,
Nor is there singing school but studying
Monuments of its own magnificence;
15 And therefore I have sailed the seas and come
To the holy city of Byzantium.

III

O sages standing in God's holy fire
As in the gold mosaic of a wall
Come from the holy fire, perne in a gyre,[2]
20 And be the singing-masters of my soul.
Consume my heart away; sick with desire

(*"Sailing to Byzantium"* concludes on page 558.)

---

1. Byzantium, ancient name for the city that became Constantinople and later Istanbul. For Yeats, however, it was not so much a place as an ideal, a symbol for the timeless world of art and intellect as opposed to the natural world of biological change. It was a "holy city": literally, because it was the center of Eastern Christendom; symbolically, because it fostered that development of intellect and imagination that produces artistic perfection. Byzantine art was highly stylized, abandoning all naturalistic representation.
2. perne in a gyre. A perne (or *pirn*) is a spool or bobbin; a gyre is a spiraling motion describing a cone. The image seems to be of a long file of sages, spiraling down like the thread flying off a spinning bobbin, forming ever tighter circles that narrow to a single point, the poet who is calling the sages to himself.

And fastened to a dying animal
It knows not what it is; and gather me
Into the artifice of eternity.

IV

25 Once out of nature I shall never take
My bodily form from any natural thing,
But such a form as Grecian goldsmiths make[3]
Of hammered gold and gold enameling

To keep a drowsy Emperor awake;
30 Or set upon a golden bough to sing
To lords and ladies of Byzantium
Of what is past, or passing, or to come.

1927

---

3. **such . . . make.** Yeats wrote, "I have read somewhere that in the emperor's palace at Byzantium was a tree made of gold and silver, and artificial birds that sang."

Reader's Note: "Sailing to Byzantium"

The title suggests this is a poem about a process: the word "Sailing" tells us of something continuously happening—not "I will sail" or "I once sailed," but "I am sailing." (The title for the first draft of the poem suggests this same idea in a different way: "Towards Byzantium.")

The declaration of lines 15-16, "therefore I have sailed the seas and come / To the holy city of Byzantium," might seem to contradict this suggestion, until it becomes clear that the city's name also represents a spiritual state. Though the speaker may already be physically in the city of Byzantium, he is still metaphorically on his journey "out of nature" (line 25) to the ultimate Byzantium of pure spirit, and he isn't there yet.

The fact that the speaker has not reached his goal is important. His poem illustrates how divided his feelings still are about the quest he has undertaken. He has not altogether lost as yet his love for "that sensual music" (line 7) from the land of the young. His is a heart still "sick with desire" (line 21), and at least one reason he now sails away from "the mackerel-crowded seas" (line 4) of youth is that his body ages. It is a "dying animal" (line 22) or "a tattered coat upon a stick" (line 10), and the only escape from the pain and confusion he feels because of his divided self is to cast off that "sick" heart, that "dying" body.

His mind has already perceived a fatal inadequacy in "Those dying generations" (line 3). They are so "Caught in that sensual music" that they "neglect / Monuments of unaging intellect." (lines 7-8). He determines to fix his hope on this form of permanence. These are monuments to that other aspect of self, to the soul's "own magnificence" (line 14); studying them trains the soul (line 13) to sing, and in so doing to rise above the losses of aging, singing "louder . . . / For every tatter in its mortal dress . . . " (lines 11–12). In this "singing school" (line 13) the "singing-masters" (line 20) are those "sages" (line 17) who have achieved spiritual purity. "God's holy fire" (line 17) has burned away every speck of the physical and the imperfect—to these sages the fire is but a golden backdrop, such as one sees behind the saints in Byzantine mosaics. Rather passively the poet calls to these teachers to come and "gather" (line 23) him into their form of eternity—artificial, in the sense that it is entirely the creation of human spirit. There is nothing natural about it.

The strange picture of a golden mechanical bird translates the imagery of stanza 1 into another form of being. The "birds in the trees" (line 2) now become the poet as a fabulous toy; "the young / In one another's arms" (lines 1–2) hearing their own "sensual music" become "a drowsy Emperor" (line 29) and the "lords and ladies of Byzantium" (line 31). There may be a fair bit of irony in this last stanza. Is it better to keep a "drowsy Emperor awake" than to be caught up in "that sensuous music"?

*T*he Second Coming[1]

Turning and turning in the widening gyre[2]
The falcon cannot hear the falconer;
Things fall apart; the center cannot hold;
Mere anarchy is loosed upon the world,
5 The blood-dimmed tide is loosed, and everywhere
The ceremony of innocence is drowned;
The best lack all conviction, while the worst
Are full of passionate intensity.

Surely some revelation is at hand;
10 Surely the Second Coming is at hand.
The Second Coming! Hardly are those words out
When a vast image out of *Spiritus Mundi*[3]
Troubles my sight: somewhere in sands of the
   desert
A shape with lion body and the head of a man,
15 A gaze blank and pitiless as the sun,

Is moving its slow thighs, while all about it
Reel shadows of the indignant desert birds.
The darkness drops again; but now I know
That twenty centuries of stony sleep
20 Were vexed to nightmare by a rocking cradle,
And what rough beast, its hour come round at last,
Slouches towards Bethlehem to be born?   1921

1. *The Second Coming.* In this poem Yeats borrows a Christian concept—the Second Coming of Christ at the end of the world—in order to develop his own notion of historical change.
2. *gyre* (jīr), a spiral motion.
3. *Spiritus Mundi,* "soul of the world." [Latin] Yeats believed in the existence of a "Great Memory," a collective unconscious that connected individuals with the *Spiritus Mundi,* and was a reservoir of symbolic images from the past.

Reader's Note: "The Second Coming"

By the year 1920, Yeats saw the old order of the world flying apart. The horrors of World War I were just past, and now Ireland seemed moving toward anarchy, as squads of assassins from the revolutionary Sinn Fein (shin fān) independence movement and the official Royal Irish Constabulary murdered innocent citizens in opposing terrorist campaigns. "We are," he wrote, "but weasels fighting in a hole." The end of everything he valued seemed at hand, and it made Yeats think of the Second Coming.

In the Gospels, Jesus warns his disciples that he will be crucified, but assures them that he will return again, after an uncertain length of time. Cataclysmic violence will precede this Second Coming, warning everyone that the end of the world is at hand.

Yeats intends his readers to recall this Christian tradition, clearly alluding to the destruction which foreshadows Christ's return in lines 4 to 8 and to his first coming in the reference to Bethlehem (line 22).

But Yeats was no Christian, and he alters the traditional story in a particular way, to make it fit his own theory of history. In his version it is not Jesus who returns, but rather some other divinity, too alien to be fully comprehended. The poet's knowledge of this new god comes from a vision he has had, a vision which rises out of the shared unconscious mind in which all human beings participate and to which Yeats refers by its Latin name, the *Spiritus Mundi,* the "soul of the world." The vision this creates in the poet's mind is vague but menacing—the poet tries to describe it in lines 13–18, but soon loses it, and "darkness drops again" (line 18). He is still so unsure of its meaning that he ends his poem with a question.

What he does understand is that during the past two thousand years (an even number, which seemed to Yeats a complete era in earthly history) this new beast-god has been in stony sleep (line 19), waiting to be born, and angered ("vexed") by the more gentle god of Christianity, symbolized by the "rocking cradle" (line 20) of the infant Jesus. Now this "rough beast" (line 21) is moving toward its own birth, its own, ominous Bethlehem.

Discussion

The Wild Swans at Coole

1. In what ways is the season of the year in this poem an appropriate setting for its speaker?

2. What are the crucial differences between the swans and the speaker?

Sailing to Byzantium

1. In "Sailing to Byzantium" the first two stanzas describe a country the speaker has left, and the last two describe the country (Byzantium) to which he is going. Both countries are symbolic only. Keeping this in mind, consider the following questions: **(a)** What images does Yeats use in stanza one to describe the first country? What is missing in the lives of those who live there? **(b)** Why does the speaker sail to Byzantium? What does he hope to lose before he reaches his destination? **(c)** What does the old man wish to do when he reaches Byzantium?

2. List the words and the consonant sounds Yeats repeats in the second stanza. Explain how the repeated words stress his ideas and how the sounds reinforce them. Compare the repetition here to the second stanza of "The Sorrow of Love" (first version, 1892). How has the music of Yeats's poetry, and its function, changed?

The Second Coming

1. In the first eight lines of this poem Yeats tries to describe the characteristics of our era in history. Tell what it is that terrifies him by carefully examining the words and images that he employs in the following phrases: **(a)** "the center cannot hold"; **(b)** "The blood-dimmed tide is loosed"; **(c)** "The ceremony of innocence is drowned"; **(d)** "The best lack all conviction"; **(e)** "the worst / Are full of passionate intensity."

2. What does the description of the "rough beast" suggest about its nature? What will life be like, do you think, once it becomes a god?

*T*he Sorrow of Love

The quarrel of the sparrows in the eaves,
The full round moon and the star-laden sky,
And the loud song of the ever-singing leaves
Had hid away earth's old and weary cry.

5   And then you came with those red mournful lips,
And with you came the whole of the world's
        tears,
And all the sorrows of her laboring ships,
And all the burden of her myriad years.

And now the sparrows warring in the eaves,
10 The crumbling moon, the white stars in the sky,
And the loud chanting of the unquiet leaves,
Are shaken with earth's old and weary cry.

1892

"The Sorrow of Love" from *The Variorum Edition of the Poems of W. B. Yeats* edited by Peter Allt and Russell K. Alspach (New York: Macmillan, 1957). Reprinted by permission of Michael Yeats and Macmillan London Limited.

*T*he Sorrow of Love

The brawling of a sparrow in the eaves,
The brilliant moon and all the milky sky,
And all that famous harmony of leaves,
Had blotted out man's image and his cry.

5   A girl arose that had red mournful lips
And seemed the greatness of the world in tears,
Doomed like Odysseus and the laboring ships
And proud as Priam murdered with his peers;[1]

Arose, and on the instant clamorous eaves,
10 A climbing moon upon an empty sky,
And all that lamentation of the leaves,
Could but compose man's image and his cry.   1927

From *Collected Poems* by William Butler Yeats (New York: Macmillan, 1956). Reprinted by permission of Macmillan Publishing Company, Michael B. Yeats, Anne Yeats and Macmillan, London, Limited.

1. **Odysseus . . . Priam murdered with his peers.** Odysseus (o dis′ e əs), king of Ithaca, was one of the Greek force besieging Troy in Homer's *Iliad*. His ten-years' wandering following the end of the Trojan War is the subject of Homer's *Odyssey*. Priam (pri′əm) was king of Troy, and died along with most of his nobles ("his peers") when the city was sacked by the Greeks.

Reader's Note: Yeats's Revision of ''The Sorrow of Love''

Yeats was a constant reviser of his own work, both before and after its publication, and frequently a lyric's final version is the consequence of many second thoughts. ''The Sorrow of Love'' furnishes an extreme example; the version of 1927 is virtually a new poem, compared to the original of 1892.

Yeats begins the earlier of the two with a puzzling first stanza. The sounds of leaves and sparrows, the sight of the moon and stars, have somehow hidden ''earth's old and weary cry'' (line 4). Since these things are of the earth, the poem must use the term in some special sense. That it does becomes clear with the next stanza.

The ''red mournful lips'' (line 5) refer to Maud Gonne, whose distant beauty frustrates Yeats's passion in other celebrated poems of this era including ''When You Are Old'' and ''Adam's Curse.'' Now the special meaning of the ''earth's . . . cry'' should be clear.

In the last stanza the power of earth's cry ''shakes'' the sounds and sights which once seemed to keep it hidden. The reader must infer what this shaking might be. It seems to alter the appearance of things. In stanza 1 the sparrows ''quarrel'' but in stanza 3 they are ''warring.'' The moon is ''full'' in 1, but ''crumbling'' in 3, while the leaves were, at first, ''ever-singing,'' now they are ''unquiet.'' Earth's ''old and weary cry'' has effected a fundamental shift in perception.

Thirty-five years later, much had changed. Maud Gonne, after repeatedly refusing Yeats, married John MacBride (1865–1916) in 1903. It was an unhappy union, and after two years they legally separated. She continued in her absolute dedication to revolutionary causes and in time Yeats came to associate her destructive beauty with that of Helen, who precipitated the Trojan War. Yeats married and fathered two children. But he never ceased to feel the impact of his first passion.

The 1927 version of ''The Sorrow of Love'' is not, as in 1892, directly addressed to Maud Gonne. In lines 5–6 she has become an objective symbol of the sorrow the poem describes, a figure from the past that represents a fundamental human emotion. To define her uncontrollable attraction to revolutionary agitation, as well as her self-destructive pride, the speaker compares her to Odysseus and Priam. Such allusions, typical of Yeats's later style, lift the poem into the realm of myth, and imply that great and tragic figures still appear in the modern world. The earlier version's reference to ''laboring ships'' (line 8) may have been an attempt to suggest such ideas, but now they find a clear, objective statement.

One puzzle from the first version is now gone: ''earth's . . . cry'' has become ''man's image and his cry'' (line 4). But some of the contrast between the first and third stanzas, so dramatically evident in the first version, is now gone. There is no particular difference between ''brawling'' (line 1) and ''clamorous'' (line 9) or change between ''brilliant'' (line 2) and ''climbing'' (line 10). Only the shift from ''harmony'' (line 3) to ''lamentation'' (line 11) suggests any alteration.

And indeed the conclusion of the poem may be different. The 1892 version ends with the speaker's perception of the world ''shaken'' (line 12), but in 1927 that word becomes ''compose.'' It is an ambiguous term, which can mean to create, in the sense that one composes a picture or a piece of music; or it can mean to give order and control, so that we speak of someone as ''composed.'' Both senses fit this context. The contrast between ''shaken'' and ''compose'' can thus imply a new and different way of thinking about the sorrow of love.

Girl's Song

I went out alone
To sing a song or two,
My fancy on a man,
And you know who.

5 Another came in sight
That on a stick relied
To hold himself upright;
I sat and cried.

And that was all my song—
10 When everything is told,
Saw I an old man young
Or young man old?

1932

Young Man's Song

"She will change," I cried,
"Into a withered crone."
The heart in my side,
That so still had lain,
5 In noble rage replied
And beat upon the bone:

"Uplift those eyes and throw
Those glances unafraid:
She would as bravely show
10 Did all the fabric fade;
No withered crone I saw
Before the world was made."

Abashed by that report,
For the heart cannot lie,
15 I knelt in the dirt.
And all shall bend the knee
To my offended heart
Until it pardon me.

1932

Swift's Epitaph

Jonathan Swift's tomb in St. Patrick's Cathedral in Dublin bears the Latin epitaph he composed for himself. A literal English version would be: "Here lies the body of Jonathan Swift, Dean of this Cathedral Church, where savage indignation cannot lacerate his heart anymore. Traveler, go, and imitate if you can his strenuous vindication of man's liberty." "Swift's Epitaph" is Yeats's poetic version.

Swift has sailed into his rest;
Savage indignation there
Cannot lacerate his breast.
Imitate him if you dare,
5 World-besotted traveller; he
Served human liberty.

1933

Discussion

The Sorrow of Love

1. What do "earth's old and weary cry" in the first version and "man's image and his cry" in the second describe? Discuss whether there is a shift in emphasis between the first and second versions of this line.

2. Explain what the first version means by "shaken" (line 12) and how this alters the speaker's perceptions.

3. What are the different possible meanings for the word "composed" (line 12) in the second version?

Girl's Song

The question which ends "Girl's Song" asks the reader to choose between two alternatives. Discuss the meaning the poem would have if the answer to her question were "both."

Young Man's Song

How can the woman in "Young Man's Song" "as bravely show" even after "all the fabric fade"? What could his heart have seen "Before the world was made"?

Swift's Epitaph

Why call the traveler "World-besotted"?

Composition

1. In an effort to imagine the future, Yeats's "Second Coming" describes the poet's vision of a beast, the rough god of the coming era. What do you think the future holds in store? Create your own symbolic image that will serve as an emblem for the future you think is coming.

In an essay, first describe your vision, and then explain to your reader what it means.

2. There are many different sorts of love. Look back over Yeats's poems. How does he address the woman he loves?

In an essay describe the character of the emotion you observe in Yeats's love poetry.

Joseph Conrad 1857–1924

While a number of celebrated writers at the beginning of this century lived unusual and romantic lives, Conrad's is the most exotic, the most surprising. He was born Józef Teodor Konrad Korzeniowski. His father and mother were aristocrats of a Polish nation ruled by Russia. His father was an idealistic patriot and a writer. When Conrad was four years old, the police jailed his father for subversive political activities and in May of 1862 exiled the family to a bleak town in northern Russia near the Ural Mountains. There the harsh climate permanently damaged his parents' already weakened health. In 1863 the family moved to a milder climate in a town 125 miles from Kiev, where the five-year-old Joseph learned to read French and Polish from "a good, ugly governess."

Though finally permitted to return home, the family had already suffered irremediable harm. Conrad's mother died in 1865 when he was seven, and his father died four years later.

Conrad's uncle took responsibility for this melancholy but intelligent eleven-year-old boy, who was already reading Cervantes and Dickens. Romantic adventure novels gave him the desire to escape to the sea, and for several years his uncle unsuccessfully tried to dissuade him. Finally, he gave in, and Conrad, now seventeen, joined the French merchant marine at Marseilles, feeling "like a man in a dream."

He served as apprentice and then steward on ships sailing for the West Indies and the coast of South America. Accompanying a fellow sailor, Conrad even smuggled guns to guerrilla bands in Spain in 1876. This reckless adolescence reached a climax when Conrad lost 800 francs gambling and tried to commit suicide. His uncle arrived and paid his debts, and Conrad entered into a more stable young manhood, joining the British merchant navy in June of 1878. During the next sixteen years he worked his way up to the rank of ship's captain, became a naturalized British subject, and saw the world—Australia, Singapore, Java, Siam (now Thailand), Malaysia, and Sumatra. In 1890 he made a trip—later immortalized in his novella *Heart of Darkness*—up the Congo River to Stanley Falls.

Jungle fever, contracted during this adventure, permanently weakened Conrad's health. And at the same time, a very different interest was taking him over. In 1889 he had begun writing a novel. By 1894 it was complete, and when a publisher accepted it, Conrad shifted his energies to literature.

In the next 29 years he wrote 31 volumes of fiction and reminiscence. Many of his stories and novels derive from the adventures of his young manhood, events now examined with the retrospective eye of an older, more thoughtful man—much like Marlow in "Youth." These novels of the sea, such as *Lord Jim* (1900), as well as later studies of politics such as *Nostromo* (1904), *The Secret Agent* (1907), and *Under Western Eyes* (1911) established Conrad as one of the most important English novelists of the first half of the century.

Youth

This could have occurred nowhere but in England, where men and sea interpenetrate, so to speak—the sea entering into the life of most men, and the men knowing something or everything about the sea, in the way of amusement, of travel, or of breadwinning.

We were sitting round a mahogany table that reflected the bottle, the claret-glasses, and our faces as we leaned on our elbows. There was a director of companies, an accountant, a lawyer, Marlow, and myself. The director had been a *Conway* boy,[1] the accountant had served four years at sea, the lawyer—a fine crusted Tory, High Churchman, the best of old fellows, the soul of honor—had been chief officer in the P. & O. service[2] in the good old days when mail-boats were square-rigged at least on two masts, and used to come down the China Sea before a fair monsoon with stun'-sails set alow and aloft. We all began life in the merchant service. Between the five of us there was the strong bond of the sea, and also the fellowship of the craft, which no amount of enthusiasm for yachting, cruising, and so on can give, since one is only the amusement of life and the other is life itself.

Marlow (at least I think that is how he spelt his name) told the story, or rather the chronicle, of a voyage:

"Yes, I have seen a little of the Eastern seas; but what I remember best is my first voyage there. You fellows know there are those voyages that seem ordered for the illustration of life, that might stand for a symbol of existence. You fight, work, sweat, nearly kill yourself, sometimes do kill yourself, trying to accomplish something— and you can't. Not from any fault of yours. You simply can do nothing, neither great nor little— not a thing in the world—not even marry an old maid, or get a wretched 600-ton cargo of coal to its port of destination.

"It was altogether a memorable affair. It was my first voyage to the East, and my first voyage as second mate; it was also my skipper's first command. You'll admit it was time. He was sixty if a day; a little man, with a broad, not very straight back, with bowed shoulders and one leg more bandy than the other, he had that queer twisted-about appearance you see so often in men who work in the fields. He had a nutcracker face—chin and nose trying to come together over a sunken mouth—and it was framed in iron-gray fluffy hair, that looked like a chin-strap of cotton-wool sprinkled with coal-dust. And he had blue eyes in that old face of his, which were amazingly like a boy's, with that candid expression some quite common men preserve to the end of their days by a rare internal gift of simplicity of heart and rectitude of soul. What induced him to accept me was a wonder. I had come out of a crack Australian clipper, where I had been third officer, and he seemed to have a prejudice against crack clippers as aristocratic and high-toned. He said to me, 'You know, in this ship you will have to work.' I said I had to work in every ship I had ever been in. 'Ah, but this is different, and you gentlemen out of them big ships; . . . but there! I dare say you will do. Join tomorrow.'

"I joined tomorrow. It was twenty-two years ago; and I was just twenty. How time passes! It was one of the happiest days of my life. Fancy! Second mate for the first time—a really responsible officer! I wouldn't have thrown up my new billet for a fortune. The mate looked me over carefully. He was also an old chap, but of another stamp. He had a Roman nose, a snow-white, long beard, and his name was Mahon, but he insisted that it should be pronounced Mann. He was well connected; yet there was something wrong with his luck, and he had never got on.

---

1. *a Conway boy.* The *Conway* was a training ship on which student officers for the British merchant navy gained sea experience.
2. *the P & O service,* "Pacific and Oriental," a famous British shipping line to the Far East.

"As to the captain, he had been for years in coasters, then in the Mediterranean, and last in the West Indian trade. He had never been round the Capes.[3] He could just write a kind of sketchy hand, and didn't care for writing at all. Both were thorough good seamen of course, and between those two old chaps I felt like a small boy between two grandfathers.

"The ship also was old. Her name was the *Judea*.[4] Queer name, isn't it? She belonged to a man Wilmer, Wilcox—some name like that; but he has been bankrupt and dead these twenty years or more, and his name don't matter. She had been laid up in Shadwell basin for ever so long. You may imagine her state. She was all rust, dust, grime—soot aloft, dirt on deck. To me it was like coming out of a palace into a ruined cottage. She was about 400 tons, had a primitive windlass, wooden latches to the doors, not a bit of brass about her, and a big square stern. There was on it, below her name in big letters, a lot of scrollwork, with the gilt off, and some sort of a coat of arms, with the motto 'Do or Die' underneath. I remember it took my fancy immensely. There was a touch of romance in it, something that made me love the old thing—something that appealed to my youth!

"We left London in ballast—sand ballast—to load a cargo of coal in a northern port for Bankok. Bankok! I thrilled. I had been six years at sea, but had only seen Melbourne and Sydney, very good places, charming places in their way—but Bankok!

"We worked out of the Thames under canvas, with a North Sea pilot on board. His name was Jermyn, and he dodged all day long about the galley drying his handkerchief before the stove. Apparently he never slept. He was a dismal man, with a perpetual tear sparkling at the end of his nose, who either had been in trouble, or was in trouble, or expected to be in trouble—couldn't be happy unless something went wrong. He mistrusted my youth, my commonsense, and my seamanship, and made a point of showing it in a hundred little ways. I dare say he was right. It seems to me I knew very little then, and I know not much more now; but I cherish a hate for that Jermyn to this day.

"We were a week working up as far as Yarmouth Roads,[5] and then we got into a gale—the famous October gale of twenty-two years ago. It was wind, lightning, sleet, snow, and a terrific sea. We were flying light, and you may imagine how bad it was when I tell you we had smashed bulwarks and a flooded deck. On the second night she shifted her ballast into the lee bow, and by that time we had been blown off somewhere on the Dogger Bank.[6] There was nothing for it but go below with shovels and try to right her, and there we were in that vast hold, gloomy like a cavern, the tallow dips stuck and flickering on the beams, the gale howling above, the ship tossing about like mad on her side; there we all were, Jermyn, the captain, everyone, hardly able to keep our feet, engaged on that gravedigger's work, and trying to toss shovelfuls of wet sand up to windward. At every tumble of the ship you could see vaguely in the dim light men falling down with a great flourish of shovels. One of the ship's boys (we had two), impressed by the weirdness of the scene, wept as if his heart would break. We could hear him blubbering somewhere in the shadows.

"On the third day the gale died out, and by and by a north-country tug picked us up. We took sixteen days in all to get from London to the Tyne.[7] When we got into dock we had lost our turn for loading, and they hauled us off to a tier where we remained for a month. Mrs. Beard (the captain's name was Beard) came from Colchester to see the old man. She lived on board. The crew of runners had left, and there remained only the officers, one boy, and the steward, a mulatto who answered to the name of Abraham. Mrs. Beard was an old woman, with a face all wrinkled and ruddy like a winter apple, and the figure of a young girl. She caught sight of me once, sewing on a button, and insisted on having my shirts to repair. This was something different from the

---

3. *the Capes,* the Cape of Good Hope at the southern end of Africa and Cape Horn, the southern tip of South America.

4. *Judea.* "Youth" describes almost exactly an actual experience of Conrad's during his years at sea. The real ship on which he served as second mate was called the *Palestine;* but Conrad did not alter the name of the *Palestine's* captain, Beard, or her first mate, Mahon.

5. *Yarmouth Roads.* Yarmouth is a seaport in eastern England. *Roads* (or *roadstead*) means a place near the shore where ships may anchor.

6. *Dogger Bank,* a submerged sandbank in the center of the North Sea.

7. *Tyne,* a river in northeast England. The distance from London to the mouth of the Tyne is about 300 miles.

captains' wives I had known on board crack clippers. When I brought her the shirts, she said: 'And the socks? They want mending, I am sure, and John's—Captain Beard's—things are all in order now. I would be glad of something to do.' Bless the old woman. She overhauled my outfit for me, and meantime I read for the first time *Sartor Resartus* and Burnaby's *Ride to Khiva*.[8] I didn't understand much of the first then; but I remember I preferred the soldier to the philosopher at the time; a preference which life has only confirmed. One was a man, and the other was either more—or less. However, they are both dead and Mrs. Beard is dead, and youth, strength, genius, thoughts, achievements, simple hearts—all die. . . . No matter.

"They loaded us at last. We shipped a crew. Eight able seamen and two boys. We hauled off one evening to the buoys at the dock-gates, ready to go out, and with a fair prospect of beginning the voyage next day. Mrs. Beard was to start for home by a late train. When the ship was fast we went to tea. We sat rather silent through the meal—Mahon, the old couple, and I. I finished first, and slipped away for a smoke, my cabin being in a deck-house just against the poop.[9] It was high water, blowing fresh with a drizzle; the double dock-gates were opened, and the steam-colliers were going in and out in the darkness with their lights burning bright, a great plashing of propellers, rattling of winches, and a lot of hailing on the pier-heads. I watched the procession of head-lights gliding high and of green lights gliding low in the night, when suddenly a red gleam flashed at me, vanished, came into view again, and remained. The fore-end of a steamer loomed up close. I shouted down the cabin, 'Come up, quick!' and then heard a startled voice saying afar in the dark, 'Stop her, sir.' A bell jingled. Another voice cried warningly, 'We are going right into that barque, sir.' The answer to this was a gruff 'All right,' and the next thing was a heavy crash as the steamer struck a glancing blow with the bluff of her bow about our fore-rigging. There was a moment of confusion, yelling, and running about. Steam roared. Then somebody was heard saying, 'All clear, sir.' . . . 'Are you all right?' asked the gruff voice. I had jumped forward to see the damage, and hailed back, 'I think so.' 'Easy astern,' said the gruff

voice. A bell jingled. 'What steamer is that?' screamed Mahon. By that time she was no more to us than a bulky shadow manœuvring a little way off. They shouted at us some name—a woman's name, Miranda or Melissa—or some such thing. 'This means another month in this beastly hole,' said Mahon to me, as we peered with lamps about the splintered bulwarks and broken braces. 'But where's the captain?'

"We had not heard or seen anything of him all that time. We went aft to look. A doleful voice arose hailing somewhere in the middle of the dock, '*Judea* ahoy!' . . . How the devil did he get there? . . . 'Hallo!' we shouted. 'I am adrift in our boat without oars,' he cried. A belated waterman offered his services, and Mahon struck a bargain with him for half-a-crown[10] to tow our skipper alongside; but it was Mrs. Beard that came up the ladder first. They had been floating about the dock in that mizzly cold rain for nearly an hour. I was never so surprised in my life.

"It appears that when he heard my shout 'Come up' he understood at once what was the matter, caught up his wife, ran on deck, and across, and down into our boat, which was fast to the ladder. Not bad for a sixty-year-old. Just imagine that old fellow saving heroically in his arms that old woman—the woman of his life. He set her down on a thwart and was ready to climb back on board when the painter came adrift somehow, and away they went together. Of course in the confusion we did not hear him shouting. He looked abashed. She said cheerfully, 'I suppose it does not matter my losing the train now?' 'No, Jenny—you go below and get warm,' he growled. Then to us: 'A sailor has no business with a wife—I say. There I was, out of the ship. Well, no harm done this time. Let's go and look at what that fool of a steamer smashed.'

"It wasn't much, but it delayed us three weeks. At the end of that time, the captain being

---

8. Sartor Resartus *and* Burnaby's Ride to Khiva. *Sartor Resartus* (Latin for "The Tailor Re-Tailored") is a philosophical satire by Thomas Carlyle (1795–1881). *The Ride to Khiva* is a once-popular travel book by Frederick Gustavus Burnaby (1842–1885), describing a 300-mile journey across the Russian steppes in winter.
9. poop, a raised deck at the stern of a ship, often forming the roof of a cabin.
10. half-a-crown, a British coin worth about sixty cents at the time of the story, though far larger in purchasing power.

engaged with his agents, I carried Mrs. Beard's bag to the railway-station and put her all comfy into a third-class carriage. She lowered the window to say, 'You are a good young man. If you see John—Captain Beard—without his muffler at night, just remind him from me to keep his throat well wrapped up.' 'Certainly, Mrs. Beard,' I said. 'You are a good young man: I noticed how attentive you are to John—to Captain—' The train pulled out suddenly; I took my cap off to the old woman: I never saw her again. . . . Pass the bottle.

"We went to sea next day. When we made that start for Bankok we had been already three months out of London. We had expected to be a fortnight or so—at the outside.

"It was January, and the weather was beautiful—the beautiful sunny winter weather that has more charm than in the summertime, because it is unexpected, and crisp, and you know it won't, it can't, last long. It's like a windfall, like a godsend, like an unexpected piece of luck.

"It lasted all down the North Sea, all down Channel; and it lasted till we were three hundred miles or so to the westward of the Lizards;[11] then the wind went round to the sou'west and began to pipe up. In two days it blew a gale. The *Judea*, hove to, wallowed on the Atlantic like an old candle-box. It blew day after day: it blew with spite, without interval, without mercy, without rest. The world was nothing but an immensity of great foaming waves rushing at us, under a sky low enough to touch with the hand and dirty like a smoked ceiling. In the stormy space surrounding us there was as much flying spray as air. Day after day and night after night there was nothing round the ship but the howl of the wind, the tumult of the sea, the noise of water pouring over the deck. There was no rest for her and no rest for us. She tossed, she pitched, she stood on her head, she sat on her tail, she rolled, she groaned, and we had to hold on while on deck and cling to our bunks when below, in a constant effort of body and worry of mind.

"One night Mahon spoke through the small window of my berth. It opened right into my very bed, and I was lying there sleepless, in my boots, feeling as though I had not slept for years, and could not if I tried. He said excitedly—

" 'You got the sounding-rod in here, Mar-

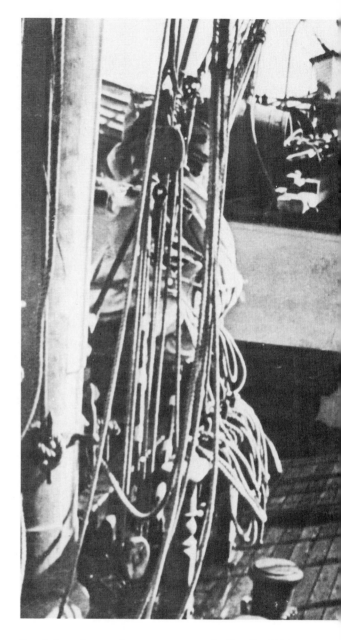

low? I can't get the pumps to suck. By God! it's no child's play.'

"I gave him the sounding-rod and lay down again, trying to think of various things—but I thought only of the pumps. When I came on deck they were still at it, and my watch relieved at the pumps. By the light of the lantern brought on deck to examine the sounding-rod I caught a glimpse of their weary, serious faces. We

11. *the Lizards,* Lizard Head, a peninsula in southwest England.

pumped all the four hours. We pumped all night, all day, all the week—watch and watch. She was working herself loose, and leaked badly—not enough to drown us at once, but enough to kill us with the work at the pumps. And while we pumped the ship was going from us piecemeal: the bulwarks went, the stanchions were torn out, the ventilators smashed, the cabin-door burst in. There was not a dry spot in the ship. She was being gutted bit by bit. The long-boat changed, as if by magic, into matchwood where she stood in her gripes.[12] I had lashed her myself, and was rather proud of my handiwork, which had withstood so long the malice of the sea. And we pumped. And there was no break in the weather. The sea was white like a sheet of foam, like a caldron of boiling milk; there was not a break in the clouds, no—not the size of a man's hand[13]—

---

12. *gripes,* the assemblage of ropes and nautical hardware used to secure a ship's boats.
13. *the size of a man's hand,* an allusion to I Kings 18:44.

no, not for so much as ten seconds. There was for us no sky, there were for us no stars, no sun, no universe—nothing but angry clouds and an infuriated sea. We pumped watch and watch, for dear life; and it seemed to last for months, for years, for all eternity, as though we had been dead and gone to a hell for sailors. We forgot the day of the week, the name of the month, what year it was, and whether we had ever been ashore. The sails blew away, she lay broadside on under a weather-cloth,[14] the ocean poured over her, and we did not care. We turned those handles, and had the eyes of idiots. As soon as we had crawled on deck I used to take a round turn with a rope about the men, the pumps, and the mainmast, and we turned, we turned incessantly, with the water to our waists, to our necks, over our heads. It was all one. We had forgotten how it felt to be dry.

"And there was somewhere in me the thought: By Jove! this is the deuce of an adventure—something you read about; and it is my first voyage as second mate—and I am only twenty—and here I am lasting it out as well as any of these men, and keeping my chaps up to the mark. I was pleased. I would not have given up the experience for worlds. I had moments of exultation. Whenever the old dismantled craft pitched heavily with her counter high in the air, she seemed to me to throw up, like an appeal, like a defiance, like a cry to the clouds without mercy, the words written on her stern: '*Judea*, London. Do or Die.'

"O youth! The strength of it, the faith of it, the imagination of it! To me she was not an old rattletrap carting about the world a lot of coal for a freight—to me she was the endeavor, the test, the trial of life. I think of her with pleasure, with affection, with regret—as you would think of someone dead you have loved. I shall never forget her. . . . Pass the bottle.

"One night when tied to the mast, as I explained, we were pumping on, deafened with the wind, and without spirit enough in us to wish ourselves dead, a heavy sea crashed aboard and swept clean over us. As soon as I got my breath I shouted, as in duty bound, 'Keep on, boys!' when suddenly I felt something hard floating on deck strike the calf of my leg. I made a grab at it and missed. It was so dark we could not see each other's faces within a foot—you understand.

"After that thump that ship kept quiet for a while, and the thing, whatever it was, struck my leg again. This time I caught it—and it was a saucepan. At first, being stupid with fatigue and thinking of nothing but the pumps, I did not understand what I had in my hand. Suddenly it dawned upon me, and I shouted, 'Boys, the house on deck is gone. Leave this, and let's look for the cook.'

"There was a deck-house forward, which contained the galley, the cook's berth, and the quarters of the crew. As we had expected for days to see it swept away, the hands had been ordered to sleep in the cabin—the only safe place in the ship. The steward, Abraham, however, persisted in clinging to his berth, stupidly, like a mule—from sheer fright I believe, like an animal that won't leave a stable falling in an earthquake. So we went to look for him. It was chancing death, since once out of our lashings we were as exposed as if on a raft. But we went. The house was shattered as if a shell had exploded inside. Most of it had gone overboard—stove, men's quarters, and their property, all was gone; but two posts, holding a portion of the bulkhead to which Abraham's bunk was attached, remained as if by a miracle. We groped in the ruins and came upon this, and there he was, sitting in his bunk, surrounded by foam and wreckage, jabbering cheerfully to himself. He was out of his mind; completely and forever mad, with this sudden shock coming upon the fag end of his endurance. We snatched him up, lugged him aft, and pitched him head-first down the cabin companion. You understand there was no time to carry him down with infinite precautions and wait to see how he got on. Those below would pick him up at the bottom of the stairs all right. We were in a hurry to go back to the pumps. That business could not wait. A bad leak is an inhuman thing.

"One would think that the sole purpose of that fiendish gale had been to make a lunatic of that poor devil of a mulatto. It eased before morning, and next day the sky cleared, and as the sea went down the leak took up. When it came to bending a fresh set of sails the crew demanded to put back—and really there was nothing else to

---

14. *a weather-cloth,* a canvas or tarpaulin used to shelter the deck from wind and rain.

do. Boats gone, decks swept clean, cabin gutted, men without a stitch but what they stood in, stores spoiled, ship strained. We put her head for home, and—would you believe it? The wind came east right in our teeth. It blew fresh, it blew continuously. We had to beat up every inch of the way, but she did not leak so badly, the water keeping comparatively smooth. Two hours' pumping in every four is no joke—but it kept her afloat as far as Falmouth.[15]

"The good people there live on casualties of the sea, and no doubt were glad to see us. A hungry crowd of shipwrights sharpened their chisels at the sight of that carcass of a ship. And, by Jove! they had pretty pickings off us before they were done. I fancy the owner was already in a tight place. There were delays. Then it was decided to take part of the cargo out and caulk her topsides. This was done, the repairs finished, cargo reshipped; a new crew came on board, and we went out—for Bankok. At the end of a week we were back again. The crew said they weren't going to Bankok—a hundred and fifty days' passage—in a something hooker[16] that wanted pumping eight hours out of the twenty-four; and the nautical papers inserted again the little paragraph: 'Judea. Barque. Tyne to Bankok; coals; put back to Falmouth leaky and with crew refusing duty.'

"There were more delays—more tinkering. The owner came down for a day, and said she was as right as a little fiddle. Poor old Captain Beard looked like the ghost of a Geordie[17] skipper—through the worry and humiliation of it. Remember he was sixty, and it was his first command. Mahon said it was a foolish business, and could end badly. I loved the ship more than ever, and wanted awfully to get to Bankok. To Bankok! Magic name, blessed name. Mesopotamia[18] wasn't a patch on it. Remember I was twenty, and it was my first second-mate's billet, and the East was waiting for me.

"We went out and anchored in the outer roads with a fresh crew—the third. She leaked worse than ever. It was as if those confounded shipwrights had actually made a hole in her. This time we did not even go outside. The crew simply refused to man the windlass.

"They towed us back to the inner harbor, and we became a fixture, a feature, an institution of the place. People pointed us out to visitors as 'That 'ere barque that's going to Bankok—has been here six months—put back three times.' On holidays the small boys pulling about in boats would hail, 'Judea, ahoy!' and if a head showed above the rail shouted, 'Where you bound to?—Bankok?' and jeered. We were only three on board. The poor old skipper mooned in the cabin. Mahon undertook the cooking, and unexpectedly developed all a Frenchman's genius for preparing nice little messes. I looked languidly after the rigging. We became citizens of Falmouth. Every shopkeeper knew us. At the barber's or tobacconist's they asked familiarly, 'Do you think you will ever get to Bankok?' Meantime the owner, the underwriters, and the charterers squabbled amongst themselves in London, and our pay went on. . . . Pass the bottle.

"It was horrid. Morally it was worse than pumping for life. It seemed as though we had been forgotten by the world, belonged to nobody, would get nowhere; it seemed that, as if bewitched, we would have to live forever and ever in that inner harbor, a derision and a byword to generations of long-shore loafers and dishonest boatmen. I obtained three months' pay and a five days' leave, and made a rush for London. It took me a day to get there and pretty well another to come back—but three months' pay went all the same. I don't know what I did with it. I went to a music-hall, I believe, lunched, dined, and supped in a swell place in Regent Street, and was back to time, with nothing but a complete set of Byron's works and a new railway rug to show for three months' work. The boatman who pulled me off to the ship said: 'Hallo! I thought you had left the old thing. *She* will never get to Bankok.' 'That's all *you* know about it,' I said scornfully—but I didn't like that prophecy at all.

"Suddenly a man, some kind of agent to somebody, appeared with full powers. He had grog-blossoms[19] all over his face, an indomitable

---

15. *Falmouth,* a seaport on the southwest coast of England.
16. *hooker,* an old-fashioned or clumsy ship.
17. *Geordie,* someone from Tyneside, the area in northeast England around the mouth of the Tyne.
18. *Mesopotamia,* David Garrick, the famous eighteenth-century English actor, said that "that blessed word Mesopotamia" in the mouth of the famous preacher George Whitefield had the power of making people laugh or cry.
19. *grog-blossoms,* a florid complexion as a result of heavy drinking (*grog* is nautical slang for rum).

energy, and was a jolly soul. We leaped into life again. A hulk came alongside, took our cargo, and then we went into dry dock to get our copper stripped. No wonder she leaked. The poor thing, strained beyond endurance by the gale, had, as if in disgust, spat out all the oakum of her lower seams. She was recaulked, new coppered, and made as tight as a bottle. We went back to the hulk and reshipped our cargo.

"Then, on a fine moonlight night, all the rats left the ship.

"We had been infested with them. They had destroyed our sails, consumed more stores than the crew, affably shared our beds and our dangers, and now, when the ship was made seaworthy, concluded to clear out. I called Mahon to enjoy the spectacle. Rat after rat appeared on our rail, took a last look over his shoulder, and leaped with a hollow thud into the empty hulk. We tried to count them, but soon lost the tale. Mahon said: 'Well, well! don't talk to me about the intelligence of rats. They ought to have left before, when we had that narrow squeak from foundering. There you have the proof how silly is the superstition about them. They leave a good ship for an old rotten hulk, where there is nothing to eat, too, the fools! . . . I don't believe they know what is safe or what is good for them, any more than you or I.'

"And after some more talk we agreed that the wisdom of rats had been grossly overrated, being in fact no greater than that of men.

"The story of the ship was known, by this, all up the Channel from Land's End to the Forelands, and we could get no crew on the south coast. They sent us one all complete from Liverpool, and we left once more—for Bankok.

"We had fair breezes, smooth water right into the tropics, and the old *Judea* lumbered along in the sunshine. When she went eight knots everything cracked aloft, and we tied our caps to our heads; but mostly she strolled on at the rate of three miles an hour. What could you expect? She was tired—that old ship. Her youth was where mine is—where yours is—you fellows who listen to this yarn; and what friend would throw your years and your weariness in your face? We didn't grumble at her. To us aft, at least, it seemed as though we had been born in her, reared in her, had lived in her for ages, had never known any

other ship. I would just as soon have abused the old village church at home for not being a cathedral.

"And for me there was also my youth to make me patient. There was all the East before me, and all life, and the thought that I had been tried in that ship and had come out pretty well. And I thought of men of old who, centuries ago, went that road in ships that sailed no better, to the land of palms, and spices, and yellow sands, and of brown nations ruled by kings more cruel than Nero the Roman, and more splendid than Solomon the Jew. The old bark lumbered on, heavy with her age and the burden of her cargo, while I lived the life of youth in ignorance and hope. She lumbered on through an interminable procession of days; and the fresh gilding flashed back at the setting sun, seemed to cry out over the darkening sea the words painted on her stern, '*Judea,* London. Do or Die.'

"Then we entered the Indian Ocean and steered northerly for Java Head. The winds were light. Weeks slipped by. She crawled on, do or die, and people at home began to think of posting us as overdue.

"One Saturday evening, I being off duty, the men asked me to give them an extra bucket of water or so—for washing clothes. As I did not wish to screw on the fresh-water pump so late, I went forward whistling, and with a key in my hand to unlock the forepeak scuttle,[20] intending to serve the water out of a spare tank we kept there.

"The smell down below was as unexpected as it was frightful. One would have thought hundreds of paraffin lamps had been flaring and smoking in that hole for days. I was glad to get out. The man with me coughed and said, 'Funny smell, sir.' I answered negligently, 'It's good for the health they say,' and walked aft.

"The first thing I did was to put my head down the square of the midship ventilator. As I lifted the lid a visible breath, something like a thin fog, a puff of faint haze, rose from the opening. The ascending air was hot, and had a heavy, sooty, paraffiny smell. I gave one sniff, and put down the lid gently. It was no use choking myself. The cargo was on fire.

---

20. *forepeak scuttle,* a small opening in the deck of a ship.

"Next day she began to smoke in earnest. You see it was to be expected, for though the coal was of a safe kind, that cargo had been so handled, so broken up with handling, that it looked more like smithy coal than anything else. Then it had been wetted—more than once. It rained all the time we were taking it back from the hulk, and now with this long passage it got heated, and there was another case of spontaneous combustion.

"The captain called us into the cabin. He had a chart spread on the table, and looked unhappy. He said, 'The coast of West Australia is near, but I mean to proceed to our destination. It is the hurricane month, too; but we will just keep her head for Bankok, and fight the fire. No more putting back anywhere, if we all get roasted. We will try first to stifle this 'ere damned combustion by want of air.'

"We tried. We battened down everything, and still she smoked. The smoke kept coming out through imperceptible crevices; it forced itself through bulkheads and covers; it oozed here and there and everywhere in slender threads, in an invisible film, in an incomprehensible manner. It made its way into the cabin, into the forecastle; it poisoned the sheltered places on the deck, it could be sniffed as high as the mainyard. It was clear that if the smoke came out the air came in. This was disheartening. This combustion refused to be stifled.

"We resolved to try water, and took the hatches off. Enormous volumes of smoke, whitish, yellowish, thick, greasy, misty, choking, ascended as high as the trucks.[21] All hands cleared out aft. Then the poisonous cloud blew away, and we went back to work in a smoke that was no thicker now than that of an ordinary factory chimney.

"We rigged the force-pump, got the hose along, and by and by it burst. Well, it was as old as the ship—a prehistoric hose, and past repair. Then we pumped with the feeble head pump, drew water with buckets, and in this way managed in time to pour lots of Indian Ocean into the main hatch. The bright stream flashed in sunshine, fell into a layer of white crawling smoke, and vanished on the black surface of coal. Steam ascended mingling with the smoke. We poured salt water as into a barrel without a bottom. It was our fate to pump in that ship, to pump out of her, to pump into her; and after keeping water out of her to save ourselves from being drowned, we frantically poured water into her to save ourselves from being burnt.

"And she crawled on, do or die, in the serene weather. The sky was a miracle of purity, a miracle of azure. The sea was polished, was blue, was pellucid, was sparkling like a precious stone, extending on all sides, all round to the horizon— as if the whole terrestrial globe had been one jewel, one colossal sapphire, a single gem fashioned into a planet. And on the luster of the great calm waters the *Judea* glided imperceptibly, enveloped in languid and unclean vapors, in a lazy cloud that drifted to leeward, light and slow; a pestiferous cloud defiling the splendor of sea and sky.

"All this time of course we saw no fire. The cargo smoldered at the bottom somewhere. Once Mahon, as we were working side by side, said to me with a queer smile: 'Now, if she only would spring a tidy leak—like that time when we first left the Channel—it would put a stopper on this fire. Wouldn't it?' I remarked irrelevantly, 'Do you remember the rats?'

"We fought the fire and sailed the ship too as carefully as though nothing had been the matter. The steward cooked and attended on us. Of the other twelve men, eight worked while four rested. Everyone took his turn, captain included. There was equality, and if not exactly fraternity, then a deal of good feeling. Sometimes a man, as he dashed a bucketful of water down the hatchway, would yell out, 'Hurrah for Bankok!' and the rest laughed. But generally we were taciturn and serious—and thirsty. Oh! how thirsty! And we had to be careful with the water. Strict allowance. The ship smoked, the sun blazed. . . . Pass the bottle.

"We tried everything. We even made an attempt to dig down to the fire. No good, of course. No man could remain more than a minute below. Mahon, who went first, fainted there, and the man who went to fetch him out did likewise. We lugged them out on deck. Then I leaped down to show how easily it could be done. They had

---

21. trucks, a small wooden cap at the top of a masthead to secure the ropes used in raising signal flags.

learned wisdom by that time, and contented themselves by fishing for me with a chain-hook tied to a broom-handle, I believe. I did not offer to go and fetch up my shovel, which was left down below.

"Things began to look bad. We put the longboat into the water. The second boat was ready to swing out. We had also another, a 14-foot thing, on davits aft, where it was quite safe.

"Then, behold, the smoke suddenly decreased. We redoubled our efforts to flood the bottom of the ship. In two days there was no smoke at all. Everybody was on the broad grin. This was on a Friday. On Saturday no work, but sailing the ship, of course, was done. The men washed their clothes and their faces for the first time in a fortnight, and had a special dinner given them. They spoke of spontaneous combustion with contempt, and implied *they* were the boys to put out combustions. Somehow we all felt as though we each had inherited a large fortune. But a beastly smell of burning hung about the ship. Captain Beard had hollow eyes and sunken cheeks. I had never noticed so much before how twisted and bowed he was. He and Mahon prowled soberly about hatches and ventilators, sniffing. It struck me suddenly poor Mahon was a very, very old chap. As to me, I was as pleased and proud as though I had helped to win a great naval battle. O! Youth!

"The night was fine. In the morning a homeward-bound ship passed us hull down—the first we had seen for months; but we were nearing the land at last, Java Head being about 190 miles off, and nearly due north.

"Next day it was my watch on deck from eight to twelve. At breakfast the captain observed, 'It's wonderful how that smell hangs about the cabin.' About ten, the mate being on the poop, I stepped down on the main-deck for a moment. The carpenter's bench stood abaft the mainmast: I leaned against it sucking at my pipe, and the carpenter, a young chap, came to talk to me. He remarked, 'I think we have done very well, haven't we?' and then I perceived with annoyance the fool was trying to tilt the bench. I said curtly, 'Don't, Chips,' and immediately became aware of a queer sensation, of an absurd delusion—I seemed somehow to be in the air. I heard all round me like a pent-up breath released—as if a thousand giants simultaneously had said Phoo!—and felt a dull concussion which made my ribs ache suddenly. No doubt about it— I was in the air, and my body was describing a short parabola. But short as it was, I had the time to think several thoughts in, as far as I can remember, the following order: 'This can't be the carpenter—What is it?—Some accident—Submarine volcano?—Coals, gas!—By Jove! we are being blown up—Everybody's dead—I am falling into the after-hatch—I see fire in it.'

"The coal-dust suspended in the air of the hold had glowed dull-red at the moment of the explosion. In the twinkling of an eye, in an infinitesimal fraction of a second since the first tilt of the bench, I was full length on the cargo. I picked myself up and scrambled out. It was quick like a rebound. The deck was a wilderness of smashed timber, lying crosswise like trees in a wood after a hurricane; an immense curtain of soiled rags waved gently before me—it was the main-sail blown to strips. I thought, The masts will be toppling over directly; and to get out of the way bolted on all fours towards the poop-ladder. The first person I saw was Mahon, with eyes like saucers, his mouth open, and the long white hair standing straight on end round his head like a silver halo. He was just about to go down when the sight of the main-deck stirring, heaving up, and changing into splinters before his eyes, petrified him on the top step. I stared at him in unbelief, and he stared at me with a queer kind of shocked curiosity. I did not know that I had no hair, no eyebrows, no eyelashes, that my young moustache was burnt off, that my face was black, one cheek laid open, my nose cut, and my chin bleeding. I had lost my cap, one of my slippers, and my shirt was torn to rags. Of all this I was not aware. I was amazed to see the ship still afloat, the poop-deck whole—and, most of all, to see anybody alive. Also the peace of the sky and the serenity of the sea were distinctly surprising. I suppose I expected to see them convulsed with horror. . . . Pass the bottle.

"There was a voice hailing the ship from somewhere—in the air, in the sky—I couldn't tell. Presently I saw the captain—and he was mad. He asked me eagerly, 'Where's the cabin-table?' and to hear such a question was a frightful shock. I had just been blown up, you understand,

and vibrated with that experience—I wasn't quite sure whether I was alive. Mahon began to stamp with both feet and yelled at him 'Good God! don't you see the deck's blown out of her?' I found my voice, and stammered out as if conscious of some gross neglect of duty, 'I don't know where the cabin-table is.' It was like an absurd dream.

"Do you know what he wanted next? Well, he wanted to trim the yards. Very placidly, and as if lost in thought, he insisted on having the foreyard squared. 'I don't know if there's anybody alive,' said Mahon, almost tearfully. 'Surely,' he said, gently, 'there will be enough left to square the foreyard.'

"The old chap, it seems, was in his own berth winding up the chronometers, when the shock sent him spinning. Immediately it occurred to him—as he said afterwards—that the ship had struck something, and he ran out into the cabin. There, he saw, the cabin-table had vanished somewhere. The deck being blown up, it had fallen down into the lazarette[22] of course. Where we had our breakfast that morning he saw only a great hole in the floor. This appeared to him so awfully mysterious, and impressed him so immensely, that what he saw and heard after he got on deck were mere trifles in comparison. And, mark, he noticed directly the wheel deserted and his barque off her course—and his only thought was to get that miserable, stripped, undecked, smoldering shell of a ship back again with her head pointing at her port of destination. Bankok! That's what he was after. I tell you this quiet, bowed, bandy-legged, almost deformed little man was immense in the singleness of his idea and in his placid ignorance of our agitation. He motioned us forward with a commanding gesture, and went to take the wheel himself.

"Yes; that was the first thing we did—trim the yards of that wreck! No one was killed, or even disabled, but everyone was more or less hurt. You should have seen them! Some were in rags, with black faces, like coal-heavers, like sweeps, and had bullet heads that seemed closely cropped, but were in fact singed to the skin. Others, of the watch below, awakened by being shot out from their collapsing bunks, shivered incessantly, and kept on groaning even as we went about our work. But they all worked. That crew of Liverpool hard cases had in them the right stuff. It's my experience they always have. It is the sea that gives it—the vastness, the loneliness surrounding their dark stolid souls. Ah! Well! we stumbled, we crept, we fell, we barked our shins on the wreckage, we hauled. The masts stood, but we did not know how much they might be charred down below. It was nearly calm, but a long swell ran from the west and made her roll. They might go at any moment. We looked at them with apprehension. One could not foresee which way they would fall.

"Then we retreated aft and looked about us. The deck was a tangle of planks on edge, of planks on end, of splinters, of ruined woodwork. The masts rose from that chaos like big trees above a matted undergrowth. The interstices of that mass of wreckage were full of something whitish, sluggish, stirring—of something that was like a greasy fog. The smoke of the invisible fire was coming up again, was trailing, like a poisonous thick mist in some valley choked with dead wood. Already lazy wisps were beginning to curl upwards amongst the mass of splinters. Here and there a piece of timber, stuck upright, resembled a post. Half of a fife-rail had been shot through the foresail, and the sky made a patch of glorious blue in the ignobly soiled canvas. A portion of several boards holding together had fallen across the rail, and one end protruded overboard, like a gangway leading upon nothing, like a gangway leading over the deep sea, leading to death—as if inviting us to walk the plank at once and be done with our ridiculous troubles. And still the air, the sky—a ghost, something invisible was hailing the ship.

"Someone had the sense to look over, and there was the helmsman, who had impulsively jumped overboard, anxious to come back. He yelled and swam lustily like a merman, keeping up with the ship. We threw him a rope, and presently he stood amongst us streaming with water and very crestfallen. The captain had surrendered the wheel, and apart, elbow on rail and chin in hand, gazed at the sea wistfully. We asked ourselves, What next? I thought, Now, this is something like. This is great. I wonder what will happen. O youth!

---

22. *lazarette*, space between decks.

"Suddenly Mahon sighted a steamer far astern. Captain Beard said, 'We may do something with her yet.' We hoisted two flags, which said in the international language of the sea, 'On fire. Want immediate assistance.' The steamer grew bigger rapidly, and by and by spoke with two flags on her foremast, 'I am coming to your assistance.'

"In half an hour she was abreast, to windward, within hail, and rolling slightly, with her engines stopped. We lost our composure, and yelled all together with excitement, 'We've been blown up.' A man in a white helmet, on the bridge, cried, 'Yes! All right! all right!' and he nodded his head, and smiled, and made soothing motions with his hand as though at a lot of frightened children. One of the boats dropped in the water, and walked towards us upon the sea with her long oars. Four Calashes[23] pulled a swinging stroke. This was my first sight of Malay seamen. I've known them since, but what struck me then was their unconcern: they came alongside, and even the bowman standing up and holding to our main-chains with the boat-hook did not deign to lift his head for a glance. I thought people who had been blown up deserved more attention.

"A little man, dry like a chip and agile like a monkey, clambered up. It was the mate of the steamer. He gave one look, and cried, 'O boys—you had better quit.'

"We were silent. He talked apart with the captain for a time,—seemed to argue with him. Then they went away together to the steamer.

"When our skipper came back we learned that the steamer was the *Somerville,* Captain Nash, from West Australia to Singapore *via* Batavia with mails, and that the agreement was she should tow us to Anjer or Batavia, if possible, where we could extinguish the fire by scuttling,[24] and then proceed on our voyage—to Bankok! The old man seemed excited. 'We will do it yet,' he said to Mahon, fiercely. He shook his fist at the sky. Nobody else said a word.

"At noon the steamer began to tow. She went ahead slim and high, and what was left of the *Judea* followed at the end of seventy fathom of tow-rope—followed her swiftly like a cloud of smoke with mastheads protruding above. We went aloft to furl the sails. We coughed on the yards, and were careful about the bunts.[25] Do you

see the lot of us there, putting a neat furl on the sails of that ship doomed to arrive nowhere? There was not a man who didn't think that at any moment the masts would topple over. From aloft we could not see the ship for smoke, and they worked carefully, passing the gaskets with even turns. 'Harbor furl—aloft there!' cried Mahon from below.

"You understand this? I don't think one of those chaps expected to get down in the usual way. When we did I heard them saying to each other, 'Well, I thought we would come down overboard, in a lump—sticks and all—blame me if I didn't.' 'That's what I was thinking to myself,' would answer wearily another battered and bandaged scarecrow. And, mind, these were men without the drilled-in habit of obedience. To an onlooker they would be a lot of profane scallywags without a redeeming point. What made them do it—what made them obey me when I, thinking consciously how fine it was, made them drop the bunt of the foresail twice to try and do it better? What? They had no professional reputation—no examples, no praise. It wasn't a sense of duty; they all knew well enough how to shirk, and laze, and dodge—when they had a mind to it—and mostly they had. Was it the two pounds ten a month that sent them there? They didn't think their pay half good enough. No; it was something in them, something inborn and subtle and everlasting. I don't say positively that the crew of a French or German merchantman wouldn't have done it, but I doubt whether it would have been done in the same way. There was a completeness in it, something solid like a principle, and masterful like an instinct—a disclosure of something secret—of that hidden something, that gift of good or evil that makes racial difference, that shapes the fate of nations.

"It was that night at ten that, for the first time since we had been fighting it, we saw the fire. The speed of the towing had fanned the smoldering destruction. A blue gleam appeared forward, shining below the wreck of the deck. It wavered

---

23. *Calashes,* in the Far East, a native sailors.
24. *scuttling,* sinking a ship by cutting a hole in the hull.
25. *bunts,* the middle part of a sail that is *furled* (rolled up around the *yard,* the beam fastened across a mast to support a sail).

in patches, it seemed to stir and creep like the light of a glowworm. I saw it first, and told Mahon. 'Then the game's up,' he said. 'We had better stop this towing, or she will burst out suddenly fore and aft before we can clear out.' We set up a yell; rang bells to attract their attention; they towed on. At last Mahon and I had to crawl forward and cut the rope with an axe. There was no time to cast off the lashings. Red tongues could be seen licking the wilderness of splinters under our feet as we made our way back to the poop.

"Of course they very soon found out in the steamer that the rope was gone. She gave a loud blast of her whistle, her lights were seen sweeping in a wide circle, she came up ranging close alongside, and stopped. We were all in a tight group on the poop looking at her. Every man had saved a little bundle or a bag. Suddenly a conical flame with a twisted top shot up forward and threw upon the black sea a circle of light, with the two vessels side by side and heaving gently in its center. Captain Beard had been sitting on the gratings still and mute for hours, but now he rose slowly and advanced in front of us, to the mizzen-shrouds. Captain Nash hailed: 'Come along! Look sharp. I have mail-bags on board. I will take you and your boats to Singapore.'

" 'Thank you! No!' said our skipper. 'We must see the last of the ship.'

" 'I can't stand by any longer,' shouted the other. 'Mails—you know.'

" 'Ay! ay! We are all right.'

" 'Very well! I'll report you in Singapore. . . . Good-bye!'

"He waved his hand. Our men dropped their bundles quietly. The steamer moved ahead, and passing out of the circle of light, vanished at once from our sight, dazzled by the fire which burned fiercely. And then I knew that I would see the East first as commander of a small boat. I thought it fine; and the fidelity to the old ship was fine. We should see the last of her. Oh, the glamor of youth! Oh, the fire of it, more dazzling than the flames of the burning ship, throwing a magic light on the wide earth, leaping audaciously to the sky, presently to be quenched by time, more cruel, more pitiless, more bitter than the sea—and like the flames of the burning ship surrounded by an impenetrable night.

"The old man warned us in his gentle and inflexible way that it was part of our duty to save for the underwriters as much as we could of the ship's gear. Accordingly we went to work aft, while she blazed forward to give us plenty of light. We lugged out a lot of rubbish. What didn't we save? An old barometer fixed with an absurd quantity of screws nearly cost me my life: a sudden rush of smoke came upon me, and I just got away in time. There were various stores, bolts of canvas, coils of rope; the poop looked like a marine bazaar, and the boats were lumbered to the gunwales. One would have thought the old man wanted to take as much as he could of his first command with him. He was very, very quiet, but off his balance evidently. Would you believe it? He wanted to take a length of old stream-cable and a kedge-anchor with him in the longboat. We said 'Ay, ay, sir,' deferentially, and on the quiet let the things slip overboard. The heavy medicine-chest went that way, two bags of green coffee, tins of paint—fancy, paint!—a whole lot of things. Then I was ordered with two hands into the boats to make a stowage and get them ready against the time it would be proper for us to leave the ship.

"We put everything straight, stepped[26] the longboat's mast for our skipper, who was to take charge of her, and I was not sorry to sit down for a moment. My face felt raw, every limb ached as if broken. I was aware of all my ribs, and would have sworn to a twist in the backbone. The boats, fast astern, lay in a deep shadow, and all around I could see the circle of the sea lighted by the fire. A gigantic flame arose forward straight and clear. It flared fierce, with noises like the whirr of wings, with rumbles as of thunder. There were cracks, detonations, and from the cone of flame the sparks flew upwards, as man is born to trouble,[27] to leaky ships, and to ships that burn.

"What bothered me was that the ship, lying broadside to the swell and to such wind as there was—a mere breath—the boats would not keep astern where they were safe, but persisted, in a pig-headed way boats have, in getting under the counter and then swinging alongside. They were knocking about dangerously and coming near the

---

26. stepped, fixed in a vertical position.
27. the sparks . . . trouble, an allusion to Job 5:7.

flame, while the ship rolled on them, and, of course, there was always the danger of the masts going over the side at any moment. I and my two boat-keepers kept them off as best we could, with oars and boat-hooks; but to be constantly at it became exasperating, since there was no reason why we should not leave at once. We could not see those on board, nor could we imagine what caused the delay. The boat-keepers were swearing feebly, and I had not only my share of the work but also had to keep at it two men who showed a constant inclination to lay themselves down and let things slide.

"At last I hailed, 'On deck there,' and someone looked over. 'We're ready here,' I said. The head disappeared, and very soon popped up again. 'The captain says, All right, sir, and to keep the boats well clear of the ship.'

"Half an hour passed. Suddenly there was a frightful racket, rattle, clanking of chain, hiss of water, and millions of sparks flew up into the shivering column of smoke that stood leaning slightly above the ship. The cat-heads had burned away, and the two red-hot anchors had gone to the bottom, tearing out after them two hundred fathom of red-hot chain. The ship trembled, the mass of flame swayed as if ready to collapse, and the fore top-gallant-mast fell. It darted down like an arrow of fire, shot under, and instantly leaping up within an oar's-length of the boats, floated quietly, very black on the luminous sea. I hailed the deck again. After some time a man in an unexpectedly cheerful but also muffled tone, as though he had been trying to speak with his mouth shut, informed me, 'Coming directly, sir,' and vanished. For a long time I heard nothing but the whirr and roar of the fire. There were also whistling sounds. The boats jumped, tugged at the painters, ran at each other playfully, knocked their sides together, or, do what we would, swung in a bunch against the ship's side. I couldn't stand it any longer, and swarming up a rope, clambered aboard over the stern.

"It was as bright as day. Coming up like this, the sheet of fire facing me was a terrifying sight, and the heat seemed hardly bearable at first. On a settee cushion dragged out of the cabin Captain Beard, his legs drawn up and one arm under his head, slept with the light playing on him. Do you know what the rest were busy about? They were sitting on deck right aft, round an open case, eating bread and cheese and drinking bottled stout.

"On the background of flames twisting in fierce tongues above their heads they seemed at home like salamanders,[28] and looked like a band of desperate pirates. The fire sparkled in the whites of their eyes, gleamed on patches of white skin seen through the torn shirts. Each had the marks as of a battle about him—bandaged heads, tied up arms, a strip of dirty rag round a knee—and each man had a bottle between his legs and a chunk of cheese in his hand. Mahon got up. With his handsome and disreputable head, his hooked profile, his long white beard, and with an uncorked bottle in his hand, he resembled one of those reckless sea-robbers of old making merry amidst violence and disaster. 'The last meal on board,' he explained solemnly. 'We had nothing to eat all day, and it was no use leaving all this.' He flourished the bottle and indicated the sleeping skipper. 'He said he couldn't swallow anything, so I got him to lie down,' he went on; and as I stared, 'I don't know whether you are aware, young fellow, the man had no sleep to speak of for days—and there will be dam' little sleep in the boats.' 'There will be no boats by-and-by if you fool about much longer,' I said, indignantly. I walked up to the skipper and shook him by the shoulder. At last he opened his eyes, but did not move. 'Time to leave her, sir,' I said quietly.

"He got up painfully, looked at the flames, at the sea sparkling round the ship, and black, black as ink farther away; he looked at the stars shining dim through a thin veil of smoke in a sky black, black as Erebus.[29]

"'Youngest first,' he said.

"And the ordinary seaman, wiping his mouth with the back of his hand, got up, clambered over the taffrail, and vanished. Others followed. One, on the point of going over, stopped short to drain his bottle, and with a great swing of his arm flung it at the fire. 'Take this!' he cried.

"The skipper lingered disconsolately, and we left him to commune alone for a while with his first command. Then I went up again and brought

---

28. **salamanders,** mythical animals supposed to be able to live in fire.
29. **Erebus,** in Greek mythology, the entrance to Hades, the underworld.

him away at last. It was time. The ironwork on the poop was hot to the touch.

"Then the painter of the long-boat was cut, and the three boats, tied together, drifted clear of the ship. It was just sixteen hours after the explosion when we abandoned her. Mahon had charge of the second boat, and I had the smallest—the 14-foot thing. The long-boat would have taken the lot of us; but the skipper said we must save as much property as we could—for the underwriters—and so I got my first command. I had two men with me, a bag of biscuits, a few tins of meat, and a breaker[30] of water. I was ordered to keep close to the long-boat, that in case of bad weather we might be taken into her.

"And do you know what I thought? I thought I would part company as soon as I could. I wanted to have my first command all to myself. I wasn't going to sail in a squadron if there were a chance for independent cruising. I would make land by myself. I would beat the other boats. Youth! All youth! The silly, charming, beautiful youth.

"But we did not make a start at once. We must see the last of the ship. And so the boats drifted about that night, heaving and setting on the swell. The men dozed, waked, sighed, groaned. I looked at the burning ship.

"Between the darkness of earth and heaven she was burning fiercely upon a disk of purple sea shot by the blood-red play of gleams; upon a disk

---

30. **breaker,** a small cask.

of water glittering and sinister. A high, clear flame, an immense and lonely flame, ascended from the ocean, and from its summit the black smoke poured continuously at the sky. She burned furiously; mournful and imposing like a funeral pile kindled in the night, surrounded by the sea, watched over by the stars. A magnificent death had come like a grace, like a gift, like a reward to that old ship at the end of her laborious days. The surrender of her weary ghost to the keeping of stars and sea was stirring like the sight of a glorious triumph. The masts fell just before daybreak, and for a moment there was a burst and turmoil of sparks that seemed to fill with flying fire the night patient and watchful, the vast night lying silent upon the sea. At daylight she was only a charred shell, floating still under a cloud of smoke and bearing a glowing mass of coal within.

"Then the oars were got out, and the boats forming in a line moved round her remains as if in procession—the long-boat leading. As we pulled across her stern a slim dart of fire shot out viciously at us, and suddenly she went down, head first, in a great hiss of steam. The unconsumed stern was the last to sink; but the paint had gone, had cracked, had peeled off, and there were no letters, there was no word, no stubborn device that was like her soul, to flash at the rising sun her creed and her name.

"We made our way north. A breeze sprang up, and about noon all the boats came together for the last time. I had no mast or sail in mine, but I made a mast out of a spare oar and hoisted a boat-awning for a sail, with a boat-hook for a yard. She was certainly overmasted, but I had the satisfaction of knowing that with the wind aft I could beat the other two. I had to wait for them. Then we all had a look at the captain's chart, and, after a sociable meal of hard bread and water, got our last instructions. These were simple: steer north, and keep together as much as possible, 'Be careful with that jury-rig,[31] Marlow,' said the captain; and Mahon, as I sailed proudly past his boat, wrinkled his curved nose and hailed, 'You will sail that ship of yours under water, if you don't look out, young fellow.' He was a malicious old man—and may the deep sea where he sleeps now rock him gently, rock him tenderly to the end of time!

"Before sunset a thick rain-squall passed over the two boats, which were far astern, and that was the last I saw of them for a time. Next day I sat steering my cockle-shell—my first command—with nothing but water and sky around me. I did sight in the afternoon the upper sails of a ship far away, but said nothing, and my men did not notice her. You see I was afraid she might be homeward bound, and I had no mind to turn back from the portals of the East. I was steering for Java—another blessed name—like Bankok, you know. I steered many days.

"I need not tell you what it is to be knocking about in an open boat. I remembered nights and days of calm, when we pulled, we pulled, and the boat seemed to stand still, as if bewitched within the circle of the sea horizon. I remember the heat, the deluge of rain-squalls that kept us baling for dear life (but filled our water-cask), and I remember sixteen hours on end with a mouth dry as a cinder and a steering-oar over the stern to keep my first command head on to a breaking sea. I did not know how good a man I was till then. I remember the drawn faces, the dejected figures of my two men, and I remember my youth and the feeling that will never come back any more—the feeling that I could last forever, outlast the sea, the earth, and all men; the deceitful feeling that lures us on to joys, to perils, to love, to vain effort—to death; the triumphant conviction of strength, the heat of life in the handful of dust, the glow in the heart that with every year grows dim, grows cold, grows small, and expires—and expires, too soon, too soon—before life itself.

"And this is how I see the East. I have seen its secret places and have looked into its very soul; but now I see it always from a small boat, a high outline of mountains, blue and afar in the morning; like faint mist at noon; a jagged wall of purple at sunset. I have the feel of the oar in my hand, the vision of a scorching blue sea in my eyes. And I see a bay, a wide bay, smooth as glass and polished like ice, shimmering in the dark. A red light burns far off upon the gloom of the land, and the night is soft and warm. We drag at the oars with aching arms, and suddenly a puff

---

31. *jury-rig*, a temporary rig.

of wind, a puff faint and tepid and laden with strange odors of blossoms, of aromatic wood, comes out of the still night—the first sigh of the East on my face. That I can never forget. It was impalpable and enslaving, like a charm, like a whispered promise of mysterious delight.

"We had been pulling this finishing spell for eleven hours. Two pulled, and he whose turn it was to rest sat at the tiller. We had made out the red light in that bay and steered for it, guessing it must mark some small coasting port. We passed two vessels, outlandish and high-sterned, sleeping at anchor, and, approaching the light, now very dim, ran the boat's nose against the end of a jutting wharf. We were blind with fatigue. My men dropped the oars and fell off the thwarts as if dead. I made fast to a pile. A current rippled softly. The scented obscurity of the shore was grouped into vast masses, a density of colossal clumps of vegetation, probably—mute and fantastic shapes. And at their foot the semicircle of a beach gleamed faintly, like an illusion. There was not a light, not a stir, not a sound. The mysterious East faced me, perfumed like a flower, silent like death, dark like a grave.

"And I sat weary beyond expression, exulting like a conqueror, sleepless and entranced as if before a profound, a fateful enigma.

"A splashing of oars, a measured dip reverberating on the level of water, intensified by the silence of the shore into loud claps, made me jump up. A boat, a European boat, was coming in. I invoked the name of the dead: I hailed: *Judea* ahoy! A thin shout answered.

"It was the captain. I had beaten the flagship by three hours, and I was glad to hear the old man's voice again, tremulous and tired. 'Is it you, Marlow?' 'Mind the end of that jetty, sir,' I cried.

"He approached cautiously, and brought up with the deep-sea lead line which we had saved—for the underwriters. I eased my painter and fell alongside. He sat, a broken figure at the stern, wet with dew, his hands clasped in his lap. His men were asleep already. 'I had a terrible time of it,' he murmured. 'Mahon is behind—not very far.' We conversed in whispers, in low whispers, as if afraid to wake up the land. Guns, thunder, earthquakes would not have awakened the men just then.

"Looking round as we talked, I saw away at sea a bright light travelling in the night. 'There's a steamer passing the bay,' I said. She was not passing, she was entering, and she even came close and anchored. 'I wish,' said the old man, 'you would find out whether she is English. Perhaps they could give us a passage somewhere.' He seemed nervously anxious. So by dint of punching and kicking I started one of my men into a state of somnambulism,[32] and giving him an oar, took another and pulled towards the lights of the steamer.

"There was a murmur of voices in her, metallic hollow clangs of the engine-room, footsteps on the deck. Her ports shone, round like dilated eyes. Shapes moved about, and there was a shadowy man high up on the bridge. He heard my oars.

"And then, before I could open my lips, the East spoke to me, but it was in a Western voice. A torrent of words was poured into the enigmatical, the fateful silence; outlandish, angry words, mixed with words and even whole sentences of good English, less strange but even more surprising. The voice swore and cursed violently; it riddled the solemn peace of the bay by a volley of abuse. It began by calling me Pig, and from that went crescendo into unmentionable adjectives—in English. The man up there raged aloud in two languages, and with a sincerity in his fury that almost convinced me I had, in some way, sinned against the harmony of the universe. I could hardly see him, but began to think he would work himself into a fit.

"Suddenly he ceased, and I could hear him snorting and blowing like a porpoise. I said—

" 'What steamer is this, pray?'

" 'Eh? What's this? And who are you?'

" 'Castaway crew of an English barque burnt at sea. We came here tonight. I am the second mate. The captain is in the long-boat, and wishes to know if you would give us a passage somewhere.'

" 'Oh, my goodness! I say. . . . This is the *Celestial* from Singapore on her return trip. I'll arrange with your captain in the morning, . . . and, . . . I say, . . . did you hear me just now?'

---

32. **somnambulism,** sleepwalking.

" 'I should think the whole bay heard you.'

" 'I thought you were a shore-boat. Now, look here—this infernal lazy scoundrel of a caretaker has gone to sleep again—curse him. The light is out, and I nearly ran foul of the end of this damned jetty. This is the third time he plays me this trick. Now, I ask you, can anybody stand this kind of thing? It's enough to drive a man out of his mind. I'll report him. . . . I'll get the Assistant Resident[33] to give him the sack, by . . . ! See—there's no light. It's out, isn't it? I take you to witness the light's out. There should be a light, you know. A red light on the—'

" 'There was a light,' I said, mildly.

" 'But it's out, man! What's the use of talking like this? You can see for yourself it's out—don't you? If you had to take a valuable steamer along this Godforsaken coast you would want a light, too. I'll kick him from end to end of his miserable wharf. You'll see if I don't. I will—'

" 'So I may tell my captain you'll take us?' I broke in.

" 'Yes, I'll take you. Good night,' he said, brusquely.

"I pulled back, made fast again to the jetty, and then went to sleep at last. I had faced the silence of the East. I had heard some of its language. But when I opened my eyes again the silence was as complete as though it had never been broken. I was lying in a flood of light, and the sky had never looked so far, so high, before. I opened my eyes and lay without moving.

"And then I saw the men of the East—they were looking at me. The whole length of the jetty was full of people. I saw brown, bronze, yellow faces, the black eyes, the glitter, the color of an Eastern crowd. And all these beings stared without a murmur, without a sigh, without a movement. They stared down at the boats, at the sleeping men who at night had come to them from the sea. Nothing moved. The fronds of palms stood still against the sky. Not a branch stirred along the shore, and the brown roofs of hidden houses peeped through the green foliage, through the big leaves that hung shining and still like leaves forged of heavy metal. This was the East of the ancient navigators, so old, so mysterious, resplendent and somber, living and unchanged, full of danger and promise. And these were the men. I sat up suddenly. A wave of movement passed through the crowd from end to end, passed along the heads, swayed the bodies, ran along the jetty like a ripple on the water, like a breath of wind on a field—and all was still again. I see it now—the wide sweep of the bay, the glittering sands, the wealth of green infinite and varied, the sea blue like the sea of a dream, the crowd of attentive faces, the blaze of vivid color—the water reflecting it all, the curve of the shore, the jetty, the high-sterned outlandish craft floating still, and the three boats with the tired men from the West sleeping, unconscious of the land and the people and of the violence of sunshine. They slept thrown across the thwarts, curled on bottom-boards, in the careless attitudes of death. The head of the old skipper, leaning back in the stern of the longboat, had fallen on his breast, and he looked as though he would never wake. Farther out old Mahon's face was upturned to the sky, with the long white beard spread out on his breast, as though he had been shot where he sat at the tiller; and a man, all in a heap in the bows of the boat, slept with both arms embracing the stem-head and with his cheek laid on the gunwale. The East looked at them without a sound.

"I have known its fascination since; I have seen the mysterious shores, the still water, the lands of brown nations, where a stealthy Nemesis[34] lies in wait, pursues, overtakes so many of the conquering race, who are proud of their wisdom, of their knowledge, of their strength. But for me all the East is contained in that vision of my youth. It is all in that moment when I opened my young eyes on it. I came upon it from a tussle with the sea—and I was young—and I saw it looking at me. And this is all that is left of it! Only a moment; a moment of strength, of romance, of glamor—of youth! . . . A flick of sunshine upon a strange shore, the time to remember, the time for a sigh, and—good-bye!—Night—Good-bye . . . !"

He drank.

"Ah! The good old time—the good old time. Youth and the sea. Glamor and the sea! The good, strong sea, the salt, bitter sea, that could whisper to you and roar at you and knock your breath out of you."

---

33. **Assistant Resident,** a diplomatic agent.
34. **Nemesis,** in Greek mythology, the goddess of vengeance.

He drank again.

"By all that's wonderful it is the sea, I believe, the sea itself—or is it youth alone? Who can tell? But you here—you all had something out of life: money, love—whatever one gets on shore—and, tell me, wasn't that the best time, that time when we were young at sea; young and had nothing, on the sea that gives nothing, except hard knocks—and sometimes a chance to feel your strength—that only—what you all regret?"

And we all nodded at him: the man of finance, the man of accounts, the man of law, we all nodded at him over the polished table that like a still sheet of brown water reflected our faces, lined, wrinkled; our faces marked by toil, by deceptions, by success, by love; our weary eyes looking still, looking always, looking anxiously for something out of life, that while it is expected is already gone—has passed unseen, in a sigh, in a flash—together with the youth, with the strength, with the romance of illusions.

1898

Discussion

1. Analyze the characteristics of Marlow's audience. How do they influence the way he tells his story?

2. In the fourth paragraph Marlow says some voyages "might stand for a symbol of existence." Examine his remarks in this paragraph. What does he think is characteristic of human life? How does this attitude color his subsequent narrative?

3. By contrast, how does the *Judea*'s motto suggest young Marlow's attitude?

4. What sort of relationship develops between Marlow and Mrs. Beard? After he describes seeing her off at the train station, he says, " . . . I never saw her again . . . Pass the bottle." What links these two sentences?

5. In the midst of the second storm at sea, young Marlow experienced "moments of exultation." Explain the basis for his feelings. Do you find them sensible?

6. How does the rats' abandonment of the *Judea* add to the irony of Marlow's adventure?

7. Analyze closely the evolution of perception, from confusion to understanding, in the paragraph that begins "Next day it was my watch . . ." (page 574). At first, how do his mistakes turn the scene toward comedy? Finally, at what point does Marlow's mind grasp what is happening?

8. After the deck explodes, the young Marlow expects to see the ocean "convulsed with horror," but instead he finds with amazement "the peace of the sky and the serenity of the sea." Explain the reasons for his first assumption, and the implications in what he actually perceives.

9. In the midst of the disaster Marlow learns that the crew "had in them the right stuff." He concludes, "It is the sea that gives it . . . " What does he mean by "the right stuff," and how can the sea impart this quality?

10. Why does Captain Beard try to save the ship's supplies? What does this tell you about the code he lives by?

11. As the ship goes up in flames, Marlow sees it as a metaphor. "Oh, the glamor of youth! Oh, the fire of it, more dazzling than the flames of the burning ship . . . surrounded by an impenetrable night." How does this parallel illustrate Marlow's ideas about growing up?

12. All through the story young Marlow has dreamed of reaching the East. What does he find there? What do these discoveries imply?

Composition

In "Youth" an older man looks back on his early life at sea. How does he now judge the ideas, the dreams, and the actions of the young man that he was? Find an example of his present opinion of each.

In an essay consider how the story might change if these examples were described by a young Marlow, just after the events had occurred.

Rudyard Kipling 1865–1936

The world of Kipling's youth, and the subject of his first writings, has now almost entirely disappeared. He was born in Bombay, into the world of the British Empire at its height, when the British ruled the entire subcontinent of India. In his first years a household of native servants nursed and indulged him. He spoke their tongue more readily than his own and accompanied them to places Europeans rarely saw.

To guard his health and expand his horizon, Kipling's parents took him to England in 1871. For the next six years he and his sister boarded with an English family and attended local schools. Kipling had been a spoiled and willful child and was unprepared for the tyrannous control exercised by his paid guardians. Though bitterly unhappy he kept his troubles from his parents. In 1878 they enrolled him in the United Services College, a secondary school designed to train the less than brilliant sons of not very wealthy families for careers in military service. The food was spare, the classroom education inadequate, and the bullying by older boys virtually unchecked; Kipling survived.

At seventeen he returned to India. His father had found him a job as editorial assistant for a newspaper in Lahore. Here Kipling learned the newspaper trade and began to write poems and stories to fill up the occasional empty column. He entered into the world of the colonial administrators and soldiers and began to reproduce it in his writings.

His first book, *Departmental Ditties* (1886), was something new in English literature, describing the personalities and petty aspirations of a colonial society in a strongly cadenced

*M*ary *Postgate*

Of Miss Mary Postgate, Lady McCausland wrote that she was "thoroughly conscientious, tidy, companionable, and ladylike. I am very sorry to part with her, and shall always be interested in her welfare."

Miss Fowler engaged her on this recommendation, and to her surprise, for she had had experience of companions, found that it was true. Miss Fowler was nearer sixty than fifty at the time, but though she needed care she did not exhaust her attendant's vitality. On the contrary, she gave out, stimulatingly and with reminiscences. Her father had been a minor Court official in the days when the Great Exhibition of 1851[1] had just set its

seal on Civilization made perfect. Some of Miss Fowler's tales, none the less, were not always for the young. Mary was not young, and though her speech was as colorless as her eyes or her hair, she was never shocked. She listened unflinching-

1. **The Great Exhibition of 1851,** the first international exposition, organized to promote British artistic and industrial products and celebrate British imperialism. The Crystal Palace, an immense structure of iron and glass designed by Sir Joseph Paxton, was built to house it.

verse derived from ballads and theatrical patter songs. Many of these poems are in dialect. The book sold very well. In the next years Kipling wrote a series of stories first published in newspapers and then collected in book editions sold at Indian railroad stations. These were immensely successful, and by 1889 he felt ready to move to England and challenge the literary establishment at its center.

In the 1890s, along with several collections of stories, he published the two volumes of the *Jungle Books* and the sea tale *Captains Courageous.* In 1901 his finest novel, *Kim,* appeared.

By now Kipling's works had achieved enormous popularity. His poems were recited and sung in music-halls, his stories were a prized feature of the magazines in which they appeared, and his books were best sellers. He became a public figure who frequently contributed topical poems and letters to the newspapers. His strong support for the Empire and the military, his enthusiasm for the war in South Africa and his hatred of Germany made him controversial.

"Mary Postgate"—published in May of 1915—must thus be read in its context. The Germans had just taken Belgium and were making their first bombing runs over England. Tales of rape and torture came from behind enemy lines. Powerful nations, most notably the United States, still endeavored to remain neutral. The story becomes one way Kipling could effectively speak his mind. In October of the same year he received notice that his son was missing in action. He knew the boy was dead.

Until the war ended Kipling wrote no more fiction. But in the 1920s and 1930s he continued to publish stories and poems, and in fact his latest tales may well be his best. During his lifetime Kipling made a fortune as a writer, was the respected confidant of heads of state and military leaders, and won the Nobel Prize for Literature (1907). After his death a revulsion against his belief in empire and his admiration for force damaged his literary reputation. As time passes, however, the skill and power of his writing draw more serious attention, and he again appears to be one of the finest British short-story writers of this century.

ly to every one; said at the end, "How interesting!" or "How shocking!" as the case might be, and never again referred to it, for she prided herself on a trained mind, which "did not dwell on these things." She was, too, a treasure at domestic accounts, for which the village tradesmen, with their weekly books, loved her not. Otherwise she had no enemies; provoked no jealousy even among the plainest; neither gossip nor slander had ever been traced to her; she supplied the odd place at the Rector's or the Doctor's table at half an hour's notice; she was a sort of public aunt to very many small children of the village street, whose parents, while accepting every-thing, would have been swift to resent what they called "patronage"; she served on the Village Nursing Committee as Miss Fowler's nominee when Miss Fowler was crippled by rheumatoid arthritis, and came out of six months fortnightly meetings equally respected by all the cliques.

And when Fate threw Miss Fowler's nephew, an unlovely orphan of eleven, on Miss Fowler's hands, Mary Postgate stood to her share of the business of education as practiced in private and public schools. She checked printed clothes-lists, and unitemised bills of extras; wrote to Head and House masters, matrons, nurses and doctors, and grieved or rejoiced over half-term reports. Young Wyndham Fowler repaid her in his holidays by calling her "Gatepost," "Postey," or "Packthread," by thumping her between her narrow shoulders, or by chasing her bleating, round the garden, her large mouth open, her large nose high in air, at a stiff-necked shamble very like a camel's. Later on he filled the house with clamor, argument, and harangues as to his personal needs, likes and dislikes, and the limitations of "you women," reducing Mary to tears of physical fatigue, or, when he chose to be humorous, of helpless laughter. At crises, which multiplied as he grew older, she was his ambassadress and his interpretress to Miss Fowler, who had no large sympathy with the young; a vote in his interest at the councils on his future; his sewing-woman, strictly accountable for mislaid boots and garments; always his butt and his slave.

And when he decided to become a solicitor, and had entered an office in London; when his greeting had changed from "Hullo, Postey, you old beast," to "Mornin' Packthread," there came a war which, unlike all wars that Mary could remember, did not stay decently outside England and in the newspapers, but intruded on the lives of people whom she knew. As she said to Miss Fowler, it was "most vexatious." It took the Rector's son who was going into business with his elder brother; it took the Colonel's nephew on the eve of fruit-farming in Canada; it took Mrs. Grant's son who, his mother said, was devoted to the ministry; and, very early indeed, it took Wynn Fowler, who announced on a postcard that he had joined the Flying Corps and wanted a cardigan waistcoat.

"He must go, and he must have the waistcoat," said Miss Fowler. So Mary got the proper-sized needles and wool, while Miss Fowler told the men of her establishment—two gardeners and an odd man,[2] aged sixty—that those who could join the Army had better do so. The gardeners left. Cheape, the odd man, stayed on, and was promoted to the gardener's cottage. The cook, scorning to be limited in luxuries, also left, after a spirited scene with Miss Fowler, and took the housemaid with her. Miss Fowler gazetted Nellie, Cheape's seventeen-year-old daughter to the vacant post; Mrs. Cheape to the rank of cook with occasional cleaning bouts; and the reduced establishment moved forward smoothly.

Wynn demanded an increase in his allowance. Miss Fowler, who always looked facts in the face, said, "He must have it. The chances are he won't live long to draw it, and if three hundred makes him happy—"

Wynn was grateful, and came over, in his tight-buttoned uniform, to say so. His training center was not thirty miles away, and his talk was so technical that it had to be explained by charts of the various types of machines. He gave Mary such a chart.

"And you'd better study it, Postey," he said. "You'll be seeing a lot of 'em soon." So Mary studied the chart, but when Wynn next arrived to swell and exalt himself before his womenfolk, she failed badly in cross-examination, and he rated her as in the old days.

"You *look* more or less like a human being," he said in his new Service voice. "You *must* have had a brain at some time in your past. What have you done with it? Where d'you keep it? A sheep would know more than you do, Postey. You're lamentable. You are less use than an empty tin can, you dowey old cassowary."[3]

"I suppose that's how your superior officer talks to *you?*" said Miss Fowler from her chair.

"But Postey doesn't mind," Wynn replied. "Do you, Packthread?"

"Why? Was Wynn saying anything? I shall get this right next time you come," she muttered, and knitted her pale brows again over the diagrams of Taubes, Farmans, and Zeppelins.[4]

In a few weeks the mere land and sea battles which she read to Miss Fowler after breakfast passed her like idle breath. Her heart and her interest were high in the air with Wynn, who had finished "rolling" (whatever that might be) and had gone on from a "taxi" to a machine more or less his own. One morning it circled over their very chimneys, alighted on Vegg's Heath, almost outside the garden gate, and Wynn came in, blue with cold, shouting for food. He and she drew

---

2. **odd man,** a man doing odd jobs, or occasional work.
3. **dowey old cassowary.** *Dowey* is a dialect word meaning "dull," or "dismal." A cassowary is a large, flightless Australian bird. This is more of Wynn's half-affectionate abuse.
4. **Taubes, Farmans, and Zeppelins.** The first two were types of German and French aircraft in World War I; the third was a German dirigible, a lighter-than-air craft with a rigid inner framework.

Miss Fowler's bath-chair,[5] as they had often done, along the Heath foot-path to look at the biplane. Mary observed that "it smelt very badly."

"Postey, I believe you think with your nose," said Wynn. "I know you don't with your mind. Now, what type's that?"

"I'll go and get the chart," said Mary.

"You're hopeless! You haven't the mental capacity of a white mouse," he cried, and explained the dials and the sockets for bomb-dropping till it was time to mount and ride the wet clouds once more.

"Ah!" said Mary, as the stinking thing flared upward. "Wait till our Flying Corps gets to work! Wynn says it's much safer than in the trenches."

"I wonder," said Miss Fowler. "Tell Cheape to come and tow me home again."

"It's all downhill. I can do it," said Mary, "if you put the brake on." She laid her lean self against the pushing-bar and home they trundled.

"Now, be careful you aren't heated and catch a chill," said overdressed Miss Fowler.

"Nothing makes me perspire," said Mary. As she bumped the chair under the porch she straightened her long back. The exertion had given her a color, and the wind had loosened a wisp of hair across her forehead. Miss Fowler glanced at her.

"What do you ever think of, Mary?" she demanded suddenly.

"Oh, Wynn says he wants another three pairs of stockings—as thick as we can make them."

"Yes. But I mean the things that women think about. Here you are, more than forty—"

"Forty-four," said truthful Mary.

"Well?"

"Well?" Mary offered Miss Fowler her shoulder as usual.

"And you've been with me ten years now."

"Let's see," said Mary. "Wynn was eleven when he came. He's twenty now, and I came two years before that. It must be eleven."

"Eleven! And you've never told me anything that matters in all that while. Looking back, it seems to me that *I've* done all the talking."

"I'm afraid I'm not much of a conversationalist. As Wynn says, I haven't the mind. Let me take your hat."

Miss Fowler, moving stiffly from the hip, stamped her rubber-tipped stick on the tiled hall floor. "Mary, aren't you *anything* except a companion? Would you *ever* have been anything except a companion?"

Mary hung up the garden hat on its proper peg. "No," she said after consideration. "I don't imagine I ever should. But I've no imagination, I'm afraid."

Self-Portrait by Gwen John, painted about 1900.

She fetched Miss Fowler her eleven-o'clock glass of Contrexeville.[6]

That was the wet December when it rained six inches to the month, and the women went abroad as little as might be. Wynn's flying chariot visited them several times, and for two mornings (he had warned her by postcard) Mary heard the thresh of

5. *bath-chair*, wheelchair.
6. *Contrexeville*, mineral water from a French spa.

his propellers at dawn. The second time she ran to the window, and stared at the whitening sky. A little blur passed overhead. She lifted her lean arms towards it.

That evening at six o'clock there came an announcement in an official envelope that Second Lieutenant W. Fowler had been killed during a trial flight. Death was instantaneous. She read it and carried it to Miss Fowler.

"I never expected anything else," said Miss Fowler; "but I'm sorry it happened before he had done anything."

The room was whirling round Mary Postgate, but she found herself quite steady in the midst of it.

"Yes," she said. "It's a great pity he didn't die in action after he had killed somebody."

"He was killed instantly. That's one comfort," Miss Fowler went on.

"But Wynn says the shock of a fall kills a man at once—whatever happens to the tanks," quoted Mary.

The room was coming to rest now. She heard Miss Fowler say impatiently, "But why can't we cry, Mary?" and herself replying, "There's nothing to cry for. He has done his duty as much as Mrs. Grant's son did."

"And when he died, *she* came and cried all the morning," said Miss Fowler. "This only makes me feel tired—terribly tired. Will you help me to bed, please, Mary?—And I think I'd like the hot-water bottle."

So Mary helped her and sat beside, talking of Wynn in his riotous youth.

"I believe," said Miss Fowler suddenly, "that old people and young people slip from under a stroke like this. The middle-aged feel it most."

"I expect that's true," said Mary, rising. "I'm going to put away the things in his room now. Shall we wear mourning?"

"Certainly not," said Miss Fowler. "Except, of course, at the funeral. I can't go. You will. I want you to arrange about his being buried here. What a blessing it didn't happen at Salisbury!"

Every one, from the Authorities of the Flying Corps to the Rector, was most kind and sympathetic. Mary found herself for the moment in a world where bodies were in the habit of being despatched by all sorts of conveyances to all sorts of places. And at the funeral two young men in buttoned-up uniforms stood beside the grave and spoke to her afterwards.

"You're Miss Postgate, aren't you?" said one. "Fowler told me about you. He was a good chap—a first-class fellow—a great loss."

"Great loss!" growled his companion. "We're all awfully sorry."

"How high did he fall from?" Mary whispered.

"Pretty nearly four thousand feet, I should think, didn't he? You were up that day, Monkey?"

"All of that," the other child replied. "My bar[7] made three thousand, and I wasn't as high as him by a lot."

"Then *that's* all right," said Mary. "Thank you very much."

They moved away as Mrs. Grant flung herself weeping on Mary's flat chest, under the lychgate, and cried, "*I* know how it feels! *I* know how it feels!"

"But both his parents are dead," Mary returned, as she fended her off. "Perhaps they've all met by now," she added vaguely as she escaped towards the coach.

"I've thought of that too," wailed Mrs. Grant; "but then he'll be practically a stranger to them. Quite embarrassing!"

Mary faithfully reported every detail of the ceremony to Miss Fowler, who, when she described Mrs. Grant's outburst, laughed aloud.

"Oh, how Wynn would have enjoyed it! He was always utterly unreliable at funerals. D'you remember——" And they talked of him again, each piecing out the other's gaps. "And now," said Miss Fowler, "we'll pull up the blinds and we'll have a general tidy. That always does us good. Have you seen to Wynn's things?"

"Everything—since he first came," said Mary. "He was never destructive—even with his toys."

They faced that neat room.

"It can't be natural not to cry," Mary said at last. "I'm so afraid you'll have a reaction."

"As I told you, we old people slip from under

---

7. *bar,* altimeter (works by barometric pressure).

the stroke. It's you I'm afraid for. Have you cried yet?''

"I can't. It only makes me angry with the Germans."

"That's sheer waste of vitality," said Miss Fowler. "We must live till the war's finished." She opened a full wardrobe. "Now, I've been thinking things over. This is my plan. All his civilian clothes can be given away—Belgian refugees, and so on."

Mary nodded. "Boots, collars, and gloves?"

"Yes. We don't need to keep anything except his cap and belt."

"They came back yesterday with his Flying Corps clothes"—Mary pointed to a roll on the little iron bed.

"Ah, but keep his Service things. Some one may be glad of them later. Do you remember his sizes?''

"Five feet eight and a half; thirty-six inches round the chest. But he told me he's just put on an inch and a half. I'll mark it on a label and tie it on his sleeping-bag."

"So that disposes of *that,*" said Miss Fowler, tapping the palm of one hand with the ringed third finger of the other. "What waste it all is! We'll get his old school trunk tomorrow and pack his civilian clothes."

"And the rest?" said Mary. "His books and pictures and the games and the toys—and—and the rest?"

"My plan is to burn every single thing," said Miss Fowler. "Then we shall know where they are and no one can handle them afterwards. What do you think?"

"I think that would be much the best," said Mary. "But there's such a lot of them."

"We'll burn them in the destructor," said Miss Fowler.

This was an open-air furnace for the consumption of refuse; a little circular four-foot tower of pierced brick over an iron grating. Miss Fowler had noticed the design in a gardening journal years ago, and had had it built at the bottom of the garden. It suited her tidy soul, for it saved unsightly rubbish-heaps, and the ashes lightened the stiff clay soil.

Mary considered for a moment, saw her way clear, and nodded again. They spent the evening putting away well-remembered civilian suits, underclothes that Mary had marked, and the regiments of very gaudy socks and ties. A second trunk was needed, and, after that, a little packing-case, and it was late next day when Cheape and the local carrier lifted them to the cart. The Rector luckily knew of a friend's son, about five feet eight and a half inches high, to whom a complete Flying Corps outfit would be most acceptable, and sent his gardener's son down with a barrow to take delivery of it. The cap was hung up in Miss Fowler's bedroom, the belt in Miss Postgate's; for, as Miss Fowler said, they had no desire to make tea-party talk of them.

"That disposes of *that,*" said Miss Fowler. "I'll leave the rest to you, Mary. I can't run up and down the garden. You'd better take the big clothes-basket and get Nellie to help you."

"I shall take the wheel-barrow and do it myself," said Mary, and for once in her life closed her mouth.

Miss Fowler, in moments of irritation, had called Mary deadly methodical. She put on her oldest waterproof and gardening-hat and her ever-slipping galoshes, for the weather was on the edge of more rain. She gathered firelighters from the kitchen, a half-scuttle of coals, and a faggot of brushwood. These she wheeled in the barrow down the mossed paths to the dank little laurel shrubbery where the destructor stood under the drip of three oaks. She climbed the wire fence into the Rector's glebe[8] just behind, and from his tenant's rick pulled two large armfuls of good hay, which she spread neatly on the fire-bars. Next, journey by journey, passing Miss Fowler's white face at the morning-room window each time, she brought down in the towel-covered clothes-basket, on the wheel-barrow, thumbed and used Hentys, Marryats, Levers, Stevensons, Baroness Orczys, Garvices,[9] school-books, and atlases, unrelated piles of the *Motor Cyclist,* the *Light Car,* and catalogues of Olympia Exhibitions;[10] the remnants of a fleet of sailing-ships from nine-penny cutters to a three-guinea yacht; a prep.-school dressing-gown; bats from three-and-sixpence to twenty-four shillings;

---

8. glebe (glēb), farmland belonging to a vicarage.
9. Hentys. . . .Garvices, authors of Victorian adventure stories for boys.
10. Olympia Exhibitions, exhibitions of all kinds held in a large building in West London.

cricket and tennis balls; disintegrated steam and clockwork locomotives with their twisted rails; a gray and red tin model of a submarine; a dumb gramophone and cracked records; golf-clubs that had to be broken across the knee, like his walking-sticks, and an assegai;[11] photographs of private and public school cricket and football elevens, and his O.T.C.[12] on the line of march; kodaks, and film-rolls; some pewters, and one real silver cup, for boxing competitions and Junior Hurdles; sheaves of school photographs; Miss Fowler's photograph; her own which he had borne off in fun and (good care she took not to ask!) had never returned; a playbox with a secret drawer; a load of flannels, belts, and jerseys, and a pair of spiked shoes unearthed in the attic; a packet of all the letters that Miss Fowler and she had ever written to him, kept for some absurd reason through all these years; a five-day attempt at a diary; framed pictures of racing motors in full Brooklands[13] career, and load upon load of undistinguishable wreckage of toolboxes, rabbit-hutches, electric batteries, tin soldiers, fret-saw outfits, and jigsaw puzzles.

Miss Fowler at the window watched her come and go, and said to herself, "Mary's an old woman. I never realized it before."

After lunch she recommended her to rest.

"I'm not in the least tired," said Mary. "I've got it all arranged. I'm going to the village at two o'clock for some paraffin.[14] Nellie hasn't enough, and the walk will do me good."

She made one last quest round the house before she started, and found that she had overlooked nothing. It began to mist soon as she had skirted Vegg's Heath, where Wynn used to descend—it seemed to her that she could almost hear the beat of his propellers overhead, but there was nothing to see. She hoisted her umbrella and lunged into the blind wet till she had reached the shelter of the empty village. As she came out of Mr. Kidd's shop with a bottle full of paraffin in her string shopping-bag, she met Nurse Eden, the village nurse, and fell into talk with her, as usual, about the village children. They were just parting opposite the "Royal Oak" when a gun, they fancied, was fired immediately behind the house. It was followed by a child's shriek dying into a wail.

"Accident!" said Nurse Eden promptly, and dashed through the empty bar, followed by Mary. They found Mrs. Gerritt, the publican's wife, who could only gasp and point to the yard, where a little cart-lodge was sliding sideways amid a clatter of tiles. Nurse Eden snatched up a sheet drying before the fire, ran out, lifted something from the ground, and flung the sheet around it. The sheet turned scarlet and half her uniform too, as she bore the load into the kitchen. It was little Edna Gerritt, aged nine, whom Mary had known since her perambulator days.

"Am I hurted bad?" Edna asked, and died between Nurse Eden's dripping hands. The sheet fell aside and for an instant, before she could shut her eyes, Mary saw the ripped and shredded body. "It's a wonder she spoke at all," said Nurse Eden. "What in God's name was it?"

"A bomb," said Mary.

"One o' the Zeppelins?"

"No. An aeroplane. I thought I heard it on the Heath but I fancied it was one of ours. It must have shut off its engines as it came down. That's why we didn't notice it."

"The filthy pigs!" said Nurse Eden, all white and shaken. "See the pickle I'm in! Go and tell Dr. Hennis, Miss Postgate." Nurse looked at the mother, who had dropped face down on the floor. "She's only in a fit. Turn her over."

Mary heaved Mrs. Gerritt right side up, and hurried off for the doctor. When she told her tale, he asked her to sit down in the surgery till he got her something.

"But I don't need it, I assure you," said she. "I don't think it would be wise to tell Miss Fowler about it, do you? Her heart is so irritable in this weather."

Dr. Hennis looked at her admiringly as he packed up his bag.

"No. Don't tell anybody till we're sure," he said, and hastened to the "Royal Oak," while Mary went on with the paraffin. The village behind her was as quiet as usual, for the news had not yet spread. She frowned a little to herself, her large nostrils expanded uglily and from time to time she muttered a phrase which Wynn who

---

11. assegai (as'ə gī), Zulu throwing spear, a relic of British campaigning against the Zulus, a Bantu-speaking people of South Africa, in the late 1870s.
12. O.T.C., Officers Training Corps.
13. Brooklands, a famous auto speedway in England.
14. paraffin, kerosene.

never restrained himself before his womenfolk, had applied to the enemy. "Bloody pagans! They *are* bloody pagans. But," she continued, falling back on the teaching that had made her what she was, "one mustn't let one's mind dwell on these things."

Before she reached the house Dr. Hennis, who was also a special constable, overtook her in his car.

"Oh, Miss Postgate," he said, "I wanted to tell you that the accident at the 'Royal Oak' was due to Gerritt's stable tumbling down. It's been dangerous for a long time. It ought to have been condemned."

"I thought I heard an explosion too," said Mary.

"You might have been misled by the beams snapping. I've been looking at 'em. They were dry-rotted through and through. Of course, as they broke, they would make a noise just like a gun."

"Yes?" said Mary politely.

"Poor little Edna was playing underneath it," he went on, still holding her with his eyes, "and that and the tiles cut her to pieces, you see?"

"I saw it," said Mary, shaking her head. "I heard it too."

"Well, we cannot be sure." Dr. Hennis changed his tone completely. "I know both you and Nurse Eden (I've been speaking to her) are perfectly trustworthy, and I can rely on you not to say anything—yet at least. It is no good to stir up people unless—"

"Oh, I never do—anyhow," said Mary, and Dr. Hennis went on to the country town.

After all, she told herself, it might, just possibly, have been the collapse of the old stable that had done all those things to poor little Edna. She was sorry she had even hinted at other things, but Nurse Eden was discretion itself. By the time she reached home the affair seemed increasingly remote by its very monstrosity. As she came in, Miss Fowler told her that a couple of aeroplanes had passed half an hour ago.

"I thought I heard them," she replied, "I'm going down to the garden now. I've got the paraffin."

"Yes, but—what *have* you got on your boots? They're soaking wet. Change them at once."

Not only did Mary obey but she wrapped the boots in a newspaper, and put them into the string bag with the bottle. So, armed with the longest kitchen poker, she left.

"It's raining again," was Miss Fowler's last word, "but—I know you won't be happy till that's disposed of."

"It won't take long. I've got everything down there, and I've put the lid on the destructor to keep the wet out."

The shrubbery was filling with twilight by the time she had completed her arrangements and sprinkled the sacrificial oil. As she lit the match that would burn her heart to ashes, she heard a groan or a grunt behind the dense Portugal laurels.

"Cheape?" she called impatiently, but Cheape, with his ancient lumbago, in his comfortable cottage would be the last man to profane the sanctuary. "Sheep," she concluded, and threw in the fusee.[15] The pyre went up in a roar, and the immediate flame hastened night around her.

"How Wynn would have loved this!" she thought, stepping back from the blaze.

By its light she saw, half hidden behind a laurel not five paces away, a bareheaded man sitting very stiffly at the foot of one of the oaks. A broken branch lay across his lap—one booted leg protruding from beneath it. His head moved ceaselessly from side to side, but his body was as still as the tree's trunk. He was dressed—she moved sideways to look more closely—in a uniform something like Wynn's, with a flap buttoned across the chest. For an instant she had some idea that it might be one of the young flying men she had met at the funeral. But their heads were dark and glossy. This man's was as pale as a baby's, and so closely cropped that she could see the disgusting pinky skin beneath. His lips moved.

"What do you say?" Mary moved towards him and stooped.

"Laty! Laty! Laty!" he muttered, while his hands picked at the dead wet leaves. There was no doubt as to his nationality. It made her so angry that she strode back to the destructor, though it was still too hot to use the poker there. Wynn's books seemed to be catching well. She

---

15. *fusee* (fū zē′), match.

looked up at the oak behind the man; several of the light upper and two or three rotten lower branches had broken and scattered their rubbish on the shrubbery path. On the lowest fork a helmet with dependent strings, showed like a bird's-nest in the light of a long-tongued flame. Evidently this person had fallen through the tree. Wynn had told her that it was quite possible for people to fall out of aeroplanes. Wynn told her too, that trees were useful things to break an aviator's fall, but in this case the aviator must have been broken or he would have moved from his queer position. He seemed helpless except for his horrible rolling head. On the other hand, she could see a pistol case at his belt—and Mary loathed pistols. Months ago, after reading certain Belgian reports together, she and Miss Fowler had had dealings with one—a huge revolver with flat-nosed bullets, which latter, Wynn said, were forbidden by the rules of war to be used against civilized enemies. "They're good enough for us," Miss Fowler had replied. "Show Mary how it works." And Wynn, laughing at the mere possibility of any such need, had led the craven winking Mary into the Rector's disused quarry, and had shown her how to fire the terrible machine. It lay now in the top-left-hand drawer of her toilet-table—a memento not included in the burning. Wynn would be pleased to see how she was not afraid.

She slipped up to the house to get it. When she came through the rain, the eyes in the head were alive with expectation. The mouth even tried to smile. But at sight of the revolver its corners went down just like Edna Gerritt's. A tear trickled from one eye, and the head rolled from shoulder to shoulder as though trying to point out something.

"Cassée. Tout cassée,"[16] it whimpered.

"What do you say?" said Mary disgustedly, keeping well to one side, though only the head moved.

"Cassée," it repeated. "Che me rends. Le médicin! Toctor!"[17]

"Nein!" said she, bringing all her small German to bear with the big pistol. "Ich haben der todt Kinder gesehn."[18]

The head was still. Mary's hand dropped. She had been careful to keep her finger off the trigger for fear of accidents. After a few moments' waiting, she returned to the destructor, where the flames were falling, and churned up Wynn's charring books with the poker. Again the head groaned for the doctor.

"Stop that!" said Mary, and stamped her foot. "Stop that, you bloody pagan!"

The words came quite smoothly and naturally. They were Wynn's own words, and Wynn was a gentleman who for no consideration on earth would have torn little Edna into those vividly colored strips and strings. But this thing hunched under the oak-tree had done that thing. It was no question of reading horrors out of newspapers to Miss Fowler. Mary had seen it with her own eyes on the "Royal Oak" kitchen table. She must not allow her mind to dwell upon it. Now Wynn was dead, and everything connected with him was lumping and rustling and tinkling under her busy poker into red black dust and grey leaves of ash. The thing beneath the oak would die too. Mary had seen death more than once. She came of a family that had a knack of dying under, as she told Miss Fowler, "most distressing circumstances." She would stay where she was till she was entirely satisfied that It was dead—dead as dear papa in the late 'eighties; aunt Mary in 'eighty-nine; mamma in 'ninety-one; cousin Dick in 'ninety-five; Lady McCausland's housemaid in 'ninety-nine; Lady McCausland's sister in nineteen hundred and one; Wynn buried five days ago; and Edna Gerritt still wait ing for decent earth to hide her. As she thought—her underlip caught up by one faded canine, brows knit and nostrils wide—she wielded the poker with lunges that jarred the grating at the bottom, and careful scrapes round the brick-work above. She looked at her wristwatch. It was getting on to half-past four, and the rain was coming down in earnest. Tea would be at five. If It did not die before that time, she would be soaked and would have to change. Meantime, and this occupied her, Wynn's things were burning well in spite of the hissing wet though now and again a book-back with a quite distinguishable title would be heaved up out of the mass. The exercise of stoking had given her a glow which seemed to

---

16. *"Cassée. Tout cassée."* "Broken, all broken." [French]
17. *"Che me rends. Le médicin! Toctor!"* The wounded German aviator employs a mixture of French and (accented) English to say, "I give up. Doctor! Doctor!"
18. *"Nein! . . . gesehn."* Mary responds (in very ungrammatical German), "No, I have seen the dead child."

reach to the marrow of her bones. She hummed—Mary never had a voice—to herself. She had never believed in all those advanced views—though Miss Fowler herself leaned a little that way—of woman's work in the world; but now she saw there was much to be said for them. This, for instance, was *her* work—work which no man, least of all Dr. Hennis, would ever have done. A man, at such a crisis, would be what Wynn called a "sportsman"; would leave everything to fetch help, and would certainly bring It into the house. Now a woman's business was to make a happy home for—for a husband and children. Failing these—it was not a thing one should allow one's mind to dwell upon—but—

"Stop it!" Mary cried once more across the shadows. "Nein, I tell you! Ich haben der todt Kinder gesehn."

But it was a fact. A woman who had missed these things could still be useful—more useful than a man in certain respects. She thumped like a pavior[19] through the settling ashes at the secret thrill of it. The rain was damping the fire, but she could feel—it was too dark to see—that her work was done. There was a dull red glow at the bottom of the destructor, not enough to char the wooden lid if she slipped it half over against the driving wet. This arranged, she leaned on the poker and waited, while an increasing rapture laid hold on her. She ceased to think. She gave herself up to feel. Her long pleasure was broken by a sound that she had waited for in agony several times in her life. She leaned forward and listened, smiling. There could be no mistake. She closed her eyes and drank it in. Once it ceased abruptly.

"Go on," she murmured, half aloud. "That isn't the end."

Then the end came very distinctly in a lull between two rain-gusts. Mary Postgate drew her breath short between her teeth and shivered from head to foot. *"That's* all right," said she contentedly, and went up to the house, where she scandalized the whole routine by taking a luxurious hot bath before tea, and came down looking, as Miss Fowler said when she saw her lying all relaxed on the other sofa, "quite handsome!"

1915

---

19. *pavior* (pāv′yẻr), a street paver who rams down cobblestones.

Discussion

1. Characterize the way Miss Fowler and Wynn treat Mary Postgate. How does she react to their treatment?

2. When Mary fails to pass Wynn's cross-examination identifying enemy aircraft, he accuses her of being "less use than an empty tin can . . ." How did you react to the remark at this point in the story? What details led you to your reaction?

3. Explain why Miss Fowler and Mary react in such an unexpected way to the news of Wynn's death.

4. Several times Miss Fowler uses the phrase, "that disposes of *that*." What does she mean, and how does this provide a clue to her inner feelings?

5. What does the list of Wynn's things Mary prepares to burn tell us about him? What does it suggest she has lost in his death?

6. Why does Dr. Hennis go out of his way to insist that Edna's death "was due to Geritt's stable tumbling down"? What is the point of including this scene in the story?

7. Explain why Kipling has the German aviator fall near the fire.

8. Why does Mary let the aviator die? What effect does it have on her?

Composition

Mary Postgate finally dies, and a successor must now cart her old belongings out to the destructor for burning.

In an essay, describe what she finds as she cleans out Mary's room, and explain how each article tells us something about its owner's character.

H. G. Wells 1866–1946

Herbert George Wells was a self-made man, who began life as a shop clerk and ended it as the author of 114 books, a writer so influential in the first half of this century that, as George Orwell put it, "The minds of all of us, and therefore the physical world, would be perceptibly different if Wells had never existed."

Wells's parents were lower-middle class, his father a shopkeeper, his mother a lady's maid. When he was born they were trying for a more genteel life by running a china shop in a London suburb. Wells attended what he later called "a beastly little private school" that gave him only a smattering of knowledge. When he was fourteen he became an apprentice to a draper (dealer in cloth or dry goods). This meant long days working in a basement. His mother, meanwhile, had obtained a position as housekeeper in a country estate, and on holidays her son joined her in the servants' quarters, getting glimpses of life above stairs. The apprenticeship to the draper didn't last, and from his fourteenth to his eighteenth year Wells went from one job to another. In 1884 he won a scholarship to a London college and began training to be a science teacher. There he studied with the biologist T. H. Huxley and read widely in science and philosophy. But a characteristic restlessness overtook him and Wells failed his final examination in 1887. Ill with tuberculosis, frustrated with the private tutoring jobs his failure had forced him to take, Wells began to write short essays on science for popular magazines. They led to his first success, in 1896, the science fantasy *The Time Machine.*

While *The Time Machine* can be called one of the first science-fiction novels in English, it

The Door in the Wall

I

One confidential evening, not three months ago, Lionel Wallace told me this story of the Door in the Wall. And at the time I thought that so far as he was concerned it was a true story.

He told it me with such a direct simplicity of conviction that I could not do otherwise than believe in him. But in the morning, in my own flat, I woke to a different atmosphere, and as I lay in bed and recalled the things he had told me, stripped of the glamor of his earnest slow voice, denuded of the focussed shaded table light, the shadowy atmosphere that wrapped about him and the pleasant bright things, the dessert and glasses and napery of the dinner we had shared, making them for the time a bright little world quite cut off from everyday realities, I saw it all as frankly incredible. "He was mystifying!" I said, and then: "How well he did it! . . . It isn't quite the thing I should have expected him, of all people, to do well."

is very different from the work of the nineteenth-century French writer of science fiction, Jules Verne. Typically Verne begins with a likely invention, such as the submarine, and then works out exactly how it would function. By contrast, Wells's time machine is a creation of pure fantasy, whose operating principles the story never tries to explain. Wells's interest is not technological, but social; his subject is the world he is living in and its potential for improvement. The time machine simply permits his narrator to examine these matters from a fresh perspective by visiting a world of the future in which present problems reach an extreme.

It was a very successful book, and in the next few years Wells wrote a series of "scientific romances" which have enjoyed continued popularity into our own day: *The Island of Dr. Moreau* (1896), *The Invisible Man* (1897), *The War of the Worlds* (1898), and *The First Men on the Moon* (1901). At the same time Wells was writing short stories such as "The Door in the Wall," which also grew out of his knack for integrating something odd or fantastic into an otherwise ordinary world. He "found that, taking almost anything as a starting point and letting my thoughts play about with it, there would presently come out of the darkness, in a manner quite inexplicable, some absurd little nucleus. Little men in canoes upon sunlit oceans would come floating out of nothingness, incubating the eggs of prehistoric monsters unawares . . . "

The success of Wells's tales catapulted him into wealth, celebrity, and respectability. He continued to write rapidly, turning to studies of contemporary society in brilliant novels like *Kipps* (1905), in which he drew on his own unhappy adolescence, and *Tono-Bungay* (1909), a humorous satire on the dishonest promotion of patent medicine. But he found himself attracted more and more to the role of social prophet, and for much of the rest of his life his writing became devoted to telling people what the future could be like. Wells believed that the intelligent use of scientific knowledge would create a utopian society. Such optimism appeared to contradict his despairing predictions of aerial warfare, tanks, and the atomic bomb. But there was no contradiction in his valedictory, *Mind at the End of Its Tether* (1945), written during World War II and predicting the extinction of humanity.

Afterwards, as I sat up in bed and sipped my morning tea, I found myself trying to account for the flavor of reality that perplexed me in his impossible reminiscences, by supposing they did in some way suggest, present, convey—I hardly know which word to use—experiences it was otherwise impossible to tell.

Well, I don't resort to that explanation now. I have got over my intervening doubts. I believe now, as I believed at the moment of telling, that Wallace did to the very best of his ability strip the truth of his secret for me. But whether he himself saw, or only thought he saw, whether he himself was the possessor of an inestimable privilege, or the victim of a fantastic dream, I cannot pretend to guess. Even the facts of his death, which ended my doubts forever, throw no light on that. That much the reader must judge for himself.

I forget now what chance comment or criticism of mine moved so reticent a man to confide in me. He was, I think, defending himself against an imputation of slackness and unreliability I had made in relation to a great public movement in which he had disappointed me. But he plunged suddenly. "I have," he said, "a preoccupation—"

"I know," he went on, after a pause that he devoted to the study of his cigar ash, "I have been negligent. The fact is—it isn't a case of ghosts or apparitions—but—it's an odd thing to tell of, Redmond—I am haunted. I am haunted by something—that rather takes the light out of things, that fills me with longings . . ."

He paused, checked by that English shyness

that so often overcomes us when we would speak of moving or grave or beautiful things. "You were at Saint Athelstan's all through," he said, and for a moment that seemed to me quite irrelevant. "Well"—and he paused. Then very haltingly at first, but afterwards more easily, he began to tell of the thing that was hidden in his life, the haunting memory of a beauty and a happiness that filled his heart with insatiable longings that made all the interests and spectacle of worldly life seem dull and tedious and vain to him.

Now that I have the clue to it, the thing seems written visibly in his face. I have a photograph in which that look of detachment has been caught and intensified. It reminds me of what a woman once said of him—a woman who had loved him greatly. "Suddenly," she said, "the interest goes out of him. He forgets you. He doesn't care a rap for you—under his very nose . . . . ."

Yet the interest was not always out of him, and when he was holding his attention to a thing Wallace could contrive to be an extremely successful man. His career, indeed, is set with successes. He left me behind him long ago; he soared up over my head, and cut a figure in the world that I couldn't cut—anyhow. He was still a year short of forty, and they say now that he would have been in office and very probably in the new Cabinet if he had lived. At school he always beat me without effort—as it were by nature. We were at school together at Saint Athelstan's College in West Kensington for almost all our school time. He came into the school as my co-equal, but he left far above me, in a blaze of scholarships and brilliant performance. Yet I think I made a fair average running. And it was at school I heard first of the Door in the Wall—that I was to hear of a second time only a month before his death.

To him at least the Door in the Wall was a real door leading through a real wall to immortal realities. Of that I am now quite assured.

And it came into his life early, when he was a little fellow between five and six. I remember how, as he sat making his confession to me with a slow gravity, he reasoned and reckoned the date of it. "There was," he said, "a crimson Virginia creeper in it—all one bright uniform crimson in a clear amber sunshine against a white wall. That came into the impression somehow, though I don't clearly remember how, and there were

horse-chestnut leaves upon the clean pavement outside the green door. They were blotched yellow and green, you know, not brown nor dirty, so that they must have been new fallen. I take it that means October. I look out for horse-chestnut leaves every year, and I ought to know.

"If I'm right in that, I was about five years and four months old."

He was, he said, rather a precocious little boy—he learned to talk at an abnormally early age, and he was so sane and "old-fashioned," as people say, that he was permitted an amount of initiative that most children scarcely attain by seven or eight. His mother died when he was born, and he was under the less vigilant and authoritative care of a nursery governess. His father was a stern, preoccupied lawyer, who gave him little attention, and expected great things of him. For all his brightness he found life a little grey and dull I think. And one day he wandered.

He could not recall the particular neglect that enabled him to get away, nor the course he took among the West Kensington roads. All that had faded among the incurable blurs of memory. But the white wall and the green door stood out quite distinctly.

As his memory of that remote childish experience ran, he did at the very first sight of that door experience a peculiar emotion, an attraction, a desire to get to the door and open it and walk in. And at the same time he had the clearest conviction that either it was unwise or it was wrong of him—he could not tell which—to yield to this attraction. He insisted upon it as a curious thing that he knew from the very beginning—unless memory has played him the queerest trick—that the door was unfastened, and that he could go in as he chose.

I seem to see the figure of that little boy, drawn and repelled. And it was very clear in his mind, too, though why it should be so was never explained, that his father would be very angry if he went through that door.

Wallace described all these moments of hesitation to me with the utmost particularity. He went right past the door, and then, with his hands in his pockets, and making an infantile attempt to whistle, strolled right along beyond the end of the wall. There he recalls a number of mean, dirty shops, and particularly that of a plumber and decorator, with a dusty disorder of earthenware pipes, sheet lead ball taps, pattern books of wallpaper, and tins of enamel. He stood pretending to examine these things, and coveting, passionately desiring the green door.

Then, he said, he had a gust of emotion. He made a run for it, lest hesitation should grip him again, he went plump with outstretched hand through the green door and let it slam behind him. And so, in a trice, he came into the garden that has haunted all his life.

It was very difficult for Wallace to give me his full sense of that garden into which he came.

There was something in the very air of it that exhilarated, that gave one a sense of lightness and good happening and well being; there was something in the sight of it that made all its color clean and perfect and subtly luminous. In the instant of coming into it one was exquisitely glad—as only in rare moments and when one is young and joyful one can be glad in this world. And everything was beautiful there. . . .

Wallace mused before he went on telling me. "You see," he said, with the doubtful inflection of a man who pauses at incredible things, "there were two great panthers there . . . Yes, spotted panthers. And I was not afraid. There was a long wide path with marble-edged flower borders on either side, and these two huge velvety beasts were playing there with a ball. One looked up and came towards me, a little curious as it seemed. It came right up to me, rubbed its soft round ear very gently against the small hand I held out and purred. It was, I tell you, an enchanted garden. I know. And the size? Oh! it stretched far and wide, this way and that. I believe there were hills far away. Heaven knows where West Kensington had suddenly got to. And somehow it was just like coming home.

"You know, in the very moment the door swung to behind me, I forgot the road with its fallen chestnut leaves, its cabs and tradesmen's carts, I forgot the sort of gravitational pull back to the discipline and obedience of home, I forgot all hesitations and fear, forgot discretion, forgot all the intimate realities of this life. I became in a moment a very glad and wonder-happy little boy—in another world. It was a world with a different quality, a warmer, more penetrating and mellower light, with a faint clear gladness in its air, and wisps of sun-touched cloud in the blueness of its sky. And before me ran this long wide path, invitingly, with weedless beds on either side, rich with untended flowers, and these two great panthers. I put my little hands fearlessly on their soft fur, and caressed their round ears and the sensitive corners under their ears, and played with them, and it was as though they welcomed me home. There was a keen sense of homecoming in my mind, and when presently a tall, fair girl appeared in the pathway and came to meet me, smiling, and said, "Well?" to me, and lifted me, and kissed me, and put me down, and led me by the hand, there was no amazement, but only an impression of delightful rightness, of being reminded of happy things that had in some strange way been overlooked. There were broad steps, I remember, that came into view between spikes of delphinium, and up these we went to a great avenue between very old and shady dark trees. All down this avenue, you know, between the red chapped stems, were marble seats of honor and statuary, and very tame and friendly white doves . . . . .

"And along this avenue my girl-friend led me, looking down—I recall the pleasant lines, the finely-modelled chin of her sweet kind face—asking me questions in a soft, agreeable voice, and telling me things, pleasant things I know, though what they were I was never able to recall . . . And presently a little Capuchin monkey, very clean, with a fur of ruddy brown and kindly hazel eyes, came down a tree to us and ran beside me, looking up at me and grinning, and presently leapt to my shoulder. So we went on our way in great happiness. . . ."

He paused.

"Go on," I said.

"I remember little things. We passed an old man musing among laurels, I remember, and a place gay with paroquets, and came through a broad shaded colonnade to a spacious cool palace, full of pleasant fountains, full of beautiful things, full of the quality and promise of heart's desire. And there were many things and many people, some that still seem to stand out clearly and some that are a little vague, but all these people were beautiful and kind. In some way—I don't know how—it was conveyed to me that they all were kind to me, glad to have me there, and filling me with gladness by their gestures, by the touch of their hands, by the welcome and love in their eyes. Yes—"

He mused for awhile. "Playmates I found there. That was very much to me, because I was a lonely little boy. They played delightful games in a grass-covered court where there was a sun-dial set about with flowers. And as one played one loved. . . .

"But—it's odd—there's a gap in my memory. I don't remember the games we played. I never remembered. Afterwards, as a child, I spent long hours trying, even with tears, to recall the form of that happiness. I wanted to play it all over again—in my nursery—by myself. No! All I remember is the happiness and two dear playfellows who were most with me. . . . Then presently came a somber dark woman, with a grave, pale face and dreamy eyes, a somber woman wearing a soft long robe of pale purple, who carried a book and beckoned and took me aside with her into a gallery above a hall—though my playmates were loth to have me go, and ceased their game and stood watching as I was carried away. 'Come back to us!' they cried. 'Come back to us soon!' I looked up at her face, but she heeded them not at all. Her face was very gentle and grave. She took me to a seat in the gallery, and I stood beside her, ready to look at her book as she opened it upon her knee. The pages fell open. She pointed, and I looked, marvelling, for in the living pages of that book I saw myself; it was a story about myself, and in it were all the things that had happened to me since ever I was born. . . .

"It was wonderful to me, because the pages of that book were not pictures, you understand, but realities."

Wallace paused gravely—looked at me doubtfully.

"Go on," I said. "I understand."

"They were realities—yes, they must have been; people moved and things came and went in them; my dear mother, whom I had near forgotten; then my father, stern and upright, the servants, the nursery, all the familiar things of home. Then the front door and the busy streets, with traffic to and fro: I looked and marvelled, and looked half doubtfully again into the woman's face and turned the pages over, skipping this

and that, to see more of this book, and more, and so at last I came to myself hovering and hesitating outside the green door in the long white wall, and felt again the conflict and the fear.

" 'And next?' I cried, and would have turned on, but the cool hand of the grave woman delayed me.

" 'Next?' I insisted, and struggled gently with her hand, pulling up her fingers with all my childish strength, and as she yielded and the page came over she bent down upon me like a shadow and kissed my brow.

"But the page did not show the enchanted garden, nor the panthers, nor the girl who had led me by the hand, nor the playfellows who had been so loth to let me go. It showed a long grey street in West Kensington, on that chill hour of afternoon before the lamps are lit, and I was there, a wretched little figure, weeping aloud, for all that I could do to restrain myself, and I was weeping because I could not return to my dear playfellows who had called after me, 'Come back to us! Come back to us soon!' I was there. This was no page in a book, but harsh reality; that enchanted place and the restraining hand of the grave mother at whose knee I stood had gone—whither have they gone?"

He halted again, and remained for a time, staring into the fire.

"Oh! the wretchedness of that return!" he murmured.

"Well?" I said after a minute or so.

"Poor little wretch I was—brought back to this grey world again! As I realised the fulness of what had happened to me, I gave way to quite ungovernable grief. And the shame and humiliation of that public weeping and my disgraceful homecoming remain with me still. I see again the benevolent-looking old gentleman in gold spectacles who stopped and spoke to me—prodding me first with his umbrella. 'Poor little chap,' said he; 'and are you lost then?'—and me a London boy of five or more! And he must needs bring in a kindly young policeman and make a crowd of me, and so march me home. Sobbing, conspicuous, and frightened, I came from the enchanted garden to the steps of my father's house.

"That is as well as I can remember my vision of that garden—the garden that haunts me still. Of course, I can convey nothing of that indescribable quality of translucent unreality, that difference from the common things of experience that hung about it all; but that—that is what happened. If it was a dream, I am sure it was a daytime and altogether extraordinary dream. . . . H'm!—naturally there followed a terrible questioning, by my aunt, my father, the nurse, the governess—everyone. . . .

"I tried to tell them, and my father gave me my first thrashing for telling lies. When afterwards I tried to tell my aunt, she punished me again for my wicked persistence. Then, as I said, everyone was forbidden to listen to me, to hear a word about it. Even my fairy tale books were taken away from me for a time—because I was 'too imaginative.' Eh? Yes, they did that! My father belonged to the old school. . . . And my story was driven back upon myself. I whispered it to my pillow—my pillow that was often damp and salt to my whispering lips with childish tears. And I added always to my official and less fervent prayers this one heartfelt request: 'Please God I may dream of the garden. Oh! take me back to my garden! Take me back to my garden!'

"I dreamt often of the garden. I may have added to it, I may have changed it; I do not know. . . . All this you understand is an attempt to reconstruct from fragmentary memories a very early experience. Between that and the other consecutive memories of my boyhood there is a gulf. A time came when it seemed impossible I should ever speak of that wonder glimpse again."

I asked an obvious question.

"No," he said. "I don't remember that I ever attempted to find my way back to the garden in those early years. This seems odd to me now, but I think that very probably a closer watch was kept on my movements after this misadventure to prevent my going astray. No, it wasn't until you knew me that I tried for the garden again. And I believe there was a period—incredible as it seems now—when I forgot the garden altogether—when I was about eight or nine it may have been. Do you remember me as a kid at Saint Athelstan's?"

"Rather!"

"I didn't show any signs did I in those days of having a secret dream?"

II

He looked up with a sudden smile.

"Did you ever play North-West Passage with me? . . . No, of course you didn't come my way!"

"It was the sort of game," he went on, "that every imaginative child plays all day. The idea was the discovery of a North-West Passage to school. The way to school was plain enough; the game consisted in finding some way that wasn't plain, starting off ten minutes early in some almost hopeless direction, and working one's way round through unaccustomed streets to my goal. And one day I got entangled among some rather low-class streets on the other side of Campden Hill, and I began to think that for once the game would be against me and that I should get to school late. I tried rather desperately a street that seemed a *cul de sac,* and found a passage at the end. I hurried through that with renewed hope. 'I shall do it yet,' I said, and passed a row of frowsy little shops that were inexplicably familiar to me, and behold! there was my long white wall and the green door that led to the enchanted garden!

"The thing whacked upon me suddenly. Then, after all, that garden, that wonderful garden, wasn't a dream!" . . .

He paused.

"I suppose my second experience with the green door marks the world of difference there is between the busy life of a schoolboy and the infinite leisure of a child. Anyhow, this second time I didn't for a moment think of going in straight away. You see . . . For one thing my mind was full of the idea of getting to school in time—set on not breaking my record for punctuality. I must surely have felt *some* little desire at least to try the door—yes, I must have felt that. . . . But I seem to remember the attraction of the door mainly as another obstacle to my overmastering determination to get to school. I was immediately interested by this discovery I had made, of course—I went on with my mind full of it—but I went on. It didn't check me. I ran past tugging out my watch, found I had ten minutes still to spare, and then I was going downhill into familiar surroundings. I got to school, breathless, it is true, and wet with perspiration, but in time. I can remember hanging up my coat and hat . . . Went right by it and left it behind me. Odd, eh?"

He looked at me thoughtfully. "Of course, I didn't know then that it wouldn't always be there. School boys have limited imaginations. I supposed I thought it was an awfully jolly thing to have it there, to know my way back to it, but there was the school tugging at me. I expect I was a good deal distraught and inattentive that morning, recalling what I could of the beautiful strange people I should presently see again. Oddly enough I had no doubt in my mind that they would be glad to see me . . . Yes, I must have thought of the garden that morning just as a jolly sort of place to which one might resort in the interludes of a strenuous scholastic career.

"I didn't go that day at all. The next day was a half holiday, and that may have weighed with me. Perhaps, too, my state of inattention brought down impositions upon me and docked the margin of time necessary for the detour. I don't know. What I do know is that in the meantime the enchanted garden was so much upon my mind that I could not keep it to myself.

"I told—What was his name?—a ferrety-looking youngster we used to call Squiff."

"Young Hopkins," said I.

"Hopkins it was. I did not like telling him, I had a feeling that in some way it was against the rules to tell him, but I did. He was walking part of the way home with me; he was talkative, and if we had not talked about the enchanted garden we should have talked of something else, and it was intolerable to me to think about any other subject. So I blabbed.

"Well, he told my secret. The next day in the play interval I found myself surrounded by half a dozen bigger boys, half teasing and wholly curious to hear more of the enchanted garden. There was that big Fawcett—you remember him?—and Carnaby and Morley Reynolds. You weren't there by any chance? No, I think I should have remembered if you were. . . . .

"A boy is a creature of odd feelings. I was, I really believe, in spite of my secret self-disgust, a little flattered to have the attention of these big fellows. I remember particularly a moment of pleasure caused by the praise of Crawshaw—you remember Crawshaw major, the son of Crawshaw the composer?—who said it was the best lie he had ever heard. But at the same time there was

a really painful undertow of shame at telling what I felt was indeed a sacred secret. That beast Fawcett made a joke about the girl in green—."

Wallace's voice sank with the keen memory of that shame. "I pretended not to hear," he said. "Well, then Carnaby suddenly called me a young liar and disputed with me when I said the thing was true. I said I knew where to find the green door, could lead them all there in ten minutes. Carnaby became outrageously virtuous, and said I'd have to—and bear out my words or suffer. Did you ever have Carnaby twist your arm? Then perhaps you'll understand how it went with me. I swore my story was true. There was nobody in the school then to save a chap from Carnaby though Crawshaw put in a word or so. Carnaby had got his game. I grew excited and red-eared, and a little frightened, I behaved altogether like a silly little chap, and the outcome of it all was that instead of starting alone for my enchanted garden, I led the way presently—cheeks flushed, ears hot, eyes smarting, and my soul one burning misery and shame—for a party of six mocking, curious and threatening schoolfellows.

"We never found the white wall and the green door . . ."

"You mean?—"

"I mean I couldn't find it. I would have found it if I could.

"And afterwards when I could go alone I couldn't find it. I never found it. I seem now to have been always looking for it through my schoolboy days, but I've never come upon it again."

"Did the fellows—make it disagreeable?"

"Beastly . . . . . Carnaby held a council over me for wanton lying. I remember how I sneaked home and upstairs to hide the marks of my blubbering. But when I cried myself to sleep at last it wasn't for Carnaby, but for the garden, for the beautiful afternoon I had hoped for, for the sweet friendly women and the waiting playfellows and the game I had hoped to learn again, that beautiful forgotten game. . . .

"I believed firmly that if I had not told—. . . I had bad times after that—crying at night and wool-gathering by day. For two terms I slackened and had bad reports. Do you remember? Of course you would! It was you—your beating me in mathematics that brought me back to the grind again.''

III

For a time my friend stared silently into the red heart of the fire. Then he said: ''I never saw it again until I was seventeen.

''It leapt upon me for the third time—as I was driving to Paddington on my way to Oxford and a scholarship. I had just one momentary glimpse. I was leaning over the apron of my hansom smoking a cigarette, and no doubt thinking myself no end of a man of the world, and suddenly there was the door, the wall, the dear sense of unforgettable and still attainable things.

''We clattered by—I too taken by surprise to stop my cab until we were well past and round a corner. Then I had a queer moment, a double and divergent movement of my will: I tapped the little door in the roof of the cab, and brought my arm down to pull out my watch. 'Yes, sir!' said the cabman, smartly. 'Er—well—it's nothing,' I cried. '*My* mistake! We haven't much time! Go on!' and he went on. . . .

''I got my scholarship. And the night after I was told of that I sat over my fire in my little upper room, my study, in my father's house, with his praise—his rare praise—and his sound counsels ringing in my ears, and I smoked my favorite pipe—the formidable bulldog of adolescence—and thought of that door in the long white wall. 'If I had stopped,' I thought, 'I should have missed my scholarship, I should have missed Oxford—muddled all the fine career before me! I begin to see things better!' I fell musing deeply, but I did not doubt then this career of mine was a thing that merited sacrifice.

''Those dear friends and that clear atmosphere seemed very sweet to me, very fine, but remote. My grip was fixing now upon the world. I saw another door opening—the door of my career.''

He stared again into the fire. Its red lights picked out a stubborn strength in his face for just one flickering moment, and then it vanished again.

''Well,'' he said and sighed, ''I have served that career. I have done—much work, much hard work. But I have dreamt of the enchanted garden a thousand dreams, and seen its door, or at least glimpsed its door, four times since then. Yes—four times. For a while this world was so bright and interesting, seemed so full of meaning and opportunity that the half-effaced charm of the garden was by comparison gentle and remote. Who wants to pat panthers on the way to dinner with pretty women and distinguished men? I came down to London from Oxford, a man of bold promise that I have done something to redeem. Something—and yet there have been disappointments. . . .

''Twice I have been in love—I will not dwell on that—but once, as I went to someone who, I know, doubted whether I dared to come, I took a short cut at a venture through an unfrequented road near Earl's Court, and so happened on a white wall and a familiar green door. 'Odd!' said I to myself, 'but I thought this place was on Campden Hill. It's the place I never could find somehow—like counting Stonehenge[1]—the place of that queer daydream of mine.' And I went by it intent upon my purpose. It had no appeal to me that afternoon.

''I had just a moment's impulse to try the door, three steps aside were needed at the most—though I was sure enough in my heart that it would open to me—and then I thought that doing so might delay me on the way to that appointment in which I thought my honor was involved. Afterwards I was sorry for my punctuality—I might at least have peeped in I thought, and waved a hand to those panthers, but I knew enough by this time not to seek again belatedly that which is not found by seeking. Yes, that time made me very sorry. . . .

''Years of hard work after that and never a sight of the door. It's only recently it has come back to me. With it there has come a sense as though some thin tarnish had spread itself over my world. I began to think of it as a sorrowful and bitter thing that I should never see that door again. Perhaps I was suffering a little from overwork—perhaps it was what I've heard spoken of as the feeling of forty. I don't know. But certainly the keen brightness that makes effort easy has gone out of things recently, and that just at a time

---

1. **Stonehenge** (stŏn'henj), a prehistoric ruin on Salisbury Plain in southwestern England, consisting of a circular arrangement of huge upright stone slabs.

with all these new political developments—when I ought to be working. Odd, isn't it? But I do begin to find life toilsome, its rewards, as I come near them, cheap. I began a little while ago to want the garden quite badly. Yes—and I've seen it three times.''

"The garden?''

"No—the door! And I haven't gone in!''

He leaned over the table to me, with an enormous sorrow in his voice as he spoke. "Thrice I have had my chance—*thrice*! If ever that door offers itself to me again, I swore, I will go in out of this dust and heat, out of this dry glitter of vanity, out of these toilsome futilities. I will go and never return. This time I will stay. . . . I swore it and when the time came—*I didn't go.*

"Three times in one year have I passed that door and failed to enter. Three times in the last year.

"The first time was on the night of the snatch division[2] on the Tenants' Redemption Bill, on which the Government was saved by a majority of three. You remember? No one on our side—perhaps very few on the opposite side—expected the end that night. Then the debate collapsed like eggshells. I and Hotchkiss were dining with his cousin at Brentford, we were both unpaired, and we were called up by telephone, and set off at once in his cousin's motor. We got in barely in time, and on the way we passed my wall and door—livid in the moonlight, blotched with hot yellow as the glare of our lamps lit it, but unmistakable. 'My God!' cried I. 'What?' said Hotchkiss. 'Nothing!' I answered, and the moment passed.

" 'I've made a great sacrifice,' I told the whip[3] as I got in. 'They all have,' he said, and hurried by.

"I do not see how I could have done otherwise then. And the next occasion was as I rushed to my father's bedside to bid that stern old man farewell. Then, too, the claims of life were imperative. But the third time was different; it happened a week ago. It fills me with hot remorse to recall it. I was with Gurker and Ralphs—it's no secret now you know that I've had my talk with Gurker. We had been dining at Frobisher's, and the talk had become intimate between us. The question of my place in the reconstructed ministry lay always just over the boundary of the dis-

cussion. Yes—yes. That's all settled. It needn't be talked about yet, but there's no reason to keep a secret from you. . . . Yes—thanks! thanks! But let me tell you my story.

"Then, on that night things were very much in the air. My position was a very delicate one. I was keenly anxious to get some definite word from Gurker, but was hampered by Ralphs's presence. I was using the best power of my brain to keep that light and careless talk not too obviously directed to the point that concerns me. I had to. Ralphs's behavior since has more than justified my caution. . . . Ralphs, I knew, would leave us beyond the Kensington High Street, and then I could surprise Gurker by a sudden frankness. One has sometimes to resort to these little devices. . . . And then it was that in the margin of my field of vision I became aware once more of the white wall, the green door before us down the road.

"We passed it talking. I passed it. I can still see the shadow of Gurker's marked profile, his opera hat tilted forward over his prominent nose, the many folds of his neck wrap going before my shadow and Ralphs's as we sauntered past.

"I passed within twenty inches of the door. 'If I say goodnight to them, and go in,' I asked myself, 'what will happen?' And I was all a-tingle for that word with Gurker.

"I could not answer that question in the tangle of my other problems. 'They will think me mad,' I thought. 'And suppose I vanish now!—Amazing disappearance of a prominent politician!' That weighed with me. A thousand inconceivably petty worldlinesses weighed with me in that crisis.''

Then he turned on me with a sorrowful smile, and, speaking slowly; "Here I am!'' he said.

"Here I am!'' he repeated, "and my chance has gone from me. Three times in one year the door has been offered me—the door that goes into peace, into delight, into a beauty beyond dreaming, a kindness no man on earth can know. And I have rejected it, Redmond, and it has gone—''

"How do you know?''

---

2. **snatch division,** surprise vote.
3. **whip,** party official whose job it is to see that other party members in a lawmaking body are present for important votes and other business.

Photograph by Alvin Langdon Coburn (1882–1966), the frontispiece of an early illustrated edition of Wells's stories (1911).

"I know. I know. I am left now to work it out, to stick to the tasks that held me so strongly when my moments came. You say, I have success—this vulgar, tawdry, irksome, envied thing. I have it." He had a walnut in his big hand. "If that was my success," he said, and crushed it, and held it out for me to see.

"Let me tell you something, Redmond. This loss is destroying me. For two months, for ten weeks nearly now, I have done no work at all, except the most necessary and urgent duties. My soul is full of inappeasable regrets. At nights—when it is less likely I shall be recognized—I go out. I wander. Yes. I wonder what people would think of that if they knew. A Cabinet Minister, the responsible head of that most vital of all departments, wandering alone—grieving—sometimes near audibly lamenting—for a door, for a garden!"

IV

I can see now his rather pallid face, and the unfamiliar somber fire that had come into his eyes. I see him very vividly tonight. I sit recalling his words, his tones, and last evening's *Westminster Gazette* still lies on my sofa, containing the notice of his death. At lunch today the club was busy with him and the strange riddle of his fate.

They found his body very early yesterday morning in a deep excavation near East Kensington Station. It is one of two shafts that have been made in connection with an extension of the railway southward. It is protected from the intrusion of the public by a hoarding[4] upon the high road, in which a small doorway has been cut for the convenience of some of the workmen who live in that direction. The doorway was left unfastened through a misunderstanding between two gangers,[5] and through it he made his way. . . .

My mind is darkened with questions and riddles.

It would seem he walked all the way from the House that night—he has frequently walked home during the past Session—and so it is I figure his dark form coming along the late and empty streets, wrapped up, intent. And then did the pale electric lights near the station cheat the rough planking into a semblance of white? Did that fatal unfastened door awaken some memory?

Was there, after all, ever any green door in the wall at all?

I do not know. I have told his story as he told it to me. There are times when I believe that Wallace was no more than the victim of the coincidence between a rare but not unprecedented type of hallucination and a careless trap, but that indeed is not my profoundest belief. You may think me superstitious if you will, and foolish; but, indeed, I am more than half convinced that he had in truth, an abnormal gift, and a sense, something—I know not what—that in the guise of wall and door offered him an outlet, a secret and peculiar passage of escape into another and altogether more beautiful world. At any rate, you will say, it betrayed him in the end. But did it betray him? There you touch the inmost mystery of these dreamers, these men of vision and the imagination. We see our world fair and common, the hoarding and the pit. By our daylight standard he walked out of security into darkness, danger and death. But did he see like that?

1906

---

4. *hoarding,* a board fence erected around a construction site.
5. *gangers,* workmen.

Discussion

1. Why does Wells use a character such as Redmond to tell the story of Lionel Wallace and the Door in the Wall?

2. In his description of the garden, Wallace emphasizes the gentleness and friendliness of the people and the animals. Why do you think this is so important to him?

3. Why does the child's insistence on turning the page expel him from the garden?

4. In what ways do the subsequent appearances of the Door connect with Wallace's own life?

5. The narrator says of the Door, that "it betrayed him in the end." What does he mean? And—as the narrator himself wonders—was this in fact the case?

Composition

"The Door in the Wall" describes the secret dream of a man of wealth and power. Make an informal list of what you think are the most important and revealing characteristics of his ideal world.

In an essay consider the characteristics of this dream, and what has caused Lionel Wallace to have such a dream.

Saki 1870–1916

Born Hector Hugh Munro, "Saki" embodied the cosmopolitan flair, the satiric wit, and the premature end of his generation. Munro's father was the inspector general of the Burmese police, and Munro was born in Burma. When his mother died two years later, Hector, his elder brother, and his sister went back to England to be reared by their grandmother and two sternly forbidding aunts. The boy's resentment at their discipline emerged years later in stories which satirize the conventional, the self-righteous, and the cruel.

Munro was a delicate child, given to reading and sketching. He attended local schools and then boarded for two years at Bedford Grammar School. He never went to college. Instead, his father, now retired, returned to Europe to take his children on a tour of Germany, Austria, and Switzerland, after which they settled in the English countryside, where for two years the father directed the final phase of his son's education.

In 1893, aged 22, Munro tried to follow his father's footsteps, enlisting in the Burmese Police. But he could not take the climate, and after one year and seven bouts of fever he returned to England. Now, with his father's financial support, Munro determined to try a different sort of career, and for the next several years he did historical research at the British Museum for a book, finally published in 1900, *The Rise of the Russian Empire*. Critics and readers were not impressed either by its relatively brief (334-page) treatment of a complex subject, or by Munro's sometimes lurid descriptions of battles and torture.

So in 1901 he sought yet another role to play, and this time was more successful. In conjunction with a well-known cartoonist, he began writing political satire for the *Westminster Gazette*. To preserve his anonymity Munro took the pen name "Saki" from the cupbearer in the Persian poem *The Rubáiyát of Omar Khayyám*. Munro knew politics and brought to

bear on it a mordant wit that delighted readers. Within a year he was gathering his first pieces into a paperback book that sold well.

Then in 1902 Munro left England to become a foreign correspondent for the *Morning Post*. During the next six years he reported from the Balkans, Poland, Russia, and, finally, Paris. At the same time he was sending a series of comic short stories back to English newspapers, and published his first book of them in 1904.

Munro returned home in 1908, bought a house outside of London, and settled into a relatively quiet life, writing during the day, playing bridge evenings at his club. In his short stories he exhibits a sparkling wit, a careless cruelty, and some deep insights into the malicious side of human nature. In "Tobermory," the marvel of the talking cat is not as important as the threat caused by the cat's knowledge of the hypocrisies and social indiscretions of the members of the house party.

But this tranquil, productive life soon came to an end. In August 1914, on first hearing that England was at war with Germany, Munro enlisted in the army. He was 43 years old. Refusing an officer's commission, Munro faced trench warfare in France at the end of 1915 as a regular infantryman. After a year of brave service he was killed in combat.

Tobermory

It was a chill, rain-washed afternoon of a late August day, that indefinite season when partridges are still in security or cold storage, and there is nothing to hunt—unless one is bounded on the north by the Bristol Channel, in which case one may lawfully gallop after fat red stags. Lady Blemley's house-party was not bounded on the north by the Bristol Channel, hence there was a full gathering of her guests round the tea table on this particular afternoon. And, in spite of the blankness of the season and the triteness of the occasion, there was no trace in the company of that fatigued restlessness which means a dread of the pianola and a subdued hankering for auction bridge. The undisguised open-mouthed attention of the entire party was fixed on the homely negative personality of Mr. Cornelius Appin. Of all her guests, he was the one who had come to Lady Blemley with the vaguest reputation. Some one had said he was "clever," and he had got his invitation in the moderate expectation, on the part of his hostess, that some portion at least of his cleverness would be contributed to the general entertainment. Until tea-time that day she had been unable to discover in what direction, if any, his cleverness lay. He was neither a wit nor a croquet champion, a hypnotic force nor a begetter of amateur theatricals. Neither did his exterior suggest the sort of man in whom women are willing to pardon a generous measure of mental deficiency. He had subsided into mere Mr. Appin, and the Cornelius seemed a piece of transparent baptismal bluff. And now he was claiming to have launched on the world a discovery beside which the invention of gunpowder, of the printing-press, and of steam locomotion were inconsiderable trifles. Science had made bewildering strides in many directions during recent decades, but this thing seemed to belong to the domain of miracle rather than to scientific achievement.

"And do you really ask us to believe," Sir Wilfrid was saying, "that you have discovered a means for instructing animals in the art of human speech, and that dear old Tobermory has proved your first successful pupil?"

"It is a problem at which I have worked for the last seventeen years," said Mr. Appin, "but only during the last eight or nine months have I been rewarded with glimmerings of success. Of course I have experimented with thousands of animals, but latterly only with cats, those wonderful creatures which have assimilated themselves so marvellously with our civilization while retaining all their highly developed feral instincts. Here and there among cats one comes across an outstanding superior intellect, just as one does among the ruck of human beings, and when I made the acquaintance of Tobermory a week ago I saw at once that I was in contact with a 'Beyond-cat' of extraordinary intelligence. I had gone far along the road to success in recent experiments; with Tobermory, as you call him, I have reached the goal."

Mr. Appin concluded his remarkable statement in a voice which he strove to divest of a triumphant inflection. No one said "Rats," though Clovis's lips moved in a monosyllabic contortion which probably invoked those rodents of disbelief.

"And do you mean to say," asked Miss Resker, after a slight pause, "that you have taught Tobermory to say and understand easy sentences of one syllable?"

"My dear Miss Resker," said the wonder-worker patiently, "one teaches little children and savages and backward adults in that piecemeal fashion; when one has once solved the problem of making a beginning with an animal of highly developed intelligence one has no need for those halting methods. Tobermory can speak our language with perfect correctness."

This time Clovis very distinctly said, "Beyond-rats!" Sir Wilfrid was more polite, but equally sceptical.

"Hadn't we better have the cat in and judge for ourselves?" suggested Lady Blemley.

Sir Wilfrid went in search of the animal, and the company settled themselves down to the languid expectation of witnessing some more or less adroit drawing-room ventriloquism.

In a minute Sir Wilfrid was back in the room, his face white beneath its tan and his eyes dilated with excitement.

"By Gad, it's true!"

His agitation was unmistakably genuine, and his hearers started forward in a thrill of awakened interest.

Collapsing into an armchair he continued breathlessly: "I found him dozing in the smoking-room, and called out to him to come for his tea. He blinked at me in his usual way, and I said, 'Come on, Toby; don't keep us waiting'; and, by Gad! he drawled out in a most horribly natural voice that he'd come when he dashed well pleased! I nearly jumped out of my skin!"

Appin had preached to absolutely incredulous hearers; Sir Wilfrid's statement carried instant conviction. A Babel-like chorus of startled exclamation arose, amid which the scientist sat mutely enjoying the first fruit of his stupendous discovery.

In the midst of the clamour Tobermory entered the room and made his way with velvet tread and studied unconcern across to the group seated round the tea table.

A sudden hush of awkwardness and constraint fell on the company. Somehow there seemed an element of embarrassment in addressing on equal terms a domestic cat of acknowledged mental ability.

"Will you have some milk, Tobermory?" asked Lady Blemley in a rather strained voice.

"I don't mind if I do," was the response, couched in a tone of even indifference. A shiver of suppressed excitement went through the listeners, and Lady Blemley might be excused for pouring out the saucerful of milk rather unsteadily.

"I'm afraid I've spilt a good deal of it," she said apologetically.

"After all, it's not my Axminster,"[1] was Tobermory's rejoinder.

Another silence fell on the group, and then Miss Resker, in her best district-visitor manner, asked if the human language had been difficult to learn. Tobermory looked squarely at her for a moment and then fixed his gaze serenely on the middle distance. It was obvious that boring questions lay outside his scheme of life.

"What do you think of human intelligence?" asked Mavis Pellington lamely.

"Of whose intelligence in particular?" asked Tobermory coldly.

"Oh, well, mine for instance," said Mavis, with a feeble laugh.

"You put me in an embarrassing position," said Tobermory, whose tone and attitude certainly did not suggest a shred of embarrassment. "When your inclusion in this house-party was suggested Sir Wilfrid protested that you were the most brainless woman of his acquaintance, and that there was a wide distinction between hospitality and the care of the feeble-minded. Lady Blemley replied that your lack of brain-power was the precise quality which had earned you your invitation, as you were the only person she could think of who might be idiotic enough to buy their old car. You know, the one they call 'The Envy of Sisyphus,'[2] because it goes quite nicely uphill if you push it."

Lady Blemley's protestations would have had greater effect if she had not casually suggested to Mavis only that morning that the car in question would be just the thing for her down at her Devonshire home.

Major Barfield plunged in heavily to effect a diversion.

"How about your carryings-on with the tortoiseshell puss up at the stables, eh?"

The moment he had said it everyone realized the blunder.

"One does not usually discuss these matters in public," said Tobermory frigidly. "From a slight observation of your ways since you've been in this house I should imagine you'd find it inconvenient if I were to shift the conversation on to your own little affairs."

The panic which ensued was not confined to the Major.

"Would you like to go and see if cook has got your dinner ready?" suggested Lady Blemley

---

1. **Axminster,** a kind of carpet with a finely tufted, velvetlike pile.

2. **'The Envy of Sisyphus.'** Sisyphus (sis′e fəs) is a trickster from Greek mythology. He was finally punished in the Underworld for his crimes, being compelled to roll a great rock up a hill, where, nearing the top, it would break away and roll to the bottom.

hurriedly, affecting to ignore the fact that it wanted at least two hours to Tobermory's dinnertime.

"Thanks," said Tobermory, "not quite so soon after my tea. I don't want to die of indigestion."

"Cats have nine lives, you know," said Sir Wilfrid heartily.

"Possibly," answered Tobermory; "but only one liver."

"Adelaide!" said Mrs. Cornett, "do you mean to encourage that cat to go out and gossip about us in the servants' hall?"

The panic had indeed become general. A narrow ornamental balustrade ran in front of most of the bedroom windows at the Towers, and it was recalled with dismay that this had formed a favorite promenade for Tobermory at all hours, whence he could watch the pigeons—and heaven knew what else besides. If he intended to become reminiscent in his present outspoken strain the effect would be something more than disconcerting. Mrs. Cornett, who spent much time at her toilet table, and whose complexion was reputed to be of a nomadic though punctual disposition, looked as ill at ease as the Major. Miss Scrawen, who wrote fiercely sensuous poetry and led a blameless life, merely displayed irritation; if you are methodical and virtuous in private you don't necessarily want everyone to know it. Bertie van Tahn, who was so depraved at seventeen that he had long ago given up trying to be any worse, turned a dull shade of gardenia white, but he did not commit the error of dashing out of the room like Odo Finsberry, a young gentleman who was understood to be reading for the Church and who was possibly disturbed at the thought of scandals he might hear concerning other people. Clovis had the presence of mind to maintain a composed exterior; privately he was calculating how long it would take to procure a box of fancy mice through the agency of the *Exchange and Mart* as a species of hush-money.

Even in a delicate situation like the present, Agnes Resker could not endure to remain too long in the background.

"Why did I ever come down here?" she asked dramatically.

Tobermory immediately accepted the opening.

"Judging by what you said to Mrs. Cornett on the croquet-lawn yesterday, you were out for food. You described the Blemleys as the dullest people to stay with that you knew, but said they were clever enough to employ a first-rate cook; otherwise they'd find it difficult to get anyone to come down a second time."

"There's not a word of truth in it! I appeal to Mrs. Cornett—" exclaimed the discomfited Agnes.

"Mrs. Cornett repeated your remark afterwards to Bertie van Tahn," continued Tobermory, "and said, 'That woman is a regular Hunger Marcher; she'd go anywhere for four square meals a day,' and Bertie van Tahn said—"

At this point the chronicle mercifully ceased. Tobermory had caught a glimpse of the big yellow Tom from the Rectory working his way through the shrubbery towards the stable wing. In a flash he had vanished through the open French window.

With the disappearance of his too brilliant pupil Cornelius Appin found himself beset by a hurricane of bitter upbraiding, anxious inquiry, and frightened entreaty. The responsibility for the situation lay with him, and he must prevent matters from becoming worse. Could Tobermory impart his dangerous gift to other cats? was the first question he had to answer. It was possible, he replied, that he might have initiated his intimate friend the stable puss into his new accomplishment, but it was unlikely that his teaching could have taken a wider range as yet.

"Then," said Mrs. Cornett, "Tobermory may be a valuable cat and a great pet; but I'm sure you'll agree, Adelaide, that both he and the stable cat must be done away with without delay."

"You don't suppose I've enjoyed the last quarter of an hour, do you?" said Lady Blemley bitterly. "My husband and I are very fond of Tobermory—at least, we were before this horrible accomplishment was infused into him; but now, of course, the only thing is to have him destroyed as soon as possible."

"We can put some strychnine in the scraps he always gets at dinnertime," said Sir Wilfrid, "and I will go and drown the stable cat myself. The coachman will be very sore at losing his pet, but I'll say a very catching form of mange has

© Ray Reiss

broken out in both cats and we're afraid of it spreading to the kennels.''

"But my great discovery!" expostulated Mr. Appin; "after all my years of research and experiment—"

"You can go and experiment on the short-horns at the farm, who are under proper control," said Mrs. Cornett, "or the elephants at the Zoological Gardens. They're said to be highly intelligent, and they have this recommendation, that they don't come creeping about our bedrooms and under chairs, and so forth."

An archangel ecstatically proclaiming the Millennium, and finding that it clashed unpardonably with Henley[3] and would have to be indefinitely postponed, could hardly have felt more crestfallen than Cornelius Appin at the reception of his wonderful achievement. Public opinion, however, was against him—in fact, had the general voice been consulted on the subject it is probable that a strong minority vote would have been in

---

3. Henley, a place on the Thames River in Oxfordshire, the site of an annual regatta since 1839.

favour of including him in the strychnine diet.

Defective train arrangements and a nervous desire to see matters brought to a finish prevented an immediate dispersal of the party, but dinner that evening was not a social success. Sir Wilfrid had had rather a trying time with the stable cat and subsequently with the coachman. Agnes Resker ostentatiously limited her repast to a morsel of dry toast, which she bit as though it were a personal enemy; while Mavis Pellington maintained a vindictive silence throughout the meal. Lady Blemley kept up a flow of what she hoped was conversation, but her attention was fixed on the doorway. A plateful of carefully dosed fish scraps was in readiness on the sideboard, but sweets and savory and dessert went their way, and no Tobermory appeared either in the dining-room or kitchen.

The sepulchral dinner was cheerful compared with the subsequent vigil in the smoking-room. Eating and drinking had at least supplied a distraction and cloak to the prevailing embarrassment. Bridge was out of the question in the general tension of nerves and tempers, and after Odo Finsberry had given a lugubrious rendering of "Melisande in the Wood," to a frigid audience, music was tacitly avoided. At eleven the servants went to bed, announcing that the small window in the pantry had been left open as usual for Tobermory's private use. The guests read steadily through the current batch of magazines, and fell back gradually on the "Badminton Library" and bound volumes of *Punch*. Lady Blemley made periodic visits to the pantry, returning each time with an expression of listless depression which forestalled questioning.

At two o'clock Clovis broke the dominating silence.

"He won't turn up tonight. He's probably in the local newspaper office at the present moment, dictating the first instalment of his reminiscences. Lady What's-her-name's book won't be in it. It will be the event of the day."

Having made this contribution to the general cheerfulness, Clovis went to bed. At long intervals the various members of the house-party followed his example.

The servants taking round the early tea made a uniform announcement in reply to a uniform question. Tobermory had not returned.

Breakfast was, if anything, a more unpleasant function than dinner had been, but before its conclusion the situation was relieved. Tobermory's corpse was brought in from the shrubbery, where a gardener had just discovered it. From the bites on his throat and the yellow fur which coated his claws it was evident that he had fallen in unequal combat with the big Tom from the Rectory.

By midday most of the guests had quitted the Towers, and after lunch Lady Blemley had sufficiently recovered her spirits to write an extremely nasty letter to the Rectory about the loss of her valuable pet.

Tobermory had been Appin's one successful pupil, and he was destined to have no successor. A few weeks later an elephant in the Dresden Zoological Garden, which had shown no previous signs of irritability, broke loose and killed an Englishman who had apparently been teasing it. The victim's name was variously reported in the papers as Oppin and Eppelin, but his front name was faithfully rendered Cornelius.

"If he was trying German irregular verbs on the poor beast," said Clovis, "he deserved all he got."

1911

Discussion

1. How does the first paragraph of "Tobermory" satirize a particular social world?
2. Why was Cornelius Appin invited to Lady Blemley's house party?
3. What does Tobermory reveal about human nature?
4. The tale ends with Appin's death. Given the way it is described, how should the reader react? In what ways does this death complete Saki's satire?

Composition

Before his untimely death, Cornelius Appin also trained one of the dogs in your neighborhood to speak.

In a brief sketch, explain what happened.

George Bernard Shaw
1856–1950

England's most significant dramatist since the Renaissance was an Irishman, born into an unhappy Dublin family in 1856. His father drank, and the little money he made kept the family in genteel poverty. Shaw's mother and older sister, seeking some sort of a profession, took vocal lessons from a local musician named George Vandaleur Lee, and he moved in with the family in 1865, much to the scandal of the neighbors.

Shaw's parents seem to have ignored him. He remembered his childhood as "rich only in dreams, frightful and loveless in realities." They gave him only a sketchy education in local schools (1867–1869) where he did poorly. At the age of fifteen he started work as clerk for a real-estate office, staying there four years.

In 1872 Vandaleur Lee went to London and soon after Mrs. Shaw and her daughter followed him. Shaw joined them in 1876. He had no clear sense of his goals in life. He wrote music criticism under Lee's name (1876–1878), sold telephones for the Edison Company (1879), and tried to write fiction, producing five novels no one would publish (1879–1883).

By his own account, Shaw's life changed dramatically in 1882 when he heard a lecture by the American political theorist Henry George. It set Shaw to reading Karl Marx's *Das Capital* and thinking about the problems of capitalist societies. "My life," he said later, "has been spent mostly in big modern towns, where my sense of beauty has been starved, whilst my intellect has been gorged with problems." In 1884, along with a cluster of friends, Shaw helped found the Fabian Society, and for the rest of his life he remained deeply involved in efforts to alter British society through the peaceful redistribution of wealth.

In time, Shaw came to think he might make the theater serve as a vehicle for his ideas, and his first play, *Widowers' Houses,* about slum landlords, premiered in 1892. An early review called it "The most daring play submitted of

late years. . ." In 1893 he pushed further, in *Mrs. Warren's Profession,* a serious discussion of prostitution. The official censor refused it a performance license.

But Shaw was convinced now of his calling, despite the reproach of some critics and the erratic enthusiasms of London audiences. He became deeply involved in the production of his works, choosing leading actors, superintending the rehearsals, and dictating how long the plays would run. In 1898 he began a lifelong practice of publishing his play texts, then a very uncommon practice. To the book editions he added lengthy stage directions, as well as prefaces and epilogues which further elaborated his ideas, thus creating in the print version what he called a "theatre of the mind."

Shaw's characters are vehicles for mounting his satirical assaults on social conventions. The long intellectual dialogues are never dull because of Shaw's genius for making iconoclastic statements in a highly entertaining and witty manner. In 1925 he was awarded the Nobel Prize. Perhaps not to disappoint his many admirers and enemies, who had become accustomed to his outrageous public utterances, he rejected it. The award, according to Shaw, was akin to throwing a lifebelt to a swimmer after he had succeeded in reaching dry land. Later he accepted the prize and awarded the money to the Anglo-Swedish Literary Society.

(Shaw introduction concludes on page 612.)

In his private life Shaw contradicted the belief that genius is intolerant, egotistical, and tortured. Kindhearted, generous, tolerant, and free from envy and malice, he never refused help to less successful authors or those who had fallen on hard times—even those who had criticized him in their writings. But his true greatness lay in his talent to entertain people and, at the same time, awaken their consciences.

The title alludes to a story from classical myth, retold in Ovid's *Metamorphoses*. Pygmalion, a sensitive young sculptor, is "shocked at the vices / Nature has given the female disposition . . ." and decides to live alone. He carves a statue depicting a woman with "greater beauty / Than any girl could have, and fell in love / With his own workmanship . . ." Venus, goddess of love, pities him, and brings the statue to life as a real woman, Galatea.

The play *Pygmalion* echoes with other stories as well: the tale of Cinderella, the poor, forgotten servant girl who turns into a princess; and also Mary Shelley's *Frankenstein*, in which an overly ambitious scientist's experiments (note how frequently that word appears in Shaw's play) create a being different from other living things who has nowhere to go. (See "Shaw and Smollett," page 649.)

Shaw's "Preface" to *Pygmalion* ignores all of this, and discusses instead the problem of language in England. So diverse are the dialects people use, that "it is impossible for an Englishman to open his mouth without making some other Englishman despise him." Shaw blames this on the alphabet, and argues that a new, more accurate one is a necessity. Thus, "The reformer we need most today is an energetic phonetic enthusiast: that is why I have made such a one the hero of a popular play." But behind this issue is a larger and more serious one which concerned the thinkers of Shaw's day, as England moved toward popular democracy. How can the gaps between social classes be bridged, and the nation brought together? Language is one obstacle. But, as *Pygmalion* indicates, it is by no means the only one.

Pygmalion

CAST OF CHARACTERS

THE DAUGHTER—Miss Eynsford Hill (Clara)

THE MOTHER—Mrs. Eynsford Hill

FREDDY—Mr. Eynsford Hill, *her son*

THE FLOWER GIRL—Eliza (Liza) Doolittle

THE GENTLEMAN—Colonel Pickering

THE NOTE TAKER—Henry Higgins, *a professor of phonetics*

A BYSTANDER

A SARCASTIC BYSTANDER

GENERAL BYSTANDERS

MRS. PEARCE, *Henry Higgins's housekeeper*

ALFRED DOOLITTLE, *Eliza's father*

MRS. HIGGINS, *Henry Higgins's mother*

THE PARLOR-MAID

The illustrations accompanying *Pygmalion* are photographs of the 1974 London production starring Alec McCowen as Higgins, Diana Rigg as Liza Doolittle, Jack May as Colonel Pickering, and Bob Hoskins as Alfred Doolittle.

Act One

London at 11:15 P.M. Torrents of heavy summer rain. Cab whistles blowing frantically in all directions. Pedestrians running for shelter into the portico of St. Paul's Church (not Wren's cathedral but Inigo Jones's church in Covent Garden[1] vegetable market), among them a lady and her daughter in evening dress. They are all peering out gloomily at the rain, except one man

---

1. *Covent Garden,* chief fruit, vegetable, and flower-market district of London. It originally was a "convent garden" attached to Westminster Abbey. The area also includes St. Paul's Church, designed by the English architect Inigo Jones (1573–1652), and the Covent Garden Opera House.

with his back turned to the rest, who seems wholly preoccupied with a notebook in which he is writing busily.

The church clock strikes the first quarter.

THE DAUGHTER *(in the space between the central pillars, close to the one on her left)*. I'm getting chilled to the bone. What can Freddy be doing all this time? He's been gone twenty minutes.

THE MOTHER *(on her daughter's right)*. Not so long. But he ought to have got us a cab by this.

A BYSTANDER *(on the lady's right)*. He wont[2] get no cab not until half-past eleven, missus, when they come back after dropping their theater fares.

THE MOTHER. But we must have a cab. We cant stand here until half-past eleven. It's too bad.

THE BYSTANDER. Well, it aint my fault, missus.

THE DAUGHTER. If Freddy had a bit of gumption, he would have got one at the theater door.

THE MOTHER. What could he have done, poor boy?

THE DAUGHTER. Other people got cabs. Why couldnt he?

FREDDY *rushes in out of the rain from the Southampton Street side, and comes between them closing a dripping umbrella. He is a young man of twenty, in evening dress, very wet round the ankles.*

THE DAUGHTER. Well, havnt you got a cab?

FREDDY. Theres not one to be had for love or money.

THE MOTHER. Oh, Freddy, there must be one. You cant have tried.

THE DAUGHTER. It's too tiresome. Do you expect us to go and get one ourselves?

FREDDY. I tell you theyre all engaged. The rain was so sudden: nobody was prepared; and everybody had to take a cab. Ive been to Charing Cross one way and nearly to Ludgate Circus the other; and they were all engaged.

THE MOTHER. Did you try Trafalgar Square?

FREDDY. There wasnt one at Trafalgar Square.

THE DAUGHTER. Did you try?

FREDDY. I tried as far as Charing Cross Station. Did you expect me to walk to Hammersmith?

THE DAUGHTER. You havnt tried at all.

THE MOTHER. You really are very helpless, Freddy. Go again; and dont come back until you have found a cab.

FREDDY. I shall simply get soaked for nothing.

THE DAUGHTER. And what about us? Are we to stay here all night in this draft, with next to nothing on? You selfish pig—

FREDDY. Oh, very well: I'll go; I'll go. *(He opens his umbrella and dashes off Strandwards,[3] but comes into collision with a flower girl, who is hurrying in for shelter, knocking her basket out of her hands. A blinding flash of lightning, followed instantly by a rattling peal of thunder, orchestrates the incident.)*

THE FLOWER GIRL. Nah then, Freddy: look wh' y' gowin, deah.

FREDDY. Sorry. *(He rushes off.)*

THE FLOWER GIRL *(picking up her scattered flowers and replacing them in the basket)*. Theres menners f' yer! Te-oo banches o voylets trod into the mad. *(She sits down on the plinth[4] of the column, sorting her flowers, on the lady's right. She is not at all a romantic figure. She is perhaps eighteen, perhaps twenty, hardly older. She wears a little sailor hat of black straw that has long been exposed to the dust and soot of London and has seldom if ever been brushed. Her hair needs washing rather badly: its mousy color can hardly be natural. She wears a shoddy black coat that reaches nearly to her knees and is shaped to her waist. She has a brown skirt with a coarse apron. Her boots are much the worse for wear. She is no doubt as clean as she can afford to be; but compared to the ladies she is very dirty. Her features are no worse than theirs; but their condition leaves something to be desired; and she needs the services of a dentist.)*

THE MOTHER. How do you know that my son's name is Freddy, pray?

THE FLOWER GIRL. Ow, eez ye-ooa san, is e? Wal, fewd dan y' de-ooty bawmz a mather should, eed now bettern to spawl a pore gel's

---

flahrzn than ran awy athaht pyin. Will ye-oo py me f' them? *(Here, with apologies, this desperate attempt to represent her dialect without a phonetic alphabet must be abandoned as unintelligible outside London.)*

THE DAUGHTER. Do nothing of the sort, mother. The idea!

THE MOTHER. Please allow me, Clara. Have you any pennies?

THE DAUGHTER. No. Ive nothing smaller than sixpence.

THE FLOWER GIRL *(hopefully)*. I can give you change for a tanner,[5] kind lady.

THE MOTHER *(to* CLARA*)*. Give it to me. *(*CLARA *parts reluctantly.)* Now *(To the girl)* this is for your flowers.

THE FLOWER GIRL. Thank you kindly, lady.

THE DAUGHTER. Make her give you the change. These things are only a penny a bunch.

THE MOTHER. Do hold your tongue, Clara. *(To the girl)* You can keep the change.

THE FLOWER GIRL. Oh, thank you, lady.

THE MOTHER. Now tell me how you know that young gentleman's name.

THE FLOWER GIRL. I didnt.

THE MOTHER. I heard you call him by it. Dont try to deceive me.

THE FLOWER GIRL *(protesting)*. Who's trying to deceive you? I called him Freddy or Charlie same as you might yourself if you was talking to a stranger and wished to be pleasant.

THE DAUGHTER. Sixpence thrown away! Really, mamma, you might have spared Freddy that. *(She retreats in disgust behind the pillar.)*

An elderly gentleman of the amiable military type rushes into the shelter, and closes a dripping umbrella. He is in the same plight as FREDDY, *very wet about the ankles. He is in evening dress, with a light overcoat. He takes the place left vacant by the daughter's retirement.*

THE GENTLEMAN. Phew!

THE MOTHER *(to* THE GENTLEMAN*)*. Oh, sir, is there any sign of its stopping?

THE GENTLEMAN. I'm afraid not. It started worse than ever about two minutes ago. *(He goes to the plinth beside* THE FLOWER GIRL; *puts up his foot on it; and stoops to turn down his trouser ends.)*

THE MOTHER. Oh dear! *(She retires sadly and joins her daughter.)*

THE FLOWER GIRL *(taking advantage of the military gentleman's proximity to establish friendly relations with him)*. If it's worse, it's a sign it's nearly over. So cheer up, Captain; and buy a flower off a poor girl.

THE GENTLEMAN. I'm sorry. I havnt any change.

THE FLOWER GIRL. I can give you change, Captain.

THE GENTLEMAN. For a sovereign? Ive nothing less.

THE FLOWER GIRL. Garn! Oh do buy a flower off me, Captain. I can change half-a-crown. Take this for tuppence.

THE GENTLEMAN. Now dont be troublesome: theres a good girl. *(Trying his pockets)* I really havnt any change—Stop: heres three hapence, if thats any use to you. *(He retreats to the other pillar.)*

THE FLOWER GIRL *(disappointed, but thinking three half-pence better than nothing)*. Thank you, sir.

THE BYSTANDER *(to the girl)*. You be careful: give him a flower for it. Theres a bloke here behind taking down every blessed word youre saying. *(All turn to the man who is taking notes.)*

THE FLOWER GIRL *(springing up terrified)*. I aint done nothing wrong by speaking to the gentleman. Ive a right to sell flowers if I keep off the kerb. *(Hysterically)* I'm a respectable girl: so help me, I never spoke to him except to ask him to buy a flower off me. *(General hubbub, mostly sympathetic to* THE FLOWER GIRL, *but deprecating her excessive sensibility. Cries of* Dont start hollerin. Who's hurting you? Nobody's going to touch you. Whats the good of fussing? Steady on. Easy easy, etc., *come from the elderly staid spectators, who pat her comfortingly. Less patient ones bid her shut her head, or ask her roughly what is wrong with her. A remoter group, not knowing what the matter is, crowd in and increase the noise with question and answer:* Whats the row? What she do? Where is he? A tec[6] taking her down. What! him? Yes: him over there: Took money off the gentleman, etc.*)*

THE FLOWER GIRL *(breaking through them to*

---

5. *tanner,* sixpence. [Slang]
6. *tec,* detective. [Slang]

the gentleman, crying wildly). Oh, sir, dont let him charge me.[7] You dunno what it means to me. Theyll take away my character and drive me on the streets for speaking to gentlemen. They—

THE NOTE TAKER *(coming forward on her right, the rest crowding after him).* There, there, there, there! who's hurting you, you silly girl? What do you take me for?

THE BYSTANDER. It's all right: he's a gentleman: look at his boots. *(Explaining to* THE NOTE TAKER*)* She thought you was a copper's nark, sir.

THE NOTE TAKER *(with quick interest).* Whats a copper's nark?

THE BYSTANDER *(inapt at definition).* It's a— well, it's a copper's nark, as you might say. What else would you call it? A sort of inform-er.

THE FLOWER GIRL *(still hysterical).* I take my Bible oath I never said a word—

THE NOTE TAKER *(overbearing but good-humored).* Oh, shut up, shut up. Do I look like a policeman?

THE FLOWER GIRL *(far from reassured).* Then what did you take down my words for? How do I know whether you took me down right? You just show me what youve wrote about me. *(*THE NOTE TAKER *opens his book and holds it steadily under her nose, though the pressure of the mob trying to read it over his shoulders would upset a weaker man.)* Whats that? That aint proper writing. I cant read that.

THE NOTE TAKER. I can. *(Reads, reproducing her pronunciation exactly)* "Cheer ap, Keptin; n' baw ya flahr orf a pore gel."

THE FLOWER GIRL *(much distressed).* It's because I called him Captain. I meant no harm. *(To* THE GENTLEMAN*)* Oh, sir, dont let him lay a charge agen me for a word like that. You—

THE GENTLEMAN. Charge! I make no charge. *(To* THE NOTE TAKER*)* Really, sir, if you are a detective, you need not begin protecting me against molestation by young women until I ask you. Anybody could see that the girl meant no harm.

THE BYSTANDERS GENERALLY *(demonstrating against police espionage).* Course they could. What business is it of yours? You mind your own affairs. He wants promotion, he does.

Taking down people's words! Girl never said a word to him. What harm if she did? Nice thing a girl cant shelter from the rain without being insulted, etc., etc., etc. *(She is conducted by the more sympathetic demonstrators back to her plinth, where she resumes her seat and struggles with her emotion.)*

THE BYSTANDER. He aint a tec. He's a blooming busybody: thats what he is. I tell you, look at his boots.

THE NOTE TAKER *(turning on him genially).* And how are all your people down at Selsey?

THE BYSTANDER *(suspiciously).* Who told you my people come from Selsey?

THE NOTE TAKER. Never you mind. They did. *(To the girl)* How do you come to be up so far east? You were born in Lisson Grove.

THE FLOWER GIRL *(appalled).* Oh, what harm is there in my leaving Lisson Grove? It wasnt fit for a pig to live in; and I had to pay four-and-six a week. *(In tears)* Oh, boo—hoo—oo—

THE NOTE TAKER. Live where you like; but stop that noise.

THE GENTLEMAN *(to the girl).* Come, come! he cant touch you: you have a right to live where you please.

A SARCASTIC BYSTANDER *(thrusting himself between* THE NOTE TAKER *and* THE GENTLEMAN*).* Park Lane, for instance. I'd like to go into the Housing Question with you, I would.

THE FLOWER GIRL *(subsiding into a brooding melancholy over her basket, and talking very low-spiritedly to herself).* I'm a good girl, I am.

THE SARCASTIC BYSTANDER *(not attending to her).* Do you know where *I* come from?

THE NOTE TAKER *(promptly).* Hoxton. *Titterings. Popular interest in* THE NOTE TAKER*'s performance increases.*

THE SARCASTIC ONE *(amazed).* Well, who said I didnt? Bly me! You know everything, you do.

THE FLOWER GIRL *(still nursing her sense of injury).* Aint no call to meddle with me, he aint.

THE BYSTANDER *(to her).* Of course he aint. Dont you stand it from him. *(To* THE NOTE TAKER*)* See here: what call have you to know about

---

7. *charge me,* bring an accusation against me.

people what never offered to meddle with you?

THE FLOWER GIRL. Let him say what he likes. I dont want to have no truck with him.

THE BYSTANDER. You take us for dirt under your feet, dont you? Catch you taking liberties with a gentleman!

THE SARCASTIC BYSTANDER. Yes: tell him where he come from if you want to go fortune-telling.

THE NOTE TAKER. Cheltenham, Harrow,[8] Cambridge, and India.

THE GENTLEMAN. Quite right. (*Great laughter. Reaction in* THE NOTE TAKER's *favor. Exclamations of* He knows all about it. Told him proper. Hear him tell the toff[9] where he come from? etc.)

THE GENTLEMAN. May I ask, sir, do you do this for your living at a music-hall?

THE NOTE TAKER. Ive thought of that. Perhaps I shall some day.

The rain has stopped; and the persons on the outside of the crowd begin to drop off.

THE FLOWER GIRL (*resenting the reaction*). He's no gentleman, he aint, to interfere with a poor girl.

THE DAUGHTER (*out of patience, pushing her way rudely to the front and displacing* THE GENTLEMAN, *who politely retires to the other side of the pillar*). What on earth is Freddy doing? I

---

8. Cheltenham . . . India. Cheltenham and Harrow are exclusive preparatory schools.
9. toff, dandy. [Slang]

shall get pneumownia if I stay in this draft any longer.

THE NOTE TAKER (*to himself, hastily making a note of her pronunciation of "monia"*). Earlscourt.

THE DAUGHTER (*violently*). Will you please keep your impertinent remarks to yourself.

THE NOTE TAKER. Did I say that out loud? I didnt mean to. I beg your pardon. Your mother's Epsom, unmistakably.

THE MOTHER (*advancing between her daughter and* THE NOTE TAKER). How very curious! I was brought up in Largelady Park, near Epsom.

THE NOTE TAKER (*uproariously amused*). Ha! Ha! What a devil of a name! Excuse me. (*To* THE DAUGHTER) You want a cab, do you?

THE DAUGHTER. Dont dare speak to me.

THE MOTHER. Oh please, please, Clara. (*Her daughter repudiates her with an angry shrug and retires haughtily.*) We should be so grateful to you, sir, if you found us a cab. (THE NOTE TAKER *produces a whistle.*) Oh, thank you. (*She joins her daughter.*)

THE NOTE TAKER *blows a piercing blast.*

THE SARCASTIC BYSTANDER. There! I knowed he was a plain-clothes copper.

THE BYSTANDER. That aint a police whistle: thats a sporting whistle.

THE FLOWER GIRL (*still preoccupied with her wounded feelings*). He's no right to take away my character. My character is the same to me as any lady's.

THE NOTE TAKER. I dont know whether youve noticed it; but the rain stopped about two minutes ago.

THE BYSTANDER. So it has. Why didnt you say so before? and us losing our time listening to your silliness! (*He walks off towards the Strand.*)

THE SARCASTIC BYSTANDER. I can tell where you come from. You come from Anwell.[10] Go back there.

THE NOTE TAKER (*helpfully*). Hanwell.

THE SARCASTIC BYSTANDER (*affecting great distinction of speech*). Thenk you, teacher. Haw haw! So long. (*He touches his hat with mock respect and strolls off.*)

THE FLOWER GIRL. Frightening people like that! How would he like it himself?

THE MOTHER. It's quite fine now, Clara. We can walk to a motor bus. Come. (*She gathers her skirts above her ankles and hurries off towards the Strand.*)

THE DAUGHTER. But the cab—(*her mother is out of hearing*). Oh, how tiresome! (*She follows angrily.*)

All the rest have gone except THE NOTE TAKER, THE GENTLEMAN, *and* THE FLOWER GIRL, *who sits arranging her basket and still pitying herself in murmurs.*

THE FLOWER GIRL. Poor girl! Hard enough for her to live without being worrited and chivied.

THE GENTLEMAN (*returning to his former place on* THE NOTE TAKER*'s left*). How do you do it, if I may ask?

THE NOTE TAKER. Simply phonetics. The science of speech. Thats my profession: also my hobby. Happy is the man who can make a living by his hobby! You can spot an Irishman or a Yorkshireman by his brogue. *I* can place any man within six miles. I can place him within two miles in London. Sometimes within two streets.

THE FLOWER GIRL. Ought to be ashamed of himself, unmanly coward!

THE GENTLEMAN. But is there a living in that?

THE NOTE TAKER. Oh yes. Quite a fat one. This is an age of upstarts. Men begin in Kentish Town with £80 a year, and end in Park Lane with a hundred thousand. They want to drop Kentish Town; but they give themselves away every time they open their mouths. Now I can teach them—

THE FLOWER GIRL. Let him mind his own business and leave a poor girl—

THE NOTE TAKER (*explosively*). Woman: cease this detestable boohooing instantly; or else seek the shelter of some other place of worship.

THE FLOWER GIRL (*with feeble defiance*). Ive a right to be here if I like, same as you.

THE NOTE TAKER. A woman who utters such depressing and disgusting sounds has no right to be anywhere—no right to live. Remember that you are a human being with a soul and the divine gift of articulate speech: that your native language is the language of Shakespear and Milton and The Bible: and dont sit there crooning like a bilious pigeon.

---

10. *Anwell*, Hanwell, an insane asylum.

THE FLOWER GIRL (*quite overwhelmed, looking up at him in mingled wonder and deprecation without daring to raise her head*). Ah-ah-ah-ow-ow-ow-oo!

THE NOTE TAKER (*whipping out his book*). Heavens! what a sound! (*He writes; then holds out the book and reads, reproducing her vowels exactly.*) Ah-ah-ah-ow-ow-ow-oo!

THE FLOWER GIRL (*tickled by the performance, and laughing in spite of herself*). Garn!

THE NOTE TAKER. You see this creature with her kerbstone English: the English that will keep her in the gutter to the end of her days. Well, sir, in three months I could pass that girl off as a duchess at an ambassador's garden party. I could even get her a place as lady's maid or shop assistant, which requires better English.

THE FLOWER GIRL. What's that you say?

THE NOTE TAKER. Yes, you squashed cabbage leaf, you disgrace to the noble architecture of these columns, you incarnate insult to the English language: I could pass you off as the Queen of Sheba. (*To* THE GENTLEMAN) Can you believe that?

THE GENTLEMAN. Of course I can. I am myself a student of Indian dialects; and—

THE NOTE TAKER (*eagerly*). Are you? Do you know Colonel Pickering, the author of Spoken Sanscrit?

THE GENTLEMAN. I am Colonel Pickering. Who are you?

THE NOTE TAKER. Henry Higgins, author of Higgins's Universal Alphabet.

PICKERING (*with enthusiasm*). I came from India to meet you.

HIGGINS. I was going to India to meet you.

PICKERING. Where do you live?

HIGGINS. 27A Wimpole Street. Come and see me tomorrow.

PICKERING. I'm at the Carlton. Come with me now and lets have a jaw over some supper.

HIGGINS. Right you are.

THE FLOWER GIRL (*to* PICKERING, *as he passes her*). Buy a flower, kind gentleman. I'm short for my lodging.

PICKERING. I really havnt any change. I'm sorry (*he goes away*).

HIGGINS (*shocked at the girl's mendacity*). Liar. You said you could change half-a-crown.

THE FLOWER GIRL (*rising in desperation*). You ought to be stuffed with nails, you ought. (*Flinging the basket at his feet*) Take the whole blooming basket for sixpence.

The church clock strikes the second quarter.

HIGGINS (*hearing in it the voice of God, rebuking him for his Pharisaic*[11] *want of charity to the poor girl*). A reminder. (*He raises his hat solemnly; then throws a handful of money into the basket and follows* PICKERING.)

THE FLOWER GIRL (*picking up a half-crown*). Ah-ow-ooh! (*Picking up a couple of florins*) Aaah-ow-ooh! (*Picking up several coins*) Aaaaaah-ow-ooh! (*Picking up a half-sovereign*) Aaaaaaaaaaaah-ow-ooh!!!

FREDDY (*springing out of a taxicab*). Got one at last. Hallo! (*To the girl*) Where are the two ladies that were here?

THE FLOWER GIRL. They walked to the bus when the rain stopped.

FREDDY. And left me with a cab on my hands! Damnation!

THE FLOWER GIRL (*with grandeur*). Never mind, young man. I'm going home in a taxi. (*She sails off to the cab. The driver puts his hand behind him and holds the door firmly shut against her. Quite understanding his mistrust, she shews him her handful of money*). Eightpence aint no object to me, Charlie. (*He grins and opens the door.*) Angel Court, Drury Lane, round the corner of Mickle-John's oil shop. Lets see how fast you can make her hop it. (*She gets in and pulls the door to with a slam as the taxicab starts.*)

FREDDY. Well, I'm dashed.

Act Two

Next day at 11 A.M. HIGGINS's *laboratory in Wimpole Street. It is a room on the first floor, looking on the street, and was meant for the drawing room. The double doors are in the middle of the back wall; and persons entering find in the corner to their right two tall file cabinets at*

---

11. **Pharisaic,** self-righteous. The Pharisees were a strict Jewish sect at the time of Jesus.

right angles to one another against the walls. In this corner stands a flat writing table, on which are a phonograph, a laryngoscope, a row of tiny organ pipes with bellows, a set of lamp chimneys for singing flames with burners attached to a gas plug in the wall by an indiarubber tube, several tuning-forks of different sizes, a life size image of half a human head, shewing in section the vocal organs, and a box containing a supply of wax cylinders for the phonograph.

Further down the room, on the same side, is a fireplace, with a comfortable leather-covered easy-chair at the side of the hearth nearest the door, and a coal-scuttle. There is a clock on the mantelpiece. Between the fireplace and the phonograph table is a stand for newspapers.

On the other side of the central door, to the left of the visitor, is a cabinet of shallow drawers. On it is a telephone and the telephone directory. The corner beyond, and most of the side wall, is occupied by a grand piano, with the keyboard at the end furthest from the door, and a bench for the player extending the full length of the keyboard. On the piano is a dessert dish heaped with fruit and sweets, mostly chocolates.

The middle of the room is clear. Besides the easy-chair, the piano bench, and two chairs at the phonograph table, there is one stray chair. It stands near the fireplace. On the walls, engravings: mostly Piranesis and mezzotint portraits.[1] No paintings.

PICKERING is seated at the table, putting down some cards and a tuning-fork which he has been using. HIGGINS is standing up near him, closing two or three file drawers which are hanging out. He appears in the morning light as a robust, vital, appetizing sort of man of forty or thereabouts, dressed in a professional-looking black frockcoat with a white linen collar and black silk tie. He is of the energetic, scientific type, heartily, even violently interested in everything that can be studied as a scientific subject, and careless about himself and other people, including their feelings. He is, in fact, but for his years and size, rather like a very impetuous baby "taking notice" eagerly and loudly, and requiring almost as much watching to keep him out of unintended mischief. His manner varies from genial bullying when he is in a good humor to stormy petulance when anything goes wrong; but he is so entirely frank and void of malice that he remains likeable even in his least reasonable moments.

HIGGINS (as he shuts the last drawer). Well, I think thats the whole show.
PICKERING. It's really amazing. I havnt taken half of it in, you know.
HIGGINS. Would you like to go over any of it again?
PICKERING (rising and coming to the fireplace, where he plants himself with his back to the fire). No, thank you; not now. I'm quite done up for this morning.
HIGGINS (following him, and standing beside him on his left). Tired of listening to sounds?
PICKERING. Yes. It's a fearful strain. I rather fancied myself because I can pronounce twenty-four distinct vowel sounds; but your hundred and thirty beat me. I cant hear a bit of difference between most of them.
HIGGINS (chuckling, and going over to the piano to eat sweets). Oh, that comes with practice. You hear no difference at first; but you keep on listening, and presently you find theyre all as different as A from B. (MRS. PEARCE looks in: she is HIGGINS's housekeeper.) Whats the matter?
MRS. PEARCE (hesitating, evidently perplexed). A young woman wants to see you, sir.
HIGGINS. A young woman! What does she want?
MRS. PEARCE. Well, sir, she says youll be glad to see her when you know what she's come about. She's quite a common girl, sir. Very common indeed. I should have sent her away, only I thought perhaps you wanted her to talk into your machines. I hope Ive not done wrong; but really you see such queer people sometimes—youll excuse me, I'm sure, sir—
HIGGINS. Oh, thats all right, Mrs. Pearce. Has she an interesting accent?
MRS. PEARCE. Oh, something dreadful, sir, really. I dont know how you can take an interest in it.
HIGGINS (to PICKERING). Lets have her up. Shew her up, Mrs. Pearce. (He rushes across to his

---

1. **Piranesis and mezzotint portraits.** Giovanni Battista Piranesi (1720–1778) was an Italian graphic artist noted for his large prints of buildings of classical and post-classical Rome. A mezzotint is a picture engraved on a roughened copper or steel plate.

working table and picks out a cylinder to use on the phonograph).

MRS. PEARCE *(only half resigned to it).* Very well, sir. It's for you to say. *(She goes downstairs.)*

HIGGINS. This is rather a bit of luck. I'll shew you how I make records. We'll set her talking; and I'll take it down first in Bell's Visible Speech; then in broad Romic; and then we'll get her on the phonograph so that you can turn her on as often as you like with the written transcript before you.

MRS. PEARCE *(returning).* This is the young woman, sir.

THE FLOWER GIRL *enters in state. She has a hat with three ostrich feathers, orange, sky-blue, and red. She has a nearly clean apron, and the shoddy coat has been tidied a little. The pathos of this deplorable figure, with its innocent vanity and consequential air, touches* PICKERING, *who has already straightened himself in the presence of* MRS. PEARCE. *But as to* HIGGINS, *the only distinction he makes between men and women is that when he is neither bullying nor exclaiming to the heavens against some feather-weight cross, he coaxes women as a child coaxes its nurse when it wants to get anything out of her.*

HIGGINS *(brusquely, recognizing her with unconcealed disappointment, and at once, babylike, making an intolerable grievance of it).* Why,

this is the girl I jotted down last night. She's no use: Ive got all the records I want of the Lisson Grove lingo; and I'm not going to waste another cylinder on it. *(To the girl)* Be off with you: I dont want you.

THE FLOWER GIRL. Dont you be so saucy. You aint heard what I come for yet. *(To* MRS. PEARCE, *who is waiting at the door for further instructions)* Did you tell him I come in a taxi?

MRS. PEARCE. Nonsense, girl! what do you think a gentleman like Mr. Higgins cares what you came in?

THE FLOWER GIRL. Oh, we are proud! He aint above giving lessons, not him: I heard him say so. Well, I aint come here to ask for any compliment; and if my money's not good enough I can go elsewhere.

HIGGINS. Good enough for what?

THE FLOWER GIRL. Good enough for ye-oo. Now you know, dont you? I'm come to have lessons, I am. And to pay for em too: make no mistake.

HIGGINS *(stupent[2]).* Well!!! *(Recovering his breath with a gasp)* What do you expect me to say to you?

THE FLOWER GIRL. Well, if you was a gentleman, you might ask me to sit down, I think. Dont I tell you I'm bringing you business?

---

2. *stupent,* dumfounded.

HIGGINS. Pickering: shall we ask this baggage to sit down, or shall we throw her out of the window?

THE FLOWER GIRL (*running away in terror to the piano, where she turns at bay*). Ah-ah-oh-ow-ow-ow-oo! (*Wounded and whimpering*) I wont be called a baggage when Ive offered to pay like any lady.

Motionless, the two men stare at her from the other side of the room, amazed.

PICKERING (*gently*). What is it you want, my girl?

THE FLOWER GIRL. I want to be a lady in a flower shop stead of selling at the corner of Tottenham Court Road. But they wont take me unless I can talk more genteel. He said he could teach me. Well, here I am ready to pay him—not asking any favor—and he treats me as if I was dirt.

MRS. PEARCE. How can you be such a foolish ignorant girl as to think you could afford to pay Mr. Higgins?

THE FLOWER GIRL. Why shouldnt I? I know what lessons cost as well as you do; and I'm ready to pay.

HIGGINS. How much?

THE FLOWER GIRL (*coming back to him, triumphant*). Now youre talking! I thought youd come off it when you saw a chance of getting back a bit of what you chucked at me last night. (*Confidentially*) Youd had a drop in,[3] hadnt you?

HIGGINS (*peremptorily*). Sit down.

THE FLOWER GIRL. Oh, if youre going to make a compliment of it—

HIGGINS (*thundering at her*). Sit down.

MRS. PEARCE (*severely*). Sit down, girl. Do as youre told.

THE FLOWER GIRL. Ah-ah-ah-ow-ow-oo! (*She stands, half rebellious, half bewildered.*)

PICKERING (*very courteous*). Wont you sit down? (*He places the stray chair near the hearthrug between himself and* HIGGINS.)

THE FLOWER GIRL (*coyly*). Dont mind if I do. (*She sits down.* PICKERING *returns to the hearthrug.*)

HIGGINS. Whats your name?

THE FLOWER GIRL. Liza Doolittle.

HIGGINS (*declaiming gravely*).

Eliza, Elizabeth, Betsy and Bess,

They went to the woods to get a bird's nes':

PICKERING. They found a nest with four eggs in it:

HIGGINS. They took one apiece, and left three in it.

They laugh heartily at their own wit.

LIZA. Oh, dont be silly.

MRS. PEARCE (*placing herself behind* ELIZA's *chair*). You mustnt speak to the gentleman like that.

LIZA. Well, why wont he speak sensible to me?

HIGGINS. Come back to business. How much do you propose to pay me for the lessons?

LIZA. Oh, I know whats right. A lady friend of mine gets French lessons for eighteenpence an hour from a real French gentleman. Well, you wouldnt have the face to ask me the same for teaching me my own language as you would for French; so I wont give more than a shilling. Take it or leave it.

HIGGINS (*walking up and down the room, rattling his keys and his cash in his pockets*). You know, Pickering, if you consider a shilling, not as a simple shilling, but as a percentage of this girl's income, it works out as fully equivalent to sixty or seventy guineas from a millionaire.

PICKERING. How so?

HIGGINS. Figure it out. A millionaire has about £150 a day. She earns about half-a-crown.

LIZA (*haughtily*). Who told you I only—

HIGGINS (*continuing*). She offers me two-fifths of her day's income for a lesson. Two-fifths of a millionaire's income for a day would be somewhere about £60. It's handsome. By George, it's enormous! it's the biggest offer I ever had.

LIZA (*rising, terrified*). Sixty pounds! What are you talking about? I never offered you sixty pounds. Where would I get—

HIGGINS. Hold your tongue.

LIZA (*weeping*). But I aint got sixty pounds. Oh—

MRS. PEARCE. Dont cry, you silly girl. Sit down. Nobody is going to touch your money.

HIGGINS. Somebody is going to touch you; with a broomstick, if you dont stop snivelling. Sit down.

---

3. *had a drop in,* had been drinking. [Slang]

LIZA (*obeying slowly*). Ah-ah-ah-ow-oo-o! One would think you was my father.

HIGGINS. If I decide to teach you, I'll be worse than two fathers to you. Here! (*He offers her his silk handkerchief.*)

LIZA. Whats this for?

HIGGINS. To wipe your eyes. To wipe any part of your face that feels moist. Remember: thats your handkerchief; and thats your sleeve. Dont mistake the one for the other if you wish to become a lady in a shop.

LIZA, *utterly bewildered, stares helplessly at him.*

MRS. PEARCE. It's no use talking to her like that, Mr. Higgins: she doesn't understand you. Besides, youre quite wrong: she doesnt do it that way at all. (*She takes the handkerchief.*)

LIZA (*snatching it*). Here! You give me that handkerchief. He give it to me, not to you.

PICKERING (*laughing*). He did. I think it must be regarded as her property, Mrs. Pearce.

MRS. PEARCE (*resigning herself*). Serve you right, Mr. Higgins.

PICKERING. Higgins: I'm interested. What about the ambassador's garden party? I'll say youre the greatest teacher alive if you make that good. I'll bet you all the expenses of the experiment you cant do it. And I'll pay for the lessons.

LIZA. Oh, you are real good. Thank you, Captain.

HIGGINS (*tempted, looking at her*). It's almost irresistible. She's so deliciously low—so horribly dirty—

LIZA (*protesting extremely*). Ah-ah-ah-ah-ow-ow-oo-oo!!! I aint dirty: I washed my face and hands afore I come, I did.

PICKERING. Youre certainly not going to turn her head with flattery, Higgins.

MRS. PEARCE (*uneasy*). Oh, dont say that, sir: theres more ways than one of turning a girl's head; and nobody can do it better than Mr. Higgins, though he may not always mean it. I do hope, sir, you wont encourage him to do anything foolish.

HIGGINS (*becoming excited as the idea grows on him*). What is life but a series of inspired follies? The difficulty is to find them to do. Never lose a chance: it doesnt come every day. I shall make a duchess of this draggletailed guttersnipe.

LIZA (*strongly deprecating this view of her*). Ah-ah-ah-ow-ow-oo!

HIGGINS (*carried away*). Yes: in six months—in three if she has a good ear and a quick tongue—I'll take her anywhere and pass her off as anything. We'll start today: now! this moment! Take her away and clean her, Mrs. Pearce.

Monkey Brand, if it wont come off any other way. Is there a good fire in the kitchen?

MRS. PEARCE (*protesting*). Yes; but—

HIGGINS (*storming on*). Take all her clothes off and burn them. Ring up Whiteley or somebody for new ones. Wrap her up in brown paper til they come.

LIZA. Youre no gentleman, youre not, to talk of such things. I'm a good girl, I am; and I know what the like of you are, I do.

HIGGINS. We want none of your Lisson Grove prudery here, young woman. Youve got to learn to behave like a duchess. Take her away, Mrs. Pearce. If she gives you any trouble, wallop her.

LIZA (*springing up and running between* PICKERING *and* MRS. PEARCE *for protection*). No! I'll call the police, I will.

MRS. PEARCE. But Ive no place to put her.

HIGGINS. Put her in the dustbin.

LIZA. Ah-ah-ah-ow-ow-oo!

PICKERING. Oh come, Higgins! be reasonable.

MRS. PEARCE (*resolutely*). You must be reasonable, Mr. Higgins: really you must. You cant walk over everybody like this.

HIGGINS, *thus scolded, subsides. The hurricane is succeeded by a zephyr of amiable surprise.*

HIGGINS (*with professional exquisiteness of modulation*). *I* walk over everybody! My dear Mrs. Pearce, my dear Pickering, I never had the slightest intention of walking over anyone. All I propose is that we should be kind to this poor girl. We must help her to prepare and fit herself for her new station in life. If I did not express myself clearly it was because I did not wish to hurt her delicacy, or yours.

LIZA, *reassured, steals back to her chair.*

MRS. PEARCE (*to* PICKERING). Well, did you ever hear anything like that, sir?

PICKERING (*laughing heartily*). Never, Mrs. Pearce: never.

HIGGINS (*patiently*). Whats the matter?

MRS. PEARCE. Well, the matter is, sir, that you cant take a girl up like that as if you were picking up a pebble on the beach.

HIGGINS. Why not?

MRS. PEARCE. Why not! But you dont know anything about her. What about her parents? She may be married.

LIZA. Garn!

HIGGINS. There! As the girl very properly says, Garn! Married indeed! Dont you know that a woman of that class looks a worn out drudge of fifty a year after she's married?

LIZA. Whood marry me?

HIGGINS (*suddenly resorting to the most thrillingly beautiful low tones in his best elocutionary style*). By George, Eliza, the streets will be strewn with the bodies of men shooting themselves for your sake before Ive done with you.

MRS. PEARCE. Nonsense, sir. You mustnt talk like that to her.

LIZA (*rising and squaring herself determinedly*). I'm going away. He's off his chump, he is. I dont want no balmies teaching me.

HIGGINS (*wounded in his tenderest point by her insensibility to his elocution*). Oh, indeed! I'm mad, am I? Very well, Mrs. Pearce: you neednt order the new clothes for her. Throw her out.

LIZA (*whimpering*). Nah-ow. You got no right to touch me.

MRS. PEARCE. You see now what comes of being saucy. (*Indicating the door*) This way, please.

LIZA (*almost in tears*). I didnt want no clothes. I wouldnt have taken them. (*She throws away the handkerchief.*) I can buy my own clothes.

HIGGINS (*deftly retrieving the handkerchief and intercepting her on her reluctant way to the door*). Youre an ungrateful wicked girl. This is my return for offering to take you out of the gutter and dress you beautifully and make a lady of you.

MRS. PEARCE. Stop, Mr. Higgins. I wont allow it. It's you that are wicked. Go home to your parents, girl; and tell them to take better care of you.

LIZA. I aint got no parents. They told me I was big enough to earn my own living and turned me out.

MRS. PEARCE. Wheres your mother?

LIZA. I aint got no mother. Her that turned me out was my sixth stepmother. But I done without them. And I'm a good girl, I am.

HIGGINS. Very well, then, what on earth is all this fuss about? The girl doesnt belong to anybody—is no use to anybody but me. (*He goes to MRS. PEARCE *and begins coaxing.)* You can adopt her, Mrs. Pearce: I'm sure a daughter would be a great amusement to you. Now dont make any more fuss. Take her downstairs; and—

MRS. PEARCE. But whats to become of her? Is she to be paid anything? Do be sensible, sir.

HIGGINS. Oh, pay her whatever is necessary: put it down in the housekeeping book. *(Impatiently)* What on earth will she want with money? She'll have her food and her clothes. She'll only drink if you give her money.

LIZA *(turning on him).* Oh you are a brute. It's a lie: nobody ever saw the sign of liquor on me. *(To* PICKERING) Oh, sir: you're a gentleman: don't let him speak to me like that.

PICKERING *(in good-humored remonstrance).* Does it occur to you, Higgins, that the girl has some feelings?

HIGGINS *(looking critically at her).* Oh no, I dont think so. Not any feelings that we need bother about. *(Cheerily)* Have you, Eliza?

LIZA. I got my feelings same as anyone else.

HIGGINS *(to* PICKERING, *reflectively).* You see the difficulty?

PICKERING. Eh? What difficulty?

HIGGINS. To get her to talk grammar. The mere pronunciation is easy enough.

LIZA. I dont want to talk grammar. I want to talk like a lady in a flower-shop.

MRS. PEARCE. Will you please keep to the point, Mr. Higgins? I want to know on what terms the girl is to be here. Is she to have any wages? And what is to become of her when youve finished your teaching? You must look ahead a little.

HIGGINS *(impatiently).* Whats to become of her if I leave her in the gutter? Tell me that, Mrs. Pearce.

MRS. PEARCE. Thats her own business, not yours, Mr. Higgins.

HIGGINS. Well, when Ive done with her, we can throw her back into the gutter; and then it will be her own business again; so thats all right.

LIZA. Oh, youve no feeling heart in you: you dont care for nothing but yourself. *(She rises and takes the floor resolutely.)* Here! Ive had enough of this. I'm going. *(Making for the door.)* You ought to be ashamed of yourself, you ought.

HIGGINS *(snatching a chocolate cream from the piano, his eyes suddenly beginning to twinkle with mischief).* Have some chocolates, Eliza.

LIZA *(halting, tempted).* How do I know what might be in them? Ive heard of girls being drugged by the like of you.

HIGGINS *whips out his penknife; cuts a chocolate in two; puts one half into his mouth and bolts it; and offers her the other half.*

HIGGINS. Pledge of good faith, Eliza. I eat one half: you eat the other. (LIZA *opens her mouth to retort: he pops the half chocolate into it.)* You shall have boxes of them, barrels of them, every day. You shall live on them. Eh?

LIZA *(who has disposed of the chocolate after being nearly choked by it).* I wouldnt have ate it, only I'm too ladylike to take it out of my mouth.

HIGGINS. Listen, Eliza. I think you said you came in a taxi.

LIZA. Well, what if I did? Ive as good a right to take a taxi as anyone else.

HIGGINS. You have, Eliza; and in future you shall have as many taxis as you want. You shall go up and down and round the town in a taxi every day. Think of that, Eliza.

MRS. PEARCE. Mr. Higgins: youre tempting the girl. It's not right. She should think of the future.

HIGGINS. At her age! Nonsense! Time enough to think of the future when you havnt any future to think of. No, Eliza: do as this lady does: think of other people's futures; but never think of your own. Think of chocolates, and taxis, and gold, and diamonds.

LIZA. No: I dont want no gold and no diamonds. I'm a good girl, I am. *(She sits down again, with an attempt at dignity.)*

HIGGINS. You shall remain so, Eliza, under the care of Mrs. Pearce. And you shall marry an officer in the Guards, with a beautiful moustache: the son of a marquis, who will disinherit him for marrying you, but will relent when he sees your beauty and goodness—

PICKERING. Excuse me, Higgins; but I really must interfere. Mrs. Pearce is quite right. If this girl is to put herself in your hands for six months for an experiment in teaching, she must understand thoroughly what she's doing.

HIGGINS. How can she? She's incapable of understanding anything. Besides, do any of us understand what we are doing? If we did, would we ever do it?

PICKERING. Very clever, Higgins; but not to the present point. *(To* ELIZA) Miss Doolittle—

LIZA *(overwhelmed)*. Ah-ah-ow-oo!

HIGGINS. There! Thats all youll get out of Eliza. Ah-ah-ow-oo! No use explaining. As a military man you ought to know that. Give her her orders: thats what she wants. Eliza: you are to live here for the next six months, learning how to speak beautifully, like a lady in a florist's shop. If youre good and do whatever youre told, you shall sleep in a proper bedroom, and have lots to eat, and money to buy chocolates and take rides in taxis. If youre naughty and idle you will sleep in the back kitchen among the black beetles, and be walloped by Mrs. Pearce with a broomstick. At the end of six months you shall go to Buckingham Palace in a carriage, beautifully dressed. If the King finds out youre not a lady, you will be taken by the police to the Tower of London, where your head will be cut off as a warning to other presumptuous flower girls. If you are not found out, you shall have a present of seven-and-six-pence to start life with as a lady in a shop. If you refuse this offer you will be a most ungrateful and wicked girl; and the angels will weep for you. *(To* PICKERING) Now are you satisfied, Pickering? *(To* MRS. PEARCE) Can I put it more plainly and fairly, Mrs. Pearce?

MRS. PEARCE *(patiently)*. I think youd better let me speak to the girl properly in private. I dont know that I can take charge of her or consent to the arrangement at all. Of course I know you dont mean her any harm; but when you get what you call interested in people's accents, you never think or care what may happen to them or you. Come with me, Eliza.

HIGGINS. Thats all right. Thank you, Mrs. Pearce. Bundle her off to the bathroom.

LIZA *(rising reluctantly and suspiciously)*. Youre a great bully, you are. I wont stay here if I dont like. I wont let nobody wallop me. I never asked to go to Bucknam Palace, I didnt. I was never in trouble with the police, not me. I'm a good girl—

MRS. PEARCE. Dont answer back, girl. You dont understand the gentleman. Come with me.

(She leads the way to the door, and holds it open for ELIZA.)

LIZA *(as she goes out)*. Well, what I say is right. I wont go near the King, not if I'm going to have my head cut off. If I'd known what I was letting myself in for, I wouldnt have come here. I always been a good girl; and I never offered to say a word to him; and I dont owe him nothing; and I dont care; and I wont be put upon; and I have my feelings the same as anyone else—

MRS. PEARCE *shuts the door; and* ELIZA's *plaints are no longer audible.* PICKERING *comes from the hearth to the chair and sits astride it with his arms on the back.*

PICKERING. Excuse the straight question, Higgins. Are you a man of good character where women are concerned?

HIGGINS *(moodily)*. Have you ever met a man of good character where women are concerned?

PICKERING. Yes: very frequently.

HIGGINS *(dogmatically, lifting himself on his hands to the level of the piano, and sitting on it with a bounce)*. Well, I havnt. I find that the moment I let a woman make friends with me, she becomes jealous, exacting, suspicious, and a damned nuisance. I find that the moment I let myself make friends with a woman, I become selfish and tyrannical. Women upset everything. When you let them into your life, you find that the woman is driving at one thing and youre driving at another.

PICKERING. At what, for example?

HIGGINS *(coming off the piano restlessly)*. Oh, Lord knows! I suppose the woman wants to live her own life; and the man wants to live his; and each tries to drag the other on to the wrong track. One wants to go north and the other south; and the result is that both have to go east, though they both hate the east wind. *(He sits down on the bench at the keyboard.)* So here I am, a confirmed old bachelor, and likely to remain so.

PICKERING *(rising and standing over him gravely)*. Come, Higgins! You know what I mean. If I'm to be in this business I shall feel responsible for that girl. I hope it's understood that no advantage is to be taken of her position.

HIGGINS. What! That thing! Sacred, I assure you. *(Rising to explain)* You see, she'll be a pupil; and teaching would be impossible unless pupils were sacred. Ive taught scores of American millionairesses how to speak English: the best-looking women in the world. I'm seasoned. They might as well be blocks of wood. *I* might as well be a block of wood. It's—

MRS. PEARCE *opens the door. She has* ELIZA's *hat in her hand.* PICKERING *retires to the easy-chair at the hearth and sits down.*

HIGGINS *(eagerly)*. Well, Mrs. Pearce: is it all right?

MRS. PEARCE *(at the door)*. I just wish to trouble you with a word, if I may, Mr. Higgins.

HIGGINS. Yes, certainly. Come in. *(She comes forward.)* Dont burn that, Mrs. Pearce. I'll keep it as a curiosity. *(He takes the hat.)*

MRS. PEARCE. Handle it carefully, sir, please. I had to promise her not to burn it; but I had better put it in the oven for a while.

HIGGINS *(putting it down hastily on the piano)*. Oh! thank you. Well, what have you to say to me?

PICKERING. Am I in the way?

MRS. PEARCE. Not at all, sir. Mr. Higgins: will you please be very particular what you say before the girl?

HIGGINS *(sternly)*. Of course. I'm always particular about what I say. Why do you say this to me?

MRS. PEARCE *(unmoved)*. No, sir: youre not at all particular when youve mislaid anything or when you get a little impatient. Now it doesnt matter before me: I'm used to it. But you really must not swear before the girl.

HIGGINS *(indignantly)*. I swear! *(Most emphatically)*. I never swear. I detest the habit. What the devil do you mean?

MRS. PEARCE *(stolidly)*. Thats what I mean, sir. You swear a great deal too much. I dont mind your damning and blasting, and what the devil and where the devil and who the devil—

HIGGINS. Mrs. Pearce: this language from your lips! Really!

MRS. PEARCE *(not to be put off)*. —but there is a certain word I must ask you not to use. The girl has just used it herself because the bath was too hot. It begins with the same letter as bath. She knows no better: she learnt it at her mother's knee. But she must not hear it from your lips.

HIGGINS *(loftily)*. I cannot charge myself with

having ever uttered it, Mrs. Pearce. *(She looks at him steadfastly. He adds, hiding an uneasy conscience with a judicial air)* Except perhaps in a moment of extreme and justifiable excitement.

MRS. PEARCE. Only this morning, sir, you applied it to your boots, to the butter, and to the brown bread.

HIGGINS. Oh, that! Mere alliteration, Mrs. Pearce, natural to a poet.

MRS. PEARCE. Well, sir, whatever you choose to call it, I beg you not to let the girl hear you repeat it.

HIGGINS. Oh, very well, very well. Is that all?

MRS. PEARCE. No, sir. We shall have to be very particular with this girl as to personal cleanliness.

HIGGINS. Certainly. Quite right. Most important.

MRS. PEARCE. I mean not to be slovenly about her dress or untidy in leaving things about.

HIGGINS *(going to her solemnly)*. Just so. I intended to call your attention to that. *(He passes on to* PICKERING, *who is enjoying the conversation immensely.)* It is these little things that matter, Pickering. Take care of the pence and the pounds will take care of themselves is as true of personal habits as of money. *(He comes to anchor on the hearthrug, with the air of a man in an unassailable position.)*

MRS. PEARCE. Yes, sir. Then might I ask you not to come down to breakfast in your dressing-gown, or at any rate not to use it as a napkin to the extent you do, sir. And if you would be so good as not to eat everything off the same plate, and to remember not to put the porridge saucepan out of your hand on the clean table-cloth, it would be a better example to the girl. You know you nearly choked yourself with a fishbone in the jam only last week.

HIGGINS *(routed from the hearthrug and drifting back to the piano).* I may do these things sometimes in absence of mind; but surely I dont do them habitually. *(Angrily)* By the way: my dressing-gown smells most damnably of benzine.

MRS. PEARCE. No doubt it does, Mr. Higgins. But if you will wipe your fingers—

HIGGINS *(yelling).* Oh very well, very well: I'll wipe them in my hair in future.

MRS. PEARCE. I hope youre not offended, Mr. Higgins.

HIGGINS *(shocked at finding himself thought capable of an unamiable sentiment).* Not at all, not at all. Youre quite right, Mrs. Pearce: I shall be particularly careful before the girl. Is that all?

MRS. PEARCE. No sir. Might she use some of those Japanese dresses you brought from abroad? I really cant put her back into her old things.

HIGGINS. Certainly. Anything you like. Is that all?

MRS. PEARCE. Thank you, sir. Thats all. *(She goes out.)*

HIGGINS. You know, Pickering, that woman has the most extraordinary ideas about me. Here I am, a shy, diffident sort of man. Ive never been able to feel really grown-up and tremendous, like other chaps. And yet she's firmly persuaded that I'm an arbitrary overbearing bossing kind of person. I cant account for it.

MRS. PEARCE *returns.*

MRS. PEARCE. If you please, sir, the trouble's beginning already. Theres a dustman[4] downstairs, Alfred Doolittle, wants to see you. He says you have his daughter here.

PICKERING *(rising).* Phew! I say!

HIGGINS *(promptly).* Send the blackguard up.

MRS. PEARCE. Oh, very well, sir. *(She goes out.)*

PICKERING. He may not be a blackguard, Higgins.

HIGGINS. Nonsense. Of course he's a blackguard.

PICKERING. Whether he is or not, I'm afraid we shall have some trouble with him.

HIGGINS *(confidently).* Oh no: I think not. If theres any trouble he shall have it with me, not I with him. And we are sure to get something interesting out of him.

PICKERING. About the girl?

HIGGINS. No. I mean his dialect.

PICKERING. Oh!

MRS. PEARCE *(at the door).* Doolittle, sir. *(She admits* DOOLITTLE *and retires.)*

ALFRED DOOLITTLE *is an elderly but vigorous dustman, clad in the costume of his profession, including a hat with a black brim covering his neck and shoulders. He has well marked and rather interesting features, and seems equally free from fear and conscience. He has a remarkably expressive voice, the result of a habit of giving vent to his feelings without reserve. His present pose is that of wounded honor and stern resolution.*

DOOLITTLE *(at the door, uncertain which of the two gentlemen is his man).* Professor Iggins?

HIGGINS. Here. Good morning. Sit down.

DOOLITTLE. Morning, Governor. *(He sits down magisterially.)* I come about a very serious matter, Governor.

HIGGINS *(to* PICKERING*).* Brought up in Hounslow. Mother Welsh, I should think. (DOOLITTLE *opens his mouth, amazed.* HIGGINS *continues.)* What do you want, Doolittle?

DOOLITTLE *(menacingly).* I want my daughter: thats what I want. See?

HIGGINS. Of course you do. Youre her father, arnt you? You dont suppose anyone else wants her, do you? I'm glad to see you have some spark of family feeling left. She's upstairs. Take her away at once.

DOOLITTLE *(rising, fearfully taken aback).* What!

HIGGINS. Take her away. Do you suppose I'm going to keep your daughter for you?

---

4. *dustman,* a trash or garbage collector.

DOOLITTLE (remonstrating). Now, now, look here, Governor. Is this reasonable? Is it fairity to take advantage of a man like this? The girl belongs to me. You got her. Where do I come in? (He sits down again.)

HIGGINS. Your daughter had the audacity to come to my house and ask me to teach her how to speak properly so that she could get a place in a flower-shop. This gentleman and my house-keeper have been here all the time. (Bullying him) How dare you come here and attempt to blackmail me? You sent her here on purpose.

DOOLITTLE (protesting). No, Governor.

HIGGINS. You must have. How else could you possibly know that she is here?

DOOLITTLE. Dont take a man up like that, Governor.

HIGGINS. The police shall take you up. This is a plant—a plot to extort money by threats. I shall telephone for the police. (He goes resolutely to the telephone and opens the directory.)

DOOLITTLE. Have I asked you for a brass farthing? I leave it to the gentleman here: have I said a word about money?

HIGGINS (throwing the book aside and marching down on DOOLITTLE with a poser). What else did you come for?

DOOLITTLE (sweetly). Well, what would a man come for? Be human, Governor.

HIGGINS (disarmed). Alfred: did you put her up to it?

DOOLITTLE. So help me, Governor, I never did. I take my Bible oath I aint seen the girl these two months past.

HIGGINS. Then how did you know she was here?

DOOLITTLE ("most musical, most melancholy").[5] I'll tell you, Governor, if you'll only let me get a word in. I'm willing to tell you. I'm wanting to tell you. I'm waiting to tell you.

HIGGINS. Pickering: this chap has a certain natural gift of rhetoric. Observe the rhythm of his native woodnotes wild. "I'm willing to tell you: I'm wanting to tell you: I'm waiting to tell you." Sentimental rhetoric! thats the Welsh strain in him. It also accounts for his mendacity and dishonesty.

PICKERING. Oh, please, Higgins: I'm west country[6] myself. (To DOOLITTLE) How did you know the girl was here if you didnt send her?

DOOLITTLE. It was like this, Governor. The girl took a boy in the taxi to give him a jaunt. Son of her landlady, he is. He hung about on the chance of her giving him another ride home. Well, she sent him back for her luggage when she heard you was willing for her to stop here. I met the boy at the corner of Long Acre and Endell Street.

HIGGINS. Public house. Yes?

DOOLITTLE. The poor man's club, Governor: why shouldnt I?

PICKERING. Do let him tell his story, Higgins.

DOOLITTLE. He told me what was up. And I ask you, what was my feelings and my duty as a father? I says to the boy, "You bring me the luggage," I says—

PICKERING. Why didnt you go for it yourself?

DOOLITTLE. Landlady wouldnt have trusted me with it, Governor. She's that kind of woman: you know. I had to give the boy a penny afore he trusted me with it, the little swine. I brought it to her just to oblige you like, and make myself agreeable. Thats all.

HIGGINS. How much luggage?

DOOLITTLE. Musical instrument, Governor. A few pictures, a trifle of jewelry, and a birdcage. She said she didnt want no clothes. What was I to think from that, Governor? I ask you as a parent what was I to think?

HIGGINS. So you came to rescue her from worse than death, eh?

DOOLITTLE (appreciatively: relieved at being so well understood). Just so, Governor. Thats right.

PICKERING. But why did you bring her luggage if you intended to take her away?

DOOLITTLE. Have I said a word about taking her away? Have I now?

HIGGINS (determinedly). Youre going to take her away, double quick. (He crosses to the hearth and rings the bell.)

DOOLITTLE (rising). No, Governor, Dont say that. I'm not the man to stand in my girl's light. Heres a career opening for her, as you might say; and—

---

5. "most . . . melancholy," a line from Milton's poem "Il Penseroso."
6. west country, the counties in the region southwest of London, especially the remoter ones, like Devon and Cornwall.

MRS. PEARCE *opens the door and awaits orders.*

HIGGINS. Mrs. Pearce: this is Eliza's father. He has come to take her away. Give her to him. *(He goes back to the piano, with an air of washing his hands of the whole affair.)*

DOOLITTLE. No. This is a misunderstanding. Listen here—

MRS. PEARCE. He cant take her away, Mr. Higgins: how can he? You told me to burn her clothes.

DOOLITTLE. Thats right. I cant carry the girl through the streets like a blooming monkey, can I? I put it to you.

HIGGINS. You have put it to me that you want your daughter. Take your daughter. If she has no clothes go out and buy her some.

DOOLITTLE *(desperate)*. Wheres the clothes she come in? Did I burn them or did your missus here?

MRS. PEARCE. I am the housekeeper, if you please. I have sent for some clothes for your girl. When they come you can take her away. You can wait in the kitchen. This way, please. DOOLITTLE, *much troubled, accompanies her to the door; then hesitates; finally turns confidently to* HIGGINS.

DOOLITTLE. Listen here, Governor. You and me is men of the world, aint we?

HIGGINS. Oh! Men of the world, are we? Youd better go, Mrs. Pearce.

MRS. PEARCE. I think so, indeed, sir. *(She goes, with dignity.)*

PICKERING. The floor is yours, Mr. Doolittle.

DOOLITTLE *(to* PICKERING*)*. I thank you, Governor. *(To* HIGGINS, *who takes refuge on the piano bench, a little overwhelmed by the proximity of his visitor; for* DOOLITTLE *has a professional flavor of dust about him.)* Well, the truth is, Ive taken a sort of fancy to you, Governor; and if you want the girl, I'm not so set on having her back home again but what I might be open to an arrangement. Regarded in the light of a young woman, she's a fine handsome girl. As a daughter she's not worth her keep; and so I tell you straight. All I ask is my rights as a father; and youre the last man alive to expect me to let her go for nothing; for I can see youre one of the straight sort, Governor. Well, whats a five-pound note to you? And whats Eliza to me? *(He returns to his chair and sits down judicially.)*

PICKERING. I think you ought to know, Doolittle, that Mr. Higgins's intentions are entirely honorable.

DOOLITTLE. Course they are, Governor. If I thought they wasnt, I'd ask fifty.

HIGGINS *(revolted)*. Do you mean to say that you would sell your daughter for £50?

DOOLITTLE. Not in a general way I wouldnt; but to oblige a gentleman like you I'd do a good deal, I do assure you.

PICKERING. Have you no morals, man?

DOOLITTLE *(unabashed)*. Cant afford them, Governor. Neither could you if you was as poor as me. Not that I mean any harm, you know. But if Liza is going to have a bit out of this, why not me too?

HIGGINS *(troubled)*. I dont know what to do, Pickering. There can be no question that as a matter of morals it's a positive crime to give this chap a farthing. And yet I feel a sort of rough justice in his claim.

DOOLITTLE. Thats it, Governor. Thats all I say. A father's heart, as it were.

PICKERING. Well, I know the feeling; but really it seems hardly right—

DOOLITTLE. Dont say that, Governor. Dont look at it that way. What am I, Governors both? I ask you, what am I? I'm one of the undeserving poor: thats what I am. Think of what that means to a man. It means that he's up agen middle-class morality all the time. If theres anything going, and I put in for a bit of it, it's always the same story: "Youre undeserving; so you cant have it." But my needs is as great as the most deserving widow's that ever got money out of six different charities in one week for the death of the same husband. I dont need less than a deserving man: I need more. I dont eat less hearty than him; and I drink a lot more. I want a bit of amusement, cause I'm a thinking man. I want cheerfulness and a song and a band when I feel low. Well, they charge me just the same for everything as they charge the deserving. What is middle-class morality? Just an excuse for never giving me anything. Therefore, I ask you, as two gentlemen, not to play that game on me. I'm playing straight with you. I aint pretending to be deserving. I'm undeserving; and I mean to go on being undeserving. I like it; and thats the truth. Will you take advantage of a man's nature to do him out of the price of his own daughter what he's brought up and fed and clothed by the sweat of his brow until she's growed big enough to be interesting to you two gentlemen? Is five pounds unreasonable? I put it to you; and I leave it to you.

HIGGINS (*rising, and going over to* PICKERING). Pickering: if we were to take this man in hand for three months, he could choose between a seat in the Cabinet and a popular pulpit in Wales.

PICKERING. What do you say to that, Doolittle?

DOOLITTLE. Not me, Governor, thank you kindly. Ive heard all the preachers and all the prime ministers—for I'm a thinking man and game for politics or religion or social reform same as all the other amusements—and I tell you it's a dog's life any way you look at it. Undeserving poverty is my line. Taking one station in society with another, it's—it's—well, it's the only one that has any ginger in it, to my taste.

HIGGINS. I suppose we must give him a fiver.

PICKERING. He'll make a bad use of it, I'm afraid.

DOOLITTLE. Not me, Governor, so help me I wont. Dont you be afraid that I'll save it and spare it and live idle on it. There wont be a penny of it left by Monday: I'll have to go to work same as if I'd never had it. It wont pauperize me, you bet. Just one good spree for myself and the missus, giving pleasure to ourselves and employment to others, and satisfaction to you to think it's not been throwed away. You couldnt spend it better.

HIGGINS (*taking out his pocket book and coming between* DOOLITTLE *and the piano*). This is irresistible. Lets give him ten. (*He offers two notes to the dustman.*)

DOOLITTLE. No, Governor. She wouldnt have the heart to spend ten; and perhaps I shouldnt neither. Ten pounds is a lot of money: it makes a man feel prudent like; and then goodbye to happiness. You give me what I ask you, Governor: not a penny more, and not a penny less.

PICKERING. Why dont you marry that missus of yours? I rather draw the line at encouraging that sort of immorality.

DOOLITTLE. Tell her so, Governor; tell her so. I'm willing. It's me that suffers by it. Ive no hold on her. I got to be agreeable to her. I got to give her presents. I got to buy her clothes something sinful. I'm a slave to that woman, Governor, just because I'm not her lawful husband. And she knows it too. Catch her marrying me! Take my advice, Governor: marry Eliza while she's young and dont know no better. If you dont youll be sorry for it after. If you do, she'll be sorry for it after; but better her than you, because youre a man, and she's only a woman and dont know how to be happy anyhow.

HIGGINS. Pickering: if we listen to this man another minute, we shall have no convictions left.

(*To* DOOLITTLE) Five pounds I think you said.

DOOLITTLE. Thank you kindly, Governor.

HIGGINS. Youre sure you wont take ten?

DOOLITTLE. Not now. Another time, Governor.

HIGGINS (*handing him a five-pound note*). Here you are.

DOOLITTLE. Thank you, Governor. Good morning. (*He hurries to the door, anxious to get away with his booty. When he opens it he is confronted with a dainty and exquisitely clean young Japanese lady in a simple blue cotton kimono printed cunningly with small white jasmine blossoms.* MRS. PEARCE *is with her. He gets out of her way deferentially and apologizes.*) Beg pardon, miss.

THE JAPANESE LADY. Garn! Dont you know your own daughter?

DOOLITTLE		*exclaiming*	Bly me! it's Eliza!
HIGGINS	}	*simul-*	Whats that! This!
PICKERING		*taneously*	By Jove!

LIZA. Dont I look silly?

HIGGINS. Silly?

MRS. PEARCE (*at the door*). Now Mr. Higgins, please dont say anything to make the girl conceited about herself.

HIGGINS (*conscientiously*). Oh! Quite right, Mrs. Pearce. (*To* ELIZA) Yes: damned silly.

MRS. PEARCE. Please, sir.

HIGGINS (*correcting himself*). I mean extremely silly.

LIZA. I should look all right with my hat on. (*She takes up her hat; puts it on; and walks across the room to the fireplace with a fashionable air.*)

HIGGINS. A new fashion, by George! And it ought to look horrible!

DOOLITTLE (*with fatherly pride*). Well, I never thought she'd clean up as good looking as that, Governor. She's a credit to me, aint she?

LIZA. I tell you, it's easy to clean up here. Hot and cold water on tap, just as much as you like, there is. Woolly towels, there is; and a towel horse so hot, it burns your fingers. Soft brushes to scrub yourself, and a wooden bowl of soap smelling like primroses. Now I know why ladies is so clean. Washing's a treat for them. Wish they saw what it is for the like of me!

HIGGINS. I'm glad the bathroom met with your approval.

LIZA. It didnt: not all of it; and I dont care who hears me say it. Mrs. Pearce knows.

HIGGINS. What was wrong, Mrs. Pearce?

MRS. PEARCE (*blandly*). Oh, nothing, sir. It doesnt matter.

LIZA. I had a good mind to break it. I didn't know which way to look. But I hung a towel over it, I did.

HIGGINS. Over what?

MRS. PEARCE. Over the looking glass, sir.

HIGGINS. Doolittle: you have brought your daughter up too strictly.

DOOLITTLE. Me! I never brought her up at all, except to give her a lick of a strap now and again. Dont put it on me, Governor. She aint accustomed to it, you see: thats all. But she'll soon pick up your free-and-easy ways.

LIZA. I'm a good girl, I am; and I wont pick up no free-and-easy ways.

HIGGINS. Eliza: if you say again that youre a good girl, your father shall take you home.

LIZA. Not him. You dont know my father. All he come here for was to touch you for some money to get drunk on.

DOOLITTLE. Well, what else would I want money for? To put into the plate in church, I suppose. (*She puts out her tongue at him. He is so incensed by this that* PICKERING *presently finds it necessary to step between them.*) Dont you give me none of your lip; and dont let me hear you giving this gentleman any of it neither, or youll hear from me about it. See?

HIGGINS. Have you any further advice to give her before you go, Doolittle? Your blessing, for instance.

DOOLITTLE. No, Governor, I aint such a mug as to put up my children to all I know myself. Hard enough to hold them in without that. If you want Eliza's mind improved, Governor, you do it yourself with a strap. So long, gentlemen. (*He turns to go.*)

HIGGINS (*impressively*). Stop. Youll come regularly to see your daughter. It's your duty, you know. My brother is a clergyman; and he could help you in your talks with her.

DOOLITTLE (*evasively*). Certainly. I'll come, Governor. Not just this week, because I have a job at a distance. But later on you may depend on me. Afternoon, gentlemen. Afternoon, maam. (*He takes off his hat to* MRS. PEARCE, *who disdains the salutation and goes out. He winks at* HIGGINS, *thinking him probably a fellow-sufferer from* MRS. PEARCE'*s difficult disposition, and follows her.*)

LIZA. Dont you believe the old liar. He'd as soon

you set a bull-dog on him as a clergyman. You wont see him again in a hurry.

HIGGINS. I dont want to, Eliza. Do you?

LIZA. Not me. I dont want never to see him again, I dont. He's a disgrace to me, he is, collecting dust, instead of working at his trade.

PICKERING. What is his trade, Eliza?

LIZA. Taking money out of other people's pockets into his own. His proper trade's a navvy;[7] and he works at it sometimes too—for exercise—and earns good money at it. Aint you going to call me Miss Doolittle any more?

PICKERING. I beg your pardon, Miss Doolittle. It was a slip of the tongue.

LIZA. Oh, I dont mind; only it sounded so genteel. I should just like to take a taxi to the corner of Tottenham Court Road and get out there and tell it to wait for me, just to put the girls in their place a bit. I wouldnt speak to them, you know.

PICKERING. Better wait til we get you something really fashionable.

HIGGINS. Besides, you shouldnt cut[8] your old friends now that you have risen in the world. Thats what we call snobbery.

LIZA. You dont call the like of them my friends now, I should hope. Theyve took it out of me often enough with their ridicule when they had the chance; and now I mean to get a bit of my own back. But if I'm to have fashionable clothes, I'll wait. I should like to have some. Mrs. Pearce says youre going to give me some to wear in bed at night different to what I wear in the daytime; but it do seem a waste of money when you could get something to shew. Besides, I never could fancy changing into cold things on a winter night.

MRS. PEARCE (coming back). Now, Eliza. The new things have come for you to try on.

LIZA. Ah-ow-oo-ooh! (She rushes out.)

MRS. PEARCE (following her). Oh, dont rush about like that, girl. (She shuts the door behind her.)

HIGGINS. Pickering: we have taken on a stiff job.

PICKERING (with conviction). Higgins: we have.

---

7. *navvy,* unskilled laborer, especially one doing excavation or construction work.
8. *cut,* refuse to recognize socially.

Act Three

It is MRS. HIGGINS's *at-home*[1] *day. Nobody has yet arrived. Her drawing room, in a flat on Chelsea Embankment,*[2] *has three windows looking on the river; and the ceiling is not so lofty as it would be in an older house of the same pretension. The windows are open, giving access to a balcony with flowers in pots. If you stand with your face to the windows, you have the fireplace on your left and the door in the right-hand wall close to the corner nearest the windows.*

MRS. HIGGINS *was brought up on Morris and Burne-Jones;*[3] *and her room, which is very unlike her son's room in Wimpole Street, is not crowded with furniture and little tables and nicknacks. In the middle of the room there is a big ottoman; and this, with the carpet, the Morris wallpapers, and the Morris chintz window curtains and brocade covers of the ottoman and its cushions, supply all the ornament, and are much too handsome to be hidden by odds and ends of useless things. A few good oil paintings from the exhibitions in the Grosvenor Gallery thirty years ago (the Burne-Jones, not the Whistler side of them) are on the walls. The only landscape is a Cecil Lawson on the scale of a Rubens.*[4] *There is a portrait of* MRS. HIGGINS *as she was when she defied fashion in her youth in one of the beautiful Rossettian*[5] *costumes which, when caricatured by people who did not understand, led to the absurdities of popular estheticism in the eighteen-seventies.*

In the corner diagonally opposite the door MRS. HIGGINS, *now over sixty and long past taking the trouble to dress out of the fashion, sits writing at an elegantly simple writing-table with a bell button within reach of her hand. There is a Chippendale chair further back in the room*

---

1. **at-home day,** the day one receives callers.
2. **Chelsea Embankment.** Chelsea is a pleasant residential district along the bank of the Thames.
3. **Morris and Burne-Jones.** William Morris and Edward Burne-Jones were members of a decorating firm noted for fine carvings, stained glass, metalwork, wallpapers, chintzes, tiles, and carpets.
4. **Cecil Lawson . . . Rubens.** Cecil Lawson (1851–1882) was an English landscape painter. Peter Paul Rubens (1577–1640) was a Flemish painter known for his large canvases.
5. **Rossettian,** inspired by the paintings of Dante Gabriel Rossetti (1828–1882), whose work often pictures women in flowing robes.

between her and the window nearest her side. At the other side of the room, further forward, is an Elizabethan chair roughly carved in the taste of Inigo Jones. On the same side a piano in a decorated case. The corner between the fireplace and the window is occupied by a divan cushioned in Morris chintz.

It is between four and five in the afternoon.

The door is opened violently; and HIGGINS *enters with his hat on.*

MRS. HIGGINS (*dismayed*). Henry (*scolding him*)! What are you doing here to-day? It is my at-home day: you promised not to come. (*As he bends to kiss her, she takes his hat off, and presents it to him.*)

HIGGINS. Oh, bother! (*He throws the hat down on the table.*)

MRS. HIGGINS. Go home at once.

HIGGINS (*kissing her*). I know, mother. I came on purpose.

MRS. HIGGINS. But you mustnt. I'm serious, Henry. You offend all my friends: they stop coming whenever they meet you.

HIGGINS. Nonsense! I know I have no small talk; but people dont mind. (*He sits on the settee.*)

MRS. HIGGINS. Oh! dont they? Small talk indeed! What about your large talk? Really, dear, you mustnt stay.

HIGGINS. I must. Ive a job for you. A phonetic job.

MRS. HIGGINS. No use, dear. I'm sorry; but I cant get round your vowels; and though I like to get pretty postcards in your patent shorthand, I always have to read the copies in ordinary writing you so thoughtfully send me.

HIGGINS. Well, this isnt a phonetic job.

MRS. HIGGINS. You said it was.

HIGGINS. Not your part of it. Ive picked up a girl.

MRS. HIGGINS. Does that mean that some girl has picked you up?

HIGGINS. Not at all. I don't mean a love affair.

MRS. HIGGINS. What a pity!

HIGGINS. Why?

MRS. HIGGINS. Well, you never fall in love with anyone under forty-five. When will you discover that there are some rather nice-looking young women about?

HIGGINS. Oh, I cant be bothered with young women. My idea of a lovable woman is something as like you as possible. I shall never get into the way of seriously liking young women: some habits lie too deep to be changed. (*Rising abruptly and walking about, jingling his money and his keys in his trouser pockets*) Besides, theyre all idiots.

MRS. HIGGINS. Do you know what you would do if you really loved me, Henry?

HIGGINS. Oh bother! What? Marry, I suppose?

MRS. HIGGINS. No. Stop fidgeting and take your hands out of your pockets. (*With a gesture of despair, he obeys and sits down again.*) Thats a good boy. Now tell me about the girl.

HIGGINS. She's coming to see you.

MRS. HIGGINS. I dont remember asking her.

HIGGINS. You didnt. *I* asked her. If youd known her you wouldnt have asked her.

MRS. HIGGINS. Indeed! Why?

HIGGINS. Well, it's like this. She's a common flower girl. I picked her off the kerbstone.

MRS. HIGGINS. And invited her to my at-home!

HIGGINS (*rising and coming to her to coax her*). Oh, thatll be all right. Ive taught her to speak properly; and she has strict orders as to her behavior. She's to keep to two subjects: the weather and everybody's health—Fine day and How do you do, you know—and not to let herself go on things in general. That will be safe.

MRS. HIGGINS. Safe! To talk about our health! about our insides! perhaps about our outsides! How could you be so silly, Henry?

HIGGINS (*impatiently*). Well, she must talk about something. (*He controls himself and sits down again.*) Oh, she'll be all right: dont you fuss. Pickering is in it with me. Ive a sort of bet on that I'll pass her off as a duchess in six months. I started on her some months ago; and she's getting on like a house on fire. I shall win my bet. She has a quick ear; and she's been easier to teach than my middle class pupils because she's had to learn a complete new language. She talks English almost as you talk French.

MRS. HIGGINS. Thats satisfactory, at all events.

HIGGINS. Well, it is and it isnt.

MRS. HIGGINS. What does that mean?

HIGGINS. You see, Ive got her pronunciation all right; but you have to consider not only how a girl pronounces, but what she pronounces; and thats where—

They are interrupted by THE PARLOR-MAID, *announcing guests.*

THE PARLOR-MAID. Mrs. and Miss Eynsford Hill. *(She withdraws).*

HIGGINS. Oh Lord! *(He rises; snatches his hat from the table; and makes for the door; but before he reaches it his mother introduces him.)* MRS. *and* MISS EYNSFORD HILL *are the mother and daughter who sheltered from the rain in Covent Garden. The mother is well bred, quiet, and has the habitual anxiety of straitened means. The daughter has acquired a gay air of being very much at home in society: the bravado of genteel poverty.*

MRS. EYNSFORD HILL *(to* MRS. HIGGINS*).* How do you do? *(They shake hands.)*

MISS EYNSFORD HILL. How d'you do? *(She shakes.)*

MRS. HIGGINS *(introducing).* My son Henry.

MRS. EYNSFORD HILL. Your celebrated son! I have so longed to meet you, Professor Higgins.

HIGGINS. *(glumly, making no movement in her direction).* Delighted. *(He backs against the piano and bows brusquely.)*

MISS EYNSFORD HILL *(going to him with confident familiarity).* How do you do?

HIGGINS *(staring at her).* Ive seen you before somewhere. I havnt the ghost of a notion where; but Ive heard your voice. *(Drearily)* It doesnt matter. Youd better sit down.

MRS. HIGGINS. I'm sorry to say that my celebrated son has no manners. You mustnt mind him.

MISS EYNSFORD HILL *(gaily).* I dont. *(She sits in the Elizabethan chair.)*

MRS. EYNSFORD HILL *(a little bewildered).* Not at all. *(She sits on the ottoman between her daughter and* MRS. HIGGINS, *who has turned her chair away from the writing-table.)*

HIGGINS. Oh, have I been rude? I didnt mean to be.

He goes to the central window, through which, with his back to the company, he contemplates the river and the flowers in Battersea Park on the opposite bank as if they were a frozen desert.

THE PARLOR-MAID *returns, ushering in* PICKERING.

THE PARLOR-MAID. Colonel Pickering. *(She withdraws.)*

PICKERING. How do you do, Mrs. Higgins?

MRS. HIGGINS. So glad youve come. Do you know Mrs. Eynsford Hill—Miss Eynsford Hill? *(Exchange of bows. The Colonel brings the Chippendale chair a little forward between* MRS. HILL *and* MRS. HIGGINS, *and sits down.)*

PICKERING. Has Henry told you what weve come for?

HIGGINS *(over his shoulder).* We were interrupted: damn it!

MRS. HIGGINS. Oh Henry, Henry, really!

MRS. EYNSFORD HILL *(half rising).* Are we in the way?

MRS. HIGGINS *(rising and making her sit down again).* No, no. You couldnt have come more fortunately: we want you to meet a friend of ours.

HIGGINS *(turning hopefully).* Yes, by George! We want two or three people. Youll do as well as anybody else.

THE PARLOR-MAID *returns, ushering* FREDDY.

THE PARLOR-MAID. Mr. Eynsford Hill.

HIGGINS *(almost audibly, past endurance).* God of Heaven! another of them.

FREDDY *(shaking hands with* MRS. HIGGINS*).* Ahdedo?

MRS. HIGGINS. Very good of you to come. *(Introducing)* Colonel Pickering.

FREDDY *(bowing).* Ahdedo?

MRS. HIGGINS. I dont think you know my son, Professor Higgins.

FREDDY *(going to* HIGGINS*).* Ahdedo?

HIGGINS *(looking at him much as if he were a pickpocket).* I'll take my oath Ive met you before somewhere. Where was it?

FREDDY. I dont think so.

HIGGINS *(resignedly).* It dont matter, anyhow. Sit down. *(He shakes* FREDDY's *hand, and almost slings him on to the ottoman with his face to the windows; then comes round to the other side of it.)*

HIGGINS. Well, here we are, anyhow! *(He sits down on the ottoman next* MRS. EYNSFORD HILL, *on her left).* And now, what the devil are we going to talk about until Eliza comes?

MRS. HIGGINS. Henry: you are the life and soul of the Royal Society's soirees; but really youre rather trying on more commonplace occasions.

HIGGINS. Am I? Very sorry. (*Beaming suddenly*) I suppose I am, you know. (*Uproariously*) Ha, ha!

MISS EYNSFORD HILL (*who considers* HIGGINS *quite eligible matrimonially*). I sympathize. *I* havnt any small talk. If people would only be frank and say what they really think!

HIGGINS (*relapsing into gloom*). Lord forbid!

MRS. EYNSFORD HILL (*taking up her daughter's cue*). But why?

HIGGINS. What they think they ought to think is bad enough, Lord knows; but what they really think would break up the whole show. Do you suppose it would be really agreeable if I were to come out now with what *I* really think?

MISS EYNSFORD HILL (*gaily*). Is it so very cynical?

HIGGINS. Cynical! Who the dickens said it was cynical? I mean it wouldnt be decent.

MRS. EYNSFORD HILL (*seriously*). Oh! I'm sure you dont mean that, Mr. Higgins.

HIGGINS. You see, we're all savages, more or less. We're supposed to be civilized and cultured—to know all about poetry and philosophy and art and science, and so on; but how many of us know even the meanings of these names? (*To* MISS HILL) What do you know of poetry? (*To* MRS. HILL) What do you know of science? (*Indicating* FREDDY) What does he know of art or science or anything else? What the devil do you imagine I know of philosophy?

MRS. HIGGINS (*warningly*). Or of manners, Henry?

THE PARLOR-MAID (*opening the door*). Miss Doolittle. (*She withdraws.*)

HIGGINS (*rising hastily and running to* MRS. HIGGINS). Here she is, mother. (*He stands on tiptoe and makes signs over his mother's head to* ELIZA *to indicate to her which lady is her hostess.*)

ELIZA, *who is exquisitely dressed, produces an impression of such remarkable distinction and beauty as she enters that they all rise, quite fluttered. Guided by* HIGGINS'*s signals, she comes to* MRS. HIGGINS *with studied grace.*

LIZA (*speaking with pedantic correctness of pronunciation and great beauty of tone*). How do you do, Mrs. Higgins? (*She gasps slightly in making sure of the* H *in* HIGGINS, *but is quite*

successful.*) Mr. Higgins told me I might come.

MRS. HIGGINS (*cordially*). Quite right: I'm very glad indeed to see you.

PICKERING. How do you do, Miss Doolittle?

LIZA (*shaking hands with him*). Colonel Pickering, is it not?

MRS. EYNSFORD HILL. I feel sure we have met before, Miss Doolittle. I remember your eyes.

LIZA. How do you do? (*She sits down on the ottoman gracefully in the place just left vacant by* HIGGINS.)

MRS. EYNSFORD HILL (*introducing*). My daughter Clara.

LIZA. How do you do?

CLARA (*impulsively*). How do you do? (*She sits down on the ottoman beside* ELIZA, *devouring her with her eyes.*)

FREDDY (*coming to their side of the ottoman*). Ive certainly had the pleasure.

MRS. EYNSFORD HILL (*introducing*). My son Freddy.

LIZA. How do you do?

FREDDY *bows and sits down in the Elizabethan chair, infatuated.*

HIGGINS (*suddenly*). By George, yes: it all comes back to me! (*They stare at him.*) Covent Garden! (*Lamentably*) What a damned thing!

MRS. HIGGINS. Henry, please! (*He is about to sit on the edge of the table.*) Dont sit on my writing-table: youll break it.

HIGGINS (*sulkily*). Sorry.

He goes to the divan, stumbling into the fender and over the fire-irons on his way; extricating himself with muttered imprecations; and finishing his disastrous journey by throwing himself so impatiently on the divan that he almost breaks it. MRS. HIGGINS *looks at him, but controls herself and says nothing.*

A long and painful pause ensues.

MRS. HIGGINS (*at last, conversationally*). Will it rain, do you think?

LIZA. The shallow depression in the west of these islands is likely to move slowly in an easterly direction. There are no indications of any great change in the barometrical situation.

FREDDY. Ha! ha! how awfully funny!

LIZA. What is wrong with that, young man? I bet I got it right.

FREDDY. Killing!

MRS. EYNSFORD HILL. I'm sure I hope it wont turn cold. Theres so much influenza about. It runs right through our whole family regularly every spring.

LIZA (*darkly*). My aunt died of influenza: so they said.

MRS. EYNSFORD HILL (*clicks her tongue sympathetically*)!!!

LIZA (*in the same tragic tone*). But it's my belief they done the old woman in.

MRS. HIGGINS (*puzzled*). Done her in?

LIZA. Y-e-e-e-es, Lord love you! Why should she die of influenza? She come through diphtheria right enough the year before. I saw her with my own eyes. Fairly blue with it, she was. They all thought she was dead; but my father he kept ladling gin down her throat til she came to so sudden that she bit the bowl off the spoon.

MRS. EYNSFORD HILL (*startled*). Dear me!

LIZA (*piling up the indictment*). What call would a woman with that strength in her have to die of influenza? What become of her new straw hat that should have come to me? Somebody pinched it; and what I say is, them as pinched it done her in.

MRS. EYNSFORD HILL. What does doing her in mean?

HIGGINS (*hastily*). Oh, thats the new small talk. To do a person in means to kill them.

MRS. EYNSFORD HILL (*to* ELIZA, *horrified*). You surely dont believe that your aunt was killed?

LIZA. Do I not! Them she lived with would have killed her for a hat-pin, let alone a hat.

MRS. EYNSFORD HILL. But it cant have been right for your father to pour spirits down her throat like that. It might have killed her.

LIZA. Not her. Gin was mother's milk to her. Besides, he'd poured so much down his own throat that he knew the good of it.

MRS. EYNSFORD HILL. Do you mean that he drank?

LIZA. Drank! My word! Something chronic.

MRS. EYNSFORD HILL. How dreadful for you!

LIZA. Not a bit. It never did him no harm what I could see. But then he did not keep it up regular. (*Cheerfully*) On the burst, as you might say, from time to time. And always more agreeable when he had a drop in. When he was out of work, my mother used to give him fourpence and tell him to go out and not come back until he'd drunk himself cheerful and loving-like. Theres lots of women has to make their husbands drunk to make them fit to live with. (*Now quite at her ease*) You see, it's like this. If a man has a bit of a conscience, it always takes him when he's sober; and then it makes him low-spirited. A drop of booze just takes that off and makes him happy. (*To* FREDDY, *who is in convulsions of suppressed laughter*) Here! what are you sniggering at?

FREDDY. The new small talk. You do it so awfully well.

LIZA. If I was doing it proper, what was you laughing at? *(To* HIGGINS*)* Have I said anything I oughtnt?

MRS. HIGGINS *(interposing).* Not at all, Miss Doolittle.

LIZA. Well, thats a mercy, anyhow. *(Expansively)* What I always say is—

HIGGINS *(rising and looking at his watch).* Ahem!

LIZA *(looking round at him; taking the hint; and rising).* Well: I must go. *(They all rise,* FREDDY *goes to the door.)* So pleased to have met you. Goodbye. *(She shakes hands with* MRS. HIGGINS.*)*

MRS. HIGGINS. Goodbye.

LIZA. Goodbye, Colonel Pickering.

PICKERING. Goodbye, Miss Doolittle. *(They shake hands.)*

LIZA *(nodding to the others).* Goodbye, all.

FREDDY *(opening the door for her).* Are you walking across the Park, Miss Doolittle? If so—

LIZA. Walk! Not bloody likely. *(Sensation)* I am going in a taxi. *(She goes out.)*

PICKERING *gasps and sits down.* FREDDY *goes out on the balcony to catch another glimpse of* ELIZA.

MRS. EYNSFORD HILL *(suffering from shock).* Well, I really cant get used to the new ways.

CLARA *(throwing herself discontentedly into the Elizabethan chair).* Oh, it's all right, mamma, quite right. People will think we never go anywhere or see anybody if you are so old-fashioned.

MRS. EYNSFORD HILL. I daresay I am very old-fashioned; but I do hope you wont begin using that expression, Clara. I have got accustomed to hear you talking about men as rotters, and calling everything filthy and beastly; though I do think it horrible and unladylike. But this last is really too much. Dont you think so, Colonel Pickering?

PICKERING. Dont ask me. Ive been away in India for several years; and manners have changed so much that I sometimes dont know whether I'm at a respectable dinner-table or in a ship's forecastle.

CLARA. It's all a matter of habit. Theres no right or wrong in it. Nobody means anything by it.

And it's so quaint, and gives such a smart emphasis to things that are not in themselves very witty. I find the new small talk delightful and quite innocent.

MRS. EYNSFORD HILL *(rising).* Well, after that, I think it's time for us to go.

PICKERING *and* HIGGINS *rise.*

CLARA *(rising).* Oh yes: we have three at-homes to go to still. Goodbye, Mrs. Higgins. Goodbye, Colonel Pickering. Goodbye, Professor Higgins.

HIGGINS *(coming grimly at her from the divan, and accompanying her to the door).* Goodbye. Be sure you try on that small talk at the three at-homes. Dont be nervous about it. Pitch it in strong.

CLARA *(all smiles).* I will. Goodbye. Such nonsense, all this early Victorian prudery!

HIGGINS *(tempting her).* Such damned nonsense!

CLARA. Such bloody nonsense!

MRS. EYNSFORD HILL *(convulsively).* Clara!

CLARA. Ha! ha! *(She goes out radiant, conscious of being thoroughly up to date, and is heard descending the stairs in a stream of silvery laughter.)*

FREDDY *(to the heavens at large).* Well, I ask you—*(He gives it up, and comes to* MRS. HIGGINS.*)* Goodbye.

MRS. HIGGINS *(shaking hands).* Goodbye. Would you like to meet Miss Doolittle again?

FREDDY *(eagerly).* Yes, I should, most awfully.

MRS. HIGGINS. Well, you know my days.

FREDDY. Yes. Thanks awfully. Goodbye. *(He goes out.)*

MRS. EYNSFORD HILL. Goodbye, Mr. Higgins.

HIGGINS. Goodbye. Goodbye.

MRS. EYNSFORD HILL *(to* PICKERING*).* It's no use. I shall never be able to bring myself to use that word.

PICKERING. Dont. It's not compulsory, you know. Youll get on quite well without it.

MRS. EYNSFORD HILL. Only, Clara is so down on me if I am not positively reeking with the latest slang. Goodbye.

PICKERING. Goodbye.

(They shake hands.)

MRS. EYNSFORD HILL *(to* MRS. HIGGINS*).* You mustnt mind Clara. *(*PICKERING, *catching from her lowered tone that this is not meant for him* *to hear, discreetly joins* HIGGINS *at the window.)* We're so poor! and she gets so few parties, poor child! She doesn't quite know. *(*MRS. HIGGINS, *seeing that her eyes are moist, takes her hand sympathetically and goes with her to the door.)* But the boy is nice. Dont you think so?

MRS. HIGGINS. Oh, quite nice. I shall always be delighted to see him.

MRS. EYNSFORD HILL. Thank you, dear. Goodbye. *(She goes out.)*

HIGGINS *(eagerly).* Well? Is Eliza presentable? *(He swoops on his mother and drags her to the ottoman, where she sits down in* ELIZA's *place with her son on her left.)*

PICKERING *returns to his chair on her right.*

MRS. HIGGINS. You silly boy, of course she's not presentable. She's a triumph of your art and of her dressmaker's; but if you suppose for a moment that she doesnt give herself away in every sentence she utters, you must be perfectly cracked about her.

PICKERING. But dont you think something might be done? I mean something to eliminate the sanguinary[6] element from her conversation.

MRS. HIGGINS. Not as long as she is in Henry's hands.

HIGGINS *(aggrieved).* Do you mean that my language is improper?

MRS. HIGGINS. No, dearest: it would be quite proper—say on a canal barge; but it would not be proper for her at a garden party.

HIGGINS *(deeply injured).* Well I must say—

PICKERING *(interrupting him).* Come, Higgins: you must learn to know yourself. I havnt heard such language as yours since we used to review the volunteers in Hyde Park twenty years ago.

HIGGINS *(sulkily).* Oh, well, if you say so, I suppose I dont always talk like a bishop.

MRS. HIGGINS *(quieting* HENRY *with a touch).* Colonel Pickering: will you tell me what is the exact state of things in Wimpole Street?

PICKERING *(cheerfully: as if this completely changed the subject).* Well, I have come to live there with Henry. We work together at my Indian Dialects; and we think it more convenient—

MRS. HIGGINS. Quite so. I know all about that: it's

an excellent arrangement. But where does this girl live?

HIGGINS. With us, of course. Where should she live?

MRS. HIGGINS. But on what terms? Is she a servant? If not, what is she?

PICKERING *(slowly).* I think I know what you mean, Mrs. Higgins.

HIGGINS. Well, dash me if *I* do! Ive had to work at the girl every day for months to get her to her present pitch. Besides, she's useful. She knows where my things are, and remembers my appointments and so forth.

MRS. HIGGINS. How does your housekeeper get on with her?

HIGGINS. Mrs. Pearce? Oh, she's jolly glad to get so much taken off her hands; for before Eliza came, she used to have to find things and remind me of my appointments. But she's got some silly bee in her bonnet about Eliza. She keeps saying "You dont think, sir": doesnt she, Pick?

PICKERING. Yes: thats the formula. "You dont think, sir." Thats the end of every conversation about Eliza.

HIGGINS. As if I ever stop thinking about the girl and her confounded vowels and consonants. I'm worn out, thinking about her, and watching her lips and her teeth and her tongue, not to mention her soul, which is the quaintest of the lot.

MRS. HIGGINS. You certainly are a pretty pair of babies, playing with your live doll.

HIGGINS. Playing! The hardest job I ever tackled: make no mistake about that, mother. But you have no idea how frightfully interesting it is to take a human being and change her into a quite different human being by creating a new speech for her. It's filling up the deepest gulf that separates class from class and soul from soul.

PICKERING *(drawing his chair closer to* MRS. HIGGINS *and bending over to her eagerly).* Yes: it's enormously interesting. I assure you, Mrs. Higgins, we take Eliza very seriously. Every week—every day almost—there is some new change. *(Closer again)* We keep records of every stage—dozens of gramophone disks and photographs—

---

6. *sanguinary,* a reference to Liza's use of the slang word *bloody*

HIGGINS (*assailing her at the other ear*). Yes, by George: it's the most absorbing experiment I ever tackled. She regularly fills our lives up: doesnt she, Pick?

PICKERING. We're always talking Eliza.

HIGGINS. Teaching Eliza.

PICKERING. Dressing Eliza.

MRS. HIGGINS. What!

HIGGINS. Inventing new Elizas.

HIGGINS. (*speaking together*).
You know, she has the most extraordinary quickness of ear:

PICKERING.
I assure you, my dear Mrs. Higgins, that girl

HIGGINS.
just like a parrot. Ive tried her with every

PICKERING.
is a genius. She can play the piano quite beautifully.

HIGGINS.
possible sort of sound that a human being can make—

PICKERING.
We have taken her to classical concerts and to music

HIGGINS.
Continental dialects, African dialects, Hottentot

PICKERING.
halls; and it's all the same to her: she plays everything

HIGGINS.
clicks, things it took me years to get hold of; and

PICKERING.
she hears right off when she comes home, whether it's

HIGGINS.
she picks them up like a shot, right away, as if she had

PICKERING.
Beethoven and Brahms or Lehar and Lionel Monckton;[7]

HIGGINS.
PICKERING.
been at it all her life.
though six months ago, she'd never as much as touched a piano—

MRS. HIGGINS (*putting her fingers in her ears, as they are by this time shouting one another down with an intolerable noise*). Sh-sh-sh-sh! (*They stop.*)

PICKERING. I beg your pardon. (*He draws his chair back apologetically.*)

HIGGINS. Sorry. When Pickering starts shouting nobody can get a word in edgeways.

MRS. HIGGINS. Be quiet, Henry. Colonel Pickering: dont you realize that when Eliza walked into Wimpole Street, something walked in with her?

PICKERING. Her father did. But Henry soon got rid of him.

MRS. HIGGINS. It would have been more to the point if her mother had. But as her mother didnt something else did.

PICKERING. But what?

MRS. HIGGINS (*unconsciously dating herself by the word*). A problem.

PICKERING. Oh, I see. The problem of how to pass her off as a lady.

HIGGINS. I'll solve that problem. Ive half solved it already.

MRS. HIGGINS. No, you two infinitely stupid male creatures; the problem of what is to be done with her afterwards.

HIGGINS. I dont see anything in that. She can go her own way, with all the advantages I have given her.

MRS. HIGGINS. The advantages of that poor woman who was here just now! The manners and habits that disqualify a fine lady from earning her own living without giving her a fine lady's income! Is that what you mean?

PICKERING (*indulgently, being rather bored*). Oh, that will be all right, Mrs. Higgins. (*He rises to go.*)

HIGGINS (*rising also*). We'll find her some light employment.

PICKERING. She's happy enough. Dont you worry about her. Goodbye. (*He shakes hands as if he were consoling a frightened child, and makes for the door.*)

HIGGINS. Anyhow, theres no good bothering now. The thing's done. Goodbye, mother. (*He kisses her, and follows* PICKERING.)

PICKERING (*turning for a final consolation*). There are plenty of openings. We'll do whats right. Goodbye.

HIGGINS (*to* PICKERING *as they go out together*).

---

7. **Lehar and Lionel Monckton,** popular composers of light music.

Let's take her to the Shakespear exhibition at Earls Court.

PICKERING. Yes: lets. Her remarks will be delicious.

HIGGINS. She'll mimic all the people for us when we get home.

PICKERING. Ripping. (*Both are heard laughing as they go downstairs.*)

MRS. HIGGINS (*rises with an impatient bounce, and returns to her work at the writing-table. She sweeps a litter of disarranged papers out of her way; snatches a sheet of paper from her stationery case; and tries resolutely to write. At the third line she gives it up; flings down her pen; grips the table angrily and exclaims*). Oh, men! men!! men!!!*

Act Four

The Wimpole Street laboratory. Midnight. Nobody in the room. The clock on the mantelpiece strikes twelve. The fire is not alight: it is a summer night.

Presently HIGGINS *and* PICKERING *are heard on the stairs.*

HIGGINS (*calling down to* PICKERING). I say, Pick: lock up, will you? I shant be going out again.

PICKERING. Right. Can Mrs. Pearce go to bed? We dont want anything more, do we?

HIGGINS. Lord, no!

ELIZA *opens the door and is seen on the lighted landing in all the finery in which she has just won* HIGGINS's *bet for him. She comes to the hearth, and switches on the electric lights there. She is tired: her pallor contrasts strongly with her dark eyes and hair; and her expression is almost tragic. She takes off her cloak; puts her fan and flowers on the piano; and sits down on the bench, brooding and silent.* HIGGINS, *in evening dress, with overcoat and hat, comes in, carrying a smoking jacket which he has picked up downstairs. He takes off the hat and overcoat; throws them carelessly on the newspaper stand; disposes of his coat in the same way; puts on the smoking jacket; and throws himself wearily into the easy-chair at the hearth.* PICKERING, *similarly attired, comes in.*

He also takes off his hat and overcoat, and is about to throw them on HIGGINS's *when he hesitates.*

PICKERING. I say: Mrs. Pearce will row if we leave these things lying about in the drawing room.

HIGGINS. Oh, chuck them over the bannisters into the hall. She'll find them there in the morning and put them away all right. She'll think we were drunk.

PICKERING. We are, slightly. Are there any letters?

HIGGINS. I didnt look. (PICKERING *takes the overcoats and goes downstairs.* HIGGINS *begins half singing half yawning an air from* La Fanciulla del Golden West.[1] *Suddenly he stops and exclaims*) I wonder where the devil my slippers are!

ELIZA *looks at him darkly; then rises suddenly and leaves the room.*

HIGGINS *yawns again, and resumes his song.*

PICKERING *returns, with the contents of the letter-box in his hand.*

PICKERING. Only circulars, and this coroneted billet-doux[2] for you. (*He throws the circulars into the fender, and posts himself on the hearthrug, with his back to the grate.*)

HIGGINS (*glancing at the billet-doux*). Money-lender. (*He throws the letter after the circulars.*) ELIZA *returns with a pair of large down-at-heel slippers. She places them on the carpet before* HIGGINS, *and sits as before without a word.*

HIGGINS (*yawning again*). Oh Lord! What an evening! What a crew! What a silly tomfoolery! (*He raises his shoe to unlace it, and catches sight of the slippers. He stops unlacing and looks at them as if they had appeared there of their own accord.*) Oh! Theyre there, are they?

PICKERING (*stretching himself*). Well, I feel a bit tired. It's been a long day. The garden party, a dinner party, and the opera! Rather too much of a good thing. But youve won your bet, Hig-

---

1. *La Fanciulla del Golden West,* The Girl of the Golden West, an opera by Puccini that opened in New York in 1910.
2. *coroneted billet-doux.* A billet-doux (bil'ā dü') is a love letter. This one bears a coronet, or crown, indicating that it is from someone of noble birth; but Higgins's response seems to indicate that the writer is an upstart.

gins. Eliza did the trick, and something to spare, eh?

HIGGINS (*fervently*). Thank God it's over!

ELIZA *flinches violently; but they take no notice of her; and she recovers herself and sits stonily as before.*

PICKERING. Were you nervous at the garden party! *I* was. Eliza didnt seem a bit nervous.

HIGGINS. Oh, she wasnt nervous. I knew she'd be all right. No: it's the strain of putting the job through all these months that has told on me. It was interesting enough at first, while we were at the phonetics; but after that I got deadly sick of it. If I hadnt backed myself to do it I should have chucked the whole thing up two months ago. It was a silly notion: the whole thing has been a bore.

PICKERING. Oh come! the garden party was frightfully exciting. My heart began beating like anything.

HIGGINS. Yes, for the first three minutes. But when I saw we were going to win hands down, I felt like a bear in a cage, hanging about doing nothing. The dinner was worse: sitting gorging there for over an hour, with nobody but a damned fool of a fashionable woman to talk to! I tell you, Pickering, never again for me. No more artificial duchesses. The whole thing has been simple purgatory.

PICKERING. Youve never been broken in properly to the social routine. (*Strolling over to the piano*) I rather enjoy dipping into it occasionally myself: it makes me feel young again. Anyhow, it was a great success: an immense success. I was quite frightened once or twice because Eliza was doing it so well. You see, lots of the real people cant do it at all: theyre such fools that they think style comes by nature to people in their position; and so they never learn. Theres always something professional about doing a thing superlatively well.

HIGGINS. Yes: thats what drives me mad: the silly people dont know their own silly business. (*Rising*) However, it's over and done with; and now I can go to bed at last without dreading tomorrow.

ELIZA's *beauty becomes murderous.*

PICKERING. I think I shall turn in too. Still, it's been a great occasion: a triumph for you. Goodnight. (*He goes.*)

HIGGINS (*following him*). Goodnight. (*Over his shoulder, at the door*) Put out the lights, Eliza; and tell Mrs. Pearce not to make coffee for me in the morning: I'll take tea. (*He goes out.*)

ELIZA *tries to control herself and feel indifferent as she rises and walks across to the hearth to switch off the lights. By the time she gets there she is on the point of screaming. She sits down in* HIGGINS's *chair and holds on hard to the arms. Finally she gives way and flings herself furiously on the floor, raging.*

HIGGINS (*in despairing wrath outside*). What the devil have I done with my slippers? (*He appears at the door.*)

LIZA (*snatching up the slippers, and hurling them at him one after the other with all her force*). There are your slippers. And there. Take your slippers; and may you never have a day's luck with them!

HIGGINS (*astounded*). What on earth—! (*He comes to her.*) What's the matter? Get up. (*He pulls her up.*) Anything wrong?

LIZA (*breathless*). Nothing wrong—with you. Ive won your bet for you, havnt I? Thats enough for you. *I* dont matter, I suppose.

HIGGINS. You won my bet! You! Presumptuous insect! *I* won it. What did you throw those slippers at me for?

LIZA. Because I wanted to smash your face. I'd like to kill you, you selfish brute. Why didnt you leave me where you picked me out of—in the gutter? You thank God it's all over, and that now you can throw me back again there, do you? (*She crisps her fingers*[3] *frantically.*)

HIGGINS (*looking at her in cool wonder*). The creature is nervous, after all.

LIZA (*gives a suffocated scream of fury, and instinctively darts her nails at his face*)!!

HIGGINS (*catching her wrists*). Ah! would you? Claws in, you cat. How dare you show your temper to me? Sit down and be quiet. (*He throws her roughly into the easy-chair.*)

LIZA (*crushed by superior strength and weight*). Whats to become of me? Whats to become of me?

HIGGINS. How the devil do I know whats to become of you? What does it matter what becomes of you?

---

3. **crisps her fingers,** clenches and relaxes her fists.

LIZA. You dont care. I know you dont care. You wouldnt care if I was dead. I'm nothing to you—not so much as them slippers.

HIGGINS (*thundering*). Those slippers.

LIZA (*with bitter submission*). Those slippers. I didnt think it made any difference now.

A pause. ELIZA *hopeless and crushed.* HIGGINS *a little uneasy.*

HIGGINS (*in his loftiest manner*). Why have you begun going on like this? May I ask whether you complain of your treatment here?

LIZA. No.

HIGGINS. Has anybody behaved badly to you? Colonel Pickering? Mrs. Pearce? Any of the servants?

LIZA. No.

HIGGINS. I presume you dont pretend that *I* have treated you badly?

LIZA. No.

HIGGINS. I am glad to hear it. (*He moderates his tone.*) Perhaps youre tired after the strain of the day. Will you have a glass of champagne? (*He moves toward the door.*)

LIZA. No. (*Recollecting her manners*) Thank you.

HIGGINS (*good-humored again*). This has been coming on you for some days. I suppose it was natural for you to be anxious about the garden party. But thats all over now. (*He pats her kindly on the shoulder. She writhes.*) Theres nothing more to worry about.

LIZA. No. Nothing more for you to worry about. (*She suddenly rises and gets away from him by going to the piano bench, where she sits and hides her face.*) Oh God! I wish I was dead.

HIGGINS (*staring after her in sincere surprise*). Why? In heaven's name, why? (*Reasonably, going to her*) Listen to me, Eliza. All this irritation is purely subjective.

LIZA. I dont understand. I'm too ignorant.

HIGGINS. It's only imagination. Low spirits and nothing else. Nobody's hurting you. Nothing's wrong. You go to bed like a good girl and sleep it off. Have a little cry and say your prayers: that will make you comfortable.

LIZA. I heard your prayers. "Thank God it's all over!"

HIGGINS (*impatiently*). Well, dont you thank God it's all over? Now you are free and can do what you like.

LIZA (*pulling herself together in desperation*). What am I fit for? What have you left me fit for? Where am I to go? What am I to do? Whats to become of me?

HIGGINS (*enlightened, but not at all impressed*). Oh thats whats worrying you, is it? (*He thrusts his hands into his pockets, and walks about in his usual manner, rattling the contents of his pockets, as if condescending to a trivial subject out of pure kindness.*) I shouldnt bother about it if I were you. I should imagine you wont have much difficulty in settling yourself somewhere or other, though I hadnt quite realized that you were going away. (*She looks quickly at him: he does not look at her, but examines the dessert stand on the piano and decides that he will eat an apple.*) You might marry, you know. (*He bites a large piece out of the apple and munches it noisily.*) You see, Eliza, all men are not confirmed old bachelors like me and the Colonel. Most men are the marrying sort (poor devils!); and youre not bad-looking: it's quite a pleasure to look at you sometimes—not now, of course, because youre crying and looking as ugly as the very devil; but when youre all right and quite yourself, youre what I should call attractive. That is, to the people in the marrying line, you understand. You go to bed and have a good nice rest; and then get up and look at yourself in the glass; and you wont feel so cheap.

ELIZA *again looks at him, speechless, and does not stir.*

The look is quite lost on him: he eats his apple with a dreamy expression of happiness, as it is quite a good one.

HIGGINS (*a genial afterthought occurring to him*). I daresay my mother could find some chap or other who would do very well.

LIZA. We were above that at the corner of Tottenham Court Road.

HIGGINS (*waking up*). What do you mean?

LIZA. I sold flowers. I didnt sell myself. Now youve made a lady of me I'm not fit to sell anything else. I wish youd left me where you found me.

HIGGINS (*slinging the core of the apple decisively into the grate*). Tosh, Eliza. Dont you insult human relations by dragging all this cant about buying and selling into it. You neednt marry the fellow if you dont like him.

LIZA. What else am I to do?

HIGGINS. Oh, lots of things. What about your old idea of a florist's shop? Pickering could set you up in one: he's lots of money. (*Chuckling*) He'll have to pay for all those togs you have been wearing to-day; and that, with the hire of the jewellery you will make a big hole in two hundred pounds. Why, six months ago you would have thought it the millennium to have a flower shop of your own. Come! youll be all right. I must clear off to bed: I'm devilish sleepy. By the way, I came down for something: I forget what it was.

LIZA. Your slippers.

HIGGINS. Oh yes, of course. You shied them at me. (*He picks them up, and is going out when she rises and speaks to him.*)

LIZA. Before you go, sir—

HIGGINS (*dropping the slippers in his surprise at her calling him* sir). Eh?

LIZA. Do my clothes belong to me or to Colonel Pickering?

HIGGINS (*coming back into the room as if her question were the very climax of unreason*). What the devil use would they be to Pickering?

LIZA. He might want them for the next girl you pick up to experiment on.

HIGGINS (*shocked and hurt*). Is that the way you feel towards us?

LIZA. I dont want to hear anything more about that. All I want to know is whether anything belongs to me. My own clothes were burnt.

HIGGINS. But what does it matter? Why need you start bothering about that in the middle of the night?

LIZA. I want to know what I may take away with me. I dont want to be accused of stealing.

HIGGINS (*now deeply wounded*). Stealing! You shouldnt have said that, Eliza. That shews a want of feeling.

LIZA. I'm sorry. I'm only a common ignorant girl; and in my station I have to be careful. There cant be any feelings between the like of you and the like of me. Please will you tell me what belongs to me and what doesnt?

HIGGINS (*very sulky*). You may take the whole damned houseful if you like. Except the jewels. Theyre hired. Will that satisfy you? (*He turns on his heel and is about to go in extreme dudgeon.*)

LIZA (*drinking in his emotion like nectar, and nagging him to provoke a further supply*). Stop, please. (*She takes off her jewels.*) Will you take these to your room and keep them safe? I dont want to run the risk of their being missing.

HIGGINS (*furious*). Hand them over. (*She puts them into his hands.*) If these belonged to me instead of to the jeweller, I'd ram them down your ungrateful throat. (*He perfunctorily thrusts them into his pockets, unconsciously decorating himself with the protruding ends of the chains.*)

LIZA (*taking a ring off*). This ring isnt the jeweller's: it's the one you bought me in Brighton. I dont want it now. (HIGGINS *dashes the ring violently into the fireplace, and turns on her so threateningly that she crouches over the piano with her hands over her face, and exclaims*) Dont you hit me.

HIGGINS. Hit you! You infamous creature, how dare you accuse me of such a thing? It is you who have hit me. You have wounded me to the heart.

LIZA (*thrilling with hidden joy*). I'm glad. Ive got a little of my own back, anyhow.

HIGGINS (*with dignity, in his finest professional style*). You have caused me to lose my temper: a thing that has hardly ever happened to me before. I prefer to say nothing more tonight. I am going to bed.

LIZA (*pertly*). Youd better leave a note for Mrs. Pearce about the coffee; for she wont be told by me.

HIGGINS (*formally*). Damn Mrs. Pearce; and damn the coffee; and damn you; and damn my own folly in having lavished hard-earned knowledge and the treasure of my regard and intimacy on a heartless guttersnipe. (*He goes out with impressive decorum, and spoils it by slamming the door savagely.*)

ELIZA *goes down on her knees on the hearthrug to look for the ring.*

Act Five

MRS. HIGGINS's *drawing room. She is at her writing-table as before.* THE PARLOR-MAID *comes in.*

THE PARLOR-MAID *(at the door)*. Mr. Henry, maam, is downstairs with Colonel Pickering.

MRS. HIGGINS. Well, show them up.

THE PARLOR-MAID. Theyre using the telephone, maam. Telephoning to the police, I think.

MRS. HIGGINS. What!

THE PARLOR-MAID *(coming further in and lowering her voice)*. Mr. Henry is in a state, maam. I thought I'd better tell you.

MRS. HIGGINS. If you had told me that Mr. Henry was not in a state it would have been more surprising. Tell them to come up when theyve finished with the police. I suppose he's lost something.

THE PARLOR-MAID. Yes, maam *(going)*.

MRS. HIGGINS. Go upstairs and tell Miss Doolittle that Mr. Henry and the Colonel are here. Ask her not to come down til I send for her.

THE PARLOR-MAID. Yes, maam.

HIGGINS *bursts in. He is, as* THE PARLOR-MAID *has said, in a state.*

HIGGINS. Look here, mother: heres a confounded thing!

MRS. HIGGINS. Yes, dear. Good morning. *(He checks his impatience and kisses her, whilst* THE PARLOR-MAID *goes out)*. What is it?

HIGGINS. Eliza's bolted.

MRS. HIGGINS *(calmly continuing her writing)*. You must have frightened her.

HIGGINS. Frightened her! nonsense! She was left last night, as usual, to turn out the lights and all that; and instead of going to bed she changed her clothes and went right off: her bed wasn't slept in. She came in a cab for her things before seven this morning; and that fool Mrs. Pearce let her have them without telling me a word about it. What am I to do?

MRS. HIGGINS. Do without, I'm afraid, Henry. The girl has a perfect right to leave if she chooses.

HIGGINS *(wandering distractedly across the room)*. But I cant find anything. I dont know what appointments Ive got. I'm—(PICKERING *comes in.* MRS. HIGGINS *puts down her pen and turns away from the writing-table.)*

PICKERING *(shaking hands)*. Good morning, Mrs. Higgins. Has Henry told you? *(He sits down on the ottoman.)*

HIGGINS. What does that ass of an inspector say? Have you offered a reward?

MRS. HIGGINS *(rising in indignant amazement)*. You dont mean to say you have set the police after Eliza.

HIGGINS. Of course. What are the police for? What else could we do? *(He sits in the Elizabethan chair.)*

PICKERING. The inspector made a lot of difficulties. I really think he suspected us of some improper purpose.

MRS. HIGGINS. Well, of course he did. What right have you to go to the police and give the girl's name as if she were a thief, or a lost umbrella, or something? Really! *(She sits down again, deeply vexed.)*

HIGGINS. But we want to find her.

PICKERING. We cant let her go like this, you know, Mrs. Higgins. What were we to do?

MRS. HIGGINS. You have no more sense, either of you, than two children. Why—

THE PARLOR-MAID *comes in and breaks off the conversation.*

THE PARLOR-MAID. Mr. Henry: a gentleman wants to see you very particular. He's been sent on from Wimpole Street.

HIGGINS. Oh, bother! I cant see anyone now. Who is it?

THE PARLOR-MAID. A Mr. Doolittle, sir.

PICKERING. Doolittle! Do you mean the dustman?

THE PARLOR-MAID. Dustman! Oh no, sir: a gentleman.

HIGGINS *(springing up excitedly)*. By George, Pick, it's some relative of hers that she's gone to. Somebody we know nothing about. *(To* THE PARLOR-MAID) Send him up, quick.

THE PARLOR-MAID. Yes, sir. *(She goes.)*

HIGGINS *(eagerly, going to his mother)*. Genteel relatives! now we shall hear something. *(He sits down in the Chippendale chair.)*

MRS. HIGGINS. Do you know any of her people?

PICKERING. Only her father: the fellow we told you about.

THE PARLOR-MAID (*announcing.*) Mr. Doolittle. (*She withdraws.*)

DOOLITTLE *enters. He is resplendently dressed as for a fashionable wedding, and might, in fact, be the bridegroom. A flower in his button-hole, a dazzling silk hat, and patent leather shoes complete the effect. He is too concerned with the business he has come on to notice* MRS. HIGGINS. *He walks straight to* HIGGINS, *and accosts him with vehement reproach.*

DOOLITTLE (*indicating his own person*). See here! Do you see this? You done this.

HIGGINS. Done what, man?

DOOLITTLE. This, I tell you. Look at it. Look at this hat. Look at this coat.

PICKERING. Has Eliza been buying you clothes?

DOOLITTLE. Eliza! not she. Not half. Why would she buy me clothes?

MRS. HIGGINS. Good morning, Mr. Doolittle. Wont you sit down?

DOOLITTLE (*taken aback as he becomes conscious that he has forgotten his hostess*). Asking your pardon, maam. (*He approaches her and shakes her proffered hand.*) Thank you. (*He sits down on the ottoman, on* PICKERING'S *right.*) I am that full of what has happened to me that I cant think of anything else.

HIGGINS. What the dickens has happened to you?

DOOLITTLE. I shouldnt mind if it had only happened to me: anything might happen to anybody and nobody to blame but Providence, as you might say. But this is something that you done to me: yes, you, Enry Iggins.

HIGGINS. Have you found Eliza? Thats the point.

DOOLITTLE. Have you lost her?

HIGGINS. Yes.

DOOLITTLE. You have all the luck, you have. I aint found her; but she'll find me quick enough now after what you done to me.

MRS. HIGGINS. But what has my son done to you, Mr. Doolittle?

DOOLITTLE. Done to me! Ruined me. Destroyed my happiness. Tied me up and delivered me into the hands of middle-class morality.

HIGGINS (*rising intolerantly and standing over* DOOLITTLE). Youre raving. Youre drunk. Youre mad. I gave you five pounds. After that I had two conversations with you, at half-a-crown an hour. Ive never seen you since.

DOOLITTLE. Oh! Drunk! am I? Mad? am I? Tell me this. Did you or did you not write a letter to an old blighter in America that was giving five millions to found Moral Reform Societies all over the world, and that wanted you to invent a universal language for him?

HIGGINS. What! Ezra D. Wannafeller! He's dead. (*He sits down again carelessly.*)

DOOLITTLE. Yes: he's dead; and I'm done for. Now did you or did you not write a letter to him to say that the most original moralist at present in England, to the best of your knowledge, was Alfred Doolittle, a common dustman.

HIGGINS. Oh, after your last visit I remember making some silly joke of the kind.

DOOLITTLE. Ah! you may well call it a silly joke. It put the lid on me right enough. Just give him the chance he wanted to show that Americans is not like us: that they recognize and respect merit in every class of life, however humble. Them words is in his blooming will, in which, Henry Higgins, thanks to your silly joking, he leaves me a share in his Pre-digested Cheese Trust worth three thousand a year on condition that I lecture for his Wannafeller Moral Reform and World League as often as they ask me up to six times a year.

HIGGINS. The devil he does! Whew! (*Brightening suddenly*) What a lark!

PICKERING. A safe thing for you, Doolittle. They wont ask you twice.

DOOLITTLE. It aint the lecturing I mind. I'll lecture them blue in the face, I will, and not turn a hair. It's making a gentleman of me that I object to. Who asked him to make a gentleman of me? I was happy. I was free. I touched pretty nigh everybody for money when I wanted it, same as I touched you, Enry Iggins. Now I am worrited; tied neck and heels; and everybody touches me for money. It's a fine thing for you, says my solicitor. Is it? says I. You mean it's a good thing for you, I says. When I was a poor man and had a solicitor once when they found a pram in the dust cart, he got me off, and got shut of me and got me shut of him as quick as he could. Same with the doctors: used to shove me out of the hospital before I could hardly stand on my legs, and nothing to pay. Now they finds out that I'm not a healthy man and cant live unless they looks after me twice a day. In the house I'm not let do a hand's turn for myself: somebody else must do it and touch me for it. A year ago I hadnt a relative in the world except two or three that wouldnt speak to me. Now Ive fifty, and not a decent week's wages among the lot of them. I have to live for others and not for myself: thats middle-class morality. You talk of losing Eliza. Dont you be anxious: I bet she's on my doorstep by this: she that could support herself easy by selling flowers if I wasnt respectable. And the next one to touch me will be you, Enry Iggins. I'll have to learn to speak middle-class language from you, instead of speaking proper English. Thats where youll come in; and I daresay thats what you done it for.

MRS. HIGGINS. But, my dear Mr. Doolittle, you need not suffer all this if you are really in earnest. Nobody can force you to accept this bequest. You can repudiate it. Isnt that so, Colonel Pickering?

PICKERING. I believe so.

DOOLITTLE (*softening his manner in deference to her sex*). Thats the tragedy of it, maam. It's easy to say chuck it; but I havnt the nerve. Which of us has? We're all intimidated. Intimidated, maam: thats what we are. What is there for me if I chuck it but the workhouse in my old age? I have to dye my hair already to keep my job as a dustman. If I was one of the deserving poor, and had put by a bit, I could chuck it; but then why should I, acause the deserving poor might as well be millionaires for all the happiness they ever has. They dont know what happiness is. But I, as one of the undeserving poor, have nothing between me and the pauper's uniform but this here blasted three thousand a year that shoves me into the middle class. (Excuse the expression, maam: youd use it yourself if you had my provocation.) Theyve got you every way you turn: it's a choice between the Skilly of the workhouse and the Char Bydis of the middle class;[1] and I havnt the nerve for the workhouse. Intimidated: thats what I am. Broke. Brought up. Happier men than me will call for my dust, and touch me for their tip; and I'll look on helpless, and envy them. And thats what your son has brought me to. (*He is overcome by emotion.*)

MRS. HIGGINS. Well, I'm very glad youre not going to do anything foolish, Mr. Doolittle. For this solves the problem of Eliza's future. You can provide for her now.

DOOLITTLE (*with melancholy resignation*). Yes, maam: I'm expected to provide for everyone now, out of three thousand a year.

HIGGINS (*jumping up*). Nonsense! he cant provide for her. He shant provide for her. She doesnt belong to him. I paid him five pounds for her. Doolittle: either youre an honest man or a rogue.

DOOLITTLE (*tolerantly*). A little of both, Henry, like the rest of us: a little of both.

HIGGINS. Well, you took that money for the girl; and you have no right to take her as well.

MRS. HIGGINS. Henry: dont be absurd. If you want to know where Eliza is, she is upstairs.

HIGGINS (*amazed*). Upstairs!!! Then I shall jolly soon fetch her downstairs. (*He makes resolutely for the door.*)

MRS. HIGGINS (*rising and following him*). Be quiet, Henry. Sit down.

HIGGINS. I—

MRS. HIGGINS. Sit down, dear; and listen to me.

HIGGINS. Oh very well, very well, very well. (*He throws himself ungraciously on the ottoman, with his face towards the windows.*) But I think you might have told us this half an hour ago.

MRS. HIGGINS. Eliza came to me this morning. She told me of the brutal way you two treated her.

HIGGINS (*bounding up again*). What!

PICKERING (*rising also*). My dear Mrs. Higgins, she's been telling you stories. We didn't treat her brutally. We hardly said a word to her; and we parted on particularly good terms. (*Turning on* HIGGINS) Higgins: did you bully her after I went to bed?

HIGGINS. Just the other way about. She threw my slippers in my face. She behaved in the most outrageous way. I never gave her the slightest provocation. The slippers came bang into my face the moment I entered the room—before I

---

1. **Skilly . . . Char Bydis of the middle class.** Doolittle is referring to Scylla (sil'ə) and Charybdis (kə rib'dis). In the narrow strait that separates Italy and Sicily there is a dangerous rock and a whirlpool, which the ancient Greeks named Scylla and Charybdis. The expression "to be between Scylla and Charybdis" means to be between two evils, either one of which can be safely avoided only by risking the other.

had uttered a word. And used perfectly awful language.

PICKERING (*astonished*). But why? What did we do to her?

MRS. HIGGINS. I think I know pretty well what you did. The girl is naturally rather affectionate, I think. Isnt she, Mr. Doolittle?

DOOLITTLE. Very tender-hearted, maam. Takes after me.

MRS. HIGGINS. Just so. She had become attached to you both. She worked very hard for you, Henry! I dont think you quite realize what anything in the nature of brain work means to a girl like that. Well, it seems that when the great day of trial came, and she did this wonderful thing for you without making a single mistake, you two sat there and never said a word to her, but talked together of how glad you were that it was all over and how you had been bored with the whole thing. And then you were surprised because she threw your slippers at you! *I* should have thrown the fire-irons at you.

HIGGINS. We said nothing except that we were tired and wanted to go to bed. Did we, Pick?

PICKERING (*shrugging his shoulders*). That was all.

MRS. HIGGINS (*ironically*). Quite sure?

PICKERING. Absolutely. Really, that was all.

MRS. HIGGINS. You didnt thank her, or pet her, or admire her, or tell her how splendid she'd been.

HIGGINS (*impatiently*). But she knew all about that. We didnt make speeches to her, if thats what you mean.

PICKERING (*conscience stricken*). Perhaps we were a little inconsiderate. Is she very angry?

MRS. HIGGINS (*returning to her place at the writing-table*). Well, I'm afraid she wont go back to Wimpole Street, especially now that Mr. Doolittle is able to keep up the position you have thrust on her; but she says she is quite willing to meet you on friendly terms and to let bygones be bygones.

HIGGINS (*furious*). Is she, by George? Ho!

MRS. HIGGINS. If you promise to behave yourself, Henry, I'll ask her to come down. If not, go home; for you have taken up quite enough of my time.

HIGGINS. Oh, all right. Very well. Pick: you behave yourself. Let us put on our best Sunday manners for this creature that we picked out of the mud. *(He flings himself sulkily into the Elizabethan chair.)*

DOOLITTLE *(remonstrating)*. Now, now, Enry Iggins! have some consideration for my feelings as a middle-class man.

MRS. HIGGINS. Remember your promise, Henry. *(She presses the bell-button on the writing-table.)* Mr. Doolittle: will you be so good as to step out on the balcony for a moment. I dont want Eliza to have the shock of your news until she has made it up with these two gentlemen. Would you mind?

DOOLITTLE. As you wish, lady. Anything to help Henry to keep her off my hands. *(He disappears through the window.)*

THE PARLOR-MAID *answers the bell.* PICKERING *sits down in* DOOLITTLE's *place.*

MRS. HIGGINS. Ask Miss Doolittle to come down, please.

THE PARLOR-MAID. Yes, maam. *(She goes out.)*

MRS. HIGGINS. Now, Henry: be good.

HIGGINS. I am behaving myself perfectly.

PICKERING. He is doing his best, Mrs. Higgins. *A pause.* HIGGINS *throws back his head; stretches out his legs; and begins to whistle.*

MRS. HIGGINS. Henry, dearest, you dont look at all nice in that attitude.

HIGGINS *(pulling himself together)*. I was not trying to look nice, mother.

MRS. HIGGINS. It doesnt matter, dear. I only wanted to make you speak.

HIGGINS. Why?

MRS. HIGGINS. Because you cant speak and whistle at the same time.

HIGGINS *groans. Another very trying pause.*

HIGGINS *(springing up, out of patience)*. Where the devil is that girl? Are we to wait here all day?

ELIZA *enters, sunny, self-possessed, and giving a staggeringly convincing exhibition of ease of manner. She carries a little work-basket, and is very much at home.* PICKERING *is too much taken aback to rise.*

LIZA. How do you do, Professor Higgins? Are you quite well?

HIGGINS *(choking)*. Am I—*(He can say no more.)*

LIZA. But of course you are: you are never ill. So glad to see you again, Colonel Pickering. *(He rises hastily; and they shake hands.)* Quite

chilly this morning, isnt it? *(She sits down on his left. He sits beside her.)*

HIGGINS. Dont you dare try this game on me. I taught it to you; and it doesnt take me in. Get up and come home; and dont be a fool.

ELIZA *takes a piece of needlework from her basket, and begins to stitch at it, without taking the least notice of this outburst.*

MRS. HIGGINS. Very nicely put, indeed, Henry. No woman could resist such an invitation.

HIGGINS. You let her alone, mother. Let her speak for herself. You will jolly soon see whether she has an idea that I havnt put into her head or a word that I havnt put into her mouth. I tell you I have created this thing out of the squashed cabbage leaves of Covent Garden; and now she pretends to play the fine lady with me.

MRS. HIGGINS *(placidly)*. Yes, dear; but youll sit down, wont you?

HIGGINS *sits down again, savagely.*

LIZA *(to* PICKERING, *taking no apparent notice of* HIGGINS, *and working away deftly)*. Will you drop me altogether now that the experiment is over, Colonel Pickering?

PICKERING. Oh dont. You mustnt think of it as an experiment. It shocks me, somehow.

LIZA. Oh, I'm only a squashed cabbage leaf—

PICKERING *(impulsively)*. No.

LIZA *(continuing quietly)*—but I owe so much to you that I should be very unhappy if you forgot me.

PICKERING. It's very kind of you to say so, Miss Doolittle.

LIZA. It's not because you paid for my dresses. I know you are generous to everybody with money. But it was from you that I learnt really nice manners; and that is what makes one a lady, isn't it? You see it was so difficult for me with the example of Professor Higgins always before me. I was brought up to be just like him, unable to control myself, and using bad language on the slightest provocation. And I should never have known that ladies and gentlemen didnt behave like that if you hadnt been there.

HIGGINS. Well!!

PICKERING. Oh, thats only his way, you know. He doesnt mean it.

LIZA. Oh, *I* didnt mean it either, when I was a

flower girl. It was only my way. But you see I did it; and thats what makes the difference after all.

PICKERING. No doubt. Still, he taught you to speak; and I couldn't have done that, you know.

LIZA *(trivially)*. Of course: that is his profession.

HIGGINS. Damnation!

LIZA *(continuing)*. It was just like learning to dance in the fashionable way: there was nothing more than that in it. But do you know what began my real education?

PICKERING. What?

LIZA *(stopping her work for a moment)*. Your calling me Miss Doolittle that day when I first came to Wimpole Street. That was the beginning of self-respect for me. *(She resumes her stitching.)* And there were a hundred little things you never noticed, because they came naturally to you. Things about standing up and taking off your hat and opening doors—

PICKERING. Oh, that was nothing.

LIZA. Yes: things that showed you thought and felt about me as if I were something better than a scullery-maid; though of course I know you would have been just the same to a scullery-maid if she had been let into the drawing room. You never took off your boots in the dining room when I was there.

PICKERING. You mustnt mind that. Higgins takes off his boots all over the place.

LIZA. I know. I am not blaming him. It is his way, isnt it? But it made such a difference to me that you didnt do it. You see, really and truly, apart from the things anyone can pick up (the dressing and the proper way of speaking, and so on), the difference between a lady and a flower girl is not how she behaves, but how she's treated. I shall always be a flower girl to Professor Higgins, because he always treats me as a flower girl, and always will; but I know I can be a lady to you, because you always treat me as a lady, and always will.

MRS. HIGGINS. Please dont grind your teeth, Henry.

PICKERING. Well, this is really very nice of you, Miss Doolittle.

LIZA. I should like you to call me Eliza, now, if you would.

PICKERING. Thank you, Eliza, of course.

LIZA. And I should like Professor Higgins to call me Miss Doolittle.

HIGGINS. I'll see you damned first.

MRS. HIGGINS. Henry! Henry!

PICKERING (*laughing*). Why dont you slang back at him? Dont stand it. It would do him a lot of good.

LIZA. I cant. I could have done it once; but now I cant go back to it. You told me, you know, that when a child is brought to a foreign country, it picks up the language in a few weeks, and forgets its own. Well, I am a child in your country. I have forgotten my own language, and can speak nothing but yours. Thats the real break-off with the corner of Tottenham Court Road. Leaving Wimpole Street finishes it.

PICKERING (*much alarmed*). Oh! but youre coming back to Wimpole Street, arnt you? Youll forgive Higgins?

HIGGINS (*rising*). Forgive! Will she, by George! Let her go. Let her find out how she can get on without us. She will relapse into the gutter in three weeks without me at her elbow.

DOOLITTLE *appears at the center window. With a look of dignified reproach at* HIGGINS,

he comes slowly and silently to his daughter, who, with her back to the window, is unconscious of his approach.

PICKERING. He's incorrigible, Eliza. You wont relapse, will you?

LIZA. No: not now. Never again. I have learnt my lesson. I dont believe I could utter one of the old sounds if I tried. (DOOLITTLE *touches her on her left shoulder. She drops her work, losing her self-possession utterly at the spectacle of her father's splendor.*) A-a-a-a-a-ah-ow-ooh!

HIGGINS (*with a crow of triumph*). Aha! Just so. A-a-a-a-ahowooh! A-a-a-a-ahowooh! A-a-a-a-ahowooh! Victory! Victory! (*He throws himself on the divan, folding his arms, and spraddling arrogantly.*)

DOOLITTLE. Can you blame the girl? Dont look at me like that, Eliza. It aint my fault. Ive come into some money.

LIZA. You must have touched a millionaire this time, dad.

DOOLITTLE. I have. But I'm dressed something special today. I'm going to St. George's, Hanover Square.[2] Your stepmother is going to marry me.

LIZA (*angrily*). Youre going to let yourself down to marry that low common woman!

PICKERING (*quietly*). He ought to, Eliza. (*To* DOOLITTLE) Why has she changed her mind?

DOOLITTLE (*sadly*). Intimidated, Governor. Intimidated. Middle-class morality claims its victim. Wont you put on your hat, Liza, and come and see me turned off?

LIZA. If the Colonel says I must, I—I'll (*almost sobbing*) I'll demean myself. And get insulted for my pains, like enough.

DOOLITTLE. Dont be afraid: she never comes to words with anyone now, poor woman! respectability has broke all the spirit out of her.

PICKERING (*squeezing* ELIZA's *elbow gently*). Be kind to them, Eliza. Make the best of it.

LIZA (*forcing a little smile for him through her vexation*). Oh well, just to shew theres no ill feeling. I'll be back in a moment. (*She goes out.*)

DOOLITTLE (*sitting down beside* PICKERING). I feel uncommon nervous about the ceremony,

---

2. **St. George's, Hanover Square,** a church where many fashionable weddings took place.

Colonel. I wish youd come and see me through it.

PICKERING. But youve been through it before, man. You were married to Eliza's mother.

DOOLITTLE. Who told you that, Colonel?

PICKERING. Well, nobody told me. But I concluded—naturally—

DOOLITTLE. No: that aint the natural way, Colonel: it's only the middle-class way. My way was always the undeserving way. But dont say nothing to Eliza. She dont know: I always had a delicacy about telling her.

PICKERING. Quite right. We'll leave it so, if you dont mind.

DOOLITTLE. And youll come to the church, Colonel, and put me through straight?

PICKERING. With pleasure. As far as a bachelor can.

MRS. HIGGINS. May I come, Mr. Doolittle? I should be very sorry to miss your wedding.

DOOLITTLE. I should indeed be honored by your condescension, maam; and my poor old woman would take it as a tremenjous compliment. She's been very low, thinking of the happy days that are no more.

MRS. HIGGINS (*rising*). I'll order the carriage and get ready. (*The men rise, except* HIGGINS.) I shant be more than fifteen minutes. (*As she goes to the door* ELIZA *comes in, hatted and buttoning her gloves.*) I'm going to the church to see your father married, Eliza. You had better come in the brougham[3] with me. Colonel Pickering can go on with the bridegroom.

MRS. HIGGINS *goes out.* ELIZA *comes to the middle of the room between the center window and the ottoman.* PICKERING *joins her.*

DOOLITTLE. Bridegroom! What a word! It makes a man realize his position, somehow. (*He takes up his hat and goes towards the door.*)

PICKERING. Before I go, Eliza, do forgive him and come back to us.

LIZA. I dont think papa would allow me. Would you, dad?

DOOLITTLE (*sad but magnanimous*). They played you off very cunning, Eliza, them two sportsmen. If it had been only one of them, you could have nailed him. But you see, there was two; and one of them chaperoned the other, as you might say. (*To* PICKERING) It was artful of you, Colonel; but I bear no malice: I should have done the same myself. I been the victim of one woman after another all my life; and I dont grudge you two getting the better of Eliza. I shant interfere. It's time for us to go, Colonel. So long, Henry. See you in St. George's, Eliza. (*He goes out.*)

PICKERING (*coaxing*). Do stay with us, Eliza. (*He follows* DOOLITTLE.)

ELIZA *goes out on the balcony to avoid being alone with* HIGGINS. *He rises and joins her there. She immediately comes back into the room and makes for the door; but he goes along the balcony quickly and gets his back to the door before she reaches it.*

HIGGINS. Well, Eliza, youve had a bit of your own back, as you call it. Have you had enough? and are you going to be reasonable? Or do you want any more?

LIZA. You want me back only to pick up your slippers and put up with your tempers and fetch and carry for you.

HIGGINS. I havnt said I wanted you back at all.

LIZA. Oh, indeed. Then what are we talking about?

HIGGINS. About you, not about me. If you come back I shall treat you just as I have always treated you. I cant change my nature; and I dont intend to change my manners. My manners are exactly the same as Colonel Pickering's.

LIZA. Thats not true. He treats a flower girl as if she was a duchess.

HIGGINS. And I treat a duchess as if she was a flower girl.

LIZA. I see. (*She turns away composedly, and sits on the ottoman, facing the window.*) The same to everybody.

HIGGINS. Just so.

LIZA. Like father.

HIGGINS (*grinning, a little taken down*). Without accepting the comparison at all points, Eliza, it's quite true that your father is not a snob, and that he will be quite at home in any station of life to which his eccentric destiny may call him. (*Seriously*) The great secret, Eliza, is not having bad manners or good manners or any other particular sort of manners, but having the same

---

3. **brougham** (brŭm, brō'əm), a closed carriage or automobile, having an outside seat for the driver.

manner for all human souls: in short, behaving as if you were in Heaven, where there are no third-class carriages, and one soul is as good as another.

LIZA. Amen. You are a born preacher.

HIGGINS *(irritated)*. The question is not whether I treat you rudely, but whether you ever heard me treat anyone else better.

LIZA *(with sudden sincerity)*. I dont care how you treat me. I dont mind your swearing at me. I dont mind a black eye: Ive had one before this. But *(standing up and facing him)* I wont be passed over.

HIGGINS. Then get out of my way; for I wont stop for you. You talk about me as if I were a motor bus.

LIZA. So you are a motor bus: all bounce and go, and no consideration for anyone. But I can do without you: dont think I cant.

HIGGINS. I know you can. I told you you could.

LIZA *(wounded, getting away from him to the other side of the ottoman with her face to the hearth)*. I know you did, you brute. You wanted to get rid of me.

HIGGINS. Liar.

LIZA. Thank you. *(She sits down with dignity.)*

HIGGINS. You never asked yourself, I suppose, whether *I* could do without you.

LIZA *(earnestly)*. Dont you try to get round me. Youll have to do without me.

HIGGINS *(arrogant)*. I can do without anybody. I have my own soul: my own spark of divine fire. But *(with sudden humility)* I shall miss you, Eliza. *(He sits down near her on the ottoman.)* I have learnt something from your idiotic notions: I confess that humbly and gratefully. And I have grown accustomed to your voice and appearance. I like them, rather.

LIZA. Well, you have both of them on your gramophone and in your book of photographs. When you feel lonely without me, you can turn the machine on. It's got no feelings to hurt.

HIGGINS. I cant turn your soul on. Leave me those feelings; and you can take away the voice and the face. They are not you.

LIZA. Oh, you are a devil. You can twist the heart in a girl as easy as some could twist her arms to hurt her. Mrs. Pearce warned me. Time and again she has wanted to leave you; and you always got round her at the last minute. And

you dont care a bit for her. And you dont care a bit for me.

HIGGINS. I care for life, for humanity; and you are a part of it that has come my way and been built into my house. What more can you or anyone ask?

LIZA. I wont care for anybody that doesnt care for me.

HIGGINS. Commercial principles, Eliza. Like *(reproducing her Covent Garden pronunciation with professional exactness)* s'yollin voylets *(selling violets)*, isn't it?

LIZA. Dont sneer at me. It's mean to sneer at me.

HIGGINS. I have never sneered in my life. Sneering doesnt become either the human face or the human soul. I am expressing my righteous contempt for Commercialism. I dont and wont trade in affection. You call me a brute because you couldnt buy a claim on me by fetching my slippers and finding my spectacles. You were a fool: I think a woman fetching a man's slippers is a disgusting sight: did I ever fetch your slippers? I think a good deal more of you for throwing them in my face. No use slaving for me and then saying you want to be cared for: who cares for a slave? If you come back, come back for the sake of good fellowship; for youll get nothing else. Youve had a thousand times as much out of me as I have out of you; and if you dare to set up your little dog's tricks of fetching and carrying slippers against my creation of a Duchess Eliza, I'll slam the door in your silly face.

LIZA. What did you do it for if you didnt care for me?

HIGGINS *(heartily)*. Why, because it was my job.

LIZA. You never thought of the trouble it would make for me.

HIGGINS. Would the world ever have been made if its maker had been afraid of making trouble? Making life means making trouble. Theres only one way of escaping trouble; and thats killing things. Cowards, you notice, are always shrieking to have troublesome people killed.

LIZA. I'm no preacher: I dont notice things like that. I notice that you dont notice me.

HIGGINS *(jumping up and walking about intolerantly)*. Eliza: youre an idiot. I waste the treasures of my Miltonic mind by spreading them before you. Once for all, understand that I go my way and do my work without caring twopence what happens to either of us. I am not intimidated, like your father and your stepmother. So you can come back or go to the devil: which you please.

LIZA. What am I to come back for?

HIGGINS *(bouncing up on his knees on the ottoman and leaning over it to her)*. For the fun of it. Thats why I took you on.

LIZA *(with averted face)*. And you may throw me out to-morrow if I dont do everything you want me to?

HIGGINS. Yes; and you may walk out tomorrow if I dont do everything you want me to.

LIZA. And live with my stepmother?

HIGGINS. Yes, or sell flowers.

LIZA. Oh! if I only could go back to my flower basket! I should be independent of both you and father and all the world! Why did you take my independence from me? Why did I give it up? I'm a slave now, for all my fine clothes.

HIGGINS. Not a bit. I'll adopt you as my daughter and settle money on you if you like. Or would you rather marry Pickering?

LIZA *(looking fiercely round at him)*. I wouldnt marry you if you asked me; and youre nearer my age than what he is.

HIGGINS *(gently)*. Than he is: not "than what he is."

LIZA *(losing her temper and rising)*. I'll talk as I like. Youre not my teacher now.

HIGGINS *(reflectively)*. I dont suppose Pickering would, though. He's as confirmed an old bachelor as I am.

LIZA. Thats not what I want; and dont you think it. Ive always had chaps enough wanting me that way. Freddy Hill writes to me twice and three times a day, sheets and sheets.

HIGGINS *(disagreeably surprised)*. Damn his impudence! *(He recoils and finds himself sitting on his heels.)*

LIZA. He has a right to if he likes, poor lad. And he does love me.

HIGGINS *(getting off the ottoman)*. You have no right to encourage him.

LIZA. Every girl has a right to be loved.

HIGGINS. What! By fools like that?

LIZA. Freddy's not a fool. And if he's weak and poor and wants me, maybe he'd make me happier than my betters that bully me and dont want me.

HIGGINS. Can he make anything of you? Thats the point.

LIZA. Perhaps I could make something of him. But I never thought of us making anything of one another; and you never think of anything else. I only want to be natural.

HIGGINS. In short, you want me to be as infatuated about you as Freddy? Is that it?

LIZA. No I dont. Thats not the sort of feeling I want from you. And dont you be too sure of yourself or of me. I could have been a bad girl if I'd liked. Ive seen more of some things than you, for all your learning. Girls like me can drag gentlemen down to make love to them easy enough. And they wish each other dead the next minute.

HIGGINS. Of course they do. Then what in thunder are we quarrelling about?

LIZA *(much troubled)*. I want a little kindness. I know I'm a common ignorant girl, and you a book-learned gentleman; but I'm not dirt under your feet. What I done *(correcting herself)* what I did was not for the dresses and the taxis: I did it because we were pleasant together and I come—came—to care for you; not to want you to make love to me, and not forgetting the difference between us, but more friendly like.

HIGGINS. Well, of course. Thats just how I feel. And how Pickering feels. Eliza: youre a fool.

LIZA. Thats not a proper answer to give me. *(She sinks on the chair at the writing-table in tears.)*

HIGGINS. It's all youll get until you stop being a common idiot. If youre going to be a lady, youll have to give up feeling neglected if the men you know dont spend half their time snivelling over you and the other half giving you black eyes. If you cant stand the coldness of my sort of life, and the strain of it, go back to the gutter. Work til you are more a brute than a human being; and then cuddle and squabble and drink til you fall asleep. Oh, it's a fine life, the life of the gutter. It's real: it's warm: it's violent: you can feel it through the thickest skin: you can taste it and smell it without any training or any work. Not like Science and Literature and Classical Music and Philosophy and Art. You find me cold, unfeeling, selfish, dont you? Very well: be off with you to the sort of people you like. Marry some sentimental hog or other with lots of money, and a thick pair of lips to kiss you with and a thick pair of boots to kick you with. If you cant appreciate what youve got, youd better get what you can appreciate.

LIZA (*desperate*). Oh, you are a cruel tyrant. I cant talk to you: you turn everything against me: I'm always in the wrong. But you know very well all the time that youre nothing but a bully. You know I cant go back to the gutter, as you call it, and that I have no real friends in the world but you and the Colonel. You know well I couldnt bear to live with a low common man after you two; and it's wicked and cruel of you to insult me by pretending I could. You think I must go back to Wimpole Street because I have nowhere else to go but father's. But dont you be too sure that you have me under your feet to be trampled on and talked down. I'll marry Freddy, I will, as soon as he's able to support me.

HIGGINS (*sitting down beside her*). Rubbish! you shall marry an ambassador. You shall marry the Governor-General of India or the Lord-Lieutenant of Ireland, or somebody who wants a deputy-queen. I'm not going to have my masterpiece thrown away on Freddy.

LIZA. You think I like you to say that. But I havent forgot what you said a minute ago; and I wont be coaxed round as if I was a baby or a puppy. If I cant have kindness, I'll have independence.

HIGGINS. Independence? That's middle-class blasphemy. We are all dependent on one another, every soul of us on earth.

LIZA (*rising determinedly*). I'll let you see whether I'm dependent on you. If you can preach, I can teach. I'll go and be a teacher.

HIGGINS. Whatll you teach, in heaven's name?

LIZA. What you taught me. I'll teach phonetics.

HIGGINS. Ha! ha! ha!

LIZA. I'll offer myself as an assistant to Professor Nepean.

HIGGINS (*rising in a fury*). What! That impostor! that humbug! that toadying ignoramus! Teach him my methods! my discoveries! You take one step in his direction and I'll wring your neck. (*He lays hands on her.*) Do you hear?

LIZA (*defiantly non-resistant*). Wring away. What do I care? I knew youd strike me some day. (*He lets her go, stamping with rage at having forgotten himself, and recoils so hastily that he stumbles back into his seat on the ottoman.*) Aha! Now I know how to deal with you. What a fool I was not to think of it before! You cant take away the knowledge you gave me. You said I had a finer ear than you. And I can be civil and kind to people, which is more than you can. Aha! (*Purposely dropping her aitches to annoy him*) Thats done you, Enry Iggins, it has. Now I dont care that (*snapping her fingers*) for your bullying and your big talk. I'll advertize it in the papers that your duchess is only a flower girl that you taught, and that she'll teach anybody to be a duchess just the same in six months for a thousand guineas. Oh, when I think of myself crawling under your feet and being trampled on and called names, when all the time I had only to lift up my finger to be as good as you, I could just kick myself.

HIGGINS (*wondering at her*). You damned impudent slut, you! But it's better than snivelling; better than fetching slippers and finding spectacles, isnt it? (*Rising*) By George, Eliza, I said I'd make a woman of you; and I have. I like you like this.

LIZA. Yes: you turn round and make up to me now that I'm not afraid of you, and can do without you.

HIGGINS. Of course I do, you little fool. Five minutes ago you were like a millstone round my neck. Now youre a tower of strength: a consort battleship. You and I and Pickering will be three old bachelors together instead of only two men and a silly girl.

MRS. HIGGINS *returns, dressed for the wedding.* ELIZA *instantly becomes cool and elegant.*

MRS. HIGGINS. The carriage is waiting, Eliza. Are you ready?

LIZA. Quite. Is the Professor coming?

MRS. HIGGINS. Certainly not. He cant behave himself in church. He makes remarks out loud all the time on the clergyman's pronunciation.

LIZA. Then I shall not see you again, Professor. Goodbye. (*She goes to the door.*)

MRS. HIGGINS (*coming to* HIGGINS). Goodbye, dear.

HIGGINS. Goodbye, mother. (*He is about to kiss her, when he recollects something.*) Oh, by the way, Eliza, order a ham and a Stilton cheese, will you? And buy me a pair of reindeer gloves, number eights, and a tie to match that new suit of mine. You can choose the color. (*His cheerful, careless, vigorous voice shows that he is incorrigible.*)

LIZA (*disdainfully*). Number eights are too small for you if you want them lined with lamb's wool. You have three new ties that you have forgotten in the drawer of your washstand. Colonel Pickering prefers double Gloucester to Stilton; and you dont notice the difference. I telephoned Mrs. Pearce this morning not to forget the ham. What you are to do without me I cannot imagine. (*She sweeps out.*)

MRS. HIGGINS. I'm afraid youve spoilt that girl, Henry. I should be uneasy about you and her if she were less fond of Colonel Pickering.

HIGGINS. Pickering! Nonsense; she's going to marry Freddy. Ha ha! Freddy! Freddy!! Ha ha ha ha ha!!!!! (*He roars with laughter as the play ends.*)

Epilogue

The rest of the story need not be shewn in action, and indeed, would hardly need telling if our imaginations were not so enfeebled by their lazy dependence on the ready-mades and reach-me-downs of the ragshop in which Romance keeps its stock of "happy endings" to misfit all stories. Now, the history of Eliza Doolittle, though called a romance because the transfiguration it records seems exceedingly improbable, is common enough. Such transfigurations have been achieved by hundreds of resolutely ambitious young women since Nell Gwynne[1] set them the example by playing queens and fascinating kings in the theater in which she began by selling oranges. Nevertheless, people in all directions have assumed, for no other reason than that she became the heroine of a romance, that she must have married the hero of it. This is unbearable, not only because her little drama, if acted on such a thoughtless assumption, must be spoiled, but because the true sequel is patent to anyone with a sense of human nature in general, and of feminine instinct in particular.

Eliza, in telling Higgins she would not marry him if he asked her, was not coquetting: she was announcing a well-considered decision. When a bachelor interests, and dominates, and teaches, and becomes important to a spinster, as Higgins with Eliza, she always, if she has character enough to be capable of it, considers very seriously indeed whether she will play for becoming that bachelor's wife, especially if he is so little interested in marriage that a determined and devoted woman might capture him if she set herself resolutely to do it. Her decision will depend a good deal on whether she is really free to choose; and that, again, will depend on her age and income. If she is at the end of her youth, and has no security for her livelihood, she will marry him because she must marry anybody who will provide for her. But at Eliza's age a good-looking girl does not feel that pressure: she feels free to pick and choose. She is therefore guided by her instinct in the matter. Eliza's instinct tells her not to marry Higgins. It does not tell her to give him up. It is not in the slightest doubt as to his remaining one of the strongest personal interests in her life. It would be very sorely strained if there was another woman likely to supplant her with him. But as she feels sure of him on that last point, she has no doubt at all as to her course, and would not have any, even if the difference of twenty years in age, which seems so great to youth, did not exist between them.

As our own instincts are not appealed to by her conclusion, let us see whether we cannot discover some reason in it. When Higgins excused his indifference to young women on the ground that they had an irresistible rival in his mother, he gave the clue to his inveterate old-bachelordom.

The case is uncommon only to the extent that remarkable mothers are uncommon. If an imaginative boy has a sufficiently rich mother who has intelligence, personal grace, dignity of character without harshness, and a cultivated sense of the best art of her time to enable her to make her house beautiful, she sets a standard for him against which very few women can struggle, besides effecting for him a disengagement of his affections, his sense of beauty, and his idealism from his specifically sexual impulses. This makes him a standing puzzle to the huge number of uncultivated people who have been brought up in tasteless homes by commonplace or disagreeable parents, and to whom, consequently, literature, painting, sculpture, music, and affectionate personal relations come as modes of sex if they come at all. The word passion means nothing else to them; and that Higgins could have a passion for phonetics and idealize his mother instead of Eliza, would seem to them absurd and unnatural. Nevertheless, when we look round and see that hardly anyone is too ugly or disagreeable to find a wife or a husband if he or she wants one, whilst many old maids and bachelors are above the average in quality and culture, we cannot help suspecting that the disentanglement of sex from the associations with which it is so commonly confused, a disentanglement which persons of genius achieve by sheer intellectual analysis, is sometimes produced or aided by parental fascination.

Now, though Eliza was incapable of thus explaining to herself Higgins's formidable powers of resistance to the charm that prostrated Freddy at the first glance, she was instinctively aware that she could never obtain a complete grip of him, or come between him and his mother (the first necessity of the married woman). To put it shortly, she knew that for some mysterious reason he had not the makings of a married man in him, according to her conception of a husband as one to whom she would be his nearest and fondest and warmest interest. Even had there been no mother-rival, she would still have refused to accept an interest in herself that was secondary to philosophic interests. Had Mrs. Higgins died,

---

1. **Nell Gwynne** (1650–1687), an actress who became the mistress of Charles II.

there would still have been Milton and the Universal Alphabet. Landor's[2] remark that to those who have the greatest power of loving, love is a secondary affair, would not have recommended Landor to Eliza. Put that along with her resentment of Higgins's domineering superiority, and her mistrust of his coaxing cleverness in getting round her and evading her wrath when he had gone too far with his impetuous bullying, and you will see that Eliza's instinct had good grounds for warning her not to marry her Pygmalion.

And now, whom did Eliza marry? For if Higgins was a predestinate old bachelor, she was most certainly not a predestinate old maid. Well, that can be told very shortly to those who have not guessed it from the indications she has herself given them.

Almost immediately after Eliza is stung into proclaiming her considered determination not to marry Higgins, she mentions the fact that young Mr. Frederick Eynsford Hill is pouring out his love for her daily through the post. Now Freddy is young, practically twenty years younger than Higgins: he is a gentleman (or, as Eliza would qualify him, a toff), and speaks like one; he is nicely dressed, is treated by the Colonel as an equal, loves her unaffectedly, and is not her master, nor ever likely to dominate her in spite of his advantage of social standing. Eliza has no use for the foolish romantic tradition that all women love to be mastered, if not actually bullied and beaten. "When you go to women," says Nietzsche,[3] "take your whip with you." Sensible despots have never confined that precaution to women: they have taken their whips with them when they have dealt with men, and been slavishly idealized by the men over whom they have flourished the whip much more than by women. No doubt there are slavish women as well as slavish men: and women, like men, admire those that are stronger than themselves. But to admire a strong person and to live under that strong person's thumb are two different things. The weak may not be admired and hero-worshiped; but they are by no means disliked or shunned; and they never seem to have the least difficulty in marrying people who are too good for them. They may fail in emergencies; but life is not one long emergency: it is mostly a string of situations for which no exceptional strength is needed, and

with which even rather weak people can cope if they have a stronger partner to help them out. Accordingly, it is a truth everywhere in evidence that strong people, masculine or feminine, not only do not marry stronger people, but do not shew any preference for them in selecting their friends. When a lion meets another with a louder roar "the first lion thinks the last a bore." The man or woman who feels strong enough for two, seeks for every other quality in a partner than strength.

The converse is also true. Weak people want to marry strong people who do not frighten them too much; and this often leads them to make the mistake we describe metaphorically as "biting off more than they can chew." They want too much for too little; and when the bargain is unreasonable beyond all bearing, the union becomes impossible: it ends in the weaker party being either discarded or borne as a cross, which is worse. People who are not only weak, but silly or obtuse as well, are often in these difficulties.

This being the state of human affairs, what is Eliza fairly sure to do when she is placed between Freddy and Higgins? Will she look forward to a lifetime of fetching Higgins's slippers or to a lifetime of Freddy fetching hers? There can be no doubt about the answer. Unless Freddy is biologically repulsive to her, and Higgins biologically attractive to a degree that overwhelms all her other instincts, she will, if she marries either of them, marry Freddy.

And that is just what Eliza did.

Complications ensued; but they were economic, not romantic. Freddy had no money and no occupation. His mother's jointure, a last relic of the opulence of Largelady Park, had enabled her to struggle along in Earlscourt with an air of gentility, but not to procure any serious secondary education for her children, much less give the boy a profession. A clerkship at thirty shillings a week was beneath Freddy's dignity, and extremely distasteful to him besides. His prospects consisted of a hope that if he kept up appearances somebody would do something for him. The something appeared vaguely to his imagination as a private secretaryship or a sinecure of some

2. **Landor,** Walter Savage Landor (1775–1864), English writer.
3. **Nietzsche** (nē′chə), Friedrich Wilhelm Nietzsche (1844–1900), German philosopher and writer.

sort. To his mother it perhaps appeared as a marriage to some lady of means who could not resist her boy's niceness. Fancy her feelings when he married a flower girl who had become déclassée[4] under extraordinary circumstances which were now notorious!

It is true that Eliza's situation did not seem wholly ineligible. Her father, though formerly a dustman, and now fantastically disclassed, had become extremely popular in the smartest society by a social talent which triumphed over every prejudice and every disadvantage. Rejected by the middle class, which he loathed, he had shot up at once into the highest circles by his wit, his dustmanship (which he carried like a banner), and his Nietzschean transcendence of good and evil. At intimate ducal dinners he sat on the right hand of the Duchess; and in country houses he smoked in the pantry and was made much of by the butler when he was not feeding in the dining room and being consulted by cabinet ministers. But he found it almost as hard to do all this on three thousand a year as Mrs. Eynsford Hill to live in Earlscourt on an income so pitiably smaller that I have not the heart to disclose its exact figure. He absolutely refused to add the last straw to his burden by contributing to Eliza's support.

Thus Freddy and Eliza, now Mr. and Mrs. Eynsford Hill, would have spent a penniless honeymoon but for a wedding present of £500 from the Colonel to Eliza. It lasted a long time because Freddy did not know how to spend money, never having had any to spend, and Eliza, socially trained by a pair of old bachelors, wore her clothes as long as they held together and looked pretty, without the least regard to their being many months out of fashion. Still, £500 will not last two young people for ever; and they both knew, and Eliza felt as well, that they must shift for themselves in the end. She could quarter herself on Wimpole Street because it had come to be her home; but she was quite aware that she ought not to quarter Freddy there, and that it would not be good for his character if she did.

Not that the Wimpole Street bachelors objected. When she consulted them, Higgins declined to be bothered about her housing problem when that solution was so simple. Eliza's desire to have Freddy in the house with her seemed of no more importance than if she had wanted an extra piece of bedroom furniture. Pleas as to Freddy's character, and the moral obligation on him to earn his own living, were lost on Higgins. He denied that Freddy had any character, and declared that if he tried to do any useful work some competent person would have the trouble of undoing it: a procedure involving a net loss to the community, and great unhappiness to Freddy himself, who was obviously intended by Nature for such light work as amusing Eliza, which, Higgins declared, was a much more useful and honorable occupation than working in the city. When Eliza referred again to her project of teaching phonetics, Higgins abated not a jot of his violent opposition to it. He said she was not within ten years of being qualified to meddle with his pet subject; and as it was evident that the Colonel agreed with him, she felt she could not go against them in this grave matter, and that she had no right, without Higgins's consent, to exploit the knowledge he had given her; for his knowledge seemed to her as much his private property as his watch: Eliza was no communist. Besides, she was superstitiously devoted to them both, more entirely and frankly after her marriage than before it.

It was the Colonel who finally solved the problem, which had cost him much perplexed cogitation. He one day asked Eliza, rather shyly, whether she had quite given up her notion of keeping a flower shop. She replied that she had thought of it, but had put it out of her head, because the Colonel had said, that day at Mrs. Higgins's, that it would never do. The Colonel confessed that when he said that, he had not quite recovered from the dazzling impression of the day before. They broke the matter to Higgins that evening. The sole comment vouchsafed by him very nearly led to a serious quarrel with Eliza. It was to the effect that she would have in Freddy an ideal errand boy.

Freddy himself was next sounded on the subject. He said he had been thinking of a shop himself; though it had presented itself to his pennilessness as a small place in which Eliza should sell tobacco at one counter whilst he sold news-

---

4. *déclassée*, changed (generally reduced) in rank or social position.

papers at the opposite one. But he agreed that it would be extraordinarily jolly to go early every morning with Eliza to Covent Garden and buy flowers on the scene of their first meeting: a sentiment which earned him many kisses from his wife. . . .

Now here is a last opportunity for romance. Would you not like to be assured that the shop was an immense success, thanks to Eliza's charms and her early business experience in Covent Garden? Alas! the truth is the truth: the shop did not pay for a long time, simply because Eliza and her Freddy did not know how to keep it. True, Eliza had not to begin at the very beginning: she knew the names and prices of the cheaper flowers; and her elation was unbounded when she found that Freddy, like all youths educated at cheap, pretentious, and thoroughly inefficient schools, knew a little Latin. It was very little, but enough to make him appear to her a Porson or Bentley,[5] and to put him at his ease with botanical nomenclature. Unfortunately he knew nothing else; and Eliza, though she could count money up to eighteen shillings or so, and had acquired a certain familiarity with the language of Milton from her struggles to qualify herself for winning Higgins's bet, could not write out a bill without utterly disgracing the establishment. Freddy's power of stating in Latin that Balbus built a wall and that Gaul was divided into three parts[6] did not carry with it the slightest knowledge of accounts or business: Colonel Pickering had to explain to him what a cheque book and a bank account meant. And the pair were by no means easily teachable. Freddy backed up Eliza in her obstinate refusal to believe that they could save money by engaging a bookkeeper with some knowledge of the business. How, they argued, could you possibly save money by going to extra expense when you already could not make both ends meet? But the Colonel, after making the ends meet over and over again, at last gently insisted; and Eliza, humbled to the dust by having to beg from him so often, and stung by the uproarious derision of Higgins, to whom the notion of Freddy succeeding at anything was a joke that never palled, grasped the fact that business, like phonetics, has to be learned.

On the piteous spectacle of the pair spending their evenings in shorthand schools and polytechnic classes, learning bookkeeping and typewriting with incipient junior clerks, male and female, from the elementary schools, let me not dwell. There were even classes at the London School of Economics,[7] and a humble personal appeal to the director of that institution to recommend a course bearing on the flower business. He, being a humorist, explained to them the method of the celebrated Dickensian essay on Chinese Metaphysics by the gentleman who read an article on China and an article on Metaphysics and combined the information. He suggested that they should combine the London School with Kew Gardens. Eliza, to whom the procedure of the Dickensian gentleman seemed perfectly correct (as in fact it was) and not in the least funny (which was only her ignorance), took his advice with entire gravity. But the effort that cost her the deepest humiliation was a request to Higgins, whose pet artistic fancy, next to Milton's verse, was calligraphy, and who himself wrote a most beautiful Italian hand, that he would teach her to write. He declared that she was congenitally incapable of forming a single letter worthy of the least of Milton's words; but she persisted; and again he suddenly threw himself into the task of teaching her with a combination of stormy intensity, concentrated patience, and occasional bursts of interesting disquisition on the beauty and nobility, the august mission and destiny, of human handwriting. Eliza ended by acquiring an extremely uncommercial script which was a positive extension of her personal beauty, and spending three times as much on stationery as anyone else because certain qualities and shapes of paper became indispensable to her. She could not even address an envelope in the usual way because it made the margins all wrong.

Their commercial schooldays were a period of disgrace and despair for the young couple. They seemed to be learning nothing about flower shops. At last they gave it up as hopeless, and shook the dust of the shorthand schools, and the

---

5. **Porson or Bentley.** Richard Porson (1759–1808), professor of Greek at Cambridge University, was a famous English scholar. Richard Bentley (1662–1742) was a well-known classical scholar.
6. **Balbus . . . three parts,** schoolboy exercises in Latin.
7. **the London School of Economics,** founded by the Fabian Socialists Beatrice and Sidney Webb in 1895 to expand public education.

polytechnics, and the London School of Economics from their feet for ever. Besides, the business was in some mysterious way beginning to take care of itself. They had somehow forgotten their objections to employing other people. They came to the conclusion that their own way was the best, and that they had really a remarkable talent for business. The Colonel, who had been compelled for some years to keep a sufficient sum on current account at his bankers to make up their deficits, found that the provision was unnecessary: the young people were prospering. It is true that there was not quite fair play between them and their competitors in trade. Their weekends in the country cost them nothing, and saved them the price of their Sunday dinners; for the motor car was the Colonel's; and he and Higgins paid the hotel bills. Mr. F. Hill, florist and greengrocer (they soon discovered that there was money in asparagus; and asparagus led to other vegetables), had an air which stamped the business as classy; and in private life he was still Frederick Eynsford Hill, Esquire. Not that there was any swank about him: nobody but Eliza knew that he had been christened Frederick Challoner. Eliza herself swanked like anything.

That is all. That is how it turned out. It is astonishing how much Eliza still manages to meddle in housekeeping at Wimpole Street in spite of the shop and her own family. And it is notable that though she never nags her husband, and frankly loves the Colonel as if she were his favorite daughter, she has never got out of the habit of nagging Higgins that was established on the fatal night when she won his bet for him. She snaps his head off on the faintest provocation, or on none.

He no longer dares to tease her by assuming an abysmal inferiority of Freddy's mind to his own. He storms and bullies and derides: but she stands up to him so ruthlessly that the Colonel has to ask her from time to time to be kinder to Higgins; and it is the only request of his that brings a mulish expression into her face. Nothing but some emergency or calamity great enough to break down all likes and dislikes, and throw them both back on their common humanity—and may they be spared any such trial!—will ever alter this. She knows that Higgins does not need her, just as her father did not need her. The very scrupulousness with which he told her that day that he had become used to having her there, and dependent on her for all sorts of little services, and that he should miss her if she went away (it would never have occurred to Freddy or the Colonel to say anything of the sort) deepens her inner certainty that she is "no more to him than them slippers"; yet she has a sense, too, that his indifference is deeper than the infatuation of commoner souls. She is immensely interested in him. She has even secret mischievous moments in which she wishes she could get him alone, on a desert island, away from all ties and with nobody else in the world to consider, and just drag him off his pedestal and see him making love like any common man. We all have private imaginations of that sort. But when it comes to business, to the life that she really leads as distinguished from the life of dreams and fancies, she likes Freddy and she likes the Colonel; and she does not like Higgins and Mr. Doolittle. Galatea never does quite like Pygmalion: his relation to her is too godlike to be altogether agreeable.

1913

Discussion

Act One

1. In what ways does the summer rain help to begin the action of the play?

2. What clues identify the social class of the following characters: **(a)** Mrs. Eynsford Hill; **(b)** The Bystander; **(c)** The Flower Girl?

3. How do people react to the specialized knowledge of the Note Taker? What might be the cause of their reaction?

4. Why does Liza continue to hang around the scene, even after she's been frightened?

5. How do you react to the sudden news that Pickering has come from India to meet Higgins? Do you think Shaw intended the playgoer to believe in the literal possibility of this coincidental meeting?

6. Why does Higgins throw Liza a handful of coins? What does this suggest about his character? How does Liza's reaction to this windfall illustrate her personality?

Act Two

1. When Liza appears the next morning, she is prepared "to pay like any lady." Explain how this illustrates her notion of upper-class life, and, further, her own sense of herself.

2. Liza won't sit down until Higgins speaks courteously to her. What fundamental trait of her character does this demonstrate?

3. Shaw invents considerable stage business using Higgins's handkerchief. Trace what it means as it moves from one character to another.

4. How do Higgins's remarks reflect rather commonplace attitudes people have toward the poor?

5. In what way does Higgins's use of the chocolates serve as a warning about the future?

6. Mrs. Pearce indulges in her own, rather strict instructions to Higgins. What do they tell us about the way he lives? How does this undermine his assumptions about class differences?

7. Explain how Mr. Doolittle redefines a series of conventional ideas: **(a)** "rights of a father"; **(b)** "having morals"; **(c)** "undeserving poor"; **(d)** "bad use" of five pounds. How would his ideas strike the typical middle-class theater audience?

8. Why is everyone so surprised when Liza returns from her bath? How does this prepare the way for the audience to accept the results of her later training?

Act Three

1. How does the first scene illustrate Higgins's distinction between "how a girl pronounces, [and] what she pronounces. . . ."?

2. The stage directions for Liza's entrance tell us she "produces an impression of . . . remarkable distinction and beauty. . . ." How does this serve Shaw's thematic purpose?

3. During the tea, who has the better manners, and who talks more properly, Higgins or Liza? What is the point of this contrast?

4. Why does Clara choose to say "bloody nonsense!" at the end of her visit?

Act Four

1. As the act begins, Higgins takes off his coat and hat and casually throws them onto the newspaper stand. How does this gesture serve as a key to his present mood?

2. Higgins and Pickering indulge in a long conversation about their success, while Liza sits, silent. How do the words of the dialogue draw the attention of the audience to her? How ought the actress to play Liza as the men talk?

3. Analyze the significance of Liza "hurling" the slippers at Higgins.

4. When Higgins suggests that his mother could find a husband for Liza, her response is, "We were above that at the corner of Tottenham Court Road." What does she mean?

5. Higgins believes he could bridge the gap between social classes by teaching Liza to speak properly. Now, however, she insists that "in my station I have to be careful. There cant be any feeling between the like of you and the like of me." Has Higgins's own conduct proved his high hopes for social mobility to be false? Explain.

(Discussion concludes on page 664.)

6. How intense is the pain Higgins feels when he complains Liza has "wounded me to the heart"?

7. Liza gives back the ring Higgins bought her at the seaside town of Brighton. He hurls it into the fireplace. As the act ends, Liza is "down on her knees on the hearthrug to look for the ring." Explain the symbolic force of these carefully worked-out details.

Act Five

1. How does Mr. Doolittle's "success" act as a comic parallel to Liza's?

2. What does "middle-class" morality mean in Mr. Doolittle's new life?

3. In what ways does Shaw use Mrs. Higgins in this last act?

4. It takes Liza a long time to come downstairs. During the interval, Higgins sprawls, whistles, and groans. What is Liza doing?

5. Liza enters into a long conversation with Pickering. How does it parallel the conversation between Higgins and Pickering in Act Four? What does Higgins do while they talk?

6. In her new self-knowledge, how does Liza define the difference between social classes?

7. Just what is it that Higgins offers to Liza when he invites her to "come back for the sake of good fellowship. . . ."?

8. Higgins contrasts "the coldness of my sort of life" with marriage to "some sentimental hog . . . with lots of money, and a thick pair of lips to kiss you with. . . ." What is his sort of life? Are his reactions to Liza's speculations about Freddy consistent with this picture of himself?

9. What is it about Liza that gets Higgins to say, finally, "I like you like this"?

10. What is the meaning of Higgins's final laughter?

Composition

1. What separates people now? Is it still differences in speech, or are there other, more significant factors that divide us now? Choose what you consider to be the two or three major things separating people in contemporary society.

Write an essay in which you compare the social divisions of 1912 and the present.

2. Looking back over *Pygmalion,* select the two actions that most completely typify Higgins and Pickering.

Using these typical actions, compare and contrast the personalities of Higgins and Pickering.

3. Several days after his own marriage, Doolittle begins thinking about Liza and her dilemma. Imagine his reactions to the alternatives of life with Freddy and life with Higgins.

Write a letter in which Doolittle advises Liza on what to do next.

4. Evaluate the arguments Shaw employs in the *Epilogue* to prove that Liza could never marry Higgins. Divide them into two groups—those that persuade you and those that do not.

In an essay, evaluate Shaw's ideas and then give your own conclusion on this question.

Vocabulary
Roots

Use the Glossary to answer the following questions about the structure of the words given below. Read each clue and then write on your paper the matching word from the list.

> deprecate
> incense
> infatuate
> magnanimous
> perfunctory

1. Which word has a root that describes an act that is often performed in church?
2. Which has a root that describes how a light might burn?
3. Which is formed from two roots that mean something large but invisible?
4. Which has a root that can mean something done to criminals?
5. Which has a root with a meaning that might describe a dunce?

The Changing English Language

In 1879 Dr. James Augustus Henry Murray (1837–1915), the President of the Philological Society, began work on the Society's monumental dictionary project. The Philological Society had been organized in 1842. Beginning with some 200 members, the Society's purpose was to investigate the history and structure of language. Up to this time, no English dictionary had included organized and detailed information on the history of words. To correct this deficiency, the Society resolved in January, 1858, to prepare a new dictionary that would display the entire history of every word that was or had been in the English language.

For the next twenty years, first under the editorship of Herbert Coleridge (great-nephew of Samuel Taylor Coleridge), and later of F. J. Furnivall, materials toward the new dictionary were gathered by a large number of volunteer readers, who scoured English literature in search of quotations displaying the meanings of words at different historical periods. (There were a number of

American volunteers, and Coleridge at one point suggested that they confine themselves to the literature of the eighteenth century, but his proposal was not closely followed.)

One basic question Murray had to consider during his early years as editor was "What is the English language?" He saw it not as a vocabulary defined by the speech habits of a single class or ethnic group, but rather like a grouping in botany or zoology, its typical species related to other species in which the features characteristic of the group become less and less distinct. The organic grouping that formed the English language he saw as composed of a central core of thousands of words constituting the common vocabulary of the language and linked on every side to more specialized vocabularies. He illustrated this with a diagram:

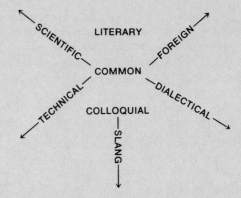

Under Murray, who was the first full-time editor the Society was able to employ, the dictionary project went forward far more swiftly. By April 19, 1882, the first copy was ready for the printer, and by November, 1883, the first volume, *A–B,* was out. Nevertheless, Murray did not live to see the completion of the project. He died in July, 1915 (shortly after completing work on the section *Trink-Turndown*). It was not until June 6, 1928, seventy years since the Philological Society had begun work on its new dictionary "on historical principles," that a banquet was held to celebrate the completion of the project, now known as the *Oxford English Dictionary.*

Content Review

1. Contrast the ways Hardy and Shaw describe the exploitation of the poor by those more well-off.

2. What false upper-class values do Saki and Shaw attack through satire?

3. In what ways does Shaw's Liza represent a new kind of woman? How does Mary Postgate resemble her?

4. What kinds of love do the poems of the era describe?

5. Contrast Hardy's treatment of war in his poetry with Kipling's in "Mary Postgate."

6. What forms of consolation do Housman and Yeats find for the fact of impending death?

7. What meaning do Hopkins and Conrad find in nature?

8. Describe how characters in stories by Conrad and Kipling experience the fundamental loneliness of human life.

9. What sorts of revelation come from the visionary experiences described by Hardy, Wells, and Yeats?

10. What emotions do Conrad's Marlow and Wells's Lionel Wallace feel when they think about the past?

Concept Review: Interpretation of New Material

When George Bernard Shaw's first plays were appearing in London, the most celebrated playwright of the moment was a fellow Irishman, Oscar Wilde. His masterpiece, *The Importance of Being Earnest* (1895), uses highly artificial dialogue to satirize social hypocrisy. In the following scene Jack Worthing, desperately in love with Gwendolen, must face her mother, the indomitable Lady Bracknell, who has just heard of their intention to marry.

from The Importance of Being Earnest • *Oscar Wilde*

LADY BRACKNELL *(sitting down).* You can take a seat, Mr. Worthing. *(Looks in her pocket for notebook and pencil.)*

JACK. Thank you, Lady Bracknell, I prefer standing.

LADY BRACKNELL *(pencil and notebook in hand).* I feel bound to tell you that you are not down on my list of eligible young men, although I have the same list as the dear Duchess of Bolton has. We work together, in fact. However, I am quite ready to enter your name, should your answers be what a really affectionate mother requires. Do you smoke?

JACK. Well, yes, I must admit I smoke.

LADY BRACKNELL. I am glad to hear it. A man should always have an occupation of some kind. There are far too many idle men in London as it is. How old are you?

JACK. Twenty-nine.

LADY BRACKNELL. A very good age to be married at. I have always been of opinion that a man who desires to get married should know either everything or nothing. Which do you know?

JACK *(after some hesitation).* I know nothing, Lady Bracknell.

LADY BRACKNELL. I am pleased to hear it. I do not approve of anything that tampers with natural ignorance. Ignorance is like a delicate exotic fruit; touch it and the bloom is gone. The whole theory of modern education is radically unsound. Fortunately in England, at any rate, education produces no effect whatsoever. If it did, it would

Judi Dench as Lady Bracknell in a 1982 National Theatre production.

prove a serious danger to the upper classes, and probably lead to acts of violence in Grosvenor Square.[1] What is your income?

JACK. Between seven and eight thousand a year.

LADY BRACKNELL (*makes a note in her book*). In land, or in investments?

JACK. In investments, chiefly.

LADY BRACKNELL. That is satisfactory. What between the duties expected of one during one's lifetime, and the duties exacted from one after one's death, land has ceased to be either a profit or a pleasure. It gives one position, and prevents one from keeping it up. That's all that can be said about land.

JACK. I have a country house with some land, of course, attached to it, about fifteen hundred acres, I believe; but I don't depend on that for my real income. In fact, as far as I can make out, the poachers are the only people who make anything out of it.

1. *Grosvenor Square*, an area in the West End, the fashionable residential part of London.

LADY BRACKNELL. A country house! How many bedrooms? Well, that point can be cleared up afterwards. You have a town house, I hope? A girl with a simple, unspoiled nature, like Gwendolen, could hardly be expected to reside in the country.

JACK. Well, I own a house in Belgrave Square, but it is let by the year to Lady Bloxham. Of course, I can get it back whenever I like, at six months' notice.

LADY BRACKNELL. Lady Bloxham? I don't know her.

JACK. Oh, she goes about very little. She is a lady considerably advanced in years.

LADY BRACKNELL. Ah, nowadays that is no guarantee of respectability of character. What number in Belgrave Square?

JACK. 149.

LADY BRACKNELL (*shaking her head*). The unfashionable side. I thought there was something. However, that could easily be altered.

JACK. Do you mean the fashion, or the side?

LADY BRACKNELL (*sternly*). Both, if necessary, I presume. What are your politics?

JACK. Well, I am afraid I really have none. I am a Liberal Unionist.

LADY BRACKNELL. Oh, they count as Tories.[2] They dine with us. Or come in the evening,[3] at any rate. Now to minor matters. Are your parents living?

JACK. I have lost both my parents.

LADY BRACKNELL. Both? . . . That seems like carelessness. Who was your father? He was evidently a man of some wealth. Was he born in what the radical papers call the purple of commerce, or did he rise from the ranks of the aristocracy?

JACK. I am afraid I really don't know. The fact is, Lady Bracknell, I said I had lost my parents. It would be nearer the truth to say that my parents seem to have lost me . . . I don't actually know who I am by birth. I was . . . well, I was found.

LADY BRACKNELL. Found!

JACK. The late Mr. Thomas Cardew, an old gentleman of a very charitable and kindly disposition, found me, and gave me the name of Worthing, because he happened to have a first class ticket for Worthing in his pocket at the time. Worthing is a place in Sussex. It is a seaside resort.

LADY BRACKNELL. Where did the charitable gentleman who had a first class ticket for this seaside resort find you?

JACK (*gravely*). In a handbag.

LADY BRACKNELL. A handbag?

JACK (*very seriously*). Yes, Lady Bracknell. I was in a handbag—a somewhat large, black leather handbag, with handles to it—an ordinary handbag in fact.

LADY BRACKNELL. In what locality did this Mr. James, or Thomas, Cardew come across this ordinary handbag?

JACK. In the cloakroom at Victoria Station. It was given to him in mistake for his own.

LADY BRACKNELL. The cloakroom at Victoria Station?

JACK. Yes. The Brighton line.

LADY BRACKNELL. The line is immaterial. Mr. Worthing, I confess I feel somewhat bewildered by what you have just told me. To be born, or at any rate bred, in a handbag, whether it had handles or not, seems to me to display a contempt for the ordinary decencies of family life that remind one of the worst excesses of the French Revolution. And I presume you know what that unfortunate movement led to? As for the particular locality in which the handbag was found, a cloakroom at a railway station might serve to conceal a social indiscretion—has probably, indeed, been used for that purpose before now—but it could hardly be regarded as an assured basis for a recognized position in good society.

JACK. May I ask you then what you would advise me to do? I need hardly say I would do anything in the world to ensure Gwendolen's happiness.

LADY BRACKNELL. I would strongly advise you, Mr. Worthing, to try and acquire some relations as soon as possible, and to make a definite effort to produce at any rate one parent, of either sex, before the season is quite over.

JACK. Well, I don't see how I could possibly manage to do that. I can produce the handbag at any moment. It is in my dressing room at home. I really think that should satisfy you, Lady Bracknell.

LADY BRACKNELL. Me, sir! What has it to do with me? You can hardly imagine that I and Lord

---

2. *Liberal Unionist . . . Tories.* The Liberal Party split in 1886 over the question of Irish Home Rule, some of the Liberals siding with the Conservatives, or Tories, who supported continued union of Ireland with England.

3. *come in the evening.* Lady Bracknell suggests that the Liberal Unionists (as only partial Tories) are not quite socially acceptable. She may not want them as dinner guests, but is willing to have them visit her during the evening.

Bracknell would dream of allowing our only daughter—a girl brought up with the utmost care—to marry into a cloakroom, and form an alliance with a parcel? Good morning, Mr. Worthing!

(LADY BRACKNELL sweeps out in majestic indignation.)   1895

On a separate sheet of paper, write your answers to the following questions. Do not write in your book.

1. Is Jack on Lady Bracknell's list of eligible young men?

2. What reason does Lady Bracknell give for approving of Jack's smoking?

3. In Lady Bracknell's terms, does Jack know "everything or nothing"?

4. To what does Lady Bracknell compare ignorance?

5. Does Jack's income derive chiefly from land or investments?

6. According to Jack, who are the only people who make anything out of his estate?

7. Where did Mr. Cardew find Jack?

8. What is Lady Bracknell's final advice to Jack?

9. What is the **tone** of this passage?

10. Compare the attitude toward the social establishment expressed here with that in *Pygmalion*.

Composition Review

You may choose any *one* of the following assignments. Assume that you are writing for your classmates.

1. Both *Pygmalion* and "Tobermory" describe, among other things, people with money and "good breeding." Choose one such person from each work and look for the ways each unintentionally reveals weaknesses and imperfections.

Then in an essay discuss how both works use unconscious self-revelation as a way to poke fun at the "better" classes.

2. Skim "Youth" looking for the most important examples of young Marlow's dreams and ideals.

Then write an essay describing and evaluating his youthful spirit.

3. Choose two characters from stories or poems who seem to be the victims of fate.

Then write an essay tracing the chain of fateful circumstances in their lives that propels them toward their fate.

4. Poets at the turn of the century continue to write about nature—but what does it mean to them now? Choose two nature poems from this unit. What kind of scenes do they describe, and what conclusions does each seem to imply?

Using your answers as a basis, write an essay discussing how poets used nature in the era of new directions.

5. Examine "Adam's Curse" and outline its major ideas and how they interconnect.

Then write a prose essay that in your own words restates the poem's argument.

6. Locate those crucial moments in "Mary Postgate" that prepare the story's protagonist for her final, dramatic decision.

Then in an essay use them to illustrate how the story influences Mary to act as she does.

7. Choose two poems from this unit that express quiet indignation. Define for yourself the source of their anger and the ways they suggest it.

Use your conclusions in an essay describing and comparing the two poems.

8. Compare the destinations of "Sailing to Byzantium" and "Youth."

In an essay discuss the ways both works could typify an older person's vision.

9. Housman's old man advises to give "not your heart away." Choose examples from two other works in this unit which seem to justify what he says.

Use them to illustrate an essay that describes the retreat from emotional commitment in the literature of this era.

Amongst the Nerves of the World by C. R. W. Nevinson, painted c. 1930.
A view looking east on Fleet Street toward St. Paul's.

• Joyce: *A Portrait of the Artist
    as a Young Man*

• Lawrence: *Sons and Lovers*

    • Owen: *Poems*

    • Eliot: *Prufrock*

World War I

    Irish Free State •
    established

Joyce: •
Dubliners

    Joyce: *Ulysses* •

    Eliot: *The Waste Land* •

• Woolf: *Mrs. Dalloway*

    • The General Strike

    • Women get the vote

    • Waugh: *Decline and Fall*

    The Great Depression

    • Auden: *Poems*

• Thomas: *Twenty-five Poems*

    • Greene: *Brighton Rock*

    • Joyce:
        Finnegans Wake

    World War II

    Eliot: *Four Quartets* •

• Orwell:
    Animal Farm

• Indian
independence

Auden: •
*The Age of
Anxiety*

1915   **1925**   **1935**   **1945**

Unit 8   1915–

The **T**wentieth Century

Larkin: *The Whitsun Weddings* •

Larkin: *High Windows* •

• Orwell:
Nineteen Eighty-Four

• Greene: *The Honorary Consul*

• Winston Churchill dies

• North Sea oil
discovered

• Elizabeth II's Silver Jubilee

• Larkin: *The Less Deceived*

• Ulster troubles begin

Greene: •
A Burnt-Out Case

• Golding:
Rites of Passage

Golding: •
Lord of the Flies

• Pinter: *The Homecoming*

• Osborne: *Look Back in Anger*

Hughes: *Crow* •

The Falklands War •

• Beckett: *Waiting for Godot*

• Hughes: *The Hawk in the Rain*

• Ulster troubles begin

Thomas: •
Under Milk Wood

National Theatre founded •

Golding awarded Nobel Prize •

Pinter: •
The Caretaker

England joins •
the Common Market

1955　　　　　**1965**　　　　　**1975**　　　　　**1985**

Background: The Twentieth Century 1915–

During World War II British civilians heroically endured months of intensive bombing and the threat of invasion; but it is World War I, "the Great War," that must nevertheless be regarded as the cultural watershed for twentieth-century England. Fought mainly in Europe and the Middle East from 1914 to 1918, the war involved on one side the Central Powers—principally Germany, Austria-Hungary, and Turkey—and on the other the Allied Powers—principally Great Britain (and the Commonwealth nations), France, Russia, and (after 1917) the United States. For the British, the chief battlefield was northern France, which became "the Western Front," where vast armies contended in huge, prolonged military actions—called *battles* by the historians, but unlike anything in previous European warfare—resulting in millions of dead and wounded. An ugly and futile bloodbath that decimated a generation, the war precipitated massive social and political changes and shattered romanticized conceptions of war, heroic behavior, and national purpose.

Reflecting on the period from 1901 to 1914, the poet Philip Larkin wrote: "Never such innocence again." Though the quiet surface of Edwardian England was troubled by industrial unrest, the threat of civil war in Ireland, and intensified agitation by the women's suffrage movement, ordinary British people still felt secure in their national identity and their country's position as the most powerful nation in the world. Since England had not been involved in a conflict with a major power since the Crimean War (1854–1856), and had experienced the Boer War (1899–1902) as remote, if unsettling, there was also a universal innocence about the nature of modern warfare.

The First World War

On August 4, 1914, the day war broke out, cheering crowds gathered outside Buckingham Palace, while young men, ardent for what they viewed as the coming test of their manhood in combat, lined up at the recruiting stations to be among the first to enlist. This universal readiness to court death and danger, spawned by the long peace, is everywhere apparent in the letters, poems, and memoirs of the young men of the period. Rupert Brooke, the most popular poet of the prewar era, urged "Come and die. It'll be great fun!" Among the middle and upper classes, the war was generally regarded as a new kind of "game," to be undertaken in the same spirit of gentlemanly competitiveness as cricket or rugby.

But after only six months of fighting, the war had become a murderous stalemate conducted from trenches. A vast system of underground fortifications stretched from the North Sea to the Alps, and the soldiers of the two sides faced each other across a wilderness of shell craters and barbed wire called "No Man's Land." The trenches were muddy tunnels with only the sight of the sky, in the words of one writer, "to persuade a man that he was not already lost in a common grave." Generals calculated in advance the number of men who would be sacrificed in an attack, then sent their troops in waves to face enemy machine guns. In 1916, during the eagerly anticipated Battle of the Somme, 60,000 British soldiers were killed or wounded the first day. In the Third Battle of Ypres, 370,000 British soldiers, mired in the mud of No Man's Land created by days of bombardment, were killed, wounded, or frozen to death. (Even during the quietest periods, some 7,000 British soldiers were killed or wounded daily on the Western Front; these losses were referred to as "wastage" by army commanders.) By 1917, the war had come to be, according to one writer, "an enormous carnival of death. Nothing else in the history of Europe, not even the Black Death, had produced such an extravagance of corpses. . . . It was the extinction of the fittest—and for what discernible purpose?"

That a radical transformation in the language,

tone, and subject matter of literature was taking place began to be apparent after 1916 in the poetry produced by the young men serving in the front lines. Back in 1914, as illustrated by the opening lines of Rupert Brooke's famous sonnet "The Soldier," the prevailing tone of poetry was still lofty and romantic: "If I should die, think only this of me: / That there's some corner of a foreign field / That is forever England." How different in tone are these lines by a later soldier-poet, Edgell Rickword, describing a dead comrade: "I knew a man, he was my chum, / but he grew darker day by day, / and would not brush the flies away."

Rejecting high-sounding abstractions like "glory," "sacrifice," and "honor" that no longer held any meaning for them, many of the soldier-poets adopted a colloquial, concrete, realistic style, bitter and deeply ironical in tone. Siegfried Sassoon, the most widely-read poet of the war, bitterly satirized generals, politicians, and a civilian population that exhorted the young to fight for their country, while remaining largely ignorant of the slaughter and suffering; those who, in the words of another soldier-poet, Wilfred Owen, "tell with such high zest / To children ardent for some desperate glory, / The old Lie: Dulce et decorum est / Pro patria mori." ("It is sweet and fitting to die for one's country.") Owen was encouraged by

Sassoon, whom he idolized, and imbued by him with a compelling sense of mission to tell the truth about modern warfare. Killed one week before the Armistice in 1918, he produced in his last year of life a haunting and accomplished group of savagely ironical poems whose dominant themes are the hideousness and senselessness of the slaughter on the Western Front. Perhaps the most important poet produced by the war, he is also, in the words of Dylan Thomas, "a poet of all times, all places, and all wars."

The Postwar Period

The 1920s were not a tranquil period for Britain. Massive unemployment was created by the return of hundreds of thousands of veterans to civilian life, and bitter labor disputes were the result. Ramsay MacDonald (1866–1937) became the first Labour Party prime minister in January, 1924; but Labour was defeated at the polls later that year and Stanley Baldwin (1867–1947), a Conservative, became prime minister. Another setback for Labour was the General Strike (May 3–13, 1926), an unsuccessful attempt to support striking coal miners that resulted in retaliatory legislation against trade unions. Baldwin and the Conservatives, who governed England from 1924–

Enthusiastic crowds at a Southwark recruiting station in December, 1915.

1929, were no more successful than their predecessors in dealing with the country's critical economic problems.

Poet, critic, and dramatist, T. S. Eliot, an American expatriate who became a British subject, was the leading spokesman for the modernist poetry that emerged in the 1920s, a poetry characterized by intellectual complexity, allusiveness, precise use of images, and an extreme pessimism. Like the soldier-poets, Eliot turned his back on what he viewed as the inflated rhetoric of the Victorians and insisted on the use of common speech in poetry, as Wordsworth and Coleridge had done earlier. In a famous essay on the metaphysical poets, Eliot argued that, between the time of John Donne and the Victorian period, a "dissociation of sensibility" had occurred; that is, a separation of thought and feeling that modern poetry should seek to bridge through the use of the carefully chosen sensory image—the "objective correlative," in Eliot's phrase. The influence of his poetry—both its technique and its pessimism—was widespread. His most famous work, *The Waste Land* (1922), a highly complex and allusive poem, was seen as a grim metaphor for postwar society.

The revolution in poetry had its counterpart in fiction. The novelists of the eighteenth and nineteenth centuries had written within a defined social context to an audience that shared similar values and beliefs. Modernist writers perceived human beings as living in private worlds and therefore took as their task the illumination of individual experience. Influenced by the work of the noted psychologist Sigmund Freud (1856–1939), novelists like James Joyce and Virginia Woolf attempted to reproduce the authentic character of human subjectivity, the so-called "stream of consciousness." Joyce's *Ulysses* (1922), probably the most influential novel of our time, employs a variety of prose styles and a story line that exactly parallels that of Homer's *Odyssey* to recount the events of a single day (June 16, 1904) in the life of a Dublin man, Leopold Bloom. In *Ulysses* Joyce creates both a microscopically accurate picture of Irish life and a mythical overview of human affairs.

Though a novelist of more narrow limits than Joyce, Virginia Woolf developed a strikingly original and poetic style to convey the inner consciousness of her characters. In novels like *Mrs. Dalloway, To the Lighthouse,* and *The Waves,* she rejected the narrative practice of setting down a series of happenings in chronological sequence as a violation of the truth of human experience: "Life is not a series of gig-lamps symmetrically arranged: life is a luminous halo, a semi-transparent envelope surrounding us from the beginning of consciousness to the end."

The novels of D. H. Lawrence are more traditional in form than those of Joyce and Woolf, but similarly focused on the inner lives of characters and their felt response to experience. In novels like *Sons and Lovers, The Rainbow,* and *Women in Love,* he explores the frequently ambivalent relationship existing between the sexes, one of intense antagonism, yet mutual dependence and need. Other major themes that dominate his fiction are the conflict between the physical and intellectual sides of human experience and the destruction of the natural world and spontaneous feeling by an encroaching industrial society.

The 1930s and '40s

A worldwide economic depression, the rise of totalitarian powers, the Second World War, and Great Britain's diminished importance in the postwar world, darkened the 1930s and '40s, and gave impetus to a literature focused on ideas, social criticism, and ideological debate. It was inevitable that the world depression that began in the late 1920s would have catastrophic effects in highly industrialized and heavily populated Britain. In two years exports and imports declined 35 percent, and three million unemployed roamed the streets of factory towns.

The Spanish Civil War (1936–1939), with Nazi Germany and Fascist Italy assisting one side, and Communist Russia the other, polarized opinion in Britain, with many writers, artists, and intellectuals joining the fight. By the late 1930s there had been some improvement in economic conditions, and Great Britain's foreign policy began to take precedence over its domestic policy. The Second World War, which began in September, 1939, with Hitler's invasion of Poland, was initially a series of disasters for Britain and her allies. During 1939 and 1940 Nazi Germany mastered Europe. Only

Britain, now under the able wartime leadership of Winston Churchill (1874–1965) remained to oppose Hitler. But Britons heroically withstood the bombardment of their cities, and with the entry of the United States into the war, and the failure of the German invasion of Russia, the tide began to turn. Although Britain and her allies were eventually victorious, the postwar years were extremely hard. The country was nearly bankrupt and recovery was slow.

Of the new poets writing during this period, the most important and influential was W. H. Auden. During the 1930s, which he characterized as a "low, dishonest decade," Auden was the acknowledged leader of a circle of writers that included Louis MacNeice, Stephen Spender, and C. Day Lewis, who aligned themselves with the political left and attempted to expose the social and economic ills of "this country of ours where nobody is well." Although they saw themselves as the creators of a new poetic tradition, the influence of Hopkins, Yeats, and Eliot on these young writers is unmistakable, especially in their use of precise and suggestive images, ironic understatement, and plain speech. Another leftist social critic of the period was George Orwell, who exposed the plight of the English working class in books like *Down and Out in Paris and London* and *The Road to Wigan Pier.*

Contemporary England

The war years, with the fear of a German invasion and the aerial bombardments of heavily industrialized areas, united the country and forged a spirit of camaraderie among the British that breached (but did not destroy) class barriers and resulted in a landslide victory for the Labour Party in the first postwar election. The new government consolidated the "welfare state," in which the social services were revised and expanded. With bipartisan support the National Health Service Act was passed, providing for the nationalization of hospitals and free medical care for the whole population.

Perhaps England's most notable postwar achievement was the peaceful liquidation of its once vast empire. This imperial loss, coupled with domestic economic problems, caused British

statesmen to develop a new posture in world affairs. Seeking closer ties with Europe, England accepted an invitation to join the Common Market, a decision taken despite a split in public opinion regarding its future impact on the country's domestic economy.

Some of the poetry of the 1940s, notably the work of Dylan Thomas, was marked by an extravagant, romantic rhetoric. Philip Larkin was in the forefront of the poets of the 1950s who rejected what they viewed as the romantic excesses of Thomas and the overly cerebral poetry of earlier poets like Eliot, in favor of plain statements and traditional forms. In his evocation of the gray landscape of a welfare state, Larkin writes from the viewpoint of a curiously passionless outsider, forever conscious of the narrow bounds of human possibilities. In contrast, the work of Ted Hughes powerfully evokes the world of nature, using a richly textured pattern of metaphor and mythic suggestiveness for its effects.

English drama experienced a renaissance in the 1950s and 1960s, stimulated by the presence of large numbers of first-rate actors and directors and the works of playwrights like John Osborne, John Arden, Harold Pinter, Tom Stoppard, and Edward Bond. Osborne's *Look Back in Anger* (1956) articulated the complaints of the working class against a social system that inhibits upward mobility and personal fulfillment, and launched a movement of socially conscious writers, the "angry young men." In contrast, the work of Harold Pinter, perhaps the most important postwar dramatist in England, is antirealist. Characters move in a nightmarish environment of menace, devoid of communication and love.

Though immensely varied and radically experimental, the literature of the twentieth century is similar to that of previous periods in its overall pattern of continuity and change. While developing new techniques to reflect present realities, modern writers have shown their indebtedness to such past masters as Shakespeare and Donne, Austen and Dickens, Hopkins, Hardy, and Yeats. However, in their rejection of false language and sentiments, in their ironic portrayal of contemporary existence, and in their search for personal identity and meaning in human life, they are the spiritual descendants of the generation whose innocence was lost in the trenches of World War I.

Siegfried Sassoon 1886–1967

Siegfried Sassoon's prewar life, richly described in his memoirs, was one of "cultivated idleness," taken up with hunting, book-collecting, and the writing of exquisite verses in the Georgian style (typical of the immediate prewar era) that focused on images of rural England as a source of patriotic ideals. Robert Graves, in his autobiography *Goodbye to All That*, tells of meeting Sassoon in France and showing him the initial drafts of his first book of poems: "He frowned and said that war should not be written about in such a realistic way. In return, he showed me some of his own poems. One of them began: 'Return to greet me, colors that were my joy, / Not in the woeful crimson of men slain . . .' Sassoon had not yet been in the trenches. I told him, in my old-soldier manner, that he would soon change his style."

The change from conventional idealist to satiric realist, brought about by his personal experiences at the front, is strikingly apparent in Sassoon's two collections of war poems, *The Old Huntsman* (1917) and *Counter-Attack* (1918). Known to his company as "Mad Jack," Sassoon fought with exceptional bravery in France, was awarded two medals, and rose to the rank of captain. By summer of 1917, however, he was convinced that the war was being unjustifiably prolonged and issued a statement reproduced by the press calling for an instant negotiated peace. Instead of being court-mar-

tialed as he had hoped, he was judged temporarily insane and hospitalized. During one of his hospital stays he met Wilfred Owen, whom he encouraged in his writing.

Though a poet of more limited range than Owen, Sassoon was the most widely-read poet of World War I and a master of satiric verse. His war poems are characterized by a direct, epigrammatic, colloquial style and a tone of intense anger and bitterness toward civilians, journalists, and politicians ignorant of the hell soldiers were going through. After the war, Sassoon produced poetry of inferior quality, but continued to write enlightening autobiographies and memoirs. He was also instrumental in bringing Wilfred Owen to the attention of the reading public.

*B*ase Details

If I were fierce, and bald, and short of breath,
  I'd live with scarlet Majors[1] at the Base,
And speed glum heroes up the line to death.
  You'd see me with my puffy petulant face,
5 Guzzling and gulping in the best hotel,
  Reading the Roll of Honor. "Poor young chap,"
I'd say—"I used to know his father well;
  Yes, we've lost heavily in this last scrap."
And when the war is done and youth stone dead,
10 I'd toddle safely home and die—in bed.   1918

---

1. scarlet Majors. The Staff officers serving in safety and relative comfort behind the lines wore cap-bands and lapel-tabs of bright red; line officers serving at the front wore khaki tabs.

Suicide in the Trenches

I knew a simple soldier boy
Who grinned at life in empty joy,
Slept soundly through the lonesome dark,
And whistled early with the lark.

5 In winter trenches, cowed and glum,
With crumps[1] and lice and lack of rum,
He put a bullet through his brain.
No one spoke of him again.

. . .

You smug-faced crowds with kindling eye
10 Who cheer when soldier lads march by,
Sneak home and pray you'll never know
The hell where youth and laughter go.

1918

"Base Details," "Suicide in the Trenches," and "Does It Matter?" from *Collected Poems* by Siegfried Sassoon. Copyright 1918 by E. P. Dutton. Copyright © 1946 by Siegfried Sassoon. Reprinted by permission of Viking Penguin Inc. and George Sassoon.

1. *crumps*, soldiers' slang for exploding shells, from the sound made by them.

Does It Matter?

Does it matter?—losing your legs? . . .
For people will always be kind,
And you need not show that you mind
When the others come in after hunting
5 To gobble their muffins and eggs.

Does it matter?—losing your sight? . . .
There's such splendid work for the blind;
And people will always be kind,
As you sit on the terrace remembering
10 And turning your face to the light.

Do they matter?—those dreams from the
     pit? . . .
You can drink and forget and be glad,
And people won't say that you're mad;
For they'll know you've fought for your
     country
15 And no one will worry a bit.

1918

Discussion

Base Details

1. What kind of people are military leaders of World War I shown to have been?

2. Explain the "double meaning" of the title.

Suicide in the Trenches

1. (a) Judging from the few details we are given, why did the "soldier boy" kill himself? (b) What words in the first stanza show the boy to have been innocent and naive?

2. Why are the "smug-faced" advised to "sneak home and pray"?

3. Describe the tone of each of the three stanzas of the poem.

Does It Matter?

1. (a) What three losses does the poem discuss? (b) What is the tone of the answers that are given to the repeated question "Does it matter?" Explain your answer.

2. What individuals and attitudes are the focus of the poem's satiric attack?

Wilfred Owen 1893–1918

Wilfred Owen went to France in December of 1916, in time to participate in some of the hardest fighting during the cold winter of 1917. In June of 1917, he was hospitalized following a nervous collapse and remained in England until September of 1918, when he volunteered to return to the front, though convinced he was fated to die. This year of reprieve enabled Owen to develop a supportive friendship with his literary idol, Siegfried Sassoon, and gave him the necessary time to carry out his self-assigned mission to tell the truth about modern warfare.

In the famous Preface to the collection of poems he planned, Owen wrote: "Above all I am not concerned with Poetry. . . . My subject is War, and the pity of War. . . . The Poetry is in the pity." The truth is that he was deeply concerned about his craft but had come to reject the romantic poetic tradition he had formerly worked in as false to facts and feelings. His esthetic conversion is evident in a letter home on February 4th, 1917, in which he described "the universal pervasion of Ugliness. Hideous landscapes, vile noises, foul language . . . everything unnatural, broken, blasted; the distortion of the dead, whose unburiable bodies sit outside the dug-outs all day, all night, the most execrable sights on earth. In poetry we call them the most glorious." Owen's poetry, in contrast, is startlingly blunt, ironic, and graphically explicit in its physical description of the daily "crucifixion" of youth on the battlefield. It is also stylistically distinctive in its use of multiple sound effects achieved through the employment of assonance, alliteration, and **consonance.**

One week before the Armistice of 1918 and two weeks after being decorated for gallantry, Wilfred Owen was killed by machine-gun fire. He had published only four poems during his lifetime and was unknown as a poet, except to a few friends. Through the efforts of his mother and friends, eight of Owen's poems were published in assorted periodicals in 1919, followed, in 1920, by the publication of his collected poems, edited by Siegfried Sassoon. They have come to be praised as the work of the finest poet of World War I and of a major writer of this century.

*D*ulce et Decorum Est

Bent double, like old beggars under sacks,
Knock-kneed, coughing like hags, we cursed
    through sludge,
Till on the haunting flares we turned our backs
And towards our distant rest began to trudge.
5 Men marched asleep. Many had lost their boots
But limped on, blood-shod. All went lame; all
    blind;
Drunk with fatigue; deaf even to the hoots

Of tired, outstripped Five-Nines[1] that dropped
   behind.

Gas! GAS! Quick, boys!—An ecstasy of
   fumbling,
10 Fitting the clumsy helmets just in time;
But someone still was yelling out and stumbling
And flound'ring like a man in fire or lime . . .
Dim, through the misty panes and thick green
   light,
As under a green sea, I saw him drowning.

15 In all my dreams, before my helpless sight,
He plunges at me, guttering, choking,
   drowning.

If in some smothering dreams you too could
   pace
Behind the wagon that we flung him in,
And watch the white eyes writhing in his face,
20 His hanging face, like a devil's sick of sin;
If you could hear, at every jolt, the blood
Come gargling from the froth-corrupted lungs,
Obscene as cancer, bitter as the cud
Of vile, incurable sores on innocent tongues,—
25 My friend, you would not tell with such high
   zest
To children ardent for some desperate glory,
The old Lie: Dulce et decorum est
Pro patria mori.[2]
1917   1920

"Dulce et Decorum Est," "Anthem for Doomed Youth," "Arms and the Boy" by Wilfred Owen, *Collected Poems of Wilfred Owen.* Copyright © 1963 Chatto & Windus, Ltd. Reprinted by permission of New Directions Publishing Corporation.

1. **Five-Nines,** shells containing poison gas. The subject of this poem is a gas attack. The use of poison gas on the Western Front, first by the Germans and then the Allies, was widely viewed as immoral.
2. **Dulce . . . mori** (dŭl′chā et də côr′əm est prō pä′trē ə môr′ē), "It is sweet and honorable to die for one's country," a quotation from one of Horace's *Odes* well known to British schoolboys.

Anthem for Doomed Youth

What passing-bells[1] for these who die as cattle?
   Only the monstrous anger of the guns.
   Only the stuttering rifles' rapid rattle
Can patter out their hasty orisons.[2]
5 No mockeries now for them; no prayers nor bells,
   Nor any voice of mourning save the choirs,—
The shrill, demented choirs of wailing shells;
   And bugles calling for them from sad shires.[3]

What candles may be held to speed them all?
10   Not in the hands of boys, but in their eyes
Shall shine the holy glimmers of good-byes.
   The pallor of girls' brows shall be their pall;
Their flowers the tenderness of patient minds,
And each slow dusk a drawing-down of blinds.
1917   1920

---

1. **passing-bells,** church bells rung for the dying or the dead.
2. **orisons** (ôr′ə zənz), prayers.
3. **bugles . . . shires,** played at funeral services held for them in their home counties (shires).

Arms and the Boy[1]

Let the boy try along this bayonet-blade
How cold steel is, and keen with hunger of blood;
Blue with all malice, like a madman's flash;
And thinly drawn with famishing for flesh.

5 Lend him to stroke these blind, blunt bullet-leads
Which long to nuzzle in the hearts of lads,
Or give him cartridges of fine zinc teeth,
Sharp with the sharpness of grief and death.

For his teeth seem for laughing round an apple.
10 There lurk no claws behind his fingers supple;
And God will grow no talons at his heels,
Nor antlers through the thickness of his curls.
1918   1920

---

1. **Arms . . . Boy.** The title is an ironic play on the opening words of Virgil's *Aeneid*: "Of arms and the man I sing . . ."

In his book *The Great War and Modern Memory*, literary historian Paul Fussell observes that one of the casualties of World War I was the system of "high" diction relating to warfare to which several generations of readers had become accustomed. "The tutors in this special diction had been the boys' books of George Alfred Henty; the male romances of Rider Haggard; the poems of Robert Bridges; and especially the Arthurian poems of Tennyson and the pseudo-medieval romances of William Morris." As examples of this "high" diction, Fussell offers a series of equivalents:

A friend is a . . . . *comrade*
A horse is a . . . . *steed*, or *charger*
The enemy is . . . . *the foe*, or *the host*
Danger is . . . . *peril*
To conquer is to . . . . *vanquish*
To be earnestly brave is to be . . . . *gallant*

To be cheerfully brave is to be . . . . *plucky*
To be stolidly brave is to be . . . . *staunch*
The dead on the battlefield are . . . . . . *the fallen*
The front is . . . . *the field*
Obedient soldiers are . . . . *the brave*
Warfare is . . . . *strife*
To die is to . . . . *perish*
The draft-notice is . . . . *the summons*
To enlist is to . . . . *join the colors*
One's death is one's . . . . *fate*
The sky is . . . . *the heavens*
What is contemptible is . . . . *base*
The legs and arms of young men are . . . . *limbs*
Dead bodies constitute . . . . *ashes*, or *dust*
The blood of young men is . . . *"the red / Sweet wine of youth"*—R. Brooke

From *The Great War and Modern Memory* by Paul Fussell. Copyright © 1975 by Oxford University Press, Inc. Reprinted by permission.

Disabled

He sat in a wheeled chair, waiting for dark,
And shivered in his ghastly suit of grey,
Legless, sewn short at elbow. Through the park
Voices of boys rang saddening like a hymn,
5 Voices of play and pleasure after day,
Till gathering sleep had mothered them from him.

About this time Town used to swing so gay
When glow-lamps budded in the light blue trees,
and girls glanced lovelier as the air grew dim,—
10 In the old times, before he threw away his knees.
Now he will never feel again how slim
Girls' waists are, or how warm their subtle hands;
All of them touch him like some queer disease.

There was an artist silly for his face,
15 For it was younger than his youth, last year.
Now, he is old; his back will never brace;
He's lost his color very far from here,
Poured it down shell-holes till the veins ran dry,
And half his lifetime lapsed in the hot race,
20 And leap of purple spurted from his thigh.

One time he liked a blood-smear down his leg,
After the matches, carried shoulder-high.
It was after football, when he'd drunk a peg,
He thought he'd better join.—He wonders why.
25 Someone had said he'd look a god in kilts,
That's why; and may be, too, to please his Meg;
Aye, that was it, to please the giddy jilts[1]
He asked to join. He didn't have to beg;

Smiling they wrote his lie; aged nineteen years.
30 Germans he scarcely thought of; all their guilt,
And Austria's, did not move him. And no fears
Of Fear came yet. He thought of jewelled hilts
For daggers in plaid socks; of smart salutes;
And care of arms; and leave; and pay arrears;
35 *Esprit de corps;*[2] and hints for young recruits.
And soon, he was drafted out with drums and
 cheers.

Some cheered him home, but not as crowds
 cheer Goal.
Only a solemn man who brought him fruits
Thanked him; and then inquired about his soul.

40 Now, he will spend a few sick years in
 Institutes,
And do what things the rules consider wise,
And take whatever pity they may dole.
Tonight he noticed how the women's eyes
Passed from him to the strong men that were
 whole.
45 How cold and late it is! Why don't they come
And put him into bed? Why don't they come?
1917   1920

"Disabled" by Wilfred Owen, *Collected Poems of Wilfred Owen.*
Copyright © 1963 Chatto & Windus, Ltd. Reprinted by permission of New Directions Publishing Corporation.

1. *jilts,* girls.
2. *Esprit de corps* (e sprē′ də kôr′), group spirit, morale. [French]

Discussion

Dulce et Decorum Est

1. What effect is achieved by the arrangement of details in this poem?

2. What explicit horrors of life in the front lines does the poem itemize?

3. What world does Owen ironically recall in the Latin quotation with which the poem concludes? (See footnote 2.)

Anthem for Doomed Youth

1. (a) Why, according to the poem, would the traditional funeral rituals, such as prayers, bells, and choir singing, be "mockeries" for soldiers killed at the front? **(b)** What does the poem state the soldiers are experiencing in place of these rituals?

2. (a) Point out ways in which Owen has created special sound effects, as befits an "anthem." **(b)** What point is he trying to make by using the word "anthem," given the kind of "music" he creates?

Arms and the Boy

1. What, specifically, is the boy being asked to do in stanzas one and two?

2. (a) According to the last stanza, just what would have to happen to the boy for him to use bullets and bayonets as they were intended? **(b)** How do the images of the poem support this idea?

3. The title is an **allusion** to the opening line ("Of arms and the man I sing. . .") of Virgil's heroic epic *The Aeneid.* Why does Owen want the reader to make a connection between his work and Virgil's?

Disabled

1. How severe are the injuries of the boy described? What details lend pathos to his present situation?

2. What two main contrasts are developed in the poem? For what effect?

3. (a) Contrast the young man's motives for enlisting with the reality he experienced. **(b)** What accounts for his particularly bitter attitude toward women?

Composition

One of the chief literary strategies employed by Sassoon and Owen is **irony.** Their subjects, their imagery, their diction, even the titles of their poems all contribute to an ironic effect. Select a poem by one or the other and examine the use of irony in it.

Write a brief essay on the use of irony in the poem you have chosen.

Vera Brittain 1893–1970

The product of an Edwardian middle-class background, Vera Brittain broke away from her sheltered family life in 1915 to serve four trying years as a Red Cross nurse in army hospitals in London, Malta, and France. After the Armistice she returned to Oxford to complete her studies and eventually launch a career as a writer and social activist. While at Somerville (one of Oxford's few women's colleges), she began her friendship with the novelist Winifred Holtby, which she later described in *Testament of Friendship.*

For almost ten years after the Armistice, Brittain struggled to find the appropriate medium through which to convey the impact of World War I on her own life and on the lives of the men and women of her generation. She first contemplated writing a novel, then reproducing the diary she had kept from 1913 to 1918, using fictitious names for the people mentioned. Finally she resolved that the truth of the experience could only be revealed by setting her personal story against the larger background of war and social change. The subtitle of *Testament of Youth*—"An Autobiographical Study of the Years 1900–1925"—emphasizes her intent to present history through an account of personal life.

A best seller when it was first published in 1933, *Testament of Youth* is especially significant for what it reveals about the upbringing of middle-class women in Edwardian England and about women's participation in and response to the events of 1914–1918. In the Foreward to her book, Brittain declares that what she has written "constitutes, in effect, the indictment of a civilization." She is particularly critical of her age for denying women equal opportunities for education and work, for engaging in an endless and futile war that slaughtered many of England's most promising youth, and for failing to prepare young people to deal with reality and change. As she poignantly recounts, World War I shattered an entire generation so that nothing could ever again be the same.

Part I of *Testament of Youth* covers the years 1900 to Christmas, 1915, and describes Brittain's childhood, her education, and her relationship with Roland Leighton, a brilliant and sensitive school friend of her brother Edward. On the historical level, this opening section describes the impact of the first year of war on English society. The precocious daughter of provincial, middle-class parents, Brittain spent the first eighteen years of her life sheltered, chaperoned, and intellectually thwarted. Like other girls of her class and time, she was admonished to avoid conversation alone with boys, to wear flowing skirts and high-necked blouses, and to aspire to matrimony and motherhood. While being courted by Roland Leighton, she was constantly supervised, her letters opened, her daily actions closely scrutinized. Since her parents believed only boys should seek higher education, Brittain was forced to wage a lengthy campaign to persuade them to allow her to spend a year preparing for the rigorous entrance and scholarship examinations for Oxford. When war broke out, Vera had just received her acceptance to Oxford and was preoccupied by her budding romance with Leighton. Not surprisingly, her first reaction to the news of the outbreak of war was that the timing could not have been more inconvenient.

from *Testament of Youth*

When the Great War broke out, it came to me not as a superlative tragedy, but as an interruption of the most exasperating kind to my personal plans. . . .

It would not, I think, be possible for any present-day girl of the same age even to imagine how abysmally ignorant, how romantically idealistic, and how utterly unsophisticated my more sensitive contemporaries and I were at that time. The naïveties of the diary which I began to write consistently soon after leaving school, and kept up until more than half way through the War, must be read in order to be believed. My "Reflective Record, 1913," is endorsed on its title page with the following comprehensive aspirations:

"To extend love, to promote thought, to lighten suffering, to combat indifference, to inspire activity."

"To know everything of something and something of everything."

My diary for August 3rd, 1914, contains a most incongruous mixture of war and tennis.

The day was Bank Holiday,[1] and a tennis tournament had been arranged at the Buxton Club. I had promised to play with my discouraged but still faithful suitor,[2] and did not in the least want to forgo the amusement that I knew this partnership would afford me—particularly as the events reported in the newspapers seemed too incredible to be taken quite seriously.

"I do not know," I wrote in my diary, "how we all managed to play tennis so calmly and take quite an interest in the result. I suppose it is because we all know so little of the real meaning of war that we are so indifferent. B. and I had to owe 30. It was good handicapping as we had a very close game with everybody." . . .

After that[3] events moved, even in Buxton, very quickly. The German cousins of some local acquaintances left the town in a panic. My parents rushed over in the car to familiar shops in Macclesfield and Leek, where they laid in stores of cheese, bacon, and butter under the generally shared impression that by next week we might all be besieged by the Germans. Wild rumors circulated from mouth to mouth; they were more plentiful than the newspapers, over which a free fight broke out on the station platform every time a batch came by train from London or Manchester. Our elderly cook, who had three Reservist sons, dissolved into continuous tears and was too much upset to prepare the meals with her usual competence; her young daughter-in-law, who had had a baby only the previous Friday, became hysterical and had to be forcibly restrained from getting up and following her husband to the station. One or two Buxton girls were hurriedly married to officers summoned to unknown destinations. Pandemonium swept over the town. Holiday trippers wrestled with one another for the *Daily Mail;* habitually quiet and respectable citizens struggled like wolves for the provisions in the food-shops, and vented upon the distracted assistants their dismay at learning that all prices had suddenly gone up.

My diary for those few days reflects *The Times*[4] in its most pontifical mood. "Germany has broken treaty after treaty, and disregarded every honorable tie with other nations. . . . Germany has destroyed the tottering hopes of peace. . . . The great fear is that our bungling Government will declare England's neutrality. . . . If we at this critical juncture refuse to help our friend France, we should be guilty of the grossest treachery."

I prefer to think that my real sentiments were more truly represented by an entry written nearly a month later after the fabulously optimistic

---

1. Bank Holiday, any day except Saturday or Sunday on which banks are legally closed. August 3, 1914 was a Monday.
2. suitor, not Roland Leighton, but an earlier male friend.
3. that, August 4, when at midnight, since the Germans had not responded to an English ultimatum that they withdraw from Belgium, the English entered the war.
4. The Times, of London, England's most influential newspaper.

reports of the Battle of Le Cateau.[5] I had been over to Newcastle-under-Lyme to visit the family dentist, and afterwards sat for an hour in a tree-shadowed walk called The Brampton and meditated on the War. It was one of those shimmering autumn days when every leaf and flower seems to scintillate with light, and I found it "very hard to believe that not far away men were being slain ruthlessly, and their poor disfigured bodies heaped together and crowded in ghastly indiscrimination into quickly provided common graves as though they were nameless vermin. . . . It is impossible," I concluded, "to find any satisfaction in the thought of 25,000 slaughtered Germans, left to mutilation and decay; the destruction of men as though beasts, whether they be English, French, German, or anything else, seems a crime to the whole march of civilization." . . .

My father vehemently forbade Edward, who was still under military age, to join anything whatsoever. Having himself escaped immersion in the public-school tradition, which stood for militaristic heroism unimpaired by the damping exercise of reason, he withheld his permission for any kind of military training, and ended by taking Edward daily to the mills to divert his mind from the War. Needless to say, these uncongenial expeditions entirely failed of their desired effect, and constant explosions—to which, having inherited so many of my father's characteristics, I seemed only to add by my presence—made our house quite intolerable. A new one boiled up after each of Edward's tentative efforts at defiance, and these were numerous, for his enforced subservience seemed to him synonymous with everlasting disgrace. One vague application for a commission which he sent to a Notts and Derby regiment actually was forwarded to the War Office—"from which," I related with ingenuous optimism, "we are expecting to hear every post."

When my father discovered this exercise of initiative, his wrath and anxiety reached the point of effervescence. Work of any kind was quite impossible in the midst of so much chaos and apprehension, and letters to Edward from Roland, describing his endeavors to get a commission in a Norfolk regiment, did nothing to ease the perpetual tension. Even after the result of my Oxford Senior[6] came through, I abandoned in despair the Greek textbooks that Roland had lent me. I even took to knitting for the soldiers, though only for a very short time; utterly incompetent at all forms of needlework, I found the simplest bed-socks and sleeping-helmets altogether beyond me. "Oh, how I wish I could wake up in the morning," concludes one typical day's entry describing these commotions, "to find this terrible war the dream it seems to me to be!"

At the beginning of 1915 I was more deeply and ardently in love than I have ever been or am ever likely to be, yet at that time Roland and I had hardly been alone together, and never at all without the constant possibility of observation and interruption. In Buxton our occasional walks had always been taken either through the town in full view of my family's inquisitive acquaintances, or as one half of a quartet whose other members kept us continually in sight. At Uppingham[7] every conversation that we had was exposed to inspection and facetious remark by schoolmasters or relatives. In London we could only meet under the benevolent but embarrassingly interested eyes of an aunt. Consequently, by the middle of that January, our desire to see one another alone had passed beyond the bounds of toleration.

In my closely supervised life, a secret visit to London was impossible even en route for Oxford; I knew that I should be seen off by a train which had been discussed for days and, as usual, have my ticket taken for me. But Leicester was a conceivable rendezvous, for I had been that way before, even though from Buxton the obvious route was via Birmingham. So for my family's benefit, I invented some objectionable students, likely to travel by Birmingham, whom I wanted to avoid. Roland, in similar mood, wrote that if he could not get leave he would come without it.

When the morning arrived, my mother decided that I seemed what she called "nervy," and insisted upon accompanying me to Miller's Dale, the junction at which travellers from Buxton change to the main line. I began in despair to

---

5. **Le Cateau,** August 26, 1914, a costly British victory.
6. **Oxford Senior,** an entrance exam.
7. **Uppingham,** the private school attended by Edward Brittain and his friends.

wonder whether she would elect to come with me all the way to Oxford, but I finally escaped without her suspecting that I had any intention other than that of catching the first available train from Leicester. The usual telegram was demanded, but I protested that at Oxford station there was always such a rush for a cab that I couldn't possibly find time to telegraph until after tea.

At Leicester, Roland, who had started from Peterborough soon after dawn, was waiting for me with another sheaf of pale pink roses. He looked tired, and said he had had a cold; actually, it was incipient influenza and he ought to have been in bed, but I did not discover this till afterwards.

To be alone with one another after so much observation was quite overwhelming, and for a time conversation in the Grand Hotel lounge moved somewhat spasmodically. But constraint disappeared when he told me with obvious pride that he had asked his own colonel for permission to interview the colonel of the 5th Norfolks, who were stationed some distance away and were shortly going to the front, with a view to getting a transfer.

"Next time I see the C.O.," he announced, "I shall tell him the colonel of the 5th was away. I shall say I spent the whole day looking for him—so after lunch I'm coming with you to Oxford."

I tried to subdue my leaping joy by a protest about his cold, but as we both knew this to be insincere it was quite ineffective. I only stipulated that when we arrived he must lose me at the station; "chap. rules," even more Victorian than the social code of Buxton, made it inexpedient for a woman student to be seen in Oxford with a young man who was not her brother.

So we found an empty first-class carriage and travelled together from Leicester to Oxford. It was a queer journey; the memory of its profound unsatisfactoriness remains with me still. I had not realized before that to be alone together would bring, all too quickly, the knowledge that being alone together was not enough. It was an intolerable realization, for I knew too that death might so easily overtake us before there could be anything more. I was dependent, he had only his pay, and we were both so distressingly young.

Thus a new constraint arose between ·us

which again made it difficult to talk. We tried to discuss impersonally the places that we wanted to see when it was possible to travel once more; we'd go to Florence together, he said, directly the War was over.

"But," I objected—my age-perspective being somewhat different from that of to-day—"it wouldn't be proper until I'm at least thirty."

"Don't worry," he replied persuasively. "I'm sure I can arrange for it to be 'proper' before you get to that age!"

And then, somehow, we found ourselves suddenly admitting that each had kept the other's letters right from the beginning. We were now only a few miles from Oxford, and it was the first real thing that we had said. As we sat together silently watching the crimson sun set over the flooded land, some quality in his nearness became so unbearable that, all unsophisticated as I was, I felt afraid. I tried to explain it to myself afterwards by a familiar quotation: "There is no beauty that hath not some strangeness in the proportion."[8]

> Like so many of the idealistic but naive young men of his generation, Roland Leighton regarded going to war as a duty, a test of heroism, and a potentially glamorous adventure. In a letter to Brittain describing his determination to secure a commission, he wrote: "I feel that I am meant to take an active part in this War. It is to me a very fascinating thing—something, if very horrible, yet very ennobling and very beautiful, something whose elemental reality raises it above the reach of all cold theorizing." On Wednesday, March 31, 1915, Vera saw Roland off to the front and returned home to the dreary realization that the war was beginning to overshadow everything in her life—school, personal relationships, ambitions, and dreams.

The next day I saw him off, although he had said that he would rather I didn't come. In the

---

8. *"There . . . proportion."* Brittain is slightly misquoting from Sir Francis Bacon's essay "Of Beauty." Bacon actually wrote, "There is no excellent beauty that hath not some strangeness in the proportion."

early morning we walked to the station beneath a dazzling sun, but the platform from which his train went out was dark and very cold. In the railway carriage we sat hand in hand until the whistle blew. We never kissed and never said a word. I got down from the carriage still clasping his hand, and held it until the gathering speed of the train made me let go. He leaned through the window looking at me with sad, heavy eyes, and I watched the train wind out of the station and swing round the curve until there was nothing left but the snowy distance, and the sun shining harshly on the bright, empty rails.

When I got back to the house, where everyone mercifully left me to myself, I realized that my hands were nearly frozen. Vaguely resenting the physical discomfort, I crouched beside the morning-room fire for almost an hour, unable to believe that I could ever again suffer such acute and conscious agony of mind. On every side there seemed to be cause for despair and no way out of it. I tried not to think because thought was intolerable, yet every effort to stop my mind from working only led to a fresh outburst of miserable speculation. I tried to read; I tried to look at the gaunt white hills across the valley, but nothing was any good, so in the end I just stayed huddled by the fire, immersed in a mood of blank hopelessness in which years seemed to have passed since the morning.

At last I fell asleep for some moments, and awoke feeling better; I was, I suppose, too young for hope to be extinguished for very long. Perhaps, I thought, Wordsworth or Browning or Shelley would have some consolation to offer; all through the War poetry was the only form of literature that I could read for comfort, and the only kind that I ever attempted to write. So I turned at once to Shelley's "Adonais,"[9] only to be provoked to new anguish by the words:

O gentle child, beautiful as thou wert,
Why didst thou leave the trodden paths of men
Too soon, and with weak hands though mighty
   heart
Dare the unpastured dragon in his den?

But the lovely cadences stirred me at last to articulateness; there was no one to whom I wanted to talk, but at least I could tell my diary a good deal of the sorrow that seemed so fathomless. . . .

That morning (April 17, 1915) I left the reassuring study of *The Times* to take part in one of the first national "flag-days" organized during the War. As I wandered with my basket of primroses up and down the Buxton streets, blindingly white as they always became in the midday sunshine, my thoughts swung dizzily between the conviction that Roland would return and the certainty that he could never possibly come back. I had little patience to spare for my mother's middle-aged acquaintances, who patronized me as they bought my primroses, and congratulated me on putting aside my "studies" to "do my bit in this terrible War." I took their pennies with scant ceremony, and one by one thrust them with a noisy clatter into my tin.

"Those who are old and think this War so terrible do not know what it means to us who are young," I soliloquized angrily. "When I think how suddenly, instantly, a chance bullet may put an end to that brilliant life, may cut it off in its youth and mighty promise, faith in the 'increasing purpose' of the ages grows dim."

The fight around Hill 60 which was gradually developing, assisted by the unfamiliar horror of gas attacks, into the Second Battle of Ypres,[10] did nothing to restore my faith in the benevolent intentions of Providence. With that Easter vacation began the wearing anxiety of waiting for letters which for me was to last, with only brief intervals, for more than three years, and which, I think, made all non-combatants feel more distracted than anything else in the War. Even when the letters came they were four days old, and the writer since sending them had had time to die over and over again. My diary, with its long-drawn-out record of days upon days of miserable speculation, still gives a melancholy impression of that nerve-racking suspense.

"Morning," it observes, "creeps on into afternoon, and afternoon passes into evening, while I go from one occupation to another, in apparent unconcern—but all the time this gnawing anxiety beneath it all."

---

9. Shelley's "Adonais," the pastoral elegy composed in 1821 by Percy Shelley in honor of John Keats, who had died that year at the age of 25.
10. Second Battle of Ypres (ē′prə), beginning April 22, 1915. This was the first action in which poison gas was used.

(Left to right) Edward Brittain, Roland Leighton, and Victor Richardson at Uppingham School O.T.C. camp in July, 1915.

Ordinary household sounds became a torment. The clock, marking off each hour of dread, struck into the immobility of tension with the shattering effect of a thunderclap. Every ring at the door suggested a telegram, every telephone call a long-distance message giving bad news. With some of us the effect of this prolonged apprehension still lingers on; even now I cannot work comfortably in a room from which it is possible to hear the front-door bell.

Having successfully completed her first-year exams at Oxford, Vera dropped all studies to commence training as a Red Cross nurse in Devonshire Hospital. In August, Roland returned home on leave, a sadly strained reunion for the young lovers, despite their becoming officially engaged. Frustrated and depressed by lack of privacy and the brevity of their time together, they parted in a mood of despair and foreboding that was to persist in the grim weeks following Roland's return to France.

As September wore on and the Battle of Loos[11] came nearer, an anxious stillness seemed to settle upon the country, making everyone taut and breathless. The Press and personal letters from France were alike full of anticipation and suspense. Roland wrote vaguely but significantly of movements of troops, of great changes impending, and seemed more obsessed with the idea of death than ever before. One letter, describing how he had superintended the reconstruction of some old trenches, was grim with a disgust and bitterness that I had never known him put into words:

"The dugouts have been nearly all blown in, the wire entanglements are a wreck, and in among the chaos of twisted iron and splintered timber and shapeless earth are the fleshless, blackened bones of simple men who poured out their red, sweet wine of youth[12] unknowing, for nothing more tangible than Honor or their Country's Glory or another's Lust of Power. Let him who thinks War is a glorious, golden thing, who loves to roll forth stirring words of exhortation, invoking Honor and Praise and Valor and Love of Country with as thoughtless and fervid a faith as inspired the priests of Baal to call on their own slumbering deity, let him but look at a little pile of sodden grey rags that cover half a skull and a shin-bone and what might have been Its ribs, or at this skeleton lying on its side, resting half crouching as it fell, perfect but that it is headless, and with the tattered clothing still draped round it; and let him realize how grand and glorious a thing it is to have distilled all Youth and Joy and Life into a fetid heap of hideous putrescence! Who is there who has known and seen who can say that Victory is worth the death of even one of these?"

Had there really been a time, I wondered, when I believed that it was?

"When I think of these things," I told him in reply, "I feel that that awful Abstraction, the Unknown God, must be some dread and wrathful deity before whom I can only kneel and plead for mercy, perhaps in the words of a quaint hymn of George Herbert's[13] that we used to sing at Oxford:

Throw away Thy wrath!
Throw away Thy rod!
O my God
Take the gentle path!"

In October, Vera received orders to report to First London General Hospital, Camberwell, an army hospital to which she had applied, lying about her age. Here she experienced miserable living conditions, twelve-hour workdays, and daily exposure to grisly wounds in the surgical wards, in addition to incessant anxiety over Roland's safety and the possible weakening of their love by separation and war. The last week of 1915 she spent in nervous, yet ecstatic anticipation of Roland's leave on December 25, Christmas Day.

Certainly the stage seemed perfectly set for his leave. Now that my parents had at last migrated temporarily to the Grand Hotel at Brighton, our two families were so near; the Matron had promised yet again that my own week's holiday should coincide with his, and even Edward wrote cheerfully for once to say that as soon as the actual date was known, he and Victor[14] would both be able to get leave at the same time.

"Very wet and muddy and many of the communication trenches are quite impassable," ran a letter from Roland written on December 9th. "Three men were killed the other day by a dugout falling in on top of them and one man was drowned in a sump hole. The whole of one's world, at least of one's visible and palpable world, is mud in various stages of solidity or stickiness. . . . I can be perfectly certain about the date of my leave by tomorrow morning and will let you know."

And, when the final information did come, hurriedly written in pencil on a thin slip of paper torn from his Field Service notebook, it brought

---

11. **Battle of Loos,** beginning September 25, 1915.
12. **red, sweet wine of youth.** Here Leighton ironically quotes a famous line from Rupert Brooke's poem "The Dead." See "The Language of Heroism," page 680.
13. **hymn of George Herbert's,** "Discipline," by the seventeenth-century religious poet George Herbert (see pages 253–255).
14. **Victor,** another school friend of Edward Brittain's.

the enchanted day still nearer than I had dared to hope.

"Shall be home on leave from 24th Dec.–31st. Land Christmas Day. R."

Even to the unusual concession of a leave which began on Christmas morning after night-duty the Matron proved amenable, and in the encouraging quietness of the winter's war, with no Loos in prospect, no great push in the west even possible, I dared to glorify my days—or rather my nights—by looking forward. In the pleasant peace of Ward 25, where all the patients, now well on the road to health, slept soundly, the sympathetic Scottish Sister teased me a little for my irrepressible excitement.

"I suppose you won't be thinking of going off and getting married? A couple of babies like you!"

It was a new and breath-taking thought, a flame to which Roland's mother—who approved of early marriages and believed that ways and means could be left to look after themselves far better than the average materialistic parent supposed—added fuel when she hinted mysteriously, on a day off which I spent in Brighton, that *this* time Roland might not be content to leave things as they were. . . . Suppose, I meditated, kneeling in the darkness beside the comforting glow of the stove in the silent ward, that during this leave we *did* marry as suddenly, as, in the last one, we became "officially" engaged? Of course it would be what the world would call—or did call before the War—a "foolish" marriage. But now that the War seemed likely to be endless, and the chance of making a "wise" marriage had become, for most people, so very remote, the world was growing more tolerant. No one—not even my family now, I thought—would hold out against us, even though we hadn't a penny beyond our pay. What if, after all, we did marry thus foolishly? When the War was over we could still go back to Oxford, and learn to be writers—or even lecturers; if we were determined enough about it we could return there, even though—oh, devastating, sweet speculation!—I might have had a baby.

I had never much cared for babies or had anything to do with them; before that time I had always been too ambitious, too much interested in too many projects, to become acutely con-

scious of a maternal instinct. But on those quiet evenings of night-duty as Christmas approached, I would come, half asleep, as near to praying as I had been at any time, even when Roland first went to France or in the days following Loos.

"Oh, God!" my half-articulate thoughts would run, "do let us get married and let me have a baby—something that is Roland's very own, something of himself to remember him by if he goes. . . . It shan't be a burden to his people or mine for a moment longer than I can help, I promise. I'll go on doing war-work and give it all my pay during the War—and as soon as ever the War's over I'll go back to Oxford and take my Finals so that I can get a job and support it. So *do* let me have a baby, dear God!"

Directly after breakfast, sent on my way by exuberant good wishes from Betty and Marjorie and many of the others, I went down to Brighton. All day I waited there for a telephone message or a telegram, sitting drowsily in the lounge of the Grand Hotel, or walking up and down the promenade, watching the grey sea tossing rough with white surf-crested waves, and wondering still what kind of crossing he had had or was having.

When, by ten o'clock at night, no news had come, I concluded that the complications of telegraph and telephone on a combined Sunday and Christmas Day had made communication impossible. So, unable to fight sleep any longer after a night and a day of wakefulness, I went to bed a little disappointed, but still unperturbed. Roland's family, at their Keymer cottage, kept an even longer vigil; they sat up till nearly midnight over their Christmas dinner in the hope that he would join them, and, in their dramatic, impulsive fashion, they drank a toast to the Dead.

The next morning I had just finished dressing, and was putting the final touches to the pastel-blue crêpe-de-Chine blouse, when the expected message came to say that I was wanted on the telephone. Believing that I was at last to hear the voice for which I had waited for twenty-four hours, I dashed joyously into the corridor. But the message was not from Roland but from Clare;[15] it was not to say that he had arrived home that morning, but to tell me that he had died of

---

15. *Clare*, Roland Leighton's sister.

wounds at a Casualty Clearing Station on December 23rd.

Section II of *Testament of Youth* depicts Vera's life during the grimmest war years, 1916 to the Armistice of 1918. Plunged into anguish and nightmarish confusion by the death of Roland, Vera suffered through months of loneliness, strained communication with family and friends, and unresolved perplexity about the meaning of Roland's death.

Whenever I think of the weeks that followed the news of Roland's death, a series of pictures, disconnected but crystal clear, unroll themselves like a kaleidoscope through my mind.

A solitary cup of coffee stands before me on a hotel breakfast-table; I try to drink it, but fail ignominiously.

Outside, in front of the promenade, dismal grey waves tumble angrily over one another on the windy Brighton shore, and, like a slaughtered animal that still twists after life has been extinguished, I go on mechanically worrying because his channel-crossing must have been so rough.

It is Sunday, and I am out for a solitary walk through the dreary streets of Camberwell before going to bed after the night's work. In front of me on the frozen pavement a long red worm wriggles slimily. I remember that, after our death, worms destroy this body—however lovely, however beloved—and I run from the obscene thing in horror.

It is Wednesday, and I am walking up the Brixton Road on a mild, fresh morning of early spring. Half-consciously I am repeating a line from Rupert Brooke: ''The deep night, and birds singing, and clouds flying . . .'' For a moment I have become conscious of the old joy in rain-washed skies and scuttling, fleecy clouds, when suddenly I remember—Roland is dead and I am not keeping faith with him; it is mean and cruel, even for a second, to feel glad to be alive.

In Sussex, by the end of January, the season was already on its upward grade; catkins hung bronze from the bare, black branches, and in the damp lanes between Hassocks and Keymer the birds sang loudly. How I hated them as I walked back to the station one late afternoon, when a red sunset turned the puddles on the road into gleaming pools of blood, and a new horror of mud and death darkened my mind with its dreadful obsession. Roland, I reflected bitterly, was now part of the corrupt clay into which war had transformed the fertile soil of France; he would never again know the smell of a wet evening in early spring.

I had arrived at the cottage that morning to find his mother and sister standing in helpless distress in the midst of his returned kit, which was lying, just opened, all over the floor. The garments sent back included the outfit that he had been wearing when he was hit. I wondered, and I wonder still, why it was thought necessary to return such relics—the tunic torn back and front by the bullet, a khaki vest dark and stiff with blood, and a pair of blood-stained breeches slit open at the top by someone obviously in a violent hurry. Those gruesome rags made me realize, as I had never realized before, all that France really meant. Eighteen months afterwards the smell of Etaples village, though fainter and more diffused, brought back to me the memory of those poor remnants of patriotism.

''Everything,'' I wrote later to Edward, ''was damp and worn and simply caked with mud. And I was glad that neither you nor Victor nor anyone who may some day go to the front was there to see. If you had been, you would have been overwhelmed by the horror of war without its glory. For though he had only worn the things when living, the smell of those clothes was the smell of graveyards and the Dead. The mud of France which covered them was not ordinary mud; it had not the usual clean pure smell of earth, but it was as though it were saturated with dead bodies— dead that had been dead a long, long time . . . . There was his cap, bent in and shapeless out of recognition—the soft cap he wore rakishly on the back of his head—with the badge thickly coated with mud. He must have fallen on top of it, or perhaps one of the people who fetched him in trampled on it.''

What actually happened to the clothes I never knew, but, incongruously enough, it was amid this heap of horror and decay that we found, surrounded by torn bills and letters, the black manuscript notebook containing his poems. On the fly-leaf he had copied a few lines written by John Masefield[16] on the subject of patriotism:

"It is not a song in the street and a wreath on a column and a flag flying from a window and a pro-Boer under a pump.[17] It is a thing very holy and very terrible, like life itself. It is a burden to be borne, a thing to labor for and to suffer for and to die for, a thing which gives no happiness and no pleasantness—but a hard life, an unknown grave, and the respect and bowed heads of those who follow."

The months of unrelieved pain and hopelessness following the death of Roland were further darkened by the departure of Vera's brother Edward for the front in February of 1916 and his later wounding in action, for which he earned the Military Cross. In September, Vera was assigned to eight months of duty on the island of Malta, where the remoteness of the war and exposure to daily sunshine effected a resurgence of hopefulness and personal vitality. In April, 1917, news of the blinding of her and Edward's beloved friend Victor by a bullet in the head abruptly ended Vera's "interval of heaven" and sent her swiftly back to England on a quixotic mission to marry and care for her disabled friend in symbolic tribute to Roland. Shortly after her return, Victor died. Another dear friend, Geoffrey, her confidant in the weeks following Roland's death, was killed at the front. Reflecting on these overwhelming losses, Edward wrote: ". . . we have lost almost all there was to lose and what have we gained? Truly as you say has patriotism worn very threadbare. . . ." With Edward at the front, her fiancé and dearest male friends gone, Vera found life at home intolerable and requested assignment to France. In August of 1917 she crossed the channel to begin work at No. 24 General Hospital, Etaples, caring for the wounded on both sides and exposing herself to considerable personal danger.

Vera Brittain as a V.A.D. nurse.

"Never in my life have I been so absolutely filthy as I get on duty here," I wrote to my mother on December 5th in answer to her request for a description of my work.

"Sister A. has six wards and there is no V.A.D.[18] in the next-door one, only an orderly, so neither she nor he spend very much time in here.

---

16. *John Masefield* (1878–1967), English poet.
17. *a pro-Boer . . . pump.* Public opinion had been strongly divided on the subject of the Boer War (1899–1902), with a number of the British sympathetic to the Boer cause. Here Masefield alludes to the false patriotism of a mob punishing someone opposed to English imperialism by dousing them with water.
18. *V.A.D.,* a nurse of the Voluntary Aid Detachment. "Sister" is the title of a head nurse in a hospital ward.

Consequently I am Sister, V.A.D. and orderly all in one (somebody said the other day that no one less than God Almighty could give a correct definition of the job of a V.A.D.!) and after, quite apart from the nursing, I have stoked the stove all night, done two or three rounds of bed-pans and kept the kettles going and prepared feeds on exceedingly black Beatrice oil-stoves and refilled them from the steam kettles, literally wallowing in paraffin all the time, I feel as if I had been dragged through the gutter! Possibly acute surgical is the heaviest kind of work there is, but acute medical is, I think, more wearing than anything else on earth. You are kept on the go the whole time and in the end there seems nothing definite to show for it—except that one or two people are still alive who might otherwise have been dead."

The rest of my letter referred to the effect, upon ourselves, of the new offensive at Cambrai.[19]

"The hospital is very heavy now—as heavy as when I came; the fighting is continuing very long this year, and the convoys keep coming down, two or three a night. . . . Sometimes in the middle of the night we have to turn people out of bed and make them sleep on the floor to make room for more seriously ill ones that have come down from the line. We have heaps of gassed cases at present who came in a day or two ago; there are 10 in this ward alone. I wish those people who write so glibly about this being a holy War, and the orators who talk so much about going on no matter how long the War lasts and what it may mean, could see a case—to say nothing of 10 cases—of mustard gas in its early stages—could see the poor things burnt and blistered all over with great mustard-colored suppurating blisters, with blind eyes—sometimes temporarily, sometimes permanently—all sticky and stuck together, and always fighting for breath, with voices a mere whisper, saying that their throats are closing and they know they will choke. The only thing one can say is that such severe cases don't last long; either they die soon or else improve—usually the former; they certainly never reach England in the state we have them here, and yet people persist in saying that God made the War, when there are such inventions of the Devil about. . . .

While enduring front-line hardship in an understaffed and besieged camp hospital, Vera was simultaneously forced to deal with the complaints and crises of her parents, who were becoming increasingly incapable of coping with wartime stress and her extended absence. Torn between loyalty to her work and to her family, Vera painfully vacillated between intense resentment toward her parents and guilt over her inability to sympathize with anyone living outside the combat zone. In April, 1918, following her mother's collapse, Vera reluctantly returned to England to take charge of her parents' household and settle into weeks of dreary domesticity and heightened anxiety over the safety of Edward, now stationed on the Italian front.

The despondency at home was certainly making many of us in France quite alarmed: because we were women we feared perpetually that, just as our work was reaching its climax, our families would need our youth and vitality for their own support. One of my cousins, the daughter of an aunt, had already been summoned home from her canteen work in Boulogne; she was only one of many, for as the War continued to wear out strength and spirits, the middle-aged generation, having irrevocably yielded up its sons, began to lean with increasing weight upon its daughters. Thus the desperate choice between incompatible claims—by which the women of my generation, with their carefully trained consciences, have always been tormented—showed signs of afflicting us with new pertinacity. . . .

Early in April a letter arrived from my father to say that my mother had "crocked up" and had been obliged, owing to the inefficiency of the domestic help then available, to go into a nursing-home. What exactly was wrong remained unspecified, though phrases referred to "toxic heart" and "complete general breakdown." My father had temporarily closed the flat and moved into an hotel, but he did not, he told me, wish to remain there. "As your mother and I can no longer man-

---

19. **Cambrai,** beginning November 20, 1917, the first action in which a notable use was made of tanks.

age without you," he concluded, "it is now your duty to leave France immediately and return to Kensington."

I read these words with real dismay, for my father's interpretation of my duty was not, I knew only too well, in the least likely to agree with that of the Army, which had always been singularly unmoved by the worries of relatives. What was I to do? I wondered desperately. There was my family, confidently demanding my presence, and here was the offensive,[20] which made every pair of experienced hands worth ten pairs under normal conditions. I remembered how the hastily imported V.A.D.s had gone sick at the 1st London during the rush after the Somme; a great push was no time in which to teach a tyro her job. How much of my mother's breakdown was physical and how much psychological—the cumulative result of pessimism at home? It did not then occur to me that my father's sense of emergency was probably heightened by a subconscious determination to get me back to London before the Germans reached the Channel ports, as everyone in England felt certain they would. I only knew that no one in France would believe a domestic difficulty to be so insoluble; if I were dead, or a male, it would have to be settled without me. I should merely be thought to have "wind-up," to be using my mother's health as an excuse to escape the advancing enemy or the threatening air raids.

Half-frantic with the misery of conflicting obligations, I envied Edward his complete powerlessness to leave the Army whatever happened at home. Today, remembering the violent clash between family and profession, between "duty" and ambition, between conscience and achievement, which has always harassed the women now in their thirties and forties, I find myself still hoping that if the efforts of various interested parties succeed in destroying the fragile international structure built up since the Armistice, and war breaks out on a scale comparable to that of 1914, the organizers of the machine will not hesitate to conscript all women under fifty for service at home or abroad. In the long run, an irrevocable allegiance in a time of emergency makes decision easier for the older as well as for the younger generation. What exhausts women in wartime is not the strenuous and unfamiliar tasks that fall upon them, nor even the hourly dread of death for husbands or lovers or brothers or sons; it is the incessant conflict between personal and national claims which wears out their energy and breaks their spirit. . . .

It seemed to me then, with my crude judgments and black-and-white values, quite inexplicable that the older generation, which had merely looked on at the War, should break under the strain so much more quickly than those of us who had faced death or horror at first hand for months on end. Today, with middle-age just round the corner, and children who tug my anxious thoughts relentlessly back to them whenever I have to leave them for a week, I realize how completely I underestimated the effect upon the civilian population of year upon year of diminishing hope, diminishing food, diminishing light, diminishing heat, of waiting and waiting for news which was nearly always bad when it came. . . .

For some time now, my apprehensions for Edward's safety had been lulled by the long quiescence of the Italian front, which had seemed a haven of peace in contrast to our own raging vortex. Repeatedly, during the German offensive, I had thanked God and the Italians who fled at Caporetto[21] that Edward was out of it, and rejoiced that the worst I had to fear from this particular push was the comparatively trivial danger that threatened myself. But now I felt the familiar stirrings of the old tense fear which had been such a persistent companion throughout the War, and my alarm was increased when Edward asked me a week or two later to send him "a funny cat from Liberty's[22] . . . to alleviate tragedy with comedy."

On Sunday morning, June 16th, I opened the *Observer,* which appeared to be chiefly concerned with the new offensive—for the moment at a standstill—in the Noyon-Montdidier sector of the Western Front, and instantly saw at the head of a column the paragraph for which I had looked so long and so fearfully:

---

20. *the offensive,* the last great German offensive of the war, beginning March 21, 1918.
21. *Caporetto,* the rout of the Italian second army by a combined Austro-German attack, October 24, 1917.
22. *Liberty's,* a London department store.

"ITALIAN FRONT ABLAZE
GUN DUELS FROM MOUNTAIN TO SEA
BAD OPENING OF AN OFFENSIVE

"The following Italian official *communiqué* was issued yesterday:

"From dawn this morning the fire of the enemy's artillery, strongly countered by our own, was intensified from the Lagerina Valley to the sea. On the Asiago Plateau, to the east of the Brenta and on the middle Piave, the artillery struggle has assumed and maintains a character of extreme violence."

A day or two later, more details were published of the fighting in Italy, and I learnt that the Sherwood Foresters[23] had been involved in the "show" on the Plateau. After that I made no pretense at doing anything but wander restlessly round Kensington or up and down the flat, and, though my father retired glumly to bed every evening at nine o'clock, I gave up writing the semi-fictitious record which I had begun of my life in France. Somehow I couldn't bring myself even to wrap up the *Spectator* and *Saturday Review* that I sent every week to Italy, and they remained in my bedroom, silent yet eloquent witnesses to the dread which my father and I, determinedly conversing on commonplace topics, each refused to put into words.

By the following Saturday we had still heard nothing of Edward. The interval usually allowed for news of casualties after a battle was seldom so long as this, and I began, with an artificial sense of lightness unaccompanied by real conviction, to think that there was perhaps, after all, no news to come. I had just announced to my father, as we sat over tea in the dining-room, that I really must do up Edward's papers and take them to the post office before it closed for the week-end, when there came the sudden loud clattering at the front-door knocker that always meant a telegram.

For a moment I thought that my legs would not carry me, but they behaved quite normally as I got up and went to the door. I knew what was in the telegram—I had known for a week—but because the persistent hopefulness of the human heart refuses to allow intuitive certainty to persuade the reason of that which it knows, I opened and read it in a tearing anguish of suspense.

"Regret to inform you Captain E. H. Brittain M.C. killed in action Italy June 15th."

"No answer," I told the boy mechanically, and handed the telegram to my father, who had followed me into the hall. As we went back into the dining-room I saw, as though I had never seen them before, the bowl of blue delphiniums on the table; their intense color, vivid, ethereal, seemed too radiant for earthly flowers.

Then I remembered that we should have to go down to Purley and tell the news to my mother.
. . .

Long after [her father] had gone to bed and the world had grown silent, I crept into the dining-room to be alone with Edward's portrait. Carefully closing the door, I turned on the light and looked at the pale, pictured face, so dignified, so steadfast, so tragically mature. He had been through so much—far, far more than those beloved friends who had died at an earlier stage of the interminable War, leaving him alone to mourn their loss. Fate might have allowed him the little, sorry compensation of survival, the chance to make his lovely music in honor of their memory. It seemed indeed the last irony that he should have been killed by the countrymen of Fritz Kreisler,[24] the violinist whom of all others he had most greatly admired.

And suddenly, as I remembered all the dear afternoons and evenings when I had followed him on the piano as he played his violin, the sad, searching eyes of the portrait were more than I could bear, and falling on my knees before it I began to cry "Edward! Oh, Edward!" in dazed repetition, as though my persistent crying and calling would somehow bring him back. . . .

> After a summer of stagnation and grief, Vera signed on for a demeaning month of duty at St. Jude's Hospital, then moved to Queen Alexandra's Hospital, Millbank, where she stayed until April 1919, functioning like an automaton in the aftermath of Edward's death. Not surprisingly, Vera observed Armistice Day in a spirit of sorrowful reminiscence and realistic assessment of the impact of the tragic war years.

---

23. *Sherwood Foresters,* Edward Brittain's regiment.
24. *Fritz Kreisler* (1875–1962), Austrian violinist.

When the sound of victorious guns burst over London at 11 a.m. on November 11th, 1918, the men and women who looked incredulously into each other's faces did not cry jubilantly: "We've won the War!" They only said: "The War is over."

From Millbank I heard the maroons[25] crash with terrifying clearness, and, like a sleeper who is determined to go on dreaming after being told to wake up, I went on automatically washing the dressing bowls in the annex outside my hut. Deeply buried beneath my consciousness there stirred the vague memory of a letter that I had written to Roland in those legendary days when I was still at Oxford, and could spend my Sundays in thinking of him while the organ echoed grandly through New College Chapel. It had been a warm May evening, when all the city was sweet with the scent of wallflowers and lilac, and I had walked back to Micklem Hall after hearing an Occasional Oratorio by Handel,[26] which described the mustering of troops for battle, the lament for the fallen and the triumphant return of the victors.

"As I listened," I told him, "to the organ swelling forth into a final triumphant burst in the song of victory, after the solemn and mournful dirge over the dead, I thought with what mockery and irony the jubilant celebrations which will hail the coming of peace will fall upon the ears of those to whom their best will never return, upon whose sorrow victory is built, who have paid with their mourning for the others' joy. I wonder if I shall be one of those who take a happy part in the triumph—or if I shall listen to the merriment with a heart that breaks and ears that try to keep out the mirthful sounds."

And as I dried the bowls I thought: "It's come too late for me. Somehow I knew, even at Oxford, that it would. Why couldn't it have ended rationally, as it might have ended, in 1916, instead of all that trumpet-blowing against a negotiated peace, and the ferocious talk of secure civilians about marching to Berlin? It's come five months too late—or is it three years? It might have ended last June, and let Edward, at least, be saved! Only five months—it's such a little time, when Roland died nearly three years ago." . . .

Late that evening, when supper was over, a group of elated V.A.D.s who were anxious to walk through Westminster and Whitehall to Buckingham Palace prevailed upon me to join them. Outside the Admiralty a crazy group of convalescent Tommies[27] were collecting specimens of different uniforms and bundling their wearers into flagstrewn taxis; with a shout they seized two of my companions and disappeared into the clamorous crowd, waving flags and shaking rattles. Wherever we went a burst of enthusiastic cheering greeted our Red Cross uniform, and complete strangers adorned with wound stripes rushed up and shook me warmly by the hand. After the long, long blackness, it seemed like a fairy-tale to see the street lamps shining through the chill November gloom.

I detached myself from the others and walked slowly up Whitehall, with my heart sinking in a sudden cold dismay. Already this was a different world from the one that I had known during four life-long years, a world in which people would be light-hearted and forgetful, in which themselves and their careers and their amusements would blot out political ideals and great national issues. And in that brightly lit, alien world I should have no part. All those with whom I had really been intimate were gone; not one remained to share with me the heights and the depths of my memories. As the years went by and youth departed and remembrance grew dim, a deeper and ever deeper darkness would cover the young men who were once my contemporaries.

For the time I realized, with all that full realization meant, how completely everything that had hitherto made up my life had vanished with Edward and Roland, with Victor and Geoffrey. The War was over; a new age was beginning; but the dead were dead and would never return.

1933

---

25. **maroons,** fireworks that simulate the sound of cannon.
26. **Handel** (1685–1759), German composer long resident in England.
27. **Tommies,** British soldiers.

Discussion

1. How does Vera Brittain characterize herself and her entire generation in her account of how she reacted to the outbreak of war?

2. (a) Describe the mood and behavior of the general public during the first weeks of the war. **(b)** What does Brittain prefer to think were her "real sentiments" about England's involvement in the war, even before she had been personally scarred by the terrible suffering that resulted?

3. What conflict helped create the state of "perpetual tension" in the Brittain household? Was it ever satisfactorily resolved?

4. Contrast the "rules of courtship" which Vera and Roland were compelled to observe with those followed in today's society.

5. Already in her diary entry of April 17, 1915, Vera is beginning to show signs of bitterness and strain. **(a)** How does her participation in one of the first national "flagdays" deepen her sense of disillusionment with the older generation? **(b)** Why, even years later, did she find it uncomfortable to work in a room where it was "possible to hear the front-door bell"?

6. Compare Roland's description of the suffering of the men at the front and his attack on romantic attitudes toward war with Wilfred Owen's "Dulce et Decorum Est." What truth about war did they both learn as a result of personal experience at the front?

7. (a) Having been informed of Roland's Christmas leave, Vera says, "I dared to glorify my days—or rather my nights—by looking forward." What fantasies helped sustain her during the days of anxious waiting? **(b)** What circumstances lent particular irony to the phone message Vera received from Roland's sister the day after Christmas?

8. (a) What contradictory feelings following Roland's death contributed to Vera's personal torment? **(b)** What was so poignant about the kit of Roland's belongings sent home to his family? Why did the copied lines of John Masefield found in the kit seem "incongruous"?

9. Writing in the early 1930s, Brittain expresses the hope that, in any future war, women are conscripted as well as men. What personal trials caused her to feel this way?

10. What was Vera's reaction to the news of Edward's death on the Italian front?

11. (a) Describe Vera's reactions on November 11, 1918, after news of the Armistice had been announced. **(b)** What realization about the lasting impact of the war became clear to Vera that day?

Vocabulary
Antonyms, Synonyms

Determine the relationship between the two italicized words listed in each numbered item. Then select, from the pairs of words that follow, the two that are related in the same way as the words in the first pair. Example—*hot : cold* (the colon means "is related to") as (a) weather : storm; (b) day : night; (c) desert : sand. In the example, *hot* is the opposite of *cold;* therefore the correct answer is (b) day : night. There is a word in each italicized pair that you will probably have to check in the Glossary.

1. *demented : sane* as **(a)** mirth : humor; **(b)** soothe : upset; **(c)** wretched : miserable.

2. *irritable : petulant* as **(a)** coax : persuade; **(b)** quiet : noisy; **(c)** stern : gentle.

3. *quiet : pandemonium* as **(a)** carefree : playful; **(b)** smart : intelligent; **(c)** proud : humble.

4. *scintillate : glitter* as **(a)** unpleasant : painful; **(b)** brave : cowardly; **(c)** honest : sinister.

5. *oozing : suppurating* as **(a)** cheap : expensive; **(b)** ruin : destroy; **(c)** friendly : hostile.

Composition

Select one of the episodes from *Testament of Youth,* such as Vera's dread at the sound of the doorbell, the arrival of Roland's blood-stiffened clothes, or the evening of Armistice Day, as the basis of a poem. Consider the images employed by Brittain, and the mood conveyed by the passage.

Write a poem based on the passage you have chosen.

T. S. Eliot 1888–1965

On June 21, 1917, the *Times Literary Supplement* reviewed *Prufrock and Other Observations,* a volume of poems by T. S. Eliot, an American who had recently settled in London; the reviewer was unenthusiastic. Thirty-one years later, Eliot was awarded the Nobel Prize. During the intervening years he had emerged as the pivotal figure of modern English literature, the person most directly responsible for changing the course of literary style and taste. He did this through his poetry and plays, works like *The Waste Land* (1922) and *Murder in the Cathedral* (1935), which reflected disillusionment with commercial values and hunger for spiritual revitalization. He did this as well through his work as critic, editor, and publisher. He founded an influential literary journal, *The Criterion,* in 1922, and seven years later became a director of the publishers Faber and Faber, where he introduced the work of W. H. Auden (see pages 740–745) and Louis MacNeice (see pages 746–747).

Eliot famously defined his beliefs as "classicist in literature, royalist in politics, and Anglo-Catholic in religion." In his criticism he discussed his distaste for romanticism and "self-expression," never wavering in his insistence that poetry is "art"—something deliberately crafted and therefore a *patterning* of feeling rather than the feelings themselves. He turned away from the Romantics and Victorians and toward Shakespeare, the metaphysical poets of the seventeenth century, and the nineteenth-century French Symbolists, all of whom he preferred for their use of "common speech," precise sensory images, and ironic wit. While Eliot's poetry is often difficult, at times overly dry, confusingly allusive, and disconnected, every word and phrase has been calculated to directly *reveal,* rather than *explain,* an idea or emotion.

"The Love Song of J. Alfred Prufrock" was written while Eliot was still a student at Harvard. He did graduate work at Harvard, the Sorbonne in Paris, and Oxford, then settled in London, becoming a British subject in 1917. Though his writings attracted attention from the start, because of financial pressures he taught school for a time, later worked in a bank, and in 1925 joined the publishing firm of Faber and Gwyer (later Faber and Faber). During his later years, fame led Eliot into the thick of editing and publishing, though he remained personally shy, aloof, and reclusive.

Eliot's recurrent theme is the sense of loss; in the words of one critic, "the lost vision, the lost purpose, the lost meaning, the lost sense of fellowship, the lost sense of self." In 1927 Eliot became a convert to the Anglican church, and in his later poetry, most impressively in *Ash Wednesday* (1930) and *Four Quartets* (1943), he turned to the theme of spiritual recovery and renewal. His verse dramas, such as *Murder in the Cathedral, The Family Reunion* (1939), and *The Cocktail Party* (1950), contain fine passages but lack characterization and genuine dramatic vitality.

*T*he Hollow Men

Mistah Kurtz—he dead.[1]
A penny for the Old Guy[2]

I

We are the hollow men
We are the stuffed men
Leaning together
Headpiece filled with straw. Alas!
5 Our dried voices, when
We whisper together
Are quiet and meaningless
As wind in dry grass
Or rats' feet over broken glass
10 In our dry cellar

Shape without form, shade without color,
Paralyzed force, gesture without motion;

Those who have crossed
With direct eyes,[3] to death's other Kingdom[4]
15 Remember us—if at all—not as lost
Violent souls, but only
As the hollow men
The stuffed men.

II

Eyes[5] I dare not meet in dreams
20 In death's dream kingdom
These do not appear:
There, the eyes are
Sunlight on a broken column
There, is a tree swinging
25 And voices are
In the wind's singing

1. *Mistah Kurtz—he dead.* Eliot's first epigraph is a quotation from Joseph Conrad's novella *Heart of Darkness* (see page 513). Kurtz is a European trader who goes into "the heart of darkness"—the central African jungle—with European standards of life and conduct. Because he has no moral or spiritual strength to sustain him, he soon turns into a barbarian. He differs, however, from Eliot's "hollow men": he is not paralyzed, as they are, but commits acts of overwhelming evil; and he is not blind as they are, but at his death glimpses the nature of his actions when he exclaims, "The horror! The horror!" Kurtz is thus one of the "lost / Violent souls" mentioned in lines 15–16.
2. *A penny . . . Guy,* traditional cry of English children soliciting money for fireworks to celebrate Guy Fawkes Day, November 5, which commemorates the thwarting of the Gunpowder Plot of 1605 in which Guy Fawkes and other conspirators planned to blow up both Houses of Parliament (see pages 130–131). On this day straw-stuffed images of Fawkes called *guys* are burned.
3. *Those . . . direct eyes,* those who have represented something positive (direct), either for good or evil.
4. *death's other Kingdom,* the afterlife; eternity.
5. *Eyes,* the eyes of those in the afterworld who had confident faith; those who represent positive spiritual force as opposed to the spiritual stagnation or paralysis of the "hollow men."

More distant and more solemn
Than a fading star.

Let me be no nearer
30 In death's dream kingdom
Let me also wear
Such deliberate disguises
Rat's coat, crowskin, crossed staves
In a field[6]
35 Behaving as the wind behaves
No nearer—
Not that final meeting
In the twilight kingdom

III

This is the dead land
40 This is cactus land
Here the stone images
Are raised, here they receive
The supplication of a dead man's hand
Under the twinkle of a fading star.
45 Is it like this
In death's other kingdom
Waking alone
At the hour when we are
Trembling with tenderness
50 Lips that would kiss
Form prayers to broken stone.

IV

The eyes are not here
There are no eyes here
In this valley of dying stars
55 In this hollow valley
This broken jaw of our lost kingdoms

In this last of meeting places
We grope together
And avoid speech
60 Gathered on this beach of the tumid river

Sightless, unless
The eyes reappear
As the perpetual star
Multifoliate rose[7]
65 Of death's twilight kingdom
The hope only
Of empty men.

V

Here we go round the prickly pear
Prickly pear prickly pear
70 *Here we go round the prickly pear*
At five o'clock in the morning.[8]
Between the idea
And the reality
Between the motion
75 And the act
Falls the Shadow
For Thine is the Kingdom[9]

Between the conception
And the creation
80 Between the emotion
And the response
Falls the Shadow
Life is very long

Between the desire
85 And the spasm
Between the potency
And the existence
Between the essence
And the descent
90 Falls the Shadow
For Thine is the Kingdom

For Thine is
Life is
For Thine is the

95 *This is the way the world ends*
This is the way the world ends
This is the way the world ends
Not with a bang but a whimper.

1925

---

6. Rat's coat . . . in a field, a scarecrow decorated with dead rats and crows.
7. Multifoliate rose, in Dante's *Divine Comedy* a symbol of Paradise, in which the saints are the many petals of the rose.
8. Here we go . . . morning, a parody of the children's rhyme "Here we go round the mulberry bush."
9. For thine . . . kingdom, a phrase from the Lord's Prayer.

Journey of the Magi[1]

"A cold coming we had of it,
Just the worst time of the year
For a journey, and such a long journey:
The ways deep and the weather sharp,
5   The very dead of winter."[2]
And the camels galled, sore-footed,
        refractory,
Lying down in the melting snow.
There were times we regretted
The summer palaces on slopes, the terraces,
10   And the silken girls bringing sherbet.
Then the camel men cursing and grumbling
And running away, and wanting their liquor
        and women,
And the night-fires going out, and the lack of
        shelters,
And the cities hostile and the towns
        unfriendly
15   And the villages dirty and charging high
        prices:
A hard time we had of it.
At the end we preferred to travel all night,
Sleeping in snatches,
With the voices singing in our ears, saying

---

1. *Magi,* the "wise men from the east" who journeyed to Bethlehem to see the infant Jesus. (Matthew 2:1–12)
2. *"A cold . . . winter,"* adapted from a nativity sermon by the seventeenth-century preacher Lancelot Andrewes (1555–1626).

20 That this was all folly.
   Then at dawn we came down to a temperate
      valley,
   Wet, below the snow line, smelling of
      vegetation;
   With a running stream and a water mill
      beating the darkness,
   And three trees on the low sky,
25 And an old white horse galloped away in the
      meadow.
   Then we came to a tavern with vine-leaves
      over the lintel,
   Six hands at an open door dicing for pieces
      of silver,
   And feet kicking the empty wineskins.[3]
   But there was no information, and so we
      continued
30 And arrived at evening, not a moment too soon
   Finding the place; it was (you may say)
      satisfactory.

   All this was a long time ago, I remember,
   And I would do it again, but set down

   This set down
35 This: were we led all that way for
   Birth or Death? There was a Birth, certainly,
   We had evidence and no doubt. I had seen
      birth and death,
   But had thought they were different; this
      Birth was
   Hard and bitter agony for us, like Death, our
      death.
40 We returned to our places, these Kingdoms,
   But no longer at ease here, in the old
      dispensation,[4]
   With an alien people clutching their gods.
   I should be glad of another death.

                                           1927

---

3. **Then at dawn . . . wineskins.** Images in this passage suggest both renewal of life ("vegetation"; "running stream") and death, foreshadowing events in the life of Jesus. The "three trees" suggest the Crucifixion; the men "dicing for pieces of silver" recall both the thirty pieces of silver received by Judas for betraying Jesus and the gambling of the soldiers for Jesus' garments at the foot of the Cross. The white horse is mentioned in Revelation 6:2 and 19:11 in passages alluding to the end of the world.
4. **the old dispensation,** the old pagan religion.

Discussion

The Hollow Men

1. What images of human emptiness are presented in section I?

2. What indication do we have in section II that the speaker, like the other "hollow men," has given up the struggle to revitalize his life?

3. (a) In sections III and IV, what elements of the physical environment reflect the emotional and spiritual emptiness of "the hollow men"? **(b)** What is the only hope for their regeneration?

4. (a) Both the opening and closing lines of Section V parody nursery rhymes. What is the effect of these lines? **(b)** What do the fragments of the Lord's Prayer suggest about the spiritual condition of "the hollow men"?

Journey of the Magi

1. (a) Who is the speaker? **(b)** How old do you think he is?

2. The speaker's account falls into three distinct parts. What are they?

3. (a) Why does the speaker say: "this Birth was / Hard and bitter agony for us, like Death, our death"? **(b)** What does he mean when he says in the last line that he "should be glad of another death"? **(c)** Why then does he also say he "would do it again" (line 33)?

4. What did the Magi find at the end of their journey? Explain.

Composition

T. S. Eliot is a highly allusive poet; his poems frequently contain quotations from other works or echo them in some way. Using the footnotes on page 698, examine the relation of Eliot's two epigraphs for "The Hollow Men" ("Mistah Kurtz—he dead" and "A penny for the Old Guy") to the poem as a whole.

In a brief essay examine the relevance of Eliot's epigraphs.

James Joyce 1882–1941

On the basis of a few poems, a play, and four works of fiction—*Dubliners, A Portrait of the Artist as a Young Man, Ulysses,* and *Finnegans Wake*—James Joyce has come to be regarded as the most original and influential writer of the twentieth century. He was born in Dublin, the eldest of a family of ten children. His father was a civil servant, continually in financial difficulties; his mother was mild-mannered and pious. For several years Joyce attended Clongowes Wood College, a famous Jesuit boarding school, before his family's increasing poverty made this impossible. He later attended University College, Dublin, where he was a brilliant scholar, accomplished in Latin, French, Italian, and Norwegian (the last to enable him to read the plays of the Norwegian dramatist Henrik Ibsen, whom he intensely admired). It was his success in publishing a review of Ibsen's play *When We Dead Awaken* in the London *Fortnightly Review* in 1900 when he was just eighteen that confirmed Joyce in his resolution to become a writer. Disillusion-

ment with Catholicism and the cultural climate of Dublin caused him to leave Ireland for a self-imposed exile in the Italian city of Trieste, and later in Paris and Zurich. Joyce's life during these years was a continual struggle against poverty, eye diseases, and the hostility of censors. During his later years, however, he began to enjoy an international reputation as a modern literary master. He was at work on a

*A*raby

North Richmond Street, being blind, was a quiet street except at the hour when the Christian Brothers' School set the boys free. An uninhabited house of two storeys stood at the blind end, detached from its neighbors in a square ground. The other houses of the street, conscious of decent lives within them, gazed at one another with brown imperturbable faces.

The former tenant of our house, a priest, had died in the back drawing-room. Air, musty from having been long enclosed, hung in all the rooms, and the waste room behind the kitchen was littered with old useless papers. Among these I found a few paper-covered books, the pages of which were curled and damp: *The Abbot,* by Wal-

ter Scott, *The Devout Communicant* and *The Memoirs of Vidocq.*[1] I liked the last best because its leaves were yellow. The wild garden behind the house contained a central apple-tree and a few straggling bushes under one of which I found the late tenant's rusty bicycle-pump. He had

1. Vidocq. François-Eugène Vidocq (1775–1857) was an ex-thief who offered his services to Napoleon's government in 1809 and was made head of a special police force composed of former thieves. What was published as his *Memoirs* in 1828 is probably not by him.

sequel to *Finnegans Wake* when he died in Zurich in 1941.

Joyce said that his purpose in writing the short stories collected in *Dubliners* (1914) was to produce "a chapter of the moral history of my country and I chose Dublin for the scene because the city seemed to me the center of paralysis." He wanted to give "the Irish people . . . one good look at themselves in my nicely polished looking glass." The style of *Dubliners* marks a sharp break with the fiction of the nineteenth century. Joyce locates the center of the action in the minds of his characters. Incident and plot are subordinated to psychological revelation. Each word and detail has a calculated purpose, and the meaning of the story is presented as an "epiphany"—a moment of heightened awareness that can occur as a result of a trivial encounter, object, or event. *A Portrait of the Artist as a Young Man* (1916), Joyce's artistic and spiritual autobiography, represents a further working out of this narrative technique. *Ulysses* (1922), perhaps this century's most famous novel, is a dazzlingly

original attempt to tell the story of a group of Dubliners on a single day and at the same time present a symbolic view of human history. Portions of Joyce's next novel, *Finnegans Wake* (1939), appeared first in Paris in periodicals under the title *Work in Progress*. This book, which occupied Joyce for fifteen years or more, carried the strenuous stylistic experimentation of *Ulysses* even further, expressing the nightlong dream of a Dublin tavern-keeper in a complex, synthetic language created from the many languages Joyce knew. The book was directed, he said, to "that ideal reader suffering from an ideal insomnia"; though exhaustively explicated, *Finnegans Wake* remains inaccessible to the general reader.

In form and content, most of Joyce's work was controversial. During his lifetime publication was often delayed, and his works were banned, burned, pirated, and confiscated. The ruling of a U.S. federal court judge in 1933 permitting the American publication of *Ulysses* was a landmark in the fight against censorship and hastened recognition of Joyce's achievement.

been a very charitable priest; in his will he had left all his money to institutions and the furniture of his house to his sister.

When the short days of winter came, dusk fell before we had well eaten our dinners. When we met in the street the houses had grown somber. The space of sky above us was the color of ever-changing violet and towards it the lamps of the street lifted their feeble lanterns. The cold air stung us and we played till our bodies glowed. Our shouts echoed in the silent street. The career of our play brought us through the dark muddy lanes behind the houses where we ran the gauntlet of the rough tribes from the cottages, to the back doors of the dark dripping gardens where

odors arose from the ashpits, to the dark odorous stables where a coachman smoothed and combed the horse or shook music from the buckled harness. When we returned to the street, light from the kitchen windows had filled the areas. If my uncle was seen turning the corner we hid in the shadow until we had seen him safely housed. Or if Mangan's sister came out on the doorstep to call her brother in to his tea we watched her from our shadow peer up and down the street. We waited to see whether she would remain or go in and, if she remained, we left our shadow and walked up to Mangan's steps resignedly. She was waiting for us, her figure defined by the light from the half-opened door. Her brother always teased her before he obeyed and I stood by the railings looking at her. Her dress swung as she moved her body and the soft rope of her hair tossed from side to side.

Every morning I lay on the floor in the front parlor watching her door. The blind was pulled down to within an inch of the sash so that I could not be seen. When she came out on the doorstep my heart leaped. I ran to the hall, seized my books and followed her. I kept her brown figure always in my eye and, when we came near the point at which our ways diverged, I quickened my pace and passed her. This happened morning after morning. I had never spoken to her, except for a few casual words, and yet her name was like a summons to all my foolish blood.

Her image accompanied me even in places the most hostile to romance. On Saturday evenings when my aunt went marketing I had to go to carry some of the parcels. We walked through the flaring streets, jostled by drunken men and bargaining women, amid the curses of laborers, the shrill litanies of shopboys who stood on guard by the barrels of pigs' cheeks, the nasal chanting of street-singers, who sang a *come-all-you* about O'Donovan Rossa, or a ballad about the troubles in our native land. These noises converged in a single sensation of life for me: I imagined that I bore my chalice safely through a throng of foes. Her name sprang to my lips at moments in strange prayers and praises which I myself did not understand. My eyes were often full of tears (I could not tell why) and at times a flood from my heart seemed to pour itself out into my bosom. I thought little of the future. I did not know whether I would ever speak to her or not or, if I spoke to her, how I could tell her of my confused adoration. But my body was like a harp and her words and gestures were like fingers running upon the wires.

One evening I went into the back drawing-room in which the priest had died. It was a dark rainy evening and there was no sound in the house. Through one of the broken panes I heard the rain impinge upon the earth, the fine incessant needles of water playing in the sodden beds. Some distant lamp or lighted window gleamed below me. I was thankful that I could see so little. All my senses seemed to desire to veil themselves and, feeling that I was about to slip from them, I pressed the palms of my hands together until they trembled, murmuring: *"O love! O love!"* many times.

At last she spoke to me. When she addressed the first words to me I was so confused that I did not know what to answer. She asked me was I going to *Araby.* I forgot whether I answered yes or no. It would be a splendid bazaar, she said she would love to go.

"And why can't you?" I asked.

While she spoke she turned a silver bracelet round and round her wrist. She could not go, she said, because there would be a retreat that week in her convent. Her brother and two other boys were fighting for their caps and I was alone at the railings. She held one of the spikes, bowing her head towards me. The light from the lamp opposite our door caught the white curve of her neck, lit up her hair that rested there and, falling, lit up the hand upon the railing. It fell over one side of her dress and caught the white border of a petticoat, just visible as she stood at ease.

"It's well for you," she said.

"If I go," I said, "I will bring you something."

What innumerable follies laid waste my waking and sleeping thoughts after that evening! I wished to annihilate the tedious intervening days. I chafed against the work of school. At night in my bedroom and by day in the classroom her image came between me and the page I strove to read. The syllables of the word *Araby* were called to me through the silence in which my soul luxuriated and cast an eastern enchantment over me. I asked for leave to go to the bazaar on Saturday night. My aunt was surprised and hoped it was not some Freemason affair.[2] I answered few questions in class. I watched my master's face pass from amiability to sternness; he hoped I was not beginning to idle. I could not call my wandering thoughts together. I had hardly any patience with the serious work of life which, now that it stood between me and my desire, seemed to me child's play, ugly monotonous child's play.

On Saturday morning I reminded my uncle that I wished to go to the bazaar in the evening.

---

2. **Freemason affair.** The Freemasons are a worldwide secret society whose purpose is mutual aid and fellowship. The Roman Catholic Church has traditionally opposed Freemasonry.

He was fussing at the hallstand, looking for the hat-brush, and answered me curtly:

"Yes, boy, I know."

As he was in the hall I could not go into the front parlor and lie at the window. I left the house in bad humor and walked slowly towards the school. The air was pitilessly raw and already my heart misgave me.

When I came home to dinner my uncle had not yet been home. Still it was early. I sat staring at the clock for some time and, when its ticking began to irritate me, I left the room. I mounted the staircase and gained the upper part of the house. The high, cold, empty, gloomy rooms liberated me and I went from room to room singing. From the front window I saw my companions playing below in the street. Their cries reached me weakened and indistinct and, leaning my forehead against the cool glass, I looked over at the dark house where she lived. I may have stood there for an hour, seeing nothing but the brown-clad figure cast by my imagination, touched discreetly by the lamplight at the curved neck, at the hand upon the railings, and at the border below the dress.

When I came downstairs again I found Mrs. Mercer sitting at the fire. She was an old garrulous woman, a pawnbroker's widow, who collected used stamps for some pious purpose. I had to endure the gossip of the tea-table. The meal was prolonged beyond an hour and still my uncle did not come. Mrs. Mercer stood up to go: she was sorry she couldn't wait any longer, but it was after eight o'clock and she did not like to be out late, as the night air was bad for her. When she had gone I began to walk up and down the room, clenching my fists. My aunt said:

"I'm afraid you may put off your bazaar for this night of Our Lord."

At nine o'clock I heard my uncle's latchkey in the hall door. I heard him talking to himself and heard the hallstand rocking when it had received the weight of his overcoat. I could interpret these signs. When he was midway through his dinner I asked him to give me the money to go to the bazaar. He had forgotten.

"The people are in bed and after their first sleep now," he said.

I did not smile. My aunt said to him energetically:

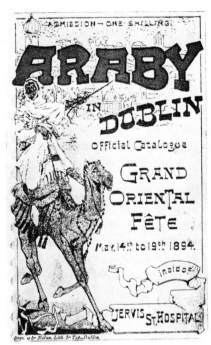

The program of the bazaar Araby in Dublin, May 14–19, 1894.

"Can't you give him the money and let him go? You've kept him late enough as it is."

My uncle said he was very sorry he had forgotten. He said he believed in the old saying: "All work and no play makes Jack a dull boy." He asked me where I was going and, when I had told him a second time he asked me did I know *The Arab's Farewell to His Steed.*[3] When I left the kitchen he was about to recite the opening lines of the piece to my aunt.

I held a florin[4] tightly in my hand as I strode down Buckingham Street towards the station. The sight of the streets thronged with buyers and glaring with gas recalled to me the purpose of my journey. I took my seat in a third-class carriage of a deserted train. After an intolerable delay the train moved out of the station slowly. It crept onward among ruinous houses and over the twinkling river. At Westland Row Station a crowd of people pressed to the carriage doors; but the porters moved them back, saying that it was a spe-

---

3. **The Arab's . . . Steed,** a famous Victorian poem by Mrs. Caroline E. S. Norton (1808–1877), "the Byron of her sex."
4. **florin,** a former English coin, worth two shillings.

cial train for the bazaar. I remained alone in the bare carriage. In a few minutes the train drew up beside an improvised wooden platform. I passed out on to the road and saw by the lighted dial of a clock that it was ten minutes to ten. In front of me was a large building which displayed the magical name.

I could not find any sixpenny entrance and, fearing that the bazaar would be closed, I passed in quickly through a turnstile, handing a shilling to a weary-looking man. I found myself in a big hall girdled at half its height by a gallery. Nearly all the stalls were closed and the greater part of the hall was in darkness. I recognised a silence like that which pervades a church after a service. I walked into the center of the bazaar timidly. A few people were gathered about the stalls which were still open. Before a curtain, over which the words *Café Chantant*[5] were written in colored lamps, two men were counting money on a salver. I listened to the fall of the coins.

Remembering with difficulty why I had come I went over to one of the stalls and examined porcelain vases and flowered tea-sets. At the door of the stall a young lady was talking and laughing with two young gentlemen. I remarked their English accents and listened vaguely to their conversation.

"O, I never said such a thing!"

"O, but you did!"

"O, but I didn't!"

"Didn't she say that?"

"Yes, I heard her."

"O, there's a . . . fib!"

Observing me the young lady came over and asked me did I wish to buy anything. The tone of her voice was not encouraging; she seemed to have spoken to me out of a sense of duty. I looked humbly at the great jars that stood like eastern guards at either side of the dark entrance to the stall and murmured:

"No, thank you."

The young lady changed the position of one of the vases and went back to the two young men. They began to talk of the same subject. Once or twice the young lady glanced at me over her shoulder.

I lingered before her stall, though I knew my stay was useless, to make my interest in her wares seem the more real. Then I turned away slowly and walked down the middle of the bazaar. I allowed the two pennies to fall against the sixpence in my pocket. I heard a voice call from one end of the gallery that the light was out. The upper part of the hall was now completely dark.

Gazing up into the darkness I saw myself as a creature driven and derided by vanity; and my eyes burned with anguish and anger.

1914

---

5. *Café Chantant*, a cafe where singers or musicians entertain.

Discussion

1. **(a)** About how old is the narrator? **(b)** How does he describe the life of the Dublin streets as he experienced it on the Saturday evenings when he accompanied his aunt on her marketing? **(c)** What idea of himself did he have on these occasions?

2. Why does the narrator offer to bring Mangan's sister a gift from the bazaar?

3. Trace the sequence of delays that thwart the narrator's aim.

4. What different things does "Araby" mean in this story?

Katherine Mansfield 1888–1923

Born Kathleen Mansfield Beauchamp, she was the daughter of a wealthy New Zealand banker, later knighted, who took her and her sisters to London to be educated at Queen's College. A talented cellist, she studied music at the Royal Academy of Music, but later realized that writing, not music, was her true calling. In 1911, through a chance meeting in Germany, she became friends with the celebrated literary critic and editor John Middleton Murry, with whom she collaborated on a short-lived literary magazine. They were married in 1918. By the end of the war, she had become a virtual invalid, moving from climate to climate for relief from incurable tuberculosis. She died in France on January 9, 1923, at the age of thirty-four.

Mansfield was strongly influenced by the short fiction of the Russian writer Chekhov, and, like him, wrote stories which depend more on atmosphere, character, and the nuances of language than on plot. Like James Joyce and Virginia Woolf in the novel, she developed a poetic and subtly crafted style to convey the inner feelings of her characters and present shifting points of view. Many of her stories center on children and on old people in isolated circumstances and are deeply affecting in their sympathetic portrayal of the lonely, the rejected, and the victimized. It has been suggested that her consciousness of the imminence of death heightened her awareness and helps account for the sensitivity for which her stories are noted.

Like Vera Brittain, Katherine Mansfield suffered the devastating loss of a brother in the war and later stated that this tragedy inspired her to dedicate her life to commemorating the "lovely time when we were both alive." The New Zealand of her childhood that she had so readily abandoned for the cosmopolitan life of England and the Continent increasingly provided the incidents and settings for her stories.

The Doll's House

When dear old Mrs. Hay went back to town after staying with the Burnells she sent the children a doll's house. It was so big that the carter and Pat carried it into the courtyard, and there it stayed, propped up on two wooden boxes beside the feed-room door. No harm could come of it; it was summer. And perhaps the smell of paint would have gone off by the time it had to be taken in. For, really, the smell of paint coming from that doll's house ("Sweet of old Mrs. Hay, of course; most sweet and generous!")—but the smell of paint was quite enough to make any one seriously ill, in Aunt Beryl's opinion. Even before the sacking was taken off. And when it was . . .

There stood the doll's house, a dark, oily, spinach green, picked out with bright yellow. Its two solid little chimneys, glued on to the roof, were painted red and white, and the door, gleaming with yellow varnish, was like a little slab of toffee. Four windows, real windows, were divided into panes by a broad streak of green. There was actually a tiny porch, too, painted yellow, with big lumps of congealed paint hanging along the edge.

But perfect, perfect little house! Who could possibly mind the smell? It was part of the joy, part of the newness.

"Open it quickly, some one!"

The hook at the side was stuck fast. Pat pried it open with his pen-knife, and the whole house-front swung back, and—there you were, gazing at one and the same moment into the drawing-room and dining-room, the kitchen and two bed-rooms. That is the way for a house to open! Why don't all houses open like that? How much more exciting than peering through the slit of a door into a mean little hall with a hatstand and two umbrellas! That is—isn't it?—what you long to know about a house when you put your hand on the knocker. Perhaps it is the way God opens houses at dead of night when He is taking a quiet turn with an angel. . . .

"O-oh!" The Burnell children sounded as though they were in despair. It was too marvel-lous; it was too much for them. They had never seen anything like it in their lives. All the rooms were papered. There were pictures on the walls, painted on the paper, with gold frames complete. Red carpet covered all the floors except the kitchen; red plush chairs in the drawing-room, green in the dining-room; tables, beds with real bedclothes, a cradle, a stove, a dresser with tiny plates and one big jug. But what Kezia liked more than anything, what she liked frightfully, was the lamp. It stood in the middle of the dining-room table, an exquisite little amber lamp with a white globe. It was even filled all ready for lighting, though, of course, you couldn't light it. But there was something inside that looked like oil, and that moved when you shook it.

The father and mother dolls, who sprawled very stiff as though they had fainted in the draw-ing-room, and their two little children asleep upstairs, were really too big for the doll's house. They didn't look as though they belonged. But the lamp was perfect. It seemed to smile at Kezia, to say, "I live here." The lamp was real.

The Burnell children could hardly walk to school fast enough the next morning. They burned to tell everybody, to describe, to—well—

to boast about their doll's house before the school-bell rang.

"I'm to tell," said Isabel, "because I'm the eldest. And you two can join in after. But I'm to tell first."

There was nothing to answer. Isabel was bossy, but she was always right, and Lottie and Kezia knew too well the powers that went with being eldest. They brushed through the thick but-tercups at the road edge and said nothing.

"And I'm to choose who's to come and see it first. Mother said I might."

For it had been arranged that while the doll's house stood in the courtyard they might ask the girls at school, two at a time, to come and look. Not to stay to tea, of course, or to come traipsing through the house. But just to stand quietly in the courtyard while Isabel pointed out the beauties, and Lottie and Kezia looked pleased. . . .

But hurry as they might, by the time they had reached the tarred palings of the boys' play-ground the bell had begun to jangle. They only just had time to whip off their hats and fall into line before the roll was called. Never mind. Isa-bel tried to make up for it by looking very impor-tant and mysterious and by whispering behind her hands to the girls near her, "Got something to tell you at playtime."

Playtime came and Isabel was surrounded. The girls of her class nearly fought to put their arms round her, to walk away with her, to beam flatteringly, to be her special friend. She held quite a court under the huge pine trees at the side of the playground. Nudging, giggling together, the little girls pressed up close. And the only two who stayed outside the ring were the two who were always outside, the little Kelveys. They knew better than to come anywhere near the Bur-nells.

For the fact was, the school the Burnell chil-dren went to was not at all the kind of place their parents would have chosen if there had been any choice. But there was none. It was the only school for miles. And the consequence was all the children in the neighborhood, the Judge's lit-tle girls, the doctor's daughters, the storekeep-er's children, the milkman's, were forced to mix together. Not to speak of there being an equal number of rude, rough little boys as well. But the line had to be drawn somewhere. It was drawn at

Doll house at Wenham built in 1884 by Benjamin Chamberlain for his daughters.

the Kelveys. Many of the children, including the Burnells, were not allowed even to speak to them. They walked past the Kelveys with their heads in the air, and as they set the fashion in all matters of behavior, the Kelveys were shunned by everybody. Even the teacher had a special voice for them, and a special smile for the other children when Lil Kelvey came up to her desk with a bunch of dreadfully common-looking flowers.

They were the daughters of a spry, hardworking little washerwoman, who went about from house to house by the day. This was awful enough. But where was Mr. Kelvey? Nobody knew for certain. But everybody said he was in prison. So they were the daughters of a washerwoman and a jailbird. Very nice company for other people's children! And they looked it. Why Mrs. Kelvey made them so conspicuous was hard to understand. The truth was they were dressed in "bits" given to her by the people for whom she worked. Lil, for instance, who was a stout, plain child, with big freckles, came to school in a dress made from a green art-serge table-cloth of the Burnells', with red plush sleeves from the Logans' curtains. Her hat, perched on top of her high forehead, was a grown-up woman's hat, once the property of Miss Lecky, the postmistress. It was turned up at the back and trimmed

with a large scarlet quill. What a little guy she looked! It was impossible not to laugh. And her little sister, our Else, wore a long white dress, rather like a nightgown, and a pair of little boy's boots. But whatever our Else wore she would have looked strange. She was a tiny wishbone of a child, with cropped hair and enormous solemn eyes—a little white owl. Nobody had ever seen her smile; she scarcely ever spoke. She went through life holding on to Lil, with a piece of Lil's shirt screwed up in her hand. Where Lil went our Else followed. In the playground, on the road going to and from school, there was Lil marching in front and our Else holding on behind. Only when she wanted anything, or when she was out of breath, our Else gave Lil a tug, a twitch, and Lil stopped and turned round. The Kelveys never failed to understand each other.

Now they hovered at the edge; you couldn't stop them listening. When the little girls turned round and sneered, Lil, as usual, gave her silly, shame-faced smile, but our Else only looked.

And Isabel's voice, so very proud, went on telling. The carpet made a great sensation, but so did the beds with real bedclothes, and the stove with an oven door.

When she finished Kezia broke in. "You've forgotten the lamp, Isabel."

"Oh, yes," said Isabel, "and there's a teeny

little lamp, all made of yellow glass, with a white globe that stands on the dining-room table. You couldn't tell it from a real one."

"The lamp's best of all," cried Kezia. She thought Isabel wasn't making half enough of the little lamp. But nobody paid any attention. Isabel was choosing the two who were to come back with them that afternoon and see it. She chose Emmie Cole and Lena Logan. But when the others knew they were all to have a chance, they couldn't be nice enough to Isabel. One by one they put their arms round Isabel's waist and walked her off. They had something to whisper to her, a secret. "Isabel's *my* friend."

Only the little Kelveys moved away forgotten; there was nothing more for them to hear.

Days passed, and as more children saw the doll's house, the fame of it spread. It became the one subject, the rage. The one question was, "Have you seen Burnells' doll house? Oh, ain't it lovely!" "Haven't you seen it? Oh, I say!"

Even the dinner hour was given up to talking about it. The little girls sat under the pines eating their thick mutton sandwiches and big slabs of johnny cake spread with butter. While always, as near as they could get, sat the Kelveys, our Else holding on to Lil, listening too, while they chewed their jam sandwiches out of a newspaper soaked with large red blobs. . . .

"Mother," said Kezia, "can't I ask the Kelveys just once?"

"Certainly not, Kezia."

"But why not?"

"Run away, Kezia; you know quite well why not."

At last everybody had seen it except them. On that day the subject rather flagged. It was the dinner hour. The children stood together under the pine trees, and suddenly, as they looked at the Kelveys eating out of their paper, always by themselves, always listening, they wanted to be horrid to them. Emmie Cole started the whisper.

"Lil Kelvey's going to be a servant when she grows up."

"O-oh, how awful!" said Isabel Burnell, and she made eyes at Emmie.

Emmie swallowed in a very meaning way and nodded to Isabel as she'd seen her mother do on those occasions.

"It's true—it's true—it's true," she said.

Then Lena Logan's little eyes snapped. "Shall I ask her?" she whispered.

"Bet you don't," said Jessie May.

"Pooh, I'm not frightened," said Lena. Suddenly she gave a little squeal and danced in front of the other girls. "Watch! Watch me! Watch me now!" said Lena. And sliding, gliding, dragging one foot, giggling behind her hand, Lena went over to the Kelveys.

Lil looked up from her dinner. She wrapped the rest quickly away. Our Else stopped chewing. What was coming now?

"Is it true you're going to be a servant when you grow up, Lil Kelvey?" shrilled Lena.

Dead silence. But instead of answering, Lil only gave her silly, shame-faced smile. She didn't seem to mind the question at all. What a sell[1] for Lena! The girls began to titter.

Lena couldn't stand that. She put her hands on her hips; she shot forward. "Yah, yer father's in prison!" she hissed, spitefully.

This was such a marvellous thing to have said that the little girls rushed away in a body, deeply, deeply excited, wild with joy. Some one found a long rope, and they began skipping. And never did they skip so high, run in and out so fast, or do such daring things as on that morning.

In the afternoon Pat called for the Burnell children with the buggy and they drove home. There were visitors. Isabel and Lottie, who liked visitors, went upstairs to change their pinafores. But Kezia thieved out[2] at the back. Nobody was about; she began to swing on the big white gates of the courtyard. Presently, looking along the road, she saw two little dots. They grew bigger, they were coming towards her. Now she could see that one was in front and one close behind. Now she could see that they were the Kelveys. Kezia stopped swinging. She slipped off the gate as if she was going to run away. Then she hesitated. The Kelveys came nearer, and beside them stalked their shadows, very long, stretching right across the road with their heads in the buttercups. Kezia clambered back on the gate; she had made up her mind; she swung out.

"Hullo," she said to the passing Kelveys.

---

1. **What a sell,** what a come-down, disappointment.
2. **thieved out,** sneaked away.

They were so astounded that they stopped. Lil gave her silly smile. Our Else stared.

"You can come and see our doll's house if you want to," said Kezia, and she dragged one toe on the ground. But at that Lil turned red and shook her head quickly.

"Why not?" asked Kezia.

Lil gasped, then she said, "Your ma told our ma you wasn't to speak to us."

"Oh, well," said Kezia. She didn't know what to reply. "It doesn't matter. You can come and see our doll's house all the same. Come on. Nobody's looking."

But Lil shook her head still harder.

"Don't you want to?" asked Kezia.

Suddenly there was a twitch, a tug at Lil's skirt. She turned round. Our Else was looking at her with big, imploring eyes; she was frowning; she wanted to go. For a moment Lil looked at our Else very doubtfully. But then our Else twitched her skirt again. She started forward. Kezia led the way. Like two little stray cats they followed across the courtyard to where the doll's house stood.

"There it is," said Kezia.

There was a pause. Lil breathed loudly, almost snorted; our Else was still as a stone.

"I'll open it for you," said Kezia kindly. She undid the hook and they looked inside.

"There's the drawing-room and the dining-room, and that's the—"

"Kezia!"

Oh, what a start they gave!

"Kezia!"

It was Aunt Beryl's voice. They turned round. At the back door stood Aunt Beryl, staring as if she couldn't believe what she saw.

"How dare you ask the little Kelveys into the courtyard?" said her cold, furious voice. "You know as well as I do, you're not allowed to talk to them. Run away, children, run away at once. And don't come back again," said Aunt Beryl. And she stepped into the yard and shooed them out as if they were chickens.

"Off you go immediately!" she called, cold and proud.

They did not need telling twice. Burning with shame, shrinking together, Lil huddling along like her mother, our Else dazed, somehow they crossed the big courtyard and squeezed through the white gate.

"Wicked, disobedient little girl!" said Aunt Beryl bitterly to Kezia, and she slammed the doll's house to.

The afternoon had been awful. A letter had come from Willie Brent, a terrifying, threatening letter, saying if she did not meet him that evening in Pulman's Bush, he'd come to the front door and ask the reason why! But now that she had frightened those little rats of Kelveys and given Kezia a good scolding, her heart felt lighter. That ghastly pressure was gone. She went back to the house humming.

When the Kelveys were well out of sight of Burnells', they sat down to rest on a big red drain-pipe by the side of the road. Lil's cheeks were still burning; she took off the hat with the quill and held it on her knee. Dreamily they looked over the hay paddocks, past the creek, to the group of wattles where Logan's cows stood waiting to be milked. What were their thoughts?

Presently our Else nudged up close to her sister. But now she had forgotten the cross lady. She put out a finger and stroked her sister's quill; she smiled her rare smile.

"I seen the little lamp," she said, softly.

Then both were silent once more.   1923

Discussion

1. (a) How do Isabel and Kezia differ in personality? (b) What is the significance of the doll's house for Isabel? What is it for Kezia?

2. (a) What are Lil and Else like? How do they relate to each other? (b) Why has the line been "drawn" to exclude the Kelveys socially?

3. (a) To what forms of social cruelty are the Kelveys subjected by the other children and by adults? (b) Is the cruelty shown by Aunt Beryl of the same quality as that shown by the little girls or is it of another type?

4. Why, when taunted by Lena about being a servant when she grows up, does Lil simply respond with "her silly, shamefaced smile"?

5. (a) How would the effect of the last statement in the story—"I seen the little lamp"—differ if spoken by Lil instead of Else? (b) What is the significance of Else's having seen the little lamp?

Virginia Woolf 1882–1941

Virginia Woolf was the daughter of Sir Leslie Stephen (1832–1904), the editor of one of the great Victorian scholarly projects, the multivolume *Dictionary of National Biography.* She was educated at home by her father and had the run of his extensive library. After his death she moved to London with her brother and sister. Their homes in the Bloomsbury district, near the British Museum, became the meeting places of a famous group of intellectuals. Among the members of the Bloomsbury Group were the economist John Maynard Keynes, the biographer Lytton Strachey, and the novelist E. M. Forster. Another member of the group was the writer Leonard Woolf, whom she married in 1912. In 1917 they founded the Hogarth Press, which published her books as well as those of a number of other important modern writers, like T. S. Eliot and E. M. Forster.

Woolf began her career as a writer doing book reviews and articles for literary journals and newspapers. At the same time she began her first novel, *The Voyage Out,* which was accepted by a publisher in 1913 but not issued until 1915. The delay was caused by one of the episodes of mental illness that were to trouble her throughout her life.

During the 1920s her work became increasingly experimental. In novels like *Mrs. Dalloway* (1925), *To the Lighthouse* (1927), and *The Waves* (1931), she rebelled against the social fiction of the prewar period with its emphasis on detailed descriptions of character and setting. Instead she attempted to express the timeless inner consciousness of her characters. Influenced by James Joyce's *Ulysses,* she used the techniques of "stream of consciousness" and "interior monologue," moving from one character to another to reveal a variety of mental responses to the same event. Another aspect of her work during this period appeared in *A Room of One's Own* (1929), a long essay in which she forcefully presented the difficulties facing the woman writer.

The outbreak of World War II was a shattering event for Woolf. Nevertheless, she managed to complete a brief, enigmatic final novel, *Between the Acts* (1941). "Written in the gloomiest days of the war," the English critic Cyril Connolly observed, "while the Spitfires and Messerschmitts fell around her Sussex home in the Battle of Britain, and published before the tide of war had turned, her book is about the eternal England, the beautiful threatened civilization which she had always loved . . ." On the morning of March 28, 1941, she walked across the water meadows to the River Ouse and drowned herself; "the one experience," she once confided to a friend, "I shall never describe."

Great Men's Houses

London, happily, is becoming full of great men's houses, bought for the nation and preserved entire with the chairs they sat on and the cups they drank from, their umbrellas and their chests of drawers. And it is no frivolous curiosity that sends us to Dickens's house and Johnson's house and Carlyle's house and Keats's house. We know them from their houses—it would seem to be a fact that writers stamp themselves upon their possessions more indelibly than other people. Of artistic taste they may have none; but they seem always to possess a much rarer and more interesting gift—a faculty for housing themselves appropriately, for making the table, the chair, the curtain, the carpet into their own image.

Take the Carlyles,[1] for instance. One hour spent in 5 Cheyne Row will tell us more about them and their lives than we can learn from all the biographies. Go down into the kitchen. There, in two seconds, one is made acquainted with a fact that escaped the attention of Froude,[2] and yet was of incalculable importance—they had no water laid on. Every drop that the Carlyles used—and they were Scots, fanatical in their cleanliness—had to be pumped by hand from a well in the kitchen. There is the well at this moment and the pump and the stone trough into which the cold water trickled. And here, too, is the wide and wasteful old grate upon which all kettles had to be boiled if they wanted a hot bath; and here is the cracked yellow tin bath, so deep and so narrow, which had to be filled with the cans of hot water that the maid first pumped and then boiled and then carried up three flights of stairs from the basement.

The high old house without water, without electric light, without gas fires, full of books and coal smoke and four-poster beds and mahogany cupboards, where two of the most nervous and exacting people of their time lived, year in year out, was served by one unfortunate maid. All through the mid-Victorian age the house was necessarily a battlefield where daily, summer and winter, mistress and maid fought against dirt and cold for cleanliness and warmth. The stairs, carved as they are and wide and dignified, seem worn by the feet of harassed women carrying tin cans. The high panelled rooms seem to echo with the sound of pumping and the swish of scrubbing. The voice of the house—and all houses have

Thomas Carlyle (and his dog "Nero") seated in the back court of the Carlyle house at 5 Cheyne Row, Chelsea, in 1857.

voices—is the voice of pumping and scrubbing, of coughing and groaning. Up in the attic under a skylight Carlyle groaned, as he wrestled with his history, on a horsehair chair, while a yellow shaft

1. **the Carlyles,** the Scottish essayist and historian Thomas Carlyle (1795–1881) and his wife Jane (1801–1866).
2. **Froude,** James Anthony Froude (1819–1894), English historian and biographer of Carlyle.

of London light fell upon his papers and the rattle of a barrel organ and the raucous shouts of street hawkers came through walls whose double thickness distorted but by no means excluded the sound. And the season of the house—for every house has its season—seems to be always the month of February, when cold and fog are in the street and torches flare and the rattle of wheels grows suddenly loud and dies away. February after February Mrs. Carlyle lay coughing in the large four-poster hung with maroon curtains in which she was born, and as she coughed the many problems of the incessant battle, against dirt, against cold, came before her. The horsehair couch needed recovering; the drawing-room paper with its small, dark pattern needed cleaning; the yellow varnish on the panels was cracked and peeling—all must be stitched, cleansed, scoured with her own hands; and had she, or had she not, demolished the bugs that bred and bred in the ancient wood panelling? So the long watches of the sleepless night passed, and then she heard Mr. Carlyle stir above her, and held her breath and wondered if Helen were up and had lit the fire and heated the water for his shaving. Another day had dawned and the pumping and the scrubbing must begin again.

Thus number 5 Cheyne Row is not so much a dwelling-place as a battlefield—the scene of labor, effort and perpetual struggle. Few of the spoils of life—its graces and its luxuries—survive to tell us that the battle was worth the effort. The relics of drawing-room and study are like the relics picked up on other battlefields. Here is a packet of old steel nibs; a broken clay pipe; a pen-holder such as schoolboys use; a few cups of white and gold china, much chipped; a horsehair sofa and a yellow tin bath. Here, too, is a cast of the thin worn hands that worked here; and of the excruciated and ravished face of Carlyle when his life was done and he lay dead here. Even the garden at the back of the house seems to be not a place of rest and recreation, but another smaller battlefield marked with a tombstone beneath which a dog lies buried. By pumping and by scrubbing, days of victory, evenings of peace and splendor were won, of course. Mrs. Carlyle sat, as we see from the picture, in a fine silk dress, in a chair pulled up to a blazing fire and had everything seemly and solid about her; but at what cost

had she won it! Her cheeks are hollow; bitterness and suffering mingle in the half-tender, half-tortured expression of the eyes. Such is the effect of a pump in the basement and a yellow tin bath up three pairs of stairs. Both husband and wife had genius; they loved each other; but what can genius and love avail against bugs and tin baths and pumps in the basement?

It is impossible not to believe that half their quarrels might have been spared and their lives immeasurably sweetened if only number 5 Cheyne Row had possessed, as the house agents put it, bath, h. and c., gas fires in the bedrooms, all modern conveniences and indoor sanitation. But then, we reflect, as we cross the worn threshold, Carlyle with hot water laid on would not have been Carlyle; and Mrs. Carlyle without bugs to kill would have been a different woman from the one we know.

An age seems to separate the house in Chelsea where the Carlyles lived from the house in Hampstead which was shared by Keats and Brown and the Brawnes.[3] If houses have their voices and places their seasons, it is always spring in Hampstead as it is always February in Cheyne Row. By some miracle, too, Hampstead has always remained not a suburb or a piece of antiquity engulfed in the modern world, but a place with a character peculiar to itself. It is not a place where one makes money, or goes when one has money to spend. The signs of discreet retirement are stamped on it. Its houses are neat boxes such as front the sea at Brighton with bow windows and balconies and deck chairs on verandahs. It has style and intention as if designed for people of modest income and some leisure who seek rest and recreation. Its prevailing colors are the pale pinks and blues that seem to harmonize with the blue sea and the white sand; and yet there is an urbanity in the style which proclaims the neighborhood of a great city. Even in the twentieth century this serenity still pervades the suburb of Hampstead. Its bow windows still look out upon vales and trees and ponds and barking dogs and couples sauntering arm in arm and pausing, here on the hilltop, to look at the distant

---

3. Keats . . . the Brawnes. The poet John Keats (see pages 402–411) and his friend Charles Brown shared a house in Hampstead next door to the one occupied by Keats's beloved, Fanny Brawne, and her mother.

John Keats in the library of his house at Hampstead, painted by his friend Joseph Severn in 1821.

domes and pinnacles of London, as they sauntered and paused and looked when Keats lived here. For Keats lived up the lane in a little white house behind wooden palings. Nothing has been much changed since his day. But as we enter the house in which Keats lived some mournful shadow seems to fall across the garden. A tree has fallen and lies propped. Waving branches cast their shadows up and down over the flat white walls of the house. Here, for all the gaiety and serenity of the neighborhood, the nightingale sang; here, if anywhere, fever and anguish had their dwelling and paced this little green plot oppressed with the sense of quick-coming death and the shortness of life and the passion of love and its misery.

Yet if Keats left any impress upon his house it is the impression not of fever, but of that clarity and dignity which come from order and self-control. The rooms are small but shapely; downstairs the long windows are so large that half the wall seems made of light. Two chairs turned together are close to the window as if someone had sat there reading and had just got up and left the room. The figure of the reader must have been splashed with shade and sun as the hanging leaves stirred in the breeze. Birds must have hopped close to his foot. The room is empty save for the two chairs, for Keats had few possessions, little furniture and not more, he said, than one hundred and fifty books. And perhaps it is because the rooms are so empty and furnished rather with light and shadow than with chairs and tables that one does not think of people, here where so many people have lived. The imagination does not evoke scenes. It does not strike one that there must have been eating and drinking here; people must have come in and out; they must have put down bags, left parcels; they must have scrubbed and cleaned and done battle with dirt and disorder and carried cans of water from the basement to the bedrooms. All the traffic of life is silenced. The voice of the house is the voice of leaves brushing in the wind; of branches stirring in the garden. Only one presence—that of Keats himself—dwells here. And even he, though his picture is on every wall, seems to come silently, on the broad shafts of light, without body or footfall. Here he sat on the chair in the window and listened without moving, and saw without starting, and turned the page without haste though his time was so short.

There is an air of heroic equanimity about the house in spite of the death masks and the brittle yellow wreaths and the other grisly memorials which remind us that Keats died young and unknown and in exile. Life goes on outside the window. Behind this calm, this rustling of leaves, one hears the far-off rattle of wheels, the bark of dogs fetching and carrying sticks from the pond. Life goes on outside the wooden paling. When we shut the gate upon the grass and the tree where the nightingale sang we find, quite rightly, the butcher delivering his meat from a small red motor van at the house next door. If we cross the road, taking care not to be cut down by some rash driver—for they drive at a great pace down these wide streets—we shall find ourselves on top of the hill and beneath shall see the whole of London lying below us. It is a view of perpetual fascination at all hours and in all seasons. One sees London as a whole—London crowded and ribbed and compact, with its dominant domes, its guardian cathedrals; its chimneys and spires; its cranes and gasometers; and the perpetual smoke which no spring or autumn ever blows away. London has lain there time out of mind scarring that stretch of earth deeper and deeper, making it more uneasy, lumped and tumultuous, branding it for ever with an indelible scar. There it lies in layers, in strata, bristling and billowing with rolls of smoke always caught on its pinnacles. And yet from Parliament Hill one can see, too, the country beyond. There are hills on the further side in whose woods birds are singing, and some stoat or rabbit pauses, in dead silence, with paw lifted to listen intently to rustlings among the leaves. To look over London from this hill Keats came and Coleridge and Shakespeare, perhaps. And here at this very moment the usual young man sits on an iron bench clasping to his arms the usual young woman.

1931

Discussion

1. One of Virginia Woolf's biographers has noted that she had a gift for finding interesting houses. According to this essay, why did she find houses so fascinating, especially those of great writers?

2. What features of the Carlyle home made her describe the place as "a battlefield" and the "season" of the house as a perpetual February?

3. (a) What probably led Woolf to choose the houses of Carlyle and Keats for description in the same essay? (b) What is her sense of the "voices" and "season" of Keats's house? Explain.

Composition

Look again at the manner in which Woolf gives a distinctive "personality" to each of the houses she describes.

Select a house that you feel has such a "personality." Using Woolf's essay as a model, write a description that captures the mood of the house you have selected and interprets the clues it provides about the character and values of its inhabitants.

D. H. Lawrence 1885–1930

Like the hero of his early novel *Sons and Lovers* (1913), David Herbert Lawrence was born in an English coal-mining town, the son of an uneducated miner and an ambitious mother who was a schoolteacher. During his childhood, the tensions and conflicts between his parents were fierce and disturbing, and, in large measure, responsible for the development of a strong attachment to his mother that later inhibited his relationships with other women. While responsive to his father's working-class values and earthiness, Lawrence was steered by his mother toward a middle-class life and strict moral behavior. Ultimately Lawrence sided with his father, opting for the primitive and instinctual, but first he had to break out of his environment.

After graduating from high school, Lawrence taught for a few years before establishing himself in London literary circles as a writer. In 1912 he declared his emancipation from the past by eloping with an aristocratic German, Frieda von Richthofen. Until his death in 1930, the Lawrences wandered the globe in search of a place undamaged by modern civilization that might also alleviate Lawrence's worsening tuberculosis. Though difficult and turbulent, these years with Frieda gave Lawrence his opportunity for self-discovery and artistic fulfillment.

Lawrence's first novel, *The White Peacock,* appeared shortly after his mother's death in 1911 and introduces two types of characters that reappear in all his later fiction: the overly intellectual, civilized individual and the more primitive, sensual man who rejects middle-class values and deplores the destruction of natural life caused by industrialization. In 1913 Lawrence's reputation began to spread with the publication of a volume of poems and the novel *Sons and Lovers,* a powerful fictional portrait of Lawrence as the incipient artist struggling to break free from his possessive mother and establish an authentic identity. *The Rainbow* (1915) relates the history of three generations of the Brangwens, a family living in rural England during the last half of the nineteenth century. *Women in Love* (1920) continues the story of the Brangwens but focuses more specifically on the quest for ideal relationships between both men and women and men with other men.

Like Joyce and Woolf, Lawrence sought in his fiction to reveal character from within, to capture the exact feelings produced by immediate experience. Detached from his characters in their conflicts, he could present their arguments without taking sides—a remarkable accomplishment for a writer of strong and passionate opinions. Lawrence's reputation as a poet continues to grow. His keen-sighted observations of nature and animals are conveyed in simple language whose artistic purity attains dignity and grandeur. *Studies in Classical American Literature* (1923) is possibly the most original collection of critical essays published in this century. Since much of his work is an exploration of the primitive and sexual in human nature, Lawrence was constantly in trouble with the censors. It was a price he was willing to pay in his revolt against puritanism, mediocrity, and the dehumanization of an industrial society.

*T*ickets, Please

There is in the Midlands a single-line tramway system which boldly leaves the county town and plunges off into the black, industrial countryside, up hill and down dale, through the long ugly villages of workmen's houses, over canals and railways, past churches perched high and nobly over the smoke and shadows, through stark, grimy cold little marketplaces, tilting away in a rush past cinemas and shops down to the hollow where the collieries are, then up again, past a little rural church, under the ash trees, on in a rush to the terminus, the last little ugly place of industry, the cold little town that shivers on the edge of the wild, gloomy country beyond. There the green and creamy colored tram-car seems to pause and purr with curious satisfaction. But in a few minutes—the clock on the turret of the Cooperative Wholesale Society's shops gives the time—away it starts once more on the adventure. Again there are the reckless swoops downhill, bouncing the loops: again the chilly wait in the hilltop marketplace: again the breathless slithering round the precipitous drop under the church: again the patient halts at the loops, waiting for the outcoming car: so on and on, for two long hours, till at last the city looms beyond the fat gasworks, the narrow factories draw near, we are in the sordid streets of the great town, once more we sidle to a standstill at our terminus, abashed by the great crimson and cream-colored city cars, but still perky, jaunty, somewhat dare-devil, green as a jaunty sprig of parsley out of a black colliery garden.

To ride on these cars is always an adventure. Since we are in war-time, the drivers are men unfit for active service: cripples and hunchbacks. So they have the spirit of the devil in them. The ride becomes a steeplechase. Hurray! we have leapt in a clear jump over the canal bridges—now for the four-lane corner. With a shriek and a trail of sparks we are clear again. To be sure, a tram often leaps the rails—but what matter! It sits in a ditch till other trams come to haul it out. It is quite common for a car, packed with one solid mass of living people, to come to a dead halt in the midst of unbroken blackness, the heart of nowhere on a dark night, and for the driver and the girl conductor to call: "All get off—car's on fire!" Instead, however, of rushing out in a panic, the passengers stolidly reply: "Get on—get on! We're not coming out. We're stopping where we are. Push on, George." So till flames actually appear.

The reason for this reluctance to dismount is that the nights are howlingly cold, black, and windswept, and a car is a haven of refuge. From village to village the miners travel, for a change of cinema, of girl, of pub. The trams are desperately packed. Who is going to risk himself in the black gulf outside, to wait perhaps an hour for another tram, then to see the forlorn notice "Depot Only," because there is something wrong! Or to greet a unit of three bright cars all so tight with people that they sail past with a howl of derision. Trams that pass in the night.

This, the most dangerous tram-service in England, as the authorities themselves declare, with pride, is entirely conducted by girls, and driven by rash young men, a little crippled, or by delicate young men, who creep forward in terror. The girls are fearless young hussies. In their ugly blue uniform, skirts up to their knees, shapeless old peaked caps on their heads, they have all the *sang-froid*[1] of an old non-commissioned officer. With a tram packed with howling colliers, roaring hymns downstairs and a sort of antiphony of obscenities upstairs, the lasses are perfectly at their ease. They pounce on the youths who try to evade their ticket-machine. They push off the men at the end of their distance. They are not going to be done in the eye—not they. They fear nobody—and everybody fears them.

"Hello, Annie!"

"Hello, Ted!"

"Oh, mind my corn, Miss Stone. It's my

"Tickets, Please" from *The Collected Stories of D. H. Lawrence,* Vol. II. Copyright 1922 by Thomas B. Seltzer. Copyright renewed 1950 by Frieda Lawrence. Reprinted by permission of Viking Penguin Inc., Laurence Pollinger Limited and the Estate of Frieda Lawrence Ravagli.

1. **sang-froid** (säN frwä′), calmness, composure; literally, "cold blood." [French]

The illustration on page 719 shows one of the first of the "clippies," the women bus conductors who replaced men during the First World War, in September, 1917.

belief you've got a heart of stone, for you've trod on it again."

"You should keep it in your pocket," replies Miss Stone, and she goes sturdily upstairs in her high boots.

"Tickets, please."

She is peremptory, suspicious, and ready to hit first. She can hold her own against ten thousand. The step of that tram-car is her Thermopylae.[2]

Therefore, there is a certain wild romance aboard these cars—and in the sturdy bosom of Annie herself. The time for soft romance is in the morning, between ten o'clock and one, when things are rather slack: that is, except marketday and Saturday. Thus Annie has time to look about her. Then she often hops off her car and into a shop where she has spied something, while the driver chats in the main road. There is very good feeling between the girls and the drivers. Are they not companions in peril, shipmates aboard this careering vessel of a tram-car, for ever rocking on the waves of a stormy land.

Then, also, during the easy hours, the inspectors are most in evidence. For some reason, everybody employed in this tram-service is young: there are no grey heads. It would not do. Therefore the inspectors are of the right age, and one, the chief, is also good-looking. See him stand on a wet, gloomy morning, in his long oilskin, his peaked cap well down over his eyes, waiting to board a car. His face ruddy, his small brown moustache is weathered, he has a faint impudent smile. Fairly tall and agile, even in his waterproof, he springs aboard a car and greets Annie.

"Hello, Annie! Keeping the wet out?"

"Trying to."

There are only two people in the car. Inspecting is soon over. Then for a long and impudent chat on the foot-board, a good, easy, twelve-mile chat.

The inspector's name is John Thomas Raynor—always called John Thomas, except sometimes, in malice, Coddy. His face sets in fury when he is addressed, from a distance, with this abbreviation. There is considerable scandal about John Thomas in half a dozen villages. He flirts with the girl conductors in the morning, and walks out with them in the dark night, when they leave their tram-car at the depot. Of course, the girls quit the service frequently. Then he flirts and walks out with the newcomer: always providing she is sufficiently attractive, and that she will consent to walk. It is remarkable, however, that most of the girls are quite comely, they are all young, and this roving life aboard the car gives them a sailor's dash and recklessness. What matter how they behave when the ship is in port? Tomorrow they will be aboard again.

Annie, however, was something of a Tartar, and her sharp tongue had kept John Thomas at arm's length for many months. Perhaps, therefore, she liked him all the more: for he always came up smiling, with impudence. She watched him vanquish one girl, then another. She could tell by the movement of his mouth and eyes, when he flirted with her in the morning, that he had been walking out with this lass, or the other, the night before. A fine cock-of-the-walk he was. She could sum him up pretty well.

In this subtle antagonism they knew each other like old friends, they were as shrewd with one another almost as man and wife. But Annie had always kept him sufficiently at arm's length. Besides, she had a boy of her own.

The Statutes fair, however, came in November, at Bestwood. It happened that Annie had the Monday night off. It was a drizzling ugly night, yet she dressed herself up and went to the fairground. She was alone, but she expected soon to find a pal of some sort.

The roundabouts were veering round and grinding out their music, the side-shows were making as much commotion as possible. In the coconut shies there were no coconuts, but artificial war-time substitutes, which the lads declared were fastened into the irons. There was a sad decline in brilliance and luxury. None the less, the ground was muddy as ever, there was the same crush, the press of faces lighted up by the flares and the electric lights, the same smell of naphtha and a few fried potatoes, and of electricity.

Who should be the first to greet Miss Annie on the showground but John Thomas. He had a

---

2. **Thermopylae** (thər mop'ə lē), a narrow mountain pass in Greece where in 480 B.C. a small force (principally Spartans) held off a huge army of Persians.

black overcoat buttoned up to his chin, and a tweed cap pulled down over his brows, his face between was ruddy and smiling and handy as ever. She knew so well the way his mouth moved.

She was very glad to have a "boy." To be at the Statutes without a fellow was no fun. Instantly, like the gallant he was, he took her on the Dragons, grim-toothed, roundabout switchbacks. It was not nearly so exciting as a tram-car actually. But, then, to be seated in a shaking, green dragon, uplifted above the sea of bubble faces, careering in a rickety fashion in the lower heavens, whilst John Thomas leaned over her, his cigarette in his mouth, was after all the right style. She was a plump, quick, alive little creature. So she was quite excited and happy.

John Thomas made her stay on for the next round. And therefore she could hardly for shame repulse him when he put his arm round her and drew her a little nearer to him, in a very warm and cuddly manner. Besides, he was fairly discreet, he kept his movement as hidden as possible. She looked down, and saw that his red, clean hand was out of sight of the crowd. And they knew each other so well. So they warmed up to the fair.

After the dragons they went on the horses. John Thomas paid each time, so she could but be complaisant. He, of course, sat astride on the outer horse—named "Black Bess"—and she sat sideways, towards him, on the inner horse—named "Wildfire." But of course John Thomas was not going to sit discreetly on "Black Bess," holding the brass bar. Round they spun and heaved, in the light. And round he swung on his wooden steed, flinging one leg across her mount, and perilously tipping up and down, across the space, half lying back, laughing at her. He was perfectly happy; she was afraid her hat was on one side, but she was excited.

He threw quoits on a table, and won for her two large, pale blue hat-pins. And then, hearing the noise of the cinemas, announcing another performance, they climbed the boards and went in.

Of course, during these performances pitch darkness falls from time to time, when the machine goes wrong. Then there is a wild whooping, and a loud smacking of simulated kisses. In these moments John Thomas drew Annie towards him. After all, he had a wonderfully warm, cozy way of holding a girl with his arm, he seemed to make such a nice fit. And, after all, it was pleasant to be so held: so very comforting and cozy and nice. He leaned over her and she felt his breath on her hair; she knew he wanted to kiss her on the lips. And, after all, he was so warm and she fitted in to him so softly. After all, she wanted him to touch her lips.

But the light sprang up; she also started electrically, and put her hat straight. He left his arm lying nonchalantly behind her. Well, it was fun, it was exciting to be at the Statutes with John Thomas.

When the cinema was over they went for a walk across the dark, damp fields. He had all the arts of love-making. He was especially good at holding a girl, when he sat with her on a stile in the black, drizzling darkness. He seemed to be holding her in space, against his own warmth and gratification. And his kisses were soft and slow and searching.

So Annie walked out with John Thomas, though she kept her own boy dangling in the distance. Some of the tram-girls chose to be huffy. But there, you must take things as you find them, in this life.

There was no mistake about it, Annie liked John Thomas a good deal. She felt so rich and warm in herself whenever he was near. And John Thomas really liked Annie, more than usual. The soft, melting way in which she could flow into a fellow, as if she melted into his very bones, was something rare and good. He fully appreciated this.

But with a developing acquaintance there began a developing intimacy. Annie wanted to consider him a person, a man: she wanted to take an intelligent interest in him, and to have an intelligent response. She did not want a mere nocturnal presence, which was what he was so far. And she prided herself that he could not leave her.

Here she made a mistake. John Thomas intended to remain a nocturnal presence; he had no idea of becoming an all-round individual to her. When she started to take an intelligent interest in him and his life and his character, he sheered off. He hated intelligent interest. And he knew that the only way to stop it was to avoid it.

The possessive female was aroused in Annie. So he left her.

It is no use saying she was not surprised. She was at first startled, thrown out of her count. For she had been so *very* sure of holding him. For a while she was staggered, and everything became uncertain to her. Then she wept with fury, indignation, desolation, and misery. Then she had a spasm of despair. And then, when he came, still impudently, on to her car, still familiar, but letting her see by the movement of his head that he had gone away to somebody else for the time being, and was enjoying pastures new, then she determined to have her own back.

She had a very shrewd idea what girls John Thomas had taken out. She went to Nora Purdy. Nora was a tall, rather pale, but well-built girl, with beautiful yellow hair. She was rather secretive.

"Hey!" said Annie, accosting her; then softly: "Who's John Thomas on with now?"

"I don't know," said Nora.

"Why, tha does," said Annie, ironically lapsing into dialect. "Tha knows as well as I do."

"Well, I do, then," said Nora. "It isn't me, so don't bother."

"It's Cissy Meakin, isn't it?"

"It is, for all I know."

"Hasn't he got a face on him!" said Annie. "I don't half like his cheek. I could knock him off the foot-board when he comes round at me."

"He'll get dropped on one of these days," said Nora.

"Ay, he will, when somebody makes up their mind to drop it on him. I should like to see him taken down a peg or two, shouldn't you?"

"I shouldn't mind," said Nora.

"You've got quite as much cause to as I have," said Annie. "But we'll drop on him one of these days, my girl. What? Don't you want to?"

"I don't mind," said Nora.

But as a matter of fact, Nora was much more vindictive than Annie.

One by one Annie went the round of the old flames. It so happened that Cissy Meakin left the tramway service in quite a short time. Her mother made her leave. Then John Thomas was on the *qui vive*. He cast his eyes over his old flock. And his eyes lighted on Annie. He thought she would be safe now. Besides, he liked her.

She arranged to walk home with him on Sunday night. It so happened that her car would be in the depot at half-past nine: the last car would come in at 10:15. So John Thomas was to wait for her there.

At the depot the girls had a little waiting-room of their own. It was quite rough, but cozy, with a fire and an oven and a mirror, and table and wooden chairs. The half-dozen girls who knew John Thomas only too well had arranged to take service this Sunday afternoon. So, as the cars began to come in, early, the girls dropped into the waiting-room. And instead of hurrying off home, they sat around the fire and had a cup of tea. Outside was the darkness and lawlessness of wartime.

John Thomas came on the car after Annie, at about a quarter to ten. He poked his head easily into the girls' waiting-room.

"Prayer-meeting?" he asked.

"Ay," said Laura Sharp. "Ladies only."

"That's me!" said John Thomas. It was one of his favorite exclamations.

"Shut the door, boy," said Muriel Baggaley.

"Oh, which side of me?" said John Thomas.

"Which tha likes," said Polly Birkin.

He had come in and closed the door behind him. The girls moved in their circle, to make a place for him near the fire. He took off his greatcoat and pushed back his hat.

"Who handles the teapot?" he said.

Nora Purdy silently poured him out a cup of tea.

"Want a bit o' my bread and drippin'?" said Muriel Baggaley to him.

"Ay, give us a bit."

And he began to eat his piece of bread.

"There's no place like home, girls," he said.

They all looked at him as he uttered this piece of impudence. He seemed to be sunning himself in the presence of so many damsels.

"Especially if you're not afraid to go home in the dark," said Laura Sharp.

"Me! By myself I am."

They sat till they heard the last tram come in. In a few minutes Emma Houselay entered.

"Come on, my old duck!" cried Polly Birkin.

"It *is* perishing," said Emma, holding her fingers to the fire.

"But—I'm afraid to, go home in, the dark," sang Laura Sharp, the tune having got into her mind.

"Who're you going with to-night, John Thomas?" asked Muriel Baggaley coolly.

"To-night?" said John Thomas. "Oh, I'm going home by myself to-night—all on my lonely-o."

"That's me!" said Nora Purdy, using his own ejaculation.

The girls laughed shrilly.

"Me as well, Nora," said John Thomas.

"Don't know what you mean," said Laura.

"Yes, I'm toddling," said he, rising and reaching for his overcoat.

"Nay," said Polly. "We're all here waiting for you."

"We've got to be up in good time in the morning," he said, in the benevolent official manner.

They all laughed.

"Nay," said Muriel. "Don't leave us all lonely, John Thomas. Take one!"

"I'll take the lot, if you like," he responded gallantly.

"That you won't, either," said Muriel. "Two's company; seven's too much of a good thing."

"Nay—take one," said Laura. "Fair and square, all above board and say which."

"Ay," cried Annie, speaking for the first time. "Pick, John Thomas; let's hear thee."

"Nay," he said. "I'm going home quiet tonight. Feeling good, for once."

"Whereabouts?" said Annie. "Take a good 'un, then. But tha's got to take one of us!"

"Nay, how can I take one," he said, laughing uneasily. "I don't want to make enemies."

"You'd only make *one*," said Annie.

"The chosen *one*," added Laura.

"Oh, my! Who said girls!" exclaimed John Thomas, again turning, as if to escape. "Well—goodnight."

"Nay, you've got to make your pick," said Muriel. "Turn your face to the wall, and say which one touches you. Go on—we shall only just touch your back—one of us. Go on—turn your face to the wall, and don't look, and say which one touches you."

He was uneasy, mistrusting them. Yet he had not the courage to break away. They pushed him to a wall and stood him there with his face to it. Behind his back they all grimaced, tittering. He looked so comical. He looked around uneasily.

"Go on!" he cried.

"You're looking—you're looking!" they shouted.

He turned his head away. And suddenly, with a movement like a swift cat, Annie went forward and fetched him a box on the side of the head that sent his cap flying and himself staggering. He started round.

But at Annie's signal they all flew at him, slapping him, pinching him, pulling his hair, though more in fun than in spite or anger. He, however, saw red. His blue eyes flamed with strange fear as well as fury, and he butted through the girls to the door. It was locked. He wrenched at it. Roused, alert, the girls stood round and looked at him. He faced them, at bay. At that moment they were rather horrifying to him, as they stood in their short uniforms. He was distinctly afraid.

"Come on, John Thomas! Come on! Choose!" said Annie.

"What are you after? Open the door," he said.

"We shan't—not till you've chosen!" said Muriel.

"Chosen what?" he said.

"Chosen the one you're going to marry," she replied.

He hesitated a moment.

"Open the blasted door," he said, "and get back to your senses." He spoke with official authority.

"You've got to choose!" cried the girls.

"Come on!" cried Annie, looking him in the eye. "Come on! Come on!"

He went forward, rather vaguely. She had taken off her belt, and swinging it, she fetched him a sharp blow over the head with the buckle end. He sprang and seized her. But immediately the other girls rushed upon him, pulling and tearing and beating him. Their blood was now thoroughly up. He was their sport now. They were going to have their own back, out of him. Strange, wild creatures, they hung on him and rushed at him to bear him down. His tunic was torn right up the back, Nora had hold at the back of his collar, and was actually strangling him. Luckily the button burst. He struggled in a wild frenzy of fury and terror, almost mad terror. His tunic was simply torn off his back, his shirt-sleeves were torn away, his arms were naked. The girls rushed at him, clenched their hands on him, and pulled at him: or they rushed at him and pushed him, butted him with all their might: or they struck him wild blows. He ducked and cringed and struck sideways. They became more intense.

At last he was down. They rushed on him, kneeling on him. He had neither breath nor strength to move. His face was bleeding with a long scratch, his brow was bruised.

Annie knelt on him, the other girls knelt and hung on to him. Their faces were flushed, their hair wild, their eyes were all glittering strangely. He lay at last quite still, with face averted, as an animal lies when it is defeated and at the mercy of the captor. Sometimes his eye glanced back at the wild faces of the girls. His breast rose heavily, his wrists were torn.

"Now, then, my fellow!" gasped Annie at length. "Now then—now—"

At the sound of her terrifying, cold triumph, he suddenly started to struggle as an animal might, but the girls threw themselves upon him with unnatural strength and power, forcing him down.

"Yes—now, then!" gasped Annie at length.

And there was a dead silence, in which the thud of heart-beating was to be heard. It was a suspense of pure silence in every soul.

"Now you know where you are," said Annie.

The sight of his white, bare arm maddened the girls. He lay in a kind of trance of fear and antagonism. They felt themselves filled with supernatural strength.

Suddenly Polly started to laugh—to giggle wildly—helplessly—and Emma and Muriel joined in. But Annie and Nora and Laura remained the same, tense, watchful, with gleaming eyes. He winced away from these eyes.

"Yes," said Annie, in a curious low tone, secret and deadly. "Yes! You've got it now. You know what you've done, don't you? You know what you've done."

He made no sound nor sign, but lay with bright, averted eyes, and averted, bleeding face.

"You ought to be *killed*, that's what you ought," said Annie, tensely. "You ought to be *killed*." And there was a terrifying lust in her voice.

Polly was ceasing to laugh, and giving long-drawn Oh-h-hs and sighs as she came to herself.

"He's got to choose," she said vaguely.

"Oh, yes, he has," said Laura, with vindictive decision.

"Do you hear—do you hear?" said Annie. And with a sharp movement, that made him wince, she turned his face to her.

"Do you hear?" she repeated, shaking him.

But he was quite dumb. She fetched him a sharp slap on the face. He started, and his eyes widened. Then his face darkened with defiance, after all.

"Do you hear?" she repeated.

He only looked at her with hostile eyes.

"Speak!" she said, putting her face devilishly near his.

"What?" he said, almost overcome.

"You've got to *choose!*" she cried, as if it were some terrible menace, and as if it hurt her that she could not exact more.

"What?" he said, in fear.

"Choose your girl, Coddy. You've got to choose her now. And you'll get your neck broken if you play any more of your tricks, my boy. You're settled now."

There was a pause. Again he averted his face. He was cunning in his overthrow. He did not give in to them really—no, not if they tore him to bits.

"All right, then," he said, "I choose Annie." His voice was strange and full of malice. Annie let go of him as if he had been a hot coal.

"He's chosen Annie!" said the girls in chorus.

"Me!" cried Annie. She was still kneeling, but away from him. He was still lying prostrate, with averted face. The girls grouped uneasily around.

"Me!" repeated Annie, with a terrible bitter accent.

Then she got up, drawing away from him with strange disgust and bitterness.

"I wouldn't touch him," she said.

But her face quivered with a kind of agony, she seemed as if she would fall. The other girls turned aside. He remained lying on the floor, with his torn clothes and bleeding, averted face.

"Oh, if he's chosen—" said Polly.

"I don't want him—he can choose again," said Annie, with the same rather bitter hopelessness.

"Get up," said Polly, lifting his shoulder. "Get up."

He rose slowly, a strange, ragged, dazed creature. The girls eyed him from a distance, curiously, furtively, dangerously.

"Who wants him?" cried Laura, roughly.

"Nobody," they answered, with contempt. Yet each one of them waited for him to look at her, hoped he would look at her. All except Annie, and something was broken in her.

He, however, kept his face closed and averted from them all. There was a silence of the end. He picked up the torn pieces of his tunic, without knowing what to do with them. The girls stood about uneasily, flushed, panting, tidying their hair and their dress unconsciously, and watching him. He looked at none of them. He espied his cap in a corner, and went and picked it up. He put it on his head, and one of the girls burst into a shrill, hysteric laugh at the sight he presented. He, however, took no heed, but went straight to where his overcoat hung on a peg. The girls moved away from contact with him as if he had been an electric wire. He put on his coat and buttoned it down. Then he rolled his tunic-rags into a bundle, and stood before the locked door, dumbly.

"Open the door, somebody," said Laura.

"Annie's got the key," said one.

Annie silently offered the key to the girls. Nora unlocked the door.

"Tit for tat, old man," she said. "Show yourself a man, and don't bear a grudge."

But without a word or sign he had opened the door and gone, his face closed, his head dropped.

"That'll learn him," said Laura.

"Coddy!" said Nora.

"Shut up, for God's sake!" cried Annie fiercely, as if in torture.

"Well, I'm about ready to go, Polly. Look sharp!" said Muriel.

The girls were all anxious to be off. They were tidying themselves hurriedly, with mute, stupefied faces.

1922

Discussion

1. **(a)** Describe the mood and tone created by the first few paragraphs of Lawrence's story. **(b)** What marked change can be noted in the style and tone of the closing episode?

2. What indications are we given that, in each other, John Thomas and Annie have found their match?

3. **(a)** Does John Thomas deserve his fate? **(b)** Is he ever in any real danger?

4. What does the fact that the story is set in wartime and the girls wear uniforms have to do with the events of the story?

5. **(a)** Why does Annie refuse John Thomas after he selects her? **(b)** At the end of the story, why do the six girls behave so strangely after they have humiliated John Thomas?

6. How do the characters and events of the story reflect the changing status of women in twentieth-century life?

"The Piano" comes from a notebook containing drafts of early poems. It is an early version of the poem eventually published as "Piano" in Lawrence's *New Poems* (1918).

The Piano

Somewhere beneath that piano's superb
    sleek black
Must hide my mother's piano, little and
    brown, with the back
That stood close to the wall, and the front's
    faded silk both torn,
And the keys with little hollows, that my
    mother's fingers had worn.

5 Softly, in the shadows, a woman is singing
    to me
Quietly, through the years I have crept back
    to see
A child sitting under the piano, in the boom
    of the shaking strings
Pressing the little poised feet of the mother
    who smiles as she sings.

The full throated woman has chosen a
    winning, living song
10 And surely the heart that is in me must
    belong
To the old Sunday evenings, when darkness
    wandered outside
And hymns gleamed on our warm lips, as we
    watched mother's fingers glide.

Or this is my sister at home in the old front
    room
Singing love's first surprised gladness, alone
    in the gloom.
15 She will start when she sees me, and
    blushing, spread out her hands
To cover my mouth's raillery, till I'm bound
    in her shame's heart-spun bands.

A woman is singing me a wild Hungarian air
And her arms, and her bosom, and the
    whole of her soul is bare,
And the great black piano is clamoring as
    my mother's never could clamor
20 And my mother's tunes are devoured of this
    music's ravaging glamor.

Piano

Softly, in the dusk, a woman is singing to
   me;
Taking me back down the vista of years, till
   I see
A child sitting under the piano, in the boom
   of the tingling strings
And pressing the small, poised feet of a
   mother who smiles as she sings.

5 In spite of myself, the insidious mastery of
   song
Betrays me back, till the heart of me weeps
   to belong
To the old Sunday evenings at home, with
   winter outside
And hymns in the cozy parlor, the tinkling
   piano our guide.

So now it is vain for the singer to burst into
   clamor
10 With the great black piano appassionato.
   The glamor
Of childish days is upon me, my manhood is
   cast
Down in the flood of remembrance, I weep
   like a child for the past.

                       1918

Discussion

1. What episode is the basis of both versions
of this poem?

2. How does the poet's presentation of his
feelings while listening to the woman playing
differ in these two versions?

Composition

Examine both versions of this poem, paying
close attention to word choice, imagery, point
of view, rhythm, tone, and the emotion com-
municated in each one.

Write a paper in which you discuss Lawrence's revision of this poem.

Snake

A snake came to my water-trough
On a hot, hot day, and I in pajamas for the heat,
To drink there.

In the deep, strange-scented shade of the
   great dark carob-tree
5 I came down the steps with my pitcher
And must wait, must stand and wait, for
   there he was at the trough before me.

He reached down from a fissure in the
   earth-wall in the gloom
And trailed his yellow-brown slackness
   soft-bellied down, over the edge of the
   stone trough
And rested his throat upon the stone bottom,
10 And where the water had dripped from the
   tap, in a small clearness,
He sipped with his straight mouth,
Softly drank through his straight gums, into
   his slack long body,
Silently.

Someone was before me at my water-trough,
15 And I, like a second comer, waiting.

He lifted his head from his drinking, as
   cattle do,
And looked at me vaguely, as drinking cattle do,
And flickered his two-forked tongue from his
   lips, and mused a moment,
And stooped and drank a little more,
20 Being earth-brown, earth-golden from the
   burning bowels of the earth
On the day of Sicilian July, with Etna[1]
   smoking.

The voice of my education said to me
He must be killed,

From *The Complete Poems of D. H. Lawrence* edited by Vivian
de Sola Pinto and Warren Roberts. Copyright © 1964 by Angelo
Ravagli and C. M. Weekley, Executors of the Estate of Frieda
Lawrence Ravagli. Reprinted by permission of Viking Penguin
Inc., Laurence Pollinger Ltd. and the Estate of Mrs. Frieda Law-
rence Ravagli.

1. Etna, an active volcano on the Mediterranean island of Sicily.

For in Sicily the black, black snakes are
    innocent, the gold are venomous.

25 And voices in me said, If you were a man
You would take a stick and break him now,
    and finish him off.
But must I confess how I liked him,
How glad I was he had come like a guest in
    quiet, to drink at my water-trough
And depart peaceful, pacified, and thankless,
30 Into the burning bowels of this earth?

Was it cowardice, that I dared not kill him?
Was it perversity, that I longed to talk to him?
Was it humility, to feel so honored?
I felt so honored.

35 And yet those voices:
If you were not afraid, you would kill him!

And truly I was afraid, I was most afraid,
But even so, honored still more
That he should seek my hospitality
40 From out the dark door of the secret earth.

He drank enough
And lifted his head, dreamily, as one who
    has drunken,
And flickered his tongue like a forked night
    on the air, so black;
Seeming to lick his lips,
45 And looked around like a god, unseeing, into
    the air,
And slowly turned his head,
And slowly, very slowly, as if thrice adream,
Proceeded to draw his slow length curving
    round
And climb again the broken bank of my
    wall-face.

50 And as he put his head into that dreadful
    hole,

And as he slowly drew up, snake-easing his
    shoulders, and entered farther,
A sort of horror, a sort of protest against his
    withdrawing into that horrid black hole,
Deliberately going into the blackness, and
    slowly drawing himself after,
Overcame me now his back was turned.

55 I looked round, I put down my pitcher,
I picked up a clumsy log
And threw it at the water-trough with a clatter.

I think it did not hit him,
But suddenly that part of him that was left
    behind convulsed in undignified haste,
60 Writhed like lightning, and was gone
Into the black hole, the earth-lipped fissure
    in the wall-front,
At which, in the intense still noon, I stared
    with fascination.

And immediately I regretted it.
I thought how paltry, how vulgar, what a
    mean act!
65 I despised myself and the voices of my
    accursed human education.

And I thought of the albatross,[2]
And I wished he would come back, my
    snake.

For he seemed to me again like a king,
Like a king in exile, uncrowned in the
    underworld,
70 Now due to be crowned again.

And so, I missed my chance with one of the
    lords
Of life.
And I have something to expiate;
A pettiness.

                     Taormina.[3]
                     1923

---

2. *the albatross,* an allusion to Coleridge's *Rime of the Ancient
Mariner,* in which a sailor shoots an albatross, a large sea bird,
and is cursed for it.
3. *Taormina* (tä ôr mē′nä), an ancient town on the east coast of
Sicily, where Lawrence was living in July, 1912, when the incident recorded in this poem took place.

Intimates

Don't you care for my love? she said
    bitterly.

I handed her the mirror, and said:
Please address these questions to the proper
    person!
Please make all requests to head-quarters!
5 In all matters of emotional importance
please approach the supreme authority
    direct!—
So I handed her the mirror.

And she would have broken it over my
    head,
but she caught sight of her own reflection
10 and that held her spellbound for two seconds
while I fled.

1932

From *The Complete Poems of D. H. Lawrence* edited by Vivian de Sola Pinto and Warren Roberts. Copyright © 1964 by Angelo Ravagli and C. M. Weekley, Executors of the Estate of Frieda Lawrence Ravagli. Reprinted by permission of Viking Penguin Inc., Laurence Pollinger Ltd. and the Estate of Mrs. Frieda Lawrence Ravagli.

Discussion

Snake

1. (a) What is the speaker's internal conflict as he watches the snake drinking at the water-trough? (b) How does he finally resolve it?

2. The speaker realizes the snake is venomous. What are his changing feelings as he observes the snake's drinking and withdrawal into "that horrid black hole"?

3. Explain what the speaker means in the last two lines.

4. The poem dramatizes the conflict between how we are taught to think about certain creatures and how we actually feel in their presence. What does the poem imply is the proper relationship of human beings to the natural world?

Discussion

Intimates

1. What criticism of the woman is implied by the speaker?

2. Does the poem offer any proof that the speaker's criticism of the woman is justified?

3. What is the tone of the poem?

4. To what *two* sets of "intimates" does the title refer?

Evelyn Waugh 1903–1966

The son of Arthur Waugh, a critic, editor, and publisher, Evelyn Waugh attended Oxford and spent brief periods studying painting and working as a schoolmaster before beginning his career as a writer. He established his reputation with a series of brilliant satirical novels that appeared in the late 1920s and the 1930s. In *Decline and Fall* (1928), *Vile Bodies* (1930), *Black Mischief* (1932), *A Handful of Dust* (1934), and *Scoop* (1938), Waugh employed a skillful, stylish prose to expose the vicious inanities of postwar England. The world of his novels is typically that of the "Bright Young People"—the liberated members of the upper classes whose escapades were a journalistic staple of the 1920s. Waugh portrays them as heartless, empty-headed worldlings who drift from house party to night club.

The disillusioning breakup of Waugh's marriage had hastened Waugh's conversion to Catholicism in 1930. During World War II he was commissioned a second lieutenant and later became a major in the commandos, serving in West Africa and Crete and as British liaison officer in Yugoslavia. The war brought a more serious tone to Waugh's fiction. *Brideshead Revisited* (1945), a nostalgic picture of aristocratic life in the first decades of the twentieth century, was, according to Waugh, "an attempt to trace the workings of the divine purpose in a pagan world." Though elitist in its outlook and lacking the satirical bite of his earlier work, *Brideshead Revisited* remains Waugh's most popular novel. *Men at Arms* (1952), *Officers and Gentlemen* (1955), and *Unconditional Surrender* (1961) form a trilogy dealing with World War II. As with *Brideshead Revisited*, the tone is a mixture of pessimism and elitist nostalgia. In addition to his novels, Waugh's travel writing—collected in *When the Going Was Good* (1946)—his diary, and his letters are all highly readable.

Winner Takes All

1

When Mrs. Kent-Cumberland's eldest son was born (in an expensive London nursing home) there was a bonfire on Tomb Beacon; it consumed three barrels of tar, an immense catafalque of timber, and, as things turned out—for the flames spread briskly in the dry gorse and loyal tenantry were too tipsy to extinguish them—the entire vegetation of Tomb Hill.

As soon as mother and child could be moved, they traveled in state to the country, where flags were hung out in the village street and a trellis arch of evergreen boughs obscured the handsome Palladian[1] entrance gates of their home. There were farmers' dinners both at Tomb and on the Kent-Cumberlands' Norfolk estate, and funds for a silver-plated tray were ungrudgingly subscribed.

The christening was celebrated by a garden-

---

1. **Palladian,** in the neoclassical style based on the writings and buildings of the Italian architect Andrea Palladio (1518–1580). Palladian architecture was very popular in England in the seventeenth and eighteenth centuries.

party. A princess stood godmother by proxy, and the boy was called Gervase Peregrine Mountjoy St. Eustace—all of them names illustrious in the family's history.

Throughout the service and the subsequent presentations he maintained an attitude of phlegmatic dignity which confirmed everyone in the high estimate they had already formed of his capabilities.

After the garden-party there were fireworks and after the fireworks a very hard week for the gardeners, cleaning up the mess. The life of the Kent-Cumberlands then resumed its normal tranquillity until nearly two years later, when, much to her annoyance, Mrs. Kent-Cumberland discovered that she was to have another baby.

The second child was born in August in a shoddy modern house on the East Coast which had been taken for the summer so that Gervase might have the benefit of sea air. Mrs. Kent-Cumberland was attended by the local doctor, who antagonized her by his middle-class accent, and proved, when it came to the point, a great deal more deft than the London specialist.

Throughout the peevish months of waiting Mrs. Kent-Cumberland had fortified herself with the hope that she would have a daughter. It would be a softening influence for Gervase, who was growing up somewhat unresponsive, to have a pretty, gentle, sympathetic sister two years younger than himself. She would come out[2] just when he was going up to Oxford and would save him from either of the dreadful extremes of evil company which threatened that stage of development—the bookworm and the hooligan. She would bring down delightful girls for Eights Week and Commem.[3] Mrs. Kent-Cumberland had it all planned out. When she was delivered of another son she named him Thomas, and fretted through her convalescence with her mind on the coming hunting season.

2

The two brothers developed into sturdy, unremarkable little boys; there was little to choose between them except their two years' difference in age. They were both sandy-haired, courageous, and well-mannered on occasions. Neither was sensitive, artistic, highly strung, or conscious of being misunderstood. Both accept-

ed the fact of Gervase's importance just as they accepted his superiority of knowledge and physique. Mrs. Kent-Cumberland was a fair-minded woman, and in the event of the two being involved in mischief, it was Gervase, as the elder, who was the more severely punished. Tom found that his obscurity was on the whole advantageous, for it excused him from the countless minor performances of ceremony which fell on Gervase.

3

At the age of seven Tom was consumed with desire for a model motor-car, an expensive toy of a size to sit in and pedal about the garden. He prayed for it steadfastly every evening and most mornings for several weeks. Christmas was approaching.

Gervase had a smart pony and was often taken hunting. Tom was alone most of the day and the motor-car occupied a great part of his thoughts. Finally he confided his ambition to an uncle. This uncle was not addicted to expensive present giving, least of all to children (for he was a man of limited means and self-indulgent habits) but something in his nephew's intensity of feeling impressed him.

"Poor little beggar," he reflected, "his brother seems to get all the fun," and when he returned to London he ordered the motor-car for Tom. It arrived some days before Christmas and was put away upstairs with other presents. On Christmas Eve Mrs. Kent-Cumberland came to inspect them. "How very kind," she said, looking at each label in turn, "how very kind."

The motor-car was by far the largest exhibit. It was pillar-box red, complete with electric lights, a hooter and a spare wheel.

"Really," she said. "How *very* kind of Ted."

Then she looked at the label more closely. "But how foolish of him. He's put *Tom's* name on it."

"There was this book for Master Gervase," said the nurse, producing a volume labelled

---

2. **come out,** be introduced to society as a debutante.
3. **Eights Week and Commem.** Two social events at Oxford. Eights Week is highlighted by a boat race between the various Oxford colleges. (The name comes from the boats' eight-man crews.) Commem is the celebration held in memory of the founders and benefactors of the university.

"Gervase with best wishes from Uncle Ted."

"Of course the parcels have been confused at the shop," said Mrs. Kent-Cumberland. "This can't have been meant for Tom. Why, it must have cost six or seven pounds."

She changed the labels and went downstairs to supervise the decoration of the Christmas tree, glad to have rectified an obvious error of justice.

Next morning the presents were revealed. "Oh, Ger. You *are* lucky," said Tom, inspecting the motor-car. "May I ride in it?"

"Yes, only be careful. Nanny says it was awfully expensive."

Tom rode it twice round the room. "May I take it in the garden sometimes?"

"Yes. You can have it when I'm hunting."

Later in the week they wrote to thank their uncle for his presents.

Gervase wrote:

Dear Uncle Ted,
Thank you for the lovely present. It's lovely.
The pony is very well. I am going to hunt again
before I go back to school.
                    Love from Gervase.

Dear Uncle Ted (wrote Tom),
Thank you ever so much for the lovely
present. It is just what I wanted. Again thanking
you very much.
                    With love from Tom.

"So that's all the thanks I get. Ungrateful little beggar," said Uncle Ted, resolving to be more economical in future.

But when Gervase went back to school he said, "You can have the motor-car, Tom, to keep."

"What, for *my own*?"

"Yes. It's a kid's toy, anyway."

And by this act of generosity he increased Tom's respect and love for him a hundredfold.

4

The war came and profoundly changed the lives of the two boys. It engendered none of the neuroses threatened by pacifists. Air raids remained among Tom's happiest memories, when the school used to be awakened in the middle of the night and hustled downstairs to the basement where, wrapped in eiderdowns, they

were regaled with cocoa and cake by the matron, who looked supremely ridiculous in a flannel nightgown. Once a Zeppelin[4] was hit in sight of the school; they all crowded to the dormitory windows to see it sinking slowly in a globe of pink flame. A very young master whose health rendered him unfit for military service danced on the headmaster's tennis court crying, "There go the baby killers." Tom made a collection of "War Relics," including a captured German helmet, shell-splinters, *The Times* for August 4th, 1914, buttons, cartridge cases, and cap badges, that was voted the best in the school.

The event which radically changed the relationship of the brothers was the death, early in 1915, of their father. Neither knew him well nor particularly liked him. He had represented the division in the House of Commons and spent much of his time in London while the children were at Tomb. They only saw him on three occasions after he joined the army. Gervase and Tom were called out of the classroom and told of his death by the headmaster's wife. They cried, since it was expected of them, and for some days were treated with marked deference by the masters and the rest of the school.

It was in the subsequent holidays that the importance of the change became apparent. Mrs. Kent-Cumberland had suddenly become more emotional and more parsimonious. She was liable to unprecedented outbursts of tears, when she would crush Gervase to her and say, "My poor fatherless boy." At other times she spoke gloomily of death duties.[5]

5

For some years in fact "Death Duties" became the refrain of the household.

When Mrs. Kent-Cumberland let the house in London and closed down a wing at Tomb, when she reduced the servants to four and the gardeners to two, when she "let the flower gardens go," when she stopped asking her brother Ted to stay, when she emptied the stables, and became almost fanatical in her reluctance to use the car, when the bath water was cold and there were no new

---

4. *Zeppelin,* a German dirigible, or rigid airship, used to bomb England during the First World War.
5. *death duties,* taxes on the estate of a deceased person.

tennis balls, when the chimneys were dirty and the lawns covered with sheep, when Gervase's castoff clothes ceased to fit Tom, when she refused him the "extra" expense at school of carpentry lessons and mid-morning milk—"Death Duties" were responsible.

"It is all for Gervase," Mrs. Kent-Cumberland used to explain. "When he inherits, he must take over free of debt, as his father did."

6

Gervase went to Eton[6] in the year of his father's death. Tom would normally have followed him two years later, but in her new mood of economy Mrs. Kent-Cumberland cancelled his entry and began canvassing her friends' opinions about the less famous, cheaper public schools. "The education is just as good," she said, "and far more suitable for a boy who has his own way to make in the world."

Tom was happy enough at the school to which he was sent. It was very bleak and very new, salubrious, progressive, prosperous in the boom that secondary education enjoyed in the years immediately following the war, and, when all was said and done, "thoroughly suitable for a boy with his own way to make in the world." He had several friends whom he was not allowed to invite to his home during the holidays. He got his House colors for swimming and fives,[7] played once or twice in the second eleven for cricket, and was a platoon commander in the O.T.C.; he was in the sixth form and passed the Higher Certificate in his last year, became a prefect and enjoyed the confidence of his house master, who spoke of him as "a very decent stamp of boy." He left school at the age of eighteen without the smallest desire to revisit it or see any of its members again.

Gervase was then at Christ Church.[8] Tom went up to visit him, but the magnificent Etonians who romped in and out of his brother's rooms scared and depressed him. Gervase was in the Bullingdon, spending money freely and enjoying himself. He gave a dinner-party in his rooms, but Tom sat in silence, drinking heavily to hide his embarrassment, and was later somberly sick in a corner of Peckwater quad. He returned to Tomb next day in the lowest spirits.

"It is not as though Tom were a scholarly boy," said Mrs. Kent-Cumberland to her friends. "I am glad he is not, of course. But if he had been, it might have been right to make the sacrifice and send him to the University. As it is, the sooner he Gets Started the better."

7

Getting Tom started, however, proved a matter of some difficulty. During the Death Duty Period, Mrs. Kent-Cumberland had cut herself off from many of her friends. Now she cast round vainly to find someone who would "put Tom into something." Chartered Accountancy, Chinese Customs, estate agencies, "the City,"[9] were suggested and abandoned. "The trouble is that he has no particular abilities," she explained. "He is the sort of boy who would be useful in anything—an all-round man—but, of course, he has no capital."

August, September, October passed; Gervase was back at Oxford, in fashionable lodgings in the High Street, but Tom remained at home without employment. Day by day he and his mother sat down together to luncheon and dinner, and his constant presence was a severe strain on Mrs. Kent-Cumberland's equability. She herself was always busy and, as she bustled about her duties, it shocked and distracted her to encounter the large figure of her younger son sprawling on the morning-room sofa or leaning against the stone parapet of the terrace and gazing out apathetically across the familiar landscape.

"Why can't you find something to *do?*" she would complain. "There are *always* things to do about a house. Heaven knows I never have a moment." And when, one afternoon, he was asked out by some neighbors and returned too late to dress for dinner, she said, "Really, Tom, I should have thought that *you* had time for that."

"It is a very serious thing," she remarked on another occasion, "for a young man of your age to get out of the habit of work. It saps his whole morale."

6. *Eton,* a famous English public school. The English public school is a private preparatory school for the sons of the upper classes.

7. *fives,* a game similar to handball.

8. *Christ Church,* an Oxford college.

9. *"the City,"* the financial district of London.

Accordingly she fell back upon the ancient country house expedient of Cataloguing the Library. This consisted of an extensive and dusty collection of books amassed by succeeding generations of a family at no time notable for their patronage of literature; it had been catalogued before, in the middle of the nineteenth century, in the spidery, spinsterish hand of a relative in reduced circumstances; since then the additions and disturbances had been negligible, but Mrs. Kent-Cumberland purchased a fumed oak cabinet and several boxes of cards and instructed Tom how she wanted the shelves re-numbered and the books twice entered under Subject and Author.

It was a system that should keep a boy employed for some time, and it was with vexation, therefore, that, a few days after the task was commenced, she paid a surprise visit to the scene of his labor and found Tom sitting, almost lying, in an arm-chair, with his feet on a rung of the library steps, reading.

"I am glad you have found something interesting," she said in a voice that conveyed very little gladness.

"Well, to tell you the truth, I think I have," said Tom, and showed her the book.

It was the manuscript journal kept by a Colonel Jasper Cumberland during the Peninsular War.[10] It had no startling literary merit, nor did its criticisms of the general staff throw any new light upon the strategy of the campaign, but it was a lively, direct, day-to-day narrative, redolent of its period; there was a sprinkling of droll anecdotes, some vigorous descriptions of fox-hunting behind the lines of Torres Vedras, of the Duke of Wellington dining in Mess, of a threatened mutiny that had not yet found its way into history, of the assault on Badajoz; there were some bawdy references to Portuguese women and some pious reflections about patriotism.

"I was wondering if it might be worth publishing," said Tom.

"I should hardly think so," replied his mother. "But I will certainly show it to Gervase when he comes home."

For the moment the discovery gave a new interest to Tom's life. He read up the history of the period and of his own family. Jasper Cumber-

land he established as a younger son of the period, who had later emigrated to Canada. There were letters from him among the archives, including the announcement of his marriage to a Papist,[11] which had clearly severed the link with his elder brother. In a case of uncatalogued miniatures in the long drawing-room, he found the portrait of a handsome whiskered soldier, which by a study of contemporary uniforms he was able to identify as the diarist.

Presently, in his round, immature handwriting, Tom began working up his notes into an essay. His mother watched his efforts with unqualified approval. She was glad to see him busy, and glad to see him taking an interest in his family's history. She had begun to fear that by sending him to a school without "tradition" she might have made a socialist of the boy. When, shortly before the Christmas vacation, work was found for Tom, she took charge of his notes. "I am sure Gervase will be extremely interested," she said. "He may even think it worth showing to a publisher."

8

The work that had been found for Tom was not immediately lucrative, but, as his mother said, it was a beginning. It was to go to Wolverhampton and learn the motor business from the bottom. The first two years were to be spent at the works, from where, if he showed talent, he might graduate to the London showrooms. His wages, at first, were thirty-five shillings a week. This was augmented by the allowance of another pound. Lodgings were found for him over a fruit shop in the outskirts of the town, and Gervase gave him his old two-seater car, in which he could travel to and from his work, and for occasional week-ends home.

It was during one of these visits that Gervase told him the good news that a London publisher had read the diary and seen possibilities in it. Six months later it appeared under the title *The Journal of an English Cavalry Officer during the Peninsular War. Edited with notes and a biographi-*

---

10. **Peninsular War** (1808–1814), the campaigns of the Napoleonic Wars fought in Spain and Portugal. The British forces were led by Arthur Wellesley, later the Duke of Wellington. The lines of Torres Vedras were barricades erected by the Duke of Wellington to protect Portugal from invasion by French armies.
11. **Papist,** Catholic.

Swansong by Neil Davenport.

cal introduction by Gervase Kent-Cumberland. The miniature portrait was prettily reproduced as a frontispiece, there was a collotype copy of a page of the original manuscript, a contemporary print of Tomb Park, and a map of the campaign. It sold nearly two thousand copies at twelve and sixpence and received two or three respectful reviews in the Saturday and Sunday papers.

The appearance of the *Journal* coincided within a few days with Gervase's twenty-first birthday. The celebrations were extravagant and prolonged, culminating in a ball at which Tom's attendance was required.

He drove over, after the works had shut down, and arrived, just in time for dinner, to find a house-party of thirty and a house entirely transformed.

His own room had been taken for a guest ("as you will only be here for one night," his mother explained). He was sent down to the Cumberland Arms, where he dressed by candlelight in a breathless little bedroom over the bar, and arrived late and slightly dishevelled at dinner, where he sat between two lovely girls who neither knew who he was nor troubled to inquire. The dancing afterwards was in a marquee built on the terrace, which a London catering firm had converted into a fair replica of a Pont Street drawing-room. Tom danced once or twice with the daughters of neighboring families whom he had known since childhood. They asked him about Wolverhampton and the works. He had to get up early next morning; at midnight he slipped away to his bed at the inn. The evening had bored him; because he was in love.

9

It had occurred to him to ask his mother whether he might bring his fiancée to the ball, but on reflection, enchanted as he was, he had realized that it would not do. The girl was named Gladys Cruttwell. She was two years older than himself; she had fluffy yellow hair which she washed at home once a week and dried before the gas fire; on the day after the shampoo it was very light and silky; towards the end of the week, darker and slightly greasy. She was a virtuous, affectionate, self-reliant, even-tempered, unintelligent, high-spirited girl, but Tom could not disguise from himself the fact that she would not go down well at Tomb.

She worked for the firm on the clerical side. Tom had noticed her on his second day, as she tripped across the yard, exactly on time, bareheaded (the day after a shampoo) in a woolen coat and skirt which she had knitted herself. He had got into conversation with her in the canteen, by making way for her at the counter with a chivalry that was not much practiced at the works. His possession of a car gave him a clear advantage over the other young men about the place.

They discovered that they lived within a few streets of one another, and it presently became Tom's practice to call for her in the mornings and take her home in the evenings. He would sit in the two-seater outside her gate, sound the horn, and she would come running down the path to meet him. As summer approached they went for drives in the evening among leafy Warwickshire lanes. In June they were engaged. Tom was exhilarated, sometimes almost dizzy at the experience, but he hesitated to tell his mother. "After all," he reflected, "it is not as though I were Gervase," but in his own heart he knew that there would be trouble.

Gladys came of a class accustomed to long engagements; marriage seemed a remote prospect; an engagement to her signified the formal recognition that she and Tom spent their spare time in one another's company. Her mother, with whom she lived, accepted him on these terms. In years to come, when Tom had got his place in the London showrooms, it would be time enough to think about marrying. But Tom was born to a less patient tradition. He began to speak about a wedding in the autumn.

"It would be lovely," said Gladys in the tones she would have employed about winning the Irish sweepstake.

He had spoken very little about his family. She understood, vaguely, that they lived in a big house, but it was a part of life that never had been real to her. She knew that there were duchesses and marchionesses in something called "Society"; they were encountered in the papers and the films. She knew there were directors with large salaries; but the fact that there were people like Gervase of Mrs. Kent-Cumberland, and that they would think of themselves as radically different from herself, had not entered her experience. When, eventually, they were brought together Mrs. Kent-Cumberland was extremely gracious and Gladys thought her a very nice old lady. But Tom knew that the meeting was proving disastrous.

"Of course," said Mrs. Kent-Cumberland, "the whole thing is quite impossible. Miss Whatever-her-name-was seemed a thoroughly nice

girl, but you are not in a position to think of marriage. Besides," she added with absolute finality, "you must not forget that if anything were to happen to Gervase you would be his heir."

So Tom was removed from the motor business and an opening found for him on a sheep farm in South Australia.

10

It would not be fair to say that in the ensuing two years Mrs. Kent-Cumberland forgot her younger son. She wrote to him every month and sent him bandana handkerchiefs for Christmas. In the first lonely days he wrote to her frequently, but when, as he grew accustomed to the new life, his letters became less frequent she did not seriously miss them. When they did arrive they were lengthy; she put them aside from her correspondence to read at leisure and, more than once, mislaid them, unopened. But whenever her acquaintances asked after Tom she loyally answered, "Doing splendidly. And enjoying himself *very much*."

She had many other things to occupy and, in some cases, distress her. Gervase was now in authority at Tomb, and the careful régime of his minority wholly reversed. There were six expensive hunters in the stable. The lawns were mown, bedrooms thrown open, additional bathrooms installed; there was even talk of constructing a swimming pool. There was constant Saturday to Monday entertaining. There was the sale, at a poor price, of two Romneys and a Hoppner.[12]

Mrs. Kent-Cumberland watched all this with mingled pride and anxiety. In particular she scrutinized the succession of girls who came to stay, in the irreconcilable, ever-present fears that Gervase would or would not marry. Either conclusion seemed perilous; a wife for Gervase must be wellborn, well conducted, rich, of stainless reputation, and affectionately disposed to Mrs. Kent-Cumberland; such a mate seemed difficult to find. The estate was clear of the mortgages necessitated by death duties, but dividends were uncertain, and though, as she frequently pointed out, she "never interfered," simple arithmetic and her own close experience of domestic man-

---

12. *two Romneys . . . Hoppner,* paintings by two English artists, George Romney (1734–1802) and John Hoppner (1758–1810).

agement convinced her that Gervase would not long be able to support the scale of living which he had introduced.

With so much on her mind, it was inevitable that Mrs. Kent-Cumberland should think a great deal about Tomb and very little about South Australia, and should be rudely shocked to read in one of Tom's letters that he was proposing to return to England on a visit, with a fiancée and a future father-in-law; that in fact he had already started, was now on the sea and due to arrive in London in a fortnight. Had she read his earlier letters with attention she might have found hints of such an attachment, but she had not done so, and the announcement came to her as a wholly unpleasant surprise.

"Your brother is coming back."

"Oh, good! When?"

"He is bringing a farmer's daughter to whom he is engaged—and the farmer. They want to come here."

"I say, that's rather a bore. Let's tell them we're having the boilers cleaned."

"You don't seem to realize that this is a serious matter, Gervase."

"Oh, well, you fix things up. I dare say it would be all right if they came next month. We've got to have the Anchorages some time. We might get both over together."

In the end it was decided that Gervase should meet the immigrants in London, vet[13] them and report to his mother whether or no they were suitable fellow-guests for the Anchorages. A week later, on his return to Tomb, his mother greeted him anxiously.

"Well? You never wrote?"

"Wrote? Why should I? I never do. I say, I haven't forgotten a birthday or anything, have I?"

"Don't be absurd, Gervase. I mean, about your brother Tom's unfortunate entanglement. Did you see the girl?"

"Oh, *that*. Yes, I went and had dinner with them. Tom's done himself quite well. Fair, rather fat, saucer-eyed, good-tempered, I should say, by her looks."

"Does she—does she speak with an Australian accent?"

"Didn't notice it."

"And the father?"

"Pompous old boy."

"Would he be all right with the Anchorages?"

"I should think he'd go down like a dinner. But they can't come. They are staying with the Chasms."

"Indeed! What an extraordinary thing. But, of course, Archie Chasm was Governor-General[14] once. Still, it shows they must be fairly respectable. Where are they staying?"

"Claridge's."[15]

"Then they must be quite rich, too. How very interesting. I will write this evening."

11

Three weeks later they arrived. Mr. MacDougal, the father, was a tall, lean man, with pince-nez and an interest in statistics. He was a territorial magnate to whom the Tomb estates appeared a cozy small-holding. He did not emphasize this in any boastful fashion, but in his statistical zeal gave Mrs. Kent-Cumberland some staggering figures. "Is Bessie your only child?" asked Mrs. Kent-Cumberland.

"My only child and heir," he replied, coming down to brass tacks at once. "I dare say you have been wondering what sort of settlement I shall be able to make on her. Now that, I regret to say, is a question I cannot answer accurately. We have good years, Mrs. Kent-Cumberland, and we have bad years. It all depends."

"But I dare say that even in bad years the income is quite considerable?"

"In a bad year," said Mr. MacDougal, "in a *very* bad year such as the present, the net profits, after all deductions have been made for running expenses, insurance, taxation, and deterioration, amount to something between"—Mrs. Kent-Cumberland listened breathlessly—"fifty and fifty-two thousand pounds. I know that is a very vague statement, but it is impossible to be more accurate until the last returns are in."

Bessie was bland and creamy. She admired everything. "It's so *antique*," she would remark with relish, whether the object of her attention was the Norman Church of Tomb, the Victorian panelling in the billiard-room, or the central-heat-

---

13. **vet,** examine.
14. ***Governor-General,** of Australia.
15. ***Claridge's,** a famous London hotel.

ing system which Gervase had recently installed. Mrs. Kent-Cumberland took a great liking to the girl.

"Thoroughly Teachable," she pronounced. "But I wonder whether she is *really* suited to Tom . . . I *wonder* . . ."

The MacDougals stayed for four days and, when they left, Mrs. Kent-Cumberland pressed them to return for a longer visit. Bessie had been enchanted with everything she saw.

"I wish we could live here," she had said to Tom on her first evening, "in this dear, quaint old house."

"Yes, darling, so do I. Of course it all belongs to Gervase, but I always look on it as my home."

"Just as we Australians look on England."

"Exactly."

She had insisted on seeing everything; the old gabled manor, once the home of the family, relegated now to the function of dower house[16] since the present mansion was built in the eighteenth century—the house of mean proportions and inconvenient offices where Mrs. Kent-Cumberland, in her moments of depression, pictured her own declining years; the mill and the quarries; the farm, which to the MacDougals seemed minute and formal as a Noah's Ark. On these expeditions it was Gervase who acted as guide. "He, of course, knows so much more about it than Tom," Mrs. Kent-Cumberland explained.

Tom, in fact, found himself very rarely alone with his fiancée. Once, when they were all together after dinner, the question of his marriage was mentioned. He asked Bessie whether, now that she had seen Tomb, she would sooner be married there, at the village church, than in London.

"Oh, there is no need to decide anything hastily," Mrs. Kent-Cumberland had said. "Let Bessie look about a little first."

When the MacDougals left, it was to go to Scotland to see the castle of their ancestors. Mr. MacDougal had traced relationship with various branches of his family, had corresponded with them intermittently, and now wished to make their acquaintance.

Bessie wrote to them all at Tomb; she wrote daily to Tom, but in her thoughts, as she lay sleepless in the appalling bed provided for her by her distant kinsmen, she was conscious for the first time of a light feeling of disappointment and uncertainty. In Australia Tom had seemed so different from everyone else, so gentle and dignified and cultured. Here in England he seemed to recede into obscurity. Everyone in England seemed to be like Tom.

And then there was the house. It was exactly the kind of house which she had always imagined English people to live in, with the dear little park—less than a thousand acres—and the soft grass and the old stone. Tom had fitted into the house. He had fitted too well; had disappeared entirely in it and become part of the background. The central place belonged to Gervase—so like Tom but more handsome; with all Tom's charm but with more personality. Beset with these thoughts, she rolled on the hard and irregular bed until dawn began to show through the lancet window of the Victorian-baronial turret. She loved that turret for all its discomfort. It was so antique.

12

Mrs. Kent-Cumberland was an active woman. It was less than ten days after the MacDougals' visit that she returned triumphantly from a day in London. After dinner, when she sat alone with Tom in the small drawing-room, she said:

"You'll be very much surprised to hear who I saw to-day. *Gladys.*"

"Gladys?"

"Gladys Cruttwell."

"Good heavens. Where on earth did you meet her?"

"It was quite by chance," said his mother vaguely. "She is working there now."

"How was she?"

"Very pretty. Prettier, if anything."

There was a pause. Mrs. Kent-Cumberland stitched away at a gros-point chair seat. "You know, dear boy, that *I never interfere,* but I have often wondered whether you treated Gladys very kindly. I know I was partly to blame, myself. But you were both very young and your prospects so uncertain. I thought a year or two of separation

---

16. **dower house.** A dower is a widow's share of her dead husband's property; a dower house is a widow's residence.

would be a good test of whether you really loved one another."

"Oh, I am sure she has forgotten about me long ago."

"Indeed, she has not, Tom. I thought she seemed a very unhappy girl."

"But how *can* you know, Mother, just seeing her casually like that?"

"We had luncheon together," said Mrs. Kent-Cumberland. "In an A.B.C.[17] shop."

Another pause.

"But, look here, I've forgotten all about her. I only care about Bessie now."

"You know, dearest boy, I never interfere. I think Bessie is a delightful girl. But are you free? Are you free in your own conscience? You know, and I do not know, on what terms you parted from Gladys."

And there returned, after a long absence, the scene which for the first few months of his Australian venture had been constantly in Tom's memory, of a tearful parting and many intemperate promises. He said nothing. "I did not tell Gladys of your engagement. I thought you had the right to do that—as best you can, in your own way. But I did tell her you were back in England and that you wished to see her. She is coming here tomorrow for a night or two. She looked in need of a holiday, poor child."

When Tom went to meet Gladys at the station they stood for some minutes on the platform not certain of the other's identity. Then their tentative signs of recognition corresponded. Gladys had been engaged twice in the past two years, and was now walking out with a motor salesman. It had been a great surprise when Mrs. Kent-Cumberland sought her out and explained that Tom had returned to England. She had not forgotten him, for she was a loyal and good-hearted girl, but she was embarrassed and touched to learn that his devotion was unshaken.

They were married two weeks later and Mrs. Kent-Cumberland undertook the delicate mission of "explaining everything" to the MacDougals.

They went to Australia, where Mr. MacDougal very magnanimously gave them a post managing one of his more remote estates. He was satisfied with Tom's work. Gladys has a large sunny bungalow and a landscape of grazing-land and wire fences. She does not see very much company nor does she particularly like what she does see. The neighboring ranchers find her very English and aloof.

Bessie and Gervase were married after six weeks' engagement. They live at Tomb. Bessie has two children and Gervase has six race-horses. Mrs. Kent-Cumberland lives in the house with them. She and Bessie rarely disagree, and, when they do, it is Mrs. Kent-Cumberland who gets her way.

The dower house is let on a long lease to a sporting manufacturer. Gervase has taken over the Hounds and spends money profusely; everyone in the neighborhood is content.   1936

---

17. **A.B.C.**, initials of the Aereated Bread Company.

Discussion

1. Who is the "winner"? Give reasons for your choice.

2. **(a)** In what ways does Gervase receive preferential treatment? **(b)** How does Mrs. Kent-Cumberland feel about her second son?

3. What finally becomes of the ancestor's journal Tom discovers and prepares for publication?

4. What is the specific reason why Tom is taken out of the motor business and sent to South Australia?

5. **(a)** Describe Mrs. Kent-Cumberland's role in the events that follow Tom's return from Australia with the MacDougals. **(b)** Why is Bessie acceptable to Mrs. Kent-Cumberland as a wife for Gervase?

Composition

Imagine Mrs. Kent-Cumberland's views on the raising of children.

Write a dialogue between her and her daughter-in-law on this subject. (Since "she and Bessie rarely disagree," it might be almost a monologue.)

W. H. Auden 1907–1973

Auden's career as a poet was a complex and influential one. From its confused, precocious beginnings in the 1920s (while he was still an undergraduate), Auden's poetry evolved through political commitment during the 1930s and '40s, to religious reflection in his later years. For more than four decades his poetry succeeded in capturing the horrors, anxieties, and hopes of the times. It was Auden who characterized the 1930s as a "low, dishonest decade" and most memorably crystallized the mood of social dissatisfaction and impending crisis that prevailed during the years leading up to the outbreak of World War II. The postwar period has come to be known as "The Age of Anxiety," from the title of a volume of his poems published in 1948.

He was born in York, the son of a distinguished physician who moved his family to Birmingham when Auden was a year old. He enjoyed a stable and comfortable childhood and acquired an interest in science (at one time intending to be a mining engineer). He was educated at Oxford where he had a great influence on a number of his fellow undergraduates, including Louis MacNeice, Stephen Spender, and C. Day Lewis. This group shared a need to create new poetic techniques to express a heightened social consciousness and a zeal for political reform.

After graduating from Oxford in 1928, Auden spent a year in Berlin, where he was strongly influenced by contemporary German literature, particularly the work of the Marxist poet and playwright Bertolt Brecht. During the early 1930s Auden taught school in England and Scotland. In 1937 he went to Spain, where he drove an ambulance for the Republicans (those loyal to Spain's leftist government). He later recalled this visit as the beginning of his disillusionment with the left and his return to Christianity.

In 1939 Auden settled in the United States, becoming an American citizen in 1946. Beginning in 1948, he divided his time between New York and Europe, summering first on the Italian island of Ischia and later in Austria. During this period Auden spent much of his time editing, translating, and collaborating with his friend the American poet Chester Kallman on a series of opera libretti. He was elected Professor of Poetry at Oxford in 1956. In 1972 he transferred his winter residence from New York to Oxford, where his old college had provided him with a small house. He died in Vienna in 1973.

Auden delighted in playing with words, in employing a variety of rhythms, and in creating striking literary effects. But he was also insistent that "Art is not enough": poetry must also fulfill a moral function, principally that of dispelling hate and promoting love. "Poetry is not concerned with telling people what to do," he once wrote, "but with extending our knowledge of good and evil . . . leading us to the point where it is possible for us to make a rational moral choice."

The Unknown Citizen

(To JS/07/M/378
This Marble Monument
Is Erected by the State)

He was found by the Bureau of Statistics to be
One against whom there was no official complaint,
And all the reports on his conduct agree
That, in the modern sense of an old-fashioned word, he was a saint,
5 For in everything he did he served the Greater Community.
Except for the War till the day he retired
He worked in a factory and never got fired,
But satisfied his employers, Fudge Motors Inc.
Yet he wasn't a scab[1] or odd in his views,
10 For his Union reports that he paid his dues,
(Our report on his Union shows it was sound)
And our Social Psychology workers found
That he was popular with his mates and liked a drink.
The Press are convinced that he bought a paper every day
15 And that his reactions to advertisements were normal in every way.
Policies taken out in his name prove that he was fully insured,
And his Health-card shows he was once in hospital but left it cured.
Both Producers Research and High-Grade Living declare
He was fully sensible to the advantages of the Instalment Plan
20 And had everything necessary to the Modern Man,
A phonograph, a radio, a car and a frigidaire.
Our researchers into Public Opinion are content
That he held the proper opinions for the time of year;
When there was peace, he was for peace; when there was war, he went.
25 He was married and added five children to the population,
Which our Eugenist[2] says was the right number for a parent of his generation,
And our teachers report that he never interfered with their education.
Was he free? Was he happy? The question is absurd:
Had anything been wrong, we should certainly have heard.

1940

---

1. scab, worker who will not join a labor union or who takes a striker's job.
2. Eugenist, an expert in eugenics, the science of improving the human race by a careful selection of parents in order to breed healthier and more intelligent children.

Who's Who

A shilling life[1] will give you all the facts:
How Father beat him, how he ran away,
What were the struggles of his youth, what acts
Made him the greatest figure of his day:
5 Of how he fought, fished, hunted, worked all night,
Though giddy, climbed new mountains; named
    a sea:
Some of the last researchers even write
Love made him weep his pints like you and me.

With all his honors on, he sighed for one
10 Who, say astonished critics, lived at home;
Did little jobs about the house with skill
And nothing else; could whistle; would sit still
Or potter round the garden; answered some
Of his long marvellous letters but kept none.

1936

1. *shilling life,* an inexpensive biography, often issued in series.

Discussion

Who's Who

1. What is the **paradox** developed in this sonnet?

2. (a) Lines 1–8 deal with the public personality of a great man; lines 9–14 deal with someone else. Who is this second person? (b) Why might the great man sigh for this person and write "long marvellous letters" to him or her? (c) Is it in keeping with the character of the recipient that none of these letters were kept?

3. Based on the suggestions in the poem, what made the great man strive so hard for fame?

The Unknown Citizen

1. (a) Why was no official complaint ever brought against the Unknown Citizen? (b) Reread the last line of the poem. Is it true?

2. (a) The poem profiles both a person and a society. What kind of world did the Unknown Citizen inhabit? (b) What aspects of this society are most bitingly satirized? (c) What literary devices have been used to create the satiric effect of the poem?

3. In the next-to-last line the poet asks, "Was he free? Was he happy?" Are these questions answered in the poem?

The Fall of Icarus by Pieter Brueghel the Elder (1525?-1569).

Musée des Beaux Arts[1]

About suffering they were never wrong,
The Old Masters: how well they understood
Its human position; how it takes place
While someone else is eating or opening a
    window or just walking dully along;
5 How, when the aged are reverently,
    passionately waiting
For the miraculous birth, there always must be
Children who did not specially want it to
    happen, skating
On a pond at the edge of the wood:
They never forgot
10 That even the dreadful martyrdom must run its
    course
Anyhow in a corner, some untidy spot
Where the dogs go on with their doggy life and
    the torturer's horse
Scratches its innocent behind on a tree.

In Brueghel's *Icarus*,[2] for instance: how
    everything turns away
15 Quite leisurely from the disaster; the
    ploughman may
Have heard the splash, the forsaken cry,
But for him it was not an important failure; the
    sun shone
As it had to on the white legs disappearing into
    the green
Water; and the expensive delicate ship that
    must have seen
20 Something amazing, a boy falling out of the
    sky,
Had somewhere to get to and sailed calmly on.

               1940

Copyright 1940 and renewed 1968 by W. H. Auden. Reprinted from *W. H. Auden: Collected Poems,* by W. H. Auden, edited by Edward Mendelson, by permission of Random House, Inc. and Faber and Faber Ltd.
1. *Musée des Beaux Arts,* the Royal Museum of Fine Arts in Brussels.
2. *Brueghel's Icarus. The Fall of Icarus* by Pieter Brueghel (pē'tər broi'gəl) was inspired by the Greek myth that relates how the cunning artisan Daedalus made wings of feathers and wax for his son Icarus and himself in order to escape imprisonment on the island of Crete. Despite his father's warnings, Icarus flew too near the sun; the wax holding the feathers of his wings together melted, and he fell into the sea and drowned.

4. Explain the double meaning of "Unknown" in the title.

Composition

1. In "The Unknown Citizen" Auden creates a satirical **elegy** to criticize certain modern values.
    Create an elegy of your own in order to attack some aspect of contemporary life of which you disapprove. Remember that your task is to condemn through the use of ironic praise.

In Memory of W. B. Yeats   *(d. Jan. 1939)*

1

He disappeared in the dead of winter:
The brooks were frozen, the airports almost deserted,
And snow disfigured the public statues;
The mercury sank in the mouth of the dying day.
5 O all the instruments agree
The day of his death was a dark cold day.

Far from his illness
The wolves ran on through the evergreen forests,
The peasant river was untempted by the fashionable quays;
10 By mourning tongues
The death of the poet was kept from his poems.

But for him it was his last afternoon as himself,
An afternoon of nurses and rumors;
The provinces of his body revolted,
15 The squares of his mind were empty,
Silence invaded the suburbs,
The current of his feeling failed: he became his admirers.

Now he is scattered among a hundred cities
And wholly given over to unfamiliar affections;
20 To find his happiness in another kind of wood
And be punished under a foreign code of conscience.
The words of a dead man
Are modified in the guts of the living.

But in the importance and noise of tomorrow
25 When the brokers are roaring like beasts on the floor of the Bourse,[1]
And the poor have the sufferings to which they are fairly accustomed,
And each in the cell of himself is almost convinced of his freedom;
A few thousand will think of this day
As one thinks of a day when one did something slightly unusual.
30 O all the instruments agree
The day of his death was a dark cold day.

2

You were silly like us: your gift survived it all;
The parish of rich women, physical decay,
Yourself; mad Ireland hurt you into poetry.
35 Now Ireland has her madness and her weather still,

---

1. **Bourse** (bûrs), the stock exchange in Paris.

For poetry makes nothing happen: it survives
In the valley of its saying where executives
Would never want to tamper; it flows south
From ranches of isolation and the busy griefs,
40 Raw towns that we believe and die in; it survives,
A way of happening, a mouth.

3

Earth, receive an honored guest;
William Yeats is laid to rest:
Let the Irish vessel lie
45 Emptied of its poetry.

Time that is intolerant
Of the brave and innocent,
And indifferent in a week
To a beautiful physique,

50 Worships language and forgives
Everyone by whom it lives;
Pardons cowardice, conceit,
Lays its honors at their feet.

Time that with this strange excuse
55 Pardoned Kipling and his views,
And will pardon Paul Claudel,[2]
Pardons him for writing well.

In the nightmare of the dark
All the dogs of Europe bark,
60 And the living nations wait,
Each sequestered in its hate;

Intellectual disgrace
Stares from every human face,
And the seas of pity lie
65 Locked and frozen in each eye.

Follow, poet, follow right
To the bottom of the night,
With your unconstraining voice
Still persuade us to rejoice;

70 With the farming of a verse
Make a vineyard of the curse,
Sing of human unsuccess
In a rapture of distress;

In the deserts of the heart
75 Let the healing fountains start,
In the prison of his days
Teach the free man how to praise.

1940

---

2. *Kipling . . . Claudel.* Kipling and the French poet and playwright Paul Claudel (1868–1955) were both criticized for their violently right-wing views.

Discussion

Musée des Beaux Arts

1. What truth about human suffering does Auden feel that the Old Masters illustrate in their paintings?

2. What details from Brueghel's painting *The Fall of Icarus* does he offer to support his view?

In Memory of W. B. Yeats

1. The traditional **elegy**, especially in its pastoral form, exalts the memory of the dead person and places him in a context in which even nature is temporarily altered by his passing.

What details about the day of Yeats's death and the effect on the general public reveal this poem to be an "anti-elegy"?

2. (a) What shift in point of view occurs in Section 2? (b) What contrast is drawn between the poet's life and his work?

3. (a) According to Section 3, what generally happens to the reputation of a great writer after his death? (b) What grim political and social conditions of the Europe of 1939 does the poem point out? (c) What role does Auden believe the poet should assume in the modern world?

Louis MacNeice 1907–1963

The personality and work of Louis MacNeice were deeply influenced by his Irish background, which he later recalled with both nostalgia and satire. He was born in Belfast, the son of a stern Church of Ireland clergyman who later became a bishop. MacNeice was educated at Marlborough School and at Oxford, where he was associated with the group of poets that included W. H. Auden, Stephen Spender, and C. Day Lewis. He differed from these writers, however, in offering no political solutions to social problems and in developing a vivid documentary style that some critics have referred to disparagingly as "journalistic poetry." Essentially, MacNeice preferred the role of "the sensitive intellectual protesting the world's disorder but offering no panacea." He was a prolific writer whose work included not only poetry and radio scripts but criticism and translations—most notably of Goethe's *Faust.*

A distinguished classics scholar, MacNeice taught Classics at Birmingham and Greek at the University of London. He later became a feature writer and producer for the BBC, where he was credited with pioneering work in radio drama. During the forties and fifties MacNeice's literary reputation declined, but has since been reevaluated to take account of his acute visual and sensory perception and skillful use of a dry, ironic, conversational voice. A tone of melancholy underlies many of MacNeice's poems and reflects his somber view of modern life.

The British Museum Reading Room

Under the hive-like dome the stooping haunted readers
Go up and down the alleys, tap the cells of knowledge—
    Honey and wax, the accumulation of years—
Some on commission, some for the love of learning,
5 Some because they have nothing better to do
Or because they hope these walls of books will deaden
    The drumming of the demon in their ears.

Cranks, hacks, poverty-stricken scholars,
In pince-nez, period hats or romantic beards

10 And cherishing their hobby or their doom.
Some are too much alive and some are asleep
Hanging like bats in a world of inverted values,
Folded up in themselves in a world which is safe and silent:
This is the British Museum Reading Room.

15 Out on the steps in the sun the pigeons are courting,
Puffing their ruffs and sweeping their tails or taking
A sun-bath at their ease
And under the totem poles—the ancient terror—
Between the enormous fluted Ionic columns
20 There seeps from heavily jowled or hawk-like foreign faces
The guttural sorrow of the refugees.

1941

T*he Snow Man*

His memory was shaped by forgetting
Into a snowman, handful by handful;
In the end two pebbles for eyes and a cherry-
wood
Pipe clamped in the thinlipped mouth.

5 But was this fellow really his past,
This white dummy in a white waste?
While the censor works, while the frost holds,
Perhaps he will pass—but then he will pass.

Yesterday was a dance of flakes
10 Waltzing down, around, and up,
But today is lull and smudge, today
Is a man with a pipe that will not draw.

Today is a legless day with head-on
Idiot eyes, a stranded deaf
15 Mute in a muted world. This lump
Is what he remembered when he forgot,

Already beginning to dribble. Tomorrow
Comes the complete forgetting, the thaw.
Or is it rather a dance of water
20 To replace, relive, that dance of white?

1961

Discussion

The British Museum Reading Room

1. To what does the speaker compare the
Reading Room and its inhabitants in stanzas
one and two?

2. For what four different reasons are the
"haunted readers" here?

3. What is the main appeal of the Reading
Room to such a diverse group of readers?

4. In stanza three, what point is MacNeice
making by his mention of "totem poles," "Ionic columns," "foreign faces," and "refugees"?

The Snow Man

1. The entire poem is a metaphor in which
the memory process is compared to a snowman, temporarily solid, then dissolving. How
does this metaphor help explain the way the
memory works?

2. (a) Who or what is the "censor" (line 7)?
(b) Explain the pun in line 8.

3. Describe the behavior of the memory
"yesterday" and "today." What is likely to happen "tomorrow"?

Sylvia Townsend Warner
1893–1978

"Dry, ironic, compassionate, a joker, a scholar," is the summary of Sylvia Townsend Warner by one recent critic. She was the only child of a housemaster at Harrow, a famous English preparatory school. In one of the autobiographical sketches that Warner occasionally contributed to *The New Yorker,* she recalls that, as an emancipated Victorian, her father "had a fine set of irrefutable doubts." Among other things, the elder Warner, as a schoolmaster, quite naturally "doubted the benefit of learning to read." He felt that the child's native capacities to see, remember, and reflect independently were lost once he or she discovered easy access to information in books: "So long after my contemporaries had become literate, I was left to be observant, retentive, and rational." She was educated at home by her parents, had the run of her father's library, and grew up solitary and precociously learned.

Her first artistic commitment was to music, not to literature. She intended to go to Vienna to study composition with Arnold Schoenberg (1874–1951), one of the leading composers of the twentieth century, but was prevented by the outbreak of World War I. Instead she became a musicologist, remaining until 1928 as one of a group of scholars editing a ten-volume collection of Tudor Church music. A meeting with the writer David Garnett led to the publication of her first book of poetry, *The Espalier* (1925), and her first novel *Lolly Willowes* (1926). *Lolly Willowes* proved popular, especially in the U.S., where it was the first choice of the new Book-of-the-Month Club, creating an American audience for her works and leading eventually to her long association with *The New Yorker* magazine.

In the 1930s Warner became convinced that the only adequate defense against the growing power of fascism was communism. She became a member of the Communist Party of Great Britain in 1935, and made several brief trips to Spain during the Civil War in support of the Loyalist cause. Outside of these trips to Spain, Warner's life was a quiet one. In the early 1930s she moved to the first of a series of cottages she occupied in the Dorset countryside. Warner continued to write fine verse—notably *Opus 7* (1931), a brilliant satirical narrative, and the posthumously published *Twelve Poems* (1980), which contains "Gloriana Dying" (see page 137). But her reputation is largely based on her polished, original prose—seven novels, many short stories, and a fine biography of English writer T. H. White.

*T*he Phoenix

Lord Strawberry, a nobleman, collected birds. He had the finest aviary in Europe, so large that eagles did not find it uncomfortable, so well laid out that both hummingbirds and snowbuntings had a climate that suited them perfectly. But for many years the finest set of apartments remained empty, with just a label saying: "PHOENIX.[1] *Habitat: Arabia.*"

Many authorities on bird life had assured Lord Strawberry that the phoenix is a fabulous bird, or that the breed was long extinct. Lord Strawberry was unconvinced: his family had always believed in phoenixes. At intervals he received from his agents (together with statements of their expenses) birds which they declared were the phoenix but which turned out to be orioles, macaws, turkey buzzards dyed orange, crossbreeds, ingeniously assembled from various plumages. Finally Lord Strawberry went to Arabia, where, after some months, he found a phoenix, won its confidence, caught it, and brought it home in perfect condition.

It was a remarkably fine phoenix, with a charming character—affable to the other birds in the aviary and much attached to Lord Strawberry. On its arrival in England it made a great stir among ornithologists, journalists, poets, and milliners, and was constantly visited. But it was not puffed up by these attentions, and when it was no longer in the news, and the visits fell off, it showed no pique or rancor. It ate well, and seemed perfectly contented.

It costs a great deal of money to keep up an aviary. When Lord Strawberry died he died penniless. The aviary came on the market. In normal times the rarer birds, and certainly the phoenix, would have been bid for by the trustees of Europe's great zoological societies or by private persons in the U.S.A.; but as it happened Lord Strawberry died just after a world war, when both money and bird-seed were hard to come by (indeed the cost of bird-seed was one of the things which had ruined Lord Strawberry). The London *Times* urged in a leader[2] that the phoenix be bought for the London Zoo, saying that a nation of bird-lovers had a moral right to own such a rarity; and a fund, called the Strawberry Phoenix Fund, was opened. Students, naturalists, and school children contributed according to their means; but their means were small, and there were no large donations. So Lord Strawberry's executors (who had the death duties[3] to consider) closed with the higher offer of Mr. Tancred Poldero, owner and proprietor of Poldero's Wizard Wonderworld.

For quite a while Mr. Poldero considered his phoenix a bargain. It was a civil and obliging bird, and adapted itself readily to its new surroundings. It did not cost much to feed, it did not mind children; and though it had no tricks, Mr. Poldero supposed it would soon pick up some. The publicity of the Strawberry Phoenix Fund was now most helpful. Almost every contributor now saved up another half-crown in order to see the phoenix. Others who had not contributed to the fund, even paid double to look at it on the five-shilling days.

But then business slackened. The phoenix was as handsome as ever, and as amiable; but, as Mr. Poldero said, it hadn't got Udge. Even at popular prices the phoenix was not really popular. It was too quiet, too classical. So people went instead to watch the antics of the baboons, or to admire the crocodile who had eaten the woman.

One day Mr. Poldero said to his manager, Mr. Ramkin:

"How long since any fool paid to look at the phoenix?"

"Matter of three weeks," replied Mr. Ramkin.

"Eating his head off," said Mr. Poldero. "Let alone the insurance. Seven shillings a week it costs me to insure that bird, and I might as well insure the Archbishop of Canterbury."

"The public don't like him. He's too quiet for

---

1. **PHOENIX** (fē′niks), a legendary bird of Arabia, reputed to live for five hundred years, then to burn itself to ashes in a fire of its own creation and rise again, its youth renewed.
2. **leader,** an editorial.
3. **death duties,** taxes on the estate of a deceased person.

them, that's the trouble. Won't mate nor nothing. And I've tried him with no end of pretty pollies, ospreys, and Cochin-Chinas, and the Lord knows what. But he won't look at them."

"Wonder if we could swap him for a livelier one," said Mr. Poldero.

"Impossible. There's only one of him at a time."

"Go on!"

"I mean it. Haven't you ever read what it says on the label?"

They went to the phoenix's cage. It flapped its wings politely, but they paid no attention. They read:

"PANSY. *Phoenix phoenixissima formosissima arabiana.* This rare and fabulous bird is UNIQUE. The World's Old Bachelor. Has no mate and doesn't want one. When old, sets fire to itself and emerges miraculously reborn. Specially imported from the East."

"I've got an idea," said Mr. Poldero. "How old do you suppose that bird is?"

"Looks in its prime to me," said Mr. Ramkin.

"Suppose," continued Mr. Poldero, "we could somehow get him alight? We'd advertize it beforehand, of course, work up interest. Then we'd have a new bird, and a bird with some romance about it, a bird with a life-story. We could sell a bird like that."

Mr. Ramkin nodded.

"I've read about it in a book," he said. "You've got to give them scented woods and what not, and they build a nest and sit down on it and catch fire spontaneous. But they won't do it till they're old. That's the snag."

"Leave that to me," said Mr. Poldero. "You get those scented woods, and I'll do the ageing."

It was not easy to age the phoenix. Its allowance of food was halved, and halved again, but though it grew thinner its eyes were undimmed and its plumage glossy as ever. The heating was turned off; but it puffed out its feathers against the cold, and seemed none the worse. Other birds were put into its cage, birds of a peevish and quarrelsome nature. They pecked and chivied it; but the phoenix was so civil and amiable that after a day or two they lost their animosity. Then Mr. Poldero tried alley cats. These could not be

won by good manners, but the phoenix darted above their heads and flapped its golden wings in their faces, and daunted them.

Mr. Poldero turned to a book on Arabia, and read that the climate was dry. "Aha!" said he. The phoenix was moved to a small cage that had a sprinkler in the ceiling. Every night the sprinkler was turned on. The phoenix began to cough. Mr. Poldero had another good idea. Daily he stationed himself in front of the cage to jeer at the bird and abuse it.

When spring was come, Mr. Poldero felt justified in beginning a publicity campaign about the ageing phoenix. The old public favorite, he said, was nearing its end. Meanwhile he tested the bird's reactions every few days by putting a few tufts of foul-smelling straw and some strands of rusty barbed wire into the cage, to see if it were interested in nesting yet. One day the phoenix began turning over the straw. Mr. Poldero signed a contract for the film rights. At last the hour seemed ripe. It was a fine Saturday evening in May. For some weeks the public interest in the ageing phoenix had been working up, and the admission charge had risen to five shillings. The enclosure was thronged. The lights and the cameras were trained on the cage, and a loud-speaker proclaimed to the audience the rarity of what was about to take place.

"The phoenix," said the loud-speaker, "is the aristocrat of bird-life. Only the rarest and most expensive specimens of oriental wood, drenched in exotic perfumes, will tempt him to construct his strange love-nest."

Now a neat assortment of twigs and shavings, strongly scented, was shoved into the cage.

"The phoenix," the loud-speaker continued, "is as capricious as Cleopatra, as luxurious as la du Barry,[4] as heady as a strain of wild gypsy music. All the fantastic pomp and passion of the ancient East, its languorous magic, its subtle cruelties . . ."

"Lawks!" cried a woman in the crowd. "He's at it!"

A quiver stirred the dulled plumage. The phoenix turned its head from side to side. It descended, staggering, from its perch. Then wear-

---

4. *la du Barry,* Countess du Barry (1746–1793), mistress of King Louis XV of France.

ily it began to pull about the twigs and shavings.

The cameras clicked, the lights blazed full on the cage. Rushing to the loud-speaker Mr. Poldero exclaimed:

"Ladies and gentlemen, this is the thrilling moment the world has breathlessly awaited. The legend of centuries is materializing before our modern eyes. The phoenix . . ."

The phoenix settled on its pyre[5] and appeared to fall asleep.

The film director said:

"Well, if it doesn't evaluate more than this, mark it instructional."

At that moment the phoenix and the pyre burst into flames. The flames streamed upwards, leaped out on every side. In a minute or two everything was burned to ashes, and some thousand people, including Mr. Poldero, perished in the blaze.

1940

---

5. **pyre** (pīr), a pile of wood for burning a dead body as a funeral rite.

Discussion

1. (a) Contrast the two owners of the phoenix and their treatment of the bird. **(b)** To what specific forms of abuse does Mr. Poldero subject the bird? Why?

2. (a) What words are used to characterize the phoenix? **(b)** Why doesn't the phoenix prove to be a popular attraction at Poldero's Wizard Wonderworld? What does this suggest about public taste?

3. (a) What is the major target of the satire in this story? **(b)** Are there any minor targets? Explain.

Composition

A number of stories involve bringing a mythological character into the modern world. In C. S. Lewis's "Forms of Things Unknown," astronauts encounter the classical monster Medusa on the moon. In T. H. White's "The Troll," a creature out of northern folklore is encountered in a present-day Swedish resort hotel. Write a story involving the discovery of some fantastic creature—a unicorn or dragon, for example—in the modern world.

Vocabulary
Context

Using context as an aid, write the most appropriate definition for each of the italicized words on a separate sheet of paper. Be sure you can pronounce and spell all the italicized words.

1. "He had the finest *aviary* in Europe, so large that eagles did not find it uncomfortable, so well laid out that both hummingbirds and snow buntings had a climate that suited them perfectly." **(a)** poultry farm; **(b)** birdhouse; **(c)** museum; **(d)** pet shop.

2. "At intervals he received from his agents (together with statements of their expenses) birds which they declared were the phoenix but which turned out to be orioles, macaws, turkey buzzards dyed orange, etc., or stuffed crossbreeds ingeniously assembled from various *plumages*." **(a)** countries; **(b)** fossils; **(c)** collectors; **(d)** feathers.

3. "On [the phoenix's] arrival in England it made a great stir among *ornithologists*, journalists, poets, and milliners, and was constantly visited." **(a)** poultry farmers; **(b)** writers; **(c)** scientists who study birds; **(d)** cooks.

4. "But [the phoenix] was not puffed up by these attentions, and when it was no longer in the news, and the visits fell off, it showed no pique or *rancor*." **(a)** hunger; **(b)** resentment; **(c)** affection; **(d)** interest.

5. "Other birds were put into [the phoenix's] cage, birds of a peevish or quarrelsome nature. They pecked and chivied it; but the phoenix was so civil and amiable that after a day or two they lost their *animosity*." **(a)** feathers; **(b)** ability to fly; **(c)** dislike; **(d)** friendliness.

George Orwell 1903–1950

Born Eric Arthur Blair, Orwell was driven by a lifelong commitment to speak out unpleasant truths, becoming the "wintry conscience of a generation." He was born in Bengal, the son of a minor Indian civil servant. Returning to England, he went to an expensive preparatory school (the "Crossgates" of "Such, Such Were the Joys," page 757). He won a scholarship to Eton, but instead of continuing on to a university, he joined the Imperial Police in Burma (see "Shooting an Elephant," page 753). In Burma his sense of justice was outraged by the corrupting effects of imperialism both on the colonizers and on the colonized. Resigning from the Imperial Police, he returned to England, determined to become a writer. Troubled by the effects of poverty on the working class, he decided to find out more about their condition, becoming a dishwasher, a farm worker, a tramp, and chronicling his experiences in *Down and Out in Paris and London* (1933).

When the Spanish Civil War broke out in 1936, Orwell, who had become a socialist, went and fought on the side of the Republicans (those loyal to Spain's leftist government) against the military revolt led by General Franco. After being wounded he returned to England, disillusioned by the brutality of communist purges in Spain, which he described in one of his finest books, *Homage to Catalonia* (1938).

Orwell wrote a series of novels in the late 1930s, concluding with *Coming Up for Air* (1939), which reveals Orwell's nostalgia for the life of an earlier England and his fear and hatred of everything that threatened it, from American-style food to the threat of fascist militarism. When the war came, Orwell was rejected for military service, and worked for a time for the BBC. During this period Orwell became an active journalist, writing many newspaper articles and reviews. Many critics locate Orwell's genius in his essays. They cover a broad spectrum of subjects, including politics, both serious and popular literature, language (see The Changing English Language, page 807), and censorship. "Good prose is like a window pane," he once observed; and his own prose style is clear and concise. What made him distinctive as a thinker was his ability to eloquently and provocatively express what many people felt obscurely and inarticulately.

While remaining a socialist, Orwell often chastised the left. The two books that made him famous, *Animal Farm* (1945) and *Nineteen Eighty-four* (1949), were both inspired by his lifelong hatred of totalitarianism. The first is a satire on Stalinist Russia in the form of a beast fable; the second is a "dystopia," a grimly realistic account of a future society in which all freedom has been extinguished. Orwell died at the age of forty-six of tuberculosis.

Shooting an Elephant

In Moulmein, in Lower Burma, I was hated by large numbers of people—the only time in my life that I have been important enough for this to happen to me. I was sub-divisional police officer of the town, and in an aimless, petty kind of way anti-European feeling was very bitter. No one had the guts to raise a riot, but if a European woman went through the bazaars alone somebody would probably spit betel juice over her dress. As a police officer I was an obvious target and was baited whenever it seemed safe to do so. When a nimble Burman tripped me up on the football field and the referee (another Burman) looked the other way, the crowd yelled with hideous laughter. This happened more than once. In the end the sneering yellow faces of young men that met me everywhere, the insults hooted after me when I was at a safe distance, got badly on my nerves. The young Buddhist priests were the worst of all. There were several thousands of them in the town and none of them seemed to have anything to do except stand on street corners and jeer at Europeans.

All this was perplexing and upsetting. For at that time I had already made up my mind that imperialism was an evil thing and the sooner I chucked up my job and got out of it the better. Theoretically—and secretly, of course—I was all for the Burmese and all against their oppressors, the British. As for the job I was doing, I hated it more bitterly than I can perhaps make clear. In a job like that you see the dirty work of Empire at close quarters. The wretched prisoners huddling in the stinking cages of the lock-ups, the grey, cowed faces of the long-term convicts, the scarred buttocks of the men who had been flogged with bamboos—all these oppressed me with an intolerable sense of guilt. But I could get nothing into perspective. I was young and ill-educated and I had had to think out my problems in the utter silence that is imposed on every Englishman in the East. I did not even know that the British Empire is dying, still less did I know that it is a great deal better than the younger empires that are going to supplant it. All I knew was that I was stuck between my hatred of the empire I served and my rage against the evil-spirited little beasts who tried to make my job impossible. With one part of my mind I thought of the British Raj[1] as an unbreakable tyranny, as something clamped down, *in saecula saeculorum,*[2] upon the will of prostrate peoples; with another part I thought that the greatest joy in the world would be to drive a bayonet into a Buddhist priest's guts. Feelings like these are the normal by-products of imperialism; ask any Anglo-Indian official, if you can catch him off duty.

One day something happened which in a roundabout way was enlightening. It was a tiny incident in itself, but it gave me a better glimpse than I had had before of the real nature of imperialism—the real motives for which despotic governments act. Early one morning the sub-inspector at a police station the other end of the town rang me up on the phone and said that an elephant was ravaging the bazaar. Would I please come and do something about it? I did not know what I could do, but I wanted to see what was happening and I got on to a pony and started out. I took my rifle, an old .44 Winchester and much too small to kill an elephant, but I thought the noise might be useful *in terrorem.* Various Burmans stopped me on the way and told me about the elephant's doings. It was not, of course, a wild elephant, but a tame one which had gone "must." It had been chained up as tame elephants always are when their attack of "must" is due, but on the previous night it had broken its chain and escaped. Its mahout,[3] the only person who could manage it when it was in that state, had set out in pursuit, but he had taken the wrong direction and was now twelve hours' journey away, and in the morning the elephant had suddenly reappeared in the town. The Burmese population had no weapons and were quite helpless against it. It had already destroyed somebody's bamboo hut, killed a cow and raided some fruit-stalls and

1. **British Raj,** the British Empire in the East, including what is now India, Pakistan, Bangladesh, and Burma. *Raj* is a Hindi word meaning "rule."
2. *in saecula saeculorum* (in sā′cü lä sā′cü lôr əm), forever. [Latin]
3. **"must . . . mahout.** Must is a frenzied state occurring periodically in male elephants; a mahout (mə hout′) is an elephant-driver.

devoured the stock; also it had met the municipal rubbish van, and, when the driver jumped out and took to his heels, had turned the van over and inflicted violence upon it.

The Burmese sub-inspector and some Indian constables were waiting for me in the quarter where the elephant had been seen. It was a very poor quarter, a labyrinth of squalid bamboo huts, thatched with palm-leaf, winding all over a steep hillside. I remember that it was a cloudy stuffy morning at the beginning of the rains. We began questioning the people as to where the elephant had gone, and, as usual, failed to get any definite information. That is invariably the case in the East; a story always sounds clear enough at a distance, but the nearer you get to the scene of events the vaguer it becomes. Some of the people said that the elephant had gone in one direction, some said that he had gone in another, some professed not even to have heard of any elephant. I had almost made up my mind that the whole story was a pack of lies, when we heard yells a little distance away. There was a loud, scandalized cry of "Go away, child! Go away this instant!" and an old woman with a switch in her hand came round a corner of a hut, violently shooing away a crowd of naked children. Some more women followed, clicking their tongues and exclaiming; evidently there was something there that the children ought not to have seen. I rounded the hut and saw a man's dead body sprawling in the mud. He was an Indian, a black Dravidian coolie, almost naked, and he could not have been dead many minutes. The people said that the elephant had come suddenly upon him round the corner of the hut, caught him with its trunk, put its foot on his back and ground him into the earth. This was the rainy season and the ground was soft, and his face had scored a trench a foot deep and a couple of yards long. He was lying on his belly with arms crucified and head sharply twisted to one side. His face was coated with mud, the eyes wide open, the teeth bared and grinning with an expression of unendurable agony. (Never tell me, by the way, that the dead look peaceful. Most of the corpses I have seen looked devilish.) The friction of the great beast's foot had stripped the skin from his back as neatly as one skins a rabbit. As soon as I saw the dead man I sent an orderly to a friend's house nearby to borrow an elephant rifle.

I had already sent back the pony, not wanting it to go mad with fright and throw me if it smelled the elephant.

The orderly came back in a few minutes with a rifle and five cartridges, and meanwhile some Burmans had arrived and told us that the elephant was in the paddy fields below, only a few hundred yards away. As I started forward practically the whole population of the quarter flocked out of their houses and followed me. They had seen the rifle and were all shouting excitedly that I was going to shoot the elephant. They had not shown much interest in the elephant when he was merely ravaging their homes, but it was different now that he was going to be shot. It was a bit of fun to them, as it would be to an English crowd; besides, they wanted the meat. It made me vaguely uneasy. I had no intention of shooting the elephant—I had merely sent for the rifle to defend myself if necessary—and it is always unnerving to have a crowd following you. I marched down the hill, looking and feeling a fool, with the rifle over my shoulder and an ever-growing army of people jostling at my heels. At the bottom, when you got away from the huts, there was a metalled road and beyond that a miry waste of paddy fields a thousand yards across, not yet ploughed but soggy from the first rains and dotted with coarse grass. The elephant was standing eighty yards from the road, his left side towards us. He took not the slightest notice of the crowd's approach. He was tearing up bunches of grass, beating them against his knees to clean them and stuffing them into his mouth.

I had halted on the road. As soon as I saw the elephant I knew with perfect certainty that I ought not to shoot him. It is a serious matter to shoot a working elephant—it is comparable to destroying a huge and costly piece of machinery—and obviously one ought not to do it if it can possibly be avoided. And at that distance, peacefully eating, the elephant looked no more dangerous than a cow. I thought then and I think now that his attack of "must" was already passing off; in which case he would merely wander harmlessly about until the mahout came back and caught him. Moreover, I did not in the least want to shoot him. I decided that I would watch him for a little while to make sure that he did not turn savage again, and then go home.

But at that moment I glanced round at the crowd that had followed me. It was an immense crowd, two thousand at the least and growing every minute. It blocked the road for a long distance on either side. I looked at the sea of yellow faces above the garish clothes—faces all happy and excited over this bit of fun, all certain that the elephant was going to be shot. They were watching me as they would watch a conjuror about to perform a trick. They did not like me, but with the magical rifle in my hands I was momentarily worth watching. And suddenly I realized that I should have to shoot the elephant after all. The people expected it of me and I had got to do it; I could feel their two thousand wills pressing me forward, irresistibly. And it was at this moment, as I stood there with the rifle in my hands, that I first grasped the hollowness, the futility of the white man's dominion in the East. Here was I, the white man with his gun, standing in front of the unarmed native crowd—seemingly the leading actor of the piece; but in reality I was only an absurd puppet pushed to and fro by the will of those yellow faces behind. I perceived in this moment that when the white man turns tyrant it is his own freedom that he destroys. He becomes a sort of hollow, posing dummy, the conventionalized figure of a sahib.[4] For it is the condition of his rule that he shall spend his life in trying to impress the "natives" and so in every crisis he has got to do what the "natives" expect of him. He wears a mask, and his face grows to fit it. I had got to shoot the elephant. I had committed myself to doing it when I sent for the rifle. A sahib has got to act like a sahib; he has got to appear resolute, to know his own mind and do definite things. To come all that way, rifle in hand, with two thousand people marching at my heels, and then to trail feebly away, having done nothing—no, that was impossible. The crowd would laugh at me. And my whole life, every white man's life in the East, was one long struggle not to be laughed at.

But I did not want to shoot the elephant. I watched him beating his bunch of grass against his knees, with that preoccupied grandmotherly air that elephants have. It seemed to me that it would be murder to shoot him. At that age I was not squeamish about killing animals, but I had never shot an elephant and never wanted to.

(Somehow it always seems worse to kill a *large* animal.) Besides, there was the beast's owner to be considered. Alive, the elephant was worth at least a hundred pounds; dead, he would only be worth the value of his tusks—five pounds, possibly. But I had got to act quickly. I turned to some experienced-looking Burmans who had been there when we arrived, and asked them how the elephant had been behaving. They all said the same thing: he took no notice of you if you left him alone, but he might charge if you went too close to him.

It was perfectly clear to me what I ought to do. I ought to walk up to within, say, twenty-five yards of the elephant and test his behavior. If he charged I could shoot, if he took no notice of me it would be safe to leave him until the mahout came back. But also I knew that I was going to do no such thing. I was a poor shot with a rifle and the ground was soft mud into which one would sink at every step. If the elephant charged and I missed him, I should have about as much chance as a toad under a steam-roller. But even then I was not thinking particularly of my own skin, only the watchful yellow faces behind. For at that moment, with the crowd watching me, I was not afraid in the ordinary sense, as I would have been if I had been alone. A white man mustn't be frightened in front of "natives"; and so, in general, he isn't frightened. The sole thought in my mind was that if anything went wrong those two thousand Burmans would see me pursued, caught, trampled on and reduced to a grinning corpse like that Indian up the hill. And if that happened it was quite probable that some of them would laugh. That would never do. There was only one alternative. I shoved the cartridges into the magazine and lay down on the road to get a better aim.

The crowd grew very still, and a deep, low, happy sigh, as of people who see the theatre curtain go up at last, breathed from innumerable throats. They were going to have their bit of fun after all. The rifle was a beautiful German thing with cross-hair sights. I did not then know that in shooting an elephant one should shoot to cut an imaginary bar running from ear-hole to ear-hole. I ought therefore, as the elephant was sideways

---

4. *sahib* (sä′ib), in British India, a European.

on, to have aimed straight at his ear-hole; actually I aimed several inches in front of this, thinking the brain would be further forward.

When I pulled the trigger I did not hear the bang or feel the kick—one never does when a shot goes home—but I heard the devilish roar of glee that went up from the crowd. In that instant, in too short a time, one would have thought, even for the bullet to get there, a mysterious, terrible change had come over the elephant. He neither stirred nor fell, but every line of his body had altered. He looked suddenly stricken, shrunken, immensely old, as though the frightful impact of the bullet had paralyzed him without knocking him down. At last, after what seemed a long time—it might have been five seconds, I dare say—he sagged flabbily to his knees. His mouth slobbered. An enormous senility seemed to have settled upon him. One could have imagined him thousands of years old. I fired again into the same spot. At the second shot he did not collapse but climbed with desperate slowness to his feet and stood weakly upright, with legs sagging and head drooping. I fired a third time. That was the shot that did for him. You could see the agony of it jolt his whole body and knock the last remnant of strength from his legs. But in falling he seemed for a moment to rise, for as his hind legs collapsed beneath him he seemed to tower upwards like a huge rock toppling, his trunk reaching skyward like a tree. He trumpeted, for the first and only time. And then down he came, his belly towards me, with a crash that seemed to shake the ground even where I lay.

I got up. The Burmans were already racing past me across the mud. It was obvious that the elephant would never rise again, but he was not dead. He was breathing very rhythmically with long rattling gasps, his great mound of a side painfully rising and falling. His mouth was wide open—I could see far down into caverns of pale pink throat. I waited a long time for him to die, but his breathing did not weaken. Finally I fired my two remaining shots into the spot where I thought his heart must be. The thick blood welled out of him like red velvet, but still he did not die. His body did not even jerk when the shots hit him, the tortured breathing continued without a pause. He was dying, very slowly and in great agony, but in some world remote from me where not even a bullet could damage him further. I felt that I had got to put an end to that dreadful noise. It seemed dreadful to see the great beast lying there, powerless to move and yet powerless to die, and not even to be able to finish him. I sent back for my small rifle and poured shot after shot into his heart and down his throat. They seemed to make no impression. The tortured gasps continued as steadily as the ticking of a clock.

In the end I could not stand it any longer and went away. I heard later that it took him half an hour to die. Burmans were arriving with dahs[5] and baskets even before I left, and I was told they had stripped his body almost to the bones by the afternoon.

Afterwards, of course, there were endless discussions about the shooting of the elephant. The owner was furious, but he was only an Indian and could do nothing. Besides, legally I had done the right thing, for a mad elephant has to be killed, like a mad dog, if its owner fails to control it. Among the Europeans opinion was divided. The older men said I was right, the younger men said it was a damn shame to shoot an elephant for killing a coolie, because an elephant was worth more than any damn Coringhee coolie. And afterwards I was very glad that the coolie had been killed; it put me legally in the right and it gave me a sufficient pretext for shooting the elephant. I often wondered whether any of the others grasped that I had done it solely to avoid looking a fool.

1936

---

5. *dah* (dä), a heavy Burmese knife.

Discussion

1. As a member of the Imperial Police in Burma, Orwell found himself hating both the empire he served and the Burmese. What accounts for this attitude?

2. (a) Why does Orwell shoot the elephant? (b) What lesson does he feel this episode offers into the "real nature of imperialism—the real motives for which despotic governments act"?

3. Explain what makes the shooting of the elephant both ironic and horrible.

from S uch, Such Were the Joys[1]

Crossgates was an expensive and snobbish school which was in process of becoming more snobbish, and, I imagine, more expensive. The public school with which it had special connections was Harrow, but during my time an increasing proportion of the boys went on to Eton.[2] Most of them were the children of rich parents, but on the whole they were the unaristocratic rich, the sort of people who live in huge shrubberied houses in Bournemouth or Richmond, and who have cars and butlers but not country estates. There were a few exotics among them—some South American boys, sons of Argentine beef barons, one or two Russians, and even a Siamese prince, or someone who was described as a prince.

Sim had two great ambitions. One was to attract titled boys to the school, and the other was to train up pupils to win scholarships at public schools,[3] above all Eton. He did, towards the end of my time, succeed in getting hold of two boys with real English titles. One of them, I remember, was a wretched little creature, almost an albino, peering upwards out of weak eyes, with a long nose at the end of which a dewdrop always seemed to be trembling. Sim always gave these boys their titles when mentioning them to a third person, and for their first few days he actually addressed them to their faces as "Lord So-and-so." Needless to say he found ways of drawing attention to them when any visitor was being shown round the school. Once, I remember, the little fair-haired boy had a choking fit at dinner, and a stream of snot ran out of his nose onto his plate in a way horrible to see. Any lesser person would have been called a dirty little beast and ordered out of the room instantly: but Sim and Bingo laughed it off in a "boys will be boys" spirit.

All the very rich boys were more or less undisguisedly favored. The school still had a faint suggestion of the Victorian "private academy" with its "parlor boarders," and when I later read about that kind of school in Thackeray[4] I immediately saw the resemblance. The rich boys had milk and biscuits in the middle of the morning, they were given riding lessons once or twice a week, Bingo mothered them and called them by their Christian names, and above all they were never caned. Apart from the South Americans, whose parents were safely distant, I doubt whether Sim ever caned any boy whose father's income was much above £2,000 a year. But he was sometimes willing to sacrifice financial profit to scholastic prestige. Occasionally, by special arrangement, he would take at greatly reduced fees some boy who seemed likely to win scholarships and thus bring credit on the school. It was on these terms that I was at Crossgates myself: otherwise my parents could not have afforded to send me to so expensive a school.

I did not at first understand that I was being taken at reduced fees; it was only when I was about eleven that Bingo and Sim began throwing the fact in my teeth. For my first two or three years I went through the ordinary educational mill: then, soon after I had started Greek (one started Latin at eight, Greek at ten), I moved into the scholarship class, which was taught, so far as classics went, largely by Sim himself. Over a period of two or three years the scholarship boys were crammed with learning as cynically as a goose is crammed for Christmas. And with what learning! This business of making a gifted boy's career depend on a competitive examination, taken when he is only twelve or thirteen, is an evil thing at best, but there do appear to be preparatory schools which send scholars to Eton, Win-

From "Such, Such Were the Joys" in *Such, Such Were the Joys* by George Orwell. Copyright 1953 by Sonia Brownell Orwell; renewed 1981 by Mrs. George K. Perutz, Mrs. Miriam Gross, Dr. Michael Dickson, Executors of the Estate of Sonia Brownell Orwell. Reprinted by permission of Harcourt Brace Jovanovich, Inc., the estate of the late Sonia Brownell Orwell and Martin Secker & Warburg Ltd.

1. **Such . . . Joys.** Orwell makes ironic use of a line from Blake's poem "The Ecchoing Green," which describes children at play.
2. **Harrow . . . Eton,** England's two most famous preparatory schools.
3. **public schools,** exclusive private preparatory schools, like Eton and Harrow.
4. **Thackeray,** William Makepeace Thackeray (1811–1863), English novelist.

chester, etc., without teaching them to see every-thing in terms of marks. At Crossgates the whole process was frankly a preparation for a sort of confidence trick. Your job was to learn exactly those things that would give an examiner the impression that you knew more than you did know, and as far as possible to avoid burdening your brain with anything else. Subjects which lacked examination-value, such as geography, were almost completely neglected, mathematics was also neglected if you were a "classical," sci-ence was not taught in any form—indeed it was so despised that even an interest in natural his-tory was discouraged—and the books you were encouraged to read in your spare time were cho-sen with one eye on the "English Paper." Latin and Greek, the main scholarship subjects, were what counted, but even these were deliberately taught in a flashy, unsound way. We never, for example, read right through even a single book of a Greek or Latin author: we merely read short passages which were picked out because they were the kind of thing likely to be set as an "un-seen translation." During the last year or so before we went up for our scholarships, most of our time was spent in simply working our way through the scholarship papers of previous years. Sim had sheaves of these in his possession, from every one of the major public schools. But the greatest outrage of all was the teaching of his-tory.

There was in those days a piece of nonsense called the Harrow History Prize, an annual com-petition for which many preparatory schools entered. At Crossgates we mugged up[5] every paper that had been set since the competition started. They were the kind of stupid question that is answered by rapping out a name or a quo-tation. Who plundered the Begams? Who was beheaded in an open boat? Who caught the Whigs bathing and ran away with their clothes? Almost all our historical teaching was on this level. His-tory was a series of unrelated, unintelligible but—in some way that was never explained to us—important facts with resounding phrases tied to them. Disraeli brought peace with honor. Clive was astonished at his moderation. Pitt called in the New World to redress the balance of the Old. And the dates, and the mnemonic devices! (Did you know, for example, that the initial letters of

"A black Negress was my aunt: there's her house behind the barn" are also the initial letters of the battles in the Wars of the Roses?) Bingo, who "took" the higher forms in history, revelled in this kind of thing. I recall positive orgies of dates, with the keener boys leaping up and down in their places in their eagerness to shout out the right answers, and at the same time not feeling the faintest interest in the meaning of the mysterious events they were naming.

"1587?"

"Massacre of St. Bartholomew!"

"1707?"

"Death of Aurangzeeb!"

"1713?"

"Treaty of Utrecht!"

"1773?"

"The Boston Tea Party!"

"1520?"

"Oh, Mum, please, Mum—"

"Please, Mum, please, Mum! Let me tell him, Mum!"

"Well; 1520?"

"Field of the Cloth of Gold!"

An so on.

But history and such secondary subjects were not bad fun. It was in "classics" that the real strain came. Looking back, I realize that I then worked harder than I have ever done since, and yet at the time it never seemed possible to make quite the effort that was demanded of one. We would sit round the long shiny table, made of some very pale-colored, hard wood, with Sim goading, threatening, exhorting, sometimes jok-ing, very occasionally praising, but always prod-ding, prodding away at one's mind to keep it up to the right pitch of concentration, as one might keep a sleepy person awake by sticking pins into him.

"Go on, you little slacker! Go on, you idle, worthless little boy! The whole trouble with you is that you're bone and horn idle. You eat too much, that's why. You wolf down enormous meals, and then when you come here you're half asleep. Go on, now, put your back into it. You're not *thinking*. Your brain doesn't sweat."

He would tap away at one's skull with his sil-ver pencil, which, in my memory, seems to have

---

5. *mugged up,* studied.

been about the size of a banana, and which certainly was heavy enough to raise a bump: or he would pull the short hairs round one's ears, or, occasionally, reach out under the table and kick one's shin. On some days nothing seemed to go right, and then it would be: "All right, then, I know what you want. You've been asking for it the whole morning. Come along, you useless little slacker. Come into the study." And then whack, whack, whack, whack, and back one would come, red-wealed and smarting—in later years Sim had abandoned his riding crop in favor of a thin rattan cane which hurt very much more—to settle down to work again. This did not happen very often, but I do remember, more than one being led out of the room in the middle of a Latin sentence, receiving a beating and then going straight ahead with the same sentence, just like that. It is a mistake to think such methods do not work. They work very well for their special purpose. Indeed, I doubt whether classical education ever has been or can be successfully carried on without corporal punishment. The boys themselves believed in its efficacy. There was a boy named Beacham, with no brains to speak of, but evidently in acute need of a scholarship. Sim was flogging him towards the goal as one might do with a foundered horse. He went up for a scholarship at Uppingham,[6] came back with a consciousness of having done badly, and a day or two later received a severe beating for idleness. "I wish I'd had that caning before I went up for the exam," he said sadly—a remark which I felt to be contemptible, but which I perfectly well understood.

---

6. *Uppingham,* a public school (the one attended by Edward Brittain and Roland Leighton—see page 684).

Eton boys outside Lords Cricket Ground during the Eton vs. Harrow cricket match in 1937.

The boys of the scholarship class were not all treated alike. If a boy were the son of rich parents to whom the saving of fees was not all-important, Sim would goad him along in a comparatively fatherly way, with jokes and digs in the ribs and perhaps an occasional tap with the pencil, but no hair-pulling and no caning. It was the poor but "clever" boys who suffered. Our brains were a gold-mine in which he had sunk money, and the dividends must be squeezed out of us. Long before I had grasped the nature of my financial relationship with Sim, I had been made to understand that I was not on the same footing as most of the other boys. In effect there were three castes in the school. There was the minority with an aristocratic or millionaire background, there were the children of the ordinary suburban rich, who made up the bulk of the school, and there were a few underlings like myself, the sons of clergymen, Indian civil servants, struggling widows and the like. These poorer ones were discouraged from going in for "extras" such as shooting and carpentry, and were humiliated over clothes and petty possessions. I never, for instance, succeeded in getting a cricket bat of my own, because "your parents wouldn't be able to afford it." This phrase pursued me throughout my schooldays. At Crossgates we were not allowed to keep the money we brought back with us, but had to "give it in" on the first day of term, and then from time to time were allowed to spend it under supervision. I and similarly placed boys were always choked off from buying expensive toys like model aeroplanes, even if the necessary money stood to our credit. Bingo, in particular, seemed to aim consciously at inculcating a humble outlook in the poorer boys. "Do you think that's the sort of thing a boy like you should buy?" I remember her saying to somebody—and she said this in front of the whole school; "You know you're not going to grow up with money, don't you? Your people aren't rich. You must learn to be sensible. Don't get above yourself!" There was also the weekly pocket-money, which we took out in sweets, dispensed by Bingo from a large table. The millionaires had sixpence a week, but the normal sum was threepence. I and one or two others were only allowed twopence. My parents had not given instructions to this effect, and the saving of a penny a week could not conceivably have made any difference to them: it was a mark of status. Worse yet was the detail of the birthday cakes. It was usual for each boy, on his birthday, to have a large iced cake with candles, which was shared out at tea between the whole school. It was provided as a matter of routine and went on his parents' bill. I never had such a cake, though my parents would have paid for it readily enough. Year after year, never daring to ask, I would miserably hope that this year a cake would appear. Once or twice I even rashly pretended to my companions that this time I *was* going to have a cake. Then came teatime, and no cake, which did not make me more popular.

Very early it was impressed upon me that I had no chance of a decent future unless I won a scholarship at a public school. Either I won my scholarship, or I must leave school at fourteen and become, in Sim's favorite phrase "a little office-boy at forty pounds a year." In my circumstances it was natural that I should believe this. Indeed, it was universally taken for granted at Crossgates that unless you went to a "good" public school (and only about fifteen schools came under this heading) you were ruined for life. It is not easy to convey to a grown-up person the sense of strain, of nerving oneself for some terrible, all-deciding combat, as the date of the examination crept nearer—eleven years old, twelve years old, then thirteen, the fatal year itself! Over a period of about two years, I do not think there was ever a day when "the exam," as I called it, was quite out of my waking thoughts. In my prayers it figured invariably: and whenever I got the bigger portion of a wishbone, or picked up a horseshoe, or bowed seven times to the new moon, or succeeded in passing through a wishing-gate without touching the sides, then the wish I earned by doing so went on "the exam" as a matter of course. And yet curiously enough I was also tormented by an almost irresistible impulse *not* to work. There were days when my heart sickened at the labors ahead of me, and I stood stupid as an animal before the most elementary difficulties. In the holidays, also, I could not work. Some of the scholarship boys received extra tuition from a certain Mr. Batchelor, a likeable, very hairy man who wore shaggy suits and lived in a typical bachelor's "den"—booklined walls, overwhelming stench of tobacco—somewhere in the town. During the holidays Mr. Batchelor used to send us extracts from Latin authors to translate, and we were supposed to send back a wad of work once a week. Somehow I could not do it. The empty paper and the black Latin dictionary lying on the table, the consciousness of a plain duty shirked, poisoned my leisure, but somehow I could not start, and by the end of the holidays I would only have sent Mr. Batchelor fifty or a hundred lines. Undoubtedly part of the reason was that Sim and his cane were far away. But in term time, also, I would go through periods of idleness and stupidity when I would sink deeper and deeper into disgrace and even achieve a sort of feeble defiance, fully conscious of my guilt and yet unable or unwilling—I could not be sure which—to do any better. Then Bingo or Sim would send for me, and this time it would not even be a caning.

Bingo would search me with her baleful eyes. (What color were those eyes, I wonder? I remember them as green, but actually no human being has green eyes. Perhaps they were hazel.) She would start off in her peculiar wheedling, bullying style, which never failed to get right through one's guard and score a hit on one's better nature.

"I don't think it's awfully decent of you to behave like this, is it? Do you think it's quite playing the game by your mother and father to go on idling your time away, week after week, month after month? Do you *want* to throw all your chances away? You know your people aren't rich, don't you? You know they can't afford the same things as other boys' parents. How are they to send you to a public school if you don't win a scholarship? I know how proud you mother is of you. Do you *want* to let her down?"

"I don't think he wants to go to a public school any longer," Sim would say, addressing himself to Bingo with a pretense that I was not there. "I think he's given up that idea. He wants to be a little office-boy at forty pounds a year."

The horrible sensation of tears—a swelling in the breast, a tickling behind the nose—would already have assailed me. Bingo would bring out her ace of trumps:

"And do you think it's quite fair to *us*, the way you're behaving? After all we've done for you? You *do* know what we've done for you, don't you?" Her eyes would pierce deep into me, and though she never said it straight out, I did know. "We've had you here all these years—we even had you here for a week in the holidays so that Mr. Batchelor could coach you. We don't *want* to have to send you away, you know, but we can't keep a boy here just to eat up our food, term after term. *I* don't think it's very straight, the way you're behaving. Do you?"

I never had any answer except a miserable "No, Mum," or "Yes, Mum" as the case might be. Evidently it was *not* straight, the way I was behaving. And at some point or other the unwanted tear would always force its way out of the corner of my eye, roll down my nose, and splash.

Bingo never said in plain words that I was a nonpaying pupil, no doubt because vague phrases like "all we've done for you" had a deeper emotional appeal. Sim, who did not aspire to be loved by his pupils, put it more brutally, though, as was usual with him, in pompous language. "You are living on my bounty" was his favorite phrase in this context. At least once I listened to these words between blows of the cane. I must say that these scenes were not frequent, and except on one occasion they did not take place in the presence of other boys. In public I was reminded that I was poor and that my parents "wouldn't be able to afford" this or that, but I was not actually reminded of my dependent position. It was a final unanswerable argument, to be brought forth like an instrument of torture when my work became exceptionally bad.

To grasp the effect of this kind of thing on a child of ten or twelve, one has to remember that the child has little sense of proportion or probability. A child may be a mass of egoism and rebelliousness, but it has not accumulated experience to give it confidence in its own judgments. On the whole it will accept what it is told, and it will believe in the most fantastic way in the knowledge and power of the adults surrounding it. Here is an example.

I have said that at Crossgates we were not allowed to keep our own money. However, it was possible to hold back a shilling or two, and sometimes I used furtively to buy sweets which I kept hidden in the loose ivy on the playing-field wall. One day when I had been sent on an errand I went into a sweetshop a mile or more from the school and bought some chocolates. As I came out of the shop I saw on the opposite pavement a small sharp-faced man who seemed to be staring very hard at my school cap. Instantly a horrible fear went through me. There could be no doubt as to who the man was. He was a spy placed there by Sim! I turned away unconcernedly, and then, as though my legs were doing it of their own accord, broke into a clumsy run. But when I got round the next corner I forced myself to walk again, for to run was a sign of guilt, and obviously there would be other spies posted here and there about the town. All that day and the next I waited for the summons to the study, and was surprised when it did not come. It did not seem to me strange that the headmaster of a private school should dispose of an army of informers, and I did not even imagine that he would have to pay them. I assumed that any adult, inside the school or outside, would collaborate voluntarily in preventing us from breaking the rules. Sim was all-powerful, and it was natural that his agents should be everywhere. When this episode happened I do not think I can have been less than twelve years old.

I hated Bingo and Sim, with a sort of shamefaced, remorseful hatred, but it did not occur to me to doubt their judgment. When they told me that I must either win a public school scholarship or become an office-boy at fourteen, I believed that those were the unavoidable alternatives before me. And above all, I believed Bingo and Sim when they told me they were my benefactors. I see now, of course, that from Sim's point of view I was a good speculation. He sank money in me, and he looked to get it back in the form of

prestige. If I had "gone off," as promising boys sometimes do, I imagine that he would have got rid of me swiftly. As it was I won him two scholarships[7] when the time came, and no doubt he made full use of them in his prospectuses. But it is difficult for a child to realize that a school is primarily a commercial venture. A child believes that the school exists to educate and that the schoolmaster disciplines him either for his own good, or from a love of bullying. Sim and Bingo had chosen to befriend me, and their friendship included canings, reproaches, and humiliations, which were good for me and saved me from an office stool. That was their version, and I believed in it. It was therefore clear that I owed them a vast debt of gratitude. But I was *not* grateful, as I very well knew. On the contrary, I hated both of them. I could not control my subjective feelings, and I could not conceal them from myself. But it is wicked, is it not, to hate your benefactors? So I was taught, and so I believed. A child accepts the codes of behavior that are presented to it, even when it breaks them. From the age of eight, or even earlier, the consciousness of sin was never far away from me. If I contrived to seem callous and defiant, it was only a thin cover over a mass of shame and dismay. All through my boyhood I had a profound conviction that I was no good, that I was wasting my time, wrecking my talents, behaving with monstrous folly and wickedness and ingratitude—and all this, it seemed, was inescapable, because I lived among laws which were absolute, like the law of gravity, but which it was not possible for me to keep.

1952

---

7. *two scholarships,* to Eton and Winchester; Orwell went to Eton.

Discussion

1. What were Sim's "two great ambitions" for Crossgates?

2. (a) Describe the school's "three castes." (b) In what ways were the rich students favored?

3. What psychological methods did Sim and Bingo employ to motivate young Orwell? What do you think of these methods?

4. Explain how the school's preoccupation with winning scholarships actually inhibited real education.

5. How did Orwell really feel about Sim and Bingo?

Stevie Smith 1902–1971

When *Novel on Yellow Paper* by "Stevie Smith" appeared in 1936, there was uncertainty for a time as to who this individual was. The poet Robert Nicols wrote Virginia Woolf telling her he was certain that *she* was Stevie Smith, and that the new book was her best novel yet. Eventually the author's identity was established, and this led to the publication of her first book of poetry, *A Good Time Was Had by All* (1937). The literary reputation established with these books has grown slowly but steadily since.

Born in the Yorkshire city of Hull, she lived most of her life in the London suburb of Palmer's Green, sharing a small, unfashionable house with her beloved aunt, whom she dubbed "the Lion of Hull." "Very few in this suburb know me as Stevie Smith, & I should like to keep it that way," she wrote in 1956. Christened "Florence Margaret," she acquired her nickname at the age of about twenty. She was horseback riding with a friend, and some boys called to her, "Come on Steve," (after the famous jockey Steve Donoghue) and the name stuck.

After attending the progressive North London Collegiate School for Girls, she went to work instead of continuing on to a university, becoming a secretary in a magazine publishing company, work she apparently enjoyed and continued until her aunt became bed-ridden and required her constant care. She published two more novels, *Over the Frontier* (1938) and *The Holiday* (1949); a number of books of poetry, including *Tender Only to One* (1938), *Har-old's Leap* (1950), *Not Waving but Drowning* (1957), and *The Frog Prince and Other Poems* (1966); as well as several books of her curious drawings, notably *Some Are More Human Than Others* (1958). *Me Again* (1981) collects some of her short stories, essays, reviews, and letters, as well as previously unpublished poems and drawings.

In her poetry, she made use of nursery rhymes, popular songs, even hymns, employing clever twists and witty verbal maneuvers to create verse that is fresh and immediately engaging. While many of her poems are lightly humorous, even zany, they also reveal an underlying preoccupation with death, and, occasionally, a chilling fascination with the gruesome and macabre. Every collection of her poetry included a sampling of her odd drawings, like the one that accompanies "The Frog Prince," page 764.

*T*he Frog Prince

I am a frog
I live under a spell
I live at the bottom
Of a green well

5 And here I must wait
Until a maiden places me
On her royal pillow
And kisses me
In her father's palace.

10 The story is familiar
Everybody knows it well
But do other enchanted people feel as
    nervous
As I do? The stories do not tell,

Ask if they will be happier
15 When the changes come,
As already they are fairly happy
In a frog's doom?

I have been a frog now
For a hundred years
20 And in all this time
I have not shed many tears.

I am happy, I like the life,
Can swim for many a mile
(When I have hopped to the river)
25 And am for ever agile.

And the quietness,
Yes, I like to be quiet
I am habituated
To a quiet life,

30 But always when I think these thoughts
As I sit in my well
Another thought comes to me and says:
It is part of the spell

To be happy
35 To work up contentment
To make much of being a frog
To fear disenchantment

Says, It will be *heavenly*
To be set free
40 Cries, *Heavenly* the girl who disenchants
And the royal times, *heavenly,*
And I think it will be.

Come then, royal girl and royal times,
Come quickly,
45 I can be happy until you come
But I cannot be heavenly,
Only disenchanted people
Can be heavenly.   1937

Not Waving but Drowning

Nobody heard him, the dead man,
But still he lay moaning:
I was much farther out than you thought
And not waving but drowning.

5 Poor chap, he always loved larking
And now he's dead
It must have been too cold for him his heart gave way,
They said.

Oh no no no, it was too cold always
10 (Still the dead one lay moaning)
I was much too far out all my life
And not waving but drowning.

1957

Discussion

The Frog Prince

1. Why does the Frog Prince feel "nervous" (lines 12–13)?

2. What aspects of a frog's life has he come to enjoy?

3. How do the last four lines, especially the ambiguous use of *disenchanted*, explain why the Frog Prince is nevertheless eager for the maiden to come quickly and break the spell of enchantment?

Not Waving but Drowning

1. What two kinds of "drowning" are described in the poem?

2. What social criticism is implied by the repetition of the line "not waving but drowning" and the repeated references to the "cold"?

Dylan Thomas 1914–1953

As a result of his exuberant lifestyle, highly popular public readings, and widely publicized death in 1953 at the age of thirty-nine, Dylan Thomas became a celebrity whose public personality temporarily threatened to overshadow his poetry. No modern poet has generated such an outpouring of emotion, gossip, reminiscence, and criticism, nor attained his level as a "cult" figure. One of his biographers explains that Thomas met the need of his society for a romantic rebel: "He was an answer to the machine; his poems contain few images drawn from the twentieth century." Now that time has faded the public legend he can more truly be seen as the greatest lyric poet of his generation and a dramatist and essayist of original humor and charm.

Dylan Thomas was born in Swansea, Wales, a place he periodically fled but which provided the setting and stimulus of his best work. His father was a schoolteacher and poet whose readings of Shakespeare, the Bible, and other poets stimulated Thomas's early fascination with words. When later asked how he had come to write poetry, Thomas would recall his joy in nursery rhymes, stating that "what the words stood for, symbolized, or meant, was of very secondary importance; what mattered was the *sound* of them as I heard them for the first time on the lips of the remote and incomprehensible grown-ups who seemed, for some reason, to be living in my world." Thomas left school at 16 and spent fifteen months as a newspaper reporter, but poetry writing, which he had been doing since he was a small boy, was more to his taste. He published his first volume of poetry at nineteen and continued to publish well-received books of verse during the 1930s. *Portrait of the Artist as a Young Dog*, a collection of stories about his childhood and youth, appeared in 1940. Another book of boyhood reminiscences, *Quite Early One Morning* (1954), and a verse play, *Under Milk Wood* (1954), were published after his death. During World War II Thomas worked for the BBC as a documentary film editor and also as a radio broadcaster; his magnificent Welsh voice enchanted listeners, also his generous inclusion of the works of other poets in his readings.

In a letter to a friend, Thomas wrote: "I like things that are difficult to write and difficult to understand . . . I like contradicting my images, saying two things at once in one word, four in two and one in six." Not surprisingly, many of Thomas's poems are frustratingly difficult, especially those in his first two collections, *Eighteen Poems* (1934) and *Twenty-Five Poems* (1936). *Deaths and Entrances* (1946), his most famous collection of poems, reveals a movement away from obscurity to a simpler, more direct, yet ceremonial style. While the young Dylan Thomas was obsessed with mortality, an awareness that "the force" that gives life to plants and people is also the "destroyer," the later Thomas came to the realization that ". . . death shall have no dominion" in a cosmos in which all living things exist in a perpetual cycle of change and rebirth.

Fern Hill

Now as I was young and easy under the apple boughs
About the lilting house and happy as the grass was green,
    The night above the dingle starry,
        Time let me hail and climb
5   Golden in the heydays of his eyes,
And honored among wagons I was prince of the apple towns
And once below a time I lordly had the trees and leaves
        Trail with daisies and barley
    Down the rivers of the windfall light.

10 And as I was green and carefree, famous among the barns
About the happy yard and singing as the farm was home,
        In the sun that is young once only,
            Time let me play and be
        Golden in the mercy of his means,
15 And green and golden I was huntsman and herdsman, the calves
Sang to my horn, the foxes on the hills barked clear and cold,
            And the sabbath rang slowly
        In the pebbles of the holy streams.

All the sun long it was running, it was lovely, the hay
20 Fields high as the house, the tunes from the chimneys, it was air
        And playing, lovely and watery
            And fire green as grass.
        And nightly under the simple stars
As I rode to sleep the owls were bearing the farm away,
25 All the moon long I heard, blessed among stables, the night-jars
        Flying with the ricks, and the horses
            Flashing into the dark.

And then to awake, and the farm, like a wanderer white
With the dew, come back, the cock on his shoulder: it was all
30   Shining, it was Adam and maiden,
            The sky gathered again
        And the sun grew round that very day.
So it must have been after the birth of the simple light
In the first, spinning place, the spellbound horses walking warm
35   Out of the whinnying green stable
            On to the fields of praise.

And honored among foxes and pheasants by the gay house
Under the new made clouds and happy as the heart was long,
        In the sun born over and over,
40   I ran my heedless ways,
        My wishes raced through the house high hay
And nothing I cared, at my sky blue trades, that time allows
In all his tuneful turning so few and such morning songs
        Before the children green and golden
45   Follow him out of grace.

Nothing I cared, in the lamb white days, that time would take me
Up to the swallow thronged loft by the shadow of my hand,
        In the moon that is always rising,
            Nor that riding to sleep
50   I should hear him fly with the high fields
And wake to the farm forever fled from the childless land.
Oh as I was young and easy in the mercy of his means,
            Time held me green and dying
        Though I sang in my chains like the sea.

1946

If one sought to describe this poem within the compass of a single phrase, it might be called "an elegy in praise of lost youth." Lament and celebration sound throughout the work: the latter strongly at the beginning, the former gaining tone as the poem progresses.

But, as with all great threnodies (lamentations) in English—with Milton's *Lycidas,* Gray's *Elegy,* Shelley's *Adonais,* and Arnold's *Thyrsis*—the particularity of the cause of grief is lost in a sorrow which speaks for all men. Nostalgic recollection of a child's farm holiday is the leaping-off point for the poem; but—once launched—so intense and poignant a memory overtakes the poet, that his words convey more than a merely topographical homesickness. The farm becomes Eden before the Fall, and time the angel with a flaming sword.

But no such intrusive personification operates within the poem. The farm is invested with a light as radiant as the unforfeited Garden, and time exercises its function as irrevocably as God's excluding angel. So, though at the end we are faced with nothing worse than a farmstead which cannot be revisited, in actual poetic terms we have experienced the states of innocence and eternity, and been subjected to corruption, time, and change.

The poem is constructed from six nine-line stanzas, with only an infrequent rhyme. The absence of rhyme suffices to make the lyrically undulating lines more natural. The artifice and architectonic of the poem consists not in the usual technical devices, but in the repetition, in later stanzas, of *motifs* established in the first. These *motifs* are not worked out with any mechanical regularity; and their place and precedence in the poem are not formally observed. The *motifs* I find to be mainly three: that of the unwitting situation of childhood; that of the delight in this situation; that of time's operation, by which the situation becomes a fate.

*D*o Not Go Gentle into That Good Night

Do not go gentle into that good night,
Old age should burn and rave at close of day;
Rage, rage against the dying of the light.

Though wise men at their end know dark is right,
5 Because their words had forked no lightning they
Do not go gentle into that good night.

Good men, the last wave by, crying how bright

Their frail deeds might have danced in a green bay,
Rage, rage against the dying of the light.

10 Wild men who caught and sang the sun in flight,
And learn, too late, they grieved it on its way,
Do not go gentle into that good night.

Grave men, near death, who see with blinding sight
Blind eyes could blaze like meteors and be gay,
15 Rage, rage against the dying of the light.

And you, my father, there on the sad height,
Curse, bless, me now with your fierce tears, I pray.
Do not go gentle into that good night.
Rage, rage against the dying of the light.

1951   1957

Discussion

Fern Hill

1. In addition to the "I" of the poem, Time is the dominant presence, personified in three distinct forms. (a) What view of Time is developed in the first four stanzas? (b) How is this treatment of Time appropriate for childhood? (c) In what form is Time personified in stanza five and what action is Time performing? What period of a person's life does this stanza describe? (d) What final image of Time is presented in the concluding lines of the poem?

2. (a) What details of his childhood does the poet recall? (b) What do they reveal about the way children characteristically perceive the world?

3. (a) When he was a child, what did the speaker believe happened to the farm every night when he went to bed? the next morning? (b) Why, in describing this outlook, has the poet made reference to the Garden of Eden? (c) Symbolically, what happens to the farm in the last stanza? Why is such a happening inevitable?

4. (a) What color scheme is carried out in the poem, and how does it help to reinforce the overall theme? (b) Point out the instances of fresh treatment of clichés. (c) How has the poem been enhanced by the use of **assonance**?

Discussion

Do Not Go Gentle into That Good Night

1. When Dylan Thomas wrote his poem, his father was seriously ill with heart trouble and had only a short time to live. Publication of the poem was withheld until after the father's death. (a) How does the poet advise his father to react to death? (b) Stanzas two through five mention four kinds of men. How does each react to death, and why do they behave as they do? (c) What similar "fact of life" does the reaction to death of all these men serve to illustrate? (d) Why does the son ask his dying father both to "curse" and "bless" him?

2. Because of the restrictions imposed by the **villanelle** form, the words of the poem necessarily carry a cargo of double meanings. Pick out words and phrases that are clearly ambiguous and explain the two meanings intended.

3. Identify the **pun** and explain the **paradox** present in stanza five.

4. How do the words "Do not go gentle" change in meaning as they are repeated throughout the course of the poem?

Graham Greene 1904–

A great-nephew of Robert Louis Stevenson, Greene was the son of the headmaster of a school in Hertfordshire. He attended his father's school until, unhappy at the contrast between the comforts of his home life and the cruelties of the classroom, he ran away. He was sent for treatment to a psychoanalyst in whose London home he lived for six months, a period he later described as one of the happiest in his life.

Greene went to Oxford, publishing a book of poetry, *Babbling April* (1925), in the year he graduated. During the next two years he married, became a journalist (eventually joining the staff of the London *Times*), and converted to Roman Catholicism. After the publication of his first novel, *The Man Within* (1929), he left *The Times*, becoming a free-lance writer and reviewer.

Greene is both a prolific writer and an experienced traveler, and over the years his novels have been set in a number of exotic places: *Stamboul Train* (1932) on the Orient Express; *The Power and the Glory* (1940) in Mexico; *The Heart of the Matter* (1948) in Nigeria; *The Quiet American* (1956) in Vietnam; *A Burnt-Out Case* (1961) in Central Africa; *The Comedians* (1966) in Haiti; *The Honorary Consul* (1973) in Argentina.

Two important influences on Greene's writing have been his Catholicism and the cinema. As a Catholic, Greene reflects on his religious convictions and probes the nature of good and evil on both the personal and doctrinal level. Greene has done excellent work both as a film critic and as a screenwriter—*The Third Man* (1949)—and his narrative method and imagery often reveal the influence of the cinema.

Greene has made a classification of his fiction into "entertainments" and "novels." The former are, for the most part, literary thrillers, such as *A Gun for Sale* (1936), *The Ministry of Fear* (1943), and *The Third Man*. His more serious works, including *Brighton Rock* (1938), *The Power and the Glory, The Heart of the Matter, The End of the Affair* (1948), and *A Burnt-Out Case,* are set, in the words of one recent critic, in "hell . . . a hideously negative and at the same time vividly realized place." In Greene's world, evil is omnipresent, and he makes it felt. Both novels and entertainments are marked by careful plotting and characterization, and an economy and precision of language.

A Shocking Accident

1

Jerome was called into his housemaster's room in the break between the second and the third class on a Thursday morning. He had no fear of trouble, for he was a warden—the name that the proprietor and headmaster of a rather expensive preparatory school had chosen to give to approved, reliable boys in the lower forms[1] (from a warden one became a guardian and finally before leaving, it was hoped for Marlborough or Rugby,[2] a crusader). The housemaster, Mr Wordsworth, sat behind his desk with an appearance of perplexity and apprehension. Jerome had the odd impression when he entered that he was a cause of fear.

"Sit down, Jerome," Mr. Wordsworth said. "All going well with the trigonometry?"

"Yes, sir."

"I've had a telephone call, Jerome. From your aunt. I'm afraid I have bad news for you."

"Yes, sir?"

"Your father has had an accident."

"Oh."

Mr. Wordsworth looked at him with some surprise. "A serious accident."

"Yes, sir?"

Jerome worshipped his father: the verb is exact. As man re-creates God, so Jerome re-created his father—from a restless widowed author into a mysterious adventurer who travelled in far places—Nice, Beirut, Majorca, even the Canaries. The time had arrived about his eighth birthday when Jerome believed that his father either "ran guns" or was a member of the British Secret Service. Now it occurred to him that his father might have been wounded in "a hail of machine-gun bullets."

Mr. Wordsworth played with the ruler on his desk. He seemed at a loss how to continue. He said, "You know your father was in Naples?"

"Yes, sir."

"Your aunt heard from the hospital today."

"Oh."

Mr. Wordsworth said with desperation, "It was a street accident."

"Yes, sir?" It seemed quite likely to Jerome that they would call it a street accident. The police of course had fired first; his father would not take human life except as a last resort.

"I'm afraid your father was very seriously hurt indeed."

"Oh."

"In fact, Jerome, he died yesterday. Quite without pain."

"Did they shoot him through the heart?"

"I beg your pardon. What did you say, Jerome?"

"Did they shoot him through the heart?"

"Nobody shot him, Jerome. A pig fell on him." An inexplicable convulsion took place in the nerves of Mr. Wordsworth's face; it really looked for a moment as though he were going to laugh. He closed his eyes, composed his features and said rapidly as though it were necessary to expel the story as quickly as possible, "Your father was walking along a street in Naples when a pig fell on him. A shocking accident. Apparently in the poorer quarters of Naples they keep pigs on their balconies. This one was on the fifth floor. It had grown too fat. The balcony broke. The pig fell on your father."

Mr. Wordsworth left his desk rapidly and went to the window, turning his back on Jerome. He shook a little with emotion.

Jerome said, "What happened to the pig?"

2

This was not callousness on the part of Jerome, as it was interpreted by Mr. Wordsworth to his colleagues (he even discussed with them whether, perhaps, Jerome was yet fitted to be a warden). Jerome was only attempting to visualize the strange scene to get the details right. Nor was Jerome a boy who cried; he was a boy who brooded, and it never occurred to him at his preparatory school that the circumstances of his father's death were comic—they were still part of the mystery of life. It was later, in his first term at his public school, when he told the story to his best friend, that he began to realize how it affected others. Naturally after that disclosure he was known, rather unreasonably, as Pig.

Unfortunately his aunt had no sense of humor. There was an enlarged snapshot of his father on the piano; a large sad man in an unsuitable dark suit posed in Capri[3] with an umbrella (to guard him against sunstroke), the Faraglione rocks forming the background. By the age of sixteen Jerome was well aware that the portrait looked more like the author of *Sunshine and*

---

1. **lower forms,** lower grades.
2. **Marlborough or Rugby,** two famous public schools. The well-known English public schools—like Marlborough and Rugby—are private boarding schools for the sons of wealthy people.
3. **Capri,** an island in the Bay of Naples.

Shade and *Rambles in the Balearics* than an agent of the Secret Service. All the same he loved the memory of his father: he still possessed an album filled with picture-postcards (the stamps had been soaked off long ago for his other collection), and it pained him when his aunt embarked with strangers on the story of his father's death.

"A shocking accident," she would begin, and the stranger would compose his or her features into the correct shape for interest and commiseration. Both reactions, of course, were false, but it was terrible for Jerome to see how suddenly, midway in her rambling discourse, the interest would become genuine. "I can't think how such things can be allowed in a civilized country," his aunt would say. "I suppose one has to regard Italy as civilized. One is prepared for all kinds of things abroad, of course, and my brother was a great traveller. He always carried a water-filter with him. It was far less expensive, you know, than buying all those bottles of mineral water. My brother always said that his filter paid for his dinner wine. You can see from that what a careful man he was, but who could possibly have expected when he was walking along the Via Dottore Manuele Panucci on his way to the Hydrographic Museum that a pig would fall on him?" That was the moment when the interest became genuine.

Jerome's father had not been a very distinguished writer, but the time always seems to come, after an author's death, when somebody thinks it worth his while to write a letter to the *Times Literary Supplement* announcing the preparation of a biography and asking to see any letters or documents or receive any anecdotes from friends of the dead man. Most of the biographies, of course, never appear—one wonders whether the whole thing may not be an obscure form of blackmail and whether many a potential writer of a biography or thesis finds the means in this way to finish his education at Kansas or Nottingham. Jerome, however, as a chartered accountant, lived far from the literary world. He did not realize how small the menace really was, or that the danger period for someone of his father's obscur-

A scene from *A Shocking Accident,* a short film based on Graham Greene's story, which won the 1983 Academy Award as the best live action short film.

ity had long passed. Sometimes he rehearsed the method of recounting his father's death so as to reduce the comic element to its smallest dimensions—it would be of no use to refuse information, for in that case the biographer would undoubtedly visit his aunt who was living to a great old age with no sign of flagging.

It seemed to Jerome that there were two possible methods—the first led gently up to the accident, so that by the time it was described the listener was so well prepared that the death came really as an anti-climax. The chief danger of laughter in such a story was always surprise. When he rehearsed this method Jerome began boringly enough.

"You know Naples and those high tenement buildings? Somebody once told me that the Neapolitan always feels at home in New York just as the man from Turin feels at home in London because the river runs in much the same way in both cities. Where was I? Oh, yes. Naples, of course. You'd be surprised in the poorer quarters what things they keep on the balconies of those sky-scraping tenements—not washing, you know, or bedding, but things like livestock, chickens or even pigs. Of course the pigs get no exercise whatever and fatten all the quicker." He could imagine how his hearer's eyes would have glazed by this time. "I've no idea, have you, how heavy a pig can be, but these old buildings are all badly in need of repair. A balcony on the fifth floor gave way under one of those pigs. It struck the third floor balcony on its way down and sort of ricochetted into the street. My father was on the way to the Hydrographic Museum when the pig hit him. Coming from that height and that angle it broke his neck." This was really a masterly attempt to make an intrinsically interesting subject boring.

The other method Jerome rehearsed had the virtue of brevity.

"My father was killed by a pig."

"Really? In India?"

"No, in Italy."

"How interesting. I never realized there was pig-sticking[4] in Italy. Was your father keen on polo?"

In course of time, neither too early nor too late, rather as though, in his capacity as a chartered accountant, Jerome had studied the statis-

tics and taken the average, he became engaged to be married: to a pleasant fresh-faced girl of twenty-five whose father was a doctor in Pinner. Her name was Sally, her favorite author was still Hugh Walpole,[5] and she had adored babies ever since she had been given a doll at the age of five which moved its eyes and made water. Their relationship was contented rather than exciting, as became the love-affair of a chartered accountant; it would never have done if it had interfered with the figures.

One thought worried Jerome, however. Now that within a year he might himself become a father, his love for the dead man increased; he realized what affection had gone into the picture-postcards. He felt a longing to protect his memory, and uncertain whether this quiet love of his would survive if Sally were so insensitive as to laugh when she heard the story of his father's death. Inevitably she would hear it when Jerome brought her to dinner with his aunt. Several times he tried to tell her himself, as she was naturally anxious to know all she could that concerned him.

"You were very small when your father died?"

"Just nine."

"Poor little boy," she said.

"I was at school. They broke the news to me."

"Did you take it very hard?"

"I can't remember."

"You never told me how it happened."

"It was very sudden. A street accident."

"You'll never drive fast, will you, Jemmy?" (She had begun to call him "Jemmy.") It was too late then to try the second method—the one he thought of as the pig-sticking one.

They were going to marry quietly in a registry-office and have their honeymoon at Torquay. He avoided taking her to see his aunt until a week before the wedding, but then the night came, and he could not have told himself whether his apprehension was more for his father's memory or the security of his own love.

---

4. **pig-sticking,** the hunting of wild boars with a spear, especially in India.
5. **Hugh Walpole** (1884–1941), a popular English novelist of the 1920s and 1930s. Greene is suggesting that Sally is a person of conventional tastes.

The moment came all too soon. "Is that Jemmy's father?" Sally asked, picking up the portrait of the man with the umbrella.

"Yes, dear. How did you guess?"

"He has Jemmy's eyes and brow, hasn't he?"

"Has Jerome lent you his books?"

"No."

"I will give you a set for your wedding. He wrote so tenderly about his travels. My own favorite is *Nooks and Crannies*. He would have had a great future. It made that shocking accident all the worse."

"Yes?"

Jerome longed to leave the room and not see that loved face crinkle with irresistible amusement.

"I had so many letters from his readers after the pig fell on him." She had never been so abrupt before.

And then the miracle happened. Sally did not laugh. Sally sat with open eyes of horror while his aunt told her the story, and at the end, "How horrible," Sally said. "It makes you think, doesn't it? Happening like that. Out of a clear sky."

Jerome's heart sang with joy. It was as though she had appeased his fear for ever. In the taxi going home he kissed her with more passion than he had ever shown and she returned it. There were babies in her pale blue pupils, babies that rolled their eyes and made water.

"A week today," Jerome said, and she squeezed his hand. "Penny for your thoughts, my darling."

"I was wondering," Sally said, "what happened to the poor pig?"

"They almost certainly had it for dinner," Jerome said happily and kissed the dear child again.

1967

Discussion

1. Aren't all accidents "shocking"? Why is Greene's title an apt one for this story?

2. Is Jerome's question—"What happened to the pig?"—a sincere or facetious response to the report of his father's death?

3. What indications are we given that Jerome's father was not the idealized adventurer his son had made him out to be?

4. **(a)** What two methods of narrating the facts of his father's death does Jerome perfect? **(b)** Although Jerome chooses a different career than his father, do their personalities have something in common? Explain.

Frank O'Connor 1903–1966

In his autobiography, *An Only Child,* Frank O'Connor traces his life from his birth in a slum in Cork to his release in 1923 from imprisonment as a revolutionary during the civil war that followed the establishment of the Irish Free State two years earlier. Born Michael O'Donovan, his early life was hard, unhappy, and poverty-stricken. His father was a laborer, his mother a cleaning woman, and lack of money a perpetual problem. O'Connor states that he received no education worth mentioning. Nevertheless, he was able to look back on his Irish childhood with humor and compassion—qualities that are dominant in most of his stories.

O'Connor learned Gaelic from his grandmother, and his knowledge of this language enabled him to collaborate with William Butler Yeats on translations of Gaelic poems. He began writing as a boy, but was undecided whether to become a painter or a writer. He abandoned painting, he claimed, because it was too expensive. O'Connor toured Ireland on a bicycle, thereby becoming more intimately acquainted with the manners and speech of the Irish people and storing up scenes and subjects that would later appear in his many stories. Of these stories, Yeats once said, "O'Connor was doing for Ireland what Chekhov did for Russia."

O'Connor served for several years as director of the Abbey Theatre, and became a member of the Irish Academy of Letters. In 1952 he moved permanently to the United States, where he published *The Stories of Frank O'Connor* and other collections, wrote for *The New Yorker,* and taught writing courses at Stanford, Harvard, and Northwestern. *The Lonely Voice* (1962) is a lucid and sensitive study of the short story that also reveals his talent as a teacher and critic.

My Oedipus Complex[1]

Father was in the army all through the war—the first war, I mean—so, up to the age of five, I never saw much of him, and what I saw did not worry me. Sometimes I woke and there was a big figure in khaki peering down at me in the candlelight. Somtimes in the early morning I heard the

1. Oedipus (ed'ə pəs, ē'də pəs) **Complex,** (in psychoanalysis) a strong childhood attachment for the parent of the opposite sex, often accompanied by a feeling of rivalry, hostility, or fear toward the other parent.

slamming of the front door and the clatter of nailed boots down the cobbles of the lane. These were Father's entrances and exits. Like Santa Claus he came and went mysteriously.

In fact, I rather liked his visits, though it was an uncomfortable squeeze between Mother and him when I got into the big bed in the early morning. He smoked, which gave him a pleasant musty smell, and shaved, an operation of astounding interest. Each time he left a trail of souvenirs—model tanks and Gurkha knives with handles made of bullet cases, and German helmets and cap badges and button-sticks, and all sorts of military equipment—carefully stowed away in a long box on top of the wardrobe, in case they ever came in handy. There was a bit of the magpie about Father; he expected everything to come in handy. When his back was turned, Mother let me get a chair and rummage through his treasures. She didn't seem to think so highly of them as he did.

The war was the most peaceful period of my life. The window of my attic faced southeast. My mother had curtained it, but that had small effect. I always woke with the first light and, with all the responsibilities of the previous day melted, feeling myself rather like the sun, ready to illumine and rejoice. Life never seemed so simple and clear and full of possibilities as then. I put my feet out from under the clothes—I called them Mrs. Left and Mrs. Right—and invented dramatic situations for them in which they discussed the problems of the day. At least Mrs. Right did; she was very demonstrative, but I hadn't the same control of Mrs. Left, so she mostly contented herself with nodding agreement.

They discussed what Mother and I should do during the day, what Santa Claus should give a fellow for Christmas, and what steps should be taken to brighten the home. There was that little matter of the baby, for instance. Mother and I could never agree about that. Ours was the only house in the terrace without a new baby, and Mother said we couldn't afford one till Father came back from the war because they cost seventeen and six. That showed how simple she was. The Geneys up the road had a baby, and everyone knew they couldn't afford seventeen and six. It was probably a cheap baby, and Mother wanted something really good, but I felt she was

too exclusive. The Geneys' baby would have done us fine.

Having settled my plans for the day, I got up, put a chair under the attic window, and lifted the frame high enough to stick out my head. The window overlooked the front gardens of the terrace behind ours, and beyond these it looked over a deep valley to the tall, red-brick houses terraced up the opposite hillside, which were all still in shadow, while those at our side of the valley were all lit up, though with long strange shadows that made them seem unfamiliar; rigid and painted.

After that I went into Mother's room and climbed into the big bed. She woke and I began to tell her of my schemes. By this time, though I never seem to have noticed it, I was petrified in my nightshirt, and I thawed as I talked until, the last frost melted, I fell asleep beside her and woke again only when I heard her below in the kitchen, making the breakfast.

After breakfast we went into town; heard Mass at St. Augustine's and said a prayer for Father, and did the shopping. If the afternoon was fine we either went for a walk in the country or a visit to Mother's great friend in the convent, Mother St. Dominic. Mother had them all praying for Father, and every night, going to bed, I asked God to send him back safe from the war to us. Little, indeed, did I know what I was praying for!

One morning, I got into the big bed, and there, sure enough, was Father in his usual Santa Claus manner, but later, instead of uniform, he put on his best blue suit, and Mother was as pleased as anything. I saw nothing to be pleased about, because, out of uniform, Father was altogether less interesting, but she only beamed, and explained that our prayers had been answered, and off we went to Mass to thank God for having brought Father safely home.

The irony of it! That very day when he came in to dinner he took off his boots and put on his slippers, donned the dirty old cap he wore about the house to save him from colds, crossed his legs, and began to talk gravely to Mother, who looked anxious. Naturally, I disliked her looking anxious, because it destroyed her good looks, so I interrupted him.

"Just a moment, Larry!" she said gently.

This was only what she said when we had boring visitors, so I attached no importance to it and went on talking.

"Do be quiet, Larry!" she said impatiently. "Don't you hear me talking to Daddy?"

This was the first time I had heard those ominous words, "talking to Daddy," and I couldn't help feeling that if this was how God answered prayers, he couldn't listen to them very attentively.

"Why are you talking to Daddy?" I asked with as great a show of indifference as I could muster.

"Because Daddy and I have business to discuss. Now, don't interrupt again!"

In the afternoon, at Mother's request, Father took me for a walk. This time we went into town instead of out to the country, and I thought at first, in my usual optimistic way, that it might be an improvement. It was nothing of the sort. Father and I had quite different notions of a walk in town. He had no proper interest in trams, ships, and horses, and the only thing that seemed to divert him was talking to fellows as old as himself. When I wanted to stop he simply went on, dragging me behind him by the hand; when he wanted to stop I had no alternative but to do the same. I noticed that it seemed to be a sign that he wanted to stop for a long time whenever he leaned against a wall. The second time I saw him do it I got wild. He seemed to be settling himself forever. I pulled him by the coat and trousers, but, unlike Mother who, if you were too persistent, got into a wax and said: "Larry, if you don't behave yourself, I'll give you a good slap," Father had an extraordinary capacity for amiable inattention. I sized him up and wondered would I cry, but he seemed to be too remote to be annoyed even by that. Really, it was like going for a walk with a mountain! He either ignored the wrenching and pummeling entirely, or else glanced down with a grin of amusement from his peak. I had never met anyone so absorbed in himself as he seemed.

At teatime, "talking to Daddy" began again, complicated this time by the fact that he had an evening paper, and every few minutes he put it down and told Mother something new out of it. I felt this was foul play. Man for man, I was prepared to compete with him any time for Mother's attention, but when he had it all made up for him by other people it left me no chance. Several times I tried to change the subject without success.

"You must be quiet while Daddy is reading, Larry," Mother said impatiently.

It was clear that she either genuinely liked talking to Father better than talking to me, or else that he had some terrible hold on her which made her afraid to admit the truth.

"Mummy," I said that night when she was tucking me up, "do you think if I prayed hard God would send Daddy back to the war?"

She seemed to think about that for a moment.

"No, dear," she said with a smile. "I don't think he would."

"Why wouldn't he, Mummy?"

"Because there isn't a war any longer, dear."

"But, Mummy, couldn't God make another war, if he liked?"

"He wouldn't like to, dear. It's not God who makes wars, but bad people."

"Oh!" I said.

I was disappointed about that. I began to think that God wasn't quite what he was cracked up to be.

Next morning I woke at my usual hour, feeling like a bottle of champagne. I put out my feet and invented a long conversation in which Mrs. Right talked of the trouble she had with her own father till she put him in the Home. I didn't quite know what the Home was but it sounded the right place for Father. Then I got my chair and stuck my head out of the attic window. Dawn was just breaking, with a guilty air that made me feel I had caught it in the act. My head bursting with stories and schemes, I stumbled in next door, and in the half-darkness scrambled into the big bed. There was no room at Mother's side so I had to get between her and Father. For the time being I had forgotten about him, and for several minutes I sat bolt upright, racking my brains to know what I could do with him. He was taking up more than his fair share of the bed, and I couldn't get comfortable, so I gave him several kicks that made him grunt and stretch. He made room all right, though. Mother waked and felt for me. I settled back comfortably in the warmth of the bed with my thumb in my mouth.

"Mummy!" I hummed, loudly and contentedly.

"Sssh! dear," she whispered. "Don't wake Daddy!"

This was a new development, which threatened to be even more serious than "talking to Daddy." Life without my early-morning conferences was unthinkable.

"Why?" I asked severely.

"Because poor Daddy is tired."

This seemed to me a quite inadequate reason, and I was sickened by the sentimentality of her "poor Daddy." I never liked that sort of gush; it always struck me as insincere.

"Oh!" I said lightly. Then in my most winning tone: "Do you know where I want to go with you today, Mummy?"

"No, dear," she sighed.

"I want to go down the Glen and fish for thornybacks with my new net, and then I want to go out to the Fox and Hounds, and—"

"Don't-wake-Daddy!" she hissed angrily, clapping her hand across my mouth.

But it was too late. He was awake, or nearly so. He grunted and reached for the matches. Then he stared incredulously at his watch.

"Like a cup of tea, dear?" asked Mother in a meek, hushed voice I had never heard her use before. It sounded almost as though she were afraid.

"Tea?" he exclaimed indignantly. "Do you know what the time is?"

"And after that I want to go up the Rathcooney Road," I said loudly, afraid I'd forget something in all those interruptions.

"Go to sleep at once, Larry!" she said sharply.

I began to snivel. I couldn't concentrate, the way that pair went on, and smothering my early-morning schemes was like burying a family from the cradle.

Father said nothing, but lit his pipe and sucked it, looking out into the shadows without minding Mother or me. I knew he was mad. Every time I made a remark Mother hushed me irritably. I was mortified. I felt it wasn't fair; there was even something sinister in it. Every time I had pointed out to her the waste of making two beds when we could both sleep in one, she had told me it was healthier like that, and now here was this man, this stranger, sleeping with her without the least regard for her health!

He got up early and made tea, but though he brought Mother a cup he brought none for me.

"Mummy," I shouted, "I want a cup of tea, too."

"Yes, dear," she said patiently. "You can drink from Mummy's saucer."

That settled it. Either Father or I would have to leave the house. I didn't want to drink from Mother's saucer; I wanted to be treated as an equal in my own home, so, just to spite her, I drank it all and left none for her. She took that quietly, too.

But that night when she was putting me to bed she said gently: "Larry, I want you to promise me something."

"What is it?" I asked.

"Not to come in and disturb poor Daddy in the morning. Promise?"

"Poor Daddy" again! I was becoming suspicious of everything involving that quite impossible man.

"Why?" I asked.

"Because poor Daddy is worried and tired and he doesn't sleep well."

"Why doesn't he, Mummy?"

"Well, you know, don't you, that while he was at the war Mummy got the pennies from the Post Office?"

"From Miss MacCarthy?"

"That's right. But now, you see, Miss MacCarthy hasn't any more pennies, so Daddy must go out and find us some. You know what would happen if he couldn't?"

"No," I said, "tell us."

"Well, I think we might have to go out and beg for them like the poor old woman on Fridays. We wouldn't like that, would we?"

"No," I agreed. "We wouldn't."

"So you'll promise not to come in and wake him?"

"Promise."

Mind you, I meant that. I knew pennies were a serious matter, and I was all against having to go out and beg like the old woman on Fridays. Mother laid out all my toys in a complete ring round the bed so that, whatever way I got out, I was bound to fall over one of them.

When I woke I remembered my promise all

right. I got up and sat on the floor and played—for hours, it seemed to me. Then I got my chair and looked out the attic window for more hours. I wished it was time for Father to wake; I wished someone would make me a cup of tea. I didn't feel in the least like the sun; instead, I was bored and so very, very cold! I simply longed for the warmth and depth of the big featherbed.

At last I could stand it no longer. I went into the next room. As there was still no room at Mother's side I climbed over her and she woke with a start.

"Larry," she whispered, gripping my arm very tightly, "what did you promise?"

"But I did, Mummy," I wailed, caught in the very act. "I was quiet for ever so long."

"Oh, dear, and you're perished!" she said sadly, feeling me all over. "Now, if I let you stay will you promise not to talk?"

"But I want to talk, Mummy," I wailed.

"That has nothing to do with it," she said with a firmness that was new to me. "Daddy wants to sleep. Now, do you understand that?"

I understood it only too well. I wanted to talk, he wanted to sleep—whose house was it, any-way?

"Mummy," I said with equal firmness, "I think it would be healthier for Daddy to sleep in his own bed."

That seemed to stagger her, because she said nothing for a while.

"Now, once for all," she went on, "you're to be perfectly quiet or go back to your own bed. Which is it to be?"

The injustice of it got me down. I had convicted her out of her own mouth of inconsistency and unreasonableness, and she hadn't even attempted to reply. Full of spite, I gave Father a kick, which she didn't notice but which made him grunt and open his eyes in alarm.

"What time is it?" he asked in a panic-stricken voice, not looking at Mother but the door, as if he saw someone there.

"It's early yet," she replied soothingly. "It's only the child. Go to sleep again. . . . Now, Larry," she added, getting out of bed, "you've wakened Daddy and you must go back."

This time, for all her quiet air, I knew she meant it, and knew that my principal rights and privileges were as good as lost unless I asserted them at once. As she lifted me, I gave a screech, enough to wake the dead, not to mind Father. He groaned.

"That damn child! Doesn't he ever sleep?"

"It's only a habit, dear," she said quietly, though I could see she was vexed.

"Well, it's time he got out of it," shouted Father, beginning to heave in the bed. He suddenly gathered all the bedclothes about him, turned to the wall, and then looked back over his shoulder with nothing showing only two small, spiteful, dark eyes. The man looked very wicked.

To open the bedroom door, Mother had to let me down, and I broke free and dashed for the farthest corner, screeching. Father sat bolt upright in bed.

"Shut up, you little puppy!" he said in a choking voice.

I was so astonished that I stopped screeching. Never, never had anyone spoken to me in that tone before. I looked at him incredulously and saw his face convulsed with rage. It was only then that I fully realized how God had codded me, listening to my prayers for the safe return of this monster.

"Shut up, you!" I bawled, beside myself.

"What's that you said?" shouted Father, making a wild leap out of bed.

"Mick, Mick!" cried Mother. "Don't you see the child isn't used to you?"

"I see he's better fed than taught," snarled Father, waving his arms wildly. "He wants his bottom smacked."

All his previous shouting was as nothing to these obscene words referring to my person. They really made my blood boil.

"Smack your own!" I screamed hysterically. "Smack your own! Shut up! Shut up!"

At this he lost his patience and let fly at me. He did it with the lack of conviction you'd expect of a man under Mother's horrified eyes, and it ended up as a mere tap, but the sheer indignity of being struck at all by a stranger, a total stranger who had cajoled his way back from the war into our big bed as a result of my innocent intercession, made me completely dotty. I shrieked and shrieked, and danced in my bare feet, and Father, looking awkward and hairy in nothing but a short grey army shirt, glared down at me like a mountain out for murder. I think it must have been then that I realized he was jealous too. And there stood Mother in her nightdress, looking as if her heart was broken between us. I hoped she felt as she looked. It seemed to me that she deserved it all.

From that morning out my life was a hell. Father and I were enemies, open and avowed. We conducted a series of skirmishes against one another, he trying to steal my time with Mother and I his. When she was sitting on my bed, telling me a story, he took to looking for some pair of old boots which he alleged he had left behind him at the beginning of the war. While he talked to Mother I played loudly with my toys to show my total lack of concern. He created a terrible scene one evening when he came in from work and found me at his box, playing with his regimental badges, Gurkha knives and buttonsticks. Mother got up and took the box from me.

"You mustn't play with Daddy's toys unless he lets you, Larry," she said severely. "Daddy doesn't play with yours."

For some reason Father looked at her as if she had struck him and then turned away with a scowl.

"Those are not toys," he growled, taking down the box again to see had I lifted anything. "Some of those curios are very rare and valuable."

But as time went on I saw more and more how he managed to alienate Mother and me. What made it worse was that I couldn't grasp his method or see what attraction he had for Mother. In every possible way he was less winning than I. He had a common accent and made noises at his tea. I thought for a while that it might be the newspapers she was interested in, so I made up bits of news of my own to read to her. Then I thought it might be the smoking, which I personally thought attractive, and took his pipes and went round the house dribbling into them till he caught me. I even made noises at my tea, but Mother only told me I was disgusting. It all seemed to hinge round that unhealthy habit of sleeping together, so I made a point of dropping into their bedroom and nosing round, talking to myself, so that they wouldn't know I was watching them, but they were never up to anything that I could see. In the end it beat me. It seemed to depend on being grownup and giving people rings, and I realized I'd have to wait.

But at the same time I wanted him to see that I was only waiting, not giving up the fight. One evening when he was being particularly obnoxious, chattering away and well above my head, I let him have it.

"Mummy," I said, "do you know what I'm going to do when I grow up?"

"No, dear," she replied. "What?"

"I'm going to marry you," I said quietly.

Father gave a great guffaw out of him, but he didn't take me in. I knew it must only be pretense. And Mother, in spite of everything was pleased. I felt she was probably relieved to know that one day Father's hold on her would be broken.

"Won't that be nice?" she said with a smile.

"It'll be very nice," I said confidently. "Because we're going to have lots and lots of babies."

"That's right, dear," she said placidly. "I think we'll have one soon, and then you'll have plenty of company."

I was no end pleased about that because it showed that in spite of the way she gave in to Father she still considered my wishes. Besides, it would put the Geneys in their place.

It didn't turn out like that, though. To begin with, she was very preoccupied—I supposed about where she would get the seventeen and six—and though Father took to staying out late in the evenings it did me no particular good. She stopped taking me for walks, became as touchy as blazes, and smacked me for nothing at all. Sometimes I wished I'd never mentioned the confounded baby—I seemed to have a genius for bringing calamity on myself.

And calamity it was! Sonny arrived in the most appalling hullabaloo—even that much he couldn't do without a fuss—and from the first moment I disliked him. He was a difficult child—so far as I was concerned he was always difficult—and demanded far too much attention. Mother was simply silly about him, and couldn't see when he was only showing off. As company he was worse than useless. He slept all day, and I had to go round the house on tiptoe to avoid waking him. It wasn't any longer a question of not waking Father. The slogan now was "Don't-wake-Sonny!" I couldn't understand why the child wouldn't sleep at the proper time, so whenever Mother's back was turned I woke him. Sometimes to keep him awake I pinched him as well. Mother caught me at it one day and gave me a most unmerciful flaking.

One evening, when Father was coming in from work, I was playing trains in the front garden. I let on not to notice him; instead, I pretended to be talking to myself, and said in a loud voice: "If another bloody baby comes into this house, I'm going out."

Father stopped dead and looked at me over his shoulder.

"What's that you said?" he asked sternly.

"I was only talking to myself," I replied, trying to conceal my panic. "It's private."

He turned and went in without a word. Mind you, I intended it as a solemn warning, but its effect was quite different. Father started being quite nice to me. I could understand that, of course. Mother was quite sickening about Sonny. Even at mealtimes she'd get up and gawk at him in the cradle with an idiotic smile, and tell Father to do the same. He was always polite about it, but he looked so puzzled you could see he didn't know what she was talking about. He complained of the way Sonny cried at night, but she only got cross and said that Sonny never cried except when there was something up with him—which

was a flaming lie, because Sonny never had anything up with him, and only cried for attention. It was really painful to see how simple-minded she was. Father wasn't attractive, but he had a fine intelligence. He saw through Sonny, and now he knew that I saw through him as well.

One night I woke with a start. There was someone beside me in the bed. For one wild moment I felt sure it must be Mother, having come to her senses and left Father for good, but then I heard Sonny in convulsions in the next room, and Mother saying: "There! There! There!" and I knew it wasn't she. It was Father. He was lying next to me, wide awake, breathing hard and apparently mad as hell.

After a while it came to me what he was mad about. It was his turn now. After turning me out of the big bed, he had been turned out himself. Mother had no consideration now for anyone but that poisonous pup, Sonny. I couldn't help feeling sorry for Father. I had been through it all myself, and even at that age I was magnanimous. I began to stroke him down and say: "There! There!" He wasn't exactly responsive.

"Aren't you asleep either?" he snarled.

"Ah, come on and put your arm around us, can't you?" I said, and he did, in a sort of way. Gingerly, I suppose, is how you'd describe it. He was very bony but better than nothing. He

At Christmas he went out of his way to buy me a really nice model railway.

1952

Discussion

1. What is the basic source of conflict between father and son in O'Connor's story?

2. Why, according to the narrator, was the war "the most peaceful period" of his life?

3. **(a)** What tactics does the child employ in the battle with his father for the mother's attention? **(b)** How successful is he in these efforts?

4. What happens when the family triangle is squared by the arrival of Sonny?

5. Much of the humor in this story depends on the narrator's innocence and the irony that stems from his naivete. Give some key examples of this.

6. What does the title contribute to the overall effect of the story?

Philip Larkin 1922–

Larkin was born in Coventry and educated at Oxford on a scholarship. His first book of poems, *The North Ship,* while apprentice work, was notably free of the studied bookishness and apocalyptic rhetoric that characterized much English verse in the 1940s. Two novels, *Jill* (1946) and *A Girl in Winter* (1947), followed. While admired by some of Larkin's contemporaries, these early books went largely unnoticed. It was not until *The Less Deceived* (1955), appearing at a time when a reaction to the extravagances of the verse of the 1940s was underway, that Larkin's quiet, anti-romantic style suddenly gained him wide attention and quickly established him as one of the most important postwar English poets.

Larkin has said that the verse of Thomas Hardy, with its commonplace subjects and its quiet pessimistic tone, influenced him greatly. Like Hardy, Larkin typically uses traditional poetic forms, short lines, and a simple, often colloquial, diction. He is not a prolific poet, publishing only two major collections, *The Whitsun*

Weddings (1964) and *High Windows* (1974), since *The Less Deceived;* but the quality of his work has remained high.

In addition to his poetry and novels, Larkin has written jazz criticism for the London *Daily Telegraph* and edited a controversial anthology, *The Oxford Book of Twentieth-Century English Verse* (1973). He is the librarian of the University of Hull, in Yorkshire.

*A*t Grass

The eye can hardly pick them out
From the cold shade they shelter in,
Till wind distresses tail and mane;
Then one crops grass, and moves about
5 —The other seeming to look on—
And stands anonymous again.

Yet fifteen years ago, perhaps
Two dozen distances sufficed
To fable them: faint afternoons
10 Of Cups and Stakes and Handicaps,
Whereby their names were artificed
To inlay faded, classic Junes—

Silks at the start: against the sky
Numbers and parasols: outside,

15 Squadrons of empty cars, and heat,
And littered grass: then the long cry
Hanging unhushed till it subside
To stop-press columns[1] on the street.

Do memories plague their ears like flies?
20 They shake their heads. Dusk brims the shadows.
Summer by summer all stole away,
The starting-gates, the crowds and cries—
All but the unmolesting meadows,
Almanacked, their names live; they

"At Grass" by Philip Larkin from *The Less Deceived,* reprinted by permission of the Marvell Press, England.

1. stop-press columns, containing late-breaking stories in a newspaper, like racing results.

25 Have slipped their names, and stand at ease,
Or gallop for what must be joy,
And not a fieldglass sees them home,
Or curious stop-watch prophesies:
Only the groom, and the groom's boy,
30 With bridles in the evening come.

1955

Discussion

1. Explain how the words "anonymous" and "fabled" define the principal contrast developed in the poem.

2. What details suggest the popularity of horse racing in England?

3. Explain the lines "they / Have slipped their names."

4. Do the retired racehorses seem satisfied with their fate? Cite evidence from the poem to support your answer.

Homage to a Government

Next year we are to bring the soldiers home
For lack of money, and it is all right.
Places they guarded, or kept orderly,
Must guard themselves, and keep themselves
    orderly.
5 We want the money for ourselves at home
Instead of working. And this is all right.

It's hard to say who wanted it to happen,
But now it's been decided nobody minds.
The places are a long way off, not here,

10 Which is all right, and from what we hear
The soldiers there only made trouble happen.
Next year we shall be easier in our minds.

Next year we shall be living in a country
That brought its soldiers home for lack of money.
15 The statues will be standing in the same
Tree-muffled squares, and look nearly the same.
Our children will not know it's a different country.
All we can hope to leave them now is money.

1974

Discussion

1. What historical process is being examined in this poem?

2. What is the reaction of the speaker in the poem to this process?

3. What phrase is repeated (with slight variations) three times in the poem? What effect does this repetition have?

4. Does the poet really intend a "homage"? What is the tone of the poem?

5. Does the poem defend imperialism or attack its critics? Explain.

*T*he Explosion

On the day of the explosion
Shadows pointed towards the pithead:
In the sun the slagheap slept.

Down the lane came men in pitboots
5 Coughing oath-edged talk and pipe-smoke,
Shouldering off the freshened silence.

One chased after rabbits; lost them;
Came back with a nest of lark's eggs;
Showed them; lodged them in the grasses.

10 So they passed in beards and moleskins,
Fathers, brothers, nicknames, laughter,
Through the tall gates standing open.

At noon, there came a tremor; cows
Stopped chewing for a second; sun,
15 Scarfed as in a heat-haze, dimmed.

The dead go on before us, they
Are sitting in God's house in comfort,
We shall see them face to face—

Plain as lettering in the chapels
20 It was said, and for a second
Wives saw men of the explosion

Larger than in life they managed—
Gold as on a coin, or walking
Somehow from the sun towards them,

25 One showing the eggs unbroken.   1974

Discussion

1. Describe the three different scenes pictured in the poem.
2. What truth of human experience does the poem illustrate?
3. (a) What is ironic about the incident with the lark's eggs? (b) What is the meaning of the last line?
4. How do the women react to the words of the funeral service?

Composition

Examine how Larkin uses irony in "Homage to a Government" to display certain attitudes he dislikes.

Write an ironic "homage" to some person or institution.

Ted Hughes 1930–

Ted Hughes was born in Yorkshire and grew up in the West Country. He took a degree at Cambridge, where he was primarily interested in folklore and anthropology. In 1956 he married an American poet, the late Sylvia Plath. His first book of poetry, *The Hawk in the Rain,* appeared the following year.

Much of Hughes's poetry deals with the natural world. He frequently writes of the savagery and cunning of animals and of similar qualities in human beings. His viewpoint is always unsentimental, sometimes to the point of harshness. His work shows a variety of influences: folklore, mythology, anthropology, as well as the poetry of Thomas Hardy, D. H. Lawrence, and Robert Graves.

Hughes's second book of poetry, *Lupercal,* won England's prestigious Hawthornden Prize in 1961. *Wodwo* (1967) was a compilation of both poetry and prose, including short stories and a radio play. *Crow* (1970), a cycle of poems in which Hughes attempts to create a fragmentary mythology centered on a trickster figure drawn from primitive mythology, became something of a best-seller (at least for books of verse).

In addition to verse, Hughes has written a number of plays, and several books for children.

Some critics have attacked Hughes for the grimness of his poetic subject matter and the violence of his language. His admirers contend, however, that his language is vibrant and passionate, and that his recognition of violence in man and nature is a valid perception.

Pike

Pike, three inches long, perfect
Pike in all parts, green tigering the gold.
Killers from the egg: the malevolent aged grin.
They dance on the surface among the flies.

5 Or move, stunned by their own grandeur,
Over a bed of emerald, silhouette
Of submarine delicacy and horror.
A hundred feet long in their world.

In ponds, under the heat-struck lily pads—
10 Gloom of their stillness:

Logged on last year's black leaves, watching
     upwards.
Or hung in an amber cavern of weeds

The jaws' hooked clamp and fangs
Not to be changed at this date;
15 A life subdued to its instrument;
The gills kneading quietly, and the pectorals.

Three we kept behind glass,
Jungled in weed: three inches, four,
And four and a half: fed fry to them—
20 Suddenly there were two. Finally one

With a sag belly and the grin it was born with.
And indeed they spare nobody.
Two, six pounds each, over two feet long,
High and dry and dead in the willow-herb—

25 One jammed past its gills down the other's gullet:
The outside eye stared: as a vice locks—

The same iron in this eye
Though its film shrank in death.

A pond I fished, fifty yards across,
30 Whose lilies and muscular tench
Had outlasted every visible stone
Of the monastery that planted them—

Stilled legendary depth:
It was as deep as England. It held
35 Pike too immense to stir, so immense and old
That past nightfall I dared not cast

But silently cast and fished
With the hair frozen on my head
For what might move, for what eye might move.
40 The still splashes on the dark pond,

Owls hushing the floating woods
Frail on my ear against the dream
Darkness beneath night's darkness had freed,
That rose slowly towards me, watching.
1959

*B*ullfrog

With their lithe, long, strong legs,
Some frogs are able
To thump upon double-
Bass strings, though pond water deadens and clogs.

5 But you, bullfrog, you pump out
Whole fogs full of horn—a threat
As of a liner looming. True
That, first hearing you
Disgorging your gouts of darkness like a wounded god,
10 Not utterly fantastically, I expected
(As in some antique tale depicted)
A broken-down bull up to its belly in mud,
Sucking black swamp up, belching out black cloud

And a squall of gudgeon and lilies.
                                        A surprise

15 Now, to see you, a boy's prize,
No bigger than a rat, with all dumb silence
In your little old woman hands.   1959

Fern

Here is the fern's frond, unfurling a gesture,
Like a conductor whose music will now be pause
And the one note of silence
To which the whole earth dances gravely.

5 The mouse's ear unfurls its trust,
The spider takes up her bequest,
And the retina
Reins the creation with a bridle of water.

And, among them, the fern
10 Dances gravely, like the plume
Of a warrior returning, under the low hills,

Into his own kingdom.

1967

Discussion

Pike

1. Why, though only "three inches long," are baby pike already "a hundred feet long in their world"?

2. How does the line "A life subdued to its instrument" explain the dread pike inspire?

3. (a) What happened to the three pike "kept behind glass"? **(b)** How is their behavior representative of all pike?

4. What is significant about the fishing described in the last four stanzas?

5. What "dream" has darkness "freed" that leaves the poet's hair "frozen on my head" (standing on end)?

Bullfrog

1. (a) Contrast the description of the bullfrog in the first fourteen lines of the poem with that in the last three. **(b)** What is the poet recalling in this poem?

2. (a) To what does the poet compare the noise of the bullfrog? **(b)** To what does the poet compare the bullfrog itself?

Fern

1. (a) What three other natural things does the poet link with the fern's frond? **(b)** What common qualities do these four things share?

2. What words suggest the cyclic "roundness" of the rhythms of nature?

John Mortimer 1923–

Mortimer has had distinguished careers as both a lawyer and a writer. The only child of gifted and affluent parents, he was educated at Harrow and Oxford. When Mortimer was thirteen, his father, a successful lawyer, became totally blind. Since his father was determined to continue his legal practice, Mortimer read aloud to him legal briefs and literature, his initiation into what were to become his dual careers.

In the late 1940s Mortimer began to practice law; his first novels also began to appear: *Charade* (1947), *Rumming Park* (1948), and *Answer Yes or No* (1950). In the mid-1950s he began to write one-act plays for radio. It was the success of his third play, *The Dock Brief* (1957), that caused him to abandon novel writing for plays. *The Dock Brief* won an award for radio drama in 1958 and was later adapted for television and the movies. Mortimer's first full-length play was *The Wrong Side of the Park* (1960), followed by *Two Stars for Comfort* (1962).

During the 1960s Mortimer the lawyer came to be regarded as Britain's foremost legal spokesman for civil rights and free speech. In 1966 he became a Queen's Counsel, the title given to lawyers who appear only in major court cases.

During the late 1970s his two careers memorably combined in the creation of Horace Rumpole, a fictional barrister (a lawyer who pleads cases in an English court; the barrister works with a *solicitor,* who handles the legal research). Rumpole, modeled on Mortimer's father, is an endearing eccentric with a taste for wine, poetry, and pleading. So far Rumpole has appeared in a novel, several collections of short stories, and a television miniseries.

The Dock Brief

Scene One

A cell. The walls are gray and fade upwards into the shadows, so that the ceiling is not seen, and it might even be possible to escape upwards. The door is Right. Back stage is a high, barred window through which the sky looks very blue. Under the window is a stool. Against the Left wall is a bench with a wooden cupboard next to it. On the cupboard a wash basin, a towel, and a Bible.

A small fat prisoner is standing on the stool on tip toes, his hands in his pockets. His eyes are on the sky.

Bolts shoot back. The door opens. MORGEN-HALL *strides in. He is dressed in a black gown and bands, an aged barrister[1] with the appearance of a dusty vulture. He speaks off stage, to the warder.*

MORGENHALL (*to an unseen warder*). Is this where. . . . you keep Mr. Fowle? Good, excellent. Then leave us alone like a kind fellow. Would you mind closing the door? These old places are so drafty.

(*The door closes. The bolts shoot back.*)

Mr. Fowle. . . . Where are you, Mr. Fowle? Not escaped, I pray. Good Heavens man, come down. Come down, Mr. Fowle.

(*He darts at him, and there is a struggle as he pulls down the bewildered* FOWLE.)

I haven't hurt you?

(FOWLE: *negative-sounding noise.*)

I was suddenly anxious. A man in your unfortunate position. Desperate measures. And I couldn't bear to lose you. . . . No, don't stand up. It's difficult for you without braces, or a belt, I can see. And no tie, no shoe-laces. I'm so glad they're looking after you. You must forgive me if I frightened you just a little, Mr. Fowle. It was when I saw you up by that window. . . .

FOWLE (*a hoarse and sad voice*). Epping Forest.

MORGENHALL. What did you say?

FOWLE. I think you can see Epping Forest.

MORGENHALL. No doubt you can. But why, my dear chap, why should you want to?

FOWLE. It's the home stretch.

MORGENHALL. Very well.

FOWLE. I thought I could get a glimpse of the green. Between the chimneys and that shed. . . .

(FOWLE *starts to climb up again. A brief renewed struggle.*)

MORGENHALL. No, get down. It's not wise to be up there, forever trying to look out. There's a drafty, sneeping wind. Treacherous.

FOWLE. Treacherous?

MORGENHALL. I'm afraid so. You never know

what a mean, sneeping wind can do. Catch you by the throat, start a sneeze, then a dry tickle on the chest. I don't want anything to catch you like that before. . . .

FOWLE. Before what?

MORGENHALL. You're much better sitting quietly down there in the warm. Just sit quietly and I'll introduce myself.

FOWLE. I am tired.

MORGENHALL. I'm Wilfred Morgenhall.

FOWLE. Wilfred?

MORGENHALL. Morgenhall. The barrister.

FOWLE. The barrister?

MORGENHALL. Perfectly so. . . .

FOWLE. I'm sorry.

MORGENHALL. Why?

FOWLE. A barrister. That's very bad.

MORGENHALL. I don't know. Why's it so bad?

FOWLE. When a gentleman of your stamp goes wrong. A long fall.

MORGENHALL. What can you mean?

FOWLE. Different for an individual like me. I only kept a small seed shop.

MORGENHALL. Seed shop? My poor fellow. We mustn't let this unfortunate little case confuse us. We're going to remain very calm, very lucid. We're going to come to important decisions. Now, do me a favor, Mr. Fowle, no more seed shops.

FOWLE. Birdseed, of course. Individuals down our way kept birds mostly. Canaries and budgies. The budgies talked. Lot of lonely people down our way. They kept them for the talk.

MORGENHALL. Mr. Fowle. I'm a barrister.

FOWLE. Tragic.

MORGENHALL. I know the law.

FOWLE. It's trapped you.

MORGENHALL. I'm here to help you.

FOWLE. We'll help each other.

(*Pause.*)

MORGENHALL (*laughs uncontrollably*). I see. Mr. Fowle. I see where you've been bewildered. You think I'm in trouble as well. Then I've got good news for you at last. I'm free. Oh yes. I can leave here when I like.

FOWLE. You can?

MORGENHALL. The police are my friends.

---

1. *black gown and bands . . . barrister.* A barrister is a lawyer who can plead in any court. The barrister dresses in a black gown and *bands*, a collar having two strips in front.

FOWLE. They are?

MORGENHALL. And I've never felt better in my life. There now. That's relieved you, hasn't it? I'm not in any trouble.

FOWLE. Family all well?

MORGENHALL. I never married.

FOWLE. Rent paid up?

MORGENHALL. A week or two owing perhaps. Temporary lull in business. This case will end all that.

FOWLE. Which case?

MORGENHALL. Your case.

FOWLE. My. . . .?

MORGENHALL. Case.

FOWLE. Oh that—it's not important.

MORGENHALL. Not?

FOWLE. I don't care about it to any large extent. Not as at present advised.

MORGENHALL. Mr. Fowle. How could you say that?

FOWLE. The flavor's gone out of it.

MORGENHALL. But we're only at the beginning.

FOWLE. I can't believe it's me concerned. . . .

MORGENHALL. But it is you, Mr. Fowle. You mustn't let yourself forget that. You see, that's why you're here. . . .

FOWLE. I can't seem to bother with it.

MORGENHALL. Can you be so busy?

FOWLE. Slopping in, slopping out. Peering at the old forest. It fills in the day.

MORGENHALL. You seem, if I may say so, to have adopted an unpleasantly selfish attitude.

FOWLE. Selfish?

MORGENHALL. Dog in the manger.

FOWLE. In the?

MORGENHALL. Unenthusiastic.

FOWLE. You're speaking quite frankly, I well appreciate. . . .

MORGENHALL. I'm sorry, Fowle. You made me say it. There's so much of this about nowadays. There's so much ready-made entertainment. Free billiards, National Health.[2] Television. There's not the spirit abroad there used to be.

FOWLE. You feel that?

MORGENHALL. Whatever I've done I've always been mustard keen on my work. I've never lost the vision, Fowle. In all my disappointments I've never lost the love of the job.

FOWLE. The position in life you've obtained to.

MORGENHALL. Years of study I had to put in. It didn't just drop in my lap.

FOWLE. I've never studied. . . .

MORGENHALL. Year after year, Fowle, my window at college was alight until two A.M. There I sat among my books. I fed mainly on herrings. . . .

FOWLE. Lean years?

MORGENHALL. And black tea. No subsidized biscuits then, Fowle, no County Council tobacco, just work. . . .

FOWLE. Book work, almost entirely? I'm only assuming that, of course.

MORGENHALL. Want to hear some Latin?

FOWLE. Only if you have time.

MORGENHALL. Actus non sit reus nisi mens sit rea. Filius nullius. In flagrante delicto.[3] Understand it?

FOWLE. I'm no scholar.

MORGENHALL. You most certainly are not. But I had to be, we all had to be in my day. Then we'd sit for the examinations, Mods, Smalls, Greats, Tripos, Little Goes,[4] week after week, rowing men fainting, Indian students vomiting with fear, and no creeping out for a peep at the book under the pretext of a pump ship or getting a glance at the other fellow's celluloid cuff. . . .

FOWLE. That would be unheard of?

MORGENHALL. Then weeks, months of waiting. Nerve racking. Go up to the Lake District. Pace the mountains, play draughts, forget to huff. Then comes the fatal postcard.

FOWLE. What's it say?

MORGENHALL. Satisfied the examiners.

FOWLE. At last!

MORGENHALL. Don't rejoice so soon. True enough I felt I'd turned a corner, got a fur hood, bumped on the head with a Bible. Bachelor of Law sounded sweet in my ears. I thought of celebrating, a few kindred spirits round for a light ale. Told the only lady in my life that in five years' time perhaps. . . .

FOWLE. You'd arrived.

MORGENHALL. That's what I thought when they

---

2. **National Health,** the British public health system, created by the Labour government in 1946.

3. **Actus . . . delicto,** Latin legal jargon. The last phrase means "in the very act" (literally, "while the crime is blazing").

4. **Mods . . . Little Goes,** various examinations at Oxford and Cambridge.

painted my name up on my London chambers. I sat down to fill in the time until they sent my first brief in a real case. I sat down to do the crossword puzzle while I waited. Five years later, Fowle, what was I doing. . . .

FOWLE. A little charge of High Treason?

MORGENHALL. I was still doing the crossword puzzle.

FOWLE. But better at it?

MORGENHALL. Not much. Not very much. As the years pass there come to be clues you no longer understand.

FOWLE. So all that training?

MORGENHALL. Wasted. The talents rust.

FOWLE. And the lady?

MORGENHALL. Drove an ambulance in the 1914.[5] A stray piece of shrapnel took her. I don't care to talk of it.

FOWLE. Tragic.

MORGENHALL. What was?

FOWLE. Tragic my wife was never called up.

MORGENHALL. You mustn't talk like that, Fowle, your poor wife.

FOWLE. Don't let's carry on about me.

MORGENHALL. But we must carry on about you. That's what I'm here for.

FOWLE. You're here to?

MORGENHALL. Defend you.

FOWLE. Can't be done.

MORGENHALL. Why ever not?

FOWLE. I know who killed her.

MORGENHALL. Who?

FOWLE. Me.

(Pause.)

MORGENHALL *(considerable thought before he says).* Mr. Fowle, I have all the respect in the world for your opinions, but we must face this. You're a man of very little education. . . .

FOWLE. That's true.

MORGENHALL. One has only to glance at you. At those curious lobes to your ears. At the line of your hair. At the strange way your eyebrows connect in the middle, to see that you're a person of very limited intelligence.

FOWLE. Agreed, quite frankly.

MORGENHALL. You think you killed your wife.

FOWLE. Seems so to me.

MORGENHALL. Mr. Fowle. Look at yourself objectively. On questions of birdseed I have no doubt you may be infallible—but on a vital

point like this might you not be mistaken. . . . Don't answer. . . .

FOWLE. Why not, sir?

MORGENHALL. Before you drop the bomb of a reply, consider who will be wounded. Are the innocent to suffer?

FOWLE. I only want to be honest.

MORGENHALL. But you're a criminal, Mr. Fowle. You've broken through the narrow fabric of honesty. You are free to be kind, human, to do good.

FOWLE. But what I did to her. . . .

MORGENHALL. She's passed, you know, out of your life. You've set up new relationships. You've picked out me.

FOWLE. Picked out?

MORGENHALL. Selected.

FOWLE. But I didn't know. . . .

MORGENHALL. No, Mr. Fowle. That's the whole beauty of it. You didn't know me. You came to me under a system of chance invented, like the football pools, to even out the harsh inequality of a world where you have to deserve success. You, Mr. Fowle, are my first Dock Brief.

FOWLE. Your Dock?

MORGENHALL. Brief.

FOWLE. You couldn't explain?

MORGENHALL. Of course. Prisoners with no money and no friends exist. Luckily, you're one of them. They're entitled to choose any barrister sitting in Court to defend them. The barrister, however old, gets a brief, and is remunerated on a modest scale. Busy lawyers, wealthy lawyers, men with other interests, creep out of Court bent double when the Dock Brief is chosen. We regulars who are not busy sit on. I've been a regular for years. It's not etiquette, you see, even if you want the work, to wave at the prisoner, or whistle, or try to catch his eye by hoisting any sort of little flag.

FOWLE. Didn't know.

MORGENHALL. But you *can* choose the most advantageous seat. The seat any criminal would naturally point at. It's the seat under the window and for ten years my old friend Tuppy Morgan bagged it each day at ten. He sat there, reading Horace, and writing to his innumerable aunts, and almost once a year a

---

5. *1914,* the First World War.

criminal pointed him out. Oh, Mr. Fowle, Tuppy was a limpet on that seat. But this morning, something, possibly a cold, perhaps death, kept him indoors. So I had his place. And you spotted me, no doubt.

FOWLE. Spotted you?

MORGENHALL. My glasses polished. My profile drawn and learned in front of the great window.

A scene from a 1962 film based on *The Dock Brief*, starring Peter Sellers as Morgenhall and Richard Attenborough as Fowle.

FOWLE. I never noticed.

MORGENHALL. But when they asked you to choose a lawyer?

FOWLE. I shut my eyes and pointed—I've picked horses that way, and football teams. Never did me any good, though, by any stretch of the imagination.

MORGENHALL. So even you, Mr. Fowle, didn't choose me?

FOWLE. Not altogether.

MORGENHALL. The law's a haphazard business.

FOWLE. It does seem chancy.

MORGENHALL. Years of training, and then to be picked out like a football pool.

FOWLE. Don't take it badly, sir.

MORGENHALL. Of course, you've been fortunate.

FOWLE. So unusual. I was never one to draw the free bird at Christmas, or guess the weight of the cake. Now I'm sorry I told you.

MORGENHALL. Never mind. You hurt me temporarily, Fowle, I must confess. It might have been kinder to have kept me in ignorance. But now it's done. Let's get down to business. And, Fowle—

FOWLE. Yes, sir.

MORGENHALL. Remember you're dealing with a fellow man. A man no longer young. Remember the hopes I've pinned on you and try. . . .

FOWLE. Try?

MORGENHALL. Try to spare me more pain.

FOWLE. I will, sir. Of course I will.

MORGENHALL. Now. Let's get our minds in order.

FOWLE. Sort things out.

MORGENHALL. Exactly. Now, this wife of yours.

FOWLE. Doris?

MORGENHALL. Doris. A bitter, unsympathetic woman?

FOWLE. She was always cheerful. She loved jokes.

MORGENHALL. Oh, Fowle. Do be very careful.

FOWLE. I will, sir. But if you'd known Doris. . . . She laughed harder than she worked. "Thank God," she'd say, "for my old English sense of fun."

MORGENHALL. What sort of jokes, Fowle, did this Doris appreciate?

FOWLE. All sorts. Pictures in the paper. Jokes on the wireless set. Laughs out of crackers,[6] she'd keep them from Christmas to Christmas and trot them out in August.

MORGENHALL. You couldn't share it?

FOWLE. Not to that extent. I often missed the funny point.

MORGENHALL. Then you'd quarrel?

FOWLE. "Don't look so miserable, it may never happen." She said that every night when I came home. "Where'd you get that miserable expression from?"

MORGENHALL. I can see it now. There is a kind of Sunday evening appearance to you.

FOWLE. I was quite happy. But it was always "Cat got your tongue?" "Where's the funeral?" "Play us a tune on that old fiddle face of yours. Lucky there's one of us here that can see the funny side." Then we had to have our tea with the wireless on, so that she'd pick up the phrases.

MORGENHALL. You're not a wireless lover?

FOWLE. I couldn't always laugh. And she'd be doubled up across the table, gasping as if her lungs were full of water. "Laugh," she'd call, "Laugh, damn you. What've you got to be so miserable about?" Then she'd go under, bubbling like a drowning woman.

MORGENHALL. Made meals difficult?

FOWLE. Indigestible. I would have laughed, but the jokes never tickled me.

MORGENHALL. They tickled her?

FOWLE. Anything did. Anything a little comic. Our names were misfortunate.

MORGENHALL. Your names?

FOWLE. Fowle. Going down the aisle she said: "Now we're cock and hen, aren't we, old bird?" Coming away, it was "Now I'm Mrs. Fowle, you'll have to play fair with me." She laughed so hard we couldn't get her straightened up for the photograph.

MORGENHALL. Fond of puns, I gather you're trying to say.

FOWLE. Of any sort of joke. I had a little aviary at the bottom of my garden. As she got funnier so I spent more time with my birds. Budgerigars are small parrots. Circles round their eyes give them a sad, tired look.

MORGENHALL. You found them sympathetic?

FOWLE. Restful. Until one of them spoke out at me.

MORGENHALL. Spoke—what words?

FOWLE. "Don't look so miserable, it may never happen."

MORGENHALL. The bird said that?

FOWLE. She taught it during the day when I was out at work. It didn't mean to irritate.

MORGENHALL. It was wrong of her of course. To lead on your bird like that.

---

6. *crackers,* Christmas crackers, tiny firecrackers.

FOWLE. But it wasn't him that brought me to it. It was Bateson, the lodger.

MORGENHALL. Another man?

FOWLE. At long last.

MORGENHALL. I can see it now. A crime of passion. An unfaithful wife. *In flagrante.* . . . Of course, you don't know what that means. We'll reduce it to manslaughter right away. A wronged husband and there's never a dry eye in the jury-box. You came in and caught them.

FOWLE. Always laughing together.

MORGENHALL. Maddening.

FOWLE. He knew more jokes than she did.

MORGENHALL. Stealing her before your eyes?

FOWLE. That's what I thought. He was a big man. Ex-police. Said he'd been the scream of the station. I picked him for her specially. In the chitty I put up in the local sweet shop, I wrote: "Humorous type of lodger wanted."

MORGENHALL. But wasn't that a risk?

FOWLE. Slight, perhaps. But it went all right. Two days after he came he poised a bag of flour to fall on her in the kitchen. Then she sewed up the legs of his pajamas. They had to hold on to each other so as not to fall over laughing. "Look at old misery standing there," she said. "He can never see anything subtle."

MORGENHALL. Galling for you. Terribly galling.

FOWLE. I thought all was well. I spent more time with the birds. I'd come home late and always be careful to scrunch the gravel at the front door. I went to bed early and left them with the Light Program. On Sunday mornings I fed the budgies and suggested he took her tea in bed. "Laughter," she read out from her horoscope, "leads to love, even for those born under the sign of the Virgin."

MORGENHALL. You trusted them. They deceived you.

FOWLE. They deceived me all right. And I trusted them. Especially after I'd seen her on his knee and them both looking at the cartoons from one wrapping of chips.[7]

MORGENHALL. Mr. Fowle. I'm not quite getting the drift of your evidence. My hope is—your thought may not prove a shade too involved for our literal-minded judge. Old Tommy Banter was a Rugger blue in '98.[8] He never rose to

chess and his draughts had a brutal, unintelligent quality.

FOWLE. When he'd first put his knee under her I thought he'd do the decent thing. I thought I'd have peace in my little house at last. The wireless set dead silent. The end of all that happy laughter. No sound but the twitter from the end of the garden and the squeak of my own foot on the linoleum.

MORGENHALL. You wanted. . . .

FOWLE. I heard them whispering together and my hopes raised high. Then I came back and he was gone.

MORGENHALL. She'd. . . .

FOWLE. Turned him out. Because he was getting over familiar. "I couldn't have that," she said. "I may like my laugh, but thank God, I'm still respectable. No thank you, there's safety in marriage. So I'm stuck with you, fiddle face. Let's play a tune on it, shall we?" She'd sent him away, my last hope.

MORGENHALL. So you. . . .

FOWLE. I realize I did wrong.

MORGENHALL. You could have left.

FOWLE. Who'd have fed the birds? That thought was uppermost.

MORGENHALL. So it's not a crime of passion?

FOWLE. Not if you put it like that.

MORGENHALL. Mr. Fowle. I've worked and waited for you. Now, you're the only case I've got, *and* the most difficult.

FOWLE. I'm sorry.

MORGENHALL. A man could crack his head against a case like you and still be far from a solution. Can't you see how twelve honest hearts will snap like steel when they learn you ended up your wife because she *wouldn't* leave you?

FOWLE. If she had left, there wouldn't have been the need.

MORGENHALL. There's no doubt about it. As I look at you now, I see you're an unsympathetic figure.

FOWLE. There it is.

MORGENHALL. It'll need a brilliant stroke to save you. An unexpected move—something pulled out of a hat—I've got it. Something really exciting. The surprise witness.

---

7. *chips,* French fries (wrapped in newspaper).
8. *Rugger blue in '98,* a varsity rugby player.

FOWLE. Witness?

MORGENHALL. Picture the scene, Mr. Fowle. The Court room silent. The jury about to sink you. The prosecution flushed with victory. And then I rise, my voice a hoarse whisper, exhausted by that long trial. "My Lord. If your Lordship pleases."

FOWLE. What are you saying?

MORGENHALL. Do you expect me to do this off the cuff, Fowle, with no sort of rehearsal?

FOWLE. No. . . .

MORGENHALL. Take the stool and co-operate, man. Now, that towel over your head, please, to simulate the dirty gray wig—already you appear anonymous and vaguely alarming.

(MORGENHALL *arranges* FOWLE *on the stool. Drapes the towel over his head.*)

Now, my dear Fowle, forget your personality. You're Sir Tommy Banter, living with a widowed sister in a draughty great morgue on Wimbledon Common. Digestion, bad. Politics, an independent moral conservative. Favorite author, doesn't read. Diversions, snooker in the basement of the morgue, peeping at the lovers on the Common and money being given away on the television. In love with capital punishment, corporal punishment, and a younger brother who is accomplished at embroidery. A small, alarmed man, frightened of the great dog he lives with to give him the air of a country squire. Served with distinction in the Great War at sentencing soldiers to long terms of imprisonment. A man without friends, unexpectedly adored by a great-niece, three years old.

FOWLE. I am?

MORGENHALL. Him.

FOWLE. It feels strange.

MORGENHALL. Now, my Lord. I ask your Lordship's leave to call the surprise witness.

FOWLE. Certainly.

MORGENHALL. What?

FOWLE. Certainly.

MORGENHALL. For Heaven's sake, Fowle, this is like practicing bull-fights with a kitten. Here's an irregular application by the defense, something that might twist the trial in the prisoner's favor and prevent you catching the connection at Charing Cross.[9] Your breakfast's like a leadweight on your chest, your sister, plunging at

Spot last night, ripped the cloth. The dog bit your ankle on the way downstairs. No, blind yourself with rage and terrible justice.

FOWLE. No. You can't call the surprise witness.

MORGENHALL. That's better. Oh, my Lord. If your Lordship would listen to me.

FOWLE. Certainly not. You've had your chance. Let's get on with it.

MORGENHALL. My Lord. Justice must not only be done, but must clearly be seen to be done. No one knows, as yet, what my surprise witness will say. Perhaps he'll say the prisoner is guilty in his black heart as your Lordship thinks. But perhaps, gentlemen of the jury, we have trapped an innocent. If so, shall we deny him the one door through which he might walk to freedom? The public outcry would never die down.

FOWLE (*snatching off the towel and rising angrily to his feet*). Hear, hear!

MORGENHALL. What's that?

FOWLE. The public outcry.

MORGENHALL. Excellent. Now, towel back on. You're the judge.

FOWLE (*as the Judge*). Silence! I'll have all those noisy people put out. Very well. Call the witness. But keep it short.

MORGENHALL. Wonderful. Very good. Now. Deathly silence as the witness walks through the breathless crowds. Let's see the surprise witness. Take the towel off.

FOWLE (*moves from the stool and, standing very straight says*). I swear to tell the truth. . . .

MORGENHALL. You've got a real feeling for the Law. A pity you came to it so late in life.

FOWLE. The whole truth.

MORGENHALL. Now, what's your name?

FOWLE (*absent minded*). Herbert Fowle.

MORGENHALL. No, no. You're the witness.

FOWLE. Martin Jones.

MORGENHALL. Excellent. Now, you know Herbert Fowle?

FOWLE. All my life.

MORGENHALL. Always found him respectable?

FOWLE. Very quiet spoken man, and clean living.

---

9. **Charing Cross,** a London train station.

MORGENHALL. Where was he when this crime took place?

FOWLE. He was. . . .

MORGENHALL. Just a moment. My Lord, will you sharpen a pencil and note this down?

FOWLE. You'd dare to say that? To him?

MORGENHALL. Fearlessness, Mr. Fowle. The first essential in an advocate. Is your Lordship's pencil poised?

FOWLE (as Judge). Yes, yes. Get on with it.

MORGENHALL. Where was he?

FOWLE (as Witness). In my house.

MORGENHALL. All the evening?

FOWLE. Playing whist. I went to collect him and we left Mrs. Fowle well and happy. I returned with him and she'd been removed to the Country and General.

MORGENHALL. Panic stirs the prosecution benches. The prosecutor tries a few fumbling questions. But you stand your ground, don't you?

FOWLE. Certainly.

MORGENHALL. My Lord. I demand the prisoner be released.

FOWLE (as Judge). Certainly. Can't think what all this fuss has been about. Release the prisoner, and reduce all police officers in Court to the rank of P.C.

(Pause.)

MORGENHALL. Fowle.

FOWLE. Yes, sir.

MORGENHALL. Aren't you going to thank me?

FOWLE. I don't know what I can say.

MORGENHALL. Words don't come easily to you, do they?

FOWLE. Very hard.

MORGENHALL. You could just stand and stammer in a touching way and offer me that old gold watch of your father's.

FOWLE. But. . . .

MORGENHALL. Well, I think we've pulled your chestnut out of the fire. We'll just have to make sure of this fellow Jones.

FOWLE. But. . . .

MORGENHALL. Fowle, you're a good simple chap, but there's no need to interrupt my thinking.

FOWLE. I was only reminding you. . . .

MORGENHALL. Well, what?

FOWLE. We have no Jones.

MORGENHALL. Carried off in a cold spell? Then

we can get his statement in under the Evidence Act.

FOWLE. He never lived. We made him up.

(Pause.)

MORGENHALL. Fowle.

FOWLE. Yes, sir.

MORGENHALL. It's a remarkable thing, but with no legal training, I think you've put your finger on a fatal weakness in our defense.

FOWLE. I was afraid it might be so.

MORGENHALL. It is so.

FOWLE. Then we'd better just give in.

MORGENHALL. Give in? We do not give in. When my life depends on this case.

FOWLE. I forgot. Then, we must try.

MORGENHALL. Yes. Brain! Brain! Go to work. It'll come to me, you know, in an illuminating flash. Hard, relentless brain work. This is the way I go at the crosswords and I never give up. I have it. Bateson!

FOWLE. The lodger?

MORGENHALL. Bateson, the lodger. I never liked him. Under a ruthless cross-examination, you know, he might confess that it was he. Do you see a flash?

FOWLE. You look much happier.

MORGENHALL. I am much happier. And when I begin my ruthless cross-examination. . . .

FOWLE. Would you care to try it?

MORGENHALL. Mr. Fowle. You and I are learning to muck in splendidly together over this. Mr. Bateson.

FOWLE (as Bateson, lounging in an imaginary witness box with his hands in his pockets). Yes. Sir?

MORGENHALL. Perhaps, when you address the Court you'd be good enough to take your hands out of your pockets. Not you Mr. Fowle, of course. You became on very friendly terms with the prisoner's wife?

FOWLE. We had one or two good old laughs together.

MORGENHALL. Was the association entirely innocent?

FOWLE. Innocent laughs. Jokes without offense. The cracker or Christmas card variety. No jokes that would have shamed a postcard.

MORGENHALL. And to tell those innocent jokes, did you have to sit very close to Mrs. Fowle?

FOWLE. How do you mean?

MORGENHALL. Did you have to sit beneath her?

FOWLE. I don't understand.

MORGENHALL. Did she perch upon your knee?

FOWLE (horrified intake of breath).

MORGENHALL. What was that?

FOWLE. Shocked breathing from the jury, sir.

MORGENHALL. Having its effect, eh? Now, Mr. Bateson. Will you kindly answer my question.

FOWLE. You're trying to trap me.

MORGENHALL. Not trying, Bateson, succeeding.

FOWLE. Well, she may have rested on my knee. Once or twice.

MORGENHALL. And you loved her, guiltily?

FOWLE. I may have done.

MORGENHALL. And planned to take her away with you?

FOWLE. I did ask her.

MORGENHALL. And when she refused. . . .

FOWLE (as Judge). Just a moment. Where's all this leading?

MORGENHALL. Your Lordship asks me! My Lord, it is our case that it was this man, Bateson, enraged by the refusal of the prisoner's wife to follow him, who struck. . . . You see where we've got to?

FOWLE. I do.

MORGENHALL. Masterly. I think you'll have to agree with me?

FOWLE. Of course.

MORGENHALL. No flaws in this one?

FOWLE. Not really a flaw, sir. Perhaps a little hitch.

MORGENHALL. A hitch. Go on. Break it down.

FOWLE. No, sir, really. Not after you've been so kind.

MORGENHALL. Never mind. All my life I've stood against the winds of criticism and neglect. My gown may be a little tattered, my cuffs frayed. There may be a hole in my sock for the drafts to get at me. Quite often, on my way to Court, I notice that my left shoe lets in water. I am used to hardship. Speak on, Mr. Fowle.

FOWLE. Soon as he left my house, Bateson was stopped by an officer. He'd lifted an alarm clock off me, and the remains of a bottle of port. They booked him straight away.

MORGENHALL. You mean, there wasn't time?

FOWLE. Hardly. Two hours later the next door observed Mrs. Fowle at the washing. Then I came home.

MORGENHALL. Fowle. Do you want to help me?

FOWLE. Of course. Haven't I shown it?

MORGENHALL. But you will go on putting all these difficulties in my way.

FOWLE. I knew you'd be upset.

MORGENHALL. Not really. After all, I'm a grown up, even an old man. At my age one expects little gratitude. There's a cat I feed each day at my lodgings, a waitress in the lunch room here who always gets that sixpence under my plate. In ten, twenty years' time, will they remember me? Oh, I'm not bitter. But a little help, just a very little encouragement. . . .

FOWLE. But you'll win this case. A brilliant mind like yours.

MORGENHALL. Yes. Thank God. It's very brilliant.

FOWLE. And all that training.

MORGENHALL. Years of it. Hard, hard training.

FOWLE. You'll solve it, sir.

(Pause.)

MORGENHALL. Fowle. Do you know what I've heard Tuppy Morgan say? After all, he's sat here, year in, year out, as long as anyone can remember, in Court, waiting for the Dock Brief himself. Wilfred, he's frequently told me, if they ever give you a brief, old fellow, attack the medical evidence. Remember, the jury's full of rheumatism and arthritis and shocking gastric troubles. They love to see a medical man put through it. Always go for a doctor.

FOWLE (eagerly). You'd like to try?

MORGENHALL. Shall we?

FOWLE. I'd enjoy it.

MORGENHALL. Doctor. Did you say the lady died of heart failure?

FOWLE (as Doctor). No.

MORGENHALL. Come, Doctor. Don't fence with me. Her heart wasn't normal when you examined her, was it?

FOWLE. She was dead.

MORGENHALL. So it had stopped.

FOWLE. Yes.

MORGENHALL. Then her heart had failed?

FOWLE. Well. . . .

MORGENHALL. So she died of heart failure?

FOWLE. But. . . .

MORGENHALL. And heart failure might have been

brought on by a fit, I say a fit of laughter, at a curiously rich joke on the wireless?

FOWLE. Whew.

(FOWLE claps softly. Pause.)

MORGENHALL. Thank you, Fowle. It was kind but, I thought, hollow. I don't believe my attack on the doctor was convincing.

FOWLE. Perhaps a bit unlikely. But clever. . . .

MORGENHALL. Too clever. No. We're not going to win this on science, Fowle. Science must be thrown away. As I asked those questions, I saw I wasn't even convincing you of your own innocence. But you respond to emotion, Fowle, as I do, the magic of oratory, the wonderful power of words.

FOWLE. Now you're talking.

MORGENHALL. I'm going to talk.

FOWLE. I wish I could hear some of it. Words as grand as print.

MORGENHALL. A golden tongue. A voice like a lyre to charm you out of hell.

FOWLE. Now you've commenced to wander away from all I've understood.

MORGENHALL. I was drawing on the riches of my classical education which comforts me on buses, waiting at surgeries, or in prison cells. But I shall speak to the jury simply, without classical allusions. I shall say. . . .

FOWLE. Yes.

MORGENHALL. I shall say. . . .

FOWLE. What?

MORGENHALL. I had it on the tip of my tongue.

FOWLE. Oh.

MORGENHALL. I shan't disappoint you. I shall speak for a day, perhaps two days. At the end I shall say. . . .

FOWLE. Yes. Just the closing words.

MORGENHALL. The closing words.

FOWLE. To clinch the argument.

MORGENHALL. Yes. The final, irrefutable argument.

FOWLE. If I could only hear.

MORGENHALL. You shall, Fowle. You shall hear it. In Court. It'll come out in Court, and when I sink back in my seat, trembling, and wipe the real tears off my glasses. . . .

FOWLE. The judge's summing up.

MORGENHALL. What will Tommy say?

FOWLE *(as Judge).* Members of the jury. . . .

MORGENHALL. Struggling with emotion as well.

FOWLE. I can't add anything to the words of the barrister. Go out and consider your verdict.

MORGENHALL. Have they left the box?

FOWLE. Only a formality.

MORGENHALL. I see. I wonder how long they'll be out. *(Pause.)* They're out a long time.

FOWLE. Of course, it must seem long to you. The suspense.

MORGENHALL. I hope they won't disagree.

FOWLE. I don't see how they can.

(Pause.)

MORGENHALL. Fowle.

FOWLE. Yes, sir.

MORGENHALL. Shall we just take a peep into the jury room.

FOWLE. I wish we could.

MORGENHALL. Let's. Let me see, you're the foreman?

FOWLE. I take it we're all agreed, chaps. So let's sit here and have a short smoke.

(They sit on the bench together.)

MORGENHALL. An excellent idea. The barrister saved him.

FOWLE. That wonderful speech. I had a bit of doubt before I heard the speech.

MORGENHALL. No doubt now, have you?

FOWLE. Certainly not.

(They light imaginary pipes.)

Care for a fill of mine?

MORGENHALL. Thank you so much. Match?

FOWLE. Here you are.

MORGENHALL. I say, you don't think the poor fellow's in any doubt, do you?

FOWLE. No. He must know he'll get off. After the speech I mean.

MORGENHALL. I mean, I wouldn't like him to be on pins. . . .

FOWLE. Think we ought to go back and reassure him?

(They move off the bench.)

MORGENHALL. As you wish. Careful that pipe doesn't start a fire in your pocket. *(As Clerk of Court).* Gentlemen of the jury. Have you considered your verdict?

FOWLE. We have.

MORGENHALL. And do you find the prisoner guilty or not guilty?

FOWLE. Not guilty, my Lord.

MORGENHALL. Hooray!

FOWLE *(as Judge).* Now, if there's any sort of

Mafeking around,[10] I'll have the Court closed.

MORGENHALL. So I'm surrounded, mobbed. Tuppy Morgan wrings my hand and says it was lucky he left the seat. The judge sends me a letter of congratulation. The journalists dart off to their little telephones. And what now: "Of course they'd make you a judge but you're probably too busy. . . ." There's a queue of solicitors on the stairs. . . . My old clerk writes on my next brief, a thousand guineas to divorce a duchess. There are questions of new clothes, laying down the port. Oh, Mr. Fowle, the change in life you've brought me.

FOWLE. It will be your greatest day.

MORGENHALL. Yes, Mr. Fowle. My greatest day.

(The bolts shoot back, the door opens slowly.)

What's that? I said we weren't to be interrupted. It's drafty in here with that door open. Close it, there's a good chap, do.

FOWLE. I think, you know, they must want us for the trial.

(FOWLE goes through the door. MORGENHALL follows with a dramatic sweep of his gown.)

The curtain falls.

Scene Two

When the curtain rises again the sky through the windows shows that it is late afternoon. The door is unlocked and MORGENHALL enters. He is without his wig and gown. More agitated than ever, he speaks to the Warder, off stage.

MORGENHALL. He's not here at the moment—he's not. . . .? Oh, I'm so glad. Just out temporarily? With the governor? Then, I'll wait for him. Poor soul. How's he taking it? You're not allowed to answer questions? The regulations, I suppose. Well, you must obey the regulations. I'll just sit down here and wait for Mr. Fowle.

(The door closes.)

(He whistles. Whistling stops.) May it please you, my Lord, *members* of the jury. I should have said, may it please you, my *Lord,* members of the jury. I should have said. . . .

(He begins to walk up and down.)

Members of the jury. Is there one of you who doesn't crave for peace . . . crave for peace. The silence of an undisturbed life, the dignity of an existence without dependents . . . without jokes. Have you never been tempted?

I should have said. . . .

Members of the *jury.* You and I are men of the world. If your Lordship would kindly not interrupt my speech to the jury. I'm obliged. Members of the jury, before I was so rudely interrupted.

I might have said. . . .

Look at the prisoner, members of the jury. Has he hurt you, done you the slightest harm? Is he not the mildest of men? He merely took it upon himself to regulate his domestic affairs. An Englishman's home is his castle. Do any of you feel a primitive urge, members of the jury, to be revenged on this gentle bird fancier. . . .

Members of the jury, I see I'm affecting your emotions but let us consider the weight of the evidence . . .

I might have said that!

I might have said. . . . *(with distress)* I might have said something. . . .

(The door opens. FOWLE enters. He is smiling to himself, but as soon as he sees MORGENHALL he looks serious and solicitous.)

FOWLE. I was hoping you'd find time to drop in, sir. I'm afraid you're upset.

MORGENHALL. No, no, my dear chap. Not at all upset.

FOWLE. The result of the trial's upset you.

MORGENHALL. I feel a little dashed. A little out of sorts.

FOWLE. It was disappointing for you.

MORGENHALL. A touch of disappointment. But there'll be other cases. There may be other cases.

FOWLE. But you'd built such high hopes on this particular one.

---

10. **Mafeking** (maf′ə king) **around,** celebrating boisterously, as the British did on May 17, 1900, when word arrived of the relief of the town of Mafeking in South Africa during the Boer War.

MORGENHALL. Well, there it is, Fowle.

FOWLE. It doesn't do to expect too much of a particular thing.

MORGENHALL. You're right, of course.

FOWLE. Year after year I used to look forward keenly to the feathered friends fanciers' annual do. Invariably it took the form of a dinner.

MORGENHALL. Your yearly treat?

FOWLE. Exactly. All I had in the enjoyment line. Each year I built high hopes on it. June 13th, I'd say, now there's an evening to look forward to.

MORGENHALL. Something to live for?

FOWLE. In a way. But when it came, you know, it was never up to it. Your collar was always too tight, or the food was inadequate, or someone had a nasty scene with the fancier in the chair. So, on June 14th, I always said to myself: Thank God for a night at home.

MORGENHALL. It came and went and your life didn't change?

FOWLE. No, quite frankly.

MORGENHALL. And this case has left me just as I was before.

FOWLE. Don't say that.

MORGENHALL. Tuppy Morgan's back in his old seat under the window. The judge never congratulated me. No one's rung up to offer me a brief. I thought my old clerk looked coldly at me, and there was a titter in the luncheon room when I ordered my usual roll and tomato soup.

FOWLE. But I. . . .

MORGENHALL. And you're not left in a very favorable position.

FOWLE. Don't say that, sir. It's not so bad for me. After all, I had no education.

MORGENHALL. So many years before I could master the Roman Law relating to the ownership of chariots. . . .

FOWLE. Wasted, you think?

MORGENHALL. I feel so.

FOWLE. But without that rich background, would an individual have been able to sway the Court as you did?

MORGENHALL. Sway?

FOWLE. The Court.

MORGENHALL. Did I do that?

FOWLE. It struck me you did.

MORGENHALL. Indeed. . . .

FOWLE. It's turned out masterly.

MORGENHALL. Mr. Fowle, you're trying to be kind. When I was a child I played French cricket with an uncle who deliberately allowed the ball to strike his legs. At the age of seven that irked me. At sixty-three I can face the difficulties of accurate batting. . . .

FOWLE. But no, sir. I really mean it. I owe it all to you. Where I am.

MORGENHALL. I'm afraid near the end.

FOWLE. Just commencing.

MORGENHALL. I lost, Mr. Fowle. You may not be aware of it. It may not have been hammered home to you yet. But your case is lost.

FOWLE. But there are ways and ways of losing.

MORGENHALL. That's true, of course.

FOWLE. I noticed your artfulness right at the start, when the policeman gave evidence. You pulled out that red handkerchief, slowly and deliberately, like a conjuring trick.

MORGENHALL. And blew?

FOWLE. A sad, terrible trumpet.

MORGENHALL. Unnerved him, I thought.

FOWLE. He never recovered. There was no call to ask questions after that.

MORGENHALL. And then they called that doctor.

FOWLE. You were right not to bother with him.

MORGENHALL. Tactics, you see. We'd decided not to trouble with science.

FOWLE. So we had. And with Bateson. . . .

MORGENHALL. No, Fowle. I must beware of your flattery, I think I might have asked Bateson. . . .

FOWLE. It wouldn't have made a farthing's difference. A glance told them he was a demon.

MORGENHALL. He stood there, so big and red, with his no tie and dirty collar. I rose up to question him and suddenly it seemed as if there were no reason for us to converse. I remembered what you said about his jokes, his familiarity with your wife. What had he and I in common? I turned from him in disgust. I think that jury guessed the reason for my silence with friend Bateson.

FOWLE. I think they did!

MORGENHALL. But when it came to the speech.

FOWLE. The best stroke of all.

MORGENHALL. I can't agree. You no longer carry me with you.

FOWLE. Said from the heart.

MORGENHALL. I'm sure of it. But not, dare I say, altogether justified? We can't pretend, can we, Mr. Fowle, that the speech was a success?

FOWLE. It won the day.

MORGENHALL. I beg you not to be under any illusions. They found you guilty.

FOWLE. I was forgetting. But that masterly speech . . .

MORGENHALL. I can't be hoodwinked.

FOWLE. But you don't know. . . .

MORGENHALL. I stood up, Mr. Fowle, and it was the moment I'd waited for. Ambition had driven me to it, the moment when I was alone with what I wanted. Everyone turned to me, twelve blank faces in the jury box, eager to have the grumpy looks wiped off them. The judge was silent. The prosecutor courteously pretended to be asleep. I only had to open my mouth and pour words out. What stopped me?

FOWLE. What?

MORGENHALL. Fear. That's what's suggested. That's what the clerks tittered to the waitresses in Friday's luncheon room. Old Wilf Morgenhall was in a funk.

FOWLE. More shame on them. . . .

MORGENHALL. But it wasn't so. Nor did my mind go blank. When I rose I knew exactly what I was going to say.

FOWLE. Then, why?

MORGENHALL. Not say it—you were going to say?

FOWLE. It had struck me—

MORGENHALL. It must have, Fowle. It must have struck many people. You'll forgive a reminiscence. . . .

FOWLE. Glad of one.

MORGENHALL. The lady I happened to mention yesterday. I don't of course, often speak of her. . . .

FOWLE. She, who, in the 1914. . . .?

MORGENHALL. Exactly. But I lost her long before that. For years, you know, Mr. Fowle, this particular lady and I met at tea parties, tennis, and so on. Then, one evening, I walked home with her. We stood on Vauxhall Bridge, a warm Summer night, and silence fell. It was the moment when I should have spoken, the obvious moment. Then, something overcame me, it wasn't shyness or fear then, but a tre-

mendous exhaustion. I was tired out by the long wait, and when the opportunity came—all I could think of was sleep.

FOWLE. It's a relief. . . .

MORGENHALL. To go home alone. To undress, clean your teeth, knock out your pipe, not to bother with failure or success.

FOWLE. So yesterday. . . .

MORGENHALL. I had lived through that moment so many times. It happened every day in my mind, daydreaming on buses, or in the doctor's surgery. When it came, I was tired of it. The exhaustion came over me. I wanted it to be all over. I wanted to be alone in my room, in the darkness, with a soft pillow round my ears. . . . So I failed.

FOWLE. Don't say it.

MORGENHALL. Being too tired to make my daydream public. It's a nice day. Summer's coming.

FOWLE. No, don't sir. Not too near the window.

MORGENHALL. Why not, Mr. Fowle?

FOWLE. I was concerned. A man in your position might be desperate. . . .

MORGENHALL. You say you can see the forest?

FOWLE. Just a splash of it.

MORGENHALL. I think I shall retire from the bar.

FOWLE. Don't say it, sir. After that rigorous training.

MORGENHALL. Well, there it is. I think I shall retire.

FOWLE. But cheer up, sir. As you said, other cases, other days. Let's take this calmly, sir. Let's be very lucid, as you put it in your own statement.

MORGENHALL. Other cases? I'm getting on, you know. Tuppy Morgan's back in his place. I doubt if the Dock Brief will come round again.

FOWLE. But there'll be something.

MORGENHALL. What can there be? Unless?

FOWLE. Yes, sir?

MORGENHALL. There would be another brief if. . . .

FOWLE. Yes?

MORGENHALL. I advised you to appeal. . . .

FOWLE. Ah, now that, misfortunately. . . .

MORGENHALL. There's a different atmosphere

there, up in the Appeal Court, Fowle. It's far from the rough and tumble, question and answer, swear on the Bible and lie your way out of it. It's quiet up there, pure Law, of course. Yes. I believe I'm cut out for the Court of Appeal. . . .

FOWLE. But you see. . . .

MORGENHALL. A big, quiet Court in the early Summer afternoon. Piles of books, and when you put one down the dust and powdered leather rises and makes the ushers sneeze. The clock ticks. Three old judges in scarlet take snuff with trembling hands. You'll sit in the dock and not follow a legal word. And I'll give them all my Law and get you off on a technicality.

FOWLE. But today. . . .

MORGENHALL. Now, if I may remind your Lordships of Prickle against the Haverfordwest Justices *ex parte* Anger, reported in 96 Moor's Ecclesiastical at page a thousand and three. Have your Lordships the report? Lord Bradwell, C. J., says, at the foot of the page. "The guilty intention is a deep foundation stone in the wall of our jurisprudence. So if it be that Prickle did run the bailiff through with his poignard taking him for a stray dog or cat, it seems there would be well raised the plea of autrefois mistake. But, contra, if he thought him to be his neighbor's cat, then, as my Brother Breadwinkle has well said in Lord Roche and Anderson, there might fall out a constructive larceny and felo in rem." Oh, Mr. Fowle, I have some of these fine cases by heart.

FOWLE. Above me, I'm afraid, you're going now.

MORGENHALL. Of course I am. These cases always bore the prisoner until they're upheld or overruled and he comes out dead or alive at the end of it all.

FOWLE. I'd like to hear you reading them, though. . . .

MORGENHALL. You would. I'll be followed to Court by my clerk, an old tortoise burdened by the weight of authorities. Then he'll lay them out in a fine buff and half calf row,[11] a letter from a clergyman I correspond with in Wales torn to mark each place. A glass of water, a dry cough and the "My respectful submission."

FOWLE. And that, of course, is. . . .

MORGENHALL. That the judge misdirected himself. He forgot the rule in Rimmer's case, he confused his *mens sana*, he displaced the burden of proof, he played fast and loose with all reasonable doubt, he kicked the presumption of innocence round like a football.

FOWLE. Strong words.

MORGENHALL. I shan't let Tommy Banter off lightly.

FOWLE. The judge?

MORGENHALL. Thoroughly unscholarly. Not a word of Latin in the whole summing up.

FOWLE. Not up to you, of course.

MORGENHALL. Thank God, I kept my books. There have been times, Fowle, when I was tempted, pricked and harried for rent perhaps, to have my clerk barter the whole lot away for the few pounds they offer for centuries of entombed law. But I stuck to them. I still have my Swabey and Tristram, my Pod's *Privy Council*, my Spinks *Prize Cases*. I shall open them up and say . . . I shall say. . . .

FOWLE. It's no good.

MORGENHALL. What's no good?

FOWLE. It's no good appealing.

MORGENHALL. No good?

FOWLE. No good at all.

MORGENHALL. Mr. Fowle. I've worked hard for you.

FOWLE. True enough.

MORGENHALL. And I mean to go on working.

FOWLE. It's a great comfort. . . .

MORGENHALL. In the course of our close, and may I say it? yes, our happy collaboration on this little crime of yours, I've become almost fond of you.

FOWLE. Thank you, sir.

MORGENHALL. At first, I have to admit it, I was put off by your somewhat furtive and repulsive appearance. It's happened before. I saw, I quite agree, only the outer husk, and what I saw was a small man marked by all the physical signs of confirmed criminality.

FOWLE. No oil painting?

MORGENHALL. Let's agree on that at once.

FOWLE. The wife thought so, too.

MORGENHALL. Enough of her, poor woman.

FOWLE. Oh, agreed.

---

11. *fine buff and half calf row,* a row of finely bound legal books.

MORGENHALL. My first solicitude for your well-being, let's face up to this as well, had a selfish element. You were my very own case, and I didn't want to lose you.

FOWLE. Natural feelings. But still. . . .

MORGENHALL. I haven't wounded you?

FOWLE. Nothing fatal.

MORGENHALL. I'm glad. Because, you know, as we worked on this case together, an affection sprang up. . . .

FOWLE. Mutual.

MORGENHALL. You seemed to have a real desire to help, and, if I may say so, an instinctive taste for the law.

FOWLE. A man can't go through this sort of thing without getting legal interests.

MORGENHALL. Quite so. And of course, as a self-made man, that's to your credit. But I did notice, just at the start, some flaws in you as a client.

FOWLE. Flaws?

MORGENHALL. You may not care to admit it. But let's be honest. After all, we don't want to look on the dreary side; but you may not be with us for very long. . . .

FOWLE. That's what I was trying to say. . . .

MORGENHALL. Please, Mr. Fowle, no interruptions until we've cleared this out of the way. Now didn't you, just at the beginning, put unnecesary difficulties before us?

FOWLE. Did I?

MORGENHALL. I well remember, before I got a bit of keenness into you, that you seemed about to admit your guilt.

FOWLE. Oh. . . .

MORGENHALL. Just a little obstinate, wasn't it?

FOWLE. I dare say. . . .

MORGENHALL. And now, when I've worked for fifty years to get the Law at my finger-tips, I hear you mutter, "No appeal."

FOWLE. No appeal!

MORGENHALL. Mr. Fowle. . . .

FOWLE. Yesterday you asked me to spare you pain, sir. This is going to be very hard for me.

MORGENHALL. What?

FOWLE. As you say, we've worked together, and I've had the pleasure of watching the ticking over of a legal mind. If you'd call any afternoon I'd be pleased to repay the compliment by showing you my birds. . . .

MORGENHALL. Not in this world you must realize, unless we appeal.

FOWLE. You see, this morning I saw the Governor.

MORGENHALL. You had some complaint?

FOWLE. I don't want to boast, but the truth is . . . he sent for me.

MORGENHALL. You went in fear. . . .

FOWLE. And trembling. But he turned out a very gentlemanly sort of individual. Ex-Army, I should imagine. All the ornaments of a gentleman. Wife and children in a tinted photo framed on the desk, handsome oil painting of a prize pig over the mantelpiece. Healthy red face. Strong smell of scented soap. . . .

MORGENHALL. But grow to the point. . . .

FOWLE. I'm telling you. "Well, Fowle" he says, "Sit down do. I'm just finishing this letter." So I sat and looked out of his windows. Big wide windows in the Governor's office, and the view. . . .

MORGENHALL. Fowle. If this anecdote has any point, be a good little chap, reach it.

FOWLE. Of course it has, where was I?

MORGENHALL. Admiring the view as usual.

FOWLE. Panoramic it was. Well, this Governor individual, finishing his letter, lit up one of those flat type of Egyptian cigarettes. "Well, Fowle," he said. . . .

MORGENHALL. Yes, yes. It's not necessary, Fowle, to reproduce every word of this conversation. Give us the gist, just the meat, you understand. Leave out the trimmings.

FOWLE. Trimmings there weren't. He put it quite bluntly.

MORGENHALL. What did he put?

FOWLE. "Well, Fowle, this may surprise you. But the Home Office[12] was on the telephone about you this morning." Isn't that a Government department?

MORGENHALL. Yes, yes, and well. . . .

FOWLE. It seems they do, in his words, come through from time to time, and just on business, of course, on that blower.[13] And quite

---

12. Home Office, the department of the British government responsible for domestic affairs not specifically assigned to other departments (which includes matters pertaining to prisons and prisoners).

13. blower, telephone.[Slang]

frankly, he admitted he was as shocked as I was. But the drill is, as he phrased it, a reprieve.

MORGENHALL. A . . .?

FOWLE. It's all over. I'm free. It seems that trial was no good at all. . . .

MORGENHALL. No good. But why?

FOWLE. Oh, no particular reason.

MORGENHALL. There must be a reason. Nothing passes in the Law without a reason.

FOWLE. You won't care to know.

MORGENHALL. Tell me.

FOWLE. You're too busy to wait. . . .

MORGENHALL. Tell me, Mr. Fowle. I beg of you. Tell me directly why this Governor, who knows nothing of the Law, should have called our one and only trial together "No good."

FOWLE. You yourself taught me not to scatter information like bombs.

MORGENHALL. Mr. Fowle. You must answer my question. My legal career may depend on it. If I'm not to have wasted my life on useless trials.

FOWLE. You want to hear?

MORGENHALL. Certainly.

FOWLE. He may not have been serious. There was a twinkle, most likely, in his eye.

MORGENHALL. But he said . . .

FOWLE. That the barrister they chose for me was no good. An old crock, in his words. No good at all. That he never said a word in my defense. So my case never got to the jury. He said the whole business was ever so null and void, but I'd better be careful in the future. . . .

(MORGENHALL *runs across the cell, mounts the stool, begins to undo his tie.*)

No! Mr. Morgenhall! Come down from there! No, sir! Don't do it.

(*They struggle.* FOWLE *brings* MORGENHALL *to earth.*)

Don't you see? If I'd had a barrister who asked questions and made clever speeches I'd be as dead as mutton. Your artfulness saved me. . . .

MORGENHALL. My. . . .

FOWLE. The artful way you handled it. The dumb tactics. They paid off! I'm alive!

MORGENHALL. There is that. . . .

FOWLE. And so are you.

MORGENHALL. We both are?

FOWLE. I'm free.

MORGENHALL. To go back to your birds. I suppose. . . .

FOWLE. Yes, Mr. Morgenhall?

MORGENHALL. It's unlikely you'll marry again.

FOWLE. Unlikely.

(*Long pause.*)

MORGENHALL. But you have the clear appearance of a criminal. I suppose it's not impossible that you might commit some rather more trivial offense.

FOWLE. A man can't live, Mr. Morgenhall, without committing some trivial offenses. Almost daily.

MORGENHALL. Then we may meet again. You may need my services. . . .

FOWLE. Constantly.

MORGENHALL. The future may not be so black. . . .

FOWLE. The sun's shining.

MORGENHALL. Can we go?

FOWLE. I think the door's been open some time.

(*He tries it. It is unbolted and swings open.*)

After you, Mr. Morgenhall, please.

MORGENHALL. No, no.

FOWLE. A man of your education should go first.

MORGENHALL. I think you should lead the way, Mr. Fowle, and as your legal adviser I will follow at a discreet distance, to straighten out such little tangles as you may hope to leave in your wake. Let's go.

(MORGENHALL: *whistles his fragment of tune.* FOWLE: *his whistles join* MORGENHALL's. *Whistling they leave the cell,* MORGENHALL *executing, as he leaves, the steps of a small delighted dance.*)

Slow curtain

1958

Discussion

Scene One

1. In the introduction to his *Three Plays*, John Mortimer states: "Comedy [is], to my mind, the only thing worth writing in this despairing age, provided the comedy is truly on the side of the lonely, the neglected, the unsuccessful . . . ." To which group do Morgenhall and Fowle belong? From the facts given, reconstruct the kind of lives they have lived.

2. (a) Why does Morgenhall tell Fowle "And I couldn't bear to lose you . . ."? Is the statement true? **(b)** Morgenhall believes Fowle picked him as his attorney because of his distinguished and learned appearance. What is the real story?

3. After hearing Fowle's account of the events leading up to the murder, Morgenhall admits that Fowle is "an unsympathetic figure," one for whom the jury is likely to feel little compassion. **(a)** What specific actions of his wife does Fowle state drove him to murder her? **(b)** Why does Morgenhall conclude Fowle will be an "unsympathetic figure" to any jury? **(c)** Why are we never told *how* Fowle murdered his wife?

4. (a) In a rehearsal of the trial, Morgenhall has Fowle improvise the testimony of three people in addition to the words of the judge. Who are these people and what "little hitch" in each line of defense is shown up by this performance? What do they see as their one hope of acquittal? **(b)** At one point Morgenhall calls Fowle "a good simple chap." Why is this comment ironical? Explain.

Scene Two

1. Contrast what actually takes place at the trial with the earlier rehearsal. How does Morgenhall's repeated line "I might have said . . ." provide a summary of lost opportunity?

2. Describe the relationship of Morgenhall and Fowle in this scene. How have their roles been reversed?

3. (a) By what "ironic twist" is Fowle freed? **(b)** To what does he attribute his freedom?

4. (a) What is Morgenhall's explanation for his failure to act in the courtroom? How does his behavior in court also help explain his failed romance and unsuccessful career? **(b)** Does Morgenhall appear to have learned from his explanation of his failures? Explain.

The Play in Review

1. After Morgenhall tells Fowle at the beginning of Scene One that he has come to help him, Fowle replies: "We'll help each other." What are the most important things they do for each other through the course of the play? Is their relationship likely to continue?

2. (a) Explain how the play combines elements of both comedy and tragedy. **(b)** What does the play appear to be saying about man's ability to face reality?

3. Several lines of the play acquire special force through the deliberate use of double meanings. Explain in what two ways we are intended to interpret each of the following lines of dialogue: **(a)** "I see where you've been bewildered. You think I'm in trouble as well." **(b)** "As the years pass there come to be clues you no longer understand." **(c)** "Give in? We do not give in. When my life depends on this case." **(d)** "Mr. Fowle. You must answer my question. My legal career may depend on it. If I'm not to have wasted my life on useless trials."

Composition

Think about the character of Morgenhall. What does he look like? What sort of life has he had? How do other people regard him? How does the playwright seem to want us to feel about this character?

Write a character sketch of Morgenhall, contrasting what he fantasizes himself to be and what he really is. (See *Prewriting* and *Analyzing Literature* in Composition Guide.)

The Changing English Language

In the twentieth century the English language has continued to grow and change. The *Oxford English Dictionary*, published in ten volumes from 1884 to 1928 (see page 665), had swelled to twelve volumes and a supplement by 1933. The word *head* now had more than forty meanings; the word *green* had more than fifty. New words continued to be added to the language. Two world wars provided such terms as *zeppelin, U-boat, blitzkrieg, jeep, concentration camp,* and *A-bomb*; from the sciences came *neurosis, antibiotic, radio, television,* and *transistor*; from the arts came *montage, surrealism,* and *absurdist*.

As the language continued to change, words took on new meanings. *Scan* once meant to study with great care; now it means to glance at hastily. *Sophistication*, once a term of condemnation, now signifies approval. Some words once frowned on in polite society are now acceptable. To have described an act of courage as being *plucky* would have been considered vulgar in Victorian drawing rooms. And to have used the word *gutsy* would have branded the speaker as a social outcast.

The widespread use of manipulative language by propagandists and advertisers disturbed many people. Probably the best-known analyst of the corruption of English by politicians and salesmen in the recent past was George Orwell (see pages 752-762). In essays like "Politics and the English Language" he protested against bad language habits that corrupt thinking: "Modern writing at its worst does not consist in picking out words for the sake of their meaning and inventing images in order to make the meaning clearer. It consists in gumming together long strips of words which have already been set in order by someone else, and making the results presentable by sheer humbug."

Orwell's novel *Nineteen Eighty-four*, depicts a slave society ruled by a self-perpetuating elite. The official language is named *Newspeak*. Each year words are eliminated from its vocabulary. The purpose of impoverishing the language is to

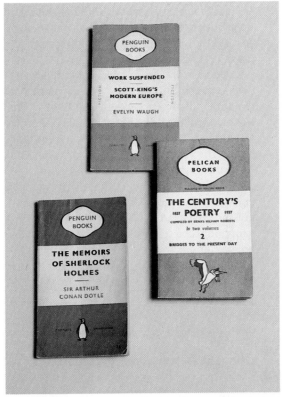

The appearance in the 1930s of the first paperbacks had a major impact on the reading habits of the British public.

narrow the range of thought of the citizens, so that it will become increasingly difficult for them to express, or even to form, an unorthodox concept. Ultimately, they will cease to think altogether. In order to create more mental confusion in the citizens, the elite promotes the practice of *doublethink*, the ability to hold two contradictory beliefs simultaneously. Such words as *Newspeak* and *doublethink* have themselves now passed into the language. Perhaps Orwell's bleak fantasy should be seen more as a warning than a prediction. But in a world replete with official euphemism, in which murder is referred to as "termination with extreme prejudice," Orwell's admonition to rid ourselves of bad language habits, like euphemism, as "a necessary first step toward political regeneration," is useful.

The  *wentieth Century*

Content Review

1. (a) What attitudes toward warfare did writers like Siegfried Sassoon, Wilfred Owen, and Vera Brittain seek to refute? **(b)** What view of war did they present in place of these attitudes?

2. Social criticism is apparent in much of twentieth-century writing. What aspects of contemporary life are attacked in **(a)** Eliot's "The Hollow Men"; **(b)** Waugh's "Winner Takes All"; **(c)** Auden's "The Unknown Citizen"; **(d)** Warner's "The Phoenix"; **(e)** Orwell's "Such, Such Were the Joys"?

3. Virginia Woolf infers that there is a close connection between "great men" and the houses they lived in. What insights does she gain about the Carlyles from seeing their house? About John Keats from seeing his?

4. Children are pivotal characters in a number of the selections in this unit. What problems are confronted by **(a)** the narrator in Joyce's "Araby"; **(b)** the Kelvey sisters in Mansfield's "The Doll's House"; **(c)** Jerome in Greene's "A Shocking Accident"; **(d)** Larry in O'Connor's "My Oedipus Complex"?

5. What attitude toward British imperialism is reflected in **(a)** Orwell's "Shooting an Elephant"; **(b)** Larkin's "Homage to a Government"?

6. Discuss the approach to the elegy form in **(a)** Owen's "Anthem for Doomed Youth"; **(b)** Auden's "The Unknown Citizen"; **(c)** Thomas's "Do Not Go Gentle into That Good Night."

7. Contrast the treatment of natural subjects in **(a)** Lawrence's "Snake"; **(b)** Stevie Smith's "The Frog Prince"; **(c)** Thomas's "Fern Hill"; **(d)** Larkin's "At Grass"; **(e)** any of the Hughes poems.

Concept Review: Interpretation of New Material

Eveline • *James Joyce*

She sat at the window watching the evening invade the avenue. Her head was leaned against the window curtains and in her nostrils was the odor of dusty cretonne. She was tired.

Few people passed. The man out of the last house passed on his way home; she heard his footsteps clacking along the concrete pavement and afterwards crunching on the cinder path before the new red houses. One time there used to be a field there in which they used to play every evening with other people's children. Then a man from Belfast bought the field and built houses in it—not like their little brown houses but bright brick houses with shining roofs. The children of the avenue used to play together in that field— the Devines, the Waters, the Dunns, little Keogh the cripple, she and her brothers and sisters. Ernest, however, never played: he was too grown up. Her father used often to hunt them in out of the field with his blackthorn stick; but usually little Keogh used to keep *nix*[1] and call out when he saw her father coming. Still they seemed to have been rather happy then. Her father was not so

1. *nix,* an old slang word, originally used by thieves to refer to the member of a gang who kept watch.

bad then; and besides, her mother was alive. That was a long time ago; she and her brothers and sisters were all grown up; her mother was dead. Tizzie Dunn was dead, too, and the Waters had gone back to England. Everything changes. Now she was going to go away like the others, to leave her home.

Home! She looked round the room, reviewing all its familiar objects which she had dusted once a week for so many years, wondering where on earth all the dust came from. Perhaps she would never see again those familiar objects from which she had never dreamed of being divided. And yet during all those years she had never found out the name of the priest whose yellowing photograph hung on the wall above the broken harmonium beside the colored print of the promises made to Blessed Margaret Mary Alacoque.[2] He had been a school friend of her father. Whenever he showed the photograph to a visitor her father used to pass it with a casual word: "He is in Melbourne now."

She had consented to go away, to leave her home. Was that wise? She tried to weigh each side of the question. In her home anyway she had shelter and food; she had those whom she had known all her life about her. Of course she had to work hard, both in the house and at business. What would they say of her in the Stores[3] when they found out that she had run away with a fellow? Say she was a fool, perhaps; and her place would be filled up by advertisement. Miss Gavan would be glad. She had always had an edge on her, especially whenever there were people listening.

"Miss Hill, don't you see these ladies are waiting?"

"Look lively, Miss Hill, please."

She would not cry many tears at leaving the Stores.

But in her new home, in a distant unknown country, it would not be like that. Then she would be married—she, Eveline. People would treat her with respect then. She would not be treated as her mother had been. Even now, though she was over nineteen, she sometimes felt herself in danger of her father's violence. She knew it was that that had given her the palpitations. When they were growing up he had never gone for her, like he used to go for Harry and Ernest, because she

was a girl; but latterly he had begun to threaten her and say what he would do to her only for her dead mother's sake. And now she had nobody to protect her. Ernest was dead and Harry, who was in the church decorating business, was nearly always down somewhere in the country. Besides, the invariable squabble for money on Saturday nights had begun to weary her unspeakably. She always gave her entire wages—seven shillings—and Harry always sent up what he could but the trouble was to get any money from her father. He said she used to squander the money, that she had no head, that he wasn't going to give her his hard-earned money to throw about the streets, and much more, for he was usually fairly bad on Saturday night. In the end he would give her the money and ask her had she any intention of buying Sunday's dinner. Then she had to rush out as quickly as she could and do her marketing, holding her black leather purse tightly in her hand as she elbowed her way through the crowds and returning home late under her load of provisions. She had hard work to keep the house together and to see that the two young children who had been left to her charge went to school regularly and got their meals regularly. It was hard work—a hard life—but now that she was about to leave it she did not find it a wholly undesirable life.

She was about to explore another life with Frank. Frank was very kind, manly, openhearted. She was to go away with him by the night boat to be his wife and to live with him in Buenos Aires where he had a home waiting for her. How well she remembered the first time she had seen him; he was lodging in a house on the main road where she used to visit. It seemed a few weeks ago. He was standing at the gate, his peaked cap pushed back on his head and his hair tumbled forward over a face of bronze. Then they had come to know each other. He used to meet her outside the Stores every evening and see her home. He took her to see The Bohemian Girl[4] and she felt elated as she sat in an unaccustomed part of the theater with him. He was awfully fond

---

2. Blessed . . . Alacoque (1647-1690), a French nun who experienced four visions of Jesus Christ between 1673 and 1675. Her visions and teaching have had considerable effect on the devotional life of Roman Catholics.
3. the Stores, a department store.
4. The Bohemian Girl, an opera (1843) by the Irish-born composer Michael Balfe (1808-1870).

of music and sang a little. People knew that they were courting and, when he sang about the lass that loves a sailor, she always felt pleasantly confused. He used to call her Poppens out of fun. First of all it had been an excitement for her to have a fellow and then she had begun to like him. He had tales of distant countries. He had started as a deck boy at a pound a month on a ship of the Allan Line going out to Canada. He told her the names of the ships he had been on and the names of the different services. He had sailed through the Straits of Magellan and he told her stories of the terrible Patagonians.[5] He had fallen on his feet in Buenos Aires, he said, and had come over to the old country just for a holiday. Of course, her father had found out the affair and had forbidden her to have anything to say to him.

"I know these sailor chaps," he said.

One day he had quarreled with Frank and after that she had to meet her lover secretly.

The evening deepened in the avenue. The white of two letters in her lap grew indistinct. One was to Harry; the other was to her father. Ernest had been her favorite but she liked Harry too. Her father was becoming old lately, she noticed; he would miss her. Sometimes he could be very nice. Not long before, when she had been laid up for a day, he had read her out a ghost story and made toast for her at the fire. Another day, when their mother was alive, they had all gone for a picnic to the Hill of Howth.[6] She remembered her father putting on her mother's bonnet to make the children laugh.

Her time was running out but she continued to sit by the window, leaning her head against the window curtain, inhaling the odor of dusty cretonne. Down far in the avenue she could hear a street organ playing. She knew the air. Strange that it should come that very night to remind her of the promise to her mother, her promise to keep the home together as long as she could. She remembered the last night of her mother's illness; she was again in the close dark room at the other side of the hall and outside she heard a melancholy air of Italy. The organ player had been ordered to go away and given sixpence. She remembered her father strutting back into the sickroom saying: "Damned Italians! coming over here!"

As she mused the pitiful vision of her mother's life laid its spell on the very quick of her being—that life of commonplace sacrifices closing in final craziness. She trembled as she heard again her mother's voice saying constantly with foolish insistence: "Derevaun Seraun! Derevaun Seraun!"[7]

She stood up in a sudden impulse of terror. Escape! She must escape! Frank would save her. He would give her life, perhaps love, too. But she wanted to live. Why should she be unhappy? She had a right to happiness. Frank would take her in his arms, fold her in his arms. He would save her.

She stood among the swaying crowd in the station at the North Wall. He held her hand and she knew that he was speaking to her, saying something about the passage over and over again. The station was full of soldiers with brown baggages. Through the wide doors of the sheds she caught a glimpse of the black mass of the boat, lying in beside the quay wall, with illumined portholes. She answered nothing. She felt her cheek pale and cold and, out of a maze of distress, she prayed to God to direct her, to show her what was her duty. The boat blew a long mournful whistle into the mist. If she went, tomorrow she would be on the sea with Frank, steaming toward Buenos Aires. Their passage had been booked. Could she still draw back after all he had done for her? Her distress awoke a nausea in her body and she kept moving her lips in silent fervent prayer.

A bell clanged upon her heart. She felt him seize her hand:

"Come!"

All the seas of the world tumbled about her heart. He was drawing her into them: he would drown her. She gripped with both hands at the iron railing.

"Come!"

No! No! No! It was impossible. Her hands clutched the iron in frenzy. Amid the seas she sent a cry of anguish.

"Eveline! Evvy!"

He rushed beyond the barrier and called to her

---

5. **Patagonians,** primitive people inhabiting the desolate southern part of South America.
6. **Hill of Howth,** a hill on a peninsula that forms the north shore of Dublin Bay.
7. **"Deveraun . . . Seraun,"** possibly corrupt Gaelic for "the end of pleasure is pain."

to follow. He was shouted at to go on but he still called to her. She set her white face to him, passive, like a helpless animal. Her eyes gave him no sign of love or farewell or recognition.

1914

Write the answers to the following questions on a separate sheet of paper. Do not write in your book.

1. (a) Where is Eveline as the story opens? **(b)** How is she feeling?

2. (a) What sort of home does she have? **(b)** What sort of neighborhood does she live in?

3. (a) Is she married? **(b)** What does she do for a living?

4. What characteristics of Eveline's father make him difficult to live with?

5. (a) What reasons does Eveline have for wanting to leave home? **(b)** What reasons has she for wanting to stay?

6. (a) What does Frank do for a living? **(b)** What does he take Eveline to see?

7. Why does Eveline have to meet Frank secretly?

8. How does the memory of her mother affect her?

9. What is the final scene of the story?

10. Where is Eveline and Frank's passage booked for?

Composition Review

You may choose any *one* of the following assignments. Assume that you are writing for your classmates.

1. While Wilfred Owen and Siegfried Sassoon both write of warfare, and have an overall similarity of tone (ironic rather than romantic), they also differ in a number of important ways. Consider the quantity and character of the imagery in each one's verse. Which is a more gifted satirist? Whose language is more elevated, more traditionally "poetical"?

Write an essay in which you contrast the literary styles of Owen and Sassoon.

2. Examine the attitudes toward faith, despair, and the life of the spirit in T. S. Eliot's "The Hollow Men" and "Journey of the Magi."

Write an essay comparing and contrasting Eliot's treatment of these issues in the two poems.

3. Compare the portrayal of life in Dublin in Joyce's "Araby" and "Eveline" and the efforts of the principal characters in these two stories to glamorize or escape that existence.

Write an essay speculating on which of these two characters—the narrator in "Araby" or Eveline—appears to have the better chance for a different life in the future.

4. Both the fire that destroys Poldero's Wizard Wonderworld in Warner's "The Phoenix"

and Jerome's father's mishap in Greene's "A Shocking Accident" are the sort of items that fill up the back pages of newspapers.

Write up either episode as a brief news story.

5. Examine the attitudes toward time expressed in Dylan Thomas's "Fern Hill" and "Do Not Go Gentle Into That Good Night."

Write an essay comparing the attitudes toward time expressed in these two poems.

6. Recollections of childhood appear in a number of the selections in this unit. The mood of these memories ranges from Dylan Thomas's celebratory "Fern Hill" to Orwell's satiric "Such, Such Were the Joys."

Write a sketch of some period of your own childhood, in whatever mood its recollection arouses in you.

7. Both D. H. Lawrence and Ted Hughes make a significant use of subjects from nature.

Write an essay comparing the treatment of subjects from nature in the poems of Lawrence and Hughes.

8. The "outsider" is a characteristic figure in twentieth-century literature.

Write an essay in which you compare the treatment of this figure in Stevie Smith's "Not Waving but Drowning" and John Mortimer's "The Dock Brief."

Definitions of Literary Terms

Words within entries in SMALL CAPITAL LETTERS refer you to other entries in the *Definitions of Literary Terms*. Numbers after a title or example refer to pages in the text where the selection referred to can be found.

alexandrine (See HEXAMETER.)

allegory (al′ə gôr′ē), a NARRATIVE either in VERSE or prose, in which characters, action, and sometimes SETTING represent abstract concepts apart from the literal meaning of the story. The underlying meaning has moral, social, religious, or political significance, and the characters are often PERSONIFICATIONS of abstract ideas such as charity, hope, greed, or envy. Spenser's *The Faerie Queene,* page 144, is a good example of allegory.

alliteration (ə lit′ə rā′shən), the repetition of consonant sounds at the beginnings of words or within words, particularly in accented syllables. It can be used to reinforce meaning, unify thought, or simply for musical effect. "Grim and greedy the gruesome monster. . . ." *(Beowulf,* page 8, line 80.)

allusion (ə lü′zhən), a brief reference to a person, event, or place, real or fictitious, or to a work of art. In Dryden's "To the Memory of Mr. Oldham," page 281, the reference to Marcellus, the promising young nephew of the emperor Augustus who died before he could succeed his uncle, is an allusion. In Auden's "Musée des Beaux Arts," page 743, there is an allusion to *Icarus,* a painting by Brueghel and to the Greek MYTH which inspired the painting.

analogy (ə nal′ə jē), a comparison made between two items, situations, or ideas that are somewhat alike but unlike in most respects. Frequently an unfamiliar or complex object or idea will be explained through comparison to a familiar or simpler one. In "Of Studies," page 235, Bacon makes an analogy between the growth of natural human abilities and that of plants in nature.

anapest (an′ə pest), a three-syllable metrical FOOT consisting of two unaccented syllables followed by an accented syllable. In the following line, the feet are divided by slashes, and since there are four feet, the line can be described as *anapestic* TETRAMETER.

> Lĭke ă chíld / frŏm thĕ wómb, / lĭke ă ghóst /
> frŏm thĕ tómb . . .
>
> Shelley, "Cloud"

anastrophe (ə nas′trə fē), inversion of the usual order of the parts of a sentence, primarily for emphasis or to achieve a certain rhythm or rhyme. "About the woodlands I will go" ("Loveliest of Trees," page 548) is a reversal or inversion of the normal order of subject-verb-object (complement), "I will go about the woodlands."

antagonist (an tag′ə nist), a character in a story or play who opposes the chief character or PROTAGONIST. In *Beowulf,* page 7, Grendel is an antagonist, as is Satan in *Paradise Lost,* page 258.

aphorism (af′ə riz′əm), a brief saying embodying a moral, such as Pope's "Know then thyself, presume not God to scan; / The proper study of mankind is Man," from *An Essay on Man*, page 327.

apostrophe (ə pos′trə fē), a figure of speech in which an absent person, an abstract concept, or an inanimate object is directly addressed. "Milton! thou shouldst be living at this hour . . ." is an example of the first (Wordsworth's "London, 1802," page 376); "Death, be not proud . . ." is an example of the second (Donne, page 241); and "O sylvan Wye! thou wanderer through the woods . . ." is an example of the third (Wordsworth's "Tintern Abbey," page 372).

archetype (är′kə tīp), an image, story-pattern, or character type which recurs frequently in literature and evokes strong, often unconscious, associations in the reader. For example, the wicked witch, the enchanted prince, and the sleeping beauty are character types widely dispersed throughout folk tales and literature. "Kubla Khan," page 385, derives much of its power from its use of archetypal images such as the "deep romantic chasm," the "demon lover," the "sacred river," "ancestral voices prophesying war," and the "damsel with a dulcimer." The story of a hero who undertakes a dangerous quest (see *Beowulf,* page 7, or *Sir Gawain and the Green Knight,* page 119) is a recurrent story pattern.

argument, a prose summary or synopsis of what is in a poem or play, both with regard to PLOT and meaning. Shaw's Epilogue to *Pygmalion* (page 657) may be regarded as an argument.

assonance (as′n əns), the repetition of similar vowel

sounds followed by different consonant sounds in stressed syllables or words. It is often used instead of RHYME. *Hate* and *great* are examples of rhyme; *hate* and *grade* are examples of assonance. In ". . . that hoard, and sleep, and feed, and know not me" the words *sleep, feed,* and *me* are assonant ("Ulysses" by Tennyson, page 446).

atmosphere, the MOOD of a literary work. An author establishes atmosphere partly through description of SETTING or landscape, and partly by the objects chosen to be described, as in the first eighteen lines of the *Prologue* to *The Canterbury Tales,* page 74, where an atmosphere of rebirth and renewal is created by Chaucer.

autobiography (See BIOGRAPHY.)

ballad, a NARRATIVE passed on in the oral tradition. It often makes use of repetition and dialogue. See "Sir Patrick Spence," page 68. A ballad whose author is unknown is called a *folk ballad.* If the author is known, the ballad is called a *literary ballad.*

ballad stanza, a STANZA usually consisting of four alternating lines of IAMBIC TETRAMETER and TRIMETER and rhyming the second and fourth lines.

> The wind sae cauld blew south and north,
> And blew into the floor;
> Quoth our goodman to our goodwife,
> "Gae out and bar the door."

> "Get Up and Bar the Door," page 69

biography, any account of a person's life. See Johnson's *Life of Milton,* page 332, or Boswell's *Life of Johnson,* page 338. AUTOBIOGRAPHY is the story of all or part of a person's life written by the person who lived it. See Vera Brittain's *Testament of Youth,* page 683.

blank verse, unrhymed IAMBIC PENTAMETER, a line of five feet. The Shakespeare play, page 160, and Milton's *Paradise Lost,* page 258, are written in blank verse.

> Ĭ máy / ăssért / Etēr- / năl Próv- / ĭdénce,
> Ănd jús- / tĭfý / thĕ wáys / ŏf Gód / tŏ mén.

> Milton, *Paradise Lost,* page 260, lines 25–26

burlesque (See SATIRE.)

cacophony (kə kofʹə nē), a succession of harsh, discordant sounds in either poetry or prose, used to achieve a specific effect. Note the harshness of sound and difficulty of articulation in these lines:

> And all is seared with trade; bleared, smeared
>   with toil;
> And wears man's smudge and shares man's smell:
>   the soil
> Is bare now, nor can foot feel, being shod.

> Hopkins, "God's Grandeur," page 542

caesura (si zhŭrʹə, si zyürʹə), a pause usually near the middle in a line of verse, usually indicated by the sense of the line, and often greater than a normal pause. For purposes of study, the mark indicating a caesura is two short vertical lines (‖). A caesura can be indicated by punctuation, the grammatical construction of a sentence, or the placement of lines on a page. It is used to add variety to regular METER and therefore to add emphasis to certain words.

> Born but to die, ‖ and reas'ning but to err;
> Alike in ignorance, ‖ his reason such,
> Whether he thinks too little, ‖ or too much:
> Chaos of thought and passion, ‖ all confused;
> Still by himself abused, ‖ or disabused . . .

> Pope, from *An Essay on Man,* page 327

The caesura was a particularly important device in Anglo-Saxon poetry, where each line had a caesura in the middle, but it is a technique used in most forms of poetry, such as the SONNET, the HEROIC COUPLET, and BLANK VERSE.

caricature (karʹə kə chŭr), exaggeration of prominent features of appearance or character. See, for example, the characters of the Murdstones in the excerpt from *David Copperfield,* page 473.

carpe diem (kärʹpe dēʹəm), Latin for "seize the day," the name applied to a THEME frequently found in LYRIC poetry: enjoy life's pleasures while you are able. See "To the Virgins, To Make Much of Time," page 247.

catastrophe, the final stage of a tragedy in which the hero meets his unhappy fate. See the final act of the Shakespeare play, page 160.

characterization, the method an author uses to acquaint a reader with his or her characters. A character's physical traits and personality may be described, as are those of John Thomas in "Tickets, Please," page 718; a character's speech and behavior may be described, as are those of the father in "My Oedipus Complex," page 776; or the thoughts and feelings of a character or the reactions of other characters to an individual may be shown, as in "A Shocking Accident," page 771. Any or all of these methods may be used in the same work.

cliché (klē shāʹ), an expression or phrase that is so overused as to become trite and meaningless: *white as snow, black as coal, cold as ice* are examples. A line from a famous writer may be quoted so often that it becomes a cliché.

climax, as a term of dramatic structure, the decisive or turning point in a story or play when the action changes course and begins to resolve itself. In *Hamlet,* the hesitation and failure of the hero to kill Claudius at prayer in Act Three is often regarded as the climax of the play. In *Macbeth,* the banquet scene in Act Three where the ghost of Banquo appears to Macbeth is often regarded as the climax. Not every story or play has this kind of dramatic climax. Sometimes a character may simply resolve a problem in his or her mind. At times there is no resolution of the PLOT; the climax then comes when a character realizes that a resolution is impossible. (See also PLOT.) The term is also used to mean the point of greatest interest in a work, where the reader or audience has the most intense emotional response.

comedy, a play written primarily to amuse the audience. In addition to arousing laughter, comic writing often appeals to the intellect. Thus the comic mode has often been used to "instruct" the audience about the follies of certain social conventions and human foibles, as is done in *Pygmalion,* page 612. When so used, the comedy tends toward SATIRE.

comedy of ideas, a comedy in which the humor lies in ideas more than in situations. See *Pygmalion,* page 612.

conceit, an elaborate and surprising *figure of speech* comparing two very dissimilar things. It usually involves intellectual cleverness and ingenuity. In the last three STANZAS of "A Valediction: Forbidding Mourning," page 239, Donne compares his soul and that of his love to the two legs or branches of a draftsman's compass used to make a circle. The previously unseen likeness as developed by the poet helps us to see and understand the subject described (the relationship of the lovers' souls) more clearly.

conflict, the struggle between two opposing forces. The four basic kinds of conflict are: (1) a person against another person or opponent (*Beowulf,* page 7, or "My Oedipus Complex," page 776); (2) a person against nature ("The Seafarer," page 57); (3) a person against society (*Pygmalion,* page 612); and (4) two elements within a person struggling for mastery (Joyce's "Eveline," page 808).

connotation (kon′ə tā′shən), the emotional associations surrounding a word, as opposed to its literal meaning or DENOTATION. Some connotations are fairly general, others quite personal. Shakespeare's Sonnet 30, page 158, uses the connotative powers of language to create a mood of longing for lost beauties of the past that survive only in the poet's memory. Many of the words used by Shakespeare in this sonnet suggest associations that cluster around a sense of loss.

consonance (kon′sə nəns), the repetition of consonant sounds that are preceded by different vowel sounds.

> For*l*orn! the very word is like a be*ll*
> To to*ll* me back from thee to my so*l*e se*l*f.
>
> Keats, "Ode to a Nightingale," page 406

Consonance is an effective device for linking sound, mood, and meaning. In the lines above, the *l* sounds reinforce the melancholy mood.

couplet, a pair of rhyming lines with identical meter.

> Know then thyself, presume not God to scan;
> The proper study of mankind is man.
>
> Pope, from *An Essay on Man,* page 327

dactyl (dak′tl), a three-syllable metrical FOOT consisting of an accented syllable followed by two unaccented syllables. In the following lines the feet are divided by slashes, and since there are six feet, the basic RHYTHM is *dactylic* HEXAMETER.

> Loosing his / arms from her / waist he flew /
> upward, a- / waiting the / sea beast.
>
> Charles Kingsley, *Andromeda*

denotation (dē nō tā′shən), the strict, literal meaning of a word. (See CONNOTATION.)

denouement (dā′nü män′), the resolution of the PLOT. The word is derived from a French word meaning literally "to untie."

dialogue, the conversation between two or more people in a literary work. Dialogue can serve many purposes, among them: (1) CHARACTERIZATION of those speaking and those spoken about, as in "A Shocking Accident," page 771; (2) the creation of MOOD or ATMOSPHERE, as in "The Withered Arm," page 516; (3) the advancement of the PLOT, as in "Tobermory," page 606; and (4) the development of a THEME, as in "Tickets, Please," page 718.

diary, a record of daily happenings written by a person for his or her own use. The diarist is moved by a need to record daily routine and confess innermost thoughts. The diary makes up in immediacy and frankness what it lacks in artistic shape and coherence. See the *Diary* of Pepys, page 283.

diction, the author's choice of words or phrases in a literary work. This choice involves both the CONNOTATION and DENOTATION of a word as well as levels of usage. In *Pygmalion,* page 612, the playwright makes use of a wide variety of dictions when he has each character speak in a way that is appropriate to his or her education and background.

dramatic convention, any of several devices which the audience accepts as a substitution for reality in a dramatic work. For instance, the audience accepts that an interval between acts may represent hours, days, weeks, months, or years; that a bare stage may be a meadow; that an invisible scaffold rather than a house supports a balcony; that an audible dialogue is supposed to represent whispered conversation; or that a rosy spotlight signals the dawn.

dramatic irony (See IRONY.)

dramatic monologue (mon′l ôg), a LYRIC poem in which the speaker addresses someone whose replies are not recorded. Sometimes the one addressed seems to be present, sometimes not. See "Porphyria's Lover," page 461, or "My Last Duchess," page 462.

elegy, a solemn, reflective poem, usually about death, written in a formal style. See Gray's "Elegy Written in a Country Churchyard," page 344.

end rhyme, the rhyming of words at the ends of lines of poetry. (See RHYME.)

end-stopped line, a line of poetry that contains a complete thought, thus necessitating the use of a semicolon, colon, or period at the end:

> Know then thyself, presume not God to scan;
> The proper study of mankind is Man.

> Pope, from *An Essay on Man*, page 327

(See also RUN-ON LINE.)

epic, a long NARRATIVE poem (originally handed down in oral tradition, later a literary form) dealing with great heroes and adventures, having a national, worldwide, or cosmic setting, involving supernatural forces, and written in a deliberately ceremonial STYLE. See *Beowulf*, page 7, or *Paradise Lost*, page 258.

epigram, any short, witty verse or saying, often ending with a wry twist.

> 'Tis with our judgments as our watches; none
> Go just alike, yet each believes his own.

> Pope, *An Essay on Criticism*

epilogue, concluding section added to a work, serving to round out or interpret it. See the Epilogue to *Pygmalion*, page 657.

epistle, in general, any letter; specifically, a long, formal, and instructional composition, in prose or verse. Pope's *Essay on Man* (page 327) consists of four verse epistles.

essay, a brief composition that presents a personal point of view. An essay may present a viewpoint through formal analysis and argument, as in "Of Studies," page 235, or it may be more informal in style, as in "Great Men's Houses," page 713.

euphony (yü′fə nē), a combination of pleasing sounds in poetry or prose.

> I cannot see what flowers are at my feet,
>   Nor what soft incense hangs upon the boughs,
> But, in embalmèd darkness, guess each sweet
>   Wherewith the seasonable month endows
> The grass, the thicket, and the fruit tree wild . . .

> Keats, "Ode to a Nightingale," page 406

(See also CACOPHONY.)

extended metaphor, a figure of speech that is developed at great length, often through a whole work or a great part of it. It is common in poetry but is used in prose as well. Wyatt's "Whoso List to Hunt," page 132, contains an extended metaphor, with the hunter representing the love-struck poet and the deer representing the poet's beloved. (See METAPHOR.)

fable, a brief tale, in which the characters are often animals, told to point out a moral truth.

fantasy, a work that takes place in an unreal world, concerns incredible characters, or employs physical and scientific principles not yet discovered. Thus, there are elements of fantasy in *The Faerie Queene*, page

144, "A Voyage to Brobdingnag," page 294, and "Tobermory," page 606.

figurative language, language used in a nonliteral way to express a suitable relationship between essentially unlike things. The more common figures of speech are SIMILE, METAPHOR, PERSONIFICATION, HYPERBOLE, and SYNECHDOCHE.

flashback, interruption of the narrative to show an episode that happened before that particular point in the story.

foil, a character whose traits are the opposite of those of another character and who thus points up the strengths of weaknesses of another character. Henry Higgins and Liza Doolittle are foils to one another in *Pygmalion*, page 612.

folk ballad (See BALLAD.)

folk epic, an EPIC of plural or doubtful authorship, or one whose authorship is more appropriately attributable to a community than to an individual. The *Beowulf*-poet (page 6) probably used an existing folk epic as the basis for his poem.

folklore, the customs, legends, songs, and tales of a people or nation. The popular ballads, page 66, are examples of folklore.

foot, a group of syllables in VERSE usually consisting of one accented syllable and the unaccented syllable(s) associated with it. (A foot may occasionally, for variety, have two accented syllables—see SPONDEE—or two unaccented syllables—the *pyrrhic*.) In the following lines the feet are divided by slashes:

> Come líve/ with me / and bé / my Lóve,
> And wé / will all / the pléa- / sures próve.

> Marlowe, "The Passionate Shepherd," page 142

The most common line lengths are five feet (PENTAMETER), four feet (TETRAMETER), and three feet (TRIMETER). The quoted lines above are IAMBIC TETRAMETER. (See also RHYTHM.)

foreshadowing, a hint given to the reader of what is to come. In "Sir Patrick Spence," page 68, the reader begins to suspect at least as early as line 16 that disaster awaits the title character.

frame, a NARRATIVE device presenting a story or group of stories within the frame of a larger narrative. The frame provides continuity for the group of stories. The pilgrimage in Chaucer's *The Canterbury Tales*, page 73, is the frame unifying the stories told by the pilgrims.

free verse, a type of poetry that differs from conventional VERSE forms in being "free" from a fixed pattern of METER and RHYME, but using RHYTHM and other poetic devices. See Eliot's "The Hollow Men," page 698.

genre (zhän′rə), a form or type of literary work. For example, the novel, the short story, and the poem are all genres. The term is a very loose one, however, so that subheadings under these would themselves also be called genres, for instance, EPIC.

heroic couplet, a pair of rhymed verse lines in IAMBIC PENTAMETER.

> The hungry judges soon the sentence sign,
> And wretches hang that jurymen may dine . . .
>
> Pope, *The Rape of the Lock*, page 322, lines 149–150

heroic simile, a SIMILE sustained for several lines and suggesting the heroic in nature or quality. See *Paradise Lost*, page 261, lines 100–113.

hexameter (hek sam′ə tər), a verse line of six feet. Spenser, in *The Faerie Queene*, uses a STANZA consisting of nine lines, the first eight of which are IAMBIC PENTAMETER and the last of which is an alexandrine.

> Mŏst loăth- / sŏme, filt̆h- / y̆, fóul, /
>
> ănd fúll / ŏf víle / dĭsdaín.
>
> Spenser, *The Faerie Queene*, page 144

homily (hom′ə lī), a sermon, or serious moral talk. See "Meditation 17," page 241.

hyperbole (hī pėr′bə lē), a figure of speech involving great exaggeration. The effect may be serious or comic. Byron uses hyperbole for comic effect in *Don Juan* (see stanza 17, page 391).

iambic pentameter (ī am′bik pen tam′ə tər), a line of verse having five metrical feet; each FOOT consists of one unaccented syllable followed by one accented syllable. Iambic pentameter is the most common meter in English poetry.

> Fŏr Gód's / săke, hóld / yŏur tóngue, /
> ănd lét / m̆e lóve . . .
>
> Donne, "The Canonization"

imagery, the sensory details that provide vividness in a literary work and tend to arouse emotions or feelings in a reader which abstract language does not. Shakespeare's Sonnet 130, page 159, is rich in specific, concrete details that appeal to the senses.

inference, a reasonable conclusion about the behavior of a character or the meaning of an event drawn from the limited information presented by the author.

in medias res (in mā′dē äs räs′), Latin for "in the middle of things." In a traditional EPIC the opening scene often begins in the middle of the action. *Paradise Lost*, page 258, opens with Satan and his angels already defeated and in Hell; later in the poem the story of the battle between Satan and the forces of Heaven, which led to this defeat, is told. This device may be used in any NARRATIVE form, not just the epic.

internal rhyme, rhyming words or accented syllables within a line which may or may not have a rhyme at the end of the line as well: "We three shall flee across the sea to Italy."

inversion (See ANASTROPHE.)

invocation (in′və kā′shən), the call on a deity or muse (classical goddess that inspired a poet) for help and inspiration found at the beginning of traditional EPIC poems. Milton, in *Paradise Lost*, page 258, instead of invoking one of the traditional muses of poetry calls upon the "Heavenly Muse."

irony, the term used to describe a contrast between what appears to be and what really is. In *verbal irony*, the intended meaning of a statement or work is different from (often the opposite of) what the statement or work literally says, as in Swift's "A Modest Proposal," page 307. *Understatement*, in which an opinion is expressed less emphatically than it might be, is a form of verbal irony, often used for humorous or cutting effect; for example, Johnson's remark in his "Letter to Chesterfield," page 331: "To be so distinguished [by Chesterfield's praise of Johnson's *Dictionary* in the press] is an honor which, being very little accustomed to favors from the great, I know not well how to receive." *Irony of situation* refers to an occurrence that is contrary to what is expected or intended, as in Hardy's "Ah, Are You Digging on My Grave?" page 536. *Dramatic irony* refers to a situation in which events or facts not known to a character on stage or in a fictional work are known to another character and the audience or reader. In *The Rape of the Lock*, page 319, events known to the sylph Ariel and to the reader are unknown to Belinda.

journal, a formal record of a person's daily experiences. It is less intimate or personal than a DIARY and more chronological than an autobiography. See *Journal of the Plague Year*, page 349, for a fictional attempt to create the impression of an actual journal.

kenning, metaphorical compound word used as a poetic device. In *Beowulf*, page 7, there are many examples of kennings. The king is the "ring-giver," the rough sea is the "whale-road," and the calm sea is the "swan-road."

literary ballad (See BALLAD.)

lyric, a poem, usually short, that expresses some basic emotion or state of mind. It usually creates a single impression and is highly personal. It may be rhymed or unrhymed. SONNETS are lyric poems. Other examples of lyrics are Burns's "A Red, Red Rose," page 362, and most of the shorter poems of the Romantics.

main idea (See THEME.)

masque, an amateur dramatic court entertainment with fine costumes and scenery, frequently given in England in the 1500s and 1600s, and the play written for such an entertainment.

maxim (See APHORISM.)

memoir (mem′wär, mem′wôr), a form of autobiography that is more concerned with personalities, events, and actions of public importance than with the private life of the writer. "Shooting on Elephant," page 753, is an example of memoir.

metaphor, a figure of speech involving an implied comparison. In "Meditation 17," page 241, Donne compares the individual to a chapter in a book and, later, to a piece of a continent. (See also SIMILE and FIGURATIVE LANGUAGE.)

metaphysical (met′ə fiz′ə kəl) **poetry,** poetry exhibiting a highly intellectual style that is witty, subtle, and sometimes fantastic, particularly in the use of CONCEITS. See especially the work of Donne, page 237.

meter, the pattern of stressed and unstressed syllables in poetry. (See RHYTHM.)

metonymy (mə ton′ə mē), a figure of speech in which a specific term naming an object is substituted for another word with which it is closely associated. For example, in Genesis, Chapters 1–3, page 230, it is said, "In the sweat of thy face shalt thou eat bread," in which the term "sweat" represents hard physical labor.

mock epic, a SATIRE using the form and style of an EPIC poem to treat a trivial incident. *The Rape of the Lock,* page 319, is a mock epic.

monologue (See SOLILOQUY and DRAMATIC MONOLOGUE.)

mood, the overall ATMOSPHERE or prevailing emotional aura of a work. "Kubla Khan," page 385, might be described as having a hypnotic, dreamlike atmosphere or mood. (See TONE for a comparison.)

motif (mō tēf′), a character, incident, idea, or object that recurs in various works or in various parts of the same work. In Shakespeare's sonnets, page 156, the nature and effect of time is a recurrent motif.

myth, a traditional story connected with the religion of a people, usually attempting to account for something in nature. Milton's *Paradise Lost,* page 258, has mythic elements in its attempts to interpret aspects of the universe.

narrative, a story or account of an event or a series of events. It may be told either in poetry or prose; it may be either fictional or true. Defoe's *Journal of the Plague Year,* page 349, is a narrative, as is *Paradise Lost,* page 258.

narrator, the teller of a story. The teller may be a character in the story, as in "My Oedipus Complex," page 776; the author himself, as in *Such, Such Were the Joys,* page 757; or an anonymous voice outside the story, as in "A Shocking Accident," page 771. A narrator's attitude toward his or her subject is capable of much variation; it can range from one of apparent indifference to one of extreme conviction and feeling. (See also PERSONA and POINT OF VIEW.)

naturalism, writing that depicts events as rigidly determined by the forces of heredity and environment. The world described tends to be bleak. There are elements of naturalism in the work of Thomas Hardy, George Eliot, and D. H. Lawrence.

neo-classicism, writing that shows the influence of the Greek and Roman classics. The term is often applied to English literature of the eighteenth century. (See Unit 4, page 272.)

novel, a long work of NARRATIVE prose fiction dealing with characters, situations, and SETTINGS that imitate those of real life. Among the authors in this text who have written novels are Charles Dickens, George Eliot, Thomas Hardy, Joseph Conrad, D. H. Lawrence, James Joyce, Virginia Woolf, and Graham Greene.

ode, a long LYRIC poem, formal in style and complex in form, often written in commemoration or celebration of a special quality, object, or occasion. See "Ode to the West Wind," page 400, "Ode on a Grecian Urn," page 408, and "Ode to a Nightingale," page 406.

onomatopoeia (on′ə mat′ə pē′ə), word(s) used in such a way that the sound of the word(s) imitates the sound of the thing spoken of. Some single words in which sound suggests meaning: "hiss," "smack," "buzz," and "hum." An example where sound echoes sense throughout the whole phrase: "The murmurous haunt of flies on summer eves." ("Ode to a Nightingale," page 406.)

ottava rima (ō tä′vä rē′mə), a STANZA pattern consisting of eight IAMBIC PENTAMETER lines rhyming *abababcc. Don Juan,* page 390, is written in ottava rima.

parable, a brief fictional work which concretely illustrates an abstract idea or teaches some lesson or truth. It differs from a FABLE in that the characters in it are generally people rather than animals; it differs from an ALLEGORY in that its characters do not necessarily represent abstract qualities. *The Wife of Bath's Tale,* page 103, has elements of the parable.

paradox, a statement, often metaphorical, that seems to be self-contradictory but which has valid meaning:

> When I lie tangled in her hair
> And fettered to her eye,
> The birds that wanton in the air
> Know no such liberty.
>
> Lovelace, "To Althea, from Prison," page 249

parody (See SATIRE.)

pastoral poetry, a conventional form of LYRIC poetry presenting an idealized picture of rural life. See "The Passionate Shepherd to His Love," page 142.

pentameter (pen tam′ə tər), a metrical line of five feet. (See also FOOT.)

> Whĕn tŏ / thĕ sḗs- / sĭŏns ŏf / swḕet sĭ- /
>
> lĕnt thṓught . . .
>
> Shakespeare, Sonnet 30, page 158

persona (pər sō′nə), the mask or voice of the author or the author's creation in a particular work. Jonathan Swift is of course the author of the excerpt from *Gulliver's Travels,* page 294, but even though the narrative is told from the *first-person* POINT OF VIEW, we are not to assume that Swift is expressing his personal opinions. Rather, he has created a persona in the form of a narrator, Lemuel Gulliver. "A Shocking Accident," page 771, is told from the *omniscient* POINT OF VIEW, but Greene has assumed a voice or persona—detached, witty, ironic—in telling the story. (See also NARRATOR and POINT OF VIEW.)

personification (pər son'ə fə kā'shən), the representation of abstractions, ideas, animals, or inanimate objects as human beings by endowing them with human qualities. Death is personified in Donne's Holy Sonnet 10, page 241. Personification is one kind of FIGURATIVE LANGUAGE.

Petrarchan sonnet (See SONNET.)

plot, in the simplest sense, a series of happenings in a literary work; but it is often used to refer to the action as it is organized around a CONFLICT and builds through complication to a CLIMAX followed by a DENOUEMENT or resolution. See the Shakespeare play, page 160.

point of view, the relation between the teller of the story and the characters in it. The teller, or NARRATOR, may be a character in the story, in which case it is told from the *first-person* point of view, as in the excerpt from *David Copperfield,* page 473. A writer who describes, in the *third person,* the thoughts and actions of any or all of the characters as the need arises is said to use the *omniscient* (om nish'ənt) point of view, as in "Tickets, Please," page 718. A writer who, in the *third person,* follows along with one character and tends to view events from that person's perspective is said to use a *limited omniscient* point of view, as in "Eveline," page 808. An author who describes only what can be seen, like a newspaper reporter, is said to use the *dramatic* point of view. (See also NARRATOR and PERSONA.)

prologue, section which precedes the main body of a work and serves as an introduction. See the *Prologue* to *The Canterbury Tales,* page 74.

protagonist (prō tag'ə nist), the leading character in a literary work. David Copperfield is the protagonist of the excerpt from *David Copperfield,* page 473. (See ANTAGONIST.)

pun, a play on words; a humorous use of a word where it can have different meanings, or of two or more words with the same or nearly the same sound but different meanings. For example, Alexander Pope wrote an epigram that was engraved on the collar of a dog that Pope presented to the king: "I am his Highness's *dog* at Kew; / Pray tell me sir, whose *dog* are you?" The word *dog* is played on in this couplet; it has a literal meaning in the first line and a figurative meaning (worthless person, or wretch) in the second.

quatrain (kwot'rān), verse STANZA of four lines. This stanza may take many forms, according to line lengths and RHYME patterns.

> Gather ye rosebuds while ye may,
>   Old time is still a-flying;
> And this same flower that smiles today
>   Tomorrow will be dying.
>
> Robert Herrick, "To the Virgins," page 247.

realism, a way of representing life that emphasizes ordinary people in everyday experiences. "My Oedipus Complex," page 776, provides an example of realism.

refrain, the repetition of one or more lines in each STANZA of a poem. See "Edward," page 67.

rhyme, exact repetition of sounds in at least the final accented syllables of two or more words.

> Hither the heroes and the nymphs resort,
> To taste awhile the pleasures of a court.
>
> Pope, *The Rape of the Lock,* page 322,
>   lines 137–138

(See also RHYME SCHEME, INTERNAL RHYME, END RHYME, and SLANT RHYME.)

rhyme scheme, any pattern of rhyme in a STANZA. For purposes of study, the pattern is labeled as shown below, with the first rhyme labeled *a,* as are all the words rhyming with it; the second rhyme labeled *b,* the third rhyme *c,* and so on.

> Queen and huntress, chaste and fair,   *a*
> Now the sun is laid to sleep,   *b*
> Seated in thy silver chair   *a*
> State in wonted manner keep;   *b*
>   Hesperus entreats thy light,   *c*
>   Goddess excellently bright.   *c*
>
>   Jonson, "To Cynthia," page 244

rhythm, the arrangement of stressed and unstressed sounds in speech or writing into patterns. Rhythm, or meter, may be regular or it may vary within a line or work. The four most common meters are IAMB or *iambus* ($\smile$ /), TROCHEE (/ $\smile$), ANAPEST ($\smile\smile$/), and DACTYL (/$\smile\smile$).

romance, a long narrative in VERSE or prose that originated in the Middle Ages. Its main elements are adventure, love, and magic. There are elements of romance in "The Day of Destiny," page 112, *Sir Gawain and the Green Knight,* page 119, and *The Faerie Queene,* page 144, particularly in its ATMOSPHERE and SETTING.

romanticism, unlike REALISM, tends to portray the uncommon. The material selected tends to deal with extraordinary people in unusual experiences. In romantic literature there is often a stress on the past and an emphasis on nature. See Unit 5 for many examples of romanticism.

run-on line, a line in which the thought continues beyond the end of the poetic line. There should be no pause after *thine* in the first line below:

> For sure our souls were near allied, and thine
> Cast in the same poetic mold with mine.
>
> Dryden, "To the Memory of Mr. Oldham," page 281

sarcasm (sar′kaz′əm), the use of language to hurt or ridicule. It is less subtle in TONE than IRONY. Boswell, in the *Life of Johnson,* page 338 (headnote), reports that when he first met Johnson he said (knowing Johnson's aversion to Scotland): "I do indeed come from Scotland, but I cannot help it." To which Johnson replied: "That, Sir, I find is what a very great many of your countrymen cannot help." Johnson's retort is an example of sarcasm.

satire, the technique that employs wit to ridicule a subject, usually some social institution or human foible, with the intention to inspire reform. SARCASM and IRONY are often used in writing satire. BURLESQUE and PARODY are closely related to satire. Burlesque is a literary or dramatic work that ridicules people, actions, or their literary works by mimicry and exaggeration. Parody, a kind of burlesque, is humorous imitation of serious writing, usually for the purpose of making the style of an author appear ridiculous. Swift's poetry and prose, page 290, Byron's *Don Juan,* page 390, and Shaw's *Pygmalion,* page 612, all provide good examples of satire.

scansion (skan′shən), the marking off of lines of poetry into feet, indicating the stressed and unstressed syllables. (See RHYTHM and FOOT.)

setting, the time (both time of day and period in history) and place in which the action of a narrative occurs. The setting may be suggested through dialogue and action, or it may be described by the NARRATOR or one of the characters. Setting contributes strongly to the MOOD or ATMOSPHERE and plausibility of a work. Setting is important in "Lines Composed a Few Miles Above Tintern Abbey," page 372.

Shakespearean sonnet (See SONNET.)

simile (sim′ə lē), a *figure of speech* involving a comparison using *like* or *as:*

> And now, like amorous birds of prey,
> Rather at once our time devour . . .
>
> Marvell, "To His Coy Mistress," page 250

In this example the similarity between the lovers and the birds of prey is their hungry appetite. (See METAPHOR for comparison.)

slant rhyme, rhyme in which the vowel sounds are not quite identical, as in the first and third lines below.

> And I untightened next the tress
>   About her neck; her cheek once more
> Blushed bright beneath my burning kiss:
>   I propped her head up as before,
>   Only, this time my shoulder bore . . .
>
> Browning, "Porphyria's Lover," page 461

soliloquy (sə lil′ə kwē), a DRAMATIC CONVENTION that allows a character alone on stage to speak his or her thoughts aloud. If someone else is on stage, and the character's words are unheard, the soliloquy becomes an *aside.* See the Shakespeare play, page 160, for examples. (Compare with DRAMATIC MONOLOGUE.)

sonnet, a LYRIC poem with a traditional form of fourteen IAMBIC PENTAMETER lines. Sonnets fall into two groups, according to their RHYME SCHEMES. The *Italian* or *Petrarchan* sonnet (after the Italian poet Petrarch) is usually rhymed *abbaabba / cdecde* (with variations permitted in the *cdecde* rhyme scheme). It forms basically a two-part poem of eight lines *(octave)* and six lines *(sestet)* respectively. These two parts are played off against each other in a great variety of ways. See "Whoso List to Hunt," page 132. The *English* or *Shakespearean* sonnet is usually rhymed *abab / cdcd / efef / gg,* presenting a four-part structure in which an idea or theme is developed in three stages and then brought to a conclusion in the COUPLET. See Shakespeare's sonnets, page 156.

speaker (SEE NARRATOR.)

Spenserian stanza (See HEXAMETER.)

spondee (spon′dē), a metrical FOOT of two accented syllables (//). It serves occasionally as a substitute foot to vary the meter, as in the third foot below.

> As yĕt / bŭt knóck, / bréathe, shíne, / ănd
> séek / tŏ ménd . . .
>
> Donne, Holy Sonnet 14, page 241

The opposite of the spondee is the *pyrrhic,* a metrical foot of two unaccented syllables (˘˘). It is rare in English poetry and is not even accepted as a foot by some experts.

sprung rhythm, metrical form which consists of scanning the accented or stressed syllables without regard to the number of unstressed syllables in a FOOT. A foot may have from one to four syllables, with the accent always on the first syllable of the foot. The term was invented and the technique developed by Gerard Manley Hopkins. The following line is scanned according to Hopkins's theory:

> Ánd fŏr áll / thís, / náture ĭs / névĕr /
> spént . . .
>
> Hopkins, "God's Grandeur," page 542

The first foot has three syllables, the second foot one, the third foot three, the fourth foot two, and the fifth foot one, with the accent on the first syllable of each foot.

stanza, a group of lines which are set off and form a division in a poem, sometimes linked with other stanzas by RHYME. Hopkins's "Pied Beauty," page 541, has two stanzas.

stereotype (ster′ē ə tīp′, stir′ē ə tīp), a conventional character, PLOT, or SETTING, which thus possesses little or no individuality, but which may be used for a purpose. The character of Murdstone in *David Copperfield* in many ways fits the stereotype of a villain.

stream of consciousness, the recording or re-creation of a character's flow of thought. Raw images, perceptions, memories come and go in seemingly random, but actually controlled, fashion, much as they do in people's minds.

style, the distinctive handling of language by an author. It involves the specific choices made with regard to DICTION, syntax, FIGURATIVE LANGUAGE, etc. For a comparison of two very different styles, see Wordsworth's "Ode on Intimations of Immortality" (page 377) with Pope's *The Rape of the Lock* (page 319).

subject, the topic about which an author is writing. (See THEME for a comparison.)

surrealism (sə rē′ə liz′əm), a term used in both painting and literature to apply to incongruous and dreamlike IMAGERY and sequences which are associated with the unconscious. "The Hollow Men," page 698, contains examples of surrealism.

symbol, something relatively concrete, such as an object, action, character, or scene, which signifies something relatively abstract, such as a concept or idea. In "Sailing to Byzantium," page 556, the city is a symbol of the ideal unity of all aspects of life—religious, aesthetic, practical, intellectual.

synecdoche (si nek′də kē), a *figure of speech* in which a part stands for the whole, as in "hired *hands.*" *Hands* (the part) stands for the whole (those who do manual labor—labor with their hands). The term also refers to a figurative expression in which the whole stands for a part, as in "call the *law.*" *Law* (the whole) represents the police (a part of the whole system of law).

tercet (tèr′sit), also called *triplet* a STANZA of three rhyming lines.

> Whenas in silks my Julia goes,
> Then, then (methinks) how sweetly flows
> That liquefaction of her clothes.
>
> Herrick, "Upon Julia's Clothes," page 247

terza rima (ter′tsä rē′mä), a verse form with a three-line STANZA rhyming *aba, bcb, cdc,* etc.

> Thou who didst waken from his summer dreams
> The blue Mediterranean, where he lay,
> Lulled by the coil of his crystalline streams,
>
> Beside a pumice isle in Baiae's bay,
> And saw in sleep old palaces and towers
> Quivering within the wave's intenser day . . .
>
> Shelley, "Ode to the West Wind," page 400

tetrameter (te tram′ə tər), a metrical line of four feet.

> Hăd wĕ / bŭt world / ĕnough, / ănd time . . .
>
> Marvell, "To His Coy Mistress," page 250

theme, the main idea or underlying meaning of a literary work. A theme may be directly stated but more often is implied. In "The Doll's House," page 707, the TOPIC or subject is described, at least in part, in the title, but an important theme is the pain of childhood.

tone, the author's attitude toward his or her subject matter and toward the audience. In the *Prologue* to *The Canterbury Tales,* page 74, Chaucer's tone is both sympathetic and ironic. He pretends to be an innocent observer, supplying details about each pilgrim in haphazard manner; yet these details, when carefully weighed, have a telling ironic force. The irony, however, is blended with humor and compassion.

topic, the subject about which an author writes. (See THEME.)

tragedy, dramatic or narrative writing in which the main character suffers disaster after a serious and significant struggle but faces his or her downfall in such a way as to attain heroic stature. See Shakespeare play, page 160.

trimeter (trim′ə tər), metrical line of three feet.

> Dŏwn tŏ / ă sun- / lĕss séa.
>
> Coleridge, "Kubla Khan," page 385

triplet (See TERCET.)

trochee (trō′kē), metrical foot made up of one accented syllable followed by an unaccented syllable.

> Dŏuble, / dŏuble / toĭl ănd / trŏuble;
> Fĭre / bŭrn ănd / caldrŏn / bŭbble.
>
> *Macbeth,* Act Four, Scene 1

verbal irony (See IRONY.)

verse, in its most general sense a synonym for poetry. Verse may also be used to refer to poetry carefully composed as to RHYTHM and RHYME SCHEME, but of inferior literary value. Sometimes the word *verse* is used to mean a line or STANZA of poetry.

vignette (vi nyet′), a literary sketch or verbal description, a brief incident or scene. "Great Men's Houses," page 713, may be considered a vignette.

villanelle, a form of poetry normally consisting of nineteen lines, written in five TERCETS and a final QUATRAIN, rhyming *aba aba aba aba aba abaa.* See Dylan Thomas's "Do Not Go Gentle into That Good Night," page 769.

voice (See PERSONA.)

Composition Guide

This Guide offers practical advice for writing many of the composition assignments in this book. These articles by themselves will not make you a better writer, but they will give you useful tips and techniques. The articles emphasize that writing is a process that begins before your pen touches paper and ends only with a revised, edited, and proofread composition.

This Guide includes the following articles:

Prewriting	821
Revising	822
Analyzing Literature	823
Making Comparisons and Contrasts	824
Evaluating Your Evidence	826
Defending Your Position	827
Developing Your Style	828

Prewriting

In writing a paper, it is often the planning, rather than the actual writing, that will take up more of your time. As with any fairly involved process, writing requires careful preparation. The steps you will go through in planning your composition will take time. However, if you skip the planning when preparing a paper, your first draft is likely to be poorly organized. Take the writing process one step at a time.

1. Understand the assignment. A "defend your position" assignment, for example, expects you to present a controlling idea and evidence to support it; be sure to do both. Note the details of the assignment and ask questions about anything you don't understand.

2. Think. Most of your writing assignments will be based on selections you have read. Spend a day thinking over the assignment and becoming familiar with the selection. Once you are familiar with the selection, try brainstorming. For example, what do you think of the

barrister Morgenhall in *The Dock Brief?* Write down every word, idea, fact, example, or opinion that occurs to you. Don't stop to edit, consider, evaluate; just put your ideas on paper.

3. Who is your audience? What is your purpose? To be effective, a writer must always be conscious that different groups of readers require different approaches. All of us make these kinds of adjustments when we speak to one another, but often forget to do so when we write. Your audience and your purpose will influence your tone, vocabulary, choice of details, level of complexity, and a great deal more.

4. Talk it over. One of the best ways to get a handle on your ideas is to talk them over with friends. You might use class discussions to refine your ideas. Having others ask questions and make suggestions will help you to develop your ideas.

5. Plan ahead. Outlining is worth a try. An outline will tell you where to go and when to stop. You might simply list key words or ideas in a logical sequence, or you might arrange your ideas in a two-level order of headings and subpoints. It will keep track of what is more and less important and help you give equal ideas equal attention. A detailed outlining of ideas before you write will help to give your paper focus and continuity.

6. Write a rough draft. Try to write out your first draft quickly so that you can get your main ideas down on paper. Rewriting and polishing can come later. During the first writing, don't bother with misspellings, punctuation, or even a few sentences that seem awkward and unclear. When you've completed your rough draft, you're ready for what many writers consider to be real writing: revising.

Revising

Experienced writers know that revising is a necessary part of the writing process. True, an occasional Mozart comes along who never leaves a smudge on the musical score, but most of us are like Beethoven, whose heavily reworked scores testify to hours of intensive revision. Every writer must be ready to write—and rewrite—until finally an inner voice cries, "Enough!" or the deadline arrives.

Is there a strategy for revision? A checklist that reminds you what to look for when reading over your manuscript can be very helpful, especially a series of questions such as the following:

1. Is the controlling idea of the paper clearly stated in the first paragraph?

2. Does the paper have a sense of progression, a steady movement toward the most important ideas, which should always be saved for last?

3. Does the paper read well aloud? Where could sentences be combined, *and*'s be eliminated, or similar sentence openings be changed to reduce choppiness and monotony?

4. What needs to be cut? (Be ruthless! Don't use four words, such as "due to the fact," where you could use one—"because." Strike out any sentence that doesn't illuminate your subject, or that repeats what you have just said.)

5. Are your paragraphs proportional? Except when used for surprise effect, a paragraph of two sentences next to one of ten or twelve

sentences implies a need for more detail or better organization of material.

6. Are the opening and closing paragraphs forceful, interesting, and complementary? (Make sure that the last paragraph is not simply a restatement of the first paragraph but a summation and resolution of all that has been discussed.)

7. Which sentences, now in passive voice, could be more effectively phrased in active voice? (Not "The murder of King Duncan is carried out by Macbeth and Lady Macbeth during the dark hours after midnight" but rather, "Macbeth and Lady Macbeth carry out the murder of King Duncan during the dark hours after midnight.")

Editing and Proofreading

Before typing your paper in its final form, you should edit it carefully to catch errors in grammar, mechanics, or usage.

1. Are all the words spelled correctly?

2. Is all of the punctuation logical and helpful in making the meaning clear?

3. Have you used capitals, italics, numerals, and abbreviations correctly?

4. Have you checked pronouns and verbs for common errors, such as faulty agreement, incorrect pronoun form or reference, incorrect form of the verb?

5. Can you spot any errors in word choice or usage?

Your last task before handing in your paper

is to proofread the completed manuscript to catch whatever errors might have slipped in while you were typing. Make certain that letters have not been switched around or words omitted, repeated, or misspelled. You should also make sure that you have followed the rules for manuscript form prescribed at your school.

Analyzing Literature

The success of any writing assignment based on a literary work depends on your ability to read closely and carefully. Consider, for example, topics such as the following:

Write a critical analysis of Keats's "Ode to a Nightingale."

Characterize Morgenhall of John Mortimer's *The Dock Brief.*

Identify and discuss the targets of social criticism in Chaucer's *Prologue* to *The Canterbury Tales.*

In addition to the conventional skills of composition, questions like these demand skill in drawing inferences, perceiving tone, interpreting figurative language and allusion, and selecting pertinent quotations and supportive detail.

1. Master the subject. Before getting down to the actual planning of your paper, expect to do several readings of the text you are analyzing. Be thorough and persistent:

• *Look up the meaning of unfamiliar words.* Consider both the denotations and connotations of the words used. For example, in "Ode to a Nightingale," Keats's use of words like *incense* and *embalmèd* conveys not only an impression of fragrance (denotation) but also an atmosphere of death (connotation).
• *Paraphrase passages containing figures of speech, allusions, or symbols.* A paraphrase of the metaphoric lines in Keats's ode, "Still wouldst thou sing, and I have ears in vain— / To thy high requiem become a sod," might be worded this way: Were the poet to die, the bird's song would continue, but the poet would no longer be alive to hear it.
• *Study the relationship of the parts to the whole.* Every literary work has a distinctive design, an organizational structure that supports and complements the ideas expressed. You should therefore carefully study the relationship of the various stanzas, speeches, or episodes to the overall work. To characterize Morgenhall of *The Dock Brief,* for example, you would have to take into account the way the two leading characters reverse roles in each scene: in Scene One, Morgenhall hopes to save a man charged with murdering his wife; in Scene Two, the client strives to save Morgenhall from possible suicide and despair.
• *Pay particular attention to the progression of ideas.* In most literary works you will be able to trace a clearly developed change either in character, situation, feeling, or viewpoint. Keats's ode, for example, traces the poet's efforts to escape into the timeless—and painless—realm of immortal beauty but ends with the poet returned to a state of mind even more "forlorn" than before, a progression that accentuates the pathos of the human condition.
• *Determine the tone of the overall work— light, serious, satiric, and so on.* Tone is a writer's technique for signaling to the reader an attitude toward a character, idea, or situation. In the *Prologue* to *The Canterbury Tales,* for example, Chaucer's tone is ironic, but so blended with humor and compassion that the reader feels drawn to his characters in spite of their faults. What could be taken as deeply tragic in *The Dock Brief* is rendered humorous and uplifting by means of witty, light-hearted dialogue.

• *Pay attention to the title.* While many titles, such as *Beowulf, Macbeth,* or *Hamlet,* simply name the main character of the work, many other titles have ironic or symbolic meaning. The title *Pygmalion* is an allusion to a Greek myth and signals that the play will describe a transformation from something lowly to something sublime. The title of "My Oedipus Complex" plays ironically upon a psychoanalytic term that is itself an allusion to Greek drama and myth. In writing about literature, the place to begin may very well be the title, which can often unlock the meaning of the overall work.

• *Focus on the selection.* Pay attention to the selection itself, for example the "Ode to a Nightingale," and not on how it reminds you of the time you heard a bird singing.

2. Gather evidence. As you read, jot down key words, important passages, author comments, or any other kind of details that relate to your subject and that you might choose to incorporate into your paper. Use file cards, if possible, since they facilitate classification and organization of information.

3. Formulate a controlling idea. After careful study of the text and your notecards, decide upon a central idea—a unifying generalization—that you intend to develop in your paper. For a critical analysis of Keats's ode, for example, you might decide on this kind of controlling idea: While the nightingale's song inspires temporary happiness by providing insight into the immortality of nature and beauty, paradoxically it also causes the poet increased pain by reminding him, through contrast, of the reality of human suffering, including his own. Don't be afraid to be independent in your ideas—as long as you can back them up. Literary interpretations are not judged as right or wrong, but as well or poorly supported.

4. Take charge of your material. You may decide to work through a poem line by line, or trace a writer's use of symbol or theme. No matter what the approach, your paper should fall into a rhythm of assertion and support, a statement followed by evidence. Conveniently, your evidence is the selection itself.

A major temptation for anyone writing a paper based on a literary work is to string together a mass of quotations as a virtuous demonstration of diligence. This kind of quoting is doomed to failure for several reasons. First, your commentary, not a mass of citation, should be the major focus of the paper. Second, quotations require a "frame"—an introduction and a follow-up explanation. They can never stand alone.

You would do well, then, to observe the following guidelines for cited material:

• *Be sparing in the use of very long quotations.*
• *Introduce a quotation in such a way that the reader feels compelled to read it.*
• *Always explain your quote.*
• *When citing a sequence of poetic lines not set up in stanza form, use slash marks to separate the lines.* For example: "Forlorn! the very word is like a bell / To toll me back from thee to my sole self."

Making Comparisons and Contrasts

Discovering likenesses and differences is the starting point of all learning, from an infant's distinguishing among sounds to the mature reader's approach to the analysis of characters and ideas in stories, novels, poems, and plays. To answer a question such as, "Does Macbeth qualify as a tragic hero?" you would probably think of other dramatic protagonists, such as Hamlet, Brutus, or Romeo, against whom Macbeth could be measured. Making comparisons and contrasts is thus a process of discovery, a way of deepening your understanding of characters and ideas in literature.

In writing a comparative analysis, the place to begin is with several readings of the work or works to be discussed. Then you need to gather evidence and choose a method of organization.

1. Establish points of comparison. You first need to set up points of comparison, issues, or categories that apply to each of your subjects. For example, suppose your assignment is the following: "Compare Colonel Pickering and Professor Higgins in their influence on Liza's development from flower girl to lady." The areas of comparison for Colonel Pickering and Professor Higgins might be these:

—initial reaction to Liza
—role in Liza's linguistic development
—personal treatment of Liza
—Liza's judgment of Higgins and Pickering

As you proceed you may decide to drop some categories and substitute others, but keep in mind that the main purpose of these categories is to keep you organized and efficient as you search for usable information.

2. Make lists. Under each category you have chosen, list all the similarities and differences you can find. At this stage, don't stop to evaluate the evidence; that can come later. But try to keep equivalent points on the same line and in parallel form:

—Liza's judgment of Higgins and Pickering

Higgins:	Pickering:
crude	courteous
inconsiderate	thoughtful
self-centered	concerned about Liza

This way you are more likely to use parallel structure when you start writing your paper.

3. Formulate a controlling idea. After you have drawn up a generous list of similarities and differences, you are ready to evaluate your material. What conclusion can be drawn from the accumulated evidence? A paper comparing Professor Higgins and Colonel Pickering in

their influence on Liza might perhaps be developed around the idea, "While Higgins was responsible for teaching Liza standard English and superficial manners, to Colonel Pickering must go the credit for turning Liza into a 'lady,' " or, "Pickering is the real Pygmalion of the play." Whatever you choose, try to devise a controlling idea that enables you to make the most complete use of the information you have assembled.

4. Select a method of organization. For comparison and contrast, you have several ways to organize your paper:

- *Whole-to-whole*. With this method of organization, you completely discuss one of your subjects first, then give comparable treatment to your second subject, bringing the two together in a final paragraph.
- *Likenesses—differences*. You could choose to discuss all the similarities of your subjects, then all their differences, placing the more important discussion last.
- *Item-by-item*. In this approach you take up each item on your list one by one, setting them down in sentence form. For example: "Professor Higgins's treatment of Liza is characteristically rude and inconsiderate. Colonel Pickering, on the other hand, is consistently courteous, thoughtful, and kind. While Higgins is mainly concerned about his personal success, Pickering hopes to make Liza a success," and so forth. This item-by-item approach, however, should not be used for the entire paper, since it can quickly become boring and repetitive.

5. Provide sturdy bridges between ideas. Papers of comparison and contrast carry the reader back and forth between ideas by means of carefully constructed bridges, transitions that make the journey smooth and interesting. The building blocks include words like "similar to," "on the other hand," "in contrast," and so on. The challenge is to keep the transitions from dominating or dulling the paper through wordiness or repetition. Strive to make your reader pay attention to your ideas, not to the apparatus that supports them.

Evaluating Your Evidence

Many writing assignments based on literary works require you to take a stand on an issue and defend your opinion. For example:

> "The Pardoner's Tale" has been called one of the greatest short stories ever written. Explain why you agree or disagree with this assessment.
>
> Some readers think that the monsters in *Beowulf* turn an otherwise serious work into a story for children. Argue for or against this viewpoint.

In writing on either of these topics, what evidence should you choose to build your case?

1. Differentiate between fact and opinion. The best evidence is always facts and information that can be defended by logic or reference to specific statements and actions in the text being studied. Stay away from statements of opinion that have no factual or textual basis. Some opinions, of course, are better than others; especially valuable are opinions that are more likely to be objective and authoritative, for example, those of literary scholars and historians.

Which of the following statements could best develop the *Beowulf* topic?

> While the monsters in *Beowulf* are related to the creatures of fairy tales, Beowulf's adventures with Grendel, the monster's mother, and the dragon involve such basic concerns as the mystery of evil, loyalty, courage, and death.

> Far from making it a story for children, the monsters in *Beowulf* are not nearly as interesting and frightening as those in some television programs for children.

The first statement is preferable to the second, which relies completely on personal opinion. While the first uses evidence in the text as the basis for opinion, the second statement leads away from the text to an unsupportable generalization. The second statement also gives the writer no direction for the rest of the paper.

2. Subordinate plot summary to interpretation. Make sure in your writing that you provide a balanced mix of plot summary and interpretation. Plot summary alone proves nothing. In writing about Grendel, for example, you would not only have to tell what he does in the poem, but also describe the significance of his encounters with humankind and infer the nature of Grendel from his actions.

One technique to ensure that interpretation is not being neglected is to ask "so what?" each time plot summary is used, then check to see whether that question has been adequately answered. For example:

- *Plot summary:* Grendel raids and ravages the kingdom.
- *Interpretation (answer to "so what?"):* Among the motives for Grendel's acts of destruction are jealousy of humanity's fellowship and retribution for humanity's neglect of the world of grief and woe.

3. Support your generalizations. Pack your paper with details. Every valid "for example" adds value to your paper. During the rough draft stage, it is better to have more details rather than fewer, since you can always come back and weed out what seems excessive or less relevant. Also pay particular attention to your paragraphs. A tiny paragraph sandwiched between long sections is usually an indication of an unsupported generalization. If you can't find evidence to support it, you should probably eliminate it from the paper.

4. Use evidence responsibly. Misreading or superficial analysis of the text can lead to poor selection of evidence and use of illogical details. The following guidelines may help you avoid such pitfalls:

- *Doublecheck your inferences.* For example, just because many of the characters in *Beowulf*, including Beowulf himself, are described as boasting, speaking brave words, and seeking for fame, this should not lead the reader to assume that these characters are being described negatively. Too much evidence in the poem suggests that brave words spoken in the quest for fame in Anglo-Saxon culture meant something other than vain blustering or foolish behavior.

- *Define the tone accurately.* Be sensitive to the author's use of irony, understatement, or hyperbole (exaggeration). When Beowulf, for example, addresses the king's rude retainer as "My good friend Unferth," we are meant to understand that Unferth is anything but Beowulf's friend and that the description of him as such is an example of irony.
- *Keep details in context.* Often the temptation is strong to build a case on a single quotation or episode without considering all that has come before and after. The result is unconscious slanting, a distortion of the facts through interpreting them out of context or ignoring

other information that changes or contradicts the point you want to make. For example, at one point it is said of Beowulf that "The warrior staggered, for all his strength, / Dismayed and shaken and borne to earth" (lines 1038–1039). Any reader who relied on this episode alone to define Beowulf's character would be in an awkward position, since the context proves Beowulf to be heroic.

Overall, evaluating evidence is a three-step procedure:

First, decide on the major points you wish to make in your paper.

Second, find valid details in the text to support each point.

Third, analyze and interpret these details so that they prove the point you are making.

Defending Your Position

Who is to blame for the evil of Frankenstein's monster?

Suppose your assignment is to answer the above question in a paper stating your opinion and giving reasons to support your opinion. Once you have decided upon the main points you wish to make and have assembled the evidence to build your case, you are ready to consider how your paper should be organized.

1. Use deduction or induction. In defending your viewpoint, you have two organizational strategies from which to choose: *deduction* and *induction.*

When using *deduction,* the writer states the thesis (controlling idea) in the first paragraph, then provides a series of proofs in support of this idea. For example:

- *Controlling idea:* Society is to blame for the evil behavior of Frankenstein's monster.
- *Supporting details:* X
  X
  X
  X

When using *induction,* the writer provides a series of examples, reasons, and proofs that lead up to the controlling idea (thesis), which is stated in the last paragraph, sometimes as the last sentence. The organizational pattern is thus the exact reverse of deduction:

- *Supporting details:* X
  X
  X
  X
- *Controlling idea:* Society is to blame for the evil behavior of Frankenstein's monster.

While you are likely to use the deductive approach for most of your writing, the inductive method has the advantage of building suspense and sustaining reader interest to the last. It also highlights your main idea and provides a strong conclusion to your paper.

2. Arrange details in order of importance. Before preparing an outline, number your ideas in their order of importance—least important to most important. Whether proceeding deductively or inductively, take up your most important point last. This way your argument becomes progressively stronger as the reader moves from point to point, and the writing gains direction and momentum.

3. Make necessary concessions. When defending an opinion, try to anticipate any opposing viewpoints that could be brought up to refute or weaken your position. Concede any point that you cannot defend, then go on to prove that your case is solid in spite of these concessions.

For example, in arguing that society is to blame for the evil behavior of Frankenstein's monster, a concession paragraph might read as follows:

"Granted, the monster is extraordinarily grotesque, so constructed as to inspire horror and revulsion by his physical presence. Even Dr. Frankenstein, his creator, so abhors the sight of the creature that he runs out of the laboratory in horror, hoping it will go away. The monster's actions are also exceptionally savage and vindictive, including the murder of Frankenstein's brother, his bride, and his closest friend. Nevertheless, the evidence of the novel points overwhelmingly to society as being to blame for the monster's fiendish behavior."

Having thus stolen the thunder from the opposition by eliminating their major arguments against you, you are in an even stronger position to proceed with your case.

4. Stay in focus. In a paper of opinion, your purpose is to win assent to your viewpoint—to win the case. Thus, you need to maintain a clear and consistent focus on your subject and avoid bringing in unrelated facts and information. For example, a discussion of Dr. Frankenstein's methods of constructing the monster or of his friendship with Clerval may be interesting, but hardly relevant to an analysis of the role of society in transforming the creature into a fiend.

5. Connect sentences and paragraphs. Make your transitions explicit through repetition of key terms and use of transitional words, such as "furthermore," "in addition," "above all." For longer papers you may need to use an occasional transitional paragraph, which sums up what has been previously emphasized and moves the paper forward to new ideas. Above all, keep in mind that the writer's primary task is to develop a sequence of coherent paragraphs in which every sentence contributes to the continuity and flow of thought.

Developing Your Style

"Style is the man," the old saying goes, but what does it mean? Each individual has a distinctive way of expressing himself, whether in dress, speech, or other personal behavior. Style is reflected in the way we walk, place furniture in a room, or serve a meal. Style is also the way we arrange words on the page, the revelation of our character and personality through how we express our ideas, feelings, and dreams.

But what if the style is wordy, wooden, or unwieldy, the sentences pedestrian and repetitive, or, even worse, pretentious or weighed down by jargon? For any writer, developing an

effective writing style is a lifelong process, an achievement. Few people write clearly, colorfully, and distinctively without extensive practice, revision, and conscious application of acquired skills.

1. Find your own voice. Use words and images that are natural and clear to you, not something you think sounds intellectually impressive or sophisticated. Don't be afraid to be yourself, to say what you believe (and not what you think your teacher expects), to draw on the rich verbal resources you already have at your command (but beware of words you learned yesterday). Simplicity and honesty have always been the hallmarks of good style.

2. Strive for flair. The writers of the late nineteenth century made much of the quest for perfection of style. Oscar Wilde reported that he once spent an entire morning putting in a comma and all afternoon taking it out. This is an amusing story but a poor example for busy writers. The painstaking search for the exact word, the right image, and the telling detail is, of course, an essential part of the writer's task. Even the most bland and ordinary style can be enlivened by application of the following techniques:

• *A startling or highly dramatic opening sentence.* Consider the first sentence of George Orwell's essay "Shooting an Elephant": "In Moulmein, in Lower Burma, I was hated by large numbers of people—the only time in my life that I have been important enough for this to happen to me." Obviously the writer has been successful in causing the reader to read on.

• *Fresh images and figures of speech that circumvent cliché.* In "Such, Such Were the Joys," George Orwell uses striking similes and metaphors: "Over a period of two or three years the scholarship boys were crammed with learning as cynically as a goose is crammed for Christmas"; "Our brains were a gold-mine in which he [the schoolmaster] had sunk money, and the dividends must be squeezed out of us." To increase your verbal fluency, try coming up with one or more fresh comparisons for each of the following:

a. neat as	c. wild as	e. quick as
b. dark as	d. blue as	f. mad as

• *A heavy concentration of strong and vivid verbs.* Almost any sentence in Virginia Woolf's "Great Men's Houses" reveals her rich use of action-revealing verbs, for example: "Up in the attic under a skylight Carlyle groaned, as he wrestled with his history, on a horsehair chair, while a yellow shaft of London light fell upon his papers and the rattle of a barrel organ and the raucous shouts of street hawkers came through walls whose double thickness distorted but by no means excluded the sound."

• *Occasional long sentences constructed by means of cumulative detail.* Beginning writers are always encouraged to write crisp, compact sentences, but mature style requires the ability to write long, flowing sentences as well. Again note Virginia Woolf's skill in providing a cumulative sequence of meaningful details: "One sees London as a whole—London crowded and ribbed and compact, with its dominant domes, its guardian cathedrals; its chimneys and spires; its cranes and gasometers; and the perpetual smoke which no spring or autumn ever blows away." Or her use of the extended periodic sentence, which sustains suspense to the final word: "The high old house without water, without electric light, without gas fires, full of books and coal smoke and four-poster beds and mahogany cupboards, where two of the most nervous and exacting people of their time lived, year in year out, was served by one unfortunate maid."

Finally, remember that even the most famous writers occasionally develop blocks and experience frustration. If you take a step-by-step approach to writing, however, you will find that the result is a well-organized paper that fulfills the assignment.

Glossary

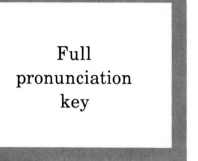

Full pronunciation key

The pronunciation of each word is shown just after the word, in this way: **ab bre vi ate** (ə brē′vē āt). The letters and signs used are pronounced as in the words below. The mark ′ is placed after a syllable with primary or heavy accent, as in the example above. The mark ′ after a syllable shows a secondary or lighter accent, as in **ab bre vi a tion** (ə brē′vē ā′shən).

Some words, taken from foreign languages, are spoken with sounds that do not otherwise occur in English. Symbols for these sounds are given in the key as "foreign sounds."

a	hat, cap	j	jam, enjoy	u	cup, butter
ā	age, face	k	kind, seek	ù	full, put
ä	father, far	l	land, coal	ü	rule, move
		m	me, am		
b	bad, rob	n	no, in		
ch	child, much	ng	long, bring	v	very, save
d	did, red			w	will, woman
		o	hot, rock	y	young, yet
e	let, best	ō	open, go	z	zero, breeze
ē	equal, be	ô	order, all	zh	measure, seizure
ėr	term, learn	oi	oil, voice		
		ou	house, out	ə	represents:
f	fat, if				a in about
g	go, bag	p	paper, cup		e in taken
h	he, how	r	run, try		i in pencil
		s	say, yes		o in lemon
i	it, pin	sh	she, rush		u in circus
ī	ice, five	t	tell, it		
		th	thin, both		
		ŦH	then, smooth		

foreign sounds

Y as in French *du.* Pronounce (ē) with the lips rounded as for (ü).

à as in French *ami.* Pronounce (ä) with the lips spread and held tense.

œ as in French *peu.* Pronounce (ā) with the lips rounded as for (ō).

N as in French *bon.* The N is not pronounced, but shows that the vowel before it is nasal.

H as in German *ach.* Pronounce (k) without closing the breath passage.

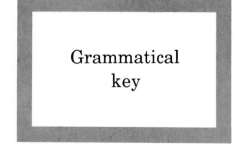

Grammatical key

adj.	adjective	*prep.*	preposition
adv.	adverb	*pron.*	pronoun
conj.	conjunction	*v.*	verb
interj.	interjection	*v.i.*	intransitive verb
n.	noun	*v.t.*	transitive verb
sing.	singular	*pl.*	plural

a baft (ə baft′), *adv.* at or toward the stern; aft. —*prep.* back of; behind. [< *a-* on + Middle English *baft* behind]

a bash (ə bash′), *v.t.* embarrass and confuse; make uneasy and somewhat ashamed; disconcert: *I was not abashed by the laughter of my classmates.* [< Old French *esbaïss-*, a form of *esbaïr* astonish]

a bate (ə bāt′), *v.*, **a bat ed**, **a bat ing.** —*v.t.* 1 lessen in force or intensity; reduce or decrease: *Soft words did not abate her fury.* 2 put an end to; stop: *abate a nuisance.* —*v.i.* become less in force or intensity; diminish: *The storm has abated.*

ab hor (ab hôr′), *v.t.*, **-horred, -hor ring.** regard with horror or disgust; hate completely; detest; loathe.

ab ject (ab′jekt, ab jekt′), *adj.* 1 so low or degraded as to be hopeless; wretched; miserable. 2 deserving contempt; despicable.

ab jure (ab jùr′), *v.t.*, **-jured, -jur ing.** 1 swear to give up; renounce. 2 retract formally or solemnly; repudiate. 3 refrain from; avoid. [< Latin *abjurare* < *ab-* away + *jurare* swear]

a bom i nate (ə bom′ə nāt), *v.t.*, **-nat ed, -nat ing.** 1 feel extreme disgust for; detest; loathe. 2 dislike: *abominate hot weather.* [< Latin *abominatum* deplored as an ill omen < *ab-* off + *ominari* prophesy < *omen* omen]

ab ste mi ous (ab stē′mē əs), *adj.* 1 sparing in eating, drinking, etc.; moderate; temperate. 2 very plain; restricted: *an abstemious diet.* [< Latin *abstemius*] —**ab ste′mi ous ly,** *adv.* —**ab ste′mi ous ness,** *n.*

ab sti nence (ab′stə nəns), *n.* 1 an abstaining; partly or entirely giving up certain pleasures, food, drink, etc. 2 Also, **total abstinence.** a refraining from drinking any alcoholic liquor.

ab struse (ab strüs′), *adj.*, **-strus er, -strus est.** hard to understand; difficult; recondite.

a bys mal (ə biz′məl), *adj.* 1 too deep or great to be measured; bottomless: *abysmal ignorance.* 2 of the lowest depths of the ocean. 3 INFORMAL. extremely bad; of very low quality. —**a bys′mal ly,** *adv.*

a byss (ə bis′), *n.* 1 a bottomless or very great depth; chasm. 2 anything too deep or great to be measured; lowest depth. 3 the chaos before the Creation. [< Greek *abyssos* < *a-* without + *byssos* bottom]

ac crue (ə krü′), *v.i.*, **-crued, -cru ing.** 1 come as a natural product or result. 2 grow or arise as the product of money invested. [< Old French *acreüe* an increase < *acreistre* to increase < Latin *accrescere* < *ad-* to + *crescere* grow] —**ac crue′ment,** *n.*

ac quit tance (ə kwit′ns), *n.* a written release from a debt or obligation.

ac ri mo ni ous (ak′rə mō′nē əs), *adj.* bitter and irritating in disposition or manner; caustic.

ad age (ad′ij), *n.* a well-known proverb.

ad a man tine (ad′ə man′tēn′, ad′ə man′tīn′), *adj.* unyielding; firm; immovable.

ad dle (ad′l), *v.*, **-dled, -dling,** *adj.* —*v.t., v.i.* 1 make or become muddled. 2 make or become rotten. —*adj.* 1 muddled; confused. 2 rotten: *addle eggs.* [Old English *adela* muck]

a droit (ə droit′), *adj.* 1 resourceful in reaching one's objective; ingenious; clever. 2 skillful in the use of the hands or body; dexterous. [< French < *à droit* rightly] —**a droit′ly,** *adv.* —**a droit′ness,** *n.*

af fec ta tion (af′ek tā′shən), *n.* 1 behavior that is not natural, but assumed to impress others; pretense. 2 mannerism, choice of language, etc., that indicates a tendency toward this.

af flict (ə flikt′), *v.t.* cause to suffer severely; trouble greatly; distress: *be afflicted with arthritis. The pangs of conscience afflicted me.* [< Latin *afflictum* dashed down, damaged < *ad-* to + *fligere* to dash]

af flic tion (ə flik′shən), *n.* 1 conditon of continued pain or distress; misery. 2 cause of continued pain or distress; misfortune.

af fright (ə frīt′), ARCHAIC. —*v.t.* excite with sudden fear; frighten. —*n.* sudden fear; fright; terror.

a gue (ā′gyü), *n.* 1 a malarial fever with chills and sweating that alternate at regular intervals. 2 any fit of shaking or shivering; chill.

a kim bo (ə kim′bō), *adj.* with the hands on the hips and the elbows bent outward. [Middle English *in kenebowe*, apparently, in keen bow, at a sharp angle]

al bi no (al bī′nō), *n., pl.* **-nos.** 1 person distinguished by the absence from birth of coloring pigment in the skin, hair, and eyes so that the skin and hair are abnormally white or milky and the eyes have a pink color with a deep-red pupil and are unable to bear ordinary light. [< Portuguese < *albo* white < Latin *albus*]

al lay (ə lā′), *v.t.*, **-layed, -lay ing.** 1 put at rest; quiet. 2 relieve (pain, trouble, thirst, etc.); alleviate. [Old English *ālecgan* < *ā-away, off* + *lecgan* to lay]

a hat	i it	oi oil	ch child	a in about
ā age	ī ice	ou out	ng long	e in taken
ä far	o hot	u cup	sh she	ə = i in pencil
e let	ō open	ù put	th thin	o in lemon
ē equal	ô order	ü rule	ŦH then	u in circus
ėr term			zh measure	< = derived from

al lu sion (ə lü′zhən), *n.* 1 act of alluding; slight or incidental mention of something. 2 a reference to a historical or literary person, event, or place, used to heighten the significance of a poetic image or a prose passage.

al lu vi al (ə lü′vē əl), *adj.* having to do with, consisting of, or formed by sand, silt, mud, etc., left by flowing water. A delta is an alluvial deposit at the mouth of a river.

am big u ous (am big′yü əs), *adj.* 1 having or permitting more than one interpretation or explanation; equivocal. 2 of doubtful position or classification. 3 not clearly defined; doubtful; uncertain.

a me na ble (ə mē′nə bəl, ə men′ə bəl), *adj.* 1 open to influence, suggestion, advice, etc.; responsive; submissive: *amenable to persuasion.* 2 accountable or answerable to some jurisdiction or authority: *People living in a country are amenable to its laws.* —**a me′na ble ness,** *n.* —**a me′na bly,** *adv.*

a miss (ə mis′), *adv.* 1 in a wrong way; wrongly. 2 **take amiss,** be offended at (something not intended to offend). —*adj.* improper; wrong. [Middle English *a mis* by mistake]

am i ty (am′ə tē), *n., pl.* **-ties.** peace and friendship, especially between nations; friendly relations; friendliness.

an ar chy (an′ər kē), *n.* 1 absence of a system of government and law. 2 disorder and confusion; lawlessness. 3 anarchism. [< Medieval Latin *anarchia* < Greek < *an-* without + *archos* ruler]

an guish (ang′gwish), *n.* 1 severe physical pain; great suffering: *the anguish of an unrelieved toothache.* 2 extreme mental pain or suffering: *the anguish of despair.* [< Old French *anguisse* < Latin *angustia* tightness < *angustus* narrow]

an i mos i ty (an′ə mos′ə tē), *n., pl.* **-ties.** keen hostile feelings; active dislike or enmity; ill will.

an nals (an′lz), *n.pl.* 1 historical events; history. 2 a written account of events year by year.

an ni hi late (ə nī′ə lāt), *v.t.*, **-lat ed, -lat ing.** destroy completely; wipe out of existence: *The flood annihilated over thirty towns and villages.* —*v.i.* cease to be; vanish; disappear: *Matter and antimatter annihilate when they collide.* [< Late Latin *annihilatum* brought to nothing <Latin *ad-* to + *nihil* nothing] —**an ni′hi la′tive,** *adj.* —**an ni′hi la′tor,** *n.*

a noint (ə noint′), *v.t.* 1 apply an ointment, oil, or similar substance to; cover or smear with oil, etc.: *Anoint sunburned arms with cold cream.* 2 consecrate by applying oil. 3 rub or smear with any other substance or liquid. —**a noint′er,** *n.* —**a noint′ ment,** *n.*

a nom a ly (ə nom′ə lē), *n., pl.* **-lies.** 1 something anomalous. 2 deviation from the rule; irregularity.

a non (ə non′), *adv.* ARCHAIC. 1 in a little while; soon. 2 at another time; again. 3 **ever and anon,** now and then. [Old English *on ān* into one]

an tiph o ny (an tif′ə nē), *n., pl.* **-nies** a responsive alternation between two groups, especially of singers.

a pace (ə pās′), *adv.* very soon; swiftly; quickly; fast.

ap os tol i cal (ap′ə stol′ə kəl), *adj.* 1 of or having to do with an apostle or apostles. 2 of the Apostles, their beliefs, teachings, time, or nature. Also, **apostolic.**

a poth e car y (ə poth′ə ker′ē), *n., pl.* **-car ies.** druggist; pharmacist. [< Late Latin *apothecarius* shopkeeper < Latin *apotheca* storehouse < Greek *apothēkē* < *apo-* from + *tithenai* put]

ap pa ri tion (ap′ə rish′ən), *n.* 1 a supernatural sight or thing; ghost or phantom. 2 the appearance of something strange, remarkable, or unexpected.

ap pas sio na to (ə pä′syä nä′tō), *adj.* (in music) with passion or strong feeling. [< Italian]

ap pease (ə pēz′), *v.t.*, **-peased, -peas ing.** 1 put an end to by satisfying (an appetite or desire): *A good dinner will appease your hunger.* 2 make calm or quiet; pacify. 3 give in to the demands of (especially those of a potential enemy).

ap pre hen si ble (ap′ri hen′sə bəl), *adj.* understandable.

ap pre hen sion (ap′ri hen′shən), *n.* **1** expectation of misfortune; dread of impending danger; fear. **2** arrest. **3** understanding.

ap pro ba tion (ap′rə bā′shən), *n.* favorable opinion; approval.

ap pur te nance (ə pėrt′n əns), *n.* addition to something more important; added thing; accessory.

ar dent (ärd′nt), *adj.* **1** glowing with passion; passionate; impassioned: *ardent love.* **2** very enthusiastic; eager: *an ardent believer in the benefits of health foods.* **3** burning; fiery; hot: *an ardent fever.* **4** glowing. —**ar′dent ly,** *adv.*

ar du ous (är′jü əs), *adj.* **1** hard to do; requiring much effort; difficult: *an arduous lesson.* **2** using up much energy; strenuous: *an arduous climb.* [< Latin *arduus* steep] —**ar′du ous ly,** *adv.* —**ar′du ous ness,** *n.*

ar raign (ə rān′), *v.t.* **1** bring before a court of law to answer an indictment. **2** call to account; find fault with; accuse. [< Anglo-French *arainer* < Old French *a-* to + *raisnier* speak]

ar rant (ar′ənt), *adj.* thoroughgoing; downright.

ar ras (ar′əs), *n.* curtain, screen, or hangings of tapestry.

ar ray (ə rā′), *n.* **1** proper order; regular arrangement; formation: *The troops marched in battle array.* **2** display of persons or things; imposing group. **3** clothes, especially for some special or festive occasion; dress; attire: *bridal array.* —*v.t.* **1** put in order for some purpose; marshal: *array troops for battle.* **2** dress in fine clothes; adorn.

ar ti fice[1] (är′tə fis), *n.* **1** a clever device or trick: *The child used every artifice to avoid going to the dentist.* **2** trickery; craft; *conduct free from artifice.* **3** skill or ingenuity. [< Latin *artificium* < *artem* art + *facere* make]

ar ti fice[2] (är′tə fis), *v.t.,* **-ficed, -fic ing.** frame or make by art.

as cend ent (ə sen′dənt), *adj.* **1** moving upward; rising. **2** superior; paramount; controlling. —*n.* position of power; controlling influence. Also, **ascendant.**

a sep tic (ə sep′tik, ā sep′tik), *adj.* free from the living germs causing infection. —**a sep′ti cal ly,** *adv.*

as per i ty (a sper′ə tē), *n., pl.* **-ties.** harshness or sharpness of temper, especially as shown in tone or manner.

as per sion (ə spėr′zhən), *n.* a damaging or false statement; slander.

as sail (ə sāl′), *v.t.* **1** attack repeatedly with violent blows. **2** attack with hostile words, arguments, or abuse. **3** (of a feeling) come over (a person) strongly; beset; trouble: *No doubts ever assail them.* —**as sail′a ble,** *adj.*

as say (ə sā′; *also especially for n.* as′ā), *v.t.* **1** examine by testing or trial; test. **2** ARCHAIC. attempt; trial. —*n.* **1** examination; test. **2** ARCHAIC. attempt; trial.

as sent (ə sent′), *v.i.* express agreement; agree; consent: *Everyone assented to the plans for the dance.* —*n.* acceptance of a proposal, statement, etc.; agreement. [< Latin *assentire* < *ad-* along with + *sentire* feel, think]

as sig na tion (as′ig nā′shən), *n.* **1** a secret meeting of lovers. **2** the appointment of a time and place for such a meeting. **3** an allotting; apportionment.

as size (ə sīz′), *n.* **1** session of a court of law. **2** assizes, *pl.* the periodic sessions of a court of law held in each county of England. [< Old French *assise,* ultimately < Latin *assidere*]

as suage (ə swāj′), *v.t.,* **-suaged, -suag ing.** **1** make (angry or excited feelings, etc.) less intense; calm or soothe. **2** make (physical or mental pain) easier or milder; relieve or lessen. **3** satisfy or appease (appetites or desires).

a sun der (ə sun′dər), *adv.* in pieces; into separate parts: *Lightning split the tree asunder.* —*adj.* apart or separate from each other: *miles asunder.*

a tro cious (ə trō′shəs), *adj.* **1** monstrously wicked or cruel; very savage or brutal; heinous: *an atrocious crime.* **2** INFORMAL. shockingly bad or unpleasant; abominable: *atrocious weather.* —**a tro′cious ly,** *adv.* —**a tro′cious ness,** *n.*

au da cious (ô dā′shəs), *adj.* **1** having the courage to take risks; recklessly daring; bold: *an audacious pilot.* **2** rudely bold; impudent. —**au da′cious ly,** *adv.* —**au da′cious ness,** *n.*

aught (ôt), *pron.* ARCHAIC. anything. Also, **ought.**

aug ment (ôg ment′), *v.t., v.i.* make or become greater in size, number, amount, or degree; increase or enlarge.

au gur (ô′gər), *n.* **1** priest in ancient Rome who made predictions and gave advice from signs and omens. **2** soothsayer; fortuneteller. —*v.t.* **1** guess from signs or omens; predict; foretell. **2** be a sign or promise of. —*v.i.* **1 augur ill,** be a bad sign. **2 augur well,** be a good sign. [< Latin]

au gur y (ô′gyər ē), *n., pl.* **-gur ies.** **1** prediction; sign; omen. **2** art or practice of foretelling events by interpreting such signs and omens as the flight of birds, thunder and lightning, etc.

au gust (ô gust′), *adj.* inspiring reverence and admiration; majestic; venerable. [< Latin *augustus* < *augere* to increase] —**au gust′ly,** *adv.* —**au gust′ness,** *n.*

aus pi cious (ô spish′əs), *adj.* **1** with signs of success; favorable. **2** prosperous; fortunate. —**aus pi′cious ly,** *adv.*

av ar ice (av′ər is), *n.* too great a desire for money or property; greed for wealth.

av a ri cious (av′ə rish′əs), *adj.* greatly desiring money or property; greedy for wealth. —**av′a ri′cious ly,** *adv.* —**av′a ri′cious ness,** *n.*

a vaunt (ə vônt′, ə vänt′), *interj.* ARCHAIC. begone! get out! go away!

a vi ar y (ā′vē er′ē), *n., pl.* **-ar ies.** house, enclosure, or large cage in which many birds, especially wild birds, are kept; birdhouse. [< Latin *aviarium* < *avis* bird]

a vouch (ə vouch′), *v.t.* **1** declare positively to be true; affirm. **2** vouch for; guarantee: *I can avouch her honesty.* **3** acknowledge; avow. [< Old French *avochier* < *a-* to + *vochier* to call] —**a vouch′ment,** *n.*

awl (ôl), *n.* a sharp-pointed tool used for making small holes in leather or wood. [Old English *æl*]

az ure (azh′ər), *n.* the clear blue color of the unclouded sky; sky blue. —*adj.* sky-blue.

badge (baj) *v.t.,.* **-badged, badging.** mark or distinguish with a badge.

bail iff (bā′lif), *n.* **1** (in England) an overseer or steward of an estate. The bailiff collects rents, directs the work of employees, etc., for the owner. **2** the chief magistrate in certain towns in England.

bait (bāt), *n.* anything, especially food, used to attract fish or other animals so that they may be caught. —*v.t.* **1** put bait on (a hook) or in (a trap). **2** tempt; attract. **3** attack; torment: *The dogs baited the bear.* **4** torment or worry by unkind or annoying remarks. [< Scandinavian (Old Icelandic) *beita* cause to bite]

bal dric (bôl′drik), *n.* belt, usually of leather and richly ornamented, hung from one shoulder to the opposite side of the body to support the wearer's sword, bugle, etc. Also, **baldrick.**

bale[1] (bāl), *n.* ARCHAIC. a great fire or burning pile.

bale[2] (bāl), *n.* ARCHAIC. **1** evil; harm. **2** sorrow; pain.

bale ful (bāl′fəl), *adj.* **1** full of hurtful or deadly influence; destructive. **2** full of misfortune; disastrous. —**bale′ful ly,** *adv.* —**bale′ful ness,** *n.*

bal last (bal′əst), *n.* **1** something heavy placed in the hold of a ship to steady it. **2** bags of sand or other heavy material carried in a balloon or dirigible to steady it or regulate its ascent.

balm (bäm, bälm), *n.* **1** a fragrant, oily, sticky substance obtained from certain kinds of trees, used to heal or to relieve pain; balsam. **2** a healing or soothing influence. **3** a fragrant ointment or oil used in anointing. **4** sweet odor; fragrance.

bane (bān), *n.* **1** cause of death, ruin, or harm. **2** destruction of any kind; ruin; harm. [Old English *bana* murderer]

bard (bärd), *n.* **1** a Celtic minstrel and poet who from earliest times to the Middle Ages sang his own poems, usually to harp accompaniment, celebrating martial exploits, etc. **2** any poet. [< Irish and Scottish Gaelic]

bark (bärk), *n.* **1** a three-masted ship, square-rigged on the first two masts and fore-and-aft-rigged on the other. **2** ARCHAIC. boat; ship. Also, **barque.**

bar on et (bar′ə nit), *n.* man in Great Britain ranking next below a baron and next above a knight. He has "Sir" before his name and "Bart." after it. EXAMPLE: Sir John Brown, Bart.

bar row (bar′ō), *n.* mound of earth or stones over an ancient grave. [Old English *beorg*]

base (bās), *adj.,* **bas er, bas est. 1** morally low or mean; selfish and cowardly: *Betraying a friend is a base action.* **2** fit for an inferior person or thing; menial; unworthy. **3** ARCHAIC. of humble birth or origin.

bea dle (bē′dl), *n.* a minor parish officer in the Church of England whose duties include keeping order and waiting on the clergy. [< Old French *bedel*]

beak er (bē′kər), *n.* **1** a large cup or drinking glass with a wide mouth. **2** contents of a beaker.

be guile (bi gīl′), *v.t.,* **-guiled, -guil ing. 1** trick or mislead (a person); deceive; delude: *Your flattery beguiled me into thinking that you were my friend.* 2 take away from deceitfully or cunningly. 3 win the attention of; entertain. 4 while away (time) pleasantly.

be hest (bi hest′), *n.* command; order.

bel dam (bel′dəm), *n.* 1 an old woman. 2 an ugly old woman; hag; witch.

be lie (bi lī′), *v.t.,* **-lied, -ly ing.** 1 give a false idea of; misrepresent: *Her frown belied her usual good nature.* 2 show to be false; prove to be mistaken. 3 fail to come up to; disappoint.

ben e dic tion (ben′ə dik′shən), *n.* 1 the asking of God's blessing, as at the end of a church service or a marriage ceremony. 2 the form or ritual of this invocation. 3 blessing.

ben e fac tor (ben′ə fak′tər, ben′ə fak′tər), *n.* person who has helped others, either by gifts of money or by some kind act. [< Late Latin < Latin *benefactum* befitted < *bene* well + *facere* do]

ben e fice (ben′ə fis), *n.* a permanent office or position in the church created by proper ecclesiastical authority and consisting of a sacred duty and the income that goes with it.

be queath (bi kwēᴛʜ′, bi kwēth′), *v.t.* 1 give or leave (especially money or other personal property) by a will. 2 hand down or leave to posterity; pass along. [Old English *becwethan* < *be-* to, for + *cwethan* say] **—be queath′er.** *n.*

be reave (bi rēv′), *v.t.,* **-reaved** or **-reft, -reav ing.** 1 leave desolate and alone: *The family was bereaved by the death of the father.* 2 deprive ruthlessly; rob: *bereaved of hope.*

be reft (bi reft′), *adj.* bereaved: *Bereft of hope and friends, the old man led a lonely life.* —*v.* a pt. and a pp. of **bereave.**

be smirch (bi smėrch′), *v.t.* 1 make dirty. 2 sully. [*be-* thoroughly + *smirch* discolor, Middle English *smorchen*]

be times (bi tīmz′), *adv.* ARCHAIC. 1 early. 2 before it is too late. 3 in a short time; soon.

be trothed (bi trōᴛʜd′, bi trôtht′), *n.* person engaged to be married. —*adj.* engaged to be married.

bide (bīd), *v.,* **bid ed** or **bode, bid ed, bid ing.** —*v.i.* 1 remain or continue in some state or action; wait: *Bide here awhile.* 2 ARCHAIC. dwell; reside. —*v.t.* ARCHAIC. put up with; endure; suffer. [Old English *bidan*]

bier (bir), *n.* 1 a moveable stand or framework on which a coffin or dead body is placed before burial. 2 such a stand together with the coffin. [Old English *bēr.* Related to *beran* BEAR.]

bil ious (bil′yəs), *adj.* 1 suffering from or caused by some trouble with bile or the liver. 2 having to do with bile. 3 peevish; bad-tempered. **—bil′ious ly,** *adv.* **—bil′ious ness,** *n.*

bit tern (bit′ərn), *n.* any of several small herons found chiefly in marshes, characterized by a peculiar booming cry.

black guard (blag′ärd, blag′ərd), *n.* a low, contemptible person; scoundrel. —*v.t.* abuse with vile language; revile. —*v.i.* behave like a blackguard.

blanch (blanch), *v.t.* make white or pale: *Old age blanched his hair.* —*v.i.* turn white or pale: *blanch with fear.*

blanc mange (blə mänzh′), *n.* a sweet dessert made of milk boiled and thickened with gelatin, cornstarch, etc., flavored and cooled in a mold. [< Old French *blanc-manger* white food]

blas phe my (blas′fə mē), *n., pl.* **-mies.** abuse or contempt for God or sacred things; profanity.

bla zon (blā′zn), *v.t.* 1 make known; proclaim: *Big posters blazoned the wonders of the coming circus.* 2 decorate; adorn. 3 describe or paint (a coat of arms). 4 display; show. —*n.* 1 coat of arms, or a shield with a coat of arms on it. 2 description or painting of a coat of arms. 3 display; show. [< Old French *blason* shield] **—bla′zon er,** *n.*

blear (blir), *adj.* 1 (of the eyes) dim from water, tears, etc. 2 indistinct; dim. —*v.t.* 1 dim (the eyes) with tears, etc. 2 blur.

blench (blench), *v.i., v.t.* turn white or pale; blanch.

blight (blīt), *n.* 1 disease of plants that causes leaves, stems, fruits, and tissues to wither and die. 2 anything that withers hope or causes destruction or ruin. 3 decay; deterioration. —*v.t.* 1 cause to wither and die. 2 destroy; ruin. —*v.i.* be blighted; suffer from blight.

blithe (blīᴛʜ, blīth), *adj.* 1 happy and cheerful; gay; joyous. 2 heedless. [Old English *blithe*] **—blithe′ly.** *adv.* **—blithe′ness,** *n.*

blithe some (blīᴛʜ′səm, blīth′səm), *adj.* blithe. **—blithe′some ly,** *adv.* **—blithe′some ness,** *n.*

bode (bōd), *v.t.,* **bod ed, bod ing.** 1 be a sign of; indicate beforehand; portend; foreshadow: *The rumble of thunder boded rain.* 2 bode ill, be a bad sign. 3 bode well, be a good sign.

bod kin (bod′kən), *n.* 1 a large, blunt needle with an eye, used

a hat	**i** it	**oi** oil	**ch** child	(a in about
ā age	**ī** ice	**ou** out	**ng** long	e in taken
ä far	**o** hot	**u** cup	**sh** she	ə = i in pencil
e let	**ō** open	**ù** put	**th** thin	o in lemon
ē equal	**ô** order	**ü** rule	**ᴛʜ** then	(u in circus
ėr term			**zh** measure	< = derived from

for drawing tape or cord through a hem, loops, etc. 2 a small dagger; stiletto. [Middle English *boydekyn* dagger]

bol ster (bōl′stər), *n.* 1 a long, firmly stuffed pillow, placed under the softer pillows on a bed or used as a back on a couch. 2 cushion or pad, often ornamental. —*v.t.* 1 support with a bolster. 2 keep from falling; support; prop. [Old English]

boon (bün), *n.* 1 great benefit; blessing: *Those warm boots were a boon to me in the cold weather.* 2 ARCHAIC. something asked for or granted as a favor. [< Scandinavian (Old Icelandic) *bōn* petition]

boor ish (bùr′ish), *adj.* like a boor; rude or rustic.[< Low German *bur* or Dutch *boer* farmer] **—boor′ish ly,** *adv.* **—boor′ish ness,** *n.*

boss (bôs, bos), *n.* a raised ornament of silver, ivory, or other material on a flat surface. [< Old French *boce* swelling, hump]

boun ty (boun′tē), *n., pl.* **-ties.** 1 a generous gift. 2 generosity in bestowing gifts; liberality. 3 reward; premium.

bourn[1] or **bourne**[1] (bôrn, bōrn), *n.* a small stream; brook.

bourn[2] or **bourne**[2] (bôrn, bōrn, bùrn), *n.* ARCHAIC. 1 boundary; limit. 2 goal; aim.[< Middle French *bourne*]

bow er (bou′ər), *n.* 1 shelter of leafy branches. 2 summerhouse or arbor. [Old English *būr* dwelling]

brace[1] (brās), **braced, brac ing.** *v.t.* 1 give strength or firmness to; support: *We braced the roof with four poles.* 2 prepare (oneself): *I braced myself for the crash.* 3 give strength and energy to; refresh: *The mountain air braced us after the long climb.*

brace[2] (brās), *n.* OBSOLETE. armor for the arm.

brand (brand), *n.* ARCHAIC. sword.

bran dish (bran′dish), *v.t.* wave or shake threateningly; flourish. —*n.* a threatening shake; flourish. [< Old French *brandiss-*, a form of *brandir* to brand < *brand* sword]

bray (brā), *n.* 1 the loud, harsh cry or noise made by a donkey. 2 a sound like this. —*v.i.* make a loud, harsh sound: *The trumpets brayed.* —*v.t.* utter in a loud, harsh sound.

bream (brēm, brim), *n., pl.* **breams** or **bream.** a yellowish freshwater fish related to the carp, common in Europe.

brief (brēf), *n.* statement of the facts and the points of law of a case to be pleaded in court.

brin ded (brin′did), *adj.* ARCHAIC. brindled; gray, tan, or tawny with darker streaks and spots.

broad (brôd), *adv.* outspokenly.

brogue (brōg), *n.* 1 an Irish accent or pronunciation of English. 2 a strongly marked accent or pronunciation peculiar to any dialect.

bruit (brüt), *v.t.* spread a report or rumor of; announce; report. —*n.* ARCHAIC. report; rumor.

buck ler (buk′lər), *n.* 1 a small, round shield used to parry blows or thrusts. 2 means of protection; defense.

bull (bùl), *n.* a formal announcement or official decree from the pope. [< Medieval Latin *bulla* < Latin, amulet, bubble]

bul wark (bùl′wərk), *n.* 1 person, thing, or idea that is a defense or protection. 2 wall of earth or other material for defense against an enemy; rampart. 3 breakwater. 4 Usually, **bulwarks,** *pl.* side of a ship extending like a fence above the deck.

bur gess (bėr′jis), *n.* citizen of an English borough.

burgh er (bėr′gər), *n.* citizen of a burgh or town; citizen.

byr ny (bėr′nē), *n.* a shirt of armor.

by word (bī′wėrd′), *n.* 1 a common saying; proverb. 2 person or thing that becomes well known as a type of some characteristic. 3 object of contempt; thing scorned. [Old English *bīword*]

ca dence (kād′ns), *n.* 1 the measure or beat of music, dancing, marching, or any movement regularly repeating itself; rhythm: *the cadence of a drum.* 2 fall of the voice. 3 a rising and falling sound; modulation.

ca jole (kə jōl′), *v.t.,* **-joled, -jol ing.** persuade by pleasant words, flattery, or false promises; coax.

ca lam i ty (kə lam′ə tē), *n., pl.* **-ties.** 1 a great misfortune, such as a flood, a fire, the loss of one's sight or hearing. **2** serious trouble; misery. [< Latin *calamitatem*]

ca lum ni ous (kə lum′nē əs), *adj.* slanderous. —**ca lum′ni ous ly,** *adv.*

cal um ny (kal′əm nē), *n., pl.* **-nies.** a false statement made to injure someone's reputation; slander. [< Latin *calumnia*]

cant (kant), *n.* **1** insincere talk; moral or religious statements that many people make, but few really believe or follow out. **2** the peculiar language of a special group, using many strange words; jargon; argot: *"Jug" is one of the words for "jail" in thieves' cant.*

ca pri cious (kə prish′əs, kə prē′shəs), *adj.* likely to change suddenly without reason; changeable; fickle: *capricious weather.* —**ca pri′cious ly,** *adv.* —**ca pri′cious ness,** *n.*

car bun cle (kär′bung kəl), *n.* a very painful, inflamed swelling under the skin caused by infection.

car di nal (kärd′n əl), *adj.* **1** of first importance; chief; principal: *The cardinal value of his plan is that it is simple.* **2** bright, rich red.

ca reer (kə rir′), *n.* **1** a general course of action or progress through life. **2** way of living; occupation; profession. **3 in full career,** at full speed; going with force: *We were in full career when we struck the post.*

car nal (kär′nl), *adj.* **1** of or connected with the appetites and passions of the body; sensual: *Gluttony and drunkenness have been called carnal vices.* **2** sexual: *carnal knowledge.* **3** worldly; not spiritual. —**car′nal ly,** *adv.*

car niv or ous (kär niv′ər əs), *adj.* **1** of or having to do with an order of mammals that feed chiefly on flesh. **2** using other animals as food; flesh-eating. —**car niv′or ous ly,** *adv.* —**car niv′or ous ness,** *n.*

ca rouse (kə rouz′), *v.,* **-roused, -rous ing,** *n.* —*v.i.* drink heavily; take part in noisy revels. —*n.* a noisy revel or drinking party. —**ca rous′er,** *n.* —**ca rous′ing ly,** *adv.*

car ri on (kar′ē ən), *n.* **1** dead and decaying flesh. **2** rottenness; filth. —*adj.* **1** dead and decaying. **2** feeding on dead and decaying flesh. **3** rotten; filthy.

case ment (kās′mənt), *n.* **1** window or part of a window which opens on hinges like a door. **2** any window. **3** a casing; covering; frame.

casque (kask), *n.* a piece of armor to cover the head; helmet.

cas ti gate (kas′tə gāt), *v.t.,* **-gat ed, -gat ing. 1** censure, chasten, or punish in order to correct. **2** criticize severely. [< Latin *castigatum* chastened < *castus* pure]

cat a falque (kat′ə falk), *n.* stand or platform to support a coffin in which a dead person lies.

cat a ract (kat′ə rakt), *n.* **1** a large, steep waterfall. **2** a violent rush or downpour of water; flood.

cat er waul (kat′ər wôl), *v.i.* howl like a cat; screech. —*n.* such a howl or screech. [Middle English *caterwrawe* < *cater* cat + *wrawe* wail, howl]

caul (kôl), *n.* ARCHAIC. a close-fitting cap of net, worn by women.

cav a lier (kav′ə lir′), *n.* **1** horseman, mounted soldier, or knight. **2** a courteous gentleman. **3** a courteous escort for a lady.

cel e brate (sel′ə brāt), *v.,* **-brat ed, -brat ing.** —*v.t.* **1** observe (a special time or day) with the proper ceremonies or festivities. **2** perform publicly with the proper ceremonies and rites. **3** praise; honor; laud. —*v.i.* observe a festival or event with ceremonies or festivities.

ce les tial (sə les′chəl), *adj.* **1** of the sky; having to do with the heavens: *The sun, moon, planets, and stars are celestial bodies.* **2** of or belonging to heaven as the place of God and the angels; heavenly; divine. **3** very good or beautiful. [< Latin *caelestis* < *caelum* heaven] —**ce les′tial ly,** *adv.*

cere ment (sir′mənt), *n.* Often, **cerements,** *pl.* cloth or garment in which a dead person is wrapped for burial.

chal ice (chal′is), *n.* **1** cup or goblet. **2** cup that holds the wine used in the Communion service.

cham ber lain (chām′bər lən), *n.* **1** person who manages the household of a sovereign or great noble. **2** a high official of a royal court. **3** treasurer: *city chamberlain.* [< Old French *chamberlenc*]

cha os (kā′os), *n.* **1** very great confusion; complete disorder: *The tornado left the town in chaos.* **2** Also, **Chaos.** the infinite space in which formless matter was thought to have existed before the ordered universe came into being. [< Latin < Greek]

charnel house, place where dead bodies or bones are laid.

char y (cher′ē, char′ē), *adj.,* **char i er, char i est. 1** showing

caution; careful; wary: *The cat was chary of getting its paws wet.* **2** shy. **3** sparing; stingy.

chasm (kaz′əm), *n.* **1** a deep opening or crack in the earth; gap. **2** a wide difference of feelings or interests between people or groups: *The chasm between England and the American colonies finally led to the Revolutionary War.* [< Latin *chasma* < Greek]

chaste (chāst), *adj.* **1** pure; virtuous. **2** decent; modest. **3** simple in taste or style; not excessively ornamented. [< Old French < Latin *castus* pure] —**chaste′ly,** *adv.* —**chaste′ness,** *n.*

chas tise (cha stīz′), *v.t.,* **-tised, -tis ing. 1** inflict punishment or suffering on to improve; punish. **2** criticize severely; rebuke. [variant of *chasten*] —**chas tise′a ble,** *adj.* —**chas tis′er,** *n.*

cher ub (cher′əb), *n., pl.* **cher u bim** for 1 and 2, **cher ubs** for 3 and 4. **1** one of the second highest order of angels. **2** picture or statue of a child with wings, or of a child's head with wings but no body. **3** a beautiful, innocent, or good child. **4** person with a chubby, innocent face. —**cher′ub like′,** *adj.*

cher u bim (cher′ə bim, cher′yə bim), *n.* **1** a pl. of **cherub** (defs. 1 and 2). **2** (formerly) cherub.

cher u bin (cher′ə bin, cher′yə bin), *n.* cherub.

chid (chid), *v.* pp. of **chide.**

chide (chīd), *v.,* **chid ed, chid, chid ing.** —*v.t.* find fault with; reproach or blame; scold. —*v.i.* find fault; speak in rebuke.

chi mer i cal (kə mer′ə kəl, kī mer′ə kəl), *adj.* **1** being or having to do with a chimera. **2** unreal; imaginary. **3** wildly fanciful; absurd; impossible: *chimerical schemes for getting rich.*

chim mer (chim′mər), *n.* DIALECT. room; chamber.

chol er (kol′ər), *n.* an irritable disposition; anger.

chol er ic (kol′ər ik), *adj.* **1** having an irritable disposition; easily made angry. **2** enraged; angry; wrathful: *a choleric outburst of temper.*

chro nom e ter (krə nom′ə tər), *n.* clock or watch that keeps very accurate time. A ship's chronometer is used in determining longitude.

cic a trice (sik′ə tris), *n.* cicatrix; a scar left by a healed wound.

cir cum scribe (sèr′kəm skrīb′, sèr′kəm skrīb), *v.t.,* **-scribed, -scrib ing. 1** draw a line around; mark the boundaries of; bound. **2** limit; restrict.

cir cum spect (sèr′kəm spekt), *adj.* watchful on all sides; cautious or prudent; careful. [< Latin *circumspectum* < *circum* around + *specere* look] —**cir′cum spect′ly,** *adv.* —**cir′cum spect′ness,** *n.*

cir cum vent (sèr′kəm vent′), *v.t.* **1** get the better of or defeat by trickery; outwit: *circumvent the law.* **2** go around. **3** catch in a trap. [< Latin *circumventum* circumvented < *circum* around + *venire* come] —**cir′cum ven′tion,** *n.*

cis tern (sis′tərn), *n.* an artificial reservoir for storing water, especially a tank below ground. [< Latin *cisterna* < *cista* box]

ci vil i ty (sə vil′ə tē), *n., pl.* **-ties. 1** polite behavior; courtesy. **2** act or expression of politeness or courtesy.

clam or ous (klam′ər əs), *adj.* **1** loud and noisy; shouting. **2** making noisy demands or complaints. —**clam′or ous ly,** *adv.*

clar i on (klar′ē ən), *adj.* clear and shrill: *a clarion call.* —*n.* **1** a trumpet with clear, shrill tones. **2** sound of or like this trumpet. [< Medieval Latin *clarionem* < Latin *clarus* clear]

cleave¹ (klēv), *v.,* **cleft** or **cleaved** or **clove, cleft** or **cleaved** or **clo ven, cleav ing.** —*v.t.* **1** cut, divide, or split open. **2** pass through; pierce; penetrate. **3** make by cutting. —*v.i.* **1** split, especially into layers. **2** pass; penetrate.

cleave² (klēv), *v.i.,* **cleaved** or (ARCHAIC) **clave, cleav ing.** hold fast; cling; adhere: *cleave to an idea.* [Old English *cleofian*]

cleft (kleft), *v.* a pt. and a pp. of **cleave¹.** —*adj.* split; divided: *a cleft stick.* —*n.* space or opening made by splitting; crack; fissure. [Old English *(ge)clyft*]

clem en cy (klem′ən sē), *n., pl.* **-cies. 1** gentleness in the use of power or authority; mercy or leniency. **2** mildness.

clepe (klēp), *v.t.,* **cleped** or **clept, clep ing.** ARCHAIC. call, name.

clout (klout), *n.* ARCHAIC. **1** cloth or rag. **2** garment.

clo ven (klō′vən), *v.* a pp. of **cleave¹.** —*adj.* split; divided.

cloy (kloi), *v.t., v.i.* **1** make or become weary by too much, too sweet, or too rich food. **2** make or become weary by too much of anything pleasant. —**cloy′ing ly,** *adv.* —**cloy′ing ness,** *n.*

cog i tate (koj′ə tāt), *v.i., v.t.,* **-tat ed, -tat ing.** think over; consider with care; meditate; ponder. [< Latin *cogitatum* tossed around < *co-* (intensive) + *agitare* agitate] —**cog′i ta′tion,** *n.*

coign of vantage, a good location for watching or doing something.

coil (koil), *n.* ARCHAIC. trouble; turmoil. [origin uncertain]

coin age (koi′nij), *n.* **1** the making of coins. **2** act or process of making up; inventing: *the coinage of new words.* **3** word, phrase, etc., invented.

col lat er al (kə lat′ər əl), *adj.* **1** related but less important; secondary; indirect. **2** side by side; parallel. **3** additional. **4** secured by stocks, bonds, etc. —*n.* stocks, bonds, etc., pledged as security for a loan. —**col lat′er al ly,** *adv.*

col lier (kol′yər), *n.* **1** ship for carrying coal. **2** a coal miner.

col lier y (kol′yər ē), *n., pl.* **-lier ies.** a coal mine and its buildings and equipment.

col lo qui al (kə lō′kwē əl), *adj.* used in everyday, informal talk, but not in formal speech or writing; conversational. Such expressions as *clip* for *punch* and *close call* for *a narrow escape* are colloquial. —**col lo′qui al ly,** *adv.*

comb er (kō′mər), *n.* **1** breaker. **2** person or thing that combs.

com bus ti ble (kəm bus′tə bəl), *adj.* capable of taking fire and burning; easily burned: *Gasoline is highly combustible.* —*n.* a combustible substance. —**com bus′ti bly,** *adv.*

come ly (kum′lē), *adj.,* **-li er, -li est. 1** pleasant to look at; attractive. **2** fitting; suitable; proper. [Old English *cȳmlic*]

com men da tion (kom′ən dā′shən), *n.* **1** praise; approval. **2** recommendation. **3** a handing over to another for safekeeping; entrusting.

com mis e rate (kə miz′ə rāt′), *v.t., v.i.,* **-rat ed, -rat ing.** feel or express sorrow for another's suffering or trouble; sympathize with; pity. —**com mis′e ra′tion,** *n.*

com mo tion (kə mō′shən), *n.* **1** violent movement; agitation; turbulence: *the commotion of the storm.* **2** bustle or stir; confusion.

com pass (kum′pəs), *v.t.* accomplish; obtain.

com pi la tion (kom′pə lā′shən), *n.* **1** act of compiling; collecting and bringing together in one list or account. **2** book, list, etc., that has been compiled.

com plai sant (kəm plā′snt, kəm plā′znt), *adj.* **1** obliging; gracious; courteous. **2** compliant. —**com plai′sant ly,** *adv.*

com pound (*adj.* kom′pound, kom pound′; *n.* kom′pound; *v.* kom pound′, kəm pound′), *adj.* **1** having more than one part. **2** formed of many similar parts combined into a single structure. —*n.* something made by combining parts; mixture. —*v.t.* **1** mix; combine. **2** add to; increase; multiply. [< Old French *compondre* put together < Latin *componere* < *com-* together + *ponere* put]

com prise (kəm prīz′), *v.t.,* **-prised, -pris ing. 1** consist of; include: *The United States comprises 50 states.* **2** make up; compose; constitute.

compt (kompt), *n.* ARCHAIC. count.

com punc tious (kəm pungk′shəs), *adj.* having or feeling compunction; regret; pricking of conscience.

con-, *prefix.* form of **com-** before *n,* as in *connote,* and before consonants except *b, h, l, m, p, r, w,* as in *concern.*

con., 1 against [for Latin *contra*]. **2** conclusion.

con cord (kon′kôrd, kong′kôrd), *n.* **1** agreement; harmony. **2** (in music) a harmonious combination of tones sounded together. **3** treaty. [< Old French *concorde* < Latin *concordia* < *com-* together + *cordis* heart]

con cu bine (kong′kyə bīn, kon′kyə bīn), *n.* woman who lives with a man without being legally married to him.

con de scen sion (kon′di sen′shən), *n.* **1** pleasantness to inferiors. **2** a haughty or patronizing attitude.

con du it (kon′dü it, kon′dit), *n.* **1** channel or pipe for carrying liquids long distances. **2** pipe or underground passage for electric wires or cables.

con fla gra tion (kon′flə grā′shən), *n.* a great and destructive fire: *A conflagration destroyed most of the city.*

con flu ence (kon′flü əns), *n.* **1** a flowing together: *the confluence of two rivers.* **2** place where two or more rivers, streams, etc., come together. **3** a coming together of people or things; throng.

con found (kon found′, kən found′ for *1, 2, 4, 5;* kon′found′ for *3*), *v.t.* **1** confuse; mix up: *The shock confounded me.* **2** surprise and puzzle. **3** damn: *Confound your impudence.* **4** ARCHAIC. make uneasy and ashamed. **5** ARCHAIC. defeat; overthrow. [< Old French *confondre* < Latin *confundere* pour together, mix up, confuse] —**con found′er,** *n.*

con fute (kən fyüt′), *v.t.,* **-fut ed, -fut ing. 1** prove (an argument, testimony, etc.) to be false or incorrect: *The lawyer confuted the testimony of the witness by showing actual photographs of the accident.* **2** prove (a person) to be wrong; overcome by argument.

con gen ial (kən jē′nyəl), *adj.* **1** having similar tastes and interests; getting on well together: *congenial companions.* **2** agreeable; suitable: *congenial work.* —**con gen′ial ly,** *adv.*

con gen i tal (kən jen′ə təl), *adj.* **1** present at birth: *a congenital deformity.* **2** inborn; deep-seated: *congenital dislikes.* [< Latin *congenitus* born with < *com-* + *genitus* born] —**con gen′i tal ly,** *adv.*

con jec ture (kən jek′chər), *n., v.,* **-tured, -tur ing.** —*n.* **1** formation of an opinion admittedly without sufficient evidence for proof; guessing. **2** a guess. —*v.t., v.i.* guess.

con ju ra tion (kon′jə rā′shən), *n.* **1** an invoking by a sacred name; conjuring. **2** the practice of magic. **3** a magic form of words used in conjuring; magic spell. **4** ARCHAIC. a solemn appeal.

con jure (kon′jər, kən jùr′), *v.t.,* **-jured, -jur ing. 1** compel (a spirit, devil, etc.) to appear or disappear by a set form of words. **2** make a solemn appeal to; request earnestly; entreat.

con sign (kən sīn′), *v.t.* **1** hand over; deliver: *The dog was consigned to the pound.* **2** send; transmit: *We will consign the goods to you by express.* **3** set apart; assign.

con so nan cy (kon′sə nən sē), *n.* **1** harmony; agreement; accordance. **2** harmony of sounds; simultaneous combination of tones in music that is agreeable to the ear. Also, **consonance.**

con ster na tion (kon′stər nā′shən), *n.* great dismay; paralyzing terror. [< Latin *consternationem* < *consternare* terrify]

con sum mate (*v.* kon′sə māt; *adj.* kən sum′it), *v.,* **-mat ed, -mat ing.** —*v.t.* bring to completion; realize; fulfill: *My ambition was consummated when I won the first prize.* —*adj.* in the highest degree; complete; perfect. —**con sum′mate ly,** *adv.*

con sum ma tion (kon′sə mā′shən), *n.* completion; fulfillment.

con tempt i ble (kən temp′tə bəl), *adj.* deserving contempt or scorn; held in contempt; mean; low; worthless: *a contemptible lie.* —**con tempt′i ble ness,** *n.* —**con tempt′i bly,** *adv.*

con tig u ous (kən tig′yü əs), *adj.* **1** in actual contact; touching: *A fence showed where the two farms were contiguous.* **2** adjoining; near. [< Latin *contiguus* < *contingere* touch closely] —**con tig′u ous ly,** *adv.* —**con tig′u ous ness,** *n.*

con ti nence (kon′tə nəns), *n.* **1** control of one's actions and feelings; self-restraint; moderation. **2** chastity.

con ti nent (kon′tə nənt), *adj.* **1** showing restraint with regard to the desires or passions; using self-control; temperate. **2** chaste. [< Latin *continentem* holding in, refraining < *com-* in + *tenere* to hold] —**con′ti nent ly,** *adv.*

con tour (kon′tùr), *n.* **1** outline of a figure. **2** line that defines or bounds anything. —*adj.* showing the outline, especially of hills, valleys, etc.

con tu me ly (kən tü′mə lē, kən tyü′mə lē; kon′tü mə lē, kon′tyə mə lē), *n., pl.* **-lies. 1** insolent contempt; insulting words or actions; humiliating treatment. **2** a humiliating insult. [< Latin *contumelia,* related to *contumacia* contumacy]

con vey ance (kən vā′əns), *n.* **1** a carrying; transmission; transportation. **2** thing that carries people and goods; vehicle. **3** communication. **4** transfer of ownership. **5** document showing such a transfer; deed.

con vo ca tion (kon′və kā′shən), *n.* **1** a calling together; assembling by a summons. **2** assembly.

con vulse (kən vuls′), *v.t.,* **-vulsed, -vuls ing. 1** shake violently. **2** cause violent disturbance; disturb violently. **3** throw into convulsions; shake with muscular spasms. **4** throw into fits of laughter; cause to shake with laughter.

con vul sion (kən vul′shən), *n.* **1** Often, **convulsions,** *pl.* a violent, involuntary contracting and relaxing of the muscles; spasm; fit. **2** a fit of laughter. **3** a violent disturbance: *The country was undergoing a political convulsion.*

con vul sive (kən vul′siv), *adj.* **1** violently disturbing. **2** having convulsions. **3** producing convulsions. —**con vul′sive ly,** *adv.* —**con vul′sive ness,** *n.*

coo lie (kü′lē), *n.* formerly, an unskilled laborer in China, India, etc., hired for very low wages. Also, **cooly.** [< Hindustani *qūlī*]

co quet (kō ket′), *v.i.,* **-quet ted, -quet ting. 1** flirt. **2** trifle.

cor dial (kôr′jəl), *adj.* **1** warm and friendly in manner; hearty; sincere: *a cordial welcome.* **2** strengthening; stimulating. —*n.* **1** food, drink, or medicine that strengthens or stimulates. **2** liqueur. —**cor′dial ly,** *adv.* —**cor′dial ness,** *n.*

a hat	i it	oi oil	ch child	a in about
ā age	ī ice	ou out	ng long	e in taken
ä far	o hot	u cup	sh she	ə = i in pencil
e let	ō open	u̇ put	th thin	o in lemon
ē equal	ô order	ü rule	ᵺ then	u in circus
ėr term			zh measure	< = derived from

cor por al (kôr′pər əl), *adj.* of the body: *corporal punishment.* [< Latin *corporalem* < *corpus* body] —**cor′por al ly,** *adv.*

cor po re al (kôr pôr′ē əl, kôr pōr′ē əl), *adj.* 1 of or for the body; bodily: *corporeal nourishment.* 2 material; tangible: *Land and money are corporeal things.* —**cor po′re al ly,** *adv.* —**cor po′re al ness,** *n.*

corse let (kôrs′lit), *n.* armor for the upper part of the body. Also, **corslet.**

coun te nance (koun′tə nəns), *n., v.,* **-nanced, -nanc ing.** —*n.* 1 expression of the face. 2 face; features. 3 approval; encouragement. 4 calmness; composure. —*v.t.* approve or encourage; sanction.

course (kôrs, kōrs), *v.,* **coursed, cours ing.** —*v.i.* 1 race; run: *The blood courses through the arteries.* 2 hunt with dogs. —*v.t.* 1 cause (dogs) to hunt for game. 2 run through.

cov ert (kuv′ərt, kō′vərt), *adj.* kept from sight; concealed; secret; hidden. —*n.* 1 a hiding place; shelter. 2 thicket in which animals hide.

cov et (kuv′it), *v.t.* desire eagerly (something that belongs to another).

cov et ous (kuv′ə təs), *adj.* desiring things that belong to others. —**cov′et ous ly,** *adv.* —**cov′et ous ness,** *n.*

cox comb (koks′kōm′), *n.* 1 a vain, empty-headed man; conceited dandy. 2 cockscomb.

coz en (kuz′n), *v.t., v.i.* deceive or trick; cheat; beguile.

cra ven (krā′vən), *adj.* cowardly. —*n.* coward. —**cra′ven ly,** *adv.* —**cra′ven ness,** *n.*

cre dent (krēd′nt), *adj.* ARCHAIC. giving credence; believing.

cre du li ty (krə dü′lə tē, krə dyü′lə tē), *n.* a too great readiness to believe.

cre scen do (krə shen′dō), *adj., adv., n., pl.* **-dos.** —*adj., adv.* (in music) with a gradual increase in force or loudness. —*n.* a gradual increase in force or loudness, especially in music.

cre tonne (kri ton′, krē′ton), *n.* a strong cotton, linen, or rayon cloth with designs printed in colors on one or both sides.

crib (krib), *v.t.,* **cribbed, crib bing.** shut up in a small space.

croft (krôft, kroft), *n.* BRITISH. 1 a small, enclosed field. 2 a very small rented farm. [Old English]

crone (krōn), *n.* a withered old woman.

crook (krůk), *n.* 1 hook; bend; curve: *a crook in a stream.* 2 a hooked, curved, or bent part: *the crook of the elbow.* 3 a shepherd's staff, curved on its upper end into a hook.

cuck old (kuk′əld), *n.* husband of an unfaithful wife. —*v.t.* make a cuckold of. [< Old French *cucuault* < *coucou* cuckoo]

cud (kud), *n.* mouthful of food brought back from the first stomach of cattle or other ruminant animals for a slow, second chewing in the mouth. [Old English *cudu, cwidu*]

cudg el (kuj′əl), *n., v.,* **-eled, -el ing** or **-elled, -el ling.** —*n.* 1 a short, thick stick used as a weapon; club. 2 **take up the cudgels for,** defend strongly. —*v.t.* beat with a cudgel. [Old English *cycgel*]

cuisse (kwis), *n.* piece of armor to protect the thigh.

cul-de-sac (kul′də sak′, kůl′də sak′), *n., pl.* **culs-de-sac** (kulz′də sak′, kůlz′də sak′), **cul-de-sacs.** street or passage open at one end only; blind alley.

cull (kul), *v.t.* 1 pick out; select: *The lawyer culled important facts from the mass of evidence.* 2 pick over; make selections from.

cum ber (kum′bər), *v.t.* encumber. —*n.* encumbrance. [< Old French *combrer* impede < *combre* barrier]

cu pid i ty (kyü pid′ə tē), *n.* eager desire to possess something; greed.

cut purse (kut′pėrs′), *n.* pickpocket.

da is (dā′is; *British* dās), *n.* a raised platform at one end of a hall or large room for a throne, seats of honor, a lectern, etc.

dal li ance (dal′ē əns), *n.* 1 a dallying; trifling. 2 flirtation.

dal li ant (dal′ē ənt), *adj.* OBSOLETE. tending to dalliance.

dam (dam), *n.* 1 the female parent of sheep, cattle, horses, or other quadrupeds. 2 a mother. [variant of *dame*]

dam sel (dam′zəl), *n.* ARCHAIC. a young girl; maiden.

das tard ly (das′tərd lē), *adj.* like a dastard; mean and cowardly; sneaking. —**das′tard li ness,** *n.*

daunt (dônt, dänt), *v.t.* 1 overcome with fear; frighten; intimidate. 2 lessen the courage of; discourage; dishearten.

daunt less (dônt′lis, dänt′lis), *adj.* not to be frightened or discouraged; brave. —**daunt′less ly,** *adv.*

dearth (dėrth), *n.* 1 too small a supply; great scarcity or lack. 2 scarcity of food; famine. [Middle English *derthe*]

dec la ma tion (dek′lə mā′shən), *n.* 1 act or art of declaiming; making formal speeches. 2 a formal speech or selection of poetry, prose, etc., for reciting. 3 loud and emotional talk.

de co rum (di kôr′əm, di kōr′əm), *n.* proper behavior; good taste in conduct, speech, dress, etc.

de cus sate (di kus′āt), *adj., v.,* **-sat ed, -sat ing.** —*adj.* 1 crossed; intersecting. 2 (of leaves, etc.) arranged along the stem in pairs, each pair at right angles to the pair next above or below. —*v.t., v.i.* to cross; intersect.

deem (dēm), *v.t., v.i.* form or have an opinion; think, believe, or consider. [Old English *dēman* < *dōm* judgment]

de fer (di fėr′), *v.i.,* **-ferred, -fer ring.** yield in judgment or opinion: *defer to one's parents' wishes.*

def er ence (def′ər əns), *n.* 1 respect for the judgment, opinion, wishes, etc., of another. 2 great respect. 3 **in deference to,** out of respect for.

def e ren tial (def′ə ren′shəl), *adj.* showing deference; respectful. —**def′e ren′tial ly,** *adv.*

de gree (di grē′), *n.* rank: *A noble is a person of high degree.*

de ject ed (di jek′tid), *adj.* in low spirits; sad; discouraged. —**de ject′ed ly,** *adv.* —**de ject′ed ness,** *n.*

de lin e ate (di lin′ē āt), *v.t.,* **-at ed, -at ing.** 1 trace the outline of. 2 draw; sketch. 3 describe in words; portray.

de lude (di lüd′), *v.t.,* **-lud ed, -lud ing.** mislead the mind or judgment of; trick or deceive. [< Latin *deludere* < *de-* to the detriment of + *ludere* to play] —**de lud′er,** *n.* —**de lud′ing ly,** *adv.*

de lu sive (di lü′siv), *adj.* misleading the mind or judgment; deceptive. —**de lu′sive ly,** *adv.* —**de lu′sive ness,** *n.*

de ment ed (di men′tid), *adj.* mentally ill; insane; crazy. [< Latin *dementem* < *de-* out + *mentem* mind] —**de ment′ed ly,** *adv.* —**de ment′ed ness,** *n.*

dep o si tion (dep′ə zish′ən, dē′pə zish′ən), *n.* 1 act of putting out of office or a position of authority; removal from power. 2 the giving of testimony under oath. 3 testimony, especially a sworn statement in writing. 4 a depositing. 5 thing deposited; deposit.

dep re cate (dep′rə kāt), *v.t.,* **-cat ed, -cat ing.** 1 express strong disapproval of: *Lovers of peace deprecate war.* 2 depreciate; belittle: *Don't deprecate the abilities of your classmates.* [< Latin *deprecatum* pleaded in excuse, averted by prayer < *de-* from, away + *precari* pray] —**dep′re cat′ing ly,** *adv.*

dep re da tion (dep′rə dā′shən), *n.* act of plundering; robbery; ravaging. [< Latin *depraedationem* < *de-* + *praeda* booty]

de ride (di rīd′), *v.t.,* **-rid ed, -rid ing.** make fun of; laugh at in scorn. [< Latin *deridere* < *de-* down + *ridere* to laugh]

de ri sion (di rizh′ən), *n.* 1 scornful laughter; ridicule. 2 object of ridicule. [< Latin *derisionem* < *deridere.* See DERIDE.]

des cant (*v.* des kant′, dis kant′; *n.* des′kant), *v.i.* talk at great length; discourse. —*n.* an extended comment; discourse.

de scry (di skrī′), *v.t.,* **-scried, -scry ing.** 1 catch sight of; be able to see; make out. 2 discover by observation; detect.

des e crate (des′ə krāt), *v.t.,* **-crat ed, -crat ing.** treat or use without respect; disregard the sacredness of; profane.

des o late (*adj.* des′ə lit; *v.* des′ə lāt), *adj., v.,* **-lat ed, -lat ing.** —*adj.* 1 laid waste; devastated; barren. 2 unhappy; forlorn; wretched. 3 left alone; solitary; lonely. 4 dreary; dismal. —*v.t.* 1 make unfit to live in; lay waste. 2 make unhappy. 3 deprive of inhabitants. [< Latin *desolatum* < *de-* + *solus* alone] —**des′o late ly,** *adv.* —**des′o late ness,** *n.*

des o la tion (des′ə lā′shən), *n.* 1 act of making desolate; devastation. 2 a ruined, lonely, or deserted condition. 3 a desolate place. 4 lonely sorrow; sadness.

de spond en cy (di spon′dən sē), *n.* loss of heart, courage, or hope; discouragement; dejection.

des pot (des′pət, des′pot), *n.* 1 monarch having unlimited power; absolute ruler. 2 any person who exercises tyrannical authority; oppressor. [< Greek *despotēs* master]

des pot ic (des pot′ik), *adj.* of a despot; having unlimited power; tyrannical. —**des pot′i cal ly,** *adv.*

des ti tute (des′tə tüt, des′tə tyüt), *adj.* 1 lacking necessary things such as food, clothing, and shelter. 2 **destitute of,** having no; without: *A bald head is destitute of hair.*

des ue tude (des′wə tüd, des′wə tyüd), *n.* disuse: *Many words once commonly used have fallen into desuetude.*

deuce (düs, dyüs), *interj.* exclamation of annoyance meaning "bad luck" or "the devil."

dex ter i ty (dek ster′ə tē), *n.* 1 skill in using the hands or body. 2 skill in using the mind; cleverness.

dex ter ous (dek′stər əs), *adj.* 1 skillful in using the hands or body. 2 having or showing skill in using the mind; clever. Also, **dextrous.** —**dex′ter ous ly,** *adv.* —**dex′ter ous ness,** *n.*

di a dem (dī′ə dem), *n.* 1 a crown. 2 an ornamental band of cloth formerly worn as a crown. 3 royal power or authority.

dif fi dent (dif′ə dənt), *adj.* lacking in self-confidence; shy. —**dif′fi dent ly,** *adv.*

di gres sion (də gresh′ən, dī gresh′ən), *n.* a digressing; turning aside from the main subject in talking or writing.

dil a to ry (dil′ə tôr′ē, dil′ə tōr′ē), *adj.* 1 tending to delay; not prompt. 2 causing delay. —**dil′a to′ri ness,** *n.*

di lec tion (də lek′shən), *n.* OBSOLETE. love.

dil i gence[1] (dil′ə jəns), *n.* constant and earnest effort to accomplish what is undertaken; industry.

dil i gence[2] (dil′ə jəns), *n.* a public stagecoach formerly used in France and other parts of Europe.

din gle (ding′gəl), *n.* a small, deep, shady valley.

dire (dīr), *adj.,* **dir er, dir est.** causing great fear or suffering; dreadful. [< Latin *dirus*] —**dire′ly,** *adv.* —**dire′ness,** *n.*

dire ful (dīr′fəl), *adj.* dire; dreadful; terrible. —**dire′ful ly,** *adv.* —**dire′ful ness,** *n.*

dirge (dèrj), *n.* a funeral song or tune. [contraction of Latin *dirige* direct! (first word in office for the dead)] —**dirge′like′,** *adj.*

dirk (dėrk), *n.* dagger. —*v.t.* stab with a dirk. [origin unknown]

dis burse (dis bėrs′), *v.t.,* **-bursed, -burs ing.** pay out; expend. [< Old French *desbourser* < *des-* dis-, away + *bourse* purse < Late Latin *bursa*] —**dis burs′er,** *n.*

dis cern (də zėrn′, də sėrn′), *v.t.* see clearly; perceive the difference between (two or more things); distinguish or recognize: *There are too many conflicting opinions for me to discern the truth.*

dis cern ment (də zėrn′mənt, də sėrn′mənt), *n.* keenness in seeing and understanding; good judgment; shrewdness.

dis con cert (dis′kən sėrt′), *v.t.* disturb the self-possession of; embarrass greatly; confuse. —**dis′con cert′ing ly,** *adv.*

dis con so late (dis kon′sə lit), *adj.* 1 without hope; forlorn; unhappy. 2 causing discomfort. —**dis con′so late ly,** *adv.*

dis count (*v.* dis′kount, dis kount′; *n., adj.* dis′kount), *v.t.* 1 deduct (a certain percentage) of the amount or cost. 2 leave out of account; disregard. —*v.i.* sell goods at a discount. —*n.* deduction from the amount or cost. —*adj.* selling goods at prices below those suggested by manufacturers.

dis course (*n.* dis′kôrs, dis′kōrs; *v.* dis kôrs′, dis kōrs′), *n., v.,* **-coursed, -cours ing.** —*n.* 1 a formal or extensive speech or writing: *Lectures and sermons are discourses.* 2 talk; conversation. —*v.i.* 1 speak or write formally or at length on some subject. 2 talk; converse. [< Latin *discursus* a running about < *dis-* + *cursus* a running]

dis gorge (dis gôrj′), *v.,* **-gorged, -gorg ing.** —*v.i.* throw up the contents; empty; discharge. —*v.t.* 1 throw out from the throat; vomit forth. 2 pour forth; discharge. 3 give up unwillingly.

di shev eled or **di shev elled** (də shev′əld), *adj.* not neat; rumpled; mussed; disordered: *disheveled appearance.*

dis perse (dis pėrs′), *v.,* **-persed, -pers ing.** —*v.t.* 1 send or drive off in different directions; scatter. 2 divide (light) into rays of different colors. —*v.i.* spread in different directions; scatter: *The crowd dispersed when it began raining.* [< Latin *dispersum* dispersed < *dis-* apart + *spargere* to scatter] —**dis pers′er,** *n.*

dis po si tion (dis′pə zish′ən), *n.* 1 one's habitual ways of acting toward others or of thinking about things; nature: *a cheerful disposition.* 2 tendency; inclination: *a disposition to argue.*

dis qui si tion (dis′kwə zish′ən), *n.* a long or formal speech or writing about a subject; dissertation.

dis sev er (di sev′ər), *v.t.* cut into parts; sever; separate. —*v.i.* separate. —**dis sev′er ment,** *n.*

dis si pate (dis′ə pāt), *v.,* **-pat ed, -pat ing.** —*v.t.* 1 spread in different directions; scatter. 2 cause to disappear; dispel. 3 spend foolishly; squander. —*v.i.* 1 scatter so as to disappear; disperse. 2 indulge excessively in sensual or foolish pleasures.

dis sol u ble (di sol′yə bəl), *adj.* capable of being dissolved.

dis tem per (dis tem′pər), *n.* 1 any sickness of the mind or body; disorder; disease. 2 disturbance. —*v.t.* make unbalanced; disturb; disorder.

dis till ment or **dis til ment** (dis til′mənt), *n.* ARCHAIC. 1 extract. 2 something distilled.

---

a hat	**i** it	**oi** oil	**ch** child	⎧ a in about
ā age	**ī** ice	**ou** out	**ng** long	⎪ e in taken
ä far	**o** hot	**u** cup	**sh** she	ə = ⎨ i in pencil
e let	**ō** open	**ù** put	**th** thin	⎪ o in lemon
ē equal	**ô** order	**ü** rule	**ᴛʜ** then	⎩ u in circus
ėr term			**zh** measure	< = derived from

dis traught (dis trôt′), *adj.* 1 in a state of mental conflict and confusion; distracted. 2 crazed.

di ver gent (də vėr′jənt, dī vėr′jənt), *adj.* diverging; different.

di verse (də vėrs′, dī vėrs′), *adj.* 1 not alike; different. 2 varied; diversified. —**di verse′ly,** *adv.* —**di verse′ness,** *n.*

doff (dof, dôf), *v.t.* 1 take off; remove: *doff one's hat.* 2 get rid of; throw aside. [contraction of *do off*]

dog mat ic (dôg mat′ik, dog mat′ik), *adj.* 1 of dogma; doctrinal. 2 positive and emphatic in asserting opinions. 3 asserted in a positive and emphatic manner: *a dogmatic statement.* —**dog mat′i cal ly,** *adv.*

dole (dōl), *n.* ARCHAIC. sorrow; grief.

dole ful (dōl′fəl), *adj.* very sad or dreary; mournful; dismal. —**dole′ful ly,** *adv.* —**dole′ful ness,** *n.*

do lor (dō′lər), *n.* sorrow; grief. [< Latin < *dolere* grieve]

dol or ous (dol′ər əs, dō′lər əs), *adj.* 1 full of or expressing sorrow; mournful. 2 causing or giving rise to sorrow; grievous; painful. —**dol′or ous ly,** *adv.* —**dol′or ous ness,** *n.*

do min ion (də min′yən), *n.* power or right of governing and controlling; rule; control.

dot ard (dō′tərd), *n.* person who is weak-minded and childish because of old age.

dot ing (dō′ting), *adj.* foolishly fond; too fond. —**dot′ing ly,** *adv.*

dou blet (dub′lit), *n.* 1 a man's close-fitting jacket. Men in Europe wore doublets from the 1400's to the 1600's. 2 pair of two similar or equal things; couple. 3 one of a pair. 4 one of two or more words in a language, derived from the same original source but coming by different routes. EXAMPLE: *fragile* and *frail.*

dow er (dou′ər), *n.* 1 a widow's share for life of her dead husband's property. 2 dowry.

dow ry (dou′rē), *n., pl.* **-ries.** 1 money or property that a woman brings to the man she marries. 2 natural gift, talent, or quality; natural endowment. Also, **dower.**

draught (draft), *n.* draft; a single act of drinking or the amount taken in a single drink.

dregs (dregz), *n. pl.* 1 the solid bits of matter that settle to the bottom of a liquid. 2 the least desirable part.

droll (drōl), *adj.* odd and amusing; quaint and laughable: *a monkey's droll tricks.* [< French *drôle*] —**droll′ness,** *n.*

dudg eon[1] (duj′ən), *n.* 1 a feeling of anger or resentment. 2 **in high dudgeon,** very angry; resentful. [origin unknown]

dudg eon[2] (duj′ən), *n.* OBSOLETE. a wooden handle on a dagger.

dul ci mer (dul′sə mər), *n.* a musical instrument with metal strings, played by striking the strings with two hammers.

dun (dun), *adj.,* **dun ner, dun nest,** *n.* —*adj.* dull, grayish-brown. —*n.* 1 a dull, grayish brown. 2 horse of a dun color. [Old English *dunn*]

du ress (dù res′, dyù res′; dùr′es, dyùr′es), *n.* 1 use of force; compulsion. The law does not require a person to fulfill a contract signed under duress. 2 imprisonment; confinement.

eaves (ēvz), *n. pl.* the lower edge of a roof that projects over the side of a building. [Old English *efes* edge]

ec cle si ast (i klē′zē ast), *n.* a member of the clergy.

ec cle si as ti cal (i klē′zē as′tə kəl), *adj.* of or having to do with the church or the clergy. —**ec cle′si as′ti cal ly,** *adv.*

ed dy (ed′ē), *n., pl.* **-dies,** *v.,* **-died, -dy ing.** —*n.* water, air, smoke, etc., moving against the main current, especially when having a whirling motion; small whirlpool or whirlwind. —*v.i., v.t.* 1 move against the main current in a whirling motion; whirl. 2 move in circles.

ef fi ca cious (ef′ə kā′shəs), *adj.* producing the desired results; effective. —**ef′fi ca′cious ly,** *adv.* —**ef′fi ca′cious ness,** *n.*

e gre gious (i grē′jəs), *adj.* 1 remarkably or extraordinarily bad; outrageous; flagrant: *an egregious blunder.* 2 remarkable; extraordinary. —**e gre′gious ly,** *adv.* —**e gre′gious ness,** *n.*

el o cu tion ar y (el′ə kyü′shə ner′ē), *adj.* of or having to do with elocution, the art of speaking or reading clearly and expressively in public.

e lude (i lüd′), *v.t.,* **e lud ed, e lud ing.** 1 avoid or escape by cleverness, quickness, etc.; slip away from; evade. 2 baffle.

e ma ci ate (i mā′shē āt), *v.t.,* **-at ed, -at ing.** make unnaturally thin; cause to lose flesh or waste away. —**e ma′ci a′tion,** *n.*

em bow er (em bou′ər), *v.t.* enclose in a shelter of leafy branches.

em i nent (em′ə nənt), *adj.* 1 above all or most others; outstanding; distinguished. 2 conspicuous; noteworthy: *The judge was a man of eminent fairness.* 3 high; lofty. 4 standing out above other things; prominent. [< Latin *eminentem* standing out, prominent < *ex-* out + *minere* jut] —**em′i nent ly,** *adv.*

em u late (em′yə lāt), *v.t.,* **-lat ed, -lat ing.** 1 copy or imitate in order to equal or excel the achievements or qualities of an admired person. 2 vie with; rival. —**em′u la′tion,** *n.*

en cum ber (en kum′bər), *v.t.* 1 hold back (from running, doing, etc.); hinder; hamper: *Heavy shoes encumber a runner in a race.* 2 block up; fill. 3 burden with weight, difficulties, cares, debt, etc.: *The farm was encumbered with a heavy mortgage.* Also, **incumber.** [< Old French *encombrer* < *en-* in + *combre* barrier]

en cum brance (en kum′brəns), *n.* 1 something useless or in the way; hindrance; burden. 2 claim, mortgage, etc., on property. Also, **incumbrance.**

en due (en dü′, en dyü′), *v.t.,* **-dued, -du ing.** 1 provide with a quality or power; furnish; supply. 2 clothe. Also, **indue.**

en gen der (en jen′dər), *v.t.* 1 bring into existence; produce; cause: *Filth engenders disease.* 2 beget: *Violence engenders violence.* [< Old French *engendrer* < Latin *ingenerare* < *in-* in + *generare* create]

e nig ma (i nig′mə), *n.* 1 a baffling or puzzling problem, situation, person, etc. 2 a puzzling statement; riddle.

en kin dle (en kin′dl), *v.t.,* **-dled, -dling.** kindle; set on fire, light, or arouse. —**en kin′dler,** *n.*

en sign (en′sīn, en′sən), *n.* a flag or banner: *The ensign of the United States is the Stars and Stripes.*

en trails (en′trālz, en′trəlz), *n.pl.* 1 the inner parts of the body of a human being or animal. 2 the intestines; bowels.

en treat (en trēt′), *v.t.* ask or keep asking earnestly; beg and pray: *The prisoners entreated their captors to let them go.*

en treat y (en trē′tē), *n., pl.* **-treat ies.** an earnest request; prayer or appeal: *I gave in to the children's entreaties.*

en voy (en′voi, än′voi), *n.* 1 messenger or representative. 2 diplomat ranking next below an ambassador and next above a minister. 3 any person sent to represent a government or ruler for diplomatic purposes.

ep i cure (ep′ə kyúr), *n.* person who has a refined taste in eating and drinking and who is very particular in choosing fine foods, wines, etc.

eq ua bil i ty (ek′wə bil′ə tē, ē′kwə bil′ə tē), *n.* equable condition or quality; evenhandedness; uniformity.

e qua nim i ty (ē′kwə nim′ə tē, ek′wə nim′ə tē), *n.* evenness of mind or temper; calmness; composure.

eq ui page (ek′wə pij), *n.* 1 carriage. 2 carriage with its horses, driver, and servants. 3 equipment; outfit. 4 articles for personal ornament or use.

e quiv o cate (i kwiv′ə kāt), *v.i.,* **-cat ed, -cat ing.** 1 use expressions of double meaning in order to mislead. 2 avoid committing oneself on some matter. —**e quiv′o cat′ing ly,** *adv.* —**e quiv′o ca′tor,** *n.*

e quiv o ca tion (i kwiv′ə kā′shən), *n.* 1 the use of expressions with double meaning in order to mislead. 2 an equivocal expression. 3 avoidance of committing oneself on some matter.

es tate (e stāt′), *n.* 1 a large piece of land belonging to a person; landed property. 2 condition or stage in life.

es thet i cism (es thet′ə siz′əm), *n.* appreciation of beauty or the cultivation of the arts.

e ther e al (i thir′ē əl), *adj.* 1 light; airy; delicate: *the ethereal beauty of a butterfly.* 2 not of the earth; heavenly. 3 of or having to do with the upper regions of space. Also, **aethereal.**

et y mol o gy (et′ə mol′ə jē), *n., pl.* **-gies.** 1 the derivation of a word. 2 account or explanation of the origin and history of a word. 3 study dealing with linguistic changes, especially with individual word origins. [< Greek *etymologia* < *etymon* the original sense or form of a word (neuter of *etymos* true, real) + *-logos* treating of]

eu ca lyp tus (yü′kə lip′təs), *n., pl.* **-tus es, -ti** (-tī). any of a genus of tall evergreen trees of the myrtle family, found mainly in Australia and neighboring islands; gum tree. It is valued for its timber and for a medicinal oil made from its leaves.

eu nuch (yü′nək), *n.* 1 a castrated man. 2 a castrated man in charge of a harem or the household of an Oriental ruler.

ev a nes cent (ev′ə nes′nt), *adj.* gradually disappearing; soon passing away; vanishing.

e ven song (ē′vən sông′, ē′vən song′), *n.* vespers.

e ven tide (ē′vən tīd′), *n.* ARCHAIC. evening.

e vince (i vins′), *v.t.,* **e vinced, e vinc ing.** 1 show clearly; manifest. 2 show that one has (a certain quality, trait, etc.).

ex alt (eg zôlt′), *v.t.* 1 make high in rank, honor, power, character, or quality; elevate. 2 fill with pride, joy, or noble feeling. 3 praise; honor; glorify. [< Latin *exaltare* < *ex-* up + *altus* high]

ex com mu ni ca tion (ek′skə myü′nə kā′shən), *n.* 1 a formal cutting off from membership in the church; prohibition from participating in any of the rites of the church. 2 an official statement announcing this.

ex cres cence (ek skres′ns), *n.* 1 an unnatural growth. Warts are excrescences on the skin. 2 a natural outgrowth. Fingernails are excrescences.

ex hil a rate (eg zil′ə rāt′), *v.t.,* **-rat ed, -rat ing.** make merry or lively; put into high spirits; cheer.

ex hort (eg zôrt′), *v.t.* urge strongly; advise or warn earnestly: *The preacher exhorted the congregation to love one another.* [< Latin *exhortari* < *ex-* thoroughly + *hortari* urge strongly]

ex hor ta tion (eg′zôr tā′shən, ek′sôr tā′shən), *n.* 1 strong urging; earnest advice or warning. 2 speech, sermon, etc., that exhorts.

ex or cist (ek′sôr sist), *n.* person who drives out (an evil spirit) by prayers, ceremonies, etc.

ex pe di ent (ek spē′dē ənt), *adj.* 1 helping to bring about a desired result; desirable or suitable under the circumstances; useful; advantageous. 2 giving or seeking personal advantage; based on self-interest. —*n.* means of bringing about a desired result: *When the truth wouldn't convince them, I used the expedient of telling a believable lie.* —**ex pe′di ent ly,** *adv.*

ex pi ate (ek′spē āt), *v.t.,* **-at ed, -at ing.** pay the penalty of; make amends for a wrong, sin, etc.; atone for.

ex pos tu late (ek spos′chə lāt), *v.i.,* **-lat ed, -lat ing.** reason earnestly with a person, protesting against something that person means to do or has done; remonstrate in a friendly way.

ex pur gate (ek′spər gāt), *v.t.,* **-gat ed, -gat ing.** remove objectionable passages or words from (a book, letter, etc.).

ex tant (ek′stənt, ek stant′), *adj.* still existing; not destroyed or lost: *Some of Washington's letters are extant.*

ex tin guish (ek sting′gwish), *v.t.* 1 put out; quench: *Water extinguished the fire.* 2 bring to an end; snuff out; destroy. 3 eclipse or obscure by superior brilliancy; outshine. 4 annul (a right, claim, etc.); nullify. [< Latin *exstinguere* < *ex-* out + *stinguere* quench] —**ex tin′guish a ble,** *adj.* —**ex tin′guish er,** *n.*

ex tort (ek stôrt′), *v.t.* obtain (money, a promise, etc.) by threats, force, fraud, or illegal use of authority. [< Latin *extortum* twisted out < *ex-* out + *torquere* twist] —**ex tort′er,** *n.*

ex ult (eg zult′), *v.i.* be very glad; rejoice greatly.

ex ul ta tion (eg′zul tā′shən, ek′sul tā′shən), *n.* an exulting; great rejoicing; triumph.

fa cade or **fa çade** (fə säd′), *n.* 1 the front part of a building. 2 any side of a building that faces a street or an open space. 3 outward appearance: *a facade of honesty.*

fa ce tious (fə sē′shəs), *adj.* 1 having the habit of joking; being slyly humorous. 2 said in fun; not to be taken seriously.

fac tion (fak′shən), *n.* 1 group of persons in a political party, church, club, etc., acting together or having a common purpose. 2 strife or quarreling among the members of a political party, church, club, neighborhood, etc.

fain (fān), ARCHAIC. —*adv.* gladly; willingly. —*adj.* 1 willing, but not eager. 2 obliged. 3 glad. 4 eager. [Old English *fægen*]

fal con (fôl′kən, fal′kən, fô′kən), *n.* any of various hawks trained to hunt and kill other birds and small game.

fal con er (fôl′kə nər, fal′kə nər, fô′kə nər), *n.* 1 person who hunts with falcons; hawker. 2 person who breeds and trains falcons for hunting.

fal la cy (fal′ə sē), *n.,pl.* **-cies.** 1 a false idea; mistaken belief; error. 2 mistake in reasoning; misleading or unsound argument.

far row (far′ō), *n.* litter of pigs. [Old English *fearh*]

far thing (fär′ᴛHing), *n.* a former British coin equal to a fourth of a British penny.

fas tid i ous (fa stid′ē əs), *adj.* hard to please; dainty in taste; easily disgusted. **—fas tid′i ous ly,** *adv.* **—fas tid′i ous ness,** *n.*

falconer (def. 1)

fast ness (fast′nis), *n.* 1 a strong, safe place; stronghold. 2 a being fast or firm; firmness. 3 a being quick or rapid; swiftness.

fath om (faᴛH′əm), *v.t.* 1 measure the depth of (water); sound. 2 get to the bottom of; understand fully. **—fath′om a ble,** *adj.*

fe al ty (fē′əl tē), *n.,pl.* **-ties.** 1 loyalty and duty owed by a vassal to his feudal lord. 2 loyalty; faithfulness; allegiance.

feign (fān), *v.t.* 1 put on a false appearance of; make believe; pretend. 2 make up to deceive; invent falsely. **—v.i.** make oneself appear; pretend (to be).

fe lic i ty (fə lis′ə tē), *n., pl.* **-ties.** 1 great happiness; bliss. 2 good fortune; blessing.

fen (fen), *n.* low, marshy land covered wholly or partially with shallow, often stagnant water. [Old English *fenn*]

fer vent (fèr′vənt), *adj.* 1 showing great warmth of feeling; very earnest; ardent. 2 hot; glowing; intense. **—fer′vent ly,** *adv.*

fer vid (fèr′vid), *adj.* 1 full of strong feeling; intensely emotional; ardent; spirited. 2 intensely hot. **—fer′vid ly,** *adv.* **—fer′-vid ness,** *n.*

fes toon (fe stün′), *n.* a string or chain of flowers, leaves, ribbons, etc., hanging in a curve between two points: *The bunting was draped on the wall in colorful festoons.* **—v.t.** 1 decorate with festoons. 2 hang in curves.

fet id (fet′id, fē′tid), *adj.* smelling very bad; stinking.

fet ter (fet′ər), *n.* 1 chain or shackle for the feet to prevent escape. 2 Usually, **fetters,** *pl.* anything that shackles or binds; restraint. **—v.t.** 1 bind with chains; chain the feet of. 2 bind; restrain: *Fetter your temper.* [Old English *feter.* Related to FOOT.]

fi del i ty (fə del′ə tē, fī del′ə tē), *n., pl.* **-ties.** 1 steadfast faithfulness; loyalty. 2 exactness, as in a copy; accuracy. 3 the ability of a radio transmitter or receiver or other device to transmit or reproduce an electric signal or sound accurately. [< Latin *fidelitatem* < *fidelis* faithful [< *fides* faith. Doublet of FEALTY.]

fil i al (fil′ē əl), *adj.* of a son or daughter; due from a son or daughter toward a mother or father; *filial affection.*

fil lip (fil′əp), *n.* 1 a quick, slight stroke with the fingernail snapped from the end of the thumb. 2 thing that rouses, revives, or stimulates: *The relishes served as a fillip to my appetite.*

fir ma ment (fèr′mə mənt), *n.* arch of the heavens; sky.

fis sure (fish′ər), *n.* 1 a long, narrow opening; split; crack. 2 a splitting apart; division into parts.

flag on (flag′ən), *n.* container for liquids, usually having a handle, a spout, and a cover.

flail (flāl), *n.* instrument for threshing grain by hand, consisting of a wooden handle at the end of which a stouter and shorter pole or club is fastened so as to swing freely. **—v.t.** 1 strike with a flail. 2 beat; thrash. [< Old French *flaiel* < Latin *flagellum* whip]

flo rin (flôr′ən, flor′ən), *n.* a former coin of Great Britain.

fold (fōld), *n.* 1 pen to keep sheep in. 2 sheep kept in a pen. **—v.t.** put or keep (sheep) in a pen.

fond (fond), *adj.* ARCHAIC. foolish.

for done (fôr dun′), *adj.* ARCHAIC. overcome with fatigue; exhausted.

for lorn (fôr lôrn′), *adj.* 1 left alone and neglected; deserted; abandoned. 2 wretched in feeling or looks; unhappy. 3 hopeless; desperate.

for spent (fôr spent′), *adj.* ARCHAIC. worn-out.

fort night (fôrt′nīt, fôrt′nit), *n.* two weeks.

foun der (foun′dər), *v.i.* 1 fill with water and sink. 2 fall down; stumble. **—v.t.** cause to fill with water and sink.

found ling (found′ling), *n.* baby or little child found abandoned.

fran chise (fran′chīz), *v.t.* set free.

fret (fret), *v.t.,v.i.,* **fret ted, fret ting.** eat or wear away.

frieze (frēz), *n.* 1 a horizontal band of decoration around a room, building, mantel, etc. 2 a horizontal band, often ornamented with sculpture, between the cornice and architrave of a building.

-ful, *suffix added to nouns to form adjectives or other nouns.* 1 full of ___: *Cheerful = full of cheer.* 2 showing ___: *Careful = showing care.* 3 having a tendency to ___: *Harmful = having a tendency to harm.* 4 enough to fill a ___: *Cupful = enough to fill a cup.* 5 that can be of ___: *Useful = that can be of use.* 6 having the qualities of ___: *Masterful = having the qualities of a master.* [Old English < adjective *full* full]

fur tive (fèr′tiv), *adj.* 1 done quickly and with stealth to avoid being noticed; secret. 2 sly; stealthy. **—fur′ tive ly,** *adv.*

fus tian (fus′chən), *n.* a coarse, heavy cloth made of cotton and flax, used for clothing in Europe throughout the Middle Ages. **—adj.** made of fustian.

fu til i ty (fyü til′ə tē), *n., pl.* **-ties.** 1 uselessness; ineffectiveness. 2 unimportance. 3 futile action, event, etc.

gain say (gān′sā′), *v.t.,* **-said, -say ing.** deny; contradict; dispute. **—gain′say′ er,** *n.*

gall[1] (gôl), *n.* 1 bile. 2 anything very bitter or harsh. 3 bitterness; hate.

gall[2] (gôl), *v.t.* 1 make sore by rubbing: *The rough strap galled the horse's skin.* 2 annoy; irritate. **—v.i.** become sore by rubbing.

gal ley (gal′ē), *n., pl.* **-leys.** kitchen of a ship or airplane.

gall ing (gô′ling), *adj.* that galls; chafing; irritating.

gal va nism (gal′və niz′əm), *n.* electricity produced by chemical action.

gam bol (gam′bəl), *n.* a running and jumping about in play; caper; frolic. **—v.i.** run and jump about in play; frolic.

gar ner (gär′nər), *v.t.* 1 gather and store away. 2 collect or deposit. **—n.** 1 storehouse for grain. 2 a store of anything.

gar nish (gär′nish), *n.* 1 something laid on or around food as a decoration: *turkey served with a garnish of parsley.* 2 decoration; trimming. **—v.t.** 1 decorate (food). 2 decorate; trim. [< Old French *garniss-,* a form of *garnir* provide, defend <Germanic. Related to WARN.]

gar ni ture (gär′nə chər), *n.* decoration; trimming; garnish.

gar ret (gar′it), *n.* 1 space in a house just below a sloping roof; attic. 2 room or apartment in such a place. [< Old French *garite* < *garir* defend]

gar ru lous (gar′ə ləs, gar′yə ləs), *adj.* 1 talking too much; talkative. 2 using too many words; wordy. [< Latin *garrulus* < *garrire* to chatter] **—gar′ ru lous ly,** *adv.* **—gar′ru lous-ness,** *n.*

gas ket (gas′kit), *n.* 1 ring or piece of rubber, soft metal, plastic, etc., packed around a pipe joint or placed between machine parts to keep a liquid or a gas from escaping. 2 cord or small rope used to secure a furled sail on a yard. [origin uncertain]

gaunt (gônt, gänt), *adj.* 1 very thin and bony; with hollow eyes and a starved look. 2 looking bare and gloomy; desolate. **—gaunt′ly,** *adv.* **—gaunt′ness,** *n.*

gaunt let (gônt′lit, gänt′lit), *n.* 1 a former punishment or torture in which the offender had to run between two rows of people who struck him or her with clubs or other weapons. 2 **run the gauntlet, a** pass between two rows of people each of whom strikes the runner as he or she passes. **b** be exposed to unfriendly attacks or severe criticism. Also, **gantlet.**

geld ing (gel′ding), *n.* a horse that has been castrated.

gen ial (jē′nyəl), *adj.* 1 smiling and pleasant; cheerful and

a hat | i it | oi oil | ch child | | a in about
ā age | ī ice | ou out | ng long | | e in taken
ä far | o hot | u cup | sh she | ə = | i in pencil
e let | ō open | ù put | th thin | | o in lemon
ē equal | ô order | ü rule | ᴛH then | | u in circus
ėr term | | | zh measure | < = derived from

genteel

friendly; kindly: *a genial welcome.* 2 helping growth; pleasantly warming; comforting: *a genial climate.* [< Latin *genialis,* literally, belonging to the genius < *genius* genius] —**ge ni al i ty** (jē′ nē al′ə tē), *n.* —**gen′ial ly,** *adv.* —**gen′ial ness,** *n.*

gen teel (jen tēl′), *adj.* 1 belonging or suited to polite society. 2 polite; well-bred; fashionable; elegant. —**gen teel′ly,** *adv.*

gib bet (jib′it), *n.* 1 an upright post with a projecting arm at the top, from which the bodies of criminals were hung after execution. 2 gallows. —*v.t.* 1 hang on a gibbet.

gibe (jīb), *v.,* **gibed, gib ing,** *n.* —*v.i.* speak in a sneering way; jeer; scoff; sneer. —*n.* a jeer; taunt; sneer. Also, **jibe.**

glean (glēn), *v.t.* 1 gather (grain) left on a field by reapers. 2 gather little by little: *glean information.* —*v.i.* gather grain left on a field by reapers. —**glean′er,** *n.*

glebe (glēb), *n.* 1 portion of land assigned to a parish church clergyman. 2 ARCHAIC. earth, soil, or land.

gloam (glōm), *n.* ARCHAIC. twilight.

goad (gōd), *n.* 1 a sharp-pointed stick for driving cattle; gad. 2 anything which drives or urges one on. —*v.t.* drive or urge on.

gob bet (gob′it), *n.* 1 lump; mass. 2 part; piece.

gorge (gôrj), *n.* ARCHAIC. throat.

gout (gout), *n.* drop, splash, or clot: *gouts of blood.*

gra da tion (grā dā′shən), *n.* 1 a change by steps or stages; gradual change. 2 step, stage, or degree in a series.

gran dam (gran′dam), *n.* ARCHAIC. 1 grandmother. 2 an old woman. [< Anglo-French *graund dame,* literally, great lady]

gran dee (gran dē′), *n.* 1 a Spanish or Portuguese nobleman of the highest rank. 2 person of high rank or great importance.

grate (grāt), *v.,* **grat ed, grat ing.** —*v.i.* have an annoying or unpleasant effect. —*v.t.* fret; annoy; irritate. [< Old French *grater* < Germanic]

greave (grēv), *n.* Often, **greaves,** *pl.* armor for the leg below the knee. [< Old French *greves,* plural]

groat (grōt), *n.* an old English silver coin worth fourpence.

grot (grot), *n.* cave or cavern.

ground (ground), *n.* piece of cloth used as background for embroidery or decoration.

grov el (gruv′əl, grov′əl), *v.i.,* **-eled, -el ing** or **-elled, -el ling.** 1 lie face downward; crawl at someone's feet; cringe. 2 abase or humble oneself.

grue some (grü′səm), *adj.* causing fear or horror; horrible; revolting. Also, **grewsome.** [Middle English *gruen* to shudder] —**grue′some ly,** *adv.* —**grue′some ness,** *n.*

gudg eon (guj′ən), *n.* a small Eurasian freshwater fish of the same family as the carp, that is often used for bait.

guer don (gėrd′n), *n., v.t.* reward. [< Old French *guerdoner* to reward < *guerdon* a reward < Old High German *widarlōn* repayment]

guile (gīl), *n.* crafty deceit; sly tricks; cunning.

guin ea (gin′ē), *n.* a former British gold coin, not made since 1813, equal to 21 shillings.

gules (gyülz), *n., adj.* (in heraldry) red.

gut ter snipe (gut′ər snīp′), *n.* 1 urchin who lives in the streets. 2 any ill-bred person.

hab er dash er (hab′ər dash′ər), *n.* dealer in the things men wear, such as hats, ties, shirts, socks, etc.

hab i ta tion (hab′ə tā′shən), *n.* 1 place to live in; home; dwelling. 2 an inhabiting.

hag (hag), *n.* 1 a very ugly old woman, especially one who is vicious or malicious. 2 witch. [Middle English *hagge*]

hal low (hal′ō), *v.t.* 1 make holy; make sacred; sanctify. 2 honor as holy or sacred. [Old English *hālgian* < *hālig* holy]

hap haz ard (hap′ haz′ərd), *adj.* not planned; random. —*adv.* by chance; at random. —*n.* chance. —**hap′haz′ard ly,** *adv.* —**hap′haz′ard ness,** *n.*

hap ly (hap′lē), *adv.* ARCHAIC. by chance.

ha rangue (hə rang′), *n., v.,* **-rangued, -rangu ing.** —*n.* 1 a noisy, vehement speech. 2 a long, pompous, formal speech. —*v.t.* address (someone) with a harangue. —*v.i.* deliver a harangue.

har bin ger (här′bən jər), *n.* one that goes ahead to announce another's coming; forerunner: *The robin is a harbinger of spring.* —*v.t.* announce beforehand; foretell. [< Old French *herbergere* provider of shelter (hence, one who goes ahead), ultimately < *herberge* lodging, of Germanic origin. Related to HARBOR.]

har mo ni ous (här mō′nē əs), *adj.* 1 agreeing in feelings, ideas, or actions; getting along well together; amicable. 2 arranged so that the parts are orderly or pleasing; going well together; congruous. 3 sweet-sounding; musical; melodious.

har mo ni um (här mō′nē əm), *n.* a small organ with metal reeds. [< French]

har row (har′ō), *n.* a heavy frame with iron teeth or upright disks, used by farmers to break up ground into fine pieces before planting seeds. —*v.t.* 1 pull a harrow over (land, etc.). 2 hurt; wound. 3 cause pain or torment to; distress.

har ry (har′ē), *v.,* **-ried, -ry ing.** —*v.t.* 1 raid and rob with violence; lay waste; pillage. 2 keep troubling; worry; torment. —*v.i.* make predatory raids. [Old English *hergian* < *here* army]

hart (härt), *n., pl.* **harts** or **hart.** a male deer, especially the male European red deer after its fifth year; stag. [Old English *heorot*]

har um-scar um (her′əm sker′əm, har′əm skar′əm), *adj.* too hasty; reckless; rash. —*n.* a reckless, rash person.

hasp (hasp), *v.t.* ARCHAIC. emclose in armor; buckle.

hatch ment (hach′mənt), *n.* a square tablet set diagonally, bearing the coat of arms of a dead person.

ha ven (hā′vən), *n.* 1 harbor or port. 2 place of shelter and safety. [Old English *hæfen*]

head stall (hed′stôl′), *n.* the part of a bridle or halter that fits around a horse's head.

heark en (här′kən), *v.i.* pay attention to what is said; listen attentively; listen. Also, **harken.**

heath (hēth), *n.* 1 open wasteland with heather or low bushes growing on it, but few or no trees; moor. 2 heather.

hea then (hē′THən), *n., pl.* **-thens** or **-then,** *adj.* —*n.* person who does not believe in the God of the Bible; person who is not a Christian, Jew, or Moslem; pagan. —**hea′then ness,** *n.*

help meet (help′mēt′), *n.* helpmate.

hem lock (hem′lok), *n.* 1 a poisonous plant of the same family as parsley, with spotted reddish-purple stems, finely divided leaves, and small white flowers. 2 poison made from it.

hent (hent), *n.* OBSOLETE. intent; purpose.

her mit age (hėr′mə tij), *n.* 1 dwelling place of a hermit. 2 a solitary or secluded dwelling place.

hie (hī), *v.,* **hied, hie ing** or **hy ing.** —*v.i.* go quickly; hasten; hurry. —*v.t.* cause to hasten. [Old English *hīgian*]

hi e rar chy (hī′ə rär′ kē), *n., pl.* **-chies.** 1 organization of persons or things arranged one above the other according to rank, class, or grade. 2 group of church officials of different ranks.

hoar (hôr′ē, hōr), *adj.* hoary.

hoar y (hôr′ē, hōr′ē), *adj.,* **hoar i er, hoar i est.** 1 white or gray. 2 white or gray with age. 3 old; ancient. —**hoar′i ness,** *n.*

holp (hōlp), *v.* ARCHAIC. a pp. of **help.**

hom i ly (hom′ə lē), *n., pl.* **-lies.** 1 sermon, usually on some part of the Bible. 2 serious moral talk or writing that warns, urges, or advises. [< Greek *homilia* < *homilos* a throng, assembly]

hood wink (hud′wingk), *v.t.* 1 mislead by a trick; deceive. 2 blindfold. —**hood′wink er,** *n.*

hos tel ry (hos′tl rē), *n., pl.* **-ries.** inn or hotel.

hul la ba loo (hul′ə bə lü′), *n., pl* **-loos.** a loud noise or disturbance; uproar.

hur dy-gur dy (hėr′dē gėr′ dē), *n., pl.* **-dies.** hand organ.

hur ly-bur ly (hėr′lē bėr′ lē), *n., pl.* **-lies.** disorder and noise; commotion; tumult.

hus band ry (huz′bən drē), *n.* 1 farming: *animal husbandry.* 2 careful management of one's affairs or resources; thrift.

hus sy (huz′ē, hus′ē), *n., pl.* **-sies.** 1 a bad-mannered or pert girl. 2 an indecent or immoral woman.

ig no ble (ig nō′bəl), *adj.* 1 without honor; disgraceful; base: *To betray a friend is ignoble.* 2 not of noble birth or position; humble. —**ig no′ble ness,** *n.* —**ig no′bly,** *adv.*

ig no min i ous (ig′nə min′ē əs), *adj.* 1 shameful; disgraceful; dishonorable. 2 contemptible. 3 lowering one's dignity; humiliating. —**ig′no min′i ous ly,** *adv.*

il lu mine (i lü′mən), *v.t.,* **-mined, -min ing.** make bright; illuminate.

im mi nent (im′ə nənt), *adj.* likely to happen soon; about to occur. —**im′mi nent ly,** *adv.*

im pal pa ble (im pal′pə bəl), *adj.* 1 that cannot be felt by touching; intangible. 2 very hard to understand; that cannot be grasped by the mind. —**im pal′pa bly,** *adv.*

840

im ped i ment (im ped′ə mənt), *n.* **1** hindrance; obstruction. **2** some physical defect, especially a defect in speech.

im per i ous (im pir′ē əs), *adj.* **1** haughty or arrogant; domineering; overbearing. **2** not to be avoided; necessary; urgent. —**im per′i ous ly**, *adv.* —**im per′i ous ness**, *n.*

im per turb a ble (im′pər tèr′bə bəl), *adj.* not easily excited or disturbed; calm. —**im′per turb′a ble ness**, *n.* —**im′per turb′a bly**, *adv.*

im pet u ous (im pech′ü əs), *adj.* acting or done with sudden or rash energy; hasty. —**im pet′u ous ly**, *adv.* —**im pet′u ous ness**, *n.*

im pe tus (im′pə təs), *n.* **1** the force with which a moving body tends to maintain its velocity and overcome resistance. **2** a driving force; cause of action or effort; incentive.

im pinge (im pinj′), *v.i.*, -**pinged**, -**ping ing**. **1** hit; strike: *Rays of light impinge on the eye.* **2** trespass; encroach; infringe.

im pi ous (im′pē əs, im pi′əs), *adj.* not pious; not having or not showing reverence for God; wicked; profane. —**im′pi ous ly**, *adv.* —**im′pi ous ness**, *n.*

im por tune (im′pôr tün′, im′pôr tyün′, im pôr′chən), *v.*, -**tuned**, -**tun ing**, *adj.* —*v.t.* ask urgently or repeatedly; annoy with pressing demands. —*adj.* importunate.

im pre ca tion (im′prə kā′shən), *n.* **1** an imprecating; cursing. **2** curse.

im preg na ble (im preg′nə bəl), *adj.* able to resist attack; not yielding to force, persuasion, etc. —**im preg′na bly**, *adv.*

im pu dent (im′pyə dənt), *adj.* shamelessly bold; very rude and insolent. —**im′pu dent ly**, *adv.*

im pu ta tion (im′pyə tā′shən), *n.* **1** an imputing. **2** a charge or hint of wrongdoing.

im pute (im pyüt′), *v.t.*, -**put ed**, -**put ing**. consider as belonging; attribute; charge to a person or a cause; blame.

in-[1], *prefix.* not; the opposite of; the absence of: *Inexpensive = not expensive. Inattention = the absence of attention.* [< Latin]

in-[2], *prefix.* in; into; on; upon: *Incase = (put) into a case. Intrust = (give) in trust.* [< Latin < *in,* preposition]

in can ta tion (in′kan tā′shən), *n.* **1** set of words spoken as a magic charm or to cast a magic spell. **2** the use of such words.

in car nate (in kär′nit, in kär′nāt), *adj.* embodied in flesh, especially in human form; personified; typified.

in cense (in sens′), *v.t.*, -**censed**, -**cens ing**. make very angry; fill with rage. [< Latin *incensum* inflamed, enraged, set on fire < *in-* (intensive) + *candere* glow white]

in cip i ent (in sip′ē ənt), *adj.* just beginning; in an early stage; commencing. —**in cip′i ent ly**, *adv.*

in co her ent (in′kō hir′ənt), *adj.* **1** having or showing no logical connection of ideas; not coherent; disconnected; confused. **2** not sticking together; loose. —**in′co her′ent ly**, *adv.*

in com mode (in′kə mōd′), *v.t.*, -**mod ed**, -**mod ing**. cause trouble, difficulty, etc., to; inconvenience.

in con gru ous (in kong′grü əs), *adj.* **1** not appropriate; out of place: *A fur coat is incongruous with a bathing suit.* **2** lacking in agreement or harmony; not consistent. —**in con′gru ous ly**, *adv.* —**in con′gru ous ness**, *n.*

in con ti nen cy (in kon′tə nən sē), *n.* lack of self-control. Also, **incontinence.**

in cor por al (in kôr′pər al), *adj.* OBSOLETE. incorporeal; not made of any material substance; insubstantial.

in cor ri gi ble (in kôr′ə jə bəl, in kor′ə jə bəl), *adj.* too firmly fixed in bad ways, an annoying habit, etc., to be reformed or changed: *an incorrigible liar.* —**in cor′ri gi bly**, *adv.*

in cred u lous (in krej′ə ləs), *adj.* **1** not ready to believe; doubting; skeptical. **2** showing a lack of belief. —**in cred′u lous ly**, *adv.*

in cu bus (ing′kyə bəs, in′kyə bəs), *n.*, *pl.* -**bi** (-bī) -**bus es**. **1** an evil spirit supposed to descend upon sleeping persons. **2** nightmare. **3** an oppressive or burdensome thing.

in cul cate (in kul′kāt, in′kul kāt), *v.t.*, -**cat ed**, -**cat ing**. impress (ideas, opinions, etc.) on the mind of another by frequent repetition; teach persistently.

in del i ble (in del′ə bəl), *adj.* that cannot be erased or removed; permanent. —**in del′i ble ness**, *n.* —**in del′i bly**, *adv.*

in di gence (in′də jəns), *n.* extreme need; poverty.

in dis sol u ble (in′di sol′yə bəl), *adj.* that cannot be dissolved, undone, or destroyed; lasting; firm. —**in′dis sol′u bly**, *adv.*

in due (in dü′, in dyü′), *v.t.*, -**dued**, -**du ing**. **1** provide with a quality or power; furnish; supply. **2** clothe. Also, **endue.**

in ex or a ble (in ek′sər ə bəl), *adj.* not influenced by pleading or entreaties; relentless; unyielding. —**in ex′or a bly**, *adv.*

a hat	i it	oi oil	ch child	⎧ a in about
ā age	ī ice	ou out	ng long	⎪ e in taken
ä far	o hot	u cup	sh she	ə = ⎨ i in pencil
e let	ō open	u̇ put	th thin	⎪ o in lemon
ē equal	ô order	ü rule	ŦH then	⎩ u in circus
ėr term			zh measure	< = derived from

in ex pe di ent (in′ik spē′dē ənt), *adj.* not expedient; not practicable, suitable, or wise. —**in′ex pe′di ent ly**, *adv.*

in ex tri ca ble (in ek′strə kə bəl), *adj.* **1** that one cannot get out of. **2** that cannot be disentangled or solved.

in fal li ble (in fal′ə bəl), *adj.* **1** free from error; that cannot be mistaken. **2** absolutely reliable; sure. —**in fal′li bly**, *adv.*

in fat u ate (in fach′ü āt), *v.t.*, -**at ed**, -**at ing**. **1** inspire with a foolish or extreme passion. **2** make foolish. [< Latin *infatuatum* made foolish < *in-* + *fatuus* foolish]

in fer nal (in fėr′nl), *adj.* **1** of or having to do with hell. **2** of the lower world which the ancient Greeks and Romans thought of as the abode of the dead. **3** fit to have come from hell; hellish; diabolical: *infernal cruelty.* [< Late Latin *infernalis* < *infernus* hell < Latin, lower < *inferus* situated below] —**in fer′nal ly**, *adv.*

in firm (in fėrm′), *adj.* **1** lacking strength or health; physically weak or feeble, especially through age. **2** without a firm purpose; not steadfast; faltering. **3** not firm, solid, or strong.

in fla gran te de lic to (in flə gran′tē di lik′tō), (in law) in the very act of committing the crime; in the performance of the deed; red-handed. [< Latin, literally, in blazing crime]

in fuse (in fyüz′), *v.t.*, -**fused**, -**fus ing**. **1** introduce as by pouring; put in; instill: *The captain infused his own courage into his soldiers.* **2** inspire: *The soldiers were infused with his courage.*

in gen ious (in jē′nyəs), *adj.* **1** skillful in making; good at inventing. **2** cleverly planned or made: *This mousetrap is a ingenious device.* [< Latin *ingeniosus* < *ingenium* natural talent < *in-* in + *gignere* beget, be born] —**in gen′ious ly**, *adv.* —**in gen′ious ness**, *n.*

in gen u ous (in jen′yü əs), *adj.* **1** free from restraint or reserve; frank and open; sincere. **2** simple and natural; innocent; naïve. [< Latin *ingenuus,* originally, native < *in-* in + *gignere* beget] —**in gen′u ous ly**, *adv.* —**in gen′u ous ness**, *n.*

in graft (in graft′), *v.t.* **1** graft (a shoot, etc.) from one tree or plant into another. **2** fix in; implant. Also, **engraft.**

in gra ti ate (in grā′shē āt), *v.t.*, -**at ed**, -**at ing**. bring (oneself) into favor; make (oneself) acceptable. —**in gra′ti at′ing ly**, *adv.*

in junc tion (in jungk′shən), *n.* **1** a formal order from a court of law ordering a person or group to do, or refrain from doing, something. **2** an authoritative or emphatic order; command.

in sa tia ble (in sā′shə bəl), *adj.* that cannot be satisfied; extremely greedy: *an insatiable appetite.* —**in sa′tia bly**, *adv.*

in scru ta ble (in skrü′tə bəl), *adj.* that cannot be understood; so mysterious or obscure that one cannot make out its meaning; incomprehensible. —**in scru′ta bly**, *adv.*

in sid i ous (in sid′ē əs), *adj.* **1** seeking to entrap or ensnare; wily or sly; crafty; tricky. **2** working secretly or subtly; developing without attracting attention: *an insidious disease.* —**in sid′i ous ly**, *adv.* —**in sid′i ous ness**, *n.*

in sip id (in sip′id), *adj.* **1** without any particular flavor; tasteless. **2** lacking interest or spirit; dull, colorless, or weak. —**in sip′id ly**, *adv.* —**in sip′id ness**, *n.*

in tem per ate (in tem′pər it), *adj.* **1** not moderate; lacking in self-control; excessive. **2** drinking too much intoxicating liquor. **3** not temperate; extreme in temperature; severe.

in ter (in tėr′), *v.t.*, -**terred**, -**ter ring**. put (a dead body) into a grave or tomb; bury.

inter-, *prefix.* **1** one with the other; with or on each other; together: *Intercommunicate = communicate with each other.* **2** between: *Interpose = put between.* **3** between or among a group: *International = between or among nations.* [< Latin < *inter* among, between, during. Related to UNDER.]

in ter ces sion (in′tər sesh′ən), *n.* **1** act or fact of interceding. **2** prayer pleading for others.

in ter dic tion (in′tər dik′shən), *n.* prohibition based on authority; formal order forbidding something.

in ter fuse (in′tər fyüz′), *v.t.*, *v.i.*, -**fused**, -**fus ing**. **1** spread through; be diffused through; permeate. **2** fuse together; blend; mix. [< Latin *interfusum* poured between < *inter-* between + *fundere* pour] —**in′ter fu′sion**, *n.*

in ter im (in′tər im), *n.* time between; the meantime. —*adj.* for the meantime; temporary.

in ter mit (in′tər mit′), *v.t., v.i.,* **-mit ted, -mit ting.** stop for a time; discontinue; suspend.

in ter sperse (in′tər spėrs′), *v.t.,* **-spersed, -spers ing.** 1 vary with something put here and there: *The grass was interspersed with beds of flowers.* 2 scatter or place here and there among other things: *Bushes were interspersed among the trees.* [< Latin *interspersum* scattered < *inter-* between + *spargere* to scatter]

in ter stice (in tėr′stis), *n., pl.* **-sti ces** (-stə sēz′). a small or narrow space between things or parts; narrow chink, crack, or opening.

in tes tate (in tes′tāt, in tes′tit), *adj.* having made no will: *die intestate.* —*n.* person who has died without making a will.

in trep id (in trep′id), *adj.* very brave; fearless; dauntless; courageous. —**in trep′id ly,** *adv.* —**in trep′id ness,** *n.*

in tre pid i ty (in′trə pid′ə tē), *n.* great bravery; dauntless courage; fearlessness.

in trin sic (in trin′sik), *adj.* 1 belonging to a thing by its very nature; essential; inherent. 2 originating or being inside the part on which it acts. —**in trin′si cal ly,** *adv.*

in ure (in yür′), *v.,* **-ured, -ur ing.** —*v.t.* toughen or harden; accustom; habituate. —*v.i.* have effect; be useful.

in vest (in vest′), *v.t.* install in office with a ceremony.

in vet er ate (in vet′ər it), *adj.* 1 confirmed in a habit, practice, feeling, etc.; habitual: *an inveterate smoker.* 2 long and firmly established; deeply rooted. —**in vet′er ate ly,** *adv.*

in vig o rate (in vig′ə rāt′), *v.t.,* **-rat ed, -rat ing.** give vigor to; fill with life and energy. —**in vig′o ra′tive,** *adj.*

in voke (in vōk′), *v.t.,* **-voked, -vok ing.** 1 call on in prayer; appeal to for help or protection. 2 appeal to for confirmation or judgment. 3 ask earnestly for; beg for.

ire (īr), *n.* anger; wrath. [< Old French < Latin *ira*]

irk (ėrk), *v.t.* cause to feel disgusted, annoyed, or troubled; weary by being tedious or disagreeable.

ir rec on cil a ble (i rek′ən sī′lə bəl, i rek′ən sī′lə bəl), *adj.* that cannot be reconciled; that cannot be made to agree; opposed: *irreconcilable enemies.* —*n.* person who persists in opposing. —**ir rec′on cil′a ble ness,** *n.* —**ir rec′on cil′a bly,** *adv.*

ir ref u ta ble (i ref′yə tə bəl, i ref′fyü′ tə bəl), *adj.* that cannot be refuted or disproved; undeniable; unanswerable. —**ir ref′u ta bly,** *adv.*

ir re me di a ble (ir′i mē′dē ə bəl), *adj.* that cannot be corrected or remedied; incurable. —**ir′re me′di a bly,** *adv.*

ir rev o ca ble (i rev′ə kə bəl), *adj.* 1 not able to be revoked; final: *an irrevocable decision.* 2 impossible to call or bring back: *the irrevocable past.* —**ir rev′o ca bly,** *adv.*

isth mus (is′məs), *n.* a narrow strip of land with water on both sides, connecting two larger bodies of land. [< Latin < Greek *isthmos*]

isthmus

ja cinth (jā′sinth, jas′inth), *n.* a reddish-orange gem.

joc und (jok′ənd, jō′kənd), *adj.* feeling, expressing, or communicating mirth or cheer; cheerful; merry; gay.

join ture (join′chər), *n.* property given to a woman at the time of her marriage.

joust (joust, just, jüst), *n.* 1 combat between two knights on horseback, armed with lances, especially as part of a tournament. 2 **jousts,** *pl.* a tournament. —*v.i.* fight with lances on horseback.

jo vi al (jō′vē əl), *adj.* good-hearted and full of fun; good-humored and merry. [< Latin. *Jovialis* of the planet Jupiter (those born under the planet's sign being supposedly cheerful) < *Jovis* Jove] —**jo′vi al ly,** *adv.* —**jo′vi al ness,** *n.*

ju bi lant (jü′bə lənt), *adj.* expressing or showing joy; rejoicing. [< Latin *jubilantem* < *jubilum* wild shout] —**ju′bi lant ly,** *adv.*

ju di cious (jü dish′əs), *adj.* having, using, or showing good judgment; wise; sensible: *A judicious historian selects and weighs facts carefully and critically.* —**ju di′cious ly,** *adv.* —**ju di′cious ness,** *n.*

junc ture (jungk′chər), *n.* 1 point or line where two things join; joint. 2 point of time, especially a critical time or state of affairs: *At this juncture we must decide what move to make next.* 3 a joining.

jur is pru dence (jür′i sprüd′ns), *n.* 1 science or philosophy of law. 2 system of laws. 3 branch of law.

ka lei do scope (kə lī′də skōp), *n.* 1 tube containing bits of colored glass and two mirrors. As it is turned, it reflects continually changing patterns. 2 a continually changing pattern or object.

ken (ken), *n., v.,* **kenned** or **kent** (kent), **ken ning.** —*n.* 1 range of sight. 2 range of knowledge. —*v.t.* SCOTTISH. know. —*v.i.* SCOTTISH. have knowledge.

kin dle (kin′dl), *v.,* **-dled, -dling.** —*v.t.* 1 set on fire; light. 2 stir up; arouse. 3 light up; brighten. —*v.i.* 1 catch fire; begin to burn. 2 become stirred up or aroused.

kirk (kėrk), *n.* SCOTLAND AND NORTH ENGLAND. church.

kite (kīt), *n.* any of various falconlike hawks usually having long, pointed wings and a long notched or forked tail.

knave (nāv), *n.* 1 a tricky, dishonest man; rogue; rascal. 2 ARCHAIC. a male servant or any man of humble birth or position.

knav er y (nā′vər ē), *n., pl.* **-er ies.** 1 behavior of a knave or rascal; trickery; dishonesty. 2 a tricky, dishonest act.

knead (nēd), *v.t.* 1 press or mix together (dough or clay) into a soft mass. 2 make or shape by kneading. 3 press and squeeze with the hands; massage.

knell (nel), *n.* 1 sound of a bell rung slowly after a death or at a funeral. 2 a warning sign of death, failure, etc. —*v.i.* 1 (of a bell) ring slowly, especially for a death or at a funeral; toll. 2 give a warning sign of death, failure, etc.

knoll (nōl), *v.i.* ARCHAIC. knell.

lab y rinth (lab′ə rinth′), *n.* 1 number of connecting passages so arranged that it is hard to find one's way from point to point; maze. 2 any confusing, complicated arrangement.

lac e rate (las′ə rāt′), *v.t.,* **-rat ed, -rat ing.** 1 tear roughly; mangle. 2 wound; hurt (the feelings, etc.).

lag gard (lag′ərd), *n.* person who moves too slowly or falls behind; backward person. —*adj.* falling behind; backward. —**lag′gard ly,** *adv.* —**lag′gard ness,** *n.*

la i ty (lā′ə tē), *n., pl.* **-ties.** the people who are not members of the clergy or of a professional class; laymen collectively.

la ment (lə ment′), *v.t.* 1 express grief for; mourn for. 2 regret. —*v.i.* express grief; mourn; weep. —*n.* 1 expression of grief or sorrow; wail. 2 poem, song, or tune that expresses grief.

lam en ta ble (lam′ən tə bəl, lə men′tə bəl), *adj.* 1 to be regretted or pitied; deplorable: *a lamentable accident.* 2 inferior; pitiful: *a lamentable fake.* —**lam′en ta bly,** *adv.*

lam en ta tion (lam′ən tā′shən), *n.* loud grief; cries of sorrow; mourning; wailing.

lan guid (lang′gwid), *adj.* 1 without energy; drooping; weak; weary: *A hot, sticky day makes a person feel languid.* 2 without interest or enthusiasm; indifferent; listless. 3 not brisk or lively; sluggish; dull. [< Latin *languidus* < *languere* be faint] —**lan′guid ly,** *adv.* —**lan′guid ness,** *n.*

lan guish (lang′gwish), *v.i.* 1 become weak or weary; lose energy; droop. 2 suffer under any unfavorable conditions. 3 grow dull, slack, or less intense. 4 long or pine *(for).* 5 assume a soft, tender look for effect.

lan guor ous (lang′gər əs), *adj.* 1 languid; without energy; weak; weary. 2 quiet; still. —**lan′guor ous ly,** *adv.*

lan yard (lan′yərd), *n.* a loose cord around the neck on which to hang a knife, whistle, etc. Also, **laniard.**

lar gess or **lar gesse** (lär′jis), *n.* 1 a generous giving. 2 a generous gift or gifts. [< Old French *largesse* < *large* generous]

lark (lärk), *n.* a merry adventure; frolic; prank. —*v.i.* have fun; play pranks; frolic. [origin uncertain]

la ryn go scope (lə ring′gə skōp), *n.* instrument with mirrors for examining the larynx.

las si tude (las′ə tüd, las′ə tyüd), *n.* lack of energy; weariness; languor. [< Latin *lassitudo* < *lassus* tired]

lat i tude (lat′ə tüd, lat′ə tyüd), *n.* room to act or think; freedom from narrow rules; scope.

lat tice (lat′is), *n., v.,* **-ticed, -tic ing.** —*n.* 1 structure of crossed wooden or metal strips with open spaces between them. **2** window, gate, etc., having a lattice. —**lat′tice like′,** *adj.*

laud a ble (lô′də bəl), *adj.* worthy of praise; commendable. —**laud′a ble ness,** *n.* —**laud′a bly,** *adv.*

lave (lāv), *v.,* **laved, lav ing.** —*v.t.* **1** wash; bathe. **2** wash or flow against: *The stream laves its banks.* —*v.i.* ARCHAIC. bathe.

lay (lā), *n.* **1** a short lyric or narrative poem to be sung. **2** song; tune. [< Old French *lai*]

lea (lē), *n.* a grassy field; meadow; pasture. [Old English *lēah*]

league (lēg), *n.* measure of distance, varying at different periods and in different countries, usually about 3 miles (5 kilometers).

lech er (lech′ər), *n.* person, especially a man, who indulges in lechery, a gross indulgence of lust.

lech er ous (lech′ər əs), *adj.* lewd; lustful. —**lech′er ous ly,** *adv.* —**lech′er ous ness,** *n.*

lee (lē), *n.* **1** shelter; protection. **2** side or part sheltered or away from the wind: *the lee of a ship.* —*adj.* sheltered or away from the wind: *the lee side of a ship.* [Old English *hlēo*]

leech (lēch), *n.* person who tries persistently to get money and favors from others without doing anything to earn them; parasite.

lees (lēz), *n.pl.* **1** the most worthless part of anything; dregs. **2** sediment deposited in the container by wine and some other liquids. [< Old French *lias,* plural of *lie,* probably < Late Latin *lia*]

lep er ous (lep′ər əs), *adj.* OBSOLETE. leprous; of or like leprosy, a chronic, infectious disease that attacks the skin and nerves, causing lumps and spots.

lese maj es ty (lēz maj′ə stē), crime or offense against the sovereign power in a state; treason. [< Middle French *lèse-majesté* < Latin *laesa majestas* insulted sovereignty]

-less, *suffix forming adjectives from verbs and nouns.* **1** without a ___; that has no ___: *Homeless = without a home.* **2** that does not ___: *Ceaseless = that does not cease.* **3** that cannot be ___ed: *Countless = that cannot be counted.* [Old English *-lēas* < *lēas* without]

lev y (lev′ē), *v.,* **lev ied, lev y ing,** *n., pl.* **lev ies.** —*v.t.* **1** order to be paid: *The government levies taxes to pay its expenses.* **2** draft or enlist (citizens) for an army. —*n.* **1** money collected by authority or force. **2** citizens drafted or enlisted for an army.

lex i con (lek′sə kən, lek′sə kon), *n.* **1** dictionary, especially of Greek, Latin, or Hebrew. **2** the vocabulary of a language or of a certain subject, group, or activity.

li ber ti cide (li bér′ti sīd), *n.* destruction of liberty.

lib er tine (lib′ər tēn′), *n.* person without moral restraints; immoral or licentious person. —*adj.* without moral restraints.

liege (lēj), *n.* in the Middle Ages: **1** lord having a right to the homage and loyal service of his vassals. **2** vassal obliged to give homage and loyal service to his lord; liegeman. —*adj.* **1** having a right to the homage and loyal service of vassals. **2** obliged to give homage and loyal service to a lord.

liege man (lēj′mən), *n., pl.* **-men.** **1** vassal. **2** a faithful follower.

lin e al (lin′ē əl), *adj.* in the direct line of descent: *A grandson is a lineal descendant of his grandfather.* —**lin′e al ly,** *adv.*

lin e a ment (lin′ē ə mənt), *n.* part or feature, especially a part or feature of a face with attention to its outline.

lin net (lin′it), *n.* a small finch of Europe, Asia, and Africa, having brown or gray plumage, the color changing at different ages and seasons. [< Middle French *linette*]

lin tel (lin′tl), *n.* a horizontal beam or stone over a door, window, etc., to support the structure above it. [< Old French, threshold, ultimately < Latin *limitem* limit]

LINTEL → ←SILL

liq ue fac tion (lik′wə fak′shən), *n.* **1** act or process of liquefying. **2** liquefied condition.

liq uor (lik′ər), *n.* OBSOLETE. fluid.

lists (lists), *n.pl.* **1** place where knights fought in tournaments or tilts. **2** any place or scene of combat. **3 enter the lists,** join in a contest; take part in a fight, argument, etc.

lit a ny (lit′n ē), *n., pl.* **-nies.** **1** prayer consisting of a series of words or requests said by a minister or priest and the congregation's responses. **2** a repeated series.

liv er y (liv′ər ē), *n., pl.* **-er ies.** **1** any special uniform provided for the servants of a household, or adopted by any group or profession. **2** any characteristic dress, garb, or outward appearance. **3** the feeding, stabling, and care of horses for pay.

liv id (liv′id), *adj.* **1** having a dull-bluish or grayish color, as from a bruise. **2** very pale. **3** flushed; reddish. **4** very angry.

loath (lōth, lōᵺ), *adj.* unwilling or reluctant; averse: *The little girl*

---

was loath to leave her mother. They were loath to admit that their son had run away. Also, **loth.** [Old English *lāth* hostile] —**loath′ness,** *n.*

lorn (lôrn), *adj.* forsaken; forlorn. —**lorn′ness,** *n.*

low (lō), *v.i., v.t.* make the sound of a cow; moo. —*n.* the sound a cow makes; mooing.

lu cid (lü′sid), *adj.* **1** marked by clearness of reasoning, expression, or arrangement; easy to follow or understand. **2** clear in intellect; rational; sane. **3** translucent; clear. —**lu′cid ly,** *adv.* —**lu′cid ness,** *n.*

lu cra tive (lü′krə tiv), *adj.* yielding gain or profit; profitable. —**lu′cra tive ly,** *adv.* —**lu′cra tive ness,** *n.*

lu gu bri ous (lü gü′brē əs, lü gyü′brē əs), *adj.* too sad; overly mournful. —**lu gu′bri ous ly,** *adv.* —**lu gu′bri ous ness,** *n.*

-ly¹, *suffix forming adverbs from adjectives.* **1** in a ___ manner: *Cheerfully = in a cheerful manner.* **2** in ___ ways or respects: *Financially = in financial respects.* **3** to a ___ degree or extent: *Greatly = to a great degree.* **4** in, to, or from a ___ direction: *Northwardly = to or from the north.* **5** in a ___ place: *Thirdly = in the third place.* **6** at a ___ time: *Recently = at a recent time.* [Old English *-līce* < *-līc* -ly]

-ly², *suffix forming adjectives from nouns.* **1** like a ___: *Ghostly = like a ghost.* **2** like that of a ___; characteristic of a ___: *Sisterly = like that of a sister.* **3** suited to a ___; fit or proper for a ___: *Gentlemanly = suited to a gentleman.* **4** of each or every ___; occurring once per ___: *Daily = of every day.* **5** being a ___; that is a ___: *Heavenly = that is a heaven.* [Old English *-līc* < *līc* body, form]

mag nan i mous (mag nan′ə məs), *adj.* **1** noble in soul or mind; generous in forgiving; free from mean or petty feelings or acts; unselfish. **2** showing or arising from a generous spirit: *a magnanimous attitude toward a conquered enemy.* [< Latin *magnanimus* < *magnus* great + *animus* spirit] —**mag nan′i mous ly,** *adv.*

mail (māl), *n.* a flexible armor made of metal rings or small loops of chain linked together, or of overlapping plates, for protecting the body against arrows, spears, etc.

mal e fac tion (mal′ə fak′shən), *n.* an evil deed; crime.

ma lev o lence (mə lev′ə ləns), *n.* the wish that evil may happen to others; ill will; spite.

ma lev o lent (mə lev′ə lənt), *adj.* wishing evil to happen to others; showing ill will; spiteful. —**ma lev′o lent ly,** *adv.*

ma li cious (mə lish′əs), *adj.* **1** showing active ill will; wishing to hurt or make suffer; spiteful. **2** proceeding from malice: *malicious mischief.* —**ma li′cious ly,** *adv.* —**ma li′cious ness,** *n.*

ma lig nant (mə lig′nənt), *adj.* **1** very evil, hateful, or malicious. **2** having an evil influence; very harmful. —**ma lig′nant ly,** *adv.*

ma lig ni ty (mə lig′nə tē), *n., pl.* **-ties.** **1** great malice; extreme hate or ill will. **2** great harmfulness; dangerous quality; deadliness. **3** a malignant feeling or act.

man ci ple (man′sə pəl), *n.* a purchasing agent for a college or other institution; steward.

man date (man′dāt, man′dit), *n.* **1** an order or command: *a royal mandate.* **2** order from a higher court or official to a lower one.

man i fold (man′ə fōld), *adj.* **1** of many kinds; many and various: *manifold duties.* **2** having many parts or forms. **3** doing many things at the same time. —*adv.* many times.

man na (man′ə), *n.* **1** (in the Bible) the food miraculously supplied to the Israelites in the wilderness. **2** food for the soul or mind. **3** any necessity unexpectedly supplied.

marge (märj), *n.* ARCHAIC. margin.

mark (märk), *n.* a former English coin.

marl (märl), *n.* a loose, crumbly soil containing clay and calcium carbonate, used as a fertilizer. —*v.t.* fertilize with marl.

mar tial (mär′shəl), *adj.* **1** of war; suitable for war. **2** such as war requires; brave; **3** given to fighting; warlike. [< Latin *Martialis* of Mars < *Mars* Mars] **—mar′tial ly,** *adv.*

mart let (märt′lit), *n.* a common European martin.

mat in (mat′n), *n.* the early morning.

mat ins (mat′nz), *n.pl.* **1** first of the seven canonical hours in the breviary of the Roman Catholic Church. **2** service for this hour, often joined to lauds. Also, **mattins** for **2.**

maw (mô), *n.* **1** mouth, throat, or gullet, especially of a meat-eating animal. **2** stomach. **3** crop of a bird.

mead (mēd), *n.* ARCHAIC. meadow. [Old English *mǣd*]

meal y (mē′lē), *adj.*, **meal i er, meal i est. 1** like meal; dry and powdery. **2** pale. **3** mealy-mouthed. **4** flecked as if with meal; spotty. **—meal′i ness,** *n.*

me an der (mē an′dər), *v.i.* **1** follow a winding course. **2** wander aimlessly. **—n. 1** a winding course. **2** aimless wandering. **3** a loop in a river or stream.

men dac i ty (men das′ə tē), *n., pl.* **-ties. 1** habit of telling lies; untruthfulness. **2** a lie: falsehood.

me ni al (mē′nē əl, mē′nyəl), *adj.* suited to or belonging to a servant; low; mean; servile. **—n.** servant who does the humblest and most unpleasant tasks. **—me′ni al ly,** *adv.*

mer ce nar y (mėr′sə ner′ē), *adj., n., pl.* **-nar ies. —adj. 1** working for money only; acting with money as the motive. **2** done for money or gain. **—n. 1** soldier serving for pay in a foreign army. **2** person who works merely for pay.

mere (mir), *n.* ARCHAIC. lake or pond. [Old English, body of water]

met a phys i cal (met′ə fiz′ə kəl), *adj.* **1** of or having to do with metaphysics. **2** highly abstract; hard to understand; abstruse. **3** ARCHAIC. supernatural. **—met′a phys′i cal ly,** *adv.*

met a phy si cian (met′ə fə zish′ən), *n.* person skilled in or familiar with metaphysics, a branch of philosophy that tries to discover and explain reality and knowledge.

mete (mēt), *v.t.*, **met ed, met ing. 1** give to each person a proper or fair share; distribute; allot. [Old English *metan*]

met tle (met′l), *n.* **1** quality of disposition or temperament. **2** spirit; courage. **3 on one's mettle,** ready to do one's best. [variant of *metal*]

met tle some (met′l səm), *adj.* full of mettle; spirited; courageous.

mew (myü), *n.* **1** sound made by a cat or kitten; meow. **2** a similar sound made by certain birds. **—v.i.** make this sound; meow. [probably imitative]

mien (mēn), *n.* manner of holding the head and body; way of acting and looking; bearing; demeanor: *the mien of a judge.*

mil len ni al (mə len′ē əl), *adj.* **1** of a thousand years. **2** like that of the millennium; fit for the millennium. **—mil len′ni al ly,** *adv.*

min ion (min′yən), *n.* **1** servant or follower willing to do whatever is ordered; servile or obsequious person. **2** a darling; favorite.

min is try (min′ə strē), *n., pl.* **-tries. 1** a ministering or serving. **2** agency; instrumentality.

mi nu ti ae (mi nü′shē ē, mi nyü′shē ē), *n.pl.* very small matters; trifling details. [< Latin, trifles, plural of *minutia* smallness < *minutum* made small]

mis-, *prefix.* **1** bad: *Misgovernment = bad government.* **2** badly: *Misbehave = behave badly.* **3** wrong: *Mispronunciation = wrong pronunciation.* **4** wrongly: *Misapply = apply wrongly.* [Old English or < Old French *mes-*]

mis al li ance (mis′ə lī′əns), *n.* an unsuitable alliance or association, especially in marriage.

mis chance (mis chans′), *n.* **1** bad luck; misfortune. **2** piece of bad luck; unlucky accident.

mis cre ant (mis′krē ənt), *n.* a base or wicked person; villain.

mis sive (mis′iv), *n.* a written message; letter.

mit i gate (mit′ə gāt), *v.t., v.i.,* **-gat ed, -gat ing.** make or become mild or milder; make or become less harsh; soften. Anger, grief, pain, punishments, heat, cold, and many other conditions may be mitigated. [< Latin *mitigatum* made gentle < *mitis* gentle]

mne mon ic (ni mon′ik), *adj.* **1** aiding the memory. **2** intended to aid the memory. **3** of or having to do with the memory.

mod i cum (mod′ə kəm), *n.* a small or moderate quantity.

mo nas tic (mə nas′tik), *adj.* **1** of monks or nuns: *the monastic vows of chastity, poverty, and obedience.* **2** of monasteries: *monastic architecture.* **—mo nas′ti cal ly,** *adv.*

mort (môrt), *n.* a great quantity.

mor ti fi ca tion (môr′tə fə kā′shən), *n.* **1** a feeling of shame; humiliation. **2** cause or source of shame or humiliation.

mor ti fy (môr′tə fī), *v.t.,* **-fied, -fy ing. 1** wound the feelings of;

make feel humbled and ashamed; humiliate. **2** overcome (bodily desires and feelings) by pain and self-denial.

mote (mōt), *n.* **1** speck of dust. **2** any very small thing.

mot ley (mot′lē), *adj.* **1** made up of parts or kinds that are different or varied: *a motley crowd.* **2** of different colors like a clown's suit.

moun te bank (moun′tə bangk), *n.* **1** person who sells quack medicines in public, appealing to the audience by tricks, stories, etc. **2** anybody who tries to deceive people by tricks, stories, etc.; charlatan.

mu lat to (mə lat′ō, myù lat′ō), *n., pl.* **-toes. 1** person having one white and one black parent. **2** any person of mixed white and black descent.

mul ti tude (mul′tə tüd, mul′tə tyüd), *n.* a great many; crowd; host. [< Latin *multitudo* < *multus* much]

mul ti tu di nous (mul′tə tüd′n əs, mul′tə tyüd′n əs), *adj.* **1** forming a multitude; very numerous; existing or occurring in great numbers. **2** including many parts, elements, items, or features. **—mul′ti tu′di nous ness,** *n.*

mu nif i cence (myü nif′ə səns), *n.* very great generosity. [< Latin *munificentia,* ultimately < *munus* gift + *facere* to make]

mus ing (myü′zing), *adj.* meditative. **—n.** meditation. **—mus′-ing ly,** *adv.*

must (must), *n.* a state of violent destructiveness, occurring periodically in male elephants. **—adj.** become violently destructive.

myr i ad (mir′ē əd), *n.* **1** ten thousand. **2** a very great number. **—adj. 1** ten thousand. **2** countless; innumerable.

myr tle (mėr′tl), *n.* any of a genus of shrubs of the myrtle family, especially an evergreen shrub of southern Europe with shiny leaves, fragrant white flowers, and black berries.

na ive ty (nä ēv′tē), *n., pl.* **-ties.** naïveté; unspoiled freshness or artlessness.

naught[1] (nôt), *n.* **1** nothing. **2** zero; 0. Also, **nought.**

naught[2] (nôt), *adv.* ARCHAIC. nothing; not at all.

nec ro man cy (nek′rə man′sē), *n.* **1** a foretelling of the future by communicating with the dead. **2** magic; sorcery.

nec tar (nek′tər), *n.* **1** (in Greek and Roman myths) the drink of the gods. **2** any delicious drink. **3** a sweet liquid found in many flowers. Bees gather nectar and make it into honey. [< Latin < Greek *nektar*] **—nec′tar like′,** *adj.*

-ness, *suffix added to adjectives to form nouns.* **1** quality or condition of being ___: *Preparedness = condition of being prepared.* **2** ___ action; ___ behavior: *Carefulness = careful action; careful behavior.* [Old English *-ness, -niss*]

ni ce ty (nī′sə tē), *n., pl.* **-ties. 1** carefulness and delicacy in handling; exactness; accuracy. **2 to a nicety,** just right.

nig gard (nig′ərd), *n.* a stingy person; miser. **—adj.** stingy.

noc tur nal (nok tėr′nl), *adj.* **1** of the night: *Stars are a nocturnal sight.* **2** in the night: *a nocturnal visitor.* **—noc tur′nal ly,** *adv.*

no mad ic (nō mad′ik), *adj.* of nomads or their life; wandering.

no men cla ture (nō′mən klā′chər, nō men′klə chər), *n.* set or system of names or terms: *the nomenclature of music.* [< Latin *nomenclatura* < *nomen* name + *calare* to call]

non cha lant (non′shə lənt, non′shə länt′), *adj.* without enthusiasm; coolly unconcerned; indifferent: *It was hard to remain nonchalant during all the excitement.* **—non′cha lant ly,** *adv.*

nose gay (nōz′gā′), *n.* bunch of flowers; bouquet. [< *nose* + obsolete *gay* something gay or pretty]

nun ner y (nun′ər ē), *n., pl.* **-ner ies.** building or buildings where nuns live; convent.

nu tri ment (nü′trə mənt, nyü′trə mənt), *n.* that which is required by an organism for life and growth; nourishment; food.

ob dur ate (ob′dər it, ob′dyər it), *adj.* **1** stubborn or unyielding; obstinate. **2** hardened in feelings or heart; not repentant. **—ob′-dur ate ly,** *adv.* **—ob′dur ate ness,** *n.*

o blique (ə blēk′; *military* ə blīk′), *adj., v.,* **o bliqued, o bliqu-ing. —adj. 1** neither perpendicular to nor parallel with a given line or surface; not straight up and down or straight across; slanting. **2** not straightforward; indirect: *She made an oblique reference to her illness, but did not mention it directly.* **—v.i., v.t.** have or take an oblique direction; slant. **—o blique′ly,** *adv.*

o bliq ui ty (ə blik′wə tē), *n., pl.* **-ties.** **1** indirectness or crookedness of thought, speech, or behavior, especially conduct that is not upright and moral. **2** inclination, or degree of inclination.

o blit e rate (ə blit′ə rāt′), *v.t.,* **-rat ed, -rat ing.** **1** remove all traces of; blot out; efface: *The heavy rain obliterated the footprints.* **2** blot out so as to leave no distinct traces; make unrecognizable.

o bliv i on (ə bliv′ē ən), *n.* **1** condition of being entirely forgotten: *Many ancient cities have long since passed into oblivion.* **2** fact of forgetting; forgetfulness. [< Latin *oblivionem* < *oblivisci* forget]

o bliv i ous (ə bliv′ē əs), *adj.* **1** not mindful; forgetful: *The book was so interesting that I was oblivious of my surroundings.* **2** bringing or causing forgetfulness. **—o bliv′i ous ly,** *adv.* **—o bliv′i ous ness,** *n.*

ob se quies (ob′sə kwēz), *n. pl.* funeral rites or ceremonies; stately funeral.

ob sti nate (ob′stə nit), *adj.* **1** not giving in; stubborn. **2** hard to control, treat, or remove; persistent. [< Latin *obstinatum* determined < *ob-* by + *stare* to stand] **—ob′sti nate ly,** *adv.*

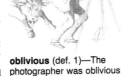

oblivious (def. 1)—The photographer was oblivious of approaching danger.

ob tuse (əb tüs′, əb tyüs′), *adj.* **1** not sharp or acute; blunt. **2** slow in understanding; insensitive; stupid. **—ob tuse′ness,** *n.*

oc cult (ə kult′, ok′ult), *adj.* **1** beyond the bounds of ordinary knowledge; mysterious. **2** outside the laws of the natural world; magical: *Astrology and alchemy are occult sciences.* **3** not disclosed; secret; revealed only to the initiated. **—n. the occult,** forces beyond ordinary knowledge supposed to involve the supernatural.

oc ta vo (ok tā′vō, ok tä′vō), *n., pl.* **-vos.** **1** the page size of a book in which each leaf is one eighth of a whole sheet of paper. **2** book having pages of this size, usually about 6 by 9 inches (15 by 23 centimeters). [< Medieval Latin *in octavo* in an eighth]

o di ous (ō′dē əs), *adj.* very displeasing; hateful; offensive. [< Latin *odiosus* < *odium* odium] **—o′di ous ly,** *adv.* **—o′di ous ness,** *n.*

of fal (ô′fəl, of′əl), *n.* **1** the waste parts of an animal killed for food. **2** garbage; refuse. [< *off* + *fall*]

of fi cious (ə fish′əs), *adj.* too ready to offer services or advice; minding other people's business; meddlesome. **—of fi′cious ly,** *adv.* **—of fi′cious ness,** *n.*

o men (ō′mən), *n.* **1** sign of what is to happen; object or event that is believed to mean good or bad fortune; augury; presage. **2** prophetic meaning; foreboding. **—v.t.** be a sign of; presage; forebode.

om i nous (om′ə nəs), *adj.* unfavorable; threatening: *ominous clouds.* **—om′i nous ly,** *adv.* **—om′i nous ness,** *n.*

om nip o tent (om nip′ə tənt), *adj.* **1** having all power; almighty. **2** having very great power or influence. **—n. the Omnipotent,** God. **—om nip′o tent ly,** *adv.*

o pi ate (ō′pē it, ō′pē āt), *n.* **1** any medical preparation containing opium or a derivative of opium and used especially to dull pain or bring sleep. **2** anything that quiets, soothes, etc.

op u lence (op′yə ləns), *n.* **1** much money or property; wealth; riches. **2** abundance; plenty.

o ra cle (ôr′ə kəl, or′ə kəl), *n.* **1** (in ancient Greece and Rome) an answer believed to be given by a god through a priest or priestess to some question. **2** place where the god was believed to give such answers. **3** the priest, priestess, or other means by which the god's answer was believed to be given. **4** a very wise person. **5** a very wise answer. [< Latin *oraculum* < *orare* speak formally]

o rac u lar (ô rak′yə lər, ō rak′yə lər), *adj.* **1** of or like an oracle. **2** with a hidden meaning that is ambiguous or difficult to make out. **3** very wise. **—o rac′u lar ly,** *adv.*

o ra to ry (ôr′ə tôr′ē, ôr′ə tōr′ē; or′ə tôr′ē, or′ə tōr′ē), *n., pl.* **-ries.** a small chapel, room, or other place set apart for private prayer. [< Late Latin *oratorium* < Latin *orare* plead, pray]

orb (ôrb), *n.* **1** anything round like a ball; sphere; globe. **2** sun, moon, planet, or star. **3** the eyeball or eye. [< Latin *orbis* circle]

or dain (ôr dān′), *v.t.* **1** establish as a law; order; fix; decide; appoint. **2** appoint or consecrate officially as a member of the clergy. **3** appoint as part of the order of the universe or of nature.

ord nance (ôrd′nəns), *n.* **1** cannon or artillery. **2** military apparatus or supplies of all kinds, such as weapons, vehicles, ammunition, etc. [variant of *ordinance*]

o ri son (ôr′ə zən, or′ə zən; ôr′ə sən, or′ə sən), *n.* prayer.

or ni thol o gist (ôr′nə thol′ə jist), *n.* an expert in ornithology,

---

a hat	i it	oi oil	ch child		a in about
ā age	ī ice	ou out	ng long		e in taken
ä far	o hot	u cup	sh she	ə =	i in pencil
e let	ō open	ù put	th thin		o in lemon
ē equal	ô order	ü rule	ŦH then		u in circus
ėr term			zh measure		< = derived from

a branch of zoology dealing with the study of birds.

ost ler (os′lər), *n.* hostler; person who takes care of horses.

ot to man (ot′ə mən), *n.* **1** a low, cushioned seat without back or arms. **2** a cushioned footstool.

o ver ture (ō′vər chər, ō′vər chùr), *n.* **1** proposal or offer. **2** a musical composition played by the orchestra as an introduction to an opera, oratorio, or other long musical composition.

pac tion (pak′shən), *n.* an agreement.

pa gan (pā′gən), *n.* person who is not a Christian, Jew, or Moslem; one who worships many gods, or no gods; heathen. The ancient Greeks and Romans were pagans.

pal frey (pôl′frē), *n., pl.* **-freys.** ARCHAIC. a gentle riding horse, especially one used by women.

palm er (pä′mər, päl′mər), *n.* **1** pilgrim returning from the Holy Land bringing a palm branch as a token. **2** any pilgrim.

palm y (pä′mē, päl′mē), *adj.,* **palm i er, palm i est.** **1** abounding in or shaded by palms. **2** flourishing; prosperous.

pal pa ble (pal′pə bəl), *adj.* **1** readily seen or heard and recognized; obvious. **2** that can be touched or felt; tangible.

pal pi ta tion (pal′pə tā′shən), *n.* **1** a very rapid beating of the heart; throb. **2** a quivering; trembling.

pal sy (pôl′zē), *n., pl.* **-sies,** *v.,* **-sied, -sy ing.** **—n.** paralysis, especially a form of paralysis occurring with Parkinson's disease. **—v.t.** afflict with palsy.

pal ter (pôl′tər), *v.i.* **1** talk or act insincerely; trifle deceitfully. **2** act carelessly; trifle. **3** haggle. [origin unknown] **—pal′ter er,** *n.*

pan de mo ni um (pan′də mō′nē əm), *n.* **1** place of wild disorder or lawless confusion. **2** wild uproar or lawlessness. **3 Pandemonium, a** abode of all the demons; hell. **b** hell's capital. In Milton's *Paradise Lost,* it is the palace built by Satan as the central part of hell. [< Greek *pan-* + *daimōn* demon]

par a gon (par′ə gon), *n.* model of excellence or perfection.

par a sol (par′ə sôl, par′ə sol), *n.* a light umbrella used as a protection from the sun.

par ley (pär′lē), *n., pl.* **-leys.** **1** conference or informal talk. **2** an informal discussion with an enemy during a truce about terms of surrender, exchange of prisoners, etc. **—v.i.** **1** discuss terms, especially with an enemy. **2** ARCHAIC. speak; talk. [< Old French *parlee,* past participle of *parler speak* < Late Latin *parabolare* < *parabola* speech, story. Doublet of PALAVER, PARABLE, PARABOLA.]

par ri cide (par′ə sīd), *n.* **1** act of killing one's parent or parents. **2** person who kills his or her parent or parents.

par si mo ni ous (pär′sə mō′nē əs), *adj.* too economical; stingy; miserly. **—par′si mo′ni ous ly,** *adv.*

par si mo ny (pär′sə mō′nē), *n.* extreme economy; stinginess. [< Latin *parsimonia* < *parcere* to spare]

par ti cle (pär′tə kəl), *n.* **1** a very little bit: *I got a particle of dust in my eye.* **2** any of the extremely small units that make up matter, such as a molecule, atom, electron, proton, or neutron. [< Latin *particula,* diminutive of *partem* part]

pate (pāt), *n.* top of the head; head: *a bald pate.* [Middle English]

pa thos (pā′thos), *n.* **1** quality in speech, writing, music, events, or a scene that arouses a feeling of pity or sadness; power of evoking tender or melancholy emotion. **2** a pathetic expression or utterance.

pa tron age (pā′trə nij, pat′rə nij), *n.* **1** regular business given to a store, hotel, etc., by customers. **2** favor, encouragement, or support given by a patron. **3** condescending favor: *an air of patronage.* **4** power to give jobs or favors: *the patronage of a congressman.* **5** political jobs or favors.

peer less (pir′lis), *adj.* without an equal; matchless. **—peer′less ly,** *adv.* **—peer′less ness,** *n.*

pelf (pelf), *n.* money or riches, thought of as bad or degrading.

pel lu cid (pə lü′sid), *adj.* **1** transparent; clear. **2** clearly expressed; easy to understand. **—pel lu′cid ly,** *adv.*

pe nal (pē′nl), *adj.* **1** of, having to do with, or given as punishment. **2** liable to be punished.

pend ent (pen′dənt), *adj.* **1** hanging; suspended. **2** overhanging. **3** pending.

pen sive (pen′siv), *adj.* **1** thoughtful in a serious or sad way. **2** melancholy. [< Old French *pensif* < *penser* think < Latin *pensare* ponder < *pendere* weigh] **—pen′sive ly,** *adv.* **—pen′sive- ness,** *n.*

pe nur i ous (pi nùr′ē əs, pi nyùr′ē əs), *adj.* **1** mean about spend- ing or giving money; stingy. **2** in a condition of penury; extremely poor. **—pe nur′i ous ly,** *adv.* **—pe nur′i ous ness,** *n.*

pen ur y (pen′yər ē), *n.* great poverty; extreme want; destitution.

per-, *prefix.* throughout; thoroughly; utterly; very: *Perfervid = very fervid. Peruse = use* (i.e., read) *thoroughly.* [< Latin, through, thoroughly, to the end, to destruction]

per chance (pər chans′), *adv.* perhaps. [< Anglo-French *par chance* by chance]

per di tion (pər dish′ən), *n.* **1** loss of one's soul and the joys of heaven; damnation. **2** hell. **3** utter loss or destruction; complete ruin.

pe remp tor y (pə remp′tər ē, per′əmp tôr′ē, per′əmp tōr′ē), *adj.* **1** leaving no choice; decisive; final; absolute: *a peremptory decree.* **2** allowing no denial or refusal: *a peremptory command.* **3** imperious; dictatorial: *a peremptory teacher.* [< Latin *peremptorius* that puts an end to, ultimately < *per-* to the end + *emere* to take] **—pe remp′tor i ly,** *adv.* **—pe remp′tor i ness,** *n.*

per fid i ous (pər fid′ē əs), *adj.* deliberately faithless; treacher- ous. **—per fid′i ous ly,** *adv.* **—per fid′i ous ness,** *n.*

per func tor y (pər fungk′tər ē), *adj.* done merely for the sake of getting rid of the duty; done from force of habit; mechanical; indifferent: *I gave my room a perfunctory cleaning.* [< Late Latin *perfunctorius* < Latin *per-* through + *fungi* execute] **—per func′- tor i ly,** *adv.* **—per func′tor i ness,** *n.*

per ni cious (pər nish′əs), *adj.* **1** that will destroy or ruin; causing great harm or damage; very injurious: *a pernicious habit.* **2** fatal; deadly. [< Latin *perniciosus,* ultimately < *per-* completely + *necis* death] **—per ni′cious ly,** *adv.* **—per ni′cious ness,** *n.*

per plex i ty (pər plek′sə tē), *n., pl.* **-ties. 1** a perplexed condi- tion; being puzzled; confusion; bewilderment. **2** an entangled or confused state. **3** something that perplexes.

per snick e ty (pər snik′ə tē), *adj.* INFORMAL. **1** overly fastidi- ous; fussy. **2** requiring precise and careful handling. Also, **per- nickety.** [origin uncertain]

per spic u ous (pər spik′yü əs), *adj.* easily understood; clear; lucid. **—per spic′u ous ly,** *adv.* **—per spic′u ous ness,** *n.*

per ti nac i ty (pėrt′n as′ə tē), *n.* great persistence; holding firmly to a purpose, action, or opinion.

pe rus al (pə rü′zəl), *n.* **1** a careful reading. **2** a detailed examination.

pe ruse (pə rüz′), *v.t.,* **-rused, -rus ing. 1** read, especially thoroughly and carefully. **2** examine in detail, in order to learn; look at with attention.

pes tif er ous (pe stif′ər əs), *adj.* **1** bringing disease or infection; pestilential. **2** bringing moral evil; pernicious. **3** troublesome; annoying. **—pes tif′er ous ly,** *adv.*

pes ti lence (pes′tl əns), *n.* **1** any infectious or contagious epidemic disease that spreads rapidly, often causing many deaths. **2** the bubonic plague.

pes ti lent (pes′tl ənt), *adj.* **1** often causing death. **2** harmful to morals; destroying peace; pernicious. **3** troublesome; annoying. [< Latin *pestilentem* < *pestis* plague]

pet ri fy (pet′rə fī), *v.,* **-fied, -fy ing. —v.t. 1** turn into stone; change (organic matter) into a substance like stone. **2** make hard as stone; stiffen; deaden. **3** paralyze with fear, horror, or surprise: *The bird was petrified as the snake came near.* **—v.i. 1** become stone or a substance like stone. **2** become rigid like stone; harden. [< French *pétrifier* < Latin *petra* stone + *facere* make]

pet u lance (pech′ə ləns), *n.* a being petulant; peevishness.

pet u lant (pech′ə lənt), *adj.* likely to have little fits of bad temper; irritable over trifles; peevish. [< Latin *petulantem*] **—pet′u lant ly,** *adv.*

phleg mat ic (fleg mat′ik), *adj.* **1** not easily aroused to feeling or action; sluggish; indifferent. **2** cool; calm.

phys ic (fiz′ik), *n., v.,* **-icked, -ick ing. —n.** medicine, especially one that acts as a laxative. **—v.t. 1** give a laxative to. **2** give medicine to. **3** act like a medicine on; cure.

phys i og no my (fiz′ē og′nə mē, fiz′ē on′ə mē), *n., pl.* **-mies.** **1** kind of features or type of face one has; one's face. **2** art of estimating character from the features of the face or the form of the body. **3** the general aspect or looks of a countryside, a situation, etc. [< Greek *physis* nature + *gnōmōn* judge < *gnōnai* recognize]

pince-nez (pans′nā′, pins′nā′), *n., pl.* **pince-nez** (pans′nāz′, pins′nāz′). eyeglasses kept in place by a spring that clips onto the bridge of the nose. [< French, pinch-nose < *pincer* to pinch + *nez* nose < Latin *nasus*]

pince-nez

pique (pēk), *n., v.,* **piqued, pi quing. —n.** a feeling of anger at being slighted; wounded pride. **—v.t. 1** cause a feeling of anger in; wound the pride of.

plaint (plānt), *n.* **1** complaint. **2** ARCHAIC. lament.

plain tive (plān′tiv), *adj.* expressive of sor- row; mournful; sad. [< Old French *plaintif* < *plaint* plaint] **—plain′tive ly,** *adv.* **—plain′tive ness,** *n.*

plight (plīt), *v.t.* promise solemnly; pledge: *plight one's loyalty.* **—n.** a solemn promise; pledge.

plum age (plü′mij), *n.* feathers of a bird: *A parrot has bright plumage.* [< Old French < *plume* plume]

ply (plī), *v.,* **plied, ply ing. —v.t. 1** work with; use: *The dressmaker plies her needle.* **2** keep up work on; work away at or on: *ply one's trade.* **3** urge again and again. **—v.i.** go back and forth regularly between certain places.

pol i tic (pol′ə tik), *adj.* **1** wise in looking out for one's own interests; prudent; shrewd. **2** showing wisdom or shrewdness. **3** scheming; crafty. **4** political **—pol′i tic ly,** *adv.*

pom mel (pum′əl, pom′əl), *n., v.,* **-meled, -mel ing** or **-melled, -mel ling. —n. 1** part of a saddle that sticks up at the front. **2** a rounded knob on the hilt of a sword, dagger, etc. **—v.t.** pummel; strike or beat.

pon der ous (pon′dər əs), *adj.* **1** very heavy. **2** heavy and clumsy: *A hippopotamus is ponderous.* **3** dull; tiresome. **—pon′- der ous ly,** *adv.* **—pon′der ous ness,** *n.*

pon tif i cal (pon tif′ə kəl), *adj.* **1** of or having to do with the pope; papal. **2** of or having to do with a bishop; episcopal. **3** pompous; dogmatic. **—pon tif′i cal ly,** *adv.*

pop in jay (pop′in jā), *n.* a vain, overly talkative person; conceited, silly person.

pop pet (pop′it), *n.* BRITISH DIALECT. a term of affection for a girl or child.

por tent (pôr′tent, pōr′tent), *n.* **1** a warning of coming evil; sign; omen. **2** ominous significance.

por ten tous (pôr ten′təs, pōr ten′təs), *adj.* **1** indicating evil to come; ominous; threatening. **2** amazing; extraordinary. **—por- ten′tous ly,** *adv.* **—por ten′tous ness,** *n.*

pos ter i ty (po ster′ə tē), *n.* **1** generations of the future: *Posterity may travel to distant planets.* **2** all of a person's descendants.

pos tern (pō′stərn, pos′tərn), *n.* **1** a small back door or gate. **2** any small or private entrance. **—adj.** rear; lesser.

post hu mous (pos′chə məs), *adj.* **1** happening after death: *posthumous fame.* **2** published after the death of the author: *a posthumous book.* **3** born after the death of the father: *a posthu- mous daughter.* **—post′hu mous ly,** *adv.*

poul tice (pōl′tis), *n., v.,* **-ticed, -tic ing. —n.** a soft, moist mass of mustard, herbs, etc., applied to the body as a medicine. **—v.t.** put a poultice on. [< Latin *pultes,* plural of *puls* mush]

pox (poks), *n.* **1** any disease characterized by eruption of pustules on the skin, such as chicken pox or smallpox. **2** syphilis.

prate (prāt), *v.,* **prat ed, prat ing,** *n.* **—v.i.** talk a great deal in a foolish way. **—v.t.** say in an empty or foolish way. **—n.** a prating; empty or foolish talk. [< Middle Dutch *praeten*]

prat tle (prat′l), *v.,* **-tled, -tling,** *n.* **—v.i. 1** talk or tell freely and carelessly, as some children do. **2** talk or tell in a foolish way. **3** babble. **—v.t.** say in a foolish or childish way. **—n. 1** childish or foolish talk. **2** babble. [< *prate*] **—prat′tler,** *n.*

pre am ble (prē′am′bəl), *n.* **1** a preliminary statement; introduc- tion to a speech or a writing. The reasons for a law and its general purpose are often stated in a preamble. **2** a preliminary or introductory fact or circumstance, especially one showing what is to follow. [< Medieval Latin *praeambulum* < Late Latin *praeambulus,* walking before < Latin *prae-* pre- + *ambulare* to walk]

pre cept (prē′sept), *n.* rule of action or behavior; guiding principle: *"If at first you don't succeed, try, try again" is a familiar precept.*

prec i pice (pres′ə pis), *n.* **1** a very steep or almost vertical face of rock; cliff or steep mountainside. **2** situation of great peril; critical position.

pre cip i tance (pri sip′ə təns), *n.* headlong haste; rashness.

pre cip i ta tion (pri sip′ə tā′shən), *n.* **1** act or state of precipitating; throwing down or falling headlong. **2** a hastening or hurrying. **3** a sudden bringing on. **4** unwise or rash rapidity; sudden haste.

pre curse (prē kėrs′), *n.* OBSOLETE. an announcing, sign, or warning of something to come.

prel a cy (prel′ə sē), *n., pl.* **-cies.** **1** position or rank of a prelate. **2** prelates. **3** church government by prelates.

prel ate (prel′it), *n.* member of the clergy of high rank, such as a bishop.

pres age (pres′ij; *also* pri sāj′ *for v.*), *n., v.,* **pre saged, pre sag ing.** —*n.* **1** sign felt as a warning; omen. **2** a feeling that something is about to happen; presentiment; foreboding. —*v.t.* **1** give warning of; predict. **2** have or give a presentiment or prophetic impression of.

pre script (*n.* prē′skript; *adj.* pri skript′, prē′skript), *n.* that which is prescribed; rule; order; direction. —*adj.* prescribed.

pre sump tu ous (pri zump′chü əs), *adj.* acting without permission or right; too bold; forward. —**pre sump′tu ous ly,** *adv.* —**pre sump′tu ous ness,** *n.*

pri mal (prī′məl), *adj.* **1** of early times; first; primeval. **2** chief; fundamental. —**pri′mal ly,** *adv.*

pri or ess (prī′ər is), *n.* head of a convent or priory for women. Prioresses usually rank below abbesses.

pris tine (pris′tēn′, pris′tən, *or* pris′tīn), *adj.* as it was in its earliest time or state; original; primitive. —**pris′tine ly,** *adv.*

prith ee (prɪᴛн′ē), *interj.* ARCHAIC. I pray thee; I ask you.

priv y (priv′ē), *adj.* **1** private. **2** ARCHAIC. secret; hidden. **3 privy to,** having secret or private knowledge of.

pro cras ti nate (prō kras′tə nāt), *v.i., v.t.,* **-nat ed, -nat ing.** put things off until later; delay, especially repeatedly. —**pro cras′ti na′tion,** *n.* —**pro cras′ti na′tor,** *n.*

pro cre ant (prō′krē ənt), *adj.* generating; having to do with procreation: *a procreant breed of birds.*

prod i gal (prod′ə gəl), *adj.* **1** given to extravagant or reckless spending; wasteful. **2** abundant; lavish. —*n.* person who is wasteful or extravagant; spendthrift.

pro di gious (prə dij′əs), *adj.* **1** very great; huge; vast. **2** wonderful; marvelous. —**pro di′gious ly,** *adv.*

prod i gy (prod′ə jē), *n., pl.* **-gies.** **1** person endowed with amazing brilliance, talent, etc., especially a remarkably talented child. **2** a marvelous example.

prof a na tion (prof′ə nā′shən), *n.* act of profaning.

pro fane (prə fān′), *adj., v.,* **-faned, -fan ing.** —*adj.* **1** characterized by contempt or disregard for God or holy things; irreverent. **2** not sacred; worldly; secular. **3** ritually unclean or polluted. —*v.t.* **1** treat (holy things) with contempt or disregard; desecrate. **2** put to wrong or unworthy use. [< Latin *profanus* not sacred < *pro-* in front (outside) of + *fanum* temple, shrine] —**pro fane′ly,** *adv.* —**pro fane′ness,** *n.*

prom on to ry (prom′ən tôr′ē, prom′ən tōr′ē), *n., pl.* **-ries.** a high point of land extending from the coast into the water; headland.

prop a gate (prop′ə gāt), *v.,* **-gat ed, -gat ing.** —*v.i.* produce offspring; reproduce. —*v.t.* **1** increase in number or intensity; multiply. **2** cause to increase in number by the production of young. **3** spread (news, knowledge, etc.); extend. **4** pass on; send further.

prop a ga tion (prop′ə gā′shən), *n.* **1** the breeding of plants or animals. **2** a spreading; getting more widely believed; making more widely known.

pro pi tious (prə pish′əs), *adj.* **1** holding well; favorable: *propitious weather for our trip.* **2** favorably inclined; gracious. [< Latin *propitius,* originally, falling forward < *pro-* forward + *petere* go toward] —**pro pi′tious ly,** *adv.* —**pro pi′tious ness,** *n.*

pros o dy (pros′ə dē), *n.* **1** the science of poetic meters and versification. **2** any system or style of versification: *Latin prosody.*

pros trate (pros′trāt), *v.,* **-trat ed, -trat ing,** *adj.* —*v.t.* **1** lay down flat; cast down. **2** make very weak or helpless; exhaust: *Sickness often prostrates people.* —*adj.* **1** lying flat with face downward. **2** lying flat: *I stumbled and fell prostrate on the floor.* **3** overcome; helpless: *a prostrate enemy.*

pros y (prō′zē), *adj.,* **pros i er, pros i est.** like prose; commonplace; dull; tiresome. —**pros′i ly,** *adv.* —**pros′i ness,** *n.*

prov i dence (prov′ə dəns), *n.* **1** God's care and help.

a hat	i it	oi oil	ch child	a in about
ā age	ī ice	ou out	ng long	e in taken
ä far	o hot	u cup	sh she	ə = { i in pencil
e let	ō open	ù put	th thin	o in lemon
ē equal	ô order	ü rule	ᴛн then	u in circus
ėr term			zh measure	< = derived from

2 Providence, God. 3 instance of God's care and help. **4** a being provident; prudence.

prov i dent (prov′ə dənt), *adj.* **1** having or showing foresight; careful in providing for the future; prudent. **2** economical; frugal.

pro vi sion al ly (prə vizh′ə nə lē), *adv.* **1** for the time being; temporarily. **2** conditionally.

psal ter y (sôl′tər ē), *n., pl.* **-ter ies.** an ancient musical instrument played by plucking the strings. [Old English *saltere*]

pub li can (pub′lə kən), *n.* **1** BRITISH. keeper of a pub. **2** a tax collector of ancient Rome.

pun gent (pun′jənt), *adj.* **1** sharply affecting the organs of taste and smell: *a pungent pickle, the pungent smell of burning leaves.* **2** sharp; biting: *pungent criticism.* **3** stimulating to the mind; keen; lively: *a pungent wit.* —**pun′gent ly,** *adv.*

pur ga tion (pėr gā′shən), *n.* a purging; cleansing.

pur ga tive (pėr′gə tiv), *n.* medicine that causes emptying of the bowels. Castor oil is a purgative. —*adj.* purging, especially causing the bowels to empty.

pur ga to ry (pėr′gə tôr′ē, pėr′gə tōr′ē), *n., pl.* **-ries.** **1** (in Roman Catholic belief) a temporary condition or place in which the souls of those who have died penitent are purified from venial sin or the effects of sin by punishment. **2** any condition or place of temporary suffering or punishment.

pur port (*v.* pər pôrt′, pər pōrt′; pėr′ pôrt, pėr′pōrt; *n.* pėr′pôrt, pėr′pōrt), *v.t.* **1** claim or profess. **2** have as its main idea; mean. —*n.* meaning; main idea. —**pur port′ed ly,** *adv.*

pur vey or (pər vā′ər), *n.* **1** person who supplies provisions. **2** person who supplies anything: *a purveyor of gossip.*

pus tule (pus′chül), *n.* a small bump on the skin, filled with pus and inflamed at the base. [< Latin *pustula*]

pu tres cence (pyü tres′ns), *n.* putrescent condition.

pu tres cent (pyü tres′nt), *adj.* **1** becoming putrid; rotting. **2** having to do with putrefaction.

pyre (pīr), *n.* **1** pile of wood for burning a dead body as a funeral rite. **2** any large pile or heap of burnable material.

quack (kwak), *n.* **1** a dishonest person who pretends to be a doctor. **2** an ignorant pretender to knowledge or skill of any sort; charlatan. —*adj.* not genuine: *a quack doctor.*

quad ru ped (kwod′rə ped), *n.* animal that has four feet. —*adj.* four-footed. [< Latin *quadrupedem* < *quadru-* four + *pedem* foot]

quail (kwāl), *v.i.* be afraid; lose courage; shrink back in fear: *quail at an angry look.*

quell (kwel), *v.t.* **1** put down (disorder, rebellion, etc.): *quell a riot.* **2** put an end to; overcome: *quell one's fears.* [Old English *cwellan* to kill] —**quell′a ble,** *adj.* —**quell′er,** *n.*

quer u lous (kwer′ə ləs, kwer′yə ləs), *adj.* complaining; fretful; peevish: *a querulous remark. Some people are very querulous when they are sick.* [< Latin *querulus* < *queri* complain] —**quer′u lous ly,** *adv.* —**quer′u lous ness,** *n.*

qui es cence (kwī es′ns), *n.* absence of activity; a quiet state; stillness.

quill (kwil), *n.* a large, stiff feather. —**quill′-like′,** *adj.*

quin tes sence (kwin tes′ns), *n.* **1** the purest form of some quality; pure essence. **2** the most perfect example of something: *Her dress was the quintessence of good taste and style.* [< Medieval Latin *qu inta essentia* fifth essence; with reference to a fifth element supposed by medieval philosophers to be more pervasive than the four elements (earth, water, fire, and air)]

qui vive? (kē vēv′), **1** who goes there? **2 on the qui vive,** watchful; alert. [< French, literally, (long) live who?; expecting such a reply as *Vive le roi!* Long live the king!]

quix ot ic (kwik sot′ik), *adj.* **1** resembling Don Quixote; extravagantly chivalrous or romantic. **2** visionary; not practical. —**quix ot′i cal ly,** *adv.*

ra di ance (rā′dē əns), *n.* **1** vivid brightness: *the radiance of the sun, the radiance of a smile.* **2** radiation.

rail (rāl), *v.i.* complain bitterly; use violent and reproachful language: *rail at one's hard luck.*

rail ler y (rā′lər ē), *n., pl.* **-ler ies.** **1** good-humored ridicule; joking; teasing. **2** a bantering remark.

rai ment (rā′mənt), *n.* ARCHAIC. clothing; garments.

ram pant (ram′pənt), *adj.* **1** growing without any check. **2** passing beyond restraint or usual limits; unchecked. **3** angry; excited; violent. **—ram′pant ly,** *adv.*

ran cor (rang′kər), *n.* bitter resentment or ill will; extreme hatred or spite. [< Late Latin, rankness < Latin *rancere* be rank]

rapt (rapt), *adj.* **1** lost in delight. **2** so busy thinking of or enjoying one thing that one does not know what else is happening. [< Latin *raptum* seized] **—rapt′ly,** *adv.* **—rapt′ness,** *n.*

rav age (rav′ij), *v.,* **-aged, -ag ing,** *n.* **—v.t.** damage greatly; lay waste; destroy: *The forest fire ravaged many miles of country.* **—n.** violence; destruction; great damage. **—rav′ag er,** *n.*

rav el (rav′əl), *v.,* **-eled, -el ing** or **-elled, -el ling,** *n.* **—v.i.** **1** fray out; separate into threads. **2** become tangled, involved, or confused. **—v.t.** **1** separate the threads of; fray. **2** make plain or clear; unravel. **—n.** an unraveled thread or fiber.

re-, *prefix.* **1** again; anew; once more: *Reappear = appear again.* **2** back: *Repay = pay back.* [< Latin *re-, red-*]

re buke (ri byük′), *v.,* **-buked, -buk ing,** *n.* **—v.t.** express disapproval of; reprove. **—n.** expression of disapproval; scolding. [< Anglo-French *rebuker* < Old French *rebuchier* < *re-* back + *buchier* to strike]

re cal ci trant (ri kal′sə trənt), *adj.* resisting authority or control; disobedient. **—n.** a recalcitrant person or animal.

re ca pit u late (rē′kə pich′ə lāt), *v.t., v.i.,* **-lat ed, -lat ing.** repeat or recite the main points of; tell briefly; sum up.

re cog ni zance (ri kog′nə zəns, ri kon′ə zəns), *n.* in law: **1** bond binding a person to do some particular act. **2** sum of money to be forfeited if the act is not performed.

rec om pense (rek′əm pens), *v.,* **-pensed, -pens ing,** *n.* **—v.t.** **1** pay (a person); pay back; reward. **2** make a fair return for (an action, anything lost, damage done, or hurt received). **—n.** **1** payment; reward. **2** return; amends. [< Late Latin *recompensare* < Latin *re-* back + *compensare* compensate]

rec on dite (rek′ən dīt, ri kon′dīt), *adj.* **1** hard to understand; profound. **2** little known; obscure. **3** hidden from view; concealed. [< Latin *reconditum* stored away < *re-* back + *com-* up + *-dere* to put] **—rec′on dite′ly,** *adv.* **—rec′on dite′ness,** *n.*

re course (rē′kôrs, rē′kōrs; ri kôrs′, ri kōrs′), *n.* **1** a turning for help or protection; appealing: *recourse to a doctor in an emergency.* **2 have recourse to,** turn to for help; appeal to.

red o lent (red′l ənt), *adj.* **1** having a pleasant smell; fragrant; aromatic. **2** smelling strongly; giving off an odor: *a house redolent of fresh paint.* **3** suggesting thoughts or feelings; reminiscent: *Rome is a city redolent of history.* [< Latin *redolentem* emitting scent < *re-, red-* back + *olere* to smell] **—red′o lent ly,** *adv.*

re dress (*v.* ri dres′; *n.* rē′dres, ri dres′), *v.t.* set right; repair; remedy. **—n.** **1** a setting right; reparation; relief: *Anyone who has been injured deserves redress.* **2** the means of a remedy. [< Middle French *redresser* < *re-* again + *dresser* straighten, arrange]

reeve (rēv), *n.* **1** the chief official of a town or district. **2** bailiff; steward; overseer. [Old English *(ge)rēfa*]

re frac tor y (ri frak′tər ē), *adj.* **1** hard to manage; stubborn; obstinate: *Mules are refractory.* **2** not yielding readily to treatment: *a refractory cough.*

re it er ate (rē it′ə rāt′), *v.t.,* **-rat ed, -rat ing.** say or do several times; repeat (an action, demand, etc.) again and again: *reiterate a command.* **—re it′e ra′tion,** *n.*

re lent less (ri lent′lis), *adj.* without pity; not relenting; unyielding. **—re lent′less ly,** *adv.* **—re lent′less ness,** *n.*

re miss (ri mis′), *adj.* **1** careless or slack in doing what one has to do; neglectful; negligent: *be remiss in one's duty.* **2** characterized by carelessness, negligence, or inattention. [< Latin *remissum* remitted] **—re miss′ly,** *adv.* **—re miss′ness,** *n.*

re mon strance (ri mon′strəns), *n.* act of remonstrating; protest; complaint.

re mon strate (ri mon′strāt), *v.i.,* **-strat ed, -strat ing.** speak, reason, or plead in complaint or protest: *The teacher remonstrated with us about our unruly behavior.*

re morse (ri môrs′), *n.* deep, painful regret for having done wrong; compunction; contrition: *I felt remorse for being rude, so I*

apologized. [< Late Latin *remorsum* tormented, bit again < Latin *re-* back + *mordere* to bite]

ren coun ter (ren koun′tər), *n.* a hostile meeting; battle.

rend (rend), *v.t.,* **rent, rend ing.** **1** pull apart violently; tear: *Wolves will rend a lamb.* **2** split: *Lightning rent the tree.* **3** disturb violently: *a mind rent by doubt.* **4** remove with force or violence.

ren dez vous (rän′də vü), *n., pl.* **-vous** (-vüz). **1** an appointment or engagement to meet at a fixed place or time; meeting by agreement. **2** a meeting place; gathering place.

rep a ra tion (rep′ə rā′shən), *n.* a giving of satisfaction or compensation for wrong or injury done.

re past (ri past′), *n.* meal; food. [< Old French, ultimately < Latin *re-* again + *pascere* to feed]

re pine (ri pīn′), *v.i.,* **-pined, -pin ing.** be discontented; fret; complain. **—re pin′er,** *n.*

re plen ish (ri plen′ish), *v.t.* fill again; provide a new supply for; renew: *replenish one's wardrobe. You had better replenish the fire.* [< Old French *repleniss-,* a form of *replenir,* fill again, ultimately < Latin *re-* again + *plenus* full] **—re plen′ish er,** *n.* **—re plen′ish ment,** *n.*

req ui em or **Req ui em** (rek′wē əm, rē′kwē əm), *n.* **1** Mass for the dead; musical church service for the dead. **2** music for it. **3** any musical service or hymn for the dead. [< Latin, accusative of *requies* rest; the first word of the Mass for the dead]

re quit al (ri kwī′tl), *n.* **1** repayment; payment; return. **2** act of requiting.

re quite (ri kwīt′), *v.t.,* **-quit ed, -quit ing.** **1** pay back; make return for: *requite kindness with love.* **2** make return to; reward: *The knight requited the boy for his warning.* **3** make retaliation for; avenge. [< *re-* + *quite,* variant of *quit*] **—re quit′er,** *n.*

re splend ent (ri splen′dənt), *adj.* very bright; shining; splendid: *the resplendent sun, a face resplendent with joy.* [< Latin *resplendentem* < *re-* back + *splendere* to shine] **—re splend′ent ly,** *adv.*

res tive (res′tiv), *adj.* **1** restless; uneasy. **2** hard to manage. **3** refusing to go ahead; balky. [< Old French *restif* motionless < *rester* remain] **—res′tive ly,** *adv.* **—res′tive ness,** *n.*

re tain er (ri tā′nər), *n.* **1** person who serves a person of rank; attendant; follower. **2** person who retains.

re tic u late (*adj.* ri tik′yə lit, ri tik′yə lāt; *v.* ri tik′yə lāt), *adj., v.,* **-lat ed, -lat ing.** **—adj.** covered with or resembling a network. *Reticulate leaves have the veins arranged like the threads of a net.* **—v.t.** cover or mark with a network. **—v.i.** form a network

rev e la tion (rev′ə lā′shən), *n.* **1** act of making known. **2** the thing made known: *Her true nature was a revelation to me.* **3** disclosure of divine truth and will to humankind. **4 Revelation,** the last book of the New Testament, supposed to have been written by the apostle John. [< Latin *revelationem* < *revelare* reveal]

rev el ry (rev′əl rē), *n., pl.* **-ries.** boisterous reveling or festivity.

re ver be rate (ri vėr′bə rāt′), *v.,* **-rat ed, -rat ing.** **—v.i.** **1** echo back. **2** be cast back; be reflected a number of times, as light or heat. **—v.t.** **1** reecho (a sound or noise). **2** cast back; reflect (light or heat). **—re ver′be ra′tion,** *n.*

ric o chet (rik′ə shā′; *British* rik′ə shet′), *n., v.,* **-cheted** (-shād′), **-chet ing** (-shā′ing) or **-chet ted** (-shet′id), **-chet ting** (-shet′ing). **—n.** the skipping or jumping motion of an object after glancing off a flat surface: *the ricochet of a flat stone off the surface of the lake.* **—v.i.** move with a skipping or jumping motion. [< French]

rill (ril), *n.* a tiny stream; little brook.

riv elled (riv′əld), *adj.* ARCHAIC. full of wrinkles or small folds.

riv en (riv′ən), *adj.* torn apart; split. **—v.** a pp. of **rive.**

ru di ment (rü′də mənt), *n.* **1** part to be learned first; beginning: *the rudiments of grammar.* **2** something in an early stage; undeveloped or imperfect form.

rue[1] (rü), *v.,* **rued, ru ing.** **—v.t.** be sorry for; regret. **—n.** sorrow; regret. [Old English *hrēowan*]

rue[2] (rü), *n.* a strong-smelling, woody herb of the same family as the citrus, with yellow flowers, and bitter leaves that were formerly much used in medicine. [< Old French < Latin *ruta*]

rue ful (rü′fəl), *adj.* **1** sorrowful; unhappy; mournful: *a rueful expression.* **2** causing sorrow or pity: *a rueful sight.* **—rue′ful ly,** *adv.*

ru mi nant (rü′mə nənt), *n.* any of a suborder of even-toed, hoofed, herbivorous mammals which chew the cud and have a stomach with four separate cavities, including cattle, deer, sheep, goats, giraffes, and camels. **—adj.** belonging to the group of ruminants. [< Latin *ruminantem* chewing a cud < *rumen* gullet]

sac ri le gious (sak′rə lij′əs, sak′rə lē′jəs), *adj.* injurious or insulting to sacred persons or things. —**sac′ri le′gious ly,** *adv.* —**sac′ri le′gious ness,** *n.*

saf fron (saf′rən), *n.* **1** an autumn crocus with purple flowers having orange-yellow stigmas. **2** an orange yellow. —*adj.* orange-yellow.

sa gac i ty (sə gas′ə tē), *n.* keen, sound judgment; mental acuteness; shrewdness.

sage (sāj), *adj.*, **sag er, sag est,** *n.* —*adj.* **1** showing wisdom or good judgment: *a sage reply.* **2** wise: *a sage adviser.* —*n.* a very wise person. —**sage′ly,** *adv.* —**sage′ness,** *n.*

sal ly (sal′ē), *v.*, **-lied, -ly ing,** *n.*, *pl.* **-lies.** —*v.i.* **1** go suddenly from a defensive position to attack an enemy; rush forth suddenly; go out. **3** set out briskly or boldly. —*n.* **1** a sudden attack on an enemy made from a defensive position; sortie. **2** a sudden rushing forth. **3** a going forth; trip; excursion. **4** a witty remark.

sa lu bri ous (sə lü′brē əs), *adj.* favorable or conducive to good health; healthful. [< Latin *salubris* < *salus* good health] —**sa lu′-bri ous ly,** *adv.* —**sa lu′bri ous ness,** *n.*

sal u tar y (sal′yə ter′ē), *adj.* **1** beneficial. **2** good for the health; wholesome. —**sal′u tar′i ly,** *adv.*

salve (sav), *n.*, *v.*, **salved, salv ing.** —*n.* **1** a soft, greasy substance put on wounds and sores; healing ointment. **2** something soothing; balm. —*v.t.* **1** put salve on. **2** smooth over; soothe.

sanc ti fy (sangk′tə fī), *v.t.*, **-fied, -fy ing.** **1** make holy; make legitimate or binding by a religious sanction: *sanctify a marriage.* **2** set apart as sacred; observe as holy.

san guine (sang′gwən), *adj.* **1** naturally cheerful and hopeful. **2** confident; hopeful. **3** having a healthy red color; ruddy. **4** (in old physiology) having an active circulation, a ruddy color, and a cheerful and ardent disposition. —**san′guine ly,** *adv.*

sa ti ate (*v.* sā′shē āt; *adj.* sā′shē it), *v.*, **-at ed, -at ing,** *adj.* —*v.t.* **1** feed fully; satisfy fully. **2** weary or disgust with too much. —*adj.* filled to satiety; satiated. —**sa′ti a′tion,** *n.*

saun ter (sôn′tər, sän′tər), *v.i.* walk along slowly and happily; stroll: *saunter in the park.* —*n.* **1** a leisurely or careless gait. **2** a stroll. [origin uncertain] —**saun′ter er,** *n.*

scarp (skärp), *n.* **1** a steep slope. **2** the inner slope or side of a ditch surrounding a fortification. —*v.t.* make into a steep slope; slope steeply. [< Italian *scarpa;* of Germanic origin]

scath er (scath′ər), *n.* OBSOLETE. criminal; thief; murderer. [Old English *sceatha*]

scep ter (sep′tər), *n.* **1** the rod or staff carried by a ruler as a symbol of royal power or authority. **2** royal or imperial power or authority; sovereignty. Also, **sceptre.**

scin til late (sin′tl āt), *v.i.*, **-lat ed, -lat ing.** sparkle; flash: *The snow scintillates in the sun like diamonds. Brilliant wit scintillates.* —**scin′til lat′ing ly,** *adv.* —**scin′til la′tor,** *n.*

scotch (skoch), *v.t.* **1** inflict such hurt upon (something regarded as dangerous) that it is made harmless for the time. **2** stamp on or stamp out (something dangerous); crush: *scotch a rumor.*

screed (skrēd), *n.* a long speech or writing.

scru ple (skrü′pəl), *n.* **1** a feeling of doubt about what one ought to do: *No scruple ever holds him back from prompt action.* **2** a feeling of uneasiness that keeps a person from doing something.

scru pu los i ty (skrü′pyə los′ə tē), *n.*, *pl.* **-ties.** **1** a being scrupulous; strict regard for what is right; scrupulous care. **2** an instance of this.

scud (skud), *v.*, **scud ded, scud ding,** *n.* —*v.i.* **1** run or move swiftly: *Clouds scudded across the sky driven by the high wind.* **2** (of a boat, etc.) run before a storm with little or no sail set. —*n.* **1** a scudding. **2** clouds or spray driven by the wind.

scul lion (skul′yən), *n.* ARCHAIC. **1** servant who does the dirty, rough work in a kitchen. **2** a low, contemptible person.

scur ril i ty (skə ril′ə tē), *n.*, *pl.* **-ties.** **1** coarse joking. **2** indecent abuse. **3** an indecent or coarse remark.

scythe (sīᴛH), *n.*, *v.*, **scythed, scyth ing.** —*n.* a long, thin, slightly curved blade on a long handle, for cutting grass, etc. —*v.t.* cut or mow with a scythe.

sear (sir), *v.t.* **1** burn or char the surface of. **2** make hard or unfeeling. **3** dry up; wither. —*v.i.* become dry, burned, or hard. —*n.* mark made by searing.

sec ond (sek′ənd), *n.* (in music) a lower tone.

sedge (sej), *n.* any of a large family of monocotyledonous herbs growing chiefly in wet places, resembling grasses but having solid, three-sided stems and small, inconspicuous flowers usually in spikes or heads. [Old English *secg*]

sem blance (sem′bləns), *n.* **1** outward appearance: *Their story*

sen tient (sen′shənt), *adj.* that can feel. —**sen′tient ly,** *adv.*

sep ul cher (sep′əl kər), *n.* **1** place of burial; tomb; grave. **2** structure or recess in some old churches in which sacred relics were deposited. —*v.t.* bury (a dead body) in a sepulcher. Also, **sepulchre.** [< Old French < Latin *sepulcrum* < *sepelire* bury]

se pul chral (sə pul′krəl), *adj.* **1** of sepulchers or tombs. **2** of burial: *sepulchral ceremonies.* **3** deep and gloomy; dismal; suggesting a tomb: *sepulchral darkness.* —**se pul′chral ly,** *adv.*

se ques ter (si kwes′tər), *v.t.* **1** remove or withdraw from public use or from public view; seclude. **2** take away (property) for a time from an owner until a debt is paid or some claim is satisfied. **3** seize by authority; take and keep.

serf (sėrf), *n.* **1** (in the feudal system) a slave who could not be sold off the land, but passed from one owner to another with the land. **2** person treated almost like a slave; person who is mistreated, underpaid, etc. [< French < Latin *servus* slave] —**serf′like′,** *adj.*

se ros i ty (si ros′ə tē), *n.* a condition characterized by an effusion of fluid.

ser ous (sir′əs), *adj.* **1** of, having to do with, or producing serum. **2** like serum; watery. Tears are drops of a serous fluid.

shal lop (shal′əp), *n.* a small, light, open boat with sail or oars. [< French *chaloupe* < Dutch *sloepe*]

shard (shärd), *n.* **1** piece of broken earthenware or pottery. **2** a broken piece; fragment. Also, **sherd.** [Old English *sceard*]

shav er (shā′vər), *n.* INFORMAL. youngster; small boy.

shin gle (shing′gəl), *n.* **1** loose stones or pebbles that lie on the seashore; coarse gravel. **2** beach or other place covered with this.

ship wright (ship′rīt′), *n.* person who builds or repairs ships.

shire (shīr), *n.* one of the counties into which Great Britain is divided, especially one whose name ends in *-shire.*

shoal (shōl), *n.* place in a sea, lake, or stream where the water is shallow. —*adj.* shallow. —*v.i.* become shallow.

shrift (shrift), *n.* ARCHAIC. **1** confession of one's sins to a priest, followed by the granting of forgiveness by the priest. **2** act of shriving. [Old English *scrift* < *scrīfan* shrive]

shriv en (shriv′ən), *v.* ARCHAIC. a pp. of **shrive,** pardon after confessing.

shroud (shroud), *n.* **1** cloth or garment in which a dead person is wrapped or dressed for burial. **2** something that covers, conceals, or veils: *The fog was a shroud over the city.* **3** Usually, **shrouds,** *pl.* rope from a mast to the side of a ship. Shrouds help support the mast. —*v.t.* **1** wrap or dress for burial. **2** cover; conceal; veil: *Their plans are shrouded in secrecy.* —**shroud′like′,** *adj.*

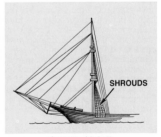

shrouds (def. 3)

silks (silks), *n. pl.* the blouse and peaked cap worn by a jockey.

si ne cure (sī′nə kyūr, sin′ə kyùr), *n.* **1** an extremely easy job; position requiring little or no work and usually paying well. **2** an ecclesiastical benefice without parish duties.

sin ew (sin′yü), *n.* **1** tendon. **2** strength; energy; force. **3** Often, **sinews,** *pl.* means of strength; source of power. —*v.t.* furnish with sinews. —**sin′ew less,** *adj.*

sink (singk), *n.* **1** drain; sewer. **2** place of vice or corruption.

sin u ous (sin′yü əs), *adj.* **1** having many curves or turns; winding: *the sinuous motion of a snake.* **2** indirect; devious. **3** untrustworthy. [< Latin *sinuosus* < *sinus* a curve] —**sin′-u ous ly,** *adv.* —**sin′u ous ness,** *n.*

a hat	**i** it	**oi** oil	**ch** child	a in about
ā age	**ī** ice	**ou** out	**ng** long	e in taken
ä far	**o** hot	**u** cup	**sh** she	ə = { i in pencil
e let	**ō** open	**ù** put	**th** thin	o in lemon
ē equal	**ô** order	**ü** rule	**ᴛH** then	u in circus
ėr term			**zh** measure	< = derived from

849

skir mish (skėr′mish), *n.* a brief fight between small groups of soldiers. —*v.i.* take part in a skirmish.

slan der (slan′dər), *n.* 1 a false statement spoken with intent to harm the reputation of another. 2 the spreading of false reports. —*v.t.* talk falsely about. —*v.i.* speak or spread slander.

sleight (slīt), *n.* 1 skill; dexterity. 2 a clever trick.

slov en ly (sluv′ən lē), *adj.*, **-li er, -li est**, *adv.* —*adj.* untidy, dirty, or careless in dress, appearance, habits, work, etc. —*adv.* in a slovenly manner. —**slov′en li ness,** *n.*

slum ber ous (slum′bər əs), *adj.* 1 sleepy; heavy with drowsiness. 2 causing or inducing sleep. 3 inactive or quiet. —**slum′ber ous ly,** *adv.*

smirch (smėrch), *v.t.* 1 make dirty; soil with soot, dirt, etc. 2 cast discredit upon; taint; tarnish. —*n.* 1 a dirty mark; stain. 2 blot on a person's reputation. [Middle English *smorchen* discolor]

smith y (smith′ē, smiŦH′ē), *n.*, *pl.* **smith ies,** *v.*, **smith ied, smith y ing.** —*n.* workshop of a smith, especially a blacksmith. —*v.t.* make or shape by forging.

smit ten (smit′n), *adj.* hard hit; struck. —*v.* a pp. of **smite,** give or strike a hard blow.

soi ree or **soi rée** (swä rā′), *n.* an evening party or social gathering. [< French *soirée* < *soir* evening]

so journ (*v.* sō′jėrn′, sō jėrn′; *n.* sō′jėrn′), *v.i.* stay for a time. —*n.* a brief stay. —**so′journ′er,** *n.*

so lic it (sə lis′it), *v.t.* 1 ask earnestly; try to get: *The tailor sent around cards soliciting trade.* 2 influence to do wrong; tempt; entice: *to solicit a judge with offers of money.* —*v.i.* make appeals or requests.

so lic i tous (sə lis′ə təs), *adj.* 1 showing care or concern; anxious; concerned: *Parents are solicitous for their children's progress in school.* 2 desirous; eager: *solicitous to please.* [< Latin *solicitus* < *sollus* all + *ciere* arouse] —**so lic′i tous ly,** *adv.* —**so lic′i tous ness,** *n.*

so lil o quize (sə lil′ə kwīz), *v.i.*, **-quized, -quiz ing.** 1 talk to oneself. 2 speak a soliloquy. —**so lil′o quiz′er,** *n.*

sol i tude (sol′ə tüd, sol′ə tyüd), *n.* 1 a being alone: *I like company and hate solitude.* 2 a lonely place. 3 loneliness.

som ber or **som bre** (som′bər), *adj.* 1 having deep shadows; dark; gloomy. 2 melancholy; dismal. —**som′ber ly, som′bre ly,** *adv.*

soph ist (sof′ist), *n.* 1 a clever but misleading reasoner. 2 Often, **Sophist.** one of a class of teachers of rhetoric, philosophy, ethics, etc., in ancient Greece.

sor cer ess (sôr′sər is), *n.* woman who practices sorcery; witch.

sot (sot), *n.* person who commonly or habitually drinks too much alcoholic liquor; confirmed drunkard. [Old English, a fool]

sov er eign (sov′rən), *n.* a former British gold coin, that was equal to 20 shillings or one pound.

span (span), *n.*, *v.*, **spanned, span ning.** —*n.* 1 part between two supports. 2 the distance between the tip of the thumb and the tip of the little finger when the hand is spread out; about 9 inches (23 centimeters). —*v.t.* 1 extend over or across. 2 measure by the hand spread out. [Old English *spann*]

spas mod ic (spaz mod′ik), *adj.* 1 having to do with, like, or characterized by a spasm or spasms. 2 occurring very irregularly; intermittent. —**spas mod′i cal ly,** *adv.*

spawn (spôn), *n.* 1 the eggs of fish, frogs, shellfish, etc. 2 the young newly hatched from such eggs. 3 offspring, especially a large number of offspring. 4 product or result. —*v.i.* (of fish, etc.) produce spawn. —*v.t.* 1 produce (spawn). 2 bring forth; give birth to.

spec ter (spek′tər), *n.* 1 phantom or ghost, especially one of a terrifying nature or appearance. 2 thing causing terror or dread. Also, **spectre.** [< Latin *spectrum* appearance]

spew (spyü), *v.t.*, *v.i.* throw out; cast forth; vomit. —*n.* something that is spewed; vomit. Also, **spue.** [Old English *spīwan*]

spin et (spin′it), *n.* 1 a compact upright piano. 2 an old-fashioned musical instrument like a small harpsichord.

splay (splā), *v.t.* 1 spread out; expand; extend. 2 make slanting; bevel. —*v.i.* 1 have or lie in a slanting direction; slope. 2 spread out; flare. —*adj.* wide and flat; turned outward.

spor tive (spôr′tiv, spōr′tiv), *adj.* playful; merry: *a sportive puppy.* —**spor′tive ly,** *adv.* —**spor′tive ness,** *n.*

sprad dle (sprad′l), *v.i.*, **-dled, -dling.** sprawl.

spright ly (sprīt′lē), *adj.*, **-li er, -li est**, *adv.* —*adj.* lively; gay. —*adv.* in a sprightly manner. Also, **spritely.** —**spright′li ness,** *n.*

sprite (sprīt), *n.* fairy. [< Old French *esprit* spirit < Latin *spiritus*]

spurn (spėrn), *v.t.* 1 refuse with scorn; scorn: *spurn a bribe, spurn an offer of friendship.* 2 strike with the foot; kick away. —*v.i.* oppose with scorn: *spurn at restraint.*

squal id (skwol′id), *adj.* 1 foul through neglect or want of cleanliness; dirty; filthy. 2 morally repulsive or wretched; degraded. —**squal′id ly,** *adv.* —**squal′id ness,** *n.*

squall (skwôl), *n.* 1 a sudden, violent gust of wind, often with rain, snow, or sleet. 2 INFORMAL. disturbance or commotion.

squeam ish (skwē′mish), *adj.* 1 too proper, modest, etc.; easily shocked; prudish. 2 too particular; too scrupulous. 3 slightly sick at one's stomach; nauseated. —**squeam′ish ly,** *adv. squal′id ly,* *adv.* —**squal′id ness,** *n.*

staff (staf), *n.*, *pl.* **staves** or **staffs.** a stick, pole, or rod used as a support, as an emblem of office, as a weapon, etc.: *The flag hangs on a staff.*

stag nant (stag′nənt), *adj.* 1 not running or flowing. 2 foul from standing still. 3 not active; sluggish; dull.

stag nate (stag′nāt), *v.*, **-nat ed, -nat ing.** —*v.i.* be or become stagnant. —*v.t.* make stagnant. [< Latin *stagnatum* made stagnant < *stagnum* standing water] —**stag na′tion,** *n.*

stal wart (stôl′wərt), *adj.* 1 strongly built; sturdy; robust. 2 strong and brave; valiant. 3 firm; steadfast. —*n.* 1 a stalwart person. 2 a loyal supporter of a political party. [Old English *stælwierthe* serviceable < *stathol* position + *wierthe* worthy] —**stal′wart ly,** *adv.* —**stal′wart ness,** *n.*

stan chion (stan′shən), *n.* an upright bar, post, or support, as for a window, a roof, or the deck of a ship.

stan dard (stan′dərd), *n.* flag, emblem, or symbol.

staves (stāvz), *n.* a pl. of **staff.**

stealth (stelth), *n.* secret or sly action: *She obtained the letter by stealth, taking it while nobody was in the room.*

stig ma (stig′mə), *n.*, *pl.* **-mas** or **-ma ta.** 1 mark of disgrace; stain or reproach on one's reputation. 2 a distinguishing mark or sign. 3 an abnormal spot or mark in the skin, especially one that bleeds or turns red.

sti pend (stī′pend), *n.* fixed or regular pay, especially for professional services; salary.

sto i cal (stō′ə kəl), *adj.* like a stoic; indifferent to pleasure and pain; self-controlled. —**sto′i cal ly,** *adv.* —**sto′i cal ness,** *n.*

stone (stōn), *n.*, *pl.* **stone.** a British unit of weight, equal to 14 pounds.

stoup (stüp), *n.* a drinking cup; flagon; tankard.

strand (strand), *n.* shore; land bordering a sea, lake, or river.

strife (strīf), *n.* 1 a quarreling; fighting: *bitter strife between rivals.* 2 a quarrel; fight. [< Old French *estrif*; of Germanic origin]

strip ling (strip′ling), *n.* boy just coming into manhood; youth; lad.

sub-, *prefix.* 1 under; below: *Subnormal = below normal.* 2 down; further; again: *Subdivide = divide again.* 3 near; nearly: *Subtropical = nearly tropical.* 4 lower; subordinate: *Subcommittee = a lower or subordinate committee.* 5 resulting from further division: *Subsection = section resulting from further division of something.* 6 slightly; somewhat: *Subacid = slightly acid.* [< Latin < *sub* under, beneath]

sub lime (sə blīm′), *adj.*, *n.*, *v.*, **-limed, -lim ing.** —*adj.* lofty or elevated in thought, feeling, language, etc.; noble; grand; exalted. —*n.* something that is lofty, noble, exalted, etc. —*v.t.* 1 make higher or nobler; make sublime. 2 purify or refine (a solid substance) by applying heat and condensing the vapor given off. —*v.i.* pass from a solid to a vapor or from a vapor to a solid without going through a liquid state.

sub or di na tion (sə bôrd′n ā′shən), *n.* 1 act of subordinating. 2 submission to authority; willingness to obey; obedience.

sub orn (sə bôrn′), *v.t.* 1 persuade, bribe, or cause (someone) to do an illegal or evil deed. 2 persuade or cause (a witness) to give false testimony in court. [< Latin *subornare* < *sub-* secretly + *ornare* equip] —**sub′or na′tion,** *n.* —**sub orn′er,** *n.*

sub serve (səb sėrv′), *v.t.*, **-served, -serv ing.** help or assist (a purpose, action, etc.): *Chewing food well subserves digestion.* [< Latin *subservire* < *sub-* under + *servire* serve]

sub ser vi ence (səb sėr′vē əns), *n.* 1 slavish politeness and obedience; tame submission; servility. 2 a being of use or service.

sub tile (sut′l, sub′təl), *adj.* subtle. —**sub′tile ly,** *adv.*

suc cor (suk′ər), *n.* person or thing that helps or assists; help; aid. —*v.t.* help, assist, or aid (a person, etc.). Also, **succour.**

sum mar i ly (sə mer′ə lē, sum′ər ə lē), *adv.* in a summary manner; briefly; without delay.

sump tu ous (sump′chü əs), *adj.* lavish and costly; magnificent; rich. —**sump′tu ous ly,** *adv.* —**sump′tu ous ness,** *n.*

sun dry (sun′drē), *adj.* several; various: *From sundry hints, I guessed his age.* [Old English *syndrig* separate < *sundor* apart]

su per flu ous (sù pėr′flü əs), *adj.* **1** more than is needed: *In writing telegrams it pays to omit superfluous words.* **2** needless; unnecessary. [< Latin *superfluus*, ultimately < *super-* over + *fluere* to flow] —**su per′flu ous ly,** *adv.* —**su per′flu ous ness,** *n.*

su per nal (sù pėr′nl), *adj.* **1** heavenly; divine. **2** lofty; exalted. [< Latin *supernus* < *super* above] —**su per′nal ly,** *adv.*

su per nu me rar y (sü′pər nü′mə rer′ē, sü′pər nyü′mə rer′ē), *adj., n., pl.* **-rar ies.** —*adj.* more than the usual or necessary number; extra. —*n.* an extra person or thing.

su pine (sü pīn′), *adj.* **1** lying flat on the back. **2** lazily inactive; listless. [< Latin *supinus*] —**su pine′ly,** *adv.*

sup plant (sə plant′), *v.t.* **1** take the place of; displace or set aside. **2** take the place of by unfair methods or by treacherous means.

sup pli cate (sup′lə kāt), *v.,* **-cat ed, -cat ing.** —*v.t.* beg humbly and earnestly: *supplicate a judge to pardon someone.* —*v.i.* pray humbly. [< Latin *supplicatum* bent down, suppliant < *sub-* down + *plicare* to bend] —**sup′pli ca′tor,** *n.*

sup po si tion (sup′ə zish′ən), *n.* **1** act of supposing. **2** thing supposed; belief; opinion.

sup pos i ti tious (sə poz′ə tish′əs), *adj.* **1** not genuine. **2** hypothetical.

sup pu rate (sup′yə rāt′), *v.i.,* **-rat ed, -rat ing.** form pus; discharge pus; fester. [< Latin *suppuratum* festered < *sub-* under + *puris* pus]

sur cease (sėr′sēs′, sər sēs′), *n.* end; cessation.

sur feit (sėr′fit), *n.* **1** too much; excess. —*v.t.* feed or supply to excess. —*v.i.* eat, drink, or indulge in something to excess.

sur mise (*v.* sər mīz′; *n.* sər mīz′, sėr′mīz′), *v.,* **-mised, -mis ing,** *n.* —*v.t., v.i.* infer or guess. —*n.* formation of an idea with little or no evidence; a guessing.

sus pi ra tion (sus′pə rā′shən), *n.* a sigh.

sus te nance (sus′tə nəns), *n.* **1** food or provisions; nourishment: *The lost campers went without sustenance for two days.* **2** means of living; support: *give money for the sustenance of the poor.*

swain (swān), *n.* ARCHAIC. **1** lover. **2** a young man who lives in the country. [< Scandinavian (Old Icelandic) *sveinn* boy]

sward (swôrd), *n.* a grassy surface; turf. [Old English *sweard* skin]

swath (swoth, swôth), *n.* **1** space covered by a single cut of a scythe or by one cut of a mowing machine. **2** row of grass, grain, etc., cut by a scythe or mowing machine. **3** a strip. **4 cut a wide swath,** make a showy display; splurge. Also, **swathe.**

swill (swil), *n.* **1** kitchen refuse, especially when partly liquid; slops. Swill is sometimes fed to pigs. **2** a deep drink. —*v.t.* **1** drink greedily. **2** fill with drink. —*v.i.* drink greedily; drink too much.

swoon (swün), *v.i.* **1** faint: *swoon at the sight of blood.* **2** fade or die away gradually. —*n.* a faint.

syl van (sil′vən), *adj.* of, in, or having woods: *live in a sylvan retreat.* Also, **silvan.** [< Latin *sylvanus, silvanus* < *silva* forest]

syn co pe (sing′kə pē), *n.* a fainting.

tab ard (tab′ərd), *n.* a coarse outer garment worn by the poor during the Middle Ages.

tac i turn (tas′ə tėrn′), *adj.* speaking very little; not fond of talking. [< Latin *taciturnus* < *tacitum* unspoken, tacit] —**tac′ i turn′ly,** *adv.*

tag (tag), *n.* a familiar quotation.

tal low (tal′ō), *n.* the hard fat from sheep, cows, etc., after it has been melted. It is used for making candles, soap, etc. —*v.t.* grease with tallow. [Middle English *talgh*] —**tal′low like′,** *adj.*

tar ry (tar′ē), *v.,* **-ried, -ry ing.** —*v.i.* **1** delay leaving; remain; stay: *We tarried an extra day to see all the sights.* **2** be tardy; hesitate: *Why do you tarry so long?* —*v.t.* ARCHAIC. wait for.

taw dry (tô′drē), *adj.,* **-dri er, -dri est.** showy and cheap; gaudy; garish. —**taw′dri ly,** *adv.* —**taw′dri ness,** *n.*

te di ous (tē′dē əs, tē′jəs), *adj.* long and tiring; boring; wearisome: *A long talk that you cannot understand is tedious.* —**te′ di ous ly,** *adv.* —**te′di ous ness,** *n.*

teem (tēm), *v.i.* be full (of); abound; swarm: *The swamp teemed with mosquitoes.* [Old English *tēman* < *tēam* progeny]

tem per ance (tem′pər əns), *n.* **1** a being moderate in action, speech, habits, etc.; self-control. **2** a being moderate in the use of alcoholic drinks.

a hat	i it	oi oil	ch child		a in about
ā age	ī ice	ou out	ng long		e in taken
ä far	o hot	u cup	sh she	ə =	i in pencil
e let	ō open	u̇ put	th thin		o in lemon
ē equal	ô order	ü rule	ᴛʜ then		u in circus
ėr term			zh measure		< = derived from

ten ant less (ten′ənt lis), *adj.* not occupied; empty.

tench (tench), *n., pl.* **tench es** or **tench.** a freshwater fish of Europe, of the same family as the carp, noted for the length of time it can live out of water. [< Old French *tenche* < Late Latin *tinca*]

ten or (ten′ər), *n.* **1** in music: **a** the highest natural adult male voice. **b** singer with such a voice. **2** the general tendency; course: *the even tenor of country life.* **3** the general meaning or drift; gist; purport: *I understand French well enough to get the tenor of his speech.*

tern (tėrn), *n.* any of a family of sea birds of the same order as the gulls but with a more slender body and bill and usually a long, forked tail. [< Scandinavian (Danish) *terne*]

thorpe (thôrp), *n.* ARCHAIC. village; hamlet.

thrall (thrôl), *n.* **1** person in bondage; slave or serf. **2** bondage; slavery. [< Scandinavian (Old Icelandic) *thræll*]

thwart (thwôrt), *v.t.* prevent from doing something, particularly by blocking the way; oppose and defeat. —*n.* **1** seat across a boat, on which a rower sits. **2** brace between the gunwales of a canoe. [< Scandinavian (Old Icelandic) *thvert* across]

thwarts (def. 2)

ti dings (tī′dingz), *n., pl.* news; information: *joyful tidings.*

tim brel (tim′brəl), *n.* a tambourine or similar instrument. [diminutive of Middle English *timbre* < Old French, drum]

tim or ous (tim′ər əs), *adj.* **1** easily frightened; timid. **2** characterized by or indicating fear. [< Latin *timor* fear < *timere* to fear] —**tim′or ous ly,** *adv.* —**tim′or ous ness,** *n.*

tinct (tingkt), *adj.* tinged. —*n.* tint; tinge. [< Latin *tinctus*]

tinc ture (tingk′chər), *n., v.,* **-tured, -tur ing.** —*n.* **1** solution of medicine in alcohol: *tincture of iodine.* **2** trace; tinge. **3** color; tint. —*v.t.* **1** give a trace or tinge to. **2** color; tint.

tip pet (tip′it), *n.* **1** scarf for the neck and shoulders with ends hanging down in front. **2** a long, narrow, hanging part of a hood, sleeve, or scarf. **3** band of silk or other material worn around the neck by certain clergymen.

tip ple (tip′əl), *v.,* **-pled, -pling,** *n.* —*v.t., v.i.* drink (alcoholic liquor) often or too much. —*n.* an alcoholic liquor. [origin uncertain] —**tip′pler,** *n.*

tithe (tīᴛʜ), *n., v.,* **tithed, tith ing.** —*n.* **1** one tenth. **2** one tenth of one's yearly income paid as a donation or tax for the support of the church. **3** any small tax. —*v.t.* put a tax or a levy of a tenth on. —*v.i.* give or pledge one tenth of one's income to the church or to charity.

tor rid (tôr′id, tor′id), *adj.* **1** very hot; burning; scorching: *torrid weather.* **2** exposed or subject to great heat: *torrid deserts.* **3** very ardent; passionate: *a torrid love scene.* [< Latin *torridus* < *torrere* to parch] —**tor′rid ly,** *adv.* —**tor′rid ness,** *n.*

To ry (tôr′ē, tōr′ē), *n., pl.* **-ries.** member of a British political party that favored royal power and the established church and opposed change.

tra duce (trə düs′, trə dyüs′), *v.t.,* **-duced, -duc ing.** speak evil of (a person) falsely; slander. [< Latin *traducere* parade in disgrace < *trans-* across + *ducere* to lead] —**tra duce′ment,** *n.*

tram mel (tram′əl), *v.t.,* **-meled, -mel ing** or **-melled, -mel ling.** **1** hinder; restrain. **2** catch in or as if in a trammel; entangle.

tran quil (trang′kwəl), *adj.,* **-quil er, -quil est** or **-quil er, -quil est.** free from agitation or disturbance; calm; peaceful; quiet. —**tran′quil ly,** *adv.* —**tran′quil ness,** *n.*

tran scend ent (tran sen′dənt), *adj.* **1** surpassing ordinary limits; excelling; superior; extraordinary. **2** above and independent of the physical universe. —**tran scend′ent ly,** *adv.*

trans fig u ra tion (tran sfig′yə rā′shən), *n.* a change in form or appearance; transformation.

transfix

trans fix (tran sfiks′), *v.t.* **1** pierce through: *The hunter transfixed the lion with a spear.* **2** fasten or fix by piercing through with something pointed; impale. **3** make motionless or helpless (with amazement, terror, grief, etc.). —**trans fix′ion,** *n.*

trans gress (trans gres′, tranz gres′), *v.i.* break a law, command, etc.; sin. —*v.t.* **1** go contrary to; sin against. **2** go beyond (a limit or bound): *transgress the bounds of good taste.* [< Latin *transgressum* gone beyond < *trans-* beyond + *gradi* to step] —**trans gres′sor,** *n.*

trans gres sion (trans gresh′ən, tranz gresh′ən), *n.* a transgressing or a being transgressed; breaking a law, command, etc.; sin.

tran si to ry (tran′sə tôr′ē, tran′sə tōr′ē), *adj.* passing soon or quickly; lasting only a short time; fleeting; transient. —**tran′si to′ri ly,** *adv.* —**tran′si to′ri ness,** *n.*

trans lu cent (tran slü′snt, tranz lü′snt), *adj.* letting light through without being transparent: *Frosted glass is translucent.* [< Latin *translucentem* < *trans-* through + *lucere* to shine] —**trans lu′cent ly,** *adv.*

tra vail (trə vāl′, trav′āl), *n.* **1** toil; labor. **2** trouble, hardship, or suffering. **3** severe pain; agony; torture. **4** the labor and pain of childbirth. —*v.i.* **1** toil; labor. **2** suffer the pains of childbirth; be in labor. [< Old French < Late Latin *trepalium* torture device, ultimately < Latin *tri-* three + *palus* stake]

trea tise (trē′tis), *n.* a formal and systematic book or writing dealing with some subject.

tre bly (treb′lē), *adv.* three times; triply.

trem u lous (trem′yə ləs), *adj.* **1** trembling; quivering: *a voice tremulous with sobs.* **2** timid; fearful. **3** that wavers; shaky: *tremulous writing.* [< Latin *tremulus* < *tremere* to tremble] —**trem′u lous ly,** *adv.* —**trem′u lous ness,** *n.*

trench ant (tren′chənt), *adj.* **1** sharp; keen; cutting: *trenchant wit.* **2** vigorous; effective: *a trenchant policy.* **3** clear-cut; distinct: *in trenchant outline against the sky.* —**trench′ant ly,** *adv.*

trib u la tion (trib′yə lā′shən), *n.* great trouble; severe trial; affliction. [< Late Latin *tribulationem* < *tribulare* oppress, press < Latin *tribulum* threshing sledge]

trib u tar y (trib′yə ter′ē), *n., pl.* **-tar ies,** *adj.* —*n.* **1** stream that flows into a larger stream or body of water. **2** person or country that pays tribute, an obligation or forced payment. —*adj.* **1** flowing into a larger stream or body of water. **2** paying tribute; required to pay tribute.

trice (trīs), *n.* **1** a very short time; moment; instant. **2 in a trice,** in an instant; immediately.

trite (trīt), *adj.*, **trit er, trit est.** worn out by use; no longer new or interesting; commonplace; hackneyed. — **trite′ly,** *adv.*

troll (trōl), *n.* (in Scandinavian folklore) an ugly dwarf or giant with supernatural powers, living underground or in caves. [< Swedish and Norwegian < Old Icelandic, giant, demon]

troth (trôth, trōth), *n.* ARCHAIC. **1** faithfulness or fidelity; loyalty. **2** promise. **3** truth. **4** betrothal. **5 plight one's troth, a** promise to marry. **b** promise to be faithful. —*v.t.* **1** promise. **2** betroth.

trun cheon (trun′chən), *n.* **1** a stick cut and shaped for use as a weapon: *a policeman's truncheon.* **2** staff of office or authority: *a herald's truncheon.* —*v.t.* beat with a truncheon; club.

tu mult (tü′mult, tyü′mult), *n.* **1** noise or uproar; commotion: *the tumult of the storm.* **2** a violent disturbance or disorder: *The cry of "Fire!" caused a tumult in the theater.* **3** a violent disturbance of mind or feeling; confusion or excitement. [< Latin *tumultus*]

tur bid (tėr′bid), *adj.* **1** muddy; thick; not clear. **2** (of air, smoke, etc.) thick; dense; dark. **3** confused; disordered.

turn cock (tėrn′kok′), *n.* OBSOLETE. a hand operated valve or fawcet.

twain (twān), *n., adj.* ARCHAIC. two. [Old English *twēgen*]

ty ro (tī′rō), *n., pl.* **-ros.** beginner in learning anything; novice. Also, **tiro.** [< Latin *tiro* recruit]

---

un-[1] *prefix.* not ___; the opposite of ___: *Unequal = not equal; the opposite of equal. Unchanged = not changed. Unjust = not just.* [Old English]

un-[2] *prefix.* do the opposite of ___; do what will reverse the act: *Unfasten = do the opposite of fasten. Uncover = do the opposite of cover.* [Old English *un-, on-*]

---

unc tion (ungk′shən), *n.* **1** an anointing with oil, ointment, or the like, for medical purposes or as a religious rite. **2** the oil, ointment, or the like, used for anointing. **3** something soothing or comforting: *the unction of flattery.* **4** fervor; earnestness. **5** affected earnestness, sentiment, etc.; smoothness and oiliness of language, manner, etc. [< Latin *unctionem* < *unguere* anoint]

up braid (up brād′), *v.t.* find fault with; blame; reprove: *The captain upbraided the guards for falling asleep.*

ur ban i ty (ėr′ban′ə tē), *n., pl.* **-ties. 1** courtesy, refinement, or elegance. **2** smooth politeness.

u sur ous (yü′zhər əs), *adj.* OBSOLETE. **1** taking extremely high or unlawful interest for the use of money. **2** of, having to do with, or of the nature of usury.

u surp (yü zėrp′, yü sėrp′), *v.t.* seize and hold (power, position, authority, etc.) by force or without right: *The king's brother tried to usurp the throne.* —*v.i.* commit usurpation. —**u surp′er,** *n.*

u sur pa tion (yü′zər pā′shən, yü′sər pā′shən), *n.* a usurping; the seizing and holding of the place or power of another by force or without right: *the usurpation of the throne by a pretender.*

---

vac il late (vas′ə lāt), *v.i., v.i.,* **-lat ed, -lat ing. 1** waver in mind or opinion: *I was vacillating between two possible choices.* **2** move first one way and then another; waver. [< Latin *vacillatum* wavered] —**vac′il lat′ing ly,** *adv.* —**vac′il la′tion,** *n.*

vale (vāl), *n.* valley. [< Old French *val* < Latin *vallis*]

van (van), *n.* the front part of an army, fleet, or other advancing group. [short for *vanguard*]

van quish (vang′kwish, van′kwish), *v.t.* **1** conquer, defeat, or overcome in battle or conflict. **2** overcome or subdue by other than physical means: *vanquish fear.*

var let (vär′lit), *n.* a low, mean fellow; rascal.

vaunt (vônt, vänt), *v.t.* boast of. —*v.i.* brag or boast.

ve he mence (vē′ə məns), *n.* vehement quality or nature; strong feeling; forcefulness; violence.

ve he ment (vē′ə mənt), *adj.* **1** having or showing strong feeling; caused by strong feeling; eager; passionate. **2** forceful; violent. [< Latin *vehementem* being carried away < *vehere* carry] —**ve′he ment ly,** *adv.*

vel li cate (vel′ə kāt), *v.,* **-cat ed, -cat ing.** —*v.t.* pluck. —*v.i.* twitch; move with convulsions.

ven e ra tion (ven′ə rā′shən), *n.* **1** a feeling of deep respect; reverence: *veneration for learning.* **2** act of venerating: *veneration of one's ancestors.* **3** condition of being venerated.

ver dur ous (vėr′jər əs), *adj.* green and fresh.

ver i ty (ver′ə tē), *n., pl.* **-ties. 1** truth. **2** a true statement or fact. **3** reality. [< Latin *veritatem* < *verus* true]

ver min (vėr′mən), *n. pl. or sing.* **1** small animals that are troublesome or destructive. Fleas, lice, bedbugs, rats, and mice are vermin. **2** very unpleasant or vile person or persons.

vex (veks), *v.t.* **1** anger by trifles; annoy; provoke. **2** worry; trouble; harass. **3** disturb by commotion; agitate: *The island was much vexed by storms.* [< Latin *vexare*] —**vex′ing ly,** *adv.*

vex a tion (vek sā′shən), *n.* **1** a vexing. **2** a being vexed: *His face showed his vexation at the delay.* **3** thing that vexes.

vex a tious (vek sā′shəs), *adj.* vexing; annoying. —**vex a′tious ly,** *adv.* —**vex a′tious ness,** *n.*

vi al (vī′əl), *n.* a small glass or plastic bottle for holding medicines or the like; phial. [variant of *phial*]

vi car i ous (vī ker′ē əs, vī ker′ē əs), *adj.* **1** done or suffered for others: *vicarious work.* **2** felt by sharing in others' experience: *The invalid received vicarious pleasure from reading travel stories.* **3** taking the place of another; doing the work of another: *a vicarious agent.* **4** delegated: *vicarious authority.* —**vi car′i ous ly,** *adv.* —**vi car′i ous ness,** *n.*

vice roy (vīs′roi), *n.* person ruling a country or province as the deputy of the sovereign. [< French *vice-roi* < *vice* vice + *roi* king]

vict ual (vit′l), *n., v.,* **-ualed, -ual ing** or **-ualled, -ual ling.** —*n.* **victuals,** *pl.* food or provisions. —*v.t.* supply with food or provisions. —*v.i.* **1** take on a supply of food or provisions: *The ship will victual before sailing.* **2** eat or feed: *sheep victualing on new grass.* [< Latin *victualia,* plural of *victualis* of food < *victus* food, sustenance < *vivere* to live]

vie (vī), *v.i.,* **vied, vy ing.** strive for superiority; contend in rivalry; compete. [short for Middle French *envier* to wager, challenge < Latin *invitare* invite] **—vi′er,** *n.*

vin di ca tion (vin′də kā′shən), *n.* a vindicating or a being vindicated; defense; justification.

vin dic tive (vin dik′tiv), *adj.* **1** feeling a strong tendency toward revenge; bearing a grudge: *A vindictive person is unforgiving.* **2** showing a strong tendency toward revenge: *a vindictive act.* [< Latin *vindicta* revenge < *vindex* avenger] **—vin dic′tive ly,** *adv.* **—vin dic′tive ness,** *n.*

vint ner (vint′nər), *n.* dealer in wine; wine merchant.

vis age (viz′ij), *n.* **1** face. **2** appearance or aspect. [< Old French < *vis* face < Latin *visus* sight < *videre* to see]

vis cous (vis′kəs), *adj.* **1** thick like heavy syrup or glue; sticky. **2** having the property of viscosity. [< Latin *viscosus* < *viscum* birdlime] **—vis′cous ly,** *adv.* **—vis′cous ness,** *n.*

vi sion ar y (vizh′ə ner′ē), *n., pl.* **-ar ies,** *adj.* **—n. 1** person given to imagining or dreaming; person who is not practical; dreamer. **2** person who sees visions. **—adj. 1** not practical; dreamy: *a visionary author.* **2** having visions; able to have visions. **—vi′sion ar′i ness,** *n.*

vo lup tu ous (və lup′chü əs), *adj.* **1** caring much for the pleasures of the senses. **2** giving pleasure to the senses: *voluptuous music, voluptuous beauty.* [< Latin *voluptuosus* < *voluptas* pleasure] **—vo lup′tu ous ly,** *adv.* **—vo lup′tu ous ness,** *n.*

vor tex (vôr′teks), *n., pl.* **-tex es** or **-ti ces. 1** a whirling mass of water, etc., that sucks everything near it toward its center; whirlpool. **2** whirl of activity or other situation from which it is hard to escape. [< Latin, variant of *vertex*]

vouch safe (vouch sāf′), *v.t.,* **-safed, -saf ing.** be willing to grant or give; deign (to do or give): *The proud man vouchsafed no reply when we spoke to him.*

wan (won), *adj.,* **wan ner, wan nest. 1** lacking natural or normal color; pale. **2** looking worn or tired; faint; weak. **—wan′ly,** *adv.*

wane (wān), *v.i.,* **waned, wan ing. 1** lose size; become smaller gradually. **2** decline in power, influence, or importance. **3** decline in strength or intensity. **4** draw to a close.

wan ton (won′tən), *adj.* **1** reckless, heartless, or malicious: *wanton cruelty.* **2** without reason or excuse: *wanton mischief.* **3** not moral; not chaste. **4** frolicsome; playful: *a wanton child.* **5** not restrained: *a wanton mood.* **—n.** a wanton person. **—v.i.** act in a wanton manner: *The wind wantoned with the leaves.* **—v.t.** waste foolishly; squander: *wanton away one's time.* **—wan′ton ly,** *adv.* **—wan′ton ness,** *n.*

ware (wer, war), *n.* Usually, **wares,** *pl.* a manufactured thing; article for sale: *The peddler sold his wares cheap.*

war rant (wôr′ənt, wor′ənt), *v.t.* **1** authorize. **2** justify. **3** promise; guarantee.

was sail (wos′əl, was′əl), *n.* **1** a drinking party; revelry with drinking of healths. **2** spiced ale or other liquor drunk at a wassail. [< Scandinavian (Old Icelandic) *ves heill* be healthy!]

wa ter man (wô′tər mən, wot′ər mən), *n., pl.* **-men. 1** boatman. **2** oarsman.

wat tle (wot′l), *n., v.,* **-tled, -tling. —n.** Also, **wattles,** *pl.* sticks interwoven with twigs or branches; framework of wicker. **—v.t.** make (a fence, wall, roof, hut, etc.) of wattle.

weal (wēl), *n.* well-being; prosperity. ARCHAIC. society; the state.

ween (wēn), *v.t., v.i.* ARCHAIC. think; suppose; believe; expect. [Old English *wēnan*]

wel ter (wel′tər), *v.i.* **1** a rolling or tumbling about. **2** a surging or confused mass. **3** confusion; commotion.

wend (wend), *v.,* **wend ed** or **went, wend ing. —v.t.** direct (one's way): *We wended our way home.* **—v.i.** go.

whelk (hwelk), *n.* pimple or pustule. [Old English *hwylca*]

a hat	**i** it	**oi** oil	**ch** child		⎧ a in about
ā age	**ī** ice	**ou** out	**ng** long		e in taken
ä far	**o** hot	**u** cup	**sh** she	**ə =** ⎨ i in pencil
e let	**ō** open	**ù** put	**th** thin		o in lemon
ē equal	**ô** order	**ü** rule	**ŦH** then		⎩ u in circus
ėr term			**zh** measure		**<** = derived from

whet (hwet), *v.t.,* **whet ted, whet ting. 1** sharpen by rubbing. **2** make keen or eager; stimulate. **3** rub vigorously together.

whet stone (hwet′stōn′), *n.* stone for sharpening knives or tools.

whew (hwyü), *v.i.* **1** whistle. **2** make a rustling noise.

whin ny (hwin′ē), *n., pl.* **-nies,** *v.,* **-nied, -ny ing. —n.** the prolonged, quavering sound that a horse makes. **—v.i.** utter a whinny or any sound like it. **—v.t.** express with such a sound.

wick et (wik′it), *n.* a small door or gate.

wight (wīt), *n.* **1** ARCHAIC. a human being; person. **2** OBSOLETE. any living being; creature. [Old English *wiht*]

wile (wīl), *n., v.,* **wiled, wil ing. —n. 1** a trick to deceive; cunning way. **2** subtle trickery; slyness; craftiness. **—v.t.** coax; lure; entice.

wim ple (wim′pəl), *n., v.,* **-pled, -pling. —n.** cloth for the head arranged in folds about the head, cheeks, chin, and neck, worn sometimes by nuns and formerly by other women. **—v.t. 1** cover with or as if with a wimple; veil. **2** cause to ripple. **3** ARCHAIC. lay in folds, as a veil. **—v.i. 1** ripple. **2** ARCHAIC. lie in folds. [Old English *wimpel*]

wist ful (wist′fəl), *adj.* longing; yearning: *A child stood looking with wistful eyes at the toys in the window.* **—wist′ful ly,** *adv.* **—wist′ful ness,** *n.*

wimple

with al (wi ŦHôl′, wi thôl′), *adv.* **1** with it all; as well; besides; also: *I am tired and hungry and hurt withal.* **2** ARCHAIC. **a** in spite of all; nevertheless. **b** therewith. **—prep.** ARCHAIC. with. [Middle English < *with + all*]

wont (wunt, wōnt, wônt), *adj.* accustomed. **—n.** custom; habit.

wont ed (wun′tid, wōn′tid, wôn′tid), *adj.* accustomed; customary; usual. **—wont′ed ly,** *adv.* **—wont′ed ness,** *n.*

wool gath er ing (wùl′gaŦH′ər ing), *n.* absorption in thinking or daydreaming; absent-mindedness. **—adj.** inattentive; absent-minded; dreamy.

yeo man (yō′mən), *n., pl.* **-men. 1** (formerly, in Great Britain) a person who owned land, but not a large amount, and usually farmed it himself. **2** ARCHAIC. servant or attendant in a royal or noble household. [Middle English *yoman*]

yoke (yōk), *n.* **1** a wooden frame to fasten two work animals together. **2** something that joins or unites. **3** something that holds people in slavery or submission.

yore (yôr, yōr), *n.* **of yore, a** now long since gone; long past: *in days of yore.* **b** of long ago; formerly; in the past: *prouder than of yore.* **—adv.** OBSOLETE. long ago; years ago.

zeal ous (zel′əs), *adj.* full of zeal; eager; earnest; enthusiastic.

zeph yr (zef′ər), *n.* **1** the west wind. **2** any soft, gentle wind; mild breeze. [< *Zephyrus*]

Index of Vocabulary Exercises

Affixes, 109, 459
Antonyms, 415, 498, 696
Context, 41, 88, 264, 314, 336, 751
Dictionary, 41, 88, 264, 314, 336, 554
Etymologies, 228 (*Macbeth*), 386
Pronunciation Key, 347
Roots, 109, 459, 664
Synonyms, 415, 498, 696

Combined Skills Exercises
    Affixes, Context, Roots, Synonyms, 159, 411
    Affixes, Context, Roots, Pronunciation Key, 228
      (*Hamlet*)

Index of Composition Assignments

Personal

Describe return to beloved place after long absence, 382
Describe familiar scene involving contrast, 435
Describe personal experience with nature, 435
Discuss childhood as Golden Age of life, 435
Use Hopkin's diction in personal description of nature, 545
Write personal reflection on the assumptions of Housman's "To an Athlete Dying Young," 549
Describe the "personality" of a house you know, 716
Write a sketch recollecting some period of your childhood, 811

Explanatory

Describe characteristics of Germanic kingship, 41
Explain a reading of the cryptogram in "The Husband's Message," 44
Describe human interdependence in *Beowulf*, 59
Explain the prevalence in Anglo-Saxon literature of the view of human life expressed by Edwin's thane, 59

Compare and contrast the views of everyday life provided by "Edward" and "Get Up and Bar the Door," 71
Discuss folk beliefs present in "Sir Patrick Spence" and "The Demon Lover," 71
Discuss development of a modern folk ballad, 71
Compare and contrast modern and medieval ballads, 71
Discuss the enduring popularity of the story of King Arthur, 116
Discuss a character from the Medieval unit relative to the code of knighthood, 123
Discuss treatment of the theme of death in medieval selections, 123
Discuss the label "The Age of Reason," 353
Discuss literary history reflected in Dryden and Gray, 353
Discuss "Age of Reason" selections relative to the moral objectives of Addison and Steele, 353
Describe the world of which Tennyson dreams in lyric 106 from *In Memoriam*, 459
Explain how unnecessary details affect one's reading of *David Copperfield*, 488
Explain what the narrator of *The Mill on the Floss* has to say about a topic, and then express your own ideas about the topic, 498

Discuss attitudes toward education of children in
Victorian selections, 509

Explain why science troubles the speaker of *In
Memoriam*, 509

Evaluate the state of solitary childhood as opposed
to close sibling attachments, 509

Prepare an indictment of one of the characters in
"The Withered Arm," 535

Describe the emotion in Yeats's love poetry, 563

Consider "Youth" narrated by a young Marlow, 583

Describe the dream of Lionel Wallace in "The Door
in the Wall," 604

Compare the social divisions of 1912 with those of
the present, 664

Trace the chain of fateful circumstance in the lives
of two characters, 669

Discuss treatment of nature in turn-of-the-century
poetry, 669

Restate the argument of "Adam's Curse" in prose,
669

Discuss the retreat from emotional commitment in
turn-of-the-century literature, 669

Speculate on the future lives of the narrator in
"Araby" and Eveline, 811

Write a ballad, 435

Write a prose monologue continuing Tennyson's
"Ulysses," 459

Write a description from a child's point of view, 488

Describe your vision of the future and explain to the
reader what it means, 563

Describe what Mary Postgate's successor finds as
she cleans out her room, and what these articles
tell about her, 593

Explain what happened to the dog in your
neighborhood trained to speak by Cornelius
Appin, 610

Write a letter in which Doolittle advises Eliza what
to do next, 664

Write a poem based on an episode from *Testament
of Youth*, 696

Write a dialogue between Mrs. Kent-Cumberland
and Bessie on the raising of children, 739

Write a satirical elegy attacking some aspect of
contemporary life, 743

Write a story about a fantastic creature in the
modern world, 751

Write an ironic "homage" to some person or
institution, 785

Write a newspaper story based on either "The
Phoenix" or "A Shocking Accident," 811

Creative

Write an informal dialogue between Hrothgar and
Beowulf, 41

Describe a contemporary monster's lair, 41

Write an interview with one of the Canterbury
pilgrims, 88

Write a letter home as one of the Canterbury
pilgrims, 88

Describe the Pardoner preaching, 94

Write an anecdote illustrating a moral text, 94

Write a Chaucerian "link," 109

Write a speech for the Wife of Bath, 109

Describe a modern parallel for the Wife of Bath, 109

Write a filmscript based on nymph-shepherd
exchange, 142

Create prosecution's arguments against Macbeth or
his wife, 229 (*Macbeth*)

Create filmscript based on a scene from *Macbeth*,
229 (*Macbeth*)

Write a soliloquy for Ophelia, 229 (*Hamlet*)

Write an editorial on the condition of Denmark, 229
(*Hamlet*)

Write a humorous soliloquy, 229 (*Hamlet*)

Write a report to Fortinbras exonerating Hamlet, 229
(*Hamlet*)

Write a brief formal essay, 236

Create a portrait of a Renaissance type, 271

Write a narrative describing the Fire of London, 289

Write a newspaper article based on *The Rape of the
Lock*, 325

Write a free-verse lyric based on Wordsworth's
"The World Is Too Much with Us," 435

Critical

Analyze female characters in *Beowulf*, 41

Analyze Wiglaf's role in *Beowulf*, 41

Write a character sketch of Beowulf, 41

Discuss fairy-tale element in *Beowulf*, 59

Compare/contrast views of death in *Beowulf* and
"The Seafarer," 59

Discuss elegiac elements in "The Wife's Lament,"
"The Husband's Message," and "The
Seafarer," 59

Analyze nature imagery in Anglo-Saxon and Celtic
poems, 59

Comment on F. N. Robinson's analysis of the
Pardoner, 94

Compare/contrast description of Arthur's court in
Malory and the *Gawain*-poet, 123

Compare/contrast the Prioress and the Wife of Bath,
123

Analyze destructive forces operating in *Macbeth*,
229 (*Macbeth*)

Discuss theme of equivocation in *Macbeth*, 229
(*Macbeth*)

Discuss recurring symbol in *Macbeth*, 229 (*Macbeth*)

Discuss deterioration of Macbeth's character, 229
(*Macbeth*)

Discuss contemporary application of theatrical
standards expressed in *Hamlet*, 229 (*Hamlet*)

Discuss Tom Stoppard's use of *Hamlet* in
Rosencrantz and Guildenstern Are Dead, 229
(*Hamlet*)

Discuss Hamlet's role as a "mirror" reflecting other characters' flaws, 229 (*Hamlet*)

Discuss role of Horatio, 229 (*Hamlet*)

Compare/contrast Claudius with Hamlet's version of him, 229 (*Hamlet*)

Describe character of Gertrude, 229 (*Hamlet*)

Discuss the effect of pride in *Paradise Lost,* 264

Discuss images of light and darkness in *Paradise Lost,* 264

Compare/contrast the language of Book I with another book of *Paradise Lost,* 264

Compare/contrast Satan with the monster from *The Faerie Queene,* 271

Discuss Coleridge's analysis of Hamlet, 271

Discuss Macbeth as an agent of disorder, 271

Compare/contrast Herrick and Lovelace with other Cavalier poets, 271

Discuss treatment of the theme of death in Donne and Jonson, 271

Discuss treatment of theme of time in Herrick, Milton, and Marvell, 271

Discuss J. Donald Adams's comment on Johnson, 343

Discuss contemporary application of Johnson's views, 343

Compare/contrast verisimilitude in Defoe and Swift, 353

Discuss satire in unit in terms of Horatian/Juvenalian distinction, 353

Discuss Blake's symbols of the lamb and the tiger, 370

Describe character of Donna Inez, Wordsworth, or Victor Frankenstein, 435

Define the madness of Porphyria's lover, and compare with that of the Duke in "My Last Duchess," 464

Compare and contrast Tennyson's King and Browning's Duke, 509

Compare and contrast the personalities of Higgins and Pickering, 664

Evaluate Shaw's ideas and give your own conclusion as to whether Liza would ever marry Higgins, 664

Discuss unconscious self-revelation in *Pygmalion* and "Tobermory," 669

Describe and evaluate Marlowe's youthful spirit in "Youth," 669

Show how crucial moments influence Mary Postgate to act as she does, 669

Compare and contrast two poems of quiet indignation, 669

Compare "Sailing to Byzantium" and "Youth," 669

Examine the use of irony in a poem by Sassoon or Owen, 681

Discuss the relevance of the epigraphs to "The Hollow Men" to the poem as a whole, 701

Discuss Lawrence's revision of "The Piano," 727

Write a character sketch of Morgenhall in *The Dock Brief,* 806

Compare and contrast the literary styles of Owen and Sassoon, 811

Compare and contrast T. S. Eliot's treatment of faith, despair, and the life of the spirit in "The Hollow Men" and "Journey of the Magi," 811

Compare treatment of the theme of time in "Fern Hill" and "Do Not Go Gentle into That Good Night," 811

Discuss treatment of natural subjects in Lawrence and Hughes, 811

Discuss treatment of the theme of the "outsider" in Stevie Smith and John Mortimer, 811

Index of Features

These features are of several types: (1) Articles headed *Comment* supply interesting additional information on periods, authors, or topics appearing in the book. (2) Articles headed *Reader's Note* provide close readings of selections in the book or detailed information on literary topics. (3) Articles headed *The Changing English Language* trace the development of the English language or discuss important language-related topics.

Comment

The Nature of Grendel, 8

Heroic Morality, 31

The Treasure of Sutton Hoo, 34

Medieval Tourists, 77

A Fifteenth-Century Valentine, 107

Elizabeth Young and Old, 136

The Death of Raleigh, 140

Sidney's Metaphor, 150

Shakespeare's Theater—The Globe, 183 (*Hamlet*); 217 (*Macbeth*)

The Witch-Scenes in *Macbeth,* 198

Hamlet, Prince of Denmark, 208

Ben Jonson's Vision of His Son, 245

Size and Scale in *Gulliver's Travels,* 299

Blake's Obscurities, 364

Coleridge's Remarks About "Kubla Khan," 386

Did Keats Make a Blunder?, 403

The Gothic Novel, 429
G. K. Chesterton on *David Copperfield*, 483
Hardy's Geography, 521
Housman on Writing His Poetry, 547
Yeats and Ronsard, 551
Yeats on the Source of "Innisfree," 552
Shaw and Smollett, 649
The Language of Heroism, 680

"The Lady of Shalott," 444
"The Passing of Arthur," 454
The Dramatic Monologue, 463
"Dover Beach," 470
Imagery in "God's Grandeur," 542
"Sailing to Byzantium," 558
"The Second Coming," 559
Yeats's Revision of "The Sorrow of Love," 561
"The Hollow Men," 700
"Fern Hill," 769

Reader's Note

The Poetry of *Beowulf*, 11
Translating *Beowulf*, 22
Sonnets and Sonnet Sequences, 135
The Spenserian Stanza, 145
Allegory, 147
"A Valediction," 240
"To His Coy Mistress," 251
Dryden and the Heroic Couplet, 281
The Rape of the Lock as a Mock Epic, 321
"Ode on a Grecian Urn," 409

The Changing English Language

The Anglo-Saxons, 55
The Medieval Period, 117
The Renaissance, 265
The Age of Reason, 348
The Romantics, 431
The Victorians, 505
New Directions, 665
The Twentieth Century, 807

Index of Authors and Titles

Adam's Curse, 553
Addison, Joseph, 312; *Will Wimble*, 312
"*Ah, Are You Digging on My Grave?*," 536
Alas, So All Things Now Do Hold Their Peace, 135
Alexander, Michael (trans.); *Beowulf* (passage), 23; *Riddles*, 45
Amoretti, 148
Anthem for Doomed Youth, 679
Araby, 702
Arcadia, 150
Argument of His Book, The, 246
Arms and the Boy, 679
Arnold, Matthew, 467; *Isolation*, 468; *Self-Dependence*, 468; *Dover Beach*, 469
Astrophel and Stella, 150
At Grass, 783
Auden, W. H., 740; *The Unknown Citizen*, 741; *Who's Who*, 742; *Musée des Beaux Arts*, 743; *In Memory of W. B. Yeats*, 744
Auld Land Syne, 362
Autobiography of John Stuart Mill, The, 506
Autumn, 154
Avarice, 254

Bacon, Sir Francis, 235; *Of Studies*, 235
Bait, The, 238
Base Details, 676

Batter my heart, three-personed God, from HOLY SONNETS, 241
Bede, 47; *The Ecclesiastical History of the English People*, 48
Beowulf (trans. Charles W. Kennedy), 7
Beowulf-poet, The, 6; *Beowulf*, 7
Bermudas, 252
Blake, William, 363; *Introduction*, from SONGS OF INNOCENCE, 364; *Introduction*, from SONGS OF EXPERIENCE, 364; *The Lamb*, 365; *The Tyger*, 365; *Holy Thursday*, from SONGS OF INNOCENCE, 366; *Holy Thursday*, from SONGS OF EXPERIENCE, 366; *The Divine Image*, 367; *The Human Abstract*, 367; *Proverbs of Hell*, from THE MARRIAGE OF HEAVEN AND HELL, 368; *A New Jerusalem*, from MILTON, 370
Boswell, James, 337; *The Life of Samuel Johnson, LL.D.*, 338
British Museum Reading Room, The, 746
Brittain, Vera, 682; *Testament of Youth*, 683
Brown Penny, 553
Browning, Elizabeth Barrett, 465; *Sonnets from the Portuguese*, 465
Browning, Robert, 460; *Porphyria's Lover*, 461; *My Last Duchess*, 462; *Prospice*, 464
Bullfrog, 786
Burns, Robert, 360; *To a Mouse*, 361; *John Anderson, My Jo*, 361; *A Red, Red Rose*, 362; *Auld Lang Syne*, 362
Byron, Lord (George Gordon), 387; *She Walks in Beauty*, 388; *So We'll Go No More A-Roving*, 388; *When We Two Parted*, 388; *Don Juan*, 390

Campion, Thomas, 152; *When to Her Lute Corinna Sings*, 152; *Now Winter Nights Enlarge*, 153; *The Man of Life Upright*, 153
Chaucer, Geoffrey, 72; *The Prologue to* THE CANTERBURY TALES, 73; *The Pardoner's Prologue*, 88; *The Pardoner's Tale*, 90; *The Wife of Bath's Prologue*, 95; *The Wife of Bath's Tale*, 103
Coghill, Nevill (trans.); *The Prologue to* THE CANTERBURY TALES, 73; *The Pardoner's Prologue*, 88; *The Pardoner's Tale*, 90; *The Wife of Bath's Prologue*, 95; *The Wife of Bath's Tale*, 103
Coleridge, Samuel Taylor, 383; *Frost at Midnight*, 384; *Kubla Khan*, 385
Composed upon Westminster Bridge, September 3, 1802 375
Conrad, Joseph, 564; *Youth*, 565
Crossley-Holland, Kevin (trans.); *Beowulf* (passage), 23
Cummings, E. E.; *i carry your heart* (Comment), 150

David Copperfield, 473
Day of Destiny, The, from MORTE DARTHUR, *112*
Death, be not proud, from HOLY SONNETS, 241
Defoe, Daniel; *A Journal of the Plague Year*, 349
Delight in Disorder, 247
Demon Lover, The, 70
De Quincey, Thomas, 412; *On the Knocking at the Gate in* MACBETH, 413
Description of a City Shower, A, 292
Diary (of Samuel Pepys), *The*, 283
Dickens, Charles, 472; *David Copperfield*, 473
Dictionary of the English Language, 329
Disabled, 680
Divine Image, The, 367
Do Not Go Gentle into That Good Night, 769
Dock Brief, The, 789
Does It Matter?, 677
Doll's House, The, 707
Don Juan, 390
Donne, John, 237; *Song*, 238; *The Bait*, 238; *A Valediction: Forbidding Mourning*, 239; *Death, be not proud*, from HOLY SONNETS, 241; *Batter my heart, three-personed God*, from HOLY SONNETS, 241; *Meditation 17*, 241
Door in the Wall, The, 594
Dover Beach, 469
Dryden, John, 278; *I Feed a Flame Within*, 279; *Song Sung by Venus in Honor of Britannia*, 279; *Mac Flecknoe*, 280; *To the Memory of Mr. Oldham*, 281
Dulce et Decorum Est, 678

Eagle of Pengwern (trans. Gwyn Williams), 53
Easter Wings, 255
Ecclesiastical History of the English People, The (trans. Leo Sherley-Price), 48
Edward, 67
Elegy Written in a Country Churchyard, 344
Eliot, George, 489; *The Mill on the Floss*, 490
Eliot, T. S., 697; *The Hollow Men*, 698; *Journey of the Magi*, 700
Elizabeth I; *When I Was Fair and Young* (Comment), 136
England in 1819, 398
Epistle to Miss Blount, 326
Essay on Man, An, 327
Eveline, 808

Even Such Is Time, 140
Explosion, The, 784

Faerie Queene, The, 144
Fern, 788
Fern Hill, 767
Flower, Robin (trans.); *Pangur Ban*, 53
Frankenstein, 417
Frog Prince, The, 764
Frost at Midnight, 384

Gawain-poet, The; *Sir Gawain and the Green Knight*, 119
Genesis, Chapters 1–3, from THE KING JAMES BIBLE, 230
Get Up and Bar the Door, 69
Girl's Song, 562
Gloriana Dying, 137
God's Grandeur, 542
Gordon, George (see Byron, Lord)
Gray, Thomas, 344; *Elegy Written in a Country Churchyard*, 344; *Sonnet on the Death of Richard West*, 347
Great Men's Houses, 713
Greene, Graham, 771; *A Shocking Accident*, 771
Gulliver's Travels, 294

Hamlet, Prince of Denmark, 160
Hardy Thomas, 516; *The Withered Arm*, 516; *The Man He Killed*, 536; *"Ah, Are You Digging on My Grave?,"* 536; *In Time of "The Breaking of Nations,"* 538; *Snow in the Suburbs*, 538
He Is Not Dead That Sometime Hath a Fall, 133
Herbert, George, 253; *Avarice*, 254; *Love (III)*, 254; *Easter Wings*, 255; *Virtue*, 255
Herrick, Robert, 246; *The Argument of His Book*, 246; *To the Virgins, To Make Much of Time*, 247; *Delight in Disorder*, 247; *Upon Julia's Clothes*, 247
Hollow Men, The, 698
Holy Thursday, from SONGS OF EXPERIENCE, 366
Holy Thursday, from SONGS OF INNOCENCE, 366
Holy Sonnets, 241
Homage to a Government, 785
Hopkins, Gerard Manley, 540; *Pied Beauty*, 541; *God's Grandeur*, 542; *Spring and Fall: To a Young Child*, 543; *Thou Art Indeed Just, Lord*, 544
Housman, A. E., 546; *When I was One-and-Twenty*, 547; *Loveliest of Trees*, 548; *To an Athlete Dying Young*, 549
Howard, Henry (see Surrey, Earl of)
Hughes, Ted, 786; *Bullfrog*, 786; *Pike*, 787; *Fern*, 788
Human Abstract, The, 367
Husband's Message, The (trans. Burton Raffel), 43

i carry your heart, 150
I Feed a Flame Within, 279
Importance of Being Earnest, The, 666
In Memoriam, 448
In Memory of W. B. Yeats, 744
In Time of "The Breaking of Nations," 538
Intimates, 729

Introduction, from SONGS OF EXPERIENCE, 364
Introduction, from SONGS OF INNOCENCE, 364
Isolation, 468
It Is a Beauteous Evening, 376

John Anderson, My Jo, 361
Johnson, Samuel, 328; *Dictionary of the English Language*, 329; *Letter to Chesterfield*, 331; *The Life of Milton*, 332; *On the Death of Dr. Robert Levet*, 335
Jonson, Ben, 243; *To Cynthia*, 244; *Still to Be Neat*, 244; *On My First Son*, 244; *Song, to Celia*, 245; *On My First Daughter*, 245
Jones, Gwyn (trans.); *The Stanzas of the Graves*, 52
Journal of the Plague Year, A, 349
Journey of the Magi, 700
Joyce, James, 702; *Araby*, 702; *Eveline*, 808

Keats, John, 402; *On First Looking into Chapman's Homer*, 403; *When I Have Fears*, 403; *La Belle Dame Sans Merci*, 404; *Ode to a Nightingale*, 406; *Ode on a Grecian Urn*, 408; *To Autumn*, 410; *This Living Hand*, 411
King James Bible, The, 230
Kipling, Rudyard, 584; *Mary Postgate*, 584
Kraken, The, 443
Kubla Khan, 385

La Belle Dame Sans Merci, 404
Lady of Shalott, The, 443
Lake Isle of Innisfree, The, 552
Lamb, The, 365
Larkin, Philip, 783; *At Grass*, 783; *The Explosion*, 784; *Homage to a Government*, 785
Lawrence, D. H., 717; *Tickets, Please*, 718; *The Piano*, 726; *Piano*, 727; *Snake*, 727; *Intimates*, 729
Let me not to the marriage of true minds, 158
Letter to Chesterfield, 331
Life of Milton, The, 332
Life of Samuel Johnson, LL.D., The, 338
Lines Composed a Few Miles Above Tintern Abbey, 372
Litany in Time of Plague, A, 155
London, 1802, 376
Love (III), 254
Lovelace, Richard, 248; *To Althea, from Prison*, 249; *To Lucasta, on Going to the Wars*, 249
Loveliest of Trees, 548
Lover's Vow, A, 134

Macbeth, 160
Mac Flecknoe, 280
MacNeice, Louis, 746; *The British Museum Reading Room*, 746; *The Snow Man*, 747
Malory, Sir Thomas, 110; *The Day of Destiny*, from MORTE DARTHUR, 112
Man He Killed, The, 536
Man of Life Upright, The, 153
Mansfield, Katherine, 707; *The Doll's House*, 707
Marlowe, Christopher, 141; *The Passionate Shepherd to His Love*, 142

Marriage of Heaven and Hell, The, 368
Marvell, Andrew, 250; *To His Coy Mistress*, 250; *Bermudas*, 252
Mary Postgate, 584
Meditation 17, 241
Meyer, Kuno (trans.); *Summer Is Gone*, 54
Mill, John Stuart; *The Autobiography of John Stuart Mill*, 506
Mill on the Floss, The, 490
Milton, 370
Milton, John, 256; *On His Having Arrived at the Age of Twenty-Three*, 257; *On His Blindness*, 257; *Paradise Lost*, 258
Modest Proposal, A, 307
Morte Darthur, 112
Mortimer, John, 789; *The Dock Brief*, 789
Musée des Beaux Arts, 743
Music, When Soft Voices Die, 398
My Heart Leaps Up, 375
My Last Duchess, 462
My mistress' eyes are nothing like the sun, 159
My Oedipus Complex, 776

Nashe, Thomas, 154; *Autumn*, 154; *A Litany in Time of Plague*, 155
New Jerusalem, A, from MILTON, 370
No longer mourn for me when I am dead, 158
Not Waving But Drowning, 765
Now Winter Nights Enlarge, 153
Nymph's Reply to the Shepherd, The, 142

O'Connor, Frank, 776; *The Viking Terror* (trans.), 54; *My Oedipus Complex*, 776
Ode on a Grecian Urn, 408
Ode on Intimations of Immortality from Recollections of Early Childhood, 377
Ode to a Nightingale, 406
Ode to the West Wind, 400
Of Studies, 235
Oft Have I Mused, 151
On First Looking into Chapman's Homer, 403
On His Blindness, 257
On His Having Arrived at the Age of Twenty-Three, 257
On My First Daughter, 245
On My First Son, 244
On the Death of Dr. Robert Levet, 335
On the Knocking at the Gate in MACBETH, 413
Orwell, George, 752; *Shooting an Elephant*, 753; *Such, Such Were the Joys*, 757
Owen, Wilfred, 678; *Dulce et Decorum Est*, 678; *Anthem for Doomed Youth*, 679; *Arms and the Boy*, 679; *Disabled*, 680
Ozymandias, 399

Pangur Ban (trans. Robin Flower), 53
Paradise Lost, 258
Pardoner's Prologue, The (trans. Nevill Coghill), 88
Pardoner's Tale, The (trans. Nevill Coghill), 90
Passing of Arthur, The, from IDYLLS OF THE KING, 452
Passionate Shepherd to His Love, The, 142
Pepys, Samuel, 282; *The Diary*, 283

Phoenix, The, 749
Piano, 727
Piano, The, 726
Pied Beauty, 541
Pike, 787
Pope, Alexander, 318; *The Rape of the Lock*, 319; *Epistle to Miss Blount*, 326; *An Essay on Man*, 327
Porphyria's Lover, 461
Praeterita, 500
Prelude, The, 432
Prologue to THE CANTERBURY TALES, *The* (trans. Nevill Coghill), 74
Prospice, 464
Proverbs of Hell, from THE MARRIAGE OF HEAVEN AND HELL, 368
Pygmalion, 612

Raffel, Burton (trans.); *Beowulf* (passage), 23; *The Husband's Message*, 43; *The Seafarer*, 57
Raleigh, Sir Walter, 138; *Sir Walter Raleigh to His Son*, 139; *To Queen Elizabeth*, 139; *What Is Our Life?*, 140; *Even Such Is Time*, 140; *The Nymph's Reply to the Shepherd*, 142
Rape of the Lock, The, 319
Red, Red Rose, A, 362
Richard II, Act Three, Scene 2, 267
Riddles (trans. J. Duncan Spaeth and Michael Alexander), 45
Ruskin, John, 499; *Praeterita*, 500

Sailing to Byzantium, 556
Saki, 605; *Tobermory*, 606
Sassoon, Siegfried, 676; *Base Details*, 676; *Suicide in the Trenches*, 677; *Does It Matter?*, 677
Satirical Elegy on the Death of a Late Famous General, A, 291
Seafarer, The (trans. Burton Raffel), 57
Second Coming, The, 559
Self-Dependence, 468
Shakespeare, William, 156; *Shall I compare thee to a summer's day?*, 156; *When in disgrace with fortune and men's eyes*, 157; *When to the sessions of sweet silent thought*, 158; *No longer mourn for me when I am dead*, 158; *That time of year thou mayst in me behold*, 158; *Let me not to the marriage of true minds*, 158; *My mistress' eyes are nothing like the sun*, 159; *Hamlet, Prince of Denmark*, 160; *Macbeth*, 160; *Richard II, Act Three, Scene 2*, 267
Shall I compare thee to a summer's day?, 156
Shaw, George Bernard, 611; *Pygmalion*, 612
Shelley, Mary, 416; *Frankenstein*, 417
Shelley, Percy Bysshe, 397; *To Wordsworth*, 398; *Music, When Soft Voices Die*, 398; *England in 1819*, 398; *Ozymandias*, 399; *Ode to the West Wind*, 400
Sherley-Price, Leo (trans.); *The Ecclesiastical History of the English People*, 48
She Walks in Beauty, 388
Shocking Accident, A, 771
Shooting an Elephant, 753
Sidney, Sir Philip, 149; *My true love hath my heart*, from ARCADIA, 150; *Sonnet 31*, from ASTROPHEL AND STELLA, 150; *Oft Have I Mused*, 151; *Thou Blind Man's Mark*, 151

Sir Gawain and the Green Knight (trans. Brian Stone), 119
Sir Patrick Spence, 68
Sir Walter Raleigh to His Son, 139
Smith, Stevie, 763; *The Frog Prince*, 764; *Not Waving But Drowning*, 765
Snake, 727
Snow in the Suburbs, 538
Snow Man, The, 747
Spenser, Edmund, 143; *The Faerie Queene*, 144; *Sonnet 30*, from AMORETTI, 148; *Sonnet 75*, from AMORETTI, 148
Spring and Fall: To a Young Child, 543
Song, 238
Song Sung by Venus in Honor of Britannia, 279
Song, to Celia, 245
Songs of Experience, 364
Songs of Innocence, 364
Sonnet on the Death of Richard West, 347
Sonnets from the Portuguese, 465
Sorrow of Love, The (1892), 560
Sorrow of Love, The (1927), 560
So We'll Go No More A-Roving, 388
Spaeth, J. Duncan (trans.); *Beowulf* (passage), 23; *Riddles*, 45
Stanzas of the Graves, The (trans. Gwyn Jones), 52
Steele, Sir Richard, 315; *Alexander Selkirk*, 315
Still to Be Neat, 244
Stone, Brian (trans.); *Sir Gawain and the Green Knight*, 119
Such, Such Were the Joys, 757
Suicide in the Trenches, 677
Summer Is Gone (trans. Kuno Meyer), 54
Surrey, Earl of (Henry Howard), 134; *A Lover's Vow*, 134; *Alas, So All Things Now Do Hold Their Peace*, 135
Swift, Jonathan, 290; *A Satirical Elegy on the Death of a Late Famous General*, 291; *A Description of a City Shower*, 292; *A Voyage to Brobdingnag*, from GULLIVER'S TRAVELS, 294; *A Modest Proposal*, 307
Swift's Epitaph, 563

Tears, Idle Tears, 448
Tennyson, Alfred, Lord, 442; *The Kraken*, 443; *The Lady of Shalott*, 443; *Ulysses*, 446; *Tears, Idle Tears*, 448; *In Memoriam*, 448; *The Passing of Arthur*, from IDYLLS OF THE KING, 452
Testament of Youth, 683
That time of year thou mayst in me behold, 158
This Living Hand, 411
Thomas, Dylan, 766; *Fern Hill*, 767; *Do Not Go Gentle into That Good Night*, 769
Thou Art Indeed Just, Lord, 544
Thou Blind Man's Mark, 151
Tickets, Please, 718
To Althea, from Prison, 249
To a Mouse, 361
To an Athlete Dying Young, 549
To Autumn, 410
To Cynthia, 244
To His Coy Mistress, 250
To Lucasta, on Going to the Wars, 249
To Queen Elizabeth, 139
To the Memory of Mr. Oldham, 281
To the Virgins, To Make Much of Time, 247
To Wordsworth, 398
Tobermory, 606
Twenty-third Psalm, The; from THE GREAT BIBLE, 234

Twenty-third Psalm, The; from THE KING JAMES BIBLE, 234
Twenty-third Psalm, The; from THE BAY PSALM BOOK, 234
Twenty-third Psalm, The; from THE NEW ENGLISH BIBLE, 234
Tyger, The, 365

Ulysses, 446
Unknown Citizen, The, 741
Upon Julia's Clothes, 247

Valediction: Forbidding Mourning, A, 239
Varium et Mutabile, 133
Viking Terror, The (trans. Frank O'Connor), 54
Virtue, 255
Voyage to Brobdingnag, A, from GULLIVER'S TRAVELS, 294

Warner, Sylvia Townsend, 748; *Gloriana Dying* (Comment), 137; *The Phoenix,* 749
Waugh, Evelyn, 730; *Winner Takes All,* 730
Wells, H. G., 594; *The Door in the Wall,* 594
What Is Our Life?, 140
When I Have Fears, 403
When I Was Fair and Young, 136
When I Was One-and-Twenty, 547
When in disgrace with fortune and men's eyes, 157
When to Her Lute Corinna Sings, 152
When to the sessions of sweet silent thought, 158
When We Two Parted, 388

When You Are Old, 551
Who's Who, 742
Whoso List to Hunt, 132
Wife of Bath's Prologue, The (trans. Nevill Coghill), 95
Wife of Bath's Tale, The (trans. Nevill Coghill), 103
Wife's Lament, The (trans. Charles W. Kennedy), 42
Wild Swans at Coole, The, 555
Wilde, Oscar; *The Importance of Being Earnest,* 666
Will Wimble, 312
Williams, Gwyn (trans); *Eagle of Pengwern,* 53
Winner Takes All, 730
Withered Arm, The, 516
Woolf, Virginia, 712; *Great Men's Houses,* 713
Wordsworth, William, 371; *Lines Composed a Few Miles Above Tintern Abbey,* 372; *My Heart Leaps Up,* 375; *Composed Upon Westminster Bridge, September 3, 1802,* 375; *It Is a Beauteous Evening,* 376; *The World Is Too Much with Us,* 376; *London, 1802,* 376; *Ode on Intimations of Immortality from Recollections of Early Childhood,* 377; *The Prelude,* 432
World Is Too Much with Us, The, 376
Wyatt, Sir Thomas, 132; *Whoso List to Hunt,* 132; *Varium et Mutabile,* 133; *He Is Not Dead That Sometime Hath a Fall,* 133

Yeats, William Butler, 550; *When You Are Old,* 551; *The Lake Isle of Innisfree,* 552; *Adam's Curse,* 553; *Brown Penny,* 553; *The Wild Swans at Coole,* 555; *Sailing to Byzantium,* 556; *The Second Coming,* 559; *The Sorrow of Love (1892),* 560; *The Sorrow of Love (1927),* 560; *Girl's Song,* 562; *Young Man's Song,* 562; *Swift's Epitaph,* 563
Young Man's Song, 562
Youth, 565

Acknowledgments

Illustration not credited is from Scott, Foresman. Source abbreviations are: British Museum for By permission of the Trustees of the British Museum; Fitzwilliam for Fitzwilliam Museum, Cambridge; National Gallery for Reproduced by courtesy of the Trustees, The National Gallery, London; Royal Collection for Royal Collection, Courtesy of Her Majesty The Queen, Copyright Reserved; Tate Gallery for The Tate Gallery, London; V and A for Victoria and Albert Museum, Crown Copyright.

Unit 1
xviii-Giraudon/Art Resource, with special authorization of the City of Bayeux; **5**-British Library; **10**-Swedish Travel Information Bureau; **19,34,35**-British Museum; **34**(1)-Gary Gianni; **45**-The Board of Trinity College, Dublin; **47,49**-British Museum; **53**-The Board of Trinity College, Dublin; **54**-Bygdoy Museum, Oslo; **56**-British Museum.

Unit 2
60-British Library; **63**-British Museum; **65**-British Library; **67**-British Museum; **69**-Burrell Collection, Glasgow Museums & Art Galleries; **72**-Bodleian Library, Oxford; **73**-The Museum of London; **75,76,78,79,83**-By permission of The Huntington Library, San Marino, California; **86**-British Library; **89,98**-By permission of The Huntington Library; **102**-British Museum; **107**-Bibliotheque Mejanes; **111**-British Museum; **113**-Courtesy of Lambeth Palace Library/Photo by John Freeman; **115**-British Library; **117**-British Museum; **119**-M805 f48 The Pierpont Morgan Library; **122**-British Library.

Unit 3
124-By courtesy of Mr. Simon Wingfield Digby, Sherborne Castle; **127**-Thyssen-Bornemisza Collection; **128,129**-From the collection of the late Captain Eric Palmer;

131,132-Royal Collection; 134-The Bettmann Archive; 136,138-National Portrait Gallery, London; 141-Masters, Fellows & Scholars of Corpus Christi College, Cambridge; 143-National Portrait Gallery, London; 148-V and A; 149-National Portrait Gallery, London; 150-V and A; 151-Royal Collection; 154-British Library; 155-The Museum of London; 157-© 1983 Cloudshooters/Laurel Spingola; 160 (*Hamlet*)-Courtesy Stacy Keach; 163 through 196 (*Macbeth*)-Harvard Theatre Collection, Angus McBean photographer; 199-© Jennifer Girard; 203, 207 and 214 through 227-Harvard Theatre Collection, Angus McBean photographer; 208 (*Hamlet*) (1) The Bettmann Archive/BBC Hulton; 208 (r) Harvard Theatre Collection; 209 (1) Still from the film *Hamlet* by courtesy of the Rank Organisation plc; 209 (r) Holte Photographics, Ltd.; 231-Glasgow Museums and Art Galleries, Stirling Maxwell Collection, Pollock House; 235-From the Gorhambury Collection by permission of the Earl of Verulam; 237-Courtesy private Scottish collection/Photo: Tom Scott; 242-Courtauld Institute of Art, University of London; 243-National Portrait Gallery, London; 246-The Bettmann Archive; 248-Dulwich College Picture Gallery; 250-Granger Collection; 253-The Bridgeman Art Library, Guildhall Art Gallery, City of London; 256-Princeton University Library; 259-British Museum; 269-Courtesy Seattle Repertory Theatre.

Unit 4

272-The Trustees of Sir John Soane's Museum; 275-Sheldonian Theatre, Oxford; 278-The Bettmann Archive; 282-National Portrait Gallery, London; 286,287-From John Leake's *An Exact Surveigh of the Streets Contained Within the Ruins of the City of London, 1669*; 290-National Portrait Gallery, London; 300,303,305-Culver Pictures; 312,315-National Portrait Gallery, London; 318-Bodleian Library, Oxford; 326-British Museum; 328-Tate Gallery; 331-National Portrait Gallery, London; 337-Scottish National Portrait Gallery/Photo: Tom Scott; 341-Granger Collection; 344-National Portrait Gallery, London; 346-From Designs by Mr. R. Bentley for Six Poems by Mr. T. Gray, London; 348-From *The Poetical Work of Alexander Pope,* ed. R. Carruthers, Vol. I, London, Ingram, Cooke & Co., 1853; 350,351-Society of Antiquaries.

Unit 5

354-Clive House Museum, Shrewsbury; 358-V and A; 360-National Portrait Gallery, London; 361-From *Keith Brockie's Wildlife Sketchbook,* copyright © 1981 by Keith Brockie, Macmillan Publishing Co., Inc. All rights reserved. 363-Fitzwilliam; 367-British Museum; 369-Tate Gallery; 370-British Museum; 371-National Portrait Gallery, London; 373-British Museum; 375-Kate Moon; 383-National Portrait Gallery, London; 385-Mansell Collection; 387-National Portrait Gallery; 389-Library of Congress; 393-Manchester, Whitworth Art Gallery; 397-National Portrait Gallery, London; 399-Photo: © Marshall Cavendish Ltd. 1979; 402-National Portrait Gallery, London; 404-Hessisches Landesmuseum; 407-National Gallery; 410-British Museum; 412-The New York Public Library, Astor, Lenox and Tilden Foundations; 416-The Bettmann Archive; 423-Culver Pictures; 423 (top) Museum of Modern Art/Film Stills Archive; (bottom) British Library; 431-British Museum.

Unit 6

436-City of Manchester Art Galleries; 439-Royal Collection; 440-The Bettmann Archive/BBC Hulton; 442-The Bettmann Archive; 447-National Gallery; 449-Tate Gallery; 457-Museo de Arte de Ponce; 460-Granger Collection; 461-Fitzwilliam; 462(t) Uffizi Gallery/Photo: Art Resource; 462(b) FOTOMAS; 465-National Portrait Gallery, London; 466-Tate Gallery; 467-Granger Collection; 469-Tate Gallery; 472,473-The Dickens House; 475,489-National Portrait Gallery, London; 495-V and A; 499-Goodspeed-Ruskin Collection/Wellesley College Collection; 501-Ashmolean Museum, Oxford; 505-Dickens House Museum.

Unit 7

510-Tate Gallery; 514-Courtesy Newberry Library, Chicago; 515-The Museum of London; 516-Fitzwilliam; 519,523 through 533-Tom Herzberg; 537-Jorge Lewinski; 540(t) Brown Brothers; 540,543-City of Manchester Art Galleries; 544-MS. Eng. misc. a.8, folio 104 recto Shanklin, Bodleian Library, Oxford; 546-National Portrait Gallery, London; 548-V and A; 550-The Bettmann Archive/BBC Hulton; 551-National Museum of Ireland; 555-V and A; 556,557-Courtesy of the Istanbul University Library. Photo: Erkin Emiroğlu; 564-Courtesy Doubleday and Company; 568,569-Peabody Museum, Salem; 579-Gary Gianni; 584-National Portrait Gallery, London; 587-Tate Gallery; 594,603-International Museum of Photography at George Eastman House; 605-E. O. Hoppe/Courtesy The Viking Press; 611-International Museum of Photography at George Eastman House; 613 through 656-Dominic Photography; 665-From *Caught in the Web of Words* by K. M. Elisabeth Murray, Yale University Press; 667-Photo: Catherine Ashmore.

Unit 8

670-Museum of London; 673-The Bettmann Archive/BBC Hulton; 676-Fitzwilliam; 678-Culver Pictures; 682 through 691-Photos from *Chronicle of Youth* by Vera Brittain, Edited by Alan Bishop, Copyright (c) 1981 by the literary executors for the Vera Brittain Estate. By permission of William Morrow & Company; 697-(c) Rollie McKenna; 698-Ann Parker/Avon Neal; 702-The Bettmann Archive, Inc.; 705-Collection of Patrick Henchy, Dublin; 707-*Portrait of Katherine Mansfield* by Anne Rice. Collection: National Art Gallery of New Zealand; 709-Courtesy of the Wenham Historical Association; 712-The Bettmann Archive/BBC Hulton; 713-National Trust; 715-National Portrait Gallery, 717-The Bettmann Archive, Inc.; 719,730-The Bettmann Archive/BBC Hulton; 735-Neil Davenport's original paintings are available through Portal Gallery Ltd., London, England, 740-UPI; 742,743-Musée Royaux des Beaux-Arts de Belgique Bruxelles; 746-The Bettmann Archive/BBC Hulton; 748-National Portrait Gallery; 752-(c) BBC; 759-Central Press Photos, Ltd.; 763-National Portrait Gallery; 766-(c) Rollie McKenna; 767-Mary Goljenboom; 771-The Bettman Archive, Inc.; 773-Courtesy Flamingo Pictures, Ltd.; 776-Elliott Erwitt/MAGNUM; 783,786-(c) Rollie McKenna; 789-(c) Camera Press Ltd.; 793-The Bettmann Archive, Inc.

Glossary

839-Karl H. Maslowski/Photo Researchers, Inc.; 842-Fairchild Aerial Survey, Inc.; 846-Brown Brothers.

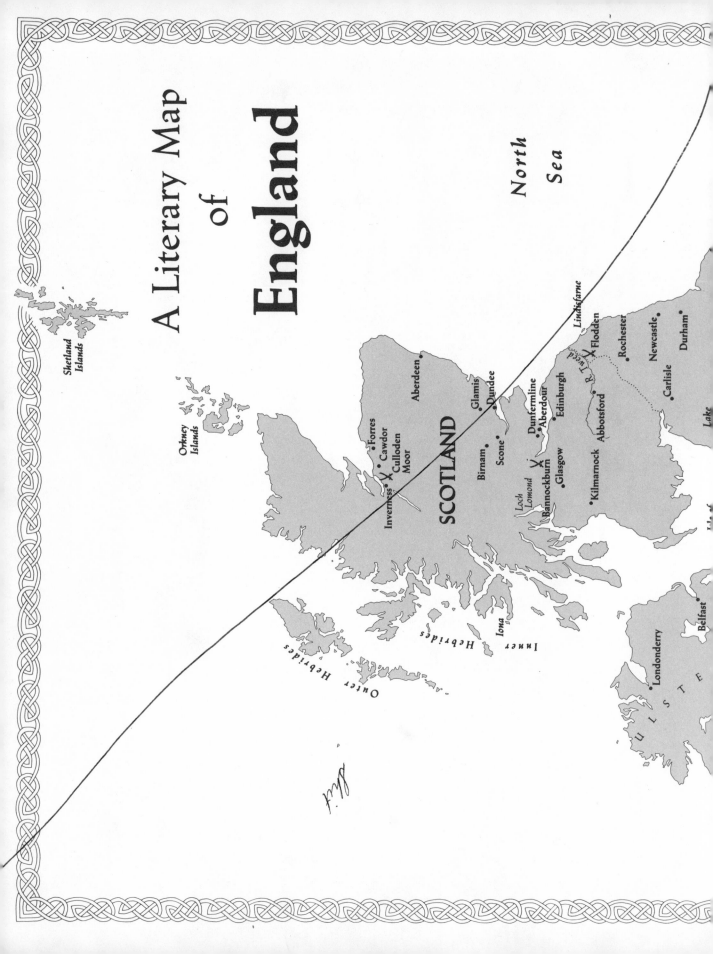

A Literary Map

of

England

North Sea

Shetland Islands

Orkney Islands

SCOTLAND

Aberdeen

Forres
Cawdor
Culloden
Moor
Inverness

Glamis
Dundee

Birnam
Scone

Dunfermline
Aberdour
Edinburgh

Loch
Lomond
Bannockburn

Glasgow
Kilmarnock

Abbotsford

R. Tweed

Lindisfarne
Flodden

Rochester
Newcastle
Durham

Carlisle

Lake

Iona

Inner Hebrides

Outer Hebrides

Londonderry

Belfast

ULSTER